2002

HISTORIC DOCUMENTS

OF

2002

2002

HISTORIC DOCUMENTS
OF
2002

Cumulative Index, 1998–2002

CQ PRESS

A Division of Congressional Quarterly Inc.

Historic Documents of 2002

Editors: Martha Gottron, John Felton, Bruce Maxwell
Production and Associate Editor: Kerry V. Kern
Indexer: Victoria Agee

"America—Still Unprepared, Still in Danger," report of an independent task force, sponsored by the Council on Foreign Relations, Gary Hart and Warren B. Rudman, cochairs. Copyright © 2002. Council on Foreign Relations Press, New York, N.Y. Reprinted with permission. [Pages 748–762.]

CQ Press
1255 22nd Street, N.W., Suite 400
Washington, D.C. 20037
(202) 729-1900; toll-free, 1-866-4CQ-PRESS (1-866-427-7737)
www.cqpress.com

Printed and bound in the United States of America

07 06 05 04 03   5 4 3 2 1

⊗ The paper used in this publication exceeds the requirements of the American National Standard for Information Sciences—Permanence of Paper for Printed Library Materials, ANSI Z39.48-1992.

The Library of Congress cataloged the first issue of this title as follows:

Historic documents. 1972—
    Washington. Congressional Quarterly Inc.

    1. United States—Politics and government—1945– —Yearbooks.
2. World politics—1945– —Yearbooks. I. Congressional Quarterly Inc.

E839.5H57   917.3′03′9205   72-97888

ISBN 1-56802-724-9
ISSN 0892-080X

PREFACE

The prospect of a war in Iraq and the aftermath of the September 11, 2001, terrorist attacks against the United States dominated international diplomacy and many aspects of U.S. domestic policy during 2002. The year was the first in decades in which international concerns regularly overrode domestic political and economic considerations in the United States.

Especially in the early months of 2002, many Americans were still in a state of shock over the September 11 terrorist attacks. The attacks—carried out through use of hijacked airplanes—killed nearly 3,000 people, destroyed the World Trade Center towers in New York City, damaged the Pentagon outside Washington, D.C., and disabused Americans of the notion that their country was safe from the troubles of the rest of the world. Months after the attacks, many Americans remained leery of air travel, and the economy continued to reel from the trauma. The administration of President George W. Bush also used its war against terrorism to justify a broad range of policies, including restrictions on civil liberties, a tougher stance against foreign enemies, and even its plan to open the Arctic National Wildlife Refuge in Alaska to oil exploration.

By far the most urgent, and controversial, outgrowth of the September 11 attacks was a decision by President Bush to use the war on terrorism to tackle the regime of Iraqi leader Saddam Hussein. Bush signaled on November 26, 2001, that he considered Iraq's government to be a supporter of terrorism because of its past (and presumed current) possession of biological and chemical weapons and its attempts to develop nuclear weapons. Bush stepped up the rhetoric against Iraq in his January 29, 2002, State of the Union address, describing Iraq, Iran, and North Korea as constituting an "axis of evil" that supported terrorism and threatened U.S. interests. From that point forward it was clear that Bush intended to use Iraq to demonstrate his determination to eliminate potential threats to U.S. security; the only questions involved when and how he would proceed.

At least for the moment, Bush answered the latter question in a speech to the United Nations General Assembly on September 12. The president denounced Iraq's government as a threat to worldwide peace and security and demanded that the UN Security Council act to enforce the numerous resolutions it had passed since 1991 requiring Baghdad to give up its weapons of mass destruction. Some of Bush's senior advisers, including Vice President

How to Use This Book

The documents are arranged in chronological order. If you know the approximate date of the report, speech, statement, court decision, or other document you are looking for, glance through the titles for that month in the table of contents.

If the table of contents does not lead you directly to the document you want, turn to the index at the end of the book. There you may find references not only to the particular document you seek but also to other entries on the same or a related subject. The index in this volume is a five-year cumulative index of *Historic Documents* covering the years 1998–2002. There is a separate volume, *Historic Documents Index, 1972–2002*, which may also be useful.

The introduction to each document is printed in italic type. The document itself, printed in roman type, follows the spelling, capitalization, and punctuation of the original or official copy. Where the full text is not given, omissions of material are indicated by the customary ellipsis points.

Internet URL addresses noting where the documents have been obtained appear at the end of each introduction. If documents were not available on the Internet, this also has been noted.

Dick Cheney and Defense Secretary Donald H. Rumsfeld, had publicly suggested that the United States should bypass the UN. In calling for action by the Security Council, Bush heeded conflicting advice from his secretary of state, Colin Powell, who had said it was important that any U.S. military action against Iraq have at least the implied blessing of the world body and broad international support.

Bush's September 12 speech set off a flurry of international diplomacy through which Powell sought to build broad support for an assertive stance against Iraq. After seven weeks of haggling over the nuance of various texts, Powell succeeded in winning unanimous support on the fifteen-member Security Council for a resolution (number 1441, adopted November 8) demanding that Baghdad provide a "full" and "complete" accounting of its prohibited missiles and weapons of mass destruction, and allow the return of UN weapons inspectors, who had left Iraq in 1998 because the government there was not cooperating. Any hopes that adoption of the latest UN decree would produce a peaceful resolution of the dispute over Iraq were quickly dashed, however. The Iraqi government on December 7 denied that it possessed prohibited weapons—a denial that carried little credibility with most world leaders—and then demonstrated only grudging cooperation with weapons inspectors sent by the United Nations, repeating a pattern from previous inspections during the 1990s.

The Bush administration in September laid out the intellectual argument for tackling suspected threats—such as Iraq's possible use of biological or chemical weapons—before, rather than after, the fact. In a National Security Strategy, approved by Bush and released September 20 by the White House, the administration argued for "preemption" as a means of heading off potential threats. The strategy embraced many other aspects of a broad foreign policy, but the advocacy of preemption attracted wide attention and was generally seen as an effort by the administration to justify a potential war in Iraq.

The intense focus on Iraq came despite the fact that the United States and its allies had not completed the work of the first element of Bush's war against terrorism: the pacification and reconstruction of Afghanistan. Less than a month after the September 11, 2001, attacks, the United States, Britain, and a few dozen allies invaded Afghanistan to root out the al Qaeda terrorist network and the Taliban government, which had offered al Qaeda an operational base there. Bush accused al Qaeda of planning and carrying out the September 11 attacks.

The military operation quickly succeeded in ousting the Taliban from power and scattering al Qaeda's thousands of fighters. Late in 2001 the United Nations brokered an agreement among Afghan factions for an interim government to be led by Hamid Karzai, a respected tribal leader who had broad support in Western capitals. At a follow-up conclave in Afghanistan in June 2002, Karzai was elected to lead the country for another two years—while a constitution was drafted for a permanent political arrangement. Even with that endorsement, Karzai remained little more than the mayor of Kabul, the national capital during 2002. Most of the rest of the country was controlled, for all practical purposes, by local warlords who had little or no loyalty to Karzai's central government. The Bush administration was reluctant to expand the international peacekeeping force that was responsible for security in the Kabul area. Washington and other Western governments also fulfilled only part of their promised contributions to rebuild Afghanistan in the wake of three decades of war. As of the end of 2002 the United States had failed to capture the two men whose charismatic leadership had turned Afghanistan into a terrorist base: al Qaeda founder Osama bin Laden and the Taliban's chief leader, known as Mullah Omar.

During the first part of the year U.S. government officials and some terrorism experts expressed hope that the Afghanistan conflict might have substantially disrupted al Qaeda's ability to plan and execute major acts of terrorism. That hope proved false on October 12, when a car bomb exploded outside two crowded seaside nightclubs on the resort island of Bali in Indonesia. More than two hundred people, about half of them Australians, died from the blast and resulting fire. In the months before the bombing the United States had tried, with little success, to get the Indonesian government to crack down on extremist Islamic groups. The bombing severely damaged the country's important tourism industry and stirred the government to action. Within two months key figures of a regional Islamist organization, with links to al Qaeda, were arrested, and some were charged with crimes in connection with the bombing.

Yet another terrorist bombing came just six weeks later, this time at a beachfront hotel in Mombasa, Kenya, patronized almost exclusively by Israelis. The explosion of a car bomb killed twelve people and injured several more, including some Israeli tourists. At almost exactly the same time, someone fired at least one surface-to-air missile at an Israeli airliner that was taking off from the nearby Mombasa airport; the missile missed the plane, which was loaded with Israeli tourists. Terrorism experts said these simultaneous attacks appeared to indicate the work of al Qaeda, which had staged similar twin attacks in the past—notably the bombings of the U.S. embassies in Nairobi, Kenya, and Dar es Salaam, Tanzania, in August 1998.

Yet another crisis emerged late in the year, just as the United Nations was beginning its debate on what to do about Iraq. The Bush administration announced in October that North Korea had admitted violating a 1994 international agreement under which it had promised to halt development of nuclear weapons. This announcement set off a round of accusations between Washington and the North Korean government in Pyongyang, which had become increasingly estranged since Bush took office. The Bush administration rejected calls for direct talks with North Korea, arguing that any diplomatic contact to resolve the dispute should be handled through talks involving other affected countries in the region, notably China, Japan, and South Korea. This argument over procedural matters led nowhere, and by year's end North Korea was openly defying the 1994 agreement and resuming operation of a reactor that had been used to produce weapons-grade plutonium for the country's small arsenal of nuclear weapons.

Elections

A coincidence of election calendars made 2002 a year of significant political turnover in several important nations. Two of the most notable elections brought to power figures who, in recent years, had been considered unacceptable by key political forces, both domestically and internationally. In October Brazilian voters elected as president Ignacio Lula de Silva, a former labor union leader far to the left of the country's political spectrum. Known as Lula, this candidate of the Workers Party benefited from widespread dissatisfaction with the uneven benefits of globalization—the opening of world economies, including Brazil's, to free trade and investment.

Unhappiness with the status quo also led to a major electoral victory in Turkey by a party with Islamist roots. In November the Justice and Development Party, headed by former Istanbul mayor Recep Tayyip Erdogan, virtually wiped out several of Turkey's long-standing secular parties and took commanding control of the parliament. Erdogan promised to honor Turkey's secular history, however, and won promises of support from leaders in Europe, as well as the Bush administration.

Another remarkable transition took place in Kenya in December, when longtime president Daniel Arap Moi reluctantly stepped aside and allowed a free election. The victor was Moi's former vice president, Mwai Kibaki, who had helped consolidate several opposition factions into a cohesive party to challenge Moi's handpicked successor. The election was more than a success for Kenya, serving as a rebuke to those who insisted African nations were not ready for true democracy.

One of those scorning democracy was the president of Zimbabwe, Robert Mugabe, who used the full range of electoral tricks to hold on to power, including repression of the opposition, disenfranchisement of voters, and even the denial of food aid for people who refused to support the government. Western leaders denounced Mugabe's reelection in March as a fraud, but many other African leaders were reluctant to criticize a colleague, especially one who had been a hero in the continent's struggle for independence from colonialism.

Mugabe pretended to hold free elections, but that could not be said for Cuban leader Fidel Castro, another dictator who held on to power despite growing public dissatisfaction. Castro welcomed former U.S. president Jimmy Carter for an extraordinary visit in May and even allowed Carter to speak to the Cuban people over national television. Carter lectured Castro on democracy and gave Cubans their first information about a homegrown petition movement for free elections. But Castro made no move to ease his grip on the island, which he had ruled for more than forty years.

War and Peace

The beleaguered peoples of four countries torn by long civil wars received good news during the year as the warring parties took important steps toward peace. The largest conflict anywhere in the world in recent decades—referred to as "Africa's First World War" for control of the Democratic Republic of the Congo—simmered down during 2002, and nearly all the participants signed peace agreements. Most of the countries that had sent soldiers to fight either for or against the Congo's government withdrew their forces during the year, but an outbreak of fighting in eastern Congo raised international concerns about the stability of the peace accord.

Two other long-term wars in Africa appeared to come to more definitive conclusions. The bigger and older conflict, in Angola, ended early in the year after the government killed longtime rebel leader Jonas Savimbi. UN-monitored efforts to restore peace appeared to be well under way by year's end. Free elections capped a much smaller—but brutal—war in the tiny West African country of Sierra Leone. Fighting between the government and a rebel group had pretty much ended the previous year, allowing the United Nations to sponsor elections in May that reelected the civilian president whom guerrilla forces had tried to oust from power.

Much work remained to bring a conclusive end to yet another long-term war, between the two major ethnic groups on the large island of Sri Lanka. The government and representatives of the guerrilla group known as the Tamil Tigers signed a cease-fire agreement in February, and both sides claimed to be committed to resolving their disputes peacefully. Even so, it was clear that overcoming the brutality of one of the world's bloodiest wars could take many years to accomplish.

U.S. Domestic Issues

Domestically, the major news story for much of the year was about corporate corruption. Starting with the collapse of the Enron energy corporation in late 2001, and running well into the summer of 2002, nearly every week brought revelations of wrongdoing of some type in the suites and board rooms of large corporations. In some cases—notably in the continuing revelations about Enron—the public learned that corporate officers had concocted false or misleading financial reports to fool investors. In many other cases, personal greed had driven actions as corporate officers took inflated salaries or stock options and bought personal luxury goods. By midyear, television frequently showed images of board chairmen, executive officers, and other high-ranking officials being taken from their homes, often in handcuffs, and into court to face charges of fraud or other wrongdoing. Congress responded with legislation aimed at regulating corporate behavior, but some of the most aggressive action was taken by state regulators, notably New York attorney general Eliot Spitzer, who cracked down on Wall Street investment houses.

The wave of corporate scandals did no favor for the U.S. economy, which was still struggling to recover from a brief recession in 2001 that was worsened by the September 11 terrorist attacks. Although inflation and interest rates remained low and growth increased, albeit sluggishly, the jobless rate hovered near 6 percent, the stock market continued its downward slide, and confidence remained low, pummeled by the corporate accounting scandals, fears of new terrorist attacks, and uncertainty over a possible war in Iraq. By year's end many public and private policymakers were openly concerned that the economy might fall back into recession, and some were even warning about a possible deflation.

Despite a growing federal budget deficit (the result of lower tax revenue and increased spending on national security) and signs that the nation's states and cities were being forced to cut back on services to maintain balanced budgets, President Bush and the Republicans insisted that the best fiscal stimulus was to make the massive tax cuts enacted in 2001 permanent and to make new cuts. (The 2001 tax legislation had specified that the cuts would continue only through the decade.) Democrats argued that more tax cuts would only deepen the federal budget deficit, which they said would lead to higher interest rates and slower economic growth. Democrats, who held a slim majority in the Senate, blocked any further tax cuts, but they were unable to push through their own legislation to help the jobless.

Democrats tried to make the faltering economy the focus of the midterm congressional elections, in which they hoped to solidify their control of the Senate and perhaps even gain control of the House. Instead the Republicans won control of the Senate and increased their margin in the House. It was a stunning defeat for the Democrats, who quickly agreed that they had lost because they failed to offer voters a coherent policy alternative. It was an even more stunning victory for the president, who had put his prestige on the line by campaigning almost nonstop in the weeks running up to the election. The GOP congressional victories bolstered not only Bush's ability to control the legislative agenda but also his own political position going into the 2004 presidential campaign season.

Remarks widely interpreted as racist forced Sen. Trent Lott, R-Miss., to resign his position as GOP leader in December. In the midst of the controversy over Lott, the Supreme Court announced that it would hear arguments in what was considered to be the most important affirmative action case since the 1970s. At issue was whether it was constitutional for a college to consider race and ethnicity as a factor in its admissions policy. In a ruling earlier in the year, the Court issued what many considered to be its most momentous decision in decades regarding separation of church and state. By a 5–4 vote, the Court upheld a voucher plan that used public funds to pay tuition for students at religious schools.

Plan of the Book

These are only some of the topics of national and international interest chosen by the editors of *Historic Documents of 2002*. This edition marks the thirty-first volume of a CQ Press project that began with *Historic Documents of 1972*. The purpose of the series is to give students, librarians, journalists, scholars, and others convenient access to documents on a wide range of topics that set forth some of the most important issues of the year. These primary sources have often been excerpted to highlight the most important parts of lengthy documents written for a specialized audience. In our judgment the official statements, news conferences, speeches, special studies, and court decisions presented here will be of lasting interest.

Each document is preceded by an introduction that provides context and background material and, when relevant, an account of continuing developments during the year. We believe these introductions will become increasingly useful as memories of current events fade.

John Felton and Martha Gottron

CONTENTS

May

June

July

August

report by the General Accounting Office submitted August 30, 2002, to the Senate Committee on Agriculture, Nutrition, and Forestry by Lawrence J. Dyckman, director of natural resources and environment at the GAO.

September

October

CONTENTS

November

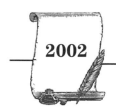

January

SUPREME COURT ON DISABILITIES IN THE WORKPLACE
January 8, 2002

The Supreme Court sharply limited the reach of the federal law protecting Americans with disabilities in the workplace during its 2001–2002 term. In two separate rulings, decided unanimously, the Court said the requirement of that law to make "reasonable accommodations" for workers with disabilities did not apply to a woman with carpal tunnel syndrome or to a man willing to take a job knowing that it could put his health at risk. In a third ruling, decided on a 5–4 vote, the court held that the Americans with Disabilities Act (ADA) did not require a company to violate its seniority system to accommodate a disabled worker. In a fourth ruling, the Court said that the ADA did not permit punitive damage awards in lawsuits filed against state and local governments.

Enacted in 1990, the ADA barred discrimination in employment, public services, and public accommodations against people with disabilities that "substantially impaired" their ability to perform "major life activities." Employers were prohibited from discriminating against people with disabilities who could, with "reasonable accommodation," perform a job. But the broadly phrased law left open to interpretation the meaning of "substantially impaired," "reasonable accommodation," and even "disability," and tens of thousands of complaints alleging discrimination were filed with the U.S. Equal Employment Opportunity Commission (EEOC) during the 1990s.

The first cases delineating the definition of disability and the scope of the protections afforded workers under the law reached the Court in 1999. In a trio of cases, the Court ruled that people with physical disabilities who could function normally with medicine or corrective devices such as glasses or hearing aids could not typically be considered "disabled" under the disability law and were thus not entitled to its protections against discrimination. Those decisions excluded from the act's protections millions of working Americans with a wide range of relatively common impairments, from diabetes and high blood pressure to vision and hearing problems and some forms of depression and anxiety. (Definition of disability, Historic Documents of 1999, p. 317)

The four cases decided in the 2001–2002 term were likely to affect millions more workers. Employers generally expressed relief that the Court was interpreting the ADA narrowly, but disability rights advocates were dismayed. "This is obviously a court that is not reading the ADA as expansively as people in the disability community would like or as major supporters in Congress thought it would be read," said Sam Bagenstos, a professor at Harvard Law School who represented the losing claimant in one of the cases. At least one justice suggested that it was Congress, not the Court, that was to blame. Justice Sandra Day O'Connor reportedly told a conference of business lawyers in March that the ADA was one of those laws that left "uncertainties as to what Congress had in mind."

Carpal Tunnel Disability

The first case to be decided, Toyota Motor Manufacturing, Kentucky, Inc. v. Williams, *involved a woman, Ella Williams, who had developed carpal tunnel syndrome, a repetitive motion disorder, in her hands and arms while working on an assembly line at a Toyota plant in Georgetown, Kentucky. The plant initially accommodated her disability by moving her to a job inspecting paint, but that job eventually changed to include wiping cars with a highlighting oil as they passed on an assembly line. That job exacerbated Williams's repetitive motion injuries, so she asked to return to her paint inspection job. When the company refused, she sued under the ADA.*

A federal court dismissed her suit, but a federal appeals court in Cincinnati ruled in her favor, holding that Williams met the definition of "disabled" because of her inability to do manual work on the assembly line. Toyota appealed to the Supreme Court.

Writing for the unanimous court on January 8, 2002, Justice O'Connor said that the appeals court had erred in determining that Williams was "substantially limited" in performing manual tasks when it considered only workplace tasks. The central question was "whether the claimant is unable to perform the variety of tasks central to most people's daily lives, not whether the claimant is unable to perform the tasks associated with her specific job." Household chores, bathing, and brushing one's teeth were the sorts of daily manual tasks that O'Connor said the appeals court should have evaluated in determining whether Williams was disabled within the meaning of the ADA.

"To be substantially limited in performing manual tasks, an individual must have an impairment that prevents or severely restricts the individual from doing activities that are of central importance to most people's daily lives," O'Connor wrote. Noting that many people recover completely from carpal tunnel syndrome, O'Connor also said the impact of the impairment must be "permanent or long-term."

Organizations representing the disabled, employees, and employers all agreed that the decision would make it much more difficult for people with workplace disability claims to win protection under the ADA. Christopher

Collins, a lawyer with a New York firm that represented businesses in ADA cases, told the Washington Post that the Court's ruling "implicitly recognized the legitimacy" of employer's skepticism about disability claims that arose from job-related injuries. "To be disabled, someone has to be disabled outside the workplace as well. In that sense, [the ruling] raises the bar and will make it more difficult for plaintiffs to demonstrate they are disabled and protected by the ADA."

Corporate Paternalism or Common Sense?

In the second case decided by a unanimous vote, the Supreme Court ruled June 11 that the ADA did not require employers to hire disabled workers whose own health or safety would be jeopardized on the job. The ruling was a substantial setback for disability rights advocates who said one of the key purposes of the ADA was to overcome the excessive corporate paternalism that kept many disabled people out of the workplace "for their own good." It should be up to the employee to decide whether to accept a job that might potentially be dangerous or even fatal, these advocates said.

Mario Echazabal worked for twenty years for a subcontractor in the coker unit of a Chevron oil refinery in El Segundo, California, doing a variety of maintenance jobs. In 1992 he applied for a job with Chevron itself. Echazabal was hired pending the results of a medical examination, but when the exam showed that he had liver disease, Chevron withdrew the offer, citing concerns that the work might exacerbate the disease and even lead to his death. Echazabal continued to work for the subcontractor without apparent ill effect and in 1995 again applied for a job with Chevron. This time Chevron not only rejected him but also pressured the subcontractor to keep Echazabal out of the refinery, saying that his liver condition made him particularly vulnerable to the toxic substances in use at the plant and that repeated exposure could prove fatal.

Echazabal sued Chevron in 1997. A federal district court sided with Chevron, but the U.S. Court of Appeals for the Ninth Circuit backed Echazabal. The appeals court ruled that the EEOC had exceeded its authority when it implemented a regulation allowing companies to refuse to hire disabled workers for jobs that might endanger them. The ADA, the appeals court said, only allowed companies to reject those disabled workers who might pose a threat to others.

A unanimous Supreme Court, however, sided with Chevron, ruling that the EEOC regulation was a reasonable interpretation of the ADA. Writing for the Court in the case of Chevron U.S.A. Inc. v. Echazabal, Justice David H. Souter acknowledged that eliminating paternalism from the workplace was a goal. But, he said, the U.S. Equal Employment Opportunity Commission reasonably interpreted the objective, not as forcing employers "to place disabled workers at a specifically demonstrated risk," but as "trying to get at refusals to give an even break to classes of disabled people while claiming to act for their own good. . . ."

Moreover, Chevron's "reasons for calling the regulation reasonable are unsurprising," Souter said. "Moral concerns aside, it wishes to avoid time *lost to sickness, excessive turnover from medical retirement or death, litigation under state tort law, and the risk of violating" federal and state occupational health and safety laws.*

Disability Rights vs. Seniority Rights

In the third case, a divided Supreme Court tried to walk a careful line between seniority rights and the ADA's requirement that employers make reasonable accommodations for disabled employees. By a 5–4 vote, the Court ruled on April 29 that in most cases where the two rights conflict, the seniority system would prevail unless the disabled worker could show special circumstances that would make an exception to the seniority system reasonable.

The case, U.S. Airways v. Barnett, concerned an airline cargo handler who had injured his back and invoked his seniority rights to move to a less strenuous job in the mailroom. When he learned that another man with more seniority planned to bid for his job, Barnett asked the airline to make an exception to the seniority rules so that he could stay in the job. U.S. Airways refused Barnett's request, arguing that making an exception to its company seniority system was an "undue hardship" that would disrupt the career plans of other workers and that Barnett's request was therefore not "reasonable." Barnett sued.

Writing for the majority, Justice Stephen G. Breyer agreed that in most cases it would be unreasonable to expect a company to violate its seniority system to accommodate the needs of a disabled worker. Noting that he could "find nothing in the [ADA] that suggests Congress intended to undermine seniority systems," Breyer said, "In our view, the seniority system will prevail in the run of cases." However, he said, the employee "remains free" to show that "special circumstances" could make an exception to the seniority system reasonable. Examples of special circumstances might be employers who make such frequent changes in the seniority system that employees' expectations that the system will be followed are diminished, and seniority systems that are already so riddled with exceptions that one more "is unlikely to matter."

Chief Justice William H. Rehnquist and Justices John Paul Stevens and Anthony M. Kennedy joined Breyer. Justice O'Connor concurred but wrote a separate opinion disagreeing with some of Breyer's reasoning. The four dissenters represented the two extremes in the case. Justice Antonin Scalia, joined by Justice Clarence Thomas, argued that the ADA did not require employers to make changes in unrelated employment policies such as seniority system; Justices Souter and Ruth Bader Ginsburg argued that the employer should be required to show that an exception to the seniority system to accommodate a disabled person was an undue hardship, rather than the employees having to show special circumstances that make the exception reasonable.

Bar on Punitive Damages

In one of the last cases of the term, the Supreme Court ruled that the ADA did not require states and local governments to pay punitive damages *for violations of the law, although they could be ordered to pay compensatory damages. The case, Barnes V. Gorman, involved a paraplegic who was arrested after an argument with a nightclub bouncer in Kansas City, Missouri. The man was injured when he was transported to the city jail in a police van that was not equipped to accommodate the disabled, and he sued the city, alleging that his injuries had made it impossible for him to continue in his full-time job. A jury awarded him $1 million in compensatory damages and $1.2 million in punitive damages. The Supreme Court overturned the punitive damages.*

The nine justices agreed that Gorman was not entitled to punitive damages in the case but did not agree on the reasoning. Writing the majority opinion, which five other justices signed, Justice Scalia said that the ADA did not specifically permit punitive awards against state or local governments and that allowing them "could well be disastrous" for state budgets. He also argued that Congress conditioned federal funding to the states and local governments on their agreement to abide by the ADA and suggested that states would not have been willing to enter such a contract had they thought they could be liable for punitive damage awards.

Following are excerpts from the case of Toyota Motor Manufacturing, Kentucky, Inc. v. Williams, *in which the Supreme Court unanimously ruled January 8, 2002, that a woman suffering from carpal tunnel syndrome that affected her ability to do her job but not other major life activities did not meet the definition of disabled under the Americans with Disabilities Act.*

The document was obtained from the Internet at supct.law .cornell.edu/supct/html/00-1089.ZS.html; accessed September 10, 2002.

No. 00–1089

Toyota Motor Manufacturing, Kentucky, Inc., Petitioner *v.* Ella Williams	On Writ of Certiorari to the United States Court of Appeals for the Sixth Circuit

[January 8, 2002]

JUSTICE O'CONNOR delivered the opinion of the Court.

Under the Americans with Disabilities Act of 1990 (ADA or Act), a physical impairment that "substantially limits one or more . . . major life activities" is a "disability." Respondent, claiming to be disabled because of her carpal tunnel syndrome and other related impairments, sued petitioner, her former employer, for failing to provide her with a reasonable accommodation as

required by the ADA. The District Court granted summary judgment to petitioner, finding that respondent's impairments did not substantially limit any
of her major life activities. The Court of Appeals for the Sixth Circuit reversed,
finding that the impairments substantially limited respondent in the major life
activity of performing manual tasks, and therefore granting partial summary
judgment to respondent on the issue of whether she was disabled under the
ADA. We conclude that the Court of Appeals did not apply the proper standard
in making this determination because it analyzed only a limited class of manual tasks and failed to ask whether respondent's impairments prevented or restricted her from performing tasks that are of central importance to most
people's daily lives.

I

Respondent began working at petitioner's automobile manufacturing plant
in Georgetown, Kentucky, in August 1990. She was soon placed on an engine
fabrication assembly line, where her duties included work with pneumatic
tools. Use of these tools eventually caused pain in respondent's hands, wrists,
and arms. She sought treatment at petitioner's in-house medical service, where
she was diagnosed with bilateral carpal tunnel syndrome and bilateral ten-
dinitis. Respondent consulted a personal physician who placed her on permanent work restrictions that precluded her from lifting more than 20 pounds
or from "frequently lifting or carrying of objects weighing up to 10 pounds,"
engaging in "constant repetitive . . . flexion or extension of [her] wrists or
elbows," performing "overhead work," or using "vibratory or pneumatic
tools."

In light of these restrictions, for the next two years petitioner assigned
respondent to various modified duty jobs. Nonetheless, respondent missed
some work for medical leave, and eventually filed a claim under the Kentucky
Workers' Compensation Act. The parties settled this claim, and respondent returned to work. She was unsatisfied by petitioner's efforts to accommodate
her work restrictions, however, and responded by bringing an action in the
United States District Court for the Eastern District of Kentucky alleging that
petitioner had violated the ADA by refusing to accommodate her disability.
That suit was also settled, and as part of the settlement, respondent returned
to work in December 1993.

Upon her return, petitioner placed respondent on a team in Quality Control
Inspection Operations (QCIO). QCIO is responsible for four tasks: (1) "assembly paint"; (2) "paint second inspection"; (3) "shell body audit"; and (4) "ED surface repair." Respondent was initially placed on a team that performed only
the first two of these tasks, and for a couple of years, she rotated on a weekly
basis between them. In assembly paint, respondent visually inspected painted
cars moving slowly down a conveyor. . . . Paint second inspection required
team members to use their hands to wipe each painted car with a glove as
it moved along a conveyor. The parties agree that respondent was physically capable of performing both of these jobs and that her performance was
satisfactory.

During the fall of 1996, petitioner announced that it wanted QCIO employees to be able to rotate through all four of the QCIO processes. Respondent therefore received training for the shell body audit job, in which team members apply a highlight oil to the hood, fender, doors, rear quarter panel, and trunk of passing cars at a rate of approximately one car per minute. The highlight oil has the viscosity of salad oil, and employees spread it on cars with a sponge attached to a block of wood. After they wipe each car with the oil, the employees visually inspect it for flaws. Wiping the cars required respondent to hold her hands and arms up around shoulder height for several hours at a time.

A short while after the shell body audit job was added to respondent's rotations, she began to experience pain in her neck and shoulders. Respondent again sought care at petitioner's in-house medical service, where she was diagnosed with myotendinitis bilateral periscapular, an inflammation of the muscles and tendons around both of her shoulder blades; myotendinitis and myositis bilateral forearms with nerve compression causing median nerve irritation; and thoracic outlet compression, a condition that causes pain in the nerves that lead to the upper extremities. Respondent requested that petitioner accommodate her medical conditions by allowing her to return to doing only her original two jobs in QCIO, which respondent claimed she could still perform without difficulty.

The parties disagree about what happened next. According to respondent, petitioner refused her request and forced her to continue working in the shell body audit job, which caused her even greater physical injury. According to petitioner, respondent simply began missing work on a regular basis. Regardless, it is clear that on December 6, 1996, the last day respondent worked at petitioner's plant, she was placed under a no-work-of-any-kind restriction by her treating physicians. On January 27, 1997, respondent received a letter from petitioner that terminated her employment, citing her poor attendance record.

Respondent filed a charge of disability discrimination with the Equal Employment Opportunity Commission (EEOC). After receiving a right to sue letter, respondent filed suit against petitioner in the United States District Court for the Eastern District of Kentucky. Her complaint alleged that petitioner had violated the ADA and the Kentucky Civil Rights Act by failing to reasonably accommodate her disability and by terminating her employment. . . .

Respondent based her claim that she was "disabled" under the ADA on the ground that her physical impairments substantially limited her in (1) manual tasks; (2) housework; (3) gardening; (4) playing with her children; (5) lifting; and (6) working, all of which, she argued, constituted major life activities under the Act. Respondent also argued, in the alternative, that she was disabled under the ADA because she had a record of a substantially limiting impairment and because she was regarded as having such an impairment.

After petitioner filed a motion for summary judgment and respondent filed a motion for partial summary judgment on her disability claims, the District Court granted summary judgment to petitioner. The court found that respondent had not been disabled, as defined by the ADA, at the time of petitioner's alleged refusal to accommodate her, and that she had therefore not been covered by the Act's protections or by the Kentucky Civil Rights Act, which is construed consistently with the ADA. The District Court held that respondent had suffered from a physical impairment, but that the impairment did not qualify as a disability because it had not "substantially limit[ed]" any "major life activit[y]." The court rejected respondent's arguments that gardening, doing housework, and playing with children are major life activities. Although the court agreed that performing manual tasks, lifting, and working are major life activities, it found the evidence insufficient to demonstrate that respondent had been substantially limited in lifting or working. The court found respondent's claim that she was substantially limited in performing manual tasks to be "irretrievably contradicted by [respondent's] continual insistence that she could perform the tasks in assembly [paint] and paint [second] inspection without difficulty." The court also found no evidence that respondent had had a record of a substantially limiting impairment, or that petitioner had regarded her as having such an impairment. . . .

Respondent appealed all but the gardening, housework, and playing-with-children rulings. The Court of Appeals for the Sixth Circuit reversed the District Court's ruling on whether respondent was disabled at the time she sought an accommodation, but affirmed the District Court's rulings on respondent's FMLA [Family and Medical Leave Act of 1993] and wrongful termination claims. The Court of Appeals held that in order for respondent to demonstrate that she was disabled due to a substantial limitation in the ability to perform manual tasks at the time of her accommodation request, she had to "show that her manual disability involve[d] a 'class' of manual activities affecting the ability to perform tasks at work." Respondent satisfied this test, according to the Court of Appeals, because her ailments "prevent[ed] her from doing the tasks associated with certain types of manual assembly line jobs, manual product handling jobs and manual building trade jobs (painting, plumbing, roofing, etc.) that require the gripping of tools and repetitive work with hands and arms extended at or above shoulder levels for extended periods of time." In reaching this conclusion, the court disregarded evidence that respondent could "ten[d] to her personal hygiene [and] carr[y] out personal or household chores," finding that such evidence "does not affect a determination that her impairment substantially limit[ed] her ability to perform the range of manual tasks associated with an assembly line job." Because the Court of Appeals concluded that respondent had been substantially limited in performing manual tasks and, for that reason, was entitled to partial summary judgment on the issue of whether she was disabled under the Act, it found that it did not need to determine whether respondent had been substantially limited in the major life activities of lifting or working, or whether she had had a "record of" a disability or had been "regarded as" disabled.

We granted certiorari to consider the proper standard for assessing whether an individual is substantially limited in performing manual tasks. We now reverse the Court of Appeals' decision to grant partial summary judgment to respondent on the issue whether she was substantially limited in performing manual tasks at the time she sought an accommodation. We express no opinion on the working, lifting, or other arguments for disability status that were preserved below but which were not ruled upon by the Court of Appeals.

II

The ADA requires covered entities, including private employers, to provide "reasonable accommodations to the known physical or mental limitations of an otherwise qualified individual with a disability who is an applicant or employee, unless such covered entity can demonstrate that the accommodation would impose an undue hardship.". . . The Act defines a "qualified individual with a disability" as "an individual with a disability who, with or without reasonable accommodation, can perform the essential functions of the employment position that such individual holds or desires." In turn, a "disability" is:

> "(A) a physical or mental impairment that substantially limits one or more of the major life activities of such individual;
> "(B) a record of such an impairment; or
> "(C) being regarded as having such an impairment."

To qualify as disabled under subsection (A) of the ADA's definition of disability, a claimant must initially prove that he or she has a physical or mental impairment. The Rehabilitation Act regulations issued by the Department of Health, Education, and Welfare (HEW) in 1977, which appear without change in the current regulations issued by the Department of Health and Human Services, define "physical impairment," the type of impairment relevant to this case, to mean "any physiological disorder or condition, cosmetic disfigurement, or anatomical loss affecting one or more of the following body systems: neurological; musculoskeletal; special sense organs; respiratory, including speech organs; cardiovascular; reproductive, digestive, genito-urinary; hemic and lymphatic; skin; and endocrine.". . .

Merely having an impairment does not make one disabled for purposes of the ADA. Claimants also need to demonstrate that the impairment limits a major life activity. The HEW Rehabilitation Act regulations provide a list of examples of "major life activities," that includes "walking, seeing, hearing," and, as relevant here, "performing manual tasks."

To qualify as disabled, a claimant must further show that the limitation on the major life activity is "substantia[l]." Unlike "physical impairment" and "major life activities," the HEW regulations do not define the term "substantially limits.". . . The EEOC, therefore, has created its own definition for purposes of the ADA. According to the EEOC regulations, "substantially limit[ed]" means "[u]nable to perform a major life activity that the average person in the general population can perform"; or "[s]ignificantly restricted as to the condition, manner or duration under which an individual can perform a particular major life activity as compared to the condition, manner, or duration under which the average person in the general population can perform that same major life activity." In determining whether an individual is substantially limited in a major life activity, the regulations instruct that the following factors should be considered: "[t]he nature and severity of the impairment;

[t]he duration or expected duration of the impairment; and [t]he permanent or long-term impact, or the expected permanent or long-term impact of or resulting from the impairment."

III

. . . The parties do not dispute that respondent's medical conditions, which include carpal tunnel syndrome, myotendinitis, and thoracic outlet compression, amount to physical impairments. The relevant question, therefore, is whether the Sixth Circuit correctly analyzed whether these impairments substantially limited respondent in the major life activity of performing manual tasks. Answering this requires us to address an issue about which the EEOC regulations are silent: what a plaintiff must demonstrate to establish a substantial limitation in the specific major life activity of performing manual tasks.

Our consideration of this issue is guided first and foremost by the words of the disability definition itself. "[S]ubstantially" in the phrase "substantially limits" suggests "considerable" or "to a large degree.". . . The word "substantial" thus clearly precludes impairments that interfere in only a minor way with the performance of manual tasks from qualifying as disabilities.

"Major" in the phrase "major life activities" means important. . . . "Major life activities" thus refers to those activities that are of central importance to daily life. In order for performing manual tasks to fit into this category–a category that includes such basic abilities as walking, seeing, and hearing—the manual tasks in question must be central to daily life. If each of the tasks included in the major life activity of performing manual tasks does not independently qualify as a major life activity, then together they must do so.

That these terms need to be interpreted strictly to create a demanding standard for qualifying as disabled is confirmed by the first section of the ADA, which lays out the legislative findings and purposes that motivate the Act. When it enacted the ADA in 1990, Congress found that "some 43,000,000 Americans have one or more physical or mental disabilities." If Congress intended everyone with a physical impairment that precluded the performance of some isolated, unimportant, or particularly difficult manual task to qualify as disabled, the number of disabled Americans would surely have been much higher. . . .

We therefore hold that to be substantially limited in performing manual tasks, an individual must have an impairment that prevents or severely restricts the individual from doing activities that are of central importance to most people's daily lives. The impairment's impact must also be permanent or long-term.

It is insufficient for individuals attempting to prove disability status under this test to merely submit evidence of a medical diagnosis of an impairment. Instead, the ADA requires those "claiming the Act's protection . . . to prove a disability by offering evidence that the extent of the limitation [caused by their impairment] in terms of their own experience . . . is substantial." That the Act defines "disability" "with respect to an individual," makes clear that Congress intended the existence of a disability to be determined in such a case-by-case manner. . . .

An individualized assessment of the effect of an impairment is particularly necessary when the impairment is one whose symptoms vary widely from person to person. Carpal tunnel syndrome, one of respondent's impairments, is just such a condition. While cases of severe carpal tunnel syndrome are characterized by muscle atrophy and extreme sensory deficits, mild cases generally do not have either of these effects and create only intermittent symptoms of numbness and tingling. Studies have further shown that, even without surgical treatment, one quarter of carpal tunnel cases resolve in one month, but that in 22 percent of cases, symptoms last for eight years or longer. . . . Given these large potential differences in the severity and duration of the effects of carpal tunnel syndrome, an individual's carpal tunnel syndrome diagnosis, on its own, does not indicate whether the individual has a disability within the meaning of the ADA.

IV

The Court of Appeals' analysis of respondent's claimed disability suggested that in order to prove a substantial limitation in the major life activity of performing manual tasks, a "plaintiff must show that her manual disability involves a 'class' of manual activities," and that those activities "affec[t] the ability to perform tasks at work." Both of these ideas lack support.

The Court of Appeals relied on our opinion in *Sutton v. United Air Lines, Inc.* [1999], for the idea that a "class" of manual activities must be implicated for an impairment to substantially limit the major life activity of performing manual tasks. But Sutton said only that "[w]hen the major life activity under consideration is that of working, the statutory phrase 'substantially limits' requires . . . that plaintiffs allege that they are unable to work in a broad class of jobs." (emphasis added). Because of the conceptual difficulties inherent in the argument that working could be a major life activity, we have been hesitant to hold as much, and we need not decide this difficult question today. In Sutton, we noted that even assuming that working is a major life activity, a claimant would be required to show an inability to work in a "broad range of jobs," rather than a specific job. But Sutton did not suggest that a class-based analysis should be applied to any major life activity other than working. Nor do the EEOC regulations. . . . Nothing in the text of the Act, our previous opinions, or the regulations suggests that a class-based framework should apply outside the context of the major life activity of working.

While the Court of Appeals in this case addressed the different major life activity of performing manual tasks, its analysis circumvented Sutton by focusing on respondent's inability to perform manual tasks associated only with her job. This was error. When addressing the major life activity of performing manual tasks, the central inquiry must be whether the claimant is unable to perform the variety of tasks central to most people's daily lives, not whether the claimant is unable to perform the tasks associated with her specific job. Otherwise, Sutton's restriction on claims of disability based on a substantial limitation in working will be rendered meaningless because an inability to perform a specific job always can be recast as an inability to perform a "class" of tasks associated with that specific job.

There is also no support in the Act, our previous opinions, or the regulations for the Court of Appeals' idea that the question of whether an impairment constitutes a disability is to be answered only by analyzing the effect of the impairment in the workplace. Indeed, the fact that the Act's definition of "disability" applies not only to Title I of the Act, which deals with employment, but also to the other portions of the Act, which deal with subjects such as public transportation, and privately provided public accommodations, demonstrates that the definition is intended to cover individuals with disabling impairments regardless of whether the individuals have any connection to a workplace.

Even more critically, the manual tasks unique to any particular job are not necessarily important parts of most people's lives. As a result, occupation-specific tasks may have only limited relevance to the manual task inquiry. In this case, "repetitive work with hands and arms extended at or above shoulder levels for extended periods of time," the manual task on which the Court of Appeals relied, is not an important part of most people's daily lives. The court, therefore, should not have considered respondent's inability to do such manual work in her specialized assembly line job as sufficient proof that she was substantially limited in performing manual tasks.

At the same time, the Court of Appeals appears to have disregarded the very type of evidence that it should have focused upon. It treated as irrelevant "[t]he fact that [respondent] can . . . ten[d] to her personal hygiene [and] carr[y] out personal or household chores." Ibid. Yet household chores, bathing, and brushing one's teeth are among the types of manual tasks of central importance to people's daily lives, and should have been part of the assessment of whether respondent was substantially limited in performing manual tasks.

The District Court noted that at the time respondent sought an accommodation from petitioner, she admitted that she was able to do the manual tasks required by her original two jobs in QCIO. In addition, according to respondent's deposition testimony, even after her condition worsened, she could still brush her teeth, wash her face, bathe, tend her flower garden, fix breakfast, do laundry, and pick up around the house. The record also indicates that her medical conditions caused her to avoid sweeping, to quit dancing, to occasionally seek help dressing, and to reduce how often she plays with her children, gardens, and drives long distances. But these changes in her life did not amount to such severe restrictions in the activities that are of central importance to most people's daily lives that they establish a manual-task disability as a matter of law. On this record, it was therefore inappropriate for the Court of Appeals to grant partial summary judgment to respondent on the issue whether she was substantially limited in performing manual tasks, and its decision to do so must be reversed. . . .

Accordingly, we reverse the Court of Appeals' judgment granting partial summary judgment to respondent and remand the case for further proceedings consistent with this opinion.

So ordered.

UNITED NATIONS REPORT ON AFGHANISTAN
January 21, 2002

Afghanistan in 2002 experienced its first full year of relative peace in more than two decades. One year after a U.S.-led invasion drove the Islamist Taliban regime and the al Qaeda terrorist network from power, Afghanistan was for all practical purposes a ward of the international community, dependent on aid agencies for emergency relief and long-term reconstruction and on the United States and its allies for security. A new Afghan government struggled to gain its footing even as warlords controlled much of the countryside, and millions of refugees returned to find their homes destroyed from decades of conflict.

By year's end, Afghanistan's future was far from clear. A reconstruction plan laid out by the United Nations in January suggested that, with substantial and sustained international support, Afghanistan could rebuild and regain a semblance of normal life as a country within a decade. But many experts—as well as ordinary Afghans—feared that Afghanistan could just as easily fall back into the cycle of regional and ethnic rivalries that had made it a breeding ground for international terrorism. In a year-end summary of the situation, the Economist *magazine said "things have not got better so much as less bad."* (Background, Historic Documents of 2001, pp. 691, 880–884)

Afghanistan's Centers of Power

Postwar Afghanistan was under the control of numerous power centers— and therefore of none of them. In theory, Afghanistan had a new "transitional" government headed by Hamid Karzai, a regional leader chosen for the post by his peers. But while Karzai commanded great respect on the international stage, his budding government had only limited authority in Kabul, the capital, and virtually no real influence in the rest of the country. By contrast, numerous warlords and regional governors ruled much of the countryside through the power of the gun; only a few of them cooperated with the Kabul government—and only whenever it was convenient to do so.

The only power with the ability to operate nearly unchallenged through-out the country was the United States military, which maintained some 9,000 combat troops and scores of aircraft in Afghanistan, at a monthly cost of about $1 billion. But Afghanistan had a long history of resisting out-side powers, and so U.S. troops were greeted in most places with suspicion and in many places with outright hostility. The International Security Assistance Force (ISAF), a UN-mandated peacekeeping force of about 4,500 troops, was limited to Kabul and environs, and numerous attempts to broaden its responsibilities sank under objections from the countries whose support was needed to finance and man it. The United Nations, through its local mission (the United Nations Assistance Mission in Afghanistan), advised the Karzai government and attempted to coordinate international aid to the country. In addition, a few dozen private and governmental agen-cies provided emergency humanitarian and long-term reconstruction aid.

Less visible, but still very influential, were Afghanistan's neighbors, sev-eral of which had developed a long-term habit of interfering in the country's affairs. The most active neighbors were Pakistan, which through its intelli-gence service continued to play Afghanistan's factions against each other, and Iran, which maintained strong links to western Afghanistan, especially to the ethnic Tajiks of Persian descent. Finally, there still were pockets of resistance from fighters of the former Taliban regime and of Osama bin Laden's al Qaeda terrorist network. Most of these fighters were in the moun-tains southwest of Kabul and in the mountainous region of the Afghanistan-Pakistan border.

Reflecting on this amalgam, and especially the continuing threat of the regional warlords, Human Rights Watch reported in November: "Far from emerging as a stable democracy, Afghanistan remains a fractured, undem-ocratic collection of 'fiefdoms' in which warlords are free to intimidate, extort, and repress local populations, while almost completely denying basic freedoms. Afghanistan, a textbook definition of a failed state under the Taliban, now runs the risk of becoming a state that fails its people, except this time on the international community's watch."

Agreement on a New Government

By far the most significant political development in Afghanistan during the year was a loya jirga, a traditional assembly, that for eleven days in June debated key issues facing the country and elected Karzai as president of a "transitional" government. The loya jirga was the second step of a multi-stage process set in motion by an agreement December 5, 2001, among lead-ing Afghan figures who met under UN auspices near Bonn, Germany. The first step had been the appointment of an interim government, headed by Karzai, which took office on December 22, 2001. That interim government was to be succeeded by the transitional government, which could hold office for two years, during which another loya jirga would be called to draft a per-manent constitution by December 2003. Elections were then to be held by June 2004 for a fully democratic government.

The loya jirga was the closest Afghanistan had ever come to democ-

racy. For several weeks beforehand, government officials and international observers had traveled the country supervising the selection of delegates representing nearly all the country's ethnic, political, and social factions. Meeting in tents supplied by the German government, the 1,600 delegates assembled on June 11 and immediately launched into a spirited debate, voicing the grievances and frustrations of a nation that had been at war for two decades. Many delegates expressed worries about the continuing influence of warlords in much of the country, while some of the 200 women delegates said too little had been done to undo the suppression of women under the previous Taliban regime.

Extensive maneuvering behind the scenes led to Karzai's overwhelming election as president on June 13. That selection left some of Karzai's fellow Pashtuns, the majority ethnic group, resentful of a process they said gave too much influence to outside powers (notably the United States) and to ethnic Tajiks whose armies controlled much of northern Afghanistan. The loya jirga was supposed to have selected a parliament and Karzai's cabinet, but delegates spent so much time arguing over procedures and other matters that Karzai cut the session short on June 21 and later appointed his own cabinet. Critics said the loya jirga process was flawed in many respects, most importantly the fact that key decisions were made in secret negotiations among powerful officials rather than in the tent where delegates were assembled.

Karzai's ability to govern was hampered by his dependence on other countries for nearly all government income and his lack of direct influence in most of the country outside Kabul. Although Karzai was an enormously popular figure able to win promises of aid from Washington, London, and other Western capitals, he was often dismissed within his country as the "mayor of Kabul."

Maintaining Security

It was perhaps inevitable that the fundamental challenge for Afghanistan, and the outside actors working there, was maintaining security, both for the new government and for ordinary Afghan citizens. Twenty-three years of conflict could not, and did not, come to a complete end after the Taliban regime collapsed in December 2001 in the face of an assault from the United States and its allies. Powerful warlords were determined to retain their influence and extend it if possible. Millions of Afghan men carried weapons, among them several thousand Taliban and al Qaeda fighters who had escaped the U.S.-led coalition and dispersed into the countryside. Moreover, ethnic and regional tensions that had fueled the previous decades of conflict remained as serious as ever and threatened to overwhelm the new government's hopes for national unity and stability.

Karzai's interim government was less than two months old when it faced the first of many frontal attacks. The aviation and tourism minister was killed in February by government security officials in what Karzai angrily called a personal vendetta. During the rest of the year several regional governors appointed by Karzai fought extensive battles with warlords.

On July 6 Karzai's vice president, Haji Abdul Qadir, was assassinated by unknown assailants in the southern city of Kandahar. That event prompted the United States to take over the role of providing personal security for Karzai. A series of bombings in Kabul during the late summer culminated with two major incidents within a few hours of each other on September 5: a car bomb exploded in Kabul, killing thirty people, and an assassination attempt was made on Karzai while he was visiting Kandahar. Karzai escaped unhurt and played down the danger he faced, but the combination of events clearly unnerved both his government and the international community.

For much of the year a principal security issue facing the world's major powers was whether to expand the ISAF peacekeeping force beyond Kabul and its vicinity. The 4,500-strong force operated under a UN Security Council mandate but was not an official UN peacekeeping operation. It began operations in December 2001 under British command, but Turkey took over command during the summer. More than a dozen countries contributed troops and equipment.

The force had been limited to the immediate area of the capital at the insistence of the United States, which said it did not want any interference with its military operations in the Afghan hinterlands and cited the impracticality of protecting such a large country with a small peacekeeping force. The Bush administration also said its priority was to train and equip an Afghan army to take over security responsibilities. In effect, the decision to limit ISAF's mandate left security for most of Afghanistan in the hands of local warlords, many of whom had been key combatants in the country's previous two decades of conflict. The United States further reinforced some of the warlords by training their forces and turning over to them tons of weapons and ammunition captured from former Taliban and al Qaeda fighters.

Citing the danger posed by conflict among the warlords, Karzai on January 30 asked the UN Security Council to expand the peacekeeping force to other regions. Karzai won the support of UN Secretary General Kofi Annan, who in March said the world needed to prevent a return to lawlessness and despair in Afghanistan by "ensuring that security is provided throughout the country, and not just in Kabul." But U.S. resistance and the reluctance of other countries to contribute additional peacekeepers to Afghanistan kept the proposal on hold for the rest of the year.

The continuing violence in Afghanistan ultimately led the Bush administration to reconsider its position. In August Pentagon officials said the United States was now willing to support an expanded force, provided that other countries supplied the money and troops for it. By mid-November the administration position had softened even further. Zalmay Khalilzad, President Bush's special envoy for Afghanistan, announced on November 15 that Washington was prepared to contribute an unspecified number of troops to an expanded peacekeeping force that would operate in other cities and regions. "I think that would facilitate reconstruction, that would give people a sense of confidence," Khalilzad said. Congress also pushed the adminis-

tration on the issue, adopting legislation in November authorizing $3.3 bil-
lion over four years for aid to Afghanistan, including $1 billion for an ex-
panded peacekeeping force. That bill contained no actual appropriations,
however.

At a NATO summit meeting in Prague on November 20, the Atlantic alliance agreed to provide security "in selected areas" but offered no details.
News reports late in the year indicated that many countries remained reluctant to provide additional troops to the Afghanistan force. Germany and
the Netherlands were scheduled to assume Turkey's leadership of the international force in February 2003.

As an alternative to an expanded ISAF, Pentagon officials in late November said teams of U.S. combat soldiers, civilian affairs specialists, and
soldiers from the new Afghan army would be deployed around the country to improve security and aid in reconstruction programs. Reporting on
that decision, the Washington Post said the initiative demonstrated "an expanded U.S. military commitment" to rebuilding Afghanistan and represented "a tacit admission that concerns about security continue to inhibit
reconstruction efforts." Officials of some international aid agencies expressed concern about the plan, however, saying that the involvement of the
U.S. military in reconstruction efforts could compromise the perceived neutrality of aid workers in the country.

Parallel to the international peacekeeping issue was a U.S.-led program
to build a new national army for Afghanistan—the first since the collapse
of a Soviet-backed regime in 1992. Annan, of the UN, called the creation of
an army "the first reconstruction project" because of the compelling need to
provide security throughout the country.

The United States in February began training about 500 soldiers to form
a national guard that was to be based in Kabul, with the principal role of
protecting the government. Then in April U.S. Army Special Forces and
French troops began training units for a national army, which ultimately
was to reach a force of 70,000. By early October about 1,200 recruits in three
battalions had graduated from the ten-week courses. Pentagon officials
established a goal of training 13,000 recruits by the end of 2003. Some
observers noted that the building of an army posed a possible danger to the
civilian government. Karzai declared himself the commander in chief, but
the de facto army commander was defense minister Mohammad Fahim, an
ethnic Tajik and one of the leading generals of the former Northern Alliance
guerrilla force. In a July 30 report, the International Crisis Group (a think
tank based in Brussels) said Fahim's willingness to accept orders from
Karzai "appears questionable" because he was determined to consolidate
his own military power.

Germany was responsible for creation of a national police force, with a
goal of training more than 1,500 officers, including women. The difficulty of
establishing a credible police force was made apparent in mid-November
when police in Kabul fired into groups of students protesting living conditions at the local university, killing three students and wounding about two
dozen others.

Hunting Taliban and al Qaeda Forces

The efforts to bring security to Afghanistan took place even as the United States continued its search-and-destroy campaign against remnants of the Taliban and al Qaeda forces. This work was slow and frustrating because thousands of armed fighters from the two factions had dispersed into Afghanistan's cities and countryside in late 2001. During the early stages of the campaign, the United States relied heavily on armed Afghan factions to root out Taliban and al Qaeda fighters hiding in remote areas. The Pakistan military had responsibility for hunting down al Qaeda fighters who had taken refuge in the caves and mountains on the Pakistan side of the border between Afghanistan and Pakistan. But these efforts bore little fruit, and by late summer the Pentagon had switched to a more intensive use of U.S. ground forces to locate Taliban and al Qaeda forces. (Al Qaeda issues, p. 990)

Late in the year U.S. officials said its campaign against the Taliban and al Qaeda fighters was nearing a successful conclusion—even though the fate of key leaders of those organizations was unknown, notably al Qaeda's head, Osama bin Laden. The U.S. claim of success also was contradicted by an upsurge in attacks against American bases and military personnel during the latter part of the year. The attacks—generally the late-night firing of Soviet-made surface-to-surface rockets—caused little damage and rarely wounded anyone. However, the widespread and frequent nature of the attacks appeared to indicate a coordinated resistance, possibly by former Taliban and al Qaeda forces, to the U.S. military presence in Afghanistan.

U.S. credibility was severely undermined by an incident that the Pentagon called a mistake. On July 1 a U.S. combat helicopter fired missiles at a village near Deh Rawud (northwest of Kandahar in south-central Afghanistan) in the belief that hostile fire had come from the vicinity. In fact, villagers were firing rifles in the air to celebrate a wedding—a common local practice. Forty people died and about fifty were wounded in the U.S. assault. The Pentagon at first denied any wrongdoing but eventually accepted responsibility for the killings. Even so, the attack reminded Afghans of their vulnerability to U.S. power and heightened resentment, in some quarters, of outside interference.

Washington's policy of working with—and even arming—regional warlords also was criticized by many observers, including human rights groups. In a November 5 report, for example, Human Rights Watch focused on the western province of Herat. There, the organization said, warlord Ismail Kahn used violence and extortion to terrorize the civilian population, virtually unchecked by the Kabul government, the UN peacekeeping force, or the U.S. military.

Refugees Return by the Thousands

Two decades of war, and more than three years of drought, had devastated Afghanistan and left millions of its citizens homeless, unemployed, sick, and facing starvation. Gathering reliable information about the state of the population was difficult, but the UN's report in January produced a litany of discouraging statistics, among them: an estimated 25 percent of Afghanistan's children died before reaching the age of five, fewer than 5 percent the country's residents had reliable access to safe drinking water; and the vast majority had no access to medical care of any kind.

As the fighting in Afghanistan eased toward the end of 2001, millions of Afghan citizens were refugees in other countries (primarily Pakistan and Iran), and more than 1 million were "internally displaced"—forced from their homes but still living within Afghanistan. Many of these homeless people had been uprooted during the previous two decades of conflict and had been living for years in camps run by the United Nations High Commission on Refugees (UNHCR) and other organizations.

UN officials estimated in January 2002 that about 800,000 refugees would return to Afghanistan during the year, but that estimate fell far short of reality. Lured by the return of relative calm, tens of thousands of refugees and internally displaced people tried to return home during the winter months, despite UN warnings that Afghanistan remained unsafe and was unprepared to deal with them.

Better weather in the spring resulted in a flood of refugees and internally displaced people trying to return home. Between April and June more than 1 million refugees returned to Afghanistan, most of them from Pakistan, overwhelming the capacity of aid agencies to deal with the influx. By year's end the total figures were impressive. According to the UNHCR, 1.8 million refugees returned to Afghanistan during 2002 (more than twice the original estimate); of these, 1.5 million came from Pakistan, 261,000 from Iran, and the rest from elsewhere in Central Asia and other countries. Even with these returns, nearly 4 million Afghans remained as refugees outside their country at the end of 2002, including about 2 million in Iran and 1.5 million in Pakistan.

Also during 2002, according to the UNHCR, about 250,000 internally displaced people returned to their homes with international assistance, and 200,000 returned home on their own. At year's end the UNHCR estimated that more than 700,000 Afghans remained displaced within the country, most of them in the southern provinces, where the drought had been most severe. Thousands of those people had fled their homes during the fighting in 2001; many thousands more were uprooted as a result of ethnic tension following the war, including ethnic Pashtuns who fled from the northern provinces because they were perceived to have been associated with the Taliban.

The good news of refugee returns had a downside, however. The sudden flood of people coming back to Afghanistan overwhelmed international agencies and the new Afghan government and outstripped the available quantities of humanitarian supplies. In addition, an estimated one-third of returning refugees and internally displaced people headed not for their original homes in the countryside but for the cities. Many ended up in Kabul, ballooning the capital's population well beyond capacity. Once there, most refugees were unable to find housing of any kind, in part because more than half the city's housing stock had been destroyed during the wars.

Attempting to discourage urbanization, the UNHCR and other agencies directed most of their relief work toward rural areas.

Thousands of the displaced people tried to make do on their own, scavenging food and finding temporary shelter in cities, in the countryside, or alongside roads. Many others lived in displacement camps. One of the largest, Maslakh, near the western city of Herat, housed about 60,000 people in what a November 14 UN report called "squalid" conditions of "makeshift shelters with just basic food and medicine." About half the people in the camp had been there for almost a year, the UN said.

Largely because of large doses of international relief aid, Afghanistan made it through the winter of 2001–2002 with little starvation. As the year progressed, aid officials said severe hunger was limited to small pockets of Afghanistan, primarily in remote mountainous regions and among traditional nomadic people. But for people in those areas it was small comfort that they were the exception. Journalists reported that some hungry Afghan families resorted to the ultimate act of desperation: selling their children for bags of wheat, beans, and other staples. "What else could I do?" a father who had traded two of his sons for food told the New York Times *in March.*

As the winter of 2002–2003 approached, the World Food Program estimated that 6 million Afghan people were vulnerable to "food insecurity," which meant that they could not be sure of obtaining enough food on a daily basis. About one-third of those people (primarily children and residents of remote areas) were listed as being the most vulnerable and in need of urgent assistance. For 2003 the UNHCR planned to help about 1.2 million refugees and 300,000 internally displaced people return to their homes in Afghanistan.

Rebuilding Society

The United Nations in January estimated that the international community would need to provide $10 billion over five years to begin rebuilding the basics of a civil society there. "The overwhelming majority of Afghans struggle to survive in miserable conditions," the UN said in a report issued January 21. "They are among the poorest and hungriest in the world."

At a conference in Tokyo in January, donor nations and organizations (including the World Bank) pledged $4.5 billion over the next five years, including $1.8 billion for 2002. The United States pledged $297 million toward the 2002 goal, but only about one-third of that amount represented new funding beyond what Washington had already promised. By contrast, the United States during 2002 spent an average of $1 billion each month on its military effort in Afghanistan, a small portion of which went for reconstruction.

No one underestimated the scope of work needed to reconstruct a country that had been systematically bombed and pillaged for more than two decades. However, even veteran aid workers expressed bewilderment at the extent of physical damage to buildings, public facilities, and land in Afghanistan. Not least of the concerns was that international efforts to reconstruct Afghanistan would have to be coordinated with a new, inexperienced *government that barely existed on paper, much less as a unified reality. Another factor was that some foreign governments (notably Japan and Saudi Arabia) were much quicker at promising aid than delivering it. By the end of August only $570 million of the $1.8 million promised for the year actually had been delivered. Ultimately, the full $1.8 billion was committed, but little of it was used to help establish Karzai's government.*

One aspect of the Afghan economy came back to life almost instantly: the cultivation of opium poppies. Afghanistan had been one of the world's major sources of opium before the Taliban succeeded in rooting out most of the production in the late 1990s. Once the Taliban were gone, farmers desperate for a reliable cash crop resumed cultivation of poppies rather than the fruits and grains that traditionally had underpinned Afghanistan's subsistence agriculture.

The problems of reconstruction were perhaps best illustrated by the halting effort to rebuild the nation's roads, nearly all of which had been destroyed as a result of combat, earthquakes, and neglect. Karzai repeatedly noted that all other reconstruction plans were doomed to failure unless Afghanistan had passable roads for the transportation of people and supplies. Despite widespread agreement with that assessment, few roads were in better shape at the end of 2002 than at the beginning of the year.

The single most visible road project—reconstruction of a highway between Kabul and Kandahar—was caught up in disputes between Karzai's government and the Asian Development Bank, which was to subsidize most of the estimated $150 million cost. When that project fell apart in the summer, the U.S. government stepped in and put the Army Corps of Engineers in charge, with additional financing from Japan and Saudi Arabia. In contrast to the halting pace of this and similar projects of Western governments, Iran quickly rebuilt the main road from the Iran-Afghanistan border to the city of Herat, earning Tehran much respect in the western part of the country.

Kabul, the capital, faced a combination of problems. Returning refugees flooded into the city in hopes of finding jobs, more than doubling the population to nearly 3 million and straining the limited supplies of food, housing, and electricity. International aid agencies took over much of the city's habitable housing stock, driving rents beyond the means of local people. The same agencies also hired thousands of Afghans as translators, drivers, and laborers at salaries that local firms and the Afghan government could not match. Confronted with government regulations on private business, many enterprising Afghans simply set up companies under the guise of nonprofit agencies, which were exempt from most taxation and rules. The net result of all these developments was that parts of Kabul began to resemble any other major international city, with fashionable shops and restaurants, while most of the city still lay in ruins, inhabited by impoverished former refugees forced to beg and scavenge for food, clothing, and fuel.

One of the most visible signs of change in Afghanistan was the new freedom of women, at least in theory. During their half-decade in power, the Taliban had enacted strict laws prohibiting girls from attending school and women from working; all females were required to wear cloaks covering their bodies from head to toe. With the collapse of the Taliban government, women suddenly were free again to take part in the country's daily life. Many women were reluctant to exercise this freedom, however—either because of family pressure or out of fear that the Taliban might return. In many areas of the country warlords, religious police, and self-appointed guardians of "civic virtue" harassed women and girls when they appeared in public. Even so, thousands of girls in Kabul and some other areas returned to makeshift schools and a substantial number of Afghan women once again joined their male counterparts in the workforce.

A major problem for Afghanistan's people was the residue of two decades of warfare in the form of unexploded land mines and bombs. Millions of pieces of unexploded and still dangerous ordnance remained scattered throughout the countryside, often buried just beneath the surface. The years of warfare had killed an estimated 2 million Afghans and left tens of thousands wounded; land mines and bombs continued to wound hundreds each week, according to relief organizations. International agencies employed several thousand local people to clear the ordnance—a task estimated to take up to twenty years.

At an international conference held in Oslo on December 17–18, donor nations pledged at least $1.2 billion for reconstruction aid to Afghanistan in 2003. The conference identified road building and the development of schools for girls as among the highest priorities for the year.

The slow pace of international aid for rebuilding the country left many Afghans frustrated, even angry. In numerous interviews with journalists, Afghan citizens recalled that politicians in Washington, London, and other capitals had made many promises when the war against the Taliban was launched in 2001. "We were hopeful that life of the poor Afghan people would change," a police investigator, Abdul Ghani, told the Associated Press in September. "But we are still waiting."

> *Following are excerpts from "Immediate and Transitional Assistance Program for the Afghan People: 2002," a report issued January 21, 2002, by the United Nations detailing the humanitarian relief and long-term reconstruction needs of Afghanistan in the wake of more than two decades of war.*
>
> ***The document was obtained from the Internet at www .reliefweb.int/library/documents/2002/un_afg_21jan.pdf; accessed October 12, 2002.***

I. Introduction

Peace and stability are at last in sight for the Afghan people. While areas of insecurity and volatility still remain, the opportunity to rally

the international community to support a coordinated relief, recovery, reconstruction, return and reintegration effort as reflected in this document, is unique and must be seized.

The devastation caused by two decades of war, missed development opportunities, and widespread human rights abuses, compounded by three years of drought that is likely to continue for another year, will necessitate sustained humanitarian action over the next year to meet the needs of an estimated 9 million Afghans. At the same time, it is now vital that immediate steps are taken to promote a return to normal life and stability and to prepare for longer-term development.

In 2002 the United Nations, international organizations and NGO [nongovernmental organization] partners will continue with a significant humanitarian programme giving millions of Afghans access to essential services. The United Nations and its partners are committed to supporting the Interim Authority in its efforts to lead Afghanistan into a new phase. The UN will strive to respond effectively to the request made in the Bonn Agreement in which the UN was urged to "reaffirm, strengthen and implement their commitment to assist with the rehabilitation, recovery and reconstruction of Afghanistan in coordination with the Interim Authority."

Recovery and the development of durable political solutions go hand in hand. Successful implementation depends on the political process and national ownership. The critical issue will be to ensure the present and future capacity of Afghans to manage recovery and reconstruction in the best interests of all parts of their population. A vital concern will be to reverse the disempowerment of women and to support them in their efforts to rebuild Afghanistan's society and economy. In addition, children must be central to this process of recovery and reconstruction in order to avert the recurrence of conflict and to maximize the chances for sustainable peace for future generations. A commitment for immediate assistance for reconstruction by the international community will be an important incentive. The quick and effective establishment and re-vitalization of basic social services can help engender support for political stability and peace, while political dialogue and reconciliation can help expand on access and opportunities for recovery. Prompt attention to, and action on, longstanding problems of discrimination, exploitation and violation of rights will signal the importance of ensuring all Afghans benefit from the new peace. A tangible "peace dividend" is essential for Afghans to unite around the peace process.

The inter-relationship between humanitarian assistance and longer-term development is critical. Both actions are mutually reinforcing and will need to be addressed concurrently. The availability of humanitarian assistance such as food and non-food items and the launching of agricultural rehabilitation interventions and sustainable livelihoods, for example, will be key to securing the return of refugees and the displaced and enabling poverty-stricken, food insecure populations to invest in productive activities.

In order to meet the immediate and longer-term needs of the people of Afghanistan, and to fulfill the objectives set by Security Council Resolution 1378, the UN is committed to a unified, integrated response. Under the overall leadership of the Special Representative of the Secretary-General (SRSG), the UN will harness its broad expertise across the political, humanitarian and development spectrum, and will ensure a comprehensive approach that includes a broad alliance of the UN system and other partners, including Afghan and international NGOs.

ITAP [Immediate and Transitional Assistance Programme for the Afghan People 2002] is, in itself, an unprecedented document, presenting for the first time a comprehensive approach for relief, recovery, and reconstruction, as well as reintegration needs of the Afghan people in 2002, including the needs of Afghans in neighbouring countries. It covers the period October 2001 to December 2002. As such it incorporates the Donor Alert and the Update issued in September and December 2001 respectively. It also incorporates those initial recovery activities outlined in the Preliminary Needs Assessment carried out by the ADB, the World Bank and UNDP [United Nations Development Programme] (on behalf of UNDG [United Nations Development Group]) which are considered critical for implementation in 2002, and for which there is an agency prepared to assume immediate project responsibility.

While the Preliminary Needs Assessment provides a framework for donor commitments over the next five years, it is not a specific programme with projects identified for immediate funding. Both the Afghan authorities, and donors, will want time to review the Needs Assessment findings, and develop detailed programmes for donor funding. However, many of the activities identified need immediate funding if the Afghan people are to see the 'peace dividend', and the Interim Authority is to have the support it needs to successfully carry out the essential tasks of the coming months. In addition, the humanitarian crisis in Afghanistan is ongoing, and there are major unmet needs, which must be met at the same time as we start on recovery. . . .

The ITAP is a key strategic tool to bring coherence in the assistance response to the Afghan crisis by the UN system as an integrated whole, together with its partners. It demonstrates that the UN is prepared to go beyond "business as usual." As well as defining the overall objectives of the assistance community and sectoral strategies, it presents a summary of the current situation and operating environment, the guiding principles by which the UN and its partners will work and the modalities for coordination and implementation.

II. The Current Situation and Challenges Ahead

The events of 11 September [2001] placed Afghanistan in the forefront of international attention, with unprecedented media coverage not only of the military campaign, but also of the plight of millions of vulnerable Afghans in Afghanistan and neighbouring countries.

The current situation faced by approximately 24 million Afghans in Afghanistan and the approximate 4 million Afghans in neighbouring countries continues to be one of the most dramatic and desperate in the world. The overwhelming majority of Afghans struggle to survive in miserable conditions. They are among the poorest and hungriest in the world. The urgent need to respond to their plight is characterized by an extremely complicated and volatile operating and planning environment.

While the humanitarian challenge is enormous, there is also an unprecedented opportunity for change with the Bonn Peace Agreement, and the establishment of the Interim Authority. We must address the challenges, and seize the opportunity at the same time, thus attempting to close the 'gap' between emergency and development response.

Human Needs

A snapshot of the current situation faced by Afghans is captured below:

- Approximately 9 million Afghans, including over 1 million internally displaced persons are in need of assistance in Afghanistan during the coming 12 months.
- Half of all Afghan children suffer from chronic malnutrition, and one out of every four children dies before reaching the age of five.
- There are some 4 million Afghan refugees, of whom the vast majority are women and children.
- The maternal mortality rate is the second highest in the world with an estimated 16,000 women dying each year from pregnancy-related causes.
- Afghanistan's grain production has fallen by more than 50% in the past two years, its livestock herds are severely depleted and its irrigation systems extensively damaged.
- Only 23 % of the population has access to safe water and only 12% to adequate sanitation.
- Afghans have suffered an abysmal human rights situation for decades. There are particular concerns for children, women and minorities, as well as specific protection concerns faced by civilians as a direct result of military or other action.
- Egregious acts of violence have been perpetrated against women. Women and girls have been excluded from educational opportunities and access to employment.
- 6% of Afghans had access to electricity in 1993, among the lowest consumption in the world.
- The primary road network has seriously deteriorated—1,700 km of 3,000 km needs re-building.
- 50% of urban housing stock is destroyed or damaged in major cities.
- Widespread environmental degradation disproportionately affects the rural poor and women.
- Three years of drought and the onset of winter have further eroded already stretched coping mechanisms. A fourth year of drought is still a possibility with the late onset of rain and snow.
- Over 800 sq km of land is unable to be put to productive use due to being contaminated by landmines and unexploded ordnance (UXO), while 150 to 300 new casualties occur each month as a result of mine/UXO accidents.
- A collapsed education system with extremely low enrolment rates and extreme imbalance between girls and boys combined with a lack of teaching capacity, a shortage of learning material and poor infrastructure.

Operating Environment

The overall operating environment for assistance agencies is rapidly changing. Prior to the 11 September attacks, the humanitarian community was engaged in a complex humanitarian aid operation designed to address the effects of war, drought, economic deterioration and widespread human rights abuses in Afghanistan. As a result of the attacks and subsequent events, the operating environment, which was already difficult, has become extremely volatile and challenging. It is now starting to stabilize, but areas of concern remain. Some of the variables are summarized below.

Consolidation of fledgling institutions of democratic decision-making created by the Bonn process: The establishment of the Interim Authority [the temporary government between December 2001 and June 2002] and eventually the Transitional Authority [which took office in June 2002] are key positive developments. The Interim Authority has the major responsibility for establishing a Loya Jurga and progressing towards a new transitional government. They will do so in the context of establishing fledgling governmental institutions, policing, army reform and a merit based civil service without yet having a fiscal base. Aid agencies are engaged in a rapid process of transition with a strong commitment to working with, and supporting the Interim Authority.

Variable security conditions: While the prospects for stability at the central level are encouraging, pockets of volatility and insecurity remain. A degree of security will be assured by the deployment of the International Security Assistance Force (ISAF) in and around Kabul, but other areas of the country will continue to suffer from lawlessness, sporadic violence, and tension between different groups. This may contribute to further displacement and impeding humanitarian access and security for humanitarian workers.

Continued need for humanitarian assistance: The prospect that a fourth year of rain failure or low rainfall will further erode coping mechanisms and the depletion of household assets and resources and lead to continuing food insecurity with a continuing need for major food distributions to food insecure areas.

External populations: Up to 20% of the Afghan people live outside the country mainly as refugees in neighbouring countries. Continuing assistance to this population will be needed as many may delay their decision to return until their physical and economic fears are resolved in Afghanistan.

Limited physical access to areas in Afghanistan refers to the ability, security conditions permitting, to reach beneficiaries. Physical access has always been difficult in Afghanistan, due to poor infrastructure, mountainous terrain and the threat of mines and unexploded ordnance. These constraints are particularly challenging for the delivery of critical assistance in remote communities.

Mines and unexploded ordnance: Newly laid land mines along the front lines and unexploded ordnance from coalition airstrikes have exacerbated Afghanistan's position as one of the most seriously mine-affected countries in the world. This problem will continue to have grave human consequences, limiting capacity for agricultural recovery and repair of infrastructure while also restricting access for humanitarian aid.

Absorptive capacity: The machinery of government remains very fragile, and in rural areas and some sectors, virtually non-existent. The absence of key services and loss of infrastructure such as health facilities, schools, transport, power and communications will continue to impede recovery. Additional stress will be placed on an already heavily over-stretched public infrastructure by large numbers of returnees. While it is critical to capitalize on the opportunities created through the establishment of a new political arrangement in Afghanistan, and to be attentive to high expectations of financial support to rebuild the country, the international community must be mindful that significant, poorly coordinated and rapid injections of funds and technical assistance have the potential to undermine the nation's reconstruction efforts to build Afghan ownership.

The factors outlined above will significantly influence the international community's engagement in Afghanistan. The key message must be that planning remains flexible and adaptable. Overall **planning assumptions** include:

- Ownership and management by the Afghan authorities will increase progressively with the investiture of the Interim Authority to be followed by the Transitional Authority.
- The drought will ease, but with still lower than normal precipitation, the consequences of the drought will be felt for several more years.
- An improved political environment will allow for substantial return of Internally Displaced Persons and refugees. It is expected that up to 1.2 million refugees and IDPs may return.
- The donor response will allow for a coordinated, effective response covering both humanitarian recovery and initial reconstruction needs.
- Political instability will continue to provide a potential threat. Parts of the country will be relatively stable allowing all actors to work effectively. There are likely to be regional variations in the levels of security and areas of instability will remain in which there will be limited access to humanitarian and development assistance. . . .

V. Sectoral Strategies and Activities for 2002

. . . [A] number of **cross-cutting themes** will underpin the activities of all agencies working in Afghanistan, to be incorporated at all stages of programming, from design to evaluation:

Governance

Effective governance is built on sound economic policy, transparent and accountable public institutions, a free media, robust and independent legal frameworks and judicial mechanisms, which, inter alia, protect and promote the rights of all citizens. Technical assistance will be provided to assist the Interim Authority to strengthen these essential elements of good governance. More widely, programmes in all sectors, including humanitarian activities, will need to take into account these wider imperatives to build an effective, transparent policy environment.

A trust fund has been established to meet the initial recurrent costs of establishing line ministries, including salaries and termination packages, as well as equipment costs, particularly in those ministries responsible for delivering social services and financial accountability. Discussions with the Interim Authority on this aspect of the Programme are currently ongoing, to determine the most essential needs. The total number of civil servants is estimated at 230,000. In addition, recurrent costs will also be paid for the national security force to consist of the army, police and intelligence service. The relevant component of the UN that will manage this support will be determined after the Security Council discussion. Such budget support will help stabilize the country to allow for a more effective recovery.

Community Empowerment and Participation

Building equitable community level governance structures is a priority, as is the reinforcement of other similar UN and NGO initiatives that empower local communities to guide and implement timely recovery efforts. Community based rehabilitation initiatives for demobilized soldiers (including child soldiers), street and working children will be supported, building on traditional protection systems and mechanisms. Youth initiatives to contribute to community rehabilitation will be promoted. Community participation will also be a key modality for programmes to reintegrate returnees, and for reconstruction of housing. The primary aim of the ITAP at the local level is to enable people to take collective decisions on issues that affect their welfare and to empower them to influence how external resources dedicated to their communities are utilized. Community-based approach should encourage the emergence of local institutions, like Community Fora, that enjoy a degree of permanence by virtue of being broad-based and owned by the people themselves. Such institutions should not be treated as a delivery arm of a project or an intervention but as bodies that function as an interface between, say, the assistance community and the people, consistent with the efforts of the Interim Authority to develop coherent political structures in Afghanistan.

Return and Reintegration of Refugees
and Internally Displaced Populations

A priority for 2002 is the need to ensure sustainable reintegration of uprooted Afghans who wish to return home. Multi-sectoral approaches, including through quick impact projects, which build the capacity of communities to absorb returning families will be required. Programmes will meet immediate needs, so that vulnerability of returnees and their communities is not increased. Programmes will also need to mesh with long term strategies for the communities in question. Mechanisms for coordination of reintegration efforts will be critical to ensure such approaches are truly multi-sectoral and coherent appropriate to communities and that they are appropriately targeted. Uncertainties around weather and the possibility of a fourth year of drought need to be balanced against the need to plan for optimum outcomes, in particular the reintegration of up to 1,200,000 refugees and IDPs.

Gender

In rebuilding Afghanistan, women will need new forms of economic security and an opportunity to reenter public and political life. A prerequisite to robust, sustainable development is that women be equal partners with men in developing strategies for reconstruction and recovery. Efforts will be needed at three levels. Firstly, strengthening the capacity of women and women's' organizations in their efforts to become equal partners in political and economic life; secondly, incorporating gender sensitive programming approaches into all activities, particularly reintegration and employment; and thirdly, practices of violence against women must be redressed at community and national level. Community empowerment will only be truly empowering if women are participating in community based activities and are able to access resources and assets equally with men.

Drug Control

Drug production in Afghanistan is undermining sustainable development. An illicit drug economy and organized crime hinder a community's efforts to seek self-reliance and security. Drug-related problems exacerbate poverty, health, and other development problems and erode the conditions for peace and sustainable human development. Thus, in the context of international assistance to Afghanistan the drug problem has to be seen as a cross-cutting issue.

The multi-dimensional nature of the drug problem implies that the problem can only be effectively addressed through a comprehensive approach that covers a wide range of thematic sectors including food security, health, education, refugees and returnees, and recovery activities. In the transition phase, humanitarian assistance can target poppy-growing communities to minimize the extent of return to poppy cultivation and to provide immediate resources to those who relied heavily on poppy cultivation. Assessment and programming studies will need to be undertaken to the major poppy growing areas to design strategies and plans to provide sustainable alternative livelihoods to poppy cultivation. The aid agencies working in the fields of food aid, healthcare, education, social work and community development, particularly income generating projects, will be instrumental in drug abuse prevention and reduction of drug related harm.

Peace building

Programmes will support efforts in peace-building and conflict prevention. A priority will be the creation of sustainable domestic capacity for peace-building. Among the specific measures and activities, the UN will work at promoting dialogue among parties with potentially conflicting interests, ensuring the provision of mechanisms for peaceful resolution of grievances, supporting the implementation of appropriate policies on issues of particular divisiveness, exchange experiences in peaceful management of disputes and instituting programmes for peace education and the creation of a culture of peace.

Human Rights

Strategic and sustainable improvement on human rights is a prerequisite for durable peace in Afghanistan. In the coming year, action is needed to address ongoing human rights concerns as well as building a foundation for an independent judicial and rule of law system that protects the rights of all Afghans. In close collaboration with the Interim authority, assistance actors will work to address the pressing human rights issues faced by a wide cross-section of Afghanistan society including deep-rooted discriminatory attitudes, policies and practices that serve to marginalize women and minorities. Action will also be needed to address human rights violations as a result of lawlessness, military action and abusive behaviour that undermines the protection of at-risk civilians including IDPs, returnees and others. Specific steps will be taken to assess existing capacity and requirements and to provide support to Afghan authorities, and the general public, particularly women, to improve understanding of human rights and to build the capacity necessary to give effect to the human rights provisions of the Bonn Agreement. The human rights activities of the assistance community set out in this text are intended to coordinate closely with and complement the comprehensive UN programme of support to implementation of the human rights provisions of the Bonn Agreement.

OHCHR [the Office of the UN High Commissioner for Human Rights] has already conducted a needs assessment exercise for a comprehensive programme of support for implementation of the human rights related provisions of the Bonn Agreement. Implementation of this project in 2002 will address, (a) delivery of human rights technical assistance/capacity building support to Government, for the establishment and activities of the Human Rights Commission and other bodies mentioned in the Bonn Agreement and to civil society; and (b), the undertaking of human rights monitoring and analysis. . . .

STATE OF THE UNION ADDRESS AND DEMOCRATIC RESPONSE
January 29, 2002

Riding a wave of popularity stemming from his handling of the September 11, 2001, terrorist attacks, President George W. Bush told Congress and the nation on January 29, 2002, to be prepared for a long and costly war against terrorism. Bush said three countries—Iraq, Iran, and North Korea—comprised an "axis of evil" that threatened the United States and the rest of the world because of their support for terrorism and their efforts to acquire weapons of mass destruction.

Concentrating primarily on security issues, Bush placed his agenda within the context of confronting what he said were "unprecedented dangers." The president said he would call on Congress to approve the largest increase in defense spending since the early 1980s. "I will not stand by, as peril draws closer and closer," he said. "The United States of America will not permit the world's most dangerous regimes to threaten us with the world's most destructive weapons."

The president's address was his first to a joint session of Congress since nine days after the terrorist attacks that killed more than 3,000 people. At that time, he promised a relentless war against all terrorist groups of "global reach," starting with the al Qaeda network that he blamed for the September 11 attacks. Just two weeks later, U.S. and allied forces launched a broad military assault that dismantled al Qaeda's infrastructure in Afghanistan and drove from power the Taliban regime that had offered shelter to al Qaeda leader Osama bin Laden and his associates. (Background, Historic Documents of 2001, pp. 614, 624, 637, 686)

Confronting an Axis of Evil

Bush had told aides after the September 11 attacks that the sudden need to confront terrorism had offered him an underlying "mission" for his presidency. He used his speech to define that mission in the broadest possible terms, wrapping nearly all his proposals with the protective packaging of the word security. *He used it twenty times in the speech (aside from the term* Social Security), *calling, in order of appearance, for: national security, homeland security, airport and border security, health security, economic security, air travel security, health security, and retirement security. For good measure, he also embraced "real security." Members of Congress responded enthusiastically, interrupting the president with applause seventy-six times.*

That the president would emphasize security and terrorism was no surprise, given that the U.S. military was still working to oust the remnants of the al Qaeda and Taliban forces from Afghanistan. What did surprise most observers was his decision to declare Iran, Iraq, and North Korea as coequal enemies with the terrorists who had recently struck directly at the United States. Using the term axis—*borrowed from World War II—the president declared that those three nations "and their terrorist allies" constituted an "axis of evil" that was "arming to threaten the peace of the world."*

In his speech, Bush offered few details to support his claim. North Korea, he said, "is a regime arming with missiles and weapons of mass destruction while starving its citizens." Iran "aggressively pursues these weapons and exports terror, while an unelected few repress the Iranian people's hope for freedom," he said. The president had a longer list of particulars against Iraq, saying the regime of Saddam Hussein had tried to develop anthrax, nerve gas, and nuclear weapons; had used poison gas against its own people; and had defied international weapons inspectors even after agreeing to disarm following the Persian Gulf War of 1991. "This is a regime with something to hide from the civilized world," the president said.

Some congressional leaders and independent foreign policy experts embraced Bush's stance on the three countries, arguing that he had focused needed attention on serious dangers. Among them was Senate Majority Leader Tom Daschle, D-S.D., who said Bush had "broad bipartisan support in his effort to ensure that we don't see another 9/11 by ignoring the perils of ignoring these three countries."

Others said Bush had endangered delicate diplomatic efforts to deal with Iran and North Korea by carelessly lumping together three countries that posed dramatically different threats. "There are elements in Iran that we want to encourage," said Rep. Doug Bereuter, R-Neb. Diplomats in many countries allied with the United States, particularly Western Europe, made similar points, suggesting that Bush's hot rhetoric may have undermined the reformist campaign of Iranian president Mohammed Khatami and blocked any chance of getting North Korea to permanently halt its nuclear weapons program.

Each of the three countries rejected the president's contentions. Iran's foreign minister, Kamal Kharrzi, sent a three-page letter to the United Nations denying that his country was developing weapons of mass destruction. The "threat or use of force against what the United States has arrogated to itself to call terrorism," he said, "undermines the global resolve to embark on a real and comprehensive war on terrorism." A progovernment newspaper in North Korea said Bush had "openly revealed his dangerous design to seize North Korea by force of arms, groundlessly linking it with terrorism." Iraq's vice president, Taha Yassin Ramadan, said the United States, not Iraq, was "the source of evil and aggression toward the whole world."

In subsequent days and weeks, administration officials provided more details to bolster the president's stance, although they did not make public any substantial evidence that the three "axis" countries had collaborated with the terrorists who attacked the United States. Some of the most specific evidence came in a CIA report delivered to Congress the day after Bush's speech. That report said Iran was "one of the most active countries" seeking to acquire weapons of mass destruction and had already stockpiled chemical weapons and was working to develop nuclear weapons. Iraq probably retained biological and chemical weapons it had produced before the Persian Gulf War and "may be attempting" to acquire technology necessary to build nuclear weapons. North Korea already had biological, chemical, and nuclear weapons, the report said, and was trying to build more. (Weapons of mass destruction, p. 437; North Korea issue, p. 731)

The president's speech set in motion what turned out to be a year-long campaign to focus international attention on Iraq. By early summer administration officials said Bush had decided on a policy of "regime change" in Iraq—in other words, forcing Iraqi leader Saddam Hussein from power. The president sought and won congressional support for his policy, in the form of a resolution passed in October that authorized him to use military force, if necessary, to disarm Iraq. Under pressure from Congress and some key allies, Bush also turned to the United Nations for support and negotiated a Security Council resolution demanding that Iraq comply with numerous previous resolutions requiring it to dismantle its weapons of mass destruction. By year's end Bush had declared that Iraq had failed to comply with the UN resolution, and he was preparing for a possible military attack early in 2003. (Iraq issues, pp. 612, 713)

Defense and Homeland Security

As he had done consistently since the September 11 attacks, Bush told the country that it was engaged in a full-scale war against terrorism. The conflict might appear to be different from previous ones, such as World War II, he said, but it was still a war that needed to be fought and won— and paid for. "It costs a lot to fight this year," the president said bluntly. "We have spent more than a billion dollars a month—over $30 million a day— and we must be prepared for future operations."

For this reason, Bush said the defense budget was his highest priority, justifying what he called "the largest increase in defense spending in two decades." That reference was to the defense buildup in President Ronald Reagan's first term (1981–1985) that generated considerable controversy in part because it was financed with borrowed money. Bush faced little opposition to his defense proposals, however, and Congress pushed through defense authorization and spending bills totaling nearly $370 billion while dozens of other pieces of legislation were stalled. Congress balked at only one major item, Bush's request for a $10 billion lump-sum contingency fund to *help pay for future antiterrorism operations, such as a war in Iraq. Even so, it appeared likely that Bush would get that money early in 2003.*

Substantially more controversy arose on the issue of "homeland security." Under pressure from Congress to improve the coordination of dozens of federal agencies responsible for various aspects of defending U.S. national territory, Bush in late 2001 created an Office of Homeland Security within the White House, headed by former Pennsylvania governor Tom Ridge. In his State of the Union address Bush said his number-two priority, after the defense budget, was to do "everything possible to protect our citizens and strengthen our nation against the ongoing threat of another attack." He mentioned four key areas: bioterrorism, emergency response, airport and border security, and improved intelligence.

For the next four months, the Bush administration and Congress wrangled over the details. Key Democrats called for creation of a cabinet-level homeland security department, but Bush resisted, saying Ridge's office was adequate. On June 6, after a Senate committee voted to create such a department, Bush suddenly reversed position and marched to the head of the parade, endorsing a massive new agency combining all or part of twenty-two federal agencies. (Homeland security, p. 530)

Prospects for quick bipartisan action foundered on the president's demand for broad discretion to hire, fire, and reassign the approximately 170,000 employees who would be integrated into the new department. After passage in the House, Bush's plan stalled in the Senate, where majority Democrats complained that the administration was trying to gut civil service protections. Ignoring his previous promises not to politicize terrorism issues, Bush used the dispute in campaigning against vulnerable Democrats during the midterm elections. That tactic contributed to the defeat of two Senate Democrats (Max Cleland of Georgia and Jean Carnahan of Missouri) and helped ensure Republicans control of the Senate for the 108th Congress in January 2003. After the election, Senate Democrats gave up the fight and gave Bush what he wanted. The president signed the homeland security bill into law (PL 107–296) on November 25. (Congressional election, p. 818)

Domestic Issues

Foreshadowing a year in which Congress would accomplish little on domestic issues, the president paid scant attention to such matters in his State of the Union address. Bush indirectly acknowledged the principal reason for this lack of focus on domestic programs: the federal budget, which just a year earlier had shown a surplus, had gone into deficit. An economic downturn and the need to increase defense spending were two of the reasons Bush cited for the deficit. The third reason went unmentioned: the $1.35 trillion, ten-year tax cut enacted at his request by Congress in 2001 would begin biting deeply into federal revenues starting in fiscal year 2004. To limit the apparent size of the tax cut, Congress had authorized it just through 2010, after which tax rates were to return to their previous levels. Bush's statement that the tax cuts would promote "long-term growth" and *should be made permanent generated the biggest cheer of the night from Republicans. The Republican-controlled House voted repeatedly to do just that, but opponents managed to block the effort in the Senate.*

The president mentioned in passing a number of other domestic initiatives, including increased funding for education programs, energy legislation, his pending request for a free hand to negotiate trade agreements, coverage under Medicare for prescription drugs, and a patients' bill of rights. Of these items, Congress enacted just one: the "fast track" or "trade promotion" authority for the negotiation of trade agreements with other countries. Congress had denied that authority to President Bill Clinton in 1995, but President Bush made just enough compromises to win it back in August.

Also relegated to a vague phrase was one of the signature items of Bush's first presidential speech to Congress on February 27, 2001: a "faith-based initiative" to allow expanded federal funding of social services provided by religious organizations. The House had approved Bush's plan in 2001, but the Senate did not act because of controversy over the mixing of politics and religion. Apparently admitting the dim prospect for full congressional approval, Bush in 2002 simply called on Congress to work on "ways to encourage the good work of charities and faith-based groups." The Senate did not act on the proposal again in 2002, and so in December Bush signed an executive order putting much of it into effect under his own authority. That order allowed religious authorities that provided social services under government contracts to discriminate in their hiring. (Bush's address to joint session of Congress, Historic Documents of 2001, p. 175)

Bush dwelled on one new proposal for a "U.S.A. Freedom Corps," which would expand on the overseas Peace Corps program and the domestic AmeriCorps and Senior Corps programs. Appealing directly to the public, the president called "for every American to commit at least two years— 4,000 hours—over the rest of your lifetime to the service of your neighborhood and your nation." Funding for Bush's proposed expansion of these volunteer programs was held up during the year because of Congress's failure to enact the necessary appropriations bills.

The president's speech came less than two months after the financial collapse of the Enron Corporation. The Houston-based energy trading company had filed for bankruptcy in December 2001, setting off a series of investigations into its questionable and possibly illegal business practices. Enron's collapse had generated widespread public unease, in large part because thousands of employees lost their life savings because their 401(k) pension plans had consisted largely of Enron stock, which became virtually worthless. Bush did not mention Enron, but without giving details he asked Congress to enact "new safeguards" so that workers would not "risk losing everything if their company fails." Referring to still-emerging reports that Enron and its accounting firm had covered up failed ventures, Bush also called for "stricter accounting standards and tougher disclosure requirements" that would make corporations "more accountable to employees and shareholders." Within weeks of Bush's speech, revelations of wrongdoing at a half-dozen other major corporations lent urgency to the matter and prompted Congress to pass legislation tightening corporate accounting and governance standards. Congress did not, however, follow through on Bush's call for legislation protecting employee savings and pension plans. (Corporate scandals, p. 391; Enron bankruptcy, Historic Documents of 2001, p. 857)

Democratic Response

Offering the official Democratic response to Bush's State of the Union address, House Minority Leader Richard Gephardt, D-Mo., sought to walk a fine line—supporting the president's war against terrorism but not embracing the totality of his program. Gephardt rendered his own thumb-nail summary of that approach: "I refuse to accept that while we stand shoulder to shoulder on the war, we should stand toe to toe on the economy." But even that summary appeared to threaten more of a confrontational approach than Gephardt's speech contained. While indirectly suggesting a difference with Bush's approach on domestic matters, Gephardt in six successive paragraphs said Democrats "want to work together" with him on issues ranging from education spending to raising the minimum wage.

Gephardt appeared to challenge the president directly only on the issue of campaign finance reform. Legislation prohibiting "soft money" contributions to political campaigns by special interest groups had been pending in Congress for years but had been opposed primarily by Republicans. As of the State of the Union address, Bush had not taken a formal position on the matter, and Gephardt directly called on the president to "stand with us to clean up the political system and get big money out of politics."

Bush ultimately stood both for and against the position Gephardt advocated. Moments before the House was to take a crucial vote February 13 on the legislation, White House spokesman Ari Fleischer said Bush believed the bill would "improve the system." That remark took the wind out of Republican opposition. Bush later called the bill "flawed" but did not try to block it during the final stages of congressional action. The ambivalence of the president's position was perhaps best signified by his refusal to hold the White House signing ceremony that was traditional for approval of such a major piece of legislation. Bush signed the bill into law (PL 107–155) on March 27 with no fanfare and no television cameras present.

> *Following are the texts of the State of the Union address delivered January 29, 2002, by President George W. Bush to a joint session of Congress and the Democratic response by Richard Gephardt, D-Mo., the House minority leader.*

> ***The documents were obtained from the Internet at www .whitehouse.gov/news/releases/2002/01/20020129–11 .html; democraticleader.house.gov/media/speeches/ readSpeech.asp?ID=53; accessed September 9, 2002.***

STATE OF THE UNION ADDRESS

Mr. Speaker, Vice President Cheney, members of Congress, distinguished guests, fellow citizens: As we gather tonight, our nation is at war, our economy is in recession, and the civilized world faces unprecedented dangers. Yet the state of our Union has never been stronger.

We last met in an hour of shock and suffering. In four short months, our nation has comforted the victims, begun to rebuild New York and the Pentagon, rallied a great coalition, captured, arrested, and rid the world of thousands of terrorists, destroyed Afghanistan's terrorist training camps, saved a people from starvation, and freed a country from brutal oppression.

The American flag flies again over our embassy in Kabul. Terrorists who once occupied Afghanistan now occupy cells at Guantanamo Bay. And terrorist leaders who urged followers to sacrifice their lives are running for their own.

America and Afghanistan are now allies against terror. We'll be partners in rebuilding that country. And this evening we welcome the distinguished interim leader of a liberated Afghanistan: Chairman Hamid Karzai.

The last time we met in this chamber, the mothers and daughters of Afghanistan were captives in their own homes, forbidden from working or going to school. Today women are free, and are part of Afghanistan's new government. And we welcome the new Minister of Women's Affairs, Doctor Sima Samar.

Our progress is a tribute to the spirit of the Afghan people, to the resolve of our coalition, and to the might of the United States military. When I called our troops into action, I did so with complete confidence in their courage and skill. And tonight, thanks to them, we are winning the war on terror. The men and women of our Armed Forces have delivered a message now clear to every enemy of the United States: Even 7,000 miles away, across oceans and continents, on mountaintops and in caves—you will not escape the justice of this nation.

For many Americans, these four months have brought sorrow, and pain that will never completely go away. Every day a retired firefighter returns to Ground Zero, to feel closer to his two sons who died there. At a memorial in New York, a little boy left his football with a note for his lost father: Dear Daddy, please take this to heaven. I don't want to play football until I can play with you again some day.

Last month, at the grave of her husband, Michael, a CIA officer and Marine who died in Mazur-e-Sharif, Shannon Spann said these words of farewell: "Semper Fi, my love." Shannon is with us tonight.

Shannon, I assure you and all who have lost a loved one that our cause is just, and our country will never forget the debt we owe Michael and all who gave their lives for freedom.

Our cause is just, and it continues. Our discoveries in Afghanistan confirmed our worst fears, and showed us the true scope of the task ahead. We have seen the depth of our enemies' hatred in videos, where they laugh about the loss of innocent life. And the depth of their hatred is equaled by the madness of the destruction they design. We have found diagrams of American nuclear power plants and public water facilities, detailed instructions for making chemical weapons, surveillance maps of American cities, and thorough descriptions of landmarks in America and throughout the world.

What we have found in Afghanistan confirms that, far from ending there, our war against terror is only beginning. Most of the 19 men who hijacked planes on September the 11th were trained in Afghanistan's camps, and so were tens of thousands of others. Thousands of dangerous killers, schooled in the methods of murder, often supported by outlaw regimes, are now spread throughout the world like ticking time bombs, set to go off without warning.

Thanks to the work of our law enforcement officials and coalition partners, hundreds of terrorists have been arrested. Yet, tens of thousands of trained terrorists are still at large. These enemies view the entire world as a battlefield, and we must pursue them wherever they are. So long as training camps operate, so long as nations harbor terrorists, freedom is at risk. And America and our allies must not, and will not, allow it.

Our nation will continue to be steadfast and patient and persistent in the pursuit of two great objectives. First, we will shut down terrorist camps, disrupt terrorist plans, and bring terrorists to justice. And, second, we must prevent the terrorists and regimes who seek chemical, biological or nuclear weapons from threatening the United States and the world.

Our military has put the terror training camps of Afghanistan out of business, yet camps still exist in at least a dozen countries. A terrorist underworld— including groups like Hamas, Hezbollah, Islamic Jihad, Jaish-i-Mohammed— operates in remote jungles and deserts, and hides in the centers of large cities.

While the most visible military action is in Afghanistan, America is acting elsewhere. We now have troops in the Philippines, helping to train that country's armed forces to go after terrorist cells that have executed an American, and still hold hostages. Our soldiers, working with the Bosnian government, seized terrorists who were plotting to bomb our embassy. Our Navy is patrolling the coast of Africa to block the shipment of weapons and the establishment of terrorist camps in Somalia.

My hope is that all nations will heed our call, and eliminate the terrorist parasites who threaten their countries and our own. Many nations are acting forcefully. Pakistan is now cracking down on terror, and I admire the strong leadership of President Musharraf.

But some governments will be timid in the face of terror. And make no mistake about it: If they do not act, America will.

Our second goal is to prevent regimes that sponsor terror from threatening America or our friends and allies with weapons of mass destruction. Some of these regimes have been pretty quiet since September the 11th. But we know their true nature. North Korea is a regime arming with missiles and weapons of mass destruction, while starving its citizens.

Iran aggressively pursues these weapons and exports terror, while an unelected few repress the Iranian people's hope for freedom.

Iraq continues to flaunt its hostility toward America and to support terror. The Iraqi regime has plotted to develop anthrax, and nerve gas, and nuclear weapons for over a decade. This is a regime that has already used poison gas to murder thousands of its own citizens—leaving the bodies of mothers huddled over their dead children. This is a regime that agreed to international inspections—then kicked out the inspectors. This is a regime that has something to hide from the civilized world.

States like these, and their terrorist allies, constitute an axis of evil, arming to threaten the peace of the world. By seeking weapons of mass destruction, these regimes pose a grave and growing danger. They could provide these arms to terrorists, giving them the means to match their hatred. They could attack our allies or attempt to blackmail the United States. In any of these cases, the price of indifference would be catastrophic.

We will work closely with our coalition to deny terrorists and their state sponsors the materials, technology, and expertise to make and deliver weapons of mass destruction. We will develop and deploy effective missile defenses to protect America and our allies from sudden attack. And all nations should know: America will do what is necessary to ensure our nation's security.

We'll be deliberate, yet time is not on our side. I will not wait on events, while dangers gather. I will not stand by, as peril draws closer and closer. The United States of America will not permit the world's most dangerous regimes to threaten us with the world's most destructive weapons.

Our war on terror is well begun, but it is only begun. This campaign may not be finished on our watch—yet it must be and it will be waged on our watch.

We can't stop short. If we stop now—leaving terror camps intact and terror states unchecked—our sense of security would be false and temporary. History has called America and our allies to action, and it is both our responsibility and our privilege to fight freedom's fight.

Our first priority must always be the security of our nation, and that will be reflected in the budget I send to Congress. My budget supports three great goals for America: We will win this war; we'll protect our homeland; and we will revive our economy.

September the 11th brought out the best in America, and the best in this Congress. And I join the American people in applauding your unity and resolve. Now Americans deserve to have this same spirit directed toward addressing problems here at home. I'm a proud member of my party—yet as we act to win the war, protect our people, and create jobs in America, we must act, first and foremost, not as Republicans, not as Democrats, but as Americans.

It costs a lot to fight this war. We have spent more than a billion dollars a month—over $30 million a day—and we must be prepared for future operations. Afghanistan proved that expensive precision weapons defeat the enemy and spare innocent lives, and we need more of them. We need to replace aging aircraft and make our military more agile, to put our troops anywhere in the world quickly and safely. Our men and women in uniform deserve the best weapons, the best equipment, the best training—and they also deserve another pay raise.

My budget includes the largest increase in defense spending in two decades—because while the price of freedom and security is high, it is never too high. Whatever it costs to defend our country, we will pay.

The next priority of my budget is to do everything possible to protect our citizens and strengthen our nation against the ongoing threat of another attack. Time and distance from the events of September the 11th will not make us safer unless we act on its lessons. America is no longer protected by vast oceans. We are protected from attack only by vigorous action abroad, and increased vigilance at home.

My budget nearly doubles funding for a sustained strategy of homeland security, focused on four key areas: bioterrorism, emergency response, airport and border security, and improved intelligence. We will develop vaccines to fight anthrax and other deadly diseases. We'll increase funding to help states and communities train and equip our heroic police and firefighters. We will improve intelligence collection and sharing, expand patrols at our borders, strengthen the security of air travel, and use technology to track the arrivals and departures of visitors to the United States.

Homeland security will make America not only stronger, but, in many ways, better. Knowledge gained from bioterrorism research will improve public health. Stronger police and fire departments will mean safer neighborhoods. Stricter border enforcement will help combat illegal drugs. And as government works to better secure our homeland, America will continue to depend on the eyes and ears of alert citizens.

A few days before Christmas, an airline flight attendant spotted a passenger lighting a match. The crew and passengers quickly subdued the man, who had been trained by al Qaeda and was armed with explosives. The people on that plane were alert and, as a result, likely saved nearly 200 lives. And tonight we welcome and thank flight attendants Hermis Moutardier and Christina Jones.

Once we have funded our national security and our homeland security, the final great priority of my budget is economic security for the American people. To achieve these great national objectives—to win the war, protect the homeland, and revitalize our economy—our budget will run a deficit that will be small and short-term, so long as Congress restrains spending and acts in a fiscally responsible manner. We have clear priorities and we must act at home with the same purpose and resolve we have shown overseas: We'll prevail in the war, and we will defeat this recession.

Americans who have lost their jobs need our help and I support extending unemployment benefits and direct assistance for health care coverage. Yet, American workers want more than unemployment checks—they want a steady paycheck. When America works, America prospers, so my economic security plan can be summed up in one word: jobs.

Good jobs begin with good schools, and here we've made a fine start. Republicans and Democrats worked together to achieve historic education reform so that no child is left behind. I was proud to work with members of both parties: [House Education Committee] Chairman John Boehner [R-Ohio] and Congressman George Miller [D-Calif.]. Senator Judd Gregg [R-N.H.]. And I was so proud of our work, I even had nice things to say about my friend, Ted

Kennedy [D-Mass.]. I know the folks at the Crawford coffee shop couldn't believe I'd say such a thing—but our work on this bill shows what is possible if we set aside posturing and focus on results.

There is more to do. We need to prepare our children to read and succeed in school with improved Head Start and early childhood development programs. We must upgrade our teacher colleges and teacher training and launch a major recruiting drive with a great goal for America: a quality teacher in every classroom.

Good jobs also depend on reliable and affordable energy. This Congress must act to encourage conservation, promote technology, build infrastructure, and it must act to increase energy production at home so America is less dependent on foreign oil.

Good jobs depend on expanded trade. Selling into new markets creates new jobs, so I ask Congress to finally approve trade promotion authority. On these two key issues, trade and energy, the House of Representatives has acted to create jobs, and I urge the Senate to pass this legislation.

Good jobs depend on sound tax policy. Last year, some in this hall thought my tax relief plan was too small; some thought it was too big. But when the checks arrived in the mail, most Americans thought tax relief was just about right. Congress listened to the people and responded by reducing tax rates, doubling the child credit, and ending the death tax. For the sake of long-term growth and to help Americans plan for the future, let's make these tax cuts permanent.

The way out of this recession, the way to create jobs, is to grow the economy by encouraging investment in factories and equipment, and by speeding up tax relief so people have more money to spend. For the sake of American workers, let's pass a stimulus package.

Good jobs must be the aim of welfare reform. As we reauthorize these important reforms, we must always remember the goal is to reduce dependency on government and offer every American the dignity of a job.

Americans know economic security can vanish in an instant without health security. I ask Congress to join me this year to enact a patients' bill of rights—to give uninsured workers credits to help buy health coverage—to approve an historic increase in the spending for veterans' health—and to give seniors a sound and modern Medicare system that includes coverage for prescription drugs.

A good job should lead to security in retirement. I ask Congress to enact new safeguards for 401K and pension plans. Employees who have worked hard and saved all their lives should not have to risk losing everything if their company fails. Through stricter accounting standards and tougher disclosure requirements, corporate America must be made more accountable to employees and shareholders and held to the highest standards of conduct.

Retirement security also depends upon keeping the commitments of Social Security, and we will. We must make Social Security financially stable and allow personal retirement accounts for younger workers who choose them.

Members, you and I will work together in the months ahead on other issues: productive farm policy—a cleaner environment—broader home ownership, especially among minorities—and ways to encourage the good work of charities and faith-based groups. I ask you to join me on these important domestic issues in the same spirit of cooperation we've applied to our war against terrorism.

During these last few months, I've been humbled and privileged to see the true character of this country in a time of testing. Our enemies believed America was weak and materialistic, that we would splinter in fear and selfishness. They were as wrong as they are evil.

The American people have responded magnificently, with courage and compassion, strength and resolve. As I have met the heroes, hugged the families, and looked into the tired faces of rescuers, I have stood in awe of the American people.

And I hope you will join me—I hope you will join me in expressing thanks to one American for the strength and calm and comfort she brings to our nation in crisis, our First Lady, Laura Bush.

None of us would ever wish the evil that was done on September the 11th. Yet after America was attacked, it was as if our entire country looked into a mirror and saw our better selves. We were reminded that we are citizens, with obligations to each other, to our country, and to history. We began to think less of the goods we can accumulate, and more about the good we can do.

For too long our culture has said, "If it feels good, do it." Now America is embracing a new ethic and a new creed: "Let's roll."

In the sacrifice of soldiers, the fierce brotherhood of firefighters, and the bravery and generosity of ordinary citizens, we have glimpsed what a new culture of responsibility could look like. We want to be a nation that serves goals larger than self. We've been offered a unique opportunity, and we must not let this moment pass.

My call tonight is for every American to commit at least two years—4,000 hours over the rest of your lifetime—to the service of your neighbors and your nation. Many are already serving, and I thank you. If you aren't sure how to help, I've got a good place to start. To sustain and extend the best that has emerged in America, I invite you to join the new USA Freedom Corps. The Freedom Corps will focus on three areas of need: responding in case of crisis at home; rebuilding our communities; and extending American compassion throughout the world.

One purpose of the USA Freedom Corps will be homeland security. America needs retired doctors and nurses who can be mobilized in major emergencies; volunteers to help police and fire departments; transportation and utility workers well-trained in spotting danger.

Our country also needs citizens working to rebuild our communities. We need mentors to love children, especially children whose parents are in prison. And we need more talented teachers in troubled schools. USA Freedom Corps will expand and improve the good efforts of AmeriCorps and Senior Corps to recruit more than 200,000 new volunteers.

And America needs citizens to extend the compassion of our country to every part of the world. So we will renew the promise of the Peace Corps, double its volunteers over the next five years—and ask it to join a new effort to encourage development and education and opportunity in the Islamic world.

This time of adversity offers a unique moment of opportunity—a moment we must seize to change our culture. Through the gathering momentum of millions of acts of service and decency and kindness, I know we can overcome evil with greater good. And we have a great opportunity during this time of war to lead the world toward the values that will bring lasting peace.

All fathers and mothers, in all societies, want their children to be educated, and live free from poverty and violence. No people on Earth yearn to be oppressed, or aspire to servitude, or eagerly await the midnight knock of the secret police.

If anyone doubts this, let them look to Afghanistan, where the Islamic "street" greeted the fall of tyranny with song and celebration. Let the skeptics look to Islam's own rich history, with its centuries of learning, and tolerance and progress. America will lead by defending liberty and justice because they are right and true and unchanging for all people everywhere.

No nation owns these aspirations, and no nation is exempt from them. We have no intention of imposing our culture. But America will always stand firm for the non-negotiable demands of human dignity: the rule of law; limits on the power of the state; respect for women; private property; free speech; equal justice; and religious tolerance.

America will take the side of brave men and women who advocate these values around the world, including the Islamic world, because we have a greater objective than eliminating threats and containing resentment. We seek a just and peaceful world beyond the war on terror.

In this moment of opportunity, a common danger is erasing old rivalries. America is working with Russia and China and India, in ways we have never before, to achieve peace and prosperity. In every region, free markets and free trade and free societies are proving their power to lift lives. Together with friends and allies from Europe to Asia, and Africa to Latin America, we will demonstrate that the forces of terror cannot stop the momentum of freedom.

The last time I spoke here, I expressed the hope that life would return to normal. In some ways, it has. In others, it never will. Those of us who have lived through these challenging times have been changed by them. We've come to know truths that we will never question: evil is real, and it must be opposed. Beyond all differences of race or creed, we are one country, mourning together and facing danger together. Deep in the American character, there is honor, and it is stronger than cynicism. And many have discovered again that even in tragedy—especially in tragedy—God is near.

In a single instant, we realized that this will be a decisive decade in the history of liberty, that we've been called to a unique role in human events. Rarely has the world faced a choice more clear or consequential.

Our enemies send other people's children on missions of suicide and murder. They embrace tyranny and death as a cause and a creed. We stand for a different choice, made long ago, on the day of our founding. We affirm it again today. We choose freedom and the dignity of every life.

Steadfast in our purpose, we now press on. We have known freedom's price. We have shown freedom's power. And in this great conflict, my fellow Americans, we will see freedom's victory.

Thank you all. May God bless.

DEMOCRATIC RESPONSE

Rep. Richard A. Gephardt, D-Mo.: Good evening.

I want to commend the President for his strong and patriotic message tonight, and I can assure you of this: there were two parties tonight in the House Chamber, but one resolve. Like generations that came before us, we will pay any price and bear any burden to make sure that this proud nation wins the first war of the 21st Century.

Tonight, we say to our men and women in uniform: thank you for your bravery, your skill and your sacrifice. When the history of this time is written, your courage will be listed in its proudest pages.

To our friends around the world, we say thank you for your aid and support. True friendship is tested not only in treaties and trade, but in times of trial.

To our enemies, we say with one voice: no act of violence—no threat will drive us apart or steer us from our course: to protect America and preserve our democracy. And make no mistake about it: we are going to hunt you down and make you pay.

Now is not a time for finger-pointing or politics as usual. The men and women who are defending our freedom are not fighting for the Democratic Party or the Republican Party. They are fighting for the greatest country that has ever existed on earth: the United States of America.

As Americans, we need to put partisanship aside and work together to solve the problems that face us. On the day after the attacks, I went to the Oval Office for a meeting with the President. I said, "Mr. President, we have to find a way to work together." I said, "we have to trust you—and you have to trust us."

Since that day, there has been no daylight between us in this war on terrorism. We have met almost every single week and built a bipartisan consensus that is helping America win this war.

We also know that to defeat terrorism, our economy must be strong. For all the things that have changed in our world over the past four months, the needs of our families have not. While our attention has shifted, our values have not.

We know that real security depends not just on justice abroad, but creating good jobs at home; not just on securing our borders, but strengthening Social Security and Medicare at home; not just on bringing governments together, but creating a government here at home that lives within its means, cuts wasteful spending, and invests in the future. Real security depends not just on meeting threats around the world, but living up to our highest values here at home.

Our values call for tax cuts that promote growth and prosperity for all Americans. Our values call for protecting Social Security—and not gambling it away on the stock market. Our values call for helping patients and older

Americans—not just big HMOs and pharmaceutical companies—ensuring that seniors don't have to choose between food and medicine. Our values call for helping workers who have lost their 401(k) plans and protecting pensions from corporate mismanagement and abuse. Our values call for helping the unemployed—not just large corporations and the most fortunate.

These same values guide us as we work toward a long-term plan for our nation. We want to roll up our sleeves and work with our President to end America's dependence on foreign oil while preserving our environment—so we don't see gas prices jump every year.

We want to work together to recruit high-quality teachers and invest more in our schools while demanding more from them. We want to say to every student who wants to go to college and every worker who wants to update their skills: the first $10,000 of your education should be tax deductible. We want to work together to raise the minimum wage—because nobody who works hard and plays by the rules should be forced to live in poverty. We want to work together to create a universal pension system that follows a worker from job to job through life and protects employees from the next Enron.

We want to work together to build our new economy, creating jobs by investing in technology so America can continue to lead the world in growth and opportunity. We want to work together to improve homeland security and protect our borders, to keep out those people who want to bring us harm—but also to celebrate our nation's diversity and welcome those hard-working immigrants who pay taxes and keep our country strong. We want to work together—as we have over the last decade—to continue to build the best-trained, best-equipped fighting force on the face of the planet.

I refuse to accept that while we stand shoulder to shoulder on the war, we should stand toe to toe on the economy. We need to find a way to respect each other, and trust each other, and work together to solve the long-term challenges America faces. I'm ready to roll up my sleeves and go to work. That's one of the reasons I have proposed that next month, a group of leaders from both parties come together at the White House for an economic growth summit to figure out how we're going to help businesses create jobs, reduce the deficit, simplify the tax code, and grow our economy.

To accomplish these goals, we need a political system that is worthy of the people of this country. In the next several weeks, the House of Representatives will once again consider campaign finance reform. If the nation's largest bankruptcy coupled with a clear example of paid political influence isn't a prime case for reform, I don't know what is. The forces aligned against this are powerful. So if you've never called or written your member of Congress, now is the time. I hope the President will stand with us to clean up the political system and get big money out of politics.

Our nation has been through a lot the past four months. If it's even possible to suggest a silver lining in this dark cloud that has fallen over our nation, it's the renewed sense of community that we have seen across America. The more we are able to turn that renewed sense of purpose into a new call for service—to encourage more Americans—young and old—to get involved—join the AmeriCorps, the Peace Corps, the military or other endeavors—the more we're going to make our nation a model for all the good things that terrorists hate us for: hope, opportunity, and freedom.

It was brought home to me how Americans are already answering that call when I spoke to a friend of mine, who is the head of a postal union. Shortly after we learned of the anthrax threat, I spoke with him and asked how he was doing. "Not well," he said. "We've lost two workers and some are sick." He said, "I went to New Jersey where they had some of the biggest problems. Because of anthrax, all the workers were working in a tent exposed to the cold—hand-sorting the mail."

He said: "I thought I was going to get an earful, but when I asked for questions, a man stood up and said, 'I have been a postal worker for 30 years. We're here and we're going to stay here. And if we've got to be outside all winter, we're going to stay here. The mail is going out. The terrorists will not win.' "

As one American said, the terrorists who attacked us wanted to teach us a lesson. They wanted us to know them. But these attacks make clear: they don't know us. They don't know what we will do to defend freedom, and they don't know what they've started. But they're beginning to find out.

As we look ahead to the future, we do so with the knowledge that we can never fully know what the men and women we lost on that day would have accomplished; we can never know what would have been the full measure of their lives, or what they would have contributed to our world if they had lived. But one thing is certain: it is up to all of us to redeem the lives they would have lived with the lives we live today; and to make the most of our time here on earth. Let us be up to that challenge.

Thank you. God Bless you and God Bless America.

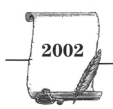

February

PRESIDENT'S ECONOMIC REPORT, ECONOMIC ADVISERS' REPORT
February 5, 2002

The American economy came out of the mild recession it had entered in 2001, but its slow and tentative emergence left consumers, investors, and businesses uncertain and wary about the future. While many of the economic fundamentals—particularly growth, inflation, and interest rates— were positive, confidence remained comparatively low, battered throughout the year by corporate accounting scandals, a plunging stock market, fears of another terrorist attack, and uncertainty over a potential war with Iraq and a confrontation with North Korea. As a result, unemployment remained stubbornly high, business investment stalled, and consumer spending grew at a pace barely strong enough to keep the economy moving.

By the end of the year many public and private policy makers and economists were openly concerned that the economy might fall back into recession. Some began to mention deflation—a reduction in the general level of prices that could further slow productivity and increase layoffs—but few thought that possibility was likely. It was unclear, however, what public policy levers remained to get the economy growing again. The Federal Reserve Board had already dropped its key interest rate target to 1.25 percent and had indicated it was unlikely to drop the rate any further. That left any further stimulative action by government to President George W. Bush and Congress. Although the Congress that would take office in 2003 would be under Republican control, it was likely that Democrats would challenge the president on his plan emphasizing tax cuts to stimulate the economy rather than immediate aid to the unemployed and to state and local governments. (2002 election, p. 818; U.S. economy, p. 877)

The rise and fall of the U.S. economy had repercussions far beyond its borders. Not only was the U.S. economy the largest in the world, but it increasingly was the only economic engine driving other national economies. In the past if the United States experienced a slowdown, Japan or Europe could often pick up the slack. But with most of those economies currently in recession or growing even more slowly than the U.S. economy, that was no

51

longer the case. While strong import demand from the United States pulled many economies affected by the Asian financial crisis of 1997–1998 from recession, the change from 15 percent growth in imports in 2000 to a decline of 3 percent in 2001 was seen as a major factor in the global slowdown. (Global economic outlook, p. 689)

Emerging from Recession

For most of the 1990s the United States, and the rest of the world, benefited from the longest and one of the most robust economic expansions in modern history. Led by investment in computers, telecommunications, information technology, and other high-tech industries, the U.S. economy added 22 million workers to the payroll during the two-term presidency of Bill Clinton. Between 1992 and 2000 inflation remained low, unemployment fell to its lowest levels in three decades, the poverty rate declined, and the federal government began to run a budget surplus for the first time in thirty years. (2000 economy, Historic Documents of 2001, p. 52)

But signs that the economy was slowing were evident for more than a year before Clinton left office. Falling stock prices, tumbling business profits, and increasing numbers of workers laid off from their jobs marked the final months of 2000. As 2001 began, the Federal Reserve Board tried to prop up the faltering economy with a series of cuts in its target for the federal funds interest rate (the interest rate financial institutions charge each other on overnight loans). During the course of the year, the Federal Reserve lowered the rate eleven times, bringing the federal funds rate from 6.5 percent at the end of 2000 to 1.75 percent on December 11, 2001, its lowest point in forty years.

The economy might well have escaped recession in 2001 had it not been for the September 11 terrorist attacks on the Pentagon and the World Trade Center. The attacks had a devastating effect on travel and tourism industries worldwide, causing high revenue losses and widespread layoffs and tipping the economy into recession. By the end of the year, consumer confidence and consumer spending were rising and the jobless rate seemed to be slowing, making analysts and policy makers cautiously optimistic that the country would emerge from its downturn in 2002. (Postattack economy, Historic Documents of 2001, p. 664)

Positive Signs of Recovery

Among the cautiously optimistic was President Bush's Council of Economic Advisers. "A recovery is in the offing," R. Glenn Hubbard, the council's chairman, told reporters February 5, 2002, upon releasing the Bush administration's first annual report to Congress on the state of the economy. The council said it expected the recovery to be slow initially but to accelerate in the middle of 2002. The council projected that real gross domestic product (GDP), the measure of overall economic growth, would increase at an annual rate of 2.7 percent and that unemployment would peak at about 6 percent in the middle of the year. Likewise, the council expected fixed investment by business to return to positive growth around the middle of the *year and to resume "rapid growth" thereafter. Consumer spending, which had been strong enough to keep the recession from becoming deeper, was expected to benefit from the $1.35 trillion tax cut bill pushed by President Bush and enacted by Congress in 2001.* (Tax cut, Historic Documents of 2001, p. 400)

In his brief accompanying report, President Bush was more circumspect, saying only that economic growth was "unacceptably slow" and that he was confident that Americans would "rise to meet the challenge."

In a demonstration of how difficult it is to predict the economic future with any certainty, the short-term expectations of the Council of Economic Advisers were largely fulfilled—but many of the expectations for the second half of the year ended up being off target. Annual real GDP growth for 2002 was likely to be close to the projection of 2.7 percent. But rather than a smooth acceleration, growth ebbed and flowed. It ran at a rate of 5 percent in the first quarter, slowed to 1.3 percent in the second quarter, accelerated to 4 percent in the third quarter, and was expected to slow again in the fourth quarter. Unemployment peaked at 6.0 percent in April and then ranged between 5.6 and 5.9 percent until November and December, when it reached 6 percent again.

Consumer spending continued in the positive range, buoyed, as it had been in 2001, by a booming housing market. Car sales also remained robust, as auto manufacturers and dealers retained the low-financing options they had introduced to lure buyers back to the auto lots after the September 11 attacks. But corporate spending did not recover. In September it fell at its fastest rate in nearly five years. By the end of the year, corporate executives and their representatives were warning that the picture was unlikely to change any time soon. The Business Roundtable (BRT), an organization representing the 200 largest U.S. corporations, reported on November 12 that 60 percent of its members expected to lay off workers in 2003 and were planning no increases in capital spending. "Our nation's economic recovery has not been strong or sustained, and the survey shows that CEOs do not expect the situation will improve significantly in 2003," said John T. Dillon, BRT chairman. FedEx Corp. chairman Frederick W. Smith said there were too many uncertainties for most corporations to consider new hiring or investment. "Until that psychology turns around, it's going to be slow," he told Washington Post *reporters and editors.*

Corporate Scandals and Bankruptcies

For much of the corporate world, the immediate uncertainties revolved around continuing low profits, the wallowing stock market, and troubles in several major industries. The long-troubled airline industry sustained two high-profile bankruptcies in 2002. U.S. Airways sought bankruptcy protection in August, while United Airlines filed for bankruptcy protection in December, after the federal government refused its request for a bailout. American, Delta, and several other major airlines announced substantial layoffs. Meanwhile, the telecommunications and "dot com" industries had still not recovered from the bursting of their stock market bubble in 1999 and

2000, and many sectors of the manufacturing industry were still trying to adjust to globalization.

Overhanging these troubles, however, was a series of corporate accounting scandals that began with the collapse of Enron Corporation in December 2001 amid allegations that the company, aided by its accountant Arthur Andersen, had used many questionable accounting practices to make its profits appear much larger than they were.

Allegations of accounting irregularities and outright fraud were reported at several other leading firms. WorldCom, the telecommunications giant, disclosed in June that it had lowered its earnings statement by $4 billion. A week later Xerox Corporation said it was lowering stated earnings by $1.4 billion. By the end of July at least fifteen major corporations and their accounting firms were under criminal and civil investigation for a variety of fraudulent or other irregular practices. Characterizing the string of revelations as "infectious greed," Federal Reserve chairman Alan Greenspan told a congressional committee in July that "lawyers, internal and external auditors, corporate boards, Wall Street security analysts, rating agencies, and large institutional holders of stock all failed for one reason or another to detect and blow the whistle on those who breached the level of trust essential to well-functioning markets."

The revelations left the stock market reeling. Standard & Poor's 500 stock index, for example, lost 30 percent of its value between the first of May and the end of July. The scandals cost millions of investors, both large and small, billions in losses, and thousands of workers lost their jobs. Many people whose 401k retirement plans were invested in the stock market watched helplessly as their pension funds were reduced or even wiped out. Congress moved quickly to approved tough new accounting regulations, but confidence in the stock market was not quick to return. Although the market regained some of the losses by year's end, investors clearly remained skittish. (Corporate scandals, p. 391)

Constrained State and Local Budgets

Another note of trouble sounded from the nation's governors, who said the states were in the worst fiscal shape since World War II, largely because of falling tax collections and mushrooming health care costs. Unlike the federal government, most states were prohibited by their constitutions from running a deficit. "Nearly every state is in crisis," the Fiscal Survey of States *for November 2002 reported. The survey, published twice a year by the National Governors Association (NGA) and the National Association of State Budget Officers, noted that spending grew only 1.3 percent in fiscal 2002 and was projected to stay at the same level in fiscal 2003, compared to 8.3 percent in fiscal 2001. Medicaid spending alone grew 13.2 percent in fiscal 2002, which meant that other programs had to be cut back. Thirty-seven states had to cut spending after their budgets for the year had been enacted.*

On the revenue side, forty-one states collected less revenue in taxes and fees than anticipated. Overall sales, personal income, and corporate income *tax collections were 9.7 percent lower than states' original estimates for the year. Twenty-three states raised taxes (mostly taxes on cigarettes) and fees for fiscal 2003 by a total of $8.3 billion. The last time such large tax increases occurred was in 1992.*

More cuts seemed inevitable for fiscal 2003, and those cuts were likely to be in programs that directly aided people, including health care and education. "You will see huge cuts in Medicaid," the federal-state health care program for the poor, predicted Raymond C. Scheppach, executive director of the NGA. Some states and local governments were warning that they might have to shorten the school year or fire teachers in order to balance their budgets.

Democrats and some Republicans in Congress were pushing the administration to include aid to state and local governments as part of a stimulus package. The Bush administration rejected these bipartisan efforts to help the states, noting that the federal government itself was facing severe budget constraints and a growing deficit.

Other Signs of Economic Hardship

Among other signs of growing economic hardship was an increase in the poverty rate. The Census Bureau reported September 24, 2002, that after falling for four years, the nation's poverty rate in 2001 rose to 11.7 percent from 11.3 percent in 2000, while median household income declined by 2.2 percent, to $42,228. Some 32.9 million people were poor in 2001—about 1.3 million more than in 2000. Most of the increase was among whites, where the poverty rate increased from 7.4 to 7.8 percent. African Americans had the highest poverty rate, at 22.7 percent. The poverty rate among children under age eighteen remained high and unchanged at 16.3 percent.

The increase in the poverty rate may have accounted for some of the increase in the number of Americans who did not have health insurance. Rising health care costs in general and prescription drug costs in particular were worrisome, particularly to those on low or fixed incomes. Soup kitchens began appearing in suburban neighborhoods for the first time, while the number of homeless began to increase, taxing already overburdened shelters in many cities. Some measures of crime, which had declined throughout the decade, began to climb again, in part, experts said, because of the tight economic situation. Higher energy prices also meant that more people were unable to afford heat at a time when states were less able to provide heating aid. (Health insurance, p. 666; crime rate, p. 784; prescription drugs, p. 945)

Preparing for War

For many businesses and individuals, concerns about the nation's economic well-being were further unsettled by periodic warnings from the Justice Department about the possibility of another terrorist attack against the United States. The ease with which everyday life in the United States could be disrupted was illustrated all too clearly in October, when two snipers brought the Washington, D.C., metropolitan area to nearly a standstill with a series of random shootings over a three-week killing spree.

Overshadowing those fears was the possibility that the United States would soon be engaged in a war with Iraq. Following his January 29 State of the Union speech, in which he identified Iraq as one of three countries comprising an "axis of evil," President Bush kept his administration focused on ousting Iraqi leader Saddam Hussein from power and using military force, if necessary, to disarm Iraq of the chemical and biological weapons the United States and other countries insisted Saddam was hiding. By the end of the year the Pentagon was engaged in a military buildup in the region that would allow a military attack on Iraq early in 2003. (Iraq, pp. 612, 713)

Late in the year North Korea—another member of Bush's axis of evil (the third was Iran)—raised international tensions when it acknowledged to U.S. officials that it had begun a program to enrich uranium for the production of nuclear weapons. U.S. demands that North Korea halt its weapons programs created the potential of yet another international standoff. (North Korea weapons program, p. 731)

In testimony before Congress on November 13, Federal Reserve chairman Greenspan cited "heightened geopolitical risks" as a main factor slowing the economic recovery. If Greenspan was right, and there seemed little doubt he was, the prospects for a speedy recovery in 2003 seemed bleak.

Following are the text of President George W. Bush's first economic report to Congress and excerpts from chapter 1 of the annual report of the Council of Economic Advisers, both submitted to Congress on February 5, 2002.

The documents were obtained from the Internet at w3 .access.gpo.gov/eop; accessed October 12, 2002.

ECONOMIC REPORT OF THE PRESIDENT

To the Congress of the United States:

Since the summer of 2000, economic growth has been unacceptably slow. This past year the inherited trends of deteriorating growth was fed by events, the most momentous of which was the terrorist attacks of September 11, 2001. The painful upshot has been the first recession in a decade. This is cause for compassion—and for action.

Our first priority was to help those Americans who were hurt most by the recession and the attacks on September 11. In the immediate aftermath of the attacks, my Administration sought to stabilize our air transportation system to keep Americans flying. Working with Congress, we provided assistance and aid to the affected areas of New York and Virginia. We sought to provide a stronger safety net for displaced workers, and we will continue these efforts.

Our economic recovery plan must be based on creating jobs in the private sector. My Administration has urged the Congress to accelerate tax relief for working Americans to speed economic growth and create jobs.

We are engaged in a war against terrorism that places new demands on our economy, and we must seek out every opportunity to build an economic foundation that will support this challenge. I am confident that Americans have proved they will rise to meet this challenge.

We must have an agenda not only for physical security, but also for economic security. Our strategy builds upon the character of Americans: removing economic barriers to their success, combining our workers and their skills with new technologies, and creating an environment where entrepreneurs and businesses large and small can grow and create jobs. Our vision must extend beyond America, engaging other countries in the virtuous cycle of free trade, raising the potential for global growth, and securing the gains from worldwide markets in goods and capitals. We must ensure that this effort builds economic bonds that encompass every American.

America faces a unique moment in history: our Nation is at war, our homeland was attacked, and our economy is in recession. In meeting these great challenges, we must draw strength from the enduring power of free markets and a free people. We must also look forward and work toward a stronger economy that will buttress the United States against an uncertain world and lift the fortunes of others worldwide.

George W. Bush
The White House
February 2002

THE ANNUAL REPORT OF THE COUNCIL OF ECONOMIC ADVISERS

Chapter 1

Restoring Prosperity

Over the past two decades, the Nation has witnessed an impressive increase in prosperity. Over 35 million jobs were created, and real income nearly doubled, producing an unprecedented standard of living. This economic success also serves as an example of what an open, free market economy—one that relies on the private sector as the engine of growth—can achieve.

A hallmark of the economy has been its ability to weather adverse economic developments in a flexible and resilient manner. This is not an accident but rather a characteristic of an economic system that relies on market forces to determine adjustments in economic activity. But such an economy, even in the presence of sound fiscal and monetary policies, is not immune to business cycles. Economic activity in 2001 is an example of how a series of adverse developments can cause setbacks on the road to greater prosperity. The last year also highlighted the value of continued efforts to strengthen the policy environment in a way that allows the private sector both to recover more quickly and flourish more strongly in the future.

Macroeconomic Performance in 2001:
Softer Economy, Harder Choices

U.S. economic growth continued to decelerate during 2001. It was apparent early in the year that policymakers would face considerable challenges as the rate of growth slowed from the rapid rates of past years. The momentum placing downward pressure on economic activity appeared to subside by midsummer, however, by which time growth of real gross domestic product (GDP) had come to a virtual standstill. Economic conditions showed some tentative signs of firming, and growth prospects were brightening. All that changed on September 11. The President, Congress, and other policymakers responded decisively to the damage and disruptions caused by the terrorist attacks, while continuing to work to strengthen the long-run economic fundamentals.

Aggregate Demand During the First Three Quarters

The deceleration of real GDP in 2001 continued a slowdown in economic activity that had begun the previous year. . . . Real GDP growth over the first three quarters remained barely positive, at 0.1 percent on an annualized basis; however, the economy steadily weakened through this period, ending with a 1.3 percent annualized contraction in real GDP in the third quarter. Although several key components of aggregate demand rose moderately, overall growth was dragged down by unusually weak investment spending. . . .

Consumption

Personal consumption expenditures grew 2.8 percent at an annual rate in the first half of 2001, followed by a 1.0 percent increase in the third quarter. . . . Consumption growth in the first three quarters was 2.2 percent—notably slower than the 4.8 percent rate of the previous 3 years.

Spending for all types of consumption slowed in 2001. Growth in spending on nondurable goods declined to a 1.1 percent annual rate through the third quarter, from a 4.5 percent rate in 1998–2000. The sharp decline in nondurable consumption is somewhat surprising, because swings in this category of consumption tend to be more muted than those in overall consumption. . . .

Growth in durable goods spending also subsided, but remained relatively strong, in the first three quarters of 2001: purchases rose 6.1 percent at an annual rate compared with 9.7 percent on average in 1998–2000. This recent strength has been atypical because, during most economic downturns, durable goods spending tends to slow more sharply than nondurable goods spending. Part of the explanation is that two key durable goods industries have proved more resilient to the slowdown than in the past. Furniture and household equipment grew robustly, as the housing sector stayed healthy in 2001. And although growth in sales of motor vehicles and parts was anemic early in the year, these sales remained remarkably high for a period of such marked slowing in overall activity.

Finally, consumption of services—the least cyclical component of consumption—grew at a 1.9 percent annual rate in the first three quarters of 2001, down from a 4.0 percent rate over 1998–2000. Medical care spending, however, continued its strong upward trend.

These patterns in consumption spending—which constitutes two-thirds of GDP—reflected several key economic crosscurrents. On the downside, the decline in equity markets and the deterioration in labor markets (discussed below) reduced wealth and consumer confidence. On the upside, housing prices continued to climb, rising at roughly an 8 percent annual rate. In addition, lower mortgage interest rates sparked the strongest wave of home refinancing ever, transforming housing equity into more liquid forms of wealth. Refinancing is estimated to have increased household liquidity (from increased cash flow and cashouts) by about $80 billion during the year. In addition, real disposable personal income, aided somewhat by provisions of the President's tax cut—reduced withholding and the payment of rebates for the new 10 percent personal income tax bracket—rose at a solid 4.5 percent annual rate during the first three quarters.

Investment Spending

Real gross private domestic investment fell at a double-digit annual rate (roughly 12 percent) in each of the first two quarters of 2001—the steepest decline in investment spending in a decade. . . . The year began with a sizable inventory liquidation, which accounted for most of the decline in gross private domestic investment in the first quarter and subtracted 2.6 percentage points from the growth rate of real GDP. Inventory reduction remained a drag on GDP growth in subsequent quarters, with manufacturing industries shedding inventories at a faster pace than wholesalers and retailers. By the end of the third quarter, the inventory-to-sales ratio had returned to a level close to the average over the previous 3 years, indicating that the downward phase of the inventory cycle may soon be ending.

Nonresidential business fixed investment contracted sharply in 2001, in stark contrast to the investment boom from 1995 to early 2000. In the first quarter this category of investment fell at only a 0.2 percent annual rate—the first decline in 9 years. In the second quarter, however, it fell at a 14.6 percent annual rate, with declines in investment in structures and in equipment and software of 12.3 percent and 15.4 percent, respectively. Investment in information processing equipment and software alone fell at a 19.5 percent rate in the second quarter. The widespread decline in business fixed investment continued in the third quarter with an 8.5 percent contraction, combining a 7.6 percent drop in structures investment with an 8.8 percent decline in equipment and software spending. Capital spending on computers and peripherals during the second and third quarters was hit particularly hard, plunging at a 28.6 percent rate.

The housing sector was a bright spot in 2001. Lower mortgage rates and rising real income helped to support rising residential investment in each of the first three quarters; growth for the period averaged 5.6 percent at an annual rate. Investment in single-family structures rose 6.0 percent, after declining during most of 2000. Investment spending on multifamily structures rose briskly at a 15.3 percent rate. Investment in residential building improvements increased at a 3.2 percent rate.

Government Spending

Government spending—Federal, State, and local levels combined—added to economic activity over the first three quarters of the year. Federal Government spending increased at a 2.9 percent annual rate during this period. In contrast, Federal spending in 2000 fell by 1.4 percent, and over 1995–2000 it grew at only a 0.1 percent average rate. Last year's increase was driven by national defense expenditure, which rose 4.4 percent through the first three quarters. Defense spending on research and development as well as personnel support accounted for most of the increase. Nondefense expenditure grew only 0.2 percent in the first three quarters of 2001.

State and local government spending increased 3.8 percent at an annual rate in the first three quarters. State and local spending has increased steadily over the past decade, averaging 2.8 percent annual growth from 1990 to 2000 and 3.2 percent from 1995 to 2000. Investment by State and local governments rose much faster (4.6 percent a year on average) than their consumption (2.8 percent) during 1995–2000. However, consumption expenditure accounts for 80 percent of State and local spending.

Net Exports

Net exports exerted a smaller drag on economic activity in 2001 than in 2000. Both imports and exports fell significantly during the year, but the drop in imports was larger. Real exports of goods and services, measured at an annual rate, declined $95.3 billion through the third quarter, mostly because of a decline in exports of capital goods—especially high-technology goods—as a result of the global economic slowdown (discussed further below). Over the same period, real imports declined $105.3 billion. Real imports of services suffered one of the largest declines on record in the third quarter, largely because international travel was disrupted in September.

Overall, net exports contributed 0.1 percentage point to real GDP growth in the first three quarters of the year. By comparison, in 2000 net exports depressed real GDP growth by 0.8 percentage point.

Preliminary Evidence on Aggregate Demand in the Fourth Quarter

The terrorist attacks of September 11 changed the direction of the macroeconomy. Before the attacks, the economy had been showing tentative signs of stabilizing after its long deceleration, and many forecasters expected real GDP growth to accelerate in the third and fourth quarters of 2001. Immediately after the attacks, however, the economy turned down because of the direct effect of the assault on the Nation's economic and financial infrastructure and because of the indirect, but more significant, effect on consumer and business confidence. The drop was sufficient to turn the sluggish period of economic activity into a recession. . . .

Beyond the initial impacts, the attacks continued to have a significant negative effect on the economy as uncertainty about the future led to a steep decline in consumer and business spending. Consumers retrenched as they mourned the loss of life and reevaluated the risks inherent in even the most mundane activities, such as shopping at malls and traveling by air. Meanwhile businesses adopted a more pessimistic outlook about the prospects for a speedy recovery. The underlying psychology was affected again in October, by the discovery of anthrax spores delivered through the mail distribution system, although the direct macroeconomic effects of this attack have been fairly limited.

Preliminary evidence indicates that economic activity at the beginning of the fourth quarter of 2001 suffered a pronounced decline. The industrial sector contracted at a faster pace in October than earlier in the year, and job losses mounted. By November, however, some tentative signs had emerged that business conditions were deteriorating at a slower pace. For example, the decline in industrial production was milder, and nondefense capital goods spending appeared to have bottomed out, with new orders recovering from the trough in September. Construction spending also performed well, as weather in the fall was unseasonably warm. By December the manufacturing sector, which had been particularly hard hit in 2001, witnessed increases in the length of the average workweek and in factory overtime. Meanwhile the Purchasing Managers' Index (PMI) of the Institute for Supply Management (formerly the National Association of Purchasing Management) rebounded sharply, with a jump to 48.2 in December from 39.8 in October. The production component of the PMI rose to 50.6 from 40.9 in October; the new orders index surged to end the year at 54.9. Moreover, industrial production in December was nearly unchanged after several months of sizable declines.

Despite the initial dropoff in consumer confidence after the terrorist attacks, consumer spending bounced back within the quarter from its September plunge. Real personal consumption expenditures on durable goods, nondurable goods, and services rose considerably in October and November. Purchases of automobiles and light trucks contributed substantially to the rebound, as consumers responded favorably to the incentive programs offered by manufacturers and dealers, such as zero-percent financing and rebates. Automobile and light truck sales surged to a record 21 million units at an annual rate in October, then moderated to something closer to the average 17-million-unit selling pace of the first three quarters. Even though nominal retail sales of goods excluding motor vehicles edged down in November and December, falling prices for energy and consumer goods suggest that real consumption spending continued to rise.

The performance of financial markets confirmed the view that economic conditions were firming in the fourth quarter. Stock market prices rebounded from a sharp decline after September 11. . . .

Labor Markets

. . . Labor markets became substantially less tight in 2001. The total unemployment rate rose from 4.0 percent in December 2000 to 5.8 percent a year later, still below the average rate for the past 20 years of 6.2 percent. The average duration of unemployment rose by 2 weeks during 2001, ending the year at 14.5 weeks. More than half of this increase occurred in the last 3 months of 2001. . . .

Inflation

Inflation remained low and stable in 2001. The consumer price index (CPI) rose only 1.6 percent during the 12 months ending in December. Consumer energy prices for fuel oil, electricity, natural gas, and gasoline tumbled 13.0 percent, reflecting a collapse in crude oil and in wellhead natural gas prices. In contrast, energy price inflation a year ago was 14.2 percent. Food prices rose 2.8 percent, the same rate as a year ago. The CPI excluding the volatile food and energy components—often referred to as the core CPI—posted another year of stable inflation. Core inflation was 2.7 percent, up somewhat from its 2.3 percent average rate over the past 4 years.

Productivity and Employment Costs

Despite the economic slowdown, nonfarm business labor productivity grew at a 1.2 percent annual rate during the first three quarters of the year. Although below the 2.4 percent average rate recorded during 1995–2000, productivity growth has been remarkably strong for this stage of the business cycle. During previous postwar recessions, productivity growth averaged 0.8 percent. Manufacturing productivity, in contrast, edged down at a 0.2 percent annual rate for the first three quarters of the year, compared with a 0.6 percent decline in the 1990–91 recession. The 2001 figure represents the first decrease in manufacturing productivity in the past 8 years, and it reflects the pronounced slump in the industrial sector that began in mid-2000. . . .

The Economic Outlook

The Administration expects that the economy will recover in 2002. The economy continues to display characteristics favorable to long-term growth: productivity growth remains strong, and inflation remains low and stable.

Near-Term Outlook: Poised for Recovery

Real GDP growth is expected to pick up early in 2002. . . . The pace is expected to be slow initially, followed by an acceleration thereafter; over the four quarters of 2002 real GDP is expected to grow 2.7 percent. The unemployment rate is projected to continue rising through the middle of 2002, when it is expected to peak around 6 percent.

As discussed earlier, the decline in aggregate demand during the past year was concentrated in inventory investment, business fixed investment, and exports. Of these downward pressures, that from inventory disinvestment is projected to reverse its course soonest and most rapidly, as the pace of liquidation is forecast to recede dramatically in the first quarter of 2002. By the end of 2001 inventories had become quite lean, making it likely that, once sales resume their growth, stockbuilding will boost real GDP growth.

Growth in business investment and exports may take longer to reassert itself. Nonresidential investment fell sharply in 2001, and some downward momentum probably remained at the start of 2002. Still, the financial foundations for investment remain positive: real short-term interest rates are low, prices of computers are again falling rapidly, and equity prices moved up during the fourth quarter. Indications late in the year suggested that these factors were contributing to an upturn in new orders for nondefense capital goods in October and November. The Administration projects that business fixed investment will return to positive growth around the middle of 2002 and resume rapid growth thereafter.

The past year's decline in exports reflects stagnating growth among the United States' trading partners. Consensus estimates of foreign growth in 2002 are anemic as well. In these circumstances any rebound in exports is likely to lag behind the expected recovery of U.S. GDP as a whole. Imports meanwhile are projected to grow faster than GDP. As a result, net exports and the current account deficit are likely to become increasingly negative during 2002.

Consumption growth slowed during the past year but has remained in positive territory. This slowing may be attributable to the decline in the stock market from its peak in March 2000. But in the absence of further stock market declines, such restraint is expected to wane. Consumption will also be supported by fiscal stimulus and interest rate cuts. The major provisions of EGTRRA [the 2001 tax cut legislation] will lower tax liabilities by about $69 billion in 2002 (up from its contribution of $57 billion in 2001).

Inflation Forecast

As measured by the GDP price index, inflation was stable at about 2.3 percent during the four quarters ending in the third quarter of 2001. The Administration expects this measure of inflation to fall to 1.9 percent over the four quarters of 2002. The unemployment rate is now above the level that the Administration considers to be the center of the range consistent with stable inflation, and capacity utilization in the industrial sector is substantially below its historical average. Despite faster-than-trend growth of output in 2003 and 2004, some downward pressure will be maintained on the inflation rate, because the unemployment rate is projected to remain high over that period. As a result, inflation in terms of the GDP price index is expected to inch down to 1.7 percent in 2003 before edging up to 1.9 percent over the forecast period.

In contrast, consumer price inflation is likely to edge up temporarily over the four quarters of 2002, to 2.4 percent, reflecting energy price fluctuations. (Petroleum-related goods make up a larger share of consumer budgets, on which the CPI is based, than of the production of final goods in the economy, on which the GDP price index is based.) In 2001 CPI inflation was held down by a 13 percent decline in energy prices. In 2002 petroleum prices are expected to stabilize, and energy price inflation is projected to be positive, but still moderate. Following a temporary increase in 2002, overall CPI inflation is projected to edge down and eventually flatten out at about 2.3 percent from 2003 forward.

Long-Term Outlook: Strengthening
the Foundation for the Future

The Administration forecasts real GDP growth to average 3.1 percent a year during the 11 years through 2012. The growth rate of the economy over the long run is determined primarily by the growth rates of its supply-side components, which include population, labor force participation, productivity, and the workweek. . . .

The Administration expects nonfarm labor productivity to grow at a 2.1 percent average pace over the forecast period, the same as over the entire period since the previous business cycle peak in the third quarter of 1990. This forecast is noticeably more conservative than the 2.6 percent average annual growth rate of actual productivity from 1995 to 2001. . . .

The Policy Outlook: An Agenda for Economic Security

The events of 2001 have brought home to us a simple lesson: We cannot be complacent about the security of American lives. Nor can we be complacent about our rate of economic growth, our gains in productivity, or our successes in the international marketplace. The war against terrorism steps up the demands on our economy. We must seek every opportunity to remove obstacles to greater efficiency and seek new ways to combine our workers' skills, our new technologies, the drive of our entrepreneurs, the efficiency of our financial markets, and the strength of our small businesses to yield faster growth. As we integrate ever more closely our own resources, so must we also extend this integration abroad, addressing the economic roots of terrorism and securing the gains from worldwide markets in goods and capital. This is our economic challenge.

The United States boasts a more rapid long-term rate of productivity growth than do other major industrialized economies. Nonetheless, the Administration is committed to seeking opportunities to enable the economy to grow even more rapidly in the future. Growth, of course, is not an end in itself. As the President has said, we seek "prosperity with a purpose." Economic growth raises standards of living and generates resources that may be devoted to a variety of activities in the market and beyond. Growth can fund environmental protection, the good works of charitable organizations, and a wide variety of nonmarket goods and services that benefit the United States, other industrialized economies, and developing economies alike.

To build upon our past success and rise to our new challenges, we must remove impediments to growth and build the institutions necessary to foster improved economic performance. For example . . . one of the President's top priorities is the U.S.-led effort toward more open global trade. Trade raises the productivity of Americans, and the United States has an opportunity to reap significant gains from future trade agreements.

Another area of interest is science and technology, long an important source of economic growth. For example, although information technology-producing industries account for roughly one-twelfth of total output, they contributed nearly a third to economic growth between 1995 and 1999. They generate some of the best and highest paying new jobs and contribute strongly to productivity growth. Technology also improves our quality of life. New agricultural technologies are increasing crop yields while reducing the need to spray herbicides and insecticides on our foods or into the atmosphere. More generally, however, it is important to establish incentives that will ensure continued growth in innovation and the new technologies that will define the 21st century. We must not only invest in basic research, but also ensure that the intellectual property of innovators is secure at home and abroad.

Getting the most out of the economy's resources also means avoiding unnecessary costs. Prominent among these are the costs—in terms of slower economic growth and waste—associated with the Federal tax code. The entire tax system would benefit from changes to address its complexity and inefficiency. With the President's leadership, progress has been made with the individual income tax by reducing marginal tax rates and improving tax fairness. Much more needs to be done, however, to ease the burden of taxation on the economy, to help it generate resources and increase productivity.

The current tax code imposes multiple layers of taxation, whose inefficiency costs may be as high as ½ percent of GDP a year, according to the Treasury Department. In addition, tax complexity is much more than an irritant around April 15: it, too, imposes real costs on taxpayers and the economy. Taxpayers bear the cost in terms of the billions of dollars they spend—on recordkeeping, tax help, and their own valuable time—trying to comply. Tax compliance costs range from $70 billion to $125 billion a year. The economy also suffers because tax complexity raises the uncertainty surrounding business decisions, wastes resources, reduces our international competitiveness, and lowers productivity. These are costs that produce few benefits. They are largely avoidable. To get the most out of our economy, we must investigate options for tax reform.

The deregulation of the economy over the past 25 years has been a tremendous source of economic flexibility and productivity growth. We must build on that success. Deregulation of several key sectors during the 1970s and 1980s has brought substantial benefits to consumers and to the economy at large. In the 20 years following the beginning of airline deregulation, the average fare declined 33 percent in real terms. Rates for long-distance telecommunications dropped 40 to 47 percent in the 10 years following deregulation of that market.

Partly because of increased competition arising from reductions in banking regulations, banks have greatly expanded the financial services they offer customers, including important new tools for diversifying risk. Together these price declines and quality improvements across a range of deregulated industries have yielded substantial economic benefits. One study estimates the combined economic benefit of deregulating just three industries—airlines, motor carriers, and railroads—at about ½ percent of GDP each year.

This important strength of our economy must be protected against unintended interference and extended to new spheres. Competition and incentives to compete are at the core of exploiting opportunities to achieve faster growth. . . . The rule of law is central to efficient markets. Today, however, frivolous lawsuits and the lure of windfall recoveries are transforming America from a lawful society to a litigious one. The litigation explosion imposes a variety of costs on all of us—as much as 2 percent of GDP by one estimate—and damages the prospects for growth. The inefficiencies in our tort system are a pure waste, an unnecessary tax on our attempts to grow faster. To reduce this wasteful distortion we must address the incentives that lead to unnecessary torts and unreasonably large settlements.

We must reexamine the provision of economic security for every individual American. . . . Personal accounts within the national retirement system would enhance the ability to diversify retirement portfolios, including diversifying part of retirement security away from the unsustainable current system. In doing so, they could for the first time provide rights of ownership, wealth accumulation, and inheritance within the Social Security framework.

We must design an efficient set of institutions that meet the short-run needs of displaced workers and move them quickly toward productive activities. The past year has displayed an extreme form of the shocks to which our economy may be subjected. The President's vision of economic security recognizes that many events impact the economy all the time. We should think comprehensively about these policies and focus our efforts on incentives for getting workers back to work, and quickly. Resources should be devoted flexibly to basic needs and retraining, without creating an incentive for unnecessarily long spells between jobs, because benefits extended under the wrong conditions create a "tax" when a new job is taken and those benefits are lost.

Finally, getting the most out of the economy will require an emphasis on efficiency in government as well. If government spending grows without discipline, billions of dollars will be siphoned away from private sector innovation, taxes will rise, and growth will suffer. The President's Management Agenda seeks to shift the emphasis of government toward results, not process. It aims to replace the present Federal Government hierarchy with a flatter, more responsive management structure and to establish a performance-based system. . . .

CENSUS SURVEY ON INTERNET USE IN THE UNITED STATES
February 5, 2002

Just two decades after the general introduction of personal computers, two-thirds of all Americans were using them at home, in school, or at work, according to a Census Bureau survey conducted in September 2001. Less than a decade after the public first became familiar with the Internet, more than half of all Americans were using it, the survey found. "Few technologies have spread as quickly, or become so widely used, as computers and the Internet," the Commerce Department said in "A Nation Online: How Americans Are Expanding Their Use of the Internet," a report based on the Census Bureau survey and released February 5, 2002. "These information technologies are rapidly becoming modern fixtures of modern social and economic life, opening opportunities and new avenues for many Americans."

The increasingly widespread use of high technology was not entirely cost-free, however. Millions of Americans—especially the underprivileged—had yet to gain access to computers and the Internet, putting them at a competitive disadvantage in the employment marketplace. Those who did use the Internet faced numerous annoyances, including viruses spread by e-mails, a surge of unsolicited e-mail messages (called "spam"), and concerns about whether their children were being unduly exposed to the Web's ubiquitous violence and pornography. (Internet pornography, p. 287)

More Americans Online

The Census Bureau asked how Americans used computers and the Internet during its "Current Population Survey" conducted in September 2001. The survey included about 57,000 households and 137,000 individuals across the country, the bureau said. The survey documented, in hard numbers, what had become obvious by the beginning of the twenty-first century: Personal computers and the Internet had become nearly as important to the daily lives of most Americans as the telephone, jet air travel, and television.

Perhaps the single most striking finding of the survey was the rapid growth in access to the Internet during the one-year period between the

Census Bureau's previous survey in 2000 and the September 2001 survey. In August 2000 the survey estimated that 116.5 million Americans over the age of three had used the Internet. Just thirteen months later the corresponding estimate was 142.8 million people. In percentage terms, Internet use grew from 44.4 percent of the population to 53.9 percent during that period.

The growth in Internet use occurred across all demographic categories measured by the Census Bureau, including age, race, income, educational attainment, and geographic location. As could be expected, the rate of Internet use corresponded with the level of family income and educational attainment. Only about 30 percent of those reporting a family income of $25,000 or less used the Internet, but more than 75 percent of those in families with incomes above $75,000 said they had used the Internet. Similarly, Internet use stood at about 40 percent for those with a high school diploma but more than 80 percent for those with a bachelor's degree.

In its survey, the Census Bureau did not ask Americans why they used the Internet. Another series of surveys conducted between March 2000 and January 2002 by the Pew Internet and American Life Project asked detailed questions about what people did on the Internet. The findings were released February 3 in "Getting Serious Online." The report described how Americans increasingly were using the Internet at work and also at home for serious research on questions of importance to them, such as looking for information about health issues. Americans also were using e-mail not just to exchange greetings and gossip but also to seek advice and express personal concerns to friends and family members, the survey showed.

On a typical day, as of March 2001 according to the report, more than 64 million Americans went online. Sending e-mail was by far the most common activity of those with Internet access (54 percent), with getting news second (26 percent). Other major Web activities were: surfing the Web for fun, looking for information about a hobby, and doing research for a job (all at about 20 percent); and looking for political news or information and checking the weather (both at 17 percent). In "Counting on the Internet," a survey published December 19, the Pew researchers found that most Americans believed they could find accurate and reliable information on the Internet. Perhaps most striking was the increasing reliance on the Internet for information about health problems. "When asked where they will go for information the next time they need health or medical information, Internet users are about as likely to say they will turn to the Internet for information as they are to contact a medical professional," the Pew study said. "Forty-six percent say they will find health care information online next time they need it and 47 percent say they will contact a medical professional."

The "Digital Divide" Issue

During the late 1990s the administration of President Bill Clinton had devoted considerable attention to the issue of a "digital divide"—the fact that poor people and racial minorities were much less likely to have access to computers and the Internet than the rest of society. Starting with the 1996 Telecommunications Act (PL 104–104), the Clinton administration and Congress took several steps to ease public access to the Internet, including federally funded programs that financed computer centers for libraries and nonprofit organizations. (Background, Historic Documents of 1999, p. 368)

By 2002 the digital divide question had become one of perception. Civil rights groups and organizations dedicated to increasing public use of the Internet noted that 40 percent or more of racial minorities and low-income people did not have computers or Internet access. The Bush administration focused instead on the strong growth in computer and Internet use among those groups, arguing that poor people and minorities were rapidly catching up with the rest of society.

The disagreement was of more than academic significance because the administration's proposed fiscal 2003 budget called for cutting more than $100 million from Clinton-era programs intended to broaden public access to the Internet. The Leadership Conference on Civil Rights Education Fund and the Benton Foundation produced their own study in July that used the Census Bureau figures and other data to challenge the administration's approach. Called "Bringing a Nation Online: The Importance of Federal Leadership," the report said the administration's position was "overly optimistic" and that "specific segments of society—particularly the underserved communities—continue to significantly lag behind and that the digital divide remains a persistent problem."

Teaching Students about Technology

Although computers were becoming common in American households and workplaces, millions of Americans had little understanding of how advanced technology worked, according to a report issued January 17 by the National Academy of Engineering and the National Research Council. "Most Americans know little about the world of technology, yet from day to day they must make critical decisions that are technologically based, such as whether to buy genetically engineered foods or transmit personal data over the Internet," the two research organizations said in "Technically Speaking: Why All Americans Need to Know More about Technology." "Moreover, the use of technology as a learning tool in the classroom is often confused with the broader concept of being technologically literate—knowing something of the nature and history of technology, as well as having a certain level of skill in using technologies and thinking critically about them." The report was based on a study sponsored by the National Science Foundation and the Battelle Memorial Institute.

The report called for a broad-based initiative to improve American's understanding of technology and ability to make wise use of it. Education about technology should begin at the kindergarten level, the report said, and "the connection between all subjects and technology should be emphasized throughout a student's education." In too many cases, educators mistook the use of computers in the classroom for education about technology issues.

Privacy, Spamming Issues

*As useful as the Internet was, its growing popularity resulted in un-
pleasant side-effects, including a deluge of spam e-mail messages, periodic
surges of computer viruses, and easy access by children to sites featuring
pornography and violence. These problems deterred some people from joining the Internet crowd, but some experts said a greater concern was that
spam and viruses were clogging the Internet and costing millions of dollars
in unnecessary expense for businesses and individuals.*

*By 2002 the prevalence of spam had become by far the most common
complaint among Internet users, according to several studies and public interest groups. Surveys conducted during 2001 and 2002 estimated that 15–
40 percent of all e-mail messages were unsolicited and unwanted by the recipients. If true, that meant spam e-mail messages numbered in the billions; a study by the IDC research firm estimated the world's total e-mail
traffic in 2002 at 31 billion messages.*

*Consumer groups and government agencies said spam was more than
simply annoying to its recipients. The Coalition Against Unsolicited Commercial E-mail, a group formed specifically to draw attention to the problem, said many spam messages made fraudulent or misleading claims,
contained pornography and other material objectionable to many recipients, took up valuable space on individual computers and system networks,
and forced recipients to spend time downloading and deleting messages
they did not want. In a July 2002 report the Federal Trade Commission
(FTC) noted that "deceptive spam is especially troublesome because it can
cheat consumers out of their money, undermine consumer confidence in online commerce and harm legitimate Internet marketers."*

*Internet users could buy software programs and services to filter out
spam messages, but experts said many of these antispam technologies were
ineffective or worked only for limited periods, until the spammers devised
new ways of getting around them. Many Internet users also were looking
to the federal government for assistance. Timothy J. Muris, chairman of the
FTC (which had primary jurisdiction over the spam issue), told a computer
industry forum in June that the commission received as many as 40,000
samples of spam each month from irate Internet users.*

*On November 13 the FTC and twelve federal, state, and local law enforce-
ment agencies in eight northeastern states announced a coordinated anti-
spamming campaign. The FTC reach settlements with four companies said
to have engaged in spamming, and it filed complaints against three others.
One of the actions involved a company that claimed to help Internet users
reduce the amount of spam they received; instead, the FTC said, the company generated even more spam e-mail to those who used its services. In
addition to the FTC actions, state and local officials in New Jersey, New York,
and the six New England states sent notices to 100 companies and individuals warning them that they faced prosecution for spamming activities.*

*Even if government regulations and lawsuits succeeded in clamping
down on U.S.-based companies that engaged in deceptive spamming, the*

international nature of the Internet would allow the offenders to simply shift their operations to another country. Only a handful of countries, primarily in Western Europe, had taken steps against fraudulent Internet activities within their borders.

Following are excerpts from "A Nation Online: How Americans Are Expanding Their Use of the Internet," a report released February 5, 2002, by the U.S. Department of Commerce.

The document was obtained from the Internet at nita.doc .gov/ntiahome/dn/index.html; accessed October 24, 2002.

Chapter 1: Overview

Americans' use of information technologies grew at phenomenal rates in 2001. This past year saw a rapid increase in computer and Internet use, not only in homes, but also at the workplace, schools, and other locations. Broadband connections, available principally through cable modems and digital subscriber lines (DSL), are making higher-speed connections available to an increasing number of Americans and expanding options for online usage.

The Department of Commerce's Census Bureau surveyed approximately 57,000 households containing more than 137,000 individuals in all 50 states and the District of Columbia and found a rapid diffusion of these technologies. At the time of the survey, September 2001, 60.2 million U.S. homes (or 56.5 percent) had a personal computer. Seven of every eight households with computers (88.1 percent) also subscribed to the Internet. As a result, more than half of U.S. households (53.9 million homes, or 50.5 percent) had Internet connections. . . . [T]his remarkable rise to over 50 percent household penetration of both computers and the Internet occurred very quickly.

On an individual (rather than household) basis, as of September 2001 two-thirds (66.8 percent) of the people in the United States used a computer at home, school and/or work. The vast majority of those who used computers (80.6 percent) were also connecting to the Internet. These two factors taken together contributed to a substantial rise in Internet use. By September 2001, 143 million people in the United States (or 53.9 percent) were using the Internet, up from 116.5 million people (or 44.5 percent) in August 2000. The widespread increase in information technologies in the United States has occurred across all 50 states. . . . [I]n August 2000, few states had more than 50 percent of their population using the Internet. By September 2001, most states had at least half of their population online.

The rapid diffusion of the Internet is not a unique U.S. phenomenon. According to data compiled by the Organization for Economic Cooperation and Development (OECD) from various nations, the rise in Internet use is truly a global phenomenon.

The spread of new technologies, such as the Internet, can be described by a variety of metrics—such as the percent of households connected and the percent of the population connected. . . . [S]electing a different basis of measurement can affect the results: in September 2001, 50.5 percent of households had Internet connections; 56.7 percent of the total U.S. population lived in households with these connections; a lower 43.6 percent of Americans were using the Internet in their homes; while 53.9 percent of the total population used the Internet at some location.

This report features data on *individuals* more than data on *households*, for several reasons. First, focusing on individuals permits us to study such factors as age, gender, education, and employment status in determining computer and Internet use. Second, Internet access is more frequently occurring outside the home, at such locations as work, schools, and libraries. And finally, a small but growing number of Internet connections are increasingly occurring over personal devices, such as wireless phones and personal digital assistants, in addition to the computer. For some variables, such as the type of home Internet connection and reasons for non-subscribership, the household remains the unit of measurement because that is the level at which the question was most appropriately asked. For purposes of historical comparisons with earlier data available only on a household basis, we also use current household data. . . .

Chapter 2: Computer and Internet Use

Increasingly, we are a nation online. Individuals continue to expand their use of computers and the Internet. As of September 2001, 174 million people or 65.6 percent of the U.S. population were computer users. One hundred forty three million people or 53.9 percent of the population used the Internet.

Both computer and Internet use have increased substantially in the past few years. Since 1997 computer use has grown at a rate of 5.3 percent on an annualized basis. Internet use has grown at a rate of 20 percent a year since 1998. In the 13 months before September 2001, over 26 million more people went online.

The demographic profile of computer and Internet users provided in this chapter reveals that growth in computer and Internet use is broadly based. In every income bracket, at every level of education, in every age group, for people of every race and among people of Hispanic origin, among both men and women, many more people use computers and the Internet now than did so in the recent past. Some people are still more likely to be Internet users than others. Individuals living in low-income households or having little education, still trail the national average. However, broad measures of Internet use in the United States suggest that over time Internet use has become more equitable.

Demographic Factors in Computer and Internet Use

Income

Family income remains an indicator of whether a person uses a computer or the Internet. Individuals who live in high-income households are more likely to be computer and Internet users than those who live in low-income households. This relationship has held true in each successive survey of computer and Internet use.

Nonetheless, both computer and Internet use have increased steadily across all income categories over time. While notable differences remain in Internet use across income categories, Internet use has grown considerably among people who live in lower income households. Among people living in the lowest income households (less than $15,000 annually), Internet use had increased from 9.2 percent in October 1997 to 25.0 percent in September 2001.

Internet use is growing faster among people in lower family income brackets. Internet use among people who live in households where family income is less than $15,000 grew at an annual rate of 25 percent between December 1998 and September 2001. Over the same period Internet use grew at an annual rate of 11 percent among people living in households where family income was $75,000 or more.

Not only did the Internet use rate grow faster for those living in lower income households, but growth also accelerated between August 2000 and September 2001 relative to December 1998 to August 2000. For people living in households in the two lowest income brackets, the Internet use rate grew faster between August 2000 and September 2001 than between December 1998 and August 2000. This acceleration in the growth of Internet use did not occur among people living in higher income households

Employment Status

Both the employed and the not employed (either unemployed or not in the labor force) saw growth in computer and Internet use rates since 1997.

People who are employed are more likely to be both computer and Internet users. In 2001, 73.2 percent of employed people (age 16 and older) were computer users and 65.4 percent were Internet users. In contrast, only 40.8 percent of people who were not employed were computer users and 36.9 were Internet users.

Age

Increases in computer and Internet use have occurred across the entire age distribution. Since December 1997, the entire age distribution has shifted upward with each new survey.

Computer and Internet use are strongly associated with the age of the individual. [C]hildren and teenagers were the most likely to be computer users. Computer use is also relatively high—about 70 percent in 2001—among people in their prime workforce years (generally people in their 20s to their 50s). Those above this age range are less likely to be computer users. This pattern is consistent in both 1997 and 2001.

Rates of Internet use show a similar pattern that holds true for each year of data. Internet use rates climb steadily as age increases for children through young adults, level off at relatively high rates for people between ages 26 and 55, and then fall among people at higher ages.

One would expect to see the current plateau for Internet use among those age 25 to 55 extend to older ages over time because the overall upward shift in the age distribution [is composed of two elements]. . . . The first is an absolute increase in Internet use by people and the second is a cohort effect. The cohort effect describes the fact that the people who are in the 55-year-old age cohort in September 2001 are not the same people who were in this age group in earlier surveys. The 55 year olds of September 2001 were mostly 51 year olds when Census first asked about Internet use in October 1997. People who used the Internet when they were younger will likely continue to do so as they age.

Gender

Males and females have had approximately equal rates of computer use since 1997. In 1997, males were more likely than females to be Internet users. Between October 1997 and August 2000, this difference disappeared. Since August 2000, males and females have had virtually identical rates of Internet use. In September 2001, the Internet use rate was 53.9 percent for males and 53.8 percent for females.

The annual growth rates from August 2000 to September 2001 were similar: 19 percent growth at an annual rate for males and 20 percent for females.

Although the aggregate rates of use and growth by gender have equalized, there are still gender-related differences in Internet use within various age groups. Women, from approximately age 20 to age 50, are more likely to be Internet users than men. From about age 60 and older, men have higher rates of Internet use than women.

Gender can also be considered in the context of household type. In previous years people who lived in single parent households (where children under the age of 18 are present) headed by women were less likely to be Internet users. The Internet use rate among people living in female-headed single parent households grew dramatically between August 2000 and September 2001, and the differential between Internet use rates between people living in male and female single parent households has largely disappeared.

However . . . people who live in households headed by married couples (where children under the age of 18 are present) are more likely than people who live in other household types to be both computer and Internet users.

Educational Attainment

Educational attainment also factors into computer and Internet use. The higher a person's level of education, the more likely he or she will be a computer or Internet user.

. . . [A]dults (age 25 and above) with education beyond college were the most likely to be both computer and Internet users each year of the survey. Those with Bachelor's degrees trailed close behind. At the opposite end of the spectrum are those adults whose highest level of education is less than high school. In September 2001, the computer use rate for the latter was 17.0 percent and the Internet use rate was 12.8.

Internet use has grown rapidly among those with lower levels of educational attainment. Internet use for adults with a Bachelor's degree and adults with and education level beyond a Bachelor's degree grew at annual rates of

13 and 9 percent, respectively from December 1998 to September 2001. Internet use among those with only a high school diploma grew at an annual rate of 30 percent over the same period.

Interrelated Demographic Factors

Descriptive statistics, such as those in this chapter, are not sufficient to determine why a certain group of individuals has higher or lower rates of computer and Internet use. One of the reasons is that demographic characteristics are often interrelated.

An individual's occupation is often associated with a certain level of education. People with higher incomes often have higher levels of education. Thus, the statistics describing how people living in low income households, or who have low levels of education, or a given occupation are less likely to be Internet users may be capturing a more complicated interaction between the demographic characteristics. For example, income and education are strongly correlated. Thus, the relationship between Internet use and educational attainment could simply reflect the fact that people with higher levels of education tend to have higher incomes.

On closer examination, however, we find that income and education have independent effects on Internet use. [P]eople who have lower levels of education but live in households with a high family incomes are less likely to be Internet users than those who have high levels of education and live in households with low family income.

Both higher income and more education are themselves correlated with occupations that tend to have greater Internet use at work. [A] person's use at work has an important relationship to whether the Internet is at home, independent of income.

Urban or Rural Location of the Household

In September 2001, people living in each urban/rural category—non-central city urban, central city urban, and rural—had higher rates of Internet use than in previous years .

Over the 1998 to 2001 period, growth in Internet use among people living in rural households has been particularly strong (24 percent at an average annual rate). Use of the Internet by people in rural households now approaches the national average. Internet use among people living in central city urban households has also grown, although not as rapidly (19 percent at an average annual rate). Internet use among people who live in non-central city urban households has grown at a slightly slower rate (18 percent at an average annual rate). Even with the slowest growth rate, however, people living in non-central city urban households used the Internet at a rate greater than the other two geographic categories in September 2001.

Race/Hispanic Origin

Since 1997, rates of computer and Internet use by individuals have increased for each broad race/Hispanic origin category.

Differences in computer and Internet use across these broad race and

Hispanic origin categories persist. In each survey, Whites and Asian American and Pacific Islanders have had higher rates of both computer and Internet use than Blacks and Hispanics. In September 2001, the computer use rates were highest for Asian American and Pacific Islanders (71.2 percent) and Whites (70.0 percent). Among Blacks, 55.7 percent were computer users. Almost half of Hispanics (48.8 percent) were computer users. During the same year, Internet use among Whites and Asian American and Pacific Islanders hovered around 60 percent, while Internet use rates for Blacks (39.8 percent) and Hispanics (31.6 percent) trailed behind.

On the other hand, Internet use has increased across all race and groups and growth in Internet use rates was faster for Blacks and Hispanics than for Whites and Asian American and Pacific Islanders. From December 1998 to September 2001, Internet use among Blacks grew at an annual rate of 31 percent. Internet use among Hispanics grew at an annual rate of 26 percent. Internet use continued to grow among Asian American and Pacific Islanders (21 percent), and Whites (19 percent), although not so rapidly as for Blacks and Hispanics. Although not so dramatic, Blacks and Hispanics also have had somewhat faster growth in computer use than Whites and Asian American and Pacific Islanders.

Growth in Internet use rates for Blacks and Hispanics also accelerated in the 2000 to 2001 period. Between August 2000 and September 2001, growth in Hispanic Internet use increased to 30 percent from the 24 percent annual rate of growth from December 1998 to August 2000. Growth in Internet use among Blacks increased to a 33 percent annual rate between August 2000 and September 2001, from the 30 percent annual rate of growth between December 1998 and August 2000. Growth rates among Whites and Asian American and Pacific Islanders were comparable during both periods.

The race and ethnic origin categories used in this analysis are broad aggregations of what can be very disparate sub-groups. Individual sub-groups may have higher or lower levels of Internet use than the aggregate. [An example is] a sub-group of the Hispanic population (those not speaking English in the home) that has much lower levels of Internet use than the aggregate Hispanic population. It is likely that each broad category has sub-groups with rates of computer and Internet use that differ dramatically from the aggregate. . . .

Chapter 3: Online Activities

As increasing numbers of Americans are going online, they are engaging in a wide variety of online activities. Nearly half (45.0 percent) of the population now uses e-mail. The September 2001 survey asked respondents to report on activities in 16 areas, compared to the nine activities measured in the August 2000 survey. This year's survey revealed that activity levels for the original nine categories continued to grow, while also reporting strong activity levels for the newly added categories.

Primary Uses by the U.S. Population

The chief uses of the Internet remained the same in September 2001 as in August 2000, but occurred at much higher levels. The predominant use continued to be e-mail or instant messaging. In September 2001, nearly half of the population used e-mail (45.2 percent, up from 35.4 percent in 2000). Searching for information also ranked high: approximately one-third of Americans used the Internet to search for product and service information (36.2 percent, up from 26.1 percent in 2000), and to search for news, weather, and sports information (33.3 percent, up from 19.2 percent in 2000).

In addition, many more Internet users reported making online purchases or conducting online banking. The August 2000 survey combined these two categories and found that 13.3 percent of online users were engaged in both activities. The September 2001 survey, however, asked about these activities separately and found that 21.0 percent made online purchases and 8.1 percent conducted banking online.

Activities Among Those Individuals Online

Looking more specifically at Internet users, e-mail easily outdistances all other online activity. Online users are also connecting to the Internet in large numbers to search for information, whether it is product/services, health, or government services. The Internet is also a source for news and sports for many online users. To the extent that product/service purchases, online trading, and online banking represent consumers engaged in e-commerce, that activity is fairly strong and growing.

Whether an Internet user engages in a certain activity varies by some, but not all, demographic factors. For example, geography has little impact on the selection of activity. The proportions of Internet users engaged in specific online activities varies little across regions, and was similar regardless of whether the Internet user lived in a rural, urban, or central city area. Household type also showed little, if any, differences. Gender, age, race, and income, however, do have some relationship with Internet users' selection of online activities. . . .

Gender

Male and female Internet users engage in some online activities at different rates. More men than women used the Internet to check news, weather, and sports (67.1 percent versus 56.7 percent respectively), but more women went online to find information on health services or practices (39.8 percent contrasted with 29.6 percent for men). A higher proportion of male Internet users use the Internet for financial purposes as compared with females: they were more than twice as likely as females to trade online (12.6 percent of males compared to 5.3 percent of females), and males were slightly more likely to bank online than female users (19.3 percent versus 16.5 percent).

A larger percentage of male Internet users reported using the Internet for entertainment-oriented activities. A higher proportion of males versus females played games online (45.3 percent versus 39.1 percent, respectively) and viewed television or movies or listened to the radio (21.9 percent versus 15.9 percent, respectively).

Men and women responded similarly for the remaining categories surveyed. For example, 82.8 percent of male Internet users e-mailed, compared to 85.1 percent of female Internet users; 16.9 percent of male Internet users searched online for jobs, compared to 16.0 percent of female Internet users; and 18.4 percent of male Internet users participated in online chat rooms or list servs, compared to 16.3 percent of female Internet users.

Age

An Internet user's age also affects online use and activities. Those 55 and older were least likely to use the Internet in many of the surveyed categories, such as playing games, job searching, participating in chat rooms or list servs, viewing television or movies, listening to the radio, or trading online. On the other hand, this age group was more likely (42.7 percent) than any other age group to check health information online. And those 55 and older showed equally strong e-mail use as any other adult age group.

Internet users in the 25–34 age group were the most likely to bank online (26.1 percent), followed by the Internet users in the 35–44 age group (21.3 percent), the 45–54 age group (17.7 percent) and the 55 and above age group (13.0 percent).

Online shopping is particularly common among 25–34 years old Internet users. About half of the people in this age group (53.0 percent) used the Internet for online shopping, as did 51.2 percent of the 35–44 year olds. . . .

Chapter 8: The Unconnected

The earlier chapters of this report have chronicled changes in the connected population: who they are, where they are, what they are doing online, what devices and connection types they are using, and where they are using the Internet. There is a sizable segment of the U.S. population (as of September 2001, 46.1 percent of persons and 49.5 percent of households), however, that does not use the Internet. This chapter profiles this "unconnected" population and explores some of the reasons why it may not be online.

The Offline Population

. . . As the analysis in Chapter 2 shows, Internet use has expanded dramatically in the United States, but a number of groups are more likely not to be Internet users. These non-users include:

- People in households with low family incomes — 75.0 percent of people who live in households where income is less than $15,000 and 66.6 percent of those in households with incomes between $15,000 and $35,000.
- Adults with low levels of overall education—60.2 percent of adults (age 25+) with only a high school degree and 87.2 percent of adults with less than a high school education.
- Hispanics—68.4 percent of all Hispanics and 85.9 percent of Hispanic households where Spanish is the only language spoken.
- Blacks—60.2 percent of Blacks.

Earlier chapters have examined the change in the online population focusing on the growth in the number of users or home connections. We gain a different perspective by looking at the rate of *decrease* in the population that is not online. In other words, we compare the change in the online population with the group initially *not online* instead of the group initially online.

Consider the non-Internet-using population by educational attainment, for example. Among people at least 25 years old with a high school education, the share not using the Internet declined from 69.4 percent in August 2000 to 60.2 in September 2001. Over the same period and age level, the share of those with a college education who were not using the Internet shrank from 27.5 percent to 19.2 percent . Thus, high school graduates had a slightly larger point change (9.2 percentage points) than college graduates (8.3 percentage points). Because so many more high school graduates were not Internet users in August 2000, the 9.2 percentage point change over the next 13 months represented a 12 percent annual rate of decline in non-Internet-users. On the other hand, so few college graduates were non-Internet-users in 2000 that their 8.2 percentage point change reflected a 28 percent annual rate of decline in non-Internet-users. When Chapter 2 examined those same point changes from the perspective of the growth in Internet users, high school graduates had a larger growth rate of Internet users than college graduates (27 percent vs. 11 percent).

The Importance of Cost to Households
Never Connected to the Internet

The cost of Internet access matters much more to households with lower incomes than to those with higher incomes. The September 2001 survey asked households without Internet subscriptions the question, "What is the main reason that you don't have the Internet at home?" Survey results indicated that the largest specific response was that the cost was "too expensive." This response was volunteered by one-fourth of these households, but much more often by lower income households than by higher income households.

. . . With successively higher income categories, fewer households report that cost is a barrier and more households are making their first connections to the Internet at home. Households with incomes below $15,000 volunteered cost as the barrier to home Internet subscriptions 34.7 percent of the time. Among households in that income category, the share of the population without home Internet subscriptions declined by only 6 percent between August 2000 and September 2001. At the other end of the spectrum, only 9.6 percent of households with incomes of at least $75,000 said that they were deterred by cost. That income level saw a 34 percent reduction in the share of households without home Internet between August 2000 and September 2001.

Among specific responses, cost rated highly across a number of demographic groups of non-Internet households. In particular, respondents for married couples or single-parent families with children, and heads of households that were younger than 45 years of age, less educated, or unemployed all identified "too expensive" as the most important reason for non-connectivity at a much higher level than the national figure of 25.3 percent. . . .

U.S. TREASURY OFFICIAL ON ECONOMIC CRISIS IN ARGENTINA
February 6, 2002

Argentina during late 2001 and early 2002 underwent what was perhaps the most dramatic economic collapse of any major country since the end of World War II. The economic meltdown left millions of Argentines destitute and led to a persistent political crisis that showed no sign of easing by the end of 2002. Early in the twentieth century Argentina had been among the world's most prosperous nations, but at the opening of the twenty-first century it had fallen into the deep poverty endemic in much of Latin America.

While the Argentinean people looked for jobs, their political leaders grew increasingly desperate in searching for short-term solutions that would put the economy back on the road to recovery. Having poured billions of dollars into failed rescue efforts in 2001, the world's key economic decision makers—particularly the U.S. government and the International Monetary Fund (IMF)—withheld further aid through most of 2002 in hopes of pressuring Argentina's leaders to adopt financial reforms. Argentina's economy appeared to improve during the second half of the year—but not before its collapse had infected some of its neighbors, including Brazil, Paraguay, and Uruguay. (Brazil election, p. 774)

What Went Wrong in Argentina

Argentina's economic distress was many decades in the making, the result of policies adopted by both democratic and dictatorial governments, as well as of forces beyond the control of a country of 37 million people. As recently as 1998, however, many experts believed the country was headed toward renewal of the world-class prosperity it had once enjoyed. Even looking back on the crisis, prominent international economists disagreed about why Argentina fell so far so fast. Some placed nearly all the blame on Argentina's political leaders, some blamed the IMF and the U.S. government, while others said many forces and actors came together to create a unique set of circumstances in Argentina.

Over the long-term, the roots of Argentina's problems could be traced back to a 1943 military coup that ultimately brought to power Juan Domingo

Peron, a populist former military officer who beguiled Argentines with promises of economic growth and social services. Peron's policies mixed elements of fascism, capitalism, and socialism but failed to keep Argentina on a level with other major economies following World War II. Peron fell from power in 1955 (although he briefly returned to office in 1973–1974), initiating three decades of political instability that ended only with the collapse of a military dictatorship in 1982. Throughout these decades Argentina's economy rarely boomed but frequently went bust, the result of lagging investment, systemic corruption in both government and business, and growing international competition for the agricultural products (such as beef and grain) that had been the country's chief source of income from foreign trade. Nearly every government tried to borrow and spend its way out of the economic doldrums, creating an enormous pile of debt and leading to hyperinflation that reached 3,000 percent in 1988.

The election in 1988 of Carlos Menem as president ushered in a new era for Argentina. A charismatic leader who carried the banner of Peron's old political party, Menem sold off businesses that had been acquired by the government since the Peron era and actively encouraged foreign investment and international trade. In essence, Menem adopted the free-market economic policies that the United States, the International Monetary Fund, and most experts were urging on all developing countries.

In April 1991 Menem's economy minister, Domingo Cavallo, designed a monetary policy that instantly ended inflation as a problem: a new currency, the peso, *was linked one-to-one to the U.S. dollar (in other words, the government set the peso value at one dollar by backing the total number of pesos with an equivalent amount of dollars). That policy made it impossible for the government to continue spending beyond its means simply by printing more money.*

While the policy cured inflation and spurred an influx of foreign investment, it led ultimately to other problems. The booming U.S. economy throughout the 1990s meant a strong dollar in comparison to most other currencies. Because the peso was linked to the soaring dollar, agricultural and industrial products from Argentina became too expensive for other countries to buy. As a result, economic growth in Argentina peaked at nearly 7 percent in 1993 but stalled in the later 1990s. Unemployment rose to more than 20 percent by 1997, leading to a series of violent protests and costing Menem's Peronist Party control of the lower house of parliament.

Hoping to stimulate growth again, Menem stepped up government spending. But because of the peso-dollar link and because tax revenues lagged, the government had to borrow, both domestically and on the international market. By the late 1990s Argentina's public and private debt had soared to more than $100 billion—a figure that might have been sustainable with a growing economy but was a mounting burden during a recession. The heavy government borrowing was made worse by a unique system under which the twenty-four provincial governments were responsible for much of Argentina's public sector spending but did not have to raise all the revenue to pay for what they spent. In effect, the central government was required to *subsidize provincial budgets over which it had little control. Michael Mussa, chief economist at the IMF until late 2001, said Argentina's total foreign debt (both public and private) more than doubled, from $62 billion in 1992 to $142 billion in 1998—a period when the gross domestic product rose by about 25 percent.*

Two international financial crises during the 1990s contributed to Argentina's woes. The first was the collapse of the Mexican peso in 1994– 1995, an event that caused many investors in the United States and other industrial countries to worry about the underlying health of all Latin American economies. The second and more serious blow to Argentina started with the East Asian financial crisis of 1997–1998. The near simultaneous run on currencies from Thailand to Indonesia had an impact worldwide on developing countries, reaching Russia and other formerly communist countries by mid-1998 and parts of Latin America, most notably Argentina and Brazil. The Brazilian government was forced to devalue its currency, the real, *in January 1999. Brazil historically was Argentina's largest market, but the collapse of the real sharply curtailed trade between the two countries because Argentina was still stuck with its peso valued at one-to-one with the U.S. dollar.* (Asian financial crisis, Historic Documents of 1998, p. 722)

Despite the increasing signs of trouble, Argentina was widely praised by world financial leaders for its adherence to free-market economic principles. In October 1998 U.S. president Bill Clinton invited President Menem to address the annual joint meeting in Washington of the IMF and the World Bank—an honor intended to establish Argentina as a positive example for other countries.

Presidential elections in October 1999 came in the midst of the worsening economic crisis. Menem had toyed with seeking a third term, but with the economy turning sour and his government besieged by mounting charges of corruption, he stepped aside. His chosen successor to lead the Peronist Party, Senator Eduardo Duhalde, lost the election to Fernando de la Rua, who led a relatively new center-left coalition called the Alliance.

The Economy Unravels

De la Rua took office in December 1999 and almost immediately found himself under enormous pressure, both domestically and internationally, to take dramatic action to revive the sagging economy. At the urging of the IMF, the government in 2000 announced severe cuts in spending on education, welfare, and other services. That step was greeted by large-scale protest demonstrations and led to the resignations of key aides, including the vice president, the economy minister, and several other cabinet members. While politically damaging to de la Rua's government, the spending cuts failed to stimulate the economy and had little impact on the growing budget deficit, which was pushing the country close to default on its public and private debt.

By late 2000 the IMF concluded that Argentina should be given what an official called "one last chance" to put its house in order. The result was a $40 billion rescue plan, announced in January 2001, consisting of about

$20 billion in loans from the IMF, the World Bank, the Inter-American Development Bank, and the Spanish government—plus an estimated $20 billion in private loans once Argentina's situation stabilized. But there was to be no stability in Argentina during 2001 or the following year. The economy continued to deteriorate, the deficit ballooned, and de la Rua repeatedly shuffled his cabinet amid controversies over imposing austerity measures.

In a desperate gamble to win new international support, de la Rua brought back Cavallo, Menem's economy minister who had designed the peso-dollar peg a decade earlier, and gave him sweeping power to deal with the growing crisis. Cavallo unilaterally announced major economic changes, including a revision of the peso-dollar peg and a debt swap that lowered current payments on Argentina's loans but at the cost of much higher payments later in the decade. Cavallo also proposed a new austerity program that was so unpopular that a general strike in July 2001 nearly shut down the entire country.

The last half of 2001 saw a rapid-fire series of events that ended in the collapse of Argentina's economy and the overthrow of its political order. At Cavallo's insistence, the IMF and U.S. government agreed in August 2001 to provide $9 billion—of which $6 billion was from previously pledged aid and $3 billion was supposedly conditioned on new steps to restructure the country's debt. But that new injection of money served only to postpone the moment when Argentina would face the reality that it could no longer make its debt payments.

De la Rua suffered a major political blow in October 2001 when the voters put the Peronist Party back in control of both houses of parliament. A run on the banks in late November led the government to close all banks, effective December 1. Unable to get access to their deposits, Argentines rioted, first in the provinces, then in Buenos Aires. The government appealed again to the IMF for yet another bailout but was rebuffed. The administration of President George W. Bush, representing the IMF's biggest shareholder, said Argentina had squandered the previous bailouts and needed to face the consequences.

A state of siege failed to calm the unrest, which peaked with wide-scale rioting on December 19, 2001, and de la Rua announced his resignation the following day. He was the second elected president to resign amid economic turmoil in a little over ten years; Raul Alfonsin had left office early in 1989, hoping that his elected successor, Menem, could calm economic fears at that time. But de la Rua's departure had no calming effect because the crisis in late 2001 was far more severe than the one a dozen years earlier. His successor, the Senate president, lasted just one day, and the Argentinean presidency became a revolving door with five men holding the post in a period of less than two weeks. In the midst of this political turmoil, Argentina suspended payment on about $95 billion in loans to private banks, a default that some economists had said for months was inevitable. In dollar terms, it was the largest single default by any government in world history.

The political crisis eased on January 1, 2002, when Peronist Party senator Duhalde—the man de la Rua had defeated in 1999—agreed to take the *presidency. Duhalde pledged to develop a "new economic model," one based largely on the policies that Argentina had followed before Menem cut back the government's role in the economy and emphasized free markets. The rioting stopped, at least temporarily, but Argentines still had no money in their pockets. More ominously, Argentine's trust in political leaders, and in the economic policies the leaders had embraced, had been shattered. "This [free market] economic model has destroyed me and destroyed the country," the* New York Times *quoted engineer Juan Patricio Longo Escalante as saying. "After all that we've been through, now we're broke, back to point zero and having to start all over again."*

Struggling Through 2002

With strong bipartisan parliamentary support for desperate action, Duhalde took numerous steps to try to quell the economic slide. He started with a series of measures that, by early February, set the peso free from its link to the U.S. dollar. Duhalde also proposed budgets that cut government spending in some areas and increased it in others—all with the intention of reviving the economy and restoring public confidence. One of the government's first efforts was to reduce political patronage, a time-honored system under which millions of dollars in spending were used by legislators to dispense favors. The government also partially eased the freeze on bank deposits, allowing Argentines to withdraw some of their peso-denominated savings but not their savings in dollars. Congress rejected a government plan to covert about 60 percent of all bank deposits into government bonds, and another run on the banks in April forced the government to close the banks once again for a week.

While the politicians battled over recovery plans, the Argentine people suffered. Unemployment rose to about 22 percent by midyear, and fully half of the country's population was declared to be living in poverty. Unable to obtain loans, hundreds of businesses went bankrupt. Inflation, which had been banished for more than a decade, briefly returned to haunt Argentina as the peso fell on international markets. Over the long term, one of the most worrisome consequences of Argentina's economic collapse was the near total failure of its banking system. Foreign banks pulled out of Argentina; domestic banks were left with virtually no capital but millions of angry depositors. Prospects for a recapitalization of the banks were slim, meaning that Argentine citizens and businesses could not obtain the loans needed to stimulate the economy.

The government missed several payments on international loans but for most of the year took extraordinary steps to stay current with its payments to the IMF and other official lenders (such as the World Bank), hoping for another rescue package from the global lenders of last resort. Negotiations between Duhalde's government and the IMF dragged on throughout the year with no successful conclusion, however. Backed by the Bush administration's resistance to additional bailouts, the IMF demanded additional cutbacks in government spending. U.S. Treasury secretary Paul O'Neill visited

Argentina in early August but offered no immediate financial assistance. Many observers saw this stance as a rebuff to Argentina, particularly since on the same trip to South America O'Neill announced $30 billion in loans for Brazil and $1.5 billion for Uruguay, both of which had suffered because of Argentina's troubles.

Frustrated by the impasse and by the continuing economic decline, Duhalde announced July 2 that he was moving up the 2003 presidential elections by six months, to April, in hopes that "a president elected by the people" could "push forward long-term measures that will bring us a sustainable economic recovery." Duhalde had already said that he would not run for the presidency, and all during 2002 he engaged in disputes with Menem, his former mentor who had made it clear he would seek the presidency again. The political uncertainly further contributed to Argentina's difficulties in obtaining more aid from the IMF and other international agencies. IMF managing director Horst Kohler said September 23 that the "core problem" was that "we cannot present to our Board an agreement where we have no indication or at least a judgment about the probabilities that what we have agreed with this President or this government will be implemented."

Unable, or unwilling, to reach an agreement with the IMF and determined to preserve the country's dwindling foreign currency reserves of less than $10 billion, Duhalde's government in November paid interest but no principal on an $805 million loan payment due the World Bank That act of desperation effectively cut Argentina off from any new international financing, including World Bank loans that the government had used to finance social programs. Argentina missed another $726 million loan payment to the World Bank on December 12.

Argentina's economic crisis eased a bit during the second half of the year, enabling Economy Minister Robert Lavagna to declare in December that the recession had ended after nearly four years. The economy had grown for three consecutive months, he said, and other encouraging signs were that bank deposits were increasing, some industries (particularly textiles and metal working) had resumed production at closed plants, and the unemployment rate fell to about 18 percent. Even so, the downturn during the first half of the year meant that Argentina's economy contracted by about 12 percent on an annual basis—putting it about 19 percent below the high point during the second quarter of 1998. The government's strategy of refusing to give into the IMF's demands for deeper spending cuts seemed to have yielded a short-term payoff. Under pressure from some of Argentina's trading partners and European countries, the IMF at year's end appeared ready to stretch out Argentina's loans, at least until after the scheduled April 2003 presidential election. Despite this progress on the economic front, the country's political scene remained chaotic. The ruling Peronist Party was badly split and no opposition candidate seemed likely to command a national majority, raising the prospect that Duhalde might postpone the election or change his mind about not running to succeed himself.

Reviewing the Lessons from Argentina

As could be expected, there was widespread debate—both in Argentina and in other countries—about who was primarily to blame for Argentina's economic collapse. In interviews and public opinion polls, the Argentine people seemed to assign equal blame to their politicians and to officials in Washington (especially at the IMF). Political leaders in Buenos Aires said their counterparts in Washington demanded too much from Argentina and provided too little help, while IMF defenders said Argentina's leaders simply refused to face the need to end a decades-long habit of spending beyond the country's means.

The dispute was of more than academic significance because it went to the heart of the role of the international community in general, and the IMF in particular, in responding to economic problems in individual countries. A similar debate erupted after the 1997–1998 East Asian financial crisis, when many critics accused the IMF of deepening the misery in many countries by forcing severe cuts in all government spending, including unemployment benefits and other "safety net" programs. As a result of the Asian crisis the IMF made numerous changes in how it handled economic emergencies. Also featured in this debate were many of the questions about the virtues and vices of globalization: the increasing connections between the world's economies, based on free market principles.

Much of the controversy focused on the issue of whether the IMF was too aggressive in pressing Argentina to cut its spending, both when the recession got under way in 1998 and after the economic collapse three years later. IMF officials said they had no choice but to push Argentina to cut spending, which they said had run out of control for many decades. If the IMF made a major mistake, it was "in failing to press Argentine authorities much harder to have a more responsible fiscal policy" when the economy was booming during the 1990s, the agency's former chief economist, Mussa, said in a paper published by the Institute for International Economics in July 2002. Argentina consistently missed its budget-cutting targets, Mussa argued, and external pressure from the IMF was needed to force the country to deal with uncontrolled spending by the provincial governments.

IMF critics rejected this argument, noting that Argentina's deficit spending, on an annual basis, was well within the bounds that the IMF set for most other countries. Joseph E. Stiglitz, a former chief economist at the World Bank who had become a harsh critic of the IMF, noted that much of Argentina's budget deficit resulted from a decision—endorsed by the IMF— to privatize the country's social security system. That step took social security revenues and expenses out of the budget and worsened the country's apparent budget deficit. Moreover, Stiglitz said, forcing Argentina to cut government spending during a recession made the downturn worse and guaranteed an eventual economic collapse.

In Washington the Bush administration clearly sided with the IMF point of view. Even so, administration officials said the IMF during the 1990s had been too willing to bail out countries with debt crises because most of the bailout money ultimately went to private investors who had taken risks in those countries. In congressional testimony on February 6, the administration's point man on the Argentine situation—John B. Taylor, undersecretary of the Treasury for international affairs—said "it is neither feasible nor desirable for official sector resources [such as IMF lending] to grow at the rate necessary to ensure that all creditors in all cases would always be able to get paid in full."

Following are excerpts from testimony delivered February 6, 2002, by John B. Taylor, the undersecretary of the Treasury for international affairs, to the Subcommittee on International Monetary Policy and Trade of the House Financial Services Committee, in which he reviewed the economic crisis in Argentina.

The document was obtained from the Internet at usinfo .state.gov/regional/ar/argentina/argentia6.htm; accessed November 4, 2002.

In order to understand the current situation in Argentina, I think it is helpful to review some of the key economic developments in Argentina during the last decade.

In the early 1990s, the government of Argentina undertook a series of important reforms in economic policy, including monetary policy, fiscal policy, structural policy, and international trade policy. Perhaps most dramatic and immediately noticeable was the change in monetary policy. A highly inflationary monetary policy was replaced by a new "convertibility law," which pegged the peso one-to-one with the dollar and largely prevented the central bank from financing the government's budget deficit by printing money. Fiscal policy was also brought into better control with a decline in deficits. On the structural side, a comprehensive privatization program was implemented through which a number of inefficient state-owned enterprises were privatized. Moreover, barriers to international trade and investment were reduced and Argentina's financial sector was opened to foreign investors.

These reforms produced very impressive results. Hyperinflation—which had risen to over 3000 percent—was brought to a quick end by the convertibility law. Economic growth turned around sharply: after falling during the 1980s, real GDP growth began increasing at over 4 percent per year. Investment and exports grew particularly rapidly. The sharp increase in economic growth was even more remarkable given the very rapid disinflation that was occurring at the same time.

However, starting in the late 1990s there were a number of policy setbacks and external shocks which sharply reduced economic growth in Argentina and ultimately led to the financial crises in 2000–2001 and the current halt to economic activity.

First, government budget deficits began to increase, an indication that discipline had begun to wane. With government spending increasing faster than tax revenues, the central government budget deficit rose to an average of 2 percent during the years in the late 1990s from 1 percent in the early 1990s. In addition to the spending increases by the central government, other factors also put pressure on the budget: federal revenue-sharing arrangements with the provinces provided little incentive to contain costs and tax compliance remained very low. These deficits could not be financed by money creation because of the convertibility law. Instead, they were financed by borrowing in both the domestic and the international capital markets; however, as the government's debt began to rise and raise questions about sustainability of the debt, risk premia rose and increased interest rates. Eventually the higher interest rates put additional pressure on the budget deficit and held back economic growth.

Second, the low inflation of the early 1990s turned into a persistent deflation which also had negative effects on economic growth. The currencies of Argentina's major trading partners in Europe and Brazil depreciated relative to the dollar, and therefore relative to the Argentine peso. This effective appreciation of the peso and deterioration in Argentina's competitiveness, along with the higher interest rates, further held back economic growth.

Third, persistent expectations of depreciation of the peso caused interest rates on peso loans to be higher than dollar interest rates. Whenever policy actions were taken that raised questions about central bank independence or about the convertibility law, market expectations of depreciation increased, causing domestic interest rates to rise further. Examples included the replacement of the governor of the central bank and the adjustment of the convertibility law to allow for a basket of euros and dollars.

As low economic growth persisted into 2000, concerns began to grow that a vicious cycle of low tax revenues and continued government spending increases would lead to rising interest rates, which would further slow the economy. Following the political turmoil in October 2000 when Vice President Alvarez resigned, Argentina's borrowing costs soared and rolling over government debt became more and more difficult. Renewed plans to reduce the budget deficit brought interest rates down temporarily, but by February 2001 it was clear that further actions needed to take place. In March 2001, a newly appointed Economy Minister Lopez Murphy announced significant reductions in government spending, but after strong political protests, he was replaced by Economy Minister Cavallo who began to introduce a number of policy changes culminating in a zero-deficit law in the summer of 2001.

Eventually, however, it became clear that these changes to the budget were not working. The government debt was becoming unsustainable in the views of many market participants, and interest rates on government debt began to increase sharply. By October it was apparent that the debt would have to be restructured and, indeed, President de la Rua took the step of announcing that such a restructuring would take place.

As the restructuring effort was underway, the uncertainty about its impact on the banking system led to increasing large deposit withdrawals from banks and international reserves began to fall. In order to stop the withdrawals and the decline in reserves, the government imposed severe restrictions on such withdrawals in December. Soon after the restrictions were imposed, social and political protests turned violent, leading to the resignation of President de la Rua and his ministers.

Economic circumstances in Argentina have deteriorated even more rapidly since the imposition of the restrictions on deposits withdrawals. The lack of a functioning payments system has led to a virtual halt of much economic activity. The shortage of liquidity is hindering economic activity and underlies much of the social frustration. The Duhalde government, which took over in January, is in the process of gradually removing these restrictions and at the same time moving to a flexible exchange-rate system.

It is, of course, up to the government of Argentina to work out the details of a set of economic policies that will increase economic growth. Indeed, it has begun to lay out the broad outlines of such a policy strategy in the last few days. The government must develop a budget that is based on realistic assumptions about economic growth and available sources of non-inflationary financing. The Central Bank must establish a transparent, rules-based monetary regime that will keep inflation low as it has been in the 1990s. The exchange-rate regime must be unified to prevent distortions. The government must initiate negotiations to restructure its private debt. And banks must be recapitalized so that lending to the private sector can resume, which in turn will strengthen growth, investment, and job creation.

During this period of time, the government of Argentina had several programs with the IMF [International Monetary Fund]. In March 2000, Argentina obtained a $7.4 billion IMF program. The Argentine government treated the program as "precautionary," meaning that the government did not intend to draw upon it. However, starting in the summer of 2000, the growing concern in financial markets (discussed above) was that the persistent Argentine recession was setting up the potential for a financial crisis.

In December 2000, Argentina drew on $2 billion from its IMF program, and the next month the IMF approved an additional $6.3 billion for Argentina's program, bringing the total program size to $13.7 billion. As a condition for the January package, the Argentine government agreed to a series of deeper structural measures in the area of fiscal, pension and health-care reforms to help develop a sustainable fiscal position in the medium term and to build investor confidence.

The January 2001 augmented program was designed to allow the Argentine government time to work on its structural reform agenda and to meet relatively relaxed fiscal deficit targets in the first half of the year. Unfortunately, Argentina missed its first-quarter fiscal targets and second-quarter structural reform benchmarks.

In August 2001, the IMF provided Argentina with further augmentation— this time, an additional $8 billion. The U.S. government made clear that IMF assistance should not be used simply to bail out bondholders, and supported the designation of part of the IMF package ($3 billion), which could be used to support a voluntary, market-based debt operation. However, when tax revenues continued to fall short and the government failed to reach an agreement to cut transfers to the provinces, it became increasingly clear that the government was not going to be able to meet its fiscal targets and had no other sources of financing. This fueled concerns about the government's ability to service its debt, particularly to domestic banks, and eventually prompted an accelerated run on the banking system.

In December, IMF staff determined that Argentina was not going to make its fiscal targets for the fourth quarter that were agreed upon in August and that its program was no longer sustainable. Thus, the IMF could not complete its review and consequently did not disburse a loan tranche in December 2001.

The U.S. government has remained in close engagement with the Argentine authorities throughout the crisis period. We have held almost daily phone conversations with economy ministry and central bank officials, and have held very frequent bilateral meetings. . . . Our discussions with the International Monetary Fund [IMF] and the government of Argentina during the last year should be viewed in the context of our overall approach to emerging markets. During the last three of four years, the flows of capital to the emerging markets have declined sharply, and it has been the intent of the Bush Administration to reverse this trend by reducing the severity and frequency of financial crises of the kind that we have seen in Argentina.

Of course, the ideal would be to prevent crises such as the one in Argentina from occurring. This requires not only early detection of policies or of external shocks that could cause crises, but also the resolve to take actions to reverse such policies or counter such shocks. The Bush Administration has encouraged the IMF to strengthen its capacity to detect potential troubles on the horizon, and to be willing to warn countries that are heading down a dangerous path to take appropriate action. The IMF needs to focus in particular on country vulnerability to "balance sheets" shocks and on the adequacy of liquid reserves to short-term external liabilities. Effective communication with markets is also key. And the IMF can be more effective and credible in undertaking these tasks if it focuses on issues that are central to its expertise—notably, strengthening monetary, fiscal, exchange rate, financial sector, and debt management policies. In the last decade, the IMF became too involved in matters outside of these core areas.

In recent years, the IMF has responded to crises with increasingly large financing packages, leading to concerns that some private creditors were acting on the assumption that their investments would be protected whenever an emerging market country got into financial trouble. We sought a more prudent approach to the use of IMF resources. This approach has been guided by the view that it is neither feasible nor desirable for official sector resources to grow at the rate necessary to ensure that all creditors in all cases would always be able to get paid in full. At the same time, we are cognizant of the risks of a sharp change in policy given the expectations that have been built into investment decisions over many years, and therefore we are moving in the direction of fewer large-scale packages.

An important change has taken place in emerging markets in recent years, and we have taken account of this change as part of our approach to emerging markets. The change is that investors are increasingly differentiating between countries and markets based on fundamental economic assessments—judgments that are facilitated by better information. This differentiation is reducing contagion from one country to another, as exemplified most recently by the relative stability in other emerging markets over the past few months despite the crisis in Argentina. Emphasis on the risk of contagion by the official sector in the past led to the expectation on the part of investors and emerging market governments that the official sector would bail them out. That encouraged excessive risk-taking and gave rise to the very conditions that made financial crises more likely. Changing this mindset has been an important priority, and, I think, an area where we have made some progress.

One important challenge that remains is to explore options to promote more orderly sovereign debt restructurings. The official sector should not encourage countries to default on their debts, but we recognize that restructuring can and will happen in certain cases. In the United States, the bankruptcy code provides a stable environment for a debtor and its creditors to negotiate a fair restructuring agreement. However, no such mechanisms exist on an international level to help ensure that if and when a sovereign debt restructuring occurs, it does so in a more orderly manner that treats creditors fairly and reduces the scope for arbitrary, unpredictable official action. Various possibilities, some IMF-centered and others based more on using existing or new contractual provisions in debt contracts to facilitate restructurings when needed, are under discussion. If those discussions can lead to a sensible, market-friendly approach which encourages creditor and debtor ownership of the process, then both creditors and debtors will benefit.

Thank you again for this opportunity to speak with you. I look forward to hearing your views and answering your questions.

SRI LANKAN GOVERNMENT AND REBELS ON CEASE-FIRE
February 22, 2002

A nineteen-year-long civil war in Sri Lanka appeared to come to an end in 2002. In a process mediated by Norway, the Sri Lankan government and a separatist rebel group known as the Tamil Tigers signed a permanent cease-fire on February 22. Ten months later, on December 5, the opposing sides agreed to the framework for a long-term political solution giving the country's Tamil minority substantial autonomy within a new federal system.

If fully implemented and followed up with the necessary constitutional changes, the peace agreements would resolve one of the longest and bloodiest ethnic conflicts anywhere in recent decades. More than 64,000 people had been killed during the fighting, and hundreds of thousands had been displaced—many leaving the island permanently. The fighting severely hindered economic growth in Sri Lanka, a land endowed with rich natural resources and famous around the world for its scenic beauty and its exports of tea, rubber, and other products.

Background to the Conflict

Sri Lanka, with 19 million people, has three major ethnic groups. The Sinhalese, most of whom are Buddhists, comprise approximately 75 percent of the population and speak a local language called Sinhala; they are descended from people who migrated to the island from northern India in ancient times. The Tamils, most of whom are Hindu, make up about 18 percent of the population and speak a language closely related to Hindi; they live in the northern and eastern parts of the island. Muslims, most of whom speak Tamil, make up about 7 percent of the population and live in the east.

Formerly known as Ceylon, Sri Lanka was under British colonial rule from the early nineteenth century until 1948. During much of that period Tamils held privileged positions as the country's middle class. After independence, the majority Sinhalese assumed the bulk of political power and reduced the Tamils' privileges. Growing Sinhalese nationalism led ulti-

mately to the establishment of Buddhism as the national religion in 1972. The socialist government, which had nationalized much of the economy, changed the country's name from Ceylon to Sri Lanka, which means "resplendent land" in Sinhala.

Four years later Tamil nationalists formed the Liberation Tigers of Tamil Eelam (generally known as the Tamil Tigers), with the stated goal of establishing an independent country in the north and east of the island. The Tigers launched their guerrilla war in 1983 and quickly became a highly disciplined military force. Partly in response to the rebellion, radical Sinhalese nationalists attacked the government for making what they considered to be too many concessions to the Tamils.

At the government's request, India sent about 50,000 troops to enforce a planned cease-fire in 1987. The Indian forces became bogged down in the conflict, however, and withdrew in 1989. Fighting between the government and the Tamil rebels continued throughout the 1990s, with each side using extreme violence to advance its cause. The Tigers adopted suicide bombing as a standard tactic, sending more than 200 explosives-laden "martyrs" to kill government officials and civilians. Among their victims were a president of Sri Lanka (killed in 1993) and the prime minister of India, Rajiv Gandhi (killed in 1991). Another Sri Lankan president, Chandrika Kumaratunga, narrowly escaped death in a suicide bombing just before winning reelection in 1999. The Tamils made widespread use of child soldiers, often forcibly taking children as young as twelve away from their parents. (Child soldiers, p. 916)

To repress the rebellion, the government essentially closed off Tamil-majority areas, a step that blocked shipments of food, medicine, and consumer goods to the residents. Some of the war's worst violence occurred in clashes between the Tamils and Muslims; in 1990, for example, the Tigers killed more than 125 Muslims as they prayed at their mosques in eastern Sri Lanka.

Several attempts to negotiate an end to the fighting during the 1990s failed, most notably in 1995 when peace talks collapsed and the government launched a massive offensive that recaptured the Tamil stronghold of Jaffna. An estimated 300,000 Tamils fled the country during the decade, most migrating to India.

The Move Toward Peace

Diplomats, journalists, outside experts, and Sri Lankan leaders said that a sudden move toward peace starting in late 2001 was the result of numerous factors that converged after nearly two decades of war. Clearly one major incentive for both sides was that the war had reached the point of stalemate. The government had failed to end the rebellion, the Tigers had failed to gain their independent state, and full victory was not foreseeable for either side.

The Tigers also were coming under increasing international pressure. India, which had once supported the movement, had declared Tiger leader

Velupillai Prabhakaran and his top associates wanted men after the 1991 assassination of Rajiv Gandhi. Other countries that had sympathized with the Tigers, or at least allowed them to collect money for their cause, gradually lost patience with the seemingly endless war. Britain, for example, had allowed the Tigers to maintain an office in London, but in February 2001 declared the Tigers a terrorist organization, closed the London office, and curtailed their fund raising in Britain.

The September 2001 terrorist attacks against the United States drew increased international attention to all groups that had used terrorism, including the Tigers. The United States already included the Tigers on its list of international terrorist organizations. After September 11 several U.S. allies followed suit, freezing Tamil bank accounts and targeting Tamil exiles in Asian and Western countries that had financially supported the rebels.

Yet another factor was the intervention by Norway, the home of the Nobel Peace prize, which had long seen itself as a potential neutral mediator in the world's conflicts. Norwegian diplomats in 1992 brought together Israeli and Palestinian leaders for negotiations that led to the 1993 Oslo peace agreement. Norway launched a peace initiative in Sri Lanka in 2000, but four attempts at serious negotiations ended in failure before the resumption of talks late in 2001. Some observers noted that Norway was not a totally disinterested party because a Norwegian energy company, Norsk Hydro, held a majority stake in Ceylon Oxygen, a major Sri Lankan employer. (Middle East peace accord, Historic Documents of 1993, p. 747)

Shifting sentiments among the non-Tamil population in Sri Lanka were demonstrated by parliamentary elections in December 2001. A coalition headed by the center-right party, the United National Front headed by Ranil Wickremesinghe, won the elections on a platform calling for renewed talks based on increased autonomy for the Tamil population in exchange for lasting peace.

Finally, it was clear that most Sri Lankan people were eager for peace. The war had severely disrupted the country's economy, in large part by discouraging tourism, previously one of Sri Lanka's most important industries. In one of their last major operations, the Tigers in 2001 destroyed most of the airport at Colombo, the capital—an act that damaged the country's links to the rest of the world. "People are tired of the war, on both sides, and I think their leaders recognize that," Norwegian negotiator Vidar Helgesen told the BBC in February.

All those factors came into play in late December 2001, when the government and Tigers agreed to a month-long cease-fire, and the government lifted a ban on goods for Tamil-controlled areas. The truce was made permanent by the February 22 agreement. Announcing the permanent cease-fire, Norwegian foreign minister Jan Petersen said the opposing sides faced "a long road" to a permanent solution. "The parties will face risks and uncertainties, and they will have to make hard choices," he said. "But no hardships are worse than those of conflict and bloodshed. No gains are greater than those of peace and prosperity."

Previous cease-fires had been temporary, but this one was open ended, essentially committing both sides to a political settlement. The truce included several "confidence-building" measures intended to make life easier for the civilian population, among them the opening of roads and railways into the conflicted areas.

One potential obstacle to peace was political strife within the Sri Lankan government. The prime minister, Wickremesinghe, appeared fully committed to the peace process that had been the key element of his political campaign. But President Kumaratunga, an intended victim of a Tamil Tiger assassination attempt just three years earlier, at times appeared less eager for a settlement. Although she technically did not control government actions, the president was commander in chief of the army and retained a wide political following. Kumaratunga pledged not to block the peace process, however, and Wickremesinghe won important backing for his stance in local elections in March, which his party won by overwhelming margins.

Negotiating a Federal Agreement

Following the cease-fire, an important second step toward peace came in March when a monitoring force led by Norway began the process of decommissioning rebel fighters and clearing roadblocks that had closed off Tamil areas. On April 10 Tiger leader Prabhakaran emerged from hiding and gave his first news conference in a dozen years. More than 300 journalists from around the world trekked to a remote Tiger jungle camp in eastern Sri Lanka to hear Prabhakaran say he was "sincerely committed" to peace. To the surprise of the reporters, Prabhakaran also said he was willing to consider a settlement that gave the Tamils autonomy but not the full independence that had long been his goal. The Tigers had abandoned violence, including the use of suicide bombers, he said: "The time has changed. We are adopting new strategies."

Low-level talks between government and rebel officials were held during the middle part of the year. On September 4 the government formally lifted a legal ban on the Tigers, a step that cleared the way for high-level political talks beginning on September 16 in Thailand. Three days of talks produced a key breakthrough: a formal announcement by the rebels that they had given up the quest for their own nation and would settle for autonomy.

Two other successful rounds of negotiations were held in November, the second of which featured a direct meeting in Oslo between Sri Lankan prime minister Wickremesinghe and the Tiger's chief negotiator, Anton Balasingham. In conjunction with the latter meeting, Britain, the European Union, the United States, and other donor nations on November 24 agreed to provide at least $60 million in development and humanitarian aid for Sri Lanka. At the donor's session, the chief U.S. representative—deputy secretary of state Richard Armitage—demanded that the Tamil Tigers renounce terrorism. With Armitage sitting in the front row, rebel diplomat Balasingham replied that the Tigers had pledged not to "resort to war or violence," but he stopped short of meeting the demand for a renunciation of terrorism.

Rebel leader Prabhakaran made a similar point in a rare radio broadcast on November 27, arguing that outside powers could not impose conditions on the peace talks. Even so, Prabhakaran clearly stated that he was willing to accept "substantial regional autonomy and self-government" rather than full independence.

On December 5, after four more days of talks in Oslo, negotiators for the government and rebels announced their most far-reaching agreement yet: a framework for a federal system of government. A joint statement said the two sides had agreed that Tamils should have the right of "internal self-determination in areas of historical habitation of the Tamil-speaking people based on a federal structure within a united Sri Lanka."

Diplomats and analysts said the details of that "federal structure" would have to be worked out in subsequent negotiations during 2003 over a new Sri Lankan constitution. To become effective, a new constitution would require approval by a two-thirds majority in the national parliament—a much larger majority than Wickremesinghe's government could reliably muster.

Despite the peace agreements and the absence of fighting, news organizations reported in late December that the Tamil Tigers were continuing to recruit soldiers, including children. Norwegian peace monitors said they had obtained information on several dozen cases in which children in Tamil-controlled areas had been forced to join the guerrillas.

Following are excerpts from the "Agreement on a Cease-Fire Between the Government of the Democratic Socialist Republic of Sri Lanka and the Liberation Tigers of Tamil Eelam," signed February 22, 2002, by representatives of the two parties following negotiations in Oslo mediated by the Norwegian foreign ministry, and excerpts from an accompanying statement by Jan Petersen, the foreign minister of Norway.

The documents were obtained from the Internet at www .usip.org/library/pa/sri_lanka/pa_sri_lanka_02222002 .html; accessed November 27, 2002.

CEASE-FIRE AGREEMENT

Preamble

The overall objective of the Government of the Democratic Socialist Republic of Sri Lanka (hereinafter referred to as the GOSL) and the Liberation Tigers of Tamil Eelam (hereinafter referred to as the LTTE) is to find a negotiated solution to the ongoing ethnic conflict in Sri Lanka.

The GOSL and the LTTE (hereinafter referred to as the Parties) recognize the importance of bringing an end to the hostilities and improving the living conditions for all inhabitants affected by the conflict. Bringing an end to the hostilities is also seen by the Parties as a means of establishing a positive atmosphere in which further steps towards negotiations on a lasting solution can be taken.

The Parties further recognize that groups that are not directly party to the conflict are also suffering the consequences of it. This is particularly the case as regards the Muslim population. Therefore, the provisions of this Agreement regarding the security of civilians and their property apply to all inhabitants.

With reference to the above, the Parties have agreed to enter into a cease-fire, refrain from conduct that could undermine the good intentions or violate the spirit of this Agreement and implement confidence-building measures as indicated in the articles below.

Article 1: Modalities of a ceasefire

The Parties have agreed to implement a ceasefire between their armed forces as follows:

1.1 A jointly agreed ceasefire between the GOSL and the LTTE shall enter into force on such date as is notified by the Norwegian Minister of Foreign Affairs in accordance with Article 4.2, hereinafter referred to as D-day.

Military operations

1.2 Neither Party shall engage in any offensive military operation. This requires the total cessation of all military action and includes, but is not limited to, such acts as:

   a. The firing of direct and indirect weapons, armed raids, ambushes, assassinations, abductions, destruction of civilian or military property, sabotage, suicide missions and activities by deep penetration units;
   b. Aerial bombardment;
   c. Offensive naval operations.

1.3 The Sri Lankan armed forces shall continue to perform their legitimate task of safeguarding the sovereignty and territorial integrity of Sri Lanka without engaging in offensive operations against the LTTE.

Separation of forces

[Paragraphs 1.4 through 1.13 dealt with specific provisions for the separation of combat units and the freedom of movement for combatants.]

Article 2: Measures to restore normalcy

The Parties shall undertake the following confidence-building measures with the aim of restoring normalcy for *all* inhabitants of Sri Lanka:

2.1 The Parties shall in accordance with international law abstain from hostile acts against the civilian population, including such acts as torture, intimidation, abduction, extortion and harassment.

2.2 The Parties shall refrain from engaging in activities or propagating ideas that could offend cultural or religious sensitivities. Places of worship (temples, churches, mosques and other holy sites, etc.) currently held by the forces of either of the Parties shall be vacated by D-day + 30 and made accessible to the public. Places of worship which are situated in "high security zones" shall be vacated by all armed personnel and maintained in good order by civilian workers, even when they are not made accessible to the public.

2.3 Beginning on the date on which this Agreement enters into force, school buildings occupied by either Party shall be vacated and returned to their intended use. This activity shall be completed by D-day + 160 at the latest.

2.4 A schedule indicating the return of all other public buildings to their intended use shall be drawn up by the Parties and published at the latest by D-day + 30.

2.5 The Parties shall review the security measures and the set-up of checkpoints, particularly in densely populated cities and towns, in order to introduce systems that will prevent harassment of the civilian population. Such systems shall be in place from D-day + 60.

2.6 The Parties agree to ensure the unimpeded flow of non-military goods to and from the LTTE-dominated areas with the exception of certain items as shown in Annex A [these items included arms and ammunition, explosives, remote control devices, and other items with potential military uses]. Quantities shall be determined by market demand. The GOSL shall regularly review the matter with the aim of gradually removing any remaining restrictions on non-military goods.

[Paragraphs 2.7 through 2.13 dealt with matters such as the movement of civilians and the reopening of roads, rail links, and fishing rights.]

Article 3: The Sri Lanka Monitoring Mission

The Parties have agreed to set up an international monitoring mission to enquire into any instance of violation of the terms and conditions of this Agreement. Both Parties shall fully cooperate to rectify any matter of conflict caused by their respective sides. The mission shall conduct international verification through on-site monitoring of the fulfilment of the commitments entered into in this Agreement as follows:

3.1 The name of the monitoring mission shall be the Sri Lanka Monitoring Mission

3.2 Subject to acceptance by the Parties, the Royal Norwegian Government (hereinafter referred to as the RNG) shall appoint the Head of the SLMM (hereinafter referred to as the HoM), who shall be the final authority regarding interpretation of this Agreement.

[Paragraphs 3.3 through 3.13 dealt with procedures for the operation of the monitoring mission and the resolution of disputes between the parties.]

Article 4: Entry into Force, Amendments and Termination of the Agreement

4.1 Each Party shall notify its consent to be bound by this Agreement through a letter to the Norwegian Minister of Foreign Affairs signed by Prime

Minister Ranil Wickremesinghe on behalf of the GOSL and by leader Velupillai Pirabaharan on behalf of the LTTE, respectively. The Agreement shall be initialled by each Party and enclosed in the above-mentioned letter.

4.2 The Agreement shall enter into force on such date as is notified by the Norwegian Minister of Foreign Affairs.

4.3 This Agreement may be amended and modified by mutual agreement of both Parties. Such amendments shall be notified in writing to the RNG.

4.4 This Agreement shall remain in force until notice of termination is given by either Party to the RNG. Such notice shall be given fourteen (14) days in advance of the effective date of termination. . . .

STATEMENT BY FOREIGN MINISTER OF NORWAY

As from 00:00 hours on 23 February 2002, a ceasefire agreement enters into force between the Government of Sri Lanka and the Liberation Tamil Tigers of Eelam (LTTE). The ceasefire document, signed by Sri Lankan Prime Minister Ranil Wickremesinghe and LTTE leader Vellipulai Prabhakaran, has been deposited with the Norwegian Government, and we have been asked to make the agreement public.

The overall objective of the parties is to find a negotiated solution to the ethnic conflict in Sri Lanka, which has cost 60,000 lives and caused widespread human suffering. The ceasefire will pave the way for further steps towards negotiations.

Through this formalized ceasefire the parties commit themselves to putting an end to the hostilities. They commit themselves to restoring normalcy for all the inhabitants of Sri Lanka, whether they are Sinhalese, Tamils, Muslims or others. And they commit themselves to accepting an international monitoring mission, led by Norway, which will conduct on-site monitoring.

Both sides have taken bold steps to conclude the ceasefire, and this agreement is a message that they are prepared to continue taking bold steps to achieve peace. They are embarking on a long road towards a political solution. It will not be easy. It will require determination and courage. The parties will face risks and uncertainties, and they will have to make hard choices. But no hardships are worse than those of conflict and bloodshed. No gains are greater than those of peace and prosperity.

On the journey to peace and prosperity, the inhabitants of Sri Lanka, and their leaders, will need the solidarity of the international community. It must mobilize political and financial support for peace and reconciliation. Norway will continue to accompany the parties in this demanding process.

I shall now provide some more detail about the ceasefire agreement.

First, it outlines the modalities of the ceasefire, including the total cessation of all offensive military operations, the separation of forces, and increased freedom of movement for unarmed troops on both sides.

Second, measures to restore normalcy for all the inhabitants of Sri Lanka—Sinhalese, Tamils, Muslims and others—putting an end to hostile acts against civilians, allowing the unimpeded flow of non-military goods, opening roads and railway lines, and a gradual easing of fishing restrictions.

Third, a small international monitoring mission, led by Norway. The mission will conduct international on-site monitoring of the fulfilment of the commitments made by the Parties. Let me underline, however, that it is up to the parties to respect the agreement and to impose sanctions on those individuals on either side who act contrary to the agreement.

COMPTROLLER GENERAL ON EMPLOYEE PENSION PLANS
February 27, 2002

The collapse in late 2001 of the giant energy trading company Enron, together with the deepening slump in the stock market, spawned a national debate about the adequacy of the nation's retirement system in general and the extent to which American workers were preparing themselves for retirement. Enron employees lost not only their jobs but also most of their retirement savings, largely because those savings were invested in Enron stock. Similar fates befell employees of several other failed or faltering companies in 2002.

At the same time, the general malaise in the stock market was cutting the value of virtually all retirement funds invested in the stock market. On December 31, 2002, the Dow Jones industrial average closed down for the third year in a row. Many workers who had planned on retiring within the next few years found that they no longer had as much saved for retirement as they had hoped and would either have to live more frugally during their "golden years" than they had expected or have to work longer than they had planned.

In the wake of the devastating losses to Enron employees, Congress quickly began to debate several controversial proposals to cap the amount of company stock an employee could hold and to limit the time a company could require an employee to hold on to their stock. Congress was unable to reach a consensus on those issues by the end of the year. An even more difficult issue was whether most workers, not just those caught in Enron-type situations, would have enough money to live on in retirement. That was an issue few politicians, or their constituents, seemed willing to confront directly.

Employer Stock Ownership

When Enron declared bankruptcy in December 2001 its employees discovered that most of their retirement savings had evaporated. Enron employees had 401(k) retirement plans under which employees could invest part of their pay in a retirement fund, which was partially matched by *company contributions. The problem was that Enron made its contribution in company stock, and many employees also invested at least part of their retirement funds in company stock. By the end of 2000, 62 percent of the assets held in Enron 401(k) plans were invested in Enron stock. Both Enron and its employees did well, at least on paper. But when Enron stock prices fell—from a high of $80 a share in January 2001 to less than 70 cents a share by the end of the year, the employees' retirement plans as well as Enron itself were all but wiped out. About 20,000 Enron employees lost an estimated $1 billion.*

In Enron's case, managers appeared to be engaged in phony accounting to keep the company's share value high and were thus deliberately misleading all investors in the company, including its employees, about Enron's true value. Shortly after the accounting scandal was revealed, Enron employees filed a class action suit alleging that Enron had violated its fiduciary duties in administering the retirement plans by not operating them solely in the best interests of the employees. Enron's management of the plans was also under investigation by the Department of Labor. (Corporate crime, p. 391)

Enron employees were not the only ones to get caught by investing retirement funds in company stock that then lost most of its value. The retirement accounts of employees of WorldCom, Global Crossing, Lucent Technologies, Nortel Networks, Qwest Communications, Rite Aid, and Providian Financial Corporation, among others, all suffered sharp losses when the companies' stock prices plunged.

In the wake of the Enron scandal, Congress immediately began to debate legislation to protect holders of 401(k) plans from suffering similar losses. Two aspects of the Enron plan that came under fire were the requirement that employers hold on to their Enron stock until they reached age fifty and a prohibition on 401(k) transactions during certain periods, generally when plan administration was being changed. Enron employees were bitterly angry that they had been blocked from making changes in their retirement accounts while Enron managers were still able to sell their Enron stock. The House passed a bill (HR 3762) in April that would allow employees to sell stock in their company in as little as three years after they received it as matching contributions.

Partisan tensions were more evident in the Senate, where Democrats pushed legislation that would not only shorten the time employees had to hold company stock but also limit the amount of employer stock that workers could acquire in their 401(k) plans. A host of experts had advised that employers be required to warn their employees about the risks of not diversifying their investments. David M. Walker, comptroller general of the United States and a former assistant secretary for pension and welfare benefit programs in the Labor Department, told the Senate Finance Committee on February 27 that "diversification of pension assets is crucially important" to balance investment risks.

But there was little support for a cap. Opponents pointed to a number of successful companies where employees held more than three-fourths of their

401(k) assets in company stock, including Procter & Gamble, Anheuser-Busch, Coca-Cola, Abbott Laboratories, and General Electric. Opponents also warned that companies that could not make their contributions to 401(k) plans in company stock might decide not to offer the plans at all. In the end Democrats compromised on legislation that was similar to the House-passed legislation, but the bill was pulled from the floor when it became apparent that it would become a magnet for unrelated, end-of-session items.

Congress dealt with the "lock-down" complaint in legislation overhauling corporate accounting practices (PL 107–204), which was signed into law July 30. The legislation required that participants in 401(k) plans be given thirty days' notice before being locked out of buying or selling in their accounts when administrative changes in the plan are ordered. Corporate executives were also barred from selling their stock during such periods.

The Broader Problems with 401(k) Plans

The retirement fund losses sustained by employees of Enron and other big companies highlighted a broader issue on which few people had been focusing: A shift in retirement plans away from defined-benefit plans in which the employer paid a guaranteed fixed benefit and assumed the investment risk, toward defined-contribution plans in which the employee assumed much of the investment risk and had no guaranteed benefit. The retirement welfare of 401(k) participants was thus much more directly dependent on the ups and downs of the stock and bond markets as well as the investors' savvy about investing.

The Labor Department reported that in 1998 (the last year for which it had data) employer-sponsored retirement accounts had assets of $4 trillion. About half were held in defined-benefit plans, which enrolled about 40 million people, with more than half still working. The other $2 trillion was held in 401(k) plans, stock bonus plans, and profit-sharing plans, for which there was no fixed or guaranteed benefit. Employees had to depend on their investments returning a sufficient amount to support their retirement. About 55 million workers participated in these plans, with 88 percent still working. Some workers participated in both defined benefit and defined contribution plans.

The 401(k) programs began in 1982 and grew quickly, helped along by the booming stock market of the 1980s and 1990s (which was kept booming in part by the growing retirement funds). By 1998, $1.5 trillion in assets was held in 401(k) plans, and roughly three of every four new dollars invested in retirement plans were being put into the popular plans. By the late 1990s companies were still contributing more to retirement plans than their workers, but the percentage was falling and experts projected that worker contributions had likely surpassed employer contributions in 1999 or 2000.

The year 2000 also marked the first time that 401(k) participants lost money in their accounts. According to Cerulli Associates, a Boston research firm, the average account declined from $46,740 at the beginning of the year *to $41,919 by the end of the year. Because those averages did not factor in any contributions made during the year, the losses, at least for some employees, were even higher. Given the continuing poor performance of the markets in 2001 and 2002, it was likely that the downward trend continued.*

To reduce some of the risk inherent in 401(k) programs, the legislative reforms considered in Congress would require employers to educate their employees about their investment choices, including telling them of the benefits of diversification. Although they were not opposed to the idea, many pension experts and advocates for retirees questioned whether employees would make much use of such information. In the opinion of one pension expert, workers were, at best, too passive and at worst self-destructive gamblers.

Several other, more controversial proposals were also offered for taking some of the risk out of the system and encouraging more workers to save for retirement. One would give companies tax incentives to encourage them to switch back to offering defined-benefit programs. That seemed unlikely as more and more companies were abandoning their defined-benefit plans for 401(k) and other plans that cost them less to administer. Another proposal would require companies to contribute to 401(k) plans for all their workers, even if individual workers did not participate. A variant would be to require all workers to enroll in 401(k) plans with the option of opting out. A more extreme proposal would have the government guarantee defined-contribution plans, as it already guaranteed defined-benefit plans. Little public debate on any of these proposals had taken place as of the end of the year.

Lack of Preparedness

The media focus on retirement funds after the Enron debacle also made clear that many workers did in fact appear to be gambling with retirement. An analysis of Census Bureau data conducted by the Congressional Research Service found that more than half of all paid workers did not own retirement savings accounts of any sort. About a third worked for employees who did not sponsor a retirement plan. But in 2001 only slightly more than half of workers who had access to employer-sponsored plans participated, according to the analysis. There were indications late in 2002 that more workers were opting out of 401(k) plans, as many were unable to afford contributions, unwilling to risk money in the ailing stock market, and untrusting of the integrity of the plans after the corporate accounting scandals.

A survey conducted by the Employee Benefit Research Institute found similar disheartening results. Seventy percent of those surveyed said they were very confident or somewhat confident that they would have enough savings to retire comfortably, yet only 67 percent said they had saved anything for retirement. Almost 50 percent of all workers had saved less than $50,000; nearly 70 percent had never tried to calculate how much money they might need in retirement. By one estimate, the average American must save at least $230,000 to be able to draw $1,000 a month to supplement Social Security benefits. "Clearly, people have not saved enough," said Michael Tanner, director of health and welfare studies at the libertarian Cato Institute.

Labor statistics indicated that many older workers were beginning to work past the traditional retirement age: 40 percent of men over age fifty-five were still working, the highest proportion since January 1984. The share of older women still in the workplace hit a record 28 percent. People were working longer for a variety of reasons, including preferring some work to all leisure. Longer life expectancy and better medical care meant that many older people were more physically capable of continuing their working lives than had been true in the past. Companies were beginning to realize that older workers offered benefits such as reliability and expertise that were sometimes lacking in younger workers. Anecdotally, however, many older Americans were remaining in or returning to the workforce because they needed the extra pay to survive.

That trend could turn out to be a bonus for the Social Security system, the federal retirement program that most workers relied upon to provide a base income during retirement. The system, which was enacted in 1935, paid minimal benefits to retirees out of funds generated by a payroll tax shared equally by the employer and the employee. The system worked well for the first few decades, preventing many older Americans from living lives of poverty. But as people began to live longer and retire earlier, the system began paying out benefits over more years than ever before. At the same time, declining fertility rates meant that fewer workers were available to pay into the system.

Policy makers had known for decades that the shrinking ratio of workers to retirees—expected to be less than two to one by 2030, when the huge baby boom generation was retired—could not sustain the system. But proposals for overhauling Social Security, including a proposal by President George W. Bush for privatizing part of the system, were so controversial that they had received only cursory exploration in Congress. "If people would work until they're 70, we wouldn't have a Social Security crisis," Richard Johnson, a senior research associate at the Urban Institute, told the Los Angeles Times. (Bush privatization plan, Historic Documents of 2001, p. 914)

> *Following is the text of testimony delivered February 27, 2002, to the Senate Finance Committee by Comptroller General David M. Walker, who discussed key issues confronting private pension plans in the wake of the collapse of the Enron Corporation.*
>
> **The document was obtained from the Internet at www.gao .gov/new.items/d02480t.pdf; accessed February 10, 2003.**

Mr. Chairman and Members of the Committee:

I am pleased to be here today to provide you with preliminary observations on some of the challenges facing our nation's private pension system. Pension income is crucial to American retirees' standard of living. About half of Americans over 65 receive payments from pensions and savings plans, and such income represents about 18 percent of their total income. Over 70 million workers participate in pension and savings plans, and such plans in 1997 represented about $3.6 trillion in retirement savings.

The federal government encourages employers to sponsor and maintain pension and savings plans for their employees. The private pension system is voluntary and consists of defined benefit plans and defined contribution plans. Defined benefit plans promise to provide a level of retirement income that is generally based on salary and years of service. Defined contribution plans are based on the contributions to and investment returns on the individual accounts. Such plans include thrift savings plans, profit-sharing plans, and employee stock ownership plans (ESOPs).

The financial collapse of the Enron Corporation and its effect on the company's workers and retirees suggests certain vulnerabilities in these selected savings mechanisms. Enron's retirement plans, which included a defined benefit cash balance plan, a defined contribution 401(k) plan, and an ESOP, caused Congress to question specifically the use of employer stock as the company match, the continued existence of floor offsets, and the practice of investment freezes or lockdowns during changes in plan administrators. The financial losses suffered by participants in Enron's retirement plans have raised questions about the benefits and limitations of such private pension and savings plans and the challenges employees face in saving for retirement through their employer-provided plans.

You asked me here today to help provide context for considering how to address the vulnerabilities the Enron case may suggest. Accordingly, I will discuss three areas that, because of the experience with Enron, appear particularly salient to policymakers' decisions: (1) the importance of investment diversification and related investor education issues; (2) the crucial role of disclosure, and what information employees need and can expect about their company and their pension plans; and (3) the importance of fiduciary rules in safeguarding employee pension assets. In discussing these three issues, I will also address certain plan design issues such as floor-offsets, using company stock in pension plans, and plan operation issues, such as investment freezes or lockdowns. My observations are based on prior GAO work, a preliminary review of Enron's and other public companies' plans, discussions with industry experts and senior regulatory officials, and my personal experience, including my former position as Assistant Secretary of Labor for Pension and Welfare Benefit Programs.

In summary, the collapse of the Enron Corporation and the accompanying loss of Enron employees' retirement savings appear to highlight vulnerabilities in the private pension system and help focus attention on strengthening several aspects of this system. Diversification of pension assets is crucially important, particularly in a world where the use of defined contribution plans-those plans in which employees bear the investment risk-is increasing. If both the employees' 401(k) contributions and the company match are largely in employer stock, as was the case at Enron, employees risk losing not only their jobs should the company go out of business, but also a significant portion of their retirement savings. The Enron situation suggests the importance of encouraging employees to diversify but any action would have to be balanced against the desires of employers and employees to maintain a portion of retirement savings in company stock. In addition, the Enron situation illustrates the need to provide employees with investment education and advice that will enable them to better manage their retirement savings.

Workers need clear and understandable information about their pension plans to make wise retirement saving decisions. While disclosure rules state that plan sponsors must provide plan participants with a summary of benefits and rights under their pension plan and notification when plan benefits are changed, such information is not always clear, particularly in describing complex plans, like floor-offset arrangements. We have also observed in earlier work that wide variation exists in the type and amounts of information workers receive about plan changes that can potentially reduce pension benefits, and enhanced disclosure requirements may be warranted. Furthermore, employees, like other investors, need reliable and understandable information about a company's financial condition and prospects.

Finally, fiduciary standards form the cornerstone of private pension protections. These standards require plan sponsors to act in a manner that is solely in the interest of plan participants and beneficiaries. In the end, investigations of Enron's actions related to its plans will determine whether plan fiduciaries acted in accordance with these responsibilities. In light of Enron, policymakers may wish to consider whether current fiduciary standards are sufficient or whether they require strengthening, and act accordingly to address these fundamental principles of pension management.

The Enron collapse provides the Congress with clear examples of issues it may wish to consider when deciding whether and how to strengthen the security of plan benefits. These issues include employees' need for enhanced education and appropriate investment advice, plan designs such as floor-offset arrangements and the use of employer stock in retirement savings plans, and plan operations, such as plan investment freezes and lockdowns. Addressing these issues will require balancing the need for greater participant protections with the potential increase in employer burden that could undermine their willingness to sponsor or contribute to such plans.

Background

The Internal Revenue Code (IRC) defines pension plans as either defined benefit or defined contribution and includes separate requirements for each type of plan. The employer, as plan sponsor, is responsible for funding the promised benefit, investing and managing the plan assets, and bearing the investment risk. If a defined benefit plan terminates with insufficient assets to pay promised benefits, the Pension Benefit Guaranty Corporation (PBGC) provides plan termination insurance to pay participants' pension benefits up to certain limits.

Under defined contribution plans, employees have individual accounts to which employers, employees, or both make periodic contributions. Plans that allow employees to choose to contribute a portion of their pre-tax compensation to the plan under section 401(k) of IRC are generally referred to as 401(k) plans. In many 401(k) plans employees can control the investments in their account while in other plans the employer controls the investments. ESOPs may also be combined with other pension plans, such as a profit-sharing plan or a 401(k) plan. Investment income earned on a 401(k) plan accumulates tax-free until an individual withdraws the funds. In a defined contribution plan, the employee bears the investment risk, and plan participants have no termination insurance.

The Internal Revenue Service (IRS) and the Pension and Welfare Benefits Administration (PWBA) of the Department of Labor (DOL) are primarily responsible for enforcing laws related to private pension plans. Under the Employee Retirement Income Security Act of 1974 (ERISA), as amended, IRS enforces coverage and participation, vesting , and funding standards that concern how plan participants become eligible to participate in benefit plans, earn rights to benefits, and reasonable assurance that plans have sufficient assets to pay promised benefits. IRS also enforces provisions of the IRC that apply to pension plans, including provisions under section 401(k) of the IRC. PWBA enforces ERISA's reporting and disclosure provisions and fiduciary standards, which concern how plans should operate in the best interest of participants.

Since the 1980's, there has been a significant shift from defined benefit plans to defined contribution pension plans. Many employers sponsor both types of plans, with the defined contribution plan supplementing the defined benefit plan. However, most of the new pension plans adopted by employers are defined contribution plans. According to the Department of Labor, employers sponsored over 660,000 defined contribution plans as of 1997 compared with about 59,000 defined benefit plans. As shown in figure 1, defined contribution plans covered about 55 million participants, while defined benefit plans covered over 40 million participants in 1997.

The number of employer-sponsored 401(k) plans has also increased substantially in recent years, increasing from over 17,000 in 1984 to over 265,000 plans in 1997. In 1997, 401(k) plans accounted for 40 percent of all employer-sponsored defined contribution plans and approximately 37 percent of all private pension plans. Approximately 33.8 million employees actively participated in a 401(k) plan, and these plans held about $1.3 trillion in assets as of 1997.

The continued growth in the number of defined contribution plans and plan assets is encouraging, but concerns remain that many workers who traditionally lack pensions may not be benefiting from these plans, and the overall percentage of workers covered by pensions has remained relatively stable for many years. Furthermore, the trend toward defined contribution plans and the increased availability of lump-sum payments from pension plans when workers change jobs raises issues of whether workers will preserve their pension benefits until retirement or outlive their retirement assets.

Similar to other large companies, Enron sponsored both a defined benefit plan and a defined contribution plan, covering over 20,000 employees. Enron's tax-qualified pension plans consisted of a 401(k)-defined contribution plan, an employee stock ownership plan, and a defined benefit cash balance plan. Under Enron's 401(k) plan, participants were allowed to contribute from 1 to 15 percent of their eligible base pay in any combination of pre-tax salary deferrals or after-tax contributions subject to certain limitations. Enron generally matched 50 percent of all participants' pre-tax contributions up to a maximum of 6 percent of an employee's base pay, with the matching contributions invested solely in the Enron Corporation Stock Fund. Participants were allowed to reallocate their company matching contributions among other investment options when they reached the age of 50.

Enron's employee stock ownership plan, like other ESOPs, was designed to encourage employee ownership in their company. The plan provided employee retirement benefits for workers' service with the company between January 1, 1987, and December 31, 1994. No new participants were allowed into the ESOP after January 1, 1995.

Finally, Enron sponsored a cash balance plan, which accrued retirement benefits to employees during their employment at Enron. An employee was eligible to be a member of the cash balance plan immediately upon being employed. According to DOL officials, the cash balance plan did not have any investments in Enron stock as of the end of 2000. If the plan is unable to pay promised benefits and is taken over by PBGC, vested participants and retirees will receive their promised benefits up to the limit guaranteed under ERISA.

Greater Diversification and Investment Sophistication May Be Needed

The Enron collapse points to the importance of prudent investment principles such as diversification, including diversification of employer matching contributions. Diversification helps individuals to mitigate the risk of holding stocks by spreading their holdings over many investments and reducing excessive exposure to any one source of risk. Many workers are covered by participant-directed 401(k) plans that allow participants to allocate the investment of their account balances among a menu of investment options, including employer stock. Additionally, many plan sponsors match participants' elective contributions with shares of employer stock.

When the employer's stock constitutes the majority of employees' account balances and is the only type of matching contribution the employer provides, employees are exposed to the possibility of losing more than their job if the company goes out of business or into serious financial decline. They are also exposed to the possibility of losing a major portion of their retirement savings. For example, DOL reports that 63 percent of Enron's 401(k) assets were invested in company stock as of the end of 2000. These concentrations are the result both of employee investment choice and employer matching with company stock. The types of losses experienced by Enron employees could have been limited if employees had diversified their account balances and if they had been able to diversify their company matching contributions more quickly.

Companies prefer to match employees' contributions with company stock for a number of reasons. First, when a company makes its matching contribution in the form of company stock, issuing the stock has little impact on the company's financial statement in the short term. Second, stock contributions are fully deductible as a business expense for tax purposes at the share price in effect when the company contributes them. Third, matching contributions in company stock puts more company shares in the hands of employees who some officials feel are less likely to sell their shares if the company's profits are less than expected or in the event of a takeover. Finally, companies point out that matching with company stock promotes a sense of employee ownership, linking the interests of employees with the company and other shareholders.

Some pension experts have said that easing employer restrictions on when employees are allowed to sell their company matching contributions would increase their ability to diversify. In 1997, a majority of the Pension and Welfare Benefits Administration Advisory Council working group on employer assets in ERISA plans recommended that participants in 401(k) plans be able to sell employer stock when they become vested in the plan. Additionally, legislation has recently been introduced that would limit the amount of employer stock that can be held in participants' 401(k) accounts and provide participants greater freedom to diversify their employer matching contributions. Proponents of allowing employees to diversify employer stock matching contributions more quickly say that this would benefit both employers and employees by maintaining the tax and financial benefits for the company while providing employees with more investment freedom and increased retirement benefit security. However, others have expressed concern that further restrictions on employer plan designs may reduce incentives for employers to sponsor plans or provide matching contributions.

Even with opportunities to diversify, studies indicate that employees will need education to improve their ability to manage their retirement savings. Numerous studies have looked at how well individuals who are currently investing understand investments and the markets. On the basis of those studies, it is clear that among those who save through their company's retirement programs or on their own, large percentages of the investing population are unsophisticated and do not fully understand the risks associated with their investment choices. For example, one study found that 47 percent of 401(k) plan participants believe that stocks are components of a money market fund, and 55 percent of those surveyed thought that they could not lose money in government bond funds. Another study on the financial literacy of mutual fund investors found that less than half of all investors correctly understood the purpose of diversification. These studies and others indicate the need for enhanced investment education about such topics as investing, the relationship between risk and return, and the potential benefits of diversification.

In addition to investor education, employees may need more individualized investment advice. Such investment advice becomes even more important as participation in 401(k) plans continues to increase. ERISA does not require plan sponsors to make investment advice available to plan participants. Under ERISA, providing investment advice results in fiduciary responsibility for those providing the advice, while providing investment education does not. ERISA does, however, establish conditions employers must meet in order to be shielded from fiduciary liability related to investment choices made by employees in their participant-directed accounts. In 1996, DOL issued guidance to employers and investment advisers on how to provide educational investment information and analysis to participants without triggering fiduciary liability. DOL recently issued guidance about investment advice making it easier for plans to use independent investment advisors to provide advice to employees in retirement plans.

Industry representatives that we spoke with said more companies are providing informational sessions with investment advisors to help employees better understand their investments and the risk of not diversifying. They also said that changes are needed under ERISA to better shield employers from fiduciary liability for investment advisors' recommendations to individual participants. ERISA currently prohibits fiduciary investment advisors from engaging in transactions with clients' plans where they have a conflict of interest, for example, when the advisors are providing other services such as plan administration. As a result, investment advisors cannot provide specific investment advice to 401(k) plan participants about their firm's investment products without approval from DOL. Various legislative proposals have been introduced that would address employers' concern about fiduciary liability when they make investment advice available to plan participants and make it easier for fiduciary investment advisors to provide investment advice to participants when they also provide other services to the participants' plan. However, concerns remain that such proposals may not adequately protect plan participants from conflicted advice.

Enhanced Disclosure Could Help Employees Understand Investment Risks They Face

Enron's failure highlights the importance of plan participants receiving clear information about their pension plan and any changes to it that could affect plan benefits. Current ERISA disclosure requirements provide only minimum guidelines that firms must follow on the type of information they provide plan participants. Improving the amount of disclosure provided to plan participants and also ensuring that such disclosure is in plain English could help participants better manage the risks they face.

Enron's pension plans illustrate the complex nature of some plan designs that may be difficult for participants to understand. For example, Enron's pension plans included a floor-offset arrangement. Such arrangements consist of separate, but associated defined benefit and defined contribution plans. The benefits accrued under one plan offset the benefit payable from the other. In 1987, Congress limited the use of such plans. However, plans in existence when the provision was enacted, including Enron's plan, were grandfathered. In addition, Enron's conversion of its defined benefit plan from one type of benefit formula to another illustrates the types of changes and their consequent affect on benefits that plan participants need to understand. Enron's defined benefit plan was converted from a final average pay formula-where the pension benefit is a percentage of the participant's final years of pay multiplied by his or her length of service-to a cash balance formula, which expresses the defined benefit as a hypothetical account balance. As we have previously reported, conversions to cash balance plans can be advantageous to certain groups of workers-for example, those who switch jobs frequently-but can lower the pension benefits of others.

The extent to which Enron employees were informed or understood the effect of the floor-offset or the conversion of their defined benefit plan to a cash balance formula is unclear. As stated in a prior GAO report on cash balance plans, we found wide variation in the type and amounts of information workers receive about plan changes and that can potentially reduce pensions benefits. Based in part on our recommendations, the Congress, under the Economics Growth and Tax Relief Reconciliation Act of 2001, required that employers provide participants more timely and clear information concerning changes to plans that could reduce their future benefits. The Treasury Department is responsible for issuing the applicable regulations implementing this requirement.

Other types of information may also be beneficial to plan participants. Currently, ERISA requires that plan administrators provide each plan participant with a summary of certain financial data reported to DOL. As we previously reported, the Secretary of Labor could require that plan administrators provide plan participants with information about the employers' financial condition and other information. Such information could enable employees to be more fully informed about their holdings and any potential risks associated with them.

ERISA Requires Fiduciaries to be Prudent and Reasonable

Under ERISA, fiduciaries are held to high but broad standards. Persons who perform certain tasks, generally involving the use of a plan's assets, become fiduciaries because of those duties. Others, such as the plan sponsor, the plan administrator, or a trustee are fiduciaries because of their position. Fiduciaries are required to act solely in the interest of plan participants and beneficiaries. They are to adhere to a standard referred to as the prudent expert rule, which requires them to act as a prudent person experienced in such matters would in similar circumstances. Fiduciaries are required to follow their plan's documents and act in accordance with the terms of the plan as it is set out. If fiduciaries do not perform their duties in accordance with ERISA standards, they may be held personally liable for any breach of their duty.

Yet, even with the high standards and broad guidance provided by ERISA, in some cases the actions of fiduciaries can seem to conflict with the best interests of plan participants. During the period when revelations about Enron's finances were contributing to the steady devaluation of Enron's stock price, Enron's plan fiduciaries imposed a lockdown on the 401(k) plan, preventing employees from making withdrawals or investment transfers. Enron imposed the lockdown to change recordkeepers, an acceptable practice. Some observers, however, have questioned whether Enron employees were sufficiently notified about the lockdown. Observers have also questioned the equity of treatment between Enron senior executives and Enron workers during the lockdown. Enron's employees were unable to make changes to their 401(k) accounts during the plan's lockdown period. However, Enron executives did not face similar restrictions on company stock not held in the plan. Fairness would suggest that company executives should face similar restrictions in their ability to sell company stock during lockdown periods when workers are unable to make 401(k) investment changes. This is especially true for those executives who serve as pension plan fiduciaries, including plan trustees.

Conclusions

The Enron collapse, although not by itself evidence that private pension law should be changed, serves to illustrate what can happen to employees' retirement savings under certain conditions. Specifically, it illustrates the importance of diversification for retirement savings as well as employees' need for enhanced education, appropriate investment advice, and greater disclosure. All of these may help them better navigate the risks they face in saving for retirement.

In addition to the broad issues of diversification and education, Enron's collapse raises questions about the relationship between various plan designs and participant benefit security. In particular, Congress may wish to consider whether further restrictions on floor-offset arrangements are warranted, whether to provide additional employee flexibility in connection with matches in the form of employer stocks, and whether to limit the amount of employer stock that can be held in certain retirement saving plans. Resolving these issues will require considering the tradeoffs between providing greater participant protections and employers' need for flexibility in plan design. Finally, Congress will have to weigh whether to rely on the broad fiduciary standards established in ERISA that currently govern fiduciary actions or to impose specific requirements that would govern certain plan administrative operations such as plan investment freezes or lockdowns.

Mr. Chairman, this concludes my statement. I would be happy to answer any questions you or other members of the Committees may have.

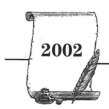

March

GAO TESTIMONY ON
ABUSE IN NURSING HOMES
March 4, 2002

The problem of abuse and neglect of nursing home residents came to the forefront of public attention in 2002, highlighted by a series of congressional hearings, newspaper investigations, and government reports. "Unlawful abuse and neglect is widespread, underreported, infrequently prosecuted, and the cause of untold suffering, injury, illness, and death," said Marie-Therese Connolly, the head of the Department of Justice's Nursing Home Initiative. According to the General Accounting Office (GAO), the investigative arm of Congress, 30 percent of the nation's 17,000 nursing homes had been cited at some point for actually harming patients or placing them at risk of death or serious injury.

The most prevalent problem was neglect, with an unknown number of nursing home residents suffering or dying unnecessarily from malnutrition, dehydration, and complications arising from untreated bedsores. But every year in every state, dozens of complaints were filed alleging physical assaults and sexual abuse against residents by nursing home staff or by other residents—assaults that often resulted in serious injury or death. Perhaps the most disturbing incidents were those that went unreported or untreated in an attempt to gloss over the wrongdoing.

Health care experts and others who examined the problem agreed that inadequate staffing in nursing homes was the main cause of these preventable deaths. Shortages of nurses and nurse aides had affected every type of health care facility in recent years, not only nursing homes. The problem was particularly acute in nursing homes, where the pay was typically low, the work often unpleasant and physically and emotionally demanding, and overtime frequently mandatory. In March the U.S. Department of Health and Human Services reported that nine of ten nursing homes did not have enough nursing staff to provide adequate care.

Although identifying the problem underlying poor quality care was comparatively easy, fixing it was much more difficult and controversial. Not only did shortages of qualified nurses and nurse aides have to be overcome, but policy decisions about who would pay for these improvements had to be negotiated between nursing home owners, many of whom were seeking a profit, and the federal and state governments. Meanwhile, families trying to find a high-quality nursing home for their loved ones could turn to an updated federal Web site, Nursing Home Compare, for assistance. As of November, consumers using the Web site would find ten indicators of care for all nursing homes in the United States and a listing of any deficiencies found during complaint investigations and annual inspections.

Dimensions of the Problem

About 3 million elderly and disabled people a year spend some time in a nursing home. On any given day an estimated 1.8 million nursing home beds were occupied, mostly by white women age seventy-five or older. Nursing home residents, generally too frail physically or mentally to care properly for themselves, received help with basic needs such as eating, dressing, and toileting. Lax attention, particularly by nurse aides, who provided much of this care, could result in malnutrition, dehydration, and bedsores, all of which could result in severe illness or death if left unattended. A national survey of more than 500,000 death certificates in 1999 found that these three maladies were listed as the cause of death in 4,138 cases. Findings from several other investigations that compared patients' medical records with death certificates suggested that the cause of death was often misstated on the certificates and that the actual number of deaths attributable to starvation, dehydration, and bedsores was much higher.

Not all cases of malnutrition, dehydration, and bedsores could be prevented. A resident might refuse to eat or drink. Disease might aggravate bedsores and interfere with proper absorption of nutrients. Residents might have living wills that bar supplemental nutrition or medical treatment under certain conditions. But medical experts estimated that these circumstances accounted for only about 15 percent of all deaths of nursing home residents from these causes. The rest most likely could have been prevented with better and more timely care. "The number of avoidable deaths of our elderly could be in the tens of thousands," Sen. John Breaux, D-La., told the St. Louis Post Dispatch *in October. Breaux headed the Senate Special Committee on Aging.*

There were also incidents of physical abuse and sexual assault. During hearings before the Senate Aging Committee in March, witnesses told of residents being hit, choked, and slammed into walls, sometimes by other residents but more often by nursing home staff. A staff member of one Florida nursing home was awaiting trial on charges that he had raped and impregnated a thirty-seven-year-old woman who had been incapacitated by a stroke. The nursing home staff did not realize the woman was pregnant until she gave birth.

No one knew with any certainty the extent of physical abuse problems in nursing homes. State surveys for July 2000 through June 2001 showed that 2.2 percent of nursing homes were cited for abuse or neglect that caused harm to a patient—about a percentage point less than the previous year.

Noting that those figures indicated that abuse was not on the rise, Alan DeFend, a spokesman for the American Health Care Association, said the "bad actions" of a small percentage of nursing homes should not be allowed to overshadow "the good works of the hundreds of thousands of health-care professionals who are providing quality compassionate care." The association represented nursing homes.

The findings of a GAO investigation, presented to the Senate Aging Committee at its March 4 hearings, said that incidents of abuse often went unreported, for many reasons, including fear of reprisals. Leslie G. Aronovitz, director of GAO's health care program dealing with administration and integrity issues, told the committee that even when abuse was reported, the complaints were often not acted on promptly, making it difficult for investigators to gather evidence. In the three states that the GAO investigated—Georgia, Illinois, and Pennsylvania—local law enforcement agencies were seldom called to nursing homes to investigate complaints of abuse, and state nursing home inspection agencies were often not promptly notified of abuse allegations. Partly as a result, few alleged abuses were ever prosecuted.

Aronovitz noted several gaps in efforts to prevent and detect abuse. For example, under federal law, each state was required to keep a registry of certified nurse aides that nursing homes were required to check before hiring aides. Aides found to be abusive were effectively excluded from the registry. The GAO found frequent and long delays in including information about abusive aides on such registries. The agency also noted that states kept track of abuse by nurse aides within the state, but not abuses committed by aides when they worked in another state. Some categories of workers, such as laundry aides and maintenance personnel, were not registered, licensed, or otherwise certified, so nursing homes could easily hire someone with a history of abuse that stopped short of a criminal record. Even a criminal background check might not reflect abuses committed in another state.

The GAO investigation also found that nursing homes were rarely sanctioned for failing to respond adequately to allegations of abuse. Of 158 cases reviewed by the GAO in the three states under investigation, twenty-six nursing homes were eventually cited for abuse-related deficiencies, but only one of these was assessed a civil monetary penalty, and that one was reduced on appeal. While some had argued that stiffer penalties for deficiencies might encourage nursing homes to do a better job in the first place, the industry contended that higher fines could put nursing homes out of business and leave residents looking for new accommodations and that it was better to require nursing homes to fix the conditions that caused the abuse.

Aronovitz made several suggestions for improvements, including: conducting more and better screening for prospective employees, involving local law enforcement in abuse complaints immediately, setting uniform definitions of abuse, and displaying telephone numbers for reporting abuse more prominently in nursing homes and in phone books. The Centers for Medicare and Medicaid Services (CMS), an agency within the Department of Health and Human Services that had responsibility for ensuring that nursing homes complied with federal standards, agreed with many of the

GAO recommendations. CMS said it would clarify its instructions to the states about definitions of abuse and notification of law enforcement officials when there was an abuse complaint. It said it would review the other recommendations as part of its overall reassessment of regulations to protect nursing home residents from abuse.

In September 2002 Senators Breaux and Orrin Hatch, R-Utah, introduced legislation designed to prevent abuse of the elderly not only in nursing homes but also in private homes and other care settings. Among its provisions was one establishing criminal penalties for individuals and nursing home facilities responsible for neglect and abuse. Another provision would require criminal background checks on all nursing home employees.

Federal Web Site on Nursing Home Quality Indicators

In November the federal government began to disclose important violations of standards on its popular and highly publicized Web site, which was designed to help consumers evaluate nursing homes. According to a report released February 21 by Rep. Henry A. Waxman, D-Calif., and Sen. Charles E. Grassley, R-Iowa, the Web site, Nursing Home Compare, included violations that were found by annual state inspections but did not include violations that were found during complaint investigations. During a fifteen-month study, conducted October 1, 2000, to December 31, 2001, the report said approximately 52,000 complaints alleging physical, mental, or sexual abuse and medical neglect were filed. Nearly half of those, some 25,000, were substantiated after investigations but none were reported on the Web site. As a result, some nursing home facilities were highly rated even though they had experienced violations of health and safety standards that resulted in serious injury, even death in a few cases. The report, "HHS Nursing Home Compare Website Has Major Flaws," was prepared by the Democratic staff of the Special Investigations Division of the House Committee on Government Reform.

At the time, Tom Scully, director of CMS, which was in charge of the Web site, said that the complaint data were not included in the Web site data largely because CMS wanted to be sure the complaints were substantiated and were not double-counted in the tallies. But he said the report "is probably a helpful prod to get us to do what we're in the process of doing anyway." In November Scully announced that the Web site now included in its nursing home reports deficiencies found as a result of complaint investigations. "I would rate this as extremely important," said Donna Lenhoff, executive director of the National Citizens' Coalition for Nursing Home Reform. "It means that consumers will be able to find out more information and they will be alerted to some of the questions they need to ask about nursing homes."

Increasing Nursing Home Staff

Most advocates for nursing home residents said the abuse problem would not diminish until nursing homes were more adequately staffed. To back up their arguments, they cited a report by the federal government finding that nine of every ten nursing homes were understaffed. The report, prepared for the CMS and released March 19, identified staffing thresholds below which it found that the quality of care suffered.

The report, "Appropriateness of Minimum Nurse Staffing Ratios in Nursing Homes: Overview of the Phase II Report," said residents in an average nursing home needed 4.1 hours of care every day, including 2.8 hours from a nurse aide and 1.3 hours from a registered nurse or licensed practical nurse. A coauthor of the report said that to meet the thresholds identified, nursing homes would need one nurse aide for every five to six patients; currently the average was one aide for every seven to fourteen patients. All told, the report said, nursing homes would need to hire between 77,000 and 137,000 registered nurses, 22,000 to 27,000 licensed practical nurses, and 181,000 to 310,000 nurse aides, and pay for each of these categories would need to increase. A severe shortages of nurses as well as cost could make it impossible for most nursing homes to meet these thresholds. The report estimated that total nursing home expenditures would need to increase 8 percent to cover the staffing increases needed to meet the thresholds.

Even as it released the report, the Bush administration said it would not set minimum staffing levels because of the costs involved and would instead rely on market forces and more efficient use of existing staff to cover the shortfall. In a cover letter signed by HHS secretary Tommy G. Thompson, the administration said "it would be improper to conclude that the staffing thresholds described" in the report "should be used as staffing standards." Other factors affecting quality of staffing needed to be addressed, the letter said, such as management, tenure, and training of staff; the nursing shortage; and operational details, such as staff mix and turnover rates.

Lenhoff, of National Citizens' Coalition for Nursing Home Reform, said that Thompson was "ignoring an overwhelming body of evidence that there is a relationship between nurse staffing levels and quality. While good management practices, training and other factors can improve care, there is no substitute for having enough qualified workers available."

Representatives of the nursing home industry agreed that many nursing homes were short-staffed and blamed the problem on the nursing shortage and on underfunding of the Medicaid and Medicare programs. Medicaid, the federal-state health care program for the poor and disabled, covered the costs of more than two-thirds of all nursing home residents, many of whom first "spent down" all their own wealth on their health care costs before becoming eligible for Medicaid. Medicare was the federal health care program for Americans over age sixty-five; it covered brief nursing home stays, typically by people requiring rehabilitation after surgery. Together the two programs paid nursing homes $58.4 billion in 2001. According to Charles H. Roadman, president and chief executive officer of the American Health Care Association, states underfunded nursing home care by $3.5 billion a year. Federal cuts in spending for the two programs exacerbated the staffing shortfall, he said. Roadman denied allegations that profit motives were a *significant cause of low staffing ratios and poor care at for-profit nursing homes.*

Other critics decried the incentive bonuses many states paid to nursing homes for keeping their costs down. In a series examining quality of care in nursing homes in Georgia, the Atlanta Journal-Constitution *found that at least one nursing home was receiving a bonus from the state Medicaid program for keeping staff and other costs low, even while state inspectors were citing the home for insufficient staff, abuse, and neglect.*

Following are excerpts from testimony delivered March 4, 2002, to the Senate Special Committee on Aging by Leslie G. Aronovitz, director of Health Care—Program Administration and Integrity Issues in the General Accounting Office. Aronovitz reported on the findings of an investigation into the handling of nursing home abuse complaints by nursing homes, state inspection agencies, law enforcement officials, and the justice system.

The document was obtained from the Internet at* www.gao .gov/new.items/d02448t.pdf; *accessed October 19, 2002.

Mr. Chairman and Members of the Committee:

I am pleased to be here today as you discuss the issue of abuse in nursing homes. The 1.5 million elderly and disabled individuals residing in U.S. nursing homes constitute a population that is highly vulnerable because of their physical and cognitive impairments. Residents typically require extensive assistance in the basic activities of daily living, such as dressing, feeding, and bathing, and many require skilled nursing or rehabilitative care. Residents with dementia may be irrational and combative. This combination of impairments heightens the residents' vulnerability to abuse and impedes efforts to substantiate allegations and build cases for prosecution.

Our work for this committee on nursing home care quality has found that oversight by federal and state authorities has increased in recent years. During these years, however, the number of homes cited for deficiencies involving actual harm to residents or placing them at risk of death or serious injury remained unacceptably high—30 percent of the nation's 17,000 nursing homes. Concerns exist that too many nursing home residents are subjected to abuse—such as pushing, slapping, beating, and sexual assault—by the individuals entrusted with their care. You therefore asked us to examine efforts by nursing home oversight authorities to protect residents against physical and sexual abuse. My remarks today will focus on (1) inherent difficulties in measuring the extent of the abuse problem, (2) gaps in efforts to prevent and deter resident abuse, and (3) the limited role of law enforcement in abuse investigations. My comments reflect the findings of a report we are issuing today. The report is based on our visits to three states with relatively large nursing home populations and discussions with officials at the Centers for Medicare and Medicaid Services (CMS)—the federal agency charged with oversight of states compliance with federal nursing home standards.

In brief, the ambiguous and hidden nature of abuse in nursing homes makes the prevalence of this offense difficult to determine. CMS defines abuse in its nursing home regulations and the states we visited maintain definition[s] consistent with the CMS definition. However, the states vary in their interpretation and application of the definitions. For example, nurse aides in two of the states we visited who struck residents were not considered abusive by state survey agency officials under certain circumstances, whereas the third state's nurse aides under similar circumstances were consistently cited for this offense. Incidents of abuse often remain hidden, moreover, because victims, witnesses, and others, including family members, are unable to file complaints or are reluctant for several reasons, including fear of reprisal. When complaints and incidents are reported, they are often not reported immediately, thus harming efforts to investigate cases and obtain necessary evidence.

Despite certain measures in place at various levels to prevent or deter resident abuse, certain gaps undermine these protections. For instance, states use a registry to keep records on nurse aides within the state, but these state registries do not include information about offenses committed by nurse aides in other states. Unlicensed or uncertified personnel, such as laundry aides and maintenance workers, are not listed with a registry or with a licensing or certification body, allowing those with a history of abuse to be employed without detection, unless they have an established criminal record. In addition, in the states we visited, nursing homes often did not notify state authorities immediately of abuse allegations. Moreover, state's efforts to inform consumers about available protections appeared limited, as the government agency pages in telephone books of several major cities we visited lacked explicitly designated phone numbers for filing nursing home complaints with the state.

Local and state enforcement authorities have played a limited role in addressing incidents of abuse. Several local police departments we interviewed had little knowledge of the state survey agencies investigation activities at nursing homes in their communities. Some noted that, by the time the police are called, others may have begun investigations, hampering police efforts to collect evidence. Even the involvement of Medicaid Fraud Control Units (MFCU)—the state law enforcement agencies with explicit responsibility for investigating allegations of patient neglect and abuse in nursing homes—is not automatic. MFCUs get involved in resident abuse cases through referrals from state survey agencies. However, as demonstrated in the states we visited, the extent to which a state's MFCU investigates cases varies according to the referral policies at each state's survey agency. Our review of alleged abuse cases suggests that the early involvement of the state MFCU can be productive in obtaining criminal convictions.

In its federal oversight role, CMS could do more to ensure that nursing home residents are protected from abuse. Requirements for screening and hiring prospective employees, involving local law enforcement promptly when incidents of abuse are alleged, and ensuring the public's access to designated telephone numbers are among the protections that CMS could strengthen. Our report makes recommendations addressing these requirements.

Background

To help ensure that nursing homes provide proper care to their residents, a combination of federal, state, and local oversight agencies and requirements is in place. At the heart of nursing home oversight activities are state survey agencies, which, under contract with the federal government, perform detailed inspections of nursing homes participating in the Medicare and Medicaid programs. The purpose of the inspections is to ensure that nursing homes comply with Medicare and Medicaid standards. CMS, in the Department of Health and Human Services (HHS), is the federal agency with which the states contract and is responsible for oversight of states' facility inspections and other nursing-home-related activities. By law, CMS sets the standards for nursing homes' participation in Medicare and Medicaid.

State survey agencies also investigate complaints of inadequate care, including allegations of physical or sexual abuse. Once aware of an abuse allegation, nursing homes are required by CMS to notify the state survey agency immediately. They must also conduct their own investigations and submit their findings in written reports to the state survey agency, which determines whether to investigate further.

Certain federal and state requirements focus on the screening of prospective nursing home employees. CMS requires nursing homes to establish policies prohibiting employment of individuals convicted of abusing nursing home residents. Although this requirement does not include offenses committed outside the nursing home, the three states we visited—Georgia, Illinois, and Pennsylvania—do not limit offenses to those committed in the nursing home setting and have broadened the list of disqualifying offenses to include kidnapping, murder, assault, battery, or forgery.

As another protective measure, federal law requires states to maintain a registry of nurse aides—specifically, all individuals who have satisfactorily completed an approved nurse aide training and competency evaluation program. This requirement is consistent with the fact that nurse aides are the primary caregivers in these facilities. Before employing an aide, nursing homes are required to check the registry to verify that the aide has passed a competency evaluation. Aides whose names are not included in a state's registry may work at a nursing home for up to 4 months to complete their training and pass a state-administered competency evaluation. CMS' nursing home regulations require states to add to the registry any findings of abuse, neglect, or theft of a resident's property that have been established against an individual. The inclusion of such a finding on a nurse aide's record constitutes a lifetime ban on nursing home employment, as CMS regulations prohibit homes from hiring individuals with these offenses. As a matter of due process, nurse aides have a right to request a hearing to rebut the allegations against them, be represented by an attorney, and appeal an unfavorable outcome. Other nursing home professionals who are suspected of abuse and who are licensed by the state, such as registered nurses, are referred to their respective state licensing boards for review and possible disciplinary action.

Among the local and state law enforcement agencies that may investigate nursing home abuse cases are the MFCUs. MFCUs are state agencies charged with conducting criminal investigations related to Medicare and Medicaid. Generally, MFCUs are located in the state attorney general's office, although they can be located in another state agency, such as the state police. Part of their mission is to investigate patient abuse in nursing homes. MFCUs typically receive abuse cases from referrals by state survey agencies. If criminal charges are brought, prosecuting attorneys within the MFCU or attorneys representing the locality take charge of the case.

Ambiguous and Hidden Nature of Nursing Home Abuse Makes Extent of Problem Difficult to Measure

The problem of nursing home abuse is difficult to quantify and is likely understated for several reasons. First, states differ in what they consider abuse, with the result that some states do not count incidents that CMS or other states would count as abuse. Second, powerful incentives exist for victims, their families, and witnesses to keep silent or delay the reporting of abuse allegations. Third, some research focuses on citations of nursing homes for abuse-related violations, which are maintained in a CMS database, but these data reflect only the extent to which facilities fail to comply with federal or state regulations. Abuse incidents that nursing homes handle properly are not counted, because no violation has been committed that warrants a citation.

States Do Not Share Common View of Resident Abuse

Some states may not be citing nurse aides for incidents that other states would consider abuse. Based on the definition of abuse in the Older Americans Act of 1965, CMS defines abuse as "the willful infliction of injury, unreasonable confinement, intimidation, or punishment with resulting physical harm, pain or mental anguish." States maintain their own definitions that are consistent with the CMS definition. Our review of case files showed that states interpret and apply these definitions differently.

For example, on the basis of the abuse cases reviewed, we noted that Georgia survey agency officials were less likely to determine that an aide had been abusive if the aide's behavior appeared to be spontaneous or the result of a "reflex" response. The Georgia officials told us that, to cite an aide for abuse, they must find that the individual's actions were intentional. They said they would view an instance in which an aide struck a combative resident in retaliation after being slapped by the resident as an unfortunate reflex response rather than an act of abuse. Among the Georgia case files we reviewed, we found 5 cases in which the aides struck back after residents hit them or otherwise made physical contact. In all five cases, Georgia officials had determined that the aides' behavior was not abusive because the residents were combative and the aides did not intend to hurt the residents.

In Pennsylvania, officials emphasized other factors to determine a finding of abuse. They said that establishing intention was important, but they would be unlikely to cite an aide for abuse unless the aide caused serious injury or obvious pain. Our review of Pennsylvania files indicated that most of the aides that were found to have been abusive had, in fact, clearly injured residents or caused them obvious pain. In several cases reviewed in which residents were bumped or slapped and reported being in pain as the result of aides' actions, the survey agency officials decided not to take action against the aides because, in their view, the residents had no apparent physical injuries.

In contrast, the Illinois survey agency considers any nonaccidental injury to be abuse. Thus, incidents not considered abusive in Georgia and Pennsylvania—reflex actions and incidents not involving serious injury or obvious pain—could be considered abusive in Illinois. In the 17 Illinois case files we reviewed involving either combative residents or residents who did not suffer serious injury, officials found that aides had been abusive. When Illinois handled a case similar to a Georgia case in which a nursing home employee witnessed a nurse aide strike a combative resident, the state not only included this information in the individual's nurse aide registry file, it also referred the matter to the state's MFCU, resulting in a criminal conviction.

CMS officials indicated that states may use different definitions of abuse, as long as the definitions are at least as inclusive as the CMS definition. The officials agreed that intent is a key factor in assessing whether an aide abused a resident but argued that intent can be formed in an instant. In their view, an aide who slaps a resident, regardless of whether it was a reflexive response, should be considered abusive. In light of these different perspectives, we have recommended that CMS clarify the definition of abuse to ensure that states cite abuse consistently and appropriately.

People May Be Unable or Reluctant to Report Abuse Allegations

The physical and mental impairments typical of the nursing home population handicap residents ability to respond to abuse. Some residents lack the ability to communicate or even realize that they have been abused, while others are reluctant to report abuse because they fear reprisal. For these reasons, elder abuse in nursing homes is likely underreported or often not reported immediately. In some cases, residents are unable to complain about what was done to them. In other cases, family members may hesitate to report their suspicions because they fear retribution or that, if reported, the resident will be asked to leave the home. In still other cases, facility staff fear losing their jobs or recrimination from coworkers, while facility management may not want to risk adverse publicity or sanctions from the state. In our file reviews, we saw evidence that family members, staff, and management did not immediately report allegations of abuse.

Data on States Nursing Home Citations Provide Little Information About Resident Abuse

Data from states' annual inspections of nursing homes, while a source of information about facility compliance with nursing home standards, provide little precision about the extent of care problems, of which resident abuse-related problems are a subset. Abuse-related violations committed by nursing homes include failure to protect residents from sexual, physical, or verbal abuse; failure to properly investigate allegations of resident abuse or to ensure that nursing home staff have been properly screened before employment; and failure to develop and implement written policies prohibiting abuse.

In 2000, we reported on the wide variation across states in surveyors' identification and classification of serious deficiencies—conditions under which residents were harmed or were in immediate jeopardy of harm or death. The extent to which abuse-related violations are counted as serious deficiencies depends on how the surveyor classifies the severity of the deficiency identified. In our analysis, the problem of "interrater reliability"—that is, individual differences among surveyors in citing homes for serious deficiencies—was one of several factors contributing to the difference of roughly 48 percentage points across states in the proportion of homes cited in 1999 and 2000 for serious deficiencies. The variation ranged from about 1 in 10 homes cited in one state to more than 1 in 2 homes cited in another.

We also found that one state's tally of nursing homes with serious deficiencies would have been highly misleading as an indicator of serious care problems. Of the homes the state surveyed during the 1999–2000 period, it found 84 to be "deficiency free." However, when we cross-checked the annual inspection results for these homes with the homes' history of complaint allegations, we found that these deficiency-free homes had received 605 complaints and that significant numbers of these complaints were substantiated when investigated. This discrepancy illustrates the difficulty of estimating the extent of resident abuse using nursing home inspection data.

Gaps Exist in Efforts to Prevent or Deter Resident Abuse

Nursing home residents inability to protect themselves accentuates the need for strong preventive measures to be in place in both nursing homes and the agencies overseeing them. Although certain measures are in place, we found them to be, in some cases, incomplete or insufficient. In the states we visited, efforts to screen employees and achieve prompt reporting fell short of creating a net sufficiently tight to protect residents from potential offenders.

Sources Used to Screen Prospective Employees Do Not Contain Complete or Up-to-Date Information

Nursing homes have available three main tools to screen prospective employees: criminal background checks conducted by local law enforcement agencies, criminal background checks conducted by the Federal Bureau of Investigation (FBI), and state registries listing information on nursing home aides, including any findings of abuse committed in the state's facilities. The information included in these sources, however, is often not complete or up to date.

State and local law enforcement officials in the three states we visited conduct background checks on prospective nursing home employees, but these checks are made only state wide. Consequently, individuals who have committed disqualifying crimes—including kidnapping, murder, assault, battery, and forgery—may be able to pass muster for employment by crossing state lines. On request, the FBI will conduct background checks outside the prospective employee's state of residence, but in some states these requests are rarely made, according to an FBI official.

Some states allow individuals to begin working before facilities complete their background checks. Pennsylvania permits new employees to work for 30 days and Illinois, for 3 months, before criminal background checks are completed. In contrast, Georgia requires that background checks be completed within 3 days of the request and interprets this requirement to mean that the checks must be completed before prospective employees may assume their duties.

Of the three states we visited, only Illinois requires that the results of criminal background checks on prospective nurse aides be reported to the state survey agency, which enters the information in the registry. A 1998 survey conducted by HHS Office of Inspector General reported that Illinois was the only state with this requirement. Nursing homes in Illinois checking the state registry are able to determine if an aide has a disqualifying conviction well before an offer of employment is made and a criminal background check is initiated. Alternatively, the survey agencies in states without this requirement do not have the information necessary to warn their respective nursing home communities about inappropriate individuals seeking employment.

Nurse aide registries, designed to maintain background information on nursing home aides, also contain information gaps that can undermine screening efforts. To cite an individual in the state's registry for a finding of abuse, authorities must first establish a finding, notify the individual of the intent to "annotate" the registry, and if the individual requests, hold a hearing to consider whether the finding is warranted. Specifically, the individual must be notified in writing of the state's intent to annotate the registry and be given 30 days from the date of the state's notice to make a written request for a hearing. Because the hearing may not be completed for several months after it is requested and decisions may not be rendered immediately, additional time may elapse. As with background checks, state registries do not track an aide's offenses committed at nursing homes in other states.

Our analysis of nurse aide records from 1999 indicated that hearings to reconsider an abuse finding added, on average, 5 to 7 months to the process of annotating an individual's record in the state registry. During this time, residents of other nursing homes were at risk because, even if an aide was terminated from one home, the individual could find new employment in other homes before the state's registry included information on the individual's offense. Thus, because of the amount of time that can elapse between the date a finding is established and the date it is published, the use of nurse aide registries as a screening tool alone is inadequate.

Facilities can screen licensed personnel, such as nurses and therapists, by checking the records of licensing boards for disciplinary actions, but screening other facility employees, such as laundry aides, security guards, and maintenance workers, is limited to criminal background checks. Unless such employees are convicted of an offense, problems with their prior behavior will not be detected. No centralized source contains a record of substantiated abuse allegations involving these individuals. Even when abuse violations identified through nursing home inspections are cited, they result in sanctions against the homes and not the employees. We identified 10 uncertified and unlicensed employees in the 158 cases we reviewed who allegedly committed abuse. One of the 10 pled guilty in court, thus establishing a criminal record. However, the disposition of five of these cases left no way to track the individuals through routine screening channels. Three of the nine—all of whom were dismissed from their positions—were investigated by law enforcement but were not prosecuted. Two others were also terminated by their nursing home employers but were not the subject of criminal investigations. (In these cases, physical abuse was alleged but the residents did not sustain apparent injuries.) The remaining four cases involved instances in which the allegations proved unfounded or the evidence was inconsistent; the individuals were thus not tracked, as appropriate.

In 1998, the HHS Office of the Inspector General recommended developing a national abuse registry and expanding state registries to include not only aides but all other nursing home employees cited for abuse offenses. A firm that CMS (then the Health Care Financing Administration) contracted with in September 2000 is currently conducting a feasibility study regarding the development of a national registry that would centralize nurse aide registry information and include information on all nursing home employees. The contractor intends to report its findings in March 2002.

Efforts to Alert Authorities of Abuse Incidents and Allegations Lack Sufficient Rigor

Enlisting the help of the facilities and the public to report incidents and allegations of abuse can supplement other efforts to protect nursing home residents. However, in the states we visited, nursing homes' performance in notifying the survey agencies promptly was well below par. In addition, access to information on phone numbers the public could use for filing complaints was limited.

In the three states we visited, nursing homes are required to notify their state survey agencies of abuse allegations immediately, which the agencies define as the day the facility becomes aware of the incident or the next day. Using this standard, we examined 111 abuse allegations filed by the three states nursing homes. We found that, for these allegations, the homes in Pennsylvania notified the state late 60 percent of the time; in Illinois, late almost half of the time; and in Georgia, late about 40 percent of the time. Each state had several cases for which homes notified the state a week or more late and in each state at least one home notified the state more than 2 weeks late. Such time lags delay efforts by the survey agencies to conduct their own prompt investigations and ensure that nursing homes are taking appropriate steps to protect residents. In these situations, residents remain vulnerable to additional abuse until corrective action is taken.

As a nursing home resident's family and friends are another essential resource for reporting abuse to the state authorities, increasing public awareness of the state's phone number for filing complaints should be a high
priority. CMS requires nursing homes to post phone numbers for making complaints to the state. However, in major cities of the states we visited, phone
numbers specifically for lodging complaints to the state survey agency were
not listed in the telephone book. This was the case in Chicago and Peoria, Illinois; in Athens and Augusta, Georgia; and in Philadelphia and Pittsburgh,
Pennsylvania.

At the same time, the telephone books we examined listed numbers in the
government agency pages for organizations that appeared to be appropriate
for reporting abuse allegations but did not have authority to take action. In the
telephone books of selected cities in the three states we visited, we identified
listings for 42 such entities that were not affiliated with the state survey agencies. Of these, six entities said they were capable of accepting and acting on
abuse allegations. These included long-term care ombudsmen and adult protective services offices. The other 36 either could not be reached or could not
accept complaints, despite having listings such as the "Senior Helpline" or the
"Fraud and Abuse Line." Sometimes these entities attempted to refer us to an
appropriate organization to report abuse, with mixed success. For example,
calls we made in Georgia resulted in four correct referrals to the state survey
agency's designated complaint intake line but also led to five incorrect referrals. Five entities offered us no referrals.

Law Enforcement's Involvement in
Protecting Residents Is Limited

The involvement of law enforcement in protecting nursing home residents
has generally been limited. Owing to the nature of the nursing home population, developing adequate evidence to investigate and prosecute abuse cases
and achieve convictions is difficult. The states we visited had different policies
for referring cases to law enforcement agencies.

Residents' Impairments Weaken Law
Enforcement's Efforts to Develop Cases

Critical evidence is often missing in elder abuse cases, precluding prosecution. Our review of states' case files included instances in which residents sustained black eyes, lacerations, and fractures but were unable or unwilling to
describe what had happened. However, despite what appeared to be signs of
abuse, investigators could neither rule out accidental injuries nor identify a
perpetrator.

The cases that are prosecuted are often weakened by the time lapse between the incident and the trial. Law enforcement officials and prosecutors indicated that the amount of time that elapses between an incident and a trial
can ruin an otherwise successful case, because witnesses cannot always retain essential details of the incident. For example, in one case we reviewed, a
victim's roommate witnessed an incident of abuse and positively identified the
abuser during the investigation. By the time of the trial nearly 5 months later,

however, the witness could no longer identify the suspect in the courtroom, prompting the judge to dismiss the charges. Law enforcement officials told us that, without testimony from either a victim or witness, conviction is unlikely. Similarly, resident victims may not survive long enough to participate in a trial. A recent study of 20 sexually abused nursing home residents revealed that 11 died within 1 year of the abuse.

Local Law Enforcement Authorities in States Visited Not Frequently Involved with Nursing Home Abuse Incidents

In the states we visited, local law enforcement authorities did not have much involvement in nursing home abuse cases. Our discussions with officials from 19 local law enforcement agencies indicate that police are rarely summoned to nursing homes to investigate allegations of abuse. Of those 19 agencies, 15 indicated that they had little or no contact with their state's survey agency regarding abuse of nursing home residents in the past year. In fact, several police departments we interviewed were unaware of the role state survey agencies play in investigating instances of resident abuse. Several of the police officials we met with noted that, even when the police are called, other entities may have begun investigating, hampering further evidence collection.

Involving law enforcement authorities does not appear to be common for abuse incidents occurring in nursing homes. Facility residents and family members may report allegations directly to the facility. There is no federal requirement compelling nursing homes that receive such complaints to contact local law enforcement, although some states, including Pennsylvania, have instituted such requirements.

MFCUs Not as Involved as Their Mission Would Suggest

The involvement of MFCUs—the state law enforcement agencies whose mission is to, among other things, investigate allegations of patient neglect and abuse in nursing homes—is not automatic. MFCUs get involved in resident abuse cases through referrals from state survey agencies. Each of the states we visited had a different referral policy. In Pennsylvania, by agreement, the state's MFCU typically investigates nursing home neglect matters, while local law enforcement agencies investigate nursing home abuse. In contrast, the survey agencies in Illinois and Georgia both refer allegations of resident abuse to their states' MFCUs, but these two states' referral policies also differ from one another.

Of the cases we reviewed in Illinois, the survey agency consistently referred all reports of physical and sexual abuse to the state's MFCU, regardless of whether the source of the report was an individual or a nursing facility. The Illinois MFCU, in turn, determined whether the cases warranted opening an investigation. The Georgia survey agency, on the other hand, screened its allegations before referring cases to the state's MFCU, basing its assessment of a case's merit on the severity of the harm done and the potential for the MFCU to obtain a criminal conviction.

Our review of case files from Illinois and Georgia suggests that the more the state's MFCU is involved in resident abuse investigations, the greater the potential to convict offenders. (This case file review consisted of only those cases that were opened in 1999 and closed at the time of our review.) The Illinois MFCU obtained 18 convictions from 50 unscreened referrals. In Georgia, however, where the survey agency tried to avoid referring weak cases to the state's MFCU, 14 of 52 cases were referred and 3 resulted in convictions. The state's small number of convictions from the cases opened in 1999 was not consistent with the expectation that prescreened cases would have greater potential for successful prosecution.

In 2000, the Georgia survey agency substantially changed its MFCU referral policy, leading to a four-fold increase in the state's total number of referrals from the previous year. The policy change followed a meeting between survey agency and MFCU officials, at which the MFCU indicated a willingness to investigate instances that the survey agency had previously assumed the MFCU would have dismissed—such as incidents involving nursing home employees slapping residents.

The timeliness of referrals made to the MFCU may also play a role in achieving favorable results. Of the 64 cases referred in the two states, we determined that the Illinois survey agency referred its cases to the MFCU earlier than did Georgia's. Illinois referred its cases, on average, within 3 days after receiving a report of abuse, whereas Georgia referred its cases, on average, 15 days after learning about an allegation.

Concluding Observations

The problem of resident abuse in nursing homes is serious but of unknown magnitude, with certain limitations in the adequacy of protections in the states we visited. Nurse aide registries provide information on only one type of employee, are difficult to keep current, and do not capture offenses committed in other states. At the same time, local law enforcement authorities are seldom involved in nursing home abuse cases and therefore are not in a position to help protect this at-risk population. MFCUs, which are likely to have expertise in investigating nursing home abuse cases, must rely on the state survey agencies to refer such cases. When a state's referral policy is overly restrictive, the MFCU is precluded from capitalizing on its potential to bring offenders to justice.

Several opportunities exist for CMS to establish new safeguards and strengthen those now in place. Our report includes recommendations for CMS to, among other things, clarify what is included in CMS definition of abuse and increase the involvement of MFCUs in examining abuse allegations. Without such improvements, vulnerable nursing home residents remain considerably ill-protected.

Mr. Chairman, this concludes my prepared remarks. I will be pleased to answer any questions you or the committee members may have.

COMMONWEALTH COMMISSION ON ELECTIONS IN ZIMBABWE
March 19, 2002

Zimbabwe—formerly one of the richest countries in Africa, with all the resources needed to develop long-term prosperity and democratic stability—descended into political crisis and economic despair during 2002. President Robert Mugabe, who had led Zimbabwe since independence in 1980, used violence, intimidation of opponents, and an apparently rigged election to maintain his hold on political power. A severe food shortage, made worse by the government's use of food as a political weapon, affected nearly half the country's 12 million people. The once prosperous economy had declined by nearly one-third since 1998, putting Zimbabwe on the bottom rung of the poorest countries in Africa.

Zimbabwe's troubles came to a head over two sets of elections during the year, both of which the government said were won by Mugabe's ruling party. Most international observers said the first election, held in March for the presidency, was rigged in Mugabe's favor. In many respects the key finding came from a forty-two-member delegation of the British Commonwealth. On March 19 the Commonwealth said it was suspending Zimbabwe's membership for one year because of the "high level of politically motivated violence" during the presidential election cycle. That conclusion was endorsed by a three-member committee that included Australian prime minister John Howard, South African president Thabo Mbeki, and Nigerian president Olusegun Obasanjo. Mugabe's ruling party also was declared the winner of legislative elections in September, when substantially less international attention was paid to Zimbabwe. (Background, Historic Documents of 2001, p. 508)

Disputed Elections

Zimbabwe's first, and by far the more controversial, election of 2002 was held March 9–11, when the presidency and numerous local offices were on the ballot. Mugabe, who had headed the government since a white minority regime was forced to give up power in 1980, was seeking a third six-year term as president. Mugabe headed the ruling political party, the Zimbabwe

African National Union-Patriotic Front (known as ZANU-PF). He faced an increasingly strong opposition from a coalition of business and labor groups known as the Movement for Democratic Change. The coalition's presidential candidate, Morgan Tsvangirai, had been the leader of an independent labor federation, the Zimbabwe Congress of Trade Unions.

Starting in 2000, the government and ZANU-PF used every means at its disposal—both legal and illegal—to thwart an electoral challenge by the opposition, according to most independent reports by organizations based in Zimbabwe and other countries. The government-dominated courts consistently ruled against the opposition on all legal questions, and voter registration and preelection procedures were stacked in favor of the governing party. Government-controlled broadcast and print media harshly attacked Tsvangirai and other opposition leaders, accusing them of treasonable acts and of doing the bidding of the white minority. The government had long sought to discourage independent observation of the election, first by banning or limiting the actions of some international observer groups and journalists, and then by threatening (and in some cases actually attacking) observers as they tried to monitor preelection campaigning or the conduct of the voting. When the government barred its delegation, the European Union on February 19 imposed limited sanctions against the Zimbabwe government, including a travel ban and freeze on assets held in Europe by Mugabe and his top aides.

According to reports by observer groups, government supporters, which included youth militias organized by the ZANU-PF, worked to intimidate opposition groups. Among other tactics, progovernment forces set up road blocks to prevent opposition supporters from attending political rallies, prevented distribution of independent newspapers in many areas, and established "no go" areas from which opposition supporters were barred (or attacked if they entered). The government also sharply reduced the number of polling stations in opposition strongholds, especially the capital, Harare, thereby creating long lines of frustrated voters. On the election days, police units attacked voters as they waited at urban polling stations, a tactic that frightened thousands of voters away from the polls. Numerous irregularities also took place during the vote counting in many districts, affording government supporters the opportunity to rig the outcome in Mugabe's favor.

The government's final results gave Mugabe 56.2 percent of the 3 million votes cast, with Tsvangirai receiving 41.9 percent. Mugabe hailed the results as a mandate, but Tsvangirai called it "the biggest electoral fraud I have ever witnessed in my life."

The majority of outside observers agreed with Tsvangirai that the election had been so flawed as to have been invalid. Perhaps the most important criticism came from the observer group sponsored by the British Commonwealth. In a preliminary report issued March 14, the Commonwealth observers argued that thousands of voters had been disenfranchised by government tactics and that the entire election had been conducted "in a climate of fear and suspicion." The group was chaired by former Nigerian president Abdulsalami Abubakar, a general who had stepped aside in 1999 to allow civilian elections in his country.

The United States also condemned Mugabe's handling of the election. In a statement made March 13, Secretary of State Colin Powell said the government's abuse of the electoral process began in the preelection period, which "was marked by a sustained government-orchestrated campaign of intimidation and violence."

Smaller observer groups from several African countries disputed the charges that the Zimbabwe election was invalid. While acknowledging procedural problems, these delegations accepted Mugabe's assertion that the voting had been free and fair, and the outcome represented the will of the people.

Mugabe remained defiant in the face of international criticism, insisting that the election had been a triumph of democracy and a reaffirmation of Zimbabwe's independence. In his inaugural speech on March 17, Mugabe said the election was a "stunning blow to imperialism," especially to Britain, the country's colonial power. "Thanks to the people of Zimbabwe for loudly saying: Never again shall Zimbabwe be a colony," he said.

A second set of elections, held September 28–29, decided about 1,400 council seats in local governments throughout Zimbabwe. Largely because of government intimidation and the violence that accompanied the March elections, opposition candidates ran in less than half the contests and only a handful were elected. Most international observers reported that the September election was just as flawed as the March election had been.

Land Reform and Economic Collapse

In the latter part of the twentieth century Zimbabwe generally was considered the breadbasket of southern Africa because its fertile farmland and skilled farmers were extraordinarily productive. Corn was the main staple food crop, while tobacco was the country's principal export crop and source of foreign currency. During the 1980s the government (with modest aid from Britain) gradually bought out many of the white farmers, who had controlled more than three-fourths of Zimbabwe's most productive farmland, and settled the farms with blacks. White farmers mounted legal challenges that slowed the land reform process in the early 1990s, but in 1997 Mugabe vowed a "fast-track" land reform program and targeted nearly 1,500 white farms for compulsory takeover. That step put Mugabe on a collision course with Britain, which refused to subsidize land takings without adequate compensation to the farmers. Many of the choicest farms were given to Mugabe's relatives and close associates (including his wife, Grace), some of whom did not farm the land but turned the estates into vacation homes.

Starting in 1998, black squatters, with tacit government backing, forcibly occupied dozens of white-owned farms. Many of the squatters claimed to be veterans of the independence struggle who were owed compensation by the government. In addition to displacing white owners, the squatters forced thousands of black workers off the farms. Without these workers, and with a long-term drought afflicting much of southern Africa, production on the farms declined sharply. By October 2001 Zimbabwe, once a net food exporter, was forced to seek international food aid.

Zimbabwe voters in February 2000 rejected a draft constitution allowing the government to seize white-owned farms without any compensation to the owners, but the government disregarded the vote and quickly adopted legislation putting the policy into practice. Also in 2000, the Movement for Democratic Change mounted a strong challenge in parliamentary elections but fell just short of winning a majority because of procedural advantages held by Mugabe's ruling party.

The rate and violence of farm seizures increased dramatically just before and after the March 2002 presidential election, when war veterans and other militants associated with ZANU-PF drove more than 200 white farmers off their land. The legislature in May adopted the Land Acquisition and Amendment bill, which legalized the seizure of equipment owned by white farmers and created a streamlined process for evicting those farmers from their land—starting with a ban on the planting of crops. The government ordered about 2,900 white farmers to leave their farms by August 8; most defied the order, and several hundred were arrested.

Food and export crop production plummeted as a result of these land seizures and a continuing drought. The 2002 corn crop was less than half the previous year's level, forcing the country to rely heavily on imports and donations to feed nearly half of its 12.5 million people, according to the United Nations World Food Program. Food shortages were exacerbated in some areas by the government's reported policy of using food supplies to reward its friends and punish its enemies. In a September 16 report, a team from Refugees International said it had received numerous reports that "people are denied food for political reasons," including the government's allocation of food "based on political affiliation." Journalists and other observers reported numerous cases in which government agencies denied food aid to anyone unable to prove membership in the ruling party.

In addition to falling agricultural production, Zimbabwe's economy was battered by declining production in the nation's mines and by a near-total collapse of tourism. As of mid-2002 unemployment was estimated at more than 60 percent, inflation was raging at an annual rate of more than 100 percent, and the country's gross domestic product had declined by nearly 30 percent during the previous two years. In a October 17 report, the International Crisis Group (a Brussels-based think tank) said Mugabe's party had established a "mafia economy" in which party leaders, government officials, and high-ranking military officers had been given profitable farms and businesses or lucrative contracts—often at the expense of political enemies. Ironically, the report said, Mugabe relied heavily on corrupt white Zimbabweans who conducted much of the government's business, especially overseas.

Yet another major factor in Zimbabwe's decline was the AIDS epidemic. According to United Nations figures, about 25 percent of the population was infected with HIV/AIDS, one of the highest rates in the world. Deaths and ill-

ness caused by AIDS severely crippled the economy and put an enormous strain on the country's health care infrastructure. Refugees International reported that an estimated half-million children had lost at least one parent to the epidemic, but the government had no workable policy to care for AIDS orphans. (Worldwide AIDS epidemic, p. 469)

The International Role

Mugabe's actions put his fellow African leaders in a difficult position. Having embraced democracy—at least in theory if not fully in practice— African leaders reportedly were embarrassed by Mugabe's desperate efforts to cling to power. Even so, Mugabe for decades had been hailed in the region as a hero of African liberation because of his leadership role in the struggle against the white minority regime in Zimbabwe, then known as Rhodesia. Many African leaders deeply resented the international pressure on Mugabe, especially from Britain (one of the continent's chief colonial powers) and the United States, which they believed was acting as a neocolonial force through its unilateral diplomatic and military positions on many key issues of the day. The South African government, in particular, found itself caught between demands by Western countries and its longstanding close relationship with Mugabe. Both South Africa and Zimbabwe had been run by white minority regimes for most of the twentieth century, and the current leaders of both countries had been deeply involved in the long and bloody struggles against those regimes.

Some observers said Western insistence that African governments take a strong public stance against Mugabe had been counterproductive. Public pressure from London, Washington, and other capitals made it appear that African leaders were merely doing the West's bidding when they criticized Mugabe, the International Crisis Group said in its October 17 report. "Independent, meaningful action by South Africa and other key African states would be more likely if their policies were no longer the target of public pressure from the West," the report said. For their part, senior South African officials made it clear that they were tired of Western pressure. Meeting in Johannesburg on November 15 with her counterpart from Zimbabwe, South African foreign minister Nkosazana Zuma called on Western countries to ease their sanctions against Zimbabwe. "We don't think that's a situation which should continue for a long time," she said of the penalties against Mugabe's government.

> *Following are excerpts from the "Report of the Commonwealth Observer Group," issued in London on March 19, 2002, detailing the results of the March 2002 presidential election in Zimbabwe. General Abdulsalami Abubakar, a former president of Nigeria, chaired the observer delegation that produced the report.*

> **The documents was obtained from the Internet at www.thecommonwealth.org/docs/reports/zimbabwecogreport.doc; accessed October 13, 2002.**

Chapter Six: The Campaign

The conduct of the election campaign represents a key element in the credibility of any electoral process. The free expression of the will of the people is contingent as much upon the ability of political parties to campaign freely without fear of retribution as it is on the integrity of the polling and counting processes. For this to happen, certain fundamental freedoms must prevail and be guaranteed by law. These include freedom of speech and of the press, freedom of movement and of association, and freedom from violence and intimidation. These freedoms are also enshrined in the Constitution of Zimbabwe and in a range of international instruments to which Zimbabwe has acceded. These are the benchmarks we have used in assessing the electoral campaign for the 2002 Presidential elections in Zimbabwe.

Violence, Intimidation and Coercion

Politically motivated violence and/or the threat of it fundamentally impedes the ability of electors to participate freely in the electoral process. People can either be deterred from voting or else influenced in their choice if violence is a factor in the electoral process.

Throughout our stay in Zimbabwe, there were widespread allegations of violence and intimidation by both major political parties but more involved incidents by supporters of the ruling ZANU-PF [Zimbabwe African National Union-Patriotic Front] party and agents of the security services, against known or suspected supporters of the MDC [Movement for Democratic Change, the leading opposition party]. Members of our Group received numerous representations from the political parties and civil society organisations about specific cases of alleged violence and intimidation. However, our assessment of the level and scale of violence and intimidation during the election campaign is based largely on what members of our Group actually observed or were able to verify first hand.

On 18 February 2002, in full view of members of our Advance Team, a group of about one thousand ZANU-PF youths, armed with clubs, ran amok through the central business district of Harare attacking MDC offices and suspected MDC supporters.

It was reported and verified that on 22 February 2002, a group of about two hundred youths armed with stones and clubs attacked the MDC offices in Kwe Kwe in the Midlands, while members of the South African observer team were having a meeting with local MDC officials. The youths, suspected to be supporters of ZANU-PF, pelted the building (already destroyed in an arson attack) with rocks for fifteen minutes. They also attacked the clearly marked car of the South African observers. The youths ran away upon the arrival of the police who were alerted by the observers' driver. None of the observers was hurt but four MDC officials were injured and admitted to hospital.

On 24 February, supporters of the MDC dispersing after a rally in Chinhoyi were attacked by ZANU-PF youths in full view of international observers, including members of the Commonwealth Observer Group (COG). One of the cars used by the COG was briefly attacked outside the stadium in which the rally was held. Following the incident, the Chairman of the COG issued a statement strongly condemning the violence and calling on the authorities to take the necessary steps to ensure that voters were able to freely express their will and that all observers were able to perform the duties for which they had been invited by the Government of Zimbabwe.

Members of our Group met numerous victims of politically motivated violence. Many had bruises, scars and axe-wounds all over their bodies. One victim we observed had the letters 'MDC' carved into his back with a sharp knife. Another victim was chained alive in a coffin and threatened with drowning, while being repeatedly interrogated about the identities of local MDC operatives. Members of our team in the Midlands met a woman who had been gang raped by ZANU-PF youths because she was the sister of an MDC member. We also received a report from another observer group and ZANU-PF that some ZANU-PF youths were detained in a toilet of an MDC office without food for three days.

In Mashonaland East, the local medical authorities confirmed to our observers that there had been at least seven significant bashings of MDC supporters over the two-week period in the lead-up to the poll. Some of the victims were kept in hospital for their own protection. One of our observers was also approached by a 19-year old boy who said he had been abducted by members of the ZANU-PF youth wing and taken to one of three designated youth camps in the area. He said that while there, he was beaten on the soles of his feet for 36 hours for consorting with the MDC. Other observers noted that this particular practice was widespread.

Also in Mashonaland East, three politically-related murders were recorded in recent months, two of which were related to the MDC. One of these involved a local school principal who was taken from his schoolroom, dragged into the bush land and clubbed to death because of his strong association with the MDC in what was a traditionally strong ZANU-PF area. He was found with a ZANU-PF t-shirt pulled over his upper torso. The other was a local white farmer who, having formally joined MDC, was dragged from his farm and killed by having a block of concrete dropped on his head. In Matabeleland North, John Sabinda, a local Chairman of the MDC organisation was axed to death, while in Midlands Province, an MDC operative was beheaded with a spade.

Observers were also shown scores of MDC offices and several residences of MDC officials across the country attacked and destroyed allegedly by supporters of ZANU-PF. These included MDC offices and other buildings in Harare, Bulawayo, Kwe Kwe, Marondera and Redcliffe. In Chinhoyi, Observers were shown houses of officials of MDC and ZANU-PF, which had been petrol-bombed.

Numerous complaints have been made to members of our Group about the activities of a paramilitary youth group trained by the Government under a "National Youth Training Programme." Members of this group appear to have replaced the "War Veterans" as leading perpetrators of politically motivated violence, intimidation and abductions during this campaign, especially in the rural areas. Our observers met dozens of victims of this group and saw enough other direct evidence of their activities to be seriously concerned. Members of the youth group appeared to operate mostly at night and in uniform. Its members set up illegal roadblocks and intimidated opposition supporters, confiscated national identity cards (which were needed to be able to vote) of known or suspected MDC supporters and forced many from their homes and areas of residence.

There was also clear evidence of violence by MDC supporters against members of ZANU-PF, though these were much less in terms of numbers and scale. For example, the National Secretary-General of the War Veterans Association claimed to have been ambushed by over 70 MDC supporters and left for dead. He received a wound to his head and a knife wound to his shoulder. However the preponderance of political violence was perpetrated by ZANU-PF youths and supporters against known or suspected supporters of the MDC.

Campaign Issues/Freedom of Movement and of Association

The main themes of ZANU-PF's campaign were land and the sovereignty of the country. The party promised that if elected, it would complete its 'fast-track' land reform programme designed to acquire 9.2 million hectares of white-owed land (more if necessary) for redistribution to blacks. It accused the British Government and Zimbabwean white farmers of trying to recolonise the country, using the MDC as a front.

The MDC for its part focused on what it alleged was ZANU-PF's mismanagement of the economy and corruption. It promised a more orderly and equitable land reform programme and the withdrawal of Zimbabwean forces from the Democratic Republic of Congo. The party slogan was "change," and its appeal was for a change from the long period of ZANU-PF rule (over 20 years).

We found that the land issue dominated the campaign and believe that it was done in a manner that exacerbated racial tension in Zimbabwe.

Although there was some door-to-door campaigning, the main instrument of active campaigning remained the rally. Both ZANU-PF and the MDC held several animated and well-attended rallies across the country, culminating in 'Star Rallies' in the capital, Harare. However, ultimately, the MDC was able to hold far fewer rallies than ZANU-PF.

Our observers received numerous and widespread complaints from officials of the opposition MDC party about being refused permission by the police to hold rallies or other public meetings or having their rallies/public meetings broken up by the police on the basis of powers conferred by the Public Order and Security Act. Similar complaints were made to observers by several civil society organisations, including the Zimbabwe Council of Churches and the National Constitutional Assembly (NCA). Although the police claim that they have also refused to authorise some ZANU-PF meetings where there was a perceived threat to public order, observers did not hear any complaints in this regard from ZANU-PF officials, nor personally encounter any such cases. Our observers themselves came across numerous cases where MDC meetings were declared illegal by the police and where supporters were stopped at police or youth militia roadblocks and denied access to party meetings or rallies.

Our observers met with MDC Members of Parliament, some of whom said they had been advised by the police to leave their constituencies for the period of the campaign for their own safety, thereby effectively negating their ability to campaign for the party in their constituencies.

MDC officials complained that the cumulative effect of the Public Order and Security Act and the General Laws Amendment Act, especially the wide and discretionary powers of arrest and detention given to the police, created a climate of fear among their supporters. Many, they allege, were reluctant to attend public meetings for fear of being arrested and detained under the various provisions of the Public Order and Security Act, including for not carrying an identity card in a public place. We did not receive any similar complaints from ZANU-PF supporters.

We also noted that both main political parties resorted to littering the streets with their campaign leaflets. Some of our Observers noted that in various constituencies, MDC used littering where their party was prohibited from distributing their party posters in normal public places or where the pro-MDC newspaper, the *Daily News*, was unavailable. Other Observers noticed that on the second day of voting, the MDC violated the Electoral Act by littering entrances of most polling stations, especially in Zvimba North, Chinhoyi and Mhangure.

It was evident that the ruling party exploited its access to state resources for the benefit of its electoral campaign. At several locations, our observers saw trucks, buses and cars belonging to various government agencies being used to ferry ZANU-PF supporters to rallies. We also came across a number of cases in which ZANU-PF campaign materials and rally signs were stored in government departments and police stations. Furthermore, we were told by commercial vehicle operators that they had been compelled to display a poster of the President's picture with the words "Vote ZANU-PF" on the windscreen of their vehicles under threat of having their licences withdrawn if they refused to comply.

The Rule of Law

Deep concerns were expressed to many of our observers by opposition parties and civil society groups about political bias on the part of the police. In one particularly telling incident, two MDC Members of Parliament accused by the police of possessing offensive weapons (clubs and catapults) were paraded all day long in handcuffs and in full public view at the police station despite clearly needing medical attention following severe beating, allegedly by members of the local youth militia, outside the police station itself. Members of our observer team, who visited the area the following day, were denied access to the MPs by the police. Over thirty MDC supporters were also detained in connection with this incident. The MDC claimed the weapons were planted by ZANU-PF youths who then proceeded to attack the MPs.

Our Observers also noted a reluctance of the police to intervene to stop attacks by members of the youth militia and supporters of the ruling party against opposition supporters. The failure of the police to disperse the ZANU-PF youths who attacked the MDC office building in Harare on 18 February (a fact verified by our own observation), is a case in point. One of our observer teams was privately told by a serving police officer that instructions had been given to junior officers by their superiors not to investigate cases involving ZANU-PF supporters.

We were left in no doubt that the MDC was deeply distrustful of the police and did not feel that it enjoyed the protection of the law during the campaign. On the contrary, the party and its supporters regarded the police as part of the machinery of violence and intimidation against them. Such a situation seriously calls into question the application of the rule of law in Zimbabwe.

The News Media

The Broadcast Media

This is dominated by the state owned Zimbabwe Broadcasting Corporation, ZBC, which is the sole radio and television broadcaster in the country. Whereas its television broadcasts do not cover the whole country, the ZBC radio can be heard across the nation on shortwave and in the urban areas on FM. For many people across the country ZBC radio bulletins are their only source of news.

There is no independent broadcasting regulatory authority. Under the terms of the Broadcasting Act 1996 the Corporation is a corporate body controlled by a board appointed by the Minister of Information.

ZBC was restructured under the Broadcasting Services Act of 2001. According to the Corporation, the majority of its funding (75%) comes from advertising revenue with the balance from licence fees and sponsorships.

The news and current affairs programmes for ZBC's radio and television stations are produced by Newsnet, one of its divisions. The main nightly television news bulletin is at 8 PM.

In order to guide its producers in their election coverage ZBC produced a set of "10 Golden Rules." These rules were to fulfil its public obligation and mandate to provide regular programmes on which the parties and candidates contesting the Presidential elections, as well as members of the public, air views on policy matters. The rules stated that each party's Presidential candidate would be allocated airtime specified by the ZBC. Under the "Golden Rules," sponsored party broadcast programmes were not to be accepted and neither would political advertisements. The schedule of party political programmes was to remain the sole preserve of the ZBC.

We found the ZBC news and current affairs programmes to be very biased in favour of the ruling ZANU-PF party. Its flagship nightly one hour Newshour television programme extensively covered the rallies of the presidential candidate of the ruling party. More than a quarter of the bulletin was regularly dedicated to these rallies. In addition, coverage of the ruling party was supplemented by stories featuring other senior members of ZANU-PF. In direct contravention of its "Golden Rules," ZBC featured advertisements during the Newshour bulletin which showed footage of the civil war accompanied by statements outlining the ruling party's land policy. Land was a central issue of the campaign and one advertisement that was regularly featured on ZBC was on the theme "land is the economy and the economy is land." The advertisement culminated with a logo which is also used by the ruling party.

We also found that ZBC did not adhere to basic standards of journalism. News stories were editorialised in favour of the government while the little coverage given to the opposition was negative. Indeed, the Chief Executive of ZBC told us that they were biased because so much was at stake in this election.

The Editor of *The Sunday Mail* told one observer that the government media cannot be independent from its owners since it has to reflect its ideologies and that must be paramount.

The Print Media

The print media is dominated by the newspapers of the Zimpapers group. The English language titles in the group printed in Harare are *The Herald*, published daily with the exception of Sunday when the group publishes the *Sunday Mail*. Likewise from Bulawayo the Group publishes *The Chronicle* daily and the Sunday News and from Mutare the weekly Manica Post. In addition the group publishes *Kwayedza*, a weekly title in Shona.

Zimpapers was formerly owned by the Argus group of South Africa. At independence in 1980 a grant from the Nigerian government enabled the new Government of Zimbabwe to purchase the titles through a new trust it set up called the Mass Media Trust. Zimpapers is now a public company listed on the Stock Exchange. The majority shareholding of 51% belongs to the government controlled Mass Media Trust.

The editorial policy of the Zimpapers newspapers is to promote national unity and reconciliation. The papers strongly support the government and during the campaign carried numerous reports of the rallies by the presidential candidate of the ruling party and other senior ZANU-PF officials. Closer to the polls the papers supplemented this with full page advertisements for ZANU-PF. We were told that the party paid for these advertisements which were placed using a local advertising company that also handles copy for government departments.

The main privately owned newspaper is the *Daily News*, which is published daily except on Sunday. Other privately owned papers include *The Financial Gazette, The Zimbabwe Independent, the Standard* and the *Mirror*.

We found the print media to be polarised with the papers owned by Zimpapers strongly supporting ZANU-PF while most of the independent titles strongly support the MDC. This was clearly illustrated by the reports of crowds attending the "Star" rallies by the presidential candidates. The estimates of the size of the crowds varied by a factor of four. When questioned about why this polarisation existed the journalists from the independent media said that they were unable to get interviews and clarifications from government officials, senior ZANU-PF members and the police and therefore they conceded that their reporting could be construed as being partisan.

In the run up to polling the *Daily News* carried numerous full page advertisements in support of the MDC, while *The Herald* did likewise for ZANU-PF. Some of the advertisements and cartoons were insulting of the respective political opponents and even of foreign statesmen. A few days before voting both papers carried public education notices.

Journalists working for the independent papers told us of the harassment they encountered when they tried to report from some upcountry locations. Those from the *Daily News* told us that it was not possible to sell their paper in many locations around the country. They told us that their vendors had been beaten up and in some cases members of the public who carried the *Daily News* in some rural areas were deemed to be MDC supporters and had been assaulted. We were able to see that there are many areas in the country where the *Daily News* was not allowed to be sold whereas *The Herald* is available in all parts of the country.

In addition to this we are aware that prior to our arrival the printing press for the *Daily News* had been bombed. After the attack the paper had been limited in the number of pages it was able to print and this had an adverse effect on its ability to sell pages for advertising revenue and in the amount of news it was able to carry. During the period we were in Zimbabwe, however, the paper was almost fully operational. . . .

Conclusions and Recommendations

1. This has been one of the most keenly contested elections in the history of Zimbabwe. Following on the 2000 parliamentary election which was described as "constituting a turning point in the post-independence history of Zimbabwe," the 2002 Presidential election aroused considerable international and local interest because of the perceived consequences for Zimbabwe's political and economic future. As in 2000, the Presidential election was contested by two parties each commanding widespread popular support, as well as by three other candidates. A major feature of the election campaign was the prospect of change.

2. We were enjoined by our Terms of Reference "to observe relevant aspects of the organisation and conduct of the 2002 Presidential election" and "to consider the various factors impinging on the credibility of the electoral process as a whole." We have therefore set out in this Report to examine not only what took place on the election days (9–11 March) but the electoral system, the legal framework, the political background, and most importantly the campaign period leading up to the Presidential election.

Conclusions

3. We were deeply impressed by the determination of the people of Zimbabwe to exercise their democratic rights, very often under difficult conditions. At polling stations across the country, voters queued patiently and peacefully, and sometimes for very long hours. We were also impressed by the profes-

sionalism and conscientiousness of the majority of the polling staff, many of whom also had to work for very long hours under difficult conditions and without rest.

4. However, it was clear to us that while the actual polling and counting processes were peaceful and the secrecy of the ballot was assured, the Presidential election in Zimbabwe was marred by a high level of politically motivated violence and intimidation, which preceded the poll. While violent acts were carried out by supporters of both of the main political parties, it is our view that most of these were perpetrated by members/supporters of the ruling party against members/supporters of the opposition.

5. We were particularly concerned about the activities of paramilitary youth groups organised under a 'National Youth Training Programme,' Members of these groups were responsible for a systematic campaign of intimidation against known or suspected supporters of the main opposition party, the Movement for Democratic Change, MDC. The violence and intimidation created a climate of fear and suspicion.

6. Members of our Group found that very often the Zimbabwe Republic Police (ZRP) and other security forces did not take action to investigate reported cases of violence and intimidation, especially against known or suspected supporters of the MDC. Indeed, the ZRP appeared to be heavy-handed in dealing with the MDC and lenient towards supporters of the Zimbabwe African National Union-Patriotic Front, ZANU-PF. This failure to impartially enforce the law seriously calls into question the application of the rule of law in Zimbabwe.

7. We were concerned that the legislative framework within which the elections were conducted, particularly certain provisions of the Public Order and Security Act and the General Laws Amendment Act, was basically flawed, and prejudicially applied. Limitations on the freedom of speech, movement and of association prevented the opposition from campaigning freely.

8. We further regret the restrictions placed on civil society groups, which effectively barred this important sector from participation in the democratic process, and prevented them from carrying out much needed voter education activities, In particular we consider that unnecessary restrictions were placed on the accreditation of independent domestic observers.

9. We found that thousands of Zimbabwean citizens were disenfranchised as a result of the lack of transparency in the registration process and the wide discretionary powers of the Registrar-General in deciding who is included in or omitted from the electoral register.

10. It is our view that the ruling party used its incumbency to exploit state resources for the benefit of its electoral campaign. This was compounded by the Government's monopoly of the broadcast media—a factor which was not offset by the bias of most of the privately-owned print media in favour of the opposition MDC.

11. On polling day itself, many who wanted to cast their vote could not do so because of a significant reduction in the number of polling stations in urban areas. There was an inexplicable delay in complying with a High Court order

to extend voting to 11 March. Voting in Harare and Chitungwiza was especially slow, leading to many voters being turned away even at the end of the third day. These problems were not evident in the rural areas.

12. Taking into account all of the foregoing, and recalling our mandate, we have concluded that the conditions in Zimbabwe did not adequately allow for a free expression of will by the electors in the 2002 Presidential election.

13. We call on all Zimbabweans to put aside their differences and to work together for the future of their country. We believe national reconciliation is a priority and that the Commonwealth should assist in this process.

Recommendations

14. The Group recommends as follows:

    (a) There is an urgent need for there to be a cessation to the systematic use of violence in political campaigns, especially against the opposition party. To address this need, the political parties and the security authorities should jointly establish mechanisms and structures at central and district levels to co-ordinate and implement peace initiatives.

    (b) There is a fundamental need for there to be a clear separation of party and state in Zimbabwe and for there to be a proscription on the use of state resources for party political activity.

    (c) The Government and law enforcement agencies should strictly enforce the law in respect to all acts of political violence.

    (d) the provisions of the General Laws Amendment Act, the Public Order and Security Act and the access to information and Privacy Act which impede the freedoms of association movement and speech should be repealed.

    (e) In accordance with its commitment to all the people of Zimbabwe to assist in the development of a democratic society, the Commonwealth should continue to offer assistance to strengthen the country's democratic institutions. The Commonwealth should also offer technical and economic assistance as appropriate.

15. The Commonwealth Observer Group which was present for the June 2000 Parliamentary elections in Zimbabwe made a series of recommendations intended to assist in resolving problems which the Group had identified during its observations. A number of us were members of that 2000 COG. We regret that in effect none of our recommendations has been accepted by the Government nor by the electoral authorities. In particular, we remain strongly of the view that had a more transparent electoral process been established under a truly impartial authority, the credibility of the current Presidential election could have been considerably enhanced. The lack of such an authority inevitably raises questions over the conduct of this election.

16. We note that steps have been taken to allocate greater resources, and a role in keeping with constitutional provisions, to the Electoral Supervisory Commission (ESC). This is a move in the right direction, but there is still

a need to divorce this body from governmental control in order to ensure its independence.

17. We make the following recommendations, which we believe would assist in the conduct of future elections in Zimbabwe:

(a) There is a need to revisit the system of election administration. The responsibility is currently shared between the Elections Directorate, the Registrar-General and the Electoral Supervisory Commission. All these bodies are appointed by either the President or the Executive. There is a need to establish an Independent Electoral Commission adequately staffed and equipped to be fully responsible for all aspects of electoral administration and management.

(b) Legislation should provide for publication of a preliminary and subsequently final voter's roll in sufficient time prior to an election. Both of these lists should be made available for easily accessible public inspection, rather than only in offices of constituency registrars.

(c) All parties should subscribe to a Code of Conduct regarding the activities of political parties and candidates during the campaign and election period.

(d) Regulations governing the use of public media by the political parties and a Code of Conduct on media coverage and advertising during the campaign and election period need to be devised.

(e) There is a need to review the Constituency delimitation exercise and the number of polling stations attached to constituencies.

(f) A well-organised and ongoing voter education programme should be initiated and carried out by election officials, political parties and civil society.

18. We are grateful to the Commonwealth Secretary-General for inviting us to participate in this Commonwealth Observer Group. We recognise the importance of our mission for the Commonwealth and for Zimbabwe. In this light, we also thank the Government of Zimbabwe for having invited Commonwealth Observers to this election. We have reported what we have seen in accordance with our mandate. We feel our highest obligation is to the people of Zimbabwe.

April

DECLARATION OF CEASE-FIRE ENDING ANGOLAN CIVIL WAR
April 4, 2002

One of modern Africa's longest and bloodiest civil wars—a conflict between the government and guerrillas in Angola—came to an end in 2002. It was the third attempt in eleven years to end a war that began following Portugal's withdrawal from Angola (and its other colonies) in 1975. Unlike the previous two efforts, this one appeared likely to succeed. Jonas Savimbi, the charismatic leader of the guerrilla group, the National Union for the Total Independence of Angola (UNITA), was killed in February, and his successors signed a formal peace accord on April 4, 2002. During the following months UNITA's 80,000 fighters gave up their weapons and, along with their families, entered government-run camps.

The war spanned twenty-seven years, displaced an estimated 4.5 million people (out of a total population of about 12 million), and resulted in the deaths of between 500,000 and 1 million people. The United States was a major participant during the 1980s as a principal backer of Savimbi, while the former Soviet Union long sponsored the government.

Angola potentially was one of the wealthiest countries in Africa, with large deposits of oil, diamonds, iron ore, copper, and other natural resources. Few of those riches went to benefit the nation's people during the war, however, and instead were used to buy weapons for the opposing sides and, reportedly, to enrich their leaders. News reports during 2002 indicated that $1 billion in government oil revenues was missing—either looted by government officials or lost through ineptitude. At war's end, international agencies called Angola a humanitarian disaster zone. Nearly 3 million people remained homeless, and United Nations agencies said 2 million of them desperately needed food aid. The majority of the displaced and hungry were children, including tens of thousands orphaned by the war.

For more than a quarter century, Angola was a recurring item on the agenda of the United Nations Security Council. The collapse of a peace agreement during the 1990s led to the withdrawal of a UN peacekeeping force in 1999—a low point in the world body's attempts to contain conflicts in the developing world. With the arrival of peace, Angola in 2002 was elected for the first time to a two-year term on the Security Council, starting in January 2003. (Background, Historic Documents of 1998, p. 947; Historic Documents of 1991, p. 287)

The Long Road to Peace

Portugal's withdrawal from Angola in 1975 set off a scramble for control of the giant country among three paramilitary factions: the People's Movement for the Liberation of Angola (MPLA), which was backed by the Soviet Union; UNITA, which had backing from South Africa and the United States; and the National Front for the Liberation of Angola (FNLA), which also had U.S. support. The MPLA quickly defeated the FNLA, took full control of Luanda, the capital, and established itself as the Angolan government. Savimbi's UNITA forces continued to fight, however.

During the 1980s the Angolan war became a front in the cold war between the United States and the Soviet Union. The administration of President Ronald Reagan (1981–1989) gave strong political and military backing to Savimbi, while the Soviet Union continued its support for the Marxist government headed by Jose Eduardo dos Santos. Moscow also financed a force of about 50,000 Cuban mercenaries who fought on behalf of the government. Washington's association with Savimbi essentially was a marriage of convenience; the mercurial guerrilla leader previously had espoused Marxist ideals, had received support from China, and was useful to the United States primarily because he was fighting a Soviet-sponsored regime.

For the leaders of the two factions in Angola, the struggle eventually centered more around control of Angola's rich natural resources (especially diamonds and oil) than political ideology. The government controlled the coastal enclave of Cabinda, with its offshore oil wells operated by multinational corporations, and Savimbi controlled key diamond-mining regions in the southern and eastern provinces. Both sides used the profits from these resources to buy arms and enrich themselves rather than to improve the lives of ordinary Angolans, hundreds of thousands of whom were routinely forced to flee their homes because of fighting.

Three developments in the late 1980s and early 1990s seemed to herald an end to the war. The first was a U.S.-mediated regional agreement intended to bring peace to both Angola and neighboring Southwest Africa (now Namibia), where leftist guerrillas had been fighting South African control. That agreement led to Namibian independence in 1990, to the withdrawal of Cuban soldiers from Angola, and to U.S. termination of its support for Savimbi. During the same period, the white minority government of South Africa began the process of turning power over to the black majority—and also ended its direct involvement on UNITA'S behalf in Angola. UNITA and the dos Santos government signed a peace agreement in May 1991.

The third development came seven months after that accord: the collapse of the Soviet Union, finally ending the cold war and depriving the dos Santos regime of its major external source of support. With both sides now on their own, Savimbi and dos Santos agreed to contested presidential and legislative elections, which were held under United Nations supervision in September 1992. Dos Santos fell just short of a required 50 percent majority for the presidency, and UNITA candidates captured a small minority of seats in the legislature. The capital, Luanda, erupted into violence and Savimbi challenged the results and resumed his guerrilla war.

The new U.S. administration of President Bill Clinton (1993–2001) formally recognized the dos Santos government in 1993, and Savimbi once again announced his readiness to give up the struggle. New negotiations led to a second peace agreement, signed in Lusaka, Zambia, in October 1994. Over the next three years the two sides negotiated various political agreements. Savimbi agreed to accept the results of the September 1992 elections, the United Nations sent a 7,000-man peacekeeping force into Angola, UNITA representatives elected in 1992 took their places in the National Assembly, and the government and UNITA formed a "union and reconciliation" government.

The underlying disputes between Savimbi and the government proved too strong to permit true reconciliation, however, and Savimbi rearmed his soldiers. In late 1997 the UN Security Council imposed sanctions against UNITA for failing to respect the 1994 Lusaka peace accord. Fighting escalated during late 1998, and in February 1999 Secretary General Kofi Annan pulled the beleaguered UN peacekeepers out of Angola—a bitter admission of defeat for what had once seemed a promising prospect of peace.

After the government gained control in 2000 of two diamond-mining regions that had been Savimbi's main source of income it became only a matter of time before UNITA would collapse. In June 2001 Savimbi acknowledged defeat in the conventional military sense but said he would continue fighting a guerrilla war against the government. Shortly afterward UNITA launched kidnappings and other attacks on civilians. In August 2001 UNITA derailed a train and killed passengers trying to escape; more than 400 people died in the attack. The government responded to UNITA guerrilla tactics with "cleansing" attacks on rebel areas, depriving civilians and rebels of food and other supplies.

Savimbi's last-gasp strategy finally failed on February 22, 2002, when government forces said they killed Savimbi in a gun battle in east-central Angola. Photographs of Savimbi's bullet-riddled body confirmed the end of the guerrilla leader's long struggle. Three weeks later the Angolan army said Savimbi's chief military aide and likely successor, Antonio Dembo, also was dead.

The decimation of UNITA leadership presented the Angolan government with a fresh chance for peace, but many international observers at first doubted that dos Santos would seize it. Instead, they said, dos Santos would continue the war. For years the government had used the war as its chief rallying cry and as an excuse for its failure to use the country's wealth to improve the lives of its citizens. Dos Santos proved the doubters wrong, however, with the unveiling on March 13 of an Agenda for Peace calling for an end to the fighting and a final peace agreement. Key military aides representing

UNITA and the government met two days later, and formal cease-fire talks, begun on March 20, quickly produced an agreement.

In a broadcast speech to the nation on April 3, dos Santos pledged that "we will together turn our eyes to the resolution of the grave and dramatic problems which have accumulated for centuries of colonialism and decades of armed conflict." The next day, UNITA general Abreu Kamorteiro signed a formal peace agreement along with government commander Armando da Cruz Neto. The agreement was officially witnessed by the UN special envoy for Angola, Ibrahim Gambari, and the ambassadors of Portugal, Russia, and the United States—the "troika" of nations that had tried to guarantee implementation of the 1994 Lusaka accord. Speaking after the signing, UNITA's senior surviving general, Paulo Lukamba, said: "We start a new era, the era of cooperation. We are sure that from now on UNITA and the commanders I am leading are ready to fulfill what are our duties in this agreement."

The Peace Agreement

Technically, the April 4 peace agreement was an amendment to the Lusaka accord, the second attempt to end the war. Most provisions of the April 4 agreement dealt with treatment of the 80,000 UNITA guerrillas, who in essence were a hungry, defeated army. UNITA agreed to demobilize and disarm its fighters. In turn, the government agreed to give the fighters and up to 300,000 family members food, clothing, medical care, and vocational training to help them reenter civilian life. The government also agreed to absorb 5,000 UNITA officers and soldiers into the national army and 40 into the national police force.

These provisions were to be supervised by a joint military commission, composed of representatives from UNITA and the Angolan army. Unlike previous peace agreements, this one did not call for a large UN peacekeeping force. The reason was simple: UNITA had been defeated and its fighters were exhausted. To handle the world body's political responsibilities, the Security Council on August 15 established a new UN mission in Angola, consisting primarily of diplomats.

The United Nations objected to a major provision of the agreement providing for an amnesty, under a law passed in March by the legislature, for "all crimes committed within the framework of the armed conflict." In witnessing the April 4 signing, Gambari entered a reservation saying that the United Nations did not give legal recognition to any amnesty for genocide, crimes against humanity, and war crimes. The UN objection was a matter of principal, with no immediate effect because the world body was not planning a prosecution for the many human rights crimes committed during the Angolan war.

Under the long-dormant Lusaka agreement, a resolution of political matters following the war was left to a joint commission chaired by the United Nations. That panel held several meetings from September through November but dissolved itself on November 20 when the government and UNITA appeared to be cooperating. Annan said both parties agreed to a plan to hold a new general election in 2004.

In contrast to previous peace agreements, all fighting stopped in Angola with the signing of the April 4 cease-fire. By early July the government said more than 84,000 UNITA military personnel, including 658 foreign soldiers, had given up their weapons and assembled in thirty-six government-run "quartering areas" along with nearly 240,000 family members. The government also had to provide food and other supplies to more than 30,000 former army soldiers (and their families) whose services were no longer needed. The flood of people overwhelmed the government, which was ill-prepared to deal with the needs, but UN and international relief agencies stepped in to help keep the former combatants fed and housed. On August 2 senior government and UNITA leaders held a ceremony in Luanda to declare an official end to the war.

At year's end, the UN said 426,000 former combatants and family members were still living in the camps. Even with the international aid, UNITA officials said late in the year that hundreds of soldiers and family members had died of starvation, and others had left the camps to return to their homes. UNITA also complained that the government began moving former soldiers from the camps in November without giving them the tools and supplies they would need in civilian life.

Three major UNITA factions agreed in October to merge as a united political party, and the government formally acknowledged UNITA as a party entitled to operate throughout the country. On October 15 UNITA representatives in the national assembly took their place as the main opposition party, with longtime UNITA operative Jeronimo Wanga as the chairman. In keeping with the Lusaka accord, the government appointed three UNITA members as provincial governors and four as cabinet ministers. Finally, in December the government and UNITA agreed on a new constitution providing for a single legislative body, strong powers for the presidency, and a system for the presidential appointment of provincial governors based on which party gained the most votes in each province.

The UN Security Council on December 9 lifted all sanctions it had imposed on UNITA in 1993 for its renewal of the war. The sanctions had included an embargo on the trade in rough diamonds from UNITA-controlled zones, a freeze on all UNITA assets held abroad, restrictions on the sales of fuel and arms to the guerrillas, and a ban on international travel by UNITA officials.

Humanitarian Disaster

When the fighting stopped, at least 4 million Angolan civilians were still displaced from their homes but living within Angola, according to a May 2 report by the United Nations Office for the Coordination of Humanitarian Affairs. Another 450,000 Angolans were refugees in other countries, primarily Zambia and the Democratic Republic of the Congo. Enticed by the prospect of peace, an estimated 1.2 million displaced people and refugees returned to their homes between April 4 and the end of the year—the vast majority on their own power, without international assistance. At year's end, the UN office estimated that more than 2.8 million people remained displaced within the country and up to 400,000 remained as refugees in other countries.

While many of these people had been able to fend for themselves, about 1.8 million still needed food aid at the end of the year, the UN said, and some 300,000 more were in danger of needing aid by early 2003. Many of the needy lived in regions formerly controlled by UNITA. Most Angolans relied on subsistence agriculture for their livelihood, but millions of acres of farmland had been destroyed in the war, and farmers lost their seeds, tools, and livestock.

In addition, the UN cited reports that about 200,000 people might be in "critical distress" in inaccessible areas. Large parts of Angola were cut off because of heavy seasonal rains, and the presence of land mines and other unexploded ordnance made many areas too dangerous for relief operations. UN and relief agencies requested $386 million from donor countries for humanitarian operations in Angola during 2003. Visiting Angola in September, Secretary of State Colin Powell said the United States would provide food and other forms of aid to help the country get through its immediate crisis. But over the long term, he said, the Angolan government needed to end corruption and use its oil wealth constructively to help its people.

Children were the most seriously affected people in Angola. In a July 26 report to the Security Council, Annan said children constituted more than half of those made homeless by the war, and most children suffered from malnutrition, malaria, measles, diarrhea, respiratory ailments, or other preventable diseases. About 700,000 children had lost one or both parents, he said, and about 100,000 had been separated from their families, many ending up on city streets. The war and poor living conditions contributed to the deaths of thousands of Angolan children each year. According to UN estimates, Angola had one of the highest infant mortality rates in the world, with one child in three dying before the age of five.

The AIDS pandemic that had struck the rest of southern Africa also was becoming an increasingly severe problem in Angola. The government estimated in 2002 that nearly 9 percent of the population was infected with the HIV/AIDS virus. (AIDS pandemic, p. 469)

Famine in Southern Africa

The end of the Angolan war, and the humanitarian crisis that emerged in the war's wake, came in the context of a major famine that swept rapidly through much of southern Africa during 2002. At year's end relief agencies estimated that more than 14 million people in six countries—Lesotho, Malawi, Mozambique, Swaziland, Zambia, and Zimbabwe—were at a "severe risk" of starvation in coming months because of the famine. Zimbabwe was hardest hit, with about one-half of its 12 million people in danger. Angola was not on this list of famine countries because its humanitarian problem resulted almost exclusively from war, not the typical mix in Africa of war, poverty, failed economic policies, corruption, and floods in some years and drought in others.

Donor nations, including the United States, supplied nearly 300,000 metric tons of food aid during the last half of 2002 to alleviate the famine. The UN's World Food Program (WFP) said on December 30 that "hundreds of thousands more" tons of food would be needed in the first months of 2003, at a total cost of more than $500 million. "Our lack of resources is seriously threatening WFP's ability to feed these growing numbers of desperately hungry of people—many of whom are suffering the double blow of HIV/AIDS and food shortages, which are intrinsically linked in southern Africa," said Judith Lewis, the agency's southern Africa regional coordinator.

The southern Africa famine brought international attention to one issue that had been troubling humanitarian agencies for years: the resistance of some countries to genetically modified food provided by the United States. For decades much of the food produced in the United States and consumed by Americans had been modified through biotechnology. At the start of the twenty-first century few Americans had concerns about genetically modified food, but an increasing number of Europeans objected to what they called "Frankenfood," and some of this resistance had spread to developing countries, most notably Zambia.

Although nearly 3 million Zambians were considered at risk because of the famine, the government said in August that it would not accept U.S. food aid unless it could be proven to be safe—in other words, that it had not been genetically modified. The government of Zimbabwe also refused at least one shipment of U.S. corn (the staple crop in the region), citing concerns about safety and the possibility that Zimbabwean farmers might plant genetically modified seeds from the United States—thus endangering local strains of corn. Zimbabwe later changed its stance and accepted genetically modified food aid from the United States, but only if grains had been milled beforehand so they could not be planted. Mozambique took a similar position. Milling resolved some of the concerns about modified food, but it added to the cost of the aid and caused some delays in distribution, U.S. officials said. (Zimbabwe election, p. 133)

Following are excerpts from the Memorandum of Understanding Addendum to the Lusaka Protocol for the Cessation of Hostilities and the Resolution of the Outstanding Military Issues under the Lusaka Protocol, signed April 4, 2002, in Luanda, Angola, by representatives of the government of Angola and the National Union for the Total Independence of Angola, the guerilla group that had been fighting the government. The memorandum declared an immediate cease-fire in the war and provided for demobilization of UNITA fighters.

The document was obtained from the Internet at www .irinnews.org/IRIN/lusakaprotocol.doc; accessed January 14, 2003.

Preamble

The Delegation of the Angolan Armed Forces, mandated by the Government of the Republic of Angola;

The Delegation of the UNITA Military Forces, mandated by its Leadership Commission;

In the presence of the United Nations in Angola and of the Observer States of the Angolan Peace Process [Portugal, Russia, and the United States];

Considering that the Lusaka Protocol, signed on 20/11/94 by the Government and by UNITA, with United Nations mediation and in the presence of the Observer States of the Angolan Peace Process, the legal and political instrument for the resolution of the Angolan conflict, in the sense of securing peace and national reconciliation in the Republic of Angola, was unable to experience the positive evolution expected for its definitive conclusion;

Considering that, the growing and pressing need to secure peace and national reconciliation in the Republic of Angola, expressed and felt daily by all Angolans, has become imperative and urgent, and calls first of all for the cessation of the armed conflict between UNITA, as a political and military structure, and the Government, promoting, to this end, appropriate initiatives with creativity and flexibility, for the definitive conclusion of the implementation of the Lusaka Protocol;

Conscious of the fact that, the end of the internal conflict leads to peace and national reconciliation in the Republic of Angola and constitutes a challenge for which a determined commitment needs to be made to overcome and achieve for the benefit of the Angolan people;

Inspired by a will to confer on their relations a new and positive dimension, sustained on the fact that in the spirit of reconciliation, all Angolans need to pardon and forget the griefs resulting from the conflict and face the future with tolerance and confidence;

Accordingly, in order to implement their commitments and obligations under the Lusaka Protocol, hereby decide to adopt the Memorandum of Understanding, in the following terms:

Chapter I: Object and Principles of the Memorandum of Understanding

Object

1.1 The object of the Memorandum of Understanding is the commitment by the parties to, through their fraternal and active cooperation, guarantee the attainment and mataerialization of the cease-fire and the resolution of all pending military issues and, subsequently, the definitive resolution of the armed conflict, resumed following the total execution of the task of the formation of the FAA [Armed Forces of Angola], under the Lusaka Protocol.

1.2 The objective of the cooperation between the parties is the resolution of the negative military factors which gave rise to the blockade of the Lusaka Protocol and, subsequently, the creation of conditions for its definitive conclusion.

Fundamental Principles

1. The parties reaffirm their respect for the rule of law and for the democratic institutions in the Republic of Angola, and, accordingly, the observance of the Constitutional Law and of the remaining legislation in force in the Republic of Angola.

2. The parties reiterate their unequivocal acceptance of the validity of the relevant legal and political instruments, in particular, the Lusaka Protocol and the Resolutions of the Security Council of the United Nations, relative to the Angolan peace process.

3. The parties recognize that the respect for democracy in all fields and levels of national life is essential for peace and national reconciliation.

Chapter II: Agenda of the Memorandum of Understanding

[Points 1–3 omitted.]

4. Issues of National Reconciliation

Amnesty

2.1 The Government guarantees, in the interest of peace and national reconciliation, the approval and publication, by the competent organs and institutions of the State of the Republic of Angola, of an Amnesty Law for all crimes committed within the framework of the armed conflict between the UNITA military forces and the Government.

5. Cessation of Hostilities and Pending Military Issues under the Lusaka Protocol

1) Cease-Fire

3.1 The parties reiterate their commitment to comply scrupulously with all their commitments and obligations relative to the task of re-establishment of cease-fire. . . .

3.2 In this regard, the Government, through the General Staff of the FAA and the UNITA military forces, through the High General Staff, will issue and comply with a declaration of re-establishment of the cease-fire, with a view to ending the armed conflict, and the attainment of peace and national reconciliation.

3.3 The task of re-establishing the cease-fire, includes the following:

   a) The definitive and total cessation of military actions throughout the national territory and the non-dissemination of hostile propaganda.
   b) The non-conduct of force movements, to reinforce or occupy new military positions, as well as the non undertaking of acts of violence against the civilian populations and the destruction of property.
   c) The regular reporting on the situation of positions of the units and the other para-military structures of the UNITA military forces in zones or areas of possible military tension.

d) The guarantee of protection of persons and their property, of public resources and property, and also of the free circulation of persons and goods.

2) Disengagement, Quartering and Conclusion of the Demilitarization of UNITA Military Forces

3.4 The parties reiterate their commitment to comply scrupulously with their commitments and obligations relative to the task of quartering and conclusion of the demilitarization of the UNITA military forces.

3.5 In this regard, the Mixed Military Commission, with the support of the General Staff of FAA, will proceed to quarter and demilitarize all units and para-military structures of the UNITA military forces, including the following:

a) The reporting, by the High General Staff of the UNITA military forces, to the Mixed Military Commission, on all reliable and verifiable data, relative to the combative and numerical composition of the units and para-military structures of the UNITA military forces, and their location.

b) The establishment of monitoring mechanisms of the demilitarization process of the UNITA military forces.

c) The identification of the units and the para-military structures of the UNITA military forces, the establishment of quartering areas for the same.

d) The definition of the respective itineraries and means of movement and the conduct of the military units and para-military structures of the UNITA military forces to quartering areas.

e) The disengagement from the points of location and the movement of the units and para-military structures of the UNITA military forces to quartering areas.

f) The reception, accommodation and feeding, and the registration of the personnel of the military units and para-military structures of the UNITA military forces in the quartering areas.

g) The handing over and, in continuation, the collection, storage and subsequent destruction of the entire armament and equipment of the military units and para-military structures of the UNITA armed forces.

3) Integration of Generals, Senior Officers, Captains and Junior Officers, Sergeants and Men, from the UNITA Military Forces into the Angolan Armed Forces

3.6 The Government, in the interest of national reconciliation, will proceed, through the General Staff of FAA, to integrate the Generals, Senior Officers, Captains and Junior Officers, Sergeants and men from the UNITA military forces into the FAA, in accordance with the existing structural vacancies. . . .

[Annex 2 gave the following numbers of officers and enlisted men to be incorporated into the army: 4 generals, 8 lieutenant generals, 18 brigadier generals,

40 colonels, 60 lieutenant colonels, 100 majors, 150 captains, 200 lieutenants, 250 second lieutenants, 300 cadets, 20 sergeant majors, 30 sergeant adjutants, 50 first sergeants, 200 second sergeants, 500 corporals, and 3,077 soldiers, for a grand total of 5,007.]

4) Integration of Generals and Senior Officers from the UNITA Military Forces into the National Police

3.8 The Government, in the interest of national reconciliation, will proceed to integrate some Generals and Senior Officers from the UNITA military forces into the National Police, through the General Command of the National Police, in accordance with the existing structural vacancies. . . .

[Annex 3 gave the following numbers of personnel to be incorporated into the police: 3 sub-commissioners, 5 first superintendents, 14 superintendents, and 18 intendants, for a grand total of 40.]

5) Demobilization of the Personnel of the UNITA Military Forces and the Extinction of the UNITA Military Forces

3.10 The parties reiterate their commitment to comply scrupulously with their commitments and obligations relative to the task of demobilization of the excess personnel of the UNITA military forces and the extinction of the UNITA military forces. . . .

3.11 In this regard, the Mixed Military Commission, with the support of the United Nations, shall proceed to demobilize the excess personnel of the UNITA military forces and the extinction of the UNITA military forces, including the following;

    a) The individual demobilization of the excess personnel from the UNITA military forces.

    b) The formal and definitive extinction of the UNITA military forces.

    c) The placement of the demobilized personnel of the ex-UNITA military forces at the administrative dependency on the General Staff of FAA, through the FAA Military Regions and Operational Commands.

6) Social and Vocational Reintegration of Demobilized Personnel of the Ex-UNITA Military Forces into National Life

3.12 The parties reiterate their commitment to comply scrupulously with their commitments and obligations relative to task of social reintegration of the demobilized personnel. . . .

3.13 In this regard, the Government through the General Staff of FAA and of the competent public organs and services, with UNITA participation and with the assistance of the international community, shall proceed with the reintegration of the demobilized personnel into civil society, within a program of vocational reintegration.

3.14 The vocational reinsertion of the demobilized personnel of the ex-UNITA military forces includes the following:

a) The protection, accommodation and feeding of the personnel of the ex-UNITA military forces in the training centers.

b) The professional training of the personnel of the ex-UNITA military forces, to capacitate them for the national labor market, through a program of special and urgent social reintegration. . . .

[Chapter III listed details for the coordination and timing of various actions following the cease-fire. Chapter IV listed the final provisions.]

Annex 1: Document Relating to the Quartering of the UNITA Military Forces

The Delegation of the Angolan Armed Forces and the Delegation of the UNITA Military Forces to the Military Talks, pertaining to the quartering of the UNITA military forces, have agreed as follows:

9. General points on the quartering

(i) The quartering of the UNITA military forces must provide the living conditions necessary for the stay of the military in a total number of up to 50,000, comprising about 12 General and 47 Brigadiers, about 1,700 Senior Officers, about 17,350 Captains and Junior Officers, about 3,150 Sergeants and about 27,740 men, for the duration of a period of time from the welcoming of the personnel until their integration into FAA and the National Police and the vocation reinsertion of the demobilized personnel.

(ii) Quartering areas must have a structure of operation managed by highly qualified personnel, with capacity to quarter up to 1,600 personnel and with security and easy access.

(iii) The quartering of the UNITA military forces implies, also, on the one hand, the accommodation of 12 Generals and 47 Brigadiers, in cities close to the quartering areas and, on the other hand, the organization and securing of areas for the accommodation of the families of the military, close to the quartering areas, in a total of up to 300,000 individuals, including men, women and children.

(iv) Ensuring emergency initial assistance to the families of the military of the UNITA military forces, and the promotion of their reintegration, supported by small-scale productive ventures and provision of services, that is to say, quick income generating projects in the areas of agriculture, rural commerce and other possible areas of profitable occupation, to be guaranteed by the competent organs and entities of State administration, in close cooperation with the General Staff of FAA and with the participation of the United Nations. . . .

[The remainder of Annex 1 gave details for the management and locations of the quartering areas, along with the quartering of foreign soldiers who had been part of the UNITA military. Annex 2 detailed the numbers of UNITA officers and troops to be incorporated into the Armed Forces of Angola. Annex 3 detailed the numbers of UNITA officers to be incorporated into the national police force of Angola.]

Annex 4: Document Pertaining to the Vocational Reinsertion of Demobilized Personnel of the Ex-UNITA Military Forces into National Life

The Delegation of the Angolan Armed Forces and the Delegation of the UNITA Military Forces to the Military Talks, in the matter related to the vocational reinsertion of the demobilized personnel of the ex-UNITA military forces, have agreed as follows:

1. The vocational reinsertion of the demobilized personnel of the ex-UNITA military forces consists in their civic training, socio-economic promotion, on the part of the competent organs and entities of the State, in close cooperation with the General Staff of FAA and with support of the United Nations, considering to this purpose the pressing need to:

(i) Guarantee initial assistance to the demobilized personnel of the ex-UNITA military forces.

(ii) Guarantee general and specific training for the demobilized personnel of the ex-UNITA military forces.

(iii) Ensure their supported reintegration into national life.

2. The process of vocational reinsertion of the demobilized personnel of the ex-UNITA military forces shall be conducted through the following methods:

(i) The vocational reinsertion of the demobilized personnel of the ex-UNITA military forces as part of the national Reconstruction Service.

(ii) The vocational reintegration of the demobilized personnel of the ex-UNITA military forces, as part of the national labor market, in particular, in the public and private sectors.

(iii) The vocational reinsertion of the demobilized personnel of the ex-UNITA military forces as part of the Populations Resettlement Program. . . .

Annex 5: Document Pertaining to Considerations Regarding the Conditions for the Conclusion of the Lusaka Protocol

Considering that the UNITA military forces were integrated into a political and military organization and, that the extinction of the military component of this organization is in conformity with the law and order in the Republic of Angola;

In accordance with the spirit of the provision in Points 6 and 8 of the Declaration by the Government of March 13, 2002, and number 1.1 of Point 1 of Chapter II of the present Memorandum and, considering that its signing and implementation by the parties constitutes the conditions for the conclusion of the implementation of the Lusaka Protocol;

The Parties consider that conditions have been created to guarantee the continuity of UNITA participation in the process of conclusion of the implementation of the Lusaka Protocol.

Accordingly, they recommend to UNITA the need to rapidly establish the internal consensus necessary so that, with the Government as partner, it may participate in the process of the conclusion of the implementation of the Lusaka Protocol.

[Annex 6 reiterated provisions in the Lusaka protocol for the government to guarantee the personal security of UNITA leaders.]

PAKISTANI PRESIDENT ON
ELECTION REFERENDUM
April 5, 2002

Three years after ousting an elected civilian government, Pakistan's military leader, General Pervez Musharraf, kept his grip on power during 2002, while claiming to restore democracy. Musharraf pushed through a referendum in April that gave him five more years as president—a title he had taken for himself a year earlier. In August he issued a decree ending the constitution to ensure that he would dominate any elected civilian government. In October he allowed elections for new national and provincial parliaments. No one party emerged as the victor at the national level, but a promilitary party was put in charge of the government, giving Pakistan at least the appearance of civilian rule. However, an Islamist party won control of one provincial assembly—a first for Pakistan. (Musharraf coup, Historic Documents of 1999, p. 623)

Ever since its founding in 1948, Pakistan had undergone numerous periods of political instability and had been ruled for more than half its history by military regimes that ousted weak civilian leaders. But in 2002 the political situation in Pakistan was of urgent interest to the rest of the world, especially that country's most important patron, the United States. Following the September 11, 2001, terrorist attacks against the United States, Musharraf had sided with Washington in its war against terrorism, starting with the al Qaeda network that was responsible for the attacks. Musharraf abandoned Pakistan's support for the Islamist regime, known as the Taliban, in neighboring Afghanistan, where al Qaeda had been based. He also allowed U.S. military forces to operate from Pakistan as they attacked the Taliban and al Qaeda, eventually driving the Taliban from power in late 2001. (Events in Afghanistan, p. 15)

President George W. Bush expressed his support for Musharraf, saying in August the Pakistani leader had been "tight with us on the war against terror, and that's what I appreciate." Even so, the political situation in Pakistan posed a dilemma for the United States, which before the September 11 attacks had demanded a return to civilian rule. On the one hand, it was clear that the likely alternatives to Musharraf's military regime would be either a weak civilian government or an Islamist regime that would end Pakistani cooperation with the United States. On the other hand, Musharraf had taken little action to bring extremist factions within Pakistan under control; for example, he had not convincingly followed through on his promises to end government support of guerrilla groups that were battling India's control of the disputed province of Kashmir. (Kashmir conflict, p. 325)

Anti-Western Sentiments on the Rise

A central aspect of the year's political developments in Pakistan was the increasing role played there by fundamentalist Islamist factions. Pakistan was the world's second most populist Muslim country, after Indonesia. Pakistan's leaders always had been secular, but most had tolerated religious groups that sought to establish an Islamic state and that viscerally opposed Western influence in the country. Moreover, Pakistani governments since the late 1980s had provided weapons, training, and logistical support for Islamist guerrilla forces that were battling India's control of most of Kashmir, a Muslim-majority province disputed between India and Pakistan since the 1947 partition of the Indian subcontinent. The two countries had fought several wars over Kashmir and nearly came to blows again in late 2001 and early 2002 after Pakistan-based Kashmiri guerrillas attacked the Indian parliament, killing seven people. As a result, Musharraf came under intense pressure from the United States and India to halt all support for the Kashmiri guerrillas.

Musharraf responded in January by arresting the guerrilla group leaders and banning five of the Kashmiri groups, including the two alleged to have carried out the attack on the Indian parliament. Under his orders, the military closed some of the guerrilla training camps that it had sponsored and made at least a token effort to halt guerrilla infiltrations into Indian-controlled Kashmir. But those steps failed to satisfy India, which insisted that guerrillas continued to attack Kashmir from bases in Pakistan. Musharraf's actions also enraged leaders of the groups, as well as many religious Pakistanis who had long considered the guerrillas as heroes. Accusing him of betrayal and treason, some Pakistanis began calling their president "Busharraf" to mock his apparent willingness to do the U.S. president's bidding.

Extremists took more concrete action to protest Western influence in Pakistan. The most highly publicized was the kidnapping in January of Wall Street Journal *reporter Daniel Pearl, who had been writing about Islamist groups in Pakistan. Pearl was killed in February, and the killers videotaped his grisly death. Musharraf's government charged one group, Jaish e-Muhammad, with the crime and put one of its leaders, Ahmed Omar Saeed Sheikh, on trial. Saeed Sheikh was convicted on July 15 and sentenced to death.*

On March 17 four people, including a U.S. embassy employee and her daughter, were killed in a grenade attack on a Christian church patronized by diplomats and other foreign nationals in the capital, Islamabad. On

May 8 eleven French nationals and two Pakistanis were killed when a car bomb exploded outside the Sheraton Hotel in Karachi. The victims were engineers helping to build a submarine that Pakistan had purchased from France. A Pakistani who was the presumed suicide bomber also died in the attack. Musharraf's government blamed the attack on a radical group, Lashkar e-Jhangvi, which authorities said might also have been involved in the Daniel Pearl case. Pakistan and U.S. officials said it appeared that Jaish e-Muhammad and Lashkar e-Jhangvi were cooperating with al Qaeda fighters who had fled into Pakistan from Afghanistan during the war in late 2001.

Yet another attack came on June 14, when a car bomb was exploded outside the U.S. consulate in Karachi, killing twelve Pakistanis and wounding forty-four others. Also, in December Pakistani authorities said they had thwarted a plan by anti-American militants to ram a bomb-laden Volkswagen into a car carrying U.S. diplomats.

Presidential Referendum

Musharraf on April 5 announced his plans for the referendum on his presidency, saying he was determined to "bring real democracy" to Pakistan. Running his political campaign with military efficiency, Musharraf barred public rallies by parties opposing him but traveled to rallies around the country on his own behalf.

On the day of voting, April 30, journalists and international observers said they found numerous cases of fraud and coerced voting—including situations in which polling stations were set up in workplaces and employees were instructed by their bosses to vote "yes." The official returns showed that 56 percent of the electorate had gone to the polls, with 97.5 percent voting in favor of retaining Musharraf. The president's critics claimed that only about 10 percent of registered voters had actually cast ballots in the referendum.

Musharraf Writes New Rules

Empowered by at least the appearance of a public mandate, Musharraf next moved to set the stage for parliamentary elections, which he had promised for October, exactly three years after his coup. On July 12 Musharraf went on national television to explain proposed constitutional amendments that, among other things, gave him authority to name the prime minister and dismiss the parliament. Musharraf also issued decrees barring electoral candidacies of the two prime ministers who had served during the 1990s—Nawaz Sharif of the Pakistan Muslim League and Benazir Bhutto of the Pakistan People's Party—and requiring all candidates for parliament to hold college degrees.

Musharraf told his country that "true democracy never existed in Pakistan. If that had happened, I would not have been sitting before you." Complaining that criticism of his rule had created "a sense of uncertainty" in the country, Musharraf pledged: "I am not power hungry. I want to give power, not take it away, but we need checks and balances." Explaining that last phrase, he said the country needed "unity of command. Unless there is one man in charge on top, the government will never function."

On August 21 Musharraf announced that he had incorporated twenty-nine constitutional proposals into a formal document with the bland title of a "Legal Framework Order." Its provisions effectively legitimized his continued control of government. The order gave the president the power to disband the national government and parliament, as well as the four provincial parliaments. The order also established a National Security Council, dominated by the military, that held the final say in key decisions by the government on any security matters as well as "democracy, governance and inter-provincial harmony."

Leaders of most of the country's major political parties denounced Musharraf's constitutional changes and adopted an agreement in August pledging to try to reverse them once a new parliament was in office. Most observers said it was highly unlikely, however, that Musharraf would allow his changes to be nullified.

The U.S. government, which had kept a discreet silence in response to Musharraf's previous actions suppressing opposition, sent mixed signals about the constitutional changes. "We believe that President Musharraf wants to develop strong democratic institutions in his country," State Department spokesman Philip Reeker said on August 22. "However, we are concerned that his recent decisions could make it more difficult to build strong democratic institutions in Pakistan." President Bush expressed no such concerns, however. Speaking a few hours after Reeker, Bush praised Musharraf for siding with the United States "in the war against terror."

Parliamentary Elections

Musharraf's tactics put Pakistan's political parties in a difficult position of choosing whether to boycott the election or field candidates for a parliament that might have little real political power. In the end, all major parties chose to compete, even though the leaders of the two largest traditional parties—former prime ministers Sharif and Bhutto—were in exile, faced arrest if they returned, and were barred from again seeking public office.

Sharif, in exile with his family in Saudi Arabia, said in September he would support Bhutto, his long-time political nemesis, for prime minister. Politicians aligned with Musharraf formed a new party, called the Pakistan Muslim League-Quaid (known as the PML-Q), in an attempt to split Sharif's Pakistan Muslim League Party. Musharraf's opponents derisively offered their own name for the new party: the "King's Party." Seeking to consolidate their influence, six Islamic parties merged to form the United Action Front, which mounted a campaign based largely on anti-American slogans and opposition to Pakistan's cooperation with the U.S. war against terrorism.

Independent public opinion polls conducted during the campaign appeared to show that Musharraf still had broad public support, with 60 per-

cent or more of respondents giving him a favorable rating. Even so, many Pakistanis expressed doubts that the president would allow a return to democracy any time soon.

In the October 10 voting, the big surprise to many observers was a strong showing by the Islamic parties, which won a majority in one of the two provinces bordering Afghanistan (the Northwest Frontier) and came close to a majority in another border province, Baluchistan. Jubilant supporters called the religious alliance's strong showing a rebuke to Musharraf and a mandate for ousting the United States from Pakistan. The United Action Front's 52 seats made it the third-largest faction in the 342-seat National Assembly, behind the pro-Musharraf PML-Q, with 77 seats, and Bhutto's Pakistan People's Party, with 62 seats. Former prime minister Sharif's old Pakistan Muslim League and various minor parties took the rest of the 272 elected seats (another 70 were set aside for women and other groups).

Most international observers faulted Musharraf's government for trying to control the elections through rules that barred Bhutto, Sharif, and many other opposition candidates. The government's rules "were based on questionable legal grounds and clearly had a negative impact on the electoral process," an observer delegation from the European Union said in an October 12 report.

With no single party having anywhere near a majority, the election results meant that a government could be formed only through a coalition of two or more parties, with the pro-military PML-Q as the core. At first there was talk of the PML-Q joining forces with the coalition of religious parties, but Musharraf reportedly opposed such a deal, as did key religious leaders. A formal alliance between the PML-Q and Bhutto's party might have been possible, but Musharraf rejected Bhutto's demands that the government drop longstanding corruption charges against her and her husband. Ultimately, a political deal was struck and announced on November 21, in which some members of Bhutto's party agreed to join a coalition government in exchange for ministerial posts and other favors. Zafarullah Khan Jamali, a pro-Musharraf leader of the PML-Q, won the post of prime minister, with a razor-thin majority of 172 votes in the 342-seat parliament. A leader of the religious parties, Fazlur Rahman, came in a distant second with 86 votes.

The new government took office on November 23 at a ceremony in the presidential palace. Musharraf made it clear that the government's job would be to carry out his policies. "Whatever projects have been started should be seen through to their logical ends in these next five years so that Pakistan can progress and prosper," he said. Most observers predicted that Jamali's government would face repeated challenges because of its narrow margin.

The coalition of religious parties took control of the provincial government in the Northwest Frontier on November 25, becoming the first overtly Islamist government in Pakistan's history. The new provincial government said its first priority would be to enforce Islamic law. Some alliance leaders also said they would try to force an end to U.S. military operations in the province, where remnants of the al Qaeda terrorist network and the defeated Taliban government of Afghanistan were said to have taken refuge. Even so, national leaders insisted Pakistan would continue to cooperate with the United States, and a senior State Department official visiting Pakistan on December 17 expressed satisfaction with that cooperation.

Following are excerpts from a nationally televised address delivered April 5, 2002, by Pakistan's president, Pervez Musharraf, in which he announced plans for a referendum on allowing him to stay in office for five additional years.

The document was obtained from the Internet at www .infopak.gov.pk/President_Addresses/Address-5April.htm; accessed December 7, 2002.

My dear countrymen; ASSALAM-O-ALAIKUM

Pakistan is once again at a historic juncture. October 2002 is fast approaching and a new political era is going to commence. Some very important decisions have to be taken by me and by all of you. Genuine democracy, as I have been saying all along, which is the essence of democracy has to be introduced in Pakistan. It has to be placed on firm foundations. During the past two and a half years, we have done a lot, and in my opinion all the reforms and restructuring that we have done in various sectors will go [to] waste if we do not cap it with true democracy.

I am addressing you today, because this is a historic moment. In the past also I have, on every occasion, taken the people of Pakistan into confidence whenever any important national issue has arisen. I am aware that you have never disappointed me in the past and will not let me down in future. I am never worried about the views of any group, or any individual or for that matter any organisation. But I am always deeply concerned about your views. When I have your support, I feel confident. Therefore, in the same spirit I am talking to you today. It is my firm belief that if the intentions are good and the desire is for the betterment of Pakistan, and the people of Pakistan are with us, then I am sure that God is with us too.

We started in October 1999 with a seven point agenda. I will briefly inform you how we have progressed on each of them:

i.   Rebuild National Confidence and Morale: In my opinion we have a number of achievements in this regard. We can now see a sense of confidence among Pakistanis both at home and abroad. People now say that they are proud to be Pakistanis. With the passage of time, this will improve further.

ii. Strengthen federation, remove inter-provincial disharmony and restore national cohesion: We have successes in this too. National cohesion has taken place. Inter- provincial disharmony has been removed to a large extent. We have to do more in this regard. But I am confident that our even-handed policy towards the four provinces will further enhance inter-provincial harmony.

iii. Revive economy and restore investor confidence: We have indeed revived the economy and taken it out from a failed state situation. Investor confidence is gradually building up and will improve further.

iv. Ensure law and order and dispense speedy justice: A lot remains to be done in this regard. I will dwell upon it a little later. What we have already done to achieve this; we have undertaken far-reaching reforms and restructuring. With the passage of time further improvements will come about.

v. Depoliticise state institutions: I have no doubt whatsoever that state institutions have been depoliticised we are strictly following the policy and nothing is being done on personal whims.

vi. Devolution of power to the grass roots level: We have already done this. I will speak about it later. As you know already, the local government has been functioning since last August.

vii. Lastly, ensuring swift and across the board accountability: We have done quite a lot in this regard. We can never be fully satisfied. But whatever we have done, no government in the past or even in the future will be able to match our performance. . . .

[Musharraff then offered a detailed description of his programs to promote economic development, reform operations of the government, and alleviate poverty.]

Now let me focus on political restructuring. As to the political structure we decided to adopt a bottoms up approach from the local government to the province and then to the centre. I am of the view that local government system is real democracy and real empowerment of the people of Pakistan. This is empowerment in three areas, political, administrative and financial empowerment. We are also giving funds at the gross root levels. In addition, for the first time women have been given 33% representation in the local government levels. We are also bringing the empowerment of farmers and labourers. We are bringing the poor people into the assemblies, and into the decision making process. They will sit as equals with the rich who have been looting them in the past. This is a silent revolution. You would have heard, read and seen various opinion in this regard. But the local government system is the most important step for Pakistan. We will not allow it to be reversed. It is Pakistan's requirement. It is the requirement of the people and it must continue.

Now, we shall come to the provincial level. We are considering holding provincial elections in October. Both provincial and national elections will be held in October as I have declared again and again. However, some people try to create doubt that perhaps elections will not be held. We want to ensure maximum autonomy at the provincial level. People say that local government under devolution of power plan has undone provinces. This is wrong. This view is peddled by either those who do not understand it, or those who want to create misgivings in the minds of people. We have devolved power to the districts and now we are going to devolve power to the provinces. Provinces will get what they need. They will enjoy autonomy as enshrined in the Constitution. We will improve financial position of the provinces. We will provide funds to the provinces in accordance with Provincial Finance Award. We are trying to address the acute financial situation faced by the provinces. We want to ensure that the nation, the provinces and the districts have smooth functioning under a comprehensive plan by October. This will promote provincial harmony and any apprehensions God willing will end.

Now let us come to national level. In my view, it is important to keep democracy on [the] rails. Democracy should never derail. It must take root in Pakistan. It must function. This is what I want. I want to bring real democracy to the country because it is the only way out. I am not trying to deceive nor I am indulging in hypocrisy. Democracy is the only way and I want it.

Now the question is that democracy does not have any set rule. Democracy is not a constant factor. I have said this to foreign dignitaries. I said the same thing to the Commonwealth Secretary General when he came to see me. British model democracy cannot be introduced in Pakistan or the democracy in Zimbabwe be introduced in Pakistan or any other democracy in the East. Democracy has to be adjusted according to environment, prevailing local environment.

Democracy in Pakistan should be based on [the] environment in Pakistan. Now what is the environment in Pakistan? I will explain to you my own views in this regard. As I have always said there are four pre-requisites for the functioning of democracy. These pre-requisites have been derived from our past political history. We have to cover what has been happening here. We have to negate that. Number one is checks and balances on the power brokers of Pakistan. People are shy of naming power brokers. There have been three power brokers, namely President, Prime Minister and Chief of Army Staff. I am the Chief of Army Staff and a power broker. There should be checks and balances for me. There must be checks and balances for all the three power brokers.

I am saying this because the three power brokers have in the past committed violation. Let us not get into that debate. That is why; there should be checks and balances. This is the realistic approach.

The second thing is that national interest should be supreme. Let me ask whether governments in the past kept the national interest supreme? ... National interest was not kept in view while making laws or introducing constitutional amendments. Personal interest and political interest took precedence. Rules and regulations were manipulated and national industry was damaged for petty personal gains. . . . National interest should remain supreme above personal and political interest. I am saying this because the previous governments were not doing that.

The third point is to ensure continuity of our restructuring and reforms programmes. In my view this is in the best interest of Pakistan. This should continue. Whatever we have done in political, economic and governance areas must continue.

Finally, there was inter-provincial disharmony. Hatred against each other must end. A strong Pakistan should be governed on the basis of justice and total integration.

Now, the first three objectives including national interest, checks and balances and continuity of reforms should be institutionalized. That is why we are thinking of setting up the National Security Council. I will not go into details. You will know about its composition. People will be informed when we decide about it as was done in case of local governments.

First, we will make up our own mind and then your views will be invited. The decision will be taken after that in the interest of Pakistan. The idea is not based on any negative point of view. It is not meant to dismiss any government. The foremost objective of National Security Council should be to reinforce the government, to strengthen and to help it do what good it may be doing. You have seen the atmosphere in the Assembly where there was leg pulling so that no government could complete its five year tenure. Efforts were made to demolish the government after a year. This situation will not be allowed to repeat. The National Security Council will ensure completion of tenure of governments so that the government will focus on development of the nation.

The second aim should be checking every one including the Chief of Army Staff, Prime Minister and the President from taking any unbalanced, impulsive action. Now, someone can say that the elected government should be supreme and why the need for an undemocratic Security Council. The problem is that the elected governments have been indulging in loot and corruption. It destroyed governance. It destroyed economy. Our problem is that those who are voted into power and trusted by the people, betrayed that trust. Should there not be check on them? Check must be there. We are thinking on these lines.

There are people who say there should be no amendment in the Constitution but no responsible or educated person can say this. The Supreme Court has allowed amendments in the Constitution. However, amendments will not be based on whims. National interest will be kept in view while amending the Constitution. No Assembly brought amendments in the interest of Pakistan. Why should we not bring some amendments in the interest of Pakistan and for the promotion of the democratic environment? However, I shall take along the people while deciding on any constitutional amendments. I will invite their views and then decide. I shall not take any impulsive decision alone, nor for myself.

There is lot of talk of "power sharing" as if I am going to have powers as President of Pakistan. The problem is that everything is viewed in the negative perspective because of the pessimistic trend. Such has been our history based on fraud and hypocrisy. I want to say that I am not power hungry. I do not believe in power sharing. I am a solider and believe in the unity of command. I believe that there should be one authority to run things rightly. If there are two authorities nothing can be accomplished properly. What I want to say is that in the parliamentary system, the Prime Minister is the Chief Executive of the Country. He will have all the powers. He must run the government with all the authority. I have firm belief that the Prime Minister should have power and I

173

do not want to share this power. However, I want to have power to the extent that he dares not undo what I have done. He dare not violate national interests. He dare not reverse the reforms agenda. I want to assure that I will support the Prime Minister if he practices governance rightly and in the interest of Pakistan. I will back him up. I will strengthen him fully. That is how democracy in Pakistan will function. I cannot allow him to manipulate institutions. Banks, State Bank and nationalized banks were plundered in the past. This will not be allowed. So there is no question of sharing of power. I want to ensure checks and balances on the functioning of every one. Authority not only to govern, but also to govern well. Authority does not mean that one should indulge in corruption and loot without being challenged. We will not let this happen again. This is not democracy.

Now way forward. Ladies and Gentlemen the world has changed in the wake of September 11 events. What is our role in the changed world? I am proud to note that we have been able to raise our stature. We have saved the economy. We have preserved the national interest. This is our achievement. Now Pakistan enjoys prestige abroad.

Now, no one is saying that you are a failed state. No one is saying that we should be declared as terrorist state, a Damocles sword hanging on our heads every year. I had clearly enunciated in my 12th January speech and I will make a brief mention of it. We brought internal stability. Internal stability is important. We will establish the writ of the government and the supremacy of law. For this we will have to eliminate sectarian violence, extremism and internal terrorism. We have to address it. I had mentioned what the government was doing. We are pursuing the same path. Another factor of internal stability is our national development strategy, which we will have to pursue relentlessly. This is our way forward.

NATIONAL TASK FORCE
ON COLLEGE DRINKING
April 9, 2002

Two new studies about the incidence and consequences of underage and binge drinking showed that problems were far more serious than many people had thought. A federal task force on college drinking reported in April that an estimated 1,400 college students died each year in alcohol-related accidents, while another 500,000 were injured. Some 600,000 college students were assaulted every year by another student who had been drinking, and more than 70,000 were the victims of alcohol-related sexual abuse or date rape. According to the task force, an estimated 44 percent of college students engaged in binge drinking, which was defined as consuming five or more drinks in a row for men and four or more drinks in a row for women. A report by the National Center on Addiction and Substance Abuse (CASA) at Columbia University found that nearly one-third of all high school students admitted to binge drinking at least once a month.

Excessive and binge drinking among youth had far-ranging consequences, according to the two studies. It was implicated in date rape, unsafe sex, racial disturbances, academic problems and school dropouts, property damage, suicide, and accidental death and injury. These statistics did not factor in damage to academic achievement, health, and college facilities. There was also some evidence that excessive alcohol use could cause brain damage, including memory loss even after the effects of the alcohol had worn off and perhaps impairment to the nervous system.

According to the CASA study, alcohol was the leading drug of abuse among American teens. Eighty percent of all high school students had tried alcohol, compared with 70 percent who had smoked cigarettes and 47 percent who had used marijuana. Moreover, the proportion of children who began drinking in the eighth grade or earlier had jumped by about one-third since 1975, from 27 percent to 36 percent. The CASA study, "Teen Tipplers: America's Underage Drinking Epidemic," was released February 26, 2002.

Teenage drinking was also cited by the CASA study as the leading cause of adult alcoholism. People who began drinking before age twenty-one were more than twice as likely to develop alcohol problems as adults. Those who *began drinking before age fifteen were four times as likely to become alcoholics than those people who did not drink before age twenty-one. CASA estimated the total financial costs of underage drinking at $53 billion a year. The National Institute on Alcohol Abuse and Alcoholism estimated that the annual costs of alcohol abuse for all drinkers, adult and teenagers, was $185 billion.*

Contributors to Underage Drinking

CASA focused much of its study on underlying factors contributing to the high numbers of underage drinkers. Easy access to alcohol and parental permissiveness were two major factors in the equation. The entertainment media , the report said, often glamorized drinking, frequently associating it with wealth and sexual activity in the movies, while rarely showing the downside of alcohol abuse. The report saved some of its harshest criticism for the alcoholic beverage industry itself, claiming that it encouraged underage drinking through both its products and its marketing. According to the report, two-fifths of all teens fourteen to eighteen years old had tried the new sweet-tasting alcoholic beverages known as "malternatives" or "alcopops." The report also said the industry used marketing tactics similar to those used by cigarette makers that appealed particularly to youngsters, such as animation and animal characters, and advertised in venues likely to be seen by large numbers of teens, such as sports events. (Cigarette marketing to children, Historic Documents of 1996, p. 589)

The report said that the alcohol industry clearly had a conflict of interest in trying to reduce underage drinking. "Without sales to underage drinkers, the alcoholic beverage industry and the beer industry in particular, would experience severe economic declines and dramatic loss of profits," the report said.

The federal Task Force on College Drinking, established by the National Advisory Council on Alcohol Abuse and Alcoholism, looked at factors that contributed to excessive or binge drinking among college students. It found that students who drank the most tended to be white males, athletes, and fraternity or sorority members. The study also found that some first-year students who lived on campus were at high risk for alcohol abuse during the difficult transition from high school to college.

Task Force Recommendations

The task force looked not only at the incidence of drinking on campus, but also at ways to reduce excessive and binge drinking by changing the culture that sanctioned such behavior. Without changing the social norms and culture that supported drinking, the task force said, efforts to curb individual abuse were likely to be unsuccessful. "You have to first admit that you have the problem. Most colleges and universities don't really want to do that. Their efforts to deal with the problem are pretty half-hearted," said Robert L. Carothers, president of the University of Rhode Island and a task force member. The university had recently imposed a ban on drinking at all college functions, including faculty dinners, in an effort to reverse its reputation as a "party school."

The task force found that changing the culture of drinking required prevention programs that targeted three groups: individuals, including drinkers; the student population as a whole; and the college and its surrounding community. Focusing on the individual was crucial, the task force said, but the approach would be much more successful if the general student population and the surrounding community were targeted at the same time. Specific factors that affected the general school population as a whole were widespread availability and aggressive promotion of alcohol, large amounts of unstructured student time, inconsistent enforcement of laws and campus policies regarding use of alcohol, and a perception that heavy alcohol use was the norm. Cooperation between the college and the surrounding community was likely to have long-term benefits that could produce and enforce policies that improved the entire drinking environment.

The task force examined specific interventions that had been scientifically studied and then rated the effectiveness of each. For individual drinkers, the task force said a combination of interventions had been effective in reducing alcohol consumption. This combination included changing a person's expectations about the effects of alcohol and perceptions about the acceptability of excessive drinking, reinforced by motivation strategies that help the person change his or her behavior. But information or values clarification about the ill affects of excessive drinking, without any additional intervention to motivate a change in behavior, did not appear to be effective.

Examples of effective strategies included increased enforcement of the minimum legal drinking age, restrictions on the number of retail liquor outlets operating near campuses, and increased prices and taxes on alcoholic beverages. Among the strategies that had not yet been shown to be effective but that showed some promise were reducing end-of-week partying by reinstating classes and exams on Fridays and perhaps Saturday mornings, maintaining alcohol-free dorms, eliminating campus keg parties, regulating happy hours, refusing sponsorship gifts from the alcohol industry, and imposing an outright ban on alcohol on campus.

Survey of Attitudes on Substance Abuse

In August CASA released a report on teen attitudes about substance abuse. Interviewers spoke with 1,000 teens aged twelve to seventeen and to 541 parents, asking specifically about sibling influence on a teen's use of alcohol, drugs, or other substance abuse. Two-thirds of the teens with older brothers and sisters said those siblings would be "very angry" if they discovered the teen was using marijuana. The survey found that those teens were at a substantially lower risk of substance abuse than teens who thought their older siblings would not be very angry.

At the same time, nearly 50 percent of the teens thought their older siblings had tried illegal drugs. These teens were at higher risk for substance abuse than the average teen. Twelve percent of the teens with older siblings said that the older brother or sister had given them or encouraged them to use illegal drugs. These teens were almost twice as likely to smoke, drink, or use illegal drugs than the average teen.

The survey also found that parents had a bleak view of their ability to influence their teenage children to stay away from cigarettes, booze, and drugs. More than 30 percent said they thought parents had little influence over their teenage children, and parents were far more likely to predict that their children would use drugs than their children were. In an opening statement, Joseph A. Califano Jr., chairman and president of CASA, said that "parents who think they have no power over their teens are pulling the wool over their own eyes." Years of CASA studies showed that "parents are the most important resource we have to prevent substance abuse in our teens," Califano said.

In a related development, the outcome of a court case in Pennsylvania might have motivated some parents to think twice about permitting drinking at their teenagers' parties. In September a woman was convicted of involuntary manslaughter and later sentenced to at least three years in prison after a teenager left a party at her house drunk, crashed his car, and killed himself and two passengers. "This is a landmark case," said Wendy Hamilton, president of Mothers Against Drunk Driving. "I think this sends a very strong message to every parent in the country. There are too many adults who think that drinking underage is a rite of passage. It is not."

Alcohol Advertising

In two separate reports, the Center on Alcohol Marketing and Youth at Georgetown University reported that teenagers were often exposed to more advertisements and commercials for alcoholic beverages than adults. On September 24 the center released a study that compared 80 percent of all alcohol advertising in magazines with data on the numbers of adults and teenagers reading those magazines. The study found that adolescents ages twelve through twenty saw 45 percent more magazine ads for beer and 27 percent more ads for liquor than did adults. The second study, released on December 17, found that young people saw two beer or ale commercials on television for every three such commercials shown around programming watched primarily by adults.

Jim O'Hara, the executive director of the center, said the studies would be forwarded to the Federal Trade Commission (FTC), which in 1999 urged the alcohol beverage industry to adopt stricter guidelines to reduce marketing to people under age twenty-one. The industry regulated its own advertising, but O'Hara said the studies made clear that the industry was "falling far short of the kind of steps that the FTC said should be taken to protect youth."

Industry officials denied that it targeted its marketing to underage drinkers and rejected the findings of both studies. "The way to address illegal underage drinking is to encourage others to get behind programs that are working [to reduce underage drinking] instead of wasting valuable time censoring advertising to adults of legal drinking age," the Beer Institute said in a statement.

Following are excerpts from the report "A Call to Action: Changing the Culture of Drinking at U.S. Colleges," released April 9, 2002, by the Task Force of the National Advisory Council on Alcohol Abuse and Alcoholism, a unit of the National Institutes of Health.

The document was obtained from the Internet at www .collegedrinkingprevention.gov/images/TaskForce/ TaskForceReport.pdf; accessed October 14, 2002.

Introduction

Other than the damage and injuries that occur during spring break each year, the only consequences of college drinking that usually come to the public's attention are occasional student deaths from alcohol overuse (e.g., alcohol poisoning) or other alcohol-related tragedies. They prompt a brief flurry of media attention; then, the topic disappears until the next incident. In fact, the consequences of college drinking are much more than occasional; at least 1,400 college student deaths a year are linked to alcohol, as new research described in this report reveals. High-risk drinking also results in serious injuries, assaults, and other health and academic problems, and is a major factor in damage to institutional property. The relative scarcity of headlines about college drinking belies an important fact: the consequences of excessive college drinking are more widespread and destructive than most people realize. While only isolated incidents tend to make news, many school presidents conclude that these pervasive, albeit less obvious, problems are occurring on their campuses at the same time. It is a persistent and costly problem that affects virtually all residential colleges, college communities, and college students, whether they drink or not.

The call to action on campus has to do not so much with drinking per se, but with the consequences of excessive drinking by college students. Students who drink excessively have higher rates of injuries, assaults, academic problems, arrests, vandalism, and other health and social problems, compared with their nondrinking counterparts. They disrupt the studies and threaten the health and safety of their peers.

College Drinking Is a Culture

The tradition of drinking has developed into a kind of culture—beliefs and customs—entrenched in every level of college students' environments. Customs handed down through generations of college drinkers reinforce students' expectation that alcohol is a necessary ingredient for social success. These beliefs and the expectations they engender exert a powerful influence over students' behavior toward alcohol.

Customs that promote college drinking also are embedded in numerous levels of students' environments. The walls of college sports arenas carry advertisements from alcohol industry sponsors. Alumni carry on the alcohol tradition, perhaps less flamboyantly than during their college years, at sports events and alumni social functions. Communities permit establishments near campus to serve or sell alcohol, and these establishments depend on the college clientele for their financial success.

Students derive their expectations of alcohol from their environment and from each other, as they face the insecurity of establishing themselves in a new social milieu. Environmental and peer influences combine to create a culture of drinking. This culture actively promotes drinking, or passively promotes it, through tolerance, or even tacit approval, of college drinking as a rite of passage.

The Answer: Change the Culture.

The Question: How?

When a student dies from intoxication or another alcohol-related incident makes headlines, college drinking captures the public's attention, for a while. On the campus itself, administrators deal with the immediate problem, and campus life soon returns to normal. Generally, the incident doesn't result in effective, long-term changes that reduce the consequences of college drinking.

Among the reasons for this seeming inattention to long-term solutions is that administrators see college drinking as an unsolvable problem. When schools have made efforts to reduce drinking among their students—and many have made considerable effort—they haven't had significant, campus-wide success. With each failed effort, the image of college drinking as an intractable problem is reinforced, administrators are demoralized, and the likelihood that schools will devote resources to prevention programs decreases.

One reason for the lack of success of prevention efforts is that, for the most part, schools have not based their prevention efforts on strategies identified and tested for effectiveness by research. Research on college drinking is a relatively young field, and the data are incomplete. Until the recent formation of the Task Force on College Drinking, administrators and researchers did not typically collaborate on this topic. Without the expertise of the research community, administrators were at a disadvantage in trying to identify and implement strategies or combinations of strategies to address alcohol problems specific to their schools.

The Task Force on College Drinking brought together experienced administrators and scientists, who assessed what both schools and researchers need to do to establish effective prevention programs. On the basis of their findings, they made the recommendations contained in this report. Their recommendations focus not on how to effect some type of blanket prohibition of drinking, but on changing the culture of drinking on campuses and involving the surrounding communities.

Foremost among their recommendations is that to achieve a change in culture, schools must intervene at three levels: at the individual-student level, at the level of the entire student body, and at the community level. Research conducted to date strongly supports this three-level approach. Within this overarching structure, schools need to tailor programs to address their specific alcohol-related problems. Underlying each recommendation is the Task Force's understanding that no two schools are alike, that environmental influences as well as individual student characteristics impact alcohol consumption, and that effective strategies extend beyond the campus itself to encompass the surrounding community.

The Task Force's focus is on how to change the culture that underlies alcohol misuse and its consequences on campus, rather than on simply determining the number of negative alcohol-related incidents that occur each year. But because data on the consequences of college drinking underscore the need for effective prevention strategies, these data are included in the section that follows. The report offers (1) a general approach to incorporating prevention programs on campus, (2) specific interventions that schools can combine to meet the needs of their campuses, and (3) recommendations for future research on college drinking. . . .

Heavy Episodic Consumption of Alcohol

Data from several national surveys indicate that about four in five college students drink and that about half of college student drinkers engage in heavy episodic consumption. Recent concerns have, therefore, often focused on the practice of binge drinking, typically defined as consuming five or more drinks in a row for men, and four or more drinks in a row for women. A shorthand description of this type of heavy episodic drinking is the "5/4 definition." Approximately two of five college students—more than 40 percent—have engaged in binge drinking at least once during the past 2 weeks, according to this definition. It should be noted, however, that colleges vary widely in their binge drinking rates—from 1 percent to more than 70 percent—and a study on one campus may not apply to others.

The U.S. Surgeon General and the U.S. Department of Health and Human Services (USDHHS) have identified binge drinking among college students as a major public health problem. In "Healthy People 2010," which sets U.S. public health goals through the year 2010, the Federal government has singled out binge drinking among college students for a specific, targeted reduction (e.g., from 39 percent to 20 percent) by the year 2010. "Healthy People 2010" notes that: "Binge drinking is a national problem, especially among males and young adults." The report also observes that: "The perception that alcohol use is socially acceptable correlates with the fact that more than 80 percent of American youth consume alcohol before their 21st birthday, whereas the lack of social acceptance of other drugs correlates with comparatively lower rates of use. Similarly, widespread societal expectations that young persons will engage in binge drinking may encourage this highly dangerous form of alcohol consumption."

There is evidence that more extreme forms of drinking by college students are escalating. In one study, frequent binge drinkers (defined as three times or more in the past 2 weeks) grew from 20 percent to 23 percent between 1993 and 1999. The number of students who reported three or more incidents of intoxication in the past month also increased. It should be noted, however, that the number of college students who do not drink is also growing. In the same study, the percentage of abstainers increased from 15 to 19 percent. . . .

Factors Affecting Student Drinking

Living Arrangements

The proportion of college students who drink varies depending on where they live. Drinking rates are highest in fraternities and sororities followed by on-campus housing (e.g., dormitories, residence halls). Students who live independently off-site (e.g., in apartments) drink less, while commuting students who live with their families drink the least.

College Characteristics

Although the existing literature on the influence of collegiate environmental factors on student drinking is limited, a number of environmental influences working in concert with other factors may affect students' alcohol consumption. Colleges and universities where excessive alcohol use is more likely to occur include schools where Greek systems dominate (i.e., fraternities, sororities), schools where athletic teams are prominent, and schools located in the Northeast.

First-Year Students

Some first-year students who live on campus may be at particular risk for alcohol misuse. During their high school years, those who go on to college tend to drink less than their noncollege-bound peers. But during the first few years following high school, the heavy drinking rates of college students surpass those of their noncollege peers, and this rapid increase in heavy drinking over a relatively short period of time can contribute to difficulties with alcohol and with the college transition in general. Anecdotal evidence suggests that the first 6 weeks of enrollment are critical to first-year student success. Because many students initiate heavy drinking during these early days of college, the potential exists for excessive alcohol consumption to interfere with successful adaptation to campus life. The transition to college is often so difficult to negotiate that about one-third of first-year students fail to enroll for their second year.

Other Factors Affecting Drinking

Numerous other factors affect drinking behavior among college students. These include biological and genetic predisposition to use, belief system and personality, and expectations about the effects of alcohol. In addition to individual student characteristics, the size of a student body, geographical location, and importance of athletics on campus are also associated with consumption patterns as are external environmental variables including the pricing and availability of alcohol in the area surrounding a campus.

Although some drinking problems begin during the college years, many students entering college bring established drinking practices with them. Thirty percent of 12th-graders, for example, report binge drinking in high school, slightly more report having "been drunk," and almost three-quarters report drinking in the past year. Colleges and universities "inherit" a substantial number of drinking problems that developed earlier in adolescence.

Comparison with Noncollege Peers

College drinking occurs at a stage in life when drinking levels are generally elevated. Compared to all other age groups, the prevalence of periodic heavy or high-risk drinking is greatest among young adults aged 19 to 24; and among young adults, college students have the highest prevalence of high-risk drinking. Although their noncollegiate peers drink more often, college students tend to drink more heavily when they do drink.

Secondhand Consequences of Drinking

Students who do not drink or do not abuse alcohol experience secondhand consequences from others' excessive use. In addition to physical and sexual assault and damaged property, these consequences include unwanted sexual advances and disrupted sleep and study. The problems produced by high-risk drinking are neither victimless nor cost-free. All students—whether they misuse alcohol or not—and their parents, faculty, and members of the surrounding community experience the negative consequences wrought by the culture of drinking on U.S. campuses.

Post-College Consequences

The consequences of alcohol abuse during the college years do not end with graduation. Frequent, excessive drinking during college increases the prospects for continuing problems with alcohol and participation in other "health-compromising or illegal behaviors." On the other hand, in a prospective study of college students, researchers found that although fraternity/sorority membership is associated with high levels of alcohol consumption in college, Greek status did not predict post-college heavy drinking levels.

Overall, these data indicate that high-risk drinking exposes students, either directly or indirectly, to unacceptable risks. . . .

A Call to Action: Recommendations for Addressing Excessive College Drinking

To provide practical assistance to colleges and universities, the Task Force on College Drinking developed a series of recommendations on integrating research-based principles and practices in alcohol program planning. The Task Force also prepared recommendations specifically for researchers and NIAAA on the direction of future research and areas for potential collaboration with colleges and universities. All recommendations are based on scientific evidence, reflect a consensus among Task Force members, and represent the most objective guidance currently available on preventing risky drinking by college students. As such, the Task Force believes that these recommendations should serve as the basis for all interventions supported by national, state, and local organizations and implemented by colleges and communities.

Recommendations for Colleges and Universities

To change the culture of drinking on campus, the Task Force recommends that all colleges and universities adopt the following overarching approach to program development and then select appropriate strategies from among those presented on the following pages to tailor programs to the special needs of their schools.

Overarching Framework

The research strongly supports the use of comprehensive, integrated programs with multiple complementary components that target: (1) individuals, including at-risk or alcohol-dependent drinkers, (2) the student population as a whole, and (3) the college and the surrounding community. The 3-in-1 Framework presented here focuses simultaneously on each of the three primary audiences.

The Task Force members agreed that the 3-in-1 Framework is a useful introduction to encourage presidents, administrators, college prevention specialists, students, and community members to think in a broad and comprehensive fashion about college drinking. It is designed to encourage consideration simultaneously of multiple audiences on and off campus. The Task Force offers the 3-in-1 Framework as a starting point to develop effective and science-based prevention efforts.

The brief descriptions that follow provide the rationale for emphasizing these three targets in prevention programs aimed at high-risk student drinking and identify alternative prevention strategies that address each group.

(1) Individuals, Including At-Risk or Alcohol-Dependent Drinkers: The risk for alcohol problems exists along a continuum. Targeting only those with identified problems misses students who drink heavily or misuse alcohol occasionally (e.g., drink and drive from time to time). In fact, nondependent, high-risk drinkers account for the majority of alcohol-related problems.

It is crucial to support strategies that assist individual students identified as problem, at-risk, or alcohol-dependent drinkers. Strategies are clearly needed to engage these students as early as possible in appropriate screening and intervention services—whether provided on campus or through referral to specialized community-based services. One important effort to increase on-campus screening is National Alcohol Screening Day, an event that takes place in April each year. This program, supported by NIAAA and the Substance Abuse and Mental Health Services Administration, provides free, anonymous testing and health information at a growing number of colleges and universities.

(2) Student Body as a Whole: The key to affecting the behavior of the general student population is to address the factors that encourage high-risk drinking.

They include the:

- Widespread availability of alcoholic beverages to underage and intoxicated students;
- Aggressive social and commercial promotion of alcohol;

- Large amounts of unstructured student time;
- Inconsistent publicity and enforcement of laws and campus policies; and
- Student perceptions of heavy alcohol use as the norm.

Specific strategies useful in addressing these problem areas tend to vary by school. Examples of some of the most promising strategies appear in the section "Recommended Strategies" (please see below).

(3) College and the Surrounding Community: Mutually reinforcing interventions between the college and surrounding community can change the broader environment and help reduce alcohol abuse and alcohol-related problems over the long term. When college drinking is reframed as a community as well as a college problem, campus and community leaders are more likely to come together to address it comprehensively. The joint activities that typically result help produce policy and enforcement reforms that, in turn, affect the total drinking environment. Campus and community alliances also improve relationships overall and enable key groups such as student affairs offices, residence life directors, local police, retail alcohol outlets, and the court system to work cooperatively in resolving issues involving students.

Following are specific strategies that can be used within the 3-in-1 Framework to create programs addressing all three levels.

Recommended Strategies

The evidence supporting the substance abuse prevention strategies in the literature varies widely. These differences do not always mean that one strategy is intrinsically better than another. They may reflect the fact that some strategies have not been as thoroughly studied as others or have not been evaluated for application to college drinkers. To provide a useful list that accounts for the lack of research as well as negative findings, Task Force members placed prevention strategies in descending tiers on the basis of the evidence available to support or refute them.

Tier 1: Evidence of Effectiveness Among College Students

Strong research evidence (two or more favorable studies available) supports the strategies that follow. All strategies target individual problem, at-risk, or alcohol-dependent drinkers. Their efficacy as part of a campus-wide strategy has not been tested.

***Strategy:* Combining cognitive-behavioral skills with norms clarification and motivational enhancement interventions.** *Cognitive-behavioral skills training* strives to change an individual's dysfunctional beliefs and thinking about the use of alcohol through activities such as altering expectancies about alcohol's effects, documenting daily alcohol consumption, and learning to manage stress.

Norms or values clarification examines students' perceptions about the acceptability of abusive drinking behavior on campus and uses data to refute beliefs about the tolerance for this behavior as well as beliefs about the number of students who drink excessively and the amounts of alcohol they consume.

As its name implies, *motivational enhancement* is designed to stimulate students' intrinsic desire or motivation to change their behavior. Motivational enhancement strategies are based on the theory that individuals alone are responsible for changing their drinking behavior and complying with that decision. In motivational enhancement interventions, interviewers assess student alcohol consumption using a formal screening instrument. Results are scored and students receive nonjudgmental feedback on their personal drinking behavior in comparison with that of others and its negative consequences. Students also receive suggestions to support their decisions to change.

Research indicates that combining the three strategies is effective in reducing consumption. One example of such an approach is a program using motivational enhancement, developed by Marlatt. The program, the Alcohol Skills Training Program (ASTP), is a cognitive-behavioral alcohol prevention program that teaches students basic principles of moderate drinking and how to cope with high-risk situations for excessive alcohol consumption. The ASTP is designed for group administration and includes an alcohol expectancy challenge component. Controlled outcome studies show that the ASTP significantly reduces drinking rates and associated problems for both 1-year and 2-year follow-up periods.

Strategy: **Offering brief motivational enhancement interventions.** Students who receive brief (usually 45-minute), personalized motivational enhancement sessions, whether delivered individually or in small groups, reduce alcohol consumption. This strategy can also reduce negative consequences such as excessive drinking, driving after drinking, riding with an intoxicated driver, citations for traffic violations, and injuries. This approach has been used successfully in medical settings. An effective brief intervention has been developed at the University of Washington. This brief intervention for high-risk drinkers is based on the ASTP program and is known as the BASICS program: Brief Alcohol Screening and Intervention for College Students. BASICS is administered in the form of two individual sessions in which students are provided feedback about their drinking behavior and given the opportunity to negotiate a plan for change based on the principles of motivational interviewing. High-risk drinkers who participated in the BASICS program significantly reduced both drinking problems and alcohol consumption rates, compared to control group participants, at both the 2-year follow-up and 4-year outcome assessment periods. BASICS has also been found to be clinically significant in an analysis of individual student drinking changes over time.

Strategy: **Challenging alcohol expectancies.** This strategy works by using a combination of information and experiential learning to alter students' expectations about the effects of alcohol so they understand that drinking does not necessarily produce many of the effects they anticipate such as sociability and sexual attractiveness. The research conducted to date indicates that the positive effects of this strategy last for up to 6 weeks in men, but additional research is under way to verify and extend this approach to women and for longer time periods.

Tier 2: Evidence of Success With General Populations That Could Be Applied to College Environments

The Task Force recommends that college presidents, campus alcohol program planners, and student and community leaders explore the strategies listed below because they have been successful with similar populations, although they have not yet been comprehensively evaluated with college students. These environmental strategies are not guaranteed to alter the behavior of every college student, but they can help change those aspects of the campus and community culture that support excessive and underage alcohol use.

Strategy: **Increased enforcement of minimum drinking age laws.** The minimum legal drinking age (MLDA) law is the most well-studied alcohol control policy. Compared to other programs aimed at youth in general, increasing the legal age for purchase and consumption of alcohol has been the most successful effort to date in reducing underage drinking and alcohol-related problems. Most studies suggest that higher legal drinking ages reduce alcohol consumption, and over half found that a higher legal drinking age is associated with decreased rates of traffic crashes. Studies also indicate that policies are less effective if they are not consistently enforced. Moreover, the certainty of consequences is more important than severity in deterring undesirable behavior.

The benefits of the MLDA have occurred with minimal enforcement, yet studies of the effects of increased enforcement show that it is highly effective in reducing alcohol sales to minors. Increased enforcement—specifically compliance checks on retail alcohol outlets—typically cuts rates of sales to minors by at least half. Efforts to reduce the use of false age identification and tighter restrictions on "home delivery" of alcohol may also help enhance the effectiveness of this law.

Strategy: **Implementation, increased publicity, and enforcement of other laws to reduce alcohol-impaired driving.** Injury and deaths caused by alcohol-impaired driving and related injuries and deaths can be reduced by lowering legal blood alcohol limits to .08 percent for adult drivers; setting legal blood alcohol content (BAC) for drivers under age 21 at .02 percent or lower; using sobriety check points; providing server training intervention; and instituting administrative license revocation laws. Safety belt laws, particularly primary enforcement belt laws, have been shown in numerous studies to reduce traffic deaths and injuries. When California changed from a secondary to a primary enforcement belt law that permits police to stop vehicles and give a citation simply because an occupant was not belted, safety belt use rates increased 39 percent among drivers with BAC of .10 percent or higher compared to 23 percent overall. This indicates that primary enforcement belt laws can prevent many alcohol-related traffic fatalities. Comprehensive community interventions have also shown that increased enforcement and publicity of laws to reduce alcohol-impaired driving have produced significant reductions in the types of motor vehicle crashes most likely to involve alcohol and alcohol-related traffic deaths.

Strategy: **Restrictions on alcohol retail outlet density.** Studies of the number of alcohol licenses or outlets per population size have found a relationship between the density of alcohol outlets, consumption, and related problems such as violence, other crime, and health problems. One study, targeting college students specifically, found higher levels of drinking and binge drinking among underage and older college students when a larger number of businesses sold alcohol within one mile of campus. Numbers of outlets may be restricted directly or indirectly through policies that make licenses more difficult to obtain such as increasing the cost of a license.

Strategy: **Increased prices and excise taxes on alcoholic beverages.** A substantial body of research has shown that higher alcoholic beverage prices or taxes are associated with lower levels of alcohol consumption and alcohol-related problems. However, estimates of the extent to which consumption or problems change in response to a given price or tax change cover a fairly wide range. Some studies have examined these effects among young people separately from the general population. Most such studies have found that young people exhibit significant responses to price or tax changes, in some cases larger than responses estimated for the general population. An exception is the recent study by Dee, which found only small and statistically insignificant effects of beer taxes on teens' drinking behavior. In addition, Chaloupka and Wechsler found that higher beer prices tend to decrease drinking and binge drinking among U.S. college students, but that price is a relatively weak tool for influencing these behaviors among college students, especially males. In a study of the population aged 17 and older, Manning et al. found that consumption was responsive to price for all but the 5 percent of drinkers with the heaviest consumption, who exhibited no significant price response.

A number of studies have examined the effects of alcohol prices or taxes on traffic crash fatalities and other alcohol-related problems. Most such studies have reported that higher taxes or prices were associated with significant reductions in traffic crash fatalities or drunk driving, particularly among younger drivers and during nighttime hours. A few recent studies have questioned these findings. Dee found some evidence that beer taxes tend to reduce teen traffic fatalities, but concluded that those results were not robust and should be viewed with skepticism. Young and Likens found no significant effects of beer taxes on traffic crash fatality rates, either for young drivers or the general population. Mast et al. found mixed results, with several analyses indicating significant but relatively small effects of beer taxation on traffic fatalities. Other research has found associations between higher alcoholic beverage taxes and lower rates of some types of violent crime, reduced incidence of physical child abuse committed by women, and lower rates of sexually transmitted diseases, as well as with increases in college graduation rates.

Further research is needed to clarify the effects that alcoholic beverage prices or taxes have on different drinking behaviors, health-related outcomes, and population sub-groups, and to reconcile conflicting findings that have appeared in the literature. To date, however, the weight of evidence clearly suggests that higher prices and taxes can help to reduce alcohol consumption and alcohol-related problems.

Strategy: **Responsible beverage service policies in social and commercial settings.** Studies suggest that bartenders, waiters, and others in the hospitality industry would welcome written policies about responsible service of alcohol and training in how to implement them appropriately. Policies could include serving alcohol in standard sizes, limiting sales of pitchers, cutting off service of alcohol to intoxicated patrons, promoting alcohol-free drinks and food, and eliminating last-call announcements. Servers and other staff could receive training in skills such as slowing alcohol service, refusing service to intoxicated patrons, checking age identification, and detecting false identification. To prevent sales to underage patrons, it is important to back identification policies with penalties for noncompliance.

Strategy: **The formation of a campus and community coalition involving all major stakeholders may be critical to implement these strategies effectively.** A number of comprehensive community efforts have been designed to reduce alcohol and other substance use and related negative consequences among underaged youth, including college students, and among adults; and their outcomes demonstrate the potential effectiveness of this approach in college communities. For example, the Community Trials Program, which focused on alcohol trauma in the general population, resulted in a significant decline in emergency room admissions for alcohol-related assault. Both this program and Communities Mobilizing for Change (CMCA), which was designed specifically to reduce drinking among young people, resulted in reduced alcohol sales to minors. In the CMCA project young people ages 18 to 20 reduced their propensity to provide alcohol to other teens and were less likely to try to buy alcohol, drink in a bar, or consume alcohol. The Massachusetts Saving Lives Program, designed to reduce drunk driving and speeding in the general population, produced relative declines in alcohol-related fatal crashes involving drivers 15 to 25 years of age.

This approach reframes the issue as a community problem, not simply a college problem, brings together the range of players needed to address it, and sets the stage for cooperative action. In addition to college presidents and campus administrators, stakeholders in campus-community coalitions include student groups, faculty, staff, community leaders, law enforcement, and representatives from hospitality and alcohol beverage industries. Research shows that promoting community ownership of programs enhances success. On that basis, active campus and community coalitions can be expected to build support for addressing underage and excessive college drinking; help assure that strategies used respond to genuine community needs; maintain and, ultimately, institutionalize effective strategies; and evaluate and disseminate the results of the coalition's activities to other college communities.

Tier 3: Evidence of Logical and Theoretical Promise,
But Require More Comprehensive Evaluation

The Task Force recognizes that a number of popular strategies and policy suggestions make sense intuitively or have strong theoretical support. Many also raise researchable questions that may be crucial in reducing the consequences of college student drinking. Although the Task Force is eager to see

189

these strategies implemented and evaluated, it cautions interested schools to assemble a team of experienced researchers to assist them in the process.

The Task Force recommends that schools considering any of these strategies incorporate a strong evaluation component to test their viability in actual practice. Every strategy that appears below targets the student population as a whole.

Strategy: **Adopting campus-based policies and practices that appear to be capable of reducing high-risk alcohol use.** The following activities are particularly appealing because straightforward and relatively brief evaluations should indicate whether they would be successful in reducing high-risk drinking on a particular campus.

- Reinstating Friday classes and exams to reduce Thursday night partying; possibly scheduling Saturday morning classes.
- Implementing alcohol-free, expanded late-night student activities.
- Eliminating keg parties on campus where underage drinking is prevalent. Establishing alcohol-free dormitories.
- Employing older, salaried resident assistants or hiring adults to fulfill that role.
- Further controlling or eliminating alcohol at sports events and prohibiting tailgating parties that model heavy alcohol use.
- Refusing sponsorship gifts from the alcohol industry to avoid any perception that underage drinking is acceptable.
- Banning alcohol on campus, including at faculty and alumni events.

Strategy: **Increasing enforcement at campus-based events that promote excessive drinking.** Campus police can conduct random spot checks at events and parties on campus to ensure that alcohol service is monitored and that age identification is checked. It may be important for non-students to enforce these campus policies. Resident assistants and others charged with developing close supportive relationships with students might find it difficult to enforce alcohol-related rules and regulations consistently and uniformly.

Strategy: **Increasing publicity about and enforcement of underage drinking laws on campus and eliminating "mixed messages."** As indicated previously, active enforcement of minimum legal age drinking laws results in declines in sales to minors. Lax enforcement of State laws and local regulations on campus may send a "mixed message" to students about compliance with legally imposed drinking restrictions. Creative approaches are needed to test the feasibility of this strategy.

Strategy: **Consistently enforcing disciplinary actions associated with policy violations.** Inconsistent enforcement of alcohol-related rules may suggest to students that "rules are made to be broken." To test the effectiveness of this approach would likely require staff and faculty training, frequent communication with students, and the implementation of a research component.

Strategy: **Conducting marketing campaigns to correct student misperceptions about alcohol use.** On the basis of the premise that students overestimate the amount of drinking that occurs among their peers and then fashion their own behavior to meet this perceived norm, many schools are now actively conducting "social norming" campaigns to correct many of these misperceptions.

Strategy: **Provision of "safe rides" programs.** Safe rides attempt to prevent drinking and driving by providing either free or low-cost transportation such as taxis or van shuttles from popular student venues or events to residence halls and other safe destinations. Safe rides are usually restricted to students, faculty, staff, and a limited number of "guests." Safe rides sponsors often include student government, Greek Councils, student health centers, campus police, Mothers Against Drunk Driving chapters, and other local community organizations, agencies, and businesses. They have been criticized as potentially encouraging high-risk drinking, and this possibly should be considered in design, promotion, and monitoring.

Strategy: **Regulation of happy hours and sales.** Happy hours and price promotions—such as two drinks for the price of one or women drink for free—are associated with higher consumption among both light and heavy drinkers. Research shows that as the price of alcohol goes up, consumption rates go down, especially among younger drinkers. Because many bars surrounding campuses attract students by promoting drink specials, restrictions on happy hours have the potential to reduce excessive consumption off campus. If colleges and universities have a licensed establishment on campus, drink specials could be prohibited or promotion of alcohol-free drinks and food specials could be encouraged. In nonlicensed settings on campus that serve alcohol, event planners could opt to limit the amount of free alcohol that is available and eliminate all self-service. Schools could also limit alcohol use to weekends or after regular class hours in an effort to separate drinking from activities more closely aligned with the core academic mission.

Strategy: **Informing new students and their parents about alcohol policies and penalties before arrival and during orientation periods.** There is some anecdotal evidence that experiences during the first 6 weeks of enrollment affect subsequent success during the freshman year. Because many students begin drinking heavily during this time, they may be unable to adapt appropriately to campus life. Alerting parents and students to this possibility early on (e.g., through preadmission letters to parents and inclusion of information in orientation sessions and in presidents' and student leaders' welcoming speeches) may help prevent the development of problems during this critical, high-risk period.

Tier 4: Evidence of Ineffectiveness

The Task Force recognizes that it is difficult or impossible to "prove" that a specific intervention approach is universally ineffective. Nevertheless, when there are consistent findings across a wide variety of well-designed studies, it is possible to conclude that an approach is not likely to be effective and that limited resources should be used in other ways. Additionally, if there is strong evidence that an intervention approach is actually harmful or counterproductive, recommendations not to use it can be made based on fewer studies.

The Task Force also notes that some interventions may be ineffective when used in isolation, but might make an important contribution as part of a multi-component integrated set of programs and activities. However, until there is evidence of a complementary or synergistic effect resulting from inclusion with other strategies, college administrators are cautioned against making assumptions of effectiveness without scientific evidence.

Strategy: **Informational, knowledge-based, or values clarification interventions about alcohol and the problems related to its excessive use, when used alone.** This strategy is based on the assumption that college students excessively use alcohol because they lack knowledge or awareness of health risks and that an increase in knowledge would lead to a decrease in use. Although educational components are integral to some successful interventions, they do not appear to be effective in isolation. Despite this evidence, informational/ educational strategies are the most commonly utilized techniques for individually focused prevention on college campuses.

Strategy: **Providing blood alcohol content feedback to students.** This strategy uses breath analysis tests to provide students accurate information on their BAC. It could be used as part of a research evaluation or to dissuade students from driving while under the influence or continuing to drink past intoxication. Providing this information to students who are drinking must be approached with caution. Some researchers have found that the presence of immediate breath analysis feedback can actually encourage excessive drinking when students make a contest of achieving high BACs. If BAC feedback is to be provided in naturalistic settings, the procedure should be carefully monitored for adverse effects and adjusted as necessary. . . .

UN WORLD ASSEMBLY DECLARATION ON AGING
April 12, 2002

The population of the world is aging rapidly. In 2002 one of every ten people in the world was sixty or older. By 2050 that ratio is expected to shrink to one in five and, for the first time in history, the world would have more people over sixty—about 2 billion—than it had children under age fifteen.

This dramatic aging of the population, attributable to decreasing fertility rates combined with increased longevity, had immense implications for society worldwide, affecting traditional patterns of savings, investment, and consumption; labor markets, pensions, and retirement; family composition and living arrangements; and health care. "The pervasive implications of the aging of the world population [constitute] a profound demographic revolution, whose impact has been compared to that of globalization," said Nitin Desai, the United Nations undersecretary for economic and social affairs.

Desai's remarks came as the United Nations General Assembly prepared to convene the Second World Assembly on Aging, April 8–12, in Madrid, Spain. The first assembly, which took place in 1982 in Vienna, drew up a plan of action to guide policy and action on problems associated with aging. The Madrid assembly approved a revised plan of action intended to help governments and societies develop strategies to enable older people to continue to contribute to society to the best of their ability. Such an approach was intended not only to relieve the pressures on societies and economies of caring for an aging population, but also to make productive use of the talents and skills held by this group that might otherwise be wasted.

An Aging World Population

According to new statistics released by the United Nations on February 28, life expectancy at birth had increased about twenty years since 1950, to a current level of sixty-six years. Men who reached age sixty could expect to live another seventeen years; women, an additional twenty years.

Moreover, the older population was itself aging, with the numbers of those over eighty rising the fastest. By 2050 at least one-fifth of the older population was expected to be at least eighty years old. The number of centenarians was expected to increase to 3.2 million from its current level of about 210,000.

At the same time that the older population was rising, the working population on which the elderly relied for support was declining. The worldwide ratio of working age people (those ages fifteen to sixty-four) to those over sixty-five had already fallen, from twelve to one in 1950, to nine to one in 2000. That ratio was projected to drop even more—to four to one—by 2050. This decline in this "potential support ratio" was likely to have a substantial effect everywhere but particularly in developed nations such as the United States that traditionally relied on current workers to pay the social security benefits of retirees.

In countries with high per capita incomes, fewer older people continued to work. According to the UN statistics, only 31 percent of men over age sixty remained economically active in more developed regions, compared with 50 percent of men over sixty in less developed regions. Without policy and social change, the United States "could have 70 million baby boomers—with all that talent and experience—sitting and collecting Social Security and using Medicare for up to three decades in retirement without being a vital part of the economic activity," Robert Butler, president of the International Longevity Center-USA, told the Associated Press.

The overall aging of the population was likely to present even greater challenges to developing countries, where the proportion of older people was smaller than in developed countries but was growing at a much faster rate. In France, for example, the elderly population grew from 9 percent to 14 percent over 140 years. In developing countries, the elderly population was expected to balloon from 8 percent to 20 percent in fewer than 50 years. Such growth was expected to place serious strains on countries already struggling to provide basic services, such as health care and education, and to build the infrastructure and institutions required to support a modern economy. "In Europe, countries became rich before they became old," Mohammad Nizamuddin, director of the UN Population Fund for Asia and the Pacific, told Reuters. "But in the developing world, countries are growing old before they are rich."

No matter where they lived, the elderly faced some common problems, including poverty, abuse, and neglect. The report "Abuse Against Older Persons," issued by the United Nations a week before the Madrid conference, catalogued physical, financial, and emotional abuses of the elderly. In some societies, for example, the elderly, especially elderly women, were often blamed for disasters such as floods and epidemics. "Women have been ostracized, tortured, maimed or even killed if they failed to flee the community," the report said. The report also noted that, although underreported, neglect and abuse of the elderly occurred in the United States and other developed countries. (Nursing home abuse, p. 117)

Building a Society for All Ages

Delegates from 159 countries and numerous nongovernmental and private sector organizations attended the Second World Assembly on Aging to review and revise the plan of action adopted by the 1982 assembly. As passed by acclamation on April 12, that revised plan of action called for "secure aging," empowering older people to participate fully in all aspects of economic, political, and social life; providing opportunities for individual development throughout life; guaranteeing economic, social, and cultural rights of older people; and ensuring gender equality among older people.

The ambitious plan of action outlined 35 objectives and 239 recommendations focused on three priorities: aging and development; health and well-being throughout life; and supportive environments. The plan urged governments to incorporate the needs of the aging into their development and poverty-eradication programs. The elderly should have adequate minimum incomes, be given opportunities to work if they so desired, and be provided adequate health care, housing, and food, the plan said.

The accompanying political declaration, also adopted by acclamation on April 12, pledged governments to eliminate all forms of discrimination, including age discrimination, and to eliminate all forms of neglect, abuse, and violence. Like the plan of action, it called for quick action to eliminate the debt problems of developing countries, particularly of the poorest countries. "Unless the benefits of social and economic development are extended to all countries, a growing number of people, particularly older persons in all countries and even entire regions will be marginalized from the global economy," the declaration said.

Trends in the United States

According to the Census Bureau, 13 percent of the world's population age eighty and older lived in the United States. Only China had a greater proportion of the "oldest old." The number of Americans who were 100 or older also increased, from 37,306 people in 1990 to 50,454 people in 2000. Altogether about 12 percent of the American population—some 35 million people—were sixty-five or older in 2000. Of those 9.2 million were eighty or older.

New data released in February showed that the United States might be trying to buck the aging trend. For the first time since 1971, women in 2000 had enough children to offset deaths in the United States, according to the National Center for Health Statistics. There were 4,058,814 births recorded in the United States in 2000, 2.5 percent more than in 1999, the center said. That amounted to an average of 2.13 children for every woman during her childbearing years, considered to be fifteen through forty-nine. An average of 2.1 was considered necessary for the population to replace itself one for one. The researchers said that the strong economy of the 1990s was probably a major factor in the increase.

The only age group whose birth rate did not increase was teenagers. Births among fifteen- to nineteen-year-olds dropped to an all-time low, to

48.5 for every 1,000 women in the age group. Altogether teenage births dropped 22 percent in the 1990s. Because abortions among teenage girls also dropped during this period, the decline was attributed to postponing sex and greater use of contraceptives.

The Power of Positive Thinking

According to at least one study, having a positive attitude about aging may help maintain a person's health and well-being. In 1975 researchers from Miami University in Ohio asked 660 people who were age fifty or older their opinions on a series of statements related to aging, such as "As you get older you are less useful." More than twenty years later, they compared the answers to death rates and found that, on average, those people who had a positive attitude about aging lived seven and a half years longer than those with a negative attitude. The researchers cautioned that a good attitude, on its own, was not enough to predict a long or even a healthy life. But, they said, a person with a positive attitude about growing old was more likely to make decisions and lifestyle choices that led to good health. Conversely, negative attitudes could lead to depression, which in turn could contribute to weight gain, arthritis, or cardiovascular problems, the researchers said. The study was published in the August issue of the Journal of Personality and Social Psychology.

Following is the text of the draft Political Declaration adopted April 12, 2002, by acclamation in Madrid, Spain, at the Second World Assembly on Aging, sponsored by the United Nations.

The document was obtained from the Internet at www.un .org/ageing/coverage/index.html.

Article 1

We, the representatives of Governments meeting at this Second World Assembly on Ageing in Madrid, Spain, have decided to adopt an International Plan of Action on Ageing 2002 to respond to the opportunities and challenges of population ageing in the twenty-first century and promote the development of a society for all ages. In the context of this Plan of Action, we are committed to actions at all levels, including national and international levels, on three priority directions: older persons and development; advancing health and well being into old age; and, ensuring enabling and supportive environments.

Article 2

We celebrate rising life expectancy in many regions of the world as one of humanity's major achievements. We recognize that the world is experiencing an unprecedented demographic transformation and that by 2050 the number of persons aged 60 years and over will increase from 600 million to almost

2,000 million and the proportion of persons aged 60 years and over is expected to double from 10 per cent to 21 per cent. The increase will be greatest and most rapid in developing countries where the older population is expected to quadruple during the next 50 years. This demographic transformation challenges all our societies to promote increased opportunities, in particular for older persons to realize their potential to participate fully in all aspects of life.

Article 3

We reiterate the commitments made by our heads of State and Governments in major UN conferences and summits and their follow-up processes, and in the Millennium Declaration, with respect to the promotion of international and national environments that will foster a society for all ages. We furthermore reaffirm the Principles and Recommendations for Action of the International Plan of Action on Ageing endorsed by the United Nations General Assembly in 1982 and the United Nations Principles for Older Persons adopted by the General Assembly in 1991, which provided guidance in areas of independence, participation, care, self-fulfillment and dignity.

3 bis: We emphasize that in order to complement national efforts to fully implement the International Plan of Action on Ageing 2002, enhanced international cooperation is essential. We therefore, encourage the international community to further promote cooperation among all actors involved

Article 4 (former 5)

deleted

Article 5 (former 2)

We reaffirm the commitment to spare no effort to promote democracy, strengthen the rule of law, promote gender equality, as well as to promote and protect human rights and fundamental freedoms, including the right to development. We commit ourselves to eliminate all forms of discrimination, including age discrimination. We also recognize that persons, as they age, should enjoy a life of fulfillment, health, security and active participation in the economic, social, cultural and political life of their societies. We are determined to enhance the recognition of the dignity of older persons, and to eliminate all forms of neglect, abuse and violence.

Article 5 bis

deleted

Article 6

The modern world has unprecedented wealth and technological capacity and has presented extraordinary opportunities: to empower men and women to reach old age in better health, and with more fully realized well-being; to seek the full inclusion and participation of older persons in societies; to enable older persons to contribute more effectively to their communities and to the development of their societies; and to steadily improve care and support for older persons as they need it. We recognize that concerted action is required to transform the opportunities and the quality of life of men and women as they age and to ensure the sustainability of their support systems, thus building the foundation for a society for all ages. When ageing is embraced as an achievement, the reliance on human skills, experiences and resources of [the higher age groups is naturally recognized as an asset in the growth of mature, fully integrated, humane societies.

6 bis: At the same time, considerable obstacles to further integration and full participation in the global economy remain for developing countries, in particular the least developed countries, as well as for some countries with economies in transition. Unless the benefits of social and economic development are extended to all countries, a growing number of people, particularly older persons in all countries and even entire regions will remain marginalized from the global economy. For this reason we recognize the importance of placing ageing in development agendas, as well as strategies for the eradication of poverty and in seeking to achieve the full participation in the global economy of all developing countries.

Article 7 (former 11)

deleted

Article 8 (former 7)

We commit ourselves to the task of effectively incorporating ageing within social and economic strategies, policies and action while recognizing that specific policies will vary according to conditions within each country. We recognize the need to mainstream a gender perspective into all policies and programmes to take account of the needs and experiences of older women and men.

new 8 bis: We commit ourselves to protect and assist older persons in situations of armed conflict and foreign occupation.

Article 9 (former 8)

deleted

Article 10 (former 12)

The potential of older persons is a powerful basis for future development. This enables society to rely increasingly on the skills, experience and wisdom of older persons, not only to take the lead in their own betterment but also to participate actively in that of society as a whole.

new 10 bis: We emphasize the importance of international research on ageing and age related issues, as an important instrument for the formulation of policies on ageing, based on reliable and harmonized indicators developed by, inter alia, national and international statistical organizations.

Article 11 (new)

The expectations of older persons and the economic needs of society demand that older persons be able to participate in the economic, political, social and cultural life of their societies. Older persons should have the opportunity to work for as long as they wish and are able to, in satisfying and productive work, continuing to have access to education and training programs. The empowerment of older persons and the promotion of their full participation, are essential elements for active ageing. For older persons, appropriate sustainable social support should be provided.

Article 12

We stress the primary responsibility of governments in promoting, providing and ensuring access to basic social services, bearing in mind specific needs of older persons. To this end we need to work together with local authorities, civil society, including non-governmental organizations, private sector, volunteers and voluntary organizations, older persons themselves and associations for and of older persons, as well as families and communities.

new 12 bis: We recognize the need to achieve progressively the full realization of the right of everyone to the enjoyment of the highest attainable standard of physical and mental health. We reaffirm that the attainment of the highest possible level of health is a most important worldwide social goal, whose realization requires action of many other social and economic sectors in addition to the health sector. We commit ourselves to provide older persons with universal and equal access to healthcare and services including physical and mental health services and we recognize that the growing needs of an ageing population require additional policies, in particular care and treatment, the promotion of healthy lifestyles and supportive environments. We shall promote independence, accessibility and the empowerment of older persons to participate fully in all aspects of society. We recognize the contribution of older persons to development in their role as caregivers.

Article 13 (new)

We recognize the important role played by families, volunteers, communities, older persons organizations and other community-based organizations in providing support and informal care to older persons in addition to services provided by Governments.

Article 14

We recognize the need to strengthen solidarity among generations, and intergenerational partnerships, keeping in mind the particular needs of both older and younger ones, and encourage mutually responsive relationships between generations.

Article 15 (former 9)

Governments have the primary responsibility to provide leadership on ageing matters and on the implementation of the International Plan of Action on Ageing 2002 but effective collaboration between national and local governments, international agencies, older persons themselves and their organizations, other parts of civil society, including non-governmental organizations, and the private sector is essential. The implementation of the International Plan of Action on Ageing 2002 will require the partnership and involvement of many stakeholders: professional organizations; corporations; workers and workers organizations; cooperatives; research, academic, and other educational and religious institutions; and the media.

Article 16 (new)

We underline the important role of the United Nations system, including the regional commissions in assisting the Governments, at their request, in the implementation, follow-up and national monitoring of the International Plan of Action on Ageing 2002, taking into account the differences in economic, social and demographic conditions existing among countries and regions.

Article 17 (former 15)

We invite all people in all countries from every sector of society, individually and collectively, to join in our dedication to a shared vision of equality for persons of all ages.

U.S. GOVERNMENT, OAS ON
FAILED COUP IN VENEZUELA
April 12, 13, and 18, 2002

Even for a region accustomed to turmoil, Venezuela exhibited exception-
ally bizarre political behavior during 2002. Leftist president Hugo Chavez
was deposed in April during a coup led by business and military leaders,
but he clawed his way back to power just two days later. Former U.S. presi-
dent Jimmy Carter and the Organization of American States tried, and
failed, to negotiate a settlement between Chavez and his opponents. A broad-
based general strike starting in December put thousands of protesters on the
streets of Caracas for weeks on end and severely damaged the Venezuelan
economy. Chavez defied the protests and by year's end seemed likely to be
able to hold on to power, at least for the short term, even at the risk of long-
term economic and political damage to his country.

The Mounting Political Crisis

Venezuela during the last four decades of the twentieth century had en-
joyed one of the most stable and democratic political systems in Latin
America. In a region famous for its violent military coups, Venezuela saw
the peaceful transfer of power to nine elected presidents—seven of them
from the opposition—after the last military dictator leader was ousted in
1958. Venezuela also experienced strong economic growth in the last part of
the century, fueled almost entirely by the production of oil. But there were
darker sides to Venezuela's success. Corruption became endemic in business
and government, and the benefits of prosperity went almost entirely to a
tiny elite, while the vast majority of the country's 24 million people were
mired deep in poverty.

Seeking to capitalize on growing public discontent, Chavez—then a lieu-
tenant colonel in the army—in 1992 led an attempted coup against the
elected government but failed to win enough support from his fellow officers.
After serving a two-year prison term, an undeterred Chavez ran for the
presidency in 1998 on a platform of redistributing the country's wealth,
privatizing the state-owned oil company, and revamping the Congress to

*eliminate corruption. With his populist rhetoric Chavez scored an over-
whelming victory over the two mainstream political parties that had dominated Venezuelan politics for decades.*

*Once in office, Chavez wrote a new constitution strengthening the presi-
dency, at the expense of the legislature, and in August 2000 won a new six-
year term. Chavez used deliberately provocative rhetoric and actions to
unnerve his domestic political opponents and to annoy the international
forces he said were arrayed against him—primarily the United States.
Some of his actions appeared to be primarily for public relations purposes,
such as aligning himself with Cuban leader Fidel Castro and visiting Iran,
Iraq, and Libya. However, Chavez carefully avoided more substantive actions, such as cutting off oil exports to the United States, that would have
severely damaged Venezuela's economy and isolated the country entirely
from its neighbors.*

*By 2002 Chavez had accomplished little of his principal electoral man-
date, to improve the lives of the impoverished majority among Venezuela's
24 million people. He did succeed in boosting some social services, in part
by recruiting the military to build schools and roads, but his key initiatives to redistribute the nation's wealth were undermined by steep swings
in world prices for oil, Venezuela's principal trading commodity. Chavez's
style of governing relied heavily on presidential decrees, accompanied by
harsh rhetorical attacks against those he considered his enemies, including
business leaders, the wealthy elite, trade unions, key military leaders, and
the United States. An economic decline in 2001, caused in large part by
sagging oil prices, undermined Chavez's popularity. Opponents staged a
one-day nationwide work stoppage on December 10, 2001, followed by mass
protests in January 2002. Polls showed public support for Chavez had
dropped from 56 percent in mid-2001 to about 30 percent in early 2002.*

*Chavez provoked April's political crisis with a frontal attack on the na-
tional oil company, Petroleos de Venezuela. Calling the state-owned firm a
"state within a state," Chavez in January and February fired the company
president and key members of the board and installed officials loyal to him.
Company employees organized protests and work slowdowns that reduced
production. More important, the protests galvanized opposition to Chavez
by business and union leaders, as well as conservative officers within the
military. A national strike on behalf of the oil workers shut down much of
the country's business activity on April 9, and some military officers began
talking openly of ousting Chavez.*

A Coup and Countercoup

*A giant rally organized by the country's major business and labor groups
on April 11 sparked the events leading to a coup. An estimated 150,000 to
200,000 people gathered in downtown Caracas to demand that Chavez step
aside. The protesters were confronted by large groups of Chavez supporters,
many of them young men armed with sticks and bottles. As the anti-Chavez
protesters neared the presidential palace, gunfire erupted in several parts of
the city. By the end of the day eighteen people were dead and more than 140*

wounded. Later investigations appeared to show that most, and perhaps all, of the dead had been killed by the national guard and Chavez supporters.

Chavez went on national television to appeal for calm, but the violence and the scale of the protests gave his political opponents an opportunity to act. Many of the country's senior generals demanded that Chavez resign; among them was the army commander, General Efrain Vasquez, who told reporters: "Mr. President, I was loyal to the end, but today's deaths cannot be tolerated." The military leaders then confronted Chavez at the presidential palace and, they said, secured his resignation—or at least his willingness to leave the palace. Chavez was then taken into detention at a nearby army base. Officers said they refused a request by Chavez to be sent to exile in Cuba.

Early the next day, April 12, Pedro Carmona—the head of Fedcamaras, the country's largest business federation—appeared at defense ministry headquarters and announced that he would lead a transitional junta until new elections could be held. An economist and long-time leader of Venezuelan business groups, Carmona had been among the most vocal critics of Chavez. In what amounted to a sweeping repudiation of Chavez's tenure, Carmona said he had dissolved the Congress and Supreme Court and nullified the 1999 constitution under which Chavez had won his six-year term in office.

Chavez's supporters refused to give up, however, and staged massive protests in Caracas and other cities around the country on April 13. Word spread that—contrary to what military leaders had claimed—Chavez had not resigned and was prepared to return to power. Officers at the country's largest air force base also refused to support the coup. Late that evening, Carmona announced that he was resigning, and his place was taken by Chavez's vice president. Hours later, early in the morning of April 14, Chavez reappeared at the presidential palace and said he was again assuming the presidency. Momentarily humbled by the experience of the coup, Chavez avoided his usual rhetorical attacks on opponents and instead appealed for "understanding," saying: "I am here and I am prepared to rectify whatever I have to rectify."

The U.S. Role

The events in Venezuela prompted many questions about whether the United States had actively or tacitly encouraged the coup against Chavez. The questions were natural, given the long history of U.S. intervention against leaders in Chile, Cuba, Guatemala, Nicaragua, Panama, and other Latin American countries. U.S. officials insisted that they had played no role in the coup, and Chavez himself said Venezuela, not Washington, was responsible. Even so, the U.S. reaction to the coup clearly indicated that the Bush administration was enormously pleased by the prospect of being rid of Chavez. White House spokesman Ari Fleischer said on April 12 that Chavez was ousted "as a result of the message of the Venezuelan people." That stance was echoed by the State Department, which issued a statement charging that "undemocratic actions committed or encouraged by the

Chavez administration provoked yesterday's crisis in Venezuela." While calling for democracy, U.S. officials pointedly did not demand a reversal of the coup.

This approach by the Bush administration stood in sharp contrast to the position of key Latin leaders, many of whom shared Washington's disdain of Chavez. Mexican president Vicente Fox quickly denounced the coup and said he would not recognize the new government until new elections were held. Argentina, Paraguay, and Peru also described the regime installed by the military on April 12 as illegitimate. Peru's president, Alejandro Toledo, who had led popular protests against his own predecessor, said Venezuela's neighbors were eager to support "the rule of law" even if they disagreed with Chavez. (Peru elections, Historic Documents of 2000, p. 923)

Behind-the-scenes diplomacy at the Washington headquarters of the Organization of American States (OAS) demonstrated how differently the United States and its Latin allies viewed the coup. As events were still unfolding in Venezuela, OAS diplomats met to draft a resolution on the situation. The Bush administration reportedly lobbied for language that did not condemn the coup but called for a quick return to democracy and peace in Venezuela. Latin diplomats, however, successfully demanded stronger language, adopted on April 13, denouncing the "alteration of the constitutional regime" and subtly invoking the prospect of sanctions and other penalties if democracy was not quickly restored.

A subsequent investigation by the State Department's inspector general found no evidence that U.S. officials actively encouraged the coup. A detailed report, released July 29, said U.S. diplomats had privately discouraged opposition figures when they talked about a potential coup. But the report acknowledged that, given the history of U.S. intervention in Latin America, Washington's calls for respect for democracy "may have rung hollow in the ears of Venezuelan political and military leaders."

Taken aback by widespread criticism of its public statements after the coup, the Bush administration later in the year repeatedly warned publicly against another coup and called on all sides in Venezuela to resolve their disputes peacefully. If nothing else, these statements appeared to discourage Chavez's opponents from the belief that Washington would again approve of another move to oust him.

A Return to Confrontation

In the immediate aftermath of the coup, it appeared possible that the events of mid-April might have cleared the air in Venezuela and given the country's rival factions space to seek a reconciliation. A relaxed and unusually jovial Chavez promised to meet his opponents, and he even spoke of the United States "with love and affection." But tension soon rose again as the national assembly began a bitter debate in which pro- and anti-Chavez legislators called each other "fascists" and "killers" and traded blame for Venezuela's polarized politics. After meeting with leaders on both sides, OAS secretary-general Cesar Gaviria bluntly warned in an April 18 report: "There seems to be a widespread conviction that renewed confrontation be-

tween friends and opponents of the government is inevitable and could lead to increased social protest."

Rival street demonstrations took place in Caracas on May 1—May Day—signaling a return to the politics of public protest. A legislative investigation into the events surrounding the coup dragged on for weeks in May and June and provided a forum for both sides to ratchet up the rhetoric: Chavez said he had been victimized by a "Nazi" opposition; opponents said he should resign for the sake of the country.

As tensions mounted, former U.S. president Carter visited Venezuela in early July but failed to persuade key opposition figures to meet with Chavez. "There is a mix of opinions within the opposition," Carter said told reporters July 9. "The fact that the opposition declined my invitation to meet with the president directly is dispiriting."

With prospects for another coup diminished, key opposition leaders turned to the tactic of calling a national referendum on Chavez's rule early in 2003. Chavez, in turn, cited a provision of the constitution (which he had written) allowing a binding referendum on his tenure—but only halfway through his six-year term, or no sooner than August 2003. This dispute over the timing of a referendum became the focal point of mass demonstrations in October and November, including a protest on October 11 in which nearly 1 million people crowded the streets of Caracas to demand a new vote. About 120 military officers on October 22 took over a public square in Caracas and openly demanded that Chavez step down; the government on November 15 fired fifteen of the most senior officers in the protest. Street demonstrations by opposing factions led to frequent violent clashes over the next several weeks. In the meantime, Gaviria of the OAS held frequent meetings with the opposing sides but failed to achieve an accommodation.

A General Strike

Venezuela's crisis deepened on December 2 when Chavez's opponents began a general strike to demand that he call a nonbinding referendum on his presidency on February 2, 2003, and then schedule new elections within thirty days if he lost the vote. The opposition was led by major labor unions and the national business federation—but these groups were unable to agree on a single candidate who could oppose Chavez if new presidential elections were held.

In some respects, the strike was an immediate success. Day after day through the rest of December (with a break for Christmas), tens of thousands of anti-Chavez protesters took to the streets of Caracas and other cities to demand "Elecciones ya!" ("Elections now"). More important, workers at the state-owned oil company joined the strike, halting all exports of oil by December 6. This was a major blow to Venezuela's economy and had worldwide implications. Oil accounted for more than three-fourths of Venezuela's exports and about one-half of government revenues. Venezuela was the world's fifth largest oil exporter and the third largest source of imported oil for the United States (behind Canada and Saudi Arabia). Oil prices rose quickly on world markets, topping $30 a barrel by late December for the first *time in two years. Venezuelans were among the first to suffer; within two weeks the country's gasoline supplies had been exhausted, and Venezuela found itself dependent on modest imports from some of its neighbors.*

Despite the far-reaching economic consequences, the general strike did not produce its intended result: a concession by Chavez to the demand for an early vote. Gaviria's formal negotiations between the two sides ended when the strike began, but informal talks continued and reportedly came close to producing a deal putting the referendum dispute in the hands of Venezuela's courts. That deal collapsed on December 3, however, when Chavez angrily denounced the anchoring of a government oil tanker in support of the strike. "Assaulting PDVSA [the oil company] is like assaulting the heart of Venezuela," Chavez said in a speech broadcast on national television. "Nobody stops Venezuela."

Still smarting from international criticism of its endorsement of the April coup, the Bush administration had carefully avoided taking sides in the subsequent protests. That changed on December 12, the twelfth day of the strike, when White House spokesman Fleischer said that "the only peaceful and politically viable path to moving out of the crisis is through the holding of early elections." Fleischer's statement appeared to endorse the original call by the anti-Chavez alliance for a referendum early in 2003, However, the White House pointedly refused to endorse a new demand by the protesters that Chavez resign immediately and allow elections in February 2003. Several U.S. foreign policy experts said the administration's chief concern now seemed to be the resumption of Venezuela's oil exports—even at the cost of Chavez remaining in power.

The anti-Chavez strike continued through the rest of December and into the first weeks of January 2003, but by year's end it appeared likely that a determined Chavez would hold on to power, at least for the time being. The military, the sector of society most vital to his presidency, generally stood behind Chavez, largely because he had ousted the senior officers who had supported the April coup. Chavez also retained the intense loyalty of most of the poor majority who had seen him as their champion. Moreover, the economic disruptions caused by the strike threatened eventually to undermine public support for it—putting more pressure on the protest leaders to halt the strike than on Chavez to step down.

> *Following are three documents: A statement on April 12, 2002, by U.S. State Department deputy spokesman Phillip T. Reeker commenting on the coup in Venezuela, a resolution adopted April 13 by the Permanent Council of the Organization of American States (OAS) expressing concern about the coup, and excerpts from a report to the OAS on April 18 by its secretary general, Cesar Gaviria, upon his return from a mission to Venezuela.*
>
> **The documents were obtained from the Internet at www.state.gov/r/pa/prs/ps/2002/9316.htm; www.oas.org/ consejo/resolutions/res811.htm; and www.oas.org/**

speeches/SecGeneral/2002/eng/041802-inf_VEe.htm;
accessed November 4, 2002.

U.S. STATE DEPARTMENT STATEMENT

In recent days, we expressed our hopes that all parties in Venezuela, but especially the Chavez administration, would act with restraint and show full respect for the peaceful expression of political opinion. We are saddened at the loss of life. We wish to express our solidarity with the Venezuelan people and look forward to working with all democratic forces in Venezuela to ensure the full exercise of democratic rights. The Venezuelan military commendably refused to fire on peaceful demonstrators, and the media valiantly kept the Venezuelan public informed.

Yesterday's events in Venezuela resulted in a transitional government until new elections can be held. Though details are still unclear, undemocratic actions committed or encouraged by the Chavez administration provoked yesterday's crisis in Venezuela. According to the best information available, at this time: Yesterday, hundreds of thousands of Venezuelans gathered peacefully to seek redress of their grievances. The Chavez Government attempted to suppress peaceful demonstrations. Chavez supporters, on orders, fired on unarmed, peaceful protestors, resulting in more than 100 wounded or killed. Venezuelan military and police refused orders to fire on peaceful demonstrators and refused to support the government's role in such human rights violations. The government prevented five independent television stations from reporting on events. The results of these provocations are: Chavez resigned the presidency. Before resigning, he dismissed the Vice President and the Cabinet. A transition civilian government has promised early elections.

We have every expectation that this situation will be resolved peacefully and democratically by the Venezuelan people in accord with the principles of the Inter-American Democratic Charter. The essential elements of democracy, which have been weakened in recent months, must be restored fully. We will be consulting with our hemispheric partners, within the framework of the Inter-American Democratic Charter, to assist Venezuela.

OAS RESOLUTION

THE PERMANENT COUNCIL OF THE ORGANIZATION OF AMERICAN STATES,

CONSIDERING that the Charter of the Organization of American States recognizes that representative democracy is indispensable for the stability, peace, and development of the region, and that one of the purposes of the OAS is to promote and consolidate representative democracy, with due respect for the principle of nonintervention;

REAFFIRMING the right of the peoples of the Americas to democracy and the obligation of governments to promote and defend it;

TAKING INTO ACCOUNT that the Inter-American Democratic Charter recognizes as essential elements of representative democracy, inter alia, respect for human rights and fundamental freedoms, access to and the exercise of power in accordance with the rule of law, the holding of periodic, free, and fair elections based on secret balloting and universal suffrage as an expression of the sovereignty of the people, the pluralistic system of political parties and organizations, and the separation of powers and independence of the branches of government;

REITERATING that transparency in government activities, probity, responsible public administration on the part of governments, respect for social rights, and freedom of expression and of the press are essential components of the exercise of democracy; and that the constitutional subordination of all state institutions to the legally constituted civilian authority and respect for the rule of law on the part of all institutions and sector of society are equally essential to democracy;

BEARING IN MIND the deterioration of the institutional order and of the democratic process in Venezuela; and

CONSIDERING that an alteration of the constitutional regime has occurred in Venezuela, which seriously impairs the democratic order and justifies the application of the mechanisms provided for in Article 20 of the Inter-American Democratic Charter,

RESOLVES:

1. To condemn the alteration of constitutional order in Venezuela.
2. To condemn the deplorable acts of violence that have led to the loss of human life.
3. To express solidarity with the people of Venezuela, and support their resolve to re-establish full democracy, with guarantees for citizens and respect for fundamental freedoms, within the framework of the Inter-American DemocraticCharter.
4. To call for the normalization of the democratic institutional framework in Venezuela within the context of the Inter-American Democratic Charter.
5. To send to Venezuela, as a matter of urgency, a Mission headed by the Secretary General of the OAS, with the aim of carrying out a fact-finding mission and undertaking the necessary diplomatic initiatives, including good offices, to promote as quickly as possible the normalization of the democratic institutional framework. The Permanent Council shall be kept informed of the initiatives taken.
6. To convoke in accordance with Article 20, third paragraph, of the Inter-American Democratic Charter, a special session of the General Assembly, to be held at OAS headquarters, on Thursday, April 18, 2002, to receive the report of the Secretary General and to adopt such decisions as it may deem appropriate.
7. To continue to consider this matter.

REPORT OF OAS SECRETARY GENERAL GAVIRIA

Distinguished foreign ministers:

After my talks with the various sectors, I would like to make the following points.

The President of the Republic [Chavez] , in all of his speeches, has spoken of reflection, of rectification, of amendment. He gave assurances "that there will be no desire for reprisals, for persecution, for abuse"; that what happened serves as a "major lesson"; "that the situation calls for deep reflection"; that it is necessary to act with "patience and good sense"; that it is necessary "to correct what needs to be corrected"; that "dialogue must be reestablished."

He spoke also of "unity while respecting differences" and noted that his first step would be to convene the Federal Council of Government as the epicenter of dialogue with all sectors, so as to reach the greatest possible degree of consensus in the economic, social, and political areas. He also stated that the president-designate of Petroleos de Venezuela [PDVSA – the state owned oil company] and the junta he appointed had resigned, which would put an end to the issue that gave rise to the recent protests.

Although a good number of representatives of organizations outside the government have accepted the call of the President for dialogue, even after the fateful events of April 11 and 12, there is excessive polarization, not only among the natural political actors, such as the government, the political parties, and opposition groups, but among almost all labor, business, and civil society groups, representatives of some other branches of government, and the media. This excessive polarization has shades of intolerance that stand in the way of democratic dialogue and the quest for agreements that would provide a degree of understanding so as to maintain social harmony. There seems to be a widespread conviction that renewed confrontation between friends and opponents of the government is inevitable and could lead to increased social protest.

I also want to note the development of a dangerous practice of debate within the armed forces. Many leaders of public affairs constantly listen for what the various armed forces have to say about political developments, and even about the orders of the Commander in Chief , Constitutional President of the Republic. Some cite an article of the Constitution as grounds for such debate.

Opposition groups and other leaders of society distance themselves from constitutional standards in different ways. In particular, they express concern about the separation and independence of the branches of government and the lack of checks and balances in the specific case of Venezuela, since they believe that the leading figures were chosen by political majorities within the Assembly. The opposition representatives in the Assembly have called attention to a recent ruling by the Supreme Court of Justice which concludes that the presidential term begins in January, 2002.

Since the events mentioned earlier, there have been increased reports of human rights violations, acts of intimidation, and significant acts of vandalism and looting, and increasing numbers of persons dead or injured. This happened before, during and after the recent crisis. . . .

For those reasons, at meetings with various sectors, I took the liberty of proposing actions I believe should be taken immediately to prevent further expressions of discontent that could bring about other tragic events like those of April 11 and 12. In any case, it is important to reiterate some of the preambular and operative paragraphs of the Permanent Council resolution, especially as they regard repudiation of any breach of the constitutional order and condemnation of the violent events in which a number of people lost their lives.

The OAS, its member countries, the international community, and other organizations such as the Catholic Church, via the Conferencia Episcopal, could assist in fostering dialogue to ensure that these incidents are not repeated.

I would like to highlight, as well, some measures that must be taken to diffuse some of the more serious conflicts, to regain governability, to achieve political stability, and to foster economic recovery.

It is fundamental that all sectors of society, at least all those I have referred to, seek mechanisms or agreements which ensure that respect for the Constitution is the foundation and framework of action for everyone in Venezuelan public life.

It is imperative that an agreement be reached so that Article 350 of the Constitution is not interpreted as everyone's right to rebellion. Such an interpretation might well lead to worse violence than that which has already occurred. Everyone must do their part to reach that understanding.

It is essential that the government, opposition, social actors, human rights organizations and the media commit to rejecting any participation in political debate on the part of the military, and to supporting military regulations which penalize this behavior. It is also essential that we abandon the interpretation held by some that that article of the constitution can serve as the basis for actions of any officials of the armed forces. I would like to reiterate that if we do not move in this direction, we could see new acts of insubordination against the civilian authorities. This General Assembly should be categorical in pointing out the obligation of constitutional subordination of all state institutions to the legally constituted civilian authority, as enshrined in Art. 4 of the Democratic Charter.

It is an absolute necessity to resort only to peaceful measures. The state, and let there be no doubt about this, must retain a monopoly on the legitimate use of force. The accusations that certain sectors are jeopardizing the legitimate use of force must be investigated. In all cases, any use of force must occur under authorization and within the normative framework to which the military adheres.

It is very important for Venezuela's democracy that the investigations into the tragic events surrounding the demonstrations of April 11 are conducted in such a way that their conclusions are accepted by all and that those responsible meet head-on the full weight of the law. What I say should not be interpreted as undermining the legitimately constituted authorities. With a good dose of political will, this can be achieved. In any case, we must learn from this experience because demonstrations with hundreds of thousands of people brings enormous risks.

We have been informed that the Assembly is considering setting up a commission of 25 members would be in charge of investigating the facts. There are differences with respect to the name of such a commission, the manner of its establishment and its composition.

The government and opposition should do everything within their reach to guarantee the separation of powers and effective checks and balances. Beyond the importance of establishing the supremacy of the Constitution, it is essential to re-establish complete confidence in the rule of law and ensure that all the pillars of society are to heed it. That is spelled out in Art. 4 of the Democratic Charter.

Whatever agreement is reached among the different sectors of Venezuelan society should, as the Democratic Charter indicates, fully respect freedom of expression and therefore of the press. It should be clear that any complaint or deficiency on this should be resolved in accordance with the Declaration of Chapultepec. This Secretariat publicly expressed its confidence that the government of President Chávez would resolve in a satisfactory manner concerns about security and intimidation alleged by representatives of the media with whom I met.

On the issue of television, it is important to come to an agreement on a code of conduct which, beyond the issue of laws, ensures compatibility between public interest television transmissions and the media's normal programming.

The international community should provide support to Venezuela to ensure that political parties and other political groups or movements once again become the principle actors in Venezuelan politics. The current vacuum, which other social sectors have sought to fill, has clearly demonstrated its limitations. . . .

NASA ON GALAXY IMAGES FROM NEW HUBBLE CAMERA
April 30, 2002

*A powerful new camera installed in March aboard the Hubble space tele-
scope quickly provided the clearest images ever taken of distant galaxies.
The camera's first images, made public by the National Aeronautics and
Space Administration (NASA) on April 30, 2002, showed dramatic colli-
sions of galaxies and at least one galaxy being formed about 12 billion years
ago when the universe was relatively "young"—about 1 billion years old.*

*Scientists said they hoped images from the new camera, along with the
observations from a renovated infrared camera on Hubble, would provide
answers to some of the most intriguing questions about the universe, including when and how stars first formed.*

Repairs to Hubble

*Launched in April 1990, the Hubble had a troubled early history. NASA
learned only after Hubble was in space that its light-gathering telescope did
not work properly because of a flaw in one of its three mirrors. Astronauts
aboard the space shuttle* Endeavor *repaired the flawed telescope in December 1993.* (Hubble flaws, Historic Documents of 1990, p. 753)

*Astronauts in 1997 installed a new $110 million instrument, the Near
Infrared Camera and Multi-Object Spectrometer (called NICMOS), which
was designed to detect distant objects by the infrared heat they emit. But a
cooling system needed to maintain the camera's sensors at a frigid 351 degrees below zero Fahrenheit failed in 1999, putting NICMOS out of action.*

*Another repair mission reached Hubble in March 2002, with the goal of
replacing much of the telescope's original scientific equipment. Astronauts
aboard the space shuttle* Columbia *spent the first week of March making repairs and installing $172 million worth of new equipment on Hubble as it
made its orbit about 350 miles above Earth. The main new piece of scientific
equipment was a powerful camera called the Advanced Camera for Surveys,
a $76 million item that was expected to provide images that were ten times
clearer than those from Hubble's original main camera. Astronauts also
installed new solar panels, electrical equipment, and a new refrigeration*

system for the NICMOS infrared camera. At one point the astronauts needed to turn off the Hubble's electrical power for the first time since the 1990 launch—a move that ran the risk of permanently crippling the telescope but proved to be successful. The mission involved five lengthy space walks and was declared a complete success.

NASA's associate administrator for space science, Edward Weiler, said the improved systems should keep the Hubble working at least until 2010, five years longer than the telescope's original life expectancy. The space agency on September 16 revealed plans for Hubble's successor mission, which was to be named after former NASA administrator James Webb and was scheduled to be launched in 2010.

Despite its many problems, Hubble during its first dozen years generated a bonanza of scientific findings that forced scientists to revise many of their theories about the universe and provided information for new speculation. Some of the most important information offered new clues to one of the most basic questions in science: the age of the universe. In 1994 NASA scientists used evidence from Hubble to conclude that the universe might be 8 billion to 12 billion years old, much younger than the 15 billion to 18 billion estimate that previous research had indicated. In 1996 more findings from Hubble led two separate groups of scientists to develop estimates of 9 billion to 14 billion years, and in 1999 scientists using a separate calculation method narrowed the range to 13 billion to 14 billion years. On April 24, 2002, astronomer Harvey B. Richer of the University of British Columbia published an estimate of the universe's age of "about 13 billion years" based on the Hubble's observations of the oldest burned-out stars in the Milky Way. Several leading scientists said they accepted this estimate as the best available given current information. But some skeptics held out for different (generally older) ages for the universe, noting that Richer's findings clarified the age of the Milky Way but not the entire universe. (Universe age, Historic Documents of 1994, p. 458; Historic Documents of 1996, p. 265)

First Images from the New Hubble

The newly refurbished Hubble began sending data back to Earth almost immediately, and on April 30 NASA was able to unveil the first four images from the new Advanced Camera for Surveys. Scientists said they were thrilled with the results: "When we saw the first images, my colleagues and I were stunned," said Holland Ford, the Johns Hopkins University astronomer who led the camera team. "We underestimated how extraordinary the images would be."

The scientists said they were particularly interested in one of the images that showed a collision of two galaxies in the constellation Draco, about 420 million light-years from Earth (a light year is the distance light travels in one year on Earth, or about 6 trillion miles). Scientists named the larger of the two galaxies the "Tadpole" because a streaming mass of stars and gas gave it the appearance of a giant, 280,000 light-year-long tadpole in space. NASA said this long tail of debris was the result of "strong gravitational forces" from the collision of the two galaxies.

The image published by NASA was a composite of three images taken between April 1 and 9. To a layperson, the Tadpole made for a spectacular picture. NASA scientists were even more intrigued by what was in the background: upward of 6,000 galaxies or parts of galaxies. Scientists concluded that the light now visible from one of those galaxies, which showed up as a faint red dot, left when the universe was only about 1 billion years old. "We are now looking back in time to when the universe was young, seeing light from processes that happened billions of years ago," Ford told the New York Times. *Such images ultimately would help scientists understand more about how stars were formed, he said.*

One of the other images released by NASA showed two galaxies, which scientists called the "Mice," apparently in the process of merging about 160 million years ago. Astronomers had hypothesized that the Milky Way galaxy (home to the Earth and its solar system) might one day engage in a similar merger with the neighboring Andromeda galaxy. There is plenty of time to prepare for that event, which is estimated to occur several billion years from now.

On June 5 NASA scientists made public the first three images from the renovated NICMOS infrared camera on the Hubble. Those images cut through much of the dust that often obscures views of space objects, enabling scientists to get a much clearer view than ever before of distant stars and galaxies. Two of the images showed the emergence of young stars hundreds or even thousands of light years from Earth. The third image revealed four small galaxies in the process of merging, or colliding, to form one large galaxy about 1 billion light years from Earth.

NASA released dozens of other images from Hubble during the year, all of them providing much clearer views of distant galaxies and other formations than had ever been seen before. As with the releases in April and June, some of the most stunning images showed galaxies in the process of colliding or merging. For example, an image released on December 12 showed a group of galaxies known as Seyfert's Sextet, which NASA said appeared as "a grouping of galaxies engaging in a slow dance of destruction that will last for billions of years." The galaxies were so close together, NASA added, that gravitational forces were beginning to rip stars from them and distort their shapes. Eventually, the galaxies could be forced together into one large galaxy.

Water on Mars

Findings from another NASA mission, the Mars Global Surveyor, *led some scientists in 2000 to hypothesize that large quantities of frozen water might lie just below the surface of Mars—the one planet in the solar system, other than Earth, long thought to have some of the conditions necessary for life. Information appearing to confirm that hypothesis became available in 2002, based on findings from NASA's newest major mission, the Mars* Odyssey. *Launched in 2000, the* Odyssey *entered into an orbit just 200 miles above the Martian surface in October 2001 and began making observations with an array of scientific instruments in February 2002.* (Water on Mars, Historic Documents of 2000, p. 379)

NASA scientists published findings from the Odyssey in late May suggesting that large quantities of water ice lay buried only one to three feet below the surface of Mars. The ice was near the planet's poles, particularly in the southern hemisphere. "This is more like dirty ice rather than dirt containing ice," said William Boynton, a geochemist at the University of Arizona's Lunar and Planetary Laboratory who led the team analyzing the Odyssey's data.

The finding cheered scientists and Mars buffs who had long pressed for more intense exploration of Mars, including a manned mission. If frozen water was near the planet's surface, astronauts conceivably could use it for drinking and could split it into oxygen for breathing and hydrogen to power their spacecraft. NASA, however, was constrained by tight budgets and as of 2002 appeared unwilling to press Congress for the billions of dollars that would be needed to mount a manned mission to Mars. The European Union was considering plans for a possible manned Mars mission, which would be launched no earlier than 2025.

Pluto: A Nonplanet?

The discovery of Pluto in 1930 brought to nine the number of known planets in the solar system. For the next seven decades all models of the planetary system containing the Earth showed Pluto as a ball of rock and ice. Pluto was about the size of the Earth's moon, traveling an elliptical orbit of the Sun far beyond the other eight planets (except for periods when Neptune swung out beyond Pluto). No pictures were available, however, because Pluto was the only planet never directly observed by a spacecraft.

During the 1990s some scientists speculated that Pluto was not a planet, after all, but was merely the largest among billions of rocks in a distant region of the solar system known as the Kuiper Belt. Astronomers discovered the Kuiper Belt in 1992 and concluded that it consisted of the remains of the massive chunks of debris that ultimately formed the solar system about 5 billion years ago. According to some theories, comets originate in the Kuiper Belt.

New evidence for the theory downgrading Pluto's planetary status came on October 7, 2002, when astronomers from the California Institute of Technology reported the discovery of another large object in the Kuiper Belt, about one-half the size of Pluto. Michael Brown and Chadwick Trujillo said the Palomar Observatory in California had located a frozen body of ice and rock about 800 miles wide and orbiting the Sun about 1 billion miles beyond Pluto; it was the largest body found in the solar system since the discovery of Pluto. Brown and Chadwick proposed naming the object Quaoar, after a god worshiped by Indians who once inhabited the Los Angeles basin. The Hubble telescope confirmed the size of Quaoar.

Brown said the discovery of Quaoar provided strong evidence that Pluto was not really a planet but merely the largest of the Kuiper Belt rocks that somehow it was drawn into its own orbit of the Sun. "If Pluto were discovered today, no one would even consider calling it a planet because it's clearly a Kuiper Belt object," he said. Other scientists said objects even larger than Quaoar, or possibly larger than Pluto, might lie in the distant reaches of Kuiper Belt.

NASA had plans for a mission, called New Horizons, that would explore Pluto and a newly discovered moon (Charon) orbiting it. Under the agency's long-term plans, the mission was to be launched in 2006 and would take nearly ten years to reach Pluto. As of late 2002, however, Congress had not appropriated the $550 million to build and operate the mission.

Following is the text of an announcement made April 30, 2002, by the National Aeronautics and Space Administration concerning the first four images produced by the new Advanced Camera for Surveys, which was installed the previous month aboard the Hubble space telescope.

The document was obtained from the Internet at www.nasa .gov/releases/2002/02_074.html; accessed December 15, 2002.

"Remarkable, breathtaking" are words jubilant astronomers are using to describe the first four views of the universe taken by the Hubble Space Telescope's new Advanced Camera for Surveys, released by NASA today.

The new camera was installed on Hubble by astronauts during a shuttle mission last March, the fourth Hubble Space Telescope servicing mission. During five of the most challenging spacewalks ever attempted, the crew successfully upgraded the orbiting telescope with the new camera, a new power unit, new solar arrays and an experimental cooling unit for an infrared camera. Hubble managers say the orbiting telescope has been operating superbly since the servicing mission.

"Today marks the beginning of a new era of exploration with Hubble," said Dr. Ed Weiler, Associate Administrator for Space Science at NASA Headquarters, Washington. "Our team of scientists and engineers on the ground and the astronauts in space once again did the impossible. After 12 years in space, Hubble not only was given a major overhaul, its new camera has already shown us that, even after 12 years of great science and astounding images, we haven't seen anything yet."

Among the suite of four "suitable-for-framing" Advanced Camera for Surveys (ACS) science-demonstration pictures released today is a stunning view of a colliding galaxy, dubbed the "Tadpole," located 420 million light-years away. Unlike textbook images of stately galaxies, the "Tadpole"—with a long tail of stars—captures the essence of a dynamic, restless and violent universe, looking like a runaway pinwheel firework.

"The ACS is opening a wide new window onto the universe. These are among the best images of the distant universe humans have ever seen," said astronomer Holland Ford of Johns Hopkins University in Baltimore, lead scientist in the camera's seven-year development.

The camera's tenfold increase in efficiency will open up much anticipated new capability for discovery. "ACS will allow us to push back the frontier of the early universe. We will be able to enter the 'twilight zone' period when galaxies were just beginning to form out of the blackness following the cooling of the universe from the big bang," said Ford.

The ACS is a camera of superlatives. It is expected to surpass the sensitivity of the largest ground-based telescope to eventually see the very faintest objects ever recorded. The camera delivers a panoramic crispness comparable to that of a wide-screen movie, containing 16 million picture elements (megapixels) per image. By comparison, digital photos from typical consumer cameras are 2 to 4 megapixels.

The ACS image of the Tadpole illustrates the dramatic gains over the Wide Field Planetary Camera 2 resulting from doubling the area and resolution, and demonstrates a five- fold improvement in sensitivity. An unexpected bonus is the enormous number of galaxies in the new Hubble image beyond the Tadpole galaxy, giving it an appearance like the galaxy- filled Hubble Deep Field (HDF) image, taken in 1995. However, the ACS picture was taken in one-twelfth the time it took for the original HDF. Like the Hubble Deep Field, the ACS galaxies contain myriad shapes that are snapshots of galaxies throughout the universe's 13 billion-year evolution. The ACS images are so sharp astronomers can identify "building blocks" of galaxies, colliding galaxies and extremely distant galaxies in the field—an exquisite sampler of galaxies.

"The ACS will let us obtain the deepest image of the universe for the foreseeable future," added astronomer Garth Illingworth of the University of California, Lick Observatory, Santa Cruz, the deputy leader for the camera team.

The other pictures include a stunning collision between two spiral galaxies, dubbed "the Mice," that presage what might happen to our own Milky Way several billion years in the future when it collides with the neighboring galaxy in the constellation Andromeda. Computer simulations show that we are seeing the collision of the Mice approximately 160 million years after their closest encounter. Running the simulations forward in time shows that the two galaxies will eventually merge. A similar fate may await the Milky Way and the Andromeda galaxy.

Looking closer to home, ACS imaged the "Cone Nebula," a craggy-looking mountaintop of cold gas and dust that is a cousin to Hubble's iconic "pillars of creation" in the Eagle Nebula, photographed in 1995.

Peering into a celestial maternity ward called the M17 Swan Nebula, the ACS revealed a watercolor fantasy-world tapestry of vivid colors and glowing ridges of gas. Embedded in this crucible of star creation are embryonic planetary systems.

In addition to the ACS, spacewalking astronauts installed a new high-tech mechanical "refrigerator" on Hubble during the servicing mission. This "cryocooler" has successfully pumped most of the heat out of the interior of the Near Infrared Camera and Multi-Object Spectrometer (NICMOS), achieving and maintaining to within a few hundredths of one degree the target temperature for neon gas passing through the instrument of 70 degrees Kelvin (minus 203 degrees Centigrade or minus 333 degrees Fahrenheit).

Engineers are now in the process of checking out the operation of the resuscitated NICMOS instrument. By early June, scientists expect to release the first astronomical images taken with the NICMOS since 1998, when it was still being cooled by a rapidly depleting block of solid nitrogen ice.

The new rigid solar arrays, working with the new Power Control Unit, are generating 27 percent more electrical power than the previous arrays. This doubles the electrical power that can be allocated to the scientific instruments on Hubble. The new reaction wheel is operating normally. Nearly a month ago, the Space Telescope Imaging Spectrograph and the Wide Field and Planetary Camera 2 resumed science observations.

"This servicing mission has turned out to be an extraordinary success," said Preston Burch, Hubble Project Manager at NASA's Goddard Space Flight Center in Greenbelt, Md. "It was the most difficult and complicated Hubble servicing mission attempted to date and our observatory came through it with flying colors."

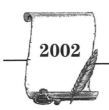

May

UN STATEMENT ON ITS
SPECIAL SESSION ON CHILDREN
May 10, 2002

Twelve years after the world's governments first pledged themselves to improving the well-being of children, delegates to the United Nations General Assembly Special Session on Children took stock of the progress that had been made and rededicated themselves to the effort of caring for the nearly 2 billion children under age eighteen worldwide. In an updated plan of action, delegations from more than 150 countries promised to take steps to provide all children with basic health care and access to quality education; to protect children against abuse, exploitation, and violence; and to combat HIV/AIDS, the autoimmune disease that was having a devastating effect on children in Sub-Saharan Africa and other regions of the world.

The document, "A World Fit for Children," was adopted by consensus at the conclusion of the three-day conference held in New York May 8–10, 2002. The special session had originally been scheduled for September 18, 2001, but was postponed in the aftermath of the terrorist attacks on the World Trade Center and the Pentagon on September 11. Adoption by consensus belied the difficult negotiations over several controversial issues, most prominently the U.S. delegation's objection to language in the document that it said implicitly endorsed abortion.

More than 3,000 delegates, including sixty-nine heads of states or governments and prime ministers or their deputies, participated in the special session, along with 1,700 delegates of nongovernmental organizations (NGOs). For the first time, children were both seen and heard at a world summit. "We are street children. We are the children of war. We are the victims and orphans of HIV/AIDS," Gabriela Azurdy Arrieta, a thirteen-year-old from Bolivia, told the opening session. "We want a world fit for children because a world fit for children is a world fit for everyone." She was one of about 400 children who were formal delegates of national or NGO delegations.

Other speakers at the assembly included United Nations Secretary General Kofi Annan; Nelson Mandela, the former president of South Africa and a worldwide symbol of civil rights; and Bill Gates, the founder of Microsoft.

Through his charitable foundation, Gates pledged $50 million for a five-year plan to fortify basic foods in developing countries with vitamins and minerals.

Progress and Problems

Since the 1990 World Summit for Children, governments, international organizations, and NGOs had made great strides in improving the lives of children. More children attended school than ever before, polio and guinea worm disease had nearly been eradicated, and 3 million fewer children died each year. Dozens of countries had succeeded in significantly reducing their rates of infant mortality, while the number of households in the developing world that used iodized salt increased from 20 percent in 1990 to more than 70 percent at the turn of the century. Iodine was a key nutrient in the prevention of mental retardation. A decline in breast-feeding also appeared to have reversed, rising from about 40 percent of all children in the developing world to 45 percent in recent years. Breast-feeding provided infants with nutrients and immunity protections that were not available in animal milk or formulas.

Malnutrition, disease, and a lack of education remained difficult problems. According to the United Nations International Children's Emergency Fund, an estimated 150 million children still suffered from malnutrition. More than 100 million—60 percent of them girls—did not attend school. Eleven million children still died before their fifth birthday; 10 million died every year from preventable causes. One of every four children were not vaccinated against common preventable diseases, such tuberculosis, measles, tetanus, and whopping cough. More than 13 million children had been orphaned by AIDS, while nearly 1.5 million had contracted HIV/AIDS. The vast majority of those children lived in Sub-Saharan Africa.

Sub-Saharan Africa also had the highest rate of child labor in the world. The International Labor Organization estimated that 29 percent of all children in the region between ages five and fourteen had to work for a living. The next highest rate was in Asia, with an estimated rate of 19 percent. As many as 1 million children were estimated to be trapped in sex work, and many of these children were also the victims of human trafficking. An estimated 300,000 children were fighting in wars and conflicts around the world. (Human trafficking, p. 332; child soldiers, p. 916)

In addition, most of the nations of the world had failed to fulfill their promise of aid to help reduce poverty and attain better living conditions for children. At the 1990 summit, industrialized nations pledged to devote an average of 0.7 percent of annual gross domestic product (GDP) for health care, education, and other developmental assistance in the developing world. Only four countries—Denmark, Netherlands, Norway, and Sweden—met that goal. The United States ranked twenty-second, with just 0.1 percent of its GDP devoted to such aid. Developing countries were supposed to invest 20 percent of their national budgets to social welfare, but the UN estimated they were actually spending only 12 to 14 percent on such efforts. Some poor countries spent three to five times as much paying off foreign debt as providing basic social services, the UN said.

The Child Rights Caucus, a coalition of more than 100 international organizations, expressed concern that the special session was in danger of making yet more promises that would not be kept. "Millions of children are today denied basic rights and suffer unconscionable abuse because governments have failed to live up to their commitments," said a representative of one member organization.

In his opening remarks on May 8, Secretary General Annan acknowledged that failure. Directly addressing the children attending the summit, Annan said that "we the grown-ups have failed you deplorably in upholding many" of the basic rights of childhood: freedom from poverty, hunger, and infectious disease; freedom from abuse and exploitation; and access to education. "We, the grown-ups, must reverse this list of failures."

Abortion, Sex Education

The final document was nearly derailed by the U.S. delegation's insistence on deleting language that it said implied support for abortion and abortion counseling. The administration of U.S. president George W. Bush particularly objected to the phrase "reproductive health services" and said at the least it wanted a footnote stating that these services did not include abortion or abortion counseling. The delegation also wanted language promoting sexual abstinence among unmarried adolescents.

Although abortion was legal in the United States, President Bush and many of his supporters were opposed to it under most circumstances. One of Bush's first actions upon taking office in 2001 was to bar federal funds from going to international family planning agencies that used their own money to perform or promote abortions overseas. The Bush administration was also on record as supporting abstinence-only sex education programs. (Funding of abortion counseling overseas, Historic Documents of 2001, p. 127)

The U.S. position was supported by the Vatican, and several Islamic nations, including Iraq and Iran. Several Catholic countries, however, broke away from the Vatican on the sensitive issue. Spain, speaking for the European Union, called for comprehensive reproductive health services and "high-quality" sex education for children. The subject was always a tricky issue because abortion was legal in some countries and illegal in others. UN documents generally tried to skirt the issue by leaving the decision to individual countries. Many delegations wanted to leave it that way. "It should be up to countries if and to what extent abortion should be featured as an element within the constellation of reproductive health services," one European delegate said.

In the end, the United States failed to win either an explicit statement barring abortions and abortion counseling for adolescents or an endorsement of sexual abstinence as the best way to prevent sexually transmitted disease and unwanted pregnancies among teenagers. But the document's original strong endorsement of sex education programs, which had been supported by a large majority of the nations participating in the session, was watered down. Aggressive promotion of the use of condoms, contraceptives, and sex education was the foundation of HIV/AIDS prevention programs in many countries. By some estimates half of all new HIV infections occurred in adolescents. The United States also persuaded the assembly to drop the word services *from the phrase "reproductive health services."*

Critics said the controversy diverted attention from the larger issues of health care and education. "The world has recognized and agreed on five previous occasions that adolescents are at great risk of HIV infection, unwanted pregnancy, and botched abortions. The Bush administration is trying to take us back to the Dark Ages," said Adrienne Germain, president of the International Women's Health Coalition. Administration officials countered that proponents of abortion rights were the ones diverting attention. "A document on children should not be focused on abortion and things like that. It should be focused on positive things," Michael J. Dennis, a human rights adviser to the U.S. State Department, told reporters.

In December the United States took a similar position on abortion and abstinence at a UN regional conference in Asia. But its efforts to change earlier agreements on family planning to bar abortion and promote abstinence were scuttled by votes of 31–1 and 32–1.

Convention on the Rights of the Child

The U.S. delegation did succeed in downplaying the status of the Convention on the Rights of the Child, a treaty intended to be the global standard for protecting child rights. It had been ratified by 191 countries since its was drawn up in 1989; only Somalia and the United States had not acted. The Clinton administration signed the convention but had never submitted it to the Senate for ratification because of opposition from those who said it interfered with the rights of parents by, for example, advocating that children have access to certain health services without first having to obtain their parents' consent. The convention also barred the death penalty for children under age eighteen, which made it inconsistent with the laws of several American states that permitted the death penalty for sixteen- and seventeen-year-olds. (Death penalty, p. 353)

Several countries and children's advocacy groups sought to give the convention momentum by having the special session endorse the treaty as the legal standard for children's rights. That did not happen. "The Convention itself has just been sidelined," said Jo Becker of Human Rights Watch.

Although the United States showed few signs that it was prepared to change its position on the Convention on the Rights of the Child, it did quietly ratify two optional protocols to the convention that it had formerly opposed. On December 23 the State Department announced that the United States was filing ratification papers with the United Nations on a protocol barring the sale of children, child pornography, and child prostitution, and another protocol on the involvement of children in armed conflict. The Senate had quietly ratified the two protocols in June with virtually no debate. The Pentagon had objected to the second protocol because it would bar send-

ing adolescents under age eighteen into combat. The United States had sent seventeen-year-olds into armed conflict in Bosnia, Somalia, and the Gulf War. Late in the year the Pentagon agreed that it would no longer send troops younger than eighteen into battle. The two protocols had entered into force earlier in the year (the one on child soldiers on February 12, and the one on child slavery on January 18).

Following are excerpts from "A World Fit for Children," a statement agreed to on May 10, 2002, by consensus of member countries of the United Nations General Assembly in its Special Session on Children.

The document was obtained from the Internet at www .unicef.org/specialsession/documentation/index.html; accessed November 30, 2002.

I. Declaration

1. Eleven years ago, at the World Summit for Children, world leaders made a joint commitment and issued an urgent, universal appeal to give every child a better future.

2. Since then, much progress has been made, as documented in the report of the Secretary-General entitled "We the Children". Millions of young lives have been saved, more children than ever are in school, more children are actively involved in decisions concerning their lives and important treaties have been concluded to protect children. However, these achievements and gains have been uneven, and many obstacles remain, particularly in developing countries. A brighter future for all has proved elusive, and overall gains have fallen short of national obligations and international commitments.

3. We, the Heads of State and Government and representatives of States participating in the special session of the General Assembly on children, reaffirming our commitment to the purposes and principles enshrined in the Charter of the United Nations are determined to seize this historic opportunity to change the world for and with children. Accordingly, we reaffirm our commitment to complete the unfinished agenda of the World Summit for Children and to address other emerging issues vital to the achievement of the longer-term goals and objectives endorsed at recent major United Nations summits and conferences, in particular the United Nations Millennium Declaration, through national action and international cooperation.

4. We reaffirm our obligation to take action to promote and protect the rights of each child—every human being below the age of 18 years including adolescents. We are determined to respect the dignity and to secure the well-being of all children. We acknowledge that the Convention on the Rights of the Child, the most universally embraced human rights treaty in history, and its Optional Protocols contain a comprehensive set of international legal

standards for the protection and well-being of children. We also recognize the importance of other international instruments relevant for children.

5. We stress our commitment to create a world fit for children in which sustainable human development, taking into account the best interests of the child, is founded on principles of democracy, equality, non-discrimination, peace and social justice and the universality, indivisibility, interdependence and interrelatedness of all human rights, including the right to development.

6. We recognize and support parents and families or, as the case may be, legal guardians as the primary caretakers of children, and we will strengthen their capacity to provide the optimum care, nurturing and protection.

7. We hereby call on all members of society to join us in a global movement that will help build a world fit for children through upholding our commitments to the following principles and objectives:

1. **Put children first.** In all actions related to children, the best interests of the child shall be a primary consideration.

2. **Eradicate poverty: invest in children.** We reaffirm our vow to break the cycle of poverty within a single generation, united in the conviction that investments in children and the realization of their rights are among the most effective ways to eradicate poverty. Immediate action must be taken to eliminate the worst forms of child labour.

3. **Leave no child behind.** Each girl and boy is born free and equal in dignity and rights; therefore, all forms of discrimination affecting children must end.

4. **Care for every child.** Children must get the best possible start in life. Their survival, protection, growth and development in good health and with proper nutrition is the essential foundation of human development. We will make concerted efforts to fight infectious diseases, tackle major causes of malnutrition and nurture children in a safe environment that enables them to be physically healthy, mentally alert, emotionally secure, socially competent and able to learn.

5. **Educate every child.** All girls and boys must have access to and complete primary education that is free, compulsory and of good quality as a cornerstone of an inclusive basic education. Gender disparities in primary and secondary education must be eliminated.

6. **Protect children from harm and exploitation.** Children must be protected against any acts of violence, abuse, exploitation and discrimination, as well as all forms of terrorism and hostage-taking.

7. **Protect children from war.** Children must be protected from the horrors of armed conflict. Children under foreign occupation must also be protected, in accordance with the provisions of international humanitarian law.

8. **Combat HIV/AIDS.** Children and their families must be protected from the devastating impact of human immunodeficiency virus/acquired immunodeficiency syndrome (HIV/AIDS).

9. **Listen to children and ensure their participation.** Children and adolescents are resourceful citizens capable of helping to build a better

future for all. We must respect their right to express themselves and to participate in all matters affecting them, in accordance with their age and maturity.

10. **Protect the Earth for children.** We must safeguard our natural environment, with its diversity of life, its beauty and its resources, all of which enhance the quality of life, for present and future generations. We will give every assistance to protect children and minimize the impact of natural disasters and environmental degradation on them.

8. We recognize that the implementation of the present Declaration and Plan of Action require not only renewed political will, but also the mobilization and allocation of additional resources at both the national and international levels, taking into account the urgency and gravity of the special needs of children.

9. In line with these principles and objectives, we adopt the Plan of Action contained in section III below, confident that together we will build a world in which all girls and boys can enjoy childhood—a time of play and learning, in which they are loved, respected and cherished, their rights are promoted and protected, without discrimination of any kind, where their safety and well-being are paramount and where they can develop in health, peace and dignity.

II. Review of progress and lessons learned

10. The World Declaration and the Plan of Action of the World Summit for Children are among the most rigorously monitored and implemented international commitments of the 1990s. Annual reviews were held at the national level and progress reports presented to the General Assembly. A mid-decade review and an extensive global end-decade review were conducted. The latter included high-level regional meetings in Beijing, Berlin, Cairo, Kathmandu and Kingston, which reviewed progress; ensured follow-up to the Summit and other major conferences; promoted renewed commitment to the achievement of the goals of the world summit; and guided actions for the future. Complementing efforts by Governments, a wide range of actors participated in the reviews, including children, young people's organizations, academic institutions, religious groups, civil society organizations, parliamentarians, the media, United Nations agencies, donors and major national and international non-governmental organizations.

11. As documented in the end-decade review of the Secretary-General on follow-up to the World Summit for Children, the 1990s was a decade of great promises and modest achievements for the world's children. On the positive side, the Summit and the entry into force of the Convention on the Rights of the Child helped accord political priority to children. A record 192 countries ratified, acceded to or signed the Convention. Some 155 countries prepared national programmes of action to implement the Summit goals. Regional commitments were made. International legal provisions and mechanisms strengthened the protection of children. Pursuit of the Summit goals has led to many tangible results for children: this year, 3 million fewer children will die than a decade ago; polio has been brought to the brink of eradication; and,

through salt iodization, 90 million newborns are protected every year from a significant loss of learning ability.

12. Yet much more needs to be done. The resources that were promised at the Summit at both the national and international levels have yet to fully materialize. Critical challenges remain: more than 10 million children die each year although most of those deaths could be prevented; 100 million children are still out of school, 60 per cent of them girls; 150 million children suffer from malnutrition; and HIV/AIDS is spreading with catastrophic speed. There is persistent poverty, exclusion and discrimination, and inadequate investment in social services. Also, debt burdens, excessive military spending, inconsistent with national security requirements, armed conflict, foreign occupation, hostage-taking and all forms of terrorism, as well as the lack of efficient use of resources, among other factors, can constrain national efforts to combat poverty and to ensure the well-being of children. The childhood of millions continues to be devastated by hazardous and exploitative labour; the sale and trafficking of children, including adolescents, and other forms of abuse, neglect, exploitation and violence.

13. The experience of the past decade has confirmed that the needs and rights of children must be a priority in all development efforts. There are many key lessons: change is possible—and children's rights are an effective rallying point; policies must address both the immediate factors affecting or excluding groups of children and the wider and deeper causes of inadequate protection and rights violations; targeted interventions that achieve rapid successes need to be pursued, with due attention to sustainability and participatory processes; and efforts should build on children's own resilience and strength. Multisectoral programmes focusing on early childhood and support to families, especially in high-risk conditions, merit special support because they provide lasting benefits for child growth, development and protection.

III. Plan of Action

A. Creating a world fit for children

14. A world fit for children is one in which all children get the best possible start in life and have access to a quality basic education, including primary education that is compulsory and available free to all, and in which all children, including adolescents, have ample opportunity to develop their individual capacities in a safe and supportive environment. We will promote the physical, psychological, spiritual, social, emotional, cognitive and cultural development of children as a matter of national and global priorities.

15. The family is the basic unit of society and as such should be strengthened. It is entitled to receive comprehensive protection and support. The primary responsibility for the protection, upbringing and development of children rests with the family. All institutions of society should respect children's rights and secure their well-being and render appropriate assistance to parents, families, legal guardians and other caregivers so that children can grow and develop in a safe and stable environment and in an atmosphere of happi-

ness, love and understanding, bearing in mind that in different cultural, social and political systems, various forms of the family exist.

16. We also recognize that a considerable number of children live without parental support, such as orphans, children living on the street, internally displaced and refugee children, children affected by trafficking and sexual and economic exploitation and children who are incarcerated. Special measures should be taken to support such children and the institutions, facilities and services that care for them, and to build and strengthen children's own abilities to protect themselves.

17. We are determined to promote access by parents, families, legal guardians, caregivers and children themselves to a full range of information and services to promote child survival, development, protection and participation.

18. Chronic poverty remains the single biggest obstacle to meeting the needs, protecting and promoting the rights of children. It must be tackled on all fronts, from the provision of basic social services to the creation of employment opportunities, from the availability of microcredit to investment in infrastructure, and from debt relief to fair trade practices. Children are hardest hit by poverty because it strikes at the very roots of their potential for development—their growing bodies and minds. Eradication of poverty and reduction of disparities must therefore be a key objective of development efforts. The goals and strategies agreed upon at recent major United Nations conferences and their follow-ups, in particular the Millennium Summit, provide a helpful international framework for national strategies for poverty reduction to fulfil and protect the rights and promote the well-being of children.

19. We recognize that globalization and interdependence are opening new opportunities through trade, investment and capital flows and advances in technology, including information technology, for the growth of the world economy, development and improvement of living standards around the world. At the same time, there remain serious challenges, including serious financial crises, insecurity, poverty, exclusion and inequality within and among societies. Considerable obstacles to further integration and full participation in the global economy remain for developing countries, in particular the least developed countries, as well as for some countries with economies in transition. Unless the benefits of social and economic development are extended to all countries, a growing number of people in all countries and even entire regions will remain marginalized from the global economy. We must act now in order to overcome those obstacles affecting peoples and countries and to realize the full potential of opportunities presented for the benefit of all, in particular children. We are committed to an open, equitable, rule-based, predictable and non-discriminatory multilateral trading and financial system. Investment in, inter alia, education and training will assist in enabling children to partake of the benefits of the breakthroughs in information and communication technologies. Globalization offers opportunities and challenges. The developing countries and countries with economies in transition face special difficulties in responding to those challenges and opportunities. Globalization should be fully inclusive and equitable, and there is a strong need for policies

and measures at the national and international levels, formulated and implemented with the full and effective participation of developing countries and countries with economies in transition to help them respond effectively to those challenges and opportunities, giving high priority to achieving progress for children.

20. Discrimination gives rise to a self-perpetuating cycle of social and economic exclusion and undermines children's ability to develop to the fullest. We will make every effort to eliminate discrimination against children, whether rooted in the child's or his or her parent's or legal guardian's race, colour, sex, language, religion, political or other opinion, national, ethnic or social origin, property, disability, birth or other status.

21. We will take all measures to ensure the full and equal enjoyment of all human rights and fundamental freedoms, including equal access to health, education and recreational services, by children with disabilities and children with special needs; to ensure the recognition of their dignity; to promote their self-reliance; and to facilitate their active participation in the community.

22. Indigenous children, children belonging to minorities and vulnerable groups, are disproportionately disadvantaged in many countries due to all forms of discrimination, including racial discrimination. We shall take appropriate measures to end discrimination, to provide special support, and to ensure equal access to services for these children.

23. The achievement of goals for children, particularly for girls, will be advanced if women fully enjoy all human rights and fundamental freedoms, including the right to development, are empowered to participate fully and equally in all spheres of society and are protected and free from all forms of violence, abuse and discrimination. We are determined to eliminate all forms of discrimination against the girl child throughout her life cycle and to provide special attention to her needs in order to promote and protect all her human rights, including the right to be free from coercion and from harmful practices and sexual exploitation. We will promote gender equality and equal access to basic social services, such as education, nutrition, health care, including sexual and reproductive health care, vaccinations, and protection from diseases representing the major causes of mortality, and will mainstream a gender perspective in all development policies and programmes.

24. We also recognize the need to address the changing role of men in society, as boys, adolescents and fathers, and the challenges faced by boys growing up in today's world. We will further promote the shared responsibility of both parents in education and in the raising of children, and will make every effort to ensure that fathers have opportunities to participate in their children's lives.

25. It is vital that national goals for children include targets for reducing disparities, in particular those which arise from discrimination on the basis of race, between girls and boys, rural and urban children, wealthy and poor children and those with and without disabilities.

26. A number of environmental problems and trends, such as global warming, ozone layer depletion, air pollution, hazardous wastes, exposure to haz-

ardous chemicals and pesticides, inadequate sanitation, poor hygiene, unsafe drinking water and food and inadequate housing, need to be addressed to ensure the health and well-being of children.

27. Adequate housing fosters family integration, contributes to social equity and strengthens the feeling of belonging, security and human solidarity, which are essential for the well-being of children. Accordingly, we will attach a high priority to overcoming the housing shortage and other infrastructure needs, particularly for children in marginalized peri-urban and remote rural areas.

28. We will take measures to manage our natural resources and protect and conserve our environment in a sustainable manner. We will work to change unsustainable patterns of production and consumption, bearing in mind principles, including, inter alia, the principle that, in view of different contributions to global and environmental degradation, States have common but differentiated responsibilities. We will help to educate all children and adults to respect the natural environment for their health and well-being.

29. The Convention on the Rights of the Child and its Optional Protocols contain a comprehensive set of international legal standards for the protection and well-being of children. We also recognize the importance of other international instruments relevant for children. The general principles of, inter alia, the best interests of the child, non-discrimination, participation and survival and development provide the framework for our actions concerning children, including adolescents. We urge all countries to consider, as a matter of priority, signing and ratifying or acceding to the Convention on the Rights of the Child, its Optional Protocols, as well as the International Labour Organization Conventions 138 and 182. We urge States Parties to fully implement their treaty obligations and to withdraw reservations incompatible with the object and purpose of the Convention and to consider reviewing reservations with a view to withdrawing them.

30. We welcome the entry into force of the Optional Protocols to the Convention on the Rights of the Child on the involvement of children in armed conflict and on the sale of children, child prostitution and child pornography, and urge States Parties to fully implement them.

31. We, the Governments participating in the special session, commit ourselves to implementing the Plan of Action through consideration of such measures as:

(a) Putting in place, as appropriate, effective national legislation, policies and action plans and allocating resources to fulfil and protect the rights and to secure the well-being of children;

(b) Establishing or strengthening national bodies, such as, inter alia, independent ombudspersons for children, where appropriate, or other institutions for the promotion and protection of the rights of the child;

(c) Developing national monitoring and evaluation systems to assess the impact of our actions on children;

(d) Enhancing widespread awareness and understanding of the rights of the child. . . .

FORMER PRESIDENT CARTER ON U.S.-CUBAN RELATIONS
May 14, 2002

Former U.S. president Jimmy Carter in May sought to break the four-decades-long stalemate in relations between Cuba and the United States—two nations separated by ninety miles of water and a vast chasm of ideological hostility left over from the cold war. Carter became the most prominent U.S. citizen to visit Cuba since Fidel Castro and his fellow communist revolutionaries took over the island in 1959. The former president told Castro to allow democracy and human rights, and in an unprecedented televised address he told the Cuban people that they deserved political freedoms. Carter also called on the United States government to end its tight economic embargo against Cuba. None of Carter's statements produced any immediate changes in government policy, either in Havana or in Washington. Even so, the forcefulness of Carter's appeals seemed bound to influence events, sooner or later, on both sides of the Florida strait.

Five months after his highly publicized visit to Cuba, Carter was awarded the Nobel Peace Prize for his lifetime of work on behalf of human rights, democracy, and other causes. The Nobel committee specifically cited Carter's key role in negotiating the 1978 Camp David peace agreement between Egypt and Israel. (Nobel Peace Prize, p. 981; Camp David agreement, Historic Documents of 1978, p. 605)

Carter's Visit to Cuba

During his presidency (1977–1981), Carter had sought a modest improvement in relations between the United States and Cuba, which had been bitter enemies since shortly after Castro's rise to power. Carter relaxed a ban on travel to Cuba by American citizens, negotiated fishing rights and maritime boundary agreements with Cuba, and convinced Castro to release several thousand political prisoners. But the cold war was still under way at the time, and there was strong resistance in both countries to any serious lessening of tension. Moreover, Castro in 1980 sent a flood of about 125,000 refugees to the United States, angering officials in Florida and Washington; among the refugees were many criminals and others (such as the mentally ill) that Castro considered undesirable. (Mariel boat lift, Historic Documents of 1980, p. 337)

In the two decades after Carter left office, the United States and Cuba remained locked in confrontation. Washington maintained tight sanctions that prohibited nearly all economic intercourse between the two countries. Congress in 1996 wrote the sanctions into law, effectively limiting the ability of any president to ease them on his own authority. For his part, Castro remained, along with North Korea's Kim Jong Il, the most unreconstructed communist leader in the world, even after the 1991 collapse of his long-time patron, the Soviet Union. (Cuba policy background, Historic Documents of 1996, p. 93)

Observers in Cuba and the United States offered numerous explanations of why Castro allowed Carter to visit—a step that Castro certainly knew would result in heightened international scrutiny of his rule. Some observers said Castro must have hoped that Carter would repeat his long-standing position of opposing the U.S. sanctions, thereby demonstrating that the sanctions policy had become controversial within the United States. By opening his country to Carter, and especially by allowing the former president to address the Cuban people directly, Castro also appeared to want to undercut his opponents' claims that Cuba was a totalitarian state.

Carter arrived in Cuba on May 12 and received Castro's pledge that he had "free and total access to anywhere you want to go." Carter had barely begun his visit when he found himself caught in a war of words between Havana and Washington. A week earlier, a senior State Department official had said that Cuba had developed a research capability for production of biological weapons and had provided similar technology to "other rogue states," including Iran and Libya. The official, Undersecretary of State John R. Bolton, implied, but did not state directly, that Cuba actually had developed biological weapons.

After touring Cuba's foremost biotechnology research center on May 13, Carter said Cuban officials had assured him that they had not developed a biological weapons program nor exported that technology to other countries. Carter also told reporters that he had specifically asked administration officials about the issue during briefings before he left for Cuba. "There were absolutely no such allegations made or questions raised [by officials in Washington]," he said. Responding to Carter, administration officials reiterated their concerns about Cuba's use of biotechnology—but appeared to back away from Bolton's implication that Cuba had produced biological weapons.

The high point of Carter's trip came on May 14, when the former president was allowed to address the Cuban people, in Spanish, over live television. Appearing before an audience (including Castro, seated in the front row) at the University of Havana, Carter bluntly called on both Cuba and the United States to develop a new relationship. "Our two nations have been trapped in a destructive state of belligerence for forty-two years," he said. "And it is time to change our relationship and the way we think and talk about each other."

The United States needed to abandon its anti-Cuba embargo, he said, because it "freezes the existing impasse, induces anger and resentment, restricts the freedoms of U.S. citizens, and makes it difficult for us to exchange ideas and respect." At the same time, Carter rejected Castro's contention that the embargo was the root cause of Cuba's economic troubles.

Although insisting that "I did not come here to interfere in Cuba's internal affairs," Carter struck directly at the most sensitive of all public questions in Cuba: the country's closed political system. Carter noted that, during the previous two decades, democracy had taken root in nearly all of Latin America. Yet, he said, "Cuba has adopted a socialist government where one political party dominates, and people are not permitted to organize any opposition movements. Your constitution recognizes freedom of speech and association, but other laws deny these freedoms to those who disagree with the government."

Carter told the Cuban people about a petition, organized by anti-Castro dissidents and signed by more than 11,000 citizens, calling on the National Assembly to hold a referendum on allowing political freedoms and human rights in Cuba. Called the Varela Project (after a famed nineteenth century Cuban priest), the petition drive was the broadest move on behalf of democracy since Castro assumed power. "When Cubans exercise this freedom to change laws peacefully by a direct vote, the world will see that Cubans, and not foreigners, will decide the future of this country," Carter said. The government had banned any mention of the petition in the mass media, however, and so Carter's praise for it must have come as a surprise to most of his audience. Even after Carter's speech, the Varela Project remained a mystery to most Cubans because no further information about it was published in the state-controlled media. Castro told ABC News in October that the government would act on the petition "in due course," but he gave no indication that he would allow the referendum.

In one small sign of a possible political opening, Cuban authorities allowed dissidents to hold small protest gatherings in Havana and other cities on December 10—International Human Rights Day. Leaders of a dissident umbrella group, the Assembly to Promote Civil Society, said it was the first time that opponents of Castro's regime had been allowed to hold simultaneous rallies in multiple places on the island.

Bush Response

Castro was not the only sitting president who was less than eager to heed Carter's advice. Just six days after Carter made his appeal in Havana for compromise steps by both Cuba and the United States, President George W. Bush made it clear that he was not ready for any conciliatory moves. In speeches in Washington and Miami on May 20, the one hundredth anniversary of Cuban independence, Bush rejected any significant change in U.S. policy toward Cuba. Bush said the embargo against Cuba would remain in place until Castro had allowed formation of opposition political parties and independent trade unions, freed allow political prisoners, and permitted international reviews of elections planned for 2003.

Speaking to a cheering throng of anti-Castro Cuban Americans in Miami, Bush said: "Mr. Castro, once, just once, show you're unafraid of a real election. Show the world you respect Cuban citizens enough to listen to their voices and count their votes. Start to release your choke hold on the working people and on enterprise. Then, and only then, will we talk about easing sanctions." Bush's visit to Miami was the highlight of a fund-raising effort for the Florida Republican Party and its candidate for governor, Jeb Bush (the president's younger bother), who was seeking reelection to a second term. Cuban Americans, many of whom took a hard line against any compromise with Castro, were significant supporters of Governor Bush.

Congressional Action

Carter's visit to Cuba, and Bush's rejection of his advice, came just as Congress was gearing up for what had become an annual debate over U.S. policy toward Cuba. Since the late 1990s, support had been growing in Congress for a new approach to Cuba. Many members of both parties noted that U.S. economic sanctions had failed, during a period of four decades, to achieve the intended purpose of forcing Castro to allow political and economic openness in Cuba. Members from agricultural states also argued that the only real effect of the sanctions was to hinder U.S. exports to Cuba of food and other products.

Calling itself the Cuba Working Group, a caucus of twenty Republicans and twenty Democrats in the House issued a report on May 15 calling U.S. policy a failure. "American policy toward Cuba lacks support among the American public, the Congress, the international community, and, most importantly, inside Cuba, among dissidents, clergy, and average Cuban citizens," the group declared. "Moreover, the U.S. policy objective of a peaceful transition to a stable, democratic form of government and respect for human rights in Cuba has gone unmet. After four decades, the U.S. embargo has failed to produce meaningful political and economic reform in Cuba."

As an alternative, the group suggested a series of incremental steps to improve relations with Cuba. The recommended steps included repealing the legal ban on travel to Cuba by U.S. citizens; ending regulations that inhibited sales to Cuba of U.S. medicine and agriculture products; repealing a $100 monthly limit on funds (called "remittances") that Cuban Americans could send to relatives in Cuba; requiring a full congressional review in 2003 of the "Helms-Burton Act" of 1996, which put the Cuba embargo into U.S. law (it previously had been only a presidential order); ending television broadcasts to Cuba of anti-Castro propaganda; and establishing educational exchange programs with Cuba, similar to the Fulbright scholarships.

Rep. William D. Delahunt, D-Mass., who cochaired the Cuba Working Group, said the policy changes would amount to "a policy of engagement. It has proven successful elsewhere in the world."

The full House on July 23 embraced key elements of the policy changes advocated by the Cuba Working Group. During consideration of the annual appropriations bill (HR 5120) for the Treasury and other agencies, the House voted by a wide margin (262–177) to eliminate restrictions on travel *to Cuba by U.S. citizens, voted by a somewhat narrower margin (251–177) to eliminate the $100 monthly limit on remittances by Cuban Americans to relatives in Cuba, and approved (by voice vote) an amendment easing the sales of food and medicines to Cuba. By a surprisingly narrow margin of 226–204, the House rejected an attempt to eliminate the entire embargo against Cuba. Taken together, these votes in the Republican-controlled House clearly demonstrated a shift in sentiment away from the hard-line policy of the previous four decades. But Bush threatened to veto any congressional measure that weakened his Cuba policy, and none of the amendments adopted by the House were included in final legislation for the year.*

Following is an English translation of the text of a speech delivered in Spanish by former president Jimmy Carter in an appearance at the University of Havana in Cuba on May 14, 2002. Carter's speech was broadcast live on Cuban television.

The document was obtained from the Internet at www .cartercenter.org/viewdoc.asp?docID=517&submenu= news; accessed October 10, 2002.

I appreciate President [Fidel] Castro's invitation for us to visit Cuba, and have been delighted with the hospitality we have received since arriving here. It is a great honor to address the Cuban people.

After a long and agonizing struggle, Cuba achieved its independence a century ago, and a complex relationship soon developed between our two countries. The great powers in Europe and Asia viewed "imperialism" as the natural order of the time and they expected the United States to colonize Cuba as the Europeans had done in Africa. The United States chose instead to help Cuba become independent, but not completely. The Platt Amendment gave my country the right to intervene in Cuba's internal affairs until President Franklin Roosevelt had the wisdom to repeal this claim in May 1934.

The dictator Fulgencio Batista was overthrown more than 43 years ago, and a few years later the Cuban revolution aligned with the Soviet Union in the Cold War. Since then, our nations have followed different philosophical and political paths.

The hard truth is that neither the United States nor Cuba has managed to define a positive and beneficial relationship. Will this new century find our neighboring people living in harmony and friendship? I have come here in search of an answer to that question.

There are some in Cuba who think the simple answer is for the United States to lift the embargo, and there are some in my country who believe the answer is for your president to step down from power and allow free elections. There is no doubt that the question deserves a more comprehensive assessment.

I have restudied the complicated history (in preparation for my conversations with President Castro), and realize that there are no simple answers.

I did not come here to interfere in Cuba's internal affairs, but to extend a hand of friendship to the Cuban people and to offer a vision of the future for our two countries and for all the Americas.

That vision includes a Cuba fully integrated into a democratic hemisphere, participating in a Free Trade Area of the Americas and with our citizens traveling without restraint to visit each other. I want a massive student exchange between our universities. I want the people of the United States and Cuba to share more than a love of baseball and wonderful music. I want us to be friends, and to respect each other.

Our two nations have been trapped in a destructive state of belligerence for 42 years, and it is time for us to change our relationship and the way we think and talk about each other. Because the United States is the most powerful nation, we should take the first step.

First, my hope is that the Congress will soon act to permit unrestricted travel between the United States and Cuba, establish open trading relationships, and repeal the embargo. I should add that these restraints are not the source of Cuba's economic problems. Cuba can trade with more than 100 countries, and buy medicines, for example, more cheaply in Mexico than in the United States. But the embargo freezes the existing impasse, induces anger and resentment, restricts the freedoms of US citizens, and makes it difficult for us to exchange ideas and respect.

Second, I hope that Cuba and the United States can resolve the forty-year-old property disputes with some creativity. In many cases, we are debating ancient claims about decrepit sugar mills, an antique telephone company, and many other obsolete holdings. Most U.S. companies have already absorbed the losses, but some others want to be paid, and many Cubans who fled the revolution retain a sentimental attachment for their homes. We resolved similar problems when I normalized relations with China in 1979. I propose that our two countries establish a blue-ribbon commission to address the legitimate concerns of all sides in a positive and constructive manner.

Third, some of those who left this beautiful island have demonstrated vividly that the key to a flourishing economy is to use individual entrepreneurial skills. But many Cubans in South Florida remain angry over their departure and their divided families. We need to define a future so they can serve as a bridge of reconciliation between Cuba and the United States.

Are such normal relationships possible? I believe they are.

Except for the stagnant relations between the United States and Cuba, the world has been changing greatly, and especially in Latin America and the Caribbean. As late as 1977, when I became President, there were only two democracies in South America, and one in Central America. Today, almost every country in the Americas is a democracy.

I am not using a U.S. definition of "democracy." The term is embedded in the Universal Declaration of Human Rights, which Cuba signed in 1948, and it was defined very precisely by all the other countries of the Americas in the Inter-American Democratic Charter last September. It is based on some simple premises: all citizens are born with the right to choose their own leaders, to define their own destiny, to speak freely, to organize political parties, trade unions and non-governmental groups, and to have fair and open trials.

Only such governments can be members of the OAS, join a Free Trade Area of the Americas, or participate in the Summits of the Americas. Today, any regime that takes power by unconstitutional means will be ostracized, as was shown in the rejection of the Venezuelan coup last month.

Democracy is a framework that permits a people to accommodate changing times and correct past mistakes. Since our independence, the United States has rid itself of slavery, granted women the right to vote, ended almost a century of legal racial discrimination, and just this year reformed its election laws to correct problems we faced in Florida eighteen months ago.

Cuba has adopted a socialist government where one political party dominates, and people are not permitted to organize any opposition movements. Your Constitution recognizes freedom of speech and association, but other laws deny these freedoms to those who disagree with the government.

My nation is hardly perfect in human rights. A very large number of our citizens are incarcerated in prison, and there is little doubt that the death penalty is imposed most harshly on those who are poor, black, or mentally ill. For more than a quarter century, we have struggled unsuccessfully to guarantee the basic right of universal health care for our people. Still, guaranteed civil liberties offer every citizen an opportunity to change these laws.

That fundamental right is also guaranteed to Cubans. It is gratifying to note that Articles 63 and 88 of your constitution allows citizens to petition the National Assembly to permit a referendum to change laws if 10,000 or more citizens sign it. I am informed that such an effort, called the Varela Project, has gathered sufficient signatures and has presented such a petition to the National Assembly. When Cubans exercise this freedom to change laws peacefully by a direct vote, the world will see that Cubans, and not foreigners, will decide the future of this country.

Cuba has superb systems of health care and universal education, but last month, most Latin American governments joined a majority in the United Nations Human Rights Commission in calling on Cuba to meet universally accepted standards in civil liberties. I would ask that you permit the International Committee of the Red Cross to visit prisons and that you would receive the UN Human Rights Commissioner to address such issues as prisoners of conscience and the treatment of inmates. These visits could help refute any unwarranted criticisms.

Public opinion surveys show that a majority of people in the United States would like to see the economic embargo ended, normal travel between our two countries, friendship between our people, and Cuba to be welcomed into the community of democracies in the Americas. At the same time, most of my fellow citizens believe that the issues of economic and political freedom need to be addressed by the Cuban people.

After 43 years of animosity, we hope that someday soon, you can reach across the great divide that separates our two countries and say, "We are ready to join the community of democracies," and I hope that Americans will soon open our arms to you and say, "We welcome you as our friends."

PROSECUTION STATEMENT IN CHURCH BOMBING TRIAL
May 14, 2002

On Sunday morning, September 15, 1963, at the height of the civil rights movement in the United States, a bomb was detonated outside a church in Birmingham, Alabama, killing four black girls. The bombing was the deadliest attack on blacks of the civil rights era and shocked the nation. Nearly thirty-nine years later, on May 22, 2002, the last of the men charged with the murders was convicted and sentenced to life in prison. Bobby Frank Cherry, now seventy-one years old, was one of four white supremacists identified as the main suspects of the crime. Two of the others were convicted; the third died without being charged.

The closing of the books on the Birmingham bombing left the June 1964 slayings of three civil rights workers in Mississippi as the last major case of the civil rights era still unresolved. The Mississippi attorney general's office had been trying for some time to build a case against an undisclosed number of suspects in the killings of civil rights workers James Chaney, Andrew Goodman, and Michael Schwerner. As in the Birmingham case, the job was made more difficult as time passed, memories faded, and witnesses died. In 1994 another major case from the civil rights era had been closed when Byron De La Beckwith was convicted in Mississippi of the 1963 murder of civil rights leader Medgar Evers. (Beckwith trial, Historic Documents of 1994, p. 100)

The bombings, beatings, and slayings that marked the civil rights era had ultimately hastened the end of segregation and helped to change societal attitudes about race and integration—the opposite effect of that intended by their perpetrators. But ugly incidents still occurred. One of the worst in recent years happened in June 1998, when James Byrd, an African American from Jasper, Texas, was beaten, chained to the back of a pickup truck, and dragged for two miles until his body literally broke apart. Three white men, known for their racist beliefs and support of the local Ku Klux Klan, were quickly arrested and convicted of murder.

The nation also still struggled with a myriad of race-related issues, from racial profiling to affirmative action. Anyone doubting that race was still a sensitive issue in America in 2002 had only to look at the controversy sur-rounding Sen. Trent Lott, R-Miss., who was forced to resign in December as the incoming Senate majority leader after making a remark that was widely construed as racist. (Lott resignation, p. 969; affirmative action, Historic Documents of 1998, p. 855)

The Birmingham Church Bombing

The bombing at the 16th Street Baptist Church in Birmingham came at the height of racial tensions in Alabama. George Wallace had been inaugurated as governor in January 1963, proclaiming "segregation now, segregation tomorrow and segregation forever." That spring, the Rev. Martin Luther King and the Southern Christian Leadership Conference decided to make Birmingham the center of a nonviolent program to protest segregation of public facilities in the South. Many of the protest marches, including the Children's Marches in May, originated from the 16th Street Baptist Church.

In June 1963 Wallace made his infamous stand at the schoolhouse door to block admission of black students to the University of Alabama. On August 28 King led the March on Washington that culminated in his "I Have a Dream" speech, delivered on the steps of the Lincoln Memorial. Two weeks later, on September 10, black children in Birmingham were admitted, under court order, to the city's previous all-white schools. The following Sunday, September 15, a dynamite bomb was set off just outside a wall of the 16th Street Baptist Church. The blast killed four black girls as they prepared for the morning service: eleven-year-old Denise McNair, and three fourteen-year-olds, Addie Mae Collins, Cynthia Wesley, and Carole Robertson. Sarah Collins, Addie's sister, lost an eye in the blast. Some twenty other people were also injured.

The killing of four girls preparing for worship horrified the nation and galvanized support for the civil rights movement. Protests spread across the country. Within two years Congress had passed two landmark pieces of civil rights legislation—the Civil Rights Act of 1964, prohibiting discrimination against African Americans and other minorities in public places, schools, and employment; and the Voting Rights Act of 1965, protecting the rights of black and other minority citizens to vote.

Long Road to Prosecution

Despite those gains, the families and friends of those killed and injured in the bombing were dismayed that the men who had set the bomb were not brought to account. Police and FBI agents had quickly identified the main suspects in the crime, but efforts to prosecute the men were repeatedly derailed. A May 1965 FBI memo to then-director J. Edgar Hoover named four former members of the Ku Klux Klan as the primary suspects in the bombing. Hoover responded that the chances for conviction were "remote" in Birmingham's highly charged racial climate, and the federal government closed its case in 1968 without bringing any charges. In 1980 the Justice Department concluded that Hoover had deliberately blocked prosecution of the four men.

The state reopened its investigation in the 1970s. One of the four men on the FBI list, Robert E. Chambliss, was convicted of murder under Alabama state law in 1977 and died in prison in 1985. Chambliss was known as "Dynamite Bob" because of his participation in several bombings. Herman Frank Cash, another prime suspect, died in 1994 without being charged.

At the urging of several black ministers, the federal government reopened its investigation in 1995. The last two men on the original FBI list, Cherry and Thomas E. Blanton, were indicted in 2000. Blanton was convicted in May 2001 and sentenced to life in prison. Cherry's trial was postponed while his mental competence to stand trial was evaluated. After psychologists testified that Cherry was faking mental illness, his trial was set for May 2002. Several other men were thought to have played minor roles in the bombing, but none were linked directly to the act itself and so were unlikely ever to be prosecuted.

The Trial

The evidence against Cherry, a retired truck driver who had moved from Birmingham to Texas in the early 1970s, was largely circumstantial, alleging that Cherry had helped build the bomb and then to detonate it. Although Cherry had never publicly admitted his guilt, the prosecution said that Cherry had often privately bragged of his role in the bombing. "Over the years, this defendant has hung this crime on his chest like a badge of honor, like a Klan medal, like a hero," said Robert Posey, assistant U.S. attorney, in his opening statement May 14.

During the trial, the prosecution called several family members and acquaintances of Cherry, who said they had heard him boast about the killings. A former wife testified that Cherry would sometimes cry about the girls that had died, even as he said that "at least they wouldn't grow up to have more black" children. Tapes secretly recorded by an FBI informant around the time of the bombings were introduced into evidence to show that Cherry had a connection with Chambliss and Blanton. The informant also testified that Cherry had said he lied to the FBI. Another witness testified that as a child playing with Cherry's son, he saw a Klansman's white robe in the Cherry house and overheard Cherry and four other men talking about integration, a bomb, and the 16th Street Baptist Church.

Cherry's defense attorneys argued that the prosecution had no hard evidence against Cherry and that its witnesses, mostly estranged family members, were not credible. In his opening statement, Mickey Johnson said the prosecution was wrongly trying to insert Cherry's hands into "blank fingerprints" that could have been filled by "hundreds if not thousands" of segregationists in the Birmingham of 1963. The prosecution, Johnson said in his closing arguments, had not shown that Cherry had actually committed the crime, only that his racist attitudes about blacks were very much the same as those of other whites.

A jury of nine whites and three blacks deliberated for less than a day before finding Cherry guilty of murder. He was automatically sentenced to life in prison. Asked by the judge if he had any comment, Cherry pointed to the prosecuting attorneys and said: "This whole bunch lied all the way through this thing. I told the truth. I don't know why I'm going to jail for nothing."

After the verdict, the sister of one of the dead girls left the courtroom in tears. "It's time, it's time," she said. For many in Birmingham, the importance of the trial went beyond the fate of a single perpetrator. "It's important to say, you can't do these kinds of deeds and walk away clean," the Rev. John Porter, a civil rights leader and retired minister from a neighboring Baptist church, told a reporter as the trial opened. "There was a time when people weren't accountable. This trial says that era is now being closed."

> *Following is the text of the opening statement for the prosecution, delivered May 14, 2002, in the trial of Bobby Frank Cherry for murdering four black girls in a bombing of the 16th Street Baptist Church in Birmingham, Alabama, on September 15, 1963. The statement was delivered by Robert Owen Posey, assistant United States attorney for the Northern District of Alabama, acting as special deputy attorney general of Alabama in this case.*

> ***The document was not available on the Internet at the time of publication.***

Introduction

Bobby Frank Cherry is charged with the bombing of the 16th Street Baptist Church on a Sunday morning in September 1963. He's charged with the murder of four of the children of that church, four children of Birmingham. I'd like to take a few minutes this morning to tell you what I expect the evidence will be, and I'd like to start by taking you back to 1963.

The History

In 1963, John F. Kennedy was President of the United States. George Wallace became Governor of Alabama for the first time in January of 1963. In his inaugural speech Wallace promised "segregation now, segregation tomorrow and segregation forever".

In the spring of 1963, Dr. Martin Luther King, Jr. and the Southern Christian Leadership Conference initiated a non-violent direct action program in Birmingham, to protest segregation of public facilities. Dr. King was arrested and put in jail. His famous "Letter From the Birmingham Jail" was dated April 16.

The 16th Street Baptist Church became a fixture of the civil rights movement. Dr. King spoke at the church. Marches sometimes originated from the church. In May we had the Children's Marches, where children joined the protests, marching from the 16th Street Baptist Church to Kelly Ingram Park.

In June of 1963, George Wallace made his stand in the schoolhouse door to oppose the admission of black students to the University of Alabama. In August, Dr. King gave his "I Have a Dream Speech" on the Capitol steps in Washington, D.C. [The speech was in fact delivered on the steps of the Lincoln Memorial.]

And then in September, 1963, in Birmingham, black children were admitted to previously all-white schools for the first time. The last time that desegregation had been attempted in Birmingham was when a black preacher named Fred Shuttlesworth tried to enroll his children in Phillips High School. They were met by a mob of Klansmen who beat Shuttlesworth to the ground. One of the men in the Klan mob was the defendant, Bobby Frank Cherry, and Cherry would later brag about how he hit Shuttlesworth in the face with a set of brass knuckles.

The Motive

The desegregation of Birmingham schools happened on September 10, 1963. Five days later, on September 15, the bomb exploded at the 16th Street Baptist Church that killed the four children.

I expect the evidence will be that it was not a coincidence that this deadly bombing occurred at the moment schools were opened to all races. It was designed as an instrument of terror to force back the tide of civil rights progress. It was done by Ku Klux Klansmen who could not stand the thought of black children going to school with white children.

Like other Klan activities, carried out under the shroud of a hooded robe, this bombing was carried out in secret. The bomb was made in secret, and it was put down at the church at a time when nobody was around to see. But as this trial progresses, I expect that the evidence will remove the shroud, will lift up that white hood, and allow this jury to see who committed this crime.

Birdwell's Testimony

I expect the evidence will be that the week before the bombing, a boy named Bobby Birdwell was playing at Bobby Frank Cherry's house in Birmingham with the defendant's son Frank. As the boys ran back and forth through the house, from the front yard to the back yard, Birdwell noticed a white hooded robe laid out in the living room. As he went through the kitchen, he saw the defendant sitting at the kitchen table with three other men. In fragments of conversation, he heard one of the men say "the bomb is ready" and "16th Street" and "church". And when the bomb exploded at the church a few days later, the image of that scene in Cherry's kitchen was burned into Birdwell's memory.

Sunday Morning

September 15, 1963, was a Sunday morning. Schools had just started back after the summer break. It was Youth Sunday at the 16th Street Baptist Church, and the youth of the church were planning to participate in the leadership of the worship service. Among the children at the church that morning were:

Carole Robertson. Carole was 14 years old. Both of her parents were teachers. She played clarinet in her school band, and was looking forward to playing at her first football game the next day.

Denise McNair was 11 years old. She was the only child of Mr. and Mrs. Chris McNair. Her parents were both teachers.

Cynthia Wesley was 14 years old. She was an only child. Her father was an elementary school principal and her mother was a teacher. She sang in the church choir.

Addie Mae Collins was 14 years old. She had come to church that day with her younger sister Sara.

Around 10:20 that morning, these five girls left their Sunday School room and went down to the ladies' lounge to freshen up and get ready for their parts in the special service. The ladies lounge was in the basement of the church, partly below ground level. On one wall there was a window that looked out onto 16th Street. There were concrete stairs outside the window. The girls could stand in the light of the window to adjust their ribbons and sashes. Sara Collins walked to a sink at the back of the lounge, and glanced back to see Denise McNair adjusting the sash on Addie's dress.

Just then, a powerful explosion rocked the church. A bomb, placed just outside the window of the ladies' lounge, blew a huge crater into the foundation of the church, and filled the lounge will flying glass and brick. The force of the explosion blew out the masonry wall opposite the window, and splintered the wood panels and stairs.

Sara Collins somehow survived the blast. As she lay in the rubble of the ladies lounge, blinded by glass in both eyes, she called out for her sister Adie. But she got no answer. Sara couldn't see that just a few feet away, her sister Addie, and Denise, and Carole and Cynthia were all dead.

In the sanctuary, the blast shattered stained glass windows, and a number of the adults were injured by flying glass. Parents were crying and searching for their children. The pastor, Rev. Haywood Cross, told them to get out of the church. One of the members, Sam Rutledge, tried to leave the church the same way he had come in that morning, by the stairs on the 16th Street side of the building. But when he came to the door at the top of the stairs, the stairs were gone. So he jumped. And then he saw that the '58 Oldsmobile he drove to church that morning had been mangled by the force of the blast.

Firemen from Station Number One, a few blocks away, felt the shock and heard the blast and came to help. Jack Crews was the lieutenant in charge of Station One's engine. When he and his men got to the church, Lt. Crews climbed down into the crater and saw the bodies, and saw that it was bad. Cynthia Wesley's body could only be identified by the shoes she was wearing.

As rescue workers uncovered the bodies of the four girls, the families of Cynthia, Carole, Denise and Adie learned the horrible news that their children had been taken from them, that someone had bombed their church on a Sunday morning.

The Investigation

After the bombing, the FBI and local law enforcement launched an intensive investigation. Bobby Frank Cherry became a suspect. He was interviewed by FBI agents on a number of occasions, beginning shortly after the bombing and continuing over a period of years. Cherry talked about his involvement in the Ku Klux Klan. He was a member of Eastview Klavern 13, a group that included Thomas Blanton and Robert Chambliss. He talked about a splinter group of Klansmen who met under the Cahaba River Bridge on Hwy. 280.

He told the FBI that he knew how to use explosives, and he described in detail the chemical ingredients for making a time-delay detonator for a bomb.

He said that the only reason he didn't bomb the church was that somebody else beat him to it.

Cherry talked a lot about the bombing. I expect the evidence to be that, over the years, the bombing of the 16th Street Baptist Church became Bobby Frank Cherry's claim to fame. He was proud of it, and he talked about it. He boasted to others that he was responsible for this bombing.

At Cherry family gatherings the bombing was a frequent topic of conversation. It was understood by most of the family that Bobby Frank Cherry was responsible. His children knew the story.

His granddaughter, Teresa, growing up in Texas, heard her grandfather brag about how he put a bomb at a church in Birmingham.

Cherry's brother-in-law, Wayne Brogdon, visited him frequently while they were both living in Chicago. Brogdon listened on many occasions to Cherry tell about how he had bombed a church in Birmingham, and about the children who were killed. Sometimes Cherry even cried when he talked about the four little girls, but then he would recover, and make some vulgar remark about their deaths.

One of Cherry's wives, named Willadean, remembers how he drove her to the church to show her where it happened.

In 1982, in Dallas, Texas, Cherry was installing carpet in an apartment building, and the son of the building manager was there working on the same apartment. As they talked they discovered that they were both from Birmingham, and Cherry proceeded to tell this man the story of how he bombed the church where four little girls were killed. The man didn't think much of it at the time. But in 1997, he saw the defendant on TV, and heard that this investigation had been reopened, and he called the FBI. And I expect that man, Wayne Gowins, will testify in this trial.

Conclusion

I expect that the testimony of Wayne Gowins and others will make it clear to you that, over the years, this defendant has hung this crime on his chest like a badge of honor, like a Klan medal, like a hero. He boasted of what he and his Klan buddies did about integration in Birmingham. He boasted about the deaths of the four little girls. He boasted about bombing a church on a Sunday morning. He said that his only regret was that more people had not been killed. Ladies and gentlemen, I submit to you that his own words convict him of this crime.

I expect that you will hear evidence from eyewitnesses to this bombing, and from explosives experts. You will hear tape recordings of conversations between this defendant and others. You'll hear statements made by this defendant to the FBI, to his family members and to others. You will hear that Bobby Frank Cherry was a part of the group of Klansmen who bombed this church. He was in the thick of it, aiding and abetting the others in the planning and execution of this crime. The judge will tell you that a person who helps in any way is guilty. The driver of the getaway car, the man who's just there ready to help if needed is guilty.

I ask you to listen carefully to the evidence, to notice how the pieces of the puzzle fit together. And at the conclusion of the evidence, we will ask you to find this defendant guilty as charged.

PRESIDENT OF SIERRA LEONE
ON THE END OF CIVIL WAR
May 19, 2002

Peaceful elections in Sierra Leone in May 2002 finally brought an end to a civil war that had been one of the world's most brutal conflicts. Battered by a decade of war, but apparently determined to put their nation back together again, Sierra Leoneans on May 14 reelected the civilian president who guerrilla forces had tried to oust from power. President Ahmed Tejan Kabbah took the oath of office May 19 and pledged to help the country "resume our status as a model of peace, stability, and democracy in the African continent."

Kabbah acknowledged that achieving that goal would be extraordinarily difficult. Since the outbreak of war in 1991, Sierra Leone had been anything but a model of peace, stability, and democracy. A rebel group, the Revolutionary United Front (RUF), aided by neighboring Liberia, had taken control of much of the country and looted the rich diamond mines of eastern Sierra Leone. The RUF appeared to be motivated more by the quest for political power and economic gain than by any particular ideology. Forcibly recruiting thousands of child soldiers, the RUF quickly developed a reputation as one of the most vicious armed groups in recent history; its trademark method of terrorizing civilian populations was to hack off the limbs of men, women, and children who stood in the way. About half of the nation's 5.2 million people were forced from their homes by the fighting, and an estimated 50,000 people were killed. No accurate count was ever made of the thousands of people who were raped or mutilated during the conflict.

The rebels and the government signed three truce accords in the late 1990s, but all agreements collapsed under the weight of continued fighting. In 2000 the RUF rebels captured 500 members of a small United Nations peacekeeping force attempting to enforce a cease-fire. The breakthrough came in May 2000 when a force of 800 British marines landed in Freetown and rescued the UN troops. At about the same time, the government captured RUF leader Foday Sankoh. Lacking Sankoh's charismatic leadership, and under pressure from the British marines and a reinforced UN contingent, the rebel force fell apart and in November 2000 signed a formal peace agreement. To enforce the agreement, the UN eventually sent 17,400 peace-keepers to Sierra Leone—by far the biggest peacekeeping mission ever for the world body. The peace accord ended the bulk of the fighting and set the stage for a process that led to the elections in May 2002.

UN officials, diplomats, and specialists on Africa said the ultimately successful international intervention in Sierra Leone offered lessons for dealing with extreme crises in other countries. One obvious lesson was that bringing peace to a small nation, such as Sierra Leone, was much easier than to a large one, such as the Democratic Republic of the Congo. Another was that international attention needed to be sustained and backed up with lots of money. The UN peacekeeping mission cost nearly $700 million annually for several years (nearly one-fourth of which was provided by the United States), and reconstruction also was expected to cost millions of dollars each year. Yet another lesson was that peacekeepers needed to be well equipped and prepared to fight. (Congo conflict, p. 546; peacekeeping background, Historic Documents of 2000, p. 642)

Peaceful Elections

The process of disarming more than 50,000 combatants from Sierra Leone's civil war came to a conclusion in January. Under UN supervision, about 47,000 former RUF fighters and several thousand members of pro-government militias handed over their arms and promised not to fight again. As an incentive to give up their weapons, the ex-fighters were given a one-time payment of about $130 and offered training in vocational skills. President Kabbah in March ended the state of emergency that had been in effect since 1998.

In the months before the election, the chief question was whether the still-imprisoned Sankoh would be allowed to run as the presidential candidate for the RUF rebel group, which had established a political party called the Revolutionary United Front Party. The government electoral commission announced on March 29 that Sankoh could not run because he had not registered to vote—something he could not do while a prisoner. The former rebels named a stand-in candidate, Pallo Bangura. The main challenger to Kabbah and his Sierra Leone People's Party turned out to be Ernest Koroma of the All People's Congress, which had been part of a junta that ruled the country before Kabbah first won the presidency in 1996.

Gangs of rock-throwing supporters of the three main political parties clashed in Freetown on May 11, just three days before the election. UN peace-keepers quickly contained the disturbance, however. On election day, voters overwhelmed the polling stations. Among them were hundreds of people whose hands had been amputated by RUF guerrillas; they voted by dipping their toes in ink and then marking ballots. UN Secretary General Kofi Annan praised the voters' "peaceful and enthusiastic participation in the elections as an eloquent testimony to Sierra Leoneans' determination to turn a page on their tragic past." More than 200 observers from the British Commonwealth, the European Union, and several African countries said the entire election process had been free and fair.

*The final tally showed that more than 80 percent of the 2.3 million regis-
tered voters went to the polls. They gave Kabbah 71 percent of the vote in the
nine-man presidential contest. Despite widespread allegations of corruption by leaders of Kabbah's party, its candidates won 83 of the 124 seats in
parliament. Perhaps just as important, the Revolutionary United Front
Party found that ten years of war had given it virtually no popular support.
Bangura, the party's presidential candidate, captured less than 2 percent of
the vote, and rebel candidates won no seats in parliament.*

*Taking the oath of office on May 19, Kabbah said his first priority would
be to combat hunger, a growing problem in country where most people were
engaged in subsistence agriculture that was disrupted by the war. Elections
for local councils were scheduled for April 2003—the first in more than
twenty-five years. UN officials expressed hope that the process would consolidate democracy as an alternative to warfare in the provinces.*

Rebuilding a War-Torn Nation

*Peace and free elections were welcome alternatives to war in Sierra
Leone, but they marked just the beginning of what was certain to be a
lengthy process of reconstructing a country whose infrastructure had been
largely destroyed. Sierra Leone had substantial mineral wealth, especially
diamonds, but the conflict traumatized the people and left them deeply
impoverished, with a per capita income among the world's lowest—less
than half a dollar a day. Corruption, a common problem in most of the
developing world, had reached epidemic proportions in Sierra Leone during the war and was a major factor discouraging international businesses
that might have considered investing there.*

*The first challenge facing the government, and the international agencies
supporting it, was to provide aid and the prospect of long-term employment
to the tens of thousands of people who fought in the war and the millions of
civilians who suffered as a consequence of it. About half of the approximately 50,000 former combatants had been reintegrated into society by late
in the year, but that still left thousands who, according to the UN, were
"increasingly restless and often resort[ed] to street protests." Most of the
civilians displaced by the war had returned to their home provinces by
year's end, but in many cases they found their homes and crop lands
destroyed.*

*The reconstruction effort received a significant boost on March 20 when
the World Bank and International Monetary Fund announced that Sierra
Leone was eligible for $950 million in debt relief under a international pro-
gram in effect since 1996. The program would allow Sierra Leone to make
investments in education, health care, and rural development programs
with money that otherwise would have been used to pay off past debts to the
World Bank and other development agencies.* (Debt relief initiative, Historic
Documents of 2000, p. 459)

*One of the painful challenges facing the country was the process of deal-
ing with the many human rights abuses committed during the war. International experts said Sierra Leone needed to confront directly the horrors*

of its past if it was to have any hope of preventing them from recurring. As part of that process, the UN and Sierra Leone on January 16 agreed to establish a war crimes tribunal, called the Special Court, to deal with serious war-time violations of international humanitarian law. The tribunal was to consider cases since November 1996, when rebels signed the first of three peace agreements. Tribunal prosecutors began work in September, and eight judges were sworn in on December 2. Two judges were from Sierra Leone and the others were from Austria, Britain, Cameroon, Canada Gambia, and Nigeria. The tribunal had a mandate to complete its work by 2005. In addition, Sierra Leone established a Truth and Reconciliation Commission to uncover the facts behind the atrocities committed during the war by all sides. Annan said this body could address one of the most destabilizing factors in the country—the "perceived lack of support provided to victims of the conflict in contrast with the assistance provided to ex-combatants."

Security Situation Still Unsettled

Sierra Leone's transition from war to peace had been made possible by military intervention from outside, but it was clear that 17,400 international peacekeepers could not stay there forever and would have to be replaced by a local security force. The British marines had been training government troops since 2000. By 2002 the government had gained working control of the Freeport area and other cities but exerted little control in rural areas, especially some of the major diamond-mining districts.

In a September 5 report to the Security Council, Annan said the UN would need to engage in a delicate balancing act as it reduced the size of its mission in Sierra Leone to "avoid creating a security vacuum in the country." He set out a series of "benchmarks" to measure progress in such tasks as rebuilding the army and police forces, the reintegration of former fighters into society, the restoration of government control over the diamond districts, and the consolidation of state authority. He called for a phased process beginning with the withdrawal of about 600 troops by the end of 2002. During 2003 remaining peacekeepers would be concentrated in the central part of the country, in the diamond regions, and along the border with Liberia. Another 4,000 troops would be withdrawn by August 2003, leaving 13,000 UN troops in key trouble spots. If conditions allowed, another 8,000 troops would be withdrawn by late 2004, and the force would hand over most of the country to the national army and police forces and concentrate in the two coastal peninsulas where Freetown and the city of Lungi are located. If all went well, Annan said, the final withdrawal of UN forces would take place at the end of 2004 or early in 2005.

The Security Council on September 24 approved the first phase of Annan's plan and extended the UN peacekeeping mandate in Sierra Leone through March 2003. The first contingent of deactivated UN peacekeepers—450 troops from Bangladesh—left Freetown on November 3. Several thousand people, many of them in tears, lined the streets to the airport as the UN forces left. Later in November, Britain withdrew the last of the marines who had been in Sierra Leone independent of the UN mission.

Neighboring Liberia Deteriorates

Perhaps the most worrisome threat to Sierra Leone's peaceful recon-struction was the festering conflict in neighboring Liberia. That country's president, Charles Taylor, had come to power in 1997 after a violent eight-year civil war that killed at least 150,000 people and left much of the coun-try in ruins. Taylor had supplied weapons to the RUF guerrillas in Sierra Leone, who paid for that support with diamonds from the mines they had seized. The UN Security Council in 2001 imposed sanctions against Taylor and his top aides in an effort to force them to stop supporting the RUF and enriching themselves with Sierra Leone's diamonds. The Security Council in May extended the sanctions for twelve months, saying that Taylor had not complied with its demands.

As peace was coming to Sierra Leone in 2000, Liberia's latent civil war erupted again. This time the fighting pitted Taylor's autocratic regime against a guerrilla force, Liberians United for Reconciliation and Democ-racy, which reportedly had support from Guinea and operated from bases in northern Liberia along the borders with Guinea and Sierra Leone. The fighting continued into 2002, and by August more than 50,000 refugees from Liberia had flooded into Sierra Leone. Fearing more serious conflict, the UN drew up contingency plans to accommodate 125,000 Liberian refu-gees. In his September 5 report to the Security Council, Annan warned that the fighting "could pose the risk of a vicious cycle of violence" in the entire West Africa region. Earlier in the year, a task force assembled by the U.S. Institute for Peace suggested that instances of "state collapse" in Liberia, Sierra Leone, and other countries had weakened stability in the region and could pose a long-term threat to U.S. security by endangering Nigeria (which supplied 10 percent of U.S. imported oil) and spawning terrorism and international criminal networks.

Ivory Coast Conflict

Yet another threat to the West Africa region was a new conflict in Ivory Coast, which for decades had been the region's bastion of economic pros-perity and stability. By year's end the conflict had drawn in France, the country's colonial power, which was seeking to prevent the violence from spiraling out of control.

Ivory Coast's unrest dated from the 1993 death of longtime ruler, Felix Houphouet-Boigny, who since independence in 1960 had held in check the fierce divisions between the populous northern region dominated by Mus-lims and the more prosperous south dominated by Christians. These latent ethnic divisions rose to the surface during the rest of the 1990s and con-tributed to a December 1999 military coup that ousted Houphouet-Boigny's successor. The coup leader, General Robert Guei, then tried to rig elections in 2000 but was forced from power by popular unrest. Laurent Gbagbo, a Christian from the south, prevailed in the violence-plagued elections, but only after the most popular leader from the north, Alassane Ouatara, was disqualified on a technicality.

On September 19, 2002, three years after the disputed elections, soldiers from the Muslim north attempted a coup against Gbagbo. The coup failed, but the rebels calling themselves the Political Movement of Ivory Coast quickly gained control of the northern half of the country, including Bouake, the second-largest city (after Abidjan, the capital). The government suggested that the rebels had support from neighboring Burkina Faso (a Muslim-majority nation); in turn vigilante groups in the south attacked many of the 3 million immigrants from Burkina Faso who worked in the country's cocoa fields.

West African leaders mediated a truce, which the two sides signed in late October, but that accord later collapsed when two other rebel groups emerged in the western part of the Ivory Coast to challenge the government. By year's end France had sent 2,500 troops to protect the 20,000 French citizens in the country and prevent the collapse of Gbagbo's government.

Controlling "Conflict Diamonds"

Liberia's trading in diamonds from Sierra Leone was only one of several situations in which African conflicts were fueled by diamond smuggling. Since 1998 news reports and official investigations had revealed that rebels groups in Angola, Congo, and several other African countries had taken control of diamond-producing areas, mined the diamonds themselves or forced others to do so, and sold the rough diamonds to middlemen who peddled them on the international market. Most reputable dealers in Antwerp and other diamond markets reportedly refused to accept these "conflict diamonds," but the lure of huge profits ensured that many unscrupulous smugglers and traders would deal in them.

After nearly three years of discussion, fifty-two nations and representatives of the legitimate diamond industry on November 5 signed an agreement intended to block the trade in conflict diamonds. Participants agreed to a set of regulations, known as the Kimberly process, under which rough, uncut diamonds exported from one country to another must be accompanied by government certification that they did not come from territory held by rebel groups. All diamond-importing countries must acknowledge the receipt of certified diamonds and refuse to accept any uncertified shipments. The agreement was to take effect January 1, 2003.

Proponents of the agreement, including the United States (the world's biggest importer of cut diamonds) said the agreement would make it much more difficult for rebel groups and unscrupulous traders to profit from conflict diamonds. Representatives of some human rights groups argued that the agreement was inadequate because it did not provide for international monitoring of the certification process by individual countries. These groups noted that many governments, such as those in Congo Republic and Liberia, had benefited from the illegal diamond trade and could not be counted on to enforce the new regulations.

Following are excerpts from a speech delivered May 19, 2002, by Ahmad Tejan Kabbah after he took the oath of office as president of Sierra Leone for a second term.

*The document was obtained from the Internet at www
.reliefweb.int/w/rwb.nsf/f303799b16d2074285256830007fb
33f/672b83bc078ebdf5c1256bc300407972?OpenDocument;
accessed November 25, 2002.*

The people have spoken. They have made what I described two weeks ago as one of the most far-reaching decisions in the current history of Sierra Leone. They have chosen the men and women whom they would like not just to lead, but more importantly to serve this nation in the next five years. They did it the democratic way—freely, transparently and peacefully.

Let me therefore start by congratulating the entire electorate for successfully demonstrating to the rest of Africa and the world at large that Sierra Leone is indeed a democracy and that we are determined to resume our status as a model of peace, stability and democracy in the African continent.

I should also like to congratulate all the political parties and their candidates, especially those who ran for the highest offices in the land as presidential and vice-presidential candidates. You should all be commended for a great effort.

In these elections that we all agreed were not a war but a friendly contest, there are no losers. As a matter of fact we should all consider ourselves winners. We are all winners because, irrespective of the results, we succeeded in making this one of the most violence-free electoral processes in Sierra Leone since independence. So to you my former contestants, be assured that there is a place for each and every one of you in the service of your country. I say this because the privilege of serving the people is not limited to a seat in Parliament, or occupancy of State House and The Lodge. You know, as I do, that there are other seats, offices and positions available in all sectors of our country from where we can each make a contribution to improving the lives of our fellow compatriots. There are also important and positive roles that each individual can play in helping us achieve that objective.

Those who care, and I have no doubt that we all do, need not be reminded that we have a lot of work to do in this country, and that no single political party, no single Government can do it alone. I would therefore like to appeal to you, whatever your party affiliation, whatever your party symbol, and whatever your ideology, to join me in building a new coalition for national development. It was our right and responsibility to vote. It is also our right and collective responsibility to work together in raising the standard of living and quality of life of all Sierra Leoneans. I trust that I can count on your cooperation.

To my fellow compatriots, I say be assured that I am aware of the heavy responsibility you have given me to serve you for another five years. By re-electing me you have made it clear that you acknowledge the great transformation that we are already experiencing, especially since the formal end of the disarmament and demobilization process. You have also made it clear that you have confidence in my experience and ability to build on the gains we have made so far. For this I am sincerely grateful.

In this connection, I should emphasize that the election is a free choice, which should not bring retribution against anyone based on the choice he or she made. Therefore, no person, no occupational group, no chiefdom or district in the country should entertain any doubt as to the attention it will get from my Government vis-à-vis others in our country. All Sierra Leone is my constituency.

Six years ago my principal objective was centred on peace—the right of every Sierra Leonean to live in peace and security. I made a pledge to do everything in my power to seek an end to the rebel war and to bring peace to our country. We have already begun to reap the benefits of this transformation. But there are other priorities on the national agenda that we must tackle more vigorously.

Fellow Sierra Leoneans, my own principal objective on this second leg of our journey together is also centred on a basic human right—the right to food. So, today, with the new mandate you have given me, I should make another pledge. This time I pledge to work harder and with greater resolve to do everything in my power to ensure that within the next five years no Sierra Leonean should go to bed hungry. We must have the capacity to feed ourselves. We will therefore place proper emphasis on agriculture. This objective is consistent with my enduring commitment to the reduction of poverty in our society and the creation of jobs and other opportunities, particularly for our women and the youth, so that they can realize their full potential.

In the next few weeks I shall present, through your new representatives in Parliament, details of my strategy for achieving this objective.

Fellow Sierra Leoneans, we all acknowledge that corruption has over a long period been eating deep into the fabric of our society. This is why I requested the help of the Government of the United Kingdom to establish the Anti-Corruption Commission. This is also why the Right Honourable Mrs. Claire Short, Minister for International Development of the United Kingdom, was here a short while ago to encourage all Sierra Leoneans to cooperate in the fight against corruption. This fight against corruption will continue to be one of my major preoccupations and I will expect you to join me in this fight.

To our friends and partners in the international community the conduct of the elections should serve as an expression of our gratitude for their support in getting us through the process peacefully. I should like to assure them that the investments they have made in Sierra Leone will continue to yield similar positive results in the near future.

As members of the international community know, the people of Sierra Leone have already demonstrated their resilience under extremely difficult circumstances. For over ten years they struggled to rid themselves of the terror and scourge of a brutal rebellion. They stood firm against the tyranny of military juntas and military/rebel regimes. They fought valiantly for the restoration of democracy. In this regard, I am sure that the people of Sierra Leone have earned the admiration of the international community. They have convinced the world that Sierra Leone is worth all the support and cooperation the international community can muster to facilitate political stability, security and sustainable development in this country.

Finally, to my fellow Sierra Leoneans, let me remind ourselves that elections, important as they are, are not an end in themselves. Now that we have reaffirmed, through the ballot box, the principle that sovereignty belongs to the people, from whom Government derives all its powers, authority and legitimacy, we should all rededicate ourselves to putting service to the interests of the nation above self-interest.

As I assume the Presidency for a second time, it is appropriate for me to renew the solemn vow I made six years ago soon after taking the oath of office:

"I vow to serve you to the best of my ability and strength, God being my helper. I promise never to sacrifice the interests of Sierra Leone or yours for any other interest or consideration, and I shall strive to ensure that all those who serve you under my direction shall do the same. And so today, and in the succeeding days, I say 'let honesty, unrelenting hard work, love and unity prevail among us.' "

STATEMENTS ON THE
INDEPENDENCE OF EAST TIMOR
May 20, 2002

East Timor, the tiny former province of Indonesia that suffered a round of extreme violence in 1999 and then came under United Nations control, gained its full independence on May 20, 2002. Four months later it became the 191st UN member. East Timor faced many challenges as an impoverished nation of fewer than 800,000 people, but its transition to independence was widely seen as one of the most important success stories in UN history. The success was all the greater because the UN had bungled its first intervention in East Timor, when the holding of a referendum on independence in 1999 led to severe violence.

Praising the determination of East Timor's people, UN Secretary General Kofi Annan told them at an independence day ceremony: "Yours has not been an easy path to independence. You should be very proud of your achievement. That a small nation is able to inspire the world and be the focus of our attention is the highest tribute that I can pay."

East Timor for 400 years was a colony of Portugal. After Portugal left in 1975, East Timor was invaded by Indonesia, which already controlled the western half of the island of Timor. During the following two decades the Indonesian military harshly suppressed a leftist independence movement in East Timor, killing or driving into exile tens of thousands of the province's people.

The 1998 overthrow of long-time Indonesian dictator Suharto created an opportunity for a peaceful solution to the conflict in East Timor. In August 1999 the UN sponsored a referendum on the future status of the province, in which about three-fourths of those who voted opted for full independence from Indonesia. Anti-independence militia groups, armed and trained by the Indonesian military, attacked independence supporters before the voting, then in a massive rampage after the voting killed an estimated 1,000 people and destroyed the vast majority of public buildings and many houses. During the violence more than 200,000 people fled across the border into Indonesian-controlled West Timor. An international peacekeep-

ing force led by Australia brought calm to East Timor in late 1999, and the UN mounted one of its most comprehensive efforts ever to rebuild a war-torn territory.

If anyone doubted that East Timor remained a deeply troubled country, those doubts were erased by two days of rioting in the capital, Dili, the first week of December 2002. A demonstration by about 500 students, protesting the arrest of one student on charges of gang violence, led to a rampage in which two people were killed and dozens of shops and buildings were damaged, including the country's only mosque and the prime minister's house. (Background, Historic Documents of 2001, p. 593, Historic Documents of 1999, p. 511)

Presidential Elections and Independence

For a people who had never experienced any form of democracy, the East Timorese suddenly found themselves going to the polls repeatedly. The first time was the 1999 independence referendum, conducted in an atmosphere of violence and hostility. Less than two years later, however, the UN in August 2001 sponsored remarkably peaceful and trouble-free elections for a constituent assembly charged with writing the territory's first constitution. The constitution was completed in March 2002; it called for a democratic state, with an elected president and a one-chamber legislature, along with an independent judiciary.

On April 14 East Timor held its first presidential election. The over-whelming winner of the two-man contest (with 82.7 percent of the vote) was Xanana Gusmao, who as leader of the pro-independence guerrilla movement Revolutionary Front for an Independent East Timor (Fretilin) had been imprisoned by Indonesia for six years until the 1999 referendum.

Gusmao had at first refused to run for the presidency, saying that former guerrilla leaders generally did not make good government officials. Gusmao ultimately relented to the demands of his supporters, but he ran as an independent, spurning the endorsement of Fretilin, which had transformed itself into East Timor's dominant political party. Gusmao criticized party leaders for enriching themselves while their constituents remained impoverished.

The election of Gusmao was the last major step in the transformation of East Timor from an embattled province of Indonesia into full statehood. That status came at the stroke of midnight on May 20, when the United Nations flag was hauled down in Dili and replaced with the brand new flag of East Timor. Later, Annan and Gusmao presided over a noon ceremony attended by international dignitaries, including former U.S. president Bill Clinton and Indonesian prime minister Megawati Sukarnoputri. Gusmao personally escorted Megawati to the ceremony, symbolizing an improvement in relations between the huge island nation and the province it had sought to control for a quarter century.

Addressing his fellow citizens for the first time as their official president, Gusmao said: "Today we are a people standing on equal footing with all other people in the world. On the celebration of independence, we wish to take upon ourselves this commitment to you: to work solely and exclusively for our people."

UN Stewardship of East Timor

In the two-plus years leading up to the May 20 independence ceremony, East Timor had been a virtual ward of the United Nations. A special mission, the United Nations Transitional Administration in East Timor (UNTAET), rebuilt East Timor's damaged buildings and public services, supervised the elections, recruited and trained thousands of public servants and technical workers, and generally served as a transitional government. In transforming East Timor UNTAET spent more than $2 billion, all of it donated by the World Bank, other international agencies, and individual countries, including Australia, Japan, and the United States. UNTAET was headed by Brazilian diplomat Sergio de Mello, who arrived shortly after the 1999 violence and then used his broad international contacts to win financial and logistical aid for East Timor.

In April 2002, shortly before it went out of business, UNTAET issued a list of its twenty-five "major achievements," starting with the establishment of an atmosphere of "peace and security" in East Timor. Other key achievements listed by the UN included the return to East Timor of most of the 200,000 refugees who had fled the 1999 violence (an estimated 50,000 remained in West Timor refugee camps as of mid-2002); the appointment of a Timorese "council of ministers" that ran the province's day-to-day government under UN supervision pending independence; the reconstruction of most schools, medical clinics, other public buildings, roads, electrical and telephone lines, and public water sources; the establishment of a police force, a small defense force, and a basic legal system; and the holding of elections leading up to independence.

De Mello said he had sought to avoid the mistakes that had plagued many previous UN efforts to bring peace and stability to war-torn areas, including Angola, Bosnia, Cambodia, Kosovo, and Rwanda. "We chose not to opt for the usual and classical peacekeeping approach: taking abuse, taking bullets, taking casualties, and not responding with enough force, not shooting to kill [when attacked]," de Mello told the Washington Post. *"The UN had done that before and we weren't going to repeat it here." The UN's one tragedy during the transition—the killing of three UN aid workers in September 2000— occurred in Indonesian-controlled West Timor, not in East Timor.* (Review of previous UN peacekeeping missions, Historic Documents of 2000, p. 642)

De Mello and other observers said a major factor in East Timor's successful transition to peace was the absence of the kind of ethnic conflict that had plagued most other UN peacekeeping operations. Nearly all East Timorese were of the same ethnic background and spoke either Portuguese or the local language, Tetum. Between Indonesia's invasion in 1975 and the 1999 referendum, the fighting in East Timor was over political issues, most importantly whether East Timor would be an independent state or would remain part of Indonesia. A central actor was the powerful Indonesian military, which sought to defeat the independence movement. The entry on the scene of international peacekeepers and the UN mission effectively eliminated the Indonesian military from the equation, enabling East Timorese to reconcile their past differences and the country to develop itself without outside intimidation.

East Timor—which had formally changed its name to Timor-Leste— became the 191st member of the United Nations on September 27, 2002.

Challenges Ahead

In an April 14 report to the UN Security Council, Annan said that all the achievements in East Timor since the 1999 violence "are at risk if they are not reinforced through a continued international presence and commitment." The tiny country faced numerous challenges, he said, notably the fact that it "is desperately poor and will remain so over the immediate future." Moreover, Annan said that key elements of a modern state were still missing or underdeveloped in East Timor, including a functioning judicial system and a police force. Annan drew particular attention to the need for a judicial system, noting that the country remained heavily dependent on foreign judges and legal experts to handle routine civil and criminal cases as well as the backlog of prosecutions stemming from the 1999 violence. Among other things, Annan said East Timor needed judges to help resolve numerous disputes over land ownership that arose during and after Indonesia controlled the territory. Until those disputes are resolved, he said, East Timor would receive little foreign investment, considered vital to its long-term economic development.

To provide the needed international support, Annan proposed that the UN establish a slimmed-down version of the mission that had run East Timor from late 1999 until early 2002. The Security Council later approved Annan's plan. Called the United Nations Mission of Support in East Timor (UNMISET), this mission's main roles were to coordinate international aid to East Timor, provide security through a peacekeeping force, and help the new government gain its footing during its first two years in office. Annan said UNMISET would gradually phase out its operations in East Timor over the next two years. The most noticeable transition would be the gradual withdrawal of the international peacekeeping force, from its high point of 8,950 troops in 2000, to 5,000 troops by November 2002, then 2,780 by July 2003, then 1,750 by December 2003, then full withdrawal by the end of June 2004. About 100 civil servants hired by the UN would remain in East Timor during the transition period, working in the country's government agencies; this was the first time that UN employees would be reporting to a national government rather than to the world body or one of its agencies.

Aside from the enthusiasm generated by the country's independence, perhaps the brightest spot in East Timor's immediate future was the prospect of relatively large revenues from oil and gas production in the Timor Sea, between East Timor and Australia. The two countries in July 2001 signed *an agreement governing development of oil and gas in two offshore fields. The agreement was converted into a full treaty after East Timor became independent. Experts estimated that East Timor would receive $2.5 billion to $3 billion in revenues over a seventeen-year period from development of gas from one field entirely within its jurisdiction; additional revenues were considered likely from other fields that East Timor shared with Australia.*

Prosecuting Rights Violators

Journalists and other observers reported that many East Timorese seemed ready to forgive their fellow citizens who had carried out the violence surrounding the 1999 independence referendum. Even so, halting efforts continued during 2002 to bring to justice the Indonesian authorities who had directed the violence and the militiamen who had carried out the most egregious crimes.

Most international attention focused on Indonesia's reluctant moves to prosecute eighteen military and civilian leaders who had armed and organized the East Timorese militias that fought the independence drive before and after the referendum. Indonesian courts handled the cases of thirteen of these leaders during 2002. Three were convicted of crimes but given relatively light sentences and allowed to remain free pending appeals. Ten others were acquitted.

In the first case, decided on August 14, an Indonesian court found the last Indonesian governor of East Timor, Jose Osorio Abilio Soares, guilty of crimes against humanity because he did nothing to stop the 1999 violence. However, the court sentenced Soares to only three years in prison, less than one-third of the ten-year sentence required under Indonesian law for the crime, and it allowed him to remain free pending an appeal. One day later, on August 15, a separate Indonesian court acquitted six military commanders of numerous charges relating to the 1999 violence. The court said it found no evidence to support the charges. Four other former security officers were acquitted on similar charges by Indonesia's human rights court on November 29.

An Indonesian court on November 27 convicted Eurico Guterres, leader of one of the most notorious pro-Indonesian militias, of human rights crimes in connection with a 1999 incident during which twelve people were killed. The court gave Guterres the minimum sentence of ten years in prison. Finally, on December 28 an Indonesian court convicted Lieutenant Colonel Sujarwo of human rights violations because he failed to prevent another incident during the 1999 violence in which at least fifteen people were killed. Sujarwo, who had commanded the Indonesian military forces in Dili, was the first Indonesian military officer convicted of charges related to the violence in East Timor. He was given a sentence of five years in prison, half the penalty requested by prosecutors.

UN officials, the United States, and international human rights organizations denounced Indonesia's handling of all these cases, saying the gov-

ernment appeared unwilling to accept full responsibility for its past actions. In a statement, Amnesty International called the trials of the six military commanders acquitted in August "seriously flawed" because the Indonesian government had failed to mount "effective prosecutions."

In East Timor, the UN in January established a Commission for Reception, Truth and Reconciliation to investigate human rights violations between 1974 (when Portugal pulled out of East Timor) and the 1999 violence. One of the commission's main tasks was to make it easier for those who had committed lesser crimes to return to their communities. Also, East Timor courts—staffed primarily by UN-hired lawyers and judges—worked on prosecuting more than 100 people thought to have been responsible for ten of the most serious crimes committed during the 1999 violence. By 2002 about half of those alleged perpetrators had been charged with crimes against humanity (including mass murder and rape); UN officials said most of the remaining were believed to be in West Timor.

Following is the text of a speech by United Nations Secretary General Kofi Annan and excerpts (prepared by the BBC) of a speech by East Timor's new president, Xanana Gusmao, both given on May 20, 2002, when East Timor attained full independence as a sovereign nation.

The documents were obtained from the Internet at www .un.org/News/Press/docs/2002/sgsm8243.doc.htm and news.bbc.co.uk/1/hi/world/asia-pacific/1997437.stm; accessed October 11, 2002.

SPEECH BY SECRETARY GENERAL ANNAN

This will not be a long speech. It cannot be. For in just a few minutes, I must stop as we reach midnight on 19 May. With the start of 20 May, you will step into a new era in your history, as an independent nation. I am deeply honoured and moved to be with you at this moment.

With the new day comes a new beginning for East Timor. Your identity as an independent people will be recognized by the whole world. I still recall the day, 45 years ago, when my own country Ghana attained its independence. Tonight, I am as excited as I was then.

At this moment, we honour every citizen of East Timor who persisted in the struggle for independence. We also remember the many who are no longer with us—but who dreamed of this moment. It is their day, too.

I salute you—people of East Timor—for the courage and perseverance you have shown. Yours has not been an easy path to independence. You should be very proud of your achievement. That a small nation is able to inspire the world and be the focus of our attention is the highest tribute that I can pay to you.

I am also deeply proud of the partnership between you—the people of East Timor—and us, the United Nations. Together, we have laid the foundations for a prosperous and democratic future.

While your determination ensured the success of your cause, you have also been helped by friends from all over the world. For the past two-and-a-half years, a global alliance of nations has come together to make this day possible.

This transitional period has been truly unique. Never before has the world united with such firm resolve to help one small nation establish itself.

Never before has the United Nations been asked to administer a territory on its way to independence. My colleagues in the United Nations Transitional Administration in East Timor (UNTAET)—led by my Special Representative Sergio Vieira de Mello—carried out this noble mission with courage and imagination.

I am proud of them, and grateful to all of them and of you for the way you have worked with them. Your independence day is a day of pride for all of us.

As you now set out to shape your own destiny, you will face trials and challenges. Independence is not an end. It is the beginning of self-rule, which requires compromise, discipline, unity and resolve. While you have succeeded in one challenge—winning your independence—this only paves the way for many more.

Those who are privileged to lead you will have to strive constantly to reduce poverty, disease and inequality; to provide education and good governance for all; and to uphold the rule of law.

And all of you who are privileged to be citizens of the new State will have to work hard for your nation, for yourselves, and for your friends and neighbours.

Controlling your own fate requires discipline and toil. Citizenship is hard work. It means that all of you must contribute your energies and ideas to the building of your nation, just as you did during your struggle for freedom.

Above all, you must remain united. Unity does not mean that only one set of beliefs is allowed, or that only one answer exists. It means celebrating a variety of views and ideas—all of which can help build a diverse and creative society.

Let me assure you that independence will not mean the end of the world's commitment to you. The United Nations will stay. Your friends around the world will continue to help. We will all work together to ensure that the first years of independence are years of stability and progress.

I have no doubt that you will fulfil your new roles—as citizens of East Timor and of the world—with spirit and great success.

I wish you a bright and secure future.

Parabens, boa sorte, e obrigado barak! Viva timor leste! [Congratulations, good luck, and thank you very much. Long live East Timor!]

SPEECH BY PRESIDENT GUSMAO

If 92 countries are gathered here today it is because the settlement of the question of East Timor was the responsibility of the international community. Therefore your presence here is the most eloquent testimony of the universal values enshrined in the charter of the United Nations and is equally an unequivocal affirmation of the rights of the fundamental rights of peoples.

To the Secretary General of the United Nations, Doctor Kofi Annan, we wish to express our most sincere gratitude for the personal commitment to the Timorese cause.

We wish to extend here a word of profound friendship to all those in the world who endeavored to understand us and above all who administered the process.

The list of acknowledgments would be long and it would make a special reference to the courage of [former Indonesian B.J.] President Habibie, the efforts of [Australian] Prime Minister John Howard and the decisiveness of [former U.S.] President [Bill] Clinton.

We warmly welcome your [Indonesian president Megawati Sukarnoputri] presence here among us, not only in your capacity as head of state of the brotherly and neighboring country which we share common borders, but also as a symbol of the democratic yearnings of the brotherly people of Indonesia.

The Indonesian people and the Timorese people have endured 24 years of difficult relations. Today we all agree that the strains in our dealings were the result of a historical mistake which now belongs to history and to the past. And this past . . . should not continue to stain our spirits or to hamper our attitudes and conduct.

I would like to pay a public tribute to the Portuguese authorities, for having turned East Timor and its people into a national cause of their own. I would also like to thank each and everyone of our brotherly Portuguese-speaking countries for their affection, their political support and solidarity, which epitomized our brotherhood and which helped strengthen our relations in difficult times.

We hope you [Portugal] and our CPLP [Community of Portuguese-Speaking Countries] brothers will stay by our side throughout this process, which is a difficult but also an exciting one, of our independence and self-determination.

Today, you are witness of the resolve to build a democratic foundations of development for the entire Timorese society. And today, you are witnesses to the hope for the future based on the active and permanent struggle against poverty in all its forms.

Today, with humility—and before the international community—we take upon ourselves the obligations towards our people. We wanted to be ourselves, we wanted to take pride in being ourselves—a people and a nation.

Today, with your assistance, we are effectively what we have always striven to be. Today we are a people standing on equal footing with all other people in the world.

To the international solidarity we extend a profound word of thanks from our people. We continue to count on you to receive other forms of support, geared towards alleviating the hardships of our most needy populations and to the strengthening of the ties of friendship among people.

Our independence will have no value if all the people in East Timor continue to live in poverty and continue to suffer all kinds of difficulties.

We gained our independence to improve our lives.

Independence! As a people, as a territory, as a nation!

One body, one mind, one wish!

FEDERAL TASK FORCE ON
SCREENING FOR DEPRESSION
May 21, 2002

A panel of independent medical experts recommended in May 2002 that primary care physicians routinely screen their adult patients for depression, a disease that is estimated to afflict nearly 20 million adults but largely goes unrecognized and untreated. Such screenings could be the first step in identifying as many as 90 percent of adult cases of depression, the task force said. The task force also said that doctors must be prepared to follow up with patients who showed signs of depression, ensuring that they received an in-depth diagnosis, proper treatment, and subsequent care.

Whether patients needing treatment for depression or other mental conditions could expect to receive quality care or could afford to pay for treatment were open questions, however. At least two other government reports issued during the year raised serious concerns about the ability of the American mental health care system to provide adequate care for the mentally ill. Congress continued to debate whether health insurance plans should be required to treat mental conditions with the same coverages and premiums as they treated physical illnesses. Many health insurance plans did not cover mental conditions at all, and many plans that did required higher premiums and copayments than they did for other medical conditions.

Depression Screenings

The recommendation that primary care doctors routinely screen their adult patients for depression was made by the U.S. Preventive Services Task Force, an independent panel of medical experts asked by the federal government to evaluate the latest medical research and make recommendations on best-practices standards for detecting a wide range of diseases, including the use of mammograms and prostate cancer screenings. (Mammograms controversy, Historic Documents of 1997, p. 142)

The task force recommended that doctors ask two questions:

- *"Over the past two weeks, have you felt down, depressed or hopeless?"*
- *"Over the past two weeks, have you felt little interest or pleasure in doing things?"*

If a patient answered yes to either question, the doctor should then use more in-depth diagnostic tools to determine whether the patient was clinically depressed. The task force said that between 5 and 9 percent of all adult patients in primary care settings suffered from depression and that routine screenings could begin to identify 90 percent of those cases. "Most patients who are depressed have some diminished function," said Alfred Berg, the chairman of the task force and a professor at the University of Washington. "They don't take pleasure in activities, they are not productive, can't concentrate, are often sleep-deprived, don't eat well, have headaches or low back pain. If you go through a formal assessment, you find the depressed patients aren't doing as well."

For patients to benefit from routine screening, however, doctors should have systems in place to provide appropriate and effective treatment and follow-up, the task force said. "Asking 'Are you depressed?' and having the patient say 'Yes,' and then moving on doesn't cut it," Berg told the Washington Post. *"You have to have access to the right therapy or medicines. Patients must have access to medicines." There should be follow-up if the patient does not show up for appointments, he added.*

The recommendation was a revision of the position the task force took in 1996, when it concluded that there was insufficient evidence to recommend either for or against routine depression screening in adults. In its May 21 recommendation, the task force said it had now concluded that there was "good evidence" not only that routine screening would improve the accurate identification of depressed patients in primary care settings, but also that these patients would respond to proper treatment, thus reducing the incidence of depression. The task force said there was still insufficient evidence to recommend routine screening of children or adolescents.

The task force gave the recommendation for adults its "B" rating, a finding of "at least fair evidence that the [screening] improves important health outcomes and concludes that benefits outweigh harms." An "A" rating is a strong recommendation that the service be provided based on "good evidence" that the service improves health and that the benefits "substantially outweigh" the dangers. "C" and "D" ratings meant that the task force found either inconclusive information or negative information about the balance between benefits and harms of the proposed service, while and "I" meant insufficient evidence to make a recommendation one way or the other.

Depression was associated with a high risk of suicide and was also linked to physical illnesses, such as cardiac disease. Women, the elderly, those with a family history of depression, the unemployed, and people with chronic diseases were all at elevated risk for depression. According to the task force, depression cost $17 billion in lost workdays every year. (Suicide prevention, Historic Documents of 2001, p. 290)

Treating Depression

According to a study published in January, the percentage of people being treated for depression tripled between 1987 and 1997, rising from 0.7 percent to 2.3 percent. The study, which was published in the Journal of the American Medical Association, *also found that the percentage of patients being treated with antidepressants, such as Prozac and Zoloft, rose from one-third in 1987 to three-fourths in 1997. The number of visits to a doctor for depression decreased by one-third.*

The researchers said the increased treatment numbers were probably not caused by an increase in the incidence of depression, but rather by an increase in the number of people seeking treatment. Although the researchers were generally encouraged that more people appeared to be seeking treatment for their depression, some were also concerned that the quality of the care had not improved. Harold Pincus, vice chairman of psychiatry at the University of Pittsburgh and a coauthor of the study, said that the best treatment generally combined antidepressant medication with long-term follow-up. But significant numbers of people received a single prescription for medication and never refilled it. Because antidepressants usually take a month or more to have any substantial effect, these patients were unlikely to be receiving much benefit from the drugs, Pincus said.

A new study of St. John's wort, a common herbal treatment for depression, found that the herb had little effect and in some cases might endanger health. The study, conducted by researchers from Duke University Medical Center, was the largest clinical trial of the effects of the herb to date. The researchers said that anyone with major or even moderately severe depression should consult a professional health care provider for advice on the best treatment.

Mental Health Parity

A legislative effort to require health insurance plans to provide greater coverage of mental illness failed in 2002. Instead, Congress cleared legislation on November 15 extending for one year an existing mental health parity law but making no changes in policy. That law, first passed in 1996, required insurance companies that covered mental illness to set the same annual and lifetime benefits for mental illness as they do for other diseases. (Mental health parity, Historic Documents of 1996, p. 389)

A coalition of nine mental health advocacy groups, led by the American Psychiatric Association, said it was pleased that the measure was extended for a year but disappointed that more sweeping changes were not made. They supported legislation by Sen. Pete V. Domenici, R-N.M., that would prevent health plans from charging higher deductibles, copayments, and out-of-pocket expenses for treatment of more than 200 mental illnesses than they charged for other illnesses. The proposed legislation would bar health plans from setting different limits on the number of visits, total days of coverage, or scope of treatment for mental and physical illness. Like current law, Domenici's plan would not have required health plans to cover mental health or add benefits, and it would have exempted companies that employed fewer than fifty workers.

Health insurers and large employers opposed the bill, saying that it would send insurance premiums soaring—as much as 10 percent, some estimated. "The Senate bill will require coverage of a range of conditions, including caffeine addiction, jet lag, religious problems, occupation problems," Karen Ignagni, president of the American Association of Health Plans, told the Washington Post. *"When members of Congress think about mental health, they think about schizophrenia. I don't think they are aware of the generalities and terms used in the Senate legislation which could increase costs for conditions that are not supported by the scientific research."*

Mental health advocacy groups challenged those cost estimates, noting that the Congressional Budget Office estimated that the Senate bill would raise costs by only 1 percent. They also rejected suggestions that mental health parity be extended only to well-recognized conditions, such as bipolar disease and major depression. A spokesman for Sen. Paul D. Wellstone, D-Minn., a cosponsor of the Senate legislation, said limited parity would be a mistake because it would "start a new form of discriminating, pitting one form of mental illness against another."

The Senate passed the Domenici bill in 2001, but it was blocked by the Republican leadership in the House. At Domenici's request, President George Bush promised to try to broker a deal to resolve the issue, but he gave only qualified support to Domenici's legislation. At a speech on mental health at the University of New Mexico on April 30, Bush said the American health system "must treat serious mental illness like any other disease," but added that "it is critical that . . . as we provide full mental health parity, that we do not significantly run up the cost of health care." Serious talks between the supporters of the Senate legislation and the House Republican leadership never got off the ground in 2002. An aide to the House GOP leadership told the Associated Press in late October that the Senate legislation would not pass in 2002 because "health care costs are just too high."

A Failed Delivery System

During his April speech in New Mexico, Bush also announced that he had named Michael F. Hogan, director of the Ohio Department of Mental Health, to chair his newly established Freedom Commission on Mental Health. The commission was asked to conduct a comprehensive study of the mental health delivery system in the United States and to advise the president on methods for improving the system.

A preliminary report released by the commission on November 1 said that the existing mental health system was an inefficient maze of programs that frustrated both people with mental illness and providers of care. The report identified several barriers that needlessly impede access to care: fragmentation and gaps in care for both adults and children, high unemployment and disability rates among people with serious mental illness, insufficient attention to older adults, and failure to make mental health and suicide prevention national priorities. David Satcher, U.S. surgeon general during the Clinton administration, had issued path-breaking reports in 1999 on both suicide and mental health in an effort to bring more public and private attention to these conditions. (Suicide, Historic Documents of 1999, p. 439; mental health, Historic Documents of 1999, p. 836)

A report released in September by the National Council on Disability, an independent federal commission, found similar failings in the public mental health system. In "The Well Being of Our Nation: An Inter-Generational Vision of Effective Mental Health Services and Supports," the council reported that state and federal mental health systems were "in crisis, unable to provide even the most basic mental health services and supports to help people with psychiatric disabilities become full members of the communities in which they live." The report said public mental health systems should "develop the expertise to deliver not just medication and counseling, but housing, transportation, and employment supports as well." The report offered several specific recommendations to help systems achieve this goal. The president's commission on mental health was expected to make its recommendations for improving the system in 2003.

Following are excerpts from "Recommendations and Rationale: Screening for Depression," a report issued May 21, 2002, by the U.S. Preventive Services Task Force, which recommended routine depression screening for all adults visiting their primary care doctors.

The document was obtained from the Internet at www .ahrq.gov/clinic/3rduspstf/depression/depressrr.htm; accessed October 21, 2002.

Summary of Recommendations

The U.S. Preventive Services Task Force (USPSTF) recommends screening adults for depression in clinical practices that have systems in place to assure accurate diagnosis, effective treatment, and followup. **B recommendation.**

The USPSTF found good evidence that screening improves the accurate identification of depressed patients in primary care settings and that treatment of depressed adults identified in primary care settings decreases clinical morbidity. Trials that have directly evaluated the effect of screening on clinical outcomes have shown mixed results. Small benefits have been observed in studies that simply feed back screening results to clinicians. Larger benefits have been observed in studies in which the communication of screening results is coordinated with effective followup and treatment. The USPSTF concluded the benefits of screening are likely to outweigh any potential harms.

The USPSTF concludes the evidence is insufficient to recommend for or against routine screening of children or adolescents for depression. **I recommendation.**

The USPSTF found limited evidence on the accuracy and reliability of screening tests in children and adolescents and limited evidence on the effectiveness of therapy in children and adolescents identified in primary care settings.

Clinical Considerations

- Many formal screening tools are available (e.g., the Zung Self-Assessment Depression Scale, Beck Depression Inventory, General Health Questionnaire [GHQ], Center for Epidemiologic Study Depression Scale [CES-D]). Asking two simple questions about mood and anhedonia ("Over the past 2 weeks, have you felt down, depressed, or hopeless?" and "Over the past 2 weeks, have you felt little interest or pleasure in doing things?") may be as effective as using longer instruments. There is little evidence to recommend one screening method over another, so clinicians can choose the method that best fits their personal preference, the patient population served, and the practice setting.

- All positive screening tests should trigger full diagnostic interviews that use standard diagnostic criteria (i.e., those from the fourth edition of *Diagnostic and Statistical Manual of Mental Disorders* [DSM-IV]) to determine the presence or absence of specific depressive disorders, such as major depression and/or dysthymia. The severity of depression and comorbid psychological problems (e.g., anxiety, panic attacks, or substance abuse) should be addressed.

- Many risk factors for depression (e.g., female sex, family history of depression, unemployment, and chronic disease) are common, but the presence of risk factors alone cannot distinguish depressed from non-depressed patients.

- The optimal interval for screening is unknown. Recurrent screening may be most productive in patients with a history of depression, unexplained somatic symptoms, comorbid psychological conditions (e.g., panic disorder or generalized anxiety), substance abuse, or chronic pain.

- Clinical practices that screen for depression should have systems in place to ensure that positive screening results are followed by accurate diagnosis, effective treatment, and careful followup. Benefits from screening are unlikely to be realized unless such systems are functioning well.

- Treatment may include antidepressants or specific psychotherapeutic approaches (e.g., cognitive behavioral therapy or brief psychosocial counseling), alone or in combination.

- The benefits of routinely screening children and adolescents for depression are not known. The existing literature suggests that screening tests perform reasonably well in adolescents and that treatments are effective, but the clinical impact of routine depression screening has not been studied in pediatric populations in primary care settings. Clinicians should remain alert for possible signs of depression in younger patients. The predictive value of positive screening tests is lower in children and adolescents than in adults, and research on the effectiveness of primary care-based interventions for depression in this age group is limited.

Scientific Evidence

Epidemiology and Clinical Consequences

Depressive disorders are common, chronic and costly. The World Health Organization identified major depression as the fourth leading cause of worldwide disease in 1990, causing more disability than either ischemic heart disease or cerebrovascular disease. In primary care settings, the point prevalence of major depression ranges from 5 percent to 9 percent among adults, and up to 50 percent of depressed patients are not recognized. Other disabling depressive illnesses include dysthymia (a chronic low-grade depression) and minor depression (an episodic, less severe illness). These two illnesses are as common as major depression in primary care settings. Depressive disorders are also relatively common in younger persons, with estimated prevalence of 0.8 percent to 2.0 percent in children and 4.5 percent in adolescents.

Accuracy and Reliability of Screening Tests

Several depression screening instruments are available; most instruments have relatively good sensitivity (80 percent to 90 percent) but only fair specificity (70 percent to 85 percent). Most instruments are easy to use and can be administered in less than 5 minutes. Shorter screening tests, including simply asking questions about depressed mood and anhedonia, appear to detect a majority of depressed patients and, in some cases, perform better than the original instrument from which they were derived.

Assuming optimal test performance and a prevalence of major depression of 5 percent to 10 percent in primary care settings, about 24 percent to 40 percent of patients who screen positive will have major depression. Some patients with "false positive" results on screening may have dysthymia or subsyndromal depressive disorders that might benefit from treatment or closer monitoring; others may have comorbid disorders such as anxiety disorder, substance abuse, panic disorder, post-traumatic stress disorder, or grief reactions; still others may have no disorder at all. The finding of a positive screen therefore requires further diagnostic questioning by the clinician to establish an appropriate diagnosis and initiate a plan for treatment and followup.

Screening instruments have been tested in children and adolescents, with sensitivity ranging from 40 percent to 100 percent and specificity from 49 percent to 100 percent. Because the underlying prevalence is much lower than in adults, the positive predictive value is low.

Effectiveness of Early Treatment

Effective treatments are available for patients with depressive illnesses detected in primary care settings. Antidepressant medications for major depression, including tricyclic antidepressants (TCAs) and selective serotonin reuptake inhibitors (SSRIs), are clearly more effective than placebo. Most of the data supporting effectiveness come from structured trials with selected populations, although more recent studies using "usual care" comparison groups and real-world settings have produced similar effects. Newer agents perform similarly to older agents.

Psychosocial and psychotherapeutic interventions are probably as effective as antidepressant medications for major depression, but they are clearly more time-intensive. The benefits of psychotherapy for other depressive illnesses are less well studied. Few studies have examined the effect of combining medications and psychotherapy.

No studies have examined treatment outcomes for children or adolescents identified by primary care clinicians through screening. Evidence for treating adolescents comes from school and community settings where SSRIs and cognitive-behavioral therapy, but not tricyclic antidepressants, appear to be effective. Whether these results can be generalized to primary care settings or to children is unclear.

Effectiveness of Screening

The review for the USPSTF identified 14 randomized, controlled trials that have examined the effectiveness of screening for depression in primary care settings. In eight studies, the only intervention was feedback of screening results to clinicians; remaining studies combined feedback with other interventions for patients or clinicians. The trials reported various outcomes, including recognition of depression, rates of treatment, and clinical improvement among patients with depression. In seven trials, routine depression screening with feedback of screening results to providers generally increased recognition of depression, especially major depression, by a factor of 2 to 3 compared with usual care. Trials that examined the effect of feedback of screening results on the proportion of depressed patients who received treatment showed mixed results: in four fair-to-good quality trials that used feedback alone, there was no significant effect on treatment rates, but four of the five trials that combined feedback with treatment advice or other system supports reported increased treatment rates in the intervention group compared with usual care. Ten trials measured the effect of screening and feedback on depression outcomes from 1 month to 2 years after the intervention. Five of these 10 studies reported significant improvements in the clinical outcomes of depressed patients, and three others reported improvements that did not reach statistical significance.

All three trials that compared the effects of integrated recognition and management programs with usual care in community primary care practices showed significantly improved patient outcomes. Integrated programs included feedback, provider and/or patient education, access to case management and/or mental health care, telephone followup, and institutional commitment to quality improvement. One trial, which included both newly detected cases of depression and patients already under treatment, showed improvement in patient symptoms at 6 months only among patients beginning a new treatment episode. No improvement was noted among patients who had recently been treated (that is, those who would have been identified without specific screening). Two trials showed improved symptoms at 12 months;

one of these also showed more employment retention in intervention compared with usual care patients. All three trials required allocation of clinic resources to detection and management programs.

On the basis of estimates from the above-mentioned trials, approximately 11 patients identified as depressed as a result of screening would need to be treated to produce one additional remission. If depression (including major depression, dysthymia, and minor depression) is present in 10 percent of primary care patients, then 110 patients would need to be screened to produce one additional remission after 6 to 12 months of treatment. The number needed to treat for benefit would be smaller for patients with major depression only, but a larger group would need to be screened to identify them.

Potential Harms of Screening and Treatment

The potential harms of screening include false-positive screening results, the inconvenience of further diagnostic work-up, the adverse effects and costs of treatment for patients who are incorrectly identified as being depressed, and potential adverse effects of labeling. None of the research reviewed provided useful empirical data regarding these potential adverse effects.

Recommendations of Others

The Canadian Task Force on Preventive Health Care (CTFPHC) found fair evidence to exclude routine screening of asymptomatic individuals for depression in 1994 but suggested that clinicians maintain a high degree of clinical suspicion for depression among their patients. The CTFPHC is currently revisiting this recommendation. The American College of Obstetricians and Gynecologists recommends that clinicians should be alert to symptoms of depression and question patients about psychosocial stressors and family history of depression when taking their history. The American Academy of Pediatrics recommends that pediatricians ask questions about depression in routine history-taking throughout adolescence. The American Medical Association recommends screening for depression among adolescents who may be at risk owing to family problems, drug or alcohol use, or other indicators of risk.

USPSTF Recommendations and Ratings

The Task Force grades its recommendations according to one of five classifications (A, B, C, D, I) reflecting the strength of evidence and magnitude of net benefit (benefits minus harms).

A. The USPSTF strongly recommends that clinicians routinely provide [the service] to eligible patients. *The USPSTF found good evidence that [the service] improves important health outcomes and concludes that benefits substantially outweigh harms.*

B. The USPSTF recommends that clinicians routinely provide [the service] to eligible patients. *The USPSTF found at least fair evidence that [the service] improves important health outcomes and concludes that benefits outweigh harms.*

C. The USPSTF makes no recommendation for or against routine provision of [the service]. *The USPSTF found at least fair evidence that [the service] can improve health outcomes but concludes that the balance of benefits and harms is too close to justify a general recommendation.*

D. The USPSTF recommends against routinely providing [the service] to asymptomatic patients. *The USPSTF found at least fair evidence that [the service] is ineffective or that harms outweigh benefits.*

I. The USPSTF concludes that the evidence is insufficient to recommend for or against routinely providing [the service]. *Evidence that the [service] is effective is lacking, of poor quality, or conflicting and the balance of benefits and harms cannot be determined.*

USPSTF Strength of Overall Evidence

The USPSTF grades the quality of the overall evidence for a service on a 3-point scale (good, fair, poor).

Good: Evidence includes consistent results from well-designed, well-conducted studies in representative populations that directly assess effects on health outcomes.

Fair: Evidence is sufficient to determine effects on health outcomes, but the strength of the evidence is limited by the number, quality, or consistency of the individual studies, generalizability to routine practice, or indirect nature of the evidence on health outcomes.

Poor: Evidence is insufficient to assess the effects on health outcomes because of limited number or power of studies, important flaws in their design or conduct, gaps in the chain of evidence, or lack of information on important health outcomes.

U.S-RUSSIAN NUCLEAR ARMS CONTROL TREATY
May 24, 2002

The United States and Russia on May 24, 2002, signed the most radical—but also most vague—treaty in the four-decades-long history of nuclear arms control. Signing the treaty in Moscow, presidents George W. Bush and Vladimir Putin pledged to reduce each nation's arsenal of strategic nuclear weapons to fewer than 2,200 deployed warheads by 2012, a dramatic reduction from the more than 10,000 long-range warheads that each nuclear superpower had deployed at the height of the cold war.

Despite the deep cutbacks it mandated, the treaty contained none of the detailed enforcement and verification provisions that had been regular features of all previous arms control agreements between Washington and Moscow. In part, this was because Bush and Putin declared that the two former enemies had become "partners and friends" who could trust each other to carry out their pledges. An equally important reason was that the Bush administration disliked being bound by treaties and wanted to be free to reconfigure the U.S. nuclear arsenal, as it saw fit, to meet changing international circumstances. The administration also planned to keep more than 2,000 warheads in storage as a "reserve."

Bush and Putin accompanied the treaty with a "joint declaration" that pledged cooperation between Washington and Moscow on a wide range of diplomatic and security issues, including the U.S. war against terrorism that followed the September 11, 2001, terrorist attacks against the United States. Proclaiming a "new strategic relationship," Bush and Putin said: "The era in which the United States and Russia saw each other as an enemy or strategic threat has ended. We are partners and we will cooperate to advance stability, security, and economic integration, and to jointly counter global challenges and to help resolve regional conflicts."

Bush submitted the Treaty Between the United States of America and the Russian Federation on Strategic Offensive Reductions (his aides called it the "Moscow treaty") to the Senate on June 20. The Senate Foreign Relations Committee conducted hearings on the treaty in July and August but took no formal action on it by year's end. The treaty had general support on Capitol

Hill, although leaders in both political parties expressed some concern about the lack of details. Putin on December 9 formally submitted the treaty to the Russian Duma, which was likely to act on it during 2003.

A New U.S.-Russian Relationship

The Moscow treaty was negotiated in the context of two significant and related developments during 2001. The first was Bush's determination, stated during his 2000 election campaign and then reiterated after he took office, to scrap the Anti-Ballistic Missile (ABM) treaty signed in 1972 by the United States and the then-Soviet Union (Russia in 1990 inherited the Soviet role in the treaty). That treaty was a cornerstone of U.S.-Soviet arms control efforts during the late twentieth century, but it also precluded one of Bush's highest priorities: development of a defense system to protect the United States against a potential intercontinental ballistic missile attack by North Korea or some other nation or group opposed to U.S. interests. Putin opposed Bush's plans but eventually conceded that he could do nothing to block them.

During U.S.-Russian negotiations on the fate of the ABM treaty, Bush and Putin in November 2001 each announced plans to cut their nuclear arsenals to about 2,000 warheads—the general range ultimately adopted in the Moscow treaty. Bush then announced on December 13, 2001, that the United States would withdraw from the treaty in six months; that action became effective in June 2002. In December Bush said the United States would begin deploying a "modest" missile defense system in 2004. Russia responded with a mild expression of "regret." (ABM withdrawal, Historic Documents of 2001, p. 927)

The second development in 2001 that strongly influenced the decision making on the Moscow treaty was the September 11 terrorist attacks against the United States. In the wake of those attacks, Bush appealed for international support for a U.S.-led war against terrorism. One of the most important responses came from Putin, who on September 24, 2001, offered political and practical backing for the U.S. war, including the use of Russian airspace for U.S. warplanes. Putin's step was a clear signal that he intended to align Russia with the West and abandon most vestiges of the cold war. Less than three months later, on December 7, the United States and its NATO allies promised to open a "new relationship" with Russia, including the formation of a joint council that would give Moscow a voice in the alliance that for a half-century had guarded Europe against Soviet expansionism. (NATO-Russia relationship, p. 885, and Historic Documents of 2001, p. 892)

Nuclear Posture Review

On January 8, 2002, as U.S. and Russian negotiators were working on the proposed new treaty, the Bush administration sent to Congress a secret document, called a Nuclear Posture Review, laying out a new strategy for the deployment and possible use of U.S. nuclear weapons. The review up-

dated the previous strategy adopted by the Clinton administration in 1994. The Defense Department on January 9 made public a brief unclassified version of the review; several key elements of the secret version were reported by news agencies in January and February.

According to published reports, the Nuclear Posture Review advocated at least three key changes from U.S. nuclear weapons policy that had been in effect throughout the cold war:

- *Nuclear weapons henceforth would be considered as just one element of a "new triad" of the U.S. weapons arsenal, rather than as a category of weapons distinct from all others. For decades, U.S. administrations had talked of a "triad" of nuclear weapons, consisting of warheads on land-based missiles, on missiles aboard submarines at sea, and aboard long-range bombers. The Bush administration's new triad consisted of: (1) all "offensive strike systems," including both nuclear warheads and nonnuclear weapons, such as long-range missiles launched by bombers and ships at sea; (2) all defensive systems, including troops at their domestic and foreign bases and new systems, such as Bush's proposed ABM program; and (3) a "revitalized defense infrastructure," including weapons laboratories, some military bases, and the civilian defense industry. Included in the third element of the triad was the prospect of resuming U.S. testing of nuclear weapons after a moratorium of nearly a dozen years. The administration's definition of a new triad was of more than just rhetorical significance. In its report, the administration said the new definition "can both reduce our dependence on nuclear weapons and improve our ability to deter attack in the face of proliferating WMD [weapons of mass destruction] capabilities. . . ."*

- *The review explicitly permitted storing, rather than eliminating, some nuclear weapons taken out of service as a result of arms control agreements. Previous administrations had negotiated treaties with the Soviet Union (and then Russia) that required both nuclear superpowers to destroy all missiles, bombers, and other weapons that were eliminated by mutual agreement. Adopting a new stance, the Bush administration said it would put out-of-service nuclear weapons into storage, where they could be used for spare parts or reserved for possible redeployment if the world situation changed dramatically.*

- *Since the onset of the cold war in the years following World War II, Washington had considered the Soviet Union its principal enemy and had targeted the vast bulk of its conventional and nuclear weapons at preventing a Soviet attack against the United States or its allies. Directly abandoning all vestiges of that policy, the Bush policy review said the United States "will no longer plan, size, or sustain its forces as though Russia presented merely a smaller version of the threat posed by the former Soviet Union." Rather than basing its military force on countering a specific threat, such as the Soviet Union or Russia, the policy review said the United States would focus on developing a broad range of military capabilities that would deter any potential aggressor and "assure friend and foe alike of U.S. resolve."*

The Nuclear Posture Review—or at least news reports about some of its secret details—produced numerous protests from some Democrats and arms control advocates in Washington, from key U.S. allies, and from Russian officials. Critics had several complaints about the document, but their underlying concern was that the Bush administration appeared to be more willing than any of its predecessors to consider using nuclear weapons, even in cases when the United States itself might not be under attack. Related to this was the administration's stated willingness to use preemptive action to head off a possible threat; the clearest expression of this policy came in a "national security strategy" issued by the White House in September. (National security, p. 633)

Some critics also said the administration really was not making the dramatic break with past policy toward Russia that it claimed. For example, Morton Halperin, who had been a senior State Department official during the Clinton administration, noted that, despite Bush's rhetoric about his friendship with Putin, Russia remained the only conceivable target for a U.S. nuclear force of 2,000 or more warheads.

Perhaps the most controversial issue was the administration's plan to store, rather than destroy, out-of-service nuclear weapons. Sen. Carl Levin, D-Mich., chairman of the Armed Services Committee, called the plan "warehoused terror rather than immediate terror." Levin and others said putting U.S. weapons in storage would encourage Russia to do the same—a prospect they called worrisome because of concerns about Russia's ability to guarantee the security of its nuclear weapons and materials. Many critics also challenged the administration's apparent willingness to consider resuming testing of current and new nuclear weapons. "Any step toward underground testing is a step in the wrong direction," said Sen. Jeff Bingaman, D-N.M., chairman of the Energy and Natural Resources Committee. Bush's father, President George H. Bush, had halted U.S. nuclear testing in 1992, but numerous officials in the second Bush administration had said new tests would be needed in the future to ensure the viability of existing weapons, as well as the functionality of any new weapons. (Protecting Russia's nuclear weapons, p. 437)

The Treaty: Cuts, but Few Details

Despite its proposed radical cutbacks, the Moscow treaty essentially was the culmination of a process that had been under way since just before the collapse of the Soviet Union at the end of 1991. The START I arms control treaty, signed in July 1991, called for each nuclear superpower to cut its strategic arsenal to 6,000 warheads—slightly more than half of what each country maintained at that time (both countries reached the 6,000 target by the end of 2001). Just before leaving office in January 1993, President George H. Bush signed the START II treaty with Russian president Boris Yeltsin. That treaty called for a limit of 3,000 to 3,500 warheads, but it was never fully ratified by either country. (START I treaty, Historic Documents of 1991, p. 475; START II treaty, Historic Documents of 1993, p. 20)

In March 1997 Yeltsin and President Bill Clinton agreed to the "framework" for a possible START III treaty; it called for each nation to reduce its nuclear arsenals to 2,000 to 2,500 warheads. Clinton and Yeltsin never completed work on a START III treaty, however, largely because both leaders encountered unrelated political problems that hindered their respective abilities to win domestic support for aggressive arms control measures. The cutbacks mandated by the 2002 Moscow treaty thus were deeper than any previous U.S.-Russian agreement, but they were in line with a trend that had started more than a decade earlier.

The 2002 Moscow treaty broke with its predecessors in one major respect. All previous nuclear arms control treaties between Washington and Moscow—starting with the Limited Test Ban Treaty of 1962 and continuing through the proposed 1993 START II treaty—were lengthy documents containing detailed provisions intended to ensure full compliance. Several of the treaties were so complex and controversial that they took years to negotiate and could be fully understood only by experts. By contrast, the treaty signed by Bush and Putin on May 24 was a scant three pages of text containing almost none of the specifics of previous agreements. The treaty imposed just one significant obligation on each country: to reduce its number of strategic nuclear warheads to the range of 1,700 to 2,200 by December 31, 2012—at which point the treaty would expire. The treaty offered no details about how the warheads were to be counted or how each country's compliance with the treaty would be verified by the other party. Instead, the treaty simply said: "Each Party shall determine for itself the composition and structure of its strategic offensive arms, based on the established aggregate limit for the number of such warheads."

For its part, the Bush administration said the United States would count only "operationally deployed" nuclear warheads toward the 2,200 limit—in other words, warheads mounted on missiles that could be fired at a moment's notice in the event of an attack. In his June 20 letter to the Senate, Bush said "a small number" of warheads would be kept in storage and would not be counted toward the treaty's limits. Secretary of State Colin Powell told the Senate Foreign Relations Committee on July 9 that the administration envisioned a total force of 4,600 active and reserve warheads by the treaty's expiration date in 2012—meaning that at least 2,400 warheads would be kept in storage, assuming that 2,200 remained on active duty.

Perhaps the treaty's most dramatic contrast with previous arms control measures was its total lack of provisions for each nation to verify the other's compliance. Previous treaties had specified complex mechanisms by which the United States and the Soviet Union (and later Russia) would ensure that the other country was actually dismantling the weapons it had promised to eliminate. Instead of such provisions, the Moscow treaty simply said the two countries would hold semiannual meetings of a Bilateral Implementation Commission, the duties of which were not specified.

Once the treaty reached the Senate, its lack of verification measures resulted in a reversal of traditional roles among proponents and opponents of arms control measures. In the past, many Republicans had refused to support nuclear arms agreements because of concerns that the United States could not absolutely verify Moscow's compliance. But those same Republicans voiced no serious objections to the Moscow treaty's silence on the verification question. Sen. Bob Graham, D-Fla., noted the irony: "It's kind of interesting to me that under President Reagan, the policy was 'trust but verify.' Now it seems to be 'trust.'"

Senior administration officials gave the Senate conflicting views on why the treaty lacked provisions on verification. Powell said the Bush administration "did not seek any new verification measures" during its negotiations with Moscow. Secretary of Defense Donald Rumsfeld said on July 17 that the administration had "repeatedly" raised verification issues but Russian officials balked.

President Bush's professed inclination to trust Putin—and his reluctance to be bound legally by treaties—were so strong that he had long opposed putting the arms control agreement in treaty form, preferring the much less formal format of an "executive agreement" that would not require approval by each country's legislature. Putin clearly wanted a treaty, and senators of both parties lobbied vigorously in favor of making the agreement a formal treaty subject to Senate approval. Secretary of State Powell reportedly backed the push for a treaty rather than an agreement, and Bush acceded to those appeals.

> *Following are two documents dated May 24, 2002: the Treaty Between the United States of America and the Russian Federation on Strategic Offensive Reductions, signed in Moscow, followed by a joint declaration on a new U.S.-Russian relationship, issued in Moscow by U.S. president George W. Bush and Russian president Vladimir Putin.*
>
> ***The documents were obtained from the Internet at www.whitehouse.gov/news/releases/2002/05/20020524-3.html and usinfo.state.gov/topical/pol/terror/02052306.htm; accessed October 13, 2002.***

STRATEGIC OFFENSIVE REDUCTIONS TREATY

The United States of America and the Russian Federation, hereinafter referred to as the Parties,

Embarking upon the path of new relations for a new century and committed to the goal of strengthening their relationship through cooperation and friendship,

Believing that new global challenges and threats require the building of a qualitatively new foundation for strategic relations between the Parties,

Desiring to establish a genuine partnership based on the principles of mutual security, cooperation, trust, openness, and predictability,

Committed to implementing significant reductions in strategic offensive arms,

Proceeding from the Joint Statements by the President of the United States of America and the President of the Russian Federation on Strategic Issues of July 22, 2001 in Genoa and on a New Relationship between the United States and Russia of November 13, 2001 in Washington,

Mindful of their obligations under the Treaty Between the United States of America and the Union of Soviet Socialist Republics on the Reduction and Limitation of Strategic Offensive Arms of July 31, 1991, hereinafter referred to as the START Treaty,

Mindful of their obligations under Article VI of the Treaty on the Non-Proliferation of Nuclear Weapons of July 1, 1968, and

Convinced that this Treaty will help to establish more favorable conditions for actively promoting security and cooperation, and enhancing international stability,

Have agreed as follows:

Article I

Each Party shall reduce and limit strategic nuclear warheads, as stated by the President of the United States of America on November 13, 2001 and as stated by the President of the Russian Federation on November 13, 2001 and December 13, 2001 respectively, so that by December 31, 2012 the aggregate number of such warheads does not exceed 1700–2200 for each Party. Each Party shall determine for itself the composition and structure of its strategic offensive arms, based on the established aggregate limit for the number of such warheads.

Article II

The Parties agree that the START Treaty remains in force in accordance with its terms.

Article III

For purposes of implementing this Treaty, the Parties shall hold meetings at least twice a year of a Bilateral Implementation Commission.

Article IV

1. This Treaty shall be subject to ratification in accordance with the constitutional procedures of each Party. This Treaty shall enter into force on the date of the exchange of instruments of ratification.
2. This Treaty shall remain in force until December 31, 2012 and may be extended by agreement of the Parties or superseded earlier by a subsequent agreement.

3. Each Party, in exercising its national sovereignty, may withdraw from this Treaty upon three months written notice to the other Party.

Article V

This Treaty shall be registered pursuant to Article 102 of the Charter of the United Nations.

Done at Moscow on May 24, 2002, in two copies, each in the English and Russian languages, both texts being equally authentic.

[Signed by Russian president Vladimir Putin and U.S. president George W. Bush.]

TEXT OF JOINT DECLARATION

The United States of America and the Russian Federation,

Recalling the accomplishments at the Ljubljana, Genoa, Shanghai, and Washington/Crawford Summits and the new spirit of cooperation already achieved;

Building on the November 13, 2001 Joint Statement on a New Relationship Between the United States and Russia, having embarked upon the path of new relations for the twenty-first century, and committed to developing a relationship based on friendship, cooperation, common values, trust, openness, and predictability;

Reaffirming our belief that new global challenges and threats require a qualitatively new foundation for our relationship;

Determined to work together, with other nations and with international organizations, to respond to these new challenges and threats, and thus contribute to a peaceful, prosperous, and free world and to strengthening strategic security;

Declare as follows:

A Foundation for Cooperation

We are achieving a new strategic relationship. The era in which the United States and Russia saw each other as an enemy or strategic threat has ended. We are partners and we will cooperate to advance stability, security, and economic integration, and to jointly counter global challenges and to help resolve regional conflicts.

To advance these objectives the United States and Russia will continue an intensive dialogue on pressing international and regional problems, both on a bilateral basis and in international fora, including in the UN Security Council, the G-8, and the OSCE [Organization for Security and Cooperation in Europe]. Where we have differences, we will work to resolve them in a spirit of mutual respect.

We will respect the essential values of democracy, human rights, free speech and free media, tolerance, the rule of law, and economic opportunity.

We recognize that the security, prosperity, and future hopes of our peoples rest on a benign security environment, the advancement of political and economic freedoms, and international cooperation.

The further development of U.S.-Russian relations and the strengthening of mutual understanding and trust will also rest on a growing network of ties between our societies and peoples. We will support growing economic interaction between the business communities of our two countries and people-to-people and cultural contacts and exchanges.

Political Cooperation

The United States and Russia are already acting as partners and friends in meeting the new challenges of the 21st century; affirming our Joint Statement of October 21, 2001, our countries are already allied in the global struggle against international terrorism.

The United States and Russia will continue to cooperate to support the Afghan people's efforts to transform Afghanistan into a stable, viable nation at peace with itself and its neighbors. Our cooperation, bilaterally and through the United Nations, the "Six-Plus-Two" diplomatic process, and in other multilateral fora, has proved important to our success so far in ridding Afghanistan of the Taliban and al-Qaida.

In Central Asia and the South Caucasus, we recognize our common interest in promoting the stability, sovereignty, and territorial integrity of all the nations of this region. The United States and Russia reject the failed model of "Great Power" rivalry that can only increase the potential for conflict in those regions. We will support economic and political development and respect for human rights while we broaden our humanitarian cooperation and cooperation on counterterrorism and counternarcotics.

The United States and Russia will cooperate to resolve regional conflicts, including those in Abkhazia [a breakaway province in Georgia] and Nagorno-Karabakh [a region of Azerbaijan disputed between Armenia and Azerbaijan], and the Transnistrian issue in Moldova. We strongly encourage the Presidents of Azerbaijan and Armenia to exhibit flexibility and a constructive approach to resolving the conflict concerning Nagorno-Karabakh. As two of the Co-Chairmen of the OSCE's Minsk Group, the United States and Russia stand ready to assist in these efforts.

On November 13, 2001, we pledged to work together to develop a new relationship between NATO and Russia that reflects the new strategic reality in the Euro-Atlantic region. We stressed that the members of NATO and Russia are increasingly allied against terrorism, regional instability, and other contemporary threats. We therefore welcome the inauguration at the May 28, 2002 NATO-Russia summit in Rome of a new NATO-Russia Council, whose members, acting in their national capacities and in a manner consistent with their respective collective commitments and obligations, will identify common approaches, take joint decisions, and bear equal responsibility, individually and jointly, for their implementation. In this context, they will observe in good faith their obligations under international law, including the UN Charter, provisions and principles contained in the Helsinki Final Act and the OSCE Charter for European Security. In the framework of the NATO-Russia Council,

NATO member states and Russia will work as equal partners in areas of common interest. They aim to stand together against common threats and risks to their security.

As co-sponsors of the Middle East peace process, the United States and Russia will continue to exert joint and parallel efforts, including in the framework of the "Quartet," to overcome the current crisis in the Middle East, to restart negotiations, and to encourage a negotiated settlement. In the Balkans, we will promote democracy, ethnic tolerance, self-sustaining peace, and long-term stability, based on respect for the sovereignty and territorial integrity of the states in the region and United Nations Security Council resolutions. The United States and Russia will continue their constructive dialogue on Iraq and welcome the continuation of special bilateral discussions that opened the way for UN Security Council adoption of the Goods Review List.

Recalling our Joint Statement of November 13, 2001 on counternarcotics cooperation, we note that illegal drug trafficking poses a threat to our peoples and to international security, and represents a substantial source of financial support for international terrorism. We are committed to intensifying cooperation against this threat, which will bolster both the security and health of the citizens of our countries.

The United States and Russia remain committed to intensifying cooperation in the fight against transnational organized crime. In this regard, we welcome the entry into force of the Treaty on Mutual Legal Assistance in Criminal Matters on January 31, 2002.

Economic Cooperation

The United States and Russia believe that successful national development in the 21st century demands respect for the discipline and practices of the free market. As we stated on November 13, 2001, an open market economy, the freedom of economic choice, and an open democratic society are the most effective means to provide for the welfare of the citizens of our countries.

The United States and Russia will endeavor to make use of the potential of world trade to expand the economic ties between the two countries, and to further integrate Russia into the world economy as a leading participant, with full rights and responsibilities, consistent with the rule of law, in the world economic system. In this connection, the sides give high priority to Russia's accession to the World Trade Organization on standard terms.

Success in our bilateral economic and trade relations demands that we move beyond the limitations of the past. We stress the importance and desirability of graduating Russia from the emigration provisions of the U.S. Trade Act of 1974, also known as the Jackson-Vanik Amendment. . . .

Preventing the Spread of Weapons of Mass Destruction: Non-Proliferation and International Terrorism

The United States and Russia will intensify joint efforts to confront the new global challenges of the twenty-first century, including combating the closely linked threats of international terrorism and the proliferation of weapons of mass destruction and their means of delivery. We believe that international terrorism represents a particular danger to international stability as shown once more by the tragic events of September 11, 2001. It is imperative that all nations of the world cooperate to combat this threat decisively. Toward this end, the United States and Russia reaffirm our commitment to work together bilaterally and multilaterally.

The United States and Russia recognize the profound importance of preventing the spread of weapons of mass destruction and missiles. The specter that such weapons could fall into the hands of terrorists and those who support them illustrates the priority all nations must give to combating proliferation.

To that end, we will work closely together, including through cooperative programs, to ensure the security of weapons of mass destruction and missile technologies, information, expertise, and material. We will also continue co-operative threat reduction programs and expand efforts to reduce weapons-usable fissile material. In that regard, we will establish joint experts groups to investigate means of increasing the amount of weapons-usable fissile material to be eliminated, and to recommend collaborative research and development efforts on advanced, proliferation-resistant nuclear reactor and fuel cycle technologies. We also intend to intensify our cooperation concerning destruc-tion of chemical weapons.

The United States and Russia will also seek broad international support for a strategy of proactive non-proliferation, including by implementing and bol-stering the Treaty on the Non-Proliferation of Nuclear Weapons and the con-ventions on the prohibition of chemical and biological weapons. The United States and Russia call on all countries to strengthen and strictly enforce export controls, interdict illegal transfers, prosecute violators, and tighten border controls to prevent and protect against proliferation of weapons of mass destruction.

Missile Defense, Further Strategic Offensive Reductions, New Consultative Mechanism on Strategic Security

The United States and Russia proceed from the Joint Statements by the President of the United States of America and the President of the Russian Federation on Strategic Issues of July 22, 2001 in Genoa and on a New Relationship Between the United States and Russia of November 13, 2001 in Washington.

The United States and Russia are taking steps to reflect, in the military field, the changed nature of the strategic relationship between them.

The United States and Russia acknowledge that today's security environ-ment is fundamentally different than during the Cold War.

In this connection, the United States and Russia have agreed to implement a number of steps aimed at strengthening confidence and increasing trans-parency in the area of missile defense, including the exchange of information on missile defense programs and tests in this area, reciprocal visits to observe missile defense tests, and observation aimed at familiarization with missile defense systems. They also intend to take the steps necessary to bring a joint center for the exchange of data from early warning systems into operation.

The United States and Russia have also agreed to study possible areas for missile defense cooperation, including the expansion of joint exercises related to missile defense, and the exploration of potential programs for the joint research and development of missile defense technologies, bearing in mind the importance of the mutual protection of classified information and the safeguarding of intellectual property rights.

The United States and Russia will, within the framework of the NATO-Russia Council, explore opportunities for intensified practical cooperation on missile defense for Europe.

The United States and Russia declare their intention to carry out strategic offensive reductions to the lowest possible levels consistent with their national security requirements and alliance obligations, and reflecting the new nature of their strategic relations.

A major step in this direction is the conclusion of the Treaty Between the United States of America and the Russian Federation on Strategic Offensive Reductions.

In this connection, both sides proceed on the basis that the Treaty Between the United States of America and the Union of Soviet Socialist Republics on the Reduction and Limitation of Strategic Offensive Arms of July 31, 1991 [the START I treaty], remains in force in accordance with its terms and that its provisions will provide the foundation for providing confidence, transparency, and predictability in further strategic offensive reductions, along with other supplementary measures, including transparency measures, to be agreed.

The United States and Russia agree that a new strategic relationship between the two countries, based on the principles of mutual security, trust, openness, cooperation, and predictability requires substantive consultation across a broad range of international security issues. To that end we have decided to:

- establish a Consultative Group for Strategic Security to be chaired by Foreign Ministers and Defense Ministers with the participation of other senior officials. This group will be the principal mechanism through which the sides strengthen mutual confidence, expand transparency, share information and plans, and discuss strategic issues of mutual interest; and
- seek ways to expand and regularize contacts between our two countries' Defense Ministries and Foreign Ministries, and our intelligence agencies.

[Signed by Russian president Vladimir Putin and U.S. president George W. Bush]

FEDERAL COURT ON INTERNET PORNOGRAPHY IN LIBRARIES
May 31, 2002

Judges, politicians, parents, and a variety of special interest groups con-
tinued to struggle during 2002 with the many legal and moral issues posed
by the explosion of pornography on the Internet. By some accounts, pornog-
raphy was one of the Internet's biggest draws—a popularity that made both
the Internet and pornography the subjects of fierce public debate.

Federal courts rendered three major decisions on Internet pornography
issues during the year, but those rulings left many questions unanswered
and provided no clear legal guidance. Two of the decisions were rendered by
the Supreme Court, which appeared to be searching for a proper balance on
the issue. All three decisions were certain to be the subject of continuing leg-
islation in Congress and litigation in the courts.

Background on Legislation

As Internet use expanded rapidly in the mid-1990s and pornography be-
came a prime attraction, Congress in several laws took steps to protect chil-
dren from viewing content that political and religious leaders considered a
social evil. Congress first confronted the pornography issue in a 1996 law
called the Community Decency Act, which was part of the Telecommunica-
tions Act of 1996 (PL 104–104). That law prohibited owners of Internet
sites from knowingly putting "patently offensive material" within the reach
of minors. In its first major decision dealing with free speech on the Inter-
net, the Supreme Court in 1997 struck down the law as unconstitutional.
(Court action, Historic Documents of 1997, p. 444)

Congress in 1998 attempted to deal with the constitutional issues raised
in the decision by passing another, the Child Online Protection Act (known
as COPA, PL 105–277). That law made it a crime to disseminate material
over the Internet that was "harmful to minors." The Supreme Court on
May 13 appeared to uphold some aspects of the law but blocked enforcement
of it pending a more thorough airing of constitutional issues.

A related question involved "virtual pornography"—the use of computer-
generated images of sexual acts. In another 1996 law, the Child Pornography

Prevention Act (PL 104–208), Congress outlawed distribution over the Internet of virtual pornography that appeared to involve children. The Supreme Court on April 16 struck down that law as unconstitutional.

Congress in 2000 passed the Children's Internet Protection Act (known as CIPA, PL 106–554), requiring libraries and schools to install antipornography filtering software on computers used by minors. Libraries and schools that failed to install the software faced the loss of federal subsidies for some information technology programs. The application of this law to libraries (though not schools) was struck down on May 31 by a three-judge federal panel in Philadelphia. The government appealed the decision, and the Supreme Court agreed in November to review it.

Libraries and Pornography

Of all the Internet-pornography issues before the courts in 2002, perhaps the most hotly contested one involved the federal government's attempt to regulate access to the Internet in public libraries. The Children's Internet Protection Act passed by Congress in December 2000 raised a host of legal and practical questions, notably free speech issues, the role of public libraries, and the practical limitations of computer software intended to "filter" out pornography and other undesirable material on the Internet.

The CIPA law, signed by President Bill Clinton, required schools and public libraries that received public funds promoting Internet access to install antipornography filtering software (called a "technology protection measure") on computers used by minors. The law imposed a deadline of July 1, 2002; schools or libraries that had not installed the software by that date risked losing information technology grants from the Education Department and special discounted rates (called the "e-rate") for their access to the Internet; the discounts were funded by a federal tax on telephone bills. According to some studies, about 14 million Americans regularly used libraries for access to the Internet, many of them people from low-income households who did not have computers at home. (Internet use, p. 67)

The American Library Association, the American Civil Liberties Union (ACLU), and other organizations filed suit in March 2001 to block application of the law to public libraries; the suit did not challenge the law's application to schools. Under a special provision in the law mandated by Congress, the suit went straight to a three-judge panel in Philadelphia that included Third U.S. Circuit Court Judge Edward R. Becker and Judges John P. Fullam and Harvey Bartle III of the district court. The panel heard legal arguments in late March and early April and rendered a unanimous decision on May 31.

In their decision in the case of American Library Association v. United States, *the judges declared themselves "sympathetic" to the goals of the law but argued that implementing it would amount to a violation of First Amendment protections of free speech. The basis of the panel's decision was that software filtering programs were so imperfect that they blocked either too much material on the Internet or not enough. The judges cited numerous examples of Internet pages that were blocked by filtering software even* though they did not contain pornography. Among the examples were Web pages giving factual medical information about human sexuality. In other cases, Internet pages containing pornography were not blocked by the software. The judges said there were many reasons for these failures, including the technical limitation that filtering software could search texts accurately but not images. In addition, the judges said filtering software simply could not keep pace with the growth of the Internet, estimated at an average of 1.5 million new pages each day. "In view of the limitations inherent in the filtering technology mandated by the CIPA, any public library that adheres to CIPA's conditions will necessarily restrict patrons' access to a substantial amount of protected speech, in violation of the First Amendment," the judges ruled.

Officials of the organizations that had challenged the law said they were pleased with the decision. "We couldn't have wanted anything better," Judith F. Krug, director of the American Library Association's office for intellectual freedom, told the New York Times. Supporters of the law expressed disappointment. Among them was the Justice Department, which on June 20 filed an appeal of the decision. The Supreme Court on November 12 agreed to consider the appeal. Several members of Congress filed bills attempting to save the CIPA law by dealing with the issues raised by the federal court, but no legislation was enacted during 2002.

Even before the federal court in Philadelphia issued its decision, a congressionally mandated study concluded that "there is no single or simple answer to controlling the access of minors to inappropriate material on the Web." The study, by the National Research Council, called for a "balanced composite" of technical, legal, economic, and educational approaches to the issue. In language that foreshadowed the judge's findings, the report said software filters can screen some pornography from children's eyes but at the risk of blocking "large amounts of appropriate material." The council also noted that a large percentage of Internet sites containing pornography originated in other countries, over which the United States had no effective control.

Ultimately, the report said, educating children was the most important step, likening the Internet to swimming pools, which can be dangerous to children. "To protect them, one can install locks, put up fences and deploy pool alarms," the report noted. "All of these measures are helpful, but by far the most important thing that one can do for one's children is to teach them to swim." The National Research Council is an arm of the National Academies of Science. Its "Youth, Pornography, and the Internet" report was released on May 2.

Virtual Pornography

The Supreme Court's decision on April 16 dealt with the narrowly drawn 1996 Child Pornography Protection Act, which sought to expand the long-standing federal prohibition on possession or distribution of pornography featuring children under the age of eighteen. The 1996 law applied that prohibition to any image that "appears to be" or "conveys the impression" of *a child "engaged in sexually explicit conduct," specifically including images created or altered by computer technology. The Free Speech Coalition, a trade association for businesses that sold pornography, challenged the law.*

In its 6–3 ruling, the Court said the law was too broad in its reach and was thus an unconstitutional infringement on free speech rights. Writing for the majority, Justice Anthony Kennedy noted that the court in 1982 had upheld a ban on pornography showing actual images of children because children had been exploited in the process. (Child pornography ban, Historic Documents of 1982, p. 675)

With "virtual pornography," the ruling said, "these images do not involve, let alone harm, any children in the production process." Sexual activity among teenagers, the opinion said, "is a fact of modern society and has been a theme in art and literature throughout the ages." In a dissent, Chief Justice William H. Rehnquist and Justice Antonin Scalia said the virtual pornography law helped meet the "compelling" need to enforce laws against child pornography.

The Justice Department drafted legislation intended to overcome the court's objections to the 1996 law, and the House of Representatives passed it (HR 4623) by a 413–8 margin on June 25. That bill expanded the definition of child pornography to include "a computer image or computer-generated image that is, or is indistinguishable from, that of a minor engaging in sexually explicit conduct." President George W. Bush endorsed the legislation and on October 23 called on the Senate to follow the lead of the House. The Senate did not act on the measure before adjourning in November.

"Community Standards" and Pornography

In its May 13 decision, the Supreme Court took a compromise position on the 1998 Child Online Protection Act, which had made it a crime to distribute over the Internet pornography that was "harmful to minors." The law did this by applying to the Internet the long-accepted "community standards" definition of pornography. The law applied only to commercial Web sites that had not made good-faith efforts to block access by children under seventeen to offensive sexual material—for example, by requiring the user to present a valid credit card number or to sign a consent form claiming that he or she was age eighteen or older. (Community standards decision, Historic Documents of 1973, p. 611)

The American Civil Liberties Union and other groups had filed suit against the government to block the law, arguing that it violated the First Amendment, just like the 1996 law that the Supreme Court had overturned. The Third Circuit Court of Appeals in Philadelphia had sided with the ACLU, ruling in June 2000 that using "community standards" to define pornography harmful to minors would allow "the most puritan of communities" to determine acceptable content for Internet sites posted anywhere in the United States.

Ruling on a Justice Department appeal of the circuit court decision, the Supreme Court took a narrow approach to the case, known as Ashcroft *v. American Civil Liberties Union. Three justices, led by Justice Clarence Thomas, said using the "community standards" measure to define harmful pornography on the Internet might be acceptable under the Constitution. Relying on the community standards device, Justice Thomas wrote, "does not by itself render the statute substantially overbroad for purposes of the First Amendment." But the Court returned the case to the Third Circuit with instructions for that court to review other legal issues, including whether Congress used too restrictive a means of trying to protect children from pornography. In the meantime, a district court's prohibition on enforcement of the law would remain in place, the Supreme Court said.*

In a concurring opinion, Justices Ruth Bader Ginsburg, David H. Souter, and Kennedy wrote that there was "a very real likelihood" that the law was constitutional but said the Court needed to "proceed with caution" on the matter. Justice John Paul Stevens dissented from the main opinion, arguing that in the context of the Internet "community standards become a sword rather than a shield."

The Court's ambivalent decision was cheered by both sides. Rep. Michael G. Oxley, R-Ohio, who was the lead sponsor of the 1998 legislation, called the decision "a clear victory for children, their parents and families, and all Americans who wish to protect young people from harmful sexual content on the World Wide Web." But ACLU attorney Ann E. Beeson interpreted the decision as saying that the law "is unenforceable by the federal government."

Following are excerpts from the preliminary statement section of the opinion, issued May 31, 2002, by a special three-judge panel of the Federal District Court for the Eastern District of Pennsylvania, in American Library Association v. United States, *in which the court found unconstitutional the Children's Internet Protection Act (PL 106–554) requiring public libraries to install anti-pornography "filtering" software on computers used by the public to access the Internet or else forfeit federal aid for Internet access programs.*

The document was obtained from the Internet at www.paed.uscourts.gov/documents/opinions/02D0414P.HTM; accessed November 15, 2002.

This case challenges an act of Congress that makes the use of filtering software by public libraries a condition of the receipt of federal funding. The Internet, as is well known, is a vast, interactive medium based on a decentralized network of computers around the world. Its most familiar feature is the World Wide Web (the "Web"), a network of computers known as servers that provide content to users. The Internet provides easy access to anyone who wishes to provide or distribute information to a worldwide audience; it is used by more than 143 million Americans. Indeed, much of the world's knowledge accumulated over centuries is available to Internet users almost instantly. Approximately 10% of the Americans who use the Internet access it at public libraries. And approximately 95% of all public libraries in the United States provide public access to the Internet.

While the beneficial effect of the Internet in expanding the amount of information available to its users is self-evident, its low entry barriers have also led to a perverse result—facilitation of the widespread dissemination of hardcore pornography within the easy reach not only of adults who have every right to access it (so long as it is not legally obscene or child pornography), but also of children and adolescents to whom it may be quite harmful. The volume of pornography on the Internet is huge, and the record before us demonstrates that public library patrons of all ages, many from ages 11 to 15, have regularly sought to access it in public library settings. There are more than 100,000 pornographic Web sites that can be accessed for free and without providing any registration information, and tens of thousands of Web sites contain child pornography.

Libraries have reacted to this situation by utilizing a number of means designed to insure that patrons avoid illegal (and unwanted) content while also enabling patrons to find the content they desire. Some libraries have trained patrons in how to use the Internet while avoiding illegal content, or have directed their patrons to "preferred" Web sites that librarians have reviewed. Other libraries have utilized such devices as recessing the computer monitors, installing privacy screens, and monitoring implemented by a "tap on the shoulder" of patrons perceived to be offending library policy. Still others, viewing the foregoing approaches as inadequate or uncomfortable (some librarians do not wish to confront patrons), have purchased commercially available software that blocks certain categories of material deemed by the library board as unsuitable for use in their facilities. Indeed, 7% of American public libraries use blocking software for adults. Although such programs are somewhat effective in blocking large quantities of pornography, they are blunt instruments that not only "underblock," i.e., fail to block access to substantial amounts of content that the library boards wish to exclude, but also, central to this litigation, "overblock," i.e., block access to large quantities of material that library boards do not wish to exclude and that is constitutionally protected.

Most of the libraries that use filtering software seek to block sexually explicit speech. While most libraries include in their physical collection copies of volumes such as *The Joy of Sex* and *The Joy of Gay Sex*, which contain quite explicit photographs and descriptions, filtering software blocks large quantities of other, comparable information about health and sexuality that adults and teenagers seek on the Web. One teenager testified that the Internet access in a public library was the only venue in which she could obtain information important to her about her own sexuality. Another library patron witness described using the Internet to research breast cancer and reconstructive surgery for his mother who had breast surgery. Even though some filtering programs contain exceptions for health and education, the exceptions do not solve the problem of overblocking constitutionally protected material. Moreover, as we explain below, the filtering software on which the parties presented evidence in this case overblocks not only information relating to health and sexuality that might be mistaken for pornography or erotica, but also vast numbers of Web pages and sites that could not even arguably be construed as harmful or inappropriate for adults or minors.

The Congress, sharing the concerns of many library boards, enacted the Children's Internet Protection Act ("CIPA"), Pub. L. No. 106-554, which makes the use of filters by a public library a condition of its receipt of two kinds of subsidies that are important (or even critical) to the budgets of many public libraries—grants under the Library Services and Technology Act . . . ("LSTA"), and so-called "E-rate discounts" for Internet access and support under the Telecommunications Act. . . . LSTA grant funds are awarded, *inter alia*, in order to: (1) assist libraries in accessing information through electronic networks, and (2) provide targeted library and information services to persons having difficulty using a library and to underserved and rural communities, including children from families with incomes below the poverty line. E-rate discounts serve the similar purpose of extending Internet access to schools and libraries in low-income communities. CIPA requires that libraries, in order to receive LSTA funds or E-rate discounts, certify that they are using a "technology protection measure" that prevents patrons from accessing "visual depictions" that are "obscene," "child pornography," or in the case of minors, "harmful to minors."

The plaintiffs, a group of libraries, library associations, library patrons, and Web site publishers, brought this suit against the United States and others alleging that CIPA is facially unconstitutional because: (1) it induces public libraries to violate their patrons' First Amendment rights contrary to the requirements of *South Dakota v. Dole*, 483 U.S. 203 (1987); and (2) it requires libraries to relinquish their First Amendment rights as a condition on the receipt of federal funds and is therefore impermissible under the doctrine of unconstitutional conditions. In arguing that CIPA will induce public libraries to violate the First Amendment, the plaintiffs contend that given the limits of the filtering technology, CIPA's conditions effectively require libraries to impose content-based restrictions on their patrons' access to constitutionally protected speech. According to the plaintiffs, these content-based restrictions are subject to strict scrutiny under public forum doctrine, *see Rosenberger v. Rector & Visitors of Univ. of Va.*, 515 U.S. 819, 837 (1995), and are therefore permissible only if they are narrowly tailored to further a compelling state interest and no less restrictive alternatives would further that interest, *see Reno v. ACLU*, 521 U.S. 844, 874 (1997). The government responds that CIPA will not induce public libraries to violate the First Amendment, since it is possible for at least some public libraries to constitutionally comply with CIPA's conditions. Even if some libraries' use of filters might violate the First Amendment, the government submits that CIPA can be facially invalidated only if it is impossible for any public library to comply with its conditions without violating the First Amendment.

Pursuant to CIPA, a three-judge Court was convened to try the issues. Following an intensive period of discovery on an expedited schedule to allow public libraries to know whether they need to certify compliance with CIPA by July 1, 2002, to receive subsidies for the upcoming year, the Court conducted an eight-day trial at which we heard 20 witnesses, and received numerous depositions, stipulations and documents. The principal focus of the trial was on the capacity of currently available filtering software. The plaintiffs adduced substantial evidence not only that filtering programs bar access to a substantial amount of speech on the Internet that is clearly constitutionally protected for adults and minors, but also that these programs are intrinsically unable to block only illegal Internet content while simultaneously allowing access to all protected speech.

As our extensive findings of fact reflect, the plaintiffs demonstrated that thousands of Web pages containing protected speech are wrongly blocked by the four leading filtering programs, and these pages represent only a fraction of Web pages wrongly blocked by the programs. The plaintiffs' evidence explained that the problems faced by the manufacturers and vendors of filtering software are legion. The Web is extremely dynamic, with an estimated 1.5 million new pages added every day and the contents of existing Web pages changing very rapidly. The category lists maintained by the blocking programs are considered to be proprietary information, and hence are unavailable to customers or the general public for review, so that public libraries that select categories when implementing filtering software do not really know what they are blocking.

There are many reasons why filtering software suffers from extensive over- and underblocking, which we will explain below in great detail. They center on the limitations on filtering companies' ability to: (1) accurately collect Web pages that potentially fall into a blocked category (e.g., pornography); (2) review and categorize Web pages that they have collected; and (3) engage in regular re-review of Web pages that they have previously reviewed. These failures spring from constraints on the technology of automated classification systems, and the limitations inherent in human review, including error, misjudgment, and scarce resources. . . . One failure of critical importance is that the automated systems that filtering companies use to collect Web pages for classification are able to search only text, not images. This is crippling to filtering companies' ability to collect pages containing "visual depictions" that are obscene, child pornography, or harmful to minors, as CIPA requires. As will appear, we find that it is currently impossible, given the Internet's size, rate of growth, rate of change, and architecture, and given the state of the art of automated classification systems, to develop a filter that neither underblocks nor overblocks a substantial amount of speech.

The government, while acknowledging that the filtering software is imperfect, maintains that it is nonetheless quite effective, and that it successfully blocks the vast majority of the Web pages that meet filtering companies' category definitions (e.g., pornography). The government contends that no more is required. In its view, so long as the filtering software selected by the libraries screens out the bulk of the Web pages proscribed by CIPA, the libraries have made a reasonable choice which suffices, under the applicable legal principles, to pass constitutional muster in the context of a facial challenge. Central to the government's position is the analogy it advances between Internet filtering and the initial decision of a library to determine which materials to purchase for its print collection. Public libraries have finite budgets and must make choices as to whether to purchase, for example, books on gardening or books on golf. Such content-based decisions, even the plaintiffs concede, are subject to rational basis review and not a stricter form of First Amendment scrutiny. In the government's view, the fact that the Internet reverses the acquisition process and requires the libraries to, in effect, purchase the entire Internet, some of which (e.g., hardcore pornography) it does not want, should not mean that it is chargeable with censorship when it filters out offending material.

The legal context in which this extensive factual record is set is complex, implicating a number of constitutional doctrines, including the constitutional limitations on Congress's spending clause power, the unconstitutional conditions doctrine, and subsidiary to these issues, the First Amendment doctrines of prior restraint, vagueness, and overbreadth. There are a number of potential entry points into the analysis, but the most logical is the spending clause jurisprudence in which the seminal case is *South Dakota v. Dole*, 483 U.S. 203 (1987). *Dole* outlines four categories of constraints on Congress's exercise of its power under the Spending Clause, but the only *Dole* condition disputed here is the fourth and last, i.e., whether CIPA requires libraries that receive LSTA funds or E-rate discounts to violate the constitutional rights of their patrons. As will appear, the question is not a simple one, and turns on the level of scrutiny applicable to a public library's content-based restrictions on patrons' Internet access. Whether such restrictions are subject to strict scrutiny, as plaintiffs contend, or only rational basis review, as the government contends, depends on public forum doctrine.

The government argues that, in providing Internet access, public libraries do not create a public forum, since public libraries may reserve the right to exclude certain speakers from availing themselves of the forum. Accordingly, the government contends that public libraries' restrictions on patrons' Internet access are subject only to rational basis review.

Plaintiffs respond that the government's ability to restrict speech on its own property, as in the case of restrictions on Internet access in public libraries, is not unlimited, and that the more widely the state facilitates the dissemination of private speech in a given forum, the more vulnerable the state's decision is to restrict access to speech in that forum. We agree with the plaintiffs that public libraries' content-based restrictions on their patrons' Internet access are subject to strict scrutiny. In providing even filtered Internet access, public libraries create a public forum open to any speaker around the world to communicate with library patrons via the Internet on a virtually unlimited number of topics. Where the state provides access to a "vast democratic forum," *Reno v. ACLU*, 521 U.S. 844, 868 (1997), open to any member of the public to speak on subjects "as diverse as human thought" (internal quotation marks and citation omitted), the state's decision selectively to exclude from the forum speech whose content the state disfavors is subject to strict scrutiny, as such exclusions risk distorting the marketplace of ideas that the state has facilitated.

Application of strict scrutiny finds further support in the extent to which public libraries' provision of Internet access uniquely promotes First Amendment values in a manner analogous to traditional public fora such as streets, sidewalks, and parks, in which content-based restrictions are always subject to strict scrutiny.

Under strict scrutiny, a public library's use of filtering software is permissible only if it is narrowly tailored to further a compelling government interest and no less restrictive alternative would serve that interest. We acknowledge that use of filtering software furthers public libraries' legitimate interests in preventing patrons from accessing visual depictions of obscenity, child pornography, or in the case of minors, material harmful to minors. Moreover, use of filters also helps prevent patrons from being unwillingly exposed to patently offensive, sexually explicit content on the Internet.

We are sympathetic to the position of the government, believing that it would be desirable if there were a means to ensure that public library patrons could share in the informational bonanza of the Internet while being insulated from materials that meet CIPA's definitions, that is, visual depictions that are obscene, child pornography, or in the case of minors, harmful to minors. Unfortunately this outcome, devoutly to be wished, is not available in this less than best of all possible worlds. No category definition used by the blocking programs is identical to the legal definitions of obscenity, child pornography, or material harmful to minors, and, at all events, filtering programs fail to block access to a substantial amount of content on the Internet that falls into the categories defined by CIPA. As will appear, we credit the testimony of plaintiffs' expert Dr. Geoffrey Nunberg [of Harvard University] that the blocking software is (at least for the foreseeable future) incapable of effectively blocking the majority of materials in the categories defined by CIPA without overblocking a substantial amount of materials. Nunberg's analysis was supported by extensive record evidence. As noted above, this inability to prevent both substantial amounts of underblocking and overblocking stems from several sources, including limitations on the technology that software filtering companies use to gather and review Web pages, limitations on resources for human review of Web pages, and the necessary error that results from human review processes.

Because the filtering software mandated by CIPA will block access to substantial amounts of constitutionally protected speech whose suppression serves no legitimate government interest, we are persuaded that a public library's use of software filters is not narrowly tailored to further any of these interests. Moreover, less restrictive alternatives exist that further the government's legitimate interest in preventing the dissemination of obscenity, child pornography, and material harmful to minors, and in preventing patrons from being unwillingly exposed to patently offensive, sexually explicit content. To prevent patrons from accessing visual depictions that are obscene and child pornography, public libraries may enforce Internet use policies that make clear to patrons that the library's Internet terminals may not be used to access illegal speech. Libraries may then impose penalties on patrons who violate these policies, ranging from a warning to notification of law enforcement, in the appropriate case. Less restrictive alternatives to filtering that further libraries' interest in preventing minors from exposure to visual depictions that are harmful to minors include requiring parental consent to or presence during unfiltered access, or restricting minors' unfiltered access to terminals within view of library staff. Finally, optional filtering, privacy screens, recessed monitors, and placement of unfiltered Internet terminals outside of sight-lines provide less restrictive alternatives for libraries to prevent patrons from being unwillingly exposed to sexually explicit content on the Internet.

In an effort to avoid the potentially fatal legal implications of the overblocking problem, the government falls back on the ability of the libraries, under CIPA's disabling provisions . . . to unblock a site that is patently proper yet improperly blocked. The evidence reflects that libraries can and do unblock the filters when a patron so requests. But it also reflects that requiring library patrons to ask for a Web site to be unblocked will deter many patrons because they are embarrassed, or desire to protect their privacy or remain anonymous. Moreover, the unblocking may take days, and may be unavailable, especially in branch libraries, which are often less well staffed than main libraries. Accordingly, CIPA's disabling provisions do not cure the constitutional deficiencies in public libraries' use of Internet filters.

Under these circumstances we are constrained to conclude that the library plaintiffs must prevail in their contention that CIPA requires them to violate the First Amendment rights of their patrons, and accordingly is facially invalid, even under the standard urged on us by the government, which would permit us to facially invalidate CIPA only if it is impossible for a single public library to comply with CIPA's conditions without violating the First Amendment. In view of the limitations inherent in the filtering technology mandated by CIPA, any public library that adheres to CIPA's conditions will necessarily restrict patrons' access to a substantial amount of protected speech, in violation of the First Amendment. . . .

For these reasons, we will enter an Order declaring Sections 1712(a)(2) and 1721(b) of the Children's Internet Protection Act, codified at 20 U.S.C. § 9134(f) and 47 U.S.C. § 254(h)(6), respectively, to be facially invalid under the First Amendment and permanently enjoining the defendants from enforcing those provisions. . . .

EPA REPORT ON
GLOBAL WARMING
May 31, 2002

The Bush administration made headway during 2002 in changing the terms of international debate on global warming—the environmental trend most scientists said could cause catastrophic climate changes during the twenty-first century. The administration promoted voluntary, rather than mandatory, measures to reduce the principal cause of global warming: the burning of coal, oil, and other fossil fuels, which produced carbon dioxide and other "greenhouse gases" that trapped heat in the Earth's upper atmosphere. The administration's position helped undermine an international drive to put into effect the 1997 Kyoto Protocol on Climate Change, a controversial treaty intended to force reductions in greenhouse gas emissions by industrial countries. As an alternative, the Bush administration successfully pushed for greater international focus on dealing with the consequences of global warming, rather than on trying to prevent it.

President George W. Bush had rejected the Kyoto Protocol in June 2001, arguing that the treaty was flawed and that complying with it would cripple the U.S. economy. The treaty would have required nearly a one-third reduction in U.S. estimated greenhouse gas emissions by 2012—a step possible only if the country radically changed its patterns of energy usage. Because the United States was by far the world's largest single producer of greenhouse gases, Bush's rejection diminished the already slim chances that the Kyoto treaty would be a significant deterrent to global warming. (Background, Historic Documents of 2001, p. 109; Kyoto Protocol, Historic Documents of 1997, p. 859)

White House Plan

When he pulled the United States out of the Kyoto treaty, Bush emphasized the uncertainties in scientific knowledge about the causes and consequences of global warming. Bush also warned that the U.S. economy would be damaged by mandatory cuts in the burning of fossil fuels. The president promised expanded research into key unanswered questions over the next decade and said his administration eventually would develop a detailed

*alternative to the treaty's provisions. The administration presented one al-
ternative on February 14, with the release of a plan on air pollution called
the Clear Skies Initiative and a global warming policy called the Global Climate Change Initiative.* (Pollution regulations, p. 894)

*As Bush had promised a year earlier, the climate change initiative con-
tained no mandatory measures and emphasized voluntary actions to limit
the U.S. impact on global warming, along with continued scientific research. The initiative offered modest incentives, including tax credits, for
businesses, governments, and individuals to take actions that reduced
greenhouse gas emissions. For example, farmers could gain tax credits for
planting trees (which absorb carbon dioxide gas), industries could gain
credits for adopting clean-fuel technologies, and consumers could gain credits for buying high-efficiency cars, furnaces, and water heaters. In addition,
the plan called for expanding an existing program under which businesses
submit reports detailing their cutbacks in greenhouse gas emissions to a
National Registry for Voluntary Emissions Reductions; in exchange those
businesses would receive emissions "credits" that could be traded with other
companies.*

*To illustrate the potential impact of its proposals, the administration
used a measurement called "greenhouse gas intensity," which put the country's total emission of greenhouse gases in economic perspective. Under this
measurement, greenhouse gases emissions (in metric tons) would be compared to the gross domestic product (GDP), with the resulting comparison
called "intensity." In 2002, for example, the White House said the United
States was expected to produce 183 metric tons of greenhouse gases for each
$1 million in GDP. The administration set a goal of reducing emissions to
151 metric tons for each $1 million in GDP by 2012: a reduction in inten-
sity of 17.5 percent (rounded up to 18 percent by the White House). This approach "quantifies our effort to reduce emissions" without hurting economic
growth, the White House report said. Many business groups, including the
Edison Electric Institute (representing power utilities), the National Mining Association, and the National Association of Manufacturers applauded
the White House proposal.*

*Environmental groups and other critics said the White House failed to
mention that, at best, its proposal would merely slow the rate of increase in
greenhouse gas emissions. This was because overall U.S. greenhouse gas
emissions would continue to increase as long as the economy expanded. The
Natural Resources Defense Council noted that the White House projected
U.S. economic growth of 38 percent during the next ten years. If that occurred, and if the administration's goal of a greenhouse gas intensity of
151 metric tons was reached, actual U.S. greenhouse gas emissions would
increase by 14 percent. Coupled with a similar increase during the 1990s,
the cumulative increase in U.S. greenhouse gas emissions between 1990
and 2012 would be about 30 percent. By contrast, the Kyoto Protocol had
called on the United States to reduce its greenhouse gas emissions by 2012
to 7 percent below the 1990 level. "The White House is using complicated
accounting measures to hide the fact that the voluntary targets they are*

*setting, if we achieve them, represent no departure whatsoever from busi-
ness as usual," said Jon Coifman of the Natural Resources Defense Council.*

EPA Report

*When he entered office in 2001 President Bush was on record as doubting
whether human activity—principally the burning of fossil fuels—was the
main reason for the warming of global temperatures that scientists had detected during the twentieth century. Along with other "global warming skeptics," Bush suggested that global warming might not even be occurring and,
if it was, nature rather than man was the principal cause. To test this assumption, the White House early in 2001 asked the National Academy of
Science to study the issue. That body produced a report in June 2001 affirming what most international scientists had been saying for years: global
warming was real, and humans were causing most of it by burning coal,
gasoline, and oil.*

*A year later, in May 2002, the administration quietly sent a detailed
report to the United Nations reaching similar conclusions. Entitled "U.S.
Climate Action Report 2002," the report was drafted by the Environmental
Protection Agency (EPA) and other bureaus and was reviewed at the White
House by the president's Council on Environmental Quality. The report
was the third in a series required by the 1992 Framework Convention on
Climate Change (known as the Rio treaty because it was negotiated at a
conference in Rio de Janeiro). That treaty was signed by Bush's father, then
president George H. Bush. The EPA posted the report on its Web site on
May 31 but made no formal announcement about it.* (Rio treaty, Historic
Documents of 1992, p. 499)

Disclosure of the report on June 3 by the New York Times *created a sen-
sation in Washington, largely because its findings appeared directly at odds
with the expressed views of the president and many of his key aides. Asked
about the report on June 3, Bush dismissed it with a curt: "I read the report
put out by the bureaucracy." White House spokesman Scott McClellan suggested the report contained nothing new and merely reinforced administration policy. McClellan also acknowledged that Bush really had not read
the 255-page report but had been told about it.*

*In essence, the report conveyed three major messages. First, global warm-
ing was for real and was caused primarily by the burning of fossil fuels.
Second, over the next several decades global warming likely would have serious consequences for the planet's environment, some of which would be
positive for humans (such as longer growing seasons in some areas) and
others of which would be negative (such as flooding of low-lying coastal
areas). Third, because global warming already was building up in the environment, humans might be able to slow the future rate of warming but
still needed to try to adapt to it.*

*Perhaps the most controversial part of the report was a discussion in
"The Science" section. "Greenhouse gases are accumulating in Earth's atmosphere as a result of human activities, causing global mean surface air temperature and subsurface ocean temperature to rise," the report said. "While*

the changes observed over the last several decades are likely due mostly to human activities, we cannot rule out that some significant part is also a reflection of natural variability." Those two sentences put the administration squarely on the side of scientists and environmentalists who had been warning about global warning for years.

The report noted that greenhouse gases emitted in the past would continue to contribute to global warming for decades to come. Future emissions would make the situation worse, the report said, noting that net U.S. greenhouse gas emissions would increase by 43 percent between 2000 and 2020.

In general the report concurred with numerous other studies that predicted wide-ranging consequences from global warming. However, after the initial furor over the report in June, the final edition of the report was changed to give more prominence to uncertainties about the impact of global warming.

Some consequences of global warming were already evident, the report noted. Glaciers in many parts of the world were melting (thus raising sea levels), and average surface air temperatures (especially in the Northern Hemisphere) had been extraordinarily high during the 1990s. Other results of global warming might take longer to become evident, the report said, and they might include reduced winter snowpacks in mountain regions, which would change the timing and cut the amount of fresh water supplies, especially to arid regions such as the western U.S. states; rising sea levels that could flood low-lying areas, such as barrier islands and coastal planes; and heat waves, which were likely to become more frequent in many areas.

These consequences would be most severe for natural ecosystems, the report said, "because generally little can be done to help them adapt to the projected rate and amount of change." But humans had the ability to adapt to a changing environment, the report added: "The question is whether we adapt poorly or well." Some of the "adaptations" mentioned in the report would have the effect of worsening global warming. For example, the report suggested that the health impacts of more frequent heat waves "can be ameliorated through such measures as the increased availability of air conditioning."

Environmental groups praised the administration for recognizing the existence of global warming but condemned its suggested response. "They're saying, 'It's true, it's happening and it's going to be bleak, but we're not going to do anything about it,' " said Susanne Moser of the Union of Concerned Scientists. Industry groups were less pleased, however, and some suggested that environmentalists within the EPA had pushed the report through the bureaucracy without the knowledge of top Bush administration officials. In numerous letters to the administration while the report was being prepared, industry groups had attempted unsuccessfully to tone down its language. Once the report was made public, the EPA made some changes that placed greater emphasize on the uncertain factors in scientific models used to make long-term weather predictions.

On a related question, the EPA report represented a significant attempt by the administration to demonstrate that its policy of voluntary restraint,

301

coupled with scientific research, ultimately would have a major impact on global warming. Environmental advocates and many scientists rejected that position, arguing that business and industry would never make sufficient voluntary changes in energy consumption unless forced to do so by government pressure in the form of regulations and mandates. These critics also argued that Bush administration taxation and subsidy policies placed far more emphasis on domestic oil, gas, and coal production than on research into renewable energy sources and other technologies that minimized the burning of fossil fuels.

During the first week of December the White House held a meeting in Washington of scientists, industry representatives, and other interested parties to discuss the government's plan for research on global warming during the next five years. That meeting featured standard arguments: Administration officials and their allies argued that drastic steps to counter global warming should not be taken until more research was conducted, while environmentalists and their allies argued that enough already was known about global warming to justify strong measures curbing greenhouse gas emissions.

Kyoto Protocol

Ever since it was negotiated in 1997, the Kyoto Protocol had been the primary focus of international disputes between those who argued for quick, aggressive action to diminish global warming and those who took a more cautious approach. The treaty was based on the assumptions that fast action was essential and that the major industrialized countries—which produced the bulk of the world's greenhouse gas emissions—needed to lead the way with mandatory cutbacks in those emissions. The treaty encouraged, but did not require, developing countries to reduce their emissions; that provision was widely criticized in industrialized countries as giving China and India (the biggest developing countries) an unfair competitive advantage.

Despite its detailed provisions, the Kyoto treaty left many important technical issues open to future negotiation. Subsequent international meetings called to resolve those issues introduced new opportunities for supporters and opponents to discuss their positions. These meetings also resulted in numerous compromises that treaty supporters said ultimately watered down major provisions, thus weakening prospects that Kyoto would have a significant impact on global warming. In 2001, for example, negotiators agreed that industrialized countries could gain "credit" toward their goals of reducing greenhouse gas emissions simply because of the presence of forests and croplands, which absorbed massive amounts of carbon dioxide.

Still more discussions were needed in 2002, with the principal action scheduled to take place at an international conference in New Delhi in late October. As that meeting opened on October 23, it was clear that the Bush administration's rejection of the Kyoto treaty had helped force a fundamental change in the world agenda on climate change. The debate over how to carry out the Kyoto treaty remained on the agenda, but it was accompanied with a new emphasis on devising ways for adapting to the inevitability of global warming.

The old issue of the Kyoto treaty was present in the form of renewed debate over the role to be played by China, India, and other developing countries. European Union (EU) delegates pressed for language calling for a process leading to future greenhouse gas cutbacks by the developing countries. The Europeans lost that argument because of strong resistance from China and India. Delegates did, however, call on countries to ratify the Kyoto treaty "in a timely manner."

The newer focus on adapting to global warming was less controversial, in large part because it served the interests of both the Bush administration and developing countries. The Bush administration wanted to shift attention away from the mandates of the Kyoto treaty, and developing countries wanted more aid to bolster their economies as they sought to catch up with the industrialized world. The final declaration adopted by the conference on November 1 said: "Adaptation to the adverse effects of climate change is of high priority for all countries. Developing countries are particularly vulnerable, especially the least developed countries and small island developing states. Adaptation requires urgent attention and action on the part of all countries. Effective and result-based measures should be supported for the development of approaches at all levels on vulnerability and adaptation, as well as capacity-building for the integration of adaptation concerns into sustainable development strategies."

Even as diplomats conducted these debates, most countries that had signed the Kyoto Protocol in 1997 or 1998 were carrying through with the process of ratifying it—actually pledging to put the treaty into effect. Two of the most important ratification steps came early in the year: Japan ratified the treaty on April 6, and the EU ratified it on May 31. In taking that step, the EU called on the United States to "reconsider its position and to return to and participate in the global framework for addressing climate change that this protocol provides."

EU ratification raised to seventy the number of countries pledging to adhere to the treaty, thus exceeding the minimum number of countries required (fifty-five) for it to take effect. The vast majority of signatories were developing nations that were not required to reduce greenhouse gas emissions under the treaty. However, the treaty was still far short on another measure. For the treaty to go into force, ratifying nations had to account for 55 percent of the world's greenhouse gas emissions as of 1990. Because the United States accounted for about 36 percent of 1990 emissions, the provision meant Russia (at about 17 percent) had to ratify the treaty before it could enter into force. Russian president Vladimir Putin promised that Moscow would ratify the treaty by early 2003. Canada, another major energy-producing country, ratified the treaty in December.

Aside from the United States, Australia was the only significant industrialized country to formally back out of the treaty. Australia signed the treaty in 1998, but Prime Minister John Howard announced on June 5 that he would not push for ratification as long as the United States stayed outside of the treaty. "For us to ratify the protocol would cost us jobs and damage our industry," Howard said. Australia was the world's leading exporter of coal, one of the fossil fuels said to be responsible for the buildup of greenhouse gases.

Consequences of Global Warming

While political leaders debated acting on global warming, numerous new studies and reports indicated that climate change already was having a significant impact on the Earth's environment. Glaciers were prominent in the year's news, with reports of exceptional melting of glaciers in Greenland, in the Andes mountains of South America, and on Kilimanjaro mountain in Tanzania. Glaciers in the coastal regions of Greenland were retreating at a rate of up to three feet each year. If that melting were to continue, sea levels probably would rise several inches during the twenty-first century, according to statements by researchers at the EPA and the National Aeronautics and Space Administration, as quoted by the Washington Post *on October 13. Most scientists agreed that global ocean levels had risen nearly eight inches during the twentieth century; most predictions were in the range of a further rise of six to twelve inches during the twenty-first century. A giant 1,250-square-mile shelf of ice (about the size of Rhode Island) broke free from Antarctica in March and shattered into thousands of icebergs; scientists said global warming was among the factors that hastened the melting of the ice shelf.*

The melting of glaciers and polar ice fed a debate among scientists about the possible impact on global ocean systems, in particular the Gulf Stream that transports warm water from the equator to the North Atlantic and in the process warms much of North America and Europe. One prominent scientist, Terrance Joyce, chairman of the Physical Oceanography Department at the Woods Hole Oceanographic Institute in Massachusetts, theorized that vast amounts of cold fresh water from melting glaciers and the arctic icecap could block the natural action (known as thermohaline pumping) that carries warm Gulf Stream water into the northern latitudes. If that were to happen, temperatures in North America and Europe could fall—even as global warming was raising temperatures elsewhere on the globe. Many other scientists disputed Joyce's theory or said it was unlikely to come to pass.

Yet another concern posited by scientists during the year was that rising temperatures in many parts of the world already were contributing to the spread of some diseases. In a study published in Science *magazine in June, researchers from Princeton University and other organizations reported evidence that disease-carrying microbes and insects, such as mosquitoes, were thriving in warmer temperatures and invading areas once off-limits to them, including mountaintops. For example, northeast Africa had experienced epidemics of the deadly Rift Valley fever (carried by mosquitoes), and oyster beds in the North Atlantic had been invaded by bacteria that formerly could not survive the cold water.*

State Actions

Many states were taking more aggressive action than the federal government to address global warming issues within their borders, according "Greenhouse and Statehouse: The Evolving State Government Role in Climate Change," a report released November 15 by the Pew Center on Global Climate Change. Written principally by Barry G. Rabe, professor of environmental policy at the University of Michigan, the study detailed both voluntary and mandatory measures that state governments had taken since the late 1990s to curb greenhouse gas emissions by business, industry, and the public.

Potentially the most far-reaching of all the state actions was legislation adopted in California during 2002 requiring a state agency, the California Air Resources Board, to develop new regulations by 2005 to reduce emissions by automobiles and trucks. The regulations would take effect in 2006 and would apply to the 2009 model year. Despite strong public support for it, the automobile industry and many other business groups heatedly opposed the bill and filed lawsuits to block its implementation. If it survived the legal challenge, the legislation might serve as a model for action by other states or even the federal government—as did previous California regulations mandating use of unleaded gasoline, catalytic converters, and clean diesel fuels.

The Pew study cited legislation and regulations in nine other states, among them Texas, which mandated that by 2010 at least 3 percent of its electricity must come from renewable energy sources, such as wind power; New Hampshire, which required emissions controls on the state's three coal-fired electric generating plants; and Massachusetts, which in 2001 included carbon dioxide (the main greenhouse gas) on a list of pollutants subject to limits imposed on six major power plants.

> Following are excerpts from the "Climate Action Report 2002," submitted by the United States on May 31, 2002, to the United Nations Framework Convention on Climate Change. Prepared by the Environmental Protection Agency and reviewed by the White House and other agencies, the report declared that human activities are contributing to global warming. This report was the third submitted to the UN since the adoption of the Framework Convention on Climate Change in 1992.

> **The document was obtained from the Internet at www.epa .gov/globalwarming/publications/car; accessed October 22, 2002.**

"The Earth's well-being is . . . an issue important to America—and it's an issue that should be important to every nation and in every part of the *world. My Administration is committed to a leadership role on the issue of climate change. We recognize our responsibility, and we will meet it—at home, in our hemisphere, and in the world."*

—George W. Bush, June 2001

Chapter 1: Introduction and Overview

With this pledge, President Bush reiterated the seriousness of climate change and ordered a Cabinet-level review of U.S. climate change policy. He requested working groups to develop innovative approaches that would: (1) be consistent with the goal of stabilizing greenhouse gas concentrations in the atmosphere; (2) be sufficiently flexible to allow for new findings; (3) support continued economic growth and prosperity; (4) provide market-based incentives; (5) incorporate technological advances; and (6) promote global participation.

The President's decision to take a deeper look at climate change policy arose from the recognition that the international dialogue begun to date lacked the requisite participatory breadth for a global response to climate change. At the 1992 Earth summit in Rio de Janeiro, the United Nations Framework Convention on Climate Change (UNFCCC) was adopted, with the ultimate objective of providing a higher quality of life for future generations. Signatories pledged to:

> *achieve . . . stabilization of greenhouse gas concentrations in the atmosphere at a level that would prevent dangerous anthropogenic interference with the climate system. Such a level should be achieved within a timeframe sufficient to allow ecosystems to adapt naturally to climate change, to ensure that food production is not threatened, and to enable economic development to proceed in a sustainable manner.*

In Rio, ambitious plans were set in motion to address climate change. However, participation in constructing measures for adapting to and mitigating the effects of climate change fell short of the breadth necessary to confront a problem that President Bush recently said has "the potential to impact every corner of the world." A global problem demands a truly participatory global response, while at the same time taking near-term action that would reduce projected growth in emissions cost-effectively and enhance our ability to cope with climate change impacts.

Based on his Cabinet's review and recommendation, President Bush recently announced a commitment to reduce greenhouse gas intensity in the United States by 18 percent over the next decade through a combination of voluntary, incentive-based, and existing mandatory measures. This represents a 4.5 percent reduction from forecast emissions in 2012, a serious, sensible, and science-based response to this global problem—despite the remaining uncertainties concerning the precise magnitude, timing, and regional patterns of climate change. The President's commitment also emphasized the need for partners in this endeavor. All countries must actively work together to achieve the long-term goal of stabilizing greenhouse gas concentrations at a level that will prevent dangerous interference with the climate system.

For our part, the United States intends to continue to be a constructive and active Party to the Framework Convention. We are leading global research efforts to enhance the understanding of the science of climate change, as called for under the Framework Convention. We lead the world in investment in climate science and in recent years have spent $1.7 billion on federal research annually. since 1990, the United States has provided over $18 billion for climate system research—more resources than any other country. In June 2001, President Bush announced a new Climate Change Research Initiative to focus on key remaining gaps in our understanding of anthropogenic climate change and its potential impacts.

As envisioned by the Framework Convention, we are helping to develop technologies to address climate change. The President has pledged to reprioritize research budgets under the National Climate Change Technology Initiative so that funds will be available to develop advanced energy and sequestration technologies. Energy policies improve efficiency and substitute cleaner fuels, while sequestration technologies will promote economic and environmentally sound methods for the capture and storage of greenhouse gases.

We plan to increase bilateral support for climate observation systems and to finance even more demonstration projects of advanced energy technologies in developing countries. President Bush's Western Hemisphere Initiative— created to enhance climate change cooperation with developing countries in the Americas and elsewhere—will also strengthen implementation of our Framework Convention commitments. In line with those commitments, we have provided over $1 billion in climate change-related assistance to developing countries over the last five years. All of this is just the beginning: we intend to strengthen our cooperation on climate science and advanced technologies around the world whenever and wherever possible.

We continue to make progress in limiting U.S. emissions of greenhouse gases by becoming more energy efficient. In the last decade, we have seen tremendous U.S. economic growth, and our level of emissions per unit of economic output has declined significantly. The President has committed the United States to continue this improvement and reduce intensity beyond forecast levels through enhanced voluntary measures. The United States is a world leader in addressing and adapting to a variety of national and global scientific problems that could be exacerbated by climate change, including malaria, hunger, malnourishment, property losses due to extreme weather events, and habitat loss and other threats to biological diversity.

Climate change is a long-term problem, decades in the making, that cannot be solved overnight. A real solution must be durable, science-based, and economically sustainable. In particular, we seek an environmentally sound approach that will not harm the U.S. economy, which remains a critically important engine of global prosperity. We believe that economic development is key to protecting the global environment. In the real world, no one will forego meeting basic family needs to protect the global commons. Environmental protection is neither achievable nor sustainable without opportunities for continued development and greater prosperity. Our objective is to ensure a long-term solution that is environmentally effective, economically efficient and sustainable, and appropriate in terms of addressing the urgent problems of today while enhancing our ability to deal with future problems. Protecting the global environment is too important a responsibility for anything less. . . .

The Science

Greenhouse gases are accumulating in Earth's atmosphere as a result of human activities, causing global mean surface air temperature and subsurface ocean temperature to rise. While the changes observed over the last several decades are likely due mostly to human activities, we cannot rule out that some significant part is also a reflection of natural variability.

Reducing the wide range of uncertainty inherent in current model predictions will require major advances in understanding and modeling of the factors that determine atmospheric concentrations of greenhouse gases and aerosols, and the feedback processes that determine the sensitivity of the climate system. Specifically, this will involve reducing uncertainty regarding:

- the future use of fossil fuels and future emissions of methane,
- the fraction of the future fossil fuel carbon that will remain in the atmosphere and provide radiative forcing versus exchange with the oceans or net exchange with the land biosphere,
- the feedbacks in the climate system that determine both the magnitude of the change and the rate of energy uptake by the oceans,
- the impacts of climate change on regional and local levels,
- the nature and causes of the natural variability of climate and its interactions with forced changes, and
- the direct and indirect effects of the changing distributions of aerosols.

Knowledge of the climate system and of projections about the future climate is derived from fundamental physics, chemistry, and observations. Data are then incorporated in global circulation models. However, model projections are limited by the paucity of data available to evaluate the ability of coupled models to simulate important aspects of climate. To overcome these limitations, it is essential to ensure the existence of a long-term observing system and to make more comprehensive regional measurements of greenhouse gases.

Evidence is also emerging that black carbon aerosols (soot), which are formed by incomplete combustion, may be a significant contributor to global warming, although their relative importance is difficult to quantify at this point. These aerosols have significant negative health impacts, particularly in developing countries.

While current analyses are unable to predict with confidence the timing, magnitude, or regional distribution of climate change, the best scientific information indicates that if greenhouse gas concentrations continue to increase, changes are likely to occur. The U.S. National Research Council has cautioned, however, that because there is considerable uncertainty in current understanding of how the climate system varies naturally and reacts to emissions of greenhouse gases and aerosols, current estimates of the magnitude of future warmings should be regarded as tentative and subject to future adjustments (either upward or downward). Moreover, there is perhaps even greater uncertainty regarding the social, environmental, and economic consequences of changes in climate.

National Circumstances: The U.S. Context

The perspective of the United States on climate change is informed by our economic prosperity, the rich diversity of our climate conditions and natural resources, and the demographic trends of over 280 million residents. Because of our diverse climatic zones, climate change will not affect the country uniformly. This diversity will also enhance our economy's resilience to future climate change.

Higher anthropogenic greenhouse gas emissions are a consequence of robust economic growth: higher incomes traditionally promote increased expenditures of energy. During the 1990s, investments in technology led to increases in energy efficiency, which partly offset the increases in greenhouse gas emissions that would normally attend strong economic growth. In addition, much of the economic growth in the United States has occurred in less energy-intensive sectors (e.g., computer technologies). Consequently, in the 1990s the direct and proportionate correlation between economic growth and greenhouse gas emissions was altered.

While the United States is the world's largest consumer of energy, it is also the world's largest producer of energy, with vast reserves of coal, natural gas, and crude oil. Nevertheless, our energy use per unit of output—i.e., the energy intensity of our economy—compares relatively well with the rest of the world. The President's new *National Energy Policy* (NEP) includes recommendations that would reduce greenhouse gas emissions by expanded use of both existing and developing technologies. The NEP's recommendations address expanded nuclear power generation; improved energy efficiency for vehicles, buildings, appliances, and industry; development of hydrogen fuels and renewable technologies; increased access to federal lands and expedited licensing practices; and expanded use of cleaner fuels, including initiatives for coal and natural gas. Tax incentives recommended in the NEP and the President's FY 2003 Budget will promote use of renewable energy forms and combined heat-and-power systems and will encourage technology development.

The nation's response to climate change—our vulnerability and our ability to adapt—is also influenced by U.S. governmental, economic, and social structures, as well as by the concerns of U.S. citizens. The political and institutional systems participating in the development and protection of environmental and natural resources in the United States are as diverse as the resources themselves.

President Bush said last year that technology offers great promise to significantly and cost-effectively reduce emissions in the long term. Our national circumstances—our prosperity and our diversity may shape our response to climate change, but our commitment to invest in innovative technologies and research will ensure the success of our response.

Greenhouse Gas Inventory

This report presents U.S. anthropogenic [man-made] greenhouse gas emission trends from 1990 through 1999 and fulfills the U.S. commitment for 2001 for an annual inventory report to the UNFCCC. . . .

Naturally occurring greenhouse gases—that is, gases that trap heat—include water vapor, carbon dioxide (CO_2), methane (CH_4), nitrous oxide (N_2O), and ozone (O_3). several classes of halogenated substances that contain fluorine, chlorine, or bromine are also greenhouse gases, but for the most part, they are solely a product of industrial activities. Chlorofluorocarbons (CFCs), hydrochlorofluorocarbons (HCFCs), and bromofluorocarbons (halons) are stratospheric ozone-depleting substances covered under the Montreal Protocol on substances That Deplete the Ozone Layer and, hence, are not included in national greenhouse gas inventories. Some other halogenated substances—hydrofluorocarbons (HFCs), perfluorocarbons (PFCs), and sulfur hexafluoride (SF_6)—do not deplete stratospheric ozone but are potent greenhouse gases and are accounted for in national greenhouse gas inventories.

Although CO_2, CH_4, and N_2O occur naturally in the atmosphere, their atmospheric concentrations have been affected by human activities. since pre-industrial time (i.e., since about 1750), concentrations of these greenhouse gases have increased by 31, 151, and 17 percent, respectively. This increase has altered the chemical composition of the Earth's atmosphere and has likely affected the global climate system.

In 1999, total U.S. greenhouse gas emissions were about 12 percent above emissions in 1990. A somewhat lower (0.9 percent) than average (1.2 percent) annual increase in emissions, especially given the robust economic growth during this period, was primarily attributable to the following factors: warmer than average summer and winter conditions, increased output from nuclear power plants, reduced CH_4 emissions from coal mines, and reduced HFC-23 by-product emissions from the chemical manufacture of HCFC-22.

As the largest source of U.S. greenhouse gas emissions, CO_2 accounted for 82 percent of total U.S. greenhouse gas emissions in 1999. Carbon dioxide from fossil fuel combustion was the dominant contributor. Emissions from this source category grew by 13 percent between 1990 and 1999.

Methane accounted for 9 percent of total U.S. greenhouse gas emissions in 1999. Landfills, livestock operations, and natural gas systems were the source of 75 percent of total CH_4 emissions. Nitrous oxide accounted for 6 percent of total U.S. greenhouse gas emissions in 1999, and agricultural soil management represented 69 percent of total N_2O emissions. The main anthropogenic activities producing N_2O in the United States were agricultural soil management, fuel combustion in motor vehicles, and adipic and nitric acid production processes. HFCs, PFCs, and SF_6 accounted for 2 percent of total U.S. greenhouse gas emissions in 1999, and substitutes for ozone-depleting substances comprised 42 percent of all HFC, PFC, and SF_6 emissions.

Evidence is also emerging that black carbon aerosols (soot), which are formed by incomplete combustion, may be a significant anthropogenic agent.

Although the U.S. greenhouse gas inventory does not cover emissions of these particles, we anticipate that U.S. research will focus more on them in coming years.

Policies and Measures

U.S. climate change programs reduced the growth of greenhouse gas emissions by an estimated 240 teragrams (million metric tons) of CO_2 equivalent in 2000 alone. This reduction helped to significantly lower (17 percent since 1990) greenhouse gases emitted per unit of gross domestic product (GDP), and thus ranks as a step forward in addressing climate change.

However, the U.S. effort was given a potentially greater boost in June 2001, when President Bush announced major new initiatives to advance climate change science and technology. These initiatives came about after government consultation with industry leaders, the scientific community, and environmental advocacy groups indicated that more could and should be done to address scientific uncertainties and encourage technological innovation.

In February 2002, the President announced a new U.S. approach to the challenge of global climate change. This approach contains policies that will harness the power of markets and technology to reduce greenhouse gas emissions. It will also create new partnerships with the developing world to reduce the greenhouse gas intensity of both the U.S. economy and economies worldwide through policies that support the economic growth that makes technological progress possible.

The U.S. plan will reduce the greenhouse gas intensity of the U.S. economy by 18 percent in ten years. This reduction exceeds the 14 percent projected reduction in greenhouse gas intensity in the absence of the additional proposed policies and measures. The new measures include an enhanced emission reduction registry; creation of transferable credits for emission reduction; tax incentives for investment in low-emission energy equipment; support for research for energy efficiency and sequestration technology; emission reduction agreements with specific industrial sectors, with particular attention to reducing transportation emissions; international outreach, in tandem with funding, to promote climate research globally; carbon sequestration on farms and forests; and, most important, review of progress in 2012 to determine if additional steps may be needed as the science justifies to achieve further reductions in our national greenhouse gas emission intensity.

The above strategies are expected to achieve emission reductions comparable to the average reductions prescribed by the Kyoto agreement, but without the threats to economic growth that rigid national emission limits would bring. The registry structure for voluntary participation of U.S. industry in reducing emissions will seek compatibility with emerging domestic and international approaches and practices, and will include provisions to ensure that early responders are not penalized in future climate actions. Furthermore, the President's approach provides a model for developing nations, setting targets that reduce greenhouse gas emissions without compromising economic growth.

Projected Greenhouse Gas Emissions

Forecasts of economic growth, energy prices, program funding, and regulatory developments were integrated to project greenhouse gas emissions levels in 2005, 2010, 2015, and 2020. When sequestration [the absorption of greenhouse gases by forests, crops, and other plants] is accounted for, total U.S. greenhouse gas emissions are projected to increase by 43 percent between 2000 and 2020. This increased growth in absolute emissions will be accompanied by a decline in emissions per unit of GDP. Note that these forecasts exclude the impact of the President's climate change initiative announced in February 2002.

Despite best efforts, the uncertainties associated with the projected levels of greenhouse gas emissions are primarily associated with forecast methodology, meteorological variations, and rates of economic growth and technological development. In addition, since the model used to generate these projections does not completely incorporate all current and future policies and measures to address greenhouse gas emissions, these measures, as well as legislative or regulatory actions not yet in force, add another layer of uncertainty to these projections.

Impacts and Adaptation

One of the weakest links in our knowledge is the connection between global and regional projections of climate change. The National Research Council's response to the President's request for a review of climate change policy specifically noted that fundamental scientific questions remain regarding the specifics of regional and local projections. Predicting the potential impacts of climate change is compounded by a lack of understanding of the sensitivity of many environmental systems and resources both managed and unmanaged to climate change. . . .

The United States is engaged in many efforts that will help our nation and the rest of the world particularly the developing world reduce vulnerability and adapt to climate change. By and large these efforts address public health and environmental problems that are of urgent concern today and that may be exacerbated by climate change. Examples include reducing the spread of malaria, increasing agricultural and forest productivity, reducing the damages from extreme weather events, and improving methods to forecast their timings and locations. Besides benefiting society in the short term, these efforts will enhance our ability to adapt to climate change in the longer term.

Challenges associated with climate change will most likely increase during the 21st century. Although changes in the environment will surely occur, our nation's economy should continue to provide the means for successful adaptation to climate changes.

Financial Resources and Transfer of Technology

To address climate change effectively, developed and developing countries must meet environmental challenges together. The United States is committed to helping developing countries and countries with economies in transition meet these challenges in ways that promote economic well-being and protect natural resources. This commitment has involved many players, ranging from government to the private sector, who have contributed significant resources to developing countries. As recognized in the UNFCCC guidelines, this assistance can take the form of hard and/or soft technology transfer.

Projects targeting hard technology transfer, such as equipment to control emissions and increase energy efficiency, can be particularly effective in reducing emissions. And projects that target the transfer of soft technologies, such as capacity building and institution strengthening through the sharing of technical expertise, can help countries reduce their vulnerability to the impacts of climate change. But whether hard or soft, technology transfer programs are most effective when they are approached collaboratively and are congruent with the development objectives and established legal framework of the target country. To this end, the United States works closely with beneficiary countries to ensure a good fit between the resources it provides and the country's needs.

Research and Systematic Observation

The United States leads the world in research on climate and other global environmental changes, funding approximately half of the world's climate change research expenditures. We intend to continue funding research in order to ensure vigorous, ongoing programs aimed at narrowing the uncertainties in our knowledge of climate change. These research programs will help advance the understanding of climate change.

The President's major new initiatives directed at addressing climate change are informed by a wealth of input and are intended to result in significant improvements in climate modeling, observation, and research efforts. The long-term vision embraced by the new initiatives is to help government, the private sector, and communities make informed management decisions regarding climate change in light of persistent uncertainties.

Education, Training, and Outreach

The United States undertakes and supports a broad range of activities aimed at enhancing public understanding and awareness of climate change. These activities range from educational initiatives sponsored by federal agencies to cooperation with independent research and academic organizations. Nongovernmental organizations, industry, and the press also play active roles in increasing public awareness and interest in climate change.

The goal of all of these endeavors—education, training, and public awareness—is to create an informed populace. The United States is committed to providing citizens with access to the information necessary to critically evaluate the consequences of policy options to address climate change in a cost-effective manner that is sustainable and effective in achieving the Framework Convention's long-term goal.

Chapter 3: Greenhouse Gas Inventory

Central to any study of climate change is the development of an emissions inventory that identifies and quantifies a country's primary anthropogenic [man-made or affected by human activities] sources and sinks of greenhouse gases. *The Inventory of U.S. Greenhouse Gas Emissions and Sinks: 1990– 1999* adheres to both (1) a comprehensive and detailed methodology for estimating sources and sinks of anthropogenic greenhouse gases, and (2) a common and consistent mechanism that enables signatory countries to the United Nations Framework Convention on Climate Change (UNFCCC) to compare the relative contribution of different emission sources and greenhouse gases to climate change. Moreover, systematically and consistently estimating national and international emissions is a prerequisite for accounting for reductions and evaluating mitigation strategies.

In June 1992, the United States signed, and later ratified in October, the UNFCCC. The objective of the UNFCCC is "to achieve . . . stabilization of greenhouse gas concentrations in the atmosphere at a level that would prevent dangerous anthropogenic interference with the climate system." By signing the Convention, Parties make commitments "to develop, periodically update, publish and make available . . . national inventories of anthropogenic emissions by sources and removals by sinks of all greenhouse gases not controlled by the Montreal Protocol, using comparable methodologies. . . ."The United States views the *Inventory of U.S. Greenhouse Gas Emissions and Sinks* as an opportunity to fulfill this commitment.

This chapter summarizes information on U.S. anthropogenic greenhouse gas emission trends from 1990 through 1999. . . .

Naturally occurring greenhouse gases include water vapor, carbon dioxide (CO_2), methane (CH_4), nitrous oxide (N_2O), and ozone (O3). several classes of halogenated substances that contain fluorine, chlorine, or bromine are also greenhouse gases, but they are, for the most part, solely a product of industrial activities. Chlorofluorocarbons (CFCs) and hydrochlorofluorocarbons (HCFCs) are halocarbons that contain chlorine, while halocarbons that contain bromine are referred to as bromofluorocarbons (i.e., halons). Because CFCs, HCFCs, and halons are stratospheric ozone-depleting substances, they are covered under the *Montreal Protocol on Substances That Deplete the Ozone Layer.* The UNFCCC defers to this earlier international treaty; consequently these gases are not included in national greenhouse gas inventories. some other fluorine-containing halogenated substances—hydrofluorocarbons (HFCs), perfluorocarbons (PFCs), and sulfur hexafluoride (SF_6)—do not deplete stratospheric ozone but are potent greenhouse gases. These latter substances are addressed by the UNFCCC and are accounted for in national greenhouse gas inventories.

There are also several gases that do not have a direct global warming effect but indirectly affect terrestrial radiation absorption by influencing the formation and destruction of tropospheric and stratospheric ozone. These gases include carbon monoxide (CO), nitrogen oxides (NOx), and non-methane volatile organic compounds (NMVOCs). Aerosols, which are extremely small particles or liquid droplets, such as those produced by sulfur dioxide (SO_2) or elemental carbon emissions, can also affect the absorptive characteristics of the atmosphere.

Although CO_2, CH_4, and N_2O occur naturally in the atmosphere, their atmospheric concentrations have been affected by human activities. since pre-industrial time (i.e., since about 1750), concentrations of these greenhouse gases have increased by 31, 151, and 17 percent, respectively. Because this build-up has altered the chemical composition of the Earth's atmosphere, it has affected the global climate system.

Beginning in the 1950s, the use of CFCs and other stratospheric ozone-depleting substances (ODSs) increased by nearly 10 percent per year until the mid-1980s, when international concern about ozone depletion led to the signing of the Montreal Protocol. since then, the production of ODSs is being phased out. In recent years, use of ODS substitutes, such as HFCs and PFCs, has grown as they begin to be phased in as replacements for CFCs and HCFCs.

Recent Trends in U.S. Greenhouse Gas Emissions

In 1999, total U.S. greenhouse gas emissions were 6,746 teragrams of CO_2 equivalents, 11.7 percent above emissions in 1990. The single-year increase in emissions from 1998 to 1999 was 0.9 percent, which was less than the 1.2 percent average annual rate of increase for 1990 through 1999. The lower than average increase in emissions, especially given the robust economic growth in 1999, was primarily attributable to the following factors: (1) warmer than normal summer and winter conditions, (2) significantly increased output from existing nuclear power plants, (3) reduced CH_4 emissions from coal mines, and (4) HFC-23 by-product emissions from the chemical manufacture of HCFC-22. . . .

The primary greenhouse gas emitted by human activities was CO_2. The largest source of CO_2, and of overall greenhouse gas emissions in the United States, was fossil fuel combustion. Emissions of CH_4 resulted primarily from decomposition of wastes in landfills, enteric fermentation associated with domestic livestock, natural gas systems, and coal mining. Most N_2O emissions were the result of agricultural soil management and mobile source fossil fuel combustion. The emissions of substitutes for ozone-depleting substances and emissions of HFC-23 during the production of HCFC-22 were the primary contributors to aggregate HFC emissions. Electrical transmission and distribution systems accounted for most sF6 emissions, while the majority of PFC emissions were a by-product of primary aluminum production.

As the largest source of U.S. greenhouse gas emissions, CO_2 from fossil fuel combustion accounted for a nearly constant 80 percent of global warming potential (GWP)-weighted emissions in the 1990s. Emissions from this source category grew by 13 percent from 1990 to 1999 and were responsible for most of the increase in national emissions during this period. The annual increase in CO_2 emissions from fossil fuel combustion was 1.2 per cent in 1999, a figure close to the source's average annual rate of 1.4 percent during the 1990s. Historically, changes in emissions from fossil fuel combustion have been the dominant factor affecting U.S. emission trends.

Changes in CO_2 emissions from fossil fuel combustion are influenced by many long-term and short-term factors, including population and economic growth, energy price fluctuations, technological changes, and seasonal temperatures. On an annual basis, the overall consumption of fossil fuels in the United States and other countries generally fluctuates in response to changes in general economic conditions, energy prices, weather, and the availability of non-fossil alternatives. For example, a year with increased consumption of goods and services, low fuel prices, severe summer and winter weather conditions, nuclear plant closures, and lower precipitation feeding hydroelectric output would be expected to have proportionally greater fossil fuel consumption than a year with poor economic performance, high fuel prices, mild temperatures, and increased output from nuclear and hydroelectric plants.

Longer-term changes in energy consumption patterns, however, tend to be more a function of changes that affect the scale of consumption (e.g., population, number of cars, and size of houses), the efficiency with which energy is used in equipment (e.g., cars, power plants, steel mills, and light bulbs), and consumer behavior (e.g., walking, bicycling, or telecommuting to work instead of driving).

Energy-related CO_2 emissions are also a function of the type of fuel or energy consumed and its carbon intensity. Producing heat or electricity using natural gas instead of coal, for example, can reduce the CO_2 emissions associated with energy consumption because of the lower carbon content of natural gas per unit of useful energy produced. . . .

Emissions of CO_2 from fossil fuel combustion grew rapidly in 1996, due primarily to two factors: (1) fuel switching by electric utilities from natural gas to more carbon-intensive coal as colder winter conditions and the associated rise in demand for natural gas from residential, commercial, and industrial customers for heating caused gas prices to rise sharply; and (2) higher consumption of petroleum fuels for transportation. Milder weather conditions in summer and winter moderated the growth in emissions in 1997; however, the shut-down of several nuclear power plants led electric utilities to increase their consumption of coal and other fuels to offset the lost capacity. In 1998, weather conditions were again a dominant factor in slowing the growth in emissions. Warm winter temperatures resulted in a significant drop in residential, commercial, and industrial natural gas consumption. This drop in emissions from natural gas used for heating was primarily offset by two factors: (1) electric utility emissions, which increased in part due to a hot summer and its associated air conditioning demand; and (2) increased gasoline consumption for transportation.

In 1999, the increase in emissions from fossil fuel combustion was caused largely by growth in petroleum consumption for transportation. In addition, heating fuel demand partly recovered in the residential, commercial, and industrial sectors as winter temperatures dropped relative to 1998, although temperatures were still warmer than normal. These increases were offset, in part, by a decline in emissions from electric utilities due primarily to: (1) an increase in net generation of electricity by nuclear plants (8 percent) to record levels, which reduced demand from fossil fuel plants; and (2) moderated summer temperatures compared to the previous year, thereby reducing electricity demand for air conditioning. Utilization of existing nuclear power plants, measured by a plant's capacity factor, increased from just over 70 percent in 1990 to over 85 percent in 1999.

Another factor that does not affect total emissions, but does affect the interpretation of emission trends, is the allocation of emissions from nonutility power producers. The Energy Information Administration (EIA) currently includes fuel consumption by nonutilities with the industrial end-use sector. In 1999, there was a large shift in generating capacity from regulated utilities to nonutilities, as restructuring legislation spurred the sale of 7 percent of utility generating capability. This shift is illustrated by the increase in industrial end-use sector emissions from coal and the associated decrease in electric utility emissions. However, emissions from the industrial end-use sector did not increase as much as would be expected, even though net generation by nonutilities increased from 11 to 15 percent of total U.S. electricity production.

Overall, from 1990 to 1999, total emissions of CO_2 and N_2O increased by 645.2 (13 percent) and 35.7 Tg CO_2 Eq. (9 percent), respectively, while CH_4 emissions decreased by 24.9 Tg CO_2 Eq. (4 percent). During the same period, aggregate weighted emissions of HFCs, PFCs, and SF_6 rose by 51.8 Tg CO_2 Eq. (62 percent). Despite being emitted in smaller quantities relative to the other principal greenhouse gases, emissions of HFCs, PFCs, and SF_6 are significant because many of them have extremely high global warming potentials and, in the cases of PFCs and SF_6, long atmospheric lifetimes. Conversely, U.S. greenhouse gas emissions were partly offset by carbon sequestration in forests and land-filled carbon, which were estimated to be 15 percent of total emissions in 1999.

Other significant trends in emissions from source categories over the nine-year period from 1990 through 1999 included the following:

- Aggregate HFC and PFC emissions resulting from the substitution of ozone-depleting substances (e.g., CFCs) increased by 55.8 Tg CO_2 Eq. This increase was partly offset, however, by reductions in PFC emissions from aluminum production (9.2 Tg CO_2 Eq. or 48 percent), and reductions in emissions of HFC-23 from the production of HCFC-22 (4.4 Tg CO_2 Eq. or 13 percent). Reductions in PFC emissions from aluminum production were the result of both voluntary industry emission reduction efforts and lower domestic aluminum production. HFC-23 emissions from the production of HCFC-22 decreased due to a reduction in the intensity of emissions from that source, despite increased HCFC-22 production.
- Emissions of N_2O from mobile combustion rose by 9.1 Tg CO_2 Eq. (17 percent), primarily due to increased rates of N_2O generation in highway vehicles.
- CH_4 emissions from coal mining dropped by 26 Tg CO_2 Eq. (30 percent) as a result of the mining of less gassy coal from underground mines and the increased use of CH_4 from degasification systems.
- N_2O emissions from agricultural soil management increased by 29.3 Tg CO_2 Eq. (11 percent), as fertilizer consumption and cultivation of nitrogen-fixing crops rose.

- By 1998, all of the three major adipic acid-producing plants had voluntarily implemented N_2O abatement technology. As a result, emissions fell by 9.3 Tg CO_2 Eq. (51 percent). The majority of this decline occurred from 1997 to 1998, despite increased production. . . .

Chapter 6: Impacts and Adaptation

In its June 2001 report, the Committee on the science of Climate Change, which was convened by the National Research Council (NRC) of the National Academy of sciences, concluded that "[h]uman-induced warming and associated sea level rises are expected to continue through the 21st century." The Committee recognized that there remains considerable uncertainty in current understanding of how climate varies naturally and will respond to projected, but uncertain, changes in the emissions of greenhouse gases and aerosols. It also noted that the "impacts of these changes will be critically dependent on the magnitude of the warming and the rate with which it occurs."

Summary of the National Assessment

To develop an initial understanding of the potential impacts of climate change for the United States during the 21st century, the U.S. Global Change Research Program has sponsored a wide-ranging set of assessment activities since the submission of the second National Communication in 1997. These activities examined regional, sectoral, and national components of the potential consequences for the environment and key societal activities in the event of changes in climate consistent with projections drawn from the Intergovernmental Panel on Climate Change (IPCC). Regional studies ranged from Alaska to the southeast and from the Northeast to the Pacific Islands. sectoral studies considered the potential influences of climate change on land cover, agriculture, forests, human health, water resources, and coastal areas and marine resources. A national overview drew together the findings to provide an integrated and comprehensive perspective.

These assessment studies recognized that definitive prediction of potential outcomes is not yet feasible as a result of the wide range of possible future levels of greenhouse gas and aerosol emissions, the range of possible climatic responses to changes in atmospheric concentration, and the range of possible environmental and societal responses. These assessments, therefore, evaluated the narrower question concerning the vulnerability of the United States to a specified range of climate warming, focusing primarily on the potential consequences of climate scenarios that project global average warming of about 2.5 to almost 4° C (about 4.5–7° F). While narrower than the IPCC's full 1.4–5.8° C (2.5–10.4° F) range of estimates of future warming, the selection of the climate scenarios that were considered recognized that it is important to treat a range of conditions about the mid-range of projected warming, which was given by the NRC as 3° C (5.4° F). similarly, assumption of a mid-range value of sea level rise of about 48 cm (19 inches) was near the middle of the IPCC's range of 9–88 cm (about 4–35 inches).

Because of these ranges and their uncertainties, and because of uncertainties in projecting potential impacts, it is important to note that this chapter cannot present absolute probabilities of what is likely to occur. Instead, it can only present judgments about the relative plausibility of outcomes in the event that the projected changes in climate that are being considered do occur. To the extent that actual emissions of greenhouse gases turn out to be lower than projected, or that climate change is at the lower end of the projected ranges and climate variability about the mean varies little from the past, the projected impacts of climate change are likely to be reduced or delayed, and continued adaptation and technological development are likely to reduce the projected impacts and costs of climate change within the United States. Even in this event, however, the long lifetimes of greenhouse gases already in the atmosphere and the momentum of the climate system are projected to cause climate to continue to change for more than a century. Conversely, if the changes in climate are toward the upper end of the projected ranges and occur rapidly or lead to unprecedented conditions, the level of disruption is likely to be increased. Because of the momentum in the climate system and natural climate variability, adapting to a changing climate is inevitable. The question is whether we adapt poorly or well. With either weak or strong warming, however, the U.S. economy should continue to grow, with impacts being reduced if actions are taken to prepare for and adapt to future changes.

Although successful U.S. adaptation to the changing climate conditions during the 20th century provides some context for evaluating potential U.S. vulnerability to projected changes, the assessments indicate that the challenge of adaptation is likely to be greater during the 21st century than in the past. Natural ecosystems appear to be the most vulnerable to climate change because generally little can be done to help them adapt to the projected rate and amount of change. sea level rise at mid-range rates is projected to cause additional loss of coastal wetlands, particularly in areas where there are obstructions to landward migration, and put coastal communities at greater risk of storm surges, especially in the south-eastern United States. Reduced snow-pack is very likely to alter the timing and amount of water supplies, potentially exacerbating water shortages, particularly throughout the western United States, if current water management practices cannot be successfully altered or modified. Increases in the heat index (which combines temperature and humidity) and in the frequency of heat waves are very likely. At a minimum, these changes will increase discomfort, particularly in cities; however, their health impacts can be ameliorated through such measures as the increased availability of air conditioning.

At the same time, greater wealth and advances in technologies are likely to help facilitate adaptation, particularly for human systems. In addition, highly managed ecosystems, such as crops and timber plantations, appear more robust than natural and lightly managed ecosystems, such as grasslands and deserts.

Some potential benefits were also identified in the assessments. For example, due to increased carbon dioxide (CO_2) in the atmosphere and an extended growing season, crop and forest productivities are likely to increase where water and nutrients are sufficient, at least for the next few decades. As a result, the potential exists for an increase in exports of some U.S. food products, depending on impacts in other food-growing regions around the world. Increases in crop production in fertile areas could cause prices to fall, benefiting consumers. Other potential benefits could include extended seasons for construction and warm-weather recreation, and reduced heating requirements and cold-weather mortality.

While most studies conducted to date have primarily had an internal focus, the United States also recognizes that its well-being is connected to the world through the global economy, the common global environment, shared resources, historic roots and continuing family relations, travel and tourism, migrating species, and more. As a result, in addition to internal impacts, the United States is likely to be affected, both directly and indirectly and both positively and detrimentally, by the potential consequences of climate change on the rest of the world. To better understand those potential consequences and the potential for adaptation worldwide, we are conducting and participating in research and assessments both within the United States and internationally. To alleviate vulnerability to adverse consequences, we are undertaking a wide range of activities that will help nationally and internationally, from developing medicines for dealing with infectious disease to promoting worldwide development through trade and assistance. . . . [T]he United States is also offering many types of assistance to the world community, believing that information about and preparation for climate change can help reduce adverse impacts. . . .

[Editor's Note: The following two paragraphs, contained within the text of the report submitted to the United Nations, were subsequently placed in boxes on the first page of Chapter 6 to give them greater prominence.]

Uncertainties in Estimates of the Timing, Magnitude, and Distribution of Future Warming

While current analyses are unable to predict with confidence the timing, magnitude, or regional distribution of climate change, the best scientific information indicates that if greenhouse gas concentrations continue to increase, changes are likely to occur. The U. S. National Research Council has cautioned, however, that "because there is considerable uncertainty in current understanding of how the climate system varies naturally and reacts to emissions of greenhouse gases and aerosols, current estimates of the magnitude of future warmings should be regarded as tentative and subject to future adjustments (either upward or downward)." Moreover, there is perhaps even greater uncertainty regarding the social, environmental, and economic consequences of changes in climate.

Uncertainties in Regional and Local Projections of Climate Change

One of the weakest links in our knowledge is the connection between global and regional predictions of climate change. The National Research Council's response to the President's request for a review of climate change policy specifically noted that fundamental scientific questions remain regarding the specifics of regional and local projections. Predicting the potential impacts of climate change is compounded by a lack of understanding of the sensitivity of many environmental systems and resources—both managed and unmanaged—to climate change.

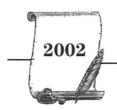
June

WHITE HOUSE STATEMENT ON CRISIS IN KASHMIR
June 5, 2002

Nuclear-armed rivals India and Pakistan marched to the brink of yet another war over the disputed province of Kashmir in April and May 2002 but then stepped back in response to intense international diplomatic pressure. Months later both countries withdrew some troops from border regions, where they had been shelling each other intermittently for about a year. Local elections in Kashmir also appeared to offer modest hope that the long dispute finally could be resolved peacefully.

Ever since Britain severed the Indian subcontinent into the two countries in 1947, India and Pakistan had disputed ownership of the province known formally as the State of Jammu and Kashmir. Even though it had a Muslim-majority population, Kashmir ended up in the hands of India, a nation dominated by Hindus, rather than Pakistan, which declared itself an Islamic republic. The two countries fought two major wars over Kashmir, in 1947–1948 and 1965, with Pakistan gaining control over about one-third of the province. But India retained most of the population of Kashmir, along with the fabled Vale (or valley) of Kashmir and the two capital cities, Srinagar and Jammu. Trained and armed by Pakistan, Islamic guerrillas in 1989 launched attacks against Indian authority in Kashmir; an estimated 35,000 to 60,000 people died in the conflict over the next dozen years.

The rivalry between India and Pakistan reached a dangerous new level in 1998 when both countries tested nuclear weapons. A subsequent move toward peace failed, and a year later the two countries fought another skirmish over Kashmir that was inconclusive but did lead to the ouster of Pakistan's elected prime minister by army chief General Pervez Musharraf. Tensions escalated again in December 2001 when Pakistan-based guerrillas attacked the Indian parliament in New Delhi, killing nine people before they were killed themselves. The two countries massed an estimated total of one million troops along the 1,800-mile border, and India threatened war unless Musharraf permanently stopped the guerrillas from carrying out attacks in Indian territory, including Kashmir. (Background, Historic Documents of 2001, p. 963)

Musharraf Crackdown

India's demand put Musharraf in an extremely difficult position. Support for Kashmiri "freedom fighters" (India called them "terrorists") had long been a central tenet of Pakistan's military. No government of Pakistan, even one led by the military, could retain public support if it was seen as weakening the country's historic claim to Kashmir. Musharraf had angered radical Islamist elements in his country by siding with Washington following the September 11, 2001, terrorist attacks against the United States. Under U.S. pressure, Musharraf abandoned Pakistani support for the Islamist regime, known as the Taliban, in neighboring Afghanistan, which in turn had provided refuge for the al Qaeda terrorist network that carried out the September 11 attacks.

Musharraf took some steps against the Kashmiri guerrillas in January, officially banning the two guerrilla groups said to have been responsible for the attack on India's parliament, Lashkar-e-Taiba and Jaish-e-Muhammed, and detaining hundreds of their fighters. Musharraf also ordered the Pakistani military and intelligence services to close some of the training camps for guerrillas in Pakistan-held Kashmir and to shut off the routes used by the guerrillas to enter Indian-controlled Kashmir. Musharraf took these steps in the context of his own plans to hold on to political power in Pakistan, first through an April referendum on extending his presidency for five years and then with parliamentary elections in October. (Pakistan elections, p. 165)

Resumption of Guerrilla Attacks

Musharraf's actions appeared to be effective for a while, but by late February Indian officials claimed that guerrilla infiltrations into Kashmir had resumed. News reports also indicated that many of the guerrillas arrested by Pakistani authorities in January had been released. Then on March 29 and 30 guerrillas began a series of attacks against civilians and Indian security forces in or near Srinagar, Kashmir's summer capital, and Jammu, the winter capital. Twenty-two people, most of them soldiers or policemen, were killed in bombings and shoot-outs, all of which Indian officials blamed on Islamic guerrillas. The most serious incident occurred at a Hindu temple in Jammu, where two attackers threw several grenades, then engaged in a gun battle with police. Four policemen, four civilians, and the two attackers were killed, according to the police.

Other incidents in mid-April killed two dozen more people and served as precursors to the deadliest attack of the year. On May 14 three armed men, disguised as soldiers, opened fire on a bus full of passengers near Jammu, killing seven. The attackers then entered the family quarters of an army camp and shot to death thirteen adults and ten children. Soldiers managed to kill the attackers. Indian officials said the Pakistan-based group Lashkar-e-Taiba was to blame, although a previously unknown group claimed responsibility.

That attack pushed tensions between India and Pakistan to the highest point since the gun battle at the Indian parliament six months earlier.

India placed full blame on the Pakistani government, which in turn denounced the attack and suggested that India had sponsored the incident in hopes of embarrassing Musharraf. The attack came on the second day of a visit to New Delhi by Christina Rocca, the U.S. assistant secretary of state for South Asia, who was attempting, with no apparent success, to calm the atmosphere between the two enemies.

Within three days, Indian and Pakistani forces were exchanging heavy mortar and gunfire across the mountainous Line of Control that divided the two parts of Kashmir. India on May 18 expelled Pakistan's ambassador to New Delhi as a sign of protest, and Indian prime minister Atal Bihari Vajpayee ostentatiously canceled a vacation so he could receive briefings from top military leaders on his "options" for a military response. In that dangerous atmosphere, a key Kashmiri moderate leader was gunned down on May 21 in Srinagar by unknown assailants. Playing their respective roles yet again, New Delhi and Islamabad each blamed the other and declared a readiness to go to war if necessary. Pakistan took a step beyond rhetoric, test firing a ballistic missile capable of carrying a nuclear bomb deep within India.

Diplomatic Intervention

This return to the real prospect of war between India and Pakistan unnerved many people in both countries but also posed a serious danger to the United States and its war against terrorists. The administration of President George W. Bush was relying heavily on Pakistan's leader, Musharraf, for help in the continuing U.S. effort to eliminate remnants of the al Qaeda terrorist network in Afghanistan and along the Afghan-Pakistan border. Pakistan had already shifted thousands of troops from the antiterror campaign to the line of confrontation with India. War between India and Pakistan over Kashmir, including possible use of nuclear weapons, would have disrupted U.S. operations in Afghanistan and might even had led to an explosion of anti-American sentiment in the region, with serious long-term consequences. The Bush administration in late May made public an assessment by the Defense Intelligence Agency that a full-scale nuclear war between India and Pakistan could kill up to 12 million people and injure millions more.

Washington pressured both sides to cool the rhetoric and allow diplomacy a chance to avoid confrontation. But history did not make the United States a totally disinterested mediator in South Asia. For most of the past half-century Washington offered diplomatic, economic, military, and political backing for Pakistan, while India was aligned during the cold war with the Soviet Union. Try as it might to put the current U.S. position in a new light, the Bush administration had an uphill struggle to overcome Indian suspicions about Washington's motives.

Bush's diplomatic task was complicated by domestic political needs of the Indian and Pakistani leaders. Formerly a fiery Hindu nationalist politician, Vajpayee had moderated his stance as prime minister and sought to *improve relations between India's Hindu majority and Muslim minority. Now ailing and nearing the end of his political career, Vajpayee was struggling to restrain the more radical elements of his Hindu nationalist party, some of whom openly called for a nuclear war against Pakistan. Disagreements among leaders of Vajpayee's coalition had been unusually pronounced since February, when hundreds of people, most of them Muslims, died in rioting between Hindus and Muslims in the western state of Gujarat. As violence also escalated in Kashmir, Vajpayee faced growing political pressure to respond militarily, if only with a "limited" air strike on the guerrilla bases under Pakistan's control.*

For his part, Musharraf was a military leader trying to refashion himself as a democrat while at the same time dampening the extreme Islamist factions in his country. As the army chief Musharraf had control of the military, but concessions to India on Kashmir might weaken his standing among more radical officers. While both Musharraf and Vajpayee had reasons for wanting to be seen by the rest of the world as a moderate, neither wanted to be remembered by future generations in his country as the man who "lost" Kashmir to the other side.

As the leader with the presumed power to stop the terrorist attacks in Kashmir, Musharraf was under more international pressure than was Vajpayee. Musharraf responded with a speech on May 27 in which he insisted, once again, that his government had stopped all guerrilla infiltration from Pakistan-controlled Kashmir into Indian-controlled Kashmir.

Four days later, the United States and several of its key allies (Australia, Britain, and Canada) urged their citizens living in India to leave because of the risk of war. That step threatened the Indian economy by casting international doubt on the country's stability. Musharraf and Vajpayee both attended an Asian summit meeting in Kazakhstan on June 4 but ignored each other, despite an attempted mediation effort by Russian president Vladimir Putin.

On June 5, as news media outlets around the world carried headlines warning of a possible nuclear war, President Bush picked up the telephone and placed separate calls to Musharraf and Vajpayee. A White House statement said Bush told Musharraf that the United States "expects Pakistan to live up to the commitment to end all support for terrorism"—meaning its backing for the guerrillas in Kashmir. The statement said Bush called on Vajpayee to "respond with de-escalatory steps"—in other words, to pull some troops back from the border region and halt any talk of destroying Pakistan with nuclear weapons. Bush thus was putting the onus on Musharraf to take the first step, while pressuring Vajpayee to offer a positive response.

Deputy Secretary of State Richard L. Armitage carried Bush's message directly to the Pakistani and Indian leaders during the next two days. Meeting in Islamabad with Musharraf on June 6, Armitage secured a verbal pledge that Pakistan would enforce a "permanent" ban on Islamic guerrillas infiltrating into Indian-held Kashmir. Armitage took that promise the next day to Vajpayee in New Delhi and urged a reciprocal action. U.S. defense secretary Donald Rumsfeld reinforced Armitage's diplomacy the fol-

lowing week in meetings with the two leaders. A key aspect of the message delivered by Armitage and Rumsfeld was a promise that the United States would stay "engaged" in South Asia; in other words, Bush had promised both India and Pakistan that he would continue to hold the other to its commitments.

The direct approach by the United States—bolstered by similar messages from Putin, European leaders, and others—appeared to have the desired effect. In the following days Indian authorities reported that the Pakistan military had sealed the border to prevent guerrilla infiltrations. Guerrilla leaders angrily confirmed that action, telling reporters on June 9 that Musharraf had summed them to a meeting in which he denied backing away from the Kashmir cause but also that he was under international pressure to halt the attacks against India. On June 10 India took symbolic steps to ease the confrontation, announcing that it was lifting a ban on flights through Indian airspace by Pakistani aircraft, returning some warships to port, and was ready to replace the ambassador to Pakistan, who had been recalled three weeks earlier.

Elections in Kashmir

The sudden easing of tension enabled New Delhi to turn its attention to plans for provincial elections in the Indian-held part of Kashmir. Along with all other Indian states, Jammu and Kashmir had its own state government responsible for local affairs. But unlike the other states, this government was headed by Muslims, reflecting the ethnic majority there. Since 1949 the Kashmiri government had been led by one family, the Abdullahs, and its India National Conference Party. The family had maintained its control with active support from successive governments in New Delhi. Charges by Kashmiri separatists that India rigged the 1987 election resulted in mass arrests of separatist leaders and led to the outbreak of the guerrilla war two years later.

India hoped to use the 2002 elections to strengthen its political hand in Kashmir by convincing moderate leaders to run for office, especially Muslims who advocated an independent Kashmir—as opposed to those who wanted to merge Kashmir with Pakistan. But that hope faded during the summer as all but a handful of separatist leaders refused to run for office. Some may have been frightened by two assassinations of moderate Muslims. The main separatist alliance, the All Parties Hurriyet Conference, urged a total boycott of the election.

In the weeks before the elections, India again accused Pakistan of allowing guerrillas to cross the border into Indian-held Kashmir. Between mid-August and the first round of elections in mid-September, Indian authorities said they had killed several dozen guerrillas in repeated battles. Robert D. Blackwill, the U.S. ambassador to India, said in September that guerrilla incursions had increased in the late summer. Dozens of people died in violence during the election cycle, many of them civilians caught in the cross-fire between guerrillas and government security forces.

Three rounds of voting for local and statewide parliamentary offices ended on October 8. Final returns, announced October 10, showed that the Abdullah family's National Conference party had failed for the first time to gain a majority in the Kashmir parliament. Omar Abdullah, the third-generation party leader who had expected to inherit his father's post as chief minister for Kashmir, was instead defeated in his district. As they always had in the past, Kashmiri separatists rejected the entire election as fraudulent, but many observers said the unexpected defeat of the ruling party would provide new legitimacy to the provincial government. That sentiment was widely echoed by voters, among them a young man named Mohammed Ayub who told the Los Angeles Times: *"I feel that my vote finally means something."*

The two opposition parties—the Congress party and the People's Democratic party—took nearly three weeks to negotiate a coalition to form a new government. The coalition took office November 2, amid a fresh round of violence, including an unsuccessful grenade attack on the new chief minister, Mufti Mohammad Sayeed of the People's Democratic Party. Sayeed promised to bring "a healing touch" to the battered territory. An early test of his policy came less than three weeks later, when guerrillas seized two Hindu temples in the Jammu area; fourteen people were killed and more than fifty wounded in the resulting gun battles between the guerrillas and security forces.

The elections had a broader impact than merely changing the government of Kashmir. Six days after results of the Kashmir voting were announced, the Indian government said it would withdraw most of the half-million troops that had been stationed along the non-Kashmir border with Pakistan. Pakistan immediately responded with its own announcement of a troop withdrawal.

> *Following is the text of a statement issued June 5, 2002, by the White House, reporting on calls by President George W. Bush to the leaders of India and Pakistan to back away from confrontation in their dispute over the state of Kashmir.*
>
> **The document was obtained from the Internet at www .whitehouse.gov/news/releases/2002/06/20020605.html; accessed December 5, 2002.**

Today, President Bush telephoned the leaders of India and Pakistan, urging them to take steps that will ease tensions in the region and reduce the risk of war—a message Deputy Secretary of State [Richard L.] Armitage and Secretary of Defense [Donald] Rumsfeld will reiterate during their trips to South Asia.

The President reiterated to President [Pervez] Musharraf that the United States expects Pakistan to live up to the commitment to end all support for terrorism. The President emphasized to Prime Minister [Atal Bihari] Vajpayee the need for India to respond with de-escalatory steps. To both leaders, the President stressed the need to choose the path of diplomacy.

South Asia is a region of tremendous potential. Armed conflict will do nothing to improve the lives of the people of India or Pakistan. It will instead blot the future of both nations. The United States is ready to help the parties in their efforts to resolve the many underlying issues that divide them.

U.S. STATE DEPARTMENT ON TRAFFICKING IN HUMANS
June 5, 2002

Governments, international organizations, and human rights monitors placed increasing focus during 2002 on global trafficking in humans—most often women and girls. Heightened attention to the problem led some governments to take legal action against criminal gangs that each year bought and sold hundreds of thousands of people and shipped them across international borders.

Forcing and tricking people into slavery are age-old practices, but experts said they became more widespread and profitable during the latter part of the twentieth century for several reasons. Globalization—the lowering of international barriers to trade and communication—led to the increased movement of people across national boundaries, including impoverished people from developing countries lured by the prospect of better lives in the industrialized world. The collapse of communism in Eastern Europe and the former Soviet Union also contributed to the growth of organized crime syndicates, which often found that trafficking in humans was easier and more profitable than narcotics or weapons. Sex tourism was another booming industry that needed a constant supply of workers, provided by criminal traffickers.

Because nearly all trafficking in humans was carried out by illegal underground organizations, no one had compiled reliable statistics on the extent of the problem. Even so, the United Nations and other organizations generally agreed that at least 700,000 people were trafficked across international borders each year; some estimates put the total figure as high as 2 million or even 4 million. Most of the victims appeared to be from Southeast Asia (primarily Thailand, the Philippines, and Cambodia) and South Asia (primarily Pakistan, India, and Bangladesh).

According to some estimates, the formerly communist countries of the Soviet Union and Eastern Europe were the fastest-growing source of people forced into international slavery. Latin America and Africa also were major sources of supply for the human trafficking business. The State Department estimated in 2000 that about 50,000 women and children were trafficked into the United States annually, most of them from Southeast Asia and the former Soviet Union. About half were forced to work in sweatshops or as domestic servants; most of the rest were forced into prostitution and other aspects of the sex industry. Tens of thousands of children also were forced into combat, most often by rebel groups. (Child soldiers, p. 916)

The United Nations General Assembly in November 2000 adopted the Protocol to Prevent, Suppress, and Punish Trafficking in Persons, Especially Women and Children. This treaty called on governments to establish criminal penalties for trafficking in humans, to protect the victims of trafficking, and to take steps to prevent trafficking in the future. The United States signed the treaty in 2000, but President George W. Bush had not submitted it to the Senate for approval as of the end of 2002. More than one hundred other countries had already signed the treaty.

State Department Report

Congress in 2000 passed legislation (PL 106–386) intended to combat trafficking in humans, both in the United States and internationally. Among other things, the law doubled the maximum prison term (to twenty years) for anyone convicted in the United States of forcing another person into slavery and required the State Department to compile an annual report on the extent of international trafficking in humans. The report was to include specific information about what countries were doing to control the problem.

The State Department's first report under the law, issued in June 2001, discussed trafficking issues in eighty-nine countries where a "significant" number of people (at least one hundred) had been trafficked in the previous year. These countries were placed into three categories: twelve "Tier 1" countries that met "minimum standards" for efforts to combat the trafficking in humans; fifty-four "Tier 2" nations that did not meet the minimum standards but were making "significant efforts" to do so; and twenty-three "Tier 3" countries that did not meet the minimum standards and were not making significant efforts to do so. Under the 2000 law, countries categorized as Tier 3 in the 2003 State Department report would be subject to U.S. sanctions, including the banning of U.S. nonhumanitarian, nontrade-related aid.

The State Department on June 5 released its 2002 report on human trafficking. It listed eighteen Tier 1 countries, fifty-three Tier 2 countries, and nineteen Tier 3 countries. The most significant changes involved the Tier 3 countries. The Tier 3 countries were: Afghanistan, Armenia, Bahrain, Belarus, Bosnia and Herzegovina, Burma, Cambodia, Greece, Indonesia, Iran, Kyrgyz Republic [Kyrgyzstan], Lebanon, Qatar, Russia, Saudi Arabia, Sudan, Tajikistan, Turkey, and the United Arab Emirates.

Eight countries that had been listed in Tier 3 in 2001 had moved up to Tier 2 in 2002: Albania, Gabon, Israel, Kazakhstan, Malaysia, Pakistan, Romania, and the Federal Republic of Yugoslavia (Serbia-Montenegro). South Korea was moved from Tier 3 to Tier 1 because of its "extraordinary strides" on the issue, the report said. In addition, five countries that had not been listed at all for 2001 were placed on the Tier 3 list for 2002: Afghanistan, Armenia, Iran, Kyrgyzstan, and Tajikistan. The report contained no information on about one-half of the 190 countries in the world. In some countries, human trafficking was not a significant problem; the State Department said it did not have sufficient reliable information to make judgments about the situation in many other countries.

Secretary of State Colin Powell said of the report: "It's a sober reminder of the reality of this modern-day form of slavery. It is a tool for our engagement with other countries, a starting point for dialogue. It's a platform for advocates. It's a coordination opportunity for regional, anti-trafficking efforts among governments. Hopefully, and most importantly, it's a freedom-promoting mechanism for individual victims of enslavement everywhere."

As with other congressionally mandated reports on internal problems in other countries, compiling the human trafficking report put the State Department in a delicate position. Some of the Tier 3 countries were longtime U.S. allies, including Greece and Turkey (both members of the NATO alliance) and Saudi Arabia, a principal source of U.S. oil. Several other countries on that list had recently become important to the United States because of their strategic role in the war against terrorism, among them Afghanistan, Indonesia, Russia, and Tajikistan.

Nancy Ely-Raphel, head of the State Department's new Office to Monitor and Combat Trafficking in Persons, said "absolutely no political considerations" entered into the selection of countries. "This is a straight-out, objective report determining whether a country is meeting the minimum standards, and whether it's making serious and sustained efforts to meet those minimum standards," she told reporters.

Human rights groups and other advocates on behalf of trafficking victims praised the State Department for taking the issue seriously. But some groups challenged specific aspects of the report, including the assessments for some countries. Critics, for example, noted that Pakistan was moved from its Tier 3 status in 2001 to Tier 2 in 2002 even though the report said Pakistan had taken only modest steps to combat trafficking. Human Rights Watch also criticized the report for failing to draw conclusions about the effectiveness of antitrafficking programs in many countries. In a June 18 letter to Secretary of State Powell, Human Rights Watch also challenged the report's lack of specific details about many countries. In that letter, LaShawn R. Jefferson, executive director of the Women's Rights Division of Human Rights Watch, noted that the report discussed corruption in Burma but provided no information describing how corruption in specific agencies contributed to human trafficking.

Rep. Chris Smith, R-N.J., who sponsored the original legislation mandating the report, said he was pleased that many countries appeared to be taking the human trafficking issue more seriously than in the past. Smith criticized the State Department for placing India, Thailand, and Vietnam in Tier 2 rather than in Tier 3. Those three countries "have serious trafficking problems in which [government] officials appear to be actively involved," Smith said.

U.S. Antitrafficking Efforts

Among the countries not rated in the State Department report was the United States—one of the world's major destinations for the trafficking of people. Department officials estimated that about 50,000 people were trafficked into the United States each year, most of them women and children who were forced to work in sex industries, in sweatshop-type factories, or on farms.

Largely as a consequence of the 2000 legislation, law enforcement agencies became more aggressive in prosecuting human trafficking cases. The government also created a new class of visas, known as the "T" visa, which could be given to as many as 5,000 victims each year who cooperated with law enforcement agencies investigating human trafficking cases. The visas would allow the victims to continue to live and work in the United States for three years, after which they would be eligible to apply for permanent resident status for themselves and for nonimmigrant status for their spouses and children. In the past, victims who reported abuses generally were deported because they were in the country illegally.

President Bush on February 13 signed an executive order establishing an Interagency Task Force to Monitor and Combat Trafficking in Persons. Chaired by the secretary of state, the task force was to oversee all U.S. government efforts on the issue. Among specific steps, the Justice Department began training federal prosecutors and other law enforcement personnel on how to deal with human trafficking cases, and the Department of Health and Human Services launched a public awareness campaign to encourage victims of trafficking to provide evidence to the government.

Bosnia and Kosovo

Two other reports issued during the year focused attention on human trafficking in Eastern Europe, especially Bosnia and Kosovo, areas of the former Yugoslavia that were under international supervision. Human trafficking was becoming an increasingly serious problem in the region despite—and in some cases because of—the presence of thousands of international peacekeepers, police officers, and civil officials.

The first report, released July 22, was commissioned by the UN and the Organization for Security and Cooperation in Europe, a multinational agency that monitored human rights and related matters. The report detailed cases in which international officials were alleged to patronize bars and brothels where women and girls had been forced to provide sexual services. "The international market for sex services as well as local demand has expanded, particularly in countries where there is a large international presence," the report said.

Human Rights Watch on November 26 released a report on its three-year investigation into human trafficking abuses in Bosnia. The organization said the report showed "how local Bosnian police officers facilitate the trafficking by creating false documents; visiting brothels to partake of free sexual services; and sometimes engaging in trafficking directly." The report also discussed cases in which international police officers working for the UN mission in Bosnia visited nightclubs as clients of trafficked women and girls and arranged to have trafficked women delivered to their homes.

Following are excerpts from the "Trafficking in Persons Report," released June 5, 2002, by the U.S. State Department. The report examined the extent to which eighty-nine countries had taken steps to halt international trafficking in humans.

The document was obtained from the Internet at www.state .gov/g/tip/rls/tiprpt/2002/; accessed October 19, 2002.

A Look at the Problem

Over the past year, at least 700,000, and possibly as many as four million men women and children worldwide were bought, sold, transported and held against their will in slave-like conditions. In this modern form of slavery, known as "trafficking in persons," traffickers use threats, intimidation and violence to force victims to engage in sex acts or to labor under conditions comparable to slavery for the traffickers' financial gain. Women, children and men are trafficked into the international sex trade for the purposes of prostitution, sex tourism and other commercial sexual services and into forced labor situations in sweatshops, construction sites and agricultural settings. The practice may take other forms as well, including the abduction of children and their conscription into government forces or rebel armies, the sale of women and children into domestic servitude, and the use of children as street beggars and camel jockeys.

Traffickers often move victims from their home communities to other areas—within their country or to foreign countries—where the victim is isolated and may be unable to speak the language or be unfamiliar with the culture. In many cases, the victims do not have immigration documents or they have fraudulent documents provided by the traffickers. Most importantly, the victims lose their support network of family and friends, thus making them more vulnerable to the traffickers' demands and threats. Victims also may be exposed to a range of health concerns, including domestic violence, alcoholism, psychological problems, HIV/AIDS and other sexually transmitted diseases. Victims in these situations do not know how to escape the violence or where to go for help. Victims may choose not to turn to authorities out of fear of being jailed or deported, especially because the governments of some countries treat victims as criminals. In other countries, there is no protection for victims who come forward to assist in the prosecution of traffickers.

Traffickers recruit and find potential victims in a number of ways. Traffickers advertise in local newspapers offering good jobs at high pay in exciting cities. They also use fraudulent employment, travel, modeling and matchmaking agencies to lure unsuspecting young men and women into the trafficking networks. In local villages, a trafficker may pose as a "friend of a friend," meet with families and convince parents that their children will be safer and better taken care of by the "friend." Traffickers often mislead parents into believing that their children will be taught a useful skill or trade—but the children end up enslaved in small shops, on farms, or in domestic servitude. Traffickers also promise parents that they will marry their daughters—but the girls are forced into prostitution. In some violent situations, traffickers may kidnap or abduct victims.

The Causes of Trafficking

Economic and political instability greatly increases the likelihood that a country will become a source of trafficking victims. In countries with chronic unemployment, widespread poverty and a lack of economic opportunities, traffickers use promises of higher wages and good working conditions in foreign countries to lure people into their networks. Victims, who want a better life for themselves and their families, are easily convinced by the traffickers' promises. Civil unrest, internal armed conflict, and natural disasters destabilize and displace populations and, in turn, increase their vulnerability to exploitation and abuse. In some countries, social or cultural practices contribute to trafficking. For example, the low status of women and girls in some societies contributes to the growing trafficking industry by not valuing their lives as highly as those of the male population. In other societies, the practice of entrusting poor children to more affluent friends or relatives may lead to abusive and exploitative situations.

In many destination countries, commercial sexual exploitation and the demands for inexpensive labor have increased over the past several decades. Many traffickers who are part of criminal networks involved in other transnational crimes have recognized that they can profit greatly by supplying people to fill these demands. Trafficking does not require a large capital investment and it frequently involves little risk of discovery by law enforcement. In addition, trafficking victims, unlike drugs, can be re-sold and used repeatedly by traffickers. In some countries, corruption contributes to the problem of trafficking, where local officials are complicit in trafficking or turn a blind eye.

Trafficking victims are often brought through "transit countries" from a source country to a destination country. Traffickers may use false documents in doing so. Weak border controls and corruption of migration officials also may further facilitate the transit of victims.

The Magnitude

Given the nature of trafficking and its often hidden face, it is extremely difficult to develop accurate statistics on the extent of the problem. According to a U.S. Government estimate based on 1997 data, 700,000 persons, mainly women and children, are trafficked across national borders worldwide each year. Other global estimates of the number of victims trafficked annually range from approximately one to four million. According to an International Organization for Migration 1997 estimate, the number of victims trafficked both internally and across national borders is four million. The United States is principally a transit and destination country for trafficking in persons. According to a 1997 estimate, some 50,000 women and children are trafficked annually for sexual exploitation into the United States.

The Trafficking Victims Protection Act of 2000

In October 2000, the Trafficking Victims Protection Act (Division A of Public Law 106-386)(the "Act") was enacted to combat trafficking, to ensure the just and effective punishment of traffickers and to protect victims. The Act added new crimes, strengthened pre-existing criminal penalties, afforded new protections to trafficking victims, and made available certain benefits and services to victims of severe forms of trafficking. With this comprehensive approach to the problem, the Act created significant mandates for several federal government agencies, including the Departments of State, Justice, Labor, Health and Human Services and the U.S. Agency for International Development. One of the State Department's responsibilities is the annual submission of a report to Congress on the status of severe forms of trafficking in persons; this is the second such report. The Act's definition of "severe forms of trafficking in persons" is in the following box, as are its definitions of other terms that are elements of that definition. For the purpose of this report, the term "trafficking" refers to "severe forms of trafficking in persons" as defined in the Act. [The Act defines "severe form of trafficking in persons" as "sex trafficking in which a commercial sex act is induced by force, fraud, or coercion, or in which the person induced to perform such act has not attained 18 years of age; or (b) the recruitment, harboring, transportation, provision, or obtaining of a person for labor or services, through the use of force, fraud or coercion for the purpose of subjection to involuntary servitude, peonage, debt bondage, or slavery."] . . .

The Report

This is the second annual report to Congress, as required by the Act, on the status of severe forms of trafficking in persons worldwide. It covers the time period of April 2001 through March 2002. . . . With this annual report, the United States seeks to bring international attention, both of governments and the general public, to the horrific practice of trafficking in persons. This report serves as a major diplomatic tool for the U.S. Government, which hopes that other governments will view this as an instrument for continued dialogue, encouragement for their current work, and an instrument to help them focus their future work on prosecution, protection, and prevention programs and policies. After the release of this year's report, the Department will continue to engage in discussions with governments about the content of the report to help strengthen cooperative efforts to eradicate trafficking. The Department will use the information gained in the compilation of this year's report to target assistance programs more effectively and to work with countries that need help in combating trafficking. Finally, the Department hopes the report will be a catalyst for government efforts to combat trafficking in persons around the world, so that this degrading practice will be eliminated. . . .

Minimum Standards

The Act defines "minimum standards for the elimination of trafficking", which are summarized as follows:

1. The government should prohibit trafficking and punish acts of trafficking.
2. The government should prescribe punishment commensurate with that for grave crimes, such as forcible sexual assault, for the knowing commission of trafficking in some of its most reprehensible forms (trafficking for sexual purposes, trafficking involving rape or kidnapping, or trafficking that causes a death).
3. For knowing commission of any act of trafficking, the government should prescribe punishment that is sufficiently stringent to deter, and that adequately reflects the offense's heinous nature.
4. The government should make serious and sustained efforts to eliminate trafficking.

The Act also sets out seven criteria that "should be considered" as indicia of the fourth point above, "serious and sustained efforts to eliminate trafficking." Summarized, they are:

1. Whether the government vigorously investigates and prosecutes acts of trafficking within its territory.
2. Whether the government protects victims of trafficking, encourages victims' assistance in investigation and prosecution, provides victims with legal alternatives to their removal to countries where they would face retribution or hardship, and ensures that victims are not inappropriately penalized solely for unlawful acts as a direct result of being trafficked.
3. Whether the government has adopted measures, such as public education, to prevent trafficking.
4. Whether the government cooperates with other governments in investigating and prosecuting trafficking.
5. Whether the government extradites persons charged with trafficking as it does with other serious crimes.
6. Whether the government monitors immigration and emigration patterns for evidence of trafficking, and whether law enforcement agencies respond appropriately to such evidence.
7. Whether the government vigorously investigates and prosecutes public officials who participate in or facilitate trafficking, and takes all appropriate measures against officials who condone trafficking.

The Act also states three factors that the Department is to consider in determining whether a country is making significant efforts to bring itself into compliance with these minimum standards. Summarized, these considerations are: 1) the extent of trafficking in the country; 2) the extent of governmental noncompliance with the minimum standards, particularly the extent to which government officials have participated in, facilitated, condoned, or are otherwise complicit in trafficking; and 3) what measures are reasonable to bring the government into compliance with the minimum standards in light of the government's resources and capabilities.

The Tiers

Tier 1

The governments of countries in **Tier 1** fully comply with the Act's minimum standards. Such governments criminalize and have successfully prosecuted trafficking, and have provided a wide range of protective services to victims. Victims are not jailed or otherwise punished solely as a result of being trafficked, and they are not summarily returned to a country where they may face hardship as a result of being trafficked. In addition, these governments sponsor or coordinate prevention campaigns aimed at stemming the flow of trafficking.

[Countries listed in Tier 1 were: Austria, Belgium, Canada, Colombia, Czech Republic, France, Germany, Hong Kong, Italy, Lithuania, Macedonia, The Netherlands, Poland, Portugal, South Korea, Spain, Switzerland, and the United Kingdom.]

Tier 2

The governments of countries in **Tier 2** do not yet fully comply with the Act's minimum standards but are making significant efforts to bring themselves into compliance with those standards. Some are strong in the prosecution of traffickers, but provide little or no assistance to victims. Others work to assist victims and punish traffickers, but have not yet taken any significant steps to prevent trafficking. Some governments are only beginning to address trafficking, but nonetheless have already taken significant steps towards the eradication of trafficking.

[Countries listed in Tier 2 were: Albania, Angola, Bangladesh, Benin, Brazil, Bulgaria, Burkina Faso, Cameroon, China, Costa Rica, Cote D'Ivoire (Ivory Coast), Dominican Republic, El Salvador, Equatorial Guinea, Estonia, Ethiopia, Gabon, Georgia, Ghana, Guatemala, Haiti, Honduras, Hungary, India, Israel, Japan, Kazakhstan, Laos, Latvia, Malaysia, Mali, Mexico, Moldova, Morocco, Nepal, Nigeria, Pakistan, Philippines, Romania, Senegal, Sierra Leone, Singapore, Slovenia, South Africa, Sri Lanka, Tanzania, Thailand, Togo, Uganda, Ukraine, Vietnam, and Yugoslavia.]

Tier 3

The governments of countries in **Tier 3** do not fully comply with the minimum standards and are not making significant efforts to bring themselves into compliance. Some of these governments refuse to acknowledge the trafficking problem within their territory. On a more positive note, several other governments in this category are beginning to take concrete steps to combat trafficking. While these steps do not yet reach the appropriate level of significance, many of these governments are on the path to placement on **Tier 2.**

[Countries listed in Tier 3 were: Afghanistan, Armenia, Bahrain, Belarus, Bosnia-Herzegovina, Burma, Cambodia, Greece, Indonesia, Iran, Kyrgyz Republic [Kyrgyzstan], Lebanon, Qatar, Russia, Saudi Arabia, Sudan, Tajikistan, Turkey, and the United Arab Emirates.]

Penalties

According to the Act, beginning with the 2003 report, countries in Tier 3 will be subject to certain sanctions, principally termination of non-humanitarian, non-trade-related assistance. Consistent with the Act, such countries also would face U.S. opposition to assistance (except for humanitarian, trade-related, and certain development-related assistance) from international financial institutions, specifically the International Monetary Fund and multilateral development banks such as the World Bank. All or part of the bilateral and multilateral assistance sanctions may be waived upon a determination by the President that the provision of such assistance to the country would promote the purposes of the Act or is otherwise in the national interest of the United States. The Act provides that the President shall waive those sanctions when necessary to avoid significant adverse effects on vulnerable populations, including women and children. . . .

Country Narratives

[Following are excerpts of the "narratives" for the nineteen countries listed in Tier 3, as well as for the nine countries that had been listed in Tier 3 in the 2001 report but were moved to a different tier in this report.]

Afghanistan (Tier 3)

Afghanistan is a country of origin and transit for women and children trafficked for the purposes of sexual exploitation and labor. Internal trafficking of women and children for purposes of sexual exploitation and forced labor also occurs. Afghanistan was under two different governments during this period: the Taliban and the Afghan Interim Authority (AIA). Until December 22, 2001, when the AIA took over there was no functioning central government. During most of 2001, the Taliban, a Pashtun-dominated fundamentalist Islamic movement, controlled approximately ninety percent of the country. Taliban forces were responsible for disappearances of women and children, many of whom were trafficked to Pakistan and the Gulf States. Under the Taliban, women and girls were subjected to rape, kidnapping, and forced marriage. Since the AIA took over, there are reports that Afghan women and children have been trafficked to Pakistan and the Middle East for purposes of sexual exploitation and forced labor. There have been numerous reports that impoverished Afghan families have sold their children for purposes of forced sexual exploitation, marriage, and labor.

Neither the Taliban nor the AIA have complied with minimum standards for the elimination of trafficking, nor did either make significant efforts to do so. The AIA was only in power for a short portion of the reporting period and a severe lack of resources and minimal governmental infrastructure have hindered the AIA from taking steps to prosecute traffickers or protect victims. During its tenure, the Taliban not only failed to take steps to combat trafficking, but also participated in trafficking. . . .

Albania (Tier 2) [Moved from Tier 3 in the 2001 report.]

Albania is a source and transit country primarily for women and girls trafficked for the purposes of sexual exploitation to Italy and Greece, and on to other EU countries, such as Belgium, France, and the Netherlands. Victims transiting Albania come mostly from Romania and Moldova, with smaller numbers from Bulgaria and Ukraine. Young boys are also reportedly trafficked from Albania to work as beggars in Italy and Greece.

The Government of Albania does not yet fully comply with minimum standards for the elimination of trafficking; however, it is making significant efforts to do so. The Penal Code prohibits trafficking. Despite a severe lack of resources, the Government arrested 96 people for trafficking crimes from December 2000 to October 2001, and the frequency of arrests continues to rise. Of these, there were at least 12 convictions, with 9 receiving minimal prison sentences. . . .

Armenia (Tier 3)

Armenia is a source country for women and girls trafficked to the United Arab Emirates, Turkey, Russia, Greece and Germany for sexual exploitation.

The Government of Armenia does not fully comply with minimum standards for the elimination of trafficking and is not making significant efforts to do so. There is no law against trafficking, but there are laws against falsification or seizure of passports and personal identification documents, pandering, and rape. . . . The government has shown signs that it recognizes a growing problem of trafficking but has not developed a national plan nor taken significant steps to counter trafficking. . . .

Bahrain (Tier 3)

Bahrain is a destination country for trafficked persons. Trafficking victims who come to Bahrain in search of work are put into situations of coerced labor and sometimes slave-like conditions, including extreme working conditions, and physical or sexual abuse. Many low-skilled foreign workers have their passports withheld, contracts altered, and suffer partial or short or long-term non-payment of salaries. Victims come primarily from India, the Philippines, Bangladesh, Indonesia, and Sri Lanka to work as domestic servants and in the construction industry.

The Government of Bahrain does not fully comply with minimum standards for the elimination of trafficking and is not making significant efforts to do so. The Penal Code does not specifically prohibit trafficking in persons. However it does outlaw forced labor, forced prostitution, and withholding of salary. . . . In terms of prevention, the government has not yet taken any action. . . .

Belarus (Tier 3)

Belarus is a country of origin and transit for women and children trafficked for purposes of sexual exploitation to Russia, Ukraine, Lithuania, Germany, Israel, Poland, Czech Republic, Turkey, Cyprus, Greece, Hungary and the Federated Republic of Yugoslavia.

The Government of Belarus does not yet fully comply with minimum standards for the elimination of trafficking and is not making significant efforts. The new criminal code penalizes trafficking and the hiring of people for exploitative purposes. To date, no trafficking cases have been prosecuted under the new criminal code. . . .

Bosnia-Herzegovina (Tier 3)

Bosnia is a destination country for women and girls trafficked into sexual exploitation mostly from Moldova, Romania, and Ukraine, and to a lesser extent, Russia, Belarus, Kazakhstan, and the Federal Republic of Yugoslavia.

The national government of Bosnia and the entity governments of the Federation and the Republika of Srpska [Serb Republic] are not fully complying with minimum standards for the elimination of trafficking and are not making significant efforts. Despite political, social, and economic troubles, Bosnian authorities have established a national action plan, are cooperating with international organizations and NGOs, and taking preliminary steps toward combating the problem. Meanwhile, the international organizations and NGOs present in Bosnia lead most of the anti-trafficking efforts. Neither the entities nor the cantons have a law that specifically prohibits trafficking; however, prosecutors can use existing laws against pimping, pandering, false imprisonment, abduction, assault, and slavery. Although some of these laws have been invoked in trafficking cases, there have been few convictions, much less significant penalties. . . .

Burma (Tier 3)

Burma is a country of origin for women and girls trafficked to Thailand, China, Taiwan, Malaysia, Pakistan, and Japan for sexual exploitation, domestic and factory work.

The Government of Burma does not fully comply with minimum standards for the elimination of trafficking and is not making significant efforts to bring itself into compliance. The government has not provided sufficient resources nor demonstrated political will to address the trafficking problem. There is no trafficking law, although there are laws against migrant smuggling and kidnapping, which can be used against traffickers. There have been some prosecutions of individuals involved in trafficking-related crimes, although punishments vary considerably. . . .

Cambodia (Tier 3)

Cambodia is a source, destination and transit country and there is internal trafficking in women and children. Victims are trafficked from Vietnam for the purpose of sexual exploitation. Cambodians are trafficked to Thailand for sexual exploitation, street begging and bonded labor.

The Government of Cambodia does not fully comply with minimum standards for the elimination of trafficking and is not making significant efforts to do so. Cambodia does not have a law against all forms of trafficking in persons, but traffickers have been prosecuted under related laws. Some traffickers were convicted during 2001 and are serving time in prison. Police actively investigate trafficking crimes and have cooperated with NGOs to rescue victims. However, corruption, lack of police training and poor implementation of laws facilitate trafficking of persons and similar crimes, such as baby selling. Although some Cambodian officials have worked to increase government efforts, a lack of resources has made progress difficult. In addition, reports of widespread and serious official corruption counter the efforts by reform-minded officials. . . .

Gabon (Tier 2) [Moved from Tier 3 in 2001 report.]

Gabon is primarily a destination country for children trafficked from other West African countries such as Benin, Togo, and Nigeria, for domestic servitude and work in the informal commercial sector. Many children are transported to the Gabonese coast by sea, only to endure long work hours, physical abuse, insufficient food, no wages, and no access to education. A significant number of these children are also sexually abused by their employers.

The Government of Gabon does not yet fully comply with minimum standards for the elimination of trafficking; however, it is making significant efforts to do so. Gabon does not have specific laws to address trafficking in persons, but draft legislation was proposed in August 2001. Other laws that can be used to prosecute trafficking, such as child abuse, are inadequate to punish traffickers. Anecdotal evidence suggests that some officials at all levels of government may employ trafficked foreign children as domestic labor, and that police and immigration officials may facilitate child trafficking. And while official government policy disapproves of trafficking, employment of trafficked children, and facilitation of trafficking in children, no government official has been formally accused of or prosecuted for trafficking or related crimes. . . .

Greece (Tier 3)

Greece is primarily a destination country and, to a lesser extent, a transit country, for women and children trafficked for the purpose of sexual exploitation. Major countries of origin include Ukraine, Russia, Bulgaria, Albania, the Federal Republic of Yugoslavia, and Romania. Women from North Africa (Tunisia and Algeria), Asia (Thailand and the Philippines), the Middle East and other countries (Moldova, Georgia, Poland, and Kazakhstan) are also trafficked to Greece.

The Government of Greece does not fully comply with minimum standards for the elimination of trafficking and is not making significant efforts to do so. The Government is now taking steps toward combating trafficking, and the Minister of Public Order described it as a first priority for the Greek police. While there is no trafficking law, slavery, pandering, and pimping laws can be used to prosecute traffickers. The Ministry of Public Order instructed all police stations to enforce existing legislation. The lack of a specific law, however, has made prosecuting traffickers difficult. . . .

Indonesia (Tier 3)

Indonesia is a source country for trafficked persons, primarily young women and girls. Foreign destinations of trafficked persons include Hong

Kong, Singapore, Taiwan, Malaysia, Brunei, Persian Gulf countries, Australia, South Korea, and Japan. Trafficking also occurs within Indonesia's borders. Victims are trafficked primarily for purposes of labor and sexual exploitation.

The Government of Indonesia does not fully comply with the minimum standards for the elimination of trafficking and is not making significant efforts. Indonesia does not have a law against all forms of trafficking in persons. Related laws are used against traffickers, but the maximum penalties are significantly less than those for rape. Judges rarely impose maximum sentences in trafficking cases. Special units within regional police headquarters handle cases of violence against women and children, including trafficking. Indonesia has increased its attention to trafficking and alien smuggling problems during the period covered by this report. Government action to combat the increasing problem, however, is hampered by insufficient funds and porous borders. Corruption among local government officials is widespread. . . .

Iran (Tier 3)

Iran is a country of origin and transit for trafficked persons. Iranian women and girls have been trafficked to the Gulf States and Turkey for purposes of commercial sexual exploitation. Boys are trafficked through Iran to the United Arab Emirates where they are forced to work as camel jockeys. Internal trafficking of women and girls for purposes of sexual exploitation also occurs.

The Government of Iran does not fully comply with minimum standards for the elimination of trafficking and is not making significant efforts to do so. Iranian law does not specifically prohibit trafficking; however, there are other statutes that could be used to prosecute traffickers. . . .

Israel (Tier 2) [Moved from Tier 3 in the 2001 report.]

Israel is a destination country for trafficked women. Women from Moldova, Russia, Ukraine, and Brazil are trafficked to Israel for the purpose of sexual exploitation.

The Government of Israel does not yet fully comply with minimum standards for the elimination of trafficking; however, it is making significant efforts to do so. The law criminalizes trafficking for the purposes of sexual exploitation. Other statutes including rape, false imprisonment, seizing a passport, exploitation, and kidnapping for prostitution may also be used in prosecuting trafficking cases. The government actively investigates trafficking cases and has successfully prosecuted traffickers. . . .

Kazakhstan (Tier 2) [Moved from Tier 3 in the 2001 report.]

Kazakhstan is a source, transit and destination country for women and men trafficked for purposes of sexual exploitation and labor. Victims are trafficked to Kazakhstan from the Kyrgyz Republic, Tajikistan, and Uzbekistan and trafficked to the United Arab Emirates, Greece, Cyprus, France, Italy, Portugal, Switzerland, Belgium, South Korea, Turkey, Israel and Albania.

The Government of Kazakhstan does not yet fully comply with minimum standards for the elimination of trafficking; however, it is making significant efforts to do so. In February 2002, a temporary measure was amended to the criminal code to cover trafficking of adults. Existing law already prohibited trafficking in children. Some actions have been brought under existing statutes or as civil actions in sexual and labor exploitation cases. The government has initiated training programs for law enforcement and is conducting random investigations of travel agencies promising work abroad. Corruption is a problem at many levels, and the government has convicted at least one customs official for taking bribes. . . .

Kyrgyz Republic [Kyrgyzstan] (Tier 3)

Kyrgyz Republic is a country of origin, transit and, to a lesser extent, destination for trafficked women, men and children. Women, mostly under 25 years old, are trafficked for prostitution to the United Arab Emirates, Turkey, China, Germany and Greece. Men are trafficked to Kazakhstan for forced labor. Women who are either destined for or transiting through Kyrgyz usually come from Uzbekistan and Tajikistan.

The Government of Kyrgyz does not fully comply with minimum standards for the elimination of trafficking and is not making significant efforts to do so. Kyrgyz does not have a law that specifically prohibits trafficking. The authorities may use other laws, such as those prohibiting rape, kidnapping and exploitation, to arrest and prosecute traffickers but the penalties for breaking those laws are frequently lighter than punishments for crimes like auto theft or drug use. In addition, the government does not actively investigate or prosecute trafficking cases. . . .

Lebanon (Tier 3)

Lebanon is a destination country for trafficked persons. Many trafficking victims come to Lebanon in search of work voluntarily and legally, but are put into situations of coerced labor, and some are put into situations with slave-like conditions, or in which they become victims of sexual exploitation. Women from Ethiopia, Sri Lanka, and the Philippines, are the primary victims of trafficking. To a lesser extent, some women from Russia, Romania, Ukraine, Moldova, and Bulgaria who have come to Lebanon end up in coercive work situations involving sexual exploitation from which they have little recourse.

The Government of Lebanon does not fully comply with minimum standards for the elimination of trafficking and is not making significant efforts to do so. Lebanon does not have legislation criminalizing trafficking in persons. However, the Penal Code does have statutes criminalizing the deprivation of personal freedom of others by abduction or other means. The government has not prosecuted any trafficking cases. Law enforcement officials are generally responsive to complaints of trafficking. However, the government has taken some measures to counter trafficking, such as the closure by the Ministry of Labor in 2001 of ten employment agencies that violated labor regulations. . . .

Malaysia (Tier 2) [Moved from Tier 3 in the 2001 report.]

Malaysia is a source and destination country for trafficked persons, primarily for the purpose of sexual exploitation. Persons trafficked into Malaysia come from Indonesia, Thailand, China, and the Philippines and a small but increasing number from Uzbekistan. Japan, Canada, the United States, Australia and Taiwan are destinations for Malaysian trafficking victims. Trafficking on a smaller scale also occurs within Malaysia's borders.

The Government of Malaysia does not yet fully comply with minimum standards for the elimination of trafficking; however, it is making significant efforts to do so. An interagency group on transnational organized crime addresses trafficking in persons, and four other interagency committees address illegal immigration, foreign labor, and border control. A separate agency investigates public corruption. There is no specific law against trafficking but applicable law criminalizes most of the acts involved in trafficking in persons. Although persons suspected of trafficking may be detained, to date there have been no prosecutions or convictions for the specific offense of trafficking. . . .

Pakistan (Tier 2) [Moved from Tier 3 in the 2001 report.]

Pakistan is a country of origin, transit, and destination for women and children trafficked for purposes of sexual exploitation and bonded labor. Internal trafficking of women and girls from rural areas to larger cities for purposes of sexual exploitation and forced labor also occurs. Afghan girls and women have been trafficked from refugee camps in Pakistan to urban areas for purposes of sexual exploitation and forced labor. Pakistan is a country of origin for young boys who are kidnapped or bought and sent to work as camel jockeys in the United Arab Emirates and Qatar. In many cases, Pakistani men and women go to the Middle East in search of work, only to be put into situations of coerced labor, slave-like conditions, or sexual exploitation. Pakistan serves as a destination point for women and children who are trafficked from Bangladesh, Afghanistan, and Central Asia for purposes of sexual exploitation and forced labor. Women and children trafficked from East Asian countries and Bangladesh to the Middle East transit through Pakistan.

The government of Pakistan does not yet fully comply with minimum standards for the elimination of trafficking; however, it is making significant efforts to do so. Pakistan has statutes in its Penal Code that criminalize kidnapping, abduction, slavery, prostitution, forced labor, and importing girls for sexual exploitation. Prosecution is possible under these existing statutes, but the government is drafting new laws that would deal more effectively with trafficking and conform its legal system to international conventions that address trafficking. Although law enforcement officials have successfully investigated and arrested traffickers, severely backlogged courts and local corruption slow convictions. The Federal Investigative Agency (FIA) has registered several cases against camel jockey traffickers that are pending in court. If prostitution is prosecuted under the Islamic law-oriented Hudood ordinances, victims are often reluctant to testify since, if the burden of proof is not met, the woman's testimony is tantamount to an admission of adultery. Open borders and corruption among border guards and law enforcement personnel allows trafficked women and girls to be brought into the country. . . .

Qatar (Tier 3)

Qatar is a destination country for trafficked persons. Women from countries in East Asia, South Asia and Africa have reported being forced into domestic servitude and sexual exploitation. Children from Sudan, Pakistan, and Bangladesh have been trafficked to Qatar and forced to work as camel jockeys.

The Government of Qatar does not fully comply with minimum standards for the elimination of trafficking and is not making significant efforts to do so. Qatari law specifically prohibits trafficking in persons. Penalties for traffickers include fines and imprisonment. Law enforcement agencies respond to complaints of trafficking by investigating them. However, the government has not prosecuted any cases against traffickers. . . .

Republic of Korea [South Korea] (Tier 1)
[Moved from Tier 3 in the 2001 report.]

The Republic of Korea is a source, transit and destination country for trafficking in persons. Koreans are trafficked to Japan and the United States for sexual exploitation. Persons from the Philippines, China, Southeast Asian countries, Russia and other countries of the former Soviet Union are trafficked to Korea or transit Korea en route to Japan and the United States.

The Government of the Republic of Korea fully complies with minimum standards for the elimination of trafficking, including making serious and sustained efforts to eliminate severe forms of trafficking in persons with respect to law enforcement, protection of victims and prevention of trafficking. Although there is no trafficking law per se, a number of provisions in the Criminal Code and the Act on Additional Punishment for Specific Crimes were used to prosecute traffickers in more than 100 cases in 2001. Additional law enforcement efforts include judicial and law enforcement training, participation in international and regional conferences on organized crime and trafficking, and cooperation with other governments on extradition. . . .

Romania (Tier 2) [Moved from Tier 3 in the 2001 report.]

Romania is a source and transit country primarily for women and girls trafficked to Bosnia, Serbia, Macedonia, Kosovo, Albania, Greece, Italy, and Turkey for the purpose of sexual exploitation.

The Government of Romania does not yet fully comply with minimum standards for the elimination of trafficking; however, it is making significant efforts to do so. The government passed a law criminalizing trafficking in persons in December 2001. The Organized Crime Directorate, the lead agency in the Human Trafficking Task Force, investigated and arrested traffickers, and the government prosecuted traffickers under kidnapping and pimping codes, convicting several traffickers. The government cooperates with other governments on investigations. . . .

Russia (Tier 3)

Russia is a country of origin for women and children trafficked to many countries throughout Europe, the Middle East and North America for purposes of sexual exploitation.

The Government of Russia does not yet fully comply with minimum standards for the elimination of trafficking and is not making significant efforts to do so. There is no law specifically against trafficking. Recruitment for prostitution is illegal but not a criminal offense. The government of Russia recognizes there is a trafficking problem and the Duma has asked the United States for cooperation in drafting anti-trafficking legislation. Existing laws which can be used against traffickers include border crossing violations, document fraud, kidnapping, forced sexual activity, fraud, organized crime and pornography statues. The government of Russia rarely vigorously investigates trafficking cases of adults and only a few related cases have been prosecuted. . . .

Saudi Arabia (Tier 3)

Saudi Arabia is a country of destination for trafficked persons. Trafficking victims who come to Saudi Arabia in search of work are put into situations of coerced labor. Victims come primarily from Sudan, Somalia, Kenya, Eritrea, Ethiopia, Bangladesh, Sri Lanka, India, Indonesia, and the Philippines to work as domestic servants and menial laborers. Many low-skilled foreign workers have their contracts altered and are subjected to extreme working conditions and physical abuse.

The Government of Saudi Arabia does not fully comply with minimum standards for the elimination of trafficking and is not making significant efforts to do so. Saudi Arabia formally abolished slavery by royal decree in 1962; however, there are no laws specifically related to trafficking. The government has an extensive system of labor courts that enforce the terms of work contracts. However, some workers are exempt from labor law, including farmers, herdsmen, drivers, and domestic servants. Regarding protection of victims, the government has made minimal efforts. . . . Government activities to prevent trafficking in persons have been minimal. . . .

Sudan (Tier 3)

Sudan is a country of destination for internationally trafficked persons, as well as a country with widespread internal trafficking. Thousands of Ugandan men, women and children, have been abducted by rebel groups to be used as sex slaves, domestic helpers, child soldiers, and forcibly conscripted soldiers. Women and children have also been subjected to intertribal abductions for domestic and sexual exploitation in the southern part of the country. There are reports of Sudanese persons being sold into slavery through Chad, to Libya.

The Government of Sudan does not fully comply with minimum standards for the elimination of trafficking and is not making significant efforts to do so. Sudan does not acknowledge the extent of the problem. Sudan tolerates abductions by government-affiliated militia as a form of remuneration for military services, and as a strategy of destabilization of the rebel-controlled areas. There are no laws that specifically address trafficking in persons. Although laws against rape, abduction, torture, and unlawful detention exist, the Government has not made an effort to investigate and prosecute any traffickers or abductors. . . .The Government has made no significant efforts toward the protection of victims or the prevention of trafficking. . . .

Tajikistan (Tier 3)

Tajikistan is a country of origin for young women trafficked to Uzbekistan, Kazakhstan, the Kyrgyz Republic, Russia, and countries of the Persian Gulf including the United Arab Emirates, Yemen, Iran and Saudi Arabia for purposes of sexual exploitation.

The Government of Tajikistan does not fully comply with minimum standards for the elimination of trafficking and is not making significant efforts to do so. Although there is a growing awareness of trafficking as a problem in Tajikistan, the government has not evidenced a willingness to address it and does not have a national plan. There is no law against trafficking, although laws against prostitution, rape, kidnapping, immigration and document fraud violations could be used against traffickers. To date, there have been no reported prosecutions of traffickers. Law enforcement officials do not vigorously investigate trafficking. Corruption is endemic. . . .

Turkey (Tier 3)

Turkey is a minor country of destination, and transit to other European destinations, for women and girls trafficked into sexual exploitation. Most come from countries of the former Soviet Union, including Azerbaijan, Georgia, Russia, Ukraine, and Moldova.

The Government of Turkey does not fully comply with minimum standards for the elimination of trafficking and is not making significant efforts to do so. Turkey has no law against trafficking, although draft anti-trafficking legislation is on the Parliamentary agenda. Other laws against organized crime, pimping, child prostitution, and forced labor can be used against traffickers. . . .Regarding prevention, the government is working on a National Action Plan to study the problem and offer remedies; however efforts thus far have been limited to a few ad hoc public education campaigns at the local level. The government's current prevention strategy involves strict regulations for immigrants, including deporting all foreigners found in commercial sex work and prohibiting their re-entry into the country; however, the government makes no effort to screen deportees for possible trafficking victims, and thus to protect trafficking victims. . . .

United Arab Emirates (Tier 3)

The United Arab Emirates is a country of destination for trafficked persons. Foreign nationals comprise about eighty-five percent of the population, and guest workers make up ninety-eight percent of the country's private sector workforce. Of these, some who come to the United Arab Emirates for unskilled or semi-skilled employment become the victims of trafficking, since they are subject to coerced labor, slave-like conditions, or sexual exploitation. Those low-skilled foreign workers forced into domestic servitude primarily come from South and Southeast Asian countries, primarily India, Sri Lanka, Indonesia, and the Philippines. Victims trafficked as domestic male servants, laborers and unskilled workers in construction and agriculture come mainly from India, Pakistan, Afghanistan, and Bangladesh. There are reports that some trafficking victims' employment contracts were altered or switched upon their arrival to the United Arab Emirates without their consent, actions against which such victims have little effective recourse. Women and girls from Azerbaijan, Kazakhstan, Ukraine, Russia, East Asia and Eastern Europe have reported being lured with the promise of legitimate jobs and then forced into sexual exploitation. Boys from Pakistan, India, Bangladesh, and Sri Lanka have been trafficked to the United Arab Emirates to work as camel jockeys.

The government of the United Arab Emirates does not fully comply with minimum standards for the elimination of trafficking and is not making significant efforts to do so. The United Arab Emirates does not have a law criminalizing trafficking in persons. Forced or compulsory labor is illegal, and labor regulations prohibit the employment of persons less than fifteen years of age. Traffickers can be prosecuted for child smuggling. The authorities have prosecuted foreign child smugglers, but do not investigate citizens involved in trafficking. The government prohibited the use of children under the age of fifteen as camel jockeys in 1993, but the Camel Racing Association, not the government, is responsible for enforcing these rules. . . .

Federal Republic of Yugoslavia (Tier 2)
[Moved from Tier 3 in the 2001 report.]

The Federal Republic of Yugoslavia is a transit country, and to a lesser extent, a source and destination country for women and girls trafficked for sexual exploitation. Victims, mostly from Moldova, Romania, Ukraine, and Bulgaria end up in Kosovo, Bosnia, Albania, and Western Europe. Roma children are also trafficked through the Federal Republic for begging and theft in Western Europe. Chinese nationals are occasionally trafficked from Serbia to Western Europe.

Neither the Government of the Federal Republic of Yugoslavia1, the Government of Serbia, nor the Government of Montenegro yet fully comply with minimum standards for the elimination of trafficking; however, they are making significant efforts to do so. The Federal Interior Ministry formed the Initial Board for Combating Trafficking in Human Beings, with representatives from all relevant federal and republic ministries, international organizations, and NGOs, and it established a high-level working group. While the lack of specific trafficking laws makes prosecution of trafficking difficult, the Serbian and Montenegrin Republic Governments are currently prosecuting under slavery, prostitution, and kidnapping laws. With foreign government consultation, the federal and republic ministries have formed a law enforcement task force that is investigating and prosecuting trafficking cases. In addition, Montenegro's security center is exchanging information with the international community in Kosovo and with Albania in trafficking case investigations. Corruption, especially at the low level, is a widespread problem. . . .

Kosovo, while technically part of Serbia, is currently being administered under the authority of the United Nations Interim Administration in Kosovo (UNMIK) pending a determination of its future status in accordance with United Nations Security Council Resolution 1244. Since the adoption of

UNSCR 1244 in June 1999, UNMIK has provided transitional administration for Kosovo. UNMIK is aware of the serious problems that exist in Kosovo concerning trafficking and is working to conduct anti-trafficking efforts. UNMIK remains the final authority in Kosovo but is turning over responsibility in most areas to Provisional Institutions of Self-government following Kosovo-wide elections last November and the formation of a coalition government. . . .

SUPREME COURT ON EXECUTION
OF THE MENTALLY RETARDED
June 20, 2002

Concerns about the death penalty continued to mount in 2002, as the legal community, politicians, and many citizens continued to react to allegations that the system was ineptly administered, racially biased, and occasionally put innocent people to death. Four death row inmates were freed in 2002 after new evidence, including DNA testing, showed either that they were innocent or had been wrongfully convicted.

Maryland became the second state, after Illinois, to declare a moratorium on the executions. A small majority of a special commission set up by the governor of Illinois to assess the fairness of the system for imposing the death penalty in that state said capital punishment should be abolished altogether. Two federal judges declared the death penalty to be unconstitutional. Lawmakers in both the House and Senate began to consider legislation intended to minimize, if not eliminate, wrongful convictions. At the end of the year the outgoing governor of Illinois was contemplating giving the state's death row inmates a blanket commutation.

The Supreme Court did not take up the fundamental issue of whether the death penalty itself was constitutional, but it did review a broad range of cases dealing with its application. Rulings in two major cases could affect hundreds of the approximately 3,000 people already on death row. In one case, Atkins v. Virginia, *the Court held that it was a violation of the Constitution's prohibition on cruel and unusual punishment to execute mentally retarded persons. In the other,* Ring v. Arizona, *it held that juries, not judges, must decide whether to impose the death penalty.*

The Court also agreed to hear several cases challenging the way the death penalty had been imposed, including a case alleging racial bias in jury selection in death penalty cases in Texas. In a second case, an inmate on Maryland's death row was seeking to have his conviction overturned on grounds that his counsel had been ineffective. Two justices, Sandra Day O'Connor and Ruth Bader Ginsburg, in 2001 had both publicly criticized the inadequacy of the representation many defense attorneys provided their clients. The Supreme Court, however, refused several opportunities to review the constitutionality of executing convicted death row inmates for crimes committed when they were sixteen or seventeen. (O'Connor, Ginsburg statements, Historic Documents of 2001, p. 387)

According to the Death Penalty Information Center, an organization opposed to the death penalty, seventy-one people were executed in 2002—five more than in 2001. Thirty-three of the executions were in Texas, and three of those were inmates who had committed their crimes when they were seventeen. Texas was the only state to execute juvenile offenders in 2002. Of the thirty-eight states that permitted capital punishment, only thirteen imposed the death penalty in 2002.

Exonerations, Overturned Convictions

Four death row inmates were exonerated in 2002, bringing to a 102 the number of people found to have been wrongfully convicted since the death penalty was reinstated in 1976. In most cases the inmates were released from death row when it was shown that prosecutors had withheld evidence that might have resulted in an acquittal or a lesser sentence. In about a dozen cases, however, including one where the inmate had already died of cancer, DNA testing proved that the inmate had not committed the crime for which he was sentenced. At least fourteen of the thirty-eight death penalty states gave inmates some access to DNA testing.

The Senate Judiciary Committee on July 18 approved the Innocence Protection Act, which would give the states incentives to preserve DNA evidence, give inmates access to that evidence, and provide qualified legal representation in capital punishment cases. Two of the panel's Republicans joined all its Democrats in support of the measure. A majority of members in the House had endorsed similar legislation, but no action was taken on the measure in 2002. One of the bill's supporters was conservative Republican Dana Rohrabacher of California, who told the Washington Post: *"I don't mind eliminating someone we know is guilty, but we need to do everything possible to determine that person is guilty."*

Illinois Report and Maryland Moratorium

A special commission established by Illinois governor George Ryan, a Republican, to study the way the death penalty was imposed in that state called for a complete overhaul of the system in a report issued April 16. Eight of the panel's fourteen members supported prohibiting the death penalty altogether. "Fix the capital punishment system or abolish it," Thomas P. Sullivan, a former U.S. attorney and the cochairman of the commission, told a news conference. "There is no other principled course."

The commission was set up by Governor Ryan in 2000 after he imposed a moratorium on executions in the state for fear the state was executing people for crimes they had not committed. Between 1977, when Illinois reinstated the death penalty, and 2000 the state had executed twelve men but released thirteen others from death row after it was proved that they had been wrongfully convicted. The commission, which included proponents and opponents of the death penalty, made eighty-five recommendations, in-

cluding reducing the number of offenses that warranted the death penalty to five from twenty; banning the death penalty for offenders convicted solely on the evidence of a single eyewitnesses, informer, or accomplice; videotaping all interrogations of suspects in capital offense cases; and creating a state-wide DNA database and independent forensics lab. Any reforms would have to be approved by the Illinois state legislature, which was not expected to take any immediate action.

On May 9 Maryland governor Parris N. Glendening declared a moratorium on executions because of doubt about the fairness of the system. Glendening, a Democrat, said he was concerned about the disproportionate number of blacks who were sentenced to death for killing whites. Nine of the thirteen men on Maryland's death row were black. Twelve of the thirteen were condemned for killing whites, even though most murder victims in Maryland were black. Glendening said he believed in the use of the "ultimate sanction" for crimes that "shock the conscience," but he said he had to "honor the responsibility I have to be absolutely certain of both the guilt of the criminal and the fairness and impartiality of the process."

Glendening said he would await the results of a study he had commissioned in 2000 before deciding whether to lift or continue the moratorium. That study was not forthcoming by the end of the year. Glendening, who was barred from seeking another term as governor, was scheduled to be replaced in January 2003 by Robert L. Ehrlich Jr., a Republican, who had said during his campaign that he would lift the moratorium, which he did soon after taking office in 2003.

Two Judges Declare Death Penalty Unconstitutional

On July 1 Jed S. Rakoff, a federal judge in Manhattan, declared the federal death penalty to be unconstitutional because it created an "undue risk" of killing innocent defendants. "By cutting off the opportunity for exonerations," the Federal Death Penalty Act, passed by Congress in 1994 "denies due process, and indeed is tantamount to foreseeable, state-sponsored murder of innocent human beings," Rakoff wrote. On December 10 a three-judge panel of the federal Court of Appeals for the Second District reversed Rakoff's ruling, saying that the same argument had been presented to, and rejected by, the Supreme Court on several past occasions. Therefore, the appeals court panel said, "We hold that the continued opportunity to exonerate oneself throughout the natural course of one's life is not a right so rooted in the traditions and conscience of our people as to be ranked as fundamental."

The case at issue involved two men alleged to have been partners in a heroin ring in the Bronx and to have brutally slain a government informant. The U.S. attorney in Manhattan had not sought the death penalty in the case but was overruled by Attorney General John Ashcroft. Since taking office in 2000, Ashcroft had been notably aggressive in seeking the death penalty in federal cases, often overruling prosecutors who had recommended seeking lesser penalties.

On September 24 a second federal judge, William Sessions of Vermont, also declared the federal death penalty to be unconstitutional because federal sentencing hearings used relaxed standards of evidence. "If the death pen-alty is to be part of our system of justice, due process of law and the fair trial guarantees of the Sixth Amendment require that standards and safeguards governing the kinds of evidence juries may consider must be rigorous, and constitutional rights and liberties scrupulously protected," Sessions wrote. His decision was being appealed.

Only two people had been executed under the federal death penalty law, Oklahoma City bomber Timothy McVeigh and Juan Garza, a drug smuggler and murderer. (McVeigh execution, Historic Documents of 2001, p. 433)

Supreme court on Mental Retardation

In 1989, the last time it ruled on the issue, the Supreme Court decided, 5–4, that there was "insufficient evidence of a national consensus against executing mentally retarded people . . . for us to conclude that it is categor-ically prohibited by the Eighth Amendment." But, wrote Justice John Paul Stevens for the six-justice majority in the Atkins *case, "much has changed since then." In 1989 only two of the thirty-eight death penalty states and the federal government barred execution of the mentally retarded. In 2002, Stevens said, sixteen more states had barred such executions, and similar legislation was pending in four other states. Moreover, Stevens said, even in those twenty states that still allowed such executions, the practice was un-common. "The practice, therefore, has become truly unusual, and it is fair to say that a national consensus has developed against it," Stevens wrote.*

"Those mentally retarded persons who meet the law's requirements for criminal responsibility should be tried and punished when they commit crimes. Because of their disabilities in areas of reasoning, judgment, and control of their impulses, however, they do not act with the level of moral culpability that characterizes the most serious adult criminal conduct," Stevens wrote for himself and Justices O'Connor, Anthony M. Kennedy, David H. Souter, Ginsburg, and Stephen G. Breyer.

"Seldom has an opinion of this Court rested so obviously upon nothing but the personal views of its members," said Justice Antonin Scalia in a sharp dissent signed by Chief Justice William H. Rehnquist and Justice Clarence Thomas. Scalia predicted that the ruling would precipitate a flood of appeals from death row inmates claiming to be retarded. Scalia's predic-tions were echoed by prosecutors around the country. The ruling is "going to create a cottage industry of psychologists . . . who will make people mentally retarded who have never been mentally retarded in their lives," said one.

Mental health experts said true retardation would be difficult to fake. The eighteen states that had the death penalty but barred execution of the men-tally retarded had generally similar definitions of the retardation: an IQ of 70 or less and deficiency in certain basic skills of daily living, communica-tions abilities, and understanding that were apparent before the person reached age eighteen. "The important thing to remember is that it's a devel-opmental disability that at a minimum appeared before adulthood," said Ruth A. Luckasson, a law professor at the University of New Mexico, "so gen-

erally what is required is a real inventory of the person's school records and past evaluative records. Usually this person's disability will have been documented from very early on."

Sentencing by Juries, Not Judges

Less than a week after it reversed itself to bar execution of the mentally retarded, the Supreme Court reversed itself to rule that juries, not judges, must determine the facts that determine whether a capital defendant is sentenced to death. The 7–2 decision was expected to affect nearly 170 people already sentenced to death in five states and possibly more than 600 people on death row in four other states.

The case arose in Arizona, which along with Colorado, Idaho, Montana, and Nebraska allowed judges to decide whether the crime a person was convicted of involved "aggravating" factors that warranted the death penalty. In four other states—Alabama, Delaware, Florida, and Indiana—the jury made recommendations to the judge, but the judge determined the sentence. (In the remaining states, the jury decided the sentence.) In 1990 the Supreme Court upheld Arizona's death-sentencing scheme. Then in 2000 the Court by a 5-4 vote struck down a state hate crime statute that allowed a judge to "enhance" a defendant's sentence beyond that authorized by the trial jury. In the case of Apprendi v. New Jersey, *the Court majority ruled that "any fact that increases the penalty for a crime beyond the prescribed statutory maximum, must be submitted to a jury and proved beyond a reasonable doubt." Two years later, a new case challenging Arizona's sentencing system came before the Court.*

In the case of Ring v. Arizona, *the trial jury sentenced Ring to life imprisonment, the maximum under state law, for a shooting death during an armed robbery. After hearing testimony at the sentencing hearing from one of Ring's co-conspirators that Ring was the gang's leader and the triggerman, the judge sentenced Ring to death. The co-conspirator had not testified at Ring's trial. By a 7–2 vote, the Supreme Court said that the Arizona death-sentencing law violated the constitutional guarantee of trial by jury. In view of the Court's holding in* Apprendi, *Justice Ginsburg wrote for the majority, the right to a jury trial "would be senselessly diminished if it encompassed the factfinding necessary to increase a defendant's sentence by two years, but not the factfinding necessary to put him to death."*

Observers immediately predicted that the decision would spark appeals from death row inmates in the nine states affected by the decision, but there were numerous questions left unanswered, including whether those convicts who had already exhausted all their appeals would be able to take advantage of the ruling.

Juvenile Executions

The Supreme Court on October 21 refused to reconsider whether to reverse a 1989 decision upholding the constitutionality of executing juvenile offenders. For the first time since 1989, four justices went on record as opposing the practice. In a dissenting opinion, the Court's four most liberal members said that execution of offenders who committed a capital crime when they were under the age of eighteen was "a relic of the past [that] is inconsistent with evolving standards of decency in civilized society." Written by Stevens and signed by Breyer, Ginsburg, and Souter, the dissent said that "we should put an end to this shameful practice."

The appeal was made by Kevin Nigel Stanford, a Kentucky man whose case in 1989 was used by the Court to uphold juvenile executions. Stanford was convicted of kidnapping, sodomizing, and shooting to death a gas station attendant when he was seventeen. Normally, an appeal to the Supreme Court was reviewed if four justices agreed that it should be. Stanford's appeal came as a request for a writ of habeas corpus, which required the consent of five justices to be reviewed. Two justices who voted to ban the death penalty for the mentally retarded, O'Connor and Kennedy, joined Rehnquist, Scalia, and Thomas to deny Stanford's request.

Opponents of the juvenile death penalty argued that teenagers under eighteen could not legally drink, vote, or sit on a jury, reflecting society's belief that most teenagers were not yet fully mature and might still be unable to make rational decisions. Opponents also argued that societal opinion was evolving toward a consensus opposed to juvenile executions. Ten of the sixteen juvenile offenders executed in the previous decade were from Texas, where the minimum age for imposing the death penalty was seventeen, as it was in four other states. Seventeen states set the minimum age at sixteen; the remaining sixteen death penalty states set the minimum age at eighteen. In recent years at least two states—Indiana and Montana—had raised their minimum age, and several other states were considering doing so. Those states that did permit the executions of sixteen- and seventeen-year-olds were seeking the death penalty in those cases less often, and juries appeared to be less willing to impose it. In 2001 only five juveniles were sentenced to death.

"Our society recognizes that juveniles are less mature, less able to exercise good judgment, more susceptible to environmental influence, so they are less culpable than adults," American Bar Association president Robert Hershon told the Christian Science Monitor *in February. "The missing element is a few more states to abolish it on their own," said Richard Dieter, executive director of the Death Penalty Information Center in Washington.*

Opponents argued that each case needed to be looked at individually. Some juveniles were just as mature as older offenders, they argued, and juries should be allowed to decide, based upon the evidence, whether a teenager knew right from wrong.

Racial Bias

The Court heard an appeal from a death row inmate in Texas who claimed Dallas County prosecutors systematically kept African Americans off the jury by using their peremptory challenges (dismissal without cause). Consideration of race in jury selection was a violation of the Fourteenth Amendment's equal protection clause. Thomas Miller-El was con-

victed in the slaying of a white hotel clerk. His attorney cited evidence of a long pattern of discrimination against blacks among the county's prosecutors, including a training manual that advised prosecutors to keep blacks off trial juries and a local newspaper story that said they had used peremptory challenges to remove 90 percent of eligible blacks from juries in fifteen death penalty cases from 1980 to 1986. One of these cases was Miller-El's, in which ten of the eleven prospective black jurors were dismissed. The eleventh said execution was too painless for killers and that they should be covered in honey and then staked over a bed of ants.

Prosecutors denied the allegations. The state argued that more blacks than whites were excluded because their answers to questions during jury selection showed they were opposed to the death penalty or were unwilling to impose it. The state said this was a race-neutral reason for using peremptory challenges. The trial judge in the case agreed that the challenges were racially neutral and thus permissible, a position that was upheld by the U.S. Court of Appeals for the Fifth Circuit.

The case of Miller-El v. Cockrell *was argued before the Supreme Court on October 16 by former solicitor general Seth Waxman and a group of former judges and prosecutors, including former FBI director William S. Sessions and former deputy attorney general Eric H. Holder Jr., who filed a friend-of-the-court brief arguing that "even the perception that racial bias is tolerated weakens public confidence that our courts can guarantee equal justice." A ruling was expected in 2003.*

Effective Representation

The Court refused, without comment, to review a ruling by the Fifth Circuit Court of Appeals that overturned the conviction of a Texas death row inmate whose court-appointed defense lawyer slept through parts of his trial. In seeking reinstatement of the conviction, Texas argued that the lawyer's behavior did not necessarily result in an unfair trial and that the Court should use the case to clarify standards for effective representation in capital punishment cases. In a separate ruling, decided by an 8–1 vote, the Court said that a convicted man did not necessarily receive an unfair trial because his defense attorney did not call any witnesses or make a closing statement at his death penalty sentencing hearing. The Court also declined to grant a new trial to a Virginia man whose defense attorney had at one point represented the victim. In the case the Court agreed to hear in its 2002–2003 term, Kevin Wiggins, a death row inmate in Maryland, challenged his sentence because his court-appointed defense attorneys failed to inform the jury information about his background that might have had a mitigating effect on his sentence.

Following are excerpts from the majority and dissenting opinions in the case of Atkins v. Virginia, *in which the Supreme Court, by a vote of 6–3, ruled on June 20, 2002, that imposing the death penalty on the mentally retarded was unconstitutional.*

*The document was obtained from the Internet at supct
.law.cornell.edu/supct/html/00-8452.ZS.html; accessed
October 9, 2002.*

No. 00–8452

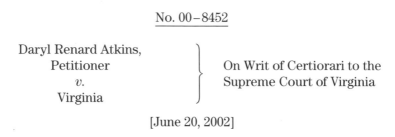

Daryl Renard Atkins,
Petitioner

v.

Virginia

On Writ of Certiorari to the
Supreme Court of Virginia

[June 20, 2002]

JUSTICE STEVENS delivered the opinion of the Court.

Those mentally retarded persons who meet the law's requirements for criminal responsibility should be tried and punished when they commit crimes. Because of their disabilities in areas of reasoning, judgment, and control of their impulses, however, they do not act with the level of moral culpability that characterizes the most serious adult criminal conduct. Moreover, their impairments can jeopardize the reliability and fairness of capital proceedings against mentally retarded defendants. Presumably for these reasons, in the 13 years since we decided *Penry v. Lynaugh* . . . (1989), the American public, legislators, scholars, and judges have deliberated over the question whether the death penalty should ever be imposed on a mentally retarded criminal. The consensus reflected in those deliberations informs our answer to the question presented by this case: whether such executions are "cruel and unusual punishments" prohibited by the Eighth Amendment to the Federal Constitution.

I

Petitioner, Daryl Renard Atkins, was convicted of abduction, armed robbery, and capital murder, and sentenced to death. At approximately midnight on August 16, 1996, Atkins and William Jones, armed with a semiautomatic handgun, abducted Eric Nesbitt, robbed him of the money on his person, drove him to an automated teller machine in his pickup truck where cameras recorded their withdrawal of additional cash, then took him to an isolated location where he was shot eight times and killed.

Jones and Atkins both testified in the guilt phase of Atkins' trial. Each confirmed most of the details in the other's account of the incident, with the important exception that each stated that the other had actually shot and killed Nesbitt. Jones' testimony, which was both more coherent and credible than Atkins', was obviously credited by the jury and was sufficient to establish Atkins' guilt. At the penalty phase of the trial, the State introduced victim impact evidence and proved two aggravating circumstances: future dangerousness and "vileness of the offense." To prove future dangerousness, the State relied on Atkins' prior felony convictions as well as the testimony of four victims of earlier robberies and assaults. To prove the second aggravator, the prosecution relied upon the trial record, including pictures of the deceased's body and the autopsy report.

In the penalty phase, the defense relied on one witness, Dr. Evan Nelson, a forensic psychologist who had evaluated Atkins before trial and concluded that he was "mildly mentally retarded." His conclusion was based on interviews with people who knew Atkins, a review of school and court records, and the administration of a standard intelligence test which indicated that Atkins had a full scale IQ of 59.

The jury sentenced Atkins to death, but the Virginia Supreme Court ordered a second sentencing hearing because the trial court had used a misleading verdict form. . . . At the resentencing, Dr. Nelson again testified. The State presented an expert rebuttal witness, Dr. Stanton Samenow, who expressed the opinion that Atkins was not mentally retarded, but rather was of "average intelligence, at least," and diagnosable as having antisocial personality disorder. . . . The jury again sentenced Atkins to death.

The Supreme Court of Virginia affirmed the imposition of the death penalty. . . . Atkins did not argue before the Virginia Supreme Court that his sentence was disproportionate to penalties imposed for similar crimes in Virginia, but he did contend "that he is mentally retarded and thus cannot be sentenced to death.". . . The majority of the state court rejected this contention, relying on our holding in *Penry.* . . . The Court was "not willing to commute Atkins' sentence of death to life imprisonment merely because of his IQ score.". . .

Justice Hassell and Justice Koontz dissented. They rejected Dr. Samenow's opinion that Atkins possesses average intelligence as "incredulous as a matter of law," and concluded that "the imposition of the sentence of death upon a criminal defendant who has the mental age of a child between the ages of 9 and 12 is excessive.". . . In their opinion, "it is indefensible to conclude that individuals who are mentally retarded are not to some degree less culpable for their criminal acts. By definition, such individuals have substantial limitations not shared by the general population. A moral and civilized society diminishes itself if its system of justice does not afford recognition and consideration of those limitations in a meaningful way.". . .

Because of the gravity of the concerns expressed by the dissenters, and in light of the dramatic shift in the state legislative landscape that has occurred in the past 13 years, we granted certiorari to revisit the issue that we first addressed in the *Penry* case. . . .

II

The Eighth Amendment succinctly prohibits "excessive" sanctions. It provides: "Excessive bail shall not be required, nor excessive fines imposed, nor cruel and unusual punishments inflicted.". . .

A claim that punishment is excessive is judged not by the standards that prevailed in 1685 when Lord Jeffreys presided over the "Bloody Assizes" or when the Bill of Rights was adopted, but rather by those that currently prevail. . . .

Proportionality review under those evolving standards should be informed by " 'objective factors to the maximum possible extent,' ". . .

We also acknowledged in *Coker* [*v. Georgia* (1977)] that the objective evidence, though of great importance, did not "wholly determine" the controversy, "for the Constitution contemplates that in the end our own judgment will be brought to bear on the question of the acceptability of the death penalty under the Eighth Amendment.". . .

Thus, in cases involving a consensus, our own judgment is "brought to bear," . . . by asking whether there is reason to disagree with the judgment reached by the citizenry and its legislators.

Guided by our approach in these cases, we shall first review the judgment of legislatures that have addressed the suitability of imposing the death penalty on the mentally retarded and then consider reasons for agreeing or disagreeing with their judgment.

III

The parties have not called our attention to any state legislative consideration of the suitability of imposing the death penalty on mentally retarded offenders prior to 1986. In that year, the public reaction to the execution of a mentally retarded murderer in Georgia apparently led to the enactment of the first state statute prohibiting such executions. In 1988, when Congress enacted legislation reinstating the federal death penalty, it expressly provided that a "sentence of death shall not be carried out upon a person who is mentally retarded." In 1989, Maryland enacted a similar prohibition. It was in that year that we decided *Penry*, and concluded that those two state enactments, "even when added to the 14 States that have rejected capital punishment completely, do not provide sufficient evidence at present of a national consensus.". . .

Much has changed since then. . . . In 1990 Kentucky and Tennessee enacted statutes similar to those in Georgia and Maryland, as did New Mexico in 1991, and Arkansas, Colorado, Washington, Indiana, and Kansas in 1993 and 1994. In 1995, when New York reinstated its death penalty, it emulated the Federal Government by expressly exempting the mentally retarded. Nebraska followed suit in 1998. There appear to have been no similar enactments during the next two years, but in 2000 and 2001 six more States—South Dakota, Arizona, Connecticut, Florida, Missouri, and North Carolina—joined the procession. The Texas Legislature unanimously adopted a similar bill, and bills have passed at least one house in other States, including Virginia and Nevada.

It is not so much the number of these States that is significant, but the consistency of the direction of change. Given the well-known fact that anticrime legislation is far more popular than legislation providing protections for persons guilty of violent crime, the large number of States prohibiting the execution of mentally retarded persons (and the complete absence of States passing legislation reinstating the power to conduct such executions) provides powerful evidence that today our society views mentally retarded offenders as categorically less culpable than the average criminal. The evidence carries even greater force when it is noted that the legislatures that have addressed the issue have voted overwhelmingly in favor of the prohibition. Moreover, even in those States that allow the execution of mentally retarded offenders, the practice is uncommon. Some States, for example New Hampshire and New Jersey, continue to authorize executions, but none have been carried out in decades. Thus there is little need to pursue legislation barring the execution of the mentally retarded in those States. And it appears that even among those States that regularly execute offenders and that have no prohibition with regard to the mentally retarded, only five have executed offenders possessing a known IQ less than 70 since we decided *Penry*. The practice, therefore, has become truly unusual, and it is fair to say that a national consensus has developed against it.

To the extent there is serious disagreement about the execution of mentally retarded offenders, it is in determining which offenders are in fact retarded. In this case, for instance, the Commonwealth of Virginia disputes that Atkins suffers from mental retardation. Not all people who claim to be mentally retarded will be so impaired as to fall within the range of mentally retarded offenders about whom there is a national consensus. As was our approach in *Ford v. Wainwright* [(1986)], with regard to insanity, "we leave to the State[s] the task of developing appropriate ways to enforce the constitutional restriction upon its execution of sentences."...

IV

This consensus unquestionably reflects widespread judgment about the relative culpability of mentally retarded offenders, and the relationship between mental retardation and the penological purposes served by the death penalty. Additionally, it suggests that some characteristics of mental retardation undermine the strength of the procedural protections that our capital jurisprudence steadfastly guards.

As discussed above, clinical definitions of mental retardation require not only subaverage intellectual functioning, but also significant limitations in adaptive skills such as communication, self-care, and self-direction that became manifest before age 18. Mentally retarded persons frequently know the difference between right and wrong and are competent to stand trial. Because of their impairments, however, by definition they have diminished capacities to understand and process information, to communicate, to abstract from mistakes and learn from experience, to engage in logical reasoning, to control impulses, and to understand the reactions of others. There is no evidence that they are more likely to engage in criminal conduct than others, but there is abundant evidence that they often act on impulse rather than pursuant to a premeditated plan, and that in group settings they are followers rather than leaders. Their deficiencies do not warrant an exemption from criminal sanctions, but they do diminish their personal culpability.

In light of these deficiencies, our death penalty jurisprudence provides two reasons consistent with the legislative consensus that the mentally retarded should be categorically excluded from execution. First, there is a serious question as to whether either justification that we have recognized as a basis for the death penalty applies to mentally retarded offenders. *Gregg v. Georgia* . . . (1976), identified "retribution and deterrence of capital crimes by prospective offenders" as the social purposes served by the death penalty. Unless the imposition of the death penalty on a mentally retarded person "measurably contributes to one or both of these goals, it 'is nothing more than the purposeless and needless imposition of pain and suffering,' and hence an unconstitutional punishment.". . .

With respect to retribution—the interest in seeing that the offender gets his "just deserts"—the severity of the appropriate punishment necessarily depends on the culpability of the offender. Since Gregg, our jurisprudence has consistently confined the imposition of the death penalty to a narrow category of the most serious crimes. For example, in *Godfrey v. Georgia* . . . (1980), we set aside a death sentence because the petitioner's crimes did not reflect "a consciousness materially more 'depraved' than that of any person guilty of murder.". . . If the culpability of the average murderer is insufficient to justify the most extreme sanction available to the State, the lesser culpability of the mentally retarded offender surely does not merit that form of retribution. Thus, pursuant to our narrowing jurisprudence, which seeks to ensure that only the most deserving of execution are put to death, an exclusion for the mentally retarded is appropriate.

With respect to deterrence—the interest in preventing capital crimes by prospective offenders—"it seems likely that 'capital punishment can serve as a deterrent only when murder is the result of premeditation and deliberation,' ". . . The theory of deterrence in capital sentencing is predicated upon the notion that the increased severity of the punishment will inhibit criminal actors from carrying out murderous conduct. Yet it is the same cognitive and behavioral impairments that make these defendants less morally culpable— for example, the diminished ability to understand and process information, to learn from experience, to engage in logical reasoning, or to control impulses— that also make it less likely that they can process the information of the possibility of execution as a penalty and, as a result, control their conduct based upon that information. Nor will exempting the mentally retarded from execution lessen the deterrent effect of the death penalty with respect to offenders who are not mentally retarded. Such individuals are unprotected by the exemption and will continue to face the threat of execution. Thus, executing the mentally retarded will not measurably further the goal of deterrence.

The reduced capacity of mentally retarded offenders provides a second justification for a categorical rule making such offenders ineligible for the death penalty. The risk "that the death penalty will be imposed in spite of factors which may call for a less severe penalty," . . . is enhanced, not only by the possibility of false confessions, but also by the lesser ability of mentally retarded defendants to make a persuasive showing of mitigation in the face of prosecutorial evidence of one or more aggravating factors. Mentally retarded defendants may be less able to give meaningful assistance to their counsel and are typically poor witnesses, and their demeanor may create an unwarranted impression of lack of remorse for their crimes. As *Penry* demonstrated, more-over, reliance on mental retardation as a mitigating factor can be a two-edged sword that may enhance the likelihood that the aggravating factor of future dangerousness will be found by the jury. . . . Mentally retarded defendants in the aggregate face a special risk of wrongful execution.

Our independent evaluation of the issue reveals no reason to disagree with the judgment of "the legislatures that have recently addressed the matter" and concluded that death is not a suitable punishment for a mentally retarded criminal. We are not persuaded that the execution of mentally retarded crimi-nals will measurably advance the deterrent or the retributive purpose of the death penalty. Construing and applying the Eighth Amendment in the light of our "evolving standards of decency," we therefore conclude that such punish-ment is excessive and that the Constitution "places a substantive restriction on the State's power to take the life" of a mentally retarded offender. . . .

The judgment of the Virginia Supreme Court is reversed and the case is re-manded for further proceedings not inconsistent with this opinion.

It is so ordered.

CHIEF JUSTICE REHNQUIST, with whom JUSTICE SCALIA and JUSTICE THOMAS join, dissenting.

The question presented by this case is whether a national consensus de-prives Virginia of the constitutional power to impose the death penalty on cap-ital murder defendants like petitioner, i.e., those defendants who indisputably are competent to stand trial, aware of the punishment they are about to suffer and why, and whose mental retardation has been found an insufficiently com-pelling reason to lessen their individual responsibility for the crime. The Court pronounces the punishment cruel and unusual primarily because 18 States re-cently have passed laws limiting the death eligibility of certain defendants based on mental retardation alone, despite the fact that the laws of 19 other States besides Virginia continue to leave the question of proper punishment to the individuated consideration of sentencing judges or juries familiar with the particular offender and his or her crime. . . .

I agree with JUSTICE SCALIA . . . (dissenting opinion), that the Court's as-sessment of the current legislative judgment regarding the execution of de-fendants like petitioner more resembles a post hoc rationalization for the majority's subjectively preferred result rather than any objective effort to as-certain the content of an evolving standard of decency. I write separately, how-ever, to call attention to the defects in the Court's decision to place weight on foreign laws, the views of professional and religious organizations, and opin-ion polls in reaching its conclusion. . . . The Court's suggestion that these sources are relevant to the constitutional question finds little support in our precedents and, in my view, is antithetical to considerations of federalism, which instruct that any "permanent prohibition upon all units of democratic government must [be apparent] in the operative acts (laws and the application of laws) that the people have approved.". . . The Court's uncritical acceptance of the opinion poll data brought to our attention, moreover, warrants addi-tional comment, because we lack sufficient information to conclude that the surveys were conducted in accordance with generally accepted scientific principles or are capable of supporting valid empirical inferences about the issue before us. . . .

In my view, . . . two sources—the work product of legislatures and sentencing jury determinations—ought to be the sole indicators by which courts ascertain the contemporary American conceptions of decency for purposes of the Eighth Amendment. They are the only objective indicia of contemporary values firmly supported by our precedents. More importantly, however, they can be reconciled with the undeniable precepts that the democratic branches of government and individual sentencing juries are, by design, better suited than courts to evaluating and giving effect to the complex societal and moral considerations that inform the selection of publicly acceptable criminal punishments. . . .

To further buttress its appraisal of contemporary societal values, the Court marshals public opinion poll results and evidence that several professional organizations and religious groups have adopted official positions opposing the imposition of the death penalty upon mentally retarded offenders. . . . In my view, none should be accorded any weight on the Eight Amendment scale when the elected representatives of a State's populace have not deemed them persuasive enough to prompt legislative action. In *Penry*, . . . we were cited similar data and declined to take them into consideration where the "public sentiment expressed in [them]" had yet to find expression in state law. . . . For the Court to rely on such data today serves only to illustrate its willingness to proscribe by judicial fiat—at the behest of private organizations speaking only for themselves—a punishment about which no across-the-board consensus has developed through the workings of normal democratic processes in the laboratories of the States. . . .

* * *

There are strong reasons for limiting our inquiry into what constitutes an evolving standard of decency under the Eighth Amendment to the laws passed by legislatures and the practices of sentencing juries in America. Here, the Court goes beyond these well-established objective indicators of contemporary values. It finds "further support to [its] conclusion" that a national consensus has developed against imposing the death penalty on all mentally retarded defendants in international opinion, the views of professional and religious organizations, and opinion polls not demonstrated to be reliable . . . . Believing this view to be seriously mistaken, I dissent.

JUSTICE SCALIA, with whom the CHIEF JUSTICE and JUSTICE THOMAS join, dissenting.

Today's decision is the pinnacle of our Eighth Amendment death-is-different jurisprudence. Not only does it, like all of that jurisprudence, find no support in the text or history of the Eighth Amendment; it does not even have support in current social attitudes regarding the conditions that render an otherwise just death penalty inappropriate. Seldom has an opinion of this Court rested so obviously upon nothing but the personal views of its members.

[Sections I, II, and III omitted.]

Today's opinion adds one more to the long list of substantive and procedural requirements impeding imposition of the death penalty imposed under this Court's assumed power to invent a death-is-different jurisprudence. None of those requirements existed when the Eighth Amendment was adopted, and some of them were not even supported by current moral consensus. They include prohibition of the death penalty for "ordinary" murder, . . . for rape of an adult woman, . . . and for felony murder absent a showing that the defendant possessed a sufficiently culpable state of mind . . ; prohibition of the death penalty for any person under the age of 16 at the time of the crime . . ; prohibition of the death penalty as the mandatory punishment for any crime . . ; a requirement that the sentencer not be given unguided discretion . . . , a requirement that the sentencer be empowered to take into account all mitigating circumstances . . ; and a requirement that the accused receive a judicial evaluation of his claim of insanity before the sentence can be executed. . . . There is something to be said for popular abolition of the death penalty; there is nothing to be said for its incremental abolition by this Court.

This newest invention promises to be more effective than any of the others in turning the process of capital trial into a game. One need only read the definitions of mental retardation adopted by the American Association of Mental Retardation and the American Psychiatric Association . . . to realize that the symptoms of this condition can readily be feigned. And whereas the capital defendant who feigns insanity risks commitment to a mental institution until he can be cured (and then tried and executed), . . . the capital defendant who feigns mental retardation risks nothing at all. The mere pendency of the present case has brought us petitions by death row inmates claiming for the first time, after multiple habeas petitions, that they are retarded. . . .

Perhaps these practical difficulties will not be experienced by the minority of capital-punishment States that have very recently changed mental retardation from a mitigating factor (to be accepted or rejected by the sentencer) to an absolute immunity. Time will tell—and the brief time those States have had the new disposition in place (an average of 6.8 years) is surely not enough. But if the practical difficulties do not appear, and if the other States share the Court's perceived moral consensus that all mental retardation renders the death penalty inappropriate for all crimes, then that majority will presumably follow suit. But there is no justification for this Court's pushing them into the experiment—and turning the experiment into a permanent practice—on constitutional pretext. Nothing has changed the accuracy of Matthew Hale's endorsement of the common law's traditional method for taking account of guilt-reducing factors, written over three centuries ago:

> "[Determination of a person's incapacity] is a matter of great difficulty, partly from the easiness of counterfeiting this disability . . . and partly from the variety of the

degrees of this infirmity, whereof some are sufficient, and some are insufficient to excuse persons in capital offenses. . . .

"Yet the law of England hath afforded the best method of trial, that is possible, of this and all other matters of fact, namely, by a jury of twelve men all concurring in the same judgment, by the testimony of witnesses . . . , and by the inspection and direction of the judge.". . .

I respectfully dissent.

PRESIDENT BUSH ON
PALESTINIAN LEADERSHIP
June 24, 2002

After trying during his first year in office to avoid direct U.S. involvement in the conflict between Israel and the Palestinians, President George W. Bush in 2002 found that he had no choice but to attempt to pressure both sides into ending the violence and trying again for a permanent peace agreement. Bush came down heavily on the side of Israel, the longtime U.S. ally that used its considerable military might to combat suicide bombings and other terrorist attacks by Palestinian militants. At the urging of Israeli prime minister Ariel Sharon, Bush told the Palestinians they needed to elect "new leadership"—in other words, replace Yasir Arafat, the aging Palestinian leader who spent most of 2002 confined, by Israel, to his West Bank compound. The president repeatedly asked Israel to withdraw its forces from the West Bank but made no serious effort to force Israeli compliance.

U.S. diplomacy, coupled with diplomatic efforts by the European Union (EU) and the United Nations, did little to reduce what had become a cycle of violence in the region. Palestinian suicide bombers and gunmen repeatedly attacked Israeli military and civilian targets, both in Israel proper and in the occupied territories, the Gaza strip and the West Bank. In response, Israel sent tanks, planes, and other heavy weapons into the occupied territories to destroy terrorist bases and impose collective punishment on entire Palestinian communities. By the end of 2002 more than 1,900 Palestinians and more than 600 Israelis had died since the current round of violence broke out in September 2000. The violence and Israeli retaliation all but destroyed the Palestinian economy, and Israel itself suffered economically. (Cycle of violence, p. 927)

Bush's diplomacy on the seemingly intractable Palestinian-Israeli conflict took place within the context of his escalating campaign of pressure against Iraqi leader Saddam Hussein. Bush in January declared Iraq to be part of an "axis of evil" (along with Iran and North Korea) and by year's end was sending a large military expedition to the Persian Gulf in anticipation of a possible war to oust Saddam. Hoping to secure Arab support for his drive against Iraq, Bush tried to prevent the Israeli-Palestinian fighting from inflaming the rapidly growing anti-American sentiment in Arab countries. (Iraq, pp. 612, 713, 927)

Shifts in U.S. Policy

Bush came to office in 2001 determined not to imitate the hands-on approach to the Middle East taken by his predecessor, Bill Clinton (1993–2001). Throughout 2001 and the early months of 2002—even as the level of violence increased in Israel and the occupied territories—Bush's administration held to a policy that the United States would "assist" the Israelis and Palestinians in finding peace but would not "insist" on any particular route to that goal. Bush sent a former Marine general, Anthony Zinni, to the region in late 2001 but quickly withdrew him when Zinni's arrival was greeted with a wave of violence. (Background, Historic Documents of 2001, p. 367)

Two developments during the early months of 2002 appeared to harden the Bush administration's already unfavorable attitude toward Arafat. The first was the January 3 seizure by Israeli commandos of a ship in the Red Sea loaded with about fifty tons of weapons. Israel immediately said the weapons were destined for Palestinians, a charge that Arafat strongly denied. Israel later produced documents appearing to show that the weapons had been ordered and paid for by Arafat's quasi-government, the Palestinian Authority.

The second development was Israel's capture in Ramallah of documents purporting to show Arafat's personal approval of payments to fifteen members of his al Fatah faction whom Israel identified as terrorists. The payments, some of them made as recently as January 2002, ranged from $350 to $600 and appeared to reinforce Israel's contention that Arafat was intimately involved in the process that led to Palestinian attacks on Israeli civilians. In June Israel gave the United States an intelligence report contending that Arafat had approved a $20,000 payment to members of the Al Aksa Martyrs Brigade, an al Fatah-affiliated group that had claimed responsibility for some of the deadliest suicide bombings.

Bolstered by evidence appearing to link the mainstream Palestinian leadership to terrorism, Sharon visited Bush at the White House on February 7 and called for direct U.S. pressure for Arafat's replacement. Bush did not adopt this approach, at first, but made clear that he disdained Arafat and preferred not to do business with him. Bush had spoken twice on the telephone with Arafat but had refused to meet him.

Saudi Peace Initiative

A reasonable prospect of peace flickered for a few weeks in late February and early March but was extinguished by the combined actions of those on both sides who seemed more interested in continuing the struggle. The hint of peace first appeared in February when Saudi Arabia's de facto ruler, Crown Prince Abdullah, told New York Times *columnist Tom Friedman that he had developed a peace plan. Under his proposal, Abdullah said, Arab countries would "normalize" relations with Israel in exchange for Israel's willingness to meet several conditions, including withdrawal from the oc-cupied territories and acceptance of a Palestinian state with Jerusalem as its capital.*

The Israeli government and the Bush administration at first played down the significance of Abdullah's proposal, but moderate Arab leaders and European diplomats seized on it as representing a potential means of exit from the region's violence and mistrust. Abdullah said he would present the plan to a summit meeting of the Arab League scheduled for late March in Beirut. Arafat, prevented by the Israeli army from leaving his Ramallah compound, wanted to attend but backed out at the last minute when Sharon's government said he would be allowed to go to Lebanon but would not be allowed back into the West Bank or any other land under Israeli control.

Abdullah outlined the plan to his Arab League colleagues on March 27. Addressing the Israeli people, he said that if their government "abandons the policy of force and oppression and embraces true peace, we will not hesitate to accept the right of the Israeli people to live in security with the people of the region."

Within hours of Abdullah's televised appeal, a Palestinian suicide bomber blew himself up at a hotel in the Israeli seaside resort town of Netanya, killing twenty-eight people and wounding about 140 others. The victims were Israelis and tourists celebrating the first night of Passover. In a statement claiming responsibility, the radical Palestinian group Hamas said the bombing was a warning both to Israel and to Arab leaders meeting in Beirut that "our Palestinian people's option is resistance and resistance only."

The bombing did not deter the Arab leaders, who the next day, March 28, adopted a resolution incorporating the essence of Abdullah's peace proposal. It called on Israel to withdraw from all territories it had occupied since the 1967 war (including Gaza, the West Bank, and the Golan Heights seized from Syria); agree to a "just solution" to the problem of some 3.6 million Palestinians considered as refugees as a result of Israel's founding in 1948; and accept a "sovereign, independent" Palestinian state located in Gaza and the West Bank, with East Jerusalem as its capital. In turn, the Arabs said they would "consider the Arab-Israeli conflict ended" and enter into a peace agreement with and establish "normal relations" with Israel. The proposal was substantially more conciliatory toward Israel than any previous statement adopted by Arab leaders acting as a group. Even so, the Arab leaders said Palestinians were justified in continuing to fight Israeli occupation of the territories; however, the leaders did not explicitly endorse suicide bombings and other forms of terrorism.

Israeli's response to the bombing and the peace initiative was a tough statement by the cabinet on March 29 promising a "wide-ranging plan of action against Palestinian terrorism" and calling Arafat "an enemy" who "will be isolated." The next day Israeli troops again surrounded Arafat's headquarters building in Ramallah and briefly cut off its water and electricity; Israel had destroyed most other Palestinian Authority buildings during raids in 2001 and earlier in 2002.

The UN Security Council on March 30 called on Israel to withdraw its forces, but Bush appeared to endorse the Israeli offensive against Arafat, cautioning Israel only that it "should make sure there is a path to peace as she secures her homeland." After yet another suicide bombing on April 1 that killed fourteen people in Haifa, Sharon stepped up his rhetoric, calling Arafat "the enemy of the entire free world" and declaring that Israel "is in a war, a war against terrorism." In following days tanks rumbled into Bethlehem, Qalqilya, Tulkarm, and other cities and towns on the West Bank to reassert Israeli de facto control.

Once again, acts of terrorism and harsh reprisals had spoken louder than calls for peace. The Saudi peace proposal simply faded into the background of resumed violence almost immediately after Arab leaders summoned the political will to endorse it.

Failed Powell Mission

Facing international criticism that his hands-off approach was undermining any prospect for peace, Bush reversed course and announced on April 4 that he was sending Secretary of State Colin Powell to the Middle East. As part of his announcement, Bush endorsed, more explicitly than had any previous U.S. president, the concept of a Palestinian state.

Bush gave Powell instructions to obtain the equivalent of a cease-fire—an agreement by Arafat to do everything possible to stop the suicide bombings and by Sharon to withdraw his tanks from Palestinian towns and villages. On his way to the region, on April 9, Powell raised expectations with a statement that he was prepared "to stay for some while" if doing so would help end the cycle of bombings and reprisals. Powell said he intended to meet with Sharon and with Arafat, as well as other leaders in the region.

Powell's mission to Israel had barely gotten underway, on April 12, when a Palestinian woman detonated a suicide bomb at a Jerusalem market, killing herself and six bystanders and wounding scores of others. A militia associated with Arafat's al Fatah faction of the Palestinian movement took responsibility for the attack. In response, Powell called on Arafat to take "a clear stand" against the suicide bombings. Arafat complied the following day with a statement condemning "all the attacks targeting civilians from both sides, and especially the attack that took place against Israeli citizens yesterday in Jerusalem." Arafat's statement also denounced Israeli "state terrorism" and singled out what he called a "massacre" of Palestinians by Israeli forces at the Jenin refugee camp and in West Bank cities. Powell met twice over the next several days with Arafat, and separately with Sharon and other Israeli officials, but he failed to win any significant concessions by either side.

Powell left the Middle East on April 17 and later said he planned to return "in the not too distant future." Powell also said the United States planned to sponsor an international conference on the Middle East early in the summer—similar to the 1991 Madrid conference that set the stage for the series of peace negotiations between Israel and the Palestinians during the 1990s. Few of they key actors in the Middle East demonstrated much enthusiasm for such a conference, however. After repeatedly postponing a date for it, Powell quietly dropped the idea and did not return to Israel during the rest of the year. (Madrid conference, Historic Documents of 1991, p. 719)

One small outcome of Powell's trip was an agreement, announced April 28, under which Israel allowed Arafat to leave his Ramallah compound temporarily. The agreement provided for U.S. and British "wardens" (unarmed civilians) to supervise the detention in Ramallah of six Palestinian men whom Israel had accused of involvement in terrorist actions. Sharon had demanded that Arafat turn the men over to the government as a price for ending his own confinement. The U.S.-brokered deal was a face-saving compromise for both sides.

Bush Calls for Replacement of Arafat

Palestinian suicide bombings eased for a bit after Powell's trip and the Israeli offensive in the West Bank, which ended on April 21. But the attacks resumed in June and the Bush administration began planning a major policy statement placing most of the blame for the situation on Arafat. Two suicide bombings in mid-June, along with Israeli evidence that Arafat's government had financed some of the bombings, reportedly contributed to a hardening attitude in the White House toward the Palestinian leader. Bush delivered his statement on the afternoon of June 24, standing in the Rose Garden of the White House surrounded by Powell and his other senior foreign policy aides.

Bush's speech broke new ground in several respects. The president embraced the idea of a Palestinian state—as he had in his April 4 speech—but he conditioned the formation of such a state on Arafat's departure as the Palestinian leader. Never mentioning Arafat by name, Bush said: "I call on the Palestinian people to elect new leaders, leaders not compromised by terror." The United States would support formation of a Palestinian state once new leaders had been elected, he said—in effect making Arafat's ouster a precondition. Administration officials later said Bush might be willing to allow Arafat to remain as a "figurehead" leader for the Palestinians, provided that an elected official, such as a prime minister, had day-to-day control of the Palestinian Authority.

Bush also suggested a two-stage approach to the formation of a Palestinian state. In the first stage, the timing of which Bush did not specify, Palestinians would be allowed a "provisional" state. Bush did not define such a state, saying only that its borders "and certain aspects of its sovereignty will be provisional." In background briefings to reporters, administration officials also were unable to provide any details for this idea. After such a state was established, Bush said, Israel and the Palestinians would negotiate a final settlement "within three years from now." One result of the negotiations would be the creation of a formal, permanent Palestinian state, he said. While vague, this suggestion bore some resemblance to the peace process initiated at Oslo, Norway, in 1993, which had envisioned a three-year process of negotiations between Israel and the Palestinians leading to a final

settlement of the most controversial issues, including the status of Jeru-
salem, the boundaries of a Palestinian state, and the fate of Palestinian
refugees. The Oslo process dragged on for seven years, not three, and even-
tually gave the Palestinians only limited control over Gaza and the West
Bank. (Oslo accord, Historic Documents of 1993, p. 747)

The president's June 24 speech also represented a break with his previous
policy of putting verbal pressure on Sharon to halt his offensives in the West
Bank. Bush said that Israel needed to withdraw to the positions it held be-
fore the Intifada started in September 2000—but only "as we make progress
toward security," a phrase that appeared to offer Sharon justification to con-
tinue military operations in the West Bank indefinitely. Bush also said Is-
raeli "settlement activity in the occupied territories must stop," but he did
not say when or under what conditions. Israel's financing of Jewish settle-
ments in the territories had fueled Palestinian resentment for more than
three decades.

Bush offered rhetorical sympathy for both Israelis and Palestinians. It
was "untenable," he said, "for Israeli citizens to live in terror." It also was
untenable, he said, "for Palestinians to live in squalor and corruption." The
president expressed sympathy for the suffering of both Israelis and Pales-
tinians. As if to counter the harsh tone of his language about Arafat and the
Palestinian leadership, he directly acknowledged the "deep anger and de-
spair" of the Palestinian people. "For decades you've been treated as pawns
in the Middle East conflict. Your interests have been held hostage to a com-
prehensive peace agreement that never seems to come, as your lives get
worse year by year. You deserve democracy and the rule of law. You deserve
an open society and a thriving economy. You deserve a life of hope for your
children. An end to occupation and a peaceful democratic Palestinian state
may seem distant, but America and our partners throughout the world
stand ready to help, help you make them possible as soon as possible."

Sharon and his aides expressed enthusiasm about Bush's speech, in
particular the call for Arafat to be removed as Palestinian leader. The
Sharon government also said it was pleased that Bush made no pressing de-
mands of Israel and instead put the burden of immediate action on the
Palestinians.

The Palestinian Authority issued a bland statement calling Bush's speech
"a serious contribution" to peace and ignoring the call for Arafat's ouster.
The day after Bush's speech, Arafat said "my people" [the Palestinians] were
"the only ones who can determine" who would lead them, not the U.S. pres-
ident. But in a clear response to U.S. pressure, Arafat's government on
June 26 announced plans for presidential and legislative elections in mid-
January 2003. Aides, and most observers, said Arafat was certain to run
for the presidency and win even though his popularity among his people
had plummeted because of his inability to establish the Palestinian state
that had long been his goal. As the violence continued later in the year, how-
ever, plans for the election were put on hold.

Senior Palestinian representatives scorned Bush's concept of a "provi-
sional" state, especially given the circumstances of frequent Israeli reoccu-

pation of territory promised the Palestinians nearly a decade earlier. "A state is a state, and you cannot be provisionally pregnant, and you cannot have a provisional state," Palestinian planning minister Nabil Shaath told CNN.

Some observers noted that Bush was demanding something of the Palestinians—an elected government with all the institutional trappings of a Western-style democracy—that existed in none of the Arab countries that were longtime U.S. allies. Hemi Salev, a political correspondent for the Israeli newspaper Maariv, *said Bush was unrealistic in his call for "Jefferson-style democracy, New England on the banks of the Jordan River."*

Martin S. Indyk, a former U.S. ambassador to Israel, praised Bush for his direct call for a new Palestinian leader. But Indyk said the president offered the Palestinian people no real incentives. "He needed to give definition to what the Palestinian state would look like, and that would give a greater sense of what they would get in return for ditching their leadership," Indyk told the New York Times. *Indyk also was one of many foreign policy analysts who expressed concern that the speech might represent a one-time nod toward the Israeli-Palestinian problem as Bush prepared to deal with what he saw as the more urgent problem of confronting Iraq.*

A detailed critique of Bush's speech came in a trio of reports issued July 16 by the International Crisis Group, a think tank based in Brussels. The lead report, "Middle East Endgame I: Getting to a Comprehensive Arab-Israeli Peace Settlement," said Bush had failed to present "clear, detailed, and comprehensive blueprints for a permanent Israel-Palestinian agreement—and for Israel-Syria and Israel-Lebanon peace treaties as well—and to press strenuously for their acceptance."

Diplomacy by the "Quartet"

In late 2001, when it first came under international pressure to resume a more forceful U.S. role in Middle East diplomacy, the Bush administration agreed to a joint diplomatic effort with the European Union, Russia, and the United Nations. Powell represented the United States, three senior European diplomats represented the EU, Foreign Minister Igor Ivanov represented Russia, and Secretary General Kofi Annan represented the UN. Calling itself the "Quartet," this group met for the first time in November 2001 and started a process of drafting recommendations for the resumption of direct talks between Israel and the Palestinians.

A series of meetings early in 2002 led to the Quartet's adoption, in July, of a set of goals reflecting much of what Bush had outlined in his June 24 speech. Among the goals were the democratic states of Israel and Palestine "living side by side in peace and security," a permanent end to violence and terrorism, an end to Israeli occupation of the West Bank and Gaza and a halt to Jewish settlements in the territories, reform of the Palestinian Authority government and the holding of Palestinian elections, and the conclusion within three years of final negotiations on all outstanding issues between Israel and the Palestinians.

Diplomats representing the Quartet put these general goals into a docu-

ment called a "roadmap" that spelled out specific steps that Israel and the Palestinians should take over the next three years. The roadmap consisted of three phases in which action by one side would be followed by reciprocal actions by the other. In the first phase, most of which would occur during 2003, the Palestinians would stop suicide bombings and other terrorist attacks against Israelis, reform the Palestinian Authority, and hold elections. Israel in turn would be required to pull its troops from the occupied territories, prohibit new or expanded Jewish settlements in the territories, and ease restrictions on Palestinians (such as road blocks that kept Palestinian workers from their jobs in Israel proper) that had contributed to the collapse of the Palestinian economy. The final settlement of issues between Israel and the Palestinians—including the formation of an independent Palestinian state—would take place in 2005.

Powell and the other senior members of the Quartet agreed informally to this roadmap on September 17, and U.S. officials presented it to Sharon during an October visit to Washington. Sharon reluctantly endorsed the plan in general but complained about specific elements, including its lack of a direct demand for the replacement of Arafat and its implication that Israel would have to withdraw completely, or nearly completely, from the territories it had occupied since the 1967 war. Later in the year, after his coalition government collapsed, Sharon asked the United States to prevent formal adoption of the plan until after Israeli elections scheduled for January 2003. The Bush administration privately agreed to that request but for nearly two months denied publicly that it had done so.

The administration's acceptance of Sharon's request for a delay drew public attention to a deepening disagreement between the United States and nearly all its European allies over how to approach Middle East issues, especially the Israeli-Palestinian conflict. For many years the European public in general, and most European leaders in particular, had been much more sympathetic toward the plight of the Palestinians—and more critical of Israeli policy—than had the U.S. public and leadership. During the 1990s the EU supplied most of the money that Arafat's Palestinian Authority had used to build its quasi-government in Gaza and the West Bank. At the same time, the United States continued its decades-long policy of giving Israel about $3 billion annually in economic and military aid, along with modest aid for the Palestinians.

During 2001 and 2002 many European politicians and foreign policy experts expressed outrage that Israel was using U.S.-supplied tanks, planes, and missiles to destroy Palestinian Authority buildings that had been financed with EU donations. Many European leaders also expressed dismay that Bush appeared to consider dealing with the Israeli-Palestinian conflict as less urgent than ousting Iraqi leader Saddam Hussein.

Disagreements between the United States and Europe came to a head— in a low-key, diplomatic sort of way—during private talks leading up to a December 20 meeting at the White House between Bush and senior representatives of the Quartet. European diplomats and the UN's Annan wanted to use the December 20 meeting as the formal unveiling of the roadmap, thus setting in motion the three-year process of reciprocal steps toward peace by the Israelis and the Palestinians. The Bush administration refused, however, finally acknowledging that Bush had promised not to pressure Sharon until after the Israeli elections. Moreover, the administration also demanded changes in the text of the roadmap that had been requested by Israel. These changes heightened the pressure on the Palestinians, for example by saying they could have a state only after they had elected a leadership "uncompromised by terror," an indirect reference to the ouster of Arafat. Another significant change also weakened the roadmap's demand for a halt to Israeli settlements in the occupied territories.

The European diplomats, Annan, and Ivanov accepted the changes during a meeting with Powell on December 20. In turn, they won the most explicit endorsement Bush had yet given to the roadmap. Meeting with the Quartet's diplomats at the White House later in the day, Bush called the plan "a way forward. It sets conditions. It's a results-oriented document. It is a way to bring people together so that they share their responsibilities." Even so, Bush said the plan was not yet complete, an indication that no action would be taken on it until after the Israeli elections. While obviously disappointed by the delay, Annan later told reporters he was pleased by "the President's strong support for the work of the Quartet and the achievement of his vision."

Following is the text of a speech delivered by President George W. Bush at the White House on June 24, 2002, in which he said Palestinians would have to elect new leaders before they could reach a peace agreement with Israel.

The document was obtained from the Internet at www .whitehouse.gov/news/releases/2002/06/20020624-3.html; accessed November 1, 2002.

For too long, the citizens of the Middle East have lived in the midst of death and fear. The hatred of a few holds the hopes of many hostage. The forces of extremism and terror are attempting to kill progress and peace by killing the innocent. And this casts a dark shadow over an entire region. For the sake of all humanity, things must change in the Middle East.

It is untenable for Israeli citizens to live in terror. It is untenable for Palestinians to live in squalor and occupation. And the current situation offers no prospect that life will improve. Israeli citizens will continue to be victimized by terrorists, and so Israel will continue to defend herself.

In the situation the Palestinian people will grow more and more miserable. My vision is two states, living side by side in peace and security. There is simply no way to achieve that peace until all parties fight terror. Yet, at this critical moment, if all parties will break with the past and set out on a new path, we can overcome the darkness with the light of hope. Peace requires a new and different Palestinian leadership, so that a Palestinian state can be born.

I call on the Palestinian people to elect new leaders, leaders not compromised by terror. I call upon them to build a practicing democracy, based on tolerance and liberty. If the Palestinian people actively pursue these goals, America and the world will actively support their efforts. If the Palestinian people meet these goals, they will be able to reach agreement with Israel and Egypt and Jordan on security and other arrangements for independence.

And when the Palestinian people have new leaders, new institutions and new security arrangements with their neighbors, the United States of America will support the creation of a Palestinian state whose borders and certain aspects of its sovereignty will be provisional until resolved as part of a final settlement in the Middle East.

In the work ahead, we all have responsibilities. The Palestinian people are gifted and capable, and I am confident they can achieve a new birth for their nation. A Palestinian state will never be created by terror—it will be built through reform. And reform must be more than cosmetic change, or veiled attempt to preserve the status quo. True reform will require entirely new political and economic institutions, based on democracy, market economics and action against terrorism.

Today, the elected Palestinian legislature has no authority, and power is concentrated in the hands of an unaccountable few. A Palestinian state can only serve its citizens with a new constitution which separates the powers of government. The Palestinian parliament should have the full authority of a legislative body. Local officials and government ministers need authority of their own and the independence to govern effectively.

The United States, along with the European Union and Arab states, will work with Palestinian leaders to create a new constitutional framework, and a working democracy for the Palestinian people. And the United States, along with others in the international community will help the Palestinians organize and monitor fair, multi-party local elections by the end of the year, with national elections to follow.

Today, the Palestinian people live in economic stagnation, made worse by official corruption. A Palestinian state will require a vibrant economy, where honest enterprise is encouraged by honest government. The United States, the international donor community and the World Bank stand ready to work with Palestinians on a major project of economic reform and development. The United States, the EU, the World Bank, the International Monetary Fund are willing to oversee reforms in Palestinian finances, encouraging transparency and independent auditing.

And the United States, along with our partners in the developed world, will increase our humanitarian assistance to relieve Palestinian suffering. Today, the Palestinian people lack effective courts of law and have no means to defend and vindicate their rights. A Palestinian state will require a system of reliable justice to punish those who prey on the innocent. The United States and members of the international community stand ready to work with Palestinian leaders to establish finance—establish finance and monitor a truly independent judiciary.

Today, Palestinian authorities are encouraging, not opposing, terrorism. This is unacceptable. And the United States will not support the establishment of a Palestinian state until its leaders engage in a sustained fight against the terrorists and dismantle their infrastructure. This will require an externally supervised effort to rebuild and reform the Palestinian security services. The security system must have clear lines of authority and accountability and a unified chain of command.

America is pursuing this reform along with key regional states. The world is prepared to help, yet ultimately these steps toward statehood depend on the Palestinian people and their leaders. If they energetically take the path of reform, the rewards can come quickly. If Palestinians embrace democracy, confront corruption and firmly reject terror, they can count on American support for the creation of a provisional state of Palestine.

With a dedicated effort, this state could rise rapidly, as it comes to terms with Israel, Egypt and Jordan on practical issues, such as security. The final borders, the capital and other aspects of this state's sovereignty will be negotiated between the parties, as part of a final settlement. Arab states have offered their help in this process, and their help is needed.

I've said in the past that nations are either with us or against us in the war on terror. To be counted on the side of peace, nations must act. Every leader actually committed to peace will end incitement to violence in official media, and publicly denounce homicide bombings. Every nation actually committed to peace will stop the flow of money, equipment and recruits to terrorist groups seeking the destruction of Israel—including Hamas, Islamic Jihad, and Hezbollah. Every nation actually committed to peace must block the shipment of Iranian supplies to these groups, and oppose regimes that promote terror, like Iraq. And Syria must choose the right side in the war on terror by closing terrorist camps and expelling terrorist organizations.

Leaders who want to be included in the peace process must show by their deeds an undivided support for peace. And as we move toward a peaceful solution, Arab states will be expected to build closer ties of diplomacy and commerce with Israel, leading to full normalization of relations between Israel and the entire Arab world.

Israel also has a large stake in the success of a democratic Palestine. Permanent occupation threatens Israel's identity and democracy. A stable, peaceful Palestinian state is necessary to achieve the security that Israel longs for. So I challenge Israel to take concrete steps to support the emergence of a viable, credible Palestinian state.

As we make progress towards security, Israel forces need to withdraw fully to positions they held prior to September 28, 2000. And consistent with the recommendations of the Mitchell Committee, Israeli settlement activity in the occupied territories must stop.

The Palestinian economy must be allowed to develop. As violence subsides, freedom of movement should be restored, permitting innocent Palestinians to resume work and normal life. Palestinian legislators and officials, humanitarian and international workers, must be allowed to go about the business of building a better future. And Israel should release frozen Palestinian revenues into honest, accountable hands.

I've asked Secretary Powell to work intensively with Middle Eastern and international leaders to realize the vision of a Palestinian state, focusing them on a comprehensive plan to support Palestinian reform and institution-building.

Ultimately, Israelis and Palestinians must address the core issues that divide them if there is to be a real peace, resolving all claims and ending the conflict between them. This means that the Israeli occupation that began in 1967 will be ended through a settlement negotiated between the parties, based on U.N. Resolutions 242 and 338, with Israeli withdrawal to secure and recognize borders.

We must also resolve questions concerning Jerusalem, the plight and future of Palestinian refugees, and a final peace between Israel and Lebanon, and Israel and a Syria that supports peace and fights terror.

All who are familiar with the history of the Middle East realize that there may be setbacks in this process. Trained and determined killers, as we have seen, want to stop it. Yet the Egyptian and Jordanian peace treaties with Israel remind us that with determined and responsible leadership progress can come quickly.

As new Palestinian institutions and new leaders emerge, demonstrating real performance on security and reform, I expect Israel to respond and work toward a final status agreement. With intensive effort by all, this agreement could be reached within three years from now. And I and my country will actively lead toward that goal.

I can understand the deep anger and anguish of the Israeli people. You've lived too long with fear and funerals, having to avoid markets and public transportation, and forced to put armed guards in kindergarten classrooms. The Palestinian Authority has rejected your offer at hand, and trafficked with terrorists. You have a right to a normal life; you have a right to security; and I deeply believe that you need a reformed, responsible Palestinian partner to achieve that security.

I can understand the deep anger and despair of the Palestinian people. For decades you've been treated as pawns in the Middle East conflict. Your interests have been held hostage to a comprehensive peace agreement that never seems to come, as your lives get worse year by year. You deserve democracy and the rule of law. You deserve an open society and a thriving economy. You deserve a life of hope for your children. An end to occupation and a peaceful democratic Palestinian state may seem distant, but America and our partners throughout the world stand ready to help, help you make them possible as soon as possible.

If liberty can blossom in the rocky soil of the West Bank and Gaza, it will inspire millions of men and women around the globe who are equally weary of poverty and oppression, equally entitled to the benefits of democratic government.

I have a hope for the people of Muslim countries. Your commitments to morality, and learning, and tolerance led to great historical achievements. And those values are alive in the Islamic world today. You have a rich culture, and you share the aspirations of men and women in every culture. Prosperity and freedom and dignity are not just American hopes, or Western hopes. They are universal, human hopes. And even in the violence and turmoil of the Middle East, America believes those hopes have the power to transform lives and nations.

This moment is both an opportunity and a test for all parties in the Middle East: an opportunity to lay the foundations for future peace; a test to show who is serious about peace and who is not. The choice here is stark and simple. The Bible says, "I have set before you life and death; therefore, choose life." The time has arrived for everyone in this conflict to choose peace, and hope, and life.

Thank you very much.

APPEALS COURT ON THE PLEDGE OF ALLEGIANCE
June 26, 2002

A three-judge panel of the federal Court of Appeals for the Ninth Circuit provoked widespread outrage following its June 26, 2002, ruling that the Pledge of Allegiance was unconstitutional. By a 2–1 vote, the panel said that the pledge's phrase "one nation, under God" was a government endorsement of religion in violation of the First Amendment. From a constitutional standpoint, Judge Alfred T. Goodwin wrote, the words "under God" were no different than stating that the United States was a nation "under Jesus," "under Vishnu," "under Zeus," or "under no god." None of these statements was "neutral with respect to religion," as required by the First Amendment, Goodwin wrote.

Reaction to the ruling was immediate and angry. "Ridiculous," President George W. Bush was reported to have said when told of the opinion. "Nuts," said Sen. Tom Daschle, D-S.D. "The worst kind of political correctness run amok," was the verdict of Sen. Kit Bond, R-Mo.

The Senate interrupted debate on a defense bill to pass a resolution condemning the court decision. The vote was 99–0. To underline their protest, senators voted from their desks, with each member rising to say "aye" as his or her name was called. The last time the Senate conducted this type of vote was in 1999, when it voted on the articles of impeachment against President Bill Clinton. Not to be outdone, House members gathered on the Capitol steps to recite the pledge in unison and to sing "God Bless America" and other patriotic songs. On June 27 the House also passed a resolution condemning the ruling, 416–3. (Clinton impeachment trial, Historic Documents of 1999, p. 15)

Attorney General John Ashcroft announced June 27 that the Justice Department would request a rehearing by a full, eleven-judge panel of the Ninth Circuit Court. California governor Gray Davis said the state would also file an appeal. Acknowledging that he knew the ruling would be an "attention-getter," Judge Goodwin announced June 27 that he was staying the ruling while other members of the court decided what to do. Even without

Goodwin's stay, the ruling would not have taken effect for several weeks, pending appeals. Even then it would affect public schools only in the nine western states under the appeals court's jurisdiction: Alaska, Arizona, California, Hawaii, Idaho, Montana, Nevada, Oregon, and Washington. By year's end, the appeals were still working their way through the process.

The panel's decision came in the midst of an upsurge in patriotic fervor following the terrorist attacks on the United States in September 2001. According to the National Conference of State Legislatures, half the states required school children to recite the pledge as part of the school day, while another half dozen recommended it. After the September 11 attacks, legislation to make recitation of the pledge mandatory was introduced in several more states.

Public furor over the decision lasted for several days. On June 27 President Bush said the circuit court judges were "out of step" with American tradition and reaffirmed his belief in a "universal God." He also said the decision showed the need for "common-sense judges who understand that our rights were derived from God. And those are the kinds of judges that I intend to put on the bench." The president raised the decision again during Fourth of July celebrations in Ripley, West Virginia. "No authority of government can ever prevent an American from pledging allegiance to this one nation under God," Bush declared. National, state, and local politicians made several statements, and the decision was the main topic of conversation on radio and television talk shows for several days.

Two weeks after the decision, Goodwin said he was somewhat surprised by how vociferous opposition to the ruling had been. Goodwin, Judge Stephen Reinhardt, who sided with Goodwin in declaring the pledge unconstitutional, and Michael A. Newdow, the plaintiff, all reportedly received death threats and other vitriolic messages in the days following the decision. Some academics and others who had supported the decision in television appearances and newspaper interviews also reported receiving hate mail.

A day after the Ninth Circuit Court panel declared the Pledge of Allegiance to be unconstitutional, the Supreme Court upheld a school voucher plan in Ohio. The Court said that the plan, which used tax funds to send children to church-run schools, did not violate the Establishment Clause. (Voucher plan, p. 406)

Amending the Pledge: Promoting Patriotism . . .

As written by Francis Bellamy in 1892, the Pledge of Allegiance read: "I pledge allegiance to my flag and to the republic for which it stands, one nation indivisible, with liberty and justice for all." In 1924 "my flag" was changed to "the flag of the United States of America." Thirty years later, at the height of the cold war, Congress added the words "under God," so that the pledge read "one nation under God, indivisible." As historian Arthur Schlesinger Jr. put it in an op-ed piece in the New York Times, the two-word addition was intended to "emphasize the antagonism between God-fearing

Americans and godless Communists." Signing the legislation, President Dwight D. Eisenhower said that "from this day forward, . . . millions of our schoolchildren will daily proclaim . . . the dedication of our nation and our people to the Almighty."

Eisenhower was correct that millions of children would stand beside their desks each day, hands over their hearts, and recite the pledge, as had millions of children before then. But the Supreme Court in 1943, before the insertion of the words "under God," had ruled that school children could not be forced to recite the pledge if to do so would conflict with their religious beliefs. "If there is any fixed star in our constitutional constellation, it is that no official, high or petty, can prescribe what shall be orthodox in politics, nationalism, religion or other matters of opinion or force citizens to confess by word or act their faith therein," Justice Robert H. Jackson wrote for the Court majority in West Virginia Board of Education v. Barnette.

. . . *Or Advancing Religion*

The 1943 case involved a family of Jehovah's Witnesses. The case before the Ninth Circuit was brought by an atheist on behalf of his eight-year-old daughter. Michael Newdow, an emergency room doctor and an attorney (who argued his own case), claimed that his daughter was injured because she was compelled to "watch and listen as her state-employed teacher in her state-run school leads her classmates in a ritual proclaiming that there is a God, and that [the United States] is 'one nation under God.' " Newdow did not seek damages but did ask that the words "under God" be deleted from the pledge.

Writing for himself and Judge Reinhardt, Goodwin said that over the last thirty years the Supreme Court had set out three tests for determining if a school district's policies violated the Establishment Clause—whether the policy advanced religion, endorsed religion, and was coercive. The pledge failed all three tests, Goodwin wrote. First, he said, "the statement that the United States is a nation 'under God' is an endorsement of religion. It is a profession of a religious belief, namely, a belief in monotheism. . . . To recite the Pledge is . . . to swear allegiance to the values for which the flag stands: unity, indivisibility, liberty, Justice, and—since 1954— monotheism."

Second, he said, the policy of reciting the pledge was coercive. Although the religious content might be minimal to some, "to an atheist or a believer in certain non-Judeo-Christian religions or philosophies, it may reasonably appear to be an attempt to enforce a 'religious orthodoxy' of monotheism, and is therefore impermissible," Goodwin wrote. Finally, Goodwin said, the legislative history of the law adding the words "under God" to the pledge "reveals that the Act's sole purpose was to advance religion, in order to differentiate the United States from nations under communist rule."

The circuit court acknowledged that the Supreme Court had upon occasion commented in dicta that the phrase "one nation under God" was not unconstitutional but pointed out that the High Court had never directly ad-

dressed the question. (Dicta, or more fully obiter dicta, *are statements made in a judicial opinion that are not essential to resolving the case before the Court.) The circuit court also noted that the Court of Appeals for the Seventh Circuit had held the phrase to be constitutional in 1992 but said that court erred because it did not apply any of the tests necessary to determine an improper establishment of religion.*

In dissent, Judge Ferdinand F. Fernandez said that a mountain was being made out of a molehill. The danger that the phrase "under God" would "bring about a theocracy or suppress somebody's beliefs is so minuscule as to be de minimis," he wrote. "The danger that phrase presents to our First Amendment freedoms is picayune at most."

Speculation on Reversal

The Ninth Circuit was the most liberal federal court of appeals, and a high proportion of its rulings had been reversed by the more conservative Supreme Court in the last few decades. Most attorneys interviewed in the days following the circuit court decision said they thought it likely that, if it took this case, the Supreme Court would reverse this decision. But many of these lawyers, both conservative and liberal, said the circuit court opinion should not be regarded as extreme but rather as a logical, even reasonable, decision based on recent Supreme Court decisions. "The majority decision is actually a very plausible reading of the Supreme Court precedents," said Eugene Volokh, a conservative law professor at UCLA.

Meanwhile, Newdow filed a new suit in federal district court in Washington, D.C., at the end of August, challenging the practice of having chaplains, who are paid with public funds, pray in Congress and minister to legislators. House and Senate chaplains made as much as $147,000 a year. Congress has had paid chaplains since its beginning in 1789. In the 1983 case of March v. Chambers, *the Supreme Court said paid chaplains were not a violation of the Establishment Clause, but Newdow argued in his court filings that rulings since then directly conflict with the 1983 decision.*

Congress in October cleared legislation reaffirming its support of the phrase "under God" in the pledge and of the national motto "In God We trust," which was printed on U.S. currency.

Following are excerpts from the opinion and dissent in the case of Newdow v. U.S. Congress et al., *in which a three-judge panel of the United States Court of Appeals for the Ninth Circuit ruled, 2–1, that the words "under God" added to the Pledge of Allegiance in 1954 were an establishment of religion in violation of the First Amendment of the Constitution.*

The document was obtained from the Internet at www.ca9.uscourts.gov/ca9/newopinions.nsf/ FE05EEE79C2A97B688256BE3007FEE32/$file/0016423 .pdf?openelement; accessed November 10, 2002.

Opinion

GOODWIN, Circuit Judge:

Michael Newdow appeals a judgment dismissing his challenge to the constitutionality of the words "under God" in the Pledge of Allegiance to the Flag. Newdow argues that the addition of these words by a 1954 federal statute to the previous version of the Pledge of Allegiance (which made no reference to God) and the daily recitation in the classroom of the Pledge of Allegiance, with the added words included, by his daughter's public school teacher are violations of the Establishment Clause of the First Amendment to the United States Constitution.

Factual and Procedural Background

Newdow is an atheist whose daughter attends public elementary school in the Elk Grove Unified School District ("EGUSD") in California. In accordance with state law and a school district rule, EGUSD teachers begin each school day by leading their students in a recitation of the Pledge of Allegiance ("the Pledge"). The California Education Code requires that public schools begin each school day with "appropriate patriotic exercises" and that "[t]he giving of the Pledge of Allegiance to the Flag of the United States of America shall satisfy" this requirement. . . .

Newdow does not allege that his daughter's teacher or school district requires his daughter to participate in reciting the Pledge. Rather, he claims that his daughter is injured when she is compelled to "watch and listen as her state-employed teacher in her state-run school leads her classmates in a ritual proclaiming that there is a God, and that our's [sic] is 'one nation under God.' "

Newdow's complaint in the district court challenged the constitutionality, under the First Amendment, of the 1954 Act, the California statute, and the school district's policy requiring teachers to lead willing students in recitation of the Pledge. He sought declaratory and injunctive relief, but did not seek damages.

The school districts and their superintendents (collectively, "school district defendants") filed a Federal Rule of Civil Procedure 12(b)(6) motion to dismiss for failure to state a claim. . . . The United States Congress, the United States, and the President of the United States (collectively, "the federal defendants") joined in the motion to dismiss filed by the school district defendants. The magistrate judge reported findings and a recommendation; District Judge Milton L. Schwartz approved the recommendation and entered a judgment of dismissal. This appeal followed.

Discussion

[Portions of the opinion concerning jurisdiction, the state of California as defendants, and Newdow's standing to sue have been omitted.]

D. Establishment Clause

The Establishment Clause of the First Amendment states that "Congress shall make no law respecting an establishment of religion," . . . a provision that "the Fourteenth Amendment makes applicable with full force to the States and their school districts." *Lee v. Weisman* . . . (1992). Over the last three decades, the Supreme Court has used three interrelated tests to analyze alleged violations of the Establishment Clause in the realm of public education: the three-prong test set forth in *Lemon v. Kurtzman* . . . (1971); the "endorsement" test, first articulated by Justice O'Connor in her concurring opinion in *Lynch* [*v. Donnelly* (1984)], and later adopted by a majority of the Court in *County of Allegheny v. ACLU* . . . (1989); and the "coercion" test first used by the Court in Lee. . . .

[The appeals court next described how the Supreme Court had applied each of these tests, including the case of *Santa Fe Independent School District v. Doe* (2000), in which the court held that the delivery of a prayer before a school football game had the unconstitutional effect of coercing those present to participate in an act of religious worship.]

We are free to apply any or all of the three tests, and to invalidate any measure that fails any one of them. The Supreme Court has not repudiated *Lemon;* in *Santa Fe*, it found that the application of each of the three tests provided an independent ground for invalidating the statute at issue in that case; and in *Lee*, the Court invalidated the policy solely on the basis of the coercion test. Although this court has typically applied the *Lemon* test to alleged Establishment Clause violations, . . . we are not required to apply it if a practice fails one of the other tests. Nevertheless, for purposes of completeness, we will analyze the school district policy and the 1954 Act under all three tests.

We first consider whether the 1954 Act and the EGUSD's policy of teacher-led Pledge recitation survive the endorsement test. The magistrate judge found that "the ceremonial reference to God in the pledge does not convey endorsement of particular religious beliefs." Supreme Court precedent does not support that conclusion.

In the context of the Pledge, the statement that the United States is a nation "under God" is an endorsement of religion. It is a profession of a religious belief, namely, a belief in monotheism. The recitation that ours is a nation "under God" is not a mere acknowledgment that many Americans believe in a deity. Nor is it merely descriptive of the undeniable historical significance of religion in the founding of the Republic. Rather, the phrase "one nation under God" in the context of the Pledge is normative. To recite the Pledge is not to describe the United States; instead, it is to swear allegiance to the values for which the flag stands: unity, indivisibility, liberty, justice, and—since 1954—monotheism. The text of the official Pledge, codified in federal law, impermissibly takes a position with respect to the purely religious question of the existence and identity of God. A profession that we are a nation "under God" is identical, for Establishment Clause purposes, to a profession that we are a nation "under Jesus," a nation "under Vishnu," a nation "under Zeus," or a nation "under no god," because none of these professions can be neutral with respect to religion. . . . Furthermore, the school district's practice of teacher-led recitation of the Pledge aims to inculcate in students a respect for the ideals set forth in the Pledge, and thus amounts to state endorsement of these ideals. Although students cannot be forced to participate in recitation of the Pledge, the school district is nonetheless conveying a message of state endorsement of a religious belief when it requires public school teachers to recite, and lead the recitation of, the current form of the Pledge. . . .

The Pledge, as currently codified, is an impermissible government endorsement of religion because it sends a message to unbelievers "that they are outsiders, not full members of the political community, and an accompanying message to adherents that they are insiders, favored members of the political community." *Lynch*, 465 U. S. at 688 (O'Connor, J., concurring). . . .

Similarly, the policy and the Act fail the coercion test. Just as in Lee, the policy and the Act place students in the untenable position of choosing between participating in an exercise with religious content or protesting. As the Court observed with respect to the graduation prayer in that case: "What to most believers may seem nothing more than a reasonable request that the nonbeliever respect their religious practices, in a school context may appear to the nonbeliever or dissenter to be an attempt to employ the machinery of the State to enforce a religious orthodoxy.". . . Although the defendants argue that the religious content of "one nation under God" is minimal, to an atheist or a believer in certain non–Judeo-Christian religions or philosophies, it may reasonably appear to be an attempt to enforce a "religious orthodoxy" of monotheism, and is therefore impermissible. The coercive effect of this policy is particularly pronounced in the school setting given the age and impressionability of schoolchildren, and their understanding that they are required to adhere to the norms set by their school, their teacher and their fellow students. . . . [T]he mere fact that a pupil is required to listen every day to the statement "one nation under God" has a coercive effect. The coercive effect of the Act is apparent from its context and legislative history, which indicate that the Act was designed to result in the daily recitation of the words "under God" in school classrooms. President Eisenhower, during the Act's signing ceremony, stated: "From this day forward, the millions of our school children will daily proclaim in every city and town, every village and rural schoolhouse, the dedication of our Nation and our people to the Almighty.". . . Therefore, the policy and the Act fail the coercion test.

Finally we turn to the *Lemon* test, the first prong of which asks if the challenged policy has a secular purpose. Historically, the primary purpose of the 1954 Act was to advance religion, in conflict with the first prong of the *Lemon* test. The federal defendants "do not dispute that the words 'under God' were intended" "to recognize a Supreme Being," at a time when the government was publicly inveighing against atheistic communism. Nonetheless, the federal defendants argue that the Pledge must be considered as a whole when assessing whether it has a secular purpose. They claim that the Pledge has the secular purpose of "solemnizing public occasions, expressing confidence in the future, and encouraging the recognition of what is worthy of appreciation in society.". . .

The flaw in defendants' argument is that it looks at the text of the Pledge "as a whole," and glosses over the 1954 Act. The problem with this approach is apparent when one considers the Court's analysis in *Wallace*. There, the Court struck down Alabama's statute mandating a moment of silence for "meditation or voluntary prayer" not because the final version "as a whole" lacked a primary secular purpose, but because the state legislature had amended the statute specifically and solely to add the words "or voluntary prayer."...

By analogy to *Wallace*, we apply the purpose prong of the *Lemon* test to the amendment that added the words "under God" to the Pledge, not to the Pledge in its final version. As was the case with the amendment to the Alabama statute in *Wallace*, the legislative history of the 1954 Act reveals that the Act's *sole* purpose was to advance religion, in order to differentiate the United States from nations under communist rule.... As the legislative history of the 1954 Act sets forth:

> At this moment of our history the principles underlying our American Government and the American way of life are under attack by a system whose philosophy is at direct odds with our own. Our American Government is founded on the concept of the individuality and the dignity of the human being. Underlying this concept is the belief that the human person is important because he was created by God and endowed by Him with certain inalienable rights which no civil authority may usurp. The inclusion of God in our pledge therefore would further acknowledge the dependence of our people and our Government upon the moral directions of the Creator. At the same time it would serve to deny the atheistic and materialistic concepts of communism with its attendant subservience of the individual.

... This language reveals that the purpose of the 1954 Act was to take a position on the question of theism, namely, to support the existence and moral authority of God, while "deny[ing] ... atheistic and materialistic concepts."... Such a purpose runs counter to the Establishment Clause, which prohibits the government's endorsement or advancement not only of one particular religion at the expense of other religions, but also of religion at the expense of atheism....

... Because the Act fails the purpose prong of *Lemon*, we need not examine the other prongs....

Similarly, the school district policy also fails the *Lemon* test. Although it survives the first prong of *Lemon* because, as even Newdow concedes, the school district had the secular purpose of fostering patriotism in enacting the policy, the policy fails the second prong.... [T]he second *Lemon* prong asks whether the challenged government action is sufficiently likely to be perceived by adherents of the controlling denominations as an endorsement, and by the nonadherents as a disapproval, of their individual religious choices."... Given the age and impressionability of schoolchildren, as discussed above, particularly within the confined environment of the classroom, the policy is highly likely to convey an impermissible message of endorsement to some and disapproval to others of their beliefs regarding the existence of a monotheistic God. Therefore the policy fails the effects prong of *Lemon*, and fails the *Lemon* test. In sum, both the policy and the Act fail the *Lemon* test as well as the endorsement and coercion tests.

In conclusion, we hold that (1) the 1954 Act adding the words "under God" to the Pledge, and (2) EGUSD's policy and practice of teacher-led recitation of the Pledge, with the added words included, violate the Establishment Clause.

The judgment of dismissal is vacated with respect to these two claims, and the cause is remanded for further proceedings consistent with our holding. Plaintiff is to recover costs on this appeal.

Reversed and Remanded.

FERNANDEZ, Circuit Judge, concurring and dissenting:

I concur in parts A, B and C of the majority opinion, but dissent as to part D.

. . . [L]egal world abstractions and ruminations aside, when all is said and done, the danger that "under God" in our Pledge of Allegiance will tend to bring about a theocracy or suppress somebody's beliefs is so minuscule as to be de minimis. The danger that phrase presents to our First Amendment freedoms is picayune at most.

Judges, including Supreme Court Justices, have recognized the lack of danger in that and similar expressions for decades, if not for centuries, as have presidents and members of our Congress. . . .

Some, who rather choke on the notion of de minimis, have resorted to the euphemism "ceremonial deism.". . . But whatever it is called (I care not), it comes to this: such phrases as "In God We Trust," or "under God" have no tendency to establish a religion in this country or to suppress anyone's exercise, or non-exercise, of religion, except in the fevered eye of persons who most fervently would like to drive all tincture of religion out of the public life of our polity. Those expressions have not caused any real harm of that sort over the years since 1791, and are not likely to do so in the future. . . .

My reading of the stelliscript suggests that upon Newdow's theory of our Constitution, accepted by my colleagues today, we will soon find ourselves prohibited from using our album of patriotic songs in many public settings. "God Bless America" and "America The Beautiful" will be gone for sure, and while use of the first three stanzas of "The Star-Spangled Banner" will still be permissible, we will be precluded from straying into the fourth. And currency beware! Judges can accept those results if they limit themselves to elements and tests, while failing to look at the good sense and principles that animated those tests in the first place. But they do so at the price of removing a vestige of the awe we all must feel at the immenseness of the universe and our own small place within it, as well as the wonder we must feel at the good fortune of our country. That will cool the febrile nerves of a few at the cost of removing the healthy glow conferred upon many citizens when the forbidden verses, or phrases, are uttered, read, or seen.

In short, I cannot accept the eliding of the simple phrase "under God" from our Pledge of Allegiance, when it is obvious that its tendency to establish religion in this country or to interfere with the free exercise (or non-exercise) of religion is de minimis.

SEC CIVIL ACTION COMPLAINT AGAINST WORLDCOM FOR FRAUD
June 26, 2002

Balance sheets, stock options, accounting standards, and other previously humdrum staples of business life suddenly became headline news and the subject of intense public controversy during 2002. Bankruptcies and scandals at giant corporations shook public confidence in corporate America and led to new legislation and business standards intended to protect investors by limiting opportunities for excessive greed in board rooms and executive suites.

Five of the ten largest bankruptcies in U.S. history occurred between late 2001 and the end of 2002. Enron, the giant Texas energy trading company, headed the parade in December 2001 with what was, at the time, the largest U.S. bankruptcy in history. Enron's fall was exceeded in July 2002 by the bankruptcy of WorldCom, the country's second-largest telecommunications company. Another telecommunications firm, Global Crossing, also headed to bankruptcy court during the year, as did United Airlines (the second-largest U.S. air carrier) and insurance giant Conseco. Other household names that fell into bankruptcy during the year included the K-Mart discount retail chain and US Airways, the sixth-largest U.S. airline. AOL-Time Warner—the result of a 1999 merger that proponents said heralded an era of "new media" dominance over magazines and books—by 2002 seemed more representative of an era of wishful thinking, its stock value having plummeted with the collapse of the "dot-com" boom. (U.S. economy, p. 877; Enron bankruptcy, Historic Documents of 2001, p. 857)

No company suffered a worse fate than Arthur Andersen, the once-prestigious accounting giant that had certified the books for Enron, World-Com, and several other troubled companies. The federal government filed a criminal charge against Arthur Anderson in April and two months later won a guilty verdict. Most of the firm's clients deserted it, and the bulk its practice was divided among other accounting firms.

Three of the bankrupt companies—Enron, WorldCom, and Global Crossing—were among a dozen or so major corporations where senior executives were accused of issuing misleading financial reports, taking

*improper or illegal loans, or simply stealing from the corporate till. Allega-
tions of corporate wrongdoing also plagued Adelphia, a major cable television provider; Tyco, a conglomerate; and numerous other large firms.*

*By the middle of the year Americans had become familiar with televised
images of once high-flying corporate executives being led, handcuffed, from
their homes following arrests. The federal government filed criminal charges
against nearly two dozen senior executives during the year and won guilty
pleas from several of them.*

*The almost nonstop onslaught of news about misdeeds in corporate
America put enormous pressure on Congress, the Bush administration, and
government regulators to take action on behalf of the public and investors.
The federal government's single biggest enforcement action was a civil
complaint filed June 26, 2002, by the Security and Exchange Commission
(SEC) alleging fraud by WorldCom. New York state attorney general Elliot
Spitzer took on Wall Street brokerage firms and won two settlements totaling
$1.4 billion.*

*President George W. Bush on March 7 sent Congress a proposal for mod-
est steps to improve corporate governance, but by that point congressional
and public opinion was demanding even tougher action. Congress eventually responded in July with a bill (PL 107–204) mandating the most important changes in federal law on corporate finances in decades; a key step
was the creation of an independent board to oversee corporate accounting
practices. The legislation offered Washington politicians a measure of protection from the wrath of voters, but critics said it would have only a modest impact because businesses had a long history of finding and exploiting
loopholes in government regulations. One unforeseen consequence of the legislation was a series of missteps by the SEC, which was supposed to implement much of it. That body's much-criticized chairman, Harvey L. Pitt, was
forced to resign in November.* (Legislation and SEC problems, p. 1032)

Sapping Public Confidence

*As a direct result of the scandals, public confidence in both corporations
and the financial markets took a beating. Numerous opinion polls showed
that corporate chief executive officers (CEOs), formerly admired for their
business and public relations savvy, had fallen in public esteem to the ranks
of used car salesmen. Just as important, millions of Americans suddenly
began to doubt the wisdom of putting their life savings into the stock markets. Analysts said this drop in investor confidence in corporate culture
contributed to the third consecutive year of declining stock values. The Dow
Jones Industrial Average fell for a third straight year for the first time since
1941, and the Standard & Poor's 500 stock index declined for the third
straight year for the first time since 1932.*

*Numerous experts said the sensational reports about corporate and in-
dividual greed tended to obscure an important truth: Company insiders
would not have been able to get away with their misdeeds if investors and
regulators had paid more attention to figures other than the short-term bottom line. During the stock market boom of the 1990s investors expected, even*

demanded, ever-rising values for their shares, and those values were largely based on reported revenues and net earnings. Few investors—whether individuals or giant institutions, such as pension funds—apparently bothered to scratch beneath the surface of quarterly and annual reports that tended to paint glowing pictures of corporate health. As a result, company insiders believed they would never be caught when they played with the books. "We turned a culture of conservatism about reported financial information into a culture of hype," former SEC chairman Richard Breeden told the Financial Times in December.

It also emerged during 2002 that some analysts for Wall Street brokerage firms who had gained fame and wealth for their supposed ability to pick high-growth stocks also had failed to do their homework. In some cases, the analysts appeared to have conspired with the companies they covered to mislead investors.

Bush administration officials, the Chamber of Commerce of the United States, and most other business groups insisted that the scandals—while damaging—showed that only a handful of unscrupulous individuals and companies were at fault. The vast majority of business people, these groups said, were honest and conscientious.

Others said the problems ran deeper. "I think it's fair to say that there was nobody in the business community who is not implicated in this in some way," Jeffrey Garten, dean of Yale University's School of Management told the Washington Post in June. "Not the executives who were under the excruciating pressure of having to meet quarterly earnings targets, no matter what. Not the lawyers and the accountants and bankers who were forced to compete furiously to get and keep clients. Not the regulators who became so intimidated by all the exuberance in the air. Certainly not the underwriters or the analysts or the credit-rating agencies or you in the press. Even those of us at business schools are implicated. It's not like the educational establishment sounded any warning. We were cheerleaders, too."

An even more succinct analysis came from the man who, perhaps more than anyone else, represented the U.S. financial establishment at the turn of the century: Federal Reserve Board Chairman Alan Greenspan. Testifying before the Senate Banking Committee on July 16, Greenspan diagnosed the problem facing corporate America as "infectious greed." Chief executive officers, he said, had created incentives for personal enrichment that "overcame the good judgment of too many corporate managers. It is not that humans have become any more greedy than in generations past. It is that the avenues to express greed had grown so enormously."

The Rise and Fall of WorldCom

In terms of numbers, the fall of WorldCom overshadowed all other corporate scandals in recent years—even including the collapse the year before of Enron, which was found to have cooked its books. WorldCom was the country's second-largest telecommunications firm, behind AT&T. It was the product of an aggressive empire-building scheme during the 1980s and 1990s led by its president and CEO, Bernard J. Ebbers, a former motel *operator with a penchant for bold deals. Ebbers and several friends in Mississippi started the company in 1983 as a discount long-distance telephone company. Over the years Ebbers used stock swaps and other techniques to acquire more than seventy other firms. Ebbers's biggest coup was his 1998 takeover of a much bigger company, MCI Communications, the country's second-largest long-distance telephone service provider. At the time the $40 billion deal was the largest corporate merger in U.S. history. That deal and others made WorldCom the world's leading carrier of Internet communications.*

The sagging technology market in 1999 and 2000 put many telecommunications firms in trouble, but WorldCom insisted it was still sound and profitable. The first major sign of trouble came March 11, 2002, when the SEC disclosed that it was investigating business practices at WorldCom, including millions of dollars of loans to Ebbers to cover his stock losses. The company announced on April 3 that it was laying off 3,700 employees (about 6 percent of its workforce) because of a sales slowdown, and the company's stock prices fell by more than one-half during the next several weeks. Ebbers abruptly resigned on April 30, reportedly under pressure from outside board members who were concerned about his debts to the company, estimated at the time at $366 million.

The company on June 25 acknowledged that it had hidden $3.85 billion worth of expenses in 2001, enabling it to post a $1.4 billion net income for the year. That figure seemed gigantic at the time, but it soon paled in comparison to the company's subsequent admissions. WorldCom increased the amount of its error to $7.6 billion on August 8 and to $9 billion on November 5.

The day after WorldCom first admitted its problem, the Securities and Exchange Commission filed suit against the company, alleging the company had fraudulently portrayed itself as a profitable company during 2001 and the first quarter of 2002. It did so, the SEC said, by falsely declaring the $3.85 billion as capital costs rather than as items that should have been levied against its balance sheet. In a statement, the SEC said these actions "were intended to mislead investors and manipulate WorldCom's earnings to keep them in line with estimates by Wall Street analysts." WorldCom's admission of improper bookkeeping and the SEC's suit helped propel corporate reform legislation through Congress early in July.

John Sidgmore, who had taken over from Ebbers as WorldCom chief executive, apologized for the company's problems and promised to cooperate with the continuing SEC investigation: "We want the bad guys exposed and the bad guys punished," he said, without giving any names. WorldCom filed for Chapter 11 bankruptcy protection on July 21, listing $107 billion in assets but saying it did not have enough cash to pay the interest on more than $41 billion in debts. The company's size made it the largest bankruptcy in U.S. history, surpassing Enron's record the previous December.

The SEC complaint and subsequent reporting by news organizations painted a picture of a company whose senior officers were obsessed with boosting the bottom line. In an extensive August 29 report, the Washington

Post *said WorldCom had developed a "grow-at-any-cost culture that made it possible for employees and managers to game the system internally and to deceive investors about the health of the business." Similar criticisms were aired in an independent report prepared by former U.S. attorney general Richard L. Thornburgh. Released November 4, the report said the company used "extraordinary and illegal steps" to conceal its frail financial picture. Thornburgh's report said the company appeared motivated by no apparent strategic vision except maintaining its stock price. Ebbers also used WorldCom to support his lavish lifestyle, leveraging his stock in the company to gain more than $1 billion in business and personal loans.*

The SEC amended its complaint on November 5, adding charges that the company had manipulated its records since at least 1999 to deceive the public about its financial soundness. The commission and the company on November 26 agreed to a settlement in which WorldCom promised to refrain from breaking securities laws, and the SEC postponed its claim for penalties until a later review of WorldCom's future behavior and progress in emerging from bankruptcy. The federal judge in New York City who was handling the case approved the agreement, but it brought objections from some investor groups that WorldCom had not been punished for its wrongdoing.

While these regulatory moves were in motion, WorldCom began the process of trying to reinvent itself as a normal company adhering to normal business rules. The board of directors in November hired as its new chairman and chief executive officer Michael D. Capellas, who had headed Compaq Computers prior to that company's merger earlier in the year with Hewlett-Packard. Capellas's chief task was to get the company out of bankruptcy in a position enabling it to compete in the depressed telecommunications market. Most of the company's remaining directors resigned on December 18 to make way for a new board to be appointed by Capellas and the company's creditors.

The two men generally considered most responsible for WorldCom's problems—former CEO Ebbers and former chief financial officer Scott D. Sullivan—faced uncertain futures as well. Ebbers had not been charged with wrongdoing as of the end of the year, but he almost certainly was liable for the millions of dollars in questionable loans he had received. Sullivan was arrested August 1 after being indicted on fraud charges, to which he pleaded not guilty. His case was pending at year's end. Two other senior officials—Donald F. Myers, the former controller, and Buford Yates Jr., the former director of accounting—pleaded guilty to fraud charges, agreed to testify against Sullivan, and were barred from working again as corporate officers.

Continuing Investigations into Enron

Enron filed for bankruptcy on December 2, 2001, after a series of downward earnings revisions pushed its stock value to less than half the price of a $1 candy bar. Investigations showed that the company's diversified empire was built almost as much on manipulated bookkeeping as on solid *business practices; its uninterrupted string of profitable quarters was the result, in large part, of the creation of off-the-books partnerships that disguised Enron's debts and inflated its revenues.*

The company managed to survive, at least through 2002, by laying off thousands of employees, selling off its most valuable assets, and focusing on what had been its core business—trading in energy futures. Bankruptcy proceedings dragged on all year and were likely to continue well into 2003, with legal and other professional fees costing more than $1 million a day. In addition to the bankruptcy case, Enron faced lawsuits from employees who charged that the company jeopardized their retirement plans, which were heavily invested in Enron stock. (Retirement plans, p. 101)

Enron's chairman and CEO, Kenneth L. Lay, resigned on January 23 but remained as a member of the board for another week before resigning that post, as well. Lay continued to maintain that he had been in the dark about the manipulations that led to the company's downfall. At the end of 2002 federal investigators were continuing a probe into the activities of Lay and his successor as chief executive, Jeffrey K. Skilling, but neither had been charged with any wrongdoing.

Both Lay and Skilling testified before congressional committees in January and February and denied any knowledge of or involvement in improper activities at Enron. Skilling testified that when he left the company in August 2001, a few weeks before it began to unravel, "I honestly, unequivocally thought the company was in good shape." Skilling's denial was rebutted by Sherron S. Watkins, an Enron vice president who had written an internal memorandum in August 2001 warning Lay of serious problems at the firm. A week after receiving that memo Lay sent a message to employees assuring them the company was in good shape. Watkins told the Senate Commerce Committee on February 26 that she believed Skilling must have approved questionable partnerships that were established to make the company's financial performance look better than it really was.

Former chief financial officer Andrew Fastow was indicted on October 30 on seventy-eight felony counts, including securities fraud, mail fraud, wire fraud, money laundering, and conspiracy based on the partnership deals. Fastow allegedly masterminded Enron's complex systems of off-the-book partnerships. In announcing the government charges on October 2, deputy attorney general Larry Thompson said Fastow and his co-conspirators "systematically and thoroughly corrupted the business of one of the largest corporations in the world." Fastow pleaded not guilty. Several lower-level Enron officials agreed to cooperate with an investigation into Fastow's activities, and two officials pleaded guilty to various charges.

Collapse of Arthur Andersen

Enron's survival, even if temporary or in a very reduced form, was better than what happened to its partner in dubious bookkeeping: the Arthur Andersen accounting firm. Widely accused of approving Enron's schemes to inflate its business worth—or at best looking the other way—the Andersen firm lost hundreds of clients early in the year. Former Federal Reserve Board chairman Paul Volcker tried to rescue Andersen but gave up on May 3, saying too many clients and partners had left for the firm to survive.

David Duncan, the firm's lead auditor at Enron, on April 10 pleaded guilty to a single felony charge of obstructing justice, in conjunction with the destruction of documents as Enron was collapsing in late 2001. Duncan was the key witness in a subsequent trial of the accounting firm, which on June 14 was found guilty of obstructing justice. District Court Judge Melinda Harmon on October 16 levied the maximum punishment against the firm: five years probation and a $500,000 fine.

Following its conviction, Andersen closed its auditing practice and most of its U.S. offices. By October only about 1,000 of the firm's 28,000 employees remained. Several of Andersen's key components had been sold to rival accounting firms.

Wall Street Brokerages

During the boom years of the 1990s analysts for Wall Street brokerage firms emerged as some of the most glamorous characters of American business. Touted by employers for their ability to "pick" rising stocks before they rose, analysts who had once labored in obscurity became rich and famous representatives of the boom years. Among the best known were Jack B. Grubman, a specialist in telecommunications firms at Salomon Smith Barney (a division of Citigroup), and Henry Blodget, a specialist in Internet companies at Merrill Lynch & Company. The brokerage firms generated sizable fees by helping companies structure new stock offerings, and their analysts earned fees for promoting stocks that seemed almost guaranteed to soar into the stratosphere.

When the stock market began to fizzle in 2000 and investors discovered that the value of some of the highly promoted companies was based more on hype than reality, the judgments of Wall Street brokerage firms came into question. Investigations, spawned in part by investor complaints, showed that Grubman's bullish ratings of WorldCom and Winstar Communications had almost certainly been influenced by his close relationships with the companies. Grubman resigned his post in August and was given a $30 million severance package by Citigroup. On December 20 Grubman agreed to pay $15 million in fines to settle charges by securities regulators. Grubman still faced civil suits filed by investors who said they had been ruined by his advice.

Blodget was under investigation by state and federal regulators at year's end. New York state attorney general Elliot L. Spitzer, who conducted an intense investigation of Merrill Lynch and other securities firms, released e-mail messages in which Blodget privately had disparaged some of the Internet firms that he was recommending publicly to investors.

Spitzer on May 20 won a settlement in which Merrill Lynch agreed to pay a $100 million civil penalty to settle charges that it had misled investors with what Spitzer called "tainted advice" about company values. Spitzer pursued the issue for the rest of the year and spearheaded negotiations among regulators and the firms for a "global settlement" of conflict-of-interest *charges against major Wall Street brokerage houses. Announced on December 20, the settlement required Wall Street's ten largest firms to pay a total fine of $1.4 billion, some of which would be used to finance independent stock research for investors. As part of the settlement, the firms agreed to several reforms intended to insulate their investment banking operations from their stock analyst functions. Among other things, the firms agreed that stock analysts would no longer be paid according to how much investment business they generated.*

Other Corporate Scandals

Other corporate scandals during the year featured a broad range of misdeeds, including insider trading, the looting of corporate treasuries by senior executives, improper bookkeeping, and questionable accounting practices. In some cases, the primary aim of corporate executives appeared to be personal enrichment; in others, executives engaged in fraudulent practices to make their companies appear much stronger financially than they really were.

Following is a summary of some of the major corporate scandals that emerged during 2002.

- *Tyco International, an industrial conglomerate of dozens of companies, escaped bankruptcy, but its high-flying CEO, Dennis Kozlowski, emerged as the year's most ridiculed poster boy of corporate greed. He resigned on June 3, one day before he was indicted on charges of evading about $1 million in sales taxes on art purchases. Subsequent investigations showed that Kozlowski had raided about $170 million from corporate accounts for his own benefit. His lavish spending put to shame even the $600 toilet seats that had gotten the Pentagon into trouble during the 1980s. Among the personal items financed by company spending were a $16.8 million Fifth Avenue apartment (along with $14 million in furnishings and renovations), a $1 million birthday party on the island of Sardinia for Kozlowski's wife, a $15,000 poodle-shaped French umbrella stand, a $6,000 shower curtain, and a $2,900 set of coat hangers.*

  An independent investigation by Tyco lawyers, reported on December 30, found that the company used numerous accounting gimmicks to improve the appearance of its financial picture. In many cases the company's actions technically fell within accounting industry standards known as "generally accepted accounting principles." Even so, they gave a misleading impression of the company's earnings and made it all but impossible for investors to understand Tyco's true worth, the report said.

  One of the most disturbing findings about Tyco was that its "lead director"—a supposedly independent board member—had solicited the company for a $20 million finder's fee for his role in arranging a business transaction. The director, Frank E. Walsh, pleaded guilty on December 17 to securities fraud and agreed to repay the $20 mil-

lion, plus a $2.5 million fine. He was the first corporate director found guilty of a crime in the year's scandals. Tyco's former chief financial officer and former general counsel also were charged in September with crimes in relation to misdeeds at the company.

- *Adelphia Communications Corp., the nation's sixth-largest cable television provider, filed for Chapter 11 bankruptcy protection on June 25 following the disclosure of more than $2 billion in off-the-books loans made to the company's founder, John J. Rigas, and members of his family. Rigas and his two sons, Michael J. and Timothy J., were arrested on July 24 and charged with bank fraud, securities fraud, and wire fraud. A federal prosecutor said they had used the company, which Rigas founded in 1952 with a $300 investment, as their "personal piggy bank." Adelphia's former vice president of finance, James Brown, in November pleaded guilty to fraud charges and agreed to testify against the Rigas family.*

- *Global Crossing, a telecommunications giant originally based on the Rochester, New York, telephone company, had become one of the country's largest fiber-optics networks. Its rapid growth came to an end with the bursting of the high-tech bubble in 1999–2000, and the company was forced into bankruptcy on January 28. It was the subject of federal investigations of accounting practices, including the use of a technique called "network capacity swaps" with other telecommunications companies—basically phony transactions that enabled the companies to inflate their revenue.*

  Global Crossing chairman Gary Winnick told a congressional committee in October that he could not remember ever having been told about potential problems at the company, which began at least as early as 2001. Despite this denial, Winnick must have learned something; before the company filed for bankruptcy, Winnick sold $734 million in Global Crossing stock. The Justice Department investigated Winnick's stock transactions and other dealings at the firm but announced in December that it would not file criminal charges.

  Two telecommunications companies based in Hong Kong and Singapore purchased Global Crossing's assets in December for about 1 percent of the company's $22 billion declared value. Winnick resigned as chairman on December 30, after placing $25 million in a trust fund for employees who had lost their life savings when the company's stock value collapsed. "You can't take the money with you," he said. "The only legacy I'm going to leave this planet with is my name." He was one of the few senior executives involved in the year's scandals to express serious regret about the losses suffered by employees and investors.

- *IMClone Systems, a biotechnology company, and Martha Stewart, the country's foremost lifestyle expert, became ensnared in the year's most famous scandal involving insider trading. Samuel Waksal, IMClone's CEO, was charged in August with insider trading after he tried to sell his own stock and tipped off family members in December 2001, shortly before the Food and Drug Administration rejected the firm's application for an experimental anticancer drug. Waksal pleaded guilty to six of the thirteen charges on October 15, 2002. In the meantime Stewart, a friend of Waksal's, came under scrutiny because of allegations that she had sold about 4,000 shares of IMClone stock just before the bad news about its drug became public. The SEC notified Stewart in September that it was investigating her for insider trading. Stewart denied any wrongdoing, but on October 3 she resigned as a member of the New York Stock Exchange board of directors, saying she did not want the publicity about her stock dealings to damage the exchange.*

- *President Bush's credibility as an advocate of corporate reform came under question in July when the news media revived reports from earlier years about some of his own practices as a businessman. In a speech on Wall Street on July 9 Bush denounced "company loans to corporate officers." Two days later the Washington Post and other news organizations reported that in 1986 and 1988 Bush had taken two low-interest loans totaling $180,375 from Harken Energy Corporation while serving as a board member of the Texas oil firm. Bush used proceeds from the loans to purchase Harken stock. The loans had been reported to the SEC and had been made public in the past but generated no controversy until the corporate scandals of 2002 drew increased public scrutiny to such practices. Bush also had been investigated in 1991 by the SEC for possible insider trading in relation to his repeated sales of Harken stock just before it fell on the markets. The SEC closed its case without bringing charges against Bush, an outcome the White House in 2002 portrayed as an exoneration. Bush said the Harken matters had been "fully vetted," but both he and Harken refused to make public the corporate records relating to his deals during his board tenure at the company from 1986 to 1993.*

- *Xerox, for years one of the country's most respected technology companies, fell behind the high-technology curve during the 1990s and had trouble playing catch-up. In April the company paid a $10 million civil fine to settle charges by the Securities and Exchange Commission that it had used various accounting tricks to inflate its pretax profits and thus defraud investors. On June 28 Xerox said it had overstated revenues since 1997 by $1.9 billion.*

- *Jack Welch, former chairman and CEO of the General Electric Co. and perhaps the most celebrated American business leader in recent decades, was caught up in the wave of attention to corporate misdeeds. Court papers filed on September 5 concerning Welch's divorce from his wife revealed that he had continued to receive generous benefits even after his retirement, including the use of a company-owned apartment in Manhattan and a corporate jet. Embarrassed by the disclosure, but insisting he had done nothing wrong, Welch later agreed to pay for his personal use of the apartment and jet.*

- *Executive compensation also emerged as a public issue. Numerous examples of excessive greed at major corporations focused unprecedented attention during the year on salaries and other payments for executives. The year's most controversial item was the increasingly widespread practice of companies using stock options to reward their executives. Stock options offered advantages to both parties: an executive got a chance to buy company stock at a low price after it had risen, and under current accounting rules the company did not have to report stock options as compensation, thus avoiding a charge against its balance sheet. The downside was that stock options gave executives an extra incentive to spruce up short-term profits so that stock values would rise—and some executives gave into the temptation to accomplish this with misleading or even false financial statements. Some members of Congress and Federal Reserve chairman Greenspan called for a halt to the practice, but Congress took no action to control stock options. A few companies, the largest of which was Coca Cola, announced that they would report stock options as expenses in the future.*

Following are excerpts from Securities and Exchange Commission v. WorldCom, Inc., a civil action complaint filed on June 26, 2002, in the U.S. District Court for the Southern District of New York, alleging fraudulent business practices at the company; and a November 26, 2002, news release by the SEC announcing a partial settlement of its case against WorldCom.

The documents were obtained from the Internet at www .sec.gov/litigation/complaints/complr17588.htm; accessed February 8, 2002.

SEC CIVIL COMPLAINT

The Securities and Exchange Commission ("the Commission") alleges for its Complaint as follows:

1. From at least the first quarter of 2001 through the first quarter of 2002, defendant WorldCom Inc. ("WorldCom") defrauded investors. In a scheme directed and approved by its senior management, WorldCom disguised its true operating performance by using undisclosed and improper accounting that materially overstated its income before income taxes and minority interests by approximately $3.055 billion in 2001 and $797 million during the first quarter of 2002.

2. By improperly transferring certain costs to its capital accounts, WorldCom falsely portrayed itself as a profitable business during 2001 and the first quarter of 2002. WorldCom's transfer of its costs to its capital accounts violated the established standards of generally accepted accounting principles

("GAAP"). WorldCom's improper transfer of certain costs to its capital accounts was not disclosed to investors in a timely fashion, and misled investors about WorldCom's reported earnings. This improper accounting action was intended to manipulate WorldCom's earnings in the year ending 2001 and in the first quarter of 2002 to keep them in line with estimates by Wall Street analysts.

3. By engaging in this conduct, WorldCom violated the anti-fraud and reporting provisions of the federal securities laws and, unless restrained and enjoined by this Court, will continue to do so. The Commission requests, among other things, that WorldCom be enjoined from further violations of the federal securities laws as alleged herein, and that it pay a monetary penalty.

The Fraudulent Scheme

4. WorldCom is a major global communications provider, operating in more than 65 countries. WorldCom provides data transmission and Internet services for businesses, and, through its MCI unit, provides telecommunications services for businesses and consumers. WorldCom became an important player in the telecommunications industry in the 1990s. However, as the economy cooled in 2001, WorldCom's earnings and profits similarly declined, making it difficult to keep WorldCom's earnings in line with expectations by industry analysts.

5. Starting at least in 2001, WorldCom engaged in an improper accounting scheme intended to manipulate its earnings to keep them in line with Wall Street's expectations, and to support WorldCom's stock price. One of WorldCom's major operating expenses was its so-called "line costs." In general, "line costs" represent fees WorldCom paid to third party telecommunication network providers for the right to access the third parties' networks. Under GAAP, these fees must be expensed and may not be capitalized. Nevertheless, beginning at least as early as the first quarter of 2001, WorldCom's senior management improperly directed the transfer of line costs to WorldCom's capital accounts in amounts sufficient to keep WorldCom's earnings in line with the analysts' consensus on WorldCom's earnings. Thus, in this manner, WorldCom materially understated its expenses, and materially overstated its earnings, thereby defrauding investors.

6. As a result of this improper accounting scheme, WorldCom materially underreported its expenses and materially overstated its earnings in its filings with the Commission, specifically, on its Form 10-K for the fiscal year ending on December 31, 2001, and on its Form 10-Q for the quarter ending on March 31, 2002.

7. In particular, WorldCom reported on its Consolidated Statement of Operations contained in its 2001 Form 10-K that its line costs for 2001 totaled $14.739 billion, and that its earnings before income taxes and minority interests totaled $2.393 billion, whereas, in truth and in fact, WorldCom's line costs for that period totaled approximately $17.794 billion, and it suffered a loss of approximately $662 million.

8. Further, WorldCom reported on its Consolidated Statement of Operations contained in its Form 10-Q for the first quarter of 2002 that its line costs

for that quarter totaled $3.479 billion, and that its income before income taxes and minority interests totaled $240 million, whereas, in truth and in fact, WorldCom's line costs for that period totaled approximately $4.276 billion and it suffered a loss of approximately $557 million.

9. WorldCom's disclosures in its 2001 Form 10-K and in its Form 10-Q for the first quarter of 2002 failed to include material facts necessary to make the statements made in light of the circumstances in which they were made not misleading. In particular, these filings failed to disclose the company's accounting treatment of its line costs, that such treatment had changed from prior periods, and that the company's line costs were actually increasing substantially as a percentage of its revenues. . . .

SEC NEWS RELEASE

The Securities and Exchange Commission announced that a judgment of permanent injunction was entered today in its pending civil enforcement action against WorldCom, Inc. This judgment settles part, but not all, of the Commission's action against WorldCom.

The judgment, signed by U.S. District Judge Jed S. Rakoff of the Southern District of New York: (1) imposes the full injunctive relief sought by the Commission, (2) orders an extensive review of the company's corporate governance systems, policies, plans, and practices, (3) orders an extensive review of the company's internal accounting control structure and policies, (4) orders that WorldCom provide reasonable training and education to certain officers and employees to minimize the possibility of future violations of the federal securities laws, and (5) provides that civil money penalties, if any, will be decided by the Court at a later date. The court reaffirmed the role of its appointed Corporate Monitor and retained jurisdiction for all purposes, including the imposition of further equitable relief and sanctions as may be determined following a hearing. WorldCom consented, without admitting or denying the allegations in the Commission's complaint, to the entry of the judgment.

The Commission's investigation into matters related to WorldCom's financial fraud is continuing.

The Commission's amended complaint alleges that WorldCom misled investors from at least as early as 1999 through the first quarter of 2002, and further states that the company has acknowledged that during that period, as a result of undisclosed and improper accounting, WorldCom materially overstated the income it reported on its financial statements by approximately $9 billion.

The judgment entered today enjoins WorldCom from violating the antifraud provisions of the federal securities laws (specifically, Section 17(a) of the Securities Act of 1933, Section 10(b) of the Securities Exchange Act of 1934 ("Exchange Act"), and Exchange Act Rule 10b-5), the reporting provisions (Section 13(a) of the Exchange Act and Rules 13a-1, 13a-13 and 12b-20 thereunder), and the books and records and internal controls provisions (Sections 13(b)(2)(A) and 13(b)(2)(B) of the Exchange Act).

The judgment further orders that the report currently being prepared by WorldCom's Special Investigative Committee be transmitted to the Corporate Monitor, Richard Breeden, upon its completion, and that Mr. Breeden shall then review the adequacy and effectiveness of WorldCom's corporate governance systems, policies, plans, and practices. This review will include but is not limited to inquiries into (1) whether WorldCom is complying with recognized standards of "best practices" with respect to corporate governance; (2) whether WorldCom has sufficient policies and safeguards in place (a) to ensure that WorldCom's Board of Directors and all committees of WorldCom's Board of Directors (including without limitation the audit committee and the compensation committee) have appropriate powers, structure, composition, and resources and (b) to prevent self-dealing by management; (3) whether WorldCom has an adequate and appropriate code of ethics and business conduct, and related compliance mechanisms; and (4) whether WorldCom has appropriate safeguards in place to prevent further violations of the federal securities laws. Following his receipt of the report of the Special Investigative Committee, the Corporate Monitor shall submit to WorldCom's Board of Directors, the Court and the Commission a report setting forth his recommendations with respect to the corporate governance issues he has reviewed. Within 60 days of the receipt of the report of the Corporate Monitor with respect to corporate governance, WorldCom's Board of Directors shall report to the Court and the Commission with respect to the decisions and actions taken as a result of each of the recommendations made by the Corporate Monitor.

The judgment further orders that WorldCom shall retain a qualified consultant, acceptable to the Commission, to perform a review of the effectiveness of WorldCom's material internal accounting control structure and policies, including those related to line costs, reserves, and capital expenditures, as well as the effectiveness and propriety of WorldCom's processes, practices and policies for ensuring that the Company's financial data is accurately reported in its public financial statements. The consultant must, within 30 days, develop a proposal for the review that is acceptable to the Commission. Any disagreements about the proposal will be resolved by the Corporate Monitor. Within 120 days after approval of the proposal, the consultant shall complete its review and submit to WorldCom's Board of Directors, the Court and the Commission, a report fully documenting the findings of its review and making specific recommendations. Within 60 days of the submission of the report, WorldCom's Board of Directors shall report to the Court and Commission with respect to the decisions and actions taken as a result of each of the recommendations made by the consultant.

The judgment further orders that WorldCom shall provide reasonable training and education to certain of its officers and employees to minimize the possibility of future violations of the federal securities laws. Completion of such training shall be mandatory for WorldCom officers and employees involved in its corporate level accounting and financial reporting functions; for those officers and employees involved in financial reporting at WorldCom's major divisions and subsidiaries (including, specifically, those officers and employees responsible for closing the books in their area of responsibility at the end of a quarterly or annual reporting period); and for senior operational officers at WorldCom's corporate, divisional and subsidiary levels. Such training and education shall include, at a minimum, components covering the following subjects: the obligations imposed by the federal securities laws; proper internal accounting controls and procedures; recognizing indications of non-GAAP (generally accepted accounting principles) accounting practices or fraud most relevant to WorldCom's business endeavors; and the obligations incumbent upon, and the responses expected of, WorldCom officers and employees upon learning of illegal or potentially illegal acts concerning the company's accounting and financial reporting. WorldCom shall consult with the Commission in designing its training and education program, and shall submit to the Commission a detailed proposal within 60 days after entry of this judgment, which describes the content and implementation of the training and education program, in a form that is acceptable to the Commission. WorldCom shall commence providing initial training and education sessions within 60 days thereafter, and shall continue to provide such training and education on an annual basis, for a minimum period of three years after entry of this judgment.

The judgment further provides that the amount of the civil penalty, if any, to be paid by WorldCom shall be determined by the Court in light of all the relevant facts and circumstances, following a hearing. At that hearing, the issues will be limited to determining the appropriateness and amount of any such civil penalty, WorldCom will be precluded from arguing that it did not violate the federal securities laws as alleged in the Commission's amended complaint, and the allegations of the complaint will be accepted as true by the Court. . . .

SUPREME COURT ON SCHOOL VOUCHERS
June 27, 2002

In a decision that many observers regarded as the most momentous ruling in decades regarding separation of church and state, the Supreme Court on June 27, 2002, upheld an Ohio voucher plan that used public funds to pay tuition for students at religious schools. The vote was 5–4, and the justices on each side drew usually firm lines in support of their opposing positions.

The decision was a turning point in a decades-long battle between proponents of school choice, who said parents should have the right to determine where their children went to school and to have that choice funded by tax money, and those who argued that the use of public fund to pay for tuition at religious schools violated the constitutional principle calling for the separation of church and state. President George W. Bush, who had supported vouchers during his 2000 presidential campaign, hailed the decision. His secretary of education, Rod Paige, said the "decision lifts the constitutional cloud that has been hanging over school choice programs for years and will open the doors of opportunity to thousands of children who need and deserve the best possible education."

After the decision was announced, spokespersons on both sides agreed that the battle over vouchers would now shift to state legislatures and local school districts. Voucher legislation had been introduced in about two-thirds of the state legislatures before the decision was announced, but the future of vouchers and similar strategies to use public funds to support school choice was far from certain. Like the Supreme Court itself, the American public was deeply divided on the issue. Voters in four states had already rejected voucher plans in statewide referendums, and both the House and Senate had rejected variations on voucher plans.

Some observers suggested that the decision might do more to support President Bush's faith-based initiative than school choice. The Bush initiative would use government funds to support church-based social welfare programs, such as counseling for drug abusers and pregnant teenagers. "If you can have vouchers for parochial school children, you can surely have vouchers for adults who need substance abuse treatment and want to get that treatment from a religious program," Kevin J. Hasson of the Becket Fund for Religious Liberty told the New York Times. *Charles C. Haynes, a senior scholar with the Freedom Forum First Amendment Center in Arlington, Virginia, agreed. "Any kind of voucher arrangements for government grants to religious groups for social services are now certainly going to be seen as not only possible but constitutional." More broadly, Haynes said, "I think this ruling signals that the court does not any longer worry too much that government money may eventually end up with religious institutions. And that is a major change. It may mark a turning point in how the government relates to religion in the United States."*

The Push for Vouchers

Some conservatives and religious leaders had long sought to use public money to pay for tuition at private and religious schools. The initial rationale, first espoused by the libertarian economist Milton Friedman in the mid-1950s, was that education for everyone would be improved if parents were given fixed sums of money—vouchers—that they could use to enroll their children in either public or private schools that met specified academic standards. Initial response to the idea was lukewarm, but it gained in popularity as public discontent with public school systems grew and as conservatives grew stronger politically. The voucher movement received a big boost during the 1980s when President Ronald Reagan endorsed a different school mechanism: tuition tax credits for private schools, including religious schools.

These proposals were opposed on several grounds. Educators, teachers unions, and parents who were satisfied with their children's public schools argued that voucher programs would drain badly needed money from public schools. Some argued that vouchers used at expensive private schools might subsidize wealthy parents who could well afford the tuition but do little to help moderate and low-income parents. But the main argument was that vouchers used to pay tuition at private religious schools amounted to an unconstitutional government subsidy of religion. As Barry Lynn, executive director of Americans United for Separation of Church and State, explained it on numerous occasions, vouchers are "nothing but a direct subsidy of the educational mission of religious denominations. And in the same way that one should not expect taxpayers to support churches, they should not be expected to support church-related educational facilities either."

Those objections were strong enough to defeat most generalized voucher or tuition tax-credit plans. Between 1970 and 2000 voters in five states— California, Colorado, Maryland, Michigan, and Washington—had rejected voucher plans. In 1999 Illinois became the first state to give parents a tax credit for private school tuition. Two other states, Arizona and Pennsylvania, allowed tax credits for donations to groups that provided scholarships to private schools. But voters in Colorado, Oregon, Utah, and the District of Columbia had all rejected tuition tax credit plans.

In the 1990s voucher supporters turned to a new constituency for support—minority parents whose children were attending failing inner-city public schools. Milwaukee became the first city to allow a limited voucher program for inner-city students from low-income families. A constitutional challenge to the plan was rejected by the Wisconsin Supreme Court in 1998, and the U.S. Supreme Court declined to review that decision. In 1999 Florida became the first state to approve a statewide voucher program for students from schools that failed to meet state performance standards and then failed to improve a year afterward.

Help for Students in Failing Schools . . .

The case that came before the Supreme Court, Zelman v. Simmons-Harris, involved a plan devised to help parents of students in the Cleveland, Ohio, school district, which had been taken over by the state in 1995 because many of its schools were failing to meet academic standards set by the state. The plan awarded tuition payments to low-income students to be used at any of a variety of schools, including public charter and magnet schools, as well as private secular and religious schools. As a practical matter, the majority of private schools that participated in the program were religious, and a group of parents challenged the voucher plan as a violation of constitutional pro-hibition on the establishment of religion.

In rejecting that challenge, the Court majority said that indirect govern-ment aid to religious schools of the sort involved in the voucher plan was permissible because the money was given to individuals who then made a "genuine and independent private choice" about where to spend it. The voucher program "permits government aid to reach religious institutions only by way of the deliberate choices of numerous individual recipients," Chief Justice William H. Rehnquist wrote for the majority. "The incidental advancement of a religious mission, or the perceived endorsement of a reli-gious message, is reasonably attributable to the individual recipient, not to the government, whose role ends with the disbursements of benefits."

Rehnquist was joined by Justices Sandra Day O'Connor, Anthony M. Kennedy, Antonin Scalia, and Clarence Thomas. O'Connor, who had been considered the key vote in this case, wrote a concurring opinion in which she fully backed the opinion written by Rehnquist and took great pains to answer each of the points raised by the dissent. Thomas also wrote a force-ful concurring opinion, declaring that vouchers were necessary to rescue minority students from dreadful schools. "The promise of public school edu-cation has failed poor inner-city blacks," Thomas wrote. "If society cannot end racial discrimination, at least it can arm minorities with the educa-tion to defend themselves from some of discrimination's effects." Thomas, the court's only African American, grew up in poverty in Savannah, Geor-gia, and credited the education he received at a Roman Catholic school there for his success.

. . . Or Impermissible Aid for Religious Schools

Writing the main dissent, Justice David H. Souter called the decision a "dramatic departure from basic principle" and "potentially tragic" in that it would force taxpayers to subsidize faiths in which they did not believe and make religion dependent on government. Souter said the majority had abandoned the principle laid down in Everson v. Board of Education *(1947), the first church-state ruling of the modern era, which held that "no tax in any amount, large or small, can be levied to support any religious activities or institutions." The majority, Souter said, misapplied its own standards of neutrality and free choice.*

Justices John Paul Stevens, Stephen G. Breyer, and Ruth Bader Ginsburg joined Souter's dissent. In a separate dissent joined by Souter and Breyer, Stevens argued that neither the plight of the Cleveland schools nor parents' voluntary choice to send their children to religious schools was relevant to the issue of whether it was constitutionally permissible for the state to fund tuition at religious schools. In another dissent joined by Stevens and Souter, Breyer stressed his concern that in a country of many different religious creeds, the decision could create "a form of religiously based conflict potentially harmful to the nation's social fabric."

Reaction

Reaction to the decision was unsurprising. Clint Bolick, vice president of the Institute for Justice, a leading supporter of vouchers, summarized the feeling of many voucher proponents: "This allows the school choice movement to shift from defense to offense." Robert Chase, president of the National Education Association, summed up the opposing side: "Just because the vouchers may be legal in some circumstances doesn't make them a good idea." Both sides agreed, however, that the decision had reinvigorated the voucher movement.

How successful such a campaign would be was problematic. Several state constitutions specifically barred states from giving money to religious schools. Public opinion polls showed that the voters were still divided over the issue. That division was reflected in Congress in 2001, where a pilot voucher program failed by 17 votes in the Senate, while an amendment containing President Bush's voucher plan fell by a wide margin of 118 votes in the House. There was also a question whether vouchers could be large enough to entice schools into the marketplace. The experience in Cleveland indicated that only inner-city Catholic schools with flagging enrollments and low-wage teachers were willing to participate in the program. If that were the case in other localities, the impact of the decision might not be as great as some had hoped.

Marc Stern, the legal director for the American Jewish Congress, said that many local governments that wanted to use vouchers for schools or other social services might find that they could not provide the range of religious and nonreligious choices that would meet the Court's standard of a "true free choice." Stern added that this fact was not likely to discourage those who favor state aid to parochial schools or faith-based programs. "All the caveats are going to be ignored because people don't read opinions. They're just going to see this as a green light," he told the New York Times. *The American Jewish Congress opposed vouchers.*

Another factor might also dampen enthusiasm for voucher programs: several studies cast doubt on their effectiveness. The General Accounting Office (GAO), the investigative arm of Congress, looked at privately funded voucher programs for low-income students in New York City, Washington, D.C., and Dayton, Ohio, and found mixed results. In New York, black students in the program generally did better in math and reading, but Hispanic students showed no improvement. In Washington, black students in the program showed some improvement at first, but by the third year their combined reading and math scores were no different than those of public school students. In Dayton, black students using the vouchers had slightly higher reading scores than their public school counterparts, but the differences were not statistically significant.

Whether their children improved in their academic performance or not, parents of voucher students told the GAO that they were more satisfied with their children's education and the safety of their school. According to the GAO, some 46,000 of the nation's 53 million school-age children participated in privately funded voucher programs. Nearly $60 million in tuition assistance was awarded solely on the basis of family income, and parents were free to decide which schools their children should attend. The report, released in late September, was entitled "School Vouchers: Characteristics of Privately Funded Programs."

In November the Miami Herald *reported that one of every four students who used a voucher to attend a private school in Florida in the fall semester had transferred back to public education. Of the 607 students that had asked for taxpayer-funded vouchers to leave their failing public school, 170 had returned to public school, many of them to their original, failing school. Many students said they were more comfortable at their old school. Some also cited problems with transportation, a more difficult curriculum, and tougher discipline.*

> *Following are excerpts from the majority opinion and a dissenting opinion in the case of* Zelman v. Simmons-Harris, *in which the Supreme Court on June 27, 2002, ruled 5–4 that a state program that allowed government-funded tuition payments to be used at religious schools was not a violation of the First Amendment's prohibition on government establishment of religion.*
>
> **The document was obtained from the Internet at supct.law .cornell.edu/supct/html/00-1751.ZS.html; accessed September 9, 2002.**

Nos. 00–1751, 00–1777, and 00–1779

Zelman, Superintendent of
Public Instruction of Ohio, et al.
v.
Simmons-Harris et al.

On Writs of Certiorari to the
United States Court of Appeals
for the Sixth Circuit

[June 27, 2002]

CHIEF JUSTICE REHNQUIST delivered the opinion of the Court.

The State of Ohio has established a pilot program designed to provide educational choices to families with children who reside in the Cleveland City School District. The question presented is whether this program offends the Establishment Clause of the United States Constitution. We hold that it does not.

There are more than 75,000 children enrolled in the Cleveland City School District. The majority of these children are from low-income and minority families. Few of these families enjoy the means to send their children to any school other than an inner-city public school. For more than a generation, however, Cleveland's public schools have been among the worst performing public schools in the Nation. In 1995, a Federal District Court declared a "crisis of magnitude" and placed the entire Cleveland school district under state control. . . . Shortly thereafter, the state auditor found that Cleveland's public schools were in the midst of a "crisis that is perhaps unprecedented in the history of American education.". . . The district had failed to meet any of the 18 state standards for minimal acceptable performance. Only 1 in 10 ninth graders could pass a basic proficiency examination, and students at all levels performed at a dismal rate compared with students in other Ohio public schools. More than two-thirds of high school students either dropped or failed out before graduation. Of those students who managed to reach their senior year, one of every four still failed to graduate. Of those students who did graduate, few could read, write, or compute at levels comparable to their counterparts in other cities.

It is against this backdrop that Ohio enacted, among other initiatives, its Pilot Project Scholarship Program. . . . The program provides financial assistance to families in any Ohio school district that is or has been "under federal court order requiring supervision and operational management of the district by the state superintendent.". . . Cleveland is the only Ohio school district to fall within that category.

The program provides two basic kinds of assistance to parents of children in a covered district. First, the program provides tuition aid for students in kindergarten through third grade, expanding each year through eighth grade, to attend a participating public or private school of their parent's choosing. . . . Second, the program provides tutorial aid for students who choose to remain enrolled in public school. . . .

The tuition aid portion of the program is designed to provide educational choices to parents who reside in a covered district. Any private school, whether religious or nonreligious, may participate in the program and accept program students so long as the school is located within the boundaries of a covered district and meets statewide educational standards. . . . Participating private schools must agree not to discriminate on the basis of race, religion, or ethnic background, or to "advocate or foster unlawful behavior or teach hatred of any person or group on the basis of race, ethnicity, national origin, or religion.". . . Any public school located in a school district adjacent to the covered district may also participate in the program. . . . Adjacent public schools are eligible to receive a $2,250 tuition grant for each program student accepted in addition to the full amount of per-pupil state funding attributable to each additional student. . . . All participating schools, whether public or private, are required to accept students in accordance with rules and procedures established by the state superintendent. . . .

Tuition aid is distributed to parents according to financial need. Families with incomes below 200% of the poverty line are given priority and are eligible to receive 90% of private school tuition up to $2,250. . . . For these lowest-income families, participating private schools may not charge a parental co-payment greater than $250. . . . For all other families, the program pays 75% of tuition costs, up to $1,875, with no co-payment cap. . . . These families receive tuition aid only if the number of available scholarships exceeds the number of low-income children who choose to participate. Where tuition aid is spent depends solely upon where parents who receive tuition aid choose to enroll their child. If parents choose a private school, checks are made payable to the parents who then endorse the checks over to the chosen school. . . .

The tutorial aid portion of the program provides tutorial assistance through grants to any student in a covered district who chooses to remain in public school. Parents arrange for registered tutors to provide assistance to their children and then submit bills for those services to the State for payment. . . . Students from low-income families receive 90% of the amount charged for such assistance up to $360. All other students receive 75% of that amount. . . . The number of tutorial assistance grants offered to students in a covered district must equal the number of tuition aid scholarships provided to students enrolled at participating private or adjacent public schools. . . .

The program has been in operation within the Cleveland City School District since the 1996–1997 school year. In the 1999–2000 school year, 56 private schools participated in the program, 46 (or 82%) of which had a religious affiliation. None of the public schools in districts adjacent to Cleveland have elected to participate. More than 3,700 students participated in the scholarship program, most of whom (96%) enrolled in religiously affiliated schools. Sixty percent of these students were from families at or below the poverty line. In the 1998–1999 school year, approximately 1,400 Cleveland public school students received tutorial aid. This number was expected to double during the 1999–2000 school year.

The program is part of a broader undertaking by the State to enhance the educational options of Cleveland's schoolchildren in response to the 1995 takeover. That undertaking includes programs governing community and magnet schools. Community schools are funded under state law but are run by their own school boards, not by local school districts. . . . These schools enjoy academic independence to hire their own teachers and to determine their own curriculum. They can have no religious affiliation and are required to accept students by lottery. During the 1999–2000 school year, there were 10 start-up community schools in the Cleveland City School District with more than 1,900 students enrolled. For each child enrolled in a community school, the school receives state funding of $4,518, twice the funding a participating program school may receive.

Magnet schools are public schools operated by a local school board that emphasize a particular subject area, teaching method, or service to students. For each student enrolled in a magnet school, the school district receives $7,746, including state funding of $4,167, the same amount received per student enrolled at a traditional public school. As of 1999, parents in Cleveland were able to choose from among 23 magnet schools, which together enrolled more than 13,000 students in kindergarten through eighth grade. These schools provide specialized teaching methods, such as Montessori, or a particularized curriculum focus, such as foreign language, computers, or the arts. . . .

In July 1999, respondents filed this action in United States District Court, seeking to enjoin the reenacted program on the ground that it violated the Establishment Clause of the United States Constitution. . . . In December 1999, the District Court granted summary judgment for respondents. . . . In December 2000, a divided panel of the Court of Appeals affirmed the judgment of the District Court, finding that the program had the "primary effect" of advancing religion in violation of the Establishment Clause. . . . The Court of Appeals stayed its mandate pending disposition in this Court. . . . We granted certiorari . . . and now reverse the Court of Appeals.

The Establishment Clause of the First Amendment, applied to the States through the Fourteenth Amendment, prevents a State from enacting laws that have the "purpose" or "effect" of advancing or inhibiting religion. . . . There is no dispute that the program challenged here was enacted for the valid secular purpose of providing educational assistance to poor children in a demonstrably failing public school system. Thus, the question presented is whether the Ohio program nonetheless has the forbidden "effect" of advancing or inhibiting religion.

To answer that question, our decisions have drawn a consistent distinction between government programs that provide aid directly to religious schools . . . and programs of true private choice, in which government aid reaches religious schools only as a result of the genuine and independent choices of private individuals. . . . While our jurisprudence with respect to the constitutionality of direct aid programs has "changed significantly" over the past two decades, . . . our jurisprudence with respect to true private choice programs has remained consistent and unbroken. Three times we have confronted Establishment Clause challenges to neutral government programs that provide aid directly to a broad class of individuals, who, in turn, direct the aid to religious schools or institutions of their own choosing. Three times we have rejected such challenges. . . .

[The next few paragraphs describe the three cases: *Mueller v. Allen* (1983);*Witters v. Washington Dept. of Servs. For Blind* (1986); and *Zobrest v. Catalina Foothills School Dist.* (1993).]

Mueller, Witters, and Zobrest thus make clear that where a government aid program is neutral with respect to religion, and provides assistance directly to a broad class of citizens who, in turn, direct government aid to religious schools wholly as a result of their own genuine and independent private choice, the program is not readily subject to challenge under the Establishment Clause. A program that shares these features permits government aid to reach religious institutions only by way of the deliberate choices of numerous individual recipients. The incidental advancement of a religious mission, or the perceived endorsement of a religious message, is reasonably attributable to the individual recipient, not to the government, whose role ends with the disbursement of benefits. . . .

We believe that the program challenged here is a program of true private choice, consistent with Mueller, Witters, and Zobrest, and thus constitutional. As was true in those cases, the Ohio program is neutral in all respects toward religion. It is part of a general and multifaceted undertaking by the State of Ohio to provide educational opportunities to the children of a failed school district. It confers educational assistance directly to a broad class of individuals defined without reference to religion, i.e., any parent of a school-age child who resides in the Cleveland City School District. The program permits the participation of all schools within the district, religious or nonreligious. Adjacent public schools also may participate and have a financial incentive to do so. Program benefits are available to participating families on neutral terms, with no reference to religion. The only preference stated anywhere in the program is a preference for low-income families, who receive greater assistance and are given priority for admission at participating schools.

There are no "financial incentive[s]" that "ske[w]" the program toward religious schools. . . . The program here in fact creates financial disincentives for religious schools, with private schools receiving only half the government assistance given to community schools and one-third the assistance given to magnet schools. Adjacent public schools, should any choose to accept program students, are also eligible to receive two to three times the state funding of a private religious school. Families too have a financial disincentive to choose a private religious school over other schools. Parents that choose to participate in the scholarship program and then to enroll their children in a private school (religious or nonreligious) must copay a portion of the school's tuition. Families that choose a community school, magnet school, or traditional public school pay nothing. Although such features of the program are not necessary to its constitutionality, they clearly dispel the claim that the program "creates . . . financial incentive[s] for parents to choose a sectarian school.". . .

Respondents suggest that even without a financial incentive for parents to choose a religious school, the program creates a "public perception that the

State is endorsing religious practices and beliefs.". . . But we have repeatedly recognized that no reasonable observer would think a neutral program of private choice, where state aid reaches religious schools solely as a result of the numerous independent decisions of private individuals, carries with it the imprimatur of government endorsement. . . .

There also is no evidence that the program fails to provide genuine opportunities for Cleveland parents to select secular educational options for their school-age children. Cleveland schoolchildren enjoy a range of educational choices: They may remain in public school as before, remain in public school with publicly funded tutoring aid, obtain a scholarship and choose a religious school, obtain a scholarship and choose a nonreligious private school, enroll in a community school, or enroll in a magnet school. That 46 of the 56 private schools now participating in the program are religious schools does not condemn it as a violation of the Establishment Clause. The Establishment Clause question is whether Ohio is coercing parents into sending their children to religious schools, and that question must be answered by evaluating all options Ohio provides Cleveland schoolchildren, only one of which is to obtain a program scholarship and then choose a religious school.

JUSTICE SOUTER speculates that because more private religious schools currently participate in the program, the program itself must somehow discourage the participation of private nonreligious schools. . . . But Cleveland's preponderance of religiously affiliated private schools certainly did not arise as a result of the program; it is a phenomenon common to many American cities. . . . To attribute constitutional significance to this figure, moreover, would lead to the absurd result that a neutral school-choice program might be permissible in some parts of Ohio, such as Columbus, where a lower percentage of private schools are religious schools, . . . but not in inner-city Cleveland, where Ohio has deemed such programs most sorely needed, but where the preponderance of religious schools happens to be greater. . . .

Respondents and JUSTICE SOUTER claim that even if we do not focus on the number of participating schools that are religious schools, we should attach constitutional significance to the fact that 96% of scholarship recipients have enrolled in religious schools. They claim that this alone proves parents lack genuine choice, even if no parent has ever said so. We need not consider this argument in detail, since it was flatly rejected in Mueller. . . . The constitutionality of a neutral educational aid program simply does not turn on whether and why, in a particular area, at a particular time, most private schools are run by religious organizations, or most recipients choose to use the aid at a religious school. . . .

This point is aptly illustrated here. The 96% figure upon which respondents and JUSTICE SOUTER rely discounts entirely (1) the more than 1,900 Cleveland children enrolled in alternative community schools, (2) the more than 13,000 children enrolled in alternative magnet schools, and (3) the more than 1,400 children enrolled in traditional public schools with tutorial assistance. . . . Including some or all of these children in the denominator of children enrolled in nontraditional schools during the 1999–2000 school year drops the percentage enrolled in religious schools from 96% to under 20%. . . .

415

In sum, the Ohio program is entirely neutral with respect to religion. It provides benefits directly to a wide spectrum of individuals, defined only by financial need and residence in a particular school district. It permits such individuals to exercise genuine choice among options public and private, secular and religious. The program is therefore a program of true private choice. In keeping with an unbroken line of decisions rejecting challenges to similar programs, we hold that the program does not offend the Establishment Clause.

The judgment of the Court of Appeals is reversed.

It is so ordered.

JUSTICE SOUTER, with whom JUSTICE STEVENS, JUSTICE GINSBURG, and JUSTICE BREYER join, dissenting.

The Court's majority holds that the Establishment Clause is no bar to Ohio's payment of tuition at private religious elementary and middle schools under a scheme that systematically provides tax money to support the schools' religious missions. The occasion for the legislation thus upheld is the condition of public education in the city of Cleveland. The record indicates that the schools are failing to serve their objective, and the vouchers in issue here are said to be needed to provide adequate alternatives to them. If there were an excuse for giving short shrift to the Establishment Clause, it would probably apply here. But there is no excuse. Constitutional limitations are placed on government to preserve constitutional values in hard cases, like these. . . . I therefore respectfully dissent.

The applicability of the Establishment Clause1 to public funding of benefits to religious schools was settled in *Everson v. Board of Ed. of Ewing* . . . (1947), which inaugurated the modern era of establishment doctrine. The Court stated the principle in words from which there was no dissent:

> "No tax in any amount, large or small, can be levied to support any religious activities or institutions, whatever they may be called, or whatever form they may adopt to teach or practice religion.". . .

The Court has never in so many words repudiated this statement, let alone, in so many words, overruled Everson.

Today, however, the majority holds that the Establishment Clause is not offended by Ohio's Pilot Project Scholarship Program, under which students may be eligible to receive as much as $2,250 in the form of tuition vouchers transferable to religious schools. In the city of Cleveland the overwhelming proportion of large appropriations for voucher money must be spent on religious schools if it is to be spent at all, and will be spent in amounts that cover almost all of tuition. The money will thus pay for eligible students' instruction not only in secular subjects but in religion as well, in schools that can fairly be characterized as founded to teach religious doctrine and to imbue teaching in all subjects with a religious dimension. Public tax money will pay at a systemic level for teaching the covenant with Israel and Mosaic law in Jewish schools, the primacy of the Apostle Peter and the Papacy in Catholic schools, the truth of reformed Christianity in Protestant schools, and the revelation to the Prophet in Muslim schools, to speak only of major religious groupings in the Republic.

How can a Court consistently leave Everson on the books and approve the Ohio vouchers? The answer is that it cannot. It is only by ignoring Everson that the majority can claim to rest on traditional law in its invocation of neutral aid provisions and private choice to sanction the Ohio law. It is, moreover, only by ignoring the meaning of neutrality and private choice themselves that the majority can even pretend to rest today's decision on those criteria.

I

The majority's statements of Establishment Clause doctrine cannot be appreciated without some historical perspective on the Court's announced limitations on government aid to religious education, and its repeated repudiation of limits previously set. My object here is not to give any nuanced exposition of the cases, . . . but to set out the broad doctrinal stages covered in the modern era, and to show that doctrinal bankruptcy has been reached today.

Viewed with the necessary generality, the cases can be categorized in three groups. In the period from 1947 to 1968, the basic principle of no aid to religion through school benefits was unquestioned. Thereafter for some 15 years, the Court termed its efforts as attempts to draw a line against aid that would be divertible to support the religious, as distinct from the secular, activity of an institutional beneficiary. Then, starting in 1983, concern with divertibility was gradually lost in favor of approving aid in amounts unlikely to afford substantial benefits to religious schools, when offered evenhandedly without regard to a recipient's religious character, and when channeled to a religious institution only by the genuinely free choice of some private individual. Now, the three stages are succeeded by a fourth, in which the substantial character of government aid is held to have no constitutional significance, and the espoused criteria of neutrality in offering aid, and private choice in directing it, are shown to be nothing but examples of verbal formalism.

[Sections A, B, and C, in which Souter reviews the development of establishment clause doctrine since the Everson case in 1947, are omitted.]

II

Although it has taken half a century since Everson to reach the majority's twin standards of neutrality and free choice, the facts show that, in the majority's hands, even these criteria cannot convincingly legitimize the Ohio scheme.

A

Consider first the criterion of neutrality. As recently as two Terms ago, a majority of the Court recognized that neutrality conceived of as evenhandedness toward aid recipients had never been treated as alone sufficient to satisfy the Establishment Clause. . . . But at least in its limited significance, formal neutrality seemed to serve some purpose. Today, however, the majority employs the neutrality criterion in a way that renders it impossible to understand.

Neutrality in this sense refers, of course, to evenhandedness in setting eligibility as between potential religious and secular recipients of public money. . . .

In order to apply the neutrality test, then, it makes sense to focus on a category of aid that may be directed to religious as well as secular schools, and ask whether the scheme favors a religious direction. Here, one would ask whether the voucher provisions, allowing for as much as $2,250 toward private school tuition (or a grant to a public school in an adjacent district), were written in a way that skewed the scheme toward benefiting religious schools.

This, however, is not what the majority asks. The majority looks not to the provisions for tuition vouchers, . . . but to every provision for educational opportunity. . . . The majority then finds confirmation that "participation of all schools" satisfies neutrality by noting that the better part of total state educational expenditure goes to public schools, . . . thus showing there is no favor of religion.

The illogic is patent. If regular, public schools (which can get no voucher payments) "participate" in a voucher scheme with schools that can, and public expenditure is still predominantly on public schools, then the majority's reasoning would find neutrality in a scheme of vouchers available for private tuition in districts with no secular private schools at all. "Neutrality" as the majority employs the term is, literally, verbal and nothing more. This, indeed, is the only way the majority can gloss over the very nonneutral feature of the total scheme covering "all schools": public tutors may receive from the State no more than $324 per child to support extra tutoring . . . whereas the tuition voucher schools (which turn out to be mostly religious) can receive up to $2,250. . . .

Why the majority does not simply accept the fact that the challenge here is to the more generous voucher scheme and judge its neutrality in relation to religious use of voucher money seems very odd. It seems odd, that is, until one recognizes that comparable schools for applying the criterion of neutrality are also the comparable schools for applying the other majority criterion, whether the immediate recipients of voucher aid have a genuinely free choice of religious and secular schools to receive the voucher money. And in applying this second criterion, the consideration of "all schools" is ostensibly helpful to the majority position.

B

The majority addresses the issue of choice the same way it addresses neutrality, by asking whether recipients or potential recipients of voucher aid have a choice of public schools among secular alternatives to religious schools. Again, however, the majority asks the wrong question and misapplies the criterion. The majority has confused choice in spending scholarships with choice from the entire menu of possible educational placements, most of them open to anyone willing to attend a public school. I say "confused" because the majority's new use of the choice criterion, which it frames negatively as "whether Ohio is coercing parents into sending their children to religious schools,". . . ignores the reason for having a private choice enquiry in the first place. Cases since Mueller have found private choice relevant under a rule that aid to religious schools can be permissible so long as it first passes through the hands of students or parents. The majority's view that all educational choices are comparable for purposes of choice thus ignores the whole point of the choice test: it is a criterion for deciding whether indirect aid to a religious school is legitimate because it passes through private hands that can spend or use the aid in a secular school. The question is whether the private hand is genuinely free to send the money in either a secular direction or a religious one. The majority now has transformed this question about private choice in channeling aid into a question about selecting from examples of state spending (on education) including direct spending on magnet and community public schools that goes through no private hands and could never reach a religious school under any circumstance. When the choice test is transformed from where to spend the money to where to go to school, it is cut loose from its very purpose.

Defining choice as choice in spending the money or channeling the aid is, moreover, necessary if the choice criterion is to function as a limiting principle at all. If "choice" is present whenever there is any educational alternative to the religious school to which vouchers can be endorsed, then there will always be a choice and the voucher can always be constitutional, even in a system in which there is not a single private secular school as an alternative to the religious school. . . . And because it is unlikely that any participating private religious school will enroll more pupils than the generally available public system, it will be easy to generate numbers suggesting that aid to religion is not the significant intent or effect of the voucher scheme. . . .

If, contrary to the majority, we ask the right question about genuine choice to use the vouchers, the answer shows that something is influencing choices in a way that aims the money in a religious direction: of 56 private schools in the district participating in the voucher program (only 53 of which accepted voucher students in 1999–2000), 46 of them are religious; 96.6% of all voucher recipients go to religious schools, only 3.4% to nonreligious ones. . . . Unfortunately for the majority position, there is no explanation for this that suggests the religious direction results simply from free choices by parents. One answer to these statistics, for example, which would be consistent with the genuine choice claimed to be operating, might be that 96.6% of families choosing to avail themselves of vouchers choose to educate their children in schools of their own religion. This would not, in my view, render the scheme constitutional, but it would speak to the majority's choice criterion. Evidence shows, however, that almost two out of three families using vouchers to send their children to religious schools did not embrace the religion of those schools. . . . The families made it clear they had not chosen the schools because they wished their children to be proselytized in a religion not their own, or in any religion, but because of educational opportunity.

Even so, the fact that some 2,270 students chose to apply their vouchers to schools of other religions . . . might be consistent with true choice if the students "chose" their religious schools over a wide array of private nonreligious options, or if it could be shown generally that Ohio's program had no effect on educational choices and thus no impermissible effect of advancing religious education. But both possibilities are contrary to fact. First, even if all existing nonreligious private schools in Cleveland were willing to accept large numbers of voucher students, only a few more than the 129 currently enrolled in such schools would be able to attend, as the total enrollment at all nonreligious private schools in Cleveland for kindergarten through eighth grade is only 510 children, . . . and there is no indication that these schools have many open seats. Second, the $2,500 cap that the program places on tuition for participating low-income pupils has the effect of curtailing the participation of nonreligious schools: "nonreligious schools with higher tuition (about $4,000) stated that they could afford to accommodate just a few voucher students." By comparison, the average tuition at participating Catholic schools in Cleveland in 1999–2000 was $1,592, almost $1,000 below the cap.

There is, in any case, no way to interpret the 96.6% of current voucher money going to religious schools as reflecting a free and genuine choice by the families that apply for vouchers. The 96.6% reflects, instead, the fact that too few nonreligious school desks are available and few but religious schools can afford to accept more than a handful of voucher students. And contrary to the majority's assertion, . . . public schools in adjacent districts hardly have a financial incentive to participate in the Ohio voucher program, and none has. For the overwhelming number of children in the voucher scheme, the only alternative to the public schools is religious. And it is entirely irrelevant that the State did not deliberately design the network of private schools for the sake of channeling money into religious institutions. The criterion is one of genuinely free choice on the part of the private individuals who choose, and a Hobson's choice is not a choice, whatever the reason for being Hobsonian.

III

I do not dissent merely because the majority has misapplied its own law, for even if I assumed arguendo that the majority's formal criteria were satisfied on the facts, today's conclusion would be profoundly at odds with the Constitution. Proof of this is clear on two levels. The first is circumstantial, in the now discarded symptom of violation, the substantial dimension of the aid. The second is direct, in the defiance of every objective supposed to be served by the bar against establishment.

A

The scale of the aid to religious schools approved today is unprecedented, both in the number of dollars and in the proportion of systemic school expenditure supported. Each measure has received attention in previous cases. On one hand, the sheer quantity of aid, when delivered to a class of religious primary and secondary schools, was suspect on the theory that the greater the aid, the greater its proportion to a religious school's existing expenditures, and the greater the likelihood that public money was supporting religious as well as secular instruction. As we said in Meek, "it would simply ignore reality to attempt to separate secular educational functions from the predominantly religious role" as the object of aid that comes in "substantial amounts.". . . . Conversely, the more "attenuated [the] financial benefit . . . that eventually flows to parochial schools," the more the Court has been willing to find a form of state aid permissible. . . .

On the other hand, the Court has found the gross amount unhelpful for Establishment Clause analysis when the aid afforded a benefit solely to one individual, however substantial as to him, but only an incidental benefit to the religious school at which the individual chose to spend the State's money. . . . When neither the design nor the implementation of an aid scheme channels a series of individual students' subsidies toward religious recipients, the relevant beneficiaries for establishment purposes, the Establishment Clause is unlikely to be implicated. The majority's reliance on the observations of five Members of the Court in Witters as to the irrelevance of substantiality of aid in that case, . . . is therefore beside the point in the matter before us, which involves considerable sums of public funds systematically distributed through thousands of students attending religious elementary and middle schools in the city of Cleveland.

The Cleveland voucher program has cost Ohio taxpayers $33 million since its implementation in 1996 ($28 million in voucher payments, $5 million in administrative costs), and its cost was expected to exceed $8 million in the 2001–2002 school year. . . . These tax-raised funds are on top of the textbooks, reading and math tutors, laboratory equipment, and the like that Ohio provides to private schools, worth roughly $600 per child. . . .

The gross amounts of public money contributed are symptomatic of the scope of what the taxpayers' money buys for a broad class of religious-school students. In paying for practically the full amount of tuition for thousands of qualifying students, the scholarships purchase everything that tuition purchases, be it instruction in math or indoctrination in faith. The consequences of "substantial" aid hypothesized in Meek are realized here: the majority makes no pretense that substantial amounts of tax money are not systematically underwriting religious practice and indoctrination.

B

It is virtually superfluous to point out that every objective underlying the prohibition of religious establishment is betrayed by this scheme, but something has to be said about the enormity of the violation. [The first of these objectives is] respect for freedom of conscience. Jefferson described it as the idea that no one "shall be compelled to . . . support any religious worship, place, or ministry whatsoever,". . . even a "teacher of his own religious persuasion,". . . and Madison thought it violated by any " 'authority which can force a citizen to contribute three pence . . . of his property for the support of any . . . establishment.' ". . .

As for the second objective, to save religion from its own corruption, Madison wrote of the " 'experience . . . that ecclesiastical establishments, instead of maintaining the purity and efficacy of Religion, have had a contrary operation.' ". . . In Madison's time, the manifestations were "pride and indolence in the Clergy; ignorance and servility in the laity[,] in both, superstition, bigotry and persecution,". . . ; in the 21st century, the risk is one of "corrosive secularism" to religious schools, . . . and the specific threat is to the primacy of the schools' mission to educate the children of the faithful according to the unaltered precepts of their faith. . . .

The risk is already being realized. In Ohio, for example, a condition of receiving government money under the program is that participating religious schools may not "discriminate on the basis of . . . religion,". . . which means the school may not give admission preferences to children who are members of the patron faith; children of a parish are generally consigned to the same admission lotteries as non-believers. . . . Nor is the State's religious antidiscrimination restriction limited to student admission policies: by its terms, a participating religious school may well be forbidden to choose a member of its own clergy to serve as teacher or principal over a layperson of a different religion claiming equal qualification for the job. . . . Indeed, a separate condition that "[t]he school . . . not . . . teach hatred of any person or group on the basis of . . . religion,". . . could be understood (or subsequently broadened) to prohibit religions from teaching traditionally legitimate articles of faith as to the error, sinfulness, or ignorance of others, if they want government money for their schools.

For perspective on this foot-in-the-door of religious regulation, it is well to remember that the money has barely begun to flow. Prior examples of aid, whether grants through individuals or in-kind assistance, were never significant enough to alter the basic fiscal structure of religious schools; state aid was welcome, but not indispensable. . . . But given the figures already involved here, there is no question that religious schools in Ohio are on the way to becoming bigger businesses with budgets enhanced to fit their new stream of tax-raised income. . . .

When government aid goes up, so does reliance on it; the only thing likely to go down is independence. If Justice Douglas in *Allen* was concerned with state agencies, influenced by powerful religious groups, choosing the textbooks that parochial schools would use, . . . how much more is there reason to wonder when dependence will become great enough to give the State of Ohio an effective veto over basic decisions on the content of curriculums? A day will come when religious schools will learn what political leverage can do, just as Ohio's politicians are now getting a lesson in the leverage exercised by religion.

Increased voucher spending is not, however, the sole portent of growing regulation of religious practice in the school, for state mandates to moderate religious teaching may well be the most obvious response to the third concern behind the ban on establishment, its inextricable link with social conflict. . . . As appropriations for religious subsidy rise, competition for the money will tap sectarian religion's capacity for discord. . . .

JUSTICE BREYER has addressed this issue in his own dissenting opinion, which I join, and here it is enough to say that the intensity of the expectable friction can be gauged by realizing that the scramble for money will energize not only contending sectarians, but taxpayers who take their liberty of conscience seriously. Religious teaching at taxpayer expense simply cannot be cordoned from taxpayer politics, and every major religion currently espouses social positions that provoke intense opposition. Not all taxpaying Protestant citizens, for example, will be content to underwrite the teaching of the Roman Catholic Church condemning the death penalty. Nor will all of America's Muslims acquiesce in paying for the endorsement of the religious Zionism taught in many religious Jewish schools, which combines "a nationalistic sentiment" in support of Israel with a "deeply religious" element. Nor will every secular taxpayer be content to support Muslim views on differential treatment of the sexes, or, for that matter, to fund the espousal of a wife's obligation of obedience to her husband, presumably taught in any schools adopting the articles of faith of the Southern Baptist Convention. Views like these, and innumerable others, have been safe in the sectarian pulpits and classrooms of this Nation not only because the Free Exercise Clause protects them directly, but because the ban on supporting religious establishment has protected free exercise, by keeping it relatively private. With the arrival of vouchers in religious schools, that privacy will go, and along with it will go confidence that religious disagreement will stay moderate.

* * *

If the divisiveness permitted by today's majority is to be avoided in the short term, it will be avoided only by action of the political branches at the state and national levels. Legislatures not driven to desperation by the problems of public education may be able to see the threat in vouchers negotiable in sectarian schools. Perhaps even cities with problems like Cleveland's will perceive the danger, now that they know a federal court will not save them from it.

My own course as a judge on the Court cannot, however, simply be to hope that the political branches will save us from the consequences of the majority's decision. Everson's statement is still the touchstone of sound law, even though the reality is that in the matter of educational aid the Establishment Clause has largely been read away. True, the majority has not approved vouchers for religious schools alone, or aid earmarked for religious instruction. But no scheme so clumsy will ever get before us, and in the cases that we may see, like these, the Establishment Clause is largely silenced. I do not have the option to leave it silent, and I hope that a future Court will reconsider today's dramatic departure from basic Establishment Clause principle.

SUPREME COURT ON
STUDENT DRUG TESTING
June 27, 2002

A divided Supreme Court ruled June 27, 2002, that a public school district's policy requiring students to undergo random drug testing as a condition for participating in extracurricular activities was not unconstitutional under the Fourth Amendment's prohibition against unreasonable searches and seizures. The ruling, which expanded a 1995 decision limiting such testing to school athletes, had potentially broad implications for the nation's 14,700 public school districts, which could decide to adopt similar policies. Several experts, including at least one of the dissenting justices, said the decision opened the door to blanket testing of all 24 million students in public middle and high schools, whether or not there was a suspicion that a student might be using drugs.

Many parents, educators, and school authorities hailed the decision as an important victory in the war against drugs. According to one respected national survey, more than half of all high school seniors and about one-quarter of all eighth graders had tried marijuana or some other illicit drug. The ruling "is a victory for common sense, and our schools will be safer as a result," said David Evans of the Drug-Free Schools Coalition.

Others said the ruling was most likely counterproductive because the prospect of having to take a drug test could discourage students from joining after-school activities. "Every available study demonstrates that the single best way to prevent drug use among students is to engage them in extracurricular activities," said Graham Boyd, an attorney for the American Civil Liberties Union (ACLU) who argued the case against testing before the Supreme Court. One study, for example, found that tenth-grade students who did not participate in after-school activities were 49 percent more likely to become drug users than students who spent one to four hours a week in extracurricular activities. Meanwhile, others said that the ruling could teach students a perverse lesson. "Drug testing presumes all students are criminals unless they can prove their innocence by producing a clean urine sample. What kind of a civics lesson is that?" asked Joe Cook, executive director of the ACLU of Louisiana.

Expanding a 1995 Ruling

The case began in Tecumseh, Oklahoma, a rural town about forty miles southeast of Oklahoma City. In 1998 the school district approved a random drug-testing policy for all middle and high school students. The only students who were tested were those who participated in interscholastic extracurricular activities, including sports, choir, Future Homemakers of America, band, and the Academic Team. To participate, students were required to take a drug test before joining and then submit to random testing at other times. Any student who refused to take the test or who tested positive more than twice could be barred from extracurricular activities for the rest of the year but would not be expelled or turned over to authorities for prosecution.

The suit challenging the law was brought by Lindsay Earls, a choir and band member and a member of the Academic Team, and another student Daniel James, who wanted to join the Academic Team. Earls, who tested negative for drugs, said that the testing invaded her privacy and that she found it humiliating to urinate into a cup in a bathroom stall with a teacher waiting outside to ensure she did not cheat. "The potential that four or five kids may use drugs is not a good enough reason to invade the privacy of all the others kids," Earls told the Washington Post.

The Tecumseh policy was broader than the student drug-testing policy upheld by the Supreme Court in 1995 in the case of Vernonia School District 47J v. Acton. *In that case, the Court ruled, 6–3, that a school district's random drug testing of middle and high school athletes was a reasonable search under the Fourth Amendment. The majority found that athletes, used to communal locker rooms, did not have the same expectation of privacy as other students; that the testing itself had only a negligible effect on students' privacy; and that athletes using drugs were a danger to themselves and others. The school's interest in detecting and preventing drug abuse among its athletes was therefore a reasonable search in furtherance of the school district's responsibilities as "guardian and tutor of the children entrusted to its care."* (Vernonia case, Historic Documents of 1995, p. 339)

A federal district court upheld the Tecumseh drug-testing program, but the Court of Appeals for the Tenth Circuit struck it down, arguing that the school district had failed to show that there was an identifiable drug problem that warranted the suspicionless drug testing.

Oral arguments before the Supreme Court on March 19 in the case of Board of Education of Independent School District No. 92 of Pottawatomie County v. Earls *were fairly testy and hinted at the eventual 5–4 vote in favor of the policy. When Earls's attorney sought to differentiate between athletes who played in potentially dangerous sports like football from choir members, Justice Antonin Scalia suggested that the attorney was trivializing the problem of drug abuse. "Do you think life and death are not involved in the fight against drugs?" he asked. Justice Stephen G. Breyer suggested that random drug testing might be no different from the metal detectors many schools used to detect guns and other weapons or even from the throat swabs a school might use to test for contagious disease.*

Justice Sandra Day O'Connor, who along with Justices John Paul Stevens and David H. Souter dissented in Vernonia, *said it was "odd to penalize" those students who joined activities such as choir and were less likely than others to be on drugs. Souter warned that the school's policy could eventually lead to testing all public school students regardless of their activities.*

Those same points were highlighted in the 5–4 decision handed down June 27. Writing for the majority, Justice Clarence Thomas said that "a student's privacy interest is limited in a public school environment where the state is responsible for maintaining discipline, health, and safety." He noted that "schoolchildren are routinely required to submit to physical examinations and vaccinations against disease. Securing order in the school environment sometimes requires that students be subjected to greater controls than those appropriate for adults." Because the school district policy stipulated that students who failed the drug test could not be expelled or prosecuted, the invasion of privacy was "not significant." Thomas said, whereas "the nationwide drug epidemic makes the war against drugs a pressing concern in every school."

Thomas dismissed the different circumstances in the Vernonia *case as "insignificant" and "not essential" to the constitutional analysis, which he said "depended primarily upon the school's custodial responsibility and authority." Noting the school district's concern about increased drug use in its schools, and the nationwide "epidemic" of drug use, Thomas said it was "entirely reasonable" for the school district to adopt the random drug-testing policy. "Indeed," he said, "it would make little sense to require a school district to wait for a substantial portion of its students to begin using drugs before it was allowed to institute a drug testing program designed to deter drug use." Thomas's opinion was joined by Chief Justice William H. Rehnquist, and Justices Scalia, Breyer, and Anthony M. Kennedy. Breyer also wrote a concurring opinion*

Writing the main dissent was Justice Ruth Bader Ginsburg, who had approved drug testing for athletes in the Vernonia *case. Ginsburg agreed that school districts were right to be concerned about students' health and that drug use was a health risk. But the risks from drug use, she said, "are present for* all *schoolchildren.* Vernonia *cannot be read to endorse invasive and suspicionless drug testing of all students, upon any evidence of drug use, solely because drugs jeopardize the life and health of those who use them. . . . Had the* Vernonia *Court agreed that public school attendance, in and of itself, permitted the State to test each student's blood or urine for drugs, the opinion in* Vernonia *could have saved many words."*

Ginsburg then argued that circumstances in the Tecumseh case were different enough to distinguish it from the Vernonia *case. In particular, she said, the school district in Tecumseh had not made a case that the danger of student drug use was immediate. "The Vernonia district sought to test a subpopulation of students distinguished by their reduced expectation of privacy, their special susceptibility to drug-related injury, and their heavy in-*

volvement with drug use," Ginsburg wrote. "The Tecumseh district seeks to test a much larger population associated with none of these factors," she said. "The particular testing program upheld today is not reasonable, it is capricious, even perverse. . . . It invades the privacy of students who need deterrence least and risks steering students at greatest risk for substance abuse away from extracurricular involvement that potentially may palliate drug problems." Ginsburg was joined by the three dissenters in Vernonia— *Stevens, Souter, and O'Connor. O'Connor also wrote a dissenting opinion, in which Souter joined.*

A Rush to Test?

Many parents and educators applauded the decision. "America's high schools are riddled with drugs, and I think this is a legitimate thing to do," said Joseph Califano, president of the Center on Addiction and Substance Abuse at Columbia University. "We've got to make our schools safe for kids and this will help. Just the possibility of a random test gives thousands of high school students a reasons to say 'No,'" he added.

Waiting to test until there was a noticeable drug problem in a school was too late, according to Calvina Fay, executive director of Drug Free America Foundation. "Drug testing has two values," Fay told the Wall Street Journal. *"It serves as a very strong deterrent and it serves as an excellent detection tool."*

Judy Appel, of the Drug Policy Alliance, disagreed, saying there was no evidence that random testing discouraged drug use. On-site drug counselors and teachers trained to spot students who showed signs of drug abuse were more effective ways to help students, she said. The alliance filed a brief in support of the students on behalf of the National Education Association and the American Academy of Pediatrics.

Whether school districts would undertake massive testing programs appeared uncertain. Lingering privacy concerns, questions about the effectiveness of testing, and the cost of the tests—ranging between $10 to and $60 each—were all factors that school districts had to consider. Surveys showed that, since the 1995 Vernonia *decision, only about 5 percent of all public schools randomly tested their athletes, while about 2 percent had testing programs for students involved in other extracurricular activities. "This is not the kind of thing that will become a standard among school districts," said Edwin Darden, a senior staff attorney for the National School Boards Association, which represented about 15,000 school districts and filed a brief in support of the Oklahoma school district. "What [the ruling] says is you can preemptively and penetratively act against drugs and it gives the local community the right to make that decision."*

Following are excerpts from the majority opinion and a dissent in the case of Board of Education of Independent School District No. 92 of Pottawatomie County v. Earls, *in which the Supreme Court, by a 5–4 vote, ruled on June 27, 2002, that a school*

*district's policy of randomly testing students engaged in extra-
curricular activities was not an unreasonable search prohibited
by the Fourth Amendment of the Constitution.*

**The document was obtained from the Internet at supct.law
.cornell.edu/supct/html/01-332.ZS.html; accessed September 9, 2002.**

No. 01–332

Board of Education of Independent School District No. 92 of Pottawatomie County, et al., petitioners, *v.* Lindsay Earls et al.	On writ of certiorari to the United States Court of Appeals for the Tenth Circuit

[June 27, 2002]

JUSTICE THOMAS delivered the opinion of the Court.

The Student Activities Drug Testing Policy implemented by the Board of
Education of Independent School District No. 92 of Pottawatomie County
(School District) requires all students who participate in competitive extracurricular activities to submit to drug testing. Because this Policy reasonably
serves the School District's important interest in detecting and preventing
drug use among its students, we hold that it is constitutional.

I

The city of Tecumseh, Oklahoma, is a rural community located approximately 40 miles southeast of Oklahoma City. The School District administers
all Tecumseh public schools. In the fall of 1998, the School District adopted
the Student Activities Drug Testing Policy (Policy), which requires all middle
and high school students to consent to drug testing in order to participate in
any extracurricular activity. In practice, the Policy has been applied only to
competitive extracurricular activities sanctioned by the Oklahoma Secondary
Schools Activities Association, such as the Academic Team, Future Farmers
of America, Future Homemakers of America, band, choir, pom pon, cheerlead-
ing, and athletics. Under the Policy, students are required to take a drug test
before participating in an extracurricular activity, must submit to random
drug testing while participating in that activity, and must agree to be tested
at any time upon reasonable suspicion. The urinalysis tests are designed to detect only the use of illegal drugs, including amphetamines, marijuana, cocaine,
opiates, and barbiturates, not medical conditions or the presence of authorized prescription medications.

At the time of their suit, both respondents attended Tecumseh High School. Respondent Lindsay Earls was a member of the show choir, the marching band, the Academic Team, and the National Honor Society. Respondent Daniel James sought to participate in the Academic Team. Together with their parents, Earls and James . . . alleged that the Policy violates the Fourth Amendment as incorporated by the Fourteenth Amendment and requested injunctive and declarative relief. They also argued that the School District failed to identify a special need for testing students who participate in extracurricular activities, and that the "Drug Testing Policy neither addresses a proven problem nor promises to bring any benefit to students or the school.". . .

Applying the principles articulated in *Vernonia School Dist. 47J v. Acton* . . . (1995), in which we upheld the suspicionless drug testing of school athletes, the United States District Court for the Western District of Oklahoma rejected respondents' claim that the Policy was unconstitutional and granted summary judgment to the School District. The court noted that "special needs" exist in the public school context and that, although the School District did "not show a drug problem of epidemic proportions," there was a history of drug abuse starting in 1970 that presented "legitimate cause for concern.". . .

The United States Court of Appeals for the Tenth Circuit reversed, holding that the Policy violated the Fourth Amendment. The Court of Appeals agreed with the District Court that the Policy must be evaluated in the "unique environment of the school setting," but reached a different conclusion as to the Policy's constitutionality. . . . Before imposing a suspicionless drug testing program, the Court of Appeals concluded that a school "must demonstrate that there is some identifiable drug abuse problem among a sufficient number of those subject to the testing, such that testing that group of students will actually redress its drug problem.". . . The Court of Appeals then held that because the School District failed to demonstrate such a problem existed among Tecumseh students participating in competitive extracurricular activities, the Policy was unconstitutional. We granted certiorari . . . , and now reverse.

II

The Fourth Amendment to the United States Constitution protects "[t]he right of the people to be secure in their persons, houses, papers, and effects, against unreasonable searches and seizures." Searches by public school officials, such as the collection of urine samples, implicate Fourth Amendment interests. . . . We must therefore review the School District's Policy for "reasonableness," which is the touchstone of the constitutionality of a governmental search. . . .

Given that the School District's Policy is not in any way related to the conduct of criminal investigations, . . . respondents do not contend that the School District requires probable cause before testing students for drug use. Respondents instead argue that drug testing must be based at least on some level of individualized suspicion. . . . It is true that we generally determine the reasonableness of a search by balancing the nature of the intrusion on the individual's privacy against the promotion of legitimate governmental interests. . . . But we have long held that "the Fourth Amendment imposes no irreducible requirement of [individualized] suspicion.". . . Therefore, in the context of safety and administrative regulations, a search unsupported by probable cause may be reasonable "when 'special needs, beyond the normal need for law enforcement, make the warrant and probable-cause requirement impracticable.'"

Significantly, this Court has previously held that "special needs" inhere in the public school context. . . . While schoolchildren do not shed their constitutional rights when they enter the schoolhouse, . . . "Fourth Amendment rights . . . are different in public schools than elsewhere; the 'reasonableness' inquiry cannot disregard the schools' custodial and tutelary responsibility for children.". . . In particular, a finding of individualized suspicion may not be necessary when a school conducts drug testing.

In *Vernonia*, this Court held that the suspicionless drug testing of athletes was constitutional. The Court, however, did not simply authorize all school drug testing, but rather conducted a fact-specific balancing of the intrusion on the children's Fourth Amendment rights against the promotion of legitimate governmental interests. . . . Applying the principles of *Vernonia* to the somewhat different facts of this case, we conclude that Tecumseh's Policy is also constitutional.

A

We first consider the nature of the privacy interest allegedly compromised by the drug testing. . . . A student's privacy interest is limited in a public school environment where the State is responsible for maintaining discipline, health, and safety. Schoolchildren are routinely required to submit to physical examinations and vaccinations against disease. . . . Securing order in the school environment sometimes requires that students be subjected to greater controls than those appropriate for adults. . . .

Respondents argue that because children participating in nonathletic extracurricular activities are not subject to regular physicals and communal undress, they have a stronger expectation of privacy than the athletes tested in *Vernonia*. . . . This distinction, however, was not essential to our decision in *Vernonia*, which depended primarily upon the school's custodial responsibility and authority.

In any event, students who participate in competitive extracurricular activities voluntarily subject themselves to many of the same intrusions on their privacy as do athletes. Some of these clubs and activities require occasional off-campus travel and communal undress. All of them have their own rules and requirements for participating students that do not apply to the student body as a whole. . . . For example, each of the competitive extracurricular activities governed by the Policy must abide by the rules of the Oklahoma Secondary Schools Activities Association, and a faculty sponsor monitors the students for compliance with the various rules dictated by the clubs and activities. . . This regulation of extracurricular activities further diminishes the expectation of privacy among schoolchildren. . . . We therefore conclude that the students affected by this Policy have a limited expectation of privacy.

B

Next, we consider the character of the intrusion imposed by the Policy. . . .

Under the Policy, a faculty monitor waits outside the closed restroom stall for the student to produce a sample and must "listen for the normal sounds of urination in order to guard against tampered specimens and to insure an accurate chain of custody.". . . The monitor then pours the sample into two bottles that are sealed and placed into a mailing pouch along with a consent form signed by the student. This procedure is virtually identical to that reviewed in *Vernonia*, except that it additionally protects privacy by allowing male students to produce their samples behind a closed stall. Given that we considered the method of collection in *Vernonia* a "negligible" intrusion, . . . the method here is even less problematic. . . .

Moreover, the test results are not turned over to any law enforcement authority. Nor do the test results here lead to the imposition of discipline or have any academic consequences. . . . Rather, the only consequence of a failed drug test is to limit the student's privilege of participating in extracurricular activities. Indeed, a student may test positive for drugs twice and still be allowed to participate in extracurricular activities. After the first positive test, the school contacts the student's parent or guardian for a meeting. The student may continue to participate in the activity if within five days of the meeting the student shows proof of receiving drug counseling and submits to a second drug test in two weeks. For the second positive test, the student is suspended from participation in all extracurricular activities for 14 days, must complete four hours of substance abuse counseling, and must submit to monthly drug tests. Only after a third positive test will the student be suspended from participating in any extracurricular activity for the remainder of the school year, or 88 school days, whichever is longer. . . .

Given the minimally intrusive nature of the sample collection and the limited uses to which the test results are put, we conclude that the invasion of students' privacy is not significant.

C

Finally, this Court must consider the nature and immediacy of the government's concerns and the efficacy of the Policy in meeting them. . . . This Court has already articulated in detail the importance of the governmental concern in preventing drug use by schoolchildren. . . . The drug abuse problem among our Nation's youth has hardly abated since *Vernonia* was decided in 1995. In fact, evidence suggests that it has only grown worse. As in *Vernonia*, "the necessity for the State to act is magnified by the fact that this evil is being visited not just upon individuals at large, but upon children for whom it has undertaken a special responsibility of care and direction.". . . The health and safety risks identified in *Vernonia* apply with equal force to Tecumseh's children. Indeed, the nationwide drug epidemic makes the war against drugs a pressing concern in every school.

Additionally, the School District in this case has presented specific evidence of drug use at Tecumseh schools. Teachers testified that they had seen students who appeared to be under the influence of drugs and that they had heard students speaking openly about using drugs. . . . A drug dog found marijuana cigarettes near the school parking lot. Police officers once found drugs or drug paraphernalia in a car driven by a Future Farmers of America member. And the school board president reported that people in the community were calling the board to discuss the "drug situation.". . . We decline to second-guess the finding of the District Court that "[v]iewing the evidence as a whole, it cannot be reasonably disputed that the [School District] was faced with a 'drug problem' when it adopted the Policy.". . .

Respondents consider the proffered evidence insufficient and argue that there is no "real and immediate interest" to justify a policy of drug testing nonathletes. . . . We have recognized, however, that "[a] demonstrated problem of drug abuse . . . [is] not in all cases necessary to the validity of a testing regime," but that some showing does "shore up an assertion of special need for a suspicionless general search program.". . . The School District has provided sufficient evidence to shore up the need for its drug testing program.

Furthermore, this Court has not required a particularized or pervasive drug problem before allowing the government to conduct suspicionless drug testing. For instance, in [*Treasury Employees v.*] *Von Raab* [(1989)] the Court upheld the drug testing of customs officials on a purely preventive basis, without any documented history of drug use by such officials. . . . In response to the lack of evidence relating to drug use, the Court noted generally that "drug abuse is one of the most serious problems confronting our society today," and that programs to prevent and detect drug use among customs officials could not be deemed unreasonable. . . . Likewise, the need to prevent and deter the substantial harm of childhood drug use provides the necessary immediacy for a school testing policy. Indeed, it would make little sense to require a school district to wait for a substantial portion of its students to begin using drugs before it was allowed to institute a drug testing program designed to deter drug use.

Given the nationwide epidemic of drug use, and the evidence of increased drug use in Tecumseh schools, it was entirely reasonable for the School District to enact this particular drug testing policy. We reject the Court of Appeals' novel test that "any district seeking to impose a random suspicionless drug testing policy as a condition to participation in a school activity must demonstrate that there is some identifiable drug abuse problem among a sufficient number of those subject to the testing, such that testing that group of students will actually redress its drug problem.". . . Among other problems, it would be difficult to administer such a test. As we cannot articulate a threshold level of drug use that would suffice to justify a drug testing program for schoolchildren, we refuse to fashion what would in effect be a constitutional quantum of drug use necessary to show a "drug problem."

Respondents also argue that the testing of nonathletes does not implicate any safety concerns, and that safety is a "crucial factor" in applying the special needs framework. . . . Respondents are correct that safety factors into the special needs analysis, but the safety interest furthered by drug testing is undoubtedly substantial for all children, athletes and nonathletes alike. We know all too well that drug use carries a variety of health risks for children, including death from overdose.

We also reject respondents' argument that drug testing must presumptively be based upon an individualized reasonable suspicion of wrongdoing because such a testing regime would be less intrusive. . . . In this context, the Fourth Amendment does not require a finding of individualized suspicion, . . . and we decline to impose such a requirement on schools attempting to prevent and detect drug use by students. Moreover, we question whether testing based on individualized suspicion in fact would be less intrusive. Such a regime would place an additional burden on public school teachers who are already tasked with the difficult job of maintaining order and discipline. A program of individualized suspicion might unfairly target members of unpopular groups. The fear of lawsuits resulting from such targeted searches may chill enforcement of the program, rendering it ineffective in combating drug use. . . .

Finally, we find that testing students who participate in extracurricular activities is a reasonably effective means of addressing the School District's legitimate concerns in preventing, deterring, and detecting drug use. While in *Vernonia* there might have been a closer fit between the testing of athletes and the trial court's finding that the drug problem was "fueled by the 'role model' effect of athletes' drug use," such a finding was not essential to the holding. . . . *Vernonia* did not require the school to test the group of students most likely to use drugs, but rather considered the constitutionality of the program in the context of the public school's custodial responsibilities. Evaluating the Policy in this context, we conclude that the drug testing of Tecumseh students who participate in extracurricular activities effectively serves the School District's interest in protecting the safety and health of its students.

III

Within the limits of the Fourth Amendment, local school boards must assess the desirability of drug testing schoolchildren. In upholding the constitutionality of the Policy, we express no opinion as to its wisdom. Rather, we hold only that Tecumseh's Policy is a reasonable means of furthering the School District's important interest in preventing and deterring drug use among its schoolchildren. Accordingly, we reverse the judgment of the Court of Appeals.

It is so ordered.

JUSTICE GINSBURG, with whom JUSTICE STEVENS, JUSTICE O'CONNOR, and JUSTICE SOUTER join, dissenting.

Seven years ago, in *Vernonia School Dist. 47J v. Acton*, . . . this Court determined that a school district's policy of randomly testing the urine of its student athletes for illicit drugs did not violate the Fourth Amendment. In so ruling, the Court emphasized that drug use "increase[d] the risk of sports-related injury" and that Vernonia's athletes were the "leaders" of an aggressive local "drug culture" that had reached "epidemic proportions.". . . Today, the Court relies upon *Vernonia* to permit a school district with a drug problem its superintendent repeatedly described as "not . . . major,". . . to test the urine of an academic team member solely by reason of her participation in a nonathletic, competitive extracurricular activity–participation associated with neither special dangers from, nor particular predilections for, drug use.

"[T]he legality of a search of a student," this Court has instructed, "should depend simply on the reasonableness, under all the circumstances, of the search.". . . Although "'special needs' inhere in the public school context,". . . those needs are not so expansive or malleable as to render reasonable any program of student drug testing a school district elects to install. The particular testing program upheld today is not reasonable, it is capricious, even perverse: Petitioners' policy targets for testing a student population least likely to be at risk from illicit drugs and their damaging effects. I therefore dissent.

I

A

. . . The *Vernonia* Court concluded that a public school district facing a disruptive and explosive drug abuse problem sparked by members of its athletic teams had "special needs" that justified suspicionless testing of district athletes as a condition of their athletic participation.

This case presents circumstances dispositively different from those of *Vernonia*. True, as the Court stresses, Tecumseh students participating in competitive extracurricular activities other than athletics share two relevant characteristics with the athletes of Vernonia. First, both groups attend public schools. . . . Concern for student health and safety is basic to the school's caretaking, and it is undeniable that "drug use carries a variety of health risks for children, including death from overdose.". . .

Those risks, however, are present for *all* schoolchildren. *Vernonia* cannot be read to endorse invasive and suspicionless drug testing of all students upon any evidence of drug use, solely because drugs jeopardize the life and health of those who use them. Many children, like many adults, engage in dangerous activities on their own time; that the children are enrolled in school scarcely allows government to monitor all such activities. If a student has a reasonable subjective expectation of privacy in the personal items she brings to school, . . . surely she has a similar expectation regarding the chemical composition of her urine. Had the *Vernonia* Court agreed that public school attendance, in and of itself, permitted the State to test each student's blood or urine for drugs, the opinion in *Vernonia* could have saved many words. . . .

The second commonality to which the Court points is the voluntary character of both interscholastic athletics and other competitive extracurricular activities. "By choosing to 'go out for the team,' [school athletes] voluntarily subject themselves to a degree of regulation even higher than that imposed on students generally.". . . Comparably, the Court today observes, "students who participate in competitive extracurricular activities voluntarily subject themselves to" additional rules not applicable to other students. . . .

The comparison is enlightening. While extracurricular activities are "voluntary" in the sense that they are not required for graduation, they are part of the school's educational program; for that reason, the petitioner (hereinafter School District) is justified in expending public resources to make them available. Participation in such activities is a key component of school life, essential in reality for students applying to college, and, for all participants, a significant contributor to the breadth and quality of the educational experience. . . . Students "volunteer" for extracurricular pursuits in the same way they might volunteer for honors classes: They subject themselves to additional requirements, but they do so in order to take full advantage of the education offered them. . . .

Voluntary participation in athletics has a distinctly different dimension: Schools regulate student athletes discretely because competitive school sports by their nature require communal undress and, more important, expose students to physical risks that schools have a duty to mitigate. For the very reason that schools cannot offer a program of competitive athletics without intimately affecting the privacy of students, *Vernonia* reasonably analogized school athletes to "adults who choose to participate in a closely regulated industry.". . . Industries fall within the closely regulated category when the nature of their activities requires substantial government oversight. . . . Interscholastic athletics similarly require close safety and health regulation; a school's choir, band, and academic team do not.

In short, *Vernonia* applied, it did not repudiate, the principle that "the legality of a search of a student should depend simply on the reasonableness, *under all the circumstances*, of the search.". . . (emphasis added). Enrollment in a public school, and election to participate in school activities beyond the bare minimum that the curriculum requires, are indeed factors relevant to reasonableness, but they do not on their own justify intrusive, suspicionless searches. *Vernonia*, accordingly, did not rest upon these factors; instead, the Court performed what today's majority aptly describes as a "fact-specific balancing,". . . Balancing of that order, applied to the facts now before the Court, should yield a result other than the one the Court announces today.

B

[In the first part of this section, Ginsburg described what the minority saw as differences in the circumstances of the *Vernonia* case and the Tecumseh case as they affected privacy of the students and the nature of the drug problem each school confronted. Ginsburg argued that the expectation of privacy for students participating in extracurricular activities had not been lowered as it was for the athletes in *Vernonia*, that the invasion of privacy was greater for the students at Tecumseh, in part because their records were not handled confidentially, and that the extent of the drug problem at Tecumseh was no where near as great as it had been at Vernonia.]

At the margins, of course, no policy of random drug testing is perfectly tailored to the harms it seeks to address. The School District cites the dangers faced by members of the band, who must "perform extremely precise routines with heavy equipment and instruments in close proximity to other students," and by Future Farmers of America, who "are required to individually control and restrain animals as large as 1500 pounds.". . . For its part, the United States acknowledges that "the linebacker faces a greater risk of serious injury if he takes the field under the influence of drugs than the drummer in the halftime band," but parries that "the risk of injury to a student who is under the influence of drugs while playing golf, cross country, or volleyball (sports covered by the policy in Vernonia) is scarcely any greater than the risk of injury to a student . . . handling a 1500-pound steer (as [Future Farmers of America] members do) or working with cutlery or other sharp instruments (as [Future Homemakers of America] members do).". . . One can demur to the Government's view of the risks drug use poses to golfers, . . . for golfers were surely as marginal among the linebackers, sprinters, and basketball players targeted for testing in Vernonia as steer-handlers are among the choristers, musicians, and academic-team members subject to urinalysis in Tecumseh. Notwithstanding nightmarish images of out-of-control flatware, livestock run amok, and colliding tubas disturbing the peace and quiet of Tecumseh, the great majority of students the School District seeks to test in truth are engaged in activities that are not safety sensitive to an unusual degree. There is a difference between imperfect tailoring and no tailoring at all.

The Vernonia district, in sum, had two good reasons for testing athletes: Sports team members faced special health risks and they "were the leaders of the drug culture.". . . No similar reason, and no other tenable justification, explains Tecumseh's decision to target for testing all participants in every competitive extracurricular activity. . . .

Nationwide, students who participate in extracurricular activities are significantly less likely to develop substance abuse problems than are their less-involved peers. . . . Even if students might be deterred from drug use in order to preserve their extracurricular eligibility, it is at least as likely that other students might forgo their extracurricular involvement in order to avoid detection of their drug use. Tecumseh's policy thus falls short doubly if deterrence is its aim: It invades the privacy of students who need deterrence least, and risks steering students at greatest risk for substance abuse away from extracurricular involvement that potentially may palliate drug problems.

To summarize, this case resembles *Vernonia* only in that the School Districts in both cases conditioned engagement in activities outside the obligatory curriculum on random subjection to urinalysis. The defining characteristics of the two programs, however, are entirely dissimilar. The Vernonia district sought to test a subpopulation of students distinguished by their reduced expectation of privacy, their special susceptibility to drug-related injury, and their heavy involvement with drug use. The Tecumseh district seeks to test a much larger population associated with none of these factors. It does so, moreover, without carefully safeguarding student confidentiality and without regard to the program's untoward effects. A program so sweeping is not sheltered by *Vernonia;* its unreasonable reach renders it impermissible under the Fourth Amendment. . . .

GROUP OF EIGHT LEADERS ON WEAPONS OF MASS DESTRUCTION
June 27, 2002

Heralding a significant policy change, President George W. Bush on June 27, 2002, joined with fellow leaders of the Group of Eight (G-8) nations in pledging to spend up to $20 billion over ten years on programs to halt the proliferation of biological, chemical, and nuclear weapons—the "weapons of mass destruction." President Bush urged international cooperation to keep such weapons out of the hands of terrorists and nations that posed a threat to international security. In a much more high-profile case, Bush also pressured the United Nations to renew a decade-long attempt to force Iraq to surrender its presumed arsenal of weapons of mass destruction. (Iraq issue, pp. 612, 713)

The $20 billion G-8 program was to be spent on programs to help Russia upgrade security measures for the gigantic arsenals of biological, chemical, and nuclear weapons that had been produced by the Soviet Union during the cold war. Russia inherited most of the weapons after the Soviet Union collapsed in 1991, but Moscow lacked the money to secure the weapons properly and to dismantle safely the weapons that were supposed to be eliminated under various arms control treaties. Western experts worried that poorly guarded Russian weapons could fall into the hands of terrorists. The United States had spent nearly $7 billion since 1992 on programs to help Russia protect and dismantle its weapons, and President Bush in 2002 pledged to spend an average of $1 billion annually over the next ten years to help finish the job. Leaders of European nations, Canada, and Japan promised to match U.S. spending for the coming decade—putting the total at $20 billion. (Background, Historic Documents of 2001, p. 17)

A New Approach by the Administration

The Bush administration's endorsement of international nonproliferation measures represented a significant change of heart from its original position upon taking office in January 2001. Early in their tenure, senior administration officials—especially in the White House and Defense Department—expressed deep skepticism about the value of arms control treaties, in particular multilateral agreements intended to halt the world-wide spread of weapons of mass destruction. The administration also proposed significant cuts in U.S. programs to help Russia protect and gradually eliminate its vast weapons arsenals. Administration officials at first played down the threat posed by such weapons and argued that, in any case, building U.S. defenses was more important than negotiating multilateral treaties or spending money on long-term programs to dismantle weapons overseas. Officials also expressed skepticism about the effectiveness of these programs.

The administration's attitude changed dramatically after the September 11, 2001, terrorist attacks against the United States. Suddenly Bush and his aides began talking in urgent terms about the danger that terrorists would pose if they managed to buy or steal weapons of mass destruction. The sense of urgency was heightened by the discovery of evidence in Afghanistan that the al Qaeda terrorist network, said to have carried out the September 11 attacks, had been actively seeking to acquire weapons of mass destruction but apparently had failed.

Bush in late 2001 agreed to congressional initiatives that added money to U.S. weapons control programs in Russia. The president's new concern was a centerpiece of his January 20, 2002, State of the Union address, in which he declared that Iran, Iraq, and North Korea constituted an "axis of evil" because they sponsored terrorism and were developing weapons of mass destruction. (State of the Union speech, p. 33)

G-8 Agreement

Early in 2002 former Sen. Sam Nunn, D-Ga., and Sen. Richard Lugar, R-Ind., the chief political advocates of U.S. nonproliferation programs in Russia, pushed Bush to expand them further by making other countries eligible for the types of arms control aid Washington had been giving Russia. Nunn and Lugar noted that nearly half of the 190 countries in the world have some capability to build weapons of mass destruction—in most cases, rudimentary chemical weapons. Lugar, a senior member of the Senate Foreign Relations Committee who was expected to become its chairman in 2003, formulated the proposition this way: "Every nation that has weapons and materials of mass destruction must account for what it has, spend its own money or obtain international technical and financial resources to safely secure what it has, and pledge that no other nation, cell, or cause will be allowed access or use."

While supporting that general proposition, the Bush administration was reluctant to broaden U.S. spending beyond the current arms control programs in Russia. The administration did agree, however, to seek international financial backing for a program to speed up work on dismantling Russia's weapons of mass destruction. Implementing such a program involved two steps: convincing other wealthy nations that it was in their interest to help Russia protect and eliminate these weapons, and getting Moscow to agree to let other nations play a role.

The administration decided that the best forum to get an agreement on such a program was at the annual series of meetings on economic and security issues held by the leaders of the Group of Eight, the world's seven leading industrialized countries—Britain, Canada, France, Germany, Italy, Japan, and the United States—plus Russia. Negotiations among G-8 officials took place during the spring and culminated in the annual G-8 summit meeting, which was held June 25–28, 2002, at the Kananaskis ski resort near Calgary in western Canada.

At the conclusion of the summit, the G-8 leaders announced what they called a "Global Partnership Against the Spread of Weapons and Materials of Mass Destruction." The basis of the agreement was a pledge by the European countries, plus Canada and Japan, to provide $10 billion over the next decade to support nonproliferation programs in Russia. This pledge matched a promise by Bush to spend an average of $1 billion annually for existing U.S. programs over the same decade. Informally, the agreement was known as "ten plus ten over ten" ($10 billion plus $10 billion over ten years).

The agreement contained few specifics, but it did amount to a significant political commitment by the G-8 leaders to a large-scale program intended to keep Russia's weapons of mass destruction out of the hands of terrorists. The G-8 leaders adopted six principles for their planned program, the first of which was sharply at odds with the Bush administration's stated views prior to the September 11 attacks. That principle called on the G-8 countries to promote "the adoption, universalization, full implementation and, where necessary, strengthening of multilateral treaties and other international instruments whose aim is to prevent the proliferation or illicit acquisition" of weapons of mass destruction.

In subsequent negotiations during 2002, the G-8 members decided that each country would negotiate its own weapons control program with Russia, rather than have the G-8 establish a new agency to coordinate the programs or create a combined fund into which countries would make contributions. Japan, for example, was expected to step up funding for an existing program to dismantle aging Russian submarines.

One central question left unsettled at the summit was how much the European countries, Canada, and Japan would contribute individually to the total $10 billion pledge. All of the countries were experiencing economic difficulties, ranging from severe recessions (in Germany and Japan) to milder downturns (Britain and France). Later announcements put the initial planned non-U.S. contributions at Britain, $750 million; Canada, $650 million; France, $750 million; Germany, $1.5 billion; Italy $1 billion; Japan, $200 million; and the European Union, $1 billion. The total of $5.85 billion fell far short of the $10 billion pledged by these countries.

As of year's end none of those countries had actually started work on any new programs in Russia. A senior State Department official told the Senate Foreign Relations Committee that the potential donor countries had yet to negotiate an "umbrella agreement" with Russia establishing the details of how new or expanded nonproliferation programs would be carried out. One obstacle was the concern in several capitals about a tendency of Russian government agencies to pose bureaucratic hurdles for such programs. For example, the United States and Japan had encountered difficulties getting adequate access to Russian weapons sites and information. Moreover, private contractors hired by these countries had faced onerous Russian taxation and regulation.

Another contentious issue was a U.S. demand that Moscow halt work by Russian commercial firms on nuclear power projects in Iran and Syria. The Bush administration charged that Russian aid would make it easier for Iran and Syria to develop nuclear weapons. The Russian government denied that charge, and the governments of Iran and Syria insisted that they were not attempting to develop nuclear weapons. Even so, the dispute interfered with efforts to build a cooperative relationship between the West and Russia on weapons issues.

Nunn-Lugar Programs

The Russian weapons-control programs sponsored by senators Nunn and Lugar had faced political obstacles in Washington ever since Congress first approved them in 1991. Most of the obstacles had been posed by conservatives who argued that U.S. aid spent to protect and dismantle old Russian weapons freed up money for Moscow to spend on new weapons. This concern had been a key ingredient in the Bush administration's early wariness about the Nunn-Lugar programs.

Even after the White House embraced the Nunn-Lugar programs following the September 11, 2001, terrorist attacks, key officials within the administration continued to express similar concerns about Russian weapons programs. As a result, Bush in April refused to sign a statement certifying that Russia was "committed" to complying with all arms control agreements it had signed. Legislation authorizing many of the Nunn-Lugar programs required such a certification before each year's funding would be spent. The president's refusal to sign the certification held up about $450 million in arms control programs run by the Defense Department and about $70 million in State Department programs. Not affected were several hundred million dollars worth of programs run by the Energy Department.

Bush's action led to a five-month political tussle involving all the arguments that had been made during the previous decade about whether and how the United States should try to help Russia control its weapons of mass destruction. The Senate voted to give the president broad authority to waive the certification requirement, but the House refused. In the end, Congress agreed to allow the Nunn-Lugar programs to proceed for the rest of fiscal year 2002 (which ended on September 30) and for all of fiscal year 2003. Effectively, that action meant that Congress and the administration would face the same issue again during 2003.

No Action on Tactical Weapons

None of the nonproliferation programs funded by the United States or other governments were intended to tackle the danger that many experts were most concerned about: the prospect of terrorists gaining control of any of Russia's estimated 20,000 tactical nuclear weapons. Tactical nuclear warheads were built during the cold war for use on short-range rockets, artillery shells, and other battlefield weapons. These weapons had never been subject to any arms control agreements between Washington and Moscow. The Russian government said it began destroying its tactical weapons in the mid-1990s but refused to give the United States any detailed information about the status of them.

Weapons experts noted that most tactical nuclear weapons were small and portable enough to be smuggled across national borders. Russia reportedly had developed bombs that could fit in a suitcase or backpack so that they could be carried behind enemy lines by special forces troops. Former senator Nunn called on the United States and Russia to give each other an "accurate accounting" of their tactical nuclear weapons and to ensure that the weapons were kept in secure storage. As of year's end, however, no official steps had been taken by any government to deal with the issue.

The "Dirty Bomb" Threat

Another threat received increased attention during 2002: the prospect that terrorists might use a "radiological" or "dirty" bomb. Such a bomb would be much easier to construct than most other types of weapons of mass destruction. Essentially, it would consist of dynamite or some other conventional explosive and radioactive material, for example pieces from the spent fuel rod of a nuclear power reactor or even material from a hospital radiology department. Detonated in a city, a dirty bomb could kill dozens or even hundreds of people with its explosive blast and could scatter radioactivity over a wide area—potentially injuring thousands of people, causing widespread panic, and contaminating property.

Weapons experts for years had talked about the potential danger of dirty bombs, but their concerns had drawn little public attention. That changed in May when U.S. authorities detained a former Chicago gang member, Jose Padilla (who called himself Abdullah al-Muhajir) as a "material witness" in the investigation of the September 11 terrorist attacks. Padilla was held in military confinement but was not formally charged with any crime, as of year's end. However, the Justice Department said it had evidence linking Padilla to the al Qaeda terrorist network and to an alleged plot to detonate a dirty bomb in the United States.

One month after the Padilla arrest, the International Atomic Energy Agency (IAEA) issued a statement noting that "more than 100 countries" may have inadequate controls over radioactive materials. The IAEA pointed specifically to the countries that had once belonged to the Soviet Union but also noted that even the U.S. government could not be sure of the safety of all radioactive materials in the country.

Only a small percentage of the "millions" of pieces of radioactive materials around the world were strong enough to cause serious harm, the IAEA said, but added: "It is these powerful sources that need to be focused on as a priority." As examples, the agency pointed to industrial and medical devices that used large amounts of radioactive material, including cobalt-60, strontium-90, caesium-137, and iridium-192.

> *Following is the text of a statement issued June 27, 2002, in Alberta, Canada, at the conclusion of the annual summit of the leaders of the Group of Eight nations, establishing what the leaders called a "global partnership against the spread of weapons and materials of mass destruction."*
>
> **The document was obtained from the Internet at www.g8 .utoronto.ca/g7/summit/2002kananaskis/arms.html; accessed November 21, 2002.**

The attacks of September 11 demonstrated that terrorists are prepared to use any means to cause terror and inflict appalling casualties on innocent people. We commit ourselves to prevent terrorists, or those that harbour them, from acquiring or developing nuclear, chemical, radiological and biological weapons; missiles; and related materials, equipment and technology. We call on all countries to join us in adopting the set of non-proliferation principles we have announced today.

In a major initiative to implement those principles, we have also decided today to launch a new G8 Global Partnership against the Spread of Weapons and Materials of Mass Destruction. Under this initiative, we will support specific cooperation projects, initially in Russia, to address non-proliferation, disarmament, counter-terrorism and nuclear safety issues. Among our priority concerns are the destruction of chemical weapons, the dismantlement of decommissioned nuclear submarines, the disposition of fissile materials and the employment of former weapons scientists. We will commit to raise up to $20 billion to support such projects over the next ten years. A range of financing options, including the option of bilateral debt for program exchanges, will be available to countries that contribute to this Global Partnership. We have adopted a set of guidelines that will form the basis for the negotiation of specific agreements for new projects, that will apply with immediate effect, to ensure effective and efficient project development, coordination and implementation. We will review over the next year the applicability of the guidelines to existing projects.

Recognizing that this Global Partnership will enhance international security and safety, we invite other countries that are prepared to adopt its common principles and guidelines to enter into discussions with us on participating in and contributing to this initiative. We will review progress on this Global Partnership at our next Summit in 2003.

The G8 Global Partnership: Principles to prevent terrorists, or those that harbour them, from gaining access to weapons or materials of mass destruction

The G8 calls on all countries to join them in commitment to the following six principles to prevent terrorists or those that harbour them from acquiring or developing nuclear, chemical, radiological and biological weapons; missiles; and related materials, equipment and technology.

1. Promote the adoption, universalization, full implementation and, where necessary, strengthening of multilateral treaties and other international instruments whose aim is to prevent the proliferation or illicit acquisition of such items; strengthen the institutions designed to implement these instruments.

2. Develop and maintain appropriate effective measures to account for and secure such items in production, use, storage and domestic and international transport; provide assistance to states lacking sufficient resources to account for and secure these items.

3. Develop and maintain appropriate effective physical protection measures applied to facilities which house such items, including defence in depth; provide assistance to states lacking sufficient resources to protect their facilities.

4. Develop and maintain effective border controls, law enforcement efforts and international cooperation to detect, deter and interdict in cases of illicit trafficking in such items, for example through installation of detection systems, training of customs and law enforcement personnel and cooperation in tracking these items; provide assistance to states lacking sufficient expertise or resources to strengthen their capacity to detect, deter and interdict in cases of illicit trafficking in these items.

5. Develop, review and maintain effective national export and transshipment controls over items on multilateral export control lists, as well as items that are not identified on such lists but which may nevertheless contribute to the development, production or use of nuclear, chemical and biological weapons and missiles, with particular consideration of end-user, catch-all and brokering aspects; provide assistance to states lacking the legal and regulatory infrastructure, implementation experience and/or resources to develop their export and transshipment control systems in this regard.

6. Adopt and strengthen efforts to manage and dispose of stocks of fissile materials designated as no longer required for defence purposes, eliminate all chemical weapons, and minimize holdings of dangerous biological pathogens and toxins, based on the recognition that the threat of terrorist acquisition is reduced as the overall quantity of such items is reduced.

The G8 Global Partnership: Guidelines for New or Expanded Cooperation Projects

The G8 will work in partnership, bilaterally and multilaterally, to develop, coordinate, implement and finance, according to their respective means, new or expanded cooperation projects to address (i) non-proliferation, (ii) disarmament, (iii) counter-terrorism and (iv) nuclear safety (including environmental) issues, with a view to enhancing strategic stability, consonant with our international security objectives and in support of the multilateral nonproliferation regimes. Each country has primary responsibility for implementing its non-proliferation, disarmament, counter-terrorism and nuclear safety obligations and requirements and commits its full cooperation within the Partnership.

Cooperation projects under this initiative will be decided and implemented, taking into account international obligations and domestic laws of participating partners, within appropriate bilateral and multilateral legal frameworks that should, as necessary, include the following elements:

    i. Mutually agreed effective monitoring, auditing and transparency measures and procedures will be required in order to ensure that cooperative activities meet agreed objectives (including irreversibility as necessary), to confirm work performance, to account for the funds expended and to provide for adequate access for donor representatives to work sites;

    ii. The projects will be implemented in an environmentally sound manner and will maintain the highest appropriate level of safety;

    iii. Clearly defined milestones will be developed for each project, including the option of suspending or terminating a project if the milestones are not met;

    iv. The material, equipment, technology, services and expertise provided will be solely for peaceful purposes and, unless otherwise agreed, will be used only for the purposes of implementing the projects and will not be transferred. Adequate measures of physical protection will also be applied to prevent theft or sabotage;

    v. All governments will take necessary steps to ensure that the support provided will be considered free technical assistance and will be exempt from taxes, duties, levies and other charges;

    vi. Procurement of goods and services will be conducted in accordance with open international practices to the extent possible, consistent with national security requirements;

    vii. All governments will take necessary steps to ensure that adequate liability protections from claims related to the cooperation will be provided for donor countries and their personnel and contractors;

    viii. Appropriate privileges and immunities will be provided for government donor representatives working on cooperation projects; and

    ix. Measures will be put in place to ensure effective protection of sensitive information and intellectual property.

Given the breadth and scope of the activities to be undertaken, the G8 will establish an appropriate mechanism for the annual review of progress under this initiative which may include consultations regarding priorities, identification of project gaps and potential overlap, and assessment of consistency of the cooperation projects with international security obligations and objectives. Specific bilateral and multilateral project implementation will be coordinated subject to arrangements appropriate to that project, including existing mechanisms.

For the purposes of these guidelines, the phrase "new or expanded cooperation projects" is defined as cooperation projects that will be initiated or enhanced on the basis of this Global Partnership. All funds disbursed or released after its announcement would be included in the total of committed resources. A range of financing options, including the option of bilateral debt for program exchanges, will be available to countries that contribute to this Global Partnership.

The Global Partnership's initial geographic focus will be on projects in Russia, which maintains primary responsibility for implementing its obligations and requirements within the Partnership.

In addition, the G8 would be willing to enter into negotiations with any other recipient countries, including those of the Former Soviet Union, prepared to adopt the guidelines, for inclusion in the Partnership.

Recognizing that the Global Partnership is designed to enhance international security and safety, the G8 invites others to contribute to and join in this initiative.

With respect to nuclear safety and security, the partners agreed to establish a new G8 Nuclear Safety and Security Group by the time of our next Summit.

GROUP OF EIGHT LEADERS
ON AID TO AFRICA
June 27, 2002

Leaders of the world's richest countries in June 2002 offered strong rhetorical support, and modest financial backing, for an ambitious plan by African leaders to reform the continent's political systems, end its wars, and adopt free market economic policies to spur development. The New Partnership for African Development (called NEPAD) was intended by its African authors as a sharp break with actions over the previous four decades since independence, during which many of the continent's fifty-three nations remained among the most poverty stricken and strife-torn in the world.

At their annual summit meeting, held June 26–27, 2002, in Alberta, Canada, the leaders of the seven wealthiest nations, plus Russia, endorsed the African partnership plan and pledged to contribute at least $6 billion annually to it, plus debt relief and trade concessions. The leaders of the Group of Eight (G-8) nations said the African plan "provides an historic opportunity to overcome obstacles to development" on the continent. The authors of the African plan had hoped for more substantial assistance from the industrialized world to offset the estimated $64 billion annual cost of promoting economic development in the region. They accepted the more modest promises of the G-8 leaders, however, and began drawing up the specifics to put their program into effect.

The G-8 summit was the second in three years to deal with economic development of the world's poorest countries. Meeting in Japan in 2000, the G-8 leaders had agreed to a UN-drafted plan to cut in half the share of the world's population living in poverty by 2015. The entire United Nations later adopted that plan as part of its "Millennium Declaration." The G-8 nations included Britain, Canada, France, Germany, Italy, Japan, and the United States—plus Russia, an economically weak nation that was invited to the summit because of its political and military power. (G-8 poverty plan, Historic Documents of 2000, p. 475; Millennium Declaration, Historic Documents of 2000, p. 700)

446

Africa Overview

A key feature of Africa's development plan was a promise by the continent's leaders to put an end to the numerous ethnic and regional wars that had killed millions of people and thwarted economic development and democracy. United Nations Secretary General Kofi Annan, a Ghanian, had told African leaders that they, and not the European imperialist powers of the nineteenth and early twentieth century, were primarily responsible for these wars. Partly in response to Annan's criticism, key African leaders, including South African president Thabo Mbeki and Senegal's new president, Abdoulaye Wade, stepped up broad-based efforts to resolve the conflicts. (Annan warnings, Historic Documents of 1998, p. 220)

For a variety of reasons, several of the most significant wars ended or appeared to be nearing an end during 2002. The biggest regional war in modern African history, for control of the Democratic Republic of the Congo, wound down with peace agreements between the Congolese government and its major opponents. Two of the continent's longest civil wars, in Angola and Sudan, also appeared to be nearing conclusion, and the relatively brief but bloody war in Sierra Leone ended with a successful election. Negotiations began in October to resolve disputes that had reduced Somalia to a patchwork of territories controlled by competing factions. Progress also came on the political front in Kenya, where the long-serving autocratic president, Daniel Arap Moi, grudgingly gave up office and allowed a free election that was won by an opposition leader. (Angola, p. 151; Congo, p. 546; Sierra Leone, p. 247; Kenya, p. 1044)

Despite these signs of progress, Africa could not quite shake itself of the demons of the past. In West Africa, age-old conflicts between Muslims and Christians erupted anew in Nigeria and Ivory Coast; the latter country, once an island of stability, found itself in the grip of a full-scale civil war at year's end. Zimbabwe, another one-time African success story, suddenly came to characterize many of the continent's persistent problems as an authoritarian president determined to hold onto power. Robert Mugabe rigged elections, intimidated the opposition, and allowed his country's economy to slide into chaos. Zimbabwe and five of its neighbors in southern Africa (Lesotho, Malawi, Mozambique, Swaziland, and Zambia) were threatened by a widespread famine, and the AIDS pandemic continued unabated, with an estimated 29 million Africans infected by the AIDS/HIV virus. (Zimbabwe, p. 133; AIDS, p. 469)

African Partnership

The peace-and-development proposal endorsed by the G-8 leaders was the culmination of a long process that began in 2000 with separate plans by Senegal's Wade and South Africa's Mbeki. In 2001 the two merged their ideas into a document, originally called the New African Initiative. G-8 leaders gave a tentative endorsement to the plan at their 2001 summit in Genoa, Italy, and promised to put Africa at the top of the agenda for their 2002 meeting. African leaders in 2001 also endorsed the plan, the name of which was later changed to the New Partnership for African Development. (Background, Historic Documents of 2001, p. 504)

The heart of the plan was a proposed deal between Africa and the world's wealthiest nations. For their part, the African leaders promised to end their regional wars, reduce corruption, embrace democracy, and adopt free market principles to govern their countries' economies. In turn, the Africans asked the United States and other wealthy countries for additional development aid and increased access to their markets for African agricultural and manufactured goods. Wade and Mbeki calculated that African nations needed an additional $64 billion each year to carry out the plan, some from increased savings and investment by Africans, but most in the form of aid, investment, debt relief, and trade concessions by the industrialized world.

A central element of the plan was a "peer review mechanism" through which African leaders would hold each other accountable for improved governance, adoption of free market economic policies, and other steps needed to modernize their societies and obtain international aid. The plan was supposed to go beyond rhetoric; for example, a country would be ineligible for aid if the military ousted elected leaders in a coup or if it invaded or supported rebel movements in other countries. Some African leaders—most notably Libyan leader Muammar Qaddafi—resisted common standards, however, calling them a neocolonial ruse by Western countries to regain control of the continent. Despite these disagreements, African leaders endorsed the NEPAD plan at a meeting on March 26, and in mid-June (ahead of the G-8 summit) they agreed to draft a formal system for monitoring each other's performance. The leaders of twelve African countries on November 4 signed an agreement establishing such a system.

The difficulty of putting peer review into practice was illustrated during the year by African reactions to the elections in Zimbabwe. Western nations and a few African leaders (notably Senegal's Wade) denounced the strong-arm tactics that President Mugabe employed to hold onto power, but most African leaders either were silent or defended Mugabe. The most prominent example was South Africa's Mbeki. Despite his eloquent pleas for Africans to embrace democracy, Mbeki refused to issue a direct condemnation of Mugabe's authoritarian approach to the ballot box.

World events also conspired to undermine support for the plan. The September 11, 2001, terrorist attacks against the United States diverted international attention toward the war against terrorism, the rebuilding of Afghanistan, and, ultimately, the determination of U.S. President George W. Bush to push Iraqi leader Saddam Hussein from power. (Afghanistan, p. 15; Iraq, pp. 612, 713; Terrorism war, p. 927)

Monterrey Summit

An important precursor to the G-8 summit was a UN-sponsored Conference on Financing for Development, held March 21–22 in Monterrey, Mexico. A week before the conference started, Bush announced plans for in-

creased U.S. aid to countries in Africa and other regions that promoted good governance and open markets and emphasized investments in education, health care, and other public service. He said a new program called the Millennium Challenge Account would boost U.S. aid spending by $5 billion to the program over a three-year period, starting in fiscal year 2004. U.S. development aid was pegged at about $10 billion in fiscal year 2002, and Bush's plan would increase the annual amount by about $1.7 billion.

If the White House expected cheers from the developing world for that proposal, it was disappointed. A broad range of critics said the suggested increase was minuscule compared to the need. Five days later, White House officials announced a "clarification" that made Bush's plan appear substantially more generous over the long term. In addition to the $5 billion increase spread over three years, the actual plan would result in a $5 billion annual increase in U.S. development aid by fiscal 2006—putting the annual total at $15 billion, 50 percent more than the fiscal 2002 amount. The White House statement blamed the original figure on a miscalculation by unnamed administration officials. That announcement brought some of the cheers the administration might have expected: "We love any kind of clarification or mistake that results in more money for poor people," said Luis Clemens, a spokesman for the British-based development and relief agency Oxfam.

At the Monterrey conference, industrialized countries, including the United States, promised to provide $12 billion in additional aid to poor countries by 2006. African leaders expressed hope that half of that amount would be dedicated to their region. In a separate announcement, Bush on June 20 said the United States would double its annual aid for education in Africa to $200 million over the next five years.

G-8 Summit Decisions

Before their meeting, the G-8 leaders received plenty of advice from development experts and prominent international officials. Two of the most important pieces of advice came from James Wolfensen, president of the World Bank, and UN Secretary General Annan. Speaking at an aid conference in Washington on June 4, Wolfensen called on the wealthy nations to concentrate increased aid on Africa. "Nowhere is the need for such help more evident than in Africa," he said. In a letter to the G-8 leaders, Annan said that while African nations bore primary responsibility for improving their lot, "even the best efforts of these countries to break out of the cycle of poverty, ignorance, disease, conflict, and environmental degradation are likely to be insufficient unless they can count on the support of the international community." The world's poor people "would therefore be bitterly disappointed if your meeting confined itself to offering them good advice and solemn exhortation, rather than pledges of action," Annan said.

Among the G-8 leaders, British prime minister Tony Blair and Canadian prime minister Jean Chretien were the principal backers of firm action. Both men lobbied their colleagues privately and publicly in the weeks before *the summit. Blair, for example, used unusually blunt language in saying the G-8 leaders had an obligation to open their markets to goods from developing countries in Africa and other regions. "It really is hypocrisy for us, the wealthy nations, to talk of our concern to alleviate poverty of the developing world while we block access to our markets," he said. In private meetings before and during the summit, however, Blair and Chretien encountered resistance. Japanese prime minister Junichiro Koizumi, whose country was still mired in a decade-long economic downturn, was reluctant to promise substantial new aid. Three of the leaders—Bush, Chretien, and French president Jacques Chirac—were unwilling to make firm commitments to reduce the agricultural subsidies demanded by farmers in their own countries.*

Four African leaders—Mbeki, Wade, Nigerian president Olusegun Obasanjo, and Algerian president Abdelaziz Bouteflika—and Annan attended the G-8 summit, held at the Kananaskis ski resort in the Canadian Rockies.

The central decision by the G-8 leaders was to promise that African nations would receive at least one-half of the $12 billion annually in additional development aid pledged at the Monterrey meeting in March. Education was to be a primary focus of the new aid, which would begin flowing by 2006 to African nations that had met the democratic and free market standards of the NEPAD plan. The G-8 leaders also agreed to add $1 billion to a program, in existence since 1996, that provided debt relief to the most debt-burdened poor countries in the world.

Less specifically, the leaders set a goal of eventually eliminating tariffs and quotas on all products from the world's poorest countries, known as the least developed countries, including those in Africa. Significantly, however, the G-8 leaders offered only the vaguest of plans to phase out export subsidies—rather than all subsidies for production—to farmers in their own countries. In fact, just six weeks before the G-8 summit, Bush signed into law a new farm bill (PL 107–171) providing $414 billion in various subsidies over ten years to American farmers. Africans and development experts had long said that agricultural subsidies in Europe and the United States effectively closed those markets to farm goods from Africa.

G-8 leaders also announced vague measures intended to help reduce conflict in Africa. These plans included the writing of regulations to curtail illegal arms sales to rebel groups by international arms brokers, and G-8 funding and training (but no troops) for an regional peacekeeping force in Africa. The leaders said they initially would focus their efforts on Angola, the Democratic Republic of the Congo, Sierra Leone, and Sudan.

In a news conference following the summit, Blair said: "Today's document will send out a signal of hope to Africa. We have agreed to help Africa help itself. This will be remembered as the summit that devoted the lion's share of its attention to Africa." Chretien made similarly optimistic statements, saying that the G-8 leaders "have acted collectively to make sure globalization benefits all and no nation is left behind." Bush left the summit early and did not comment on the agreement.

Reactions

The African leaders who developed the NEPAD plan and attended the summit had known that the G-8 leaders were not likely to agree to a massive increase in aid or to make firm promises to eliminate trade barriers. Even so, they clearly had hoped for more than they received. Nigeria's Obasanjo put the best face on the result: "This is a beginning, a departure, it's not the end," he told reporters. "If we have a good departure, the likelihood is we will have a good arrival."

Annan sought to emphasize the potential of a partnership between Africa and the G-8 nations—but used the all-important words "if" and "might." He said: "If Africans really stick to the commitments they have made in NEPAD to themselves, and to each other, and if the G-8 really carry out the action plan they are announcing today, this summit might come to be seen as a turning point in the history of Africa, and indeed of the world."

Other advocates of increased aid and trade concessions for Africa made scathing attacks on the G-8 summit. Oxfam issued a statement saying the summit had "failed to deliver the much-hyped breakthrough for Africa. A year of promises and grand intentions came to nothing as the leaders of the industrialized world agreed to an action plan lacking two key elements— action and a plan."

The United Nations General Assembly held a special meeting on the NEPAD plan on September 16. Addressing that meeting, Mbeki said African leaders were determined to keep the promises of the plan. "We stand in front of the peoples of the world to pledge that we'll honor the commitment we have made—that we'll act firmly to extricate Africa out of her long night of misery," he said. Secretary of State Colin Powell told the session that "the real test" of the African plan would come when the continent's leaders moved to carry out the governance and economic changes they had promised. "The people of Africa, and indeed the people of the world, will ultimately judge this initiative on whether its bold rhetoric and commitments are reflected in concrete action for change and greater well-being," he said.

Following is the text of the "G-8 Africa Action Plan," issued June 27, 2002, at the conclusion of the annual summit meeting of leaders of the Group of Eight nations, held in Alberta, Canada.

The document was obtained from the Internet at www .g8.gc.ca/kananaskis/afraction-en.asp; accessed November 28, 2002.

1. We, the Heads of State and Government of eight major industrialized democracies and the Representatives of the European Union, meeting with African Leaders at Kananaskis, welcome the initiative taken by African States in adopting the *New Partnership for Africa's Develop-*

ment (NEPAD), a bold and clear-sighted vision of Africa's development. We accept the invitation from African Leaders, extended first at Genoa last July and reaffirmed in the NEPAD, to build a new partnership between the countries of Africa and our own, based on mutual responsibility and respect. The NEPAD provides an historic opportunity to overcome obstacles to development in Africa.Our Africa Action Plan is the G-8's initial response, designed to encourage the imaginative effort that underlies the NEPAD and to lay a solid foundation for future cooperation.

2. The case for action is compelling. Despite its great potential and human resources, Africa continues to face some of the world's greatest callenges. The many initiatives designed to spur Africa's development have failed to deliver sustained improvements to the lives of individual women, men and children throughout Africa.

3. The *New Partnership for Africa's Development* offers something different. It is, first and foremost, a pledge by African Leaders to the people of Africa to consolidate democracy and sound economic management, and to promote peace, security and people-centred development. African Leaders have personally directed its creation and implementation. They have formally undertaken to hold each other accountable for its achievement. They have emphasized good governance and human rights as necessary preconditions for Africa's recovery. hey focus on investment-driven economic growth and economic governance as the engine for poverty reduction, and on the importance of regional and sub-regional partnerships within Africa.

4. We welcome this commitment. In support of the NEPAD objectives, we each undertake to establish enhanced partnerships with African countries whose performance reflects the NEPAD commitments. Our partners will be selected on the basis of measured results. This will lead us to focus our efforts on countries that demonstrate a political and financial commitment to good governance and the rule of law, investing in their people, and pursuing policies that spur economic growth and alleviate poverty. We will match their commitment with a commitment on our own part to promote peace and securiy in Africa, to boost expertise and capacity, to encourage trade and direct growth-oriented investment, and to provide more effective official development assistance.

5. Together, we have an unprecedented opportunity to make progress on our common goals of eradicating extreme poverty and achieving sustainable development. The new round of multilateral trade negotiations begun [in 2001] at Doha [Qatar], the Monterrey meeting on finaning for development, this G-8 Summit at Kananaskis and the World Summit on Sustainable Development in Johannesburg, are key milestones in this process.

6. NEPAD recognizes that the prime responsibility for Africa's future lies with Africa itself. We will continue to support African efforts to encourage public engagement in the NEPAD and we will continue to con-

sult with our African partners on how we can best assist their own efforts. G-8 governments are committed to mobilize and energize global action, marshal resources and expertise, and provide impetus in support of the NEPAD's objectives. As G-8 partners, we will undertake mutually reinforcin actions to help Africa accelerate growth and make lasting gains against poverty. Our Action Plan focuses on a limited number of priority areas where, collectively and individually, we can add value.

7. The African peer-review process is an innovative and potentially decisive element in the attainment of the objectives of the NEPAD. We welcome the adoption on June 11 by the NEPAD Heads of State and Government Implementation Committee of the Declaration on Democracy, Political, Economic and Corporate Governance and the African Peer Review Mechanism. The peer-review process will inform our considerations of eligibility for enhanced partnerships. We will each make our own assessments in making these partnership decisions. While we will focus particular attention on enhanced-partnership countries, we will also work with countries that do not yet meet the standards of NEPAD but which re clearly committed to and working towards its implementation. We will not work with governments which disregard the interests and dignity of their people.

8. However, as a matter of strong principle, our commitment to respond to situations of humanitarian need remains universal and is independent of particular regimes. So, too, is our commitment to addressingthe core issues of human dignity and development. The Development Goals set out in the United Nations Millennium Declaration are an important component of this engagement.

9. At Monterrey, in March 2002, we agreed to revitalize efforts to help unlock and more effectively utilize all development resources including domestic savings, trade and investment, and official development assistance. A clear link was made between good governance, sound policies, aid effectiveness and development success. In support of this strong international consensus, substantial new development assistance commitments were announced at Monterrey. By 2006, these new commitments will increase ODA [official development assistance] by a total of US$12 billion per year. Each of us will decide, in accordance with our respective priorities and procedures, how we will allocate the additional money we have pledged. Assuming strong African policy commitments, and given recent assistance trends, we believe that in aggregate half or more of our new development assistance could be directed to African nations that govern justly, invest in their own people and promote economic freedom. In this way we will support the objectives of the NEPAD. This will help ensure that no country geninely committed to poverty reduction, good governance and economic reform will be denied the chance to achieve the Millennium Goals through lack of finance.

10. We will pursue this Action Plan in our individual and collective capacities, and through the international institutions to which we belong. We warmly invite other countries to join us. We also encourage South-South cooperation and collaboration with international institutions and civil society, including the business sector, in support of the NEPAD. We will continue to maintain a constructive dialogue with our African partners in order to achieve effective implementation of our Action Plan and to support the objectives of the NEPAD. We will take the necessay steps to ensure the effective implementation of our Action Plan and will review progress at our next Summit based on a final report from our Personal Representatives for Africa.

11. To demonstrate our support for this new partnership, we make the following engagements in support of the NEPAD:

I. Promoting Peace and Security

Time and again, progress in Africa has been undermined or destroyed by conflict and insecurity. Families have been displaced and torn apart, and the use of child soldiers has robbed many individuals of the opportunity to learn, while also sowing the seeds of long-term national disruption, instability and poverty. Economic development has been deeply undermined as scarce resources needed tofight poverty have too often been wasted in deadly and costly armed conflicts. We are determined to make conflict prevention and resolution a top priority, and therefore we commit to:

1.1 Supporting African efforts to resolve the principal armed conflicts on the continent—including by:
- Providing additional support to efforts to bring peace to the Democratic Republic of the Congo and Sudan, and to consolidate peace in Angola and Sierra Leone within the next year;
- Assisting with programmes of disarmament, demobilization and reintegration; at the appropriate time,
- Taking joint action to support post-conflict development in the Great Lakes Region and Sudan; and,
- Endorsing the proposals from the UN Secretary-General to set up, with the Secretary-General and other influentil partners, contact groups and similar mechanisms to work with African countries to resolve specific African conflicts.

1.2 Providing technical and financial assistance so that, by 2010, African countries and regional and sub-regional organizations are able to engage more effectively to prevent and resolve violent conflict on the continent, and undertake peace support operations in accordance with the United Nations Charter—including by:
- Continuing to work with African partners to deliver a joint plan, by 2003, for the development of African capability to undertake peace support operations, including at the regional level;

- Training African peace support forces including through the development of regional centres of excellence for military and civilian aspects of conflict prevention and peace support, such as the Ko Annan International Peace Training Centre; and,
- Better coordinating our respective peacekeeping training initiatives.

1.3 Supporting efforts by African countries and the United Nations to better regulate the activities of arms brokers and traffickers and to eliminate the flow of illicit weapons to and within Africa—including by:
- Developing and adopting common guidelines to prevent the ilegal supply of arms to Africa; and,
- Providing assistance in regional trans-border cooperation to this end.

1.4 Supporting African efforts to eliminate and remove antipersonnel mines.

1.5 Working with African governments, civil society and others to address the linkage between armed conflict and the exploitation of natural resources—including by:
- Supporting United Nations and other initiatives to monitor and address the illegal exploitation and international transfer of natural resources from Africa which fuel armed conflicts, including mineral resources, petroleum, timber and water;
- Supporting voluntary control efforts such as the Kimberley Process for diamonds [new regulations governing trade in so-called "conflict diamonds"], and encouraging the adoption of voluntary principles of corporate social responsibility by those involved in developing Africa's national resources;
- Working to ensure better accountability and greater transparency with respect to those involved in the import or export of Africa's natural resources from areas of conflict;
- Promoting regional management of trans-boundary natural resources, including by supporting the Congo Basin Initiative and trans-border river basin commissions.

1.6 Providing more effective peace-building support to societies emerging from or seeking to prevent armed conflicts—including by:
- Supporting effective African-led reconciliation efforts, including both pre-conflict and post-conflict initiatives; and,
- Encouraging more effective coordination and cooperation among donors and international institutions in support of peace-building and conflict prevention efforts—particularly with respect to the effective disarmament, demobilizationand reintegration of former combatants, the collection and destruction of small arms, and the special needs of women and children, including child soldiers.

1.7 Working to enhance African capacities to protect and assist war-affected populations and facilitate the effective implementation in Africa of United Nations Security Council resolutions relating

to civilians, women and children in armed conflict—including by
supporting African countries hosting, assisting and protecting
large refugee populations

II. Strengthening Institutions and Governance

*The NEPAD maintains that "development is impossible in the absence of
true democracy, respect for human rights, peace and good governance". We
agree, and it has been our experience that reliable institutions and governance are a precondition or long-term or large-scale private investment.
The task of strengthening institutions and governance is thus both urgent
and of paramount importance, and for this reason, we commit to:*

**2.1 Supporting the NEPAD's priority political governance objec-
tives—including by:**
- Expanding capacity-building programmes related to political governance in Africa focusing on the NEPAD priority areas of: improving
  administrative and civil services, strengthening parliamentary oversight, promoting participatory decision-making, and judicial reform;
- Supporting African efforts to ensure that electoral processes are
  credible and transparent, and that elections are conducted in a manner that is free and fair and in accordance with the NEPAD's commitment to uphold and respect "global standards of democracy";
- Supporting African efforts to involve parliamentarians and civil society in all aspects of the NEPAD process; and,
- Supporting the reform of the security sector through assisting the
  development of an independent judiciary and democratically controlled police structures.

**2.2 Strengthening capacity-building programmes related to eco-
nomic and corporate governance in Africa focusing on the
NEPAD priority areas of implementing sound macro-economic
strategies, strengthening public financial management and accountability, protecting the integrity of monetary and financial
systems, strengthening accounting and auditing systems, and
developing an effective corporate governance framework—
including by:**
- Supporting international and African organizations such as the African Capacity Building Foundation (ACBF) and the African Regional
  Technical Assistance Centres (AFRITACs) initiative of the International Monetary Fund (IMF) in expanding regionally-oriented technical assistance and capacity-building programmes in Africa; and,
- Financing African-led research on economic governance isses
  (through the United Nations Economic Commission for Africa
  (ECA), sub-regional and regional organizations, and other African
  institutions and organizations with relevant expertise).

2.3 Supporting African peer-review arrangements—including by:
- Encouraging cooperation with respect to peer-review practices,
  modalities and experiences between the Organisation for Economic

Co-operation and Development (OECD) and the ECA, including the participation by the ECA in the OECD Development Assistance Committee (DAC) peer-review process where the countries under review so agree;

- Encouraging, where appropriate, substantive information sharing between Africa and its partners with respect to items under peer-revew; and,
- Supporting regional organizations in developing tools to facilitate peer-review processes.

2.4 Giving increased attention to and support for African efforts to promote and protect human rights—including by:

- Supporting human rights activities and national, regional and sub-regional human rights institutions in Africa;
- Supporting African efforts to implement human rights obligations undertaken by African governments; and,
- Supporting African efforts to promote reconciliation and to ensure accountability for violations of human rights and humanitarian law, including genocide, crimes against humanity and other war crimes.

2.5 Supporting African efforts to promote gender equality and the empowerment of women—including by:

- Supporting African efforts to achieve equal participation of African women in all aspects of the NEPAD process and in fulfilling the NEPAD objectives; and,
- Supporting the application of gender main-streaming in all policies and programmes.

2.6 Intensifying support for the adoption and implementation of effective measures to combat corruption, bribery and embezzlement—including by:

- Working to secure the early establishment of a UN Convention on Corruption, and the early ratification of the UN Convention Against Transnational Organized Crime;
- Strengthening and assisting the implementation and monitoring of the OECD Convention on Bribery and assisting anti-bribery and anti-corruption programmes through the international financial institutions (IFIs) and the multilateral development banks;
- Intensifying international cooperation to recover illicitly acquired financial assets;
- Supporting voluntary anti-corruption initiatives, such as the DAC Guidelines, the OECD Guidelines for Multinational Enterprises, and the UN Global Compact;
- Supporting the role of parliamentarians in addressing corruption and promoting good governance; and,
- Assisting African countries in their efforts to combat money laundering, including supporting World Bank/IMF efforts to improve co-ordination in the delivery of technical assistance to combat money laundering and terrorist financing in African countries.

III. Fostering Trade, Investment, Economic Growth and Sustainable Development

Generating economic growth is central to the NEPAD's goal of mobilizing resources for poverty reduction and development. A comprehensive effort is required to stimulate economic activity in all productive sectors while paying particular attention to sustainability and social costs and to the role of the private sector as the engine for economic growth. In this context, the particular importance of infrastructure has been emphasized by our African partners—including as a domain for public-private investment partnerships, and as a key component of regional integration and development. In order to achieve adequate growth rates, Africa must have broader access to markets. The launch of multilateral trade negotiations by World Trade Organization (WTO) members in Doha, which placed the needs and interests of developing countries at the heart of the negotiations, will help create a framework for the integration of African countries into the world trading system and the global economy, thus creating increased opportunities for trade-based growth. We are committed to the Doha development agenda and to implementing fully the WTO work programme,as well as to providing increased trade-related technical assistance to help African countries participate effectively in these negotiations. With these considerations in mind, we commit to:

3.1 Helping Africa attract investment, both from within Africa and from abroad, and implement policies conducive to economic growth—including by:
  - Supporting African initiatives aimed at improving the investment climate, including sound economic policies and efforts to improve the security of goods and transactions, consolidate property rights, modernize customs, institute needed legal and judicial reforms, and help mitigate risks for investors;
  - Facilitating the financing of private investment through increased use of development finance institutions and export credit and risk-guarantee agencies and by strengthening equivalent institutions in Africa;
  - Supporting African initiatives aimed at fostering efficient and sustainable regional financial markets and domestic savings and financing structures, including micro-credit schemes—while giving particular attention to seeing that credit and business support services meet the needs of poor women and men;
  - Enhancing international cooperation to promote greater private investment and growth in Africa, including through public-private partnerships; and,
  - Supporting the efforts of African governments to obtain sovereign credit ratings and gain access to private capital markets, including on a regional basis.

3.2 Facilitating capacity-building and the transfer of expertise for the development of infrastructure projects, with particular attention to regional initiatives.

3.3 Providing greater market access for African products—including by:

- Reaffirming our commitment to conclude negotiations no later than 1 January 2005 on further trade liberalization in the Doha round of multilateral trade negotiations taking full account of the particular circumstances, needs and requirements of developing countries, including in Africa;
- Without prejudging the outcome of the negotiations, applying our Doha commitment to comprehensive negotiations on agriculture aimed at substantial improvements in market access, reductions of all forms of export subsidies with a view to their being phased out, and substantial reductions in trade-distorting domestic support;
- Working toward the objective of duty-free and quota-free access for all products originating from the Least Developed Countries (LDCs), including African LDCs, and, to this end, each examining how to facilitate the fuller and more effective use of existing market access arrangements; and,
- Ensuring that national product standards do not unnecessarily restrict African exports and that African nations can play their full part in the relevant international standard setting systems.

3.4 Increasing the funding and improving the quality of support for trade-related technical assistance and capacity-building in Africa—including by:

- Supporting the establishment and expansion of trade-related technical assistance programmes in Africa;
- Supporting the establishment of sub-regional market and trade information offices to support trade-related technical assistance and capacity-building in Africa;
- Assisting regional organizations in their efforts to integrate trade policy into member country development plans;
- Working to increase African participation in identifying WTO-related technical assistance needs, and providing technical assistance to African countries to implement international agreements, such as the WTO agreement;
- Assisting African producers in meeting product and health standards in export markets; and,
- Providing technical assistance to help African countries engage in international negotiations, and in standard-setting systems.

3.5 Supporting African efforts to advance regional economic integration and intra-African trade—including by:

- Helping African countries develop regional institutions in key sectors affecting regional integration, including infrastructure, water, food security and energy, and sustainable management and conservation of natural resources;

- Working towards enhanced market access, on a WTO-compatible basis, for trade with African free trade areas or customs unions;
- Supporting the efforts of African countries to eliminate tariff and non-tariff barriers within Africa in a WTO-consistent manner; and,
  - Supporting efforts by African countries to work towards lowering trade barriers on imports from the rest of the world.

3.6 **Improving the effectiveness of Official Development Assistance (ODA), and strengthening ODA commitments for enhanced-partnership countries—including by:**

- Ensuring effective implementation of the OECD/DAC recommendations on untying aid to the Least Developed Countries;
- Implementing effectively the OECD agreement to ensure that export credit support to low-income countries is not used for unproductive purposes;
- Supporting efforts within the DAC to reduce aid management burdens on recipient countries and lower the transactions costs of aid;
- Taking all necessary steps to implement the pledges we made at Monterrey, including ODA level increases and aid effectiveness; and,
- Reviewing annually, within the DAC and in coordination with all relevant institutions, our progress towards the achievement in frica of the Development Goals contained in the United Nations Millennium Declaration.

IV. Implementing Debt Relief

4.1 Our aim is to assist countries through the Heavily Indebted Poor Countries (HIPC) Initiative to reduce poverty by enabling them to exit the HIPC process with a sustainable level of debt. The HIPC Initiative will reduce, by US$19 billion (net present value terms), the debt of some 22 African countries that are following sound economic policies and good governance. Combined with traditional debt relief and additional bilateral debt forgiveness, this represents a reduction of some US$30 billion—about two-thirds of their total debt burden—that will allow an important shift of resources towards education, health and other social and productive uses.

4.2 Debt relief alone, however, no matter how generous, cannot guarantee long-term debt sustainability. Sound policies, good governance, prudent new borrowing, and sound debt management by HIPCs, as well as responsible financing by creditors, will be necessary to ensure debt sustainability. We are committed to seeing that the projected shortfall in the HIPC Trust Fund is fully financed. Moreover, we remain ready, as necessary, to provide additional debt relief—so-called "topping up"—on a case-by-case basis, to countries that have suffered a fundamental change in their economic circumstances due to extraordinary external shocks. In that context these countries must continue to demonstrate a commitment to poverty reduction, sound financial management, and good governance. We will fund our share of the shortfall in the HIPC Initiative, recognizing that this shortfall will be up to US$1 billion. We call on other creditor countries to join us. Once countries exit the HIPC process, we expect they will not need additional relief under this Initiative. We support an increase in the use of grants for the poorest and debt-vulnerable countries, and look forward to its rapid adoption.

V. Expanding Knowledge: Improving and Promoting Education and Expanding Digital Opportunities

Investing in education is critical to economic and social development in Africa, and to providing Africans with greater opportunities for personal and collective advancement. Education also holds the key to important goals such as achieving full gender equality for women and girls. Yet most African countries have made poor progress towards the attainment of the Dakar Education for All (EFA) goals. In addition, the capacity of information and communications technology (ICT) to help Africa exploit digital opportunities, has not yet been realized. ICT has ben identified by the NEPAD as a targeted priority for economic and human development in Africa. With this in mind, we commit to:

5.1 **Supporting African countries in their efforts to improve the quality of education at all levels—including by:**
- Significantly increasing the support provided by our bilateral aid agencies to basic education for countries with a strong policy and financial commitment to the sector, in order to achieve the goals of universal primary education and equal access to education for girls. In that regard we will work vigorously to operationalize the G-8 Education Task Force report with a view to helping African countries which have shown through their actions a strong policy and financial commitment to education to achieve these goals; and to encourage other African countries to take the necessary steps so that they, too, can achieve universal primary education by 2015;
- Supporting the development and implementation by African countries of national educational plans that reflect the Dakar goals on Education for All, and encouraging support for those plans—particularly universal primary education—by the international community as an integral part of the national development strategies;
- Giving special emphasis and support to teacher training initiatives, in line with the NEPAD priorities, and the creation of accountability mechanisms and EFA assessment processes;
- Working with IFIs to increase their education-related spending, as a further supplement to bilateral and other efforts;
- Supporting the development of a client-driven "Education for All" Internet portal;
- Supporting programmes to encourage attendance and enhance academic performance, such as school feeding programmes; and,

461

Supporting the development of community learning centres to develop the broader educational needs of local communities.

5.2 Supporting efforts to ensure equal access to education by women and girls—including by:

- Providing scholarships and other educational support for women and girls; and,
- Supporting African efforts to break down social, cultural and other barriers to equal access by women and girls to educational opportunities.

5.3 Working with African partners to increase assistance to Africa's research and higher education capacity in enhanced-partnership countries—including by:

- Supporting the development of research centres and the establishment of chairs of excellence in areas integral to the NEPAD in Africa; and,
- Favouring the exchange of visiting academics and encouraging research partnerships between G-8/donor and African research institutions.

5.4 Helping Africa create digital opportunities—including by:

- Encouraging the Digital Opportunity Task Force (DOT Force) International e-Development Resources Network to focus on Africa, and supporting other DOT Force initiatives that can help to create digital opportunities, each building wherever possible on African initiatives already underway;
- Working towards the goal of universal access to ICT by working with African countries to improve national, regional and international telecommunications and ICT regulations and policies in order to create ICT-friendly environments;
- Encouraging and supporting the development of public-private partnerships to fast- track the development of ICT infrastructure and,
- Supporting entrepreneurship and human resource development of Africans within the ICT Sector.

5.5 Helping Africa make more effective use of ICT in the context of promoting sustainable economic, social and political development—including by:

- Supporting African initiatives to make best use of ICT to address education and health issues; and,
- Supporting African countries in increasing access to, and making the best use of, ICT in support of governance, including by supporting the development and implementation of national e-strategies and e-governance initiatives aimed at increased efficiency, effectiveness, transparency and accountability of government.

VI. Improving Health and Confronting HIV/AIDS

The persistence of diseases such as malaria and tuberculosis has remained a severe obstacle to Africa's development. To this burden has been added the devastating personal and societal costs resulting from AIDS, the consequences of which stand to undermine all efforts to promote development in Africa. The result has been a dramatic decrease in life expectancy in Africa and a significant new burden on African health systems and economies. Substantial efforts are needed to confront the health challenges that Africa faces, including the need to enhance immunization efforts directed at polio and other preventable disease. Therefore, recognizing that HIV/AIDS affects all aspects of Africa's future development and should therefore be a factor in all aspects of our support for Africa, we commit to:

6.1 Helping Africa combat the effects of HIV/AIDS—including by:
- Supporting programmes that help mothers and children infected or affected by HIV/AIDS, including children orphaned by AIDS;
- Supporting the strengthening of training facilities for the recruiting and training of health professionals;
- Supporting the development, adoption and implementation of gender-sensitive, multi-sectoral HIV/AIDS programs for prevention, care, and treatment;
- Supporting high level political engagement to increase awareness and reduce the stigma associated with HIV/AIDS;
- Supporting initiatives to improve technical capacity, including disease surveillance;
- Supporting efforts to develop strong partnerships with employers in increasing HIV/AIDS awareness and in providing support to victims and their families;
- Supporting efforts that integrate approaches that address both HIV/AIDS and tuberculosis; and,
- Helping to enhance the capacity of Africa to address the challenges that HIV/AIDS poses to peace and security in Africa.

6.2 Supporting African efforts to build sustainable health systems in order to deliver effective disease interventions—including by:
- Pressing ahead with current work with the international pharmaceutical industry, affected African countries and civil society to promote the availability of an adequate supply of life-saving medicines in an affordable and medically effective manner;
- Supporting African countries in helping to promote more effective, and cost-effective, health interventions to the most vulnerable sectors of society—including reducing maternal and infant mortality and morbidity;
- Continuing support for the [United Nations] Global Fund to Fight AIDS, Tuberculosis and Malaria, and working to ensure that the Fund continues to increase the effectiveness of its operations and learns from its experience;
- Supporting African efforts to increase Africa's access to the Global Fund and helping to enhance Africa's capacity to participate in and benefit from the Fund;

- Providing assistance to strengthen the capacity of the public sector to monitor the quality of health services offered by both public and private providers; and,
- Supporting and encouraging the twinning of hospitals and other health organizations between G-8 and African countries.

6.3 Accelerating the elimination and mitigation in Africa of polio, river blindness and other diseases or health deficiencies—including by:

- Providing, on a fair and equitable basis, sufficient resources to eliminate polio by 2005; and,
- Supporting relevant public-private partnerships for the immunization of children and the elimination of micro-nutrient deficiencies in Africa.

6.4 Supporting health research on diseases prevalent in Africa, with a view to narrowing the health research gap, including by expanding health research networks to focus on African health issues, and by making more extensive use of researchers based in Africa.

VII. Increasing Agricultural Productivity

The overwhelming majority of Africa's population is rural. Agriculture is therefore the principal economic preoccupation for most of Africa's people. Agriculture is central not only to the quality of life of most Africans, but also to the national economy of nearly all African states. Increased agricultural production, efficiency and diversification are central to the economic growth strategies of these countries. In support of the NEPAD's growth and sustainable development initiatives on agriculture, we commit to:

7.1 Making support for African agriculture a higher international priority in line with the NEPAD's framework and priorities— including by:

- Supporting the reform and financing of international institutions and research organizations that address Africa's agricultural development priority needs;
- Supporting efforts to strengthen agricultural research in Africa as well as research related to issues and aspects that are of particular importance to Africa; and,
- Working with African countries to improve the effectivenss and efficiency of ODA for agriculture, rural development and food security where there are coherent development strategies reflected in government budget priorities.

7.2 Working with African countries to reduce poverty through improved sustainable productivity and competitiveness—including by:

- Supporting the development and the responsible use of tried and tested new technology, including biotechnology, in a safe manner and adapted to the African context, to increase crop production

while protecting the environment through decreased usage of fragile land, water and agricultural chemicals;
- Studying, sharing and facilitating the responsible use of biotechnology in addressing development needs;
- Helping to improve farmers' access to key market information through the use of traditional and cutting edge communications technologies, while also building upon ongoing international collaboration that strengthens farmers' entrepreneurial skills;
- Encouraging partnerships in agriculture and water research and extension to develop, adapt and adopt appropriate demand-driven technologies, including for low-income resource-poor farmers, to increase agricultural productivity and improve ability to market agricultural, fish and food products;
- Working with African countries to promote property and resource rights;
- Supporting the main-streaming of gender issues into all agricultural and related policy together with targeted measures to ensure the rights of women for equal access to technology, technical support, land rights and credits;
- Working with African countries to support the development of agricultural infrastructure including production, transportation and markets; and,
- Working with African countries to develop sound agricultural policies that are integrated into Poverty Reduction Strategies.

7.3 Working to improve food security in Africa—including by:
- Working with African countries to integrate food security in poverty reduction efforts and promote a policy and institutional environment that enables poor people to derive better livelihoods from agriculture and rural development;
- Working with appropriate international organizations in responding to the dire food shortages in Southern Africa this year;
- Working with African countries to expand efforts to improve the quality and diversity of diets with micro-nutrients and by improving fortification technologies;
- Supporting African efforts to establish food safety and quality control systems, including helping countries develop legislation, enforcement procedures and appropriate institutional frameworks; and,
- Supporting efforts to improve and better disseminate agricultural technology.

VIII. Improving Water Resource Management

Water is essential to life. Its importance spans a wide range of critical uses—from human drinking water, to sanitation, to food security and agriculture, to economic activity, to protecting the natural environment. We have noted the importance of proper water resource management. We note also that water management is sometimes at the centre of threats to regional peace and security. We aso appreciate the importance of good water management for achieving sustainable economic growth and development, and therefore we commit to:

8. **Supporting African efforts to improve water resource development and management—including by:**
   - Supporting African efforts to promote the productive and environmentally sustainable development of water resources;
   - Supporting efforts to improve sanitation and access to potable water;
   - Mobilizing technical assistance to facilitate and accelerate the preparation of potable water and sanitation projects in both rural and urban areas, and to generate greater efficiency in these sectors; and,
   - Supporting reforms in the water sector aimed at decentralization, cost-recovery and enhanced user participation.

July

UN REPORT ON THE
GLOBAL AIDS EPIDEMIC
July 2, 2002

While much of the world focused its attentions in 2002 on preventing the spread of weapons of mass destruction by terrorists and rogue governments such as Iraq and North Korea, AIDS—the incurable acquired immuno-deficiency syndrome—and HIV, the virus that caused it, continued their deadly march across the world's continents. According to the United Nations, the epidemic was not leveling off in Africa, and it appeared poised to break out in several of the world's most populous countries, including China, India, and Indonesia. "Collectively, we have grossly, grossly under-estimated how bad this was going to be," said Peter Piot, executive director of UNAIDS, the United Nations agency that coordinated the global response to the epidemic. Piot's remarks came on July 2, 2002, as he released the UNAIDS annual report.

The UN and other agencies reported progress in the global fight against the disease, which by the end of 2002 had killed an estimated 20 million people and infected another 42 million. Several countries in Africa, Asia, and Latin America had taken steps that slowed the advance of the disease significantly. A campaign to force pharmaceutical companies to lower the price of their AIDS drugs was largely successful, although an effort to make generic drugs legally available was still under way. Public health experts were increasingly confident that a prevention package combining education and protection, if implemented comprehensively, could dramatically slow the spread of AIDS/HIV. What was missing, AIDS experts said, was the fi-nancing and sustained political commitment necessary to put effective pre-vention and treatment programs into place. Without such an effort, experts predicted that perhaps another 45 million people might be infected with HIV by 2010.

In the United States, the administration of President George W. Bush was widely criticized for not contributing more funding to the global AIDS fight. Irate demonstrators drowned out Health and Human Services Secretary Tommy G. Thompson when he tried to deliver a speech in Barcelona, Spain, at the 14th annual international AIDS conference. AIDS activists also criti-cized the administration for trying to focus AIDS prevention programs both at home and abroad on issues of moral value rather than on means of pre-venting the spread of the disease.

The Spread and Growth of the Pandemic

In 2002 an estimated 5 million people became infected with HIV, and an-other 3 million died of AIDS, about the same rate as in 2001. Some 42 mil-lion people, about half of them women, were living with HIV/AIDS. An estimated 3 million children under the age of fifteen were infected, and 14 million children had lost one or both parents to the disease. In addition to its direct human toll, the disease had severe implications for economic de-velopment, particularly in poor and low-income countries that were already struggling with high rates of unemployment and poverty and low levels of schooling and health care.

In Sub-Saharan Africa, which still had the highest HIV infection rates in the world, eleven countries were expected to have life expectancies of less than forty years—a level that was last experienced at the end of the 1800s. Botswana's life expectancy had already dropped to thirty-nine years, in-stead of the seventy-two years that would have been expected in the absence of the AIDS epidemic. Longevity was also declining in some Caribbean na-tions. Another troubling demographic change was the loss of improvements in child mortality. Those rates were now higher in Zimbabwe and South Africa than they were in 1990. It also was beginning to look increasingly likely that AIDS in Africa would kill more women than men. About 55 per-cent of all AIDS cases were women, and the rate of infection among women and young girls was rising.

The optimistic assumption that the high prevalence rates in some Afri-can countries had reached a plateau turned out to be wrong, according to the UNAIDS annual report. HIV prevalence among urban pregnant women con-tinued to rise in such countries as Botswana and Zimbabwe. Countries like Cameroon and Nigeria, where rates had been low and fairly stable for sev-eral years, were showing substantial increases. The prevalence rate among pregnant women in Cameroon was 11 percent in 2001, and some states in Nigeria were showing similar rates. AIDS experts were also closely watch-ing Ethiopia, where HIV/AIDS already seemed well embedded in the general population. An increase in infections among pregnant female refugees from Africa's many civil wars and armed conflicts was also a mounting concern. People who moved frequently from place to place, such as migrant workers, commercial travelers, and soldiers, had long been recognized as one avenue for the spread of the disease; refugee camps were now becoming another venue for AIDS transmission.

A UN report, "HIV/AIDS: China's Titanic Peril," released June 27, pre-dicted that the epidemic was about to explode in China and might reach 10 million people by 2010 unless a larger prevention effort were mounted. A CIA projection put the number at 10 million to 20 million, while the Amer-ican Enterprise Institute, a Washington think tank, estimated the number might reach 30 million. China, the world's most populous country, had only recently begun to admit that it was plagued with local epidemics, which it attributed primarily to drug users and tainted blood transfusions. The disease was also beginning to spread by sexual transmission and showing up in the general population.

Sex was a taboo subject for public discussion in China, and ignorance about how HIV was spread remained high, particularly in rural areas. Yet there were signs that at least some Chinese officials were treating the epidemic seriously. On the eve of World AIDS day in November an editorial in an English-language newspaper said that the fight against the disease "has gone beyond the confines of hospitals and clinics" and was "now a delicate social issue that needs joint efforts from all sectors of society." An event was also scheduled at the Great Hall of the People in Beijing, and rallies, exhibitions, and newspaper articles around the country sought to raise awareness about the disease and break down the stigma attached to it.

The HIV adult prevalence rate was under 1 percent in India, but in the world's second most populous country that meant an estimated 4 million people were living with the disease, nearly as many as in South Africa. Without a larger and more sustained effort to raise awareness and education among vulnerable populations, including women living in rural areas, experts predicted that the epidemic would only get worse. In the absence of a comprehensive prevention program, projections for the spread of the disease in India ranged from 9 million to 32 million by 2010.

In Indonesia AIDS workers were concerned about a sharp rise in injected drug use, until the 1990s a problem that was almost unheard of in that country. With an increase in injected drug use came an increase in HIV, with as many as one-third of the drug users already infected.

The fastest growing HIV/AIDS epidemic was in Eastern Europe and Central Asia, where at least 1.2 million people were thought to be living with the disease. Although official statistics put the number of HIV infections in Russia at about 220,000, Vadim Pokrovsky, the director of the Country's Center for AIDS Prevention and Treatment, said that the real numbers were somewhere between 800,000 and 1.2 million and could grow to as many as 5 million by 2007. Most infections were associated with intravenous drug use, which was rampant in Russia, but a growing proportion of the infections was sexually transmitted.

Russia was poorly equipped to deal with the epidemic. The country was already losing population through emigration, and it suffered other severe problems that were slowing its efforts at economic development. A World Bank study projected that if left unchecked, the epidemic could cut annual economic growth in Russia by half a percentage point by 2010 and by a full percentage point by 2020. Throughout the Russian Federation and Central Asian republics, increasing unemployment and poverty were associated with rising injected drug use and a slow but quickly growing increase in the prevalence of HIV. A fourfold increase in world production of heroin, combined with new trafficking routes across Central Asia, was contributing to the spread of the disease.

Prevention and Treatment

Two teams of experts issued separate but coordinated reports on June 28 arguing that a package of common prevention strategies could reduce the estimated number of new infections by 2010 by nearly two-thirds—if it were fully implemented. Full implementation could prevent an estimated 29 million new cases of HIV out of the 45 million projected, according to the first report. But the effort would cost $27 billion—about $1,000 for each infection averted. That would require global funding for prevention to be quadrupled quickly to $4.5 billion a year from its current level of $1.2 billion. "We can very substantially alter the course of the epidemic. None of this [projected increase] is inevitable," said Bernhard Schwartlander, a doctor and epidemiologist at the World Health Organization (WHO). The projections, which appeared in the medical journal Lancet, *were made by a group of researchers from UNAIDS, WHO, the U.S. Census Bureau, Imperial College in London, and The Futures Group International.*

In the second report, the Global HIV Prevention Working Group set out a twelve-point blueprint that it said had been effective in containing the spread of HIV. Among the strategies were mass media campaigns, condom distribution, voluntary testing and counseling, blood screening, school- and work-based education programs, treatment of other sexually transmitted diseases, peer counseling for prostitutes and homosexuals, and safe-needle programs for injecting drug addicts. The group noted that the package would work only if broad issues, such as the training of local health care workers, and broad social problems, such as women's lack of empowerment, poverty, and the stigma attached to the disease, were addressed at the same time. A key issue in any prevention strategy was access. "Estimates are that only one in five people at risk have access to prevention," said Helene Gayle, a cochair of the working group. "There's a huge gap in access to prevention when 80 percent of the people who need it are not getting it," she added. Gayle represented the Bill and Melinda Gates Foundation, which had donated sizable sums of money to HIV/AIDS treatment and prevention programs.

Major drug companies bowed to years of pressure in 2001 and agreed to drop the prices of some of their anti-AIDS drugs sold in Africa, and even cheaper generic drugs had become available in a few countries. Only a handful of people in need were benefiting from the drugs. An estimated 6 million people with AIDS in developing nations could benefit from anti-retrovirals. Yet only about 230,000 were taking the drugs, most of them in Brazil, which had defied international patent laws and made its own generic drugs that were given free to anyone who needed them. Only about 30,000 AIDS victims were on antiretrovirals in Africa, according to the aid group Médecins Sans Frontières (Doctors Without Borders). (Discounted AIDS drugs, Historic Documents of 2001, p. 441)

Access to antivirals might have been boosted by an international trade agreement that would allow poor countries to import generic versions of anti-AIDS drugs without being in violation of patent laws and intellectual property rights protected under the World Trade Organization (WTO). Under the proposed treaty, the holders of the patents on the drugs, typically large pharmaceutical companies, would not have to be consulted. But a year-long deadlock continued when the United States government on December 20 rejected the draft treaty because it covered more medicines than the United States thought necessary. The United States and other developed nations wanted the diseases covered by the treaty restricted to HIV/AIDS, malaria, tuberculosis, and other infectious diseases that threatened an epidemic of similar proportions. Developing countries, such as Brazil and China, which made generic versions of several drugs, said poor countries should be allowed to determine for themselves what constituted a health care crisis. Although it kept the treaty from going forward, the United States pledged to continue its policy of not challenging any country that broke current trade rules by importing the generic drugs to treat AIDS, tuberculosis, or malaria. WTO officials said they hoped to have the controversy resolved by early 2003.

A breakthrough of sorts came in South Africa earlier in the year, when the country's Constitutional Court April 4 upheld a lower court ruling ordering the government to begin distributing neviripine to HIV-infected pregnant women. The drug had been shown to reduce significantly the potential for mothers to transfer the virus to their babies during labor. But South African president Thabo Mbeki refused to allow its use, citing concerns about its toxicity. Two weeks after the court ruling, Mbeki and his cabinet capitulated and in a surprise announcement on April 19 said the government would offer neviripine to all poor, pregnant women infected with HIV. Former South African president Nelson Mandela and Bishop Desmond Tutu had pressed the policy shift. A pilot neviripine project reached about 90,000 women a year at eighteen clinics around the country. AIDS advocates were pleased but cautious. "Announcements get made, but practice is always what counts," one told the New York Times.

U.S. Policy, Funding Levels Criticized

On June 19 President Bush pledged $500 million over three years to provide neviripine to pregnant, HIV-infected women in several African and Caribbean countries and for other programs that would help prevent the transfer of HIV from mother to infant. The following day the Bush administration announced that it planned to spend $200 million over five years on education in Africa. Although not directly related to the AIDS epidemic, education was one of the areas that virtually everyone agreed had to be improved if AIDS prevention programs were to have widespread success.

Bush also proposed a $200 million appropriation for 2003 to the Global Fund to Fight AIDS, Tuberculosis, and Malaria, an independent private fund set up by the UN and the World Bank to collect funds from both private and public sources and funnel that funding to promising programs. UN Secretary General Kofi Annan and others had said that the fund would require between $7 billion and $10 billion a year for its work to be effective. Health and Human Services Secretary Thompson defended the $200 million

*as a "tremendously generous contribution" given other demands on the fed-
eral budget. But several Democrats disagreed. "We quite frankly look like
pikers," said Joseph Biden, chairman of the Senate Foreign Relations Committee. Late in the year, legislation authorizing nearly $4 billion in U.S.
contributions to overseas AIDS programs ran aground in the Senate after
two Republican senators anonymously placed holds on the bill, killing it for
the year. The Senate bill would have earmarked $2.2 billion in fiscal 2003–
2004 for the global AIDS fund.*

*AIDS activists shouted down Thompson at the Barcelona AIDS conference
in July to protest what they saw as U.S. failure to contribute its fair share
to the global fight against AIDS. Activists were also distressed with the administration's insistence on emphasizing sexual abstinence in sex education programs in the United States and its efforts to deemphasize the use
of condoms in U.S.-funded family-planning programs overseas. "Whenever
moral judgmentalism and squeamishness are judged by politicians to be
more important than preventing a life-threatening catastrophe, the epidemic is the winner," said the director of HIV/AIDS programs at Human
Rights Watch.* (Abstinence programs, Historic Documents of 2001, p. 456)

*Activists were also alarmed by a continuing series of audits of federally
funded HIV programs, especially after the heckling of Thompson at the
Barcelona conference. The Department of Health and Human Services said
that some of the investigations had been requested by lawmakers concerned
that the programs were distributing explicit sexual materials and downplaying the role of sexual abstinence. Although the department said the audits were meant to make the programs more efficient and better coordinated,
AIDS groups said they were having a chilling effect. "There is a fear out in
the community that if they produce something or say something inappropriate, or what is deemed as inappropriate, they will lose their funding,"
one activist told the Associated Press in September.*

> *Following is the text of "Fighting AIDS: A New Global Resolve,"
> the first chapter from the "Report on the Global HIV/AIDS Epi-
> demic 2002," the annual report of the Joint United Nations Pro-
> gramme on HIV/AIDS, released July 2, 2002.*
>
> **The document was obtained from the Internet at www
> .unaids.org/barcelona/presskit/report.html; accessed No-
> vember 28, 2002.**

In the past two years, the sense of common purpose in the worldwide
struggle against HIV/AIDS has intensified. More than at any other time in the
short history of the epidemic, the need to translate local and national examples of success into a global movement has become manifest.

The political momentum to tackle AIDS has grown. Public opinion in many countries has been mobilized by the media, nongovernmental organizations, activists, doctors, economists, and people living with HIV/AIDS. Communities and nations are progressively taking the lead in responding to the epidemic with increased political commitment, resources and institutional initiatives. But this new political resolve is not universal. An unacceptable number of governments and civil society institutions are still in a state of denial about the HIV/AIDS epidemic, and are failing to act to prevent its further spread or alleviate its impact.

By failing to act, governments and civil society are turning their backs on the possibility of success against AIDS. Where the moment of action has been seized, there is mounting evidence of inroads being made against the epidemic. Alongside the familiar achievements of Senegal, Thailand and Uganda, there are new successes on every continent. Despite emerging from genocide and conflict, Cambodia responded to the threat of HIV in the mid-1990s and has achieved marked declines in both the levels of HIV and the high-risk behaviours associated with its transmission. The infection rate among pregnant women in Cambodia declined by almost a third between 1997 and 2000. The Philippines has acted early to forestall the epidemic, keeping HIV rates low with strong prevention efforts and the mobilization of community and business organizations.

Brazil remains a leading example of the integration of comprehensive care and a renewed commitment to prevention. The numbers of new HIV infections have been kept much lower than forecast less than a decade ago, while the 1996 decision to establish a legal right to free medication has brought treatment and care to more than 100,000 HIV-positive people. As a result, the number of annual AIDS deaths in Brazil in 2000 was a third of that in 1996. The annual cost of medication (including drugs produced under licence by Brazilian manufacturers) is more than outweighed by the resulting health-care and related savings. Similar legislation-led drug-access models are being pursued across Central and South America.

In Africa, Zambia's focus on HIV prevention among youth and its efforts to involve businesses, farmers, schools and religious groups in the fight against AIDS are proving successful. The proportion of pregnant urban women aged 15–19 who were HIV-positive had fallen from 28.4% in 1993 to less than 14.8% five years later.

Examples of success come both from settings where HIV prevalence is low (and an expanding epidemic has been prevented) and from those where the impact of HIV/AIDS is already substantial. Both environments present challenges. Even where rapid increases in the epidemic are evident, yet population-wide prevalence is low, it is all too easy to marginalize HIV. For example, in the Russian Federation, the realization that the epidemic is taking hold among young people, and is not just affecting a stereotyped and stigmatized group of 'drug addicts' has been an important impetus for strengthening the national response. In heavily affected countries (e.g., in southern Africa), the challenge has been that of building the political conviction that solutions are possible in the face of the overwhelming impact of the epidemic.

Civil Society and Government Commitment

Growing political engagement in the response to AIDS is grounded in two decades of AIDS activism, led by individuals and communities whose lives have been touched by the epidemic. Organizations as diverse as the Gay Men's Health Crisis in New York, The AIDS Support Organisation in Uganda, the Save Your Generation Association in Ethiopia, Grupo Pela Vidda in Rio de Janeiro, and many hundreds of others like them, are built on the same foundations: an initially small group of people responding to the impact of AIDS by coming together to provide mutual support and take action.

An activist movement responding to AIDS now exists globally. It has many aspects: community groups providing home-based care, treatment activists working through media and the law courts to extend access to HIV drugs, networks such as the International Council of AIDS Service Organizations and its regional bodies, and associations of HIV-positive people nationally and internationally, together with positive women's networks.

The presence of nongovernmental and community-based organizations was notable at the United Nations General Assembly Special Session on HIV/AIDS in June 2001, providing a sense of urgency and conscience to Member State deliberations. The Global Fund to Fight AIDS, Tuberculosis and Malaria has modelled a new way of working by including on its Board not only nongovernmental organization representatives but also a seat for people who are themselves directly affected. The bedrock of activism, sustained in communities motivated to take action against AIDS, is key in driving political momentum locally, nationally and globally.

From within the United Nations, Secretary-General Kofi Annan has helped catalyse growing global engagement. In April 2001, at the African Summit on HIV/AIDS, Tuberculosis and Other Related Infectious Diseases, in Abuja, Nigeria, he issued a global call to action in the fight against AIDS. The personal priority he has given to AIDS has helped energize the United Nations system, as well as engage political and business leaders in the challenge.

At the Millennium Summit of the United Nations in September 2000, 43 Heads of State and Government, from both countries heavily affected and those less so, referred to AIDS as one of the most pressing problems worldwide. Presidents and prime ministers, particularly those from Africa and the Caribbean, but also those in Asia and Western and Eastern Europe, are displaying a personal commitment to the fight against AIDS. Support for expanded AIDS responses has been voiced by religious leaders and groups of all faiths—from Catholic and Protestant bishops and the Patriarch of All Russia, to associations of Imams and networks of Buddhist monks in South-East Asia.

AIDS is now a prominent issue at international gatherings—North and South. It has been on the agenda of summits and decision-making forums of the G8 and G77 nations, the Organization of American States, the Organization of African Unity, the Commonwealth of Nations, the European Union, the Association of South-East Asian Nations, and the Caribbean Community Secretariat (CARICOM). Both the World Economic Forum and the World Social Forum (in Porto Alegre) have held key sessions on AIDS and its global implications. The UN Security Council held its first-ever debate on AIDS in January 2000—the first time it had examined a health or development issue. Since then, it has held two more public debates on AIDS.

Global Priorities Are Now Clear

The new political momentum culminated in June 2001 when the membership of the United Nations met in a Special Session of the General Assembly to agree on a comprehensive and coordinated global response to the AIDS crisis. The members adopted a powerful Declaration of Commitment, and reaffirmed the pledge (made by world leaders in their Millennium Declaration) to halt and begin to reverse the spread of AIDS by 2015.

The UN General Assembly Special Session on HIV/AIDS differed from the hundreds of meetings and summits held on AIDS in the past 20 years in this crucial respect: it was a meeting of all States, acting as governments. As such, it yielded both a common mandate and a basis for political accountability. The Special Session's Declaration of Commitment, adopted unanimously, now serves as a benchmark for global action. Its targets and goals include the need to:

- secure more resources to fight AIDS, increasing annual spending to US$7–10 billion in low- and middle-income countries;
- ensure, by 2005, that a wide range of prevention programmes are available in all countries;
- by 2005, to ensure that at least 90% of young people aged 15–24 have access to information, education and services necessary to develop the life skills needed to reduce their vulnerability to HIV, and 95% by 2010;
- reduce by 25% the rate of HIV infection among young people aged 15–24 in the most affected countries by 2005 and globally by 2010;
- reduce by 20% by 2005 and 50% by 2010 the proportion of infants born with HIV;
- by 2003, enact or strengthen antidiscrimination and human rights protections for people living with HIV/AIDS and for vulnerable groups;
- by 2003, develop or strengthen participatory programmes to protect the health of those most affected by HIV/AIDS;
- empower women as an essential part of reducing vulnerability to HIV;
- by 2003, develop national strategies to strengthen health-care systems and address factors affecting the provision of HIV-related drugs, including affordability and pricing; and
- make treatment and care for people with HIV/AIDS as fundamental to the AIDS response as is prevention.

Debate at the Special Session on HIV/AIDS revealed continuing differences between States on how to respond to marginalized groups, such as men who have sex with men, injecting drug users and sex workers. Nevertheless, the Declaration expressed unanimous approval of fundamental approaches to tackling the epidemic, based on frank and forthright responses grounded in respect for human rights.

The Declaration of Commitment provides the world with a basis for effective political action and a yardstick of accountability. At international, regional and national gatherings since the Special Session, the Declaration of Commitment has served to define agendas and create a common platform for action.

Within weeks of the Special Session, implementation of the Declaration of Commitment was receiving regional attention—for example, in the Nassau Declaration on Health issued by Heads of Government of the Caribbean Community, and in regional action taken in the Commonwealth of Independent States.

Indicators, developed by the UNAIDS Secretariat and Cosponsors, together with other stakeholders, will keep track of progress on all the key elements of the Declaration of Commitment. The UN Secretary-General will report annually to the General Assembly on progress made in relation to the Declaration.

Meeting Targets

Table 1 [omitted] details the most recent baseline measures for the 25 worst-affected countries in the world, in relation to targets set in the Declaration of Commitment. These measures indicate current levels of HIV among young people, and show that young people's knowledge and awareness of HIV/AIDS will need to increase considerably if the relevant targets are to be met. The measures also reveal that levels of risky behaviour are relatively high (especially among men), while protective behaviour is generally low among men and women—areas in which substantial progress needs to be made.

The targeted reductions in the proportion of infants infected with HIV . . . can only be met if women's access to HIV testing increases significantly. Finally, the rate at which orphans attend school highlights another area where progress is required, since that rate is also an indicator of the degree to which orphans are receiving wider forms of support.

Complementing the Declaration of Commitment, a single United Nations system strategic plan was adopted for the first time in 2001, bringing together within the UN not only UNAIDS and its Cosponsors, but HIV/AIDS activities from a total of 29 UN organizations and agencies. A significant achievement in increased transparency and coordination, this plan will guide the UN system over the next five years.

Paradigm Shifts

Underpinning the renewed global resolve in tackling AIDS is a series of shifts in fundamental thinking about the epidemic.

Firstly, we now realize that the HIV/AIDS epidemic is at an early stage of development and that its long-term evolution is still unclear. Despite the epidemic's manifest potential for explosive growth within a matter of years, its overall dynamic needs to be considered in a time frame of decades.

Secondly, successful, proven approaches to HIV prevention have been identified, and the need for a particular emphasis on young people has been recognized. In every country where HIV transmission has been reduced, it has been among young people (and with their determination) that the most spectacular reductions have occurred.

Thirdly, community mobilization is the core strategy on which success against HIV has been built. Fostering such mobilization requires eliminating stigma, developing partnerships between social and government actors, and systematically involving communities and individuals infected and affected by HIV/AIDS.

Fourthly, access to comprehensive care and treatment for HIV/AIDS is not an optional luxury in global responses. Access to care is a basic necessity in programming in every setting—from the wealthiest to the poorest—and needs to encompass the full continuum, including home-based and palliative care, treatment of opportunistic infections and antiretroviral therapy.

Responding to demands for more equitable access to care is integral to creating broad, demand-driven strategies that respond to the desire by households and communities to protect themselves from HIV and its effects. Demand-driven HIV prevention is likely to succeed far more readily than supply-driven approaches.

Fifthly, addressing the economic, political, social and cultural factors that render individuals and communities vulnerable to HIV/AIDS is crucial to a sustainable and expanded international response.

The Millennium Development Goals, arising from the UN Millennium Summit of September 2000, include a commitment to halt and begin to reverse the global spread of AIDS by 2015. They also include the following goals: to halve global poverty; ensure primary-school education for all; promote gender equality and empower women; and reduce child mortality while improving maternal health. This total package is integral to success in alleviating the impact of AIDS.

Finally, lack of capacity to absorb increased resources allocated for HIV/AIDS, while posing challenges, is no reason to delay the boosting of responses in countries expressing commitment to an expanded response. Assessments of programme readiness carried out by UNAIDS, together with rapid responses to calls for proposals from the new Global Fund to Fight AIDS, Tuberculosis and Malaria, are both demonstrations of immediate and substantial unmet needs in AIDS programming in much of the world.

Building New Capacity for Success

Partnerships are emerging in response to AIDS, with increased involvement across the whole of government as well as between governments, civil society and the business sector. Trade unions and women's and youth organizations are engaging in AIDS-related activities, often for the first time. Business coalitions on AIDS have spread, especially in Asia and Africa. Globally, businesses have recognized the need for a proactive AIDS agenda, and efforts in this direction are being spearheaded by the Global Business Council on AIDS.

The International Labour Organization (ILO) became UNAIDS' eighth Co-sponsor in 2001. It has engineered a new code of conduct designed to protect and support workers with HIV/AIDS and to use workplaces more effectively in the fight against AIDS. . . .

Meanwhile, philanthropic foundations, such as the Bill and Melinda Gates Foundation, are making increasingly imaginative and generous contributions—both financial and intellectual—in prevention, in supporting care access, in reducing mother-to-child transmission, and in the search for a vaccine, among others.

Emergency responses, whether to conflict or disaster, are beginning to deal with AIDS more effectively in emergency settings, be they refugee camps or war-torn zones. The World Food Programme is lending its support to AIDS responses in its field of operations, while the International Federation of Red Cross and Red Crescent Societies has begun to tackle AIDS-related stigma, starting with its workers and volunteers.

The new paradigm in access to care is beginning to take effect, and long-standing global inequities are being challenged. From disputes before the World Trade Organization, to court cases in South Africa, debate in relation to essential medicines has been resolved in favour of lowering trade barriers to access. The principle of preferential pricing for HIV drugs for low- and middle-income countries has been largely accepted in the pharmaceutical industry. Prices have begun to drop and countries' rights to invoke compulsory or voluntary licensing arrangements on patented drugs and medications were affirmed clearly at the World Trade Organization meeting in Doha, Qatar, in late 2001. Generic versions of many antiretroviral drugs now exist. The World Health Organization has begun a process of quality assessment of HIV medicines (brand-name and generic) and is widely publishing the results in order to promote the rational use of drugs as well as affordable prices.

In Africa, where the gap between needs and resources is greatest, advances are being made in the wealthier countries (such as Botswana, Gabon and Nigeria); in those countries still with relatively small HIV-positive populations (such as Senegal); and by building outwards from existing capital-city infrastructure (in countries such as Uganda). Important progress has been made in the prevention of mother-to-child transmission. New guidelines on antiretroviral therapy and infant-feeding for HIV-infected mothers have been developed. Manufacturer Boehringer Ingelheim's offer, in July 2001, of free nevirapine for low- and middle-income countries is gradually being taken up. But this also means that voluntary counselling and testing need to go beyond the 1% of women in sub-Saharan Africa currently being reached. Antenatal care infrastructure has to expand. And safe infant-feeding by HIV-infected mothers must become an actual choice, rather than a theoretical one. Much work remains to be done, however, in transforming the successes of small pilot projects into large-scale programmes.

As with the epidemic in general, access to HIV treatment also has governance and security dimensions. Even in the poorest countries, in urban areas, in particular, there is already a huge backlog in demand for HIV treatment. If treatment remains inaccessible, or if it is only extended to small elites, social tension might be further inflamed. Already, AIDS 'miracle cures' have given rise to local instability in India, Nigeria, Thailand and elsewhere.

Paying the Bill

There has been a sea change in the understanding of the resources that are needed for an effective global response and in how to generate those funds. As agreed at the UN General Assembly, it is now clear that AIDS related spending needs to rise to US$7–10 billion to meet the main prevention and care needs of low- and middle-income countries. . . .

In creating optimal conditions for national governments to increase their AIDS efforts, more funds need to be liberated through debt relief or debt cancellation. But there is also no escaping the need for the world's high-income countries to step up their support for the world's poorer countries.

The International Conference on Financing for Development, held in Monterrey, Mexico, in March 2002, ended with a strong call to eradicate poverty, achieve sustained economic growth and promote sustainable development in the context of a fully inclusive and equitable global economic system. Its consensus statement called for substantially increased international development assistance, and pledges of increased funding were made by a number of nations. The Conference recognized the interconnectedness of domestic development, international development resources and foreign direct investment, international trade, international financial and technical cooperation, and external debt. It endorsed innovation in debt relief, as well as debt cancellation, where appropriate.

As was recognized in Conference discussions, the impacts of HIV are intimately connected with this emerging agenda of greater international coherence in financing for development. In the worst affected countries, AIDS has wiped out 50 years of development gains, measured in terms of improved life expectancy. By the same token, strengthening domestic and international financing capacities and cooperation, ranging from improved governance, to increased resource flows and more stable economic conditions, are core strategies for reducing HIV-related vulnerability and the impact of the epidemic.

Global challenges Huge global challenges still shape the context in which the world confronts the epidemic. Failure to control AIDS is an index of inequitable development and poor governance. Income inequality, gender inequality, labour migration, conflict and refugee movement all promote the spread of HIV.

Despite the widely recognized benefits of globalization, more than a billion of the world's 6 billion people still cannot fulfil their basic needs for food, water, sanitation, health care, housing and education. Worldwide, an estimated 1.1 billion people are malnourished. An estimated 1.2 billion people live on less than US$1 a day. In more than 30 of the poorest national economies (most of them in sub-Saharan Africa), real per capita incomes have been declining since the early 1980s. At the same time, pressures on States to provide basic services and infrastructure have not eased. The HIV/AIDS epidemic, along with other diseases, conflicts and droughts, is worsening matters further.

But the global response to AIDS shows that the negative effects of globalization need not be 'facts of life'. Greater access to high-income countries' markets, debt relief and more development aid will go a long way towards enabling countries to reduce poverty. High-income countries spent more than US$300 billion in 2001 on agricultural subsidies—roughly equivalent to the combined gross domestic product of all of sub-Saharan Africa. It is clear that AIDS represents a long and devastating tale of exclusion for millions of people, with or without HIV infection.

The expanding AIDS epidemic provides a compelling case for accelerating much-needed global reform in an effort to better support local responses. This can be done by:

- creating stronger international cooperation, guided by the principles of human rights;
- generating more accountability and transparency of international institutions;
- replenishing national capabilities to safeguard the right to health (including the provision of HIV prevention, access to HIV care or the development of a HIV vaccine), and enlisting the help of the business sector in such efforts;
- redressing global poverty (a driving force of the AIDS epidemic) by, among other things, increasing Official Development Assistance to at least 0.7% of gross national product (a level first agreed to by the international community in 1969 and since endorsed repeatedly, including at the 2002 Monterrey International Conference on Financing for Development); and
- above all, setting new rules of the game to ensure a more equitable distribution of the fruits of globalization.

It is true that the world cannot afford to wait until the perfect conditions exist before acting against AIDS. The fight against AIDS cannot go on hold until human security is achieved and poverty is eliminated. As Graça Machel said in her appeal to leaders at the African Development Forum 2000, "How would you react if you were told that, of your five children, two would die prematurely, but that you still had a chance to stop their deaths? Which parent wouldn't mobilize all of their financial, emotional and human resources and act immediately?" At the same time, the growing global response to AIDS needs to be bolstered by stronger human security, equality and justice. In the long run, success in the struggle against the epidemic requires a global community that acts on the basis of human concern and humane values.

There is no blueprint for bringing the epidemic under control. But the past 20 years have seen the development of tools and knowledge that we know can result in success. The world now has a road map for the fight against AIDS. Time will tell how well it is used.

UN DEVELOPMENT PROGRAM
ON THE ARAB WORLD
July 2, 2002

A lack of freedom, the prevalence of substandard education, and the sec-ond-class status of women were the three key factors that held back the Arab world, a landmark report sponsored by the United Nations concluded. The product of extensive research by Arab intellectuals, the "Arab Human De-velopment Report 2002" offered blunt answers to questions that were being raised with increasing frequency at the turn of the century: Why had Arab countries fallen behind so much of the world, and why were so many of the region's young people so angry at their leaders and the rest of the world, es-pecially the United States?

Work on the report began in 2000, but the results, published in July 2002, drew substantial attention because the questions had taken on a new ur-gency after the September 11, 2001, terrorist attacks against the United States. Carried out by nineteen young Arab men—most of them from Saudi Arabia—the September 11 attacks dramatically symbolized the anger and sense of impotence felt by many in much of the Arab world. The report did not directly address the grievances of those nineteen men or the radical ter-rorist group al Qaeda that sponsored their work, but its conclusion was a sobering one—that the basic responsibility both for creating and solving the problems of the Arab world lay within the twenty-two Arab lands, not in Washington, London, or elsewhere. (Terrorist attacks, Historic Documents of 2001, p. 614)

The Arab world is "at a crossroads," a summary of the report said. "The fundamental choice is whether its trajectory will remain marked by iner-tia, as reflected in much of the institutional context, and by ineffective poli-cies that have produced the substantial development challenges facing the region; or whether prospects for an Arab renaissance, anchored in human development, will be actively pursued."

Motivated in part by the report, the Bush administration in December launched a modest U.S.-Middle East Partnership Initiative aimed at help-ing countries in the region overcome economic stagnation and open up their political systems. However well-intended, the plan failed to compete for public attention with the contemporaneous U.S. initiative against the regime of Iraqi leader Saddam Hussein. That initiative seemed likely to result in a U.S.-led war in Iraq early in 2003—a war that many experts feared could spawn even more Arab anger. (Iraq, p. 713)

UN Report

Under the sponsorship of the UN Development Programme (UNDP) and the Arab Fund for Economic and Social Development (an Arab League agency), a team of more than twenty scholars from around the Arab world spent eighteen months examining human development in the region. The lead author was Nader Fergany, an Egyptian economist and director of the Almishkat Center for Research in Cairo. UNDP administrator Mark Malloch Brown said in an introduction the report that this "is not the grandstanding of outsiders but an honest, if controversial, view through the mirror."

Twenty-two nations were members of the Arab League, with a total population of 280 million. The countries, in North Africa, the Eastern Mediterranean, and the Persian Gulf regions, ranged in size from Qatar (with 770,000 people) to Egypt (with 70 million people), and in wealth from impoverished Somalia to the oil-rich kingdoms of Kuwait and Saudi Arabia.

The report covered the broad range of "human development" issues traditionally analyzed in such studies, among them economic development, education, health services, and population demographics. The UNDP used measures of these factors in its Human Development Index, which periodically ranked the nations of the world according to a rough gauge of well-being. The Arab authors went beyond those standard areas and explored other factors they said were indicative of the state of the their region, including political freedom, environmental degradation, and the use of technology. With these additional elements, the authors created an "Alternative Human Development Index" that showed Arab lands at an even greater disadvantage in comparison to most of the world. For example, Jordan ranked number 60 among the 111 nations in the UNDP's 1998 standard index but fell to number 68 on the broader alternative index; similarly, Egypt's ranking fell from number 75 to number 92, Kuwait from number 29 to number 70, Syria from number 70 to number 103, and Iraq from number 80 to number 110 (next to the bottom, just ahead of the Democratic Republic of the Congo). In general, both indices ranked the Arab countries in the bottom half, just ahead of or in some cases below the countries of Sub-Saharan Africa.

Arab countries had made some progress in the last half of the twentieth century, the report said. Life expectancy had increased by fifteen years during the previous three decades and, at sixty-seven years, was better than the world average; infant mortality rates had dropped substantially; and Arab lands had the lowest rate among all developing regions of extreme poverty, defined as an average income of less than $1 a day. In addition, income inequality was less pronounced in Arab countries than in most of the world.

Overall, however, the study said the Arab region "is richer than it is developed" and was hobbled by a "poverty of capabilities and poverty of opportunity." Economically, the region's shortcoming was illustrated by one startling fact, the authors said: Despite the oil wealth of about one-third of the Arab countries, the region's combined gross domestic product in 1999 was $531 billion—less than that of Spain, a country of only 40 million people. The authors largely blamed the "statist, inward-looking development models" adopted by most Arab leaders following World War II for the region's slow economic development.

The report's authors identified what they called "three deficits" as the key factors responsible for the overall poor standing of Arab countries: political freedom, women's empowerment, and knowledge. In all three areas, the authors said, Arab lands ranked below most other regions, and in the first two they were at the bottom. The report tread carefully on the influence of the one factor, aside from the Arabic language, that was common to all the Arab countries: the Islamic faith, which was held by nearly 99 percent of the region's people. The report contained few direct references to Islam, but in media interviews some of the authors pointed to indirect references in sections decrying repression of women and nonconformist opinions.

In measuring political freedom, the report used the annual rankings of Freedom House, a New York-based private organization that studied elections and democratic institutions. Arab lands fared poorly on these measures, the authors said. Many Arab countries offered some political freedoms, such as a generally free press or elections for a legislature with nominal powers. But the report said, in its understated phrasing: "The transfer of power through the ballot box is not a common phenomenon in the Arab world."

The status of women was perhaps the most sensitive issue dealt with in the report since the unequal treatment of women, in many aspects of life, was deeply rooted in the Islamic faith. Under Islamic law, women enjoyed rights equal with men only in the holding of property; in nearly all other aspects of Islamic tradition, women were subservient to men. The report did not cite religion as the cause, but it clearly stated the results: more than one-half of Arab women could neither read nor write, women had little involvement in business and almost no role in government in Arab countries, and women were valued primarily as bearers of children. In general, the report said, "society as a whole suffers when a huge proportion of its productive potential is stifled, resulting in lower family incomes and standards of living."

In discussing education in Arab countries, the report used the term knowledge *to convey a broader feeling for the region's inability to keep pace with much of the rest of the world. The report noted that during the Middle Ages the Islamic countries (including Turkey, then the base of the Ottoman empire) boasted the most advanced scientific and educational establishments in the world. But the region's quest for knowledge diminished many hundreds of years ago, the report said. Moreover, the Arab world never had* been interested in learning much of what outsiders had to offer; the report noted that over the past 1,000 years Arabs had translated about as many books as the Spanish translated in one year.

The report was chock-full of statistics, few of them flattering to the Arab world, but perhaps none was as revealing of the authors' underlying findings as a survey of Arab youth who attended a conference in Amman, Jordan, in June 2001. Those surveyed probably were not fully representative of Arab youth as a whole, the report said, but their "deep-seated concerns" and desires for the future undoubtedly expressed the feelings of many of their contemporaries in the region. Educational and job opportunities were by far the main immediate concerns of these young people. About one-half of the youths expressed a desire to emigrate to other countries, "clearly indicating their dissatisfaction with current conditions and future prospects in their home countries," the report said. Moreover, the vast majority of those wanting to emigrate cited Europe, the United States, or Canada as their favorite destinations; only about one in eight wanted to move to another Arab country. "The implicit judgment of how livable these young people consider Arab societies to be is evident," the authors said.

In recent decades many Arabs who were dissatisfied with their region's fate blamed outsiders, in particular the twentieth century colonial powers (notably Britain and France) or the United States, the world's dominant power at the beginning of the twenty-first century. The report's authors did not follow this pattern. They concluded, in an overview chapter, that Israel's occupation of Palestinian territories since 1967 had stifled the aspirations of Palestinian Arabs and had cast "a pall across the political and economic life of the entire region." But otherwise the authors said Arabs themselves were responsible for their current predicament and for changing it.

The report's prescriptions for improving life in the Arab lands flowed directly from the major problems it identified. The authors did not suggest specific programs or a detailed plan of action. They did, however, sketch out a general vision: Arab leaders needed to offer their people a greater political role, barriers to the education and advancement of women should be removed, and more resources should be put into education and the acquisition of knowledge, especially by women. In general, the report called for more cooperation among the Arab countries, offering as one example the creation of a "supranational authority" to raise money and set standards for improved educational systems in the region. One of the most urgent education tasks, the report said, was widening access by Arabs to information technology; it noted that only 1.2 percent of Arabs had access to computers and only about half of those had access to the Internet.

As could be expected, the "Arab Human Development Report 2002" generated considerable debate in the Middle East. Western-oriented Arab intellectuals and leaders generally accepted its conclusions, while more traditionally minded Arabs objected to the report's portrayal of the region as a backwater. Most commentary in Western countries was favorable. Typical was a July 5 editorial in the British newspaper, the Guardian: " [T]his re-

port's remarkable underlying message is clear. The fundamental threat to Arab societies does not emanate from the West. It arises from the ignorance, discrimination, and wasted opportunities that are the consequence of autocratic governance and corrupt or incompetent leadership. If there is anger, and there should be, let it first be directed within."

United States Initiative

Citing the UNDP report, Secretary of State Colin Powell on December 12 announced a U.S. initiative that, he said, "places the United States firmly on the side of change, on the side of reform, and on the side of a modern future for the Middle East, on the side of hope." The U.S.-Middle East Partnership, Powell said, would provide U.S. financial aid and expertise to help countries in the region reform their economies, open up their political systems, and improve education for both boys and girls. The initiative was to have a $29 million budget in fiscal year 2003, and the administration was planning on a bigger budget in future years, Powell said.

Endorsing the findings of the UN report, Powell laid special stress on improving opportunities for Arab women, noting that the "marginalization" of women was "a constant theme running through" the challenges of all Arab lands. As a pilot project, the U.S. State Department sponsored a group of fifty-five Arab women who visited the United States to observe the 2002 midterm elections.

The aim of the program was not "to say to someone, 'this is the American way, you have to do it our way,'" Powell said, but rather was to help leaders in Arab countries "look at the situation they find themselves in individually" and find solutions for their problems. Examples of specific programs to be funded by the U.S. initiative included teacher training, bolstering of Arab nongovernmental organizations, and the development of programs to combat corruption in government and business.

Arab Anger at the West

Powell insisted that the U.S. initiative to aid reform in Arab countries was not directly related to the events of September 11, 2001. He did acknowledge, however, that Washington's concern about the Arab world had taken on "new urgency" as a result of the terrorist attacks.

The reason for this sense of urgency was simple: The nineteen young Arab men who flew airplanes into American buildings, and their terrorist colleagues who attacked other Western targets, appeared to be expressing their frustration and deep anger at the West in general, the United States in particular, and the failures of their own societies as well.

Some of this hostility sprang from an Islamic fundamentalist view of the world, which held that "infidels"—the European colonial powers, the United States, the Jewish state of Israel, and autocratic, secular Arab leaders who had abandoned "true" Islam—were entirely responsible for the ills of the Middle East. Al Qaeda leader Osama bin Laden, for example, pointed specifically to the large U.S. military presence in Saudi Arabia, the birthplace of Islam, as a corrupting influence that had to be destroyed. Bin Laden also appeared to speak for millions of Arabs who were angered by what they viewed as Washington's unquestioning support for Israel in its conflict with the Palestinians.

By 2002 bin Laden had become a folk hero in much of the region; his image-adorned T-shirts worn by young men and cassettes of his sermons preaching hatred of the United States were best-sellers. Perhaps only a minority of Arabs fully shared bin Laden's bitter sentiments. Many Arabs viewed the terrorist leader as just the most recent of a series of demagogues who preached salvation but failed to deliver it. Even so, the growing popularity of his view, especially among the region's young people, pointed to deepening trouble in the future.

"Anyone who is a Muslim who says 'no' to the United States is a hero," Mazen al-Shaman, a merchant in Damascus told the New York Times *in January. "Every day you turn on the television and you see the Israelis killing Palestinians with U.S. weapons. No matter how much the United States tries to change its image in the Arab world, what we are seeing with our own eyes is much stronger."*

Such comments pointed to the growing influence of the mass media, notably satellite television networks owned by Arabs who were independent of state control, as one of the most important factors influencing popular sentiment in the Middle East. For many Arabs, especially the one-half of Arab youth who were illiterate, the networks were their only source of information about the outside world. Al Jazeera (based in Qatar) and other Arab satellite networks routinely devoted substantial parts of their broadcasts to coverage of the conflict between Israel and the Palestinians, with the Israeli military always portrayed as the aggressor. By contrast, Palestinian suicide bombers, who blew up themselves along with Israelis, were proclaimed as heroes and martyrs. (Arab-Israeli conflict, p. 369)

The Arab networks, and many Arab newspapers, also claimed that the U.S. war in Afghanistan against al Qaeda had killed thousands of innocent civilians. Another staple in 2002 was the Bush administration's campaign for "regime change" in Iraq, one consequence of which was an upsurge of sympathy in the region for Iraqi leader Saddam Hussein, previously a controversial figure among Arabs. Perhaps most striking to Americans was the widespread perception in Arab lands—fostered by television coverage— that Arabs were not responsible for the September 11 attacks in the United States. Instead, according to several public opinion surveys, many Arabs believed Jews carried out the attacks solely so Arabs would be blamed. (Afghanistan war, p. 15; Iraq, p. 612)

One manifestation of anger at the United States was a boycott of American products in Egypt, Jordan, and several other countries that had adopted elements of the Western culture of consumption. McDonald's, Starbucks, and other U.S.-based chains experienced sagging sales during the year. Arab entrepreneurs who had no direct connection to the United States but whose products appeared to be American—donuts, fried chicken, even computer software—desperately tried to prove their independence.

Anger at the United States was just part of the picture. Opinion surveys, sociological studies, and anecdotal evidence indicated a high degree of alienation in many Arab lands, especially among young people. Along with Washington, the principal targets of this alienation were the Arab governments. Some governments, described as "moderate" in the West, received substantial economic or military support from the United States and generally were sympathetic to Washington's views, among them Egypt, Jordan, Kuwait, Morocco, Saudi Arabia, and several other Persian Gulf states. Other governments historically had distanced themselves from the United States, notably Iraq, Libya and Syria. A common thread was that all these governments were autocratic to one degree or another. Also, as the "Arab Human Development Report 2002" documented, few Arab governments had provided the education, health, and other public services needed to lift their people out of poverty and ignorance. Oil, the region's one obvious source of wealth, had financed lavish lifestyles for royal families and billions of dollars worth of investments in Western ventures but almost no economic development in Arab lands.

In the past, regimes in Egypt, Syria, Tunisia, and other countries had been able to use repression to stifle dissent, which most often was articulated by Islamic groups such as the Muslim Brotherhood. But dissent continued to build, with no legitimate outlet for expression through a democratic process. By 2002, against a background of Osama bin Laden's voice calling for resistance and the United States planning a military intervention in Iraq, these governments were having more trouble keeping the lid on the boiling pot of public anger.

Following are excerpts from the "Overview" chapter of "Arab Human Development Report 2002," released July 2, 2002, by the United Nations Development Programme and the Arab Fund for Economic and Social Development. Prepared by Arab economists, sociologists, and other academic experts, the report discussed why Arab countries lagged behind much of the rest of the world and offered general suggestions for reforms.

The document was obtained from the Internet at www.undp .org/rbas/ahdr; accessed February 9, 2002.

From the Atlantic to the Gulf, people—women, men and children—are the real wealth and hope of Arab countries. Policies for development and growth in the Arab region must focus on freeing people from deprivation, in all its forms, and expanding their choices. Over the last five decades, remarkable progress has been achieved in advancing human development and reducing poverty. However, much still needs to be done to address the backlog of deprivation and imbalance.

Looking forward, much also needs to be done in order to empower the people of the Arab region to participate fully in the world of the twenty-first century. Globalization and accelerating technological advances have opened doors to unprecedented opportunities, but they have also posed a new risk: that of being left behind as the rate of change accelerates, often outpacing state capacity. Development is being reinvented by new markets (e.g., foreign exchange and capital markets), new tools (e.g., the Internet and cellular phones), new actors (e.g., non-governmental organizations, the European Union and World Trade Organization) and new rules (e.g., multilateral agreements on trade, services and intellectual property).

Challenges

Entering the new millennium, people in Arab countries face two intertwined sets of challenges to peace and to development. The first set has been made ever more conspicuous and pressing after the tragic events of 11 September 2001. These are the challenges to the pursuit of freedom from fear. Regional and external factors intersect in this realm of peace and security. The second set of challenges is equally important if not more critical.

It encompasses challenges to the achievement of freedom from want. These are the challenges faced by people and governments, states and societies as they attempt to advance human development. These challenges are fundamental, not only for their instrumental significance to development and growth but also for their intrinsic value. Equity, knowledge and the freedom and human rights integral to good governance matter for their own sake as well as for their critical role as enablers of development. They are both means and ends. They are central to both the process and the state of human development. Some key aspects of both sets of challenges are highlighted below.

Occupation Stifles Progress

Israel's illegal occupation of Arab lands is one of the most pervasive obstacles to security and progress in the region geographically (since it affects the entire region), temporally (extending over decades) and developmentally (impacting nearly all aspects of human development and human security, directly for millions and indirectly for others). The human cost extends beyond the considerable loss of lives and livelihoods of direct victims. If human development is the process of enlarging choices, if it implies that people must influence the processes that shape their lives, and if it means the full enjoyment of human rights, then nothing stifles that noble vision of development more than subjecting a people to foreign occupation.

Firstly, for Palestinians, occupation and the policies that support it, stunt their ability to grow in every conceivable way. The confiscation of Palestinian land, constraining their access to their water and other natural resources, the imposition of obstacles to the free movement of people and goods, and structural impediments to employment and economic self-management all combine to thwart the emergence of a viable economy and a secure independent state. Moreover, the expansion of illegal settlements, the frequent use of excessive force against Palestinians and the denial of their most basic human rights further circumscribe their potential to build human development. The plight of Palestinian refugees living in other countries is a further manifestation of development disfigured by occupation.

Secondly, occupation casts a pall across the political and economic life of the entire region. Among neighbouring countries, some continue to suffer themselves from Israeli occupation of parts of their lands, subjecting those people directly affected to tremendous suffering, and imposing development challenges on the rest. In most Arab states, occupation dominates national policy priorities, creates large humanitarian challenges for those receiving refugees and motivates the diversion of public investment in human development towards military spending. By symbolizing a felt and constant external threat, occupation has damaging side effects: it provides both a cause and an excuse for distorting the development agenda, disrupting national priorities and retarding political development. At certain junctures it can serve to solidify the public against an outside aggressor and justify curbing dissent at a time when democratic transition requires greater pluralism in society and more public debate on national development policies. In all these ways, occupation freezes growth, prosperity and freedom in the Arab world.

Conflicts, Sanctions and Instability Prevent Development

Political upheavals, military conflicts, sanctions and embargoes have affected many economies of the region, causing declines in productivity and disrupting markets. Some countries struggling to recover from the ravages of war have emerged with substantial debts, limiting options for public expenditure. All affected countries have emerged with compounded socio-political problems that have retarded progressive moves towards liberalization and democratization.

The direct impact of wars is registered in slowed growth, damaged infrastructure, social fragmentation and public-sector stagnation. Some countries have experienced hyperinflation, severe currency devaluations and curtailed foreign-currency earnings. Others have seen their standing in the international community collapse. Most affected countries have lost important human and capital resources critical for the renewal of stability and competitiveness.

Aspirations for Freedom and Democracy Remain Unfulfilled

There is a substantial lag between Arab countries and other regions in terms of participatory governance. The wave of democracy that transformed governance in most of Latin America and East Asia in the 1980s and Eastern Europe and much of Central Asia in the late 1980s and early 1990s has barely reached the Arab States. This freedom deficit undermines human development and is one of the most painful manifestations of lagging political development. While de jure acceptance of democracy and human rights is enshrined in constitutions, legal codes and government pronouncements, de facto implementation is often neglected and, in some cases, deliberately disregarded.

In most cases, the governance pattern is characterized by a powerful executive branch that exerts significant control over all other branches of the state, being in some cases free from institutional checks and balances. Representative democracy is not always genuine and sometimes absent. Freedoms of expression and association are frequently curtailed. Obsolete norms of legitimacy prevail.

Development Not Engendered Is Endangered

Gender inequality is the most pervasive manifestation of inequity of all kinds in any society because it typically affects half the population. There have been important quantitative improvements with respect to building women's capabilities in recent years. For example, Arab countries have shown the fastest improvements in female education of any region. Women's literacy rates have expanded threefold since 1970; female primary and secondary enrolment rates have more than doubled. However, these achievements have not succeeded in countering gender-based social attitudes and norms that exclusively stress women's reproductive role and reinforce the gender-based asymmetry of unpaid care. As a consequence, more than half of Arab women are still illiterate. The region's maternal mortality rate is double that of Latin America and the Caribbean, and four times that of East Asia.

Women also suffer from unequal citizenship and legal entitlements, often evident in voting rights and legal codes. The utilization of Arab women' s capabilities through political and economic participation remains the lowest in the world in quantitative terms, as evidenced by the very low share of women in parliaments, cabinets, and the work force and in the trend towards the feminization of unemployment. Qualitatively, women suffer from inequality of opportunity, evident in employment status, wages and gender-based occupational segregation. Society as a whole suffers when a huge proportion of its productive potential is stifled, resulting in lower family incomes and standards of living.

Bridled Minds, Shackled Potential

About 65 million adult Arabs are illiterate, two thirds of them women. Illiteracy rates are much higher than in much poorer countries. This challenge is unlikely to disappear quickly. Ten million children between 6 and 15 years of age are currently out of school; if current trends persist, this number will increase by 40 per cent by 2015. The challenge is far more than overcoming the under-supply of knowledge to people. Equally important is overcoming the under-supply of knowledgeable people, a problem exacerbated by the low quality of education together with the lack of mechanisms for intellectual capital development and use.

A major mismatch exists between the output of educational systems and labour-market needs. The mismatch is compounded by the increasingly rapid change in these needs brought about by globalization and the needs of accelerating technology.

Arab countries access to and use of cutting edge technology, exemplified by information and communication technology (ICT), is very limited. Only 0.6 per cent of the population uses the Internet and the personal computer penetration rate is only 1.2 per cent. More generally, investment in research and development does not exceed 0.5 per cent of gross national product, well below the world average. Moreover, while the production of scientific papers in the Arab region is within the range of leading third-world countries, the use of national scientific expertise is at much lower levels.

Addressing the knowledge challenge matters critically, both because knowledgeable people and a knowledge society are worthy objectives in themselves and because education and knowledge, as aspects of human capability and as proxies for increased human choice, are intrinsically linked to growth and equity. Failure to address capability deficits holds back human development in the larger sense of the concept. While the human development index (HDI) of the United Nations Development Programme (UNDP) measures some aspects of capability, it does not embrace other, wider variables such as freedom and human rights (or others such as knowledge acquisition, the institutional context and environmental responsibility). Yet the relationship between human development and human rights is of fundamental importance. It is a mutually reinforcing relationship where the common denominator is human freedom. Human development, by enhancing human capabilities, creates the ability to exercise freedom, and human rights, by providing the necessary framework, create the opportunities to exercise it. Freedom is the guarantor and the goal of both human development and human rights.

As Development Management Stumbles, Economies Falter

Improving economic governance, including management of development, is a primary challenge for Arab countries. Despite largely successful stabilization in the 1990s, evident in modest subsequent levels of inflation and budget deficits, growth continues to stagnate and to be overly vulnerable to fluctuations in oil prices. The quality of public institutions, as measured by poor cost-effectiveness and heavy regulatory burdens, is low. Critical macro variables are still under-performing, including employment, savings, productivity and non-oil exports. At about 15 per cent, average unemployment across Arab countries is among the highest rates in the developing world. Unemployment is a human-development tragedy as well as a drag on economic progress. Restoring growth will be critical to attacking it, but the economies in the region would have to grow at a minimum annual rate of five per cent to absorb the currently unemployed and provide jobs for new labour-market entrants.

Trade performance has remained sluggish and the region is still relatively closed. In some countries, tariffs are high and non-tariff barriers remain important. Throughout the 1990s, exports from the region (over 70 per cent of which are accounted for by oil and oil-related products) grew at 1.5 per cent per year, far below the global rate of six per cent. Manufacturing exports have remained stagnant and private-capital flows have lagged behind those of other regions. Arab governments are taking steps to improve this state of affairs through policy initiatives to promote trade expansion as an engine of economic (including technological) development. The creation of the Arab Free Trade Area, expanding accession to the World Trade Organization and association with the European Union are formal expressions of policies that promote trade and move towards greater integration with the global economy.

Governments have had considerable success in providing growth-support-

493

ing physical infrastructure. On the other hand, the state' s role in promoting, complementing and regulating markets for goods, services and factors of production has been both constrained and constraining. Partly as a consequence, the formal private sector's contribution to development has often been hesitant and certainly below expectations. While the share of the private sector in total investment has increased, its performance with respect to job creation and exports remains unduly limited. Markets remain incomplete. Uncorrected market failures result in inefficient outcomes.

Both growth and equity considerations make promoting dynamic private-sector development a critical priority of economic governance in Arab countries. Most countries in the region formerly adopted, and some long adhered to, now discredited statist, inward-looking development models. These models may have been appropriate in early post-independence years, but they now serve neither governments (which need rapid economic growth in order to achieve policy objectives, including human-development objectives with respect to, e.g., health care, education and provision of social safety nets) nor people (who seek more good jobs with decent wages and working conditions).

Governments in many countries have taken important steps to liberate the private sector, but a large unfinished agenda remains. Sound macroeconomic policies need to be maintained; adequate economic space needs to be provided for private initiative; central banks, banking systems in general, and financial services need to be strengthened; bureaucracy needs to be streamlined and red tape minimized. In addition, a transparent rule of law, a visibly fair and appropriately swift legal system, and an efficient and professional judiciary need to become universal; and public sector reform needs to be designed in terms of providing incentive structures to encourage private-sector investment and growth.

At the same time, beneficial regulation—for example, measures to curb monopoly, whether in the public or the private sector—needs be strengthened and enforced; graft and cronyism need to be firmly and comprehensively addressed. These and other distortions of incentive systems have human-development as well as economic-development costs in terms of denying merit its appropriate reward and discouraging human initiative.

Another area for exploration is greater regional economic cooperation. Domestic markets in many Arab economies are too small to provide the basis for dynamic, diversified and sustainable growth based on vibrant private manufacturing and services sectors. The Arab Free Trade Area is a step in the right direction, provided it lives up to its promise. However, countries may need to consider deeper integration both among themselves via moving towards a customs union or a common market and with external partners through, for example, the association agreements with the European Union that several countries have already signed. These two trends can be mutually reinforcing; the returns from association agreements can be multiplied if regional integration arrangements are in place. Finally in this connection, regional associations that address economic cooperation or shared infrastructure development need to be revitalized and supported.

The capacity of the state has fallen short of the requirement to foster rapid growth, just as it has fallen short of the demands of human development in key areas such as health and education. Financial resources have not been the binding constraint: government spending as a percentage of gross domestic product is higher than in other developing regions. While policy changes, supported by inter- and intra-sectoral reallocation of public spending, would certainly enhance effectiveness, institutional arrangements and human resources are more binding constraints. They are evident in lack of accountability, transparency and integrity, along with ineffectiveness, inefficiency and unresponsiveness to the demands of peoples and of development. . . .

Strategy

The core peace and development challenges facing the Arab people are interlinked. While issues of occupation and conflict are beyond the purview of this Report, the subsections that follow synthesize aspects of a strategy for enhancing human development.

Given the importance of capturing broader challenges to human development in its fullest sense, challenges related to increasing freedom, gender equality, knowledge acquisition and environmental choice, the Report poses the question: is it not now time to look beyond the limited measurement of human development, as reflected in the HDI? In a personal contribution to the Report, its lead author explores the parameters, methodology and impact of an alternative index that could be the starting point for further research into a more insightful approach to measuring human development.

The Arab region is living in a time of accelerating change against a backdrop of increased globalization. Success in meeting today's challenges will depend on the ability to shape, and adapt to, the demands of the new economics and the new politics. Enhanced knowledge development, broadly defined, and advances in human freedom, exemplified by political and economic participation, along with a proper appreciation of the role of culture and values, could together form the foundation of a human-development path for the Arab region that responds creatively to people's aspirations for a better life and effectively taps the forces shaping the twenty-first century.

Towards a Knowledge Society

Knowledge is a cornerstone of development, and its importance is increasing in an age of accelerating technological change and globalization. It is a public good that underpins economies, polities and societies, permeating all aspects of human activity. This Report suggests that Arab countries face a significant knowledge gap. Overcoming it will not be easy because knowledge, broadly defined, is a moving target; its frontiers are constantly expanding. To address the knowledge gap, it will be necessary to take simultaneous action in three linked and potentially synergistic areas: knowledge absorption, acquisition and communication.

The value of knowledge for development depends on its effective application. Therefore, working towards a knowledge society requires multisectoral strategies that integrate absorption, acquisition and communication—for example, through links among education systems, training systems and public- and private-sector labour-market demand. Similarly, innovators, researchers and policy analysts need to be connected with producers and policy-makers. Knowledge-development strategies need to be seen as being the concern of society as a whole and of socioeconomic actors across the board—government agencies, the private sector and civil society, particularly in local communities -thus promoting better alignment of the structure, inputs and outputs of education, training and research systems with the requirements of production, human welfare and the development process as a whole.

Knowledge absorption involves providing people with the capacity to use knowledge via education. Despite the problems noted earlier, Arab countries have made major progress in expanding education and literacy over the years. By 1995, over 90 per cent of males and 75 per cent of females were enrolled in primary schooling, and nearly 60 per cent of males and nearly 50 per cent of females were enrolled in secondary education. At the tertiary level, Arab countries outperformed all developing regions except for Latin America and the Caribbean in terms of enrolment levels for both males and females. Total enrolment for all levels rose from 31 million in 1980 to approximately 56 million in 1995. Literacy rates improved by nearly 50 per cent between 1980 and the mid-1990s. Female literacy rates have trebled since 1970.

These achievements reflect Arab governments' long-term commitment to building education systems that respond to the needs of new generations. Taken as a group, Arab countries spend a higher percentage of GDP on education than any other developing region, registering a 50 per cent increase (at current prices) between 1980 and 1995. Per capita spending on education is substantially higher than the developing-country average. Several countries in the region are undertaking major programmes of education-system reform.

Nevertheless, much remains to be done. Priorities include, inter alia, securing universal, high-quality basic education, especially for girls and other currently under-served groups; strengthening tertiary education, particularly in science and engineering; and eliminating illiteracy at one end of the education spectrum while also providing opportunities for lifetime learning for education-system graduates at the other. Lifetime learning is not a luxury; it is critical for knowledge absorption in a world of exploding new knowledge, rapid technological change and intense international competition. . . .

Effective *knowledge-acquisition strategies* may need to begin with attitudinal change, involving across-the-board commitment at all levels of society, from respect for science and knowledge, to encouraging creativity and innovation, to applying new discoveries to raise productivity and income and enhance human welfare. Attitudinal change can be supported by policies that provide incentives for enhancing both the social status and the opportunities for profit of workers in the fields of science, knowledge and innovation. Public policy also has a key role in fostering potentially productive research and development (R & D) and in supporting an environment that enables the private sector to apply new knowledge in response to market forces, e.g., by corporatizing research institutes, by offering companies incentives to contract relevant activities with public laboratories or one another, and by relying more on appropriately skilled and efficient Arab consultancy, engineering and development firms.

Knowledge acquisition entails not only building on a country's own knowledge base to generate new knowledge through R&D but also harnessing and adapting knowledge available elsewhere through openness, broadly defined, including, e.g., promoting the free flow of information and ideas, establishing constructive engagement in world markets, and attracting foreign investment. A commitment to openness is particularly important in view of the current weakness of technological development in Arab countries. This means that importing and adapting technology and internalizing it by learning-by-doing may be the most practical approach in this area, pending the establishment of the necessary conditions for dynamic local technological development, namely, a large, diverse and vibrant production system and a market large enough to justify the costs of technological development. . . .

Knowledge communication. The convergence of telecommunications and computing has vastly expanded the ability to disseminate information and reduce costs. Broadening access for all, including poor people, to ICT can greatly facilitate the acquisition and absorption of knowledge in Arab countries and offer unprecedented opportunities for education, policy formulation and implementation, and services to businesses and the poor. Strategies for knowledge communication need to be multisectoral, sensitive to the interrelationships between the sectors of communication, media and information, and open to ICT applications in fields such as education, culture and general health. Lowering the cost of Internet access is a high priority, achievable through regulatory arrangements that promote competition and prevent monopoly factors that are also of special importance in the telecommunications sector, whether public or privatized. With respect to human resources, computer-training specialists are a priority, as is training generally, especially for women, along with professional upgrading. Finally, coordination among Arab countries is important, both to ensure compatibility and connectivity among various systems and to exploit the economies of scale of regional rather than national solutions.

An Open Culture of Excellence

Culture and values are the soul of development. They provide its impetus, facilitate the means needed to further it, and substantially define people's vision of its purposes and ends. Culture and values are instrumental in the sense that they help to shape people's daily hopes, fears, ambitions, attitudes and actions, but they are also formative because they mould people's ideals and inspire their dreams for a fulfilling life for themselves and future generations. There is some debate in Arab countries about whether culture and values promote or retard development. Ultimately, however, values are not the servants of development; they are its wellspring.

Values play an especially critical role in social achievements that are not driven by narrowly economic forces, from the simple (prevention of littering) to the complex (community support for the disadvantaged and the impetus to eliminate socio-economic exclusion). Governments—Arab or otherwise—cannot decree their people's values; indeed, governments and their actions are partly formed by national cultures and values. Governments can, however, influence culture and values through leadership and example, and by shaping education and pedagogy, incentive structures in society, and use of the media. Moreover, by influencing values, they can affect the path of development.

Traditional culture and values, including traditional Arab culture and values, can be at odds with those of the globalizing world. Given rising global interdependence, the most viable response will be one of openness and constructive engagement, whereby Arab countries both contribute to and benefit from globalization. The values of democracy also have a part to play in this process of resolving differences between cultural traditionalism and global modernity. Different people will have different preferences, some welcoming global influences, others resenting their pervasive impact. In a democratic framework, citizens can decide how to appraise and influence cultural changes, taking account of a diversity of views and striking a balance between individual liberty and popular preferences in the difficult choices involved.

Several other values deserve special emphasis from a human development perspective, e.g., tolerance and respect for different cultures; respect for the rights and needs of women, young people and children; protection of the environment; support for social safety nets to protect the vulnerable; refusal to tolerate excessive unemployment; reverence for knowledge and education; and other concepts conducive to human dignity and wellbeing. Of these, respect for other cultures is particularly important in countries with minorities, as is the case in most Arab countries. Such respect needs to go beyond mere tolerance and incorporate a positive attitude to other people. States can neither legislate nor enforce such attitudes. They can, however, enshrine cultural freedom as a human right.

Values relating to gender equality and interdependence are important for human development. Respect for the rights and duties of children and young people are another value of particular relevance for dynamic and sustained human development in Arab countries. No generation of young Arabs has been as large as today's. Their vast and rapidly growing numbers, coupled with their vulnerability, make it essential to protect and nurture them. This is both their basic human right and Arab societies best investment in the future.

A Future Built by All

Human development is development of the people, for the people and by the people. If development is to be people-centred, then participatory processes need to be central to its evolution. Participation takes many forms: political, economic, social and cultural. Freedom, basic human capabilities and competitive markets are critical conditions for participation. Moreover, recognition of the multidimensional nature of the development process and the multi-stakeholder nature of societies and economies argues for strong support for pluralism and inclusion.

Political participation in Arab countries remains weak, as manifested in the lack of genuine representative democracy and restrictions on liberties. At the same time, people's aspirations for more freedom and greater participation in decision-making have grown, fueled by rising incomes, education, and information flows. The mismatch between aspirations and their fulfilment has in some cases led to alienation and its offspring apathy and discontent. Remedying this state of affairs must be a priority for national leaderships.

Moving towards pluralism, which is more conducive to genuine sustainable participation and in tune with the requirements of today's and tomorrow's world, needs to become a priority for Arab countries.

The weakening of the position of the state relative to its citizens is supporting such a shift. Two simultaneous processes are taking place. The position of the state as patron is diminishing partly as a result of the reduced benefits it can now offer in the form of guaranteed employment, subsidies and other inducements. By contrast, the power position of citizens is increasing as states increasingly depend on them for tax revenues, private-sector investment and other necessities. Moreover, human-development accomplishments that have endowed citizens, particularly the middle classes, with a new range of resources have put them in a better position to contest policies and bargain with the state.

The shortcomings of current social and economic arrangements with respect to the status of women represent a major issue for Arab countries. Women remain severely marginalized in Arab political systems and broadly discriminated against in both law and custom. Women need to be politically empowered by far greater participation. In addition, a timetable to eliminate legal discrimination should be established and followed. Adoption of the Convention on the Elimination of All Forms of Discrimination against Women (CEDAW) would be an important step in this regard. The eight Arab countries that have neither signed nor acceded to CEDAW account for nearly one third of all the countries that have not ratified the Convention. Greater transparency, disclosure and accountability can also help to advance women's political participation and reduce customary or legal discrimination.

Finally, the discrimination imposed by sexism has parallels in the prejudice implied by ageism. Both types of bias curtail the participation of two majorities in the Arab region: women and the young. Both also emanate from patriarchal dominance that exploits divergence with respect to gender and age. Predictably, discrimination is worst when the two biases overlap—in the case of young females. Ageism runs counter to the needs of the current era when technology and globalization reward innovation, flexibility and dynamism, and it deprives young people in the Arab world of opportunities to participate in and contribute to their societies' development.

People's participation in the economy also needs to be improved. Labour-force participation in the Arab countries as a group is lower than in other regions. Among the relatively small proportion of the population in the labour force, 20 million are unemployed. These problems are even more extreme with respect to women. Those fortunate enough to participate in the economy through their labour have seen its returns decline as real wages have fallen and its contribution to output fall with dwindling productivity.

Job creation, although rapid in some Arab countries from the mid-1980s to the early 1990s, has not matched the growth of the work force. Population growth is adding about six million labour-force entrants every year, a flow that is proportionately greater than in any other region. Since the unemployment rate is also one of the highest among all regions, the task of job creation is probably more formidable in the Arab region than in any other. . . .

The market is the central arena for economic participation. Free, open, competitive markets provide efficient mechanisms for economic exchange between buyers and sellers, producers and consumers, employers and workers, creditors and borrowers. Participation through free enterprise unleashes innovation and entrepreneurship. To maximize effective operation and participation, markets need to be free from arbitrary government actions and operate in the context of macroeconomic stability and an undistorted incentive system. Some Arab governments are moving in this direction by changing their roles from participants in markets to referees and by reducing public deficits and price distortions. To date, however, the pace has been slow. Governments should consider accelerating their disengagement from productive activities while strengthening their regulatory role to ensure openness and competitiveness. They should also take steps to modernize the delivery of essential public services.

As with political participation, women's economic participation remains unacceptably low, even though their capabilities have grown significantly (although still far less than is desirable). Their opportunities both to contribute to and to gain from such participation remain circumscribed by convention and legal restrictions. With respect to employment, mainstreaming gender in national development strategies and plans can set the stage for greater female participation. The feminization of unemployment can be reversed by removing gender bias in labour markets, including gender-based occupational segregation and unequal returns on education. Women' s capabilities can be better matched with labour-market demand by effectively addressing gender gaps in the quality and relevance of education and skill-training programmes.

Evidently, much remains to be done to broaden both political and economic participation in Arab countries. Some countries are already taking positive steps to increase aspects of participation; others are moving slowly, if at all. Fundamentally, raising political and economic participation is not a technical problem. Progress will depend on attitudinal change at all levels of society, from top levels of government to local communities and individual households.

A Future for All

Securing a better future for all requires putting the attack on poverty at the top of national agendas in Arab countries. The Arab region has dramatically reduced poverty and inequality in the twentieth century; it can do so again in the twenty-first. Given the political commitment, Arab countries have the resources to eradicate absolute poverty in less than a generation. Commitment, not resources, is the binding constraint. A solid, unequivocal political commitment—based on ethical, social, political and moral imperatives as well as the region' s religious and cultural traditions—to well-articulated human development objectives, including poverty reduction, is the critical ingredient for securing a brighter future for all the people of the Arab region.

The challenge of reducing poverty and inequality has become more daunting following the slowdown in economic growth since the mid-1980s and the fiscal retrenchments associated with the shift from a state-led economic model based on import substitution to a private-sector-led, outward-looking model. If poverty is to be reduced, economic growth must be accelerated. The impact of rapid growth on poverty should be particularly effective in the Arab context, where low inequality suggests that the character of growth in the past has generally been pro-poor. Nevertheless, promoting growth needs to be complemented by concerted public action if poverty-reduction efforts are to succeed. There are two reasons for this. First, such action is needed to strengthen the synergy between growth and poverty reduction, i. e., to help to increase the efficiency of translating growth into poverty reduction. Second, while growth has generally been pro-poor, it has not been automatically or consistently so.

Public action has supported pro-poor growth in the past, when a public-investment boom and rapid expansion of the public sector, coupled with large subsidy outlays financed by strategic rents from oil and geopolitics, helped to reduce poverty by increasing real wages for unskilled labour and lowering prices. Public policy also has a major role to play with respect to critical factors such as the state of the macroeconomy and the functioning of labour markets.

Another key area for public policy is the provision of social safety nets. Spending on transfer programmes needs to grow beyond its current level, which ranges from 0.2 per cent to about 1 per cent of GDP. Arguments for additionality need to be supported by greater efficiency. Transfer programmes need to be coordinated with other social programmes to avoid overlaps. Better management is needed to improve administration. Combined with better targeting, this can reduce leakage of benefits to the non-poor and cut administrative costs for needy beneficiaries.

Features of market-driven regional integration, such as migration and remittances, also have an important role. These flows have disproportionately benefited poor people, either directly through transfers or indirectly through the labour market. They need to be nurtured and sustained.

Poverty reduction will require drawing on the strengths and capabilities of a broad network of actors in government, the private sector and civil society. The role of public policy in building, utilizing and liberating people's capabilities remains critical. Governments need to provide an enabling environment for broad-based political support and mobilization for pro-poor policies and markets. This environment can be enhanced by research and policy analysis that identifies problems, diagnoses their causes and presents options for policy-makers, highlighting the tradeoffs and costs of each option. An increasingly dynamic and constructive civil society in the Arab region, including public and non-governmental think tanks and research institutions, has the potential to provide intellectual and analytical ammunition for operationalizing the commitment to a future for all, based on a comprehensive, multifaceted strategy for poverty reduction. Many of these institutions contribute to studies, reports and publications and undertake advocacy that seeks to influence national debates and impact policy. The 13 national human development reports that UNDP has supported in the region since 1994 are a case in point.

Finally, effective strategies for attacking poverty must focus not only on what needs to be done in principle but also on how to ensure that action is taken in practice. This means implementing improvements in such basic areas as promoting broad-based political participation, ensuring accountability and transparency in government, promoting a free flow of information and freedom of the press, and ensuring a strong role for community groups and NGOs in policy-making and legislative decision-making.

The legitimacy and strength of states and their institutions are inextricably linked to their capacity to mobilize and be mobilized in the fight against poverty. This implies that it will be essential to mainstream human development and poverty reduction within national economic policy, which in the past has too often sidelined them, especially in the context of structural adjustment. Countries that have reduced poverty while adjusting have shown that poverty reduction can be integral to the process and central to the goals of structural adjustment. This has now been accepted as a principle of international policy on adjustment although it is not yet always practised.

The basic priority for policy in Arab countries needs to be to create a virtuous cycle whereby economic growth promotes human development and human development in turn promotes economic growth. The starting point for this process must be a focus on people. The backlog of deprivation must be tackled if growth is to be restored on a sustainable basis. Tackling deprivation is a particularly urgent task for Arab countries with low levels of human development. The Human Development Report 1996 demonstrated that every country that succeeded in sustaining both rapid human development and rapid economic growth did so by accelerating advances in human development first, or by pursuing both objectives simultaneously. By contrast, countries that relied primarily on economic growth to reach the point where growth and human development become mutually reinforcing failed in the attempt because shortcomings in human development kept undermining their growth process.

In sum, human development is essential for sustained economic growth, and poverty reduction—the promise of a better future for all is—central to both. For Arab countries, such a future is both a moral imperative and an attainable goal as they move into the twenty-first century.

NIH ON RISKS WITH HORMONE REPLACEMENT THERAPY
July 9, 2002

Millions of older women were left in a quandary when the federal government announced July 9, 2002, that it had stopped a major clinical trial of a popular hormone pill because it appeared to elevate the risk of potentially life-threatening diseases. The pill, a combination of estrogen and progestin, had been widely prescribed for decades to ease the symptoms of menopause, including hot flashes and night sweats. Doctors also frequently prescribed the hormone combination to protect against heart disease and bone loss, long held to be two of the beneficial side-effects of the drug. The clinical trial confirmed that the hormone combination was effective in preventing bone loss, but the researchers said that the elevated risk of increased coronary heart disease, invasive breast cancer, stroke, and blood clots outweighed any benefits from the drug except those related to treating menopausal symptoms. A separate trial studying the effects of taking only estrogen was continuing.

The news dismayed and distressed many of the estimated 6 million women taking an estrogen-progestin combination. Doctors' offices and women's clinics were flooded with calls from women asking whether they should continue taking the drug or substitute something else, stop immediately, or taper off gradually. Jacques Rossouw, the acting director of the Women's Health Initiative (WHI), which was overseeing the trial, said women taking the estrogen-progestin combination should not be "unduly alarmed" by the new findings, but urged them "to have a serious talk with their doctor." Rossouw suggested that women taking the combination hormone for short-term relief from symptoms of menopause might want to continue "since the benefits are likely to outweigh the risks." Longer-term use or use for disease prevention should be reevaluated, he said.

By year's end, a consensus appeared to be forming around that advice. The United States Preventive Services Task Force, an independent body that advised the Department of Health and Human Services on best practices, recommended in October against the routine use of the combination hormone for preventing chronic conditions in postmenopausal women. But the consensus was far from unanimous. Some clinicians said that different estrogen-progestin combinations might not have the same results as Prempro, the drug used in the trial and by far the leading hormonal drug on the market. Others said lower doses might not have the same harmful effects. Still others said more research was required before firm answers on the potential benefits and harms of hormones were known. They pointed to several new studies suggesting that estrogen might be effective in slowing memory loss and the development of Alzheimer's disease and to yet other studies implicating hormones as a cause of ovarian cancer.

From Hot Flashes to Heart Attacks

Estrogen was the only drug known to be nearly universally effective in treating the symptoms of menopause, which affected about 85 percent of women sometime between the ages of forty-five and fifty-five. For many women the hot flashes, night sweats, and vaginal dryness were only mildly discomforting and disappeared within a year or two; for other women the experience could be much more intense, leading to sleeplessness, mood swings, and depression. Estrogen was first approved for treating symptoms of menopause in 1942. In the mid-1960s it was greatly popularized by a gynecologist, Robert Wilson, who flew around the country promoting his book, Feminine Forever, *and incidentally promoting the sale of Premarin, the estrogen therapy manufactured by Wyeth. Menopause, Wilson said, was a "living decay" in which women fell into a "vapid cowlike" state. That fate could be avoided, he claimed, by replacing the estrogen that a woman's body no longer produced with estrogen therapy, which would slow the aging process—a sort of fountain of youth. The not-so-subtle message was that menopausal women would be easier to live with, have fewer wrinkles, and be more sexually attractive. The message was heard. By 1975 Premarin had become the fifth leading prescription drug sold in the United States.*

In the mid-1970s studies showed that estrogen alone increased a woman's risk of developing cancer of the lining of the uterus. Wyeth responded by adding progestin, which counteracted the effects of estrogen on the uterus. Doctors began prescribing Prempro for women with uteruses, while women who had had hysterectomies could remain on estrogen alone.

At about the same time, observational studies of women taking hormones compared with women not taking them seemed to show that hormones played a beneficial role in slowing loss of bone mass, a common condition in older women that frequently led to hip and other bone fractures. Similar studies also appeared to show that women taking estrogen suffered fewer heart attacks and strokes than women who were not on hormones. Several long-term studies indicated that women on hormones might reduce their risk of heart disease by as much as 50 percent. The observational evidence seemed convincing, and bolstered by a major marketing effort on the part of Wyeth and other manufacturers, doctors began prescribing hormones to prevent heart disease, the number-one killer among women, and osteoporosis. Because studies had also shown that the hormones might cause breast cancer, women at high risk for breast cancer were usually advised not to take hor-

mone replacement therapy. Typically, however, women were advised that the benefits of taking estrogen therapy to prevent heart disease were much higher than the risks that the therapy would cause breast cancer.

In 1990 the Food and Drug Administration rejected Wyeth's request that it be allowed to label Prempro as a preventive for heart disease, saying that better data were needed. Wyeth then funded a study, known as the Heart and Estrogen/Progestin Replacement Study, or HERS, a randomized controlled study of nearly 2,800 women who already had heart disease, among whom, it was assumed, the beneficial effects of hormones would be most easily discerned. At about the same time, the National Institutes of Health (NIH) began the Women's Health Initiative, a massive, multiphase, randomized controlled study of hormone replacement therapy and its benefits or risks on health. Wyeth donated the hormone drugs used in that study.

The initial results from the HERS study, published in 1998, concluded that Prempro, and perhaps all estrogen and progestin combinations, did not reduce the risk of heart attack in older women who already had heart disease. On July 3, 2002, the results of a follow-up HERS study were published showing that hormones not only did not protect against heart disease and stroke, they also increased the risk of life-threatening blood clots and gall bladder disease.

Halting the Study

A week later, on July 9 government officials announced that it had stopped the WHI trial involving Prempro, which involved 16,608 women between the ages of fifty and seventy-nine with an intact uterus. Women enrolled in the study took daily either a placebo or 0.625 milligrams of conjugated equine estrogen plus 2.5 milligrams of medroxyprogesterone acetate. The trial, which began in 1995, was scheduled to run through 2005. In 2000 and 2002 the study's Data and Safety Monitoring Board recommended that participants be informed of a small increase in heart attacks, strokes, and blood clots among the women taking hormones, but the actual number of women experiencing such problems was within the statistical boundaries set for the study. The monitoring panel thus recommended that the trial continue since the balance between benefits and risk was still uncertain.

The situation came to a head at the monitoring board's May 31, 2002, meeting, where data showed that the increase in the number of invasive breast cancers among women taking the hormones had exceeded the statistical boundary the board had set. The board recommended that the study be stopped immediately. On July 8 study participants began receiving letters telling them that the study had been cancelled and that they should stop taking their daily dose. The health of the women in the study would continued to be monitored.

"We have long sought the answer to the question: Does postmenopausal hormone therapy prevent heart disease and, if it does, what are the risks? The bottom-line answer from WHI is that this combined form of hormone therapy is unlikely to benefit the heart, The cardiovascular and cancer risks

of estrogen plus progestin outweigh any benefits—and a 26 percent increase in breast cancer risk is too high a price to pay, even if there were a heart benefit," said Claude Lenfant, a doctor and director of the National Heart, Lung, and Blood Institute of the NIH, in a press release dated July 9. Lenfant urged women to protect against heart disease by focusing on "well-proven treatments" to prevent and control high blood pressure, high cholesterol, and obesity. "This effort could not be more important: heart disease remains the number one killer of American women," he said.

WHI acting director Rossouw stressed that while the individual risk was comparatively low, the aggregate risk was potentially significant: "The WHI results tell us that during one year, among 10,000 postmenopausal women with a uterus who are taking estrogen plus progestin, eight more will have invasive breast cancer, seven more will have a heart attack, eight more will have a stroke, and eighteen more will have blood clots, including eight with blood clots in the lungs, than will a similar group of 10,000 women not taking these hormones." Rossouw said that "was a relatively small annual increase in risk for an individual women," but even small risks add up over time. With 6 million women taking the combined drug, tens of thousands could experience these "serious adverse health events," he said. He added that the adverse effects of the hormone combination applied to all women, regardless of age, ethnicity, or health status.

The phase of the WHI trial that involved women who had had hysterectomies and were taking only estrogen continued. Some 11,000 women were participating in this study, with half randomly assigned to take Premarin and the other half a placebo.

Alternatives to Hormone Replacement

The announcement had an immediate effect on the estimated 17–20 million women on hormone replacement therapy, especially those who had been using the hormones for several years. A national survey showed that 45 percent of women born between 1897 and 1950 used hormones for at least a month and that 20 percent used them for at least five years.

Women concerned primarily about osteoporosis and bone fractures could take other drugs that have been shown to be more effective for those conditions. Merck's Fosamax and Eli Lilly's Evista were two options. A range of effective drugs was also available to treat heart conditions, including cholesterol-lowering drugs such as Lipitor and Zocor.

Women concerned that they had put themselves at greater risk for breast cancer could take some solace in studies that appeared to show the risk declining to normal levels once hormone therapy was stopped. For women on estrogen only for five years or more, the risk appeared to return to normal within four years For women on combined hormones, the risk seemed to return to normal within about six months.

There were few alternatives to estrogen for treating the symptoms of menopause that had been proven safe or effective. Women with mild discomfort could try to control the symptoms by avoiding alcohol, caffeine, and *spicy foods. Estrogen patches or creams could relieve some symptoms without having the systemic effect of hormone drugs. Antidepressants in the Prozac family showed some promise, but they needed more study for that purpose, and they had their own set of side-effect issues that had to be weighed. An estimated 30 percent of menopausal women already used some alternative therapy, ranging from acupuncture to supplements such as black cohosh, evening primrose oil, red clover, and soy protein. Many of these plants contained estrogen-like substances, called phytoestrogens. According to the National Center for Complementary and Alternative Medicine, women spent about $600 million a year on alternatives for treating menopausal symptoms.*

Reactions

Women were understandably frightened and dismayed by the cancellation of the trial and the suggestions that they reevaluate their use of hormones. Although many women decided that the benefits of eliminating night sweats and hot flashes outweighed the individual risk of heart disease, cancer, or stroke, many others decided to stop taking their hormones. Late in the year Wyeth said sales of Prempro were down 40 percent and that sales of Premarin were down 15 percent. Some women had switched to other formulations of estrogen-progestin, but overall industry statistics showed that the number of prescriptions written for hormones had dropped. At the same time, prescriptions for bone-strengthening drugs appeared to be rising.

At least two class-action suits were filed against Wyeth, one in Philadelphia and one in Chicago. Robert A. Essner, Wyeth's chief executive officer, said he doubted the suits would be successful, noting that the risk of breast cancer and other possible side-effects had long been listed on the drug's label. Wyeth already had been forced to set aside $13.2 billion to settle lawsuits by people who claimed its diet drug fen-phen had damaged heart valves.

In addition to being concerned about whether to continue using hormones, many women said they felt angry and betrayed. How could the medical establishment assure them for so long that a drug's benefits outweighed any risks only to turn around suddenly and recommend that it not be used? "We've learned a lesson the hard way," said one medical researcher in a letter to the New England Journal of Medicine. *"Until a medication is studied long term, it should not be prescribed long term for healthy women."*

Following is the text of a news release issued July 9, 2002, by the National Heart, Lung, and Blood Institute of the National Institutes of Health announcing that a clinical trial of the effects of combination hormone therapy had been halted because the risks of the drug outweighed its benefits.

The document was obtained from the Internet at www .nhlbi.nih.gov/new/press/02-07-09.htm; accessed October 18, 2002.

The National Heart, Lung, and Blood Institute (NHLBI) of the National Institutes of Health (NIH) has stopped early a major clinical trial of the risks and
benefits of combined estrogen and progestin in healthy menopausal women
due to an increased risk of invasive breast cancer. The large multi-center trial,
a component of the Women's Health Initiative (WHI), also found increases in
coronary heart disease, stroke, and pulmonary embolism in study participants
on estrogen plus progestin compared to women taking placebo pills. There
were noteworthy benefits of estrogen plus progestin, including fewer cases of
hip fractures and colon cancer, but on balance the harm was greater than the
benefit. The study, which was scheduled to run until 2005, was stopped after
an average follow-up of 5.2 years.

Participants in this component of WHI, like most women with a uterus who
take hormone therapy, were given progestin in combination with estrogen.
This practice is known to prevent endometrial cancer. A separate WHI study
of estrogen alone in women who had a hysterectomy before joining the WHI
hormone program continues unchanged because, at this point, the balance of
risks and benefits of estrogen alone is still uncertain.

The report from the WHI investigators on the estrogen plus progestin study
findings will be published in the July 17 issue of *The Journal of the American
Medical Association* (JAMA); because of the importance of the information,
the study is being released early on Tuesday, July 9, as an expedited article on
the JAMA Web site. (Full text version available to all at jama.com.)

"We have long sought the answer to the question: Does postmenopausal
hormone therapy prevent heart disease and, if it does, what are the risks? The
bottom-line answer from WHI is that this combined form of hormone therapy
is unlikely to benefit the heart. The cardiovascular and cancer risks of estrogen plus progestin outweigh any benefits—and a 26 percent increase in breast
cancer risk is too high a price to pay, even if there were a heart benefit. Similarly, the risks outweigh the benefits of fewer hip fractures," said NHLBI Director Claude Lenfant, M.D.

"Menopausal women who might have been candidates for estrogen plus
progestin should now focus on well-proven treatments to reduce the risk of
cardiovascular disease, including measures to prevent and control high blood
pressure, high blood cholesterol, and obesity. This effort could not be more
important: heart disease remains the number one killer of American women,"
added Lenfant.

The estrogen plus progestin trial of the WHI involved 16,608 women ages 50
to 79 years with an intact uterus. An important objective of the trial was to examine the effect of estrogen plus progestin on the prevention of heart disease
and hip fractures, and any associated change in risk for breast and colon cancer. The study did not address the short-term risks and benefits of hormones
for the treatment of menopausal symptoms.

About 6 million women in the U.S. are taking estrogen plus progestin for a
variety of reasons, including symptom relief, because their doctors advised it,
or for long-term health.

"Women with a uterus who are currently taking estrogen plus progestin should have a serious talk with their doctor to see if they should continue it. If they are taking this hormone combination for short-term relief of symptoms, it may be reasonable to continue since the benefits are likely to outweigh the risks. Longer term use or use for disease prevention must be re-evaluated given the multiple adverse effects noted in WHI," said Jacques Rossouw, M.D., acting director of the WHI.

According to Rossouw, the adverse effects of estrogen plus progestin applied to all women, irrespective of age, ethnicity, or prior disease status.

"When the estrogen-only trial is completed, a comparison of the results of these two trials may provide a better idea of the roles of estrogen, compared to estrogen plus progestin, in health and disease," said Marcia Stefanick, Ph.D., chair of the WHI Steering Committee and Associate Professor of Medicine, Stanford University, Palo Alto, California.

Women enrolled in the estrogen plus progestin study were randomly assigned to a daily dose of estrogen plus progestin (0.625 mg of conjugated equine estrogens plus 2.5 mg of medroxyprogesterone acetate) or to a placebo. Participants were enrolled in the study between 1993 and 1998 at over 40 clinical sites across the country.

In 2000 and again in 2001, WHI investigators complied with a recommendation from the study's Data and Safety Monitoring Board (DSMB) to inform participants of a small increase in heart attacks, strokes, and blood clots in women taking hormones. The DSMB, an independent advisory committee charged with reviewing results and ensuring participant safety, found that the actual number of women having any one of these events was small and it did not cross the statistical boundary established to ensure participant safety. Therefore, the group recommended continuing the trial due to the still uncertain balance of risks and benefits.

Then, at the DSMB's regularly scheduled meeting on May 31, 2002, the data review revealed for the first time that the number of cases of invasive breast cancer in the estrogen plus progestin group had crossed the boundary established as a signal of increased risk.

"In designing the trial and following the results, the safety of the patients was of the utmost importance," said Garnet Anderson, Ph.D., a biostatistician who led the analysis at the Fred Hutchinson Cancer Research Center, Seattle, Washington. "Because breast cancer is so serious an event, we set the bar lower to monitor for it. We pre-specified that the change in cancer rates did not have to be that large to warrant stopping the trial. And the trial was stopped at the first clear indication of increased risk," she added. She also noted that, at that point, there was no indication of increased risk for breast cancer in the estrogen-only group.

The DSMB's May 31 recommendation to stop the trial was based on the finding of increased breast cancer risk, supported by the evidence of overall health risks exceeding any benefits. Following the NHLBI's decision to stop the study, the Institute and the investigators have worked intensively to develop information materials for participants. On July 8, participants started receiving letters informing them about the results and telling them that they should stop study medications. Participants will be contacted by their clinical centers for further counseling and will continue to have clinic visits so that their health outcomes can be followed.

All WHI participants, including those in the other study components, are also receiving a newsletter with a summary of the findings and an explanation of risks and benefits.

Dr. Rossouw stressed the importance of understanding how the risk to an individual woman can be low, but the risk to the population at large can be great.

"The WHI results tell us that during 1 year, among 10,000 postmenopausal women with a uterus who are taking estrogen plus progestin, 8 more will have invasive breast cancer, 7 more will have a heart attack, 8 more will have a stroke, and 18 more will have blood clots, including 8 with blood clots in the lungs, than will a similar group of 10,000 women not taking these hormones. This is a relatively small annual increase in risk for an individual woman. Individual women who have participated in the trial and women in the population who have been on estrogen and progestin should not be unduly alarmed. However, even small individual risks over time, and on a population-wide basis, add up to tens of thousands of these serious adverse health events," explained Rossouw.

The National Cancer Institute (NCI) re-emphasized the recommendation that all women in their forties and older get screened for breast cancer with mammography every 1 to 2 years.

"Women in the WHI, women taking hormones for any reason, and any woman over 40 should remain committed to their regular program of breast cancer screening to allow the earliest possible detection of breast cancer," said Leslie Ford, M.D., associate director for clinical research in NCI's Division of Cancer Prevention.

"The reduction in colorectal cancer risk in the WHI is intriguing, but the balance of harm versus benefit does not justify any woman beginning or continuing to take estrogen plus progestin for this purpose. NCI has a number of clinical trials under way investigating new methods to detect and prevent both colorectal cancer and breast cancer that will provide critical information to help women make important health decisions," added Ford.

Specific study findings for the estrogen plus progestin group compared to placebo include:

- A 41 percent increase in strokes
- A 29 percent increase in heart attacks
- A doubling of rates of venous thromboembolism (blood clots)
- A 22 percent increase in total cardiovascular disease
- A 26 percent increase in breast cancer
- A 37 percent reduction in cases of colorectal cancer
- A one-third reduction in hip fracture rates
- A 24 percent reduction in total fractures
- No difference in total mortality (of all causes)

The WHI involves over 161,000 women who are participating in a set of clinical trials or an observational study. The clinical trials are designed to test promising but unproven preventive measures for heart disease, breast and colorectal cancer, and osteoporosis. In addition to the trials of estrogen alone and estrogen plus progestin, other trials are studying a low-fat eating pattern and calcium/Vitamin D supplementation. WHI is sponsored by NHLBI in collaboration with four other components of the NIH—the National Cancer Institute, the National Institute of Arthritis and Musculoskeletal and Skin Diseases, the National Institute on Aging, and the Office of Research on Women's Health. Note: Wyeth-Ayerst Research provided the medication (active hormones and placebo) for the estrogen plus progestin study.

PRESIDENTIAL COMMISSION ON THE ETHICS OF CLONING
July 11, 2002

Human cloning was a topic of considerable controversy in 2002. A presidential advisory panel, the U.S. Senate, and a United Nations panel all failed to reach agreement on whether scientists should be barred from cloning human embryos to harvest stem cells for use in medical research. As a result, a far less controversial ban on cloning human embryos for the purpose of producing human babies was left in limbo at the end of the year, amid reports that human clones had already been or were about to be born.

Starting with the cloning of the sheep named Dolly in 1996, researchers had successfully cloned several mammals, including cattle, pigs, goats, mice, and cats. This research was generally aimed at replicating expensively created "transgenic" animals that had been genetically modified to make them particularly useful in some way, such as for use in organ transplants. In August, for example, private researchers announced that cloned cows that produced human antibodies had been born in the United States. The antibodies might eventually be used to produce medicines to treat infectious diseases, multiple sclerosis, and perhaps even cancer. (Cloning of Dolly, Historic Documents of 1997, p. 212)

Policymakers and biomedical researchers were almost unanimously opposed to human reproductive cloning—cloning done with the intention of producing a baby that was genetically identical to another human being. The process, which was called nuclear transplantation or somatic cell nuclear transplant, involved removing the nucleus of an egg cell and replacing it with the nucleus from an adult cell. The restructured egg cell was then induced to begin dividing. If the procedure was successful, the cell would eventually divide into about 150 cells, called a "blastocyst"—an early-stage embryo that could then be implanted into a human uterus, where it could form a fetus and eventually a newborn baby.

The debate instead centered on therapeutic, or nonreproductive, human cloning. This cloning began the same way as human reproductive cloning, with the substitution of a nucleus of an adult cell for the nucleus of an egg cell and the formation of a blastocyst. Instead of being implanted into a hu-

man uterus, however, the blastocyst was used to harvest stem cells, which were unspecialized cells that could renew themselves indefinitely. For some time scientists had theorized that these cells might be used to grow replacement tissues and organs for the human body and thus allow scientists to develop treatments for numerous diseases and conditions, ranging from juvenile diabetes, to heart and kidney disease, to Parkinson's disease. Using cloned stem cells that genetically matched a human being had the further benefits of reducing the possibility of organ rejection and reducing dependence on organ donations.

Those potential benefits did not hold much sway with abortion foes who opposed the research because they equated the destruction of an embryo, however formed, to obtain the stem cells with the taking of human life. Others were morally opposed to creating a human embryo for the express purpose of destroying it. Opponents also said it would be impossible to ensure that no one used a cloned human embryo for reproductive purposes. For those reasons, opponents pressed for a ban on both reproductive and therapeutic cloning.

The main outlines of the cloning debate mirrored those that accompanied the debate in 2001 on human embryonic stem cell research. Supporters of a ban on human embryonic research had hoped they had an ally in President George W. Bush, who during his 2000 election campaign said he was flatly opposed to federal funding of such research. But in a surprise announcement August 9, 2001, Bush said he would permit limited federal funding of scientific research on about sixty lines of stem cells that were thought to have already been extracted from unused human embryos created in vitro in fertility clinics. Bush, however, remained adamantly opposed to human cloning for any reason. At a gathering of legislators, medical researchers, and bioethicists at the White House on April 10, Bush said that "advances in biomedical technology must never come at the expense of human conscience" and "therefore we much prevent human cloning by stopping it before it starts." (Bush on stem cell research, Historic Documents of 2001, p. 539)

Split Recommendation from Presidential Panel

The issue was not as clear, however, for the President's Council on Bioethics. In his August 2001 speech, Bush announced that he would form a council on bioethics to advise him, and by extension the nation, on the ethics of human cloning and stem cell research. Bush quickly named Leon R. Kass, a University of Chicago ethicist, as chairman of the panel, but little more happened until November 2001, when researchers at Advanced Cell Technology, a Massachusetts firm, announced that they had made the first human embryo clones (the clones died even before a blastocyst was formed). Bush released the names of the other seventeen members of the panel on January 16, 2002, the day before the group's first meeting. The panel consisted of a mix of scientists, lawyers, ethicists, and theologians, some of them well-known conservative thinkers.

After only a month of discussion, the panel said that it had given up any hope of reaching a consensus on the ethics of human cloning for therapeutic purposes. Instead, the advisory panel agreed to disagree. "The council, reflecting the differences of opinion in American society, is divided regarding the ethics of research involving cloned embryos," the panel said in its report, released July 11. "Yet we all agree that all parties to the debate have concerns vital to defend." Thus the panel decided to set out their differences rather than try to forge a "spurious consensus."

The panel agreed that cloning for purposes of human reproduction should be banned. Given the extremely high rates of mortality and defects among other cloned mammals, the council said, attempting to clone a human being was clearly unsafe and therefore unethical. Furthermore, even if humans could be successfully cloned, the clones were likely to encounter a range of personal and social problems, including suffering from constant comparison to the "original" and being treated more like a manufactured product than a human being. The council also worried that cloning could lead to a "new eugenics" where cloning was used to "perpetuate genetically engineered enhancements."

The panel was closely divided on the issue of therapeutic cloning. Ten of the council's eighteen members called for a four-year moratorium on all therapeutic cloning, while seven members recommended that the research be allowed to go forward under careful monitoring. One member took no position.

Another influential panel, the National Academy of Sciences Panel on Scientific and Medical Aspects of Human Cloning, issued a report on January 18 unanimously supporting a ban on cloning for purposes of reproducing humans. The panel would permit human embryo cloning for therapeutic purposes. "Human reproductive cloning should not now be practiced," the report said. "It is dangerous and likely to fail." The panel based its recommendation on animal cloning, which had shown that "only a small percentage of attempts are successful; that many of the clones die during gestation, even in late stages; that newborn clones are often abnormal; and that the procedures may carry serious risks for the mother." The panel suggested that any ban on human reproductive cloning be reviewed within five years and reconsidered only if a new scientific review showed that the procedures would be safe and effective and if a broad "national dialogue on societal, religious, and ethical issues suggests that reconsideration is warranted." The panel said any ban should be legally enforceable in both the public and private sectors and carry "substantial penalties."

Standoff in the Senate

The debate in the Senate covered the same ground, if a little more loudly and with less temperance. Two main bills were under consideration. The first (S 1829) mirrored the measure passed by the House in 2001. It would impose a penalty of at least ten years in prison and a fine of at least $1 million on anyone who attempted to create a human embryo. The second (S 2439) would make it a crime to try to create a baby through cloning or to

implant a cloned organism in a human woman, but it would permit clon-
ing to extract embryonic stem cells for biomedical research. A third bill
(S 2076) proposed banning the implantation of a cloned organism into a
human womb for purposes of creating a human being. The measure was
portrayed as a compromise, but critics said it would allow implantation of
a cloned embryo for unspecified periods of time.

Lobbying on both sides of the issue was intense. Actors Christopher
Reeve, paralyzed from a spinal cord injury, and Michael J. Fox, a victim of
Parkinson's disease, urged that therapeutic cloning be allowed to go for-
ward. "Our government is supposed to do the greatest good for the greatest
number of people," Reeve said at a Senate hearing in April. "Beyond that, we
have a moral responsibility to help others." On behalf of former president
Ronald Reagan (1981–1989), who had Alzheimer's disease, his wife, Nancy
Reagan, also urged that cloning be permitted for therapeutic purposes. The
biotechnology industry also supported therapeutic cloning, arguing that a
ban would shift the research overseas, leaving Americans behind both in
terms of potential future therapies and the money to be made from them.

An unusual coalition of antiabortion organizations, some environmen-
tal groups (such as Friends of the Earth), and some women's rights groups
supported a full ban on cloning, arguing that therapeutic cloning would
make life a commodity. "Can't they see that it's just not right to make hu-
man embryos and harvest them like crops," lamented one radio ad spon-
sored by the National Right to Life Committee.

Debate among senators was also given to dramatic and emotional state-
ment. Sen. Arlen Specter, R-Pa., a cosponsor of the bill to permit therapeu-
tic cloning, described the issue as "the most important vote involving
medical science in modern times," adding that a total ban would take the
country back to the Dark Ages. "The human body is not a commodity to be
mass-produced and stripped for its parts," countered Sen. Mary Landrieu,
D-La., a cosponsor of the bill calling for a total ban. After several months of
hearings and behind-the-scene maneuvering, the two sides had fought each
other to a standstill. Neither side had enough support to cut off a filibuster
on the Senate floor, and Senate leaders in June abandoned attempts to bring
the bills up for a vote.

The Senate debate and its lack of a resolution encouraged several state leg-
islatures to take up the issue. Many simply passed bills or resolutions urg-
ing Congress to ban either all cloning or cloning for reproductive purposes.
Iowa became the sixth state to impose a ban on all human cloning within
the state. The other five were California, Louisiana, Michigan, Rhode Is-
land, and Virginia. California became the first state to expressly permit
state and private funding for research on stem cells extracted from embryos
created in vitro and never used. Supporters of the legislation, including
Democratic governor Grey Davis, said the legislation was necessary to keep
California at the forefront of medical research. The move was motivated in
part by lack of federal funding and uncertainty over federal policy. Although
President Bush promised that scientists would have access to at least sixty

lines of stem cells, only nine stem cell lines were available by the end of 2002. The California legislation was also motivated by fears that that bio-medical researchers and their labs would move their potentially lucrative operations to Great Britain and other countries that were more open to em-bryo research. Similar legislation was under consideration in a handful of other states.

Stanford University announced in December that it was preparing to mount an effort to develop human embryonic stem cells through nuclear transfer technology, the procedure that most people referred to as therapeu-tic cloning. The leader of the project was Irving L. Weissman, a professor of medicine at Stanford who chaired the National Academy of Science's study that approved the use of cloning for therapeutic purposes. Weissman said the Stanford project was "not even close" to cloning, because it would involve the creation of only cells, not embryos. Much of the work of the project was aimed at developing a treatment for cancer.

International Cloning Ban Blocked

The United Nations also became embroiled in a cloning debate that pitted the United States against France and Germany. The three countries were also soon to be at loggerheads over the urgency of going to war with Iraq. The cloning debate centered on an international treaty to ban human reproduc-tive cloning. Such a treaty had the support of all 191 member nations, but the United States insisted that any treaty also include a ban on therapeutic cloning—a position that was supported only by the Vatican and a hand-ful of predominately Catholic countries, including Spain and some Latin American countries. That put the United States in conflict with France and Germany, who were urging a two-track approach, with the emphasis on completing a draft of a treaty banning reproductive cloning by the end of 2003 and opening it to ratification in 2004. A second treaty dealing with therapeutic cloning would be worked on simultaneously, but the timetable for completing the draft was not as urgent. (Iraq debate, p. 713)

On November 7 the United States blocked the German-French initiative on a procedural motion to guide the drafting of the treaty. The action had the effect of postponing the debate, and the drafting of the treaty, until Sep-tember 2003. "This leaves the field wide open to those working towards giving birth to a cloned human being," said the German representative, Christian Walter Much. George Annas, a professor of public health and bioethics at Boston University, put it more bluntly: "The idea of a state like the United States standing in the way of an international agreement—not because it disagrees with it but because it wants something more—is ex-tremely counterproductive and almost hypocritical."

At the end of the year, many people's worst fear—that someone would clone a human baby—may have come to fruition. Several groups had hinted that they were close to cloning a human baby. Then, on December 27, the chief executive of a company called Clonaid announced that a healthy, seven-pound baby girl named Eve had been born using cloning procedures. The company offered no proof either of the birth or the cloning, and most ex-

perts remained skeptical that such a birth had occurred. Clonaid was owned by a sect called the Raelians, who believed that extraterrestrial beings had used genetic engineering to create life on Earth.

The announcement was met with dismay and outrage. "What a sad day for science," said Robert Lanza, medical director of Advanced Cell Technology, a company that was involved with therapeutic cloning. "What they've claimed to have done is both appalling and scientifically irresponsible, and whether or not it's true, they have done a tremendous disservice to all of us in the scientific community. The backlash could cripple an area of medical research that could cure millions of people, and it would be tragic if this announcement results in a ban on all forms of cloning."

Another first in cloning was confirmed, however—the birth of an apparently healthy cloned kitten, named CopyCat, or cc for short. The kitten was the only survivor of eighty-seven embryos cloned by researchers at Texas A&M University. Their work was described in the February issue of the scientific journal Nature. *A company called Genetic Saving & Clone funded the research specifically to clone household pets and tap into a "huge interest" among pet owners. The researchers warned that a cloned pet would be "a reproduction, not a resurrection," and would not necessarily look like the original, have the same personality, or bond with the owner in the same way. For example, cc had different coloration from her genetic mother. Those cautions apparently did not daunt pet owners. The company's chief executive said he expected the demand for dog and cat clones to be "far more than we'll be able to handle for many years."*

> *Following is the text of the executive summary from "Human Cloning and Human Dignity: An Ethical Inquiry," a report of the President's Council on Bioethics released July 11, 2002.*
>
> **The document was obtained from the Internet at www .bioethics.gov/cloningreport; accessed October 31, 2002.**

For the past five years, the prospect of human cloning has been the subject of considerable public attention and sharp moral debate, both in the United States and around the world. Since the announcement in February 1997 of the first successful cloning of a mammal (Dolly the sheep), several other species of mammals have been cloned. Although a cloned human child has yet to be born, and although the animal experiments have had low rates of success, the production of functioning mammalian cloned offspring suggests that the eventual cloning of humans must be considered a serious possibility.

In November 2001, American researchers claimed to have produced the first cloned human embryos, though they reportedly reached only a six-cell stage before they stopped dividing and died. In addition, several fertility specialists, both here and abroad, have announced their intention to clone human beings. The United States Congress has twice taken up the matter, in 1998 and again in 2001–2002, with the House of Representatives in July 2001 passing a strict ban on all human cloning, including the production of cloned human embryos. As of this writing, several cloning-related bills are under consideration in the Senate. Many other nations have banned human cloning, and the United Nations is considering an international convention on the subject. Finally, two major national reports have been issued on human reproductive cloning, one by the National Bioethics Advisory Commission (NBAC) in 1997, the other by the National Academy of Sciences (NAS) in January 2002. Both the NBAC and the NAS reports called for further consideration of the ethical and social questions raised by cloning.

The debate over human cloning became further complicated in 1998 when researchers were able, for the first time, to isolate human embryonic stem cells. Many scientists believe that these versatile cells, capable of becoming any type of cell in the body, hold great promise for understanding and treating many chronic diseases and conditions. Some scientists also believe that stem cells derived from cloned human embryos, produced explicitly for such research, might prove uniquely useful for studying many genetic diseases and devising novel therapies. Public reaction to the prospect of cloning-for-biomedical-research has been mixed: some Americans support it for its medical promise; others oppose it because it requires the exploitation and destruction of nascent human life, which would be created solely for research purposes.

Human Cloning: What Is at Stake?

The intense attention given to human cloning in both its potential uses, for reproduction as well as for research, strongly suggests that people do not regard it as just another new technology. Instead, we see it as something quite different, something that touches fundamental aspects of our humanity. The notion of cloning raises issues about identity and individuality, the meaning of having children, the difference between procreation and manufacture, and the relationship between the generations. It also raises new questions about the manipulation of some human beings for the benefit of others, the freedom and value of biomedical inquiry, our obligation to heal the sick (and its limits), and the respect and protection owed to nascent human life.

Finally, the legislative debates over human cloning raise large questions about the relationship between science and society, especially about whether society can or should exercise ethical and prudential control over biomedical technology and the conduct of biomedical research. Rarely has such a seemingly small innovation raised such big questions.

The Inquiry: Our Point of Departure

As Members of the President's Council on Bioethics, we have taken up the larger ethical and social inquiry called for in the NBAC and NAS reports, with the aim of advancing public understanding and informing public policy on the matter. We have attempted to consider human cloning (both for producing children and for biomedical research) within its larger human, technological, and ethical contexts, rather than to view it as an isolated technical development. We focus first on the broad human goods that it may serve as well as threaten, rather than on the immediate impact of the technique itself. By our broad approach, our starting on the plane of human goods, and our open spirit of inquiry, we hope to contribute to a richer and deeper understanding of what human cloning means, how we should think about it, and what we should do about it.

On some matters discussed in this report, Members of the Council are not of one mind. Rather than bury these differences in search of a spurious consensus, we have sought to present all views fully and fairly, while recording our agreements as well as our genuine diversity of perspectives, including our differences on the final recommendations to be made. By this means, we hope to help policymakers and the general public appreciate more thoroughly the difficulty of the issues and the competing goods that are at stake.

Fair and Accurate Terminology

There is today much confusion about the terms used to discuss human cloning, regarding both the activity involved and the entities that result. The Council stresses the importance of striving not only for accuracy but also for fairness, especially because the choice of terms can decisively affect the way questions are posed, and hence how answers are given. We have sought terminology that most accurately conveys the descriptive reality of the matter, in order that the moral arguments can then proceed on the merits. We have resisted the temptation to solve the moral questions by artful redefinition or by denying to some morally crucial element a name that makes clear that there is a moral question to be faced.

On the basis of (1) a careful analysis of the act of cloning, and its relation to the means by which it is accomplished and the purposes it may serve, and (2) an extensive critical examination of alternative terminologies, the Council has adopted the following definitions for the most important terms in the matter of human cloning:

- *Cloning:* A form of reproduction in which offspring result not from the chance union of egg and sperm (sexual reproduction) but from the deliberate replication of the genetic makeup of another single individual (asexual reproduction).
- *Human cloning:* The asexual production of a new human organism that is, at all stages of development, genetically virtually identical to a currently existing or previously existing human being. It would be accomplished by introducing the nuclear material of a human somatic cell (donor) into an oocyte (egg) whose own nucleus has been removed or inactivated, yielding a product that has a human genetic constitution virtually identical to the donor of the somatic cell. (This procedure is known as "somatic cell nuclear transfer," or SCNT). We have declined to use the terms "reproductive cloning" and "therapeutic cloning." We have chosen instead to use the following designations:
- *Cloning-to-produce-children:* Production of a cloned human embryo, formed for the (proximate) purpose of initiating a pregnancy, with the

(ultimate) goal of producing a child who will be genetically virtually identical to a currently existing or previously existing individual.

- *Cloning-for-biomedical-research:* Production of a cloned human embryo, formed for the (proximate) purpose of using it in research or for extracting its stem cells, with the (ultimate) goals of gaining scientific knowledge of normal and abnormal development and of developing cures for human diseases.

- *Cloned human embryo:* (a) A human embryo resulting from the nuclear transfer process (as contrasted with a human embryo arising from the union of egg and sperm). (b) The immediate (and developing) product of the initial act of cloning, accomplished by successful SCNT, whether used subsequently in attempts to produce children or in biomedical research.

Scientific Background

Cloning research and stem cell research are being actively investigated and the state of the science is changing rapidly; significant new developments could change some of the interpretations in our report. At present, however, a few general points may be highlighted.

- *The technique of cloning.* The following steps have been used to produce live offspring in the mammalian species that have been successfully cloned. Obtain an egg cell from a female of a mammalian species. Remove its nuclear DNA, to produce an enucleated egg. Insert the nucleus of a donor adult cell into the enucleated egg, to produce a reconstructed egg. Activate the reconstructed egg with chemicals or electric current, to stimulate it to commence cell division. Sustain development of the cloned embryo to a suitable stage in vitro, and then transfer it to the uterus of a female host that has been suitably prepared to receive it. Bring to live birth a cloned animal that is genetically virtually identical (except for the mitochondrial DNA) to the animal that donated the adult cell nucleus.

- *Animal cloning:* low success rates, high morbidity. At least seven species of mammals (none of them primates) have been successfully cloned to produce live births. Yet the production of live cloned offspring is rare and the failure rate is high: more than 90 percent of attempts to initiate a clonal pregnancy do not result in successful live birth. Moreover, the live-born cloned animals suffer high rates of deformity and disability, both at birth and later on. Some biologists attribute these failures to errors or incompleteness of epigenetic reprogramming of the somatic cell nucleus.

- *Attempts at human cloning.* At this writing, it is uncertain whether anyone has attempted cloning-to-produce-children (although at least one physician is now claiming to have initiated several active clonal pregnancies, and others are reportedly working on it). We do not know whether a transferred cloned human embryo can progress all the way to live birth.

- *Stem cell research.* Human embryonic stem cells have been isolated from embryos (produced by IVF) at the blastocyst stage or from the germinal tissue of fetuses. Human adult stem (or multipotent) cells have been isolated from a variety of tissues. Such cell populations can be differentiated in vitro into a number of different cell types, and are currently being studied intensely for their possible uses in regenerative medicine. Most scientists working in the field believe that stem cells (both embryonic and adult) hold great promise as routes toward cures and treatments for many human diseases and disabilities. All stem cell research is at a very early stage, and it is too soon to tell which approaches will prove most useful, and for which diseases.

- *The transplant rejection problem.* To be effective as long-term treatments, cell transplantation therapies will have to overcome the immune rejection problem. Cells and tissues derived from adult stem cells and returned to the patient from whom they were taken would not be subject (at least in principle) to immune rejection.

- *Stem cells from cloned embryos.* Human embryonic stem cell preparations could potentially be produced by using somatic cell nuclear transfer to produce a cloned human embryo, and then taking it apart at the blastocyst stage and isolating stem cells. These stem cells would be genetically virtually identical to cells from the nucleus donor, and thus could potentially be of great value in biomedical research. Very little work of this sort has been done to date in animals, and there are as yet no published reports of cloned human embryos grown to the blastocyst stage. Although the promise of such research is at this time unknown, most researchers believe it will yield very useful and important knowledge, pointing toward new therapies and offering one of several possible routes to circumvent the immune rejection problem. Although some experimental results in animals are indeed encouraging, they also demonstrate some tendency even of cloned stem cells to stimulate an immune response.

- *The fate of embryos used in research.* All extractions of stem cells from human embryos, cloned or not, involve the destruction of these embryos.

The Ethics of Cloning-to-Produce-Children

Two separate national-level reports on human cloning concluded that attempts to clone a human being would be unethical at this time due to safety concerns and the likelihood of harm to those involved. The Council concurs in this conclusion. But we have extended the work of these distinguished bodies by undertaking a broad ethical examination of the merits of, and difficulties with, cloning-to-produce-children.

Cloning-to-produce-children might serve several purposes. It might allow infertile couples or others to have genetically-related children; permit couples at risk of conceiving a child with a genetic disease to avoid having an afflicted child; allow the bearing of a child who could become an ideal transplant donor for a particular patient in need; enable a parent to keep a living connection with a dead or dying child or spouse; or enable individuals or society to try to "replicate" individuals of great talent or beauty. These purposes have been defended by appeals to the goods of freedom, existence (as opposed to nonexistence), and well-being—all vitally important ideals.

A major weakness in these arguments supporting cloning-to-produce-children is that they overemphasize the freedom, desires, and control of parents, and pay insufficient attention to the well-being of the cloned child-to-be. The Council holds that, once the child-to-be is carefully considered, these arguments are not sufficient to overcome the powerful case against engaging in cloning-to-produce-children.

First, cloning-to-produce-children would violate the principles of the ethics of human research. Given the high rates of morbidity and mortality in the cloning of other mammals, we believe that cloning-to-produce-children would be extremely unsafe, and that attempts to produce a cloned child would be highly unethical. Indeed, our moral analysis of this matter leads us to conclude that this is not, as is sometimes implied, a merely temporary objection, easily removed by the improvement of technique. We offer reasons for believing that the safety risks might be enduring, and offer arguments in support of a strong conclusion: that conducting experiments in an effort to make cloning-to-produce-children less dangerous would itself be an unacceptable violation of the norms of research ethics. There seems to be no ethical way to try to discover whether cloning-to-produce-children can become safe, now or in the future.

If carefully considered, the concerns about safety also begin to reveal the ethical principles that should guide a broader assessment of cloning-to-produce-children: the principles of freedom, equality, and human dignity. To appreciate the broader human significance of cloning-to-produce-children, one needs first to reflect on the meaning of having children; the meaning of asexual, as opposed to sexual, reproduction; the importance of origins and genetic endowment for identity and sense of self; the meaning of exercising greater human control over the processes and "products" of human reproduction; and the difference between begetting and making. Reflecting on these topics, the Council has identified five categories of concern regarding cloning-to-produce-children. (Different Council Members give varying moral weight to these different concerns.)

- *Problems of identity and individuality.* Cloned children may experience serious problems of identity both because each will be genetically virtually identical to a human being who has already lived and because the expectations for their lives may be shadowed by constant comparisons to the life of the "original."
- *Concerns regarding manufacture.* Cloned children would be the first human beings whose entire genetic makeup is selected in advance. They might come to be considered more like products of a designed manufacturing process than "gifts" whom their parents are prepared to accept as they are. Such an attitude toward children could also contribute to increased commercialization and industrialization of human procreation.

- *The prospect of a new eugenics.* Cloning, if successful, might serve the ends of privately pursued eugenic enhancement, either by avoiding the genetic defects that may arise when human reproduction is left to chance, or by preserving and perpetuating outstanding genetic traits, including the possibility, someday in the future, of using cloning to perpetuate genetically engineered enhancements.
- *Troubled family relations.* By confounding and transgressing the natural boundaries between generations, cloning could strain the social ties between them. Fathers could become "twin brothers" to their "sons"; mothers could give birth to their genetic twins; and grandparents would also be the "genetic parents" of their grandchildren. Genetic relation to only one parent might produce special difficulties for family life.
- *Effects on society.* Cloning-to-produce-children would affect not only the direct participants but also the entire society that allows or supports this activity. Even if practiced on a small scale, it could affect the way society looks at children and set a precedent for future nontherapeutic interventions into the human genetic endowment or novel forms of control by one generation over the next. In the absence of wisdom regarding these matters, prudence dictates caution and restraint.

Conclusion: For some or all of these reasons, the Council is in full agreement that cloning-to-produce-children is not only unsafe but also morally unacceptable, and ought not to be attempted.

The Ethics of Cloning-for-Biomedical-Research

Ethical assessment of cloning-for-biomedical-research is far more vexing. On the one hand, such research could lead to important knowledge about human embryological development and gene action, both normal and abnormal, ultimately resulting in treatments and cures for many dreaded illnesses and disabilities. On the other hand, the research is morally controversial because it involves the deliberate production, use, and ultimate destruction of cloned human embryos, and because the cloned embryos produced for research are no different from those that could be implanted in attempts to produce cloned children. The difficulty is compounded by what are, for now, unanswerable questions as to whether the research will in fact yield the benefits hoped for, and whether other promising and morally nonproblematic approaches might yield comparable benefits. The Council, reflecting the differences of opinion in American society, is divided regarding the ethics of research involving (cloned) embryos. *Yet we agree that all parties to the debate have concerns vital to defend, vital not only to themselves but to all of us. No human being and no society can afford to be callous to the needs of suffering humanity, or cavalier about the treatment of nascent human life, or indifferent to the social effects of adopting one course of action rather than another.*

To make clear to all what is at stake in the decision, Council Members have presented, as strongly as possible, the competing ethical cases for and against cloning-for-biomedical-research in the form of first-person attempts at moral suasion. Each case has tried to address what is owed to suffering humanity, to the human embryo, and to the broader society. Within each case, supporters of the position in question speak only for themselves, and not for the Council as a whole.

A. The Moral Case for Cloning-for-Biomedical-Research

The moral case for cloning-for-biomedical-research rests on our obligation to try to relieve human suffering, an obligation that falls most powerfully on medical practitioners and biomedical researchers. We who support cloning-for-biomedical-research all agree that it may offer uniquely useful ways of investigating and possibly treating many chronic debilitating diseases and disabilities, providing aid and relief to millions. We also believe that the moral objections to this research are outweighed by the great good that may come from it. Up to this point, we who support this research all agree. But we differ among ourselves regarding the weight of the moral objections, owing to differences about the moral status of the cloned embryo. These differences of opinion are sufficient to warrant distinguishing two different moral positions within the moral case for cloning-for-biomedical-research:

Position Number One. Most Council Members who favor cloning-for-biomedical-research do so with serious moral concerns. Speaking only for ourselves, we acknowledge the following difficulties, but think that they can be addressed by setting proper boundaries.

- *Intermediate moral status.* While we take seriously concerns about the treatment of nascent human life, we believe there are sound moral reasons for not regarding the embryo in its earliest stages as the moral equivalent of a human person. We believe the embryo has a developing and intermediate moral worth that commands our special respect, but that it is morally permissible to use early-stage cloned human embryos in important research under strict regulation.
- *Deliberate creation for use.* We believe that concerns over the problem of deliberate creation of cloned embryos for use in research have merit, but when properly understood should not preclude cloning-for-biomedical-research. These embryos would not be "created for destruction," but for use in the service of life and medicine. They would be destroyed in the service of a great good, and this should not be obscured.
- *Going too far.* We acknowledge the concern that some researchers might seek to develop cloned embryos beyond the blastocyst stage, and for those of us who believe that the cloned embryo has a developing and intermediate moral status, this is a very real worry. We approve, therefore, only of research on cloned embryos that is strictly limited to the first fourteen days of development—a point near when the primitive streak is formed and before organ differentiation occurs.
- *Other moral hazards.* We believe that concerns about the exploitation of women and about the risk that cloning-for-biomedical-research could lead to cloning-to-produce-children can be adequately addressed by appropriate rules and regulations. These concerns need not frighten us into abandoning an important avenue of research.

Position Number Two. A few Council Members who favor cloning-for-biomedical-research do not share all the ethical qualms expressed above. Speaking only for ourselves, we hold that this research, at least for the purposes presently contemplated, presents no special moral problems, and therefore should be endorsed with enthusiasm as a potential new means of gaining knowledge to serve humankind. Because we accord no special moral status to the early-stage cloned embryo and believe it should be treated essentially like all other human cells, we believe that the moral issues involved in this research are no different from those that accompany any biomedical research. What is required is the usual commitment to high standards for the quality of research, scientific integrity, and the need to obtain informed consent from donors of the eggs and somatic cells used in nuclear transfer.

B. The Moral Case Against Cloning-for-Biomedical-Research

The moral case against cloning-for-biomedical-research acknowledges the possibility—though purely speculative at the moment—that medical benefits might come from this particular avenue of experimentation. But we believe it is morally wrong to exploit and destroy developing human life, even for good reasons, and that it is unwise to open the door to the many undesirable consequences that are likely to result from this research. We find it disquieting, even somewhat ignoble, to treat what are in fact seeds of the next generation as mere raw material for satisfying the needs of our own. Only for very serious reasons should progress toward increased knowledge and medical advances be slowed. But we believe that in this case such reasons are apparent.

- *Moral status of the cloned embryo.* We hold that the case for treating the early-stage embryo as simply the moral equivalent of all other human cells (Position Number Two, above) is simply mistaken: it denies the continuous history of human individuals from the embryonic to fetal to infant stages of existence; it misunderstands the meaning of potentiality; and it ignores the hazardous moral precedent that the routinized creation, use, and destruction of nascent human life would establish. We hold that the case for according the human embryo "intermediate and developing moral status" (Position Number One, above) is also unconvincing, for reasons both biological and moral. Attempts to ground the limited measure of respect owed to a maturing embryo in certain of its developmental features do not succeed, and the invoking of a "special respect" owed to nascent human life seems to have little or no operative meaning if cloned embryos may be created in bulk and used routinely with impunity. If from one perspective the view that the embryo seems to amount to little may invite a weakening of our respect, from another perspective its seeming insignificance should awaken in us a sense of shared humanity and a special obligation to protect it.
- *The exploitation of developing human life.* To engage in cloning-for-biomedical-research requires the irreversible crossing of a very significant moral boundary: the creation of human life expressly and exclusively for the purpose of its use in research, research that necessarily

involves its deliberate destruction. If we permit this research to proceed, we will effectively be endorsing the complete transformation of nascent human life into nothing more than a resource or a tool. Doing so would coarsen our moral sensibilities and make us a different society: one less humble toward that which we cannot fully understand, less willing to extend the boundaries of human respect ever outward, and more willing to transgress moral boundaries once it appears to be in our own interests to do so.

- *Moral harm to society.* Even those who are uncertain about the precise moral status of the human embryo have sound ethical-prudential reasons to oppose cloning-for-biomedical-research. Giving moral approval to such research risks significant moral harm to our society by (1) crossing the boundary from sexual to asexual reproduction, thus approving in principle the genetic manipulation and control of nascent human life; (2) opening the door to other moral hazards, such as cloning-to-produce-children or research on later-stage human embryos and fetuses; and (3) potentially putting the federal government in the novel and unsavory position of mandating the destruction of nascent human life. Because we are concerned not only with the fate of the cloned embryos but also with where this research will lead our society, we think prudence requires us not to engage in this research.

- *What we owe the suffering.* We are certainly not deaf to the voices of suffering patients; after all, each of us already shares or will share in the hardships of mortal life. We and our loved ones are all patients or potential patients. But we are not only patients, and easing suffering is not our only moral obligation. As much as we wish to alleviate suffering now and to leave our children a world where suffering can be more effectively relieved, we also want to leave them a world in which we and they want to live—a world that honors moral limits, that respects all life whether strong or weak, and that refuses to secure the good of some human beings by sacrificing the lives of others.

Public Policy Options

The Council recognizes the challenges and risks of moving from moral assessment to public policy. Reflections on the "social contract" between science and society highlight both the importance of scientific freedom and the need for boundaries. We note that other countries often treat human cloning in the context of a broad area of biomedical technology, at the intersection of reproductive technology, embryo research, and genetics, while the public policy debate in the United States has treated cloning largely on its own. We recognize the special difficulty in formulating sound public policy in this area, given that the two ethically distinct matters-cloning-to-produce-children and cloning-for-biomedical-research-will be mutually affected or implicated in any attempts to legislate about either. Nevertheless, our ethical and policy analysis leads us to the conclusion that some deliberate public policy at the federal level is needed in the area of human cloning.

We reviewed the following seven possible policy options and considered their relative strengths and weaknesses: (1) Professional self-regulation but no federal legislative action ("self-regulation"); (2) A ban on cloning-to-produce-children, with neither endorsement nor restriction of cloning-for-biomedical-research ("ban plus silence"); (3) A ban on cloning-to-produce-children, with regulation of the use of cloned embryos for biomedical research ("ban plus regulation"); (4) Governmental regulation, with no legislative prohibitions ("regulation of both"); (5) A ban on all human cloning, whether to produce children or for biomedical research ("ban on both"); (6) A ban on cloning-to-produce-children, with a moratorium or temporary ban on cloning-for-biomedical-research ("ban plus moratorium"); or (7) A moratorium or temporary ban on all human cloning, whether to produce children or for biomedical research ("moratorium on both").

The Council's Policy Recommendations

Having considered the benefits and drawbacks of each of these options, and taken into account our discussions and reflections throughout this report, the Council recommends two possible policy alternatives, each supported by a portion of the Members.

Majority Recommendation: Ten Members of the Council recommend a ban on cloning-to-produce-children combined with a four-year moratorium on cloning-for-biomedical-research. We also call for a federal review of current and projected practices of human embryo research, pre-implantation genetic diagnosis, genetic modification of human embryos and gametes, and related matters, with a view to recommending and shaping ethically sound policies for the entire field. Speaking only for ourselves, those of us who support this recommendation do so for some or all of the following reasons:

- By permanently banning cloning-to-produce-children, this policy gives force to the strong ethical verdict against cloning-to-produce-children, unanimous in this Council (and in Congress) and widely supported by the American people. And by enacting a four-year moratorium on the creation of cloned embryos, it establishes an additional safeguard not afforded by policies that would allow the production of cloned embryos to proceed without delay.

- It calls for and provides time for further democratic deliberation about cloning-for-biomedical research, a subject about which the nation is divided and where there remains great uncertainty. A national discourse on this subject has not yet taken place in full, and a moratorium, by making it impossible for either side to cling to the status-quo, would force both to make their full case before the public. By banning all cloning for a time, it allows us to seek moral consensus on whether or not we should cross a major moral boundary (creating nascent cloned human life solely for research) and prevents our crossing it without deliberate decision. It would afford time for scientific evidence, now sorely lacking, to be gathered—from animal models and other avenues of human

527

research—that might give us a better sense of whether cloning-for-biomedical-research would work as promised, and whether other morally nonproblematic approaches might be available. It would promote a fuller and better-informed public debate. And it would show respect for the deep moral concerns of the large number of Americans who have serious ethical objections to this research.

- Some of us hold that cloning-for-biomedical-research can never be ethically pursued, and endorse a moratorium to enable us to continue to make our case in a democratic way. Others of us support the moratorium because it would provide the time and incentive required to develop a system of national regulation that might come into use if, at the end of the four-year period, the moratorium were not reinstated or made permanent. Such a system could not be developed overnight, and therefore even those who support the research but want it regulated should see that at the very least a pause is required. In the absence of a moratorium, few proponents of the research would have much incentive to institute an effective regulatory system. Moreover, the very process of proposing such regulations would clarify the moral and prudential judgments involved in deciding whether and how to proceed with this research.

- A moratorium on cloning-for-biomedical-research would enable us to consider this activity in the larger context of research and technology in the areas of developmental biology, embryo research, and genetics, and to pursue a more comprehensive federal regulatory system for setting and executing policy in the entire area.

- Finally, we believe that a moratorium, rather than a lasting ban, signals a high regard for the value of biomedical research and an enduring concern for patients and families whose suffering such research may help alleviate. It would reaffirm the principle that science can progress while upholding the community's moral norms, and would therefore reaffirm the community's moral support for science and biomedical technology.

The decision before us is of great importance. Creating cloned embryos for *any* purpose requires crossing a major moral boundary, with grave risks and likely harms, and once we cross it there will be no turning back. Our society should take the time to make a judgment that is well-informed and morally sound, respectful of strongly held views, and representative of the priorities and principles of the American people. We believe this ban-plus-moratorium proposal offers the best means of achieving these goals.

This position is supported by Council Members Rebecca S. Dresser, Francis Fukuyama, Robert P. George, Mary Ann Glendon, Alfonso Gómez-Lobo, William B. Hurlbut, Leon R. Kass, Charles Krauthammer, Paul McHugh, and Gilbert C. Meilaender.

Minority Recommendation: Seven Members of the Council recommend *a ban on cloning-to-produce-children, with regulation of the use of cloned embryos for biomedical research.* Speaking only for ourselves, those of us who support this recommendation do so for some or all of the following reasons:

- By permanently banning cloning-to-produce-children, this policy gives force to the strong ethical verdict against cloning-to-produce-children, unanimous in this Council (and in Congress) and widely supported by the American people. We believe that a ban on the transfer of cloned embryos to a woman's uterus would be a sufficient and effective legal safeguard against the practice.
- *It approves cloning-for-biomedical-research and permits it to proceed without substantial delay.* This is the most important advantage of this proposal. The research shows great promise, and its actual value can only be determined by allowing it to go forward now. Regardless of how much time we allow it, no amount of experimentation with animal models can provide the needed understanding of human diseases. The special benefits from working with stem cells from cloned human embryos cannot be obtained using embryos obtained by IVF. We believe this research could provide relief to millions of Americans, and that the government should therefore support it, within sensible limits imposed by regulation.
- It would establish, *as a condition of proceeding*, the necessary regulatory protections to avoid abuses and misuses of cloned embryos. These regulations might touch on the secure handling of embryos, licensing and prior review of research projects, the protection of egg donors, and the provision of equal access to benefits.
- Some of us also believe that mechanisms to regulate cloning-for-biomedical-research should be part of a larger regulatory program governing all research involving human embryos, and that the federal government should initiate a review of present and projected practices of human embryo research, with the aim of establishing reasonable policies on the matter.

Permitting cloning-for-biomedical-research now, while governing it through a prudent and sensible regulatory regime, is the most appropriate way to allow important research to proceed while insuring that abuses are prevented. We believe that the legitimate concerns about human cloning expressed throughout this report are sufficiently addressed by this ban-plus-regulation proposal, and that the nation should affirm and support the responsible effort to find treatments and cures that might help many who are suffering.

This position is supported by Council Members Elizabeth H. Blackburn, Daniel W. Foster, Michael S. Gazzaniga, William F. May, Janet D. Rowley, Michael J. Sandel, and James Q. Wilson.

BUSH ADMINISTRATION ON HOMELAND SECURITY STRATEGY
July 16, 2002

The U.S. government in 2002 began a lengthy process of assembling a new cabinet-level Department of Homeland Security. The department was to consist of twenty-two preexisting agencies, among them the Coast Guard, the Immigration and Naturalization Service (INS), and the new Transportation Security Administration (TSA). The merger of these agencies into one department represented the federal government's most significant reorganization since the creation of the Defense Department more than fifty years earlier.

Creation of the Department of Homeland Security was a direct response to the September 11, 2001, terrorist attacks in New York City and Washington, D.C. President George W. Bush, who originally opposed the idea when it was championed by some Democrats in Congress, reversed his position in June when legislation mandating the new department picked up momentum in the Senate. The president then demanded immediate congressional action; when the Senate delayed he successfully used the issue as a partisan club against vulnerable Democrats in the midterm elections. Congress ultimately passed legislation incorporating nearly all of what the president had wanted. (September 11 attacks, Historic Documents of 2001, p. 614)

The new department was the centerpiece of a "Homeland Security Strategy" report released by the White House on July 16, 2002. That document listed dozens of specific and general ideas for protecting the United States and its citizens against terrorism and other threats. Many of the ideas would require months or even years of study before they could be adopted. Some of the proposals also were included in numerous reports issued during the year by independent organizations that studied terrorism threats to the United States and the country's vulnerabilities to terrorism. (Terrorism threats, p. 633)

Arriving at a Consensus

Bush's embrace of the idea of a homeland security department was the result of more than eight months of wrangling within his administration, nu-

merous critiques from outside experts, and political maneuvering between Democrats and Republicans. One of the president's key actions after the September 11 attacks was to establish an Office of Homeland Security within the White House. At the time the president described the office as a counterpart to the National Security Council, the White House office assigned the task of coordinating foreign and defense policy actions by such agencies as the state and defense departments.

Tom Ridge, named to be the first director of the office, had broad credibility in Congress because of his previous service as a moderate Republican member of the House and his successful tenure as governor of Pennsylvania. Even so, Ridge lacked the most important tool for political influence in Washington: budgetary control over the agencies that he was supposed to coordinate. Bush's executive order establishing the White House office said Ridge would review the budgets of those agencies, but that authority fell far short of powers necessary for him to command action as he saw fit. Moreover, as a White House official Ridge was not subject to congressional review; committees of Congress could not require him to testify before them, an independence that shielded him from direct oversight by Capitol Hill but also weakened his influence there. (Homeland security, Historic Documents of 2001, p. 637)

In the early months of 2002 Ridge repeatedly found himself under pressure from Congress because of his refusal to testify about the administration's proposed budget and other matters directly related to the war against terrorism. Members also complained that Ridge could offer no convincing explanation for why the president refused to adopt the idea of elevating his office to cabinet-level status. At the same time, congressional investigating panels and news organizations revealed that the CIA and FBI had failed to draw connections between numerous warning signs that a major terrorist plot was afoot in the United States during 2001. (Intelligence failures, p. 990)

Battered by criticism, key administration officials in April began working on a proposal to elevate Ridge's office to cabinet-level status. They worked from a host of bills introduced by members of Congress from both parties calling for such an agency, most important a proposal (S 2452) by Sen. Joseph I. Lieberman, D-Ct., who chaired the Governmental Affairs Committee and had gained national stature as Al Gore's vice presidential running mate in 2000. Lieberman's plan would have consolidated into one department the agencies responsible for border security and similar matters (including the INS, the Customs Service, the Coast Guard, and the Federal Emergency Management Agency), as well as FBI offices responsible for infrastructure and domestic preparedness. Lieberman's committee approved the measure on May 22, signaling substantial congressional support for it.

Two weeks later, on June 6, Bush abruptly reversed course and embraced an approach even broader than Lieberman's bill. Bush's reversal was his second major concession to Congress on antiterrorism matters since the September 11 attacks. In late 2001 Bush had at first insisted that expanded airport screening of passengers had to be conducted by private firms, not by government employees. That stance drew bipartisan criticism in Congress because of the poor history of many private security companies, and Bush ultimately backed down and agreed that screeners would be hired by a new government office, the TSA. In both cases Bush acted to cut his losses before the controversy could damage his image as a president taking bold action against terrorism. (Airport screener issue, Historic Documents of 2001, p. 650)

Proposal for a Homeland Security Department

Bush's plan called for a sweeping reorganization of federal agencies that had responsibilities for protecting the nation's borders, transportation services, and key infrastructure components (such as telephone lines and computer systems), along with agencies that had such tasks as responding to emergencies and assessing security threats. All or parts of twenty-two agencies would be incorporated into the new department. The administration said the agencies had a combined budget of $37.5 billion and a total of nearly 170,000 employees—although other estimates put the number of affected employees as high as 225,000. The White House said no employees would be laid off and none of the agencies would be dismantled or reduced in size. In many cases, the day-to-day duties of the agencies and their employees would not change under Bush's plan. What would change, Bush said, was the degree of coordination among them. Only two of the agencies— the Coast Guard and the Secret Service—would retain their independent identities.

One of the most important, and controversial, aspects of the proposal was that it did not fold aspects of the intelligence-gathering functions of the CIA and the FBI into the new department. Because of the failure of those agencies during 2001 to link the hints that a major terrorist plot was under way, many critics said the counterintelligence operations of both should be combined, preferably into the new department. Bush rejected that idea, however, and accepted the advice of his aides that the CIA and FBI could better coordinate their counterintelligence functions.

"The reason to create this department is not to increase the size of government, but to increase its focus and effectiveness," Bush told the nation in announcing his proposal. "This reorganization will give the good people of our government their best opportunity to succeed, by organizing our resources in a way that is thorough and unified." Bush demanded that Congress act on his proposal "quickly, this year, before the end of the congressional session."

In one sign of the haste in which the proposal was developed, the administration did not send Congress legislation for the proposal until nearly two weeks after Bush announced it—and even then the proposed bill failed to address many issues. At first it appeared that congressional review of the plan would be an enormous task because the White House counted eighty-eight committees and subcommittees that had some jurisdiction over the agencies or issues covered by the homeland security plan. Senior congres-

sional leaders initially talked about reorganizing some committees to deal with the plan, a task that itself was akin to reorganizing the federal government. "It's going to be one hell of a turf battle," said Sen. John Kyl, R-Ariz. "What committees are going to be willing to give up their jurisdiction?"

Somewhat surprisingly, the answer to Kyl's question was that many committees or subcommittees had little choice but to give into political pressure to surrender their jurisdiction, or at least the opportunity to ponder the legislation at length. In the House, the leadership used its clout to bypass the standard process by establishing a special homeland security committee headed by Majority Leader Richard K. Armey, R-Texas. That panel received recommendations from a dozen committees, some of which grumbled loudly about surrendering control and then adopted the basics of Bush's proposal. The full House adopted the measure (HR 5005) on July 26.

In the Senate the key point of resistance turned out to be a policy matter rather than one of congressional prerogatives. Democrats, who had a slender and unstable majority in the Senate, staunchly resisted Bush's demand for broad discretion to hire, fire, and write rules for employees of the new department. Lieberman's committee on July 25 produced a revised version of Lieberman's earlier bill (S 2452) that generally followed the Bush proposal for the new department but retained the right of employees to union representation in most circumstances. Bush threatened a veto of that proposal, and the bill was stalled on the Senate floor because of partisan bickering in the period leading to the midterm elections.

During the election campaign, Bush and Republicans used the Senate's failure to pass the security bill against vulnerable Democratic senators, most notably Max Cleland of Georgia, who had lost both legs and one arm in the Vietnam war. That tactic, along with other issues, resulted in the Democrats losing control of the Senate. After the election Democrats reluctantly agreed to a slightly revised version of the homeland security bill that gave unions a limited opportunity to challenge the administration's work rules. (Midterm elections, p. 818)

Bush signed the bill into law (PL 107–296) on November 25 and named Ridge as his choice to become the new department's first secretary. Ridge and other officials said putting the agency together could take a year or two. Many experts on government procedure predicted it would take many more years to straighten out the inevitable kinks in the new system, noting that administrations and Congresses tinkered with the Defense Department structure for four decades.

Homeland Security Strategy Report

As House and Senate committees were deliberating his plan for a homeland security department, Bush on July 16 made public a broad-gauge document intended to demonstrate that his administration had long-term policies for protecting the U.S. homeland, beyond creating a new federal department. The "National Strategy for Homeland Security" was one of three "strategy" documents issued by the White House in 2002; the others dealt with a national security and combating the international proliferation of weapons of mass destruction. (Weapons of mass destruction, p. 437; National security strategy, p. 633)

In a letter introducing the strategy, Bush said the document created "a comprehensive plan for using America's talents and resources to enhance our protection and reduce our vulnerability to terrorist attacks. . . . As a result of this strategy firefighters will be better equipped to fight fires, police officers better armed to fight crime, businesses better able to protect their data and information systems, and scientists better able to fight Mother Nature's deadliest diseases."

The strategy was intended as a broad-brush look at the issues involved in protecting the United States and its citizens, rather than as a series of specific legislative proposals. Its centerpiece was the president's pending proposal for the Department of Homeland Security. Many of the other items listed in the strategy were concepts offered for further study by government agencies, Congress, and outside experts. Most of the ideas had been included in previous reports by independent task forces that had studied homeland security issues during the previous decade. Moreover, several pages of the document contained a review of actions the administration had taken since the September 11 attacks. In political terms, the strategy obviously was meant to counter criticism by some Democrats that the administration was reacting to events rather than making long-term plans for homeland security. Lieberman's comment was typical of those from many members of Congress: "There's not a lot new here, but it's a very valuable statement."

The strategy offered no long-term cost estimates or information about who would pay for any of the specific proposals in it. Bush had asked Congress to appropriate $38 billion for homeland security expenses in fiscal year 2003, but the ideas presented in the strategy would have additional costs, some as early as fiscal 2003. Ridge said the strategy was vague because many of the costs were unknown, such as what would be needed to protect the Internet or food and water supplies against terrorism. Most costs would be borne by the private sector, he said, because businesses and individuals owned the vast majority of buildings, telephone lines, and similar infrastructure items that needed to be secured against attack. "This is the beginning strategy, not the end," Ridge told the Washington Post.

Most of the proposals and general ideas in the strategy were noncontroversial. Among them were deploying high-technology sensors to detect threats of nuclear and biological weapons and improving systems for emergency communications systems between federal and state governments.

Two items generated immediate controversy. One called for a "thorough review" of laws dealing with military operations within the United States "to determine whether domestic preparedness and response efforts would benefit from further involvement of military personnel, and if so how." In particular, the administration would review the 1878 Posse Comitatus Act, which prohibited the military from engaging in domestic law enforcement functions unless specifically authorized to do so by Congress. For more than a century that law ensured civilian primacy within U.S. borders, but some administration officials argued that it prevented the government from using the military's experience and personnel domestically in ways that would be compatible with civilian control of government. Just the idea of opening the question for study alarmed some members of Congress, constitutional scholars, and civil liberties advocates. "We've done very well by separating the military from law enforcement," said Senate Armed Services Committee chairman Carl Levin, of Michigan. "There would be a heavy burden for those who want to change" the law to show how a change would be beneficial.

The other controversial proposal would create minimum standards for driver's licenses, which had become the most commonly used government-issued form of identity. Some states had loose requirements for applicants to prove who they were, thus making it relatively easy for anyone, including a potential terrorist, to obtain driver's licenses using false information. Sen. Dick Durbin, D-Ill., had sponsored legislation calling for federal standards, along with a federal database of drivers license information. He noted that eighteen of the nineteen hijackers who carried out the September 11 attacks "were carrying at least one driver's license that was obtained fraudulently." But the suggestion that the federal government should set standards set off alarm bells for civil liberties advocates and some conservative groups who saw it as the first step toward a national identity card— something the administration said it did not plan. Bush had included a proposal for minimum driver's license standards in his Homeland Security Department legislation, but the House blocked it.

Other specific suggestions in the strategy included conducting an inventory of critical elements of infrastructure and developing a plan to protect them, which would be kept secret; reviewing public disclosure laws to see if they might discourage companies, such as those that produced dangerous chemicals, from sharing proprietary information with the government; and improving border patrols.

> *Following are excerpts from the National Strategy for Homeland Security, released July 16, 2002, by the White House Office of Homeland Security. The document offered proposals for protecting the United States and its citizens against terrorism and other threats.*

> **The document was obtained from the Internet at www .whitehouse.gov/homeland/book/index.html; accessed January 22, 2003.**

This document is the first *National Strategy for Homeland Security.* The purpose of the *Strategy* is to mobilize and organize our Nation to secure the

U.S. homeland from terrorist attacks. This is an exceedingly complex mission that requires coordinated and focused effort from our entire society—the federal government, state and local governments, the private sector, and the American people.

People and organizations all across the United States have taken many steps to improve our security since the September 11 attacks, but a great deal of work remains. The *National Strategy for Homeland Security* will help to prepare our Nation for the work ahead in several ways. It provides direction to the federal government departments and agencies that have a role in homeland security. It suggests steps that state and local governments, private companies and organizations, and individual Americans can take to improve our security and offers incentives for them to do so. It recommends certain actions to the Congress. In this way, the *Strategy* provides a framework for the contributions that we all can make to secure our homeland.

The *National Strategy for Homeland Security* is the beginning of what will be a long struggle to protect our Nation from terrorism. It establishes a foundation upon which to organize our efforts and provides initial guidance to prioritize the work ahead. The *Strategy* will be adjusted and amended over time. We must be prepared to adapt as our enemies in the war on terrorism alter their means of attack.

Strategic Objectives

The strategic objectives of homeland security in order of priority are to:

- Prevent terrorist attacks within the United States;
- Reduce America's vulnerability to terrorism; and
- Minimize the damage and recover from attacks that do occur.

Threat and Vulnerability

Unless we act to prevent it, a new wave of terrorism, potentially involving the world's most destructive weapons, looms in America's future. It is a challenge as formidable as any ever faced by our Nation. But we are not daunted. We possess the determination and the resources to defeat our enemies and secure our homeland against the threats they pose.

One fact dominates all homeland security threat assessments: terrorists are strategic actors. They choose their targets deliberately based on the weaknesses they observe in our defenses and our preparedness. We must defend ourselves against a wide range of means and methods of attack. Our enemies are working to obtain chemical, biological, radiological, and nuclear weapons for the purpose of wreaking unprecedented damage on America. Terrorists continue to employ conventional means of attack, while at the same time gaining expertise in less traditional means, such as cyber attacks. Our society presents an almost infinite array of potential targets that can be attacked through a variety of methods.

Our enemies seek to remain invisible, lurking in the shadows. We are actively engaged in uncovering them. Al-Qaeda remains America's most immediate and serious threat despite our success in disrupting its network in

Afghanistan and elsewhere. Other international terrorist organizations, as well as domestic terrorist groups, possess the will and capability to attack the United States.

Organizing for a Secure Homeland

In response to the homeland security challenge facing us, the President has proposed, and the Congress is presently considering, the most extensive reorganization of the federal government in the past fifty years. The establishment of a new Department of Homeland Security would ensure greater accountability over critical homeland security missions and unity of purpose among the agencies responsible for them.

American democracy is rooted in the precepts of federalism—a system of government in which our state governments share power with federal institutions. Our structure of overlapping federal, state, and local governance—our country has more than 87,000 different jurisdictions—provides unique opportunity and challenges for our homeland security efforts. The opportunity comes from the expertise and commitment of local agencies and organizations involved in homeland security. The challenge is to develop interconnected and complementary systems that are reinforcing rather than duplicative and that ensure essential requirements are met. A national strategy requires a national effort.

State and local governments have critical roles to play in homeland security. Indeed, the closest relationship the average citizen has with government is at the local level. State and local levels of government have primary responsibility for funding, preparing, and operating the emergency services that would respond in the event of a terrorist attack. Local units are the first to respond, and the last to leave the scene. All disasters are ultimately local events.

The private sector—the Nation's principal provider of goods and services and owner of 85 percent of our infrastructure—is a key homeland security partner. It has a wealth of information that is important to the task of protecting the United States from terrorism. Its creative genius will develop the information systems, vaccines, detection devices, and other technologies and innovations that will secure our homeland.

An informed and proactive citizenry is an invaluable asset for our country in times of war and peace. Volunteers enhance community coordination and action, whether at the national or local level. This coordination will prove critical as we work to build the communication and delivery systems indispensable to our national effort to detect, prevent, and, if need be, respond to terrorist attack.

Critical Mission Areas

The *National Strategy for Homeland Security* aligns and focuses homeland security functions into six critical mission areas: intelligence and warning, border and transportation security, domestic counterterrorism, protecting critical infrastructure, defending against catastrophic terrorism, and emergency preparedness and response. The first three mission areas focus primarily on preventing terrorist attacks; the next two on reducing our Nation's vulnerabilities; and the final one on minimizing the damage and recovering from attacks that do occur. The *Strategy* provides a framework to align the resources of the federal budget directly to the task of securing the homeland.

Intelligence and Warning. Terrorism depends on surprise. With it, a terrorist attack has the potential to do massive damage to an unwitting and unprepared target. Without it, the terrorists stand a good chance of being preempted by authorities, and even if they are not, the damage that results from their attacks is likely to be less severe. The United States will take every necessary action to avoid being surprised by another terrorist attack. We must have an intelligence and warning system that can detect terrorist activity before it manifests itself in an attack so that proper preemptive, preventive, and protective action can be taken.

The *National Strategy for Homeland Security* identifies five major initiatives in this area:

- Enhance the analytic capabilities of the FBI;
- Build new capabilities through the Information Analysis and Infrastructure Protection Division of the proposed Department of Homeland Security;
- Implement the Homeland Security Advisory System [the report says this system "disseminates information regarding the risk of terrorist acts to federal, state, and local authorities, the private sector and the American people"];
- Utilize dual-use analysis to prevent attacks [defined later in the report as analyzing equipment that can be converted from civilian use (an aerosol can, for example) into a weapon for a terrorist attack]; and
- Employ "red team" techniques [defined later in the report as having "certain employees responsible for viewing the United States from the perspective of the terrorists, seeking to discern and predict the methods, means and targets of the terrorists"].

Border and Transportation Security. America historically has relied heavily on two vast oceans and two friendly neighbors for border security, and on the private sector for most forms of domestic transportation security. The increasing mobility and destructive potential of modern terrorism has required the United States to rethink and renovate fundamentally its systems for border and transportation security. Indeed, we must now begin to conceive of border security and transportation security as fully integrated requirements because our domestic transportation systems are inextricably intertwined with the global transport infrastructure. Virtually every community in America is connected to the global transportation network by the seaports, airports, highways, pipelines, railroads, and waterways that move people and goods into, within, and out of the Nation. We must therefore promote the efficient and reliable flow of people, goods, and services across borders, while preventing terrorists from using transportation conveyances or systems to deliver implements of destruction.

The *National Strategy for Homeland Security* identifies six major initiatives in this area:

- Ensure accountability in border and transportation security;
- Create "smart borders" [defined later in the report as featuring "strong, advanced risk-management systems, increased use of biometric identification information, and partnerships with the private sector to allow pre-cleared goods and persons to cross borders without delay"];
- Increase the security of international shipping containers;
- Implement the Aviation and Transportation Security Act of 2001;
- Recapitalize the U.S. Coast Guard [defined later in the report as replacing ships and other equipment in the Coast Guard's "aging fleet" and making "targeted improvements in the areas of maritime domain awareness, command and control systems, and shore-side facilities"; and
- Reform immigration services.

The President proposed to Congress that the principal border and transportation security agencies—the Immigration and Naturalization Service, the U.S. Customs Service, the U.S. Coast Guard, the Animal and Plant Health Inspection Service, and the Transportation Security Agency—be transferred to the new Department of Homeland Security. This organizational reform will greatly assist in the implementation of all the above initiatives.

Domestic Counterterrorism. The attacks of September 11 and the catastrophic loss of life and property that resulted have redefined the mission of federal, state, and local law enforcement authorities. While law enforcement agencies will continue to investigate and prosecute criminal activity, they should now assign priority to preventing and interdicting terrorist activity within the United States. The Nation's state and local law enforcement officers will be critical in this effort. Our Nation will use all legal means—both traditional and nontraditional—to identify, halt, and, where appropriate, prosecute terrorists in the United States. We will pursue not only the individuals directly involved in terrorist activity but also their sources of support: the people and organizations that knowingly fund the terrorists and those that provide them with logistical assistance.

Effectively reorienting law enforcement organizations to focus on counterterrorism objectives requires decisive action in a number of areas. The *National Strategy for Homeland Security* identifies six major initiatives in this area:

- Improve intergovernmental law enforcement coordination;
- Facilitate apprehension of potential terrorists;
- Continue ongoing investigations and prosecutions;
- Complete FBI restructuring to emphasize prevention of terrorist attacks;
- Target and attack terrorist financing; and
- Track foreign terrorists and bring them to justice.

Protecting Critical Infrastructure and Key Assets. Our society and modern way of life are dependent on networks of infrastructure—both physical networks such as our energy and transportation systems and virtual networks such as the Internet. If terrorists attack one or more pieces of our critical infrastructure, they may disrupt entire systems and cause significant damage to the Nation. We must therefore improve protection of the individual pieces and interconnecting systems that make up our critical infrastructure. Protecting America's critical infrastructure and key assets will not only make us more secure from terrorist attack, but will also reduce our vulnerability to natural disasters, organized crime, and computer hackers.

America's critical infrastructure encompasses a large number of sectors. The U.S. government will seek to deny terrorists the opportunity to inflict lasting harm to our Nation by protecting the assets, systems, and functions vital to our national security, governance, public health and safety, economy, and national morale.

The *National Strategy for Homeland Security* identifies eight major initiatives in this area:

- Unify America's infrastructure protection effort in the Department of Homeland Security;
- Build and maintain a complete and accurate assessment of America's critical infrastructure and key assets;
- Enable effective partnership with state and local governments and the private sector;
- Develop a national infrastructure protection plan;
- Secure cyberspace;
- Harness the best analytic and modeling tools to develop effective protective solutions;
- Guard America's critical infrastructure and key assets against "inside" threats; and
- Partner with the international community to protect our transnational infrastructure.

Defending Against Catastrophic Threats. The expertise, technology, and material needed to build the most deadly weapons known to mankind—including chemical, biological, radiological, and nuclear weapons—are spreading inexorably. If our enemies acquire these weapons, they are likely to try to use them. The consequences of such an attack could be far more devastating than those we suffered on September 11—a chemical, biological, radiological, or nuclear terrorist attack in the United States could cause large numbers of casualties, mass psychological disruption, contamination and significant economic damage, and could overwhelm local medical capabilities.

Currently, chemical, biological, radiological, and nuclear detection capabilities are modest and response capabilities are dispersed throughout the country at every level of government. While current arrangements have proven adequate for a variety of natural disasters and even the September 11 attacks, the threat of terrorist attacks using chemical, biological, radiological, and nuclear weapons requires new approaches, a focused strategy, and a new organization.

The *National Strategy for Homeland Security* identifies six major initiatives in this area:

- Prevent terrorist use of nuclear weapons through better sensors and procedures;
- Detect chemical and biological materials and attacks;
- Improve chemical sensors and decontamination techniques;
- Develop broad spectrum vaccines, antimicrobials, and antidotes;
- Harness the scientific knowledge and tools to counter terrorism; and
- Implement the Select Agent Program [defined later in the report as regulations governing "the shipment of certain hazardous biological organisms and toxins," also known as "agents"].

Emergency Preparedness and Response. We must prepare to minimize the damage and recover from any future terrorist attacks that may occur despite our best efforts at prevention. An effective response to a major terrorist incident—as well as a natural disaster—depends on being prepared. Therefore, we need a comprehensive national system to bring together and coordinate all necessary response assets quickly and effectively. We must plan, equip, train, and exercise many different response units to mobilize without warning for any emergency.

Many pieces of this national emergency response system are already in place. America's first line of defense in the aftermath of any terrorist attack is its first responder community—police officers, firefighters, emergency medical providers, public works personnel, and emergency management officials. Nearly three million state and local first responders regularly put their lives on the line to save the lives of others and make our country safer.

Yet multiple plans currently govern the federal government's support of first responders during an incident of national significance. These plans and the government's overarching policy for counterterrorism are based on an artificial and unnecessary distinction between "crisis management" and "consequence management." Under the President's proposal, the Department of Homeland Security will consolidate federal response plans and build a national system for incident management in cooperation with state and local government. Our federal, state, and local governments would ensure that all response personnel and organizations are properly equipped, trained, and exercised to respond to all terrorist threats and attacks in the United States. Our emergency preparedness and response efforts would also engage the private sector and the American people.

The *National Strategy for Homeland Security* identifies twelve major initiatives in this area:

- Integrate separate federal response plans into a single all-discipline incident management plan;
- Create a national incident management system;
- Improve tactical counterterrorist capabilities;
- Enable seamless communication among all responders;
- Prepare health care providers for catastrophic terrorism;
- Augment America's pharmaceutical and vaccine stockpiles;
- Prepare for chemical, biological, radiological, and nuclear decontamination;

- Plan for military support to civil authorities;
- Build the Citizen Corps [defined later in the report as a national program to prepare volunteers for terrorism-related response support];
- Implement the First Responder Initiative of the Fiscal Year 2003 Budget [first responders are firefighters, police, and other emergency personnel who are the first on the scene of a fire or other incident; President Bush in January 2002 to proposed increased funding "to improve dramatically first responder preparedness for terrorist incidents and disasters"];
- Build a national training and evaluation system; and
- Enhance the victim support system [defined later in the report as when "federal agencies and provide guidance to state, local, and volunteer organizations in offering victims and their families various forms of assistance including: crisis counseling, cash grants, low-interest loans, unemployment benefits, free legal counseling, and tax refunds"].

The Foundations of Homeland Security

The *National Strategy for Homeland Security* also describes four foundations—unique American strengths that cut across all of the mission areas, across all levels of government, and across all sectors of our society. These foundations—law, science and technology, information sharing and systems, and international cooperation—provide a useful framework for evaluating our homeland security investments across the federal government.

Law. Throughout our Nation's history, we have used laws to promote and safeguard our security and our liberty. The law will both provide mechanisms for the government to act and will define the appropriate limits of action.

The *National Strategy for Homeland Security* outlines legislative actions that would help enable our country to fight the war on terrorism more effectively. New federal laws should not preempt state law unnecessarily or overly federalize the war on terrorism. We should guard scrupulously against incursions on our freedoms.

The *Strategy* identifies twelve major initiatives in this area:

Federal level

- Enable critical infrastructure information sharing;
- Streamline information sharing among intelligence and law enforcement agencies;
- Expand existing extradition authorities;
- Review authority for military assistance in domestic security;
- Revive the President's reorganization authority; and
- Provide substantial management flexibility for the Department of Homeland Security.

State level

- Coordinate suggested minimum standards for state driver's licenses;
- Enhance market capacity for terrorism insurance;
- Train for prevention of cyber attacks;
- Suppress money laundering;

- Ensure continuity of the judiciary; and
- Review quarantine authorities.

Science and Technology. The Nation's advantage in science and technology is a key to securing the homeland. New technologies for analysis, information sharing, detection of attacks, and countering chemical, biological, radiological, and nuclear weapons will help prevent and minimize the damage from future terrorist attacks. Just as science has helped us defeat past enemies overseas, so too will it help us defeat the efforts of terrorists to attack our homeland and disrupt our way of life.

The federal government is launching a systematic national effort to harness science and technology in support of homeland security. We will build a national research and development enterprise for homeland security sufficient to mitigate the risk posed by modern terrorism. The federal government will consolidate most federally funded homeland security research and development under the Department of Homeland Security to ensure strategic direction and avoid duplicative efforts. We will create and implement a long-term research and development plan that includes investment in revolutionary capabilities with high payoff potential. The federal government will also seek to harness the energy and ingenuity of the private sector to develop and produce the devices and systems needed for homeland security.

The *National Strategy for Homeland Security* identifies eleven major initiatives in this area:

- Develop chemical, biological, radiological, and nuclear countermeasures;
- Develop systems for detecting hostile intent;
- Apply biometric technology to identification devices;
- Improve the technical capabilities of first responders;
- Coordinate research and development of the homeland security apparatus;
- Establish a national laboratory for homeland security;
- Solicit independent and private analysis for science and technology research;
- Establish a mechanism for rapidly producing prototypes;
- Conduct demonstrations and pilot deployments;
- Set standards for homeland security technology; and
- Establish a system for high-risk, high-payoff homeland security research.

Information Sharing and Systems. Information systems contribute to every aspect of homeland security. Although American information technology is the most advanced in the world, our country's information systems have not adequately supported the homeland security mission. Databases used for federal law enforcement, immigration, intelligence, public health surveillance, and emergency management have not been connected in ways that allow us to comprehend where information gaps or redundancies exist. In addition, there are deficiencies in the communications systems used by states and municipalities throughout the country; most state and local first responders do not use compatible communications equipment. To secure the homeland better, we must link the vast amounts of knowledge residing within each government agency while ensuring adequate privacy.

The *National Strategy for Homeland Security* identifies five major initiatives in this area:

- Integrate information sharing across the federal government;
- Integrate information sharing across state and local governments, private industry, and citizens;
- Adopt common "meta-data" standards for electronic information relevant to homeland security;
- Improve public safety emergency communications; and
- Ensure reliable public health information.

International Cooperation. In a world where the terrorist threat pays no respect to traditional boundaries, our strategy for homeland security cannot stop at our borders. America must pursue a sustained, steadfast, and systematic international agenda to counter the global terrorist threat and improve our homeland security. Our international anti-terrorism campaign has made significant progress since September 11. The full scope of these activities will be further described in the forthcoming *National Security Strategy of the United States* and the *National Strategy for Combating Terrorism*. The *National Strategy for Homeland Security* identifies nine major initiatives in this area:

- Create "smart borders";
- Combat fraudulent travel documents;
- Increase the security of international shipping containers;
- Intensify international law enforcement cooperation;
- Help foreign nations fight terrorism;
- Expand protection of transnational critical infrastructure;
- Amplify international cooperation on homeland security science and technology;
- Improve cooperation in response to attacks; and
- Review obligations to international treaties and law.

Costs of Homeland Security

The national effort to enhance homeland security will yield tremendous benefits and entail substantial financial and other costs. Benefits include reductions in the risk of attack and their potential consequences. Costs include not only the resources we commit to homeland security but also the delays to commerce and travel. The United States spends roughly $100 billion per year on homeland security. This figure includes federal, state, and local law enforcement and emergency services, but excludes most funding for the armed forces.

The responsibility of providing homeland security is shared between federal, state and local governments, and the private sector. In many cases, sufficient incentives exist in the private market to supply protection. Government should fund only those homeland security activities that are not supplied, or are inadequately supplied, in the market. Cost sharing between different levels of government should reflect the principles of federalism. Many homeland security activities, such as intelligence gathering and border security, are properly accomplished at the federal level. In other circumstances, such as with first responder capabilities, it is more appropriate for state and local governments to handle these responsibilities.

Conclusion: Priorities for the Future

The *National Strategy for Homeland Security* sets a broad and complex agenda for the United States. The *Strategy* has defined many different goals that need to be met, programs that need to be implemented, and responsibilities that need to be fulfilled. But creating a strategy is, in many respects, about setting priorities—about recognizing that some actions are more critical or more urgent than others.

The President's Fiscal Year 2003 Budget proposal, released in February 2002, identified four priority areas for additional resources and attention in the upcoming year:

- Support first responders;
- Defend against bioterrorism;
- Secure America's borders; and
- Use 21st-century technology to secure the homeland.

Work has already begun on the President's Fiscal Year 2004 Budget. Assuming the Congress passes legislation to implement the President's proposal to create the Department of Homeland Security, the Fiscal Year 2004 Budget will fully reflect the reformed organization of the executive branch for homeland security. That budget will have an integrated and simplified structure based on the six critical mission areas defined by the *Strategy*. Furthermore, at the time the *National Strategy for Homeland Security* was published, it was expected that the Fiscal Year 2004 Budget would attach priority to the following specific items for substantial support:

- Enhance the analytic capabilities of the FBI;
- Build new capabilities through the Information Analysis and Infrastructure Protection Division of the proposed Department of Homeland Security;
- Create "smart borders";
- Improve the security of international shipping containers;
- Recapitalize the U.S. Coast Guard;
- Prevent terrorist use of nuclear weapons through better sensors and procedures;
- Develop broad spectrum vaccines, antimicrobials, and antidotes; and
- Integrate information sharing across the federal government.

In the intervening months, the executive branch will prepare detailed implementation plans for these and many other initiatives contained within the *National Strategy for Homeland Security*. These plans will ensure that the taxpayers' money is spent only in a manner that achieves specific objectives with clear performance-based measures of effectiveness.

PEACE AGREEMENT BETWEEN CONGO AND RWANDA
July 30, 2002

A series of agreements reached in 2002 offered the most serious prospect yet that a gigantic war for control of the Democratic Republic of the Congo might finally be nearing an end. Under way since 1998, the war often was referred to as "Africa's First World War" because it was a tangled complex of conflicts involving troops from six nations and a dozen or more rebel and tribal groups. Some of the participants sought political power, but key investigations by the United Nations showed that combatants also used the war to exploit Congo's riches of diamonds, gold, timber, and other natural resources for their own benefit.

By the end of 2002 the six countries that had intervened militarily in the Congo had withdrawn all, or nearly all, their troops. Still in place were thousands of fighters for rebel and tribal groups, some of which had been aligned with the outside powers. At year's end several groups were still fighting for control of territory or resources in eastern Congo, where the bulk of the war had taken place.

Estimates of the death toll from nearly four years of fighting ranged from 2 million to 3 million. The only scientific study, conducted in 2001 by the International Rescue Committee, suggested that about 2.5 million people had died in eastern Congo; tens or even hundreds of thousands likely were killed afterward. No one would ever know the precise death toll, however, because most of the fighting occurred in remote jungles out of sight of journalists, relief workers, human rights observers, and UN peacekeepers. Although it was by far the biggest war anywhere on Earth at the turn of the twenty-first century, Congo's conflict was virtually unknown in the rest of the world because it was so remote and complex.

Even beyond the carnage, the war exacted an almost unimaginable toll on the Congolese people, especially those in the eastern provinces of North Kivu, South Kivu, and the Itaru region of Orientale province. The UN High Commissioner for Refugees estimated that 20 million of Congo's 50 million people had been directly affected by the fighting.

The key to a resolution of the conflict came July 22, when the two central combatants—the governments of Congo and Rwanda—signed an agreement providing for Rwanda to withdraw militarily. Rwanda pulled nearly all its estimated 20,000 troops out of the country by late September—after bolstering allies in eastern Congo to protect its commercial interests. Uganda, which at various points had been either a partner or rival of Rwanda, also agreed in December to withdraw its last remaining troops from Congo. The two largest rebel groups in eastern Congo also agreed to lay down their arms and participate in a political process designed to lead to national elections in 2004.

The United Nations was deeply involved in efforts to negotiate peace in Congo, but it had been reluctant to commit a large peacekeeping force to monitor a country nearly as large as Western Europe. During most of 2002 the UN had about 4,200 peacekeeping troops and military observers in Congo—less than one-fourth as many peacekeepers as were monitoring a truce in Sierra Leone, a country about 3 percent the size of Congo. The UN Security Council on December 5 approved an expansion of the peacekeeping force in Congo to a maximum of 8,700 troops, but the UN had trouble getting member countries to contribute soldiers to an expanded force. (Sierra Leone, p. 247)

Reaching Deals One by One

The peace agreements in 2002 were the culmination of a long, and frequently interrupted, process led by the United Nations to end a war that had its roots in the 1994 genocide that killed hundreds of thousands of Tutsi and moderate Hutu in neighboring Rwanda. Those responsible for the killings— extremist Hutu aligned with the Rwandan government—were driven out of Rwanda by a powerful force of Rwandan Tutsi exiles who had been living in Uganda. The Tutsi exiles then established a new government in Rwanda.

In 1997 the new government of Rwanda joined with Uganda in supporting a coalition of rebels in Zaire who had been battling the corrupt regime of dictator Mobutu Sese Seko. That rebellion quickly succeeded in ousting Mobutu. A little-known leader of the rebels, Laurent Kabila, took power in Kinshasa, proclaimed himself president, and changed the country's name to the Democratic Republic of the Congo. (Rwanda genocide, Historic Documents of 1994, p. 541; Mobutu overthrow, Historic Documents of 1997, p. 877)

Little more than a year after he took power, Kabila's former allies in Rwanda and Uganda turned against him and sent their armies (along with troops from Burundi) into Congo to support rebels who had been fighting Kabila's regime. Kabila turned for support to the leftist leaders of three southern African countries, Angola, Namibia, and Zimbabwe, who sent thousands of troops to his aid. By 1999 half of Congo was controlled by Kabila and the foreign armies that supported him, and the other half (primarily in the east) was controlled by the armies of Rwanda and Uganda and a host of tribal groups. Although the war involved many large guerrilla-type battles, little of it was seen by the rest of the world. The United Nations sponsored peace talks that led to a cease-fire agreement signed in Lusaka, Zambia, in August 1999, which was to be monitored by a UN peacekeeping mission. (Cease-fire, Historic Documents of 1999, p. 645)

Despite the cease-fire, fighting continued—especially in eastern Congo— as the various parties jockeyed for position and continued to exploit Congo's vast natural resources for their own benefit. Kabila was among those pro- longing the war, in part through his refusal to participate in a UN-sponsored mediation process known as the Inter-Congolese Dialogue. The possibility of a break in the conflict emerged in January 2001 after Kabila was assas- sinated by his bodyguard. Kabila's son, Joseph, took over the government, proclaimed a desire to end the fighting, and appealed to the United States and other Western governments for support. (Background, Historic Docu- ments of 2000, p. 978; Historic Documents of 2001, p. 159)

Negotiating with the Rebels

Joseph Kabila agreed to participate in the Inter-Congolese Dialogue, and that peace process opened on February 25, 2002, in Sun City, South Africa, under UN and South African mediation. Participants included Kabila's government, representatives of major Congolese civic organizations and political parties, and the leaders of several rebel groups. Most important among the rebel groups were the Congolese Rally for Democracy (DRC), a Rwandan-backed group active in the provinces of North and South Kivu in eastern Congo, and the Uganda-supported Movement for the Liberation of Congo, which controlled most of the enormous Orientale province in the northeast.

The talks had barely started, on March 14, when Kabila's government threatened to pull out because of a military offensive in eastern Congo by Rwandan forces and their rebel allies. The UN Security Council immedi- ately passed a resolution pressuring all sides to negotiate in good faith and to halt the fighting. Further pressure came from African leaders who convened a summit meeting in Lusaka on April 3 and called on Kabila to remain in the talks. The African leaders also demanded concessions from their two colleagues who were least willing to pull out of Congo: Rwanda's president Paul Kagame and Zimbabwe's president Robert Mugabe. By that point some of the other countries involved in the war—Angola, Burundi, Namibia, and Uganda—had withdrawn at least some of their troops.

Kabila on April 15 struck a tentative political agreement with the Move- ment for the Liberation of Congo. That deal provided for Kabila to remain as head of an interim government until elections could be held in 2004. The Congolese Rally for Democracy, which had splintered into several factions, refused to accept the deal, however, and continued to battle pro-government forces and local tribal groups in the Kivu provinces. Meanwhile, a UN spe- cial envoy, Moustapha Niasse, continued negotiations among the Congolese factions in hopes of reaching a comprehensive political agreement.

The conflict in the Kivus illustrated the complexities of the Congo war, and therefore the difficulty of ending it. In a report submitted to the UN Se- curity Council on April 5, Secretary General Kofi Annan described the nu-

merous armed groups in the region as "dynamic entities." Alliances within and between the groups, he said, "are constantly shifting, and often linked to short-term goals or individual operations. The groups themselves are subject to leadership struggles linked to political, economic or other objectives. They also undergo change in the course of victory or defeat in military actions. They are in constant motion and their locations, although generally known, cannot be precisely pinpointed." This description was especially applicable to the Mai-Mai (or Mayi-Mayi), traditional warriors who used bows and arrows as well as guns and who were divided into at least four factions that repeatedly changed their alliances with other ethnic groups.

Agreements Between Congo and Rwanda and Uganda

A follow-up series of negotiations in mid-July sponsored by South Africa yielded another agreement that offered a more tangible prospect of ending the entire war. After five days of talks chaired by South African deputy president Jacob Zuma, diplomats from Congo and Rwanda on July 22 settled on a deal intended to give the conflict's principal adversaries the security guarantees they wanted. Kabila and Rwandan president Kagame signed the accord in Pretoria, South Africa, on July 30.

Under the agreement Congo agreed to disarm, disband, and turn over to the Rwandan government the militia forces that were derived from the former Hutu-dominated government of Rwanda responsible for the 1994 genocide. Kagame for several years had said his army would remain in Congo until those forces, which we viewed as a threat to his government, had been "neutralized." In return for Congo's dismantling of the former Rwandan forces, Kagame agreed to withdraw his army from eastern Congo. The Congo-Rwanda agreement was to be verified by South Africa and the United Nations. An attached timetable called for all these steps to be completed within ninety days. The agreement did not mention Rwanda's chief ally in eastern Congo, the Congolese Rally for Democracy guerillas who had refused to sign the related peace agreement in April.

Kabila said the agreement marked "a great day for the whole of Africa" and pledged to carry it out "in good faith." If the accord failed, as had previous ones, "it won't be because of a failure on the part of the DRC [Congo] government," he said. Kagame called for international support for all the countries that had been involved in the fighting, saying: "As the international community has historically been part of the problem, they must be part of the solution."

Most observers said the agreement offered the potential for a final resolution of the war—if both Congo and Rwanda strictly kept their promises. Experts called the ninety-day timetable overly optimistic but said a rigid schedule was needed to keep the pressure on Kabila and Kagame. Of the two sides, Kabila's government faced the more difficult task in rounding up and demobilizing the former Rwandan fighters who had scattered through much of Congo and even into the neighboring countries, including the Republic of Congo. On November 1 the two sides acknowledged that the three-month deadline had been too ambitious, and they agreed to a ninety-day extension.

By the end of 2002, according to UN figures, the Congolese government had disarmed and sent back to Rwanda only 430 fighters; UN officials said the process might take another two years to complete. For his part, Kagame appeared to have some confidence that his four-year occupation of eastern Congo would give him the ability to continue exploiting the region's diamonds and other natural resources.

As expected, fighting continued among various factions in eastern Congo after the peace accord, but key outside powers began carrying out their previous promises to withdraw. The United Nations reported in late August that Uganda and Zimbabwe had each withdrawn several hundred troops from Congo. Rwanda began withdrawing its troops on September 17 and said it completed the process on October 5.

Another important step came on September 6 when Kabila and Ugandan president Yoweri Museveni signed an agreement providing for Uganda to withdraw all its estimated 3,000 troops. Uganda withdrew most of its forces by late October but kept about 1,000 troops in the violence-plagued northeastern city of Bunia at the request of UN peacekeepers.

On October 18 Annan reported that more than 27,000 foreign soldiers— most of them from Rwanda—had left Congo in accordance with the various peace agreements. However, Annan questioned Rwanda's claim that it had withdrawn all its troops; he cited reports indicating that the Rwandan army "may have left significant amounts of weaponry, as well as some of its personnel" with its guerrilla allies in eastern Congo. Annan and other observers also warned that the rapid pullout of foreign troops had created a "power vacuum" in the region that armed rebel and tribal groups were seeking to exploit.

A Political Agreement

Even as fighting continued in eastern Congo, leaders of the various factions continued meeting under UN and South African supervision in an attempt to negotiate an overall political agreement. An accord finally came in Pretoria on December 17 when Kabila's government and most of the key groups that had opposed it agreed to end the war and establish a transitional government leading to elections. Among those signing the agreement were the two major rebel groups, the Congolese Rally for Democracy and the Movement for the Liberation of Congo. Kabila was to remain head of state for the interim period, with four vice presidents representing the government, the two rebel groups, and Congolese opposition political parties, which had been long suppressed by Mobutu and Kabila's father. The country would have a two-chamber legislature (a 500-member national assembly and a 120-member senate), to be elected in 2004, along with a president.

Just three days after that agreement was signed, new fighting erupted among several of the rebel factions in eastern Congo. The UN Security Council said it had received reports of a "massacre" in the Itaru region, and Annan cited reports that "tens of thousands of civilians" had been forced from their homes by the fighting. The groups signed a cease-fire agreement on De-

cember 30, but no one was ready to declare that conflict in the Congo had finally come to an end.

UN Panel on Resource Exploitation

When the Congo conflict began in 1998 it quickly became apparent that several of the major participants were using the war as a cover for their exploitation of the country's enormous natural resources. The generals of Zimbabwe's army received concessions from Laurent Kabila to extract diamonds and timber from southern Congo as payment for helping prop up his government. Rwanda and Uganda also mined diamonds and other resources.

A panel of experts appointed by the UN Security Council filed reports in 2000 and 2001 revealing some details of the looting of Congo's resources. The panel's final report, made public on October 22, 2002, was a searing indictment of governments, companies, and individuals that, the panel said, had been able to "loot and plunder the country's resources with impunity." This was possible, the panel said, because Congo lacked a government "with the authority and capacity to protect its citizens and resources."

The report specifically named the governments and armies of Rwanda and Zimbabwe, Congolese government officials, the Ugandan army, and more than four dozen individuals, including military and government officials from those countries and foreign business executives, as among the looters of Congo's resources. Several international criminal organizations, including diamond smugglers and arms dealers, also had benefited from the illegal trade in Congo's resources. The panel quoted a "reliable source" as claiming the Rwandan army had financed nearly 80 percent of its budget in 1999 with receipts from its "Congo desk," which mined Congolese diamonds and coltan (a mineral used in mobile telephones). The panel traced the dealings of one coltan trader that received "privileged access" to mines in the Congo: Eagle Wings Resources International, a Rwandan company that the panel said was a subsidiary of Trinitech International Inc., an Ohio company.

The list of prominent individuals cited by the panel included Rwandan army chief of staff James Kabarebe; Ugandan army chief of staff James Kazini; Emmerson Mnangagwa, the speaker of the Zimbabwe parliament; Katumba Mwanke, Congo's minister of the presidency (a top aide to Joseph Kabila); and Ukrainian arms trader Victor Bout. The panel also cited eighty-five multinational corporations for violating ethical guidelines, developed by the Organization for Economic Cooperation and Development, covering business operations in conflict zones. Several well-known companies were on the list, among them Anglo-American, a British mining company; Barclays Bank, a British bank; and De Beers, the South African diamond mining and trading company. Most of the individuals and organizations named in the report denied the panel's charges or refused to comment.

The panel said some of the outside powers had taken steps to ensure *that—even after they had withdrawn their armies from Congo—they would have continuing access to, or even control over, the natural resources they had been exploiting. For example, the panel said the Rwandan army had arranged for Rwandan businessmen to take control of Congolese state companies in the eastern part of the country and had placed Rwandan soldiers with key rebel groups that operated in areas where the army had been looting Congolese diamonds, cobalt, copper, timber, and other resources. In cooperation with Congo's government, Zimbabwe had transferred ownership of about $5 billion in assets from state-owned mining companies to private joint-venture firms "with no compensation or benefit to the state treasury" of Congo, the panel said.*

The panel asked the UN Security Council to impose various sanctions, including travel bans and restrictions on financial transactions, against fifty-four individuals and twenty-nine companies. The Security Council had not acted on that recommendation by year's end. UN officials said it was likely that the council in 2003 would ask the panel to continue its work and develop additional evidence against the organizations and individuals named in its report.

Kabila on November 2 dismissed the senior executives of Congo's state diamond mining company, which had been identified in the report as a central actor in illegal exports. Kabila's government denied that the firings were linked to the UN report.

Humanitarian Situation

The looting of Congo's resources was all the more serious because the country and its people had suffered from decades of corruption by the Mobutu regime, and then years of war under the Kabilas. UN agencies and international relief organizations reported that Congo barely had a functioning economy—aside from the illegal operations of Rwanda, Zimbabwe, and other powers that had intervened there. While difficult to measure because of the conflict, Congo's per capita gross domestic product was estimated in 2002 at about $100—less than 30 cents a day, one of the lowest in the world.

Annan told the Security Council in October that about 17 million Congolese needed "urgent food aid." This figure included about 2.2 million people who had been displaced from their homes; hundreds of thousands more had taken refuge in other countries, including about 400,000 in Central African Republic. A UN investigating team in August described the situation in parts of eastern Congo as a "creeping disaster" with more than 100 villages deserted and an estimated 400,000 people displaced in the region. Relief efforts were hampered not only by fighting among the armed factions but also by several episodes of harassment of relief workers and the looting of food. By early November the estimate of displaced people in eastern Congo had risen to 900,000.

Nature contributed to this man-made disaster in eastern Congo. Mount Nyiragongo volcano erupted on January 17, forcing hundreds of thousands of people in North Kivu province to flee their homes. Lava from the volcano buried about one-half of Goma, the major commercial town in the province, at the border between Congo and Rwanda.

The UN and other agencies said all sides to the conflict had committed serious human rights violations. In keeping with longstanding practice in the country, Kabila suppressed civil dissent by jailing journalists and opposition political leaders. Annan reported to the Security Council in October that human rights violations in eastern Congo "have far surpassed the predicted worst-case scenarios," with the various factions attacking each other and civilian supporters. A "cult of impunity" had developed in Congo, he said, that made it difficult to hold human rights violators accountable for their actions. Human Rights Watch on June 20 issued a report detailing what it called the "systematic" raping of women and girls by the armed factions in the eastern provinces.

Following is the text of a peace agreement between the Republic of Rwanda and the Democratic Republic of the Congo, signed July 30, 2002, by Rwandan president Paul Kagame and Congolese president Joseph Kabila. The agreement provided for the withdrawal of Rwandan armed forces from Congo, and the provision of security guarantees for both sides.

The document was obtained from the Internet at www.usip .org/library/pa/drc_rwanda/drc_rwanda_pa07302002 .html; accessed November 25, 2002.

Peace Agreement Between the Governments of the Republic of Rwanda and the Democratic Republic of the Congo on the Withdrawal of the Rwandan Troops from the Territory of the Democratic Republic of the Congo and the Dismantling of the Ex-FAR and Interahamwe Forces in the Democratic Republic of the Congo (DRC).

1. The Lusaka Ceasefire Agreement of 1999 sets out modalities for the tracking down and disarmament of ex-FAR [former Rwandan Army forces] and Interahamwe forces [Hutu extremist groups primarily responsible for the 1994 genocide in Rwanda] in the territory of the DRC. To date, it has not been possible to effectively implement the decisions relating to these armed groups.

2. The governments of the Democratic Republic of the Congo and the Republic of Rwanda have sought to find an expeditious manner of implementing these decisions.

3. The Parties acknowledge that there have been numerous attempts to implement agreements reached between them with regard to this matter. The Parties also acknowledge that the launch of the African Union, recent UN resolutions and the involvement of a third party present a window of opportunity to urgently resolve this matter.

By third party, both parties understand this to refer to the Secretary General of the United Nations and South Africa, in its dual capacity as Chairperson of the African Union and facilitator of this process.

The Parties further acknowledge that the resolution of this matter will be a process and not an event.

4. The government of the Democratic Republic of the Congo reaffirms its stated legitimate right that the forces of the government of Rwanda withdraw from the territory of the DRC without delay.

5. The government of Rwanda reaffirms its readiness to withdraw from the territory of the DRC as soon as effective measures that address its security concerns, in particular the dismantling of the ex-FAR and Interahamwe forces, have been agreed to. Withdrawal should start simultaneously with the implementation of the measures, both of which will be verified by MONUC [United Nations Mission in the Congo], JMC [a joint commission of the Congolese and Rwandan army] and the third party.

6. The Interahamwe and ex-FAR armed groups fled to various countries, including the DRC, after participating in the 1994 genocide in Rwanda. The DRC government states that it does not wish to have these armed groups present in the territory of the DRC. The DRC government does not want its territory to be used as a base for attacks against its neighbouring countries.

7. The DRC government is ready to collaborate with MONUC, the JMC and any other Force constituted by the third party, to assemble and disarm the ex-FAR and Interahamwe in the whole of the territory of the DRC.

8. In this regard, the Parties agree as follows:

8.1 The DRC government will continue with the process of tracking down and disarming the Interahamwe and ex-FAR within the territory of the DRC under its control.

8.2 The DRC government will collaborate with MONUC and the JMC in the dismantling of the ex-FAR and Interahamwe forces in the DRC.

8.3 The Rwandan government undertakes to withdraw its troops from the DRC territory, following the process outlined in paragraph 5. This will be according to measures as detailed in the implementation programme.

8.4 That MONUC, acting together with all relevant UN Agencies, should be requested to immediately set up processes to repatriate all Rwandese, ex-FAR and Interahamwe to Rwanda, including those in Kamina, in co-ordination with the governments of Rwanda and the DRC.

8.5 The governments of the DRC and Rwanda would provide the facilitator of this meeting and the UN Secretary General with all the information in their possession relating to these armed groups.

8.6 The third party will take responsibility for verifying whatever information received, through whatever measures deemed necessary.

8.7 The Parties agree to accept the verification report from the third party.

8.8 That the UN considers changing the mandate of MONUC into a Peace-keeping mission.

8.9 MONUC should immediately proceed to implement Phase 3 of its DDRR [disarmament, demobilisation, repatriation, reintegration, and resettlement] and finalise its deployment in the DRC, especially in the eastern part of the territory.

8.10 The Parties agree that their respective governments would put into place a mechanism for the normalisation of the security situation along their common border. This mechanism may include the presence of an International Force to cooperate with the two countries, in the short term, to secure their common border.

8.11 That a bilateral team, facilitated by South Africa and the UN Secretary General, work on a detailed calendar to implement this agreement.

8.12 Both Parties commit themselves to accepting the role and findings of the third party in the process of implementing this agreement, and further accept that the commitments and agreements reached in this Peace Agreement are binding.

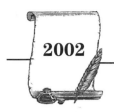

August

POINDEXTER ON PENTAGON DATA MINING SYSTEM
August 2, 2002

A Defense Department proposal for a giant computer system that could search vast amounts of personal information about Americans for clues to potential terrorist attacks generated significant controversy in late 2002. The Pentagon system—several years from completion—was one of several antiterrorism steps proposed by the Bush administration that raised concerns among some members of Congress and civil liberties groups.

Administration officials, from President George W. Bush on down, said the government had a responsibility to take tough action to prevent another terrorist attack similar to the September 11, 2001, airplane hijackings that killed early 3,000 people and destroyed the World Trade Center towers in New York City and damaged the Pentagon. These steps included the secret detention of hundreds of immigrants from Middle Eastern and South Asian countries, the use of wiretaps and other electronic surveillance measures to monitor potential terrorists in the United States, and even a nationwide search of library records to find out what terrorism suspects were reading. The administration took some of these steps under expanded law enforcement powers authorized in a law, the USA Patriot Act (PL 107–56), which was rushed through by Congress six weeks after the September 11 attacks. (Terrorist attacks, Historic Documents of 2001, pp. 614, 624, 637, 849; immigration issues, p. 764)

Critics complained that the administration was obsessed with secrecy and was undermining civil liberties that formed the bedrock of freedoms that Americans treasured. Critics also worried that Bush's talk of a long-term war against terrorism, possibly lasting many years, would result in an open-ended curtailing of civil liberties.

Opinion polls showed that most Americans did not share these concerns and, instead, put a higher priority on defeating future terrorists, even at the price of a temporary loss of some civil rights. One representative poll, reported on June 11 by the Gallup organization, CNN, and USA Today, found that only 11 percent of those surveyed thought the Bush administration had "gone too far" in restricting civil liberties; 50 percent said the administration's approach was "about right," and 25 percent said the administration hadn't gone far enough.

The United States was far from being alone in using terrorism as a reason—some said an excuse—to reduce legal and political liberties. Britain, China, Israel, Russia, Uzbekistan, and dozens of other countries cited the threat of terrorism as justifying the imposition of new limits on citizens and foreigners within their borders. Some of these countries went so far as to mimic the language the Bush administration used in its crackdown on terror. Liberian president Charles Taylor, for example, jailed three of his critics as "illegal combatants" in June, shortly after the Bush administration declared its intention to hold "enemy combatants" in prison without legal rights. The government of Eritrea cited the Bush administration's indefinite detentions of several hundred men as justification for its own jailing of a newspaper publisher.

Pentagon "Data Mining"

The Pentagon project, which involved a computer technique known as "data mining," was the brainchild of retired vice admiral John M. Poindexter, who proposed it after the September 11 terrorist attacks and began working on it at the Pentagon in January 2002. His Total Information Awareness concept was the centerpiece project of a new Information Awareness Office located in the Defense Advanced Research Projects Agency (DARPA), the Pentagon's technology research arm, best known as the home of the original Internet (then known as DarpaNet).

Reports about Poindexter's project appeared in computer industry publications as early as March, but the general interest news media paid little attention until a front-page story in the New York Times *on November 9 said the Pentagon was developing "a computer system that could create a vast electronic dragnet" of personal information. The story quoted a speech Poindexter gave on August 2 describing the project in general terms, along with the concerns of civil liberties advocates. Pentagon officials then launched a public relations campaign to quell unease about the program, which they said stemmed from the* Times' *description of a vast computer system that would obtain billions of pieces of information about the private lives of Americans. "It's absurd to think that DARPA is somehow trying to become another police agency," Edward C. "Pete" Arlidge, an undersecretary of defense, told reporters at the Pentagon on November 20.*

Arlidge and other Pentagon officials said Poindexter was developing a "concept" for a "prototype" for a computer system that would perform three tasks: translate into English giant quantities of information from foreign language publications and broadcast media (a task currently handled by human translators employed by U.S. intelligence agencies); search databases containing records such as passports, visas, work permits, drivers licenses, automobile rentals, and airline tickets and then look for patterns by comparing that information with arrest records or law enforcement agency reports of suspicious activities; and give intelligence and law enforcement agencies compilations of information that might help them detect potential terrorist attacks in advance.

In an interview with the Washington Post, *reported on November 12, Poindexter said his vision was of a system of networked computers that could draw the connections about terrorist activity that were located within vast amounts of data but not obvious to humans. "How are we going to find terrorists and preempt them, except by following their trail?" he queried.*

Arlidge said development of this three-part system was expected to take five years, and then the completed system would be turned over to law enforcement agencies. The Pentagon would not run the completed system, he said, and Poindexter "will not be involved" with its operation.

Poindexter's role in developing the system was a major point of controversy. He served as national security adviser in the mid-1980s to President Ronald Reagan (1981–1989). He was a major figure in the Iran-contra affair, an abuse-of-power scandal that emerged in 1987. In 1990 he was convicted of lying to Congress and other crimes and sentenced to six months in jail, but an appeals court overturned the conviction in 1991 because prosecutors had used evidence Poindexter had given to Congress under a grant of immunity. (Iran-contra affair, Historic Documents of 1987, p. 891)

Members of Congress and privacy and civil liberties advocates attacked the plan on several grounds, starting with Poindexter's involvement in it. Poindexter's conviction of lying to Congress "hardly makes him an ideal protector of the legal system," Sen. Bill Nelson, D-Fla., said in a Senate speech. Lee Tien, staff attorney for the Electronic Frontier Foundation, a civil liberties group, described the Pentagon program as a "dragnet database fishing expedition, trying to figure out what the 250–300 million people in the United States are doing in their daily lives, and then trying to figure out if they're bad guys." Other critics, including several well-known computer experts, predicted Poindexter's computer system would not succeed in identifying terrorist activities ahead of time. At year's end leading members of Congress in both parties said they would try to impose limits on the program—or possibly force the Pentagon to abandon it altogether—early in the 2003 session.

Domestic Spying

Federal and local law enforcement officials sought, during 2002, to remove restrictions imposed during previous decades on their ability to conduct surveillance operations against American citizens or foreigners inside the United States. Most of the restrictions were imposed, either by law or through court settlements, because of concerns that FBI agents and some local police departments had improperly spied on political dissidents, civil rights leaders, antiwar protesters and others whose only offense was their opposition to government policies. After the September 11 terrorist attacks, law enforcement officials said they needed some of the investigative tools that had been restricted because of those past abuses.

At the federal level, the most prominent issue was whether the FBI and other law enforcement agencies should be able to use secret procedures,

*established in 1978, to get authority to use wiretaps and other forms of elec-
tronic surveillance against terrorist suspects. The 1978 procedures were established in the Foreign Intelligence Surveillance Act (PL 95–511), which
was a reaction to revelations that the FBI had secretly monitored civil rights
leader Martin Luther King Jr. and other government critics. The law established a special court, the Foreign Intelligence Surveillance Court, which
had to approve requests for wiretaps used for the purpose of gaining intelligence about foreign threats to the United States. The law also established a
"wall" between counterintelligence work and routine criminal prosecutions;
this was because investigators in intelligence cases generally had an easier
time obtaining warrants for wiretaps than did investigators in criminal
cases, and legislators did not want criminal investigators pretending their
cases involved intelligence work just so they could obtain wiretaps more
easily.*

*Without any public notice, Attorney General John Ashcroft on March 6 is-
sued regulations that essentially dismantled the wall between intelligence
and criminal investigators. Ashcroft's regulations were so secret that the
Justice Department refused to give them to members of Congress, even in secret session. Ashcroft issued his regulations under a provision of the USA
Patriot Act that appeared to give federal prosecutors broader power to use
wiretaps and other espionage tactics domestically in terrorism cases.*

*At the request of three senior senators, the Foreign Intelligence Surveil-
lance Court in August released Ashcroft's regulations, along with the court's
opinion, written on May 17, that overturned them because they were "not
reasonably designed" to protect the rights of American citizens. The court's
decision offered an extraordinary public look into the work of secret wiretaps. It noted that during the Clinton administration the FBI had misrep-
resented facts in seventy-five separate requests for warrants.*

*Ashcroft appealed the court's ruling and won a major victory on No-
vember 18 when a special appellate court overturned the May 17 decision.
The appellate court, which had never before been called into action since the
1978 law was enacted, said the USA Patriot Act gave the Justice Department
wide authority to conduct wiretaps in terrorism cases. In effect, the court
ruled that the government no longer had to maintain the "wall" between domestic criminal prosecutions and intelligence gathering. "Effective counterintelligence, as we have learned, requires the wholehearted cooperation
of all the government's personnel who can be brought to the task," the court
ruled. "A standard which punishes such cooperation could well be thought
dangerous to national security." Ashcroft hailed the court ruling as "a giant
step forward" and said he would step up the use of wiretaps and other surveillance tools in counterterrorism cases.*

*In a related development, Ashcroft on May 30 issued new regulations
allowing the FBI to conduct investigations of domestic civic, political, and
religious groups even when the government had no reason to suspect wrongdoing. Ashcroft's order overturned a restriction, in place since the 1970s,
that allowed the FBI to probe such groups only when investigating an actual*

crime. That restriction—like the one limiting use of domestic wiretaps—arose because of the FBI's routine monitoring of civil rights groups and political dissidents. Ashcroft called the restriction "a competitive advantage for terrorists who skillfully utilize sophisticated techniques and modern computer systems to compile information for targeting and attacking innocent Americans." Rep. James Sensenbrenner, R-Wis., chairman of the House Judiciary Committee, expressed concern that Ashcroft took his step without notifying Congress. Sensenbrenner also said he worried about "going back to the bad old days when the FBI was spying on people like Martin Luther King."

FBI agents used the new authorities in Ashcroft's orders—as well as expanded powers granted Congress in the USA Patriot Act—to conduct nationwide sweeps for information that might be related to terrorism. The agents had a powerful tool to maintain the secrecy of their investigations: Section 215 of the Patriot Act made it a crime for anyone possessing records (such as hospitals, universities, libraries, book sellers, or video stores) to divulge an FBI request for those records.

In one well-publicized case, the FBI in late May began a nationwide search of records of companies that offered scuba diving lessons and equipment rentals. The search reportedly was prompted by information from detainees from Afghanistan indicating that terrorists might use scuba gear to carry out an attack. Dozens of companies willingly turned over their customer records, but the owners of the Reef Seekers Dive Company in Beverly Hills, California, refused in July, and the government backed down rather than take the matter to court.

Officials at several dozen libraries also were contacted by FBI agents seeking information about the reading habits of individual patrons and were warned not to reveal any information about the FBI requests. The American Library Association advised libraries to keep on file as little information as possible about its patrons and the books or other material they read.

The loosening of rules for domestic spying by federal agencies was accompanied by a similar move at the local level in some—but certainly not all—cities. The most prominent case was in New York City, where the police department went to court to undo a 1985 consent decree that prohibited the police from conducting routine surveillance—such as taking pictures and recording speeches—of political demonstrations. The decree settled a class action lawsuit stemming from police infiltration of the radical Black Panther group during the 1970s. City attorneys said that the September 11 terrorist attacks had shown that giving law enforcement officers more tools to combat terrorism was "the most vital priority" that overrode previous concerns about undermining the right of citizens to protest. A federal court in Chicago had loosened a similar consent decree that had imposed restrictions on intelligence gathering by the police in that city.

Political leaders in about two dozen other cities took the opposite approach, however, adopting resolutions and even legislation barring law enforcement officials and other employees from cooperating with federal investigations. Oakland, California; Boulder, Colorado; Flagstaff, Arizona; Santa Fe, New Mexico; and Cambridge, Massachusetts, were among the cities that adopted or in late 2002 were considering legislation resisting at least some degree of local involvement in the federal war against terrorists.

The Bush administration suffered an embarrassing defeat on a related front: a proposal by the Justice Department for a volunteer corps of citizen informants to help the government collect information about possible terrorism threats. Bush in March announced the proposal, called TIPS (for Terrorism Information and Prevention System). The Justice Department described the program as using "millions of American workers who, in the daily course of their work, are in a unique position to see potentially unusual or suspicious activity in public places." As examples, the department initially cited postal workers, utility repairmen, and others who routinely visited private homes as well as public spaces. These workers would be encouraged to report their suspicions via a toll-free TIPS line at the Justice Department.

After the proposal was widely denounced as a potential invasion of privacy, the Justice Department amended the plan to exclude workers who had access to private homes. But that change did not satisfy critics, among them House Majority Leader Richard Armey, R-Texas, who inserted language killing the entire proposal in pending legislation creating the new Homeland Security Department. The final version of the bill, signed by Bush in November, barred "any and all activities" to carry out the TIPS program. (Homeland security, p. 530)

Following are excerpts from a speech delivered August 2, 2002, by John M. Poindexter, director of the Information Awareness Office of the Defense Department, explaining an antiterrorism proposal called Total Information Awareness.

The document was obtained from the Internet at www .fas.org/irp/agency/dod/poindexter.html; accessed February 8, 2003.

Good afternoon. Today I would like to tell you about the new Information Awareness Office [IAO] and the programs we are developing. To introduce this I have a short video for you.

The world has changed dramatically since the Cold War when there existed two super powers. During the years I was in the White House it was relatively simple to identify our intelligence collection targets. It was sometimes hard to collect the intelligence, but the targets were clear. Today, we are in a world of asymmetries. The most serious asymmetric threat facing the United States is terrorism, a threat characterized by collections of people loosely organized in shadowy networks that are difficult to identify and define and whose goals are the destruction of our way of life. The intelligence collection targets are thousands of people whose identities and whereabouts we do not always know. It is somewhat analogous to the anti-submarine warfare problem of finding submarines in an ocean of noise—we must find the terrorists in a world of noise, understand what they are planning, and develop options for preventing their attacks. If we are to preserve our national security, we must figure out a way of combating this threat.

I think the solution is largely associated with information technology. We must become much more efficient and more clever in the ways we find new sources of data, mine information from the new and old, generate information, make it available for analysis, convert it to knowledge, and create actionable options. We must also break down the stovepipes—at least punch holes in them. By this, I mean we must share and collaborate between agencies, and create and support high-performance teams operating on the edges of existing organizations. Tools are needed to facilitate these collaborations, and to support these teams that work to ensure our security.

The Information Awareness Office at DARPA [Defense Advanced Research Projects Agency] is about creating technologies that would permit us have both security and privacy. More than just making sure that different databases can talk to one another, we need better ways to extract information from those unified databases, and to ensure that the private information on innocent citizens is protected. The main point is that we need a much more systematic approach. A variety of tools, processes and procedures will be required to deal with the problem, but they must be integrated by a systems approach built around a common architecture to be effective.

Total Information Awareness—a prototype system—is our answer. We must be able to detect, classify, identify, and track terrorists so that we may understand their plans and act to prevent them from being executed. To protect our rights, we must ensure that our systems track the terrorists, and those that mean us harm.

IAO programs are focused on making Total Information Awareness—TIA—real. This is a high level, visionary, functional view of the world-wide system—somewhat over simplified. One of the significant new data sources that needs to be mined to discover and track terrorists is the transaction space. If terrorist organizations are going to plan and execute attacks against the United States, their people must engage in transactions and they will leave signatures in this information space. This is a list of transaction categories, and it is meant to be inclusive. Currently, terrorists are able to move freely throughout the world, to hide when necessary, to find sponsorship and support, and to operate in small, independent cells, and to strike infrequently, exploiting weapons of mass effects and media response to influence governments. We are painfully aware of some of the tactics that they employ. This low-intensity/low-density form of warfare has an information signature. We must be able to pick this signal out of the noise. Certain agencies and apologists talk about connecting the dots, but one of the problems is to know which dots to connect. The relevant information extracted from this data must be made available in large-scale repositories with enhanced semantic content for easy analysis to accomplish this task. The transactional data will supplement our more conventional intelligence collection.

While our goal is total information awareness, there will always be uncertainty and ambiguity in trying to understand what is being planned. That's why our tools have to build models of competing hypotheses. That is, we need to bring people with diverse points of view together in a collaborative environment where there is access to all source data, discovery tools and model building tools. Collaboration has not been so important in the past when problems were less complex, but now it is essential. And tools have to make the analysis process more efficient, to properly explore the multiple possibilities.

This is the analytical environment. I could have called it the intelligence community, but in the case of counter-terrorism, it is broader to include law enforcement, friendly allies, outside experts etc. A similar environment exists for the policy and operations community, but the functions and tools are different. The mission here is to take the competing hypotheses from the analytical environment and estimate a range of plausible futures. The objective is to identify common nodes, representing situations that could occur, and to explore the probable impact of various actions or interventions that authorities might make in response to these situations.

The Information Awareness Office has a number of ongoing projects to address the functional requirements of this vision, and we will be starting new projects to complete the picture. The program managers who follow will give you the details, but I want to show you how they all fit into this system plan.

Jonathon Phillips is working on Human Identification at Distance, to achieve positive identification of humans using multi-modal biometric technologies. Such a system could be used for security systems, for example, or could be used to track potential terrorists.

Doug Dyer is starting a new program called Genisys, which addresses our database needs. This project will imagine and develop ultra-large-scale, semantically rich, easily implementable database technologies. One goal is to develop ways of treating the world-wide, distributed, legacy data bases as if they were one centralized data base, and another is to develop privacy protection technologies.

Charles Wayne leads the programs called TIDES and EARS. These projects address our needs in natural language processing, to provide discovery tools for finding information in foreign languages and converting speech to text. Automated tools are essential in order to reduce our need for expert foreign language translators and listeners in the thousands of existing human languages.

Ted Senator is the program manager for EELD, which stands for Evidence Extraction and Link Discovery. This is a key program in the area of tools for discovery of information. I will let Ted tell you the details on how this goes beyond traditional data mining techniques.

War Gaming the Asymmetric Environment is led by Larry Willis. This is an essential component of our modeling efforts. Bio-Surveillance is another of Ted Senator's programs looking at novel data sources for early warning of the release of biological agents.

Tom Armour is back on the DARPA team to extend the work on the Genoa project with a new program that we have creatively named Genoa II. I told him he had to come back to finish his work. As some of you know I've been working on Genoa for the past six years. We have transitioned some of the Genoa tools and will build on the past work primarily to address tools for collaborative reasoning, estimating plausible futures and creating actionable options for the decision maker. While the original Genoa project was aimed primarily at supporting intelligence analysis, under Genoa II we plan to focus on supporting policy and decision-making at strategic levels.

The overarching program that binds IAO's efforts together is Total Information Awareness or TIA System. The primary goal of TIA is the integration and assured transition of components developed in the programs Genoa, Genoa II, GENISYS, EELD, WAE, TIDES, HumanID and Bio-Surveillance. TIA will develop a modular system architecture using open standards that will enable a spiral development effort that will allow the insertion of new components when they are available. We will produce a complete, end-to-end, closed-loop proto-type system in a realistic environment.

. . . We will supplement the programs in IAO with commercial and other government components to rapidly implement early versions of TIA system at our R&D laboratory. We have already begun a spiral development and experiment program in conjunction with Army partners. Over the next few years we will continuously add functionality to the system as components become available.

Where will IAO's projects get data in order to develop their algorithms? To proceed with development, without intruding on domestic or foreign concerns, we are creating a data base of synthetic transactions using a simulation model. This will generate billions of transactions constituting realistic background noise. We will insert into this noise simulated transactions by a red team acting as a terrorist organization to see if we can detect and understand this activity. In the Genisys program we will be investigating the DARPA-hard problem of developing technologies that can give us the capability to detect foreign terrorist activities in this transaction space and achieve enhanced privacy for the innocents.

There are significant information policy issues related when considering data mining in actual transaction spaces. The U.S., and other countries as well, have just begun to consider some of the issues and consequences. There are ways in which technology can help preserve rights and protect people's privacy while helping to make us all safer. We are taking a number of steps to begin a reasoned discussion of the policy issues, imbued with knowledge of technology capabilities. DARPA's Information Systems and Technology panel (ISAT) has been tasked with a summer study on how we can achieve the necessary security we need and still have privacy. Discussions have been started with the National Academy of Sciences to do a longer range study on Information Policy for the InfoSpace of the Future.

We believe that total information awareness is a very difficult problem and in the tradition of the very hard problems that DARPA has addressed in the past. We think we have some very good ideas about how to solve the problem.

IAO has an open BAA [broad agency announcement] that was issued last March, and will be open for a year. We will be funding some of the good ideas that we have already received, but if you have good ideas that we haven't seen yet, please tell us about them. The BAA is on the DARPA web site.

I believe the ultimate solution to countering terrorism requires a co-evolution in 4 areas: technology, process/operations, policy and culture. Our focus is on developing the technology, the first area, and making sure that decisions in the other areas, such as policy, are knowledgeable about what is possible and what isn't. It's an exciting area, and I am proud of the contributions that we will all be collectively making to National security.

URIBE ON INAUGURATION AS PRESIDENT OF COLOMBIA
August 7, 2002

A new president took office in Colombia promising to use a "firm hand" to end guerrilla insurgencies that, along with narcotics trafficking, for decades had made Colombia one of the most violence plagued nations in all of Latin America. Alvaro Uribe, a former regional governor, was elected on May 26, 2002, on a platform promising to double the size of the army and national police to suppress leftist guerrillas and rightist paramilitaries. He replaced Andres Pastrana, who had been elected four years earlier on a promise of negotiating a peaceful resolution with the guerrillas but had failed to reach any lasting agreement.

After taking office on August 7, Uribe declared a state of emergency and imposed a tax, to be paid mostly by the wealthy, that would fund expansion of the nation's security forces. The larger of the two leftist guerrilla forces responded to Uribe by escalating its attacks, especially against civilian communities in urban areas.

The United States, which in 2000 deepened its involvement in fighting drug trafficking in Colombia, took another important step in 2002 by allowing its already extensive military aid to be used to combat the guerrillas as well as narcotics traffickers—who in many cases were one and the same. Colombia was the source of about 90 percent of the world's cocaine and of most of the heroin consumed in the United States. (U.S. aid, Historic Documents of 2000, p. 840)

Background

Colombia had suffered several waves of severe violence in the decades following World War II. Leftist guerrilla movements emerged in the early 1960s, and in subsequent decades narcotics traffickers took over large regions of the country. Largely in reaction to the guerrilla movements, large land owners in the 1980s began funding paramilitary forces to provide protection. The government succeeded during the early 1990s in dismantling two huge narcotics cartels (based in the cities of Cali and Medellin), only to stand by almost helplessly as the guerrilla and paramilitary groups took over much of the narcotics trade.

By the turn of the century the leftist guerrilla movements had coalesced into two major groups, the Revolutionary Armed Forces of Colombia (known by its Spanish acronym, FARC) with about 20,000 fighters, and the National Liberation Army (ELN), which had about 8,000 fighters. Opposing these groups—often in collaboration with the national army—was a consortium of paramilitary groups known as the United Self-Defense Forces of Colombia (AUC), many of whose leaders were former military officers. Collectively, the three groups controlled more than 40 percent of Colombia's territory. U.S. officials told Congress in 2002 that the FARC and AUC were engaged in "every facet of narcotics trafficking" and derived more than $300 million a year from it.

The violence of these groups resulted in an average of 3,500 people killed annually since the early 1990s. The guerrillas also made Colombia the kidnapping capital of the world, seizing more than 3,000 people every year, most of whom were held for ransom. More than 1 million of Colombia's 40 million people fled the country for the United States, Canada, and other safer places in Latin America. The bulk of the exiles were middle-class professionals, whose departure deepened the country's economic woes that stemmed from the violence and resulting political instability.

Seeking to break the cycle of violence, Pastrana had taken office in 1999 with a sweeping proposal, called Plan Colombia, that combined negotiating with the guerrillas and winning financial support from the United States and the European Union for a counternarcotics strategy of destroying coca and poppy plantations and offering farmers economic incentives to plant alternative crops. The administration of President Bill Clinton (1993–2001) supported Pastrana's Plan Colombia and in 2000 won congressional support for more than $1 billion in aid over two years.

Pastrana took extraordinary steps to pacify the guerrillas, most notably by ceding to the FARC a 16,000-square-mile demilitarized "safe haven" in the southern part of the country. Pastrana in effect was recognizing the fact that the guerrillas already controlled much of the territory. The difficulties Pastrana faced were evident at the outset. In January 1999 he went to a town in rebel territory for opening talks with FARC leader Manuel Marulanda (known as "Sureshot"), who failed to appear. The rebels seemed to be using the talks to consolidate control of the territory they had been ceded and to step up their business ventures of narcotics trafficking and kidnapping people for ransom. Fighting continued during 2000 and 2001, and peace negotiations went nowhere.

At the beginning of 2002 Pastrana launched one last attempt to negotiate with the FARC, and on January 20 agreed with the rebels on a timetable for future talks and renewal of the safe haven zone. But the guerrillas still were not ready for peace, and they stepped up their attacks. The breaking point came on February 20 when FARC guerrillas hijacked an airplane carrying thirty passengers so they could kidnap a senior senator, Jorge Gechem Turbay, who was a member of a family of prominent politicians and chaired the Senate's peace commission. Hours later Pastrana went on national television to announce that he was suspending all negotiations with the rebels. "Now no one believes in their willingness to reach peace," Pastrana said, indicating that he had reached a conclusion that many other Colombians had adopted months or even years earlier. Pastrana also sent the air force on bombing raids against guerrilla positions and dispatched the army to reoccupy the main towns in the safe haven. The guerrillas struck again three days later, kidnapping another prominent senator, Ingrid Betancourt, a long-time FARC opponent who was running for president. Betancourt remained in captivity for the rest of the year.

The guerrillas also launched a new line of attack against vulnerable infrastructure targets, sabotaging a dozen or more telecommunications systems and bombing dozens of electrical transmission towers and water pumping stations. FARC guerrillas, who in the past had generally limited their activities to rural areas, also moved into the cities. Their first dramatic urban offensive came on April 10 when rebels dressed in military uniforms gained access to the provincial parliament building in the city of Cali and kidnapped thirteen lawmakers, including the legislature's president, and several aides.

Uribe Wins Election

Colombia held two sets of elections in 2002, starting with elections in March for local offices and seats in both houses of Congress, the House and Senate. FARC threatened the legislative elections by killing three members of Congress, kidnapping five members (including Turbay and Betancourt), and attacking or threatening numerous others. Through violence and intimidation, the guerrillas also sought to persuade voters to stay away from the polls. The AUC paramilitary, on the other hand, fielded its own slate of candidates. Despite the violence, about 44 percent of eligible voters went to the polls, a turnout in line with previous elections. The center-left Liberal party—one of Colombia's two traditional political parties—retained its majority in both the House and Senate.

Full attention then turned to the presidential election in May, and the major question was how big a victory Uribe could achieve. Uribe was a former governor of Antioquia state whose father, a prominent rancher, had been killed by FARC guerrillas in 1983. He positioned himself as the candidate with the hardest line against the guerrillas, pledging steps to defeat them militarily. Formerly a member of the Liberal party, Uribe ran as an independent against four candidates, the most important of whom was Horacio Serpa, a former interior minister, representing the Liberal party.

Again, the guerrillas used violence to try to discourage public support for the political system. One of the worst incidents of the entire war occurred during fighting on May 1 between FARC guerrillas and rightist paramilitary forces in the town of Boyaja in Choco province, in northeastern Colombia. The guerrillas fired a gas cylinder bomb at a church where displaced people were hiding, killing 119 people, including 49 children.

Turnout for the May 26 elections was about 46 percent—slightly lower *than in previous presidential elections. Uribe captured 53 percent of the vote, avoiding a run-off for the first time since Colombia adopted its current political system in 1991. Serpa, his closest rival, received about 32 percent.*

In the weeks between the election and Uribe's inauguration on August 7, the FARC guerrillas tried another tactic to destabilize the country, issuing death threats against hundreds of local mayors unless they resigned their posts. This move generally was seen as an effort to undermine the government from the bottom up; mayors were key to organizing and funding of the local services that constituted the government in the eyes of most Colombians. Several dozen mayors resigned in the face of these threats.

In his inaugural address, Uribe repeated his campaign promises to take a more aggressive approach to the guerrillas. He said he would double the size of the army and military and would recruit 1 million civilian paid informants to give the government information about rebel activities and locations. Uribe also said he would authorize the army to recruit 15,000 peasants to fight alongside the army in their home provinces. "A whole nation is crying out for respite and security," Uribe said. "I will support and sympathize with the forces of law and order, and we will encourage our millions of civilians to join us in assisting them."

As Uribe spoke before Congress, guerrillas responded to him with one of their most direct attacks against Bogota in years. The guerrillas fired several makeshift mortars, one of which landed on the grounds of the presidential palace, injuring four police officers. Other mortars landed in poor residential neighborhoods of the capital, killing twenty-one people.

Five days later Uribe began translating his plans into action, decreeing a state of emergency that allowed the government to impose long-term curfews, limit publication of information by the news media, require citizens to tell the government of travel plans, and take other security-related steps. To pay for his expansion of security forces, Uribe also decreed a one-time tax of 1.2 percent on the net assets of individual and businesses required to file tax returns (this applied to those with at least $65,000 in net assets— about 1 percent of the total population). The government said the tax would produce $800 million, enough to pay for an additional 3,000 army troops and 10,000 police officers.

Uribe on September 11 took his most controversial decision to date, authorizing security forces to make arrests and conduct searches without obtaining warrants that were generally required. Domestic critics said the decision, combined with other steps to bolster the power of the army and police, represented a move toward a dictatorship. Human Rights Watch warned that Uribe's tactics threatened to repeat Colombia's experience during the 1980s "when similar laws combined with a lack of oversight led to egregious human rights violations." Uribe said his policy was "not to silence the critics but to confront the violence." The Colombian Supreme Court on November 28 overturned portions of Uribe's warrantless-arrest decree as unconstitutional.

During the rest of the year government security forces claimed unprecedented success in killing or capturing guerrilla and paramilitary fighters.

The claims were difficult to verify, however, because nearly all the confrontations between government and rebel forces took place in remote areas.

Uribe's initial policies achieved one success of potential significance— a cease-fire agreement by most elements of the AUC paramilitary forces, effective December 1. The AUC had been torn by internal divisions since its leader Carlos Castana, announced in July that he was retiring and the paramilitary alliance was disbanding. Castana later retracted his retirement, but on September 24 the United States announced that he, and his chief aide, Salvatore Mancuso, had been indicted on drug trafficking charges. Apparently strengthened by the U.S. indictments, Uribe won an agreement by the AUC to a two-month cease-fire and a promise that it would stop its involvement in the narcotics trade.

U.S. Involvement

When the Clinton administration embraced Pastrana's Plan Colombia in 2000, Congress imposed numerous restrictions, most important a ban on aid to the government for any military activities other than combating narcotics production and trafficking; in other words, the Colombian military could not use U.S.-financed helicopters and other military aid to fight the guerrillas directly. Congress also required the administration to promote respect for human rights in Colombia, for example by helping train personnel in the judicial system.

It was obvious from the outset that limiting U.S. aid to combating narcotics trafficking—and not to combating insurgencies—would be difficult because the two major guerrilla groups and the right-wing paramilitaries all were deeply involved in the narcotics trade. But members of Congress insisted on the limit because fighting narcotics trafficking was the highest priority for the United States and because of the Colombian military's long history of abusing the human rights of the civilian population in its battles against the guerrillas.

Following the collapse of Pastrana's peace talks with the leftist FARC guerrillas, the Bush administration in March asked Congress to drop the ban on providing aid to Colombia explicitly for counterinsurgency purposes. The administration framed its request as an antiterrorist move, arguing that the guerrillas had become more of a terrorist threat than a political threat. Fighting terrorism also had become an easy policy to sell on Capitol Hill since the September 11, 2001, terrorist attacks in New York City and Washington. The United States had placed all three Colombian armed groups on its list of "foreign terrorist organizations" but had devoted most of its aid and attention to combating the two leftist insurgencies.

Congress approved the request in July, but not before some critics warned that doing so could lead to much deeper U.S. involvement in Colombia's war. The request appeared to be "a simple word change in the law," said Rep. Nita Lowey, D-N.Y., but it was "likely to lead to huge expenditures and expanded U.S. military deployments to Colombia." Administration officials insisted that U.S. soldiers would not be sent into combat against the guerrillas.

One of the administration's first initiatives outside of combating the *narcotics trade was a $129 million program, over two years, to train and equip a Colombian army brigade to protect a pipeline that carried oil to the Caribbean coast for Occidental Petroleum and other companies. FARC guerrillas had repeatedly sabotaged the 480-mile pipeline, putting it out of service for more than half of 2001 and costing the country an estimated $500 million in revenue. Helping Colombia protect the pipeline was viewed by many in both Colombia and the United States as a significant expansion of Washington's involvement in the war.*

Under pressure from members of Congress and human rights groups, the administration briefly suspended military aid to Colombia early in the year, but reinstated it on May 1, releasing 60 percent of available funds, a step that Human Rights Watch said "sent a harmful message to the Colombia authorities, and particularly the armed forces, that human rights were less important than the ability to wage the war freely." The State Department released the remaining 40 percent of the aid on September 9.

Secretary of State Colin Powell visited Bogota on December 4 and endorsed Uribe's get-tough approach. "Our commitment has grown even stronger as we stand together against the threats of terrorism both our countries face," Powell said.

Despite the Bush administration's new emphasis on fighting terrorism in Colombia, most U.S. aid still went to combating narcotics. In fiscal year 2002 the United States provided $411 million worth of antinarcotics and military aid to Colombia. Bush requested $537 million for fiscal 2002. Congress had imposed a limit of 400 U.S. military personnel and 400 U.S. civilian contractors working with U.S. aid programs in Colombia. As of September 2002, according to Human Rights Watch, the United States had 138 temporary and permanent military personnel and civilians retained as individual contractors in Colombia.

Both the Bush administration and the Colombian government claimed during 2002 that the antinarcotics programs of Plan Colombia were beginning to succeed. Administration officials, for example, told Congress in March that the eradication of coca crops, through aerial spraying and other means, had nearly doubled between 2000 and 2001 and would double again during 2002. Even so, the administration on March 8 released a separate report indicating that coca production in Colombia continued to increase. That report, based on satellite images and other findings, estimated that 417,430 acres in Colombia were devoted to coca production in 2001, a 25 percent increase over the previous year. Some of the increase was a result of a satellite survey in 2001 of one large coca-growing area that had been obscured by cloud cover in 2000.

Following are excerpts from the speech delivered August 7, 2002, by Alvaro Uribe upon his inauguration as president of Colombia.

The document was obtained from the Internet at www .embacol.org.au/Documents/DiscursoPresidenteIngles .htm; accessed October 10, 2002.

. . . In obedience to the oath which I have just taken, which commits all my efforts and the very life which the Creator has given to me, I call on all the men and women of this country to seek again our common bond of unity, the law, democratic authority, of freedom and social justice, which we have lost in a moment of weakness in our history. Trust and solidarity have declined in our country. We look at our neighbors, and especially the State, with mistrust. Our attitude to solidarity has weakened. There is a disproportionate desire to serve one's own interest, and indifference to the fate of the community. But this, as a sign of decay in social capital, is not born of the nature of being a Colombian, which is both civic-minded and humanitarian. The reason for it is the destruction wrought by violence, of political chicanery and of corruption, which combine to cause uncertainty, poverty and inequality.

Colombia faces a series of grave difficulties. Nine million of our people live in misery, 57 percent are on the poverty line, 16 percent are unemployed and six and a half million are underemployed. The deficit represents 3 percent of our gross domestic product, and the capacity to pay public debt has reached its limit. If the same number of murders were committed here as in England, there would be 200 of them every year. One murder is serious enough, and so are 200: but we have 34,000. In kidnaps, of which between 3,000 and 3,600 are reported, we account for 60percent of all such crimes in the world. And each kidnap means suffering, the flight of capital, and unemployment.

We didn't come to complain, we got here to work.

It will be impossible to solve everything in four years, but we shall spare no effort to try. That is my duty to our youth and to future generations. It is my obligation of honor to those 80 percent of Colombians, the young now awakening to life, who need us to do whatever is right to ensure that their hopes may flower into reality. We must do our work well, and restore the faith of a people which has never bowed its head, but which does call for a steady hand at the helm and stem the tide of misery and criminal attack.

Fiscal adjustment, to put the nation's finances in order, is unavoidable. But it will be effected in such a way as to encourage economic growth and employment. Growth is the best form of fiscal adjustment, and the only lasting source of revenues for the State. The powerful, whose tenacity and success in business are good for the country, will have to bear new tax burdens. The efforts of the middle classes and the people as a whole must be rewarded by greater social investment so that we can stop them from continuing their already long years of Purgatory.

With this exceptionally delicate state of the economy, we must give encouragement to sectors of production that generate employment. When a developed country finds itself in a difficult situation, it wastes no time debating incentives: it simply designs then and puts them into practice.

Globalization, like integration of the economy, is irreversible: but the dignity of the poorer nations demands that they achieve social equity. Otherwise, their political viability could only be maintained at enormous cost to democracy and peaceful coexistence.

The Andean Community economy needs greater political will and better results. We would be wrong to think that, with the trade barriers within our region, any of our countries will be able to increase the pace of growth. The best protection within the Community is greater integration. We should all look to Mercosur, the European Union, Canada, and FTAA [the proposed Free Trade Agreement of the Americas].

We should make progress towards a harmonized and competitive exchange rate, low inflation, prudent borrowing and fiscal balance. If we can achieve that, then we can think about a single currency, our currency, which we can control ourselves.

Our borders with our neighbors are both open and closed. They are open for goods and honest men, and closed for criminals. Our work in authority will aim to prevent drugs and violence from moving into border areas. And, with the help of the government of each of those good neighbors, we will succeed in this, so that Colombia and everyone can recover peace of mind. This conflict must be stopped, or it may destabilize the whole region.

During the hand-over process I met the senior administrators of the multilateral banks, to persuade them to increase their exposure in Colombia. We need this, and we need it soon. If we use those funds properly, we will be able to continue to meet our obligations, and pay some of our overdue social debt.

Popular acceptance of our State will largely depend on our social achievements. Despite a critical shortage of funds, we will push forward with the seven tools for building equity which we explained in our manifesto: the educational revolution; broader-based social security; encouragement for the solidarity sector; social management in rural areas and of public services; support for small and medium enterprise to become a country of owners; and the quality of life in the cities.

Economic stability will depend on growth, and growth will be sustained into the longer term if it is based on a cohesive society. Economic stability is impossible without social stability.

Our State is a giant of bureaucratic inefficiency in the face of the corruption which abuses our political customs; and it is, dangerously, a dwarf in social investment. The State must promote development, guarantee social equity, and provide public order. It cannot stand in the way of private initiative, nor turn its back on the demands of society.

Our Community State will seek to ensure that funds and actions reach all, with transparency, giving people a greater part to play in the performance and supervision of public activities. The more we can encourage this participation, the more effective the effort to drive out corruption.

The State cannot ask small towns to practice austerity while those in high places waste money. As an example to all, the reforms must start in the Office of the President, Congress, pensions, salaries, the elimination of political favors, inflated payrolls, and official entertainment.

The revolution in communications will make it easier to have a smaller and less expensive Congress, with a balanced mix of representation and participation, more integrated with the public and more efficient in its work. Its independence from the Executive requires not size, but opinion, observation and control.

This afternoon a draft bill will be sent to Congress, calling for a referendum against corruption and political chicanery. This will open the door to austerity and to the transfer of funds for the revolution in opportunities, which starts with education.

We cannot fight the trade in political favors if we trade in them ourselves. The managers and directors of the regional offices of national institutions will be appointed by merit and in competition, so that all may take part in an inaugural event of equal treatment from the administration.

If our State enterprises are to continue to exist, political influence must be banished, and labor costs must be rationalized.

Our idea of democratic security requires that we work to provide the effective protection of all members of the public, regardless of political beliefs or economic standing. A whole nation is crying out for respite and security. No crime can be justified, directly or otherwise. No kidnap can be explained away by political doctrine. I understand the grief of the mother, the orphan and the displaced. As I wake every morning, I will search my soul to make sure that the acts of authority which I undertake will arise from the purest of intentions and will be performed in the noblest of ways. I will support and sympathize with the forces of law and order, and we will encourage our millions of civilians to join us in assisting them. This increases our commitment to human rights, since respect for those rights is the only way to achieve security and then, reconciliation.

When a democratic State provides effective guarantees, even if it comes to do so gradually, any violence against it is terrorism. We do not accept violence as a means of attack on the government, or as a means of defense. Both are terrorism. The only mission of the legitimate force of the State is to defend the community, and that force cannot be used to silence its critics.

Democracy is the only way in which ideas can compete. We are offering democracy, so that arms can be replaced by argument, and democratic security will be the instrument by which politics can be conducted unarmed, and with the right not to be killed. The defense of the mayors, councilors, governors, and all other representatives of the people under threat, will be the bastion of that democracy. We will not allow the long-standing struggle of the people to elect their next authority to be frustrated by the threat of a bullet.

I have asked Mr. Kofi Annan, Secretary General of the United Nations, for the good offices of his organization to seek useful dialog, based on an alleviation of the situation of our society, and this must mean a cessation of hostilities. Those who wish to enjoy freedom must allow others to enjoy peace of mind. I have asked the media to accept the prudence which this issue demands.

The world must understand that this conflict requires unconventional, imaginative and transparent solutions. The agents of violence are funded by an international criminal business—drugs. They fight with weapons not made in Colombia. No democracy can stand aside from the sufferings of the Colombian people. We will continue with Plan Colombia, adding aerial interdiction and practical substitution programs, such as payments to small-farmers for the eradication of unlawful crops and care for the restoration of our woodlands. We will follow the path already opened up in the United States, knock on doors in Europe and Asia, and reinforce our unity of purpose with our neighbors. If we do not drive out drugs, drugs will destroy our freedoms and our ecology, and the hope of living in peace will be no more than an illusion.

We want peace; not the kind of temporary reassurance that comes from insincerity, or an uneasy agreement or a tyrannical government. Temporary reassurance is not reconciliation: it is simply a suspension of violence, after which more intense violence comes back.

I receive this office as President from the hands of Andres Pastrana who has come to the end of his tasks in dignity and good faith; with much success in integrating Colombia with the rest of the world, and as a final achievement, offering good prospects that ATPA [Andean Trade Preference Area] will favor our exports.

Francisco Santos-Calderón has taken the oath as Vice-President. He has done so out of a love for this country held dear by his family, and especially by his father.

I have made an oath to the President of Congress that I will obey the Constitution and the law, and he is an honest citizen, an efficient administrator, and a man of the State. My oath carries the special meaning that for both of us in our respective territories, our word is our bond, and it is graven in stone.

I come from a mountain which taught me to love it intensely, so that I could love all Colombia in the same way. My friends up there, most of them farmers, want me to keep my eyes on Colombia. There too is my mother, always keeping me company, and my father, full of life. They would like to see me doing my duty with love—some kind of extra love—for my fellow citizens. My wife and two student children will be a constant source of support.

We will start an administration which is honest, efficient and austere. It cannot work miracles, but it will work. There is not much money, and there are many problems. But our cheerful spontaneity, intact despite all that we have suffered and our unbending determination in the face of difficulty will be invaluable. I am well aware of the size of my responsibilities, and I know that I cannot follow the right course without my compatriots—you—and your constructive criticism, your efforts and your advice.

If we can tolerate the ideas of others, promote "zero-permissiveness" for crime, and can draw on a bank of authority which can pay out, we can make a better today and a better tomorrow for creative debate.

May our love for our country be the flame of our Lord and the Virgin to guide me on the right course to steer. To overcome human vanity, and to set wrongs right.

I earnestly hope that, in four years' time, I can look all of you in the eye.

GENERAL ACCOUNTING OFFICE
ON FOOD SAFETY INSPECTIONS
August 30, 2002

The U.S. Department of Agriculture (USDA) took steps late in the year to increase its enforcement of federal meat inspections after its procedures were challenged by a hard-hitting investigative report and American consumers were faced with two of the largest recalls ever of meat and poultry. The report, prepared by the General Accounting Office (GAO), the investigative arm of Congress, detailed shortcomings by the USDA's Food Safety and Inspection Service (FSIS) that the GAO said increased the risk that contaminated food would reach the marketplace. Even before the report was officially released, a beef-packing plant in Colorado was forced to recall nearly 19 million pounds of raw ground beef that might have contained the bacteria E. coli. Two months later a poultry-packing plant in Philadelphia recalled 27 million pounds of poultry products after it was discovered that its products might have been tainted with a food-borne pathogen, listeria monocytogenes, *that had sickened several dozen people in the Northeast and killed at least eight.*

The Agriculture Department responded after each recall by tightening the inspection rules designed to detect and eliminate the potentially deadly pathogens. It also appeared likely that the USDA would seek more money in the next federal budget to increase the number of meat and poultry inspectors and to improve their training.

Meanwhile a report by the National Academy of Sciences said the U.S. food supply still remained highly vulnerable to terrorist attack and recommended that a national plan be put in place to identify and deal with threats. Concerns about the safety of the nation's food supply heightened after terrorists killed nearly 3,000 people in New York and Washington on September 11, 2001. But concrete plans for preventing deliberate biocontamination had not advanced very far by the end of 2002. (Threats to the food supply, Historic Reports of 2001, p. 698)

Tightening the Regulations

Although the United States had the safest food production system in the world, contaminated food of all sorts caused an estimated 76 million

579

illnesses a year and 5,000 deaths. Among the main contaminants were salmonella, E. coli, *and* listeria monocytogenes, *all potentially deadly pathogens
that could easily contaminate meat and poultry that were not handled carefully during the slaughtering and packing process. Until 1996 meat and
poultry were inspected using the "sniff-and-poke" test to determine fresh-
ness and cleanliness. In 1996 the Clinton administration added the Hazard
Analysis Critical Control Points (HACCP) system. Under this system, pro-
cessors were required to identify potential points in the slaughtering and
processing chain that made the meat and poultry susceptible to food-borne
pathogens and then to take steps to reduce the possibility of contamination.
The HACCP system extended sanitation beyond the meat and poultry carcasses themselves to the physical equipment in the plant, including work
surfaces, machinery, refrigeration, and drains.* (HACCP system, Historic
Documents of 1996, p. 414)

*According to the FSIS, about 5,000 meat and poultry-packing plants were
subject to USDA sanitation regulations. The FSIS had about 7,500 inspectors, 3,400 of whom stood along slaughter and production lines inspecting
carcasses by the traditional sight, touch, and smell methods, while 4,100 inspectors oversaw the HACCP systems in the plants. To make sure that the
controls were working, federal inspectors were to conduct limited testing for*
salmonella *and other microbes. There was "zero tolerance" for visible feces,
which potentially carried* E. coli—*bacteria that occurred naturally in animals' intestinal tracts.* E. coli 0157:H7 *was considered an adulterant if
found in ground beef products, while* salmonella, E. coli, *and certain strains
of* listeria *were all considered adulterants in ready-to-eat products such as
hot dogs and luncheon meats.*

*In the first years after the HACCP program was implemented, the federal
government reported that the number of food-borne illnesses had declined
significantly, with "tens of thousands of people" fewer suffering food poisoning every year. Despite that decrease, the Agriculture Department itself
reported an increase in the incidence of both* salmonella *and* E. coli. *In 1998,
two years after the HACCP was put in place, 10.8 percent of broiler chick-
ens tested positive for* salmonella. *In 2000 that percentage had dropped
to 9.1 percent, but in 2001 it shot up to 11.9 percent—the highest it had
ever been.*

*Consumer and public health advocates charged that the incidence of the
pathogens was increasing because the USDA in the George W. Bush administration was backing away from enforcing the HACCP system. For evidence they pointed to a decision by the Bush administration not to challenge
a court ruling declaring a* salmonella *performance standard to be invalid
and forbidding the USDA from shutting down any processing plant that did
not meet the performance standard. Instead it decided that inspectors would
continue to test for* salmonella. *If a plant failed two sample tests, inspectors
were supposed to conduct an in-depth review of the entire food safety process and could close down the plant if it failed to address any deficiencies.
The department said the authority to close down plants immediately after a
performance standard went unmet was not necessary to enforce sanitation*

regulations. But consumer advocates said that by abandoning the performance standard—and by not shutting down plants that failed to meet it— the USDA was giving up a powerful enforcement tool. "There has been an historic drop in pathogens on our food, and fewer people are getting sick and dying as a result," said Carol Tucker Foreman of the Consumer Federation of America. "But this administration is moving away from the regulations that were key to making this happen, and I fear the progress will eventually be reversed."

Inspecting the Inspectors

The GAO came to a similar conclusion from a different direction in its "Better USDA Oversight and Enforcement of Safety Rules Needed to Reduce Risk of Food-borne Illness," a report prepared for the Senate Agriculture Committee. The report was sent to Capitol Hill on August 30 and was officially released September 19 by Sen. Tom Harkin, D-Iowa, chairman of the Agriculture Committee.

The report found that FSIS inspectors were not consistently ensuring that the meat-packing plants were meeting federally required sanitation practices, were not consistently identifying repetitive violations of those standards, and were not consistently ensuring that plants notified of sanitation violations were taking prompt action to correct the violations. In some cases plants found to be in violation of the standards were allowed to continue operating for ten months or more while they corrected their sanitation procedures.

The GAO investigators also said that the FSIS had not assessed the scientific soundness of individual plants' HACCP plans in a timely manner, that some inspectors still did not have a clear understanding of how the standards worked or how they were to be enforced, and that FSIS managers and inspectors were "confused" about the factors to be considered in determining whether a plant was repeatedly violating the sanitation rules. Moreover, the report said, allowing plants to continue to operate while taking months to correct violations "negates an important incentive" for plants to correct the problems, increasing food safety risks. The GAO recommended a series of steps it said the Department of Agriculture should take to ensure that its inspectors were better trained and to establish clear and consistent criteria for them to follow when dealing with violations.

Two Major Recalls

As if to underline the GAO report findings, two major recalls of beef and poultry products in 2002 raised new questions about the USDA's inspection and enforcement operations. On July 19, just a week after a draft of the GAO report was leaked to the press, the Agriculture Department announced a recall of 19 million pounds of ground beef shipped from a ConAgra plant in Greeley, Colorado. Forty-two people in eight states had been sickened by E. coli found in hamburger meat that came from the plant. It was the second largest meat recall ever recorded (in 1997 Hudson Foods recalled 25 million pounds of beef). Despite the recall, problems at the Greeley plant continued.

Between August and November 18, when federal inspectors finally shut down the plant until the company corrected the violations, the plant had been cited nineteen times for allowing fecal contamination.

On September 24 the Agriculture Department announced that FSIS inspectors would begin randomly testing for E. coli at all meat-packing plants and require meatpackers to take other steps to reduce the risk of E. coli contamination. "The scientific data show that E. coli 0157:H7 is more prevalent than previously estimated," said Elsa Murano, undersecretary of agriculture with responsibility for food safety. Meatpackers said the department was setting a goal that could not possibly be met. "No policy—short of cooking—can guarantee that E. coli 0157:H7 is eliminated from ground beef in every instance," said J. Patrick Boyle, president of the American Meat Institute. "It's not a fact we try to hide."

In October the Centers for Disease Control and Prevention named Pilgrim's Pride Corp. as the "most likely source" of a listeria outbreak that had caused at least seven deaths, three miscarriages, and forty-six illnesses in several northeastern states. The company, which produced cooked sandwich meat under the brand name Wampler Foods, among others, announced on October 13 that it was recalling 27.4 million pounds of the deli products— the largest recall in U.S. history—that were manufactured at a plant outside Philadelphia. The USDA temporarily shut down the plant the same day after traces of the listeria strain were found in drains. A second plant, owned and operated by a different company, was also implicated in the same listeria outbreak.

Later investigations indicated that the Pilgrim's Pride plant's own testing showed an increase in overall listeria contamination (although not in the deadly strain traced to the outbreak), but plant managers did little to correct the problem or call it to the attention of the inspectors. An FSIS inspector later said he had been concerned about the general lack of sanitation at the plant, but that other inspectors including his chief disagreed about the seriousness of the violations. The inspector attributed some of the disagreement to confusion about what the federal regulations required of the inspectors. In November the Agriculture Department issued a new directive aimed at detecting and eliminating contamination with listeria monocytogenes. Plants that did not have an FSIS-approved testing plan in place or that refused to share the results with FSIS inspectors were to be subject to additional testing by FSIS inspectors of the final meat product, the work surfaces, and the plant environment in general. A listeria-testing standard had been drafted during the Clinton administration (1993–2001), but the Bush administration had put it on hold after it came into office in 2001.

Agroterrorism

A report by the National Academy of Sciences, released on September 19, confirmed that the nation's food supply was highly vulnerable to a terrorist attack and recommended that a national plan be put in place to identify threats. The report, prepared by the National Research Council at the request of the Department of Agriculture, said that viruses, fungi, and bacteria that caused such diseases as foot and mouth disease or "mad cow" disease were easier to obtain than biological weapons that attacked people directly and were easier to spread through wind and carrier insets. "Although an attack with such agents is high unlikely to result in famine or malnutrition," the report said, "the possible damage includes major direct and indirect costs to agricultural and national economy, adverse public-health effects, . . . loss of public confidence in the food system and in public officials, and widespread concern and confusion." (Mad cow disease, Historic Documents of 2000, p. 883)

Parts of the report, "Countering Agricultural Bioterrorism," were classified because the panel did not want its case studies to serve as a terrorism manual. The panel recommended that the government increase its efforts to understand plant and animal diseases and how they spread, establish a network of laboratories to detect and diagnose diseases, and form a nationwide system to manage and collect information on bioterrorism. The Agriculture Department's Animal and Plant Health Inspection Service was folded into the new Homeland Security Department. In March homeland security chief Tom Ridge said the administration was looking into combining the FSIS and the FDA to better prevent a terrorist attack on the food supply. But that approach, while long advocated by consumer groups and supermarket chains, was adamantly opposed by food producers. (Homeland Security Department, p. 530)

In a separate effort to protect the food supply, the Food and Drug Administration issued voluntary guidelines that it said farms, restaurants, and supermarkets should use to thwart terrorist activities. The recommendations included restricting employee access to food handling and storage areas as well as to laboratories and computer control systems, performing criminal background checks on workers, securing water sources, and monitoring salad bars and other open food displays. The only known incident of food terrorism in the United States occurred in 1984, when a cult in Oregon contaminated salad bars with Salmonella *bacteria.*

> *Following are excerpts from "Meat and Poultry: Better USDA Oversight and Enforcement of Safety Rules Needed to Reduce Risk of Food-borne Illnesses," a report by the General Accounting Office submitted August 30, 2002, to the Senate Committee on Agriculture, Nutrition, and Forestry by Lawrence J. Dyckman, director of natural resources and environment at the GAO.*
>
> **The document was obtained from the Internet at www.gao .gov/new.items/d02902.pdf; accessed January 5, 2003.**

Every year, some meat and poultry products are contaminated with microbial pathogens, such as *Salmonella* and *E. coli*, that cause foodborne illnesses and deaths. To improve the safety of meat and poultry products, and in response to recommendations from GAO and the National Academy of Sciences, the U.S. Department of Agriculture's (USDA) Food Safety and Inspection Service (FSIS) implemented additional regulatory requirements for meat and poultry plants. These requirements are intended to ensure that plants operate food safety systems that are prevention-oriented and science-based. These systems, called Hazard Analysis and Critical Control Point (HACCP) systems, were phased in from January 1998 through January 2000 at all meat and poultry slaughter and processing plants. As the foundation of the HACCP system, plants are responsible for developing HACCP plans that, among other things, identify all of the contamination hazards that are reasonably likely to occur in a plant's particular production environment, establish all of the necessary steps to control these hazards, and have valid scientific evidence to support their decisions. As a result of implementing HACCP systems over the past 5 years, plants have accepted significant new responsibilities for producing safe products, and FSIS has made major changes to the roles and responsibilities of its inspection workforce.

FSIS, through its 15 district offices across the country, oversees the activities of about 7,500 federal inspectors who review the operations of about 5,000 plants subject to the HACCP requirements nationwide. About 3,400 inspectors are stationed in plants along slaughter lines to provide traditional carcass-by-carcass inspections using sight, touch, and smell. The remaining 4,100 FSIS inspectors oversee HACCP systems in plants. As a part of their oversight, inspectors determine if plants are complying with HACCP requirements, including the requirement that their plans include the following specific components:

- A hazard analysis that identifies all the food safety hazards—biological, chemical, and physical—that are reasonably likely to occur and measures to control them.
- Critical control points in plants' processes where controls can be applied to prevent, eliminate, or reduce a food safety hazard to an acceptable level.
- Critical limits (maximum or minimum values) at which the hazard is controlled.
- Monitoring requirements to ensure that the measured values are within critical limits.
- Corrective actions to be taken if critical limits are violated.
- Verification procedures to ensure that the plants' HACCP systems result in safe products.
- Record keeping procedures for documenting HACCP requirements.

To help verify that plants' HACCP systems are effectively controlling food safety hazards, FSIS inspectors test for the presence of the pathogen *Salmonella* on raw meat and poultry in a series of samples—referred to as a "set." FSIS established limits for *Salmonella*, known as "performance standards," which vary depending on the type of product. For example, no more than 1 percent of steer carcasses sampled in a set of tests may contain *Salmonella*. In addition to limits on *Salmonella*, FSIS has established a "zero tolerance" for visible feces on carcasses at slaughter plants and considers the disease-causing pathogen *E. coli 0157:H7* an adulterant that is not allowed in ground beef. FSIS also considers *Salmonella, E. coli 0157:H7,* and *Listeria mono-cytogenes* adulterants in ready-to-eat products such as hot dogs and luncheon meats.

When FSIS inspectors find a violation of the HACCP requirements, they document the violation on a "noncompliance record" and advise the plant. FSIS writes noncompliance records to document HACCP process violations, such as a plant's failure to document its monitoring of temperatures for a cooked product, as well as for violations of the rules regarding pathogens. If the plant does not correct the violation, FSIS may take an enforcement action, such as detaining the affected meat or poultry product; slowing one or more production lines; withholding the marks showing that a product has passed USDA inspection; or suspending inspection services for one or more products or the entire plant. While inspection services are suspended, a plant cannot operate. However, FSIS may place a suspension on hold—referred to as "in abeyance"—to allow the plant to continue operating while it corrects the violation.

In 1999, we reported that weaknesses in FSIS's training for its inspectors affected its ability to ensure consistent and effective oversight of HACCP. The following year, a USDA Inspector General report identified shortcomings in plants' HACCP plans and deficiencies in FSIS's oversight of HACCP's implementation. To help address these problems, FSIS stepped up its inspector training and initiated two new review mechanisms:

- Food safety systems correlation reviews, which examine a range of inspector practices within FSIS districts to improve the effectiveness of inspections.
- In-depth verification reviews of HACCP plans in plants with serious safety problems to identify weaknesses in the scientific soundness of the plans.

FSIS also introduced consumer safety officers into its workforce with the scientific and technical expertise to, among other things, review the scientific soundness of HACCP plans.

As you requested, this report (1) assesses whether FSIS is ensuring that plants' HACCP plans meet regulatory requirements, (2) determines whether FSIS is consistently identifying repetitive violations of HACCP requirements, and (3) assesses whether FSIS is ensuring that plants take prompt and effective action to return to compliance after the agency has identified HACCP violations. As part of our review, we analyzed 1,180 noncompliance records from 16 judgmentally selected meat and poultry slaughter and processing plants where FSIS frequently found HACCP-related violations in fiscal year 2001. Our sample included different sizes of plants located in 10 different FSIS districts across the country. We also analyzed files for the 68 HACCP enforcement cases that were active in fiscal year 2001 in three FSIS districts, including the two districts with the most plants in the country. In addition, we analyzed data from the in-depth verification reviews that FSIS conducted through the end of calendar year 2001 and the food safety systems correlation reviews that it completed by May 2002. . . .

Results in Brief

FSIS is not ensuring that all plants' HACCP plans meet regulatory requirements and, as a result, consumers may be unnecessarily exposed to unsafe foods that can cause foodborne illnesses. In particular, FSIS's inspectors have not consistently identified and documented failures of plants' HACCP plans to comply with requirements. For example, FSIS's food safety systems correlation reviews in three FSIS districts found that, in about 91 percent of the plants sampled, inspectors had failed to document deficiencies in basic requirements such as the requirement that plants have adequate documentation to support the analysis of hazards in their HACCP plans. In addition, although sound science is the cornerstone of an effective HACCP plan, FSIS does not expect its inspectors to determine whether HACCP plans are based on sound science because inspectors lack the expertise to do so. FSIS has made limited progress in reviewing the scientific soundness of plants' HACCP plans. While FSIS's in-depth verification reviews have been useful in identifying numerous scientific weaknesses in HACCP plans, only about 1 percent of plants have undergone these time-and resource-intensive reviews. Similarly, consumer safety officers will improve FSIS's ability to assess the scientific adequacy of plants' HACCP plans. However, only about 6 percent of the officers that FSIS needs are on board, and FSIS managers in two large districts expressed concern that it may take years to assess the plans for all plants in their districts. Finally, we found that inspectors had not documented any HACCP violations in 55 percent of all plants during 2001; yet, when we showed these data to FSIS officials, they were surprised at the large numbers and said the absence of violations was unusual. For example, one field official said that if inspectors are finding no HACCP violations for an entire year, they may not understand their HACCP oversight responsibilities. In August 2002, FSIS told us it has developed, and would soon release, a new directive to clarify inspectors' responsibilities and new guidance for its supervisors to use to verify that inspectors are, among other things, applying appropriate inspection methods. FSIS also told us that it had introduced an interactive computer tool for inspectors and others to use to strengthen their knowledge of HACCP requirements.

FSIS is not consistently identifying repetitive violations, according to our review of 1,180 noncompliance records for fiscal year 2001. This has occurred in part because FSIS has not established specific, uniform, and clearly defined criteria for its inspectors to use in determining when a violation is repetitive. Furthermore, at the district level, FSIS officials' understanding of the criteria to consider in determining if a violation is repetitive varied. Also, in several instances, inspectors have not fully documented the basis for their decisions about repetitive violations on noncompliance records. Identifying repetitive violations, and maintaining accurate documentation on those decisions, is critical in deciding whether a HACCP plan is flawed and/or an enforcement action is needed. Moreover, we found that FSIS's inspection database did not provide summary information on repetitive violations, which could help FSIS's managers oversee inspectors' performance and plants' compliance with HACCP requirements. Summary information should also help FSIS identify common problems that may be better addressed by advising the industry to take corrective actions instead of plant-by-plant enforcement. FSIS officials agreed on the need for consistent criteria for identifying repetitive violations and expect to issue a directive with those criteria by the end of the calendar year. FSIS told us it has begun testing software that will allow its managers to extract summary data from the inspection database to help them better identify repetitive violations.

Finally, FSIS is not ensuring that plants take prompt and effective action to return to compliance after a HACCP violation has been identified. For example, FSIS has not consistently ensured that the actions that plants have taken were effective in eliminating repetitive violations, particularly those relating to "zero tolerance" for visible feces. Although plants are required to take corrective action each time a violation is cited, the number of repetitive violations in various plants—109 in one plant alone—shows that FSIS has not ensured that recurring violations were eliminated. FSIS also has not ensured that plants have taken immediate action, as required under HACCP rules, to meet the *Salmonella* performance standard. At the plants that failed two consecutive sets of tests for *Salmonella*, an average of 20 months elapsed from the date of the failure of the first set until the plants completed and passed a third set. Finally, when FSIS suspended inspections at a plant, it generally placed those suspensions in abeyance—often on the same day. This allowed the plants to operate while they took corrective actions. According to FSIS guidance, suspensions should not be held in abeyance for more than 90 days. However, nearly all the plants that were suspended in the three FSIS districts we examined had their suspensions placed in abeyance and were allowed to remain in abeyance for an average of 10 months, during which time they continued to operate. Moreover, we were generally unable to verify the time frames in which plants were expected to complete corrective actions or the actual time elapsed before the corrective actions were completed because the enforcement case files did not contain this information. The longer that FSIS allows plants to remain out of compliance with regulatory requirements, the greater the risk that unsafe food will be produced and marketed.

We are making several recommendations to the Secretary of Agriculture to ensure that (1) FSIS inspectors better ensure that plants' HACCP plans fully meet regulatory requirements, (2) FSIS inspectors and district officials have consistent criteria for identifying repetitive violations, and (3) plants act promptly and effectively to correct violations. In commenting on a draft of this report, USDA agreed with our recommendations but believes the report does not fully acknowledge FSIS's progress and efforts to ensure that all plants meet regulatory requirements. USDA described a number of actions that FSIS has recently taken or is planning to take that are consistent with our recommendations. We believe that our report reflects the status of FSIS's ongoing and planned actions. If fully carried out and given diligent management attention, these actions could go a long way toward addressing the problems we found in FSIS's oversight and enforcement of HACCP in U.S. meat and poultry plants and reducing consumers' risk of foodborne illnesses. . . .

Conclusions

Meat and poultry plants have many incentives to operate safely and certainly many appear to be doing so under HACCP. Nevertheless, FSIS's oversight and enforcement needs to be improved to ensure that it is achieving its intended food safety objectives. FSIS inspectors are currently not consistently identifying and documenting violations of HACCP regulatory requirements, and FSIS has not assessed the scientific soundness of all HACCP plans in a timely manner. Moreover, some FSIS inspectors still do not have a clear understanding of their roles, and FSIS managers have not been diligent in overseeing inspectors' activities. Finally, until consumer safety officers complete their assessments, some plants may be operating with unsound HACCP plans. These weaknesses limit the effectiveness of the HACCP system in reducing the risks posed by pathogens and contaminants on meat and poultry.

With regard to identifying repetitive violations—signs that a plant may be struggling to fully meet HACCP requirements—FSIS's inspectors and managers are confused about the factors that should be considered. Until FSIS establishes clear, consistent criteria for determining and documenting repetitive violations—and ensures that its inspectors and managers understand these criteria—serious problems may go unrecognized. The extraction of summary information on repetitive violations from FSIS's inspection database would help determine, among other things, when repetitive violations might indicate problems common to an industry sector or an FSIS district.

Finally, the longer that FSIS allows plants to remain out of compliance with HACCP requirements, the greater the risk that unsafe food will be produced. When plants do not take actions that promptly and successfully prevent repetitive violations—such as multiple recurring violations of the zero tolerance standard for visible fecal contamination—FSIS managers and officials must take enforcement actions to compel plants to revise their HACCP plans to address these problems. The system that FSIS has in place to address plants that fail *Salmonella* performance standards—allowing plants to operate while increased food safety risks persist for months and months—needs to be reexamined. Similarly, FSIS's practice of placing a plant in suspension but then immediately putting the suspension in abeyance for protracted periods of time negates an important incentive for plants to quickly correct problems. While some corrective actions could take a significant period of time to implement—and placing a suspension in abeyance might be warranted when FSIS is sure that interim actions will provide for food safety—the circumstances should be clearly established and progress closely monitored and documented to ensure that plants are returning to compliance as soon as possible.

Recommendations for Executive Action

To ensure that all HACCP plans fully meet regulatory requirements, we recommend that the Secretary of Agriculture direct FSIS to:

- provide inspectors with additional training on their roles and responsibilities under the HACCP system and use data, such as the results from the food safety system correlation reviews, to help target training to address specific weaknesses;
- develop procedures for its field supervisors and district managers to use to monitor inspector activities, including, among other things, ensuring that FSIS inspectors are consistently applying HACCP requirements;
- develop a risk-based strategy and time frames for consumer safety officers to complete their reviews of HACCP plans at all plants; and:
- develop a strategy for its supervisors, managers, and officials to systematically use data, including annual data on noncompliance records by districts, to help oversee plants' compliance with HACCP requirements.

To ensure that FSIS inspectors and district officials use consistent criteria for identifying repetitive violations of HACCP regulatory requirements, we recommend that the Secretary of Agriculture direct FSIS to:

- establish specific, uniform criteria for identifying repetitive violations;
- ensure that inspectors consistently document repetitive violations;
- modify data management systems to capture the extent to which inspectors are identifying repetitive violations at plants; and:
- develop a strategy for its supervisors, managers, and officials to systemically use available data, including summary information, to help identify repetitive violations.

To ensure that plants take prompt actions to correct violations, we recommend that the Secretary of Agriculture direct FSIS to:

- establish clear, consistent criteria for inspectors to use when considering whether to recommend suspension because of repetitive violations;
- require its inspectors to document the basis for their decision on whether or not to recommend further enforcement action based upon documented repetitive violations;
- develop guidance with specific time frames for actions to be taken at plants that fail a second set of *Salmonella* tests, including time frames for FSIS to initiate an in-depth verification review, report the results of the review, and initiate a third set of tests;
- establish, and document in enforcement case files, time frames for plants with suspensions in abeyance to implement and verify the necessary corrective actions; and:
- document in the enforcement case file how and when the district office determined that the plant had completed its corrective actions and, if the suspension is allowed to remain in abeyance for more than 90 days, the reason for the extension. . . .

September

UN SUMMIT DECLARATION ON WORLD DEVELOPMENT
September 4, 2002

A United Nations–sponsored summit sought to couple the goals of protecting the environment and ending poverty worldwide through increased economic development. The World Summit on Sustainable Development, held in Johannesburg, South Africa, from August 26 through September 4, 2002, issued an ambitious—but in many cases vaguely worded—program for improving the lives of the world's poor majority while minimizing further damage to the Earth's environment.

Unlike many similar conferences held by the UN, the summit's final declarations, issued September 4, included few specific promises. This was largely because the United States opposed international mandates for actions by individual governments and favored, instead, voluntary "partnerships" among governments, businesses, and private organizations.

The Johannesburg summit was the third major international conference in thirty years to deal with questions of development and the environment. The first, the UN Conference on the Human Environment, was held in Stockholm in 1972, just as environmental concerns were rising to the forefront in the United States and Western Europe. That conference drew attention to the importance of protecting the environment on a global scale and resulted in the creation of the UN's Environment Program, headquartered in Nairobi, Kenya. Subsequent research sponsored by the UN program and nongovernmental agencies led to the concept of "sustainable development," defined in a landmark 1987 report as "development that meets the needs of the present without compromising the ability of future generations to meet their own needs."

A second UN Conference on Environment and Development, held in Rio de Janeiro in 1992, was known as the "Earth Summit." It produced a series of agreements and treaties, including the Framework Convention on Climate Change. That treaty set voluntary guidelines by which industrialized nations promised to reduce their emissions of "greenhouse gases"—said by most scientists to be responsible for a rise in global temperatures since the beginning of the industrial revolution. Five years later most nations agreed, in the Kyoto Protocol, to strengthen the Framework Convention by imposing mandatory limits on greenhouse gas emissions. The United States ratified the Framework Convention but President George W. Bush in 2001 rejected the Kyoto Protocol as a threat to U.S. economic growth. (Global warming, p. 298; Rio summit, Historic Documents of 1992, p. 499)

Global Environment Report

Another significant development in international environmental policy in 1997 was the release of the UN Environment Program's first global assessment of the state of the Earth's natural resources. Called the Global Environment Outlook, the report focused on how poverty contributed to environmental degradation, for example by forcing millions of people in rural areas to chop down trees for fuel (leading to deforestation) and to plow up fragile soils (leading to desertification). A second report in 1999 addressed how "excessive consumption," especially in wealthy nations, contributed to stress on the environment.

The UN program issued its third Global Environment Outlook report on May 22, just as diplomats were beginning the final stage of negotiations over proposed language to be submitted to the upcoming conference in Johannesburg. Rather than focusing on a specific topic, such as poverty, this 392-page report provided a broad overview of what had happened to the environment since the 1972 Stockholm summit.

In general, the report painted a gloomy picture of the state of the Earth's land, water, and air resources. Despite increased attention paid around the world to environmental concerns, the global environment "continues to deteriorate," the report said. For example, the report estimated that 15 percent of the world's land—an area equal to Canada and the United States combined—had been degraded (and had therefore become less productive) as a result of human activities such as deforestation, overgrazing, and excessive use of fertilizers; more than one-half of the world's rivers were so seriously polluted that they endangered the lives of the people who depended on them; and air pollution damaged the health of millions of people in the "megacities" of the developing world, including Beijing, Calcutta, Mexico City, and others.

Substantial progress had been made since the 1972 Stockholm summit, the report said, particularly with the adoption by most industrialized countries of environmental regulations that curbed air and water pollution. The setting aside of protected areas, in national parks and preserves, also had preserved millions of square miles of land for future generations. Developing countries could adopt the same regulations and still achieve economic progress, the report said.

The impact of past environmental degradation would continue to be felt in coming decades no matter what kinds of policies world leaders adopted, the report said: "Much of the environmental change that will occur over the next thirty years has already been set in motion by past and current actions." As an example, more than 20 million acres of land (much of it in Africa) had been "extremely degraded" and were beyond restoration.

Even so, the report said, policies adopted in the coming decades would have future impacts on the environment, many of which might not be apparent "until long afterwards." The report did not advocate specific environmental policies but offered a series of general options, all of them based on what the authors called "a balanced approach towards sustainable development." In practical terms, the report said, "this means bringing the environment in from the margins to the heart of development."

Pressure on the United States

In the months leading up to the Johannesburg summit most attention was focused on the role of the United States, the world's single greatest economic and military power and—under President George W. Bush since 2001—a reluctant participant in UN forums that sought to impose limits on Washington's freedom of action. An important symbolic question about U.S. participation was whether Bush would attend. Bush's father, then president George H. Bush (1989–1993), had waited until the last minute to decide to attend the 1992 Rio summit; his ambivalence was widely interpreted at the time as a statement that the United States attached little importance to the summit. In 2002 administration officials made it clear well in advance that George W. Bush was unlikely to attend the Johannesburg summit.

Of greater substance was the question of whether any declarations issued by the summit would contain specific promises by the nations of the world. Such promises were known in diplomatic language as "goals and timetables." World leaders in 2000 had issued what was perhaps the most ambitious series of goals and timetables in recent history: a Millennium Declaration that called for numerous steps to reduce by half the number of people living in poverty by 2015. (Millennium Declaration, Historic Documents of 2000, p. 700)

In both public statements and private negotiations, U.S. officials made it clear that they intended to oppose specific goals and timetables at the Johannesburg summit because such promises amounted to little more than "rhetoric" that misled the world's poor people into thinking help was on the way. Officials said Washington would especially oppose any declarations at the summit that would run counter to Bush's policies, such as his rejection of the Kyoto Protocol. Representatives of most other countries took the opposite view. "We see the mistrust and disbelief in many developing countries," *Margot Wallstrom, the European Union's environment commissioner told the* New York Times. *"Targets and timetables are the only way to regain some credibility, to move from words to deeds."*

Three days after the Johannesburg summit got under way, the Bush administration's delegation made public proposals intended to portray the United States as offering "concrete action" rather than promises. Delegation leader Paula Dobriansky, the undersecretary of state for global affairs, announced a series of "partnerships" between the United States, industries, foundations, and other countries. Examples included a $15 million U.S. donation to a partnership, with an unidentified U.S. sponsor and a South African bank, to build 90,000 homes in South Africa; a "Congo Basin Forest

Partnership" that would promote the development of national parks and other protected areas in central Africa's vast but threatened forest lands; and $970 million for projects to improve access to clean water in developing countries in Africa and other regions. Dobriansky said the partnerships indicated that the United States was "the world's leader in sustainable development."

Critics, however, noted that the administration offered few details for its partnerships, in particular how much money the U.S. government would put into them. In many cases it appeared that the administration planned to pay for these partnerships by diverting funds from previously planned foreign aid programs.

Secretary of State Colin Powell, representing Bush at the close of the summit, wound up bearing the brunt of the anger of many delegates at U.S. positions. Addressing the summit on the final day, September 4, Powell was greeted by boos and catcalls when he defended the administration's approach to global warming. The objections started among environmental activists but spread to many of the delegates. Seeking to quell cries of "shame on Bush," Powell said: "Thank you, I have now heard you. I ask that you hear me."

Maneuvering at the Summit

South African president Thabo Mbeki had launched the summit with a fiery speech calling on the world's wealthy countries to assume more responsibility for promoting economic development in the world's poorest countries. "A global human society based on poverty for many and prosperity for a few, characterized by islands of wealth, surrounded by a sea of poverty, is unsustainable," he said, in an apparent effort to define the topic of the summit.

As with most such conferences, the bulk of the action took place not in forums where speeches were made but in behind-the-scenes negotiations over arcane diplomatic language intended to establish international policy. Also in keeping with such conferences, many of the disagreements broke along what was called the "North-South" divide, the "North" being the industrialized countries of Western Europe, North America, and Japan, and the "South" being most everyone else. But that traditional distinction was no longer entirely intact, since U.S. and European delegates were at odds in Johannesburg as often as they were partners.

One of the highest profile disagreements at the summit concerned a proposal by the European Union, Brazil, and several other countries to establish a specific target for increased worldwide reliance on renewable energy sources, such as solar and wind power. The U.S. delegation adamantly opposed that goal, as did representatives of nations belonging to the Organization of Petroleum Exporting Countries.

In the end, negotiations over that issue became entwined with those dealing with a seemingly separate matter: the goal of increasing worldwide access to clean water and sanitation. Along with opposing specific language on renewable energy, the United States had opposed draft language calling for a goal of cutting in half (to 2 billion) the number of people in the world lacking access to clean water and sewage treatment. Ultimately, the U.S. delegation accepted the latter goal in exchange for a willingness by the European Union to weaken its language on renewable energy. The final text called on countries to develop "advanced, cleaner, more efficient, affordable and cost-effective energy technologies"—but without any specific commitments on how or when that should happen.

A similar issue involved the status of the Kyoto Protocol, which was supposed to have been one of the focal points of the summit. An original proposal submitted by the European Union called on all nations that had signed the treaty to take the next step of ratifying it—putting it into effect—without delay. The most obvious target of that call was the United States, which helped negotiate the treaty in 1997 and signed it but had not ratified it. Because of the way the treaty was drafted, U.S. participation was vital to achieving its overall goal of preventing a worsening of global warming. Citing Bush's withdrawal from the treaty in 2001, the U.S. delegation opposed any language that could be interpreted as pressuring the United States to change its stance. After prolonged negotiations, negotiators settled on a compromise in which those nations that already had ratified the treaty "strongly urge" other nations to follow suit "in a timely manner."

Assessments of the overall accomplishments of the Johannesburg summit generally fell along predictable lines. Dobriansky and other U.S. government delegates praised the summit declarations as presenting "realistic" approaches to enhancing economic development and protecting the environment. Representatives of environmental and antipoverty organizations said they were disappointed by the summit's use of vague proclamations rather than specific goals. "When the time came for targets, timetables, and money, they let the world down," Andrew Hewitt of Oxfam International said of the leaders represented at the summit.

Following is the summary of "key outcomes" of the World Summit on Sustainable Development, held in Johannesburg, South Africa, from August 26 to September 4, 2002. The summary was prepared by the United Nations and released September 4.

The document was obtained from the Internet at www .johannesburgsummit.org/html/documents/summit_docs/ 2009_keyoutcomes_commitments.doc; accessed October 23, 2002.

Key Outcomes of the Summit

- The Summit reaffirmed sustainable development as a central element of the international agenda and gave new impetus to global action to fight poverty and protect the environment.

- The understanding of sustainable development was broadened and strengthened as a result of the Summit, particularly the important linkages between poverty, the environment and the use of natural resources.
- Governments agreed to and reaffirmed a wide range of concrete commitments and targets for action to achieve more effective implementation of sustainable development objectives.
- Energy and sanitation issues were critical elements of the negotiations and outcomes to a greater degree than in previous international meetings on sustainable development.
- Support for the establishment of a world solidarity fund for the eradication of poverty was a positive step forward.
- Africa and NEPAD [New Program for African Development, a regional plan for economic and political reform] were identified for special attention and support by the international community to better focus efforts to address the development needs of Africa.
- The views of civil society were given prominence at the Summit in recognition of the key role of civil society in implementing the outcomes and in promoting partnership initiatives. Over 8,000 civil society participants attended the Summit, reinforced by parallel events which included major groups, such as, NGOs [nongovenmental organizations], women, indigenous people, youth, farmers, trade unions, business leaders, the scientific and technological community and local authorities as well as Chief Justices from various countries.
- The concept of partnerships between governments, business and civil society was given a large boost by the Summit and the Plan of Implementation. Over 220 partnerships (with $235 million in resources) were identified in advance of the Summit and around 60 partnerships were announced during the Summit by a variety of countries.

Key Commitments, Targets and Timetables from the Johannesburg Plan of Implementation

Poverty Eradication

Halve, by the year 2015, the proportion of the world's people whose income is less than $1 a day and the proportion of people who suffer from hunger.

By 2020, achieve a significant improvement in the lives of at least 100 million slum dwellers, as proposed in the "Cities without slums" initiative.

Establish a world solidarity fund to eradicate poverty and to promote social and human development in the developing countries.

Water and Sanitation

Halve, by the year 2015, the proportion of people without access to safe drinking water.

Halve, by the year 2015, the proportion of people who do not have access to basic sanitation.

Sustainable Production and Consumption

Encourage and promote the development of a 10-year framework of programmes to accelerate the shift towards sustainable consumption and production.

Energy

Renewable energy

Diversify energy supply and substantially increase the global share of renewable energy sources in order to increase its contribution to total energy supply.

Access to energy

Improve access to reliable, affordable, economically viable, socially acceptable and environmentally sound energy services and resources, sufficient to achieve the Millenium Development Goals, including the goal of halving the proportion of people in poverty by 2015.

Energy markets

Remove market distortions including the restructuring of taxes and the phasing out of harmful subsidies.

Support efforts to improve the functioning, transparency and information about energy markets with respect to both supply and demand, with the aim of achieving greater stability and to ensure consumer access to energy services.

Energy efficiency

Establish domestic programmes for energy efficiency with the support of the international community. Accelerate the development and dissemination of energy efficiency and energy conservation technologies, including the promotion of research and development.

Chemicals

Aim, by 2020, to use and produce chemicals in ways that do not lead to significant adverse effects on human health and the environment.

Renew the commitment to the sound management of chemicals and of hazardous wastes throughout their life cycle.

Promote the ratification and implementation of relevant international instruments on chemicals and hazardous waste, including the Rotterdam Convention so that it can enter into force by 2003 and the Stockholm Convention so that it can enter into force by 2004.

Further develop a strategic approach to international chemicals management, based on the Bahia Declaration and Priorities for Action beyond 2000, by 2005.

Encourage countries to implement the new globally harmonized system for the classification and labeling of chemicals as soon as possible, with a view to having the system fully operational by 2008.

Management of the natural resource base

Water

Develop integrated water resources management and water efficiency plans by 2005.

Oceans and fisheries

Encourage the application by 2010 of the ecosystem approach for the sustainable development of the oceans.

On an urgent basis and where possible by 2015, maintain or restore depleted fish stocks to levels that can produce the maximum sustainable yield.

Put into effect the FAO [UN Food and Agriculture Organization] international plans of action by the agreed dates:

- for the management of fishing capacity by 2005; and
- to prevent, deter and eliminate illegal, unreported and unregulated fishing by 2004.

Develop and facilitate the use of diverse approaches and tools, including the ecosystem approach, the elimination of destructive fishing practices, the establishment of marine protected areas consistent with international law and based on scientific information, including representative networks by 2012.

Establish by 2004 a regular process under the United Nations for global reporting and assessment of the state of the marine environment.

Eliminate subsidies that contribute to illegal, unreported and unregulated fishing and to over-capacity.

Atmosphere

Facilitate implementation of the Montreal Protocol on Substances that Deplete the Ozone Layer by ensuring adequate replenishment of its fund by 2003/2005.

Improve access by developing countries to alternatives to ozone-depleting substances by 2010, and assist them in complying with the phase-out schedule under the Montreal Protocol.

Biodiversity

Achieve by 2010 a significant reduction in the current rate of loss of biological diversity.

Forests

Accelerate implementation of the IPF/IFF [Intergovernmental Panel on Forests and Intergovernmental Forum on Forests] proposals for action by countries and by the Collaborative Partnership on Forests, and intensify efforts on reporting to the United Nations Forum on Forests, to contribute to an assessment of progress in 2005.

Corporate responsibility

Actively promote corporate responsibility and accountability, including through the full development and effective implementation of intergovernmental agreements and measures, international initiatives and public-private partnerships, and appropriate national regulations.

Health

Enhance health education with the objective of achieving improved health literacy on a global basis by 2010.

Reduce, by 2015, mortality rates for infants and children under 5 by two thirds, and maternal mortality rates by three quarters, of the prevailing rate in 2000.

Reduce HIV prevalence among young men and women aged 15–24 by 25 per cent in the most affected countries by 2005 and globally by 2010, as well as combat malaria, tuberculosis and other diseases.

Sustainable development of small island developing States

Undertake initiatives by 2004 aimed at implementing the Global Programme of Action for the Protection of the Marine Environment from Land-based Activities to reduce, prevent and control waste and pollution and their health-related impacts.

Develop community-based initiatives on sustainable tourism by 2004.

Support the availability of adequate, affordable and environmentally sound energy services for the sustainable development of small island developing States, including through strengthening efforts on energy supply and services by 2004.

Review implementation of the Barbados Programme of Action for the Sustainable Development of Small Island Developing States in 2004.

Sustainable development for Africa

Improve sustainable agricultural productivity and food security in accordance with the Millennium Development Goals, in particular to halve by 2015 the proportion of people who suffer from hunger.

Support African countries in developing and implementing food security strategies by 2005.

Support Africa's efforts to implement NEPAD objectives on energy, which seek to secure access for at least 35 per cent of the African population within 20 years, especially in rural areas.

Means of implementation

Ensure that, by 2015, all children will be able to complete a full course of primary schooling and that girls and boys will have equal access to all levels of education relevant to national needs.

Eliminate gender disparity in primary and secondary education by 2005.

Recommend to the UN General Assembly that it consider adopting a decade of education for sustainable development, starting in 2005.

Institutional Framework for sustainable development

Adopt new measures to strengthen institutional arrangements for sustainable development at international, regional and national levels.

Enhance the role of the Commission on Sustainable Development, including through reviewing and monitoring progress in the implementation of Agenda 21 [the declaration of the 1992 Earth Summit] and fostering coherence of implementation, initiatives and partnerships.

Facilitate and promote the integration of the environmental, social and economic dimensions of sustainable development into the work programs UN regional commissions.

Establish an effective, transparent and regular inter-agency coordination mechanism on ocean and coastal issues within the United Nations system.

Take immediate steps to make progress in the formulation and elaboration of national strategies for sustainable development and begin their implementation by 2005.

Key Initiatives and Announcements from the Johannesburg Summit

Water & Sanitation

- The United States announced $970 million in investments over the next three years on water and sanitation projects.
- The European Union announced the "Water for Life" initiative that seeks to engage partners to meet goals for water and sanitation, primarily in Africa and Central Asia.
- The Asia Development Bank provided a $5 million grant to UN Habitat and $500 million in fast-track credit for the Water for Asian Cities Programme.
- The UN has received 21 other water and sanitation initiatives with at least $20 million in extra resources.

Energy

- The nine major electricity companies of the E7 [group of seven Western European countries] signed a range of agreements with the UN to facilitate technical cooperation for sustainable energy projects in developing countries.
- The European Union announced a $700 million partnership initiative on energy and the United States announced that it would invest up to $43 million in 2003.
- DESA, UNEP and the US EPA announced a partnership on Cleaner Fuels and Vehicles with broad support from confirmed partners from the private sector, the NGO community, developed and developing countries.
- The South African energy utility Eskom announced a partnership to extend modern energy services to neighboring countries.

- The United Nations Environment Programme launched a new initiative called the Global Network on Energy for Sustainable Development to promote the research, transfer and deployment of green and cleaner energy technologies to the developing world
- The UN has received 32 partnership submissions for energy projects with at least $26 million in resources.

Health

- The United States announced a commitment to spend $2.3 billion through 2003 on health, some of which was earmarked earlier for the Global Fund.
- The UN has received 16 partnership submissions for health projects with $3 million in resources.

Agriculture

- The United States will invest $90 million in 2003 for sustainable agriculture programmes.
- The UN has received 17 partnership submissions with at least $2 million in additional resources.

Biodiversity and Ecosystem Management

- Canada and Russia announced they intended to ratify the Kyoto protocol
- The United States announced $53 million for forests in 2002–2005.
- The UN has received 32 partnership initiatives with $100 million in resources.

Cross-Cutting Issues

- Agreement to the replenishment of the Global Environment Facility, with a total of $3 billion ($2.92 billion announced pre-Summit and $80 million added by EU in Johannesburg).
- Norway pledged an additional $50 million towards following up the Johannesburg commitments
- The United Kingdom announced it was doubling its assistance to Africa to £1 billion a year and raising its overall assistance for all countries by 50 per cent
- The EU announced that it will increase its development assistance with more than 22 billion euros in the years to 2006 and by more than 9 billion euros annually from 2006 onwards
- Germany announced a contribution of 500 million euros over the next five years to promote cooperation on renewable energy
- Canada announced that, as of 1 January 2003, it will eliminate tariffs and quotas on almost all products from the least developed countries, and that by 2010, it would double development assistance.
- Japan announced that it will provide at least 250 billion yen in education assistance over a five-year period and that it would extend emergency

food aid amounting to $30 million dollars to save children in southern Africa from famine

- Japan also announced it would provide cooperation in environment-related capacity building by training 5,000 people from overseas over a five-year period
- Ireland announced that it has allocated almost 8 million euros in emergency funding in response to the humanitarian needs of the African region

UN SECRETARY GENERAL ON
WORLD CRIMINAL COURT
September 10, 2002

A full half-century after it was first proposed, an international court to try cases of genocide and war crimes became official in 2002 and was expected to be in business by early 2003. But the sense of accomplishment on the part of the court's advocates was undermined by the adamant refusal of the United States to participate in its work. The administration of President George W. Bush also antagonized many U.S. allies by pressuring other countries to exempt Americans from the court's jurisdiction.

The International Criminal Court (ICC) was an outgrowth of a movement following World War II to fashion laws and procedures that might prevent a recurrence of the Holocaust—Nazi Germany's extermination of some 6 million Jews, gypsies, and other minorities. The United Nations General Assembly in 1948 adopted a treaty creating the crime of genocide, a legal concept that did not even exist prior to the war. The United States ratified that treaty in 1986, becoming one of the last major countries to do so. (Genocide treaty, Historic Documents of 1986, p. 115)

Also in 1948 the General Assembly initiated a study of whether the UN should create an "international judicial organ" to try cases of genocide and other war crimes. That study led to draft proposals for an international criminal court in 1951 and 1953 but the idea was put on hold, in part because of the difficulty of defining "aggression," at that time one of the proposed war crimes. The outbreak in 1992 of war in the former Yugoslavia, which featured horrific mass killings among three ethnic groups, prompted the UN to take another look at the proposal for an international court. Several years of study by various committees resulted in agreement, at a conference in Rome during June and July 1998, on the text of a treaty establishing such a court.

One hundred twenty countries signed the treaty when it was opened for signature in 1998, and by April 11, 2002, more than sixty countries—the minimum number required for it to go into effect on July 1—had ratified the treaty. Speaking at a September 10 ceremony marking the first official meeting of the countries that were party to the treaty, UN Secretary General

Kofi Annan hailed the new court as a place "where formerly untouchable perpetrators, regardless of their rank or status, can be held accountable for their crimes." Addressing U.S. concerns, Annan said the court "is not, and must never become, an organ for political witch hunting."

The International Criminal Court was to be seated at The Hague, the Netherlands, where the UN-sponsored International Court of Justice, generally known as the World Court, also was headquartered. The main difference between the two was that the new criminal court had jurisdiction in cases involving just three types of crimes: genocide, war crimes, and crimes against humanity. The criminal court was to have eighteen judges chosen by participating countries and a staff headed by a chief prosecutor. The World Court basically dealt with civil matters, such as disputes between countries over boundaries and fishing rights or disputes between multinational corporations. Both courts officially were independent of the United Nations and financed their operations through direct assessments of countries that participated in them.

U.S. Objections

Although it was a chief sponsor of the United Nations in 1945 and hosted its headquarters in New York City, the United States often had an uncomfortable relationship with the world body and the proposals, including treaties, that it initiated. From the UN's earliest days, some conservatives in the United States viewed it as a step toward "world government" that would undermine American sovereignty and democracy. U.S. political concerns were reinforced starting in the 1960s when many of the newly independent countries in Africa and Asia sided with the Soviet Union in votes on contentious cold war issues at the UN General Assembly. American resistance to the UN was manifested in several ways, including Congress's chronic refusal to pay some U.S. dues on time, and the languishing in the Senate for nearly four decades of the genocide treaty.

It came as no surprise, therefore, that the United States would have concerns when the UN's idea of an international criminal court resurfaced in the mid-1990s. The chief U.S. concern, expressed primarily by the Pentagon, was that U.S. soldiers, diplomats, and intelligence officials stationed overseas might be targeted for prosecution by the court. As the world's dominant military and economic power after the cold war, the United States offered an inviting target for nations or groups upset with the prevailing situation in the world. U.S. soldiers and government officials, it was feared, could face prosecution simply because they were symbols of Washington's might.

A related issue arose in the late 1990s when a Spanish prosecutor attempted, unsuccessfully, to haul former Chilean dictator Augusto Pinochet into court for the murder of civilians by his regime after he seized power in a military coup in 1973. Many Pinochet opponents had long insisted that the United States had fomented or at least supported the coup, and they put principal blame on Henry A. Kissinger, the secretary of state at the time. Even the remotest possibility that Kissinger or some other high level official—present or past—might be prosecuted for U.S. foreign policy deci-sions caused extreme anxiety in Washington.

The Clinton administration cited these concerns in 1998 when the treaty creating the International Criminal Court was completed. President Bill Clinton (1993–2001) withheld U.S. approval of the treaty until the last day it was open for signature, December 31, 2000, when he authorized a State Department diplomat to sign it. That date also was just three weeks before Clinton was due to leave office. Clinton did not send the treaty to the Senate, and he issued a statement saying he had agreed to sign it so his successor, George W. Bush, would have the option of deciding whether to pursue it.

Bush already had gone on record as opposing the treaty, and there never was any doubt that his administration would not send it to the Senate for action. On May 6, 2002, as the treaty was about to go into effect, the State Department sent a formal notice to the United Nations that the United States "does not intend to become a party" to the treaty. To reinforce the point, the letter said the United States had no legal obligations under the treaty as a consequence of the Clinton administration's signature, a step that amounted to withdrawal of the signature.

The United States was one of the few countries in the West to oppose the court, but it was not the only major country to take that position. China, In-dia, Indonesia, Iraq, Pakistan, and Turkey also had refused to sign the treaty establishing the court, and the list of countries that had signed the treaty but not ratified it as of 2002 included Egypt, Iran, Israel, Jordan, the Philip-pines, Russia, and Syria.

U.S.-Europe Conflict over Peacekeepers

Laying the groundwork for an assault on the criminal court, the Bush ad-ministration early in 2002 raised complaints about two similar tribunals the United Nations had established in the 1990s to deal with war crimes committed in the former Yugoslavia during the early 1990s and in Rwanda during the 1994 genocide. Both tribunals had moved slowly and had been criticized on various procedural grounds. The Bush administration added new pressure with a call in March for the tribunals to finish their work by the 2007–2008 session. Testifying before a House committee on March 1, Pierre-Richard Prosper, the State Department's ambassador for war crimes issues, also questioned the integrity of the tribunals, saying that "the pro-fessionalism of some [tribunal] personnel has been called into question, with allegations of mismanagement and abuse." UN officials rejected Pros-per's charges. (Yugoslav tribunal, Historic Documents of 2001, p. 826)

The new international court, Prosper said, "lacks the essential safe-guards to avoid a politicization of justice." Specifically, he said the admin-istration viewed as "insufficient" such procedures established by the treaty as a requirement that cases be submitted to a pretrial review panel. Voicing the concerns of the military, Defense Secretary Donald H. Rumsfeld said on May 6 that he feared that "renegade" prosecutors would go after U.S. ser-vicemen—a potential he said "could well create a powerful disincentive for U.S. military engagement in the world."

The Bush administration took its objections beyond the rhetorical stage on June 18. At a UN Security Council session, a State Department official warned that the United States would withdraw from international peacekeeping missions in the former Yugoslavia and other regions unless U.S. soldiers and other personnel were granted immunity from potential prosecution by the International Criminal Court. "There should be no misunderstanding that if there is not adequate protection for U.S. peacekeepers, there will be no U.S. peacekeepers," said Richard S. Williams, a U.S. representative to the UN. (Bosnia peacekeepers, Historic Documents of 2000, p. 161)

The administration took its stance less than two weeks before the treaty establishing the court went into effect and just as a UN mandate for a NATO-led peacekeeping mission in Bosnia was about to expire. The U.S. move set off an acrimonious dispute at the UN, in which even close U.S. allies criticized Washington for demanding special status. In an impassioned speech on July 10, Canadian ambassador Paul Heinbecker recited the list of state-sponsored genocides and mass killings during the twentieth century and said: "Surely, we have all learned the fundamental lesson of this bloodiest of centuries, which is that impunity from prosecution for grievous crimes must end."

That dispute at the UN finally was settled on July 13 when the Security Council voted to exempt U.S. members of peacekeeping forces from prosecution by the new court for one year. Despite the compromise, U.S. ambassador John Negroponte said the Bush administration was not prepared to back down from its opposition to the court and warned of "serious consequences" if the court tried to prosecute a U.S. citizen. "No nations should underestimate our commitment to protect our citizens," he said. President Bush kept up the theme with a speech on July 19 to U.S. soldiers who had just returned from duty in Afghanistan: "The United States cooperates with many other nations to keep the peace," he said. "But we will not submit American troops to prosecutors and judges whose jurisdiction we do not accept." The administration was not acting entirely on its own; Congress had passed legislation—the American Service Members Protection Act— that authorized the president to take "all means necessary and appropriate" to gain the release of any U.S. citizens detained by the court.

At the same time it was taking this tough line at the UN, the Bush administration launched another offensive by pressing individual nations to pledge never to extradite U.S. citizens or officials to the court. The administration won rapid agreement from Israel, one of the closest U.S. allies, and then turned its attention to other countries susceptible to persuasion, including recipients of U.S. aid and several eastern European countries whose applications for membership in the NATO alliance were pending. (NATO expansion, p. 885)

Romania, one of the NATO applicants, quickly agreed to the U.S. request— creating a new rift between the United States and the European Union (EU), which had been one of the staunchest advocates of the criminal court. Romania had also applied for membership in the EU, and its acquiescence to Washington brought a sharp reprimand from the EU's leadership in Brussels. Other eastern European nations thus found themselves in a difficult dilemma: refusing Washington's demand might jeopardize membership in NATO, which was highly prized for its political and security value, but accepting that demand might jeopardize membership in the European Union, which offered potential for stronger economic growth. (EU expansion, p. 679)

Secretary of State Colin Powell stepped up the pressure on these nations on August 19, sending them letters urging them to agree to the U.S. request "as soon as possible." U.S. diplomats also expressly told the NATO-applicant nations that the Senate might not approve their membership in the alliance unless they had agreed to exempt American personnel from jurisdiction of the criminal court, the New York Times *reported on August 31. In addition to frightening the eastern European nations, this posture further angered several European nations that had strongly supported the court, including Belgium, France, German, and Sweden.*

Signs of a possible compromise emerged in mid-September, just as the United States and its key allies were beginning negotiations at the UN over an even more contentious issue: Bush's demand for a Security Council ultimatum against Iraq. Diplomats on both sides of the Atlantic said they feared the criminal court dispute could jeopardize a unified position on forcing Iraq to give up its illegal biological, chemical, and nuclear weapons. (Iraq issue, p. 713)

Under heavy lobbying by Britain, Italy, and Spain, the EU on September 30 agreed to a position that gave the United States most of what it wanted. In effect, the fifteen current EU nations agreed among themselves not to extradite U.S. soldiers or officials to the international court, in exchange for a guarantee by Washington that any Americans suspected of war crimes would be prosecuted in the United States. The EU said each member nation was responsible for reaching a direct agreement with the United States on this question—a position that gave the eastern European nations freedom to sign such a deal if they chose. Some EU members said they had no need to sign an agreement; Germany, for example, said it already had agreements protecting the 70,000 U.S. troops stationed there.

EU officials insisted the September 30 deal would not harm the criminal court. "There is no undermining of the ICC," said Danish foreign minister Per Stig Moeller. Groups that strongly supported the new court denounced the deal, however. "Weak bilateral agreements with Washington could open the door to impunity for those accused of war crimes, crimes against humanity and genocide," said Lotte Leicht, Europe director for Human Rights Watch. "We look to every EU member state to respect their obligations to the court and reject the contracts the American side is pressing."

As of November the United States had persuaded fourteen countries to sign agreements exempting American personnel from the court's jurisdiction. They were Afghanistan, Dominican Republic, East Timor, Gambia, Honduras, Israel, Kuwait, the Marshall Islands, Mauritania, Micronesia, Palau, Romania, Tajikistan, and Uzbekistan.

Following is the text of a speech on September 10, 2002, by UN Secretary General Kofi Annan to the Assembly of States to the Rome Statute of the International Criminal Court.

The document was obtained from the Internet at www.un .org/News/Press/docs/2002/sgsm8372.doc.htm; accessed February 6, 2003.

Mr. President,

Let me first congratulate you [Prince Zeid al-Hussein of Jordan] on your election as President of the first session of the Assembly of States Parties to the Rome Statute of the International Criminal Court. I would also want to thank you for the nice words you said about me, about the Legal Office and the Secretariat and the support we have given you. I know that Mr. Corell [UN Undersecretary General for Legal Affairs Hans Corell] and the Codification Division and the entire United Nations legal team have been working very hard to make sure that the Court comes into being. You can count on my full support as you carry out your formidable responsibilities.

Martin Luther King, Jr. once said: "We shall have to repent in this generation, not so much for the evil deeds of the wicked people, but for the appalling silence of the good people."

In adopting the Rome Statute of the International Criminal Court, which entered into force on 1 July, good people spoke up—on behalf of the innocent victims of horrendous crimes, and in the name of international law. An idea that arose in the aftermath of the Holocaust and other atrocities committed during the Second World War has finally come to fruition.

In 1948, the adoption of the Universal Declaration of Human Rights and the Genocide Convention signified the beginning of a new era in the struggle for fundamental human rights and freedoms. But as the ICC takes its first steps, the quest for basic liberties has still to be won. Millions of human beings continue to be subjected to brutality of the worst sort, and denied freedoms that others take for granted. You have gathered here, in this first Assembly of States Parties, to give the ICC the operational tools which it will need to do its part to improve this sad state of affairs.

Earlier tribunals, like those of Nuremburg, Tokyo, Arusha and The Hague, were established after the fact. The ICC is different. It gives advance warning that the international community will not stand by but will be ready, immediately, if crimes within the Court's jurisdiction are committed. Indeed, by its very existence, the Court can act as a deterrent.

Countries that have established proper national criminal justice systems have nothing to fear from the Court. And those that do not yet have such a system in place can benefit from what it has to offer. But where national criminal justice systems are unwilling or unable to investigate or prosecute, the ICC will step in.

Your responsibility is to ensure that the Court begins life on secure footing. That means giving it a strong financial backing. And it means that the judges, Prosecutor and other high officials must meet the highest standards of legal rigour, human sensitivity and professional probity. States must take special care to nominate and elect to these key positions individuals who have a wealth of experience and the qualities and qualifications needed to dispense international justice fairly and with wisdom.

Above all, the independence, impartiality and the integrity of the Court must be preserved. The ICC is not—and must never become—an organ for political witch hunting. Rather, it must serve as a bastion against tyranny and lawlessness, and as a building block in the global architecture of collective security.

The Rome Statute provides a strong foundation for this work. It contains safeguards and checks and balances to ensure that justice is done and is seen to be done. And it sets out high standards of human rights, fairness and due process.

The growing number of parties to the Rome Statute is very encouraging. I urge other States to follow your example. I would like to express my great appreciation to the civil society groups and others whose advocacy has helped bring us to this day. And I would like to express the hope that non-States Parties—including those that have signed the Statute but not yet ratified it—will give the Court the support it needs to succeed.

These are daunting times for humankind. But at long last, the world has this missing link for the advancement of peace, this new institution with which to battle impunity, this court of law where formerly untouchable perpetrators, regardless of their rank or status, can be held accountable for their crimes.

The drive for justice has been an integral part of the quest for international peace. As the Court now takes up its formidable responsibilities, the United Nations looks forward to working in partnership with you in that pursuit.

PRESIDENT BUSH ON
CONFRONTING IRAQ
September 12, 2002

The Bush administration in 2002 mounted a sustained offensive to bring new international pressure against the regime of Iraqi leader Saddam Hussein, culminating in a drive at the United Nations to force Saddam to comply with numerous Security Council resolutions enacted since the 1991 Persian Gulf war. By year's end UN weapons inspectors were back in Iraq for the first time in four years, searching for biological, chemical, and possibly nuclear weapons the country had kept hidden for the previous decade.

President George W. Bush launched the campaign during his January 29 State of the Union address, in which he said Iraq, along with Iran and North Korea, constituted an "axis of evil" that posed a danger to worldwide peace and security. Bush and his aides kept up the pressure throughout the year with rhetorical blasts as well as with action, including military maneuvers that appeared to signal U.S. readiness for a war to oust Saddam from power. The administration also drafted a broad new "national security strategy" that advocated preemptive action against potential threats to U.S. interests; officials said a war against Iraq would be an example of a preemptive strike because that country might pass its weapons of mass destruction on to terrorists. (State of the Union address, p. 33; national security strategy, p. 633)

The administration's assault on Iraq met with a mixed reaction internationally. Some U.S. allies, notably Britain, readily agreed that Iraq posed an urgent danger. However, the leaders of many other countries, including most key European allies, said they did not understand Bush's sense of urgency. In the United States some members of Congress and foreign policy analysts expressed concern that a focus on Iraq could divert attention from the unfinished business of battling terrorists, including the al Qaeda network that was responsible for the September 11 terrorist attacks in New York City and Washington.

Much of the year's debate about Iraq centered on whether Bush would seek broad international support or would take unilateral action to achieve his aim of "regime change"—a euphemism for ousting Saddam from power. Bush answered that question, at least for the time being, in a September 12 speech to the United Nations General Assembly, in which he said he would ask the Security Council to give Saddam a final chance to surrender his illegal weapons of mass destruction. After weeks of negotiation, the Security Council adopted a compromise resolution on November 8, and UN inspectors returned to Iraq three weeks later. Bush also convinced Congress to give him broad authority to take military action against Iraq. (UN and congressional action, p. 713)

Bush's Sense of Urgency

After its troops were pushed out of Kuwait in the 1991 Persian Gulf War, Iraq accepted UN Security Council resolutions that, among other things, required it to give up its medium-range missiles and its stocks of biological and chemical weapons and to dismantle its program to develop nuclear weapons. During the 1990s UN inspectors destroyed Iraq's missiles and its nuclear weapons program but—because of Iraqi resistance—had only limited success in destroying the country's biological and chemical weapons. Iraq forced the inspectors to leave in December 1998, and President Bill Clinton (1993–2001) launched a missile attack that destroyed some of the country's weapons complex. (End of inspections, Historic Documents of 1998, p. 934)

After the inspectors left the outside world had no reliable information about the status of Iraq's weapons arsenal, although it was generally assumed that Saddam would try to rebuild some or all the weapons the inspectors had uncovered and destroyed. U.S. officials periodically released limited intelligence information—based mostly on satellite photographs and other circumstantial evidence—indicating that Iraq had resumed work at plants that had produced chemical weapons and ballistic missiles.

In 2001 officials in the new Bush administration began talking of the need to confront Saddam, and the level of such talk grew louder after the September 11 terrorist attacks. On November 26, 2001, Bush specifically included Iraq in a denunciation of countries that supported terrorism. "If they [countries] develop weapons of mass destruction that will be used to terrorize nations, they will be held accountable," Bush said. "And as for Mr. Saddam Hussein, he needs to let inspectors back into his country, to show us that he is not developing weapons of mass destruction." (Historic Documents of 2001, p. 849)

Bush raised the stakes with his January 29, 2002, State of the Union speech declaring Iraq to be part of an "axis of evil" along with Iran and North Korea. Administration officials said Iraq posed the most urgent problem of those three nations because of its history of developing weapons of mass destruction, of using chemical weapons at least twice (against Iran during the late stages of the 1980–1988 Iran-Iraq war and against Iraq's Kurdish minority in 1998), of invading its neighbors (Iran in 1980 and Kuwait in 1990), and its defiance of the UN weapons inspectors during the 1990s.

Following Bush's speech, administration officials talked openly, and with increasing urgency, about the need for "regime change" in Iraq. Testifying before a House committee on February 7, Secretary of State Colin Powell said the United States was committed to getting rid of Saddam, even if it had to accomplish that task alone, without the support of allies. Powell and other officials noted that the call for regime change was not new because former president Clinton and Congress had both stated that replacing Saddam was a goal of U.S. policy during the late 1990s.

Bush received strong support for his position from British prime minister Tony Blair, who echoed Washington's argument that Iraq's weapons and history of using them posed a threat to the rest of the world, Britain included. After meeting with Bush in Texas on April 8, Blair called for confronting states that supported terrorism. "If necessary, the action should be military and again, if necessary and justified, it should involve regime change," he said in a clear reference to Iraq.

This kind of talk made many other world leaders nervous, including most other European leaders. French foreign minister Hubert Vedrine, a frequent, caustic critic of U.S. foreign policy, accused Bush of adopting a "simplistic" posture. One of the most frequent criticisms of the administration was that it had not explained why confronting Iraq was so urgent. Writing in the New York Times *on September 13, former secretary of state Madeleine K. Albright voiced concern that the focus on Iraq would divert the United States from its unfinished war against terrorism, specifically the al Qaeda network: "It makes little sense now to focus the world's attention and our own military, intelligence, diplomatic, and financial resources on a plan to invade Iraq instead of on al Qaeda's ongoing plans to murder innocent people. We cannot fight a second monumental struggle without detracting from the first one."*

Even as the international debate was heating up, the UN Security Council in May faced the task of renewing the economic sanctions against Iraq that had been in effect since Iraq's invasion of Kuwait in August 1990. The sanctions were coupled with an "oil for food" program, under which Iraq was allowed to sell its oil on the world market and use the proceeds to buy food, medicine, and other supplies for civilian use. The list of supplies was carefully monitored by the United Nations in an attempt to ensure that Iraq did not use its oil profits to buy weapons or "dual use" items (such as large trucks or some types of communications equipment) that could be used either for civilian or military purposes. After extensive negotiations, the Security Council on May 14 voted to renew the sanctions and the oil-for-food program for six months, but under a new procedure it intended to reduce the bureaucratic procedures that often had delayed shipments of supplies to Iraq in the past.

Going Unilateral or Multilateral

In addition to the question of the urgency to confront Iraq, the Bush administration and some U.S. allies seemed—for much of the year—to have different positions on the utility of sending UN weapons inspectors back into Iraq. Most world leaders said the return of the inspectors should be the first step in dealing with Iraq and that any military action should come only if Iraq refused to allow them back in or refused to cooperate with them.

In Washington, State Department officials echoed that call for a return of the weapons inspectors but that view did not appear to be unanimous at senior levels of the Bush administration. Defense Secretary Donald H. Rumsfeld on April 16 expressed strong reservations that any new inspections program could be "intrusive" enough to uncover Iraq's weapons. "I just can't quite picture how intrusive something would have to be that it could offset the ease with which they [the Iraqis] have previously been able to deny and deceive [the inspectors], and which today one would think they would be vastly more skillful, having had all this time without inspectors there," he said.

Vice President Dick Cheney went even further in criticizing the call for a new weapons inspection program. Addressing the Veterans of Foreign Wars convention in Nashville on August 26, Cheney said: "A return of inspectors would provide no assurance whatsoever of his [Saddam's] compliance with U.N. resolutions. On the contrary, there is a great danger that it would provide false comfort that Saddam is somehow back in his box. Meanwhile, he would continue to plot."

In the meantime, the Bush administration leaked selected information about its plans for a potential war against Iraq. On July 5, for example, the New York Times *published details of a Pentagon "concept" for a war that would feature massive assaults against Iraq from the north, south, and west. Rumsfeld and other officials visited Qatar, Saudi Arabia, and other Middle Eastern countries that would be expected to host U.S. troops for any invasion of Iraq, and the administration held highly publicized meetings with Iraqi exile leaders. All these steps were part of an apparent campaign to convince the world, including Iraq, that the United States was serious about ousting Saddam.*

The administration's not-so-subtle planning for a war created new fears in many capitals that the United States was intending to act unilaterally, or at most with the cooperation and support of Britain and a handful of other countries. Among those expressing such concerns were some Republican allies of the administration, who cautioned that a war against Iraq could be successful over the long term only if the United States had broad international support and was committed to rebuilding Iraq once the fighting stopped.

The president's actions on other matters reinforced European views that he favored go-it-alone action in response to world challenges, rather than the multilateral, consultative approach that had become customary in Europe. This unilateral versus multilateral debate had surfaced early in 2001 when Bush announced he was withdrawing the United States from the Kyoto Protocol on global warming—a treaty his predecessor, Bill Clinton, had helped negotiate. European leaders also were angered in March, when Bush imposed tariffs on imports of specialty steel, much of it from Europe, and when he pressured Eastern European countries to support the U.S. position on a new international criminal court. (Global warming, p. 298; criminal court, p. 605)

Another issue that rubbed sensitive nerves on both sides of the Atlantic was the conflict between Israel and the Palestinians. Bush made it clear in both 2001 and 2002 that he blamed Palestinian leader Yasir Arafat for the ongoing violence that, in just two years, had killed more than 2,000 people and ended a decade's worth of diplomacy to find a peaceful solution. European leaders joined Bush in condemning Palestinian suicide bombers, but they also placed some of the blame for the violence on Israel. Many Europeans also questioned Bush's priorities: Searching for an end to Israeli-Palestinian violence was more urgent, they said, than confronting Iraqi leader Saddam Hussein.

The hawkish speech by Cheney in late August raised concerns about administration plans to a fever pitch in advance of Bush's planned speech to the UN General Assembly on September 12—the day after commemorative observances on the one-year anniversary of the terrorist attacks in New York City and Washington.

One of the world leaders most worried about unilateral action by the United States was UN Secretary General Kofi Annan who, for institutional reasons and by personal inclination, was a strong believer in multilateral action through the United Nations. On September 11 Annan took the extraordinary step of releasing an advance text of the speech he planned to give to the General Assembly the following day just before Bush's appearance. The speech was an impassioned appeal for Washington to avoid the temptation to act on its own. "When states decide to use force to deal with broader threats to international peace and security, there is no substitute for the unique legitimacy provided by the United Nations," Annan said.

In that context, Bush's speech to the UN on September 12 came as somewhat of a surprise—as well as a relief—to those who had assumed he was bent on pursuing a war regardless of the views of others. While taking a hard line against Iraq and its leader, Bush said he would work through the United Nations to put new pressure on that country to eliminate its weapons and adhere to other promises made at the conclusion of the Persian Gulf War. But Bush also described the situation as a challenge to the UN. "All the world now faces a test, and the United Nations a difficult and defining moment," he said. "Are Security Council resolutions to be honored and enforced, or cast aside without consequence? Will the United Nations serve the purpose of its founding, or will it be irrelevant?"

The speech brought wide praise, even from some foreign leaders who had been critical of what they viewed as Washington's rush to war. Norwegian prime minister Kjell Magne Bondevik praised Bush for promising that action against Iraq would be "rooted in the United Nations. I felt his speech today was more multilateral, more than I have heard from the United States in other speeches." Russian foreign minister Igor Ivanov said Bush had placed the burden on Iraq to cooperate with the UN Security Council. If Iraq did not cooperate, he said, it "will bear responsibility for possible consequences."

The Case Against Iraq

In statements by Bush and his key aides, the administration offered a long catalogue of complaints about Iraqi leader Saddam Hussein, including his dictatorial government, his abuse of the human rights of his own citizens, and his past aggressions against Iran and Kuwait. The focal point of the administration's case was the contention that Iraq still had weapons of mass destruction, was seeking to develop more weapons, and might turn some of those weapons over to terrorists, including the al Qaeda network.

The administration offered bits of evidence to support its position during the early part of the year but did not make a comprehensive presentation until September 12, the day Bush addressed the United Nations. In a twenty-one-page white paper entitled "A Decade of Deception and Defiance," the administration unleashed a torrent of complaints about Saddam Hussein's actions since the Persian Gulf War, including his defiance of sixteen Security Council resolutions and his alleged programs to build biological, chemical, and nuclear weapons.

Citing information from defectors, reports by the previous UN weapons inspectors, and U.S. intelligence sources (including spy satellites), the white paper concluded that Iraq still had biological and chemical weapons that were produced before the Persian Gulf War, was building facilities that could be used to produce new chemical weapons, had "stepped up its quest" for nuclear weapons, and was working on missiles that would exceed the ninety-mile range limit imposed by UN Security Council resolutions.

Perhaps the most controversial assertion in the report was a statement that Iraq in the previous fourteen months had "sought to buy thousands of specially designed aluminum tubes which officials believe were intended as components for centrifuges to enrich uranium" for use in nuclear weapons. The United States, according to news reports, had successfully blocked some of Iraq's attempts to buy these tubes, but some shipments had gotten through to Iraq. Experts within the administration reportedly disagreed about whether the tubes were, in fact, intended for a nuclear weapons program or for some other industrial use, including the manufacture of conventional weapons. The question was an important one because UN inspectors had concluded in the mid-1990s that Iraq had the technical ability to produce a nuclear weapon and lacked only the necessary weapons-grade fissile material, either highly enriched uranium or plutonium. If it could obtain an adequate supply of that material, Iraq could build a nuclear weapon in a matter of months, the administration said.

The administration's September 12 white paper did not mention what was perhaps the single most provocative charge that administration officials had made against Iraq: that the Baghdad government somehow supported or had a connection to the al Qaeda terrorist network. After the September 11 attacks in the United States, administration officials cited evidence that Mohammed Atta, the presumed leader of the attacks, had met earlier in 2001 with an Iraqi intelligence agent in Prague. Subsequent reports raised doubt about whether that meeting ever occurred, but administration officials continued to insist that Iraq had links to al Qaeda, perhaps through a Kurdish extremist group, Ansar al-Islam, that operated in northern Iraq. Some members of that group, or guerrillas who supported it, reportedly had received training in Afghanistan while al Qaeda was a major influence there.

The white paper mentioned Iraq's alleged involvement with other terrorist groups, including its reported payments to the families of Palestinian suicide bombers who killed Israeli soldiers and civilians, Iraq's support for several Palestinian extremist groups, and the government's support for a facility known as Salman Pak, where terrorists allegedly received training in such techniques as hijacking planes, planting explosives, and carrying out assassinations.

Following is the text of a speech by President George W. Bush to the United Nations General Assembly on September 12, 2002, in which he called for international action to force Iraq to give up its weapons of mass destruction and comply with other conditions of the cease-fire that ended the 1991 Persian Gulf War.

The document was obtained from the Internet at http:// www.whitehouse.gov/news/releases/2002/09/20020912-1 .html; accessed January 8, 2003.

Mr. Secretary General, Mr. President, distinguished delegates, and ladies and gentlemen:

We meet one year and one day after a terrorist attack brought grief to my country, and brought grief to many citizens of our world. Yesterday, we remembered the innocent lives taken that terrible morning. Today, we turn to the urgent duty of protecting other lives, without illusion and without fear.

We've accomplished much in the last year—in Afghanistan and beyond. We have much yet to do—in Afghanistan and beyond. Many nations represented here have joined in the fight against global terror, and the people of the United States are grateful.

The United Nations was born in the hope that survived a world war—the hope of a world moving toward justice, escaping old patterns of conflict and fear. The founding members resolved that the peace of the world must never again be destroyed by the will and wickedness of any man. We created the United Nations Security Council, so that, unlike the League of Nations, our deliberations would be more than talk, our resolutions would be more than wishes. After generations of deceitful dictators and broken treaties and squandered lives, we dedicated ourselves to standards of human dignity shared by all, and to a system of security defended by all.

Today, these standards, and this security, are challenged. Our commitment to human dignity is challenged by persistent poverty and raging disease. The suffering is great, and our responsibilities are clear. The United States is joining with the world to supply aid where it reaches people and lifts up lives, to extend trade and the prosperity it brings, and to bring medical care where it is desperately needed.

As a symbol of our commitment to human dignity, the United States will return to UNESCO [United Nations Educational, Scientific and Cultural Organization]. This organization has been reformed and America will participate fully in its mission to advance human rights and tolerance and learning.

Our common security is challenged by regional conflicts—ethnic and religious strife that is ancient, but not inevitable. In the Middle East, there can be no peace for either side without freedom for both sides. America stands committed to an independent and democratic Palestine, living side by side with Israel in peace and security. Like all other people, Palestinians deserve a government that serves their interests and listens to their voices. My nation will continue to encourage all parties to step up to their responsibilities as we seek a just and comprehensive settlement to the conflict.

Above all, our principles and our security are challenged today by outlaw groups and regimes that accept no law of morality and have no limit to their violent ambitions. In the attacks on America a year ago, we saw the destructive intentions of our enemies. This threat hides within many nations, including my own. In cells and camps, terrorists are plotting further destruction, and building new bases for their war against civilization. And our greatest fear is that terrorists will find a shortcut to their mad ambitions when an outlaw regime supplies them with the technologies to kill on a massive scale.

In one place—in one regime—we find all these dangers, in their most lethal and aggressive forms, exactly the kind of aggressive threat the United Nations was born to confront.

Twelve years ago, Iraq invaded Kuwait without provocation. And the regime's forces were poised to continue their march to seize other countries and their resources. Had Saddam Hussein been appeased instead of stopped, he would have endangered the peace and stability of the world. Yet this aggression was stopped—by the might of coalition forces and the will of the United Nations.

To suspend hostilities, to spare himself, Iraq's dictator accepted a series of commitments. The terms were clear, to him and to all. And he agreed to prove he is complying with every one of those obligations.

He has proven instead only his contempt for the United Nations, and for all his pledges. By breaking every pledge—by his deceptions, and by his cruelties—Saddam Hussein has made the case against himself.

In 1991, Security Council Resolution 688 demanded that the Iraqi regime cease at once the repression of its own people, including the systematic repression of minorities—which the Council said, threatened international peace and security in the region. This demand goes ignored.

Last year, the U.N. Commission on Human Rights found that Iraq continues to commit extremely grave violations of human rights, and that the regime's repression is all pervasive. Tens of thousands of political opponents and ordinary citizens have been subjected to arbitrary arrest and imprisonment, summary execution, and torture by beating and burning, electric shock, starvation, mutilation, and rape. Wives are tortured in front of their husbands, children in the presence of their parents—and all of these horrors concealed from the world by the apparatus of a totalitarian state.

In 1991, the U.N. Security Council, through Resolutions 686 and 687, demanded that Iraq return all prisoners from Kuwait and other lands. Iraq's regime agreed. It broke its promise. Last year the Secretary General's high-level coordinator for this issue reported that Kuwait, Saudi, Indian, Syrian, Lebanese, Iranian, Egyptian, Bahraini, and Omani nationals remain unaccounted for—more than 600 people. One American pilot is among them.

In 1991, the U.N. Security Council, through Resolution 687, demanded that Iraq renounce all involvement with terrorism, and permit no terrorist organizations to operate in Iraq. Iraq's regime agreed. It broke this promise. In violation of Security Council Resolution 1373, Iraq continues to shelter and support terrorist organizations that direct violence against Iran, Israel, and Western governments. Iraqi dissidents abroad are targeted for murder. In 1993, Iraq attempted to assassinate the Emir of Kuwait and a former American President. Iraq's government openly praised the attacks of September the 11th. And al Qaeda terrorists escaped from Afghanistan and are known to be in Iraq.

In 1991, the Iraqi regime agreed to destroy and stop developing all weapons of mass destruction and long-range missiles, and to prove to the world it has done so by complying with rigorous inspections. Iraq has broken every aspect of this fundamental pledge.

From 1991 to 1995, the Iraqi regime said it had no biological weapons. After a senior official in its weapons program defected and exposed this lie, the regime admitted to producing tens of thousands of liters of anthrax and other deadly biological agents for use with Scud warheads, aerial bombs, and aircraft spray tanks. U.N. inspectors believe Iraq has produced two to four times the amount of biological agents it declared, and has failed to account for more than three metric tons of material that could be used to produce biological weapons. Right now, Iraq is expanding and improving facilities that were used for the production of biological weapons.

United Nations' inspections also revealed that Iraq likely maintains stockpiles of VX, mustard and other chemical agents, and that the regime is rebuilding and expanding facilities capable of producing chemical weapons.

And in 1995, after four years of deception, Iraq finally admitted it had a crash nuclear weapons program prior to the Gulf War. We know now, were it not for that war, the regime in Iraq would likely have possessed a nuclear weapon no later than 1993.

Today, Iraq continues to withhold important information about its nuclear program—weapons design, procurement logs, experiment data, an accounting of nuclear materials and documentation of foreign assistance. Iraq employs capable nuclear scientists and technicians. It retains physical infrastructure needed to build a nuclear weapon. Iraq has made several attempts to buy high-strength aluminum tubes used to enrich uranium for a nuclear weapon. Should Iraq acquire fissile material, it would be able to build a nuclear weapon within a year. And Iraq's state-controlled media has reported numerous meetings between Saddam Hussein and his nuclear scientists, leaving little doubt about his continued appetite for these weapons.

Iraq also possesses a force of Scud-type missiles with ranges beyond the 150 kilometers permitted by the U.N. Work at testing and production facilities shows that Iraq is building more long-range missiles that it can inflict mass death throughout the region.

In 1990, after Iraq's invasion of Kuwait, the world imposed economic sanctions on Iraq. Those sanctions were maintained after the war to compel the regime's compliance with Security Council resolutions. In time, Iraq was allowed to use oil revenues to buy food. Saddam Hussein has subverted this program, working around the sanctions to buy missile technology and military materials. He blames the suffering of Iraq's people on the United Nations, even as he uses his oil wealth to build lavish palaces for himself, and to buy arms for his country. By refusing to comply with his own agreements, he bears full guilt for the hunger and misery of innocent Iraqi citizens.

In 1991, Iraq promised U.N. inspectors immediate and unrestricted access to verify Iraq's commitment to rid itself of weapons of mass destruction and long-range missiles. Iraq broke this promise, spending seven years deceiving, evading, and harassing U.N. inspectors before ceasing cooperation entirely. Just months after the 1991 cease-fire, the Security Council twice renewed its demand that the Iraqi regime cooperate fully with inspectors, condemning Iraq's serious violations of its obligations. The Security Council again renewed that demand in 1994, and twice more in 1996, deploring Iraq's clear violations of its obligations. The Security Council renewed its demand three more times in 1997, citing flagrant violations; and three more times in 1998, calling Iraq's behavior totally unacceptable. And in 1999, the demand was renewed yet again.

As we meet today, it's been almost four years since the last U.N. inspectors set foot in Iraq, four years for the Iraqi regime to plan, and to build, and to test behind the cloak of secrecy.

We know that Saddam Hussein pursued weapons of mass murder even when inspectors were in his country. Are we to assume that he stopped when they left? The history, the logic, and the facts lead to one conclusion: Saddam Hussein's regime is a grave and gathering danger. To suggest otherwise is to hope against the evidence. To assume this regime's good faith is to bet the lives of millions and the peace of the world in a reckless gamble. And this is a risk we must not take.

Delegates to the General Assembly, we have been more than patient. We've tried sanctions. We've tried the carrot of oil for food, and the stick of coalition military strikes. But Saddam Hussein has defied all these efforts and continues to develop weapons of mass destruction. The first time we may be completely certain he has a—nuclear weapons is when, God forbids, he uses one. We owe it to all our citizens to do everything in our power to prevent that day from coming.

The conduct of the Iraqi regime is a threat to the authority of the United Nations, and a threat to peace. Iraq has answered a decade of U.N. demands with a decade of defiance. All the world now faces a test, and the United Nations a difficult and defining moment. Are Security Council resolutions to be honored and enforced, or cast aside without consequence? Will the United Nations serve the purpose of its founding, or will it be irrelevant?

The United States helped found the United Nations. We want the United Nations to be effective, and respectful, and successful. We want the resolutions of the world's most important multilateral body to be enforced. And right now those resolutions are being unilaterally subverted by the Iraqi regime. Our partnership of nations can meet the test before us, by making clear what we now expect of the Iraqi regime.

If the Iraqi regime wishes peace, it will immediately and unconditionally forswear, disclose, and remove or destroy all weapons of mass destruction, long-range missiles, and all related material.

If the Iraqi regime wishes peace, it will immediately end all support for terrorism and act to suppress it, as all states are required to do by U.N. Security Council resolutions.

If the Iraqi regime wishes peace, it will cease persecution of its civilian population, including Shi'a, Sunnis, Kurds, Turkomans, and others, again as required by Security Council resolutions.

If the Iraqi regime wishes peace, it will release or account for all Gulf War personnel whose fate is still unknown. It will return the remains of any who are deceased, return stolen property, accept liability for losses resulting from the invasion of Kuwait, and fully cooperate with international efforts to resolve these issues, as required by Security Council resolutions.

If the Iraqi regime wishes peace, it will immediately end all illicit trade outside the oil-for-food program. It will accept U.N. administration of funds from that program, to ensure that the money is used fairly and promptly for the benefit of the Iraqi people.

If all these steps are taken, it will signal a new openness and accountability in Iraq. And it could open the prospect of the United Nations helping to build a government that represents all Iraqis—a government based on respect for human rights, economic liberty, and internationally supervised elections.

The United States has no quarrel with the Iraqi people; they've suffered too long in silent captivity. Liberty for the Iraqi people is a great moral cause, and a great strategic goal. The people of Iraq deserve it; the security of all nations requires it. Free societies do not intimidate through cruelty and conquest, and open societies do not threaten the world with mass murder. The United States supports political and economic liberty in a unified Iraq.

We can harbor no illusions—and that's important today to remember. Saddam Hussein attacked Iran in 1980 and Kuwait in 1990. He's fired ballistic missiles at Iran and Saudi Arabia, Bahrain, and Israel. His regime once ordered the killing of every person between the ages of 15 and 70 in certain Kurdish villages in northern Iraq. He has gassed many Iranians, and 40 Iraqi villages.

My nation will work with the U.N. Security Council to meet our common challenge. If Iraq's regime defies us again, the world must move deliberately, decisively to hold Iraq to account. We will work with the U.N. Security Council for the necessary resolutions. But the purposes of the United States should not be doubted. The Security Council resolutions will be enforced—the just demands of peace and security will be met—or action will be unavoidable. And a regime that has lost its legitimacy will also lose its power.

Events can turn in one of two ways: If we fail to act in the face of danger, the people of Iraq will continue to live in brutal submission. The regime will have new power to bully and dominate and conquer its neighbors, condemning the Middle East to more years of bloodshed and fear. The regime will remain unstable—the region will remain unstable, with little hope of freedom, and isolated from the progress of our times. With every step the Iraqi regime takes toward gaining and deploying the most terrible weapons, our own options to confront that regime will narrow. And if an emboldened regime were to supply these weapons to terrorist allies, then the attacks of September the 11th would be a prelude to far greater horrors.

If we meet our responsibilities, if we overcome this danger, we can arrive at a very different future. The people of Iraq can shake off their captivity. They can one day join a democratic Afghanistan and a democratic Palestine, inspiring reforms throughout the Muslim world. These nations can show by their example that honest government, and respect for women, and the great Islamic tradition of learning can triumph in the Middle East and beyond. And we will show that the promise of the United Nations can be fulfilled in our time.

Neither of these outcomes is certain. Both have been set before us. We must choose between a world of fear and a world of progress. We cannot stand by and do nothing while dangers gather. We must stand up for our security, and for the permanent rights and the hopes of mankind. By heritage and by choice, the United States of America will make that stand. And, delegates to the United Nations, you have the power to make that stand, as well.

Thank you very much.

FEDERAL TRADE COMMISSION ON DECEPTIVE WEIGHT-LOSS ADS
September 17, 2002

The federal government in 2002 mounted a multifaceted approach to encourage Americans to slim down because much of the population was growing fatter at an alarming pace. President George W. Bush and his wife, Laura, participated in a high-profile campaign aimed at getting adults and their children off the couch and outside exercising. The secretaries of health and human services and agriculture undertook a campaign to persuade the fast-food and restaurant industry to serve healthier foods and smaller portions. The Federal Trade Commission (FTC) began taking a closer look at advertisements for weight-loss products, finding that more than half of them made claims that were unproven and quite possibly false.

Administration officials said that these various activities were all meant to make Americans more aware of the problems of obesity. These officials noted that even small increases in physical activity and better nutrition could provide noticeable health benefits. Health care and consumer advocates generally agreed that jawboning individuals to eat less and exercise more was a good start. But many also said that some regulation of the food industry, similar to that promoted for the tobacco industry, was necessary. "It's not going to be enough to just point your finger at the American people and say 'get to it,'" Margo Wootan, director of nutrition at the Center for Science in the Public Interest, told the Christian Science Monitor *in June. "We need a comprehensive strategy." Wootan and others proposed regulating the food industry through such mechanisms as taxing soft drinks, restricting snack and other food advertising aimed at children, and restricting the use of vending machines in schools. "The kinds of things we're recommending . . . sound controversial because they're new," Wootan said. "But we're just at the beginning of the [struggle to curb obesity]. In the next few years, we'll see these ideas mainstream."*

A Problem of Epidemic Proportions

According to new data for 1999–2000 from the National Health and Nutrition Examination Survey that were published October 8 in the Journal of the American Medical Association, *64.5 percent of all adults were overweight, compared with 55.9 percent in 1988–1994. Some 30.5 percent were obese, compared with 22.9 percent in the earlier period. Extreme obesity increased to 4.7 percent in 1999–2000, from 2.9 percent in 1988–1994.*

Increases occurred among both men and women in all age groups. A higher proportion of men than women were overweight, but a higher proportion of women than men were obese. Obesity was most prevalent among black women. More than 50 percent of black women over age forty and almost 50 percent of younger black women were defined as obese. Fifteen percent of older black women were categorized as extremely obese. The weight categories were defined by the body mass index, which related height to weight and was thought to be the best quick indicator of body fat. Anyone with a body mass index of 25 or higher was defined as being overweight, a body mass index of 30 or more indicated obesity, while a body mass index of 40 or more indicated extreme obesity.

The most alarming increase was among children. Fifteen percent of all children aged six to nineteen and 10 percent of all children ages two through five were overweight. If something is not done to prevent overweight and obesity among these young children, said George L. Blackburn, chairman of nutrition medicine at Harvard Medical School, "we are going to have the first generation of children who are not going to live as long as their parents."

Overweight and obesity were associated with a variety of serious illnesses and conditions, including heart failure, stroke, diabetes, asthma, arthritis, and psychological disorders such as depression. Doctors were particularly concerned about the high incidence of overweight children. A high proportion of them was likely to become overweight or obese adults and thus at increased risk for devastating disease and illnesses. A dramatic increase in the incidence of Type 2 diabetes was showing up in children and adolescents. Type 2 diabetes, which accounted for about 95 percent of all cases of diabetes, was once considered primarily an adult disease. The federal Centers for Disease Control and Prevention (CDC) said on May 1 that other obesity-related diseases, including sleep apnea and gall bladder disease, also appeared to be worsening in children and adolescents.

Overweight and obesity were costly. By one estimate, the total cost of overweight and obesity in the United States in 2000 was estimated at $117 billion, including health care costs and costs associated with lost wages. The estimate did not include the cost of treating chronic diseases associated with overweight, which amounted to an estimated $505 billion.

A RAND study released in October said that obesity was now a more serious health problem than smoking, drinking, or poverty because it was linked to big increases in chronic health conditions and to "significantly higher" health expenditures. Compared with normal-weight individuals of the same age, gender, and social demographics, the study said obese people were likely to experience a 67 percent increase in chronic conditions (including diabetes, hypertension, heart disease, and cancer)—similar to the increase in chronic health conditions caused by aging from age thirty to age fifty. Rates of increase in chronic health conditions were 25 percent for nor-mal-weight daily smokers, 12 percent for normal-weight heavy drinkers, and 58 percent for people living in poverty. According to the study, the obese also spent more on health services and medications than either daily smok-ers or heavy drinkers. Only aging had a greater effect, and then only on spending for medications. A report issued in May by AARP (formerly the American Association of Retired Persons), the advocacy organization for older Americans, warned that increasing obesity could wipe out the health gains older Americans had made by smoking less and taking other steps to stay healthy.

Awareness Campaigns

Most obesity was preventable. The primary causes of overweight and obe-sity had long been known: overeating, eating unhealthy foods, and lack of physical exercise. Most Americans overate because food was plentiful, inex-pensive, and heavily advertised—particularly fast foods and convenience foods, which tended to be heavy on fats, sugars, and calories. Many foods targeted directly to children, such as some cereals and soft drinks, were laden with sugar. At the same time, Americans exercised less than they had in the past—their jobs were less physically demanding, their chores around home had been largely automated or mechanized, and sedentary entertain-ment such as television, movies, and the Internet had as much or more ap-peal than physical exercise.

The cure was equally simple—at least to state: Americans should eat healthy diets, consume fewer calories, and engage in more physical exer-cise. But as anyone who had tried to lose a few pounds knew, the cure was easier said than done.

In December 2001 then surgeon general David Satcher issued a call to action to individuals to eat less and get more exercise and on communities to provide an atmosphere that would make it easier for adults and chil-dren to reach and maintain healthy weights. In 2002 the federal govern-ment followed up on that call with several campaigns aimed at making Americans fitter. (Call to action, Historic Documents of 2001, p. 935)

On June 20 President Bush and wife Laura kicked off a four-day fitness campaign promoting the benefits of physical exercise by hosting a "fitness fair" on the White House lawn. "The evidence is clear: A healthier America is a stronger America," said Bush, who jogged and worked out regularly. The HealthierUS initiative called for at least half an hour of exercise every day for adults (an hour for children), eating smaller servings of healthy foods, regular preventive health screenings, and avoidance of harmful sub-stances, such as alcohol, tobacco, and illegal drugs.

The federal Centers for Disease Control and Prevention began a $125 mil-lion ad campaign to encourage kids to go out and play. Called "VERB. It's What You Do," the ads were designed to encourage children ages nine to thir-teen (known as "tweens" in the marketing world) to choose an active verb, such as run *or* jump *and then use that verb as a "launching pad to regular* *physical activity." In addition to giving tweens concrete examples of being active in "a fun, cool, and meaningful way," the ad campaign also planned to use celebrity athletes, musicians, and dancers as role models. "It's a good time to compete with all the other messages directed at this age group, which, frankly, are encouraging kids to be more sedentary," said a CDC spokesperson.*

Other initiatives included a "Walk for Better Health" campaign, aimed at promoting more physical activity among consumers and the federal work force; an action kit for community organizers interested in promoting better nutrition in school lunch programs; and a $6 million grant to 100 schools to provide fresh produce during the school day. In October Tommy G. Thompson, secretary of health and human services, and Ann M. Veneman, secretary of agriculture, met with representatives of the fast-food industry to enlist their aid in combating obesity. In particular the two lobbied for more inclusion of fruits and vegetables in meals and smaller portions. "I want more choices and healthier choices on their menus, and advertising campaigns to eat healthy," Thompson said afterward. The fast-food representatives said the industry already offered healthful choices, and that the vast majority of Americans thought the serving portions were the right size. Thompson and Veneman planned to have similar meetings with the beverage and grocery industries.

Reducing False and Misleading Weight-Loss Ads

The Federal Trade Commission weighed in September 17 with a report saying that the majority of ads for weight-loss products were misleading, exaggerated, or false, and that the number of deceptive ads was growing. The market for weight-loss products was huge. More than one-third of all Americans said they were trying to lose weight, and Americans spent nearly $35 billion annually on over-the-counter pills, patches, creams, herbal supplements, weight-loss programs, books, and videotapes promoting weight loss.

According to the FTC report, 55 percent of the ads the commission reviewed made at least one claim that was likely to be false and 40 percent made claims that were almost certainly false. Falling into that category were claims that the dieter could lose a pound or more a day over an extended time period, that the user would achieve substantial weight loss without either diet or exercise, and that dieters could lose weight while still eating all they wanted. Claims that a diet pill could allow the user to lose weight in selective parts of the body or block absorption of all fat into the body were "simply inconsistent with existing scientific knowledge," the FTC said. Popular tactics used to lure consumers included personal testimonials that were simply implausible on their face and before-and-after pictures that had been doctored. The study reviewed 300 advertisements, most of which appeared in the first half of 2001 on television, radio, the Internet, and commercial e-mail and in newspapers, magazines, infomercials, and supermarket tabloids.

The study said that deceptive advertising cost far more than the amount Americans spent buying useless and perhaps even dangerous products. Responsible producers of diet products might feel compelled to offer similar exaggerated advertising so as not to "lose market share to the hucksters who promise the impossible," the report said. Moreover, false and misleading advertising created unrealistic expectations on the part of consumers, who might spurn reasonable and proven approaches to dieting in favor of the unlikely "quick fix." The report said that "consumers who believe that it is really possible to lose a pound a day may quickly lose interest in losing a pound or less a week."

The report also said that it was "apparent that most media make little or no attempt to screen questionable ads for weight-loss products" and that "recent efforts to heighten media awareness have been largely unsuccessful." The exceptions were the major television broadcast networks, ABC, CBS, and NBC, and Good Housekeeping *magazine. The FTC called on the media to do a better job of screening the ads they run. "Reputable media should be embarrassed by some of the ads that run," said Howard Beales, director of the FTC's consumer protection bureau. "The claims are so ridiculous."*

The FTC said it would continue its enforcement efforts—the agency had filed ninety-three cases challenging false or misleading weight-loss ads since 1990—but said only the media could stop deceptive advertising before it aired. The FTC called on trade associations and self-regulatory groups to do a better job of weeding out the questionable advertising but stopped short of threatening any additional regulation.

Obesity a Global Problem

Obesity was on the increase not only in the United States but around the world. The International Obesity Task Force estimated that about 300 million of the world's 6 billion people were obese and another 750 million were overweight. The task force estimated that 22 million children under age five were overweight or obese. Overweight was the fifth most serious risk for serious health problems in high- and middle-income countries. Being underweight was a greater risk factor in middle-income countries, presenting the disturbing contrast in many countries between the malnourished poor and overweight or obese middle class. Being underweight was the leading cause of serious disease in low-income countries. Some 800 million people worldwide were estimated to be underfed.

Officials from the World Health Organization (WHO) said in May that they were talking with the food industry about ways to encourage people to control their junk food consumption and eat healthier diets. "We believe there is an enormous potential to work together [with the food industry] to solve these problems, whereas we didn't believe that in the case of the tobacco industry," said Derek Yach, WHO executive director for noncommunicable diseases and mental health. "It may very well be that they will look at advertising, but we are interested in what they will do positively with us— promoting physical activity on a worldwide scale, trying to make the less salty, less sugary, less fatty products more available and more attractive to young people." WHO planned to issue specific guidelines on reducing obesity in 2003.

Following is the executive summary from "Weight-Loss Advertising: An Analysis of Current Trends," a staff report issued September 17, 2002, by the Federal Trade Commission finding that false or misleading claims were commonly made in advertising for weight-loss products.

The document was obtained from the Internet at www.ftc .gov/bcp/reports/weightloss.pdf; accessed October 13, 2002.

This report attempts to take a comprehensive look at weight loss advertising. The need to do so is compelling. In the last decade, the number of FTC law enforcement cases involving weight loss products or services equaled those filed in the previous seven decades. Consumers spend billions of dollars a year on weight loss products and services, money wasted if spent on worthless remedies. This report highlights the scope of the problem facing consumers as they consider the thousands of purported remedies on the market, as well as the serious challenge facing law enforcement agencies attempting to prevent deceptive advertising.

According to the U.S. Surgeon General, overweight and obesity have reached epidemic proportions, afflicting 6 out of every 10 Americans. Overweight and obesity constitute the second leading cause of preventable death, after smoking, resulting in an estimated 300,000 deaths per year. The costs, direct and indirect, associated with overweight and obesity are estimated to exceed $100 billion a year.

At the same time, survey data suggest that millions of Americans are trying to lose weight. The marketplace has responded with a proliferating array of products and services, many promising miraculous, quick-fix remedies. Tens of millions of consumers have turned to over-the-counter remedies, spending billions of dollars on products and services that purport to promote weight loss. In the end, these quick-fixes do nothing to address the nation's or the individual's weight problem, and, if anything, may contribute to an already serious health crisis.

Once the province of supermarket tabloids and the back sections of certain magazines, over-the-top weight loss advertisements promising quick, easy weight loss are now pervasive in almost all media forms. At least that is the impression. But are the obviously deceptive advertisements really as widespread as they might appear watching late night television or leafing through magazines at the local newsstand? To answer this and other questions, we collected and analyzed a nonrandom sample of 300 advertisements, mostly disseminated during the first half of 2001, from broadcast and cable television, infomercials, radio, magazines, newspapers, supermarket tabloids, direct mail, commercial e-mail (spam), and Internet websites. In addition, to evaluate how weight-loss advertising has changed over the past decade, we collected ads disseminated in 1992 in eight national magazines to compare with ads appearing in 2001 in the same publications.

We conclude that false or misleading claims are common in weight-loss advertising, and, based on our comparison of 1992 magazine ads with magazines ads for 2001, the number of products and the amount of advertising, much of it deceptive, appears to have increased dramatically over the last decade.

Of particular concern in ads in 2001 are grossly exaggerated or clearly unsubstantiated performance claims. Although we did not evaluate the substantiation for specific products and advertising claims as part of this report, many of the claims we reviewed are so contrary to existing scientific evidence, or so clearly unsupported by the available evidence, that there is little doubt that they are false or deceptive. In addition to the obviously false claims, many other advertisements contain claims that appear likely to be misleading or unsubstantiated.

Falling into the too-good-to-be-true category are claims that: the user can lose a pound a day or more over extended periods of time; that substantial weight loss (without surgery) can be achieved without diet or exercise; and that users can lose weight regardless of how much they eat. Also falling into this category are claims that a diet pill can cause weight loss in selective parts of the body or block absorption of all fat in the diet. These types of claims are simply inconsistent with existing scientific knowledge.

This report catalogues the most common marketing techniques used in 300 weight loss advertisements. Nearly all of the ads reviewed used at least one and sometimes several of the following techniques, many of which should raise red flags about the veracity of the claims.

Consumer Testimonials; Before/After Photos. The headline proclaimed: "I lost 46 lbs in 30 days." Another blared, "How I lost 54 pounds without dieting or medication in less than 6 weeks!" The use of consumer testimonials is pervasive in weight-loss advertising. One hundred and ninety-five (65%) of the advertisements in the sample used consumer testimonials and 42% contained before-and-after pictures. These testimonials and photos rarely portrayed realistic weight loss. The average for the largest amount of weight loss reported in each of the 195 advertisements was 71 pounds. Fifty-seven ads reported weight loss exceeding 70 pounds, and 38 ads reported weight loss exceeding 100 pounds. The advertised weight loss ranges are, in all likelihood, simply not achievable for the products being promoted. Thirty-six ads used 71 different testimonials claiming weight loss of nearly a pound a day for time periods of 13 days or more.

Rapid Weight-loss Claims. Rapid weight-loss claims were made in 57% of the advertisements in the sample. In some cases, the falsity of such claims is obvious, as in the ad that claimed that users could lose up to 8 to 10 pounds per week while using the advertised product.

No Diet or Exercise Required. Despite the well-accepted prescription of diet and exercise for successful weight management, 42% of all of the ads reviewed promote an array of quick-fix pills, patches, potions, and programs for effortless weight loss and 64% of those ads also promised fast results. The ads claim that results can be achieved without reducing caloric intake or increasing physical activity. Some even go so far as to tell consumers "you can eat as much as you want and still lose weight."

Long-term/Permanent Weight-loss Claims. "Take it off and keep it off" (long-term/permanent weight loss) claims were used in 41% of the ads in the sample. In fact, the publicly available scientific research contains very little that would substantiate long-term or permanent weight-loss claims for most of today's popular diet products. Accordingly, long-term or permanent weight-loss claims are inherently suspect.

Clinically Proven/Doctor Approved Claims. Clinically proven and doctor approved claims are also fairly common in weight-loss advertisements, the former occurring in 40% and the latter in 25% of the ads in the sample. Some of the specific claims are virtually meaningless. For example, a representation such as, "Clinical studies show people lost 300% more weight even without dieting," may cause consumers to conclude mistakenly that the clinically proven benefits are substantial, whereas, in fact, the difference between use of the product and dieting alone could be quite small (1.5 lbs. vs. .5 lbs.). These claims do little to inform consumers and most ads fail to provide consumers with sufficient information to allow them to verify the advertisers' representations. Moreover, the Federal Trade Commission, in past law enforcement actions, has evaluated the available scientific evidence for many of the ingredients expressly advertised as clinically proven, and challenged the weight-loss efficacy claims for these ingredients.

Natural/Safe Weight-loss Claims. Safety claims are also prevalent in weight-loss advertising. Nearly half of all the ads in the sample (42%) contained specific claims that the advertised products or services are safe and 71% of those ads also claimed that the products were "all natural."

Safety claims can be difficult to evaluate, especially when so many ads fail to disclose the active ingredients in the product. On the other hand, some advertisements disclose ingredients, e. g., ephedra alkaloids, that make unqualified safety claims misleading. Nevertheless, marketers in almost half (48%) of the ads that identified ephedra as a product ingredient made safety claims. Only 30% of the ads that identified ephedra as an ingredient included a specific health warning about its potential adverse effects.

Historical Comparison. To develop a perspective on how weight-loss advertising has changed over time, this report also compares advertisements appearing in a sample of magazines published in 2001 with ads in the same magazines in 1992. Compared to 1992, readers in 2001 saw more diet ads, more often, and for more products. Specifically,

- The frequency of weight-loss advertisements in these magazines more than doubled, and
- The number of separate and distinct advertisements tripled.

Moreover, the type of weight-loss products and services advertised dramatically shifted from "meal replacements" (57%), in 1992 to dietary supplements (66%), in 2001. Meal replacement products typically facilitate the reduction of caloric intake by replacing high-calorie foods with lower-calorie substitutes, whereas dietary supplements are commonly marketed (55%) with claims that reducing caloric intake or increasing physical activity is unnecessary.

The considerable changes in the methods used to promote weight-loss products are the most revealing indication of the downward spiral to deception in weight-loss advertising. The 2001 advertisements were much more likely than the 1992 ads to use dramatic consumer testimonials and before-and-after photos, promise permanent weight loss, guarantee weight-loss success, claim that weight loss can be achieved without diet or exercise, claim that results can be achieved quickly, claim that the product is all natural, and make express or implied claims that the product is safe. Finally, although both the 1992 and 2001 examples include unobjectionable representations, as well as almost certainly false claims, the 2001 advertisements appear much more likely to make specific performance promises that are misleading.

Conclusion. The use of false or misleading claims in weight-loss advertising is rampant. Nearly 40% of the ads in our sample made at least one representation that almost certainly is false and 55% of the ads made at least one representation that is very likely to be false or, at the very least, lacks adequate substantiation. The proliferation of such ads has proceeded in the face of, and in spite of, an unprecedented level of FTC enforcement activity, including the filing of more than 80 cases during the last decade. The need for critical evaluation seems readily apparent. Government agencies with oversight over weight-loss advertising must continually reassess the effectiveness of enforcement and consumer and business education strategies. Trade associations and self-regulatory groups must do a better job of educating their members about standards for truthful advertising and enforcing those standards. The media must be encouraged to adopt meaningful clearance standards that weed out facially deceptive or misleading weight-loss claims. The past efforts of the FTC and the others to encourage the adoption of media screening standards have been largely unsuccessful. Nevertheless, as this report demonstrates, the adoption and enforcement of standards would reduce the amount of blatantly deceptive advertising disseminated to consumers and efforts to encourage the adoption of such standards should continue. Finally, individual consumers must become more knowledgeable about the importance of achieving and maintaining healthy weight, more informed about how to shop for weight-loss products and services, and more skeptical of ads promising quick-fixes.

BUSH ADMINISTRATION ON
NATIONAL SECURITY STRATEGY
September 20, 2002

Attempting to establish a new underlying basis for American foreign policy, the Bush administration in 2002 said the United States could best protect its own interests by promoting democracy and free enterprise overseas—and by taking preemptive action if necessary to defeat terrorism and tyranny. In speeches during the year and in a "National Security Strategy" made public on September 20, 2002, President George W. Bush and his aides sought to integrate into one policy two of the country's main impulses of the previous century: an idealistic desire to remake the world in America's image, along with the use of force to protect itself and advance its causes. The administration's new strategy was no mere academic formulation, however. Bush was preparing to put his policy into action early in 2003 with a war against Iraqi leader Saddam Hussein, whose defeat, the administration hoped, would launch a process promoting economic and political freedom throughout the Middle East. (Iraq, pp. 612, 713)

Both supporters and critics said Bush's strategy had the potential to become the most important development in U.S. foreign policy since the Truman administration's adoption of "containment" and "deterrence" as the means of blocking communist expansion following World War II. In various guises these policies buttressed the U.S. posture toward the rest of the world for a half-century, until the collapse of the Soviet Union's communist empire between 1989 and 1991.

Bush's new policy had no single, easily identifiable enemy, such as communism. Instead, it was directed against a broad range of threats to world peace and stability. The president focused much of his strategy on confronting terrorism but also described totalitarianism, poverty, and disease as threats to U.S. national security.

In a September 17 letter accompanying his National Security Strategy, Bush set for the United States three tasks that were stated simply but had sweeping implications. "We will defend the peace by fighting terrorists and tyrants," he said. "We will preserve the peace by building good relations among the great powers. We will extend the peace by encouraging free and open societies on every continent."

Most of the immediate commentary on Bush's strategy focused on its embrace of preemptive action against terrorists and others who directly threatened U.S. interests. The planned war in Iraq was an example of this approach. The administration also stimulated curiosity about its intentions with several statements hinting at a willingness to use nuclear weapons in some circumstances. Critics accused the administration of reckless warmongering; supporters said Bush was merely being prudent in saying he would act before the nation was attacked again.

Developing the Strategy

Bush's national security strategy was the result both of long-term thinking by many of his senior aides and the consequences of the September 11, 2001, terrorist attacks against the United States. The administration had begun to put some of the policy in place even before terrorists killed about 3,000 people in New York City and Washington, D.C., but the attacks clearly stimulated its desire for a broad review of America's policy toward the world.

When he took office in January 2001, Bush staffed the upper levels of his administration with a number of conservative intellectuals who, following the collapse of the Soviet Union a decade earlier, had advocated a fundamental rethinking of U.S. foreign policy. Deputy Secretary of Defense Paul D. Wolfowitz, Undersecretary of State John Bolton, and others had argued in policy papers and other forums that the end of the cold war offered the United States a unique, historic opportunity to reshape the course of the world for years to come. Among other things, they said Washington should consolidate its military supremacy over all conceivable rivals, should develop new offensive and defensive nuclear weapons systems, and should "finish" the job of the 1991 Persian Gulf war—in other words, oust the Iraqi leader and eliminate the biological and chemical weapons he had developed before the war. These aides also argued that the United States had allowed itself to be hamstrung by the reluctance of the United Nations and European allies to confront new dangers in the world, such as terrorism and Islamic fundamentalism. Bush's national security advisor Condoleezza Rice and Defense Secretary Donald H. Rumsfeld were known to share some of these views; Secretary of State Colin Powell appeared to be more skeptical. (Persian Gulf War, Historic Documents of 1991, p. 121)

In the first months of his administration Bush adopted some aspects of the world view of his aides. For example, he reversed a policy by his predecessor, Bill Clinton (1993–2001), of reaching out to the communist regime of North Korea, and he sped up development of a multibillion-dollar missile defense system intended to protect the United States against a limited ballistic missile attack by North Korea. (North Korea, p. 731; missile defense, p. 1026)

The September 11 terrorist attacks presented Bush with an immediate challenge and a longer-term opportunity. The challenge was to strike di-

rectly against those who carried out the attacks, and he did so by sending a large military force to drive the al Qaeda terrorist network out of Afghanistan, where it had been based. (Afghanistan, p. 15)

The longer-term opportunity for Bush was the sudden emergence in the United States of greater support for a more muscular role in the world, premised on the need to confront terrorism. Signaling the next phase in the war against terror, Bush in late 2001 began warning the Iraqi leader that the United States was prepared to force him to keep his 1991 promise to give up all weapons of mass destruction. (Warnings to Iraq, Historic Documents of 2001, p. 849)

The president escalated his rhetoric during his January 29, 2002, State of the Union address, in which he said Iran, Iraq, and North Korea constituted an "axis of evil" because they supported terrorism and were developing weapons of mass destruction. "And all nations should know: America will do what is necessary to ensure our nation's security," Bush said. "We'll be deliberate, yet time is not on our side. I will not wait on events, while dangers gather. I will not stand by, as peril draws closer and closer. The United States of America will not permit the world's most dangerous regimes to threaten us with the world's most destructive weapons." (State of the Union, p. 33)

Bush expanded on that theme with another toughly worded speech delivered June 1 at graduating ceremonies of the U.S. Military Academy at West Point. "If we wait for threats to fully materialize, we will have waited too long," he said. The old policies of containing and deterring potential foes would no longer work, he said, "when unbalanced dictators with weapons of mass destruction can deliver those weapons on missiles or secretly provide them to terrorist allies." Faced with such threats, he added, the United States had no choice but to take "preemptive action."

In that West Point speech, Bush also directly confronted criticism, both at home and abroad, of his moralistic view of the world as evidenced in his repeated use of the word evil *to describe U.S. opponents. "Some worry that it is somehow undiplomatic or impolite to speak the language of right and wrong. I disagree," he said. "Different circumstances require different methods, but not different moralities."*

During the next few months Bush and his senior aides continued to make speeches justifying the use of preemptive military strikes against terrorists and regimes who aided them. The administration specifically cited Iraq as a case in point. White House officials also told reporters early in June that the administration was developing a broad new national security strategy that expressly advocated preemption as one of the policy options open to the president.

Also in early summer officials revealed that on May 3 Rumsfeld had approved an updated Pentagon document, the "Defense Planning Guidance," describing the administration's general plans for its military services in future years. Among other things, the document placed heavy reliance on such concepts as "forward deterrence" and "unwarned attacks" against potential threats.

The administration's open talk about possible preemptive strikes sparked a debate, both nationally and internationally. While acknowledging that the September 11 terrorist attacks had changed American perceptions of current threats, both allies and critics of the administration suggested that a preemptive action should be considered only in exceptional circumstances, not as a routine matter. In a June 23 editorial, for example, the New York Times *said the United States "must take care not to set a dangerous example that might, say, tempt India to launch its own preemptive strike against Pakistan." The newspaper also warned against use of nuclear weapons in such a strike, saying they "should never be regarded as just another bigger, more effective bomb."*

Details of the Strategy

After signaling its new policy for more than three months, the administration formally enunciated its broad approach to the world in the National Security Strategy sent to Congress and made public September 20. The thirty-one page document was submitted under a 1986 Pentagon reorganization law that required an annual statement from the president on his national strategy. Most previous reports had been pro-forma efforts that were filed and quickly forgotten. The Bush administration, however, used the legislative requirement as an opportunity to make a bold statement about its intentions on a wide range of issues, from nuclear arms policy to combating AIDS in poor countries. Perhaps not coincidentally, the administration released the report just one day after Bush sent Congress a formal request for authorization to take military action against Iraq.

Despite its broad reach, much of the strategy was built around what the administration clearly viewed as the central security challenge facing the United States: terrorism. In blunt language, the strategy expanded on Bush's speech to Congress just nine days after the September 11 terrorist attacks, in which he had pledged a war "of global reach" against terrorists. This war, the strategy document said, would take place "over an extended period of time" and would involve both conventional means—such as the military attacks in Afghanistan in late 2001—and unconventional means—such as disrupting the international fund-raising of terrorist organizations. Fighting terrorism also would require "a war of ideas," the strategy said, including the support of "moderate and modern government" in the Middle East "to ensure that the conditions and ideologies that promote terrorism do not find fertile ground in any nation."

In two sections—one dealing expressly with terrorism and another discussing threats posed by weapons of mass destruction—the strategy directly said the United States would take preemptive action, if necessary, to protect itself. International law recognized a country's right to defend itself against an "imminent danger," it said, and the United States had long "maintained the option of preemptive actions to counter a sufficient threat to our national security." The strategy offered no specific cases from history nor examples of possible future action, but it did appear to set a general standard: "The greater the threat, the greater is the risk of inaction—and the more compelling the case for taking anticipatory action to defend our-selves, even if uncertainty remains as to the time and place of the enemy's attack. To forestall or prevent such hostile acts by our adversaries, the United States will, if necessary, act preemptively."

The strategy sought to allay fears of some allies that the administration's approach to the world was essentially unilateral—emphasizing U.S. inter-ests with only secondary regard for those of other countries. Even so, the United States reserved the right to act in its own best interests. "While the United States will consistently strive to enlist the support of the inter-national community, we will not hesitate to act alone, if necessary, to exer-cise our right of self-defense by acting preemptively against such terrorists, to prevent them from doing harm against our people and our country."

In just four sentences, the strategy also declared what appeared to be a policy of maintaining U.S. military superiority in the world in perpetuity. "We know from history that deterrence can fail; and we know from experi-ence that some enemies cannot be deterred," the strategy said. "The United States must and will maintain the capability to defeat any attempt by an enemy—whether a state or non-state actor—to impose its will on the United States, our allies, or our friends. We will maintain the forces sufficient to support our obligations, and to defend freedom. Our forces will be strong enough to dissuade potential adversaries from pursuing a military build-up in hopes of surpassing, or equaling, the power of the United States."

While seemingly straightforward, this statement left open such questions as who the "potential adversaries" might be, and how the United States would respond if one of them attempted to equal or surpass U.S. military might. For all practical purposes, both questions applied to China, the only rising power in the world with the near-term potential to rival the United States on a broad range of strategic and tactical military fronts. "As China builds up a massive defense structure, what do we do?" asked Lee H. Hamil-ton, director of the Woodrow Wilson International Center for Scholars and a former chairman of the House Foreign Affairs Committee. "Do we bomb them? Or does it mean that we keep increasing our own defense efforts?" The Bush strategy document did not address such questions.

Although tough-sounding rhetoric received most of the public attention paid to the strategy, other sections reflected a long-standing strain of Amer-ican idealism—in particular the view that what was good for the United States would also be good for the rest of the world. Some of the writing could easily have come from the pen of Woodrow Wilson (1913–1921), the U.S. president who sought during and after World War I to make "the world safe for democracy" and whose idealistic views for global peace had since been derided by generations of American foreign policy "realists." Another author of some of these sections could have been Jimmy Carter (1977–1981), the first president to make promoting human rights a cornerstone of U.S. policy.

The first paragraph of the main body of the report proclaimed boldly that "the United States must defend liberty and justice because these prin-ciple are right and true for all people everywhere." People in authoritarian societies worldwide had been inspired by the values of liberty enshrined in the Declaration of Independence, the strategy said, and so the United States had an obligation to "look outward for possibilities to expand liberty"—not just defend it at home.

The strategy also included impassioned language on economic justice, a theme not often featured in the policy declarations of conservative U.S. administrations. "A world where some lie in comfort and plenty, while half of the human race lives on less than $2 a day, is neither just nor stable," it declared. "Including all of the world's poor in an expanding circle of development—and opportunity—is a moral imperative and one of the top priorities of U.S. international policy." None of the strategy's prescriptions for dealing with global poverty were new, but together they presented a range of policies from across the ideological spectrum: promoting free trade and free-market economies as well as boosting development aid to help poor countries educate and provide health services for their people.

Reaction

Because the Bush administration issued the national security strategy report in the midst of its campaign to build international support for a possible war against Iraq, much of the reaction to the document reflected differing views on that issue. Administration supporters—and even some who often were at odds with Bush—praised the strategy as a carefully thought-out grounding for a long-term U.S. policy of confronting Iraq immediately and other threats in the future. Critics suggested the strategy was little more than an intellectual exercise of justifying a war that Bush was determined to fight no matter what others thought or what the consequences might be.

The debate over Bush's strategy was especially pronounced in Western Europe, where long-time U.S. allies where sharply divided about Bush's foreign policy views in general and his focus on Iraq in particular. In an editorial in its September 28 edition, the British news magazine, the Economist, *suggested that only Saddam Hussein "and any would-be emulators" should be frightened by the Bush strategy. By taking his case for action against Iraq to the United Nations, Bush had demolished the European view of him as a "Wild West cowboy," the editorial said. "It also ought to be reassuring that his new security strategy is packed to the brim with idealistic language about peace and prosperity for all, and full of declarations of intent to work with allies, reinforce nonproliferation treaties, operate through multilateral organizations, and so on."*

Critics acknowledged a U.S. right to take action to defend itself, but many said Bush's embrace of preemption as a policy option could be used by other nations to justify preemptive action against what the claimed to be a threat. This possibility was not just idle speculation, the critics said, noting that India, Indonesia, Pakistan, Russia—and even Iraq—had dressed their own, often repressive, policies in the same antiterrorism language Bush had used after the September 11 attacks.

Even some analysts who generally praised Bush's strategy said it contained some flaws, such as its repeated declaration that the United States reserved the right to act unilaterally if other nations failed to perceive the same threats. "A nation that sets itself up as an example to the world in most things will not achieve that purpose by telling the rest of the world, in some things, to shove it," Yale University historian John Lewis Gaddis wrote in the November-December issue of Foreign Policy *magazine.*

Combating Weapons of Mass Destruction

Many of the same ideas developed in the National Security Strategy were repeated in a follow-up document released by the White House on December 10: a National Strategy to Combat Weapons of Mass Destruction. A more narrowly focused, five-page document, it said the United States would take whatever steps were necessary to protect itself against biological, chemical, or nuclear weapons—called weapons of mass destruction (WMD in diplomatic-speak) because of their potential to inflict enormous casualties.

"We will not permit the world's most dangerous regimes and terrorists to threaten us with the world's most destructive weapons," the strategy document said. "We must accord the highest priority to the protection of the United States, our forces, and our friends and allies from the existing and growing WMD threat."

The document said counterproliferation and nonproliferation were the pillars of U.S. policy against such weapons. Counterproliferation, it said, meant preventing potential enemies from using mass weapons against the United States and its interests. In some cases this would mean interdicting the weapons before they could be used. Deterrence also was necessary, the strategy said, by making it clear that the United States "reserves the right to respond with overwhelming force—including through resort to all of our options—to the use of WMD against the United States, our forces abroad, and friends and allies." According to news reports, a classified version of the strategy explicitly authorized preemptive strikes against unfriendly nations or terrorist groups if they were on the verge of acquiring weapons of mass destruction or the ballistic missiles needed to carry such weapons over great distances. The Washington Post *reported on December 11 that the document specifically mentioned Iran, Iraq, Libya, North Korea, and Syria among the countries that were of special concern.*

The strategy also endorsed the diplomatic approach of nonproliferation: the use of treaties and other international commitments intended to discourage nations and groups from attempting to acquire weapons of mass destruction. The Bush administration previously had taken a mixed approach to nonproliferation, rejecting treaties on the subject that it said were flawed, and at first cutting back then embracing U.S. programs to keep the vast weapons arsenals of the former Soviet Union from falling into the hands of terrorists. (Weapons of mass destruction, p. 437)

The difficulties of carrying out the tough-minded policies embodied in the two strategy documents were illustrated in an incident in the Arabian Sea on the same day the latter strategy was released. Patrolling the region as part of an international antiterror coalition, a Spanish warship intercepted a North Korean cargo ship carrying fifteen short-range "Scud"

*missiles. The ship was held for one day but then allowed to proceed when it
was determined that the missiles had been purchased legitimately by the
government of Yemen.*

*Following are excerpts from the "National Security Strategy of
the United States of America," released by the White House on
September 20, 2002.*

***The document was obtained from the Internet at www
.whitehouse.gov/nsc/nss.html; accessed January 22, 2003.***

The great struggles of the twentieth century between liberty and totalitarianism ended with a decisive victory for the forces of freedom—and a single
sustainable model for national success: freedom, democracy, and free enterprise. In the twenty-first century, only nations that share a commitment to protecting basic human rights and guaranteeing political and economic freedom
will be able to unleash the potential of their people and assure their future
prosperity. People everywhere want to be able to speak freely; choose who
will govern them; worship as they please; educate their children—male and
female; own property; and enjoy the benefits of their labor. These values of
freedom are right and true for every person, in every society—and the duty
of protecting these values against their enemies is the common calling of freedom-loving people across the globe and across the ages.

Today, the United States enjoys a position of unparalleled military strength
and great economic and political influence. In keeping with our heritage and
principles, we do not use our strength to press for unilateral advantage. We
seek instead to create a balance of power that favors human freedom: conditions in which all nations and all societies can choose for themselves the rewards and challenges of political and economic liberty. In a world that is safe,
people will be able to make their own lives better. We will defend the peace by
fighting terrorists and tyrants. We will preserve the peace by building good relations among the great powers. We will extend the peace by encouraging free
and open societies on every continent.

Defending our Nation against its enemies is the first and fundamental commitment of the Federal Government. Today, that task has changed dramatically. Enemies in the past needed great armies and great industrial capabilities
to endanger America. Now, shadowy networks of individuals can bring great
chaos and suffering to our shores for less than it costs to purchase a single
tank. Terrorists are organized to penetrate open societies and to turn the
power of modern technologies against us.

To defeat this threat we must make use of every tool in our arsenal—military power, better homeland defenses, law enforcement, intelligence, and vigorous efforts to cut off terrorist financing. The war against terrorists of global
reach is a global enterprise of uncertain duration. America will help nations
that need our assistance in combating terror. And America will hold to ac-

count nations that are compromised by terror, including those who harbor terrorists—because the allies of terror are the enemies of civilization. The United States and countries cooperating with us must not allow the terrorists to develop new home bases. Together, we will seek to deny them sanctuary at every turn.

The gravest danger our Nation faces lies at the crossroads of radicalism and technology. Our enemies have openly declared that they are seeking weapons of mass destruction, and evidence indicates that they are doing so with determination. The United States will not allow these efforts to succeed. We will build defenses against ballistic missiles and other means of delivery. We will cooperate with other nations to deny, contain, and curtail our enemies' efforts to acquire dangerous technologies. And, as a matter of common sense and self-defense, America will act against such emerging threats before they are fully formed. We cannot defend America and our friends by hoping for the best. So we must be prepared to defeat our enemies' plans, using the best intelligence and proceeding with deliberation. History will judge harshly those who saw this coming danger but failed to act. In the new world we have entered, the only path to peace and security is the path of action.

As we defend the peace, we will also take advantage of an historic opportunity to preserve the peace. Today, the international community has the best chance since the rise of the nation-state in the seventeenth century to build a world where great powers compete in peace instead of continually prepare for war. Today, the world's great powers find ourselves on the same side—united by common dangers of terrorist violence and chaos. The United States will build on these common interests to promote global security. We are also increasingly united by common values. Russia is in the midst of a hopeful transition, reaching for its democratic future and a partner in the war on terror. Chinese leaders are discovering that economic freedom is the only source of national wealth. In time, they will find that social and political freedom is the only source of national greatness. America will encourage the advancement of democracy and economic openness in both nations, because these are the best foundations for domestic stability and international order. We will strongly resist aggression from other great powers—even as we welcome their peaceful pursuit of prosperity, trade, and cultural advancement.

Finally, the United States will use this moment of opportunity to extend the benefits of freedom across the globe. We will actively work to bring the hope of democracy, development, free markets, and free trade to every corner of the world. The events of September 11, 2001, taught us that weak states, like Afghanistan, can pose as great a danger to our national interests as strong states. Poverty does not make poor people into terrorists and murderers. Yet poverty, weak institutions, and corruption can make weak states vulnerable to terrorist networks and drug cartels within their borders.

The United States will stand beside any nation determined to build a better future by seeking the rewards of liberty for its people. Free trade and free markets have proven their ability to lift whole societies out of poverty—so the United States will work with individual nations, entire regions, and the entire global trading community to build a world that trades in freedom and therefore grows in prosperity. The United States will deliver greater development assistance through the New Millennium Challenge Account to nations that govern justly, invest in their people, and encourage economic freedom. We will also continue to lead the world in efforts to reduce the terrible toll of HIV/AIDS and other infectious diseases.

In building a balance of power that favors freedom, the United States is guided by the conviction that all nations have important responsibilities. Nations that enjoy freedom must actively fight terror. Nations that depend on international stability must help prevent the spread of weapons of mass destruction. Nations that seek international aid must govern themselves wisely, so that aid is well spent. For freedom to thrive, accountability must be expected and required.

We are also guided by the conviction that no nation can build a safer, better world alone. Alliances and multilateral institutions can multiply the strength of freedom-loving nations. The United States is committed to lasting institutions like the United Nations, the World Trade Organization, the Organization of American States, and NATO as well as other long-standing alliances. Coalitions of the willing can augment these permanent institutions. In all cases, international obligations are to be taken seriously. They are not to be undertaken symbolically to rally support for an ideal without furthering its attainment.

Freedom is the non-negotiable demand of human dignity; the birthright of every person—in every civilization. Throughout history, freedom has been threatened by war and terror; it has been challenged by the clashing wills of powerful states and the evil designs of tyrants; and it has been tested by widespread poverty and disease. Today, humanity holds in its hands the opportunity to further freedom's triumph over all these foes. The United States welcomes our responsibility to lead in this great mission.

George W. Bush
THE WHITE HOUSE
September 17, 2002

I. Overview of America's International Strategy

The United States possesses unprecedented—and unequaled—strength and influence in the world. Sustained by faith in the principles of liberty, and the value of a free society, this position comes with unparalleled responsibilities, obligations, and opportunity. The great strength of this nation must be used to promote a balance of power that favors freedom.

For most of the twentieth century, the world was divided by a great struggle over ideas: destructive totalitarian visions versus freedom and equality.

That great struggle is over. The militant visions of class, nation, and race which promised utopia and delivered misery have been defeated and discredited. America is now threatened less by conquering states than we are by failing ones. We are menaced less by fleets and armies than by catastrophic technologies in the hands of the embittered few. We must defeat these threats to our Nation, allies, and friends.

This is also a time of opportunity for America. We will work to translate this moment of influence into decades of peace, prosperity, and liberty. The U.S. national security strategy will be based on a distinctly American internationalism that reflects the union of our values and our national interests. The aim of this strategy is to help make the world not just safer but better. Our goals on the path to progress are clear: political and economic freedom, peaceful relations with other states, and respect for human dignity.

And this path is not America's alone. It is open to all.

To achieve these goals, the United States will:

- champion aspirations for human dignity;
- strengthen alliances to defeat global terrorism and work to prevent attacks against us and our friends;
- work with others to defuse regional conflicts;
- prevent our enemies from threatening us, our allies, and our friends, with weapons of mass destruction;
- ignite a new era of global economic growth through free markets and free trade;
- expand the circle of development by opening societies and building the infrastructure of democracy;
- develop agendas for cooperative action with other main centers of global power; and
- transform America's national security institutions to meet the challenges and opportunities of the twenty-first century.

II. Champion Aspirations for Human Dignity

In pursuit of our goals, our first imperative is to clarify what we stand for: the United States must defend liberty and justice because these principles are right and true for all people everywhere. No nation owns these aspirations, and no nation is exempt from them. Fathers and mothers in all societies want their children to be educated and to live free from poverty and violence. No people on earth yearn to be oppressed, aspire to servitude, or eagerly await the midnight knock of the secret police.

America must stand firmly for the nonnegotiable demands of human dignity: the rule of law; limits on the absolute power of the state; free speech; freedom of worship; equal justice; respect for women; religious and ethnic tolerance; and respect for private property.

These demands can be met in many ways. America's constitution has served us well. Many other nations, with different histories and cultures, facing different circumstances, have successfully incorporated these core principles into their own systems of governance. History has not been kind to those nations which ignored or flouted the rights and aspirations of their people.

America's experience as a great multi-ethnic democracy affirms our conviction that people of many heritages and faiths can live and prosper in peace. Our own history is a long struggle to live up to our ideals. But even in our worst moments, the principles enshrined in the Declaration of Independence were there to guide us. As a result, America is not just a stronger, but is a freer and more just society.

Today, these ideals are a lifeline to lonely defenders of liberty. And when openings arrive, we can encourage change—as we did in central and eastern Europe between 1989 and 1991, or in Belgrade in 2000. When we see democratic processes take hold among our friends in Taiwan or in the Republic of Korea, and see elected leaders replace generals in Latin America and Africa, we see examples of how authoritarian systems can evolve, marrying local history and traditions with the principles we all cherish.

Embodying lessons from our past and using the opportunity we have today, the national security strategy of the United States must start from these core beliefs and look outward for possibilities to expand liberty.

Our principles will guide our government's decisions about international cooperation, the character of our foreign assistance, and the allocation of resources. They will guide our actions and our words in international bodies. We will:

- speak out honestly about violations of the nonnegotiable demands of human dignity using our voice and vote in international institutions to advance freedom;
- use our foreign aid to promote freedom and support those who struggle non-violently for it, ensuring that nations moving toward democracy are rewarded for the steps they take;
- make freedom and the development of democratic institutions key themes in our bilateral relations, seeking solidarity and cooperation from other democracies while we press governments that deny human rights to move toward a better future; and
- take special efforts to promote freedom of religion and conscience and defend it from encroachment by repressive governments.

We will champion the cause of human dignity and oppose those who resist it.

III. Strengthen Alliances to Defeat Global Terrorism and Work to Prevent Attacks Against Us and Our Friends

The United States of America is fighting a war against terrorists of global reach. The enemy is not a single political regime or person or religion or ideology. The enemy is terrorism—premeditated, politically motivated violence perpetrated against innocents.

In many regions, legitimate grievances prevent the emergence of a lasting peace. Such grievances deserve to be, and must be, addressed within a political process. But no cause justifies terror. The United States will make no concessions to terrorist demands and strike no deals with them. We make no distinction between terrorists and those who knowingly harbor or provide aid to them.

The struggle against global terrorism is different from any other war in our history. It will be fought on many fronts against a particularly elusive enemy over an extended period of time. Progress will come through the persistent accumulation of successes—some seen, some unseen.

Today our enemies have seen the results of what civilized nations can, and will, do against regimes that harbor, support, and use terrorism to achieve their political goals. Afghanistan has been liberated; coalition forces continue to hunt down the Taliban and al-Qaida. But it is not only this battlefield on which we will engage terrorists. Thousands of trained terrorists remain at large with cells in North America, South America, Europe, Africa, the Middle East, and across Asia.

Our priority will be first to disrupt and destroy terrorist organizations of global reach and attack their leadership; command, control, and communications; material support; and finances. This will have a disabling effect upon the terrorists' ability to plan and operate.

We will continue to encourage our regional partners to take up a coordinated effort that isolates the terrorists. Once the regional campaign localizes the threat to a particular state, we will help ensure the state has the military, law enforcement, political, and financial tools necessary to finish the task.

The United States will continue to work with our allies to disrupt the financing of terrorism. We will identify and block the sources of funding for terrorism, freeze the assets of terrorists and those who support them, deny terrorists access to the international financial system, protect legitimate charities from being abused by terrorists, and prevent the movement of terrorists' assets through alternative financial networks.

However, this campaign need not be sequential to be effective, the cumulative effect across all regions will help achieve the results we seek.

We will disrupt and destroy terrorist organizations by:

- direct and continuous action using all the elements of national and international power. Our immediate focus will be those terrorist organizations of global reach and any terrorist or state sponsor of terrorism which attempts to gain or use weapons of mass destruction (WMD) or their precursors;
- defending the United States, the American people, and our interests at home and abroad by identifying and destroying the threat before it reaches our borders. While the United States will constantly strive to enlist the support of the international community, we will not hesitate to act alone, if necessary, to exercise our right of self-defense by acting pre-emptively against such terrorists, to prevent them from doing harm against our people and our country; and
- denying further sponsorship, support, and sanctuary to terrorists by convincing or compelling states to accept their sovereign responsibilities.

We will also wage a war of ideas to win the battle against international terrorism. This includes:

- using the full influence of the United States, and working closely with allies and friends, to make clear that all acts of terrorism are illegitimate so that terrorism will be viewed in the same light as slavery, piracy, or genocide: behavior that no respectable government can condone or support and all must oppose;

- supporting moderate and modern government, especially in the Muslim world, to ensure that the conditions and ideologies that promote terrorism do not find fertile ground in any nation;
- diminishing the underlying conditions that spawn terrorism by enlisting the international community to focus its efforts and resources on areas most at risk; and
- using effective public diplomacy to promote the free flow of information and ideas to kindle the hopes and aspirations of freedom of those in societies ruled by the sponsors of global terrorism.

While we recognize that our best defense is a good offense, we are also strengthening America's homeland security to protect against and deter attack.

This Administration has proposed the largest government reorganization since the Truman Administration created the National Security Council and the Department of Defense. Centered on a new Department of Homeland Security and including a new unified military command and a fundamental reordering of the FBI, our comprehensive plan to secure the homeland encompasses every level of government and the cooperation of the public and the private sector.

This strategy will turn adversity into opportunity. For example, emergency management systems will be better able to cope not just with terrorism but with all hazards. Our medical system will be strengthened to manage not just bioterror, but all infectious diseases and mass-casualty dangers. Our border controls will not just stop terrorists, but improve the efficient movement of legitimate traffic.

While our focus is protecting America, we know that to defeat terrorism in today's globalized world we need support from our allies and friends. Wherever possible, the United States will rely on regional organizations and state powers to meet their obligations to fight terrorism. Where governments find the fight against terrorism beyond their capacities, we will match their willpower and their resources with whatever help we and our allies can provide.

As we pursue the terrorists in Afghanistan, we will continue to work with international organizations such as the United Nations, as well as non-governmental organizations, and other countries to provide the humanitarian, political, economic, and security assistance necessary to rebuild Afghanistan so that it will never again abuse its people, threaten its neighbors, and provide a haven for terrorists.

In the war against global terrorism, we will never forget that we are ultimately fighting for our democratic values and way of life. Freedom and fear are at war, and there will be no quick or easy end to this conflict. In leading the campaign against terrorism, we are forging new, productive international relationships and redefining existing ones in ways that meet the challenges of the twenty-first century.

IV. Work with Others to Defuse Regional Conflicts

Concerned nations must remain actively engaged in critical regional disputes to avoid explosive escalation and minimize human suffering. In an increasingly interconnected world, regional crisis can strain our alliances, rekindle rivalries among the major powers, and create horrifying affronts to human dignity. When violence erupts and states falter, the United States will work with friends and partners to alleviate suffering and restore stability.

No doctrine can anticipate every circumstance in which U.S. action—direct or indirect—is warranted. We have finite political, economic, and military resources to meet our global priorities. The United States will approach each case with these strategic principles in mind:

- The United States should invest time and resources into building international relationships and institutions that can help manage local crises when they emerge.
- The United States should be realistic about its ability to help those who are unwilling or unready to help themselves. Where and when people are ready to do their part, we will be willing to move decisively.

The Israeli-Palestinian conflict is critical because of the toll of human suffering, because of America's close relationship with the state of Israel and key Arab states, and because of that region's importance to other global priorities of the United States. There can be no peace for either side without freedom for both sides. America stands committed to an independent and democratic Palestine, living beside Israel in peace and security. Like all other people, Palestinians deserve a government that serves their interests and listens to their voices. The United States will continue to encourage all parties to step up to their responsibilities as we seek a just and comprehensive settlement to the conflict.

The United States, the international donor community, and the World Bank stand ready to work with a reformed Palestinian government on economic development, increased humanitarian assistance, and a program to establish, finance, and monitor a truly independent judiciary. If Palestinians embrace democracy, and the rule of law, confront corruption, and firmly reject terror, they can count on American support for the creation of a Palestinian state.

Israel also has a large stake in the success of a democratic Palestine. Permanent occupation threatens Israel's identity and democracy. So the United States continues to challenge Israeli leaders to take concrete steps to support the emergence of a viable, credible Palestinian state. As there is progress towards security, Israel forces need to withdraw fully to positions they held prior to September 28, 2000. And consistent with the recommendations of the Mitchell Committee, Israeli settlement activity in the occupied territories must stop. As violence subsides, freedom of movement should be restored, permitting innocent Palestinians to resume work and normal life. The United States can play a crucial role but, ultimately, lasting peace can only come when Israelis and Palestinians resolve the issues and end the conflict between them.

In South Asia, the United States has also emphasized the need for India and Pakistan to resolve their disputes. This Administration invested time and resources building strong bilateral relations with India and Pakistan. These strong relations then gave us leverage to play a constructive role when tensions in the region became acute. With Pakistan, our bilateral relations have been bolstered by Pakistan's choice to join the war against terror and move toward building a more open and tolerant society. The Administration sees India's potential to become one of the great democratic powers of the twenty-first century and has worked hard to transform our relationship accordingly. Our involvement in this regional dispute, building on earlier investments in bilateral relations, looks first to concrete steps by India and Pakistan that can help defuse military confrontation.

Indonesia took courageous steps to create a working democracy and respect for the rule of law. By tolerating ethnic minorities, respecting the rule of law, and accepting open markets, Indonesia may be able to employ the engine of opportunity that has helped lift some of its neighbors out of poverty and desperation. It is the initiative by Indonesia that allows U.S. assistance to make a difference.

In the Western Hemisphere we have formed flexible coalitions with countries that share our priorities, particularly Mexico, Brazil, Canada, Chile, and Colombia. Together we will promote a truly democratic hemisphere where our integration advances security, prosperity, opportunity, and hope. We will work with regional institutions, such as the Summit of the Americas process, the Organization of American States (OAS), and the Defense Ministerial of the Americas for the benefit of the entire hemisphere.

Parts of Latin America confront regional conflict, especially arising from the violence of drug cartels and their accomplices. This conflict and unrestrained narcotics trafficking could imperil the health and security of the United States. Therefore we have developed an active strategy to help the Andean nations adjust their economies, enforce their laws, defeat terrorist organizations, and cut off the supply of drugs, while—as important—we work to reduce the demand for drugs in our own country.

In Colombia, we recognize the link between terrorist and extremist groups that challenge the security of the state and drug trafficking activities that help finance the operations of such groups. We are working to help Colombia defend its democratic institutions and defeat illegal armed groups of both the left and right by extending effective sovereignty over the entire national territory and provide basic security to the Colombian people.

In Africa, promise and opportunity sit side by side with disease, war, and desperate poverty. This threatens both a core value of the United States—preserving human dignity—and our strategic priority—combating global terror. American interests and American principles, therefore, lead in the same direction: we will work with others for an African continent that lives in liberty, peace, and growing prosperity. Together with our European allies, we must help strengthen Africa's fragile states, help build indigenous capability to secure porous borders, and help build up the law enforcement and intelligence infrastructure to deny havens for terrorists.

An ever more lethal environment exists in Africa as local civil wars spread beyond borders to create regional war zones. Forming coalitions of the willing and cooperative security arrangements are key to confronting these emerging transnational threats.

Africa's great size and diversity requires a security strategy that focuses on bilateral engagement and builds coalitions of the willing. This Administration will focus on three interlocking strategies for the region:

- countries with major impact on their neighborhood such as South Africa, Nigeria, Kenya, and Ethiopia are anchors for regional engagement and require focused attention;
- coordination with European allies and international institutions is essential for constructive conflict mediation and successful peace operations; and
- Africa's capable reforming states and sub-regional organizations must be strengthened as the primary means to address transnational threats on a sustained basis.

Ultimately the path of political and economic freedom presents the surest route to progress in sub-Saharan Africa, where most wars are conflicts over material resources and political access often tragically waged on the basis of ethnic and religious difference. The transition to the African Union with its stated commitment to good governance and a common responsibility for democratic political systems offers opportunities to strengthen democracy on the continent.

V. Prevent Our Enemies from Threatening Us, Our Allies, and Our Friends with Weapons of Mass Destruction

The nature of the Cold War threat required the United States—with our allies and friends—to emphasize deterrence of the enemy's use of force, producing a grim strategy of mutual assured destruction. With the collapse of the Soviet Union and the end of the Cold War, our security environment has undergone profound transformation.

Having moved from confrontation to cooperation as the hallmark of our relationship with Russia, the dividends are evident: an end to the balance of terror that divided us; an historic reduction in the nuclear arsenals on both sides; and cooperation in areas such as counterterrorism and missile defense that until recently were inconceivable.

But new deadly challenges have emerged from rogue states and terrorists. None of these contemporary threats rival the sheer destructive power that was arrayed against us by the Soviet Union. However, the nature and motivations of these new adversaries, their determination to obtain destructive powers hitherto available only to the world's strongest states, and the greater likelihood that they will use weapons of mass destruction against us, make today's security environment more complex and dangerous.

In the 1990s we witnessed the emergence of a small number of rogue states that, while different in important ways, share a number of attributes. These states:

- brutalize their own people and squander their national resources for the personal gain of the rulers;
- display no regard for international law, threaten their neighbors, and callously violate international treaties to which they are party;
- are determined to acquire weapons of mass destruction, along with other advanced military technology, to be used as threats or offensively to achieve the aggressive designs of these regimes;
- sponsor terrorism around the globe; and
- reject basic human values and hate the United States and everything for which it stands.

At the time of the Gulf War, we acquired irrefutable proof that Iraq's designs were not limited to the chemical weapons it had used against Iran and its own people, but also extended to the acquisition of nuclear weapons and biological agents. In the past decade North Korea has become the world's principal purveyor of ballistic missiles, and has tested increasingly capable missiles while developing its own WMD arsenal. Other rogue regimes seek nuclear, biological, and chemical weapons as well. These states' pursuit of, and global trade in, such weapons has become a looming threat to all nations.

We must be prepared to stop rogue states and their terrorist clients before they are able to threaten or use weapons of mass destruction against the United States and our allies and friends. Our response must take full advantage of strengthened alliances, the establishment of new partnerships with former adversaries, innovation in the use of military forces, modern technologies, including the development of an effective missile defense system, and increased emphasis on intelligence collection and analysis.

Our comprehensive strategy to combat WMD includes:

- *Proactive counterproliferation efforts.* We must deter and defend against the threat before it is unleashed. We must ensure that key capabilities—detection, active and passive defenses, and counterforce capabilities—are integrated into our defense transformation and our homeland security systems. Counterproliferation must also be integrated into the doctrine, training, and equipping of our forces and those of our allies to ensure that we can prevail in any conflict with WMD-armed adversaries.
- *Strengthened nonproliferation efforts to prevent rogue states and terrorists from acquiring the materials, technologies, and expertise necessary for weapons of mass destruction.* We will enhance diplomacy, arms control, multilateral export controls, and threat reduction assistance that impede states and terrorists seeking WMD, and when necessary, interdict enabling technologies and materials. We will continue to build coalitions to support these efforts, encouraging their increased political and financial support for nonproliferation and threat reduction programs. The recent G-8 agreement to commit up to $20 billion to a global partnership against proliferation marks a major step forward.
- *Effective consequence management to respond to the effects of WMD use, whether by terrorists or hostile states.* Minimizing the effects of

WMD use against our people will help deter those who possess such weapons and dissuade those who seek to acquire them by persuading enemies that they cannot attain their desired ends. The United States must also be prepared to respond to the effects of WMD use against our forces abroad, and to help friends and allies if they are attacked.

It has taken almost a decade for us to comprehend the true nature of this new threat. Given the goals of rogue states and terrorists, the United States can no longer solely rely on a reactive posture as we have in the past. The inability to deter a potential attacker, the immediacy of today's threats, and the magnitude of potential harm that could be caused by our adversaries' choice of weapons, do not permit that option. We cannot let our enemies strike first.

- In the Cold War, especially following the Cuban missile crisis, we faced a generally status quo, risk-averse adversary. Deterrence was an effective defense. But deterrence based only upon the threat of retaliation is less likely to work against leaders of rogue states more willing to take risks, gambling with the lives of their people, and the wealth of their nations.
- In the Cold War, weapons of mass destruction were considered weapons of last resort whose use risked the destruction of those who used them. Today, our enemies see weapons of mass destruction as weapons of choice. For rogue states these weapons are tools of intimidation and military aggression against their neighbors. These weapons may also allow these states to attempt to blackmail the United States and our allies to prevent us from deterring or repelling the aggressive behavior of rogue states. Such states also see these weapons as their best means of overcoming the conventional superiority of the United States.
- Traditional concepts of deterrence will not work against a terrorist enemy whose avowed tactics are wanton destruction and the targeting of innocents; whose so-called soldiers seek martyrdom in death and whose most potent protection is statelessness. The overlap between states that sponsor terror and those that pursue WMD compels us to action.

For centuries, international law recognized that nations need not suffer an attack before they can lawfully take action to defend themselves against forces that present an imminent danger of attack. Legal scholars and international jurists often conditioned the legitimacy of preemption on the existence of an imminent threat—most often a visible mobilization of armies, navies, and air forces preparing to attack.

We must adapt the concept of imminent threat to the capabilities and objectives of today's adversaries. Rogue states and terrorists do not seek to attack us using conventional means. They know such attacks would fail. Instead, they rely on acts of terror and, potentially, the use of weapons of mass destruction—weapons that can be easily concealed, delivered covertly, and used without warning.

The targets of these attacks are our military forces and our civilian population, in direct violation of one of the principal norms of the law of warfare. As was demonstrated by the losses on September 11, 2001, mass civilian casualties is the specific objective of terrorists and these losses would be exponentially more severe if terrorists acquired and used weapons of mass destruction.

The United States has long maintained the option of preemptive actions to counter a sufficient threat to our national security. The greater the threat, the greater is the risk of inaction—and the more compelling the case for taking anticipatory action to defend ourselves, even if uncertainty remains as to the time and place of the enemy's attack. To forestall or prevent such hostile acts by our adversaries, the United States will, if necessary, act preemptively.

The United States will not use force in all cases to preempt emerging threats, nor should nations use preemption as a pretext for aggression. Yet in an age where the enemies of civilization openly and actively seek the world's most destructive technologies, the United States cannot remain idle while dangers gather.

We will always proceed deliberately, weighing the consequences of our actions. To support preemptive options, we will:

- build better, more integrated intelligence capabilities to provide timely, accurate information on threats, wherever they may emerge;
- coordinate closely with allies to form a common assessment of the most dangerous threats; and
- continue to transform our military forces to ensure our ability to conduct rapid and precise operations to achieve decisive results.

The purpose of our actions will always be to eliminate a specific threat to the United States or our allies and friends. The reasons for our actions will be clear, the force measured, and the cause just.

VI. Ignite a New Era of Global Economic Growth through Free Markets and Free Trade

A strong world economy enhances our national security by advancing prosperity and freedom in the rest of the world. Economic growth supported by free trade and free markets creates new jobs and higher incomes. It allows people to lift their lives out of poverty, spurs economic and legal reform, and the fight against corruption, and it reinforces the habits of liberty.

We will promote economic growth and economic freedom beyond America's shores. All governments are responsible for creating their own economic policies and responding to their own economic challenges. We will use our economic engagement with other countries to underscore the benefits of policies that generate higher productivity and sustained economic growth, including:

- pro-growth legal and regulatory policies to encourage business investment, innovation, and entrepreneurial activity;
- tax policies—particularly lower marginal tax rates—that improve incentives for work and investment;
- rule of law and intolerance of corruption so that people are confident that they will be able to enjoy the fruits of their economic endeavors;

- strong financial systems that allow capital to be put to its most efficient use;
- sound fiscal policies to support business activity;
- investments in health and education that improve the well-being and skills of the labor force and population as a whole; and
- free trade that provides new avenues for growth and fosters the diffusion of technologies and ideas that increase productivity and opportunity.

The lessons of history are clear: market economies, not command-and-control economies with the heavy hand of government, are the best way to promote prosperity and reduce poverty. Policies that further strengthen market incentives and market institutions are relevant for all economies—industrialized countries, emerging markets, and the developing world.

A return to strong economic growth in Europe and Japan is vital to U.S. national security interests. We want our allies to have strong economies for their own sake, for the sake of the global economy, and for the sake of global security. European efforts to remove structural barriers in their economies are particularly important in this regard, as are Japan's efforts to end deflation and address the problems of non-performing loans in the Japanese banking system. We will continue to use our regular consultations with Japan and our European partners—including through the Group of Seven (G-7)—to discuss policies they are adopting to promote growth in their economies and support higher global economic growth.

Improving stability in emerging markets is also key to global economic growth. International flows of investment capital are needed to expand the productive potential of these economies. These flows allow emerging markets and developing countries to make the investments that raise living standards and reduce poverty. Our long-term objective should be a world in which all countries have investment-grade credit ratings that allow them access to international capital markets and to invest in their future.

We are committed to policies that will help emerging markets achieve access to larger capital flows at lower cost. To this end, we will continue to pursue reforms aimed at reducing uncertainty in financial markets. We will work actively with other countries, the International Monetary Fund (IMF), and the private sector to implement the G-7 Action Plan negotiated earlier this year for preventing financial crises and more effectively resolving them when they occur.

The best way to deal with financial crises is to prevent them from occurring, and we have encouraged the IMF to improve its efforts doing so. We will continue to work with the IMF to streamline the policy conditions for its lending and to focus its lending strategy on achieving economic growth through sound fiscal and monetary policy, exchange rate policy, and financial sector policy.

The concept of "free trade" arose as a moral principle even before it became a pillar of economics. If you can make something that others value, you should be able to sell it to them. If others make something that you value, you should be able to buy it. This is real freedom, the freedom for a person—or a nation—to make a living. To promote free trade, the United States has developed a comprehensive strategy:

- *Seize the global initiative.* The new global trade negotiations we helped launch at Doha in November 2001 will have an ambitious agenda, especially in agriculture, manufacturing, and services, targeted for completion in 2005. The United States has led the way in completing the accession of China and a democratic Taiwan to the World Trade Organization. We will assist Russia's preparations to join the WTO.

- *Press regional initiatives.* The United States and other democracies in the Western Hemisphere have agreed to create the Free Trade Area of the Americas, targeted for completion in 2005. This year the United States will advocate market-access negotiations with its partners, targeted on agriculture, industrial goods, services, investment, and government procurement. We will also offer more opportunity to the poorest continent, Africa, starting with full use of the preferences allowed in the African Growth and Opportunity Act, and leading to free trade.

- *Move ahead with bilateral free trade agreements.* Building on the free trade agreement with Jordan enacted in 2001, the Administration will work this year to complete free trade agreements with Chile and Singapore. Our aim is to achieve free trade agreements with a mix of developed and developing countries in all regions of the world. Initially, Central America, Southern Africa, Morocco, and Australia will be our principal focal points.

- *Renew the executive-congressional partnership.* Every administration's trade strategy depends on a productive partnership with Congress. After a gap of 8 years, the Administration reestablished majority support in the Congress for trade liberalization by passing Trade Promotion Authority and the other market opening measures for developing countries in the Trade Act of 2002. This Administration will work with Congress to enact new bilateral, regional, and global trade agreements that will be concluded under the recently passed Trade Promotion Authority.

- *Promote the connection between trade and development.* Trade policies can help developing countries strengthen property rights, competition, the rule of law, investment, the spread of knowledge, open societies, the efficient allocation of resources, and regional integration—all leading to growth, opportunity, and confidence in developing countries. The United States is implementing The Africa Growth and Opportunity Act to provide market-access for nearly all goods produced in the 35 countries of sub-Saharan Africa. We will make more use of this act and its equivalent for the Caribbean Basin and continue to work with multilateral and regional institutions to help poorer countries take advantage of these opportunities. Beyond market access, the most important area where trade intersects with poverty is in public health. We will ensure that the WTO intellectual property rules are flexible enough to allow developing nations to gain access to critical medicines for extraordinary dangers like HIV/AIDS, tuberculosis, and malaria.

- *Enforce trade agreements and laws against unfair practices.* Commerce depends on the rule of law; international trade depends on enforceable agreements. Our top priorities are to resolve ongoing disputes with the European Union, Canada, and Mexico and to make a global effort to address new technology, science, and health regulations that needlessly impede farm exports and improved agriculture. Laws against unfair trade practices are often abused, but the international community must be able to address genuine concerns about government subsidies and dumping. International industrial espionage which undermines fair competition must be detected and deterred.
- *Help domestic industries and workers adjust.* There is a sound statutory framework for these transitional safeguards which we have used in the agricultural sector and which we are using this year to help the American steel industry. The benefits of free trade depend upon the enforcement of fair trading practices. These safeguards help ensure that the benefits of free trade do not come at the expense of American workers. Trade adjustment assistance will help workers adapt to the change and dynamism of open markets.
- *Protect the environment and workers.* The United States must foster economic growth in ways that will provide a better life along with widening prosperity. We will incorporate labor and environmental concerns into U.S. trade negotiations, creating a healthy "network" between multilateral environmental agreements with the WTO, and use the International Labor Organization, trade preference programs, and trade talks to improve working conditions in conjunction with freer trade.
- *Enhance energy security.* We will strengthen our own energy security and the shared prosperity of the global economy by working with our allies, trading partners, and energy producers to expand the sources and types of global energy supplied, especially in the Western Hemisphere, Africa, Central Asia, and the Caspian region. We will also continue to work with our partners to develop cleaner and more energy efficient technologies.

Economic growth should be accompanied by global efforts to stabilize greenhouse gas concentrations associated with this growth, containing them at a level that prevents dangerous human interference with the global climate. Our overall objective is to reduce America's greenhouse gas emissions relative to the size of our economy, cutting such emissions per unit of economic activity by 18 percent over the next 10 years, by the year 2012. Our strategies for attaining this goal will be to:

- remain committed to the basic U. N. Framework Convention [on Climate Change] for international cooperation;
- obtain agreements with key industries to cut emissions of some of the most potent greenhouse gases and give transferable credits to companies that can show real cuts;
- develop improved standards for measuring and registering emission reductions;

- promote renewable energy production and clean coal technology, as well as nuclear power—which produces no greenhouse gas emissions, while also improving fuel economy for U.S. cars and trucks;
- increase spending on research and new conservation technologies, to a total of $4.5 billion—the largest sum being spent on climate change by any country in the world and a $700 million increase over last year's budget; and
- assist developing countries, especially the major greenhouse gas emitters such as China and India, so that they will have the tools and resources to join this effort and be able to grow along a cleaner and better path.

VII. Expand the Circle of Development by Opening Societies and Building the Infrastructure of Democracy

A world where some live in comfort and plenty, while half of the human race lives on less than $2 a day, is neither just nor stable. Including all of the world's poor in an expanding circle of development—and opportunity—is a moral imperative and one of the top priorities of U.S. international policy.

Decades of massive development assistance have failed to spur economic growth in the poorest countries. Worse, development aid has often served to prop up failed policies, relieving the pressure for reform and perpetuating misery. Results of aid are typically measured in dollars spent by donors, not in the rates of growth and poverty reduction achieved by recipients. These are the indicators of a failed strategy.

Working with other nations, the United States is confronting this failure. We forged a new consensus at the U. N. Conference on Financing for Development in Monterrey that the objectives of assistance—and the strategies to achieve those objectives—must change.

This Administration's goal is to help unleash the productive potential of individuals in all nations. Sustained growth and poverty reduction is impossible without the right national policies. Where governments have implemented real policy changes, we will provide significant new levels of assistance. The United States and other developed countries should set an ambitious and specific target: to double the size of the world's poorest economies within a decade.

The United States Government will pursue these major strategies to achieve this goal:

- *Provide resources to aid countries that have met the challenge of national reform.* We propose a 50 percent increase in the core development assistance given by the United States. While continuing our present programs, including humanitarian assistance based on need alone, these billions of new dollars will form a new Millennium Challenge Account for projects in countries whose governments rule justly, invest in their people, and encourage economic freedom. Governments must fight corruption, respect basic human rights, embrace the rule of law, invest in health care and education, follow responsible economic policies, and enable entrepreneurship. The Millennium Challenge Account will reward countries that have demonstrated real policy change and challenge those that have not to implement reforms.

- *Improve the effectiveness of the World Bank and other development banks in raising living standards.* The United States is committed to a comprehensive reform agenda for making the World Bank and the other multilateral development banks more effective in improving the lives of the world's poor. We have reversed the downward trend in U.S. contributions and proposed an 18 percent increase in the U.S. contributions to the International Development Association (IDA)—the World Bank's fund for the poorest countries—and the African Development Fund. The key to raising living standards and reducing poverty around the world is increasing productivity growth, especially in the poorest countries. We will continue to press the multilateral development banks to focus on activities that increase economic productivity, such as improvements in education, health, rule of law, and private sector development. Every project, every loan, every grant must be judged by how much it will increase productivity growth in developing countries.

- *Insist upon measurable results to ensure that development assistance is actually making a difference in the lives of the world's poor.* When it comes to economic development, what really matters is that more children are getting a better education, more people have access to health care and clean water, or more workers can find jobs to make a better future for their families. We have a moral obligation to measure the success of our development assistance by whether it is delivering results. For this reason, we will continue to demand that our own development assistance as well as assistance from the multilateral development banks has measurable goals and concrete benchmarks for achieving those goals. Thanks to U.S. leadership, the recent IDA replenishment agreement will establish a monitoring and evaluation system that measures recipient countries' progress. For the first time, donors can link a portion of their contributions to IDA to the achievement of actual development results, and part of the U.S. contribution is linked in this way. We will strive to make sure that the World Bank and other multilateral development banks build on this progress so that a focus on results is an integral part of everything that these institutions do.

- *Increase the amount of development assistance that is provided in the form of grants instead of loans.* Greater use of results-based grants is the best way to help poor countries make productive investments, particularly in the social sectors, without saddling them with ever-larger debt burdens. As a result of U.S. leadership, the recent IDA agreement provided for significant increases in grant funding for the poorest countries for education, HIV/AIDS, health, nutrition, water, sanitation, and other human needs. Our goal is to build on that progress by increasing the use of grants at the other multilateral development banks. We will also challenge universities, nonprofits, and the private sector to match government efforts by using grants to support development projects that show results.

- *Open societies to commerce and investment. Trade and investment are the real engines of economic growth.* Even if government aid increases, most money for development must come from trade, domestic capital, and foreign investment. An effective strategy must try to expand these flows as well. Free markets and free trade are key priorities of our national security strategy.

- *Secure public health.* The scale of the public health crisis in poor countries is enormous. In countries afflicted by epidemics and pandemics like HIV/AIDS, malaria, and tuberculosis, growth and development will be threatened until these scourges can be contained. Resources from the developed world are necessary but will be effective only with honest governance, which supports prevention programs and provides effective local infrastructure. The United States has strongly backed the new global fund for HIV/AIDS organized by U. N. Secretary General Kofi Annan and its focus on combining prevention with a broad strategy for treatment and care. The United States already contributes more than twice as much money to such efforts as the next largest donor. If the global fund demonstrates its promise, we will be ready to give even more.

- *Emphasize education.* Literacy and learning are the foundation of democracy and development. Only about 7 percent of World Bank resources are devoted to education. This proportion should grow. The United States will increase its own funding for education assistance by at least 20 percent with an emphasis on improving basic education and teacher training in Africa. The United States can also bring information technology to these societies, many of whose education systems have been devastated by HIV/AIDS.

- *Continue to aid agricultural development.* New technologies, including biotechnology, have enormous potential to improve crop yields in developing countries while using fewer pesticides and less water. Using sound science, the United States should help bring these benefits to the 800 million people, including 300 million children, who still suffer from hunger and malnutrition.

VIII. Develop Agendas for Cooperative Action with the Other Main Centers of Global Power

America will implement its strategies by organizing coalitions—as broad as practicable—of states able and willing to promote a balance of power that favors freedom. Effective coalition leadership requires clear priorities, an appreciation of others' interests, and consistent consultations among partners with a spirit of humility.

There is little of lasting consequence that the United States can accomplish in the world without the sustained cooperation of its allies and friends in Canada and Europe. Europe is also the seat of two of the strongest and most able international institutions in the world: the North Atlantic Treaty Organization

(NATO), which has, since its inception, been the fulcrum of transatlantic and inter-European security, and the European Union (EU), our partner in opening world trade.

The attacks of September 11 were also an attack on NATO, as NATO itself recognized when it invoked its Article V self-defense clause for the first time. NATO's core mission—collective defense of the transatlantic alliance of democracies—remains, but NATO must develop new structures and capabilities to carry out that mission under new circumstances. NATO must build a capability to field, at short notice, highly mobile, specially trained forces whenever they are needed to respond to a threat against any member of the alliance.

The alliance must be able to act wherever our interests are threatened, creating coalitions under NATO's own mandate, as well as contributing to mission-based coalitions. To achieve this, we must:

- expand NATO's membership to those democratic nations willing and able to share the burden of defending and advancing our common interests;
- ensure that the military forces of NATO nations have appropriate combat contributions to make in coalition warfare;
- develop planning processes to enable those contributions to become effective multinational fighting forces;
- take advantage of the technological opportunities and economies of scale in our defense spending to transform NATO military forces so that they dominate potential aggressors and diminish our vulnerabilities;
- streamline and increase the flexibility of command structures to meet new operational demands and the associated requirements of training, integrating, and experimenting with new force configurations; and
- maintain the ability to work and fight together as allies even as we take the necessary steps to transform and modernize our forces.

If NATO succeeds in enacting these changes, the rewards will be a partnership as central to the security and interests of its member states as was the case during the Cold War. We will sustain a common perspective on the threats to our societies and improve our ability to take common action in defense of our nations and their interests. At the same time, we welcome our European allies' efforts to forge a greater foreign policy and defense identity with the EU, and commit ourselves to close consultations to ensure that these developments work with NATO. We cannot afford to lose this opportunity to better prepare the family of transatlantic democracies for the challenges to come.

The attacks of September 11 energized America's Asian alliances. Australia invoked the ANZUS Treaty [mutual defense treaty among Australia, New Zealand, and the United States] to declare the September 11 was an attack on Australia itself, following that historic decision with the dispatch of some of the world's finest combat forces for Operation Enduring Freedom. Japan and the Republic of Korea provided unprecedented levels of military logistical support within weeks of the terrorist attack. We have deepened cooperation on counter-terrorism with our alliance partners in Thailand and the Philippines and received invaluable assistance from close friends like Singapore and New Zealand.

The war against terrorism has proven that America's alliances in Asia not only underpin regional peace and stability, but are flexible and ready to deal with new challenges. To enhance our Asian alliances and friendships, we will:

- look to Japan to continue forging a leading role in regional and global affairs based on our common interests, our common values, and our close defense and diplomatic cooperation;
- work with South Korea to maintain vigilance towards the North while preparing our alliance to make contributions to the broader stability of the region over the longer term;
- build on 50 years of U. S.-Australian alliance cooperation as we continue working together to resolve regional and global problems—as we have so many times from the Battle of the Coral Sea to Tora Bora;
- maintain forces in the region that reflect our commitments to our allies, our requirements, our technological advances, and the strategic environment; and
- build on stability provided by these alliances, as well as with institutions such as ASEAN and the Asia-Pacific Economic Cooperation forum, to develop a mix of regional and bilateral strategies to manage change in this dynamic region.

We are attentive to the possible renewal of old patterns of great power competition. Several potential great powers are now in the midst of internal transition—most importantly Russia, India, and China. In all three cases, recent developments have encouraged our hope that a truly global consensus about basic principles is slowly taking shape.

With Russia, we are already building a new strategic relationship based on a central reality of the twenty-first century: the United States and Russia are no longer strategic adversaries. The Moscow Treaty on Strategic Reductions is emblematic of this new reality and reflects a critical change in Russian thinking that promises to lead to productive, long-term relations with the Euro-Atlantic community and the United States. Russia's top leaders have a realistic assessment of their country's current weakness and the policies— internal and external—needed to reverse those weaknesses. They understand, increasingly, that Cold War approaches do not serve their national interests and that Russian and American strategic interests overlap in many areas.

United States policy seeks to use this turn in Russian thinking to refocus our relationship on emerging and potential common interests and challenges. We are broadening our already extensive cooperation in the global war on terrorism. We are facilitating Russia's entry into the World Trade Organization, without lowering standards for accession, to promote beneficial bilateral trade and investment relations. We have created the NATO-Russia Council with the goal of deepening security cooperation among Russia, our European allies, and ourselves. We will continue to bolster the independence and stability of the states of the former Soviet Union in the belief that a prosperous and stable neighborhood will reinforce Russia's growing commitment to integration into the Euro-Atlantic community.

At the same time, we are realistic about the differences that still divide us from Russia and about the time and effort it will take to build an enduring strategic partnership. Lingering distrust of our motives and policies by key Russian elites slows improvement in our relations. Russia's uneven commitment to the basic values of free-market democracy and dubious record in combating the proliferation of weapons of mass destruction remain matters of great concern. Russia's very weakness limits the opportunities for cooperation. Nevertheless, those opportunities are vastly greater now than in recent years—or even decades.

The United States has undertaken a transformation in its bilateral relationship with India based on a conviction that U.S. interests require a strong relationship with India. We are the two largest democracies, committed to political freedom protected by representative government. India is moving toward greater economic freedom as well. We have a common interest in the free flow of commerce, including through the vital sea lanes of the Indian Ocean. Finally, we share an interest in fighting terrorism and in creating a strategically stable Asia.

Differences remain, including over the development of India's nuclear and missile programs, and the pace of India's economic reforms. But while in the past these concerns may have dominated our thinking about India, today we start with a view of India as a growing world power with which we have common strategic interests. Through a strong partnership with India, we can best address any differences and shape a dynamic future.

The United States relationship with China is an important part of our strategy to promote a stable, peaceful, and prosperous Asia-Pacific region. We welcome the emergence of a strong, peaceful, and prosperous China. The democratic development of China is crucial to that future. Yet, a quarter century after beginning the process of shedding the worst features of the Communist legacy, China's leaders have not yet made the next series of fundamental choices about the character of their state. In pursuing advanced military capabilities that can threaten its neighbors in the Asia-Pacific region, China is following an outdated path that, in the end, will hamper its own pursuit of national greatness. In time, China will find that social and political freedom is the only source of that greatness.

The United States seeks a constructive relationship with a changing China. We already cooperate well where our interests overlap, including the current war on terrorism and in promoting stability on the Korean peninsula. Likewise, we have coordinated on the future of Afghanistan and have initiated a comprehensive dialogue on counterterrorism and similar transitional concerns. Shared health and environmental threats, such as the spread of HIV/AIDS, challenge us to promote jointly the welfare of our citizens.

Addressing these transnational threats will challenge China to become more open with information, promote the development of civil society, and enhance individual human rights. China has begun to take the road to political openness, permitting many personal freedoms and conducting village-level elections, yet remains strongly committed to national one-party rule by the Communist Party. To make that nation truly accountable to its citizen's needs and aspirations, however, much work remains to be done. Only by allowing the Chinese people to think, assemble, and worship freely can China reach its full potential.

Our important trade relationship will benefit from China's entry into the World Trade Organization, which will create more export opportunities and ultimately more jobs for American farmers, workers, and companies. China is our fourth largest trading partner, with over $100 billion in annual two-way trade. The power of market principles and the WTO's requirements for transparency and accountability will advance openness and the rule of law in China to help establish basic protections for commerce and for citizens. There are, however, other areas in which we have profound disagreements. Our commitment to the self-defense of Taiwan under the Taiwan Relations Act is one. Human rights is another. We expect China to adhere to its nonproliferation commitments. We will work to narrow differences where they exist, but not allow them to preclude cooperation where we agree.

The events of September 11, 2001, fundamentally changed the context for relations between the United States and other main centers of global power, and opened vast, new opportunities. With our long-standing allies in Europe and Asia, and with leaders in Russia, India, and China, we must develop active agendas of cooperation lest these relationships become routine and unproductive.

Every agency of the United States Government shares the challenge. We can build fruitful habits of consultation, quiet argument, sober analysis, and common action. In the long-term, these are the practices that will sustain the supremacy of our common principles and keep open the path of progress.

IX. Transform America's National Security Institutions to Meet the Challenges and Opportunities of the Twenty-First Century

The major institutions of American national security were designed in a different era to meet different requirements. All of them must be transformed.

It is time to reaffirm the essential role of American military strength. We must build and maintain our defenses beyond challenge. Our military's highest priority is to defend the United States. To do so effectively, our military must:

- assure our allies and friends;
- dissuade future military competition;
- deter threats against U.S. interests, allies, and friends; and
- decisively defeat any adversary if deterrence fails.

The unparalleled strength of the United States armed forces, and their forward presence, have maintained the peace in some of the world's most strategically vital regions. However, the threats and enemies we must confront have changed, and so must our forces. A military structured to deter massive Cold

War-era armies must be transformed to focus more on how an adversary might fight rather than where and when a war might occur. We will channel our energies to overcome a host of operational challenges.

The presence of American forces overseas is one of the most profound symbols of the U.S. commitments to allies and friends. Through our willingness to use force in our own defense and in defense of others, the United States demonstrates its resolve to maintain a balance of power that favors freedom. To contend with uncertainty and to meet the many security challenges we face, the United States will require bases and stations within and beyond Western Europe and Northeast Asia, as well as temporary access arrangements for the long-distance deployment of U.S. forces.

Before the war in Afghanistan, that area was low on the list of major planning contingencies. Yet, in a very short time, we had to operate across the length and breadth of that remote nation, using every branch of the armed forces. We must prepare for more such deployments by developing assets such as advanced remote sensing, long-range precision strike capabilities, and transformed maneuver and expeditionary forces. This broad portfolio of military capabilities must also include the ability to defend the homeland, conduct information operations, ensure U.S. access to distant theaters, and protect critical U.S. infrastructure and assets in outer space.

Innovation within the armed forces will rest on experimentation with new approaches to warfare, strengthening joint operations, exploiting U.S. intelligence advantages, and taking full advantage of science and technology. We must also transform the way the Department of Defense is run, especially in financial management and recruitment and retention. Finally, while maintaining near-term readiness and the ability to fight the war on terrorism, the goal must be to provide the President with a wider range of military options to discourage aggression or any form of coercion against the United States, our allies, and our friends.

We know from history that deterrence can fail; and we know from experience that some enemies cannot be deterred. The United States must and will maintain the capability to defeat any attempt by an enemy—whether a state or non-state actor—to impose its will on the United States, our allies, or our friends. We will maintain the forces sufficient to support our obligations, and to defend freedom. Our forces will be strong enough to dissuade potential adversaries from pursuing a military build-up in hopes of surpassing, or equaling, the power of the United States.

Intelligence—and how we use it—is our first line of defense against terrorists and the threat posed by hostile states. Designed around the priority of gathering enormous information about a massive, fixed object—the Soviet bloc—the intelligence community is coping with the challenge of following a far more complex and elusive set of targets.

We must transform our intelligence capabilities and build new ones to keep pace with the nature of these threats. Intelligence must be appropriately integrated with our defense and law enforcement systems and coordinated with our allies and friends. We need to protect the capabilities we have so that we do not arm our enemies with the knowledge of how best to surprise us. Those who would harm us also seek the benefit of surprise to limit our prevention and response options and to maximize injury.

We must strengthen intelligence warning and analysis to provide integrated threat assessments for national and homeland security. Since the threats inspired by foreign governments and groups may be conducted inside the United States, we must also ensure the proper fusion of information between intelligence and law enforcement.

Initiatives in this area will include:

- strengthening the authority of the Director of Central Intelligence to lead the development and actions of the Nation's foreign intelligence capabilities;
- establishing a new framework for intelligence warning that provides seamless and integrated warning across the spectrum of threats facing the nation and our allies;
- continuing to develop new methods of collecting information to sustain our intelligence advantage;
- investing in future capabilities while working to protect them through a more vigorous effort to prevent the compromise of intelligence capabilities; and
- collecting intelligence against the terrorist danger across the government with all-source analysis.

As the United States Government relies on the armed forces to defend America's interests, it must rely on diplomacy to interact with other nations. We will ensure that the Department of State receives funding sufficient to ensure the success of American diplomacy. The State Department takes the lead in managing our bilateral relationships with other governments. And in this new era, its people and institutions must be able to interact equally adroitly with non-governmental organizations and international institutions. Officials trained mainly in international politics must also extend their reach to understand complex issues of domestic governance around the world, including public health, education, law enforcement, the judiciary, and public diplomacy.

Our diplomats serve at the front line of complex negotiations, civil wars, and other humanitarian catastrophes. As humanitarian relief requirements are better understood, we must also be able to help build police forces, court systems, and legal codes, local and provincial government institutions, and electoral systems. Effective international cooperation is needed to accomplish these goals, backed by American readiness to play our part.

Just as our diplomatic institutions must adapt so that we can reach out to others, we also need a different and more comprehensive approach to public information efforts that can help people around the world learn about and understand America. The war on terrorism is not a clash of civilizations. It does, however, reveal the clash inside a civilization, a battle for the future of the Muslim world. This is a struggle of ideas and this is an area where America must excel.

We will take the actions necessary to ensure that our efforts to meet our global security commitments and protect Americans are not impaired by the potential for investigations, inquiry, or prosecution by the International Criminal Court (ICC), whose jurisdiction does not extend to Americans and which we do not accept. We will work together with other nations to avoid complications in our military operations and cooperation, through such mechanisms as multilateral and bilateral agreements that will protect U.S. nationals from the ICC. We will implement fully the American Servicemembers Protection Act, whose provisions are intended to ensure and enhance the protection of U.S. personnel and officials.

We will make hard choices in the coming year and beyond to ensure the right level and allocation of government spending on national security. The United States Government must strengthen its defenses to win this war. At home, our most important priority is to protect the homeland for the American people.

Today, the distinction between domestic and foreign affairs is diminishing. In a globalized world, events beyond America's borders have a greater impact inside them. Our society must be open to people, ideas, and goods from across the globe. The characteristics we most cherish—our freedom, our cities, our systems of movement, and modern life—are vulnerable to terrorism. This vulnerability will persist long after we bring to justice those responsible for the September 11 attacks. As time passes, individuals may gain access to means of destruction that until now could be wielded only by armies, fleets, and squadrons. This is a new condition of life. We will adjust to it and thrive—in spite of it.

In exercising our leadership, we will respect the values, judgment, and interests of our friends and partners. Still, we will be prepared to act apart when our interests and unique responsibilities require. When we disagree on particulars, we will explain forthrightly the grounds for our concerns and strive to forge viable alternatives. We will not allow such disagreements to obscure our determination to secure together, with our allies and our friends, our shared fundamental interests and values.

Ultimately, the foundation of American strength is at home. It is in the skills of our people, the dynamism of our economy, and the resilience of our institutions. A diverse, modern society has inherent, ambitious, entrepreneurial energy. Our strength comes from what we do with that energy. That is where our national security begins.

CENSUS BUREAU ON
HEALTH INSURANCE COVERAGE
September 30, 2002

After dropping for two years in a row, the number of Americans without health insurance started to climb again in 2001. According to the Census Bureau, 41.6 million Americans were uncovered in 2001—1.4 million more than in 2000. The hardest hit appeared to be middle-class workers, many of whom lost their jobs and their employer-sponsored insurance, especially in the months immediately following the September 11, 2001, terrorist attacks.

Most health policy experts predicted that the situation would get worse before it got better. A continuing lackluster economy and high unemployment along with soaring health care costs and cutbacks in public health insurance programs were expected to increase the numbers of people without insurance in 2002 and perhaps 2003. Survey after survey found that workers and their families who currently had health insurance were worried about losing it.

With the financial support of the Robert Wood Johnson Foundation, an unusual coalition of organizations that often opposed each other on health care policy issues banded together early in 2002 in an effort to push the issue of the uninsured to the top of the national political agenda. The high-powered coalition included business, professional, insurance, consumer, and labor organizations, including the Chamber of Commerce of the United States, the Business Roundtable, the American Medical Association, the Health Insurance Association of America, the AFL-CIO, Families USA, and AARP (formerly the American Association of Retired Persons). "This is the top health problem in the United States, and it's the issue of conscience in the American healthcare system," said Ron Pollack, the executive director of Families USA, a nonpartisan health care advocacy group that participated in the coalition. But Democrats and Republicans in Congress remained at loggerheads over several pieces of legislation that might have helped Americans cope with rising health care costs.

The Numbers and the Causes Behind Them

Once considered primarily a problem of the poor and the chronically un-employed, lack of health insurance was increasingly becoming a problem for the middle class. The Census Bureau data, released September 30, 2002, showed that the share of children and the poor in 2001 remained unchanged from 2000, in part because of increases in Medicaid coverage, the federal-state health insurance program for the poor. But the uninsured rate increased for all other income levels. The largest increase was among people who had incomes of $75,000 or more—800,000 people in that category were found themselves among the newly uninsured in 2001.

Most of the increase in the uninsured rate was attributable to a decline in employer-sponsored health insurance coverage. The data showed that coverage had dropped a full percentage point, from 63.6 percent in 2000 to 62.6 percent in 2001. The last time employer-sponsored coverage declined was in 1993, at the end of the last recession. The decline in coverage appeared to be concentrated among employees of small businesses.

The slow-growing economy, tightening government budgets, and mounting health care costs combined to push thousands of people off the insurance rolls. According to one estimate, more than 2 million people lost their health insurance when they lost their jobs in 2001. But the soaring costs of health care were also making insurance increasingly unaffordable for many employers and their employees. According to one preliminary estimate, company premiums were projected to increase 12–13 percent in 2002 and another 12–15 percent in 2003. Other analysts predicted premiums might jump as high as 30 or 40 percent. To cope with the rising costs, companies were increasing the share of the premiums they passed on to their employees, raising deductibles and copayments, and cutting back on benefits. According the Henry J. Kaiser Family Foundation, premiums for family coverage averaged $7,954 in 2002, with employees paying an average of $2,084 of the total—nearly $300 more than in 2001. As a result some employees could no longer afford to participate in the plans and even more were worried that they might have to drop out if their costs went much higher.

Employers were also cutting back on the medical coverage they provided for retirees. Although Medicare picked up basic expenses for people over age sixty-five, large employers had covered many of the medical expenses not covered by Medicare. A new study by Watson Wyatt Worldwide, a human resources consulting firm, said that based on actions already taken, the share of total medical expenses for retirees paid for by employers was likely to decline from its current level of more than 50 percent to less than 10 percent by 2031. The study found that about 20 percent of the companies it studied had already eliminated retiree benefits for new hires, and another 17 percent were requiring workers to pay the full premium. Still others capped their contributions for new hires and current employees. "The burden on future retirees to pay for their own medical costs is increasing dramatically and far too few employees are prepared for these looking changes," said Sylvester J. Schieber, an author of the study. (Pension plans, p. 101)

The slow economy and high health care costs were also severely constraining federal and state programs that helped the poor, the elderly, and the disabled with health care costs. At least eighteen states were expected to reduce or restrict eligibility for Medicaid. The eligibility changes were likely to leave thousands of families without health insurance. More physicians, hospitals, and health plans were dropping their Medicare patients, complaining the government reimbursements were not high enough to cover their costs. Although most people over age sixty-five were covered under Medicare, the withdrawal of health care providers left many of the elderly with fewer choices and more expensive services.

Employers and insurers were experimenting with new approaches designed to make consumers more cost conscious. One tack was to set up a tier system for prescription drugs, under which patients paid a higher proportion of the cost of brand-name drugs than generic drugs. Some plans were beginning to extend that principle to medical services, so that a routine operation would cost the patient less if it were performed in a general hospital than it would in a specialized hospital.

Another relatively new approach was the consumer-driven health plan, which combined a high-deductible health insurance plan with an employer-funded health care account that could be used to cover the "first dollar" of a qualified medical expense. Under most plans the spending accounts were not as large as the deductible, so the consumer would be liable for the difference between the costs covered by the spending account and the costs covered by the insurer. For example, an employee might have a $1,000 spending account and a $2,000 deductible, so after the spending account funds were used, the employee would be liable for the next $1,000 plus any copayment, usually 80 percent, on the remaining medical costs.

The plans were growing in popularity, particularly after the Supreme Court ruled in June that employees could roll over their unused spending account funds from year to year, giving them the potential to accumulate a sizable health care nest egg if they remained healthy. The plans were attractive to employers because it cut their costs and, for some, could help finance retirement health care benefits for their employees. One recent survey found that nearly three of every ten large employers would be offering the plan by 2003.

Consumer advocates were concerned that the plans penalized people with chronic health conditions, who ran the risk of having much higher out-of-pocket costs than they would have under most managed-care programs. While the underlying idea of the plan was to make consumers more conscious about spending on health care because they would be paying for services out of their accounts, there were concerns that at least some consumers might become too cost-conscious and forgo needed health care. Some plans were attempting to circumvent that possibility by making checkups and immunizations no-cost benefits.

Consequences of Forgoing Insurance

A report by the Institute of Medicine released in May found that the lack of health insurance resulted in delayed treatment of serious diseases, life-threatening complications, and as many as 18,000 premature deaths every year. "Because we don't see many people dying in the streets in this country, we assume that the uninsured manage to get the care they need, but the evidence refutes that assumption. The fact is that the quality and length of life are distinctly different for insured and uninsured populations," said Mary Sue Coleman, president of the Iowa Health System and cochair of the committee that wrote the report "Care Without Coverage: Too Little, Too Late."

Some of the advantages of insurance included "financial security and stability, peace of mind, alleviation of pain and suffering, improved physical function, disabilities avoided or delayed and gains in life expectancy," the report said, adding that "these benefits remain out of reach" for most uninsured Americans. The report was the second in a projected six-part series produced by the institute's Committee on the Consequences of Uninsurance. The first, released in 2001, examined the myths and realities surrounding the uninsured. The third, released in September 2002, examined the adverse effects on health if one or two members of a family lost their health insurance. (First Institute of Medicine report, Historic Documents of 2001, p. 710)

Proposals for Increasing Coverage

Virtually all parties to the debate predicted that the rising numbers of uninsured would force Congress to consider ways to improve coverage. Without change, continually rising health care costs, increasing health care needs, and budget shortfalls could increase the number of uninsured to 61 million over the next decade, according to one estimate. But there was less certainty about whether Congress would find the political will to address the problem comprehensively. Ever since 1994, when President Bill Clinton's attempt to enact universal health care ended in politically devastating failure, politicians in both parties had been reluctant to return to that issue. Instead, they tended to nibble at the edges.

With support from President George W. Bush, congressional Republicans were advocating tax credits to help individuals, families, and small businesses defray the costs of buying health insurance in the open market. Most Democrats preferred an alternative solution of expanding Medicaid or the Children's Health Insurance Program to include parents whose children were already eligible for the program. With war in Iraq looming and the federal budget deficit growing, no final action occurred in 2002 on either of those proposals or on legislation giving seniors Medicare coverage for prescription drugs. Congress was also unable to agree on additional Medicare payments to reimburse doctors, hospitals, and other providers for their services, raising the possibility that even more physicians would refuse to take Medicare patients. But Congress easily cleared legislation (PL 107–251) *extending funding for community health centers through fiscal 1996. About 40 percent of the 11 million patients who sought treatment at the centers were uninsured.* (Prescription drugs, p. 945)

House Republicans and the Bush administration were also supporting the creation of Association Health Plans (AHPs), a system that would allow small businesses to band together across state lines to buy health insurance. This alliance which would theoretically give them more clout to bargain with insurers on price and coverage levels. The House included authorization for AHPs in its version of the patients' bill of rights, which died at the end of the year. As passed the legislation would have permitted trade and professional associations such as the U.S. Chamber of Commerce or the Professional Association of Innkeepers International to sponsor and negotiate the not-for profit health care plans.

The Blue Cross and Blue Shield Association, the dominant insurer of small businesses in at least half the states, opposed the legislation. Other groups, such as the National Governors' Association, supported the concept but opposed the specific legislation because it would exempt AHPs from state regulation. There was also controversy over how many of the uninsured would be helped by such plans. The Congressional Budget Office predicted that only about 330,000 uninsured would gain coverage under the legislation, but a public policy research firm, CONSAD, estimated that the legislation would extend benefits to 4.5 million workers at affordable rates.

Oregon Health Care Initiative

Washington was not alone in its reluctance to tackle a comprehensive approach to health insurance. One state, Oregon, was usually far ahead of the crowd on health care issues, but the state's voters rejected by a 4–1 margin an initiative on the November 5 ballot that would have made medical care available to all state residents. The plan would have been funded by a progressive income and payroll tax up to 8 percent of an individual's taxable income. Those earning less than 150 percent of the poverty rate would not have been liable for the tax. In return the program in theory would have replaced all health insurance premiums, copayments, deductibles and out-of-pocket expenses for everyone already covered by health insurance plus extend coverage to hundreds of thousands of Oregon residents who did not have health insurance. The plan would have covered a full range of physical and mental health services, including long-term care and alternative forms of treatment. The plan was expected to cost about $19 billion a year.

The initiative was opposed by insurance companies and other business groups, who said the plan would run Oregon's economy into the ground. "Its sky's-the-limit coverage would mean skyrocketing costs," warned Associated Oregon Industries, which represented about 20,000 Oregon businesses. "Taxes to pay those bills will hurt individual taxpayers, cripple Oregon businesses, and cost Oregon jobs." Supporters of the initiative argued that insurance companies were opposed to the bill because it would put them out of business.

Supporters of the initiative were undaunted by its defeat. "It took decades to free slaves and give women the right to vote," said Mark Lindgren of Health Care for All Oregonians, the grass-roots group that was promoting the referendum. Several other states had been considering some sort of universal health coverage for their residents, but Oregon was the first to put the issue to the voters. Oregon was often in front of the other states on health issues. In 1994 it became the first and still only state to approve physician-assisted suicide. (Physician-assisted suicide, Historic Documents of 1994, p. 501; 1997, p. 461; 2001 p. 290)

Following are excerpts from "Health Insurance Coverage: 2001," a report released September 30, 2002, by the U.S. Census Bureau giving data on the number of Americans in 2001 without health insurance.

The document was obtained from the Internet at www .census.gov/hhes/www/hlthin01.html; accessed October 18, 2002.

Reversing two years of falling uninsured rates, the share of the population without health insurance rose in 2001. An estimated 14.6 percent of the population or 41.2 million people were without health insurance coverage during the entire year in 2001, up from 14.2 percent in 2000, an increase of 1.4 million people.

The estimates in this report are based on the 2002 Current Population Survey (CPS) Annual Demographic Supplement, conducted by the U.S. Census Bureau. Respondents provide answers to the best of their ability, but as with all surveys, the estimates may differ from the actual values. A copy of the CPS Supplement questionnaire is available electronically at *http://www.census .gov/apsd/techdoc/ cps/cps-main.html.*

Highlights

- The number and percentage of people covered by employment-based health insurance dropped in 2001, from 63.6 percent to 62.6 percent, the foundation of the overall decrease in health insurance coverage.
- The number and percentage of people covered by government health insurance programs rose in 2001, from 24.7 percent to 25.3 percent, largely from an increase in the number and percentage of people covered by medicaid (from 10.6 percent to 11.2 percent).
- The proportion of uninsured children did not change, remaining at 8.5 million in 2001, or 11.7 percent of all children.
- Although medicaid insured 13.3 million poor people, 10.1 million poor people still had no health insurance in 2001, representing 30.7 percent of the poor, unchanged from 2000.

- Hispanics (66.8 percent) were less likely than non-Hispanic Whites (90.0 percent) to be covered by health insurance. The coverage rate for Blacks in 2001 (81.0 percent) did not differ from the coverage rate for Asians and Pacific Islanders (81.8 percent).
- American Indians and Alaska Natives were less likely to have health insurance than other racial groups, based on 3-year averages (1999-2001)— 72.9 percent, compared with 80.8 percent of Blacks, 81.5 percent of Asians and Pacific Islanders, and 90.2 percent of non-Hispanic Whites. However, American Indians and Alaska Natives were more likely to have insurance than were Hispanics (67.0 percent)
- Among the entire population 18 to 64 years old, workers (both full- and part-time) were more likely to have health insurance (83.0 percent) than nonworkers (75.3 percent), but among the poor, workers were less likely to be covered (51.3 percent) than nonworkers (63.2 percent).
- Compared with 2000, the proportion who had employment-based policies in their own name fell for workers employed by firms with fewer than 25 employees, but was unchanged for those employed by larger firms.
- Young adults (18 to 24 years old) were less likely than other age groups to have health insurance coverage —71.9 percent in 2001, compared with 83.3 percent of those 25 to 64 and, reflecting widespread medicare coverage, 99.2 percent of those 65 years and over.

More people did not have health insurance in 2001.

The number of people without health insurance coverage rose to 41.2 million (14.6 percent of the population) in 2001, up 1.4 million from the previous year, when 14.2 percent of the population lacked coverage. . . . Interestingly, the number of people covered by health insurance also increased in 2001, up 1.2 million to 240.9 million (85.4 percent of the population). Both increases can be attributed in part to an overall population growth from 2000 to 2001.

A decline in employment-based insurance prompted the decrease in insurance coverage rates.

Most people (62.6 percent) were covered by a health insurance plan related to employment for some or all of 2001, a decrease of 1.0 percentage point from the previous year. The 1.1 percentage point decline in private health insurance coverage, to 70.9 percent in 2001, largely reflects the decrease in employment-based insurance.

Although it did not offset the overall decline, health insurance coverage provided by the government increased between 2000 and 2001. This increase largely reflects the increase in medicaid coverage, which rose by 0.6 percentage points to 11.2 percent in 2001. Among the entire population, 25.3 percent had government insurance, including medicare (13.5 percent), medicaid (11.2 percent), and military health care (3.4 percent). Many people carried coverage from more than one plan during the year; for example, 7.6 percent of people were covered by both private health insurance and medicare.

The uninsured rates for the poor and the near poor did not change between 2000 and 2001.

Despite the medicaid program, 10.1 million poor people, or 30.7 percent of the poor, had no health insurance of any kind during 2001. This percentage—more than double the rate for the total population—did not change significantly from the previous year. The uninsured poor comprised 24.5 percent of all uninsured people. . . .

Medicaid was the most widespread type of health insurance among the poor, with 40.5 percent (13.3 million) of those in poverty covered by medicaid for some or all of 2001. This percentage did not change from the previous year.

Among the near poor (those with a family income greater than or equal to, but less than 125 percent of, the poverty level), 26.5 percent (3.3 million people) lacked health insurance in 2001, unchanged from 2000. Although private health insurance coverage among the near poor declined in 2001—from 40.3 percent to 37.8 percent—their rate of government health insurance coverage did not change from 2000 (it was 47.1 percent in 2001).

Key demographic factors affect health insurance coverage.

Age—People 18 to 24 years old were less likely than other age groups to have health insurance coverage, with 71.9 percent covered for some or all of 2001. Because of medicare, almost all people 65 years and over (99.2 percent) had health insurance in 2001. For other age groups, health insurance coverage ranged from 76.6 percent to 88.3 percent.

Among the poor, people 18 to 64 years old had a markedly lower health insurance coverage rate (57.7 percent) in 2001 than either people under 18 (78.7 percent) or 65 years and over (97.3 percent).

Race and Hispanic origin—While the uninsured rate rose in 2001 for non-Hispanic Whites—from 9.6 percent to 10.0 percent—the uninsured rates among Blacks (19.0 percent) and among Asian and Pacific Islanders (18.2 percent) did not change from 2000. The uninsured rate among Hispanics (33.2 percent in 2001) also did not change from 2000. . . .

The CPS Annual Demographic Supplement, the source of these data, obtained interviews from 78,000 households nationwide but is not large enough to produce reliable annual estimates for American Indians and Alaska Natives. . . . The 3-year average (1999-2001) shows that 27.1 percent of American Indians and Alaska Natives were without coverage, higher than the 19.2 percent for Blacks, 18.5 percent for Asians and Pacific Islanders, and 9.8 percent for non-Hispanic Whites. However, the 3-year-average uninsured rate for Hispanics (33.0 percent) was higher than the uninsured rate for American Indians and Alaska Natives.

Comparisons of 2-year moving averages (1999-2000 and 2000-2001) show that while the uninsured rate fell for American Indians and Alaska Natives from 27.7 percent to 25.5 percent and for Blacks from 19.3 percent to 18.9 percent, uninsured rates among non- Hispanic Whites, Asian and Pacific Islanders, and Hispanics did not change.

Nativity—In 2001, the proportion of the foreign-born population without health insurance (33.4 percent) was more than double that of the native population (12.2 percent). Among the foreign born, noncitizens were much more likely than naturalized citizens to lack coverage—42.9 percent compared with 17.2 percent.

Educational attainment—Among all adults, the likelihood of being insured increased as the level of education rose. Compared with the previous year, coverage rates decreased for those with no high school diploma, those who are high school graduates only, and those with some college education but no degree. Coverage rates did not change from 2000 to 2001 for adults with an associate degree or higher.

Economic status affects health insurance coverage.

Income—The likelihood of being covered by health insurance rises with income. Among households with annual incomes of less than $25,000, the percentage with health insurance was 76.7 percent; the level rises to 92.3 percent for those with incomes of $75,000 or more. Compared with the previous year, coverage rates decreased at every level of household income.

Work experience—Of those 18 to 64 years old in 2001, full-time workers were more likely to be covered by health insurance (84.0 percent) than part-time workers (78.0 percent), and part-time workers were more likely to be insured than nonworkers (75.3 percent). /11 However, among the poor, nonworkers (63.2 percent) were more likely to be insured than part-time workers (54.0 percent), who were more likely to be insured than full-time workers (49.7 percent).

Firm size—Of the 142.6 million workers in the United States who were 18–64 years old, 56.3 percent had employment-based health insurance policies in their own name. The proportion increased with the size of the employing firm from 31.3 percent for firms with fewer than 25 employees to 69.6 percent for firms with 1000 or more employees. (These estimates do not reflect the fact that some workers were covered by another family member's employment- based policy). Compared with the previous year, the proportion who had employment-based policies in their own name decreased for workers employed by firms with fewer than 25 employees, but were unchanged for those employed by larger firms.

The uninsured rate for children did not change between 2000 and 2001.

The percentage of children (people under 18 years old) without health insurance did not change in 2001 . . . remaining at 8.5 million or 11.7 percent. A decline in employment-based health insurance coverage of children was offset by an increase in coverage by medicaid or the State Children's Health Insurance Program.

Among poor children, 21.3 percent (2.5 million children) had no health insurance during 2001, unchanged from the previous year . . . For this group, employment-based coverage decreased from 20.1 percent to 18.6 percent, while government health insurance coverage increased from 60.9 percent to 63.3 percent. Poor children made up 29.3 percent of all uninsured children in 2001.

Among near-poor children (those in families whose income was greater than or equal to, but less than 125 percent of, the poverty level), 21.6 percent (0.9 million children) were without health insurance in 2001, unchanged from 2000. For this group, private health insurance coverage decreased from 39.8 percent to 36.4 percent, but government health insurance coverage did not change.

The likelihood of health insurance coverage varies among children.

- Children 12 to 17 years old were more likely to be uninsured than those under 12—13.1 percent compared with 11.0 percent.
- The uninsured rate declined in 2001 for Hispanic children—from 25.3 percent to 24.1 percent. The uninsured rates for non-Hispanic White children (7.4 percent), Black children (13.9 percent), and Asian and Pacific Islander children (11.7 percent) were unchanged from 2000.
- While most children (68.4 percent) were covered by an employment-based or privately purchased health insurance plan in 2001, nearly one in four (22.7 percent) was covered by medicaid.
- Black children had a higher rate of medicaid coverage in 2001 than children of any other racial or ethnic group—38.3 percent, compared with 34.9 percent of Hispanic children, 18.0 percent of Asian and Pacific Islander children, and 15.3 percent of non-Hispanic White children.
- Children living in single-parent families in 2001 were less likely to be insured than children living in married-couple families—84.3 percent compared with 90.4 percent.

Some states had higher uninsured rates than others.

The proportion of people without health insurance ranged from 7.2 percent in Rhode Island to 23.2 percent in New Mexico, based on 3-year averages for 1999, 2000 and 2001. . . . Although the data presented suggest that New Mexico had the highest uninsured rate, its rate was not statistically different from the rate for Texas. Similarly, although the data suggest that Rhode Island had the lowest uninsured rate, its rate was not statistically different from the rate for Minnesota.

Comparisons of 2-year moving averages (1999–2000 and 2000–2001) show that the proportion of people without coverage fell in 14 states: Alaska, Arizona, Idaho, Louisiana, Massachusetts, Montana, Nevada, New Mexico, North Dakota, South Carolina, South Dakota, Virginia, West Virginia and Wisconsin. Meanwhile, the proportion of people without coverage rose in nine states: Arkansas, Georgia, Indiana, Missouri, Ohio, Oklahoma, Pennsylvania, Rhode Island, and Texas. . . .

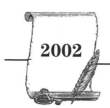

October

EU COMMISSIONER ON
ADDING TEN NEW MEMBERS
October 9, 2002

Broadening its base to take in much of the former Soviet bloc, the European Union (EU) in 2002 extended membership invitations to ten countries. The addition, during 2004, of Cyprus, the Czech Republic, Estonia, Hungary, Latvia, Lithuania, Malta, Poland, Slovakia, and Slovenia would boost total EU membership to twenty-five countries. The enlarged EU would include nearly every country in Western Europe and in the heart of Eastern Europe, which had been dominated by the Soviet Union during the last half of the twentieth century. Two other candidate countries, Bulgaria and Romania, were assured in 2002 they might be ready for admission in 2007. Turkey, whose membership application had been sitting in Europe's in-box for more than four decades, was given a consolation prize: a promise of another review of its prospects in late 2004.

A dramatic expansion of the European Union had been a foregone conclusion ever since the twin events that ended the cold war: the 1989 fall of the Berlin Wall and the 1991 collapse of the Soviet Union. But even after a decade's worth of planning and negotiations, it still was not clear by late 2002 that a bigger European Union would be a harmonious whole. Economically, most of the ten new members lagged well behind even the poorest of the fifteen older EU countries—raising serious questions about their abilities to compete in the world's most important common market. Politically, most of the new members had only limited experience with the EU's minimum requirements of democracy, the rule of law, and liberal social policies. Before formally gaining membership in 2004 they would have to finish rewriting most of their laws to conform to hundreds of EU standards on such issues as environmental policy, food safety, and workers' rights.

The EU had reached its current membership of fifteen in 1995 with the admission of Austria, Finland, and Sweden. The invitation to ten new members was an even more significant step for the union, perhaps its most important since the December 1991 summit meeting in Maastricht, the Netherlands, that led to many of the EU's institutions and policies. For Europeans, the most tangible EU institution was a common currency—the euro—which had been adopted by most member countries. At the start of 2002 the euro officially replaced the domestic currencies of those countries, consigning to the history books such former symbols of national pride as the German mark and the French franc. (Maastricht summit, Historic Documents of 1991, p. 843; Euro adoption, Historic Documents of 1999, p. 75)

If all went according to plan, the European Union was scheduled to take yet another major step in 2003 or 2004 with the adoption of a formal constitution. This document was supposed to provide a smoother system of managing the new, unwieldy agglomeration of twenty-five countries with vastly different cultures and national perspectives. Such a constitution had long been a goal for pan-European advocates of something similar to a United States of Europe. That, in fact, was one of the names under consideration for the new Europe, along with the European Community, United Europe, and the existing European Union title.

In reaching out to Eastern Europe, the EU was catching up with NATO, the cross-Atlantic alliance founded in 1949 as a military shield for Western Europe. NATO had accepted its first new members from the former Soviet bloc in 1997: the Czech Republic, Hungary, and Poland. At its summit November 2002, NATO went further, agreeing to invite seven new members including three—Estonia, Latvia, and Lithuania—that had once been part of NATO's former enemy, the Soviet Union. (NATO summit, p. 885)

The combined actions of the EU and NATO meant that, by 2004 at the latest, eighteen countries would belong to both organizations. Of NATO members, only Bulgaria, Canada, Iceland, Norway, Romania, Turkey, and the United States would remain outside of the EU as of 2004, with Bulgaria and Romania likely to join the EU three years later. Of EU members in 2004, only Austria, Cyprus, Finland, Ireland, Malta, and Sweden would remain outside of NATO.

Expanding to the East and South

The EU's membership invitation to ten countries was the culmination of a long process that had taken more than a decade. After the 1991 Maastricht summit, interested European countries were invited to apply for membership, and sixteen did so. After the applications of Austria, Finland, and Sweden were accepted in 1993 (for eventual membership in 1995), the remaining applicants went through an elaborate series of steps to show that they were on track to meet dozens of qualifying standards, most importantly that their democratic systems were entrenched and that their economies were based on free markets. By 2001 it was clear that most of the thirteen applicants would be ready for admission in what the EU called its "first wave" of expansion, scheduled to take place in time for the June 2004 elections for the European Parliament.

Even as Europe's politicians and bureaucrats were negotiating, public anxieties arose in both existing and prospective EU countries about the momentous step. Many in Western Europe feared that the EU's open borders would encourage millions of impoverished people from Eastern Europe to flood westward in search of jobs; this, it was believed, would lead to in-

creased crime, put pressure on social safety nets, and raise unemployment rates that already approached 10 percent in parts of Western Europe. Current beneficiaries of EU policies—notably farmers in France and elsewhere who received large subsidies—also were concerned that they would have to share these benefits with millions of new claimants from the East.

Likewise, many in Eastern Europe expressed hesitation about the consequences for them of entering into the continent's mainstream. Farmers in Poland—with 39 million people by far the largest of the applicant countries—worried that some of their products could not withstand competition from the heavily subsidized, highly efficient corporate farms in the West. In addition, many were angered that farmers in the new countries initially were to receive only 25 percent of the subsidies paid to farmers in existing EU member countries.

By 2002 public opinion polls showed sizable minorities in several candidate countries were inclined to reject EU membership. That was cause for concern because nine of the ten most likely new members planned referendums in 2003 on joining the union; Cyprus was the exception. In contrast to this mixed public sentiment, most political leaders in the candidate countries, across the ideological spectrum, were committed to the idea of being part of one large European family

As dates for decision making approached in 2002, EU officials took unprecedented steps to reassure both sides. The new members were offered financial incentives and a series of "safeguards" to protect their economies against crippling competition in their early years of membership. The existing EU members were told that the new countries would be examined one last time, in late 2003, to make sure they were meeting the membership requirements.

The EU's final decisions during 2002 involved several steps, each of which necessitated last-minute haggling and compromises. The first step was the requirement for an endorsement of the membership applications by the European Commission—the EU's executive branch, based in Brussels, which conducted the bulk of the negotiations with the candidate countries. In essence, the commission had the responsibility to determine whether the applicants were meeting the membership standards, including the daunting task of adopting some 80,000 pages of EU legislation known formally as "acquis communautaire."

In a landmark action, the European Commission on October 9 approved a report recommending membership for the ten applicants. The author of the report, Gunter Verheugen, the commissioner in charge of the enlargement process, said in a speech to the European Parliament that he recommended membership because "the countries earned it. Through their own efforts, they have fulfilled the accession criteria." Verheugen acknowledged that most of the candidate countries still had "shortcomings" in their economic, legal, or political systems, but those problems needed to be placed "in the context of the enormous progress made over the years."

Despite Verheugen's reassurances, some of the problems noted in his report indicated the potential for trouble in the future. Poland, for example, was admonished for its "limited" steps to deal with endemic corruption in its "political, administration, and business culture." Among other findings, Verheugen said the Czech Republic and Hungary continued to discriminate against an unpopular minority, the Roma (gypsies); and Lithuania was failing to enforce environmental laws.

Verheugen's report also discussed the three countries not included on the list for membership in 2004: Bulgaria, Romania, and Turkey. The first two, he said, had made progress, especially with the adoption of democratic political systems and the shedding of most aspects of the communist economies that had been in place until the early 1990s. If Bulgaria and Romania continued to make progress they should be ready for EU membership by 2007, the report said. Turkey also was modernizing but lagged behind EU standards on both economic and political grounds; Verheugen's report was silent on a possible membership date for Turkey.

Another hurdle for EU expansion was cleared on October 20, when voters in Ireland overwhelmingly approved the Treaty of Nice, a February 2001 agreement that revised some of the EU's procedures in anticipation of the new members. By its terms, the treaty had to be ratified by all current EU member nations before the end of 2002 so it could go into effect and thus allow the fifteen current and ten new members to adopt yet another treaty during 2003 putting the expansion in place. The fourteen other current EU members had approved the Treaty of Nice through votes in their parliaments, but Ireland had a constitutional requirement for a referendum. Irish voters had rejected the treaty in June 2001, a result the government blamed on an exceptionally low turnout. With the EU's future riding on the will of Irish voters, the Dublin government scheduled another referendum and launched a major public relations campaign on behalf of the Nice Treaty. That approach appeared to work, with the treaty winning the endorsement of 63 percent of those who voted.

European Leaders Act

The "yes" vote in Ireland left one final step in 2002 for the enlargement process: the negotiating of a financing package so the leaders of the fifteen current EU nations could give their blessing at a summit meeting in December. The key issue was a disagreement over agriculture policy among two of the EU's biggest members, France and Germany. French president Jacques Chirac, responding to his country's politically powerful farm lobby, wanted to make sure that the EU's generous subsidies to farmers would not be cut when countries with millions of new farmers (notably Poland) joined the union. German chancellor Gerhard Schroeder, whose economically troubled country was the biggest single contributor to EU coffers, wanted to cut those subsidies in the union's next budget cycle starting in 2007. The farm subsidies accounted for nearly half of the EU's total budget, which in 2002 stood at 95 billion euros (about $95 billion).

Chirac and Schroeder on October 24 reached an agreement barring future increases (even after inflation) in EU agriculture spending. Widely seen as a victory for Chirac, the deal enabled him to say he had protected French farmers. But it also allowed Schroeder to claim that he had secured a cap on German contributions to the EU budget.

On December 12 leaders of the fifteen current and ten prospective EU countries met in Copenhagen for a final round of decisions. Again, the central question was money, this time a demand by Polish prime minister Leszek Miller for more than $1 billion in additional EU aid to help the new members deal with the costs of joining. The EU already had pledged $42 billion in aid to the new members, but Miller and some of his colleagues cited continuing uncertainties among their publics about the costs and responsibilities of EU membership. Miller bargained doggedly and won $434 million in additional aid for the new members, most of which would go to Poland. With that agreement secured, EU leaders on December 13 issued the formal invitation to the ten applicants to sign a treaty in Athens in April 2003 and then to become full members on May 1, 2004.

The historic step would "bring an end to the divisions in Europe," Romano Prodi, president of the European Commission said. "For the first time in history Europe will become one, because unification is the free will of its people."

Cyprus-Turkey Issues

In another compromise at the Copenhagen summit, EU leaders agreed to look again, during their summit in December 2004, at Turkey's application for membership. If Turkey had made enough progress in meeting the union's economic and political criteria, negotiations toward its membership would begin "without delay"—meaning in 2005, with actual membership coming several years later.

Turkey's application for decades had been a thorny problem for European leaders. With about 70 million people, Turkey would be the second most populous EU member (after Germany). Moreover, Turkey was a Muslim country (in contrast to nominally Christian Europe), with an unstable democracy and a fragile economy that had undergone two serious crises in the previous five years. Turkish elections in November brought to power an Islamist party, spawning new concerns in Europe that secular rule there might be endangered after nearly eight decades. (Turkey elections, p. 906)

Moreover, Turkey was still engaged in one of Europe's most troubling international disputes—with its long-time rival, Greece, over the island of Cyprus. Since 1974 Turkey had supported a breakaway "republic" of Turkish Cypriots on the northern one-third of the island. The Greek-dominated Republic of Cyprus controlled the rest and was the only internationally recognized government on the island. Numerous diplomatic efforts over the years to negotiate a settlement of the Cyprus dispute had failed. Until 1999 Greece (an EU member) had used the dispute as a reason to block Turkey's application for membership in the EU. Later, Turkey (like Greece, a NATO member) used the Cyprus dispute to block an otherwise unrelated agreement under which NATO could loan military equipment to an emergency defense force the EU was trying to develop. (European defense force, Historic Documents of 1999, p. 817)

In 2002 the pending EU membership application of the Republic of Cyprus offered what appeared to be the best opportunity in years for diplomats to reach a solution to the Cyprus dispute. United Nations Secretary General Kofi Annan in October presented a comprehensive peace plan that offered Turkish Cypriots substantial autonomy, but not formal independence, from the Republic of Cyprus. Tactically, Annan's plan was based on the expectation that the new Turkish government—eager to win a firm date from the EU for its own membership application—would pressure Turkish Cypriot leader Rauf Denktash into taking a more flexible position than he had in the past. Similarly, Annan assumed the Cyprus government would want an agreement to ensure acceptance of its EU application.

In response to complaints from both sides in Cyprus about details of his proposal, Annan submitted a revised version on the eve of the EU summit and asked the Greek and Turkish Cypriot leaders to be in Copenhagen the next day, December 11, for a "rendezvous with history." Glafcos Clerides, president of the Republic of Cyprus, made the trip to Copenhagen along with other political leaders from the Greek side of the island. But Denktash, apparently unwilling to abandon his three-decade-long dream of a Turkish Cypriot state, flew instead to Ankara, ostensibly for a medical checkup.

The absence of a key party stalled Annan's peace plan, at least for the time being, and left Turkey's membership application as the central remaining item on the EU leaders' table. By this point the issue had become whether the EU would offer Turkey a firm date for the start of negotiations leading to membership. On Turkey's behalf, Britain and Italy demanded that Turkey be given an "early" date, in the spring of 2004, for membership talks. They were supported by the United States—not even a member of the EU—which, coincidentally, was trying to win Turkey's cooperation for an eventual war against Iraq.

The U.S. intervention in a European issue angered key EU diplomats, and it may have backfired. Over dinner the evening of December 13, the European leaders reportedly fell into a heated dispute over the propriety of Turkey's persistent lobbying and Washington's heavy-handed diplomacy. After feathers were smoothed, the leaders adopted a compromise: If Turkey was still making progress on economic and political reforms at the time of the December 2004 summit, negotiations on its membership would then begin "without delay." While it gave Turkey something close to a firm date, that compromise also meant that Ankara would have to make its case in 2004 before twenty-five members in the newly expanded European Union, rather than the fifteen who were sitting at the table in 2002.

Following is the text of a statement to the European Parliament on October 9, 2002, by Gunter Verheugen, of the European Commission, reporting on the commission's recommendation that ten countries be invited to join the European Union in 2004.

The document was obtained from the Internet at europa.eu .int/rapid/start/cgi/guesten.ksh?p_action.gettxt=gt&doc

=SPEECH/02/462\0\RAPID&lg =EN&display =;   **accessed**
December 1, 2002.

The publication of this year's progress reports and the Enlargement Strategy Paper is a milestone on the road towards achieving one of the most difficult projects that the EU [European Union] has ever undertaken. After a thorough and comprehensive analysis, the [European] Commission is now proposing that the accession negotiations with ten candidate countries be concluded by the end of the year. The reason behind this recommendation is very simple: the countries have earned it. Through their own efforts, they have fulfilled the accession criteria.

The EU's accession strategy has proved a success. It has supported the candidates in their drive to reach precisely defined goals at a number of staging posts. The most powerful motivation for achieving the necessary reforms was the clear and credible prospect of joining the EU.

The European Parliament supported us in our work with supplementary analyses and constructive criticism, and I would like to thank you for that support. As we enter the final stages, the European Parliament will play a decisive role.

Ladies and Gentlemen,

In our analysis, we draw the conclusion that Cyprus, the Czech Republic, Estonia, Hungary, Latvia, Lithuania, Malta, Poland, Slovakia and Slovenia will be able to meet all accession criteria and join the EU by the start of 2004. However, there are three major tasks to be completed in the intervening period.

First, the Treaty of Nice must be ratified. I would like to appeal to voters in Ireland, when they are deciding how to vote on the Treaty of Nice, to bear in mind that these countries' future in Europe depends on their vote. These are countries that were kept apart from us against their will and now want to join our family permanently, once and for all.

Second, we must settle the remaining unresolved issues in the accession negotiations. The main points are the "financial package", as it is known, and the institutional questions, which are of particular relevance to this House. The Member States now need to demonstrate sufficient flexibility and willingness to compromise to ensure that common positions can be reached on these unresolved issues at the summit meeting in Brussels on 24 and 25 October.

Third, the candidate countries must carry on preparing for membership even after the negotiations have closed, until they actually join the EU. In particular, they must honour the commitments that they have made to the EU during the negotiations.

Ladies and Gentlemen,

Our analysis is fair and it is based on objective criteria. It enables us to meet the EU's political objective of accession before the elections to the European Parliament in 2004, without sacrificing the requisite clarity. I can assure you that we have left nothing to chance; we have unequivocally pointed out all shortcomings that still need to be addressed and all areas where specific preparatory measures are still required.

Our analysis is based on a tried and tested method of assessing progress in terms of laws, regulations and other measures actually adopted and implemented. This time, we reviewed not just the previous year but the period since 1997, and we have included our prognosis for the run-up to accession.

We had to make a prognosis. The candidate countries are not required to complete their preparations until they join. However, we have to conclude the negotiations now, to allow enough time for the political decision process. Rest assured: our prognosis has a solid foundation. It relies on a sound knowledge of the pace and quality of the preparations in each of the ten countries.

The process of EU enlargement is a broad one. Work towards the goal of enlargement, with the stringent preparations that involves, will continue for the countries that will not be taking part in this next round.

Romania and Bulgaria have set 2007 as their indicative date for their accession. The Commission will strongly support the two countries in achieving this objective. In the meantime, we propose a gradual but substantial increase in pre-accession assistance for those countries.

Turkey has been making major and very welcome progress towards meeting the accession criteria. Our pre-accession strategy for Turkey is having exactly the effect we hoped for. With regard to democracy, the rule of law and human rights, Turkey has changed more in the last eighteen months than in the last few decades. It was too much to expect Turkey to meet all the political criteria in full this soon, and the Commission clearly states what still have to be done. We want to encourage Turkey to push ahead with its bold reforms. The door stays open for Turkey.

We therefore propose stepping up pre-accession assistance for Turkey from 2004 on, with the aim of strengthening the public administration, promoting the adoption of Community law and economic integration with the EU.

Ladies and Gentlemen,

We will continue to work towards our strategic goal of welcoming a united Cyprus as a new Member. The next few weeks will bring a "window of opportunity" for ending the decades-old conflict and providing all Cypriots with the chance of a better future. The conflict can be solved; it is a question of political will. As in the past, we will do all we can to facilitate the finding of a solution. The parties involved know that the EU intends to reach a decision in Copenhagen, and it will. I call on everyone involved to make one big final effort.

Overall, the Commission is of the opinion that all candidate countries have made significant progress towards meeting the Copenhagen criteria [EU membership requirements established at a summit meeting in 1993]. That goes not just for the adoption but also for the implementation of Community law. It has also been gratifying to see the candidate countries honouring the commitments they gave during the negotiations. We believe that all ten countries will meet all of the Copenhagen criteria in time for accession at the beginning of 2004 as planned.

All candidate countries—with the exception of Turkey—meet the political criteria already. Significant progress has been made in improving the independence, transparency and efficiency of their public administrations.

In most countries, further improvements have been made to the legal system. However, in spite of general progress with regard to the political criteria, there are still some problem areas, which we identify clearly and unambiguously. These include shortcomings in the administration, corruption, minority rights and equality issues.

The assessment of progress towards meeting the Copenhagen economic criteria must be viewed in the context of the global economy. Nevertheless, most candidate countries managed to exceed the average EU growth rate of 2.6% in the period from 1997 to 2001. Cyprus and Malta have already fulfilled all economic criteria. Estonia, Latvia, Lithuania, Poland, Slovakia, Slovenia, Hungary and the Czech Republic also have functioning market economies. These countries will be able to meet the competitiveness criteria too if they press on with their reforms with as much determination as before and focus on specific areas, named in our reports.

Bulgaria will be classed as a functioning market economy for the first time this year and it should meet the competitiveness criteria in the medium term.

Romania has also made good progress and should be classed as a functioning market economy in the medium term. Turkey too has moved towards a better-functioning market economy, despite two serious financial crises.

Most candidate countries have now adopted a large proportion of the Community acquis [a large body of EU law known formally as "acquis communautaire"]. However, they must now make further improvements to their administrative and institutional capacity.

Ladies and Gentlemen,

This year's reports reveal the areas where a special effort is still required. In particular, certain issues have still to be addressed in agriculture, regional policy, financial control and the customs union.

The Commission will continue with its regular monitoring to track developments in these and other areas over the coming months. We will produce a final comprehensive monitoring report six months before accession.

After accession, the Commission, as guardian of the Treaties, including the accession treaties, will continue to check that EU law is being properly implemented in the new Member States.

That is why we have introduced the concept of a safeguard clause, enabling us to intervene if the acquis is not implemented or in case of "disturbances" on the internal market. The safety clause is particularly important in relation to the internal market.

At this point I would just like to make one thing very clear: honouring the commitments they have given is the key to further change and successful development in the candidate countries. It is in their own interests to stay on course.

To make sure that the new Member States have the necessary administrative capacity in the next few years, we have made concrete proposals in the reports to endow the Institution Building Facility with €380 million for 2004–06. Thy particularly need to strengthen institutions dealing with justice, border controls, the customs union, veterinary services, nuclear safety and food safety.

Ladies and Gentlemen,

When we look at the progress made in the accession process to date, the picture is overwhelmingly positive and supports our timetable.

Naturally, the progress reports we are presenting today focus on areas still in need of further attention. However, this should not be taken to mean that the shortcomings were in any way predominant. The reports must be viewed in the context of the enormous of progress made over the years. The full picture emerges only when you compare what has been achieved with what has still to be done.

We must also make every effort to keep the public in the current and future Member States informed about the enlargement and to win their support for it. This remains one of the most important objectives in the next stage, up to accession and beyond.

Parliament has a decisive role to play here and I would encourage you all to contribute to the wider debate, with those in favour of enlargement but also those who are still sceptical.

It should not come as a surprise to anyone that this scepticism still exists. What worries me most is the clear lack of information in many of the Member States. Everyone in political office should understand that enlargement will become a highly topical domestic issue everywhere as soon as the treaties are signed, if not before. We must do all we can to ensure that people do not feel that if they have been backed into a corner or are having unreasonable demands placed on them when it comes to deciding on accession at national level. What is needed is information, information and more information. It is available. We just need to make sure that the public use it. The chances of a successful enlargement are slim if the public is badly informed or not informed at all.

The goal of voters from 25 Member States from northern, eastern, southern and western Europe taking part in the next set of European elections, is now within sight. Let us achieve that goal of a united, democratic Europe, together with our neighbours in central, eastern and southern Europe.

UNITED NATIONS ON THE GLOBAL ECONOMIC OUTLOOK
October 9, 2002

Predictions early in the year that the global economy was on the verge of recovery and renewed growth gave way at the end of 2002 to more pessimistic projections. The International Monetary Fund (IMF), the United Nations, and the Organization for Economic Cooperation and Development (OECD) all said the world economy was unlikely to regain any real vigor until at least mid-2003. The earlier projections had forecast recovery beginning in the last half of 2002.

In the view of most experts, several uncertainties had the potential to derail the fragile global recovery. Among these were rising geopolitical tensions, particularly over the a possible war between the United States and Iraq. These factors, combined with sluggish business capital spending, continuing deflation in the equity markets, protracted consolidation in the telecommunications sector, and rising oil prices all raised questions about the sustainability of the recovery.

The United States was widely regarded as the only economy capable of leading the world recovery. Japan, the world's second largest economy, was still mired in a ten-year recession, while Germany and much of the rest of Europe were hampered by concerns about inflation and constraints on their abilities to use fiscal and monetary policy as a stimulus. Little help was expected from Latin America, where economic and political unrest made economic recovery there precarious. Although several Asian economies appeared to be growing rapidly, none of them individually or collectively were large enough to pull the rest of the world economy along.

Meanwhile, international organizations continued to report that the benefits of a growing world economy and globalization were assisting the world's poorer countries unevenly at best. During the 1990s, according to the annual report on human development by the UN Development Programme, the number of people living in extreme poverty was reduced by nearly half in Asia. But the number grew in every other developing region—Africa, Latin America, the Middle East, eastern and central Europe, and the countries of the former Soviet Union. Extreme poverty was defined as living on less than

689

$1 a day. In October the UN Food and Agriculture Organization (FAO) reported that progress on reducing famine in the world had "virtually ground to a halt," making it highly unlikely that the UN's goal of cutting world hunger in half by 2015 would be met. "If we continue at the current pace," lamented FAO director general Jacques Diouf, "we will reach the goal more than 100 years late, closer to 2150 than to the year 2015." An estimated 25,000 people died every day from malnourishment and poverty. (UN millennium goals, Historic Documents of 2000, p. 700)

On an individual basis, an economist for the World Bank reported in January that the richest 1 percent of the world's population earned as much as the poorest 57 percent, a statistic that had remained fairly constant for several years. "We can wonder how long such huge inequalities may persist in the face of ever closer contacts, not least through television and movies, where opulent lifestyles of the rich influence expectations and often breed resentment among the poor," said Branko Milanovic in research published in the Economic Journal.

Recovery Predictions Scaled Back

The most optimistic growth projections came from the IMF, which predicted in September that the world economy would grow at a rate of 3.7 percent in 2003, down from its earlier projection of 4 percent. The most pessimistic forecast came from the OECD, the research organization of thirty industrialized economies, which anticipated growth of 1.5 percent in 2002 and 2.2 percent in 2003. The United Nations projected growth of 1.8 percent in 2002 and 2.9 percent in 2003.

In its assessment, "Global Economic Outlook," released October 9, the United Nations said that, of the five factors that were seen in April as supporting a recovery, only three remained essentially unchanged—monetary and fiscal policy stimuli, resilient consumer spending, and inventory restocking. Energy prices, which had been falling in the spring, had begun rising again as a result of uncertainty in the Middle East and turmoil in Venezuela. Business and consumer confidence, which by the spring had begun to rise from the low levels after the September 11, 2001, terrorist attacks in the United States, had once again reversed course. At the same time, the report said, the three factors that had been seen as a drag on economic recovery in the spring had not improved and in some cases had even deteriorated further. These factors were low capital spending by business, protracted consolidation in global information and communication technology, and a slump in the world's equity markets.

Since the beginning of 2002 several additional adverse factors had "exacerbated the original weaknesses in the world economy," according to the UN. These included the rising geopolitical tensions, the corporate scandals in the United States, as well as human and physical devastation caused by a number of severe floods, droughts, and other natural disasters. The report said that the strictly economic factors dragging down the global economy were principally attributable to overinvestment in manufacturing capacity in developed countries and to debt overhang and asset price deflation in the major equities markets, a significant proportion of which still needed to be worked off. The excess capacity reflected low demand not only in the home economy but also in the rest of the world as well. For many developing countries, weak overall demand had lowered prices for many of their export commodities and had reduced private capital investment, creating a vicious cycle of debt, economic contraction, a further erosion in investor confidence, and sharp increases in the costs of external financing. Several countries in Latin America, notably Argentina and Brazil, were caught in such a cycle. (Argentina, p. 80; Brazil, p. 774)

All three international organizations, to varying degrees, warned that any one of four factors might change those projections for the worse:

- *a military operation in the Middle East that might disrupt the oil supply*
- *a continued slump in the equity markets that might trap the economy in a period of low growth*
- *an abrupt drop in U.S. imports, accompanied by a devaluation of the dollar, that could trigger economic shocks elsewhere in the world*
- *continuing fragility in several economies that could touch off further debt crises*

Regional Situations in Brief

The U.S. economy—in particular, the U.S. consumer—was the main life buoy keeping the global economy afloat. After a brief recession, created in part by the September 11 terrorist attacks on New York and Washington, the U.S. economy early in 2002 had begun to show signs of recovery. Nearly all forecasters predicted that the United States would continue to lead the recovery, if only because no other country or region was likely to be in a stronger position. Among developed nations, only Canada and Australia were expected to outperform the United States in 2002 and 2003, but their economies were too small to provide the overseas investment and import demand the rest of the world needed.

Import demand remained high in the United States, fueled by consumer spending, which was in turn propelled by the lowest interest rates in more than forty years. By year's end concerns were rising that consumers were reaching their limits. In the short term any loss in consumer spending might be covered by the increase in government spending to pay for the military buildup against Iraq, a large tax cut enacted in 2001, and higher jobless benefits and other payments necessitated by the economic slowdown. After running surpluses for four straight years, the U.S. government was expected to run near-record budget deficits in 2002 and 2003 and perhaps longer. The OECD in its report gently warned about the risk of inflation given the fiscal and monetary stimulus pumped into the system. (U.S. economy, pp. 51, 877)

The economies of both Europe and Japan were expected to expand at much slower rates than the U.S. economy. European growth was sluggish,

*hampered by many factors, including inflation concerns that kept Euro-
pean interests rates higher than many experts thought desirable. In the
twelve countries that shared a common currency (the euro), constraints on
monetary and fiscal policy also reduced options for stimulating their economies. Germany, which accounted for one-third of the output of the monetary union, was bordering on another recession. Instead of taking steps to
stimulate demand, Germany was facing cuts in government spending and
possible tax increases to meet its fiscal obligations to the monetary union.
Despite reform pressure from a variety of sources, the German government
had not yet been able to clamp down on the structural problems that led to
high labor and welfare costs. The German government won some relief when
the European Central Bank cut its key interest rate half a point to 2.75 percent in early December, but some economists said the rate might have to be
cut even further. "We are very close to hitting the wall," Norbert Walter, the
chief economist at Deutsche Bank, told the* New York Times. *"2003 will be
the most challenging period of the postwar era for Germany."* (Introduction
of the euro, Historic Documents of 1999, p. 75)

*Japan in 2002 showed little sign of being able to come to grips with
the financial crisis that had kept the world's second largest economy in
recession for much of the past decade and made it the first major industrial country in recent years to suffer deflation. Any signs of strength in
the economy were attributable to export demand. Domestic demand and
business capital investment remained weak, the government remained
deeply in debt, and banks continued to hold hundreds of billions of dollars in bad loans. Most experts said Japan's economy would not revive until it had resolved the bad-loan problem. Junichiro Koizumi had pledged
just such reforms during his campaign for the prime minister's seat in
April 2001, but by the end of 2002 he appeared little closer to carrying out
reforms opposed by the entrenched banking and business community than
any of his predecessors.* (Koizumi's reform plans, Historic Documents of 2001,
p. 304)

*Another Asian economy—that of China—was the fastest growing in the
world. Growth of around 8 percent was expected in 2002, fueled by a surge
of exports, increasing foreign investment, and a housing boom. China was
now the largest export market for both South Korea and Taiwan and had
displaced Japan as Asia's largest exporter to the United States. Although
China's surge was helping its Asian neighbors, its economy—nine times
smaller than the U.S. economy—was too small to provide much of a stimulus to the entire world. The OECD and other experts warned that China's
failure to reform its state banking system to get rid of bad loans and to sell
off inefficient state enterprises could cause problems in the future.*

*One bright spot on the map was Russia. On the brink of financial catas-
trophe in 1998, the former communist country in 2002 was running a
budget surplus for the third straight year, its central bank reserves were
sufficient to meet its international debt payments, and both worker productivity and the economy were growing. The rising price of oil was a key fac-*

tor in Russia's upsurge. (Russian debt crisis, Historic Documents of 1998, p. 601)

Latin America remained in a precarious situation, as debt crises in Argentina and, to a lesser extent, in Brazil spilled over into neighboring countries. Overall most African economies were expected to grow in 2003, but great uncertainties, including political upheaval, drought, and the course of the AIDS epidemic, could easily change that forecast for individual countries or entire regions of the continent. Most countries in the Middle East grew only slowly in 2002, if they grew at all. Israel registered slower growth, and the Palestinian economy had effectively collapsed. (African development, p. 446; development in the Arab world, p. 483; Israeli-Palestinian conflict, p. 927)

Recovery Plagued by Uncertainties

At least three uncertainties that could affect the pace of global economic recovery seemed to be on almost everyone's mind. The first was the threatened U.S. military action against Iraq and its leader, Saddam Hussein. The threat had already raised the price of oil and depressed consumer and business confidence. What long-term effect the higher price of oil might have on the world economy was obviously dependent on how long it lasted and the magnitude of the price increase and supply shortage. At least one study posited that a higher price of oil sustained for six months or more could have a recessionary effect on the world economy.

A second concern was the protracted collapse of stock and other equity prices. Stock prices were down in the United States in 2002 for the third year in a row, a record rivaled only during the Great Depression of the 1930s. Falling stock prices undermined both individual and business wealth and could thus further weaken economic activity.

The third worry was the record high trade and current account deficit in the United States. The UN, the OECD, and the IMF all warned that the imbalance between the United States and the surplus countries, particularly Japan and the European Union, represented a potential source of instability in the world economy. The UN report, for one, acknowledged the "dilemma" the world faced about the United States' external deficit. On the one hand, there was concern that the larger the U.S. trade deficit, the more abrupt and disruptive any correction might be. On the other hand, the world was relying on strong U.S. import demand in the short term to carry the global economic recovery.

Following are excerpts from "Global Economic Outlook," a report prepared by the United Nations Department of Economic and Social Affairs and released October 9, 2002.

The document was obtained from the Internet at www.un .org/esa/analysis/link/1002GlobOutlook.pdf; accessed December 13, 2002.

Overview

The world economy has been undergoing a gradual recovery from the sharp global slowdown of 2001—the weakest output performance in a decade, with roughly a dozen economies falling into recession. Neither the strength nor the breadth of the upturn has, however, been satisfactory: The arrival of economic recovery at full momentum forecast at the Spring 2002 meeting appears to have been delayed by at least two quarters. In other words, the peak of the economic recovery is now seen around mid-2003 rather than in the second half of 2002 as in the April forecast. Not only that, the sustainability of the ongoing recovery remains subject to a number of uncertainties.

The latest LINK forecasting exercise reconfirms the cautious outlook made at the April 2002 LINK meeting: By taking into account a confluence of factors, the LINK baseline forecast of 1.7 per cent for 2002 reconfirms the spring forecast of 1.8 per cent for gross world product (GWP), up from 1.2 per cent in 2001, but under 3 per cent for 2003, which is slightly lower than the 3.2 per cent reported in April 2002 (table 1). This momentum should push the growth of GWP approximately back to its long-run path of annual expansion of about 3 per cent. While the turning point identified earlier has thus been confirmed, the unknowns in the global economic outlook are, as they were at the time of the Spring exercise, the strength, the sustainability, and the breadth of the ongoing economic recovery, with new uncertainties having become pervasive in the interim. [LINK was an econometric modelling system that produced a simulation of the global economy.]

The world economy at this juncture is characterized by a number of common features, albeit to varying degrees across countries: slow growth of output, benign inflation with, in fact, deflation in some economies, stagnant employment, low interest rates, worsening fiscal balances, unstable and uneven international trade, gyrating and depressed equity markets, and diverging economic performance across regions and countries.

Many economies are also increasingly constrained in their capacity to pursue further policy stimulus, either because fiscal imbalances are already large, monetary policy is already quite relaxed, or, as in the European Union (EU) countries are hitting the limits of the self-imposed policy constraints on fiscal and, for the euro-zone members, monetary policy as well.

While for most developed economies one can observe a dichotomy between resilient household consumption spending and hesitant business capital outlays, many developing countries continue to be confronted with a challenging international environment: weak external demand, prices of most non-fuel primary commodities (which are the prime export-revenue earners for many of these economies) are still hovering near their historical lows, and on the whole contracting net capital inflows to the group of developing countries and economies in transition.

At the same time, the economic recovery for a large number of economies continues to depend significantly on the health of the economy of the United States, as there is presently no other major economy that, at least in the short

694

run, could plausibly assume the role of the United States as the locomotive of global economic buoyancy.

The sluggish pace of the global economic recovery has resulted from a confluence of competing driving forces. While many of the forces analysed in the last LINK report have been confirmed, several new factors have since come to the fore.

Among the five major supportive factors identified in the last LINK report, namely, monetary-and fiscal-policy stimuli, resilient consumer spending, inventory restocking, softening energy prices, and strengthening confidence from the low levels that crystallized in the wake of the 11 September 2001 terrorist attacks, only the first three have remained all but unchanged. Energy prices are no longer supportive of economic expansion. Rather, the recent run-up in oil prices has become a constraining factor on economic buoyancy. Business and consumer confidence has in general also reversed its course.

On the other hand, the key dragging factors on global economic growth addressed in the last LINK report, namely, tepid business capital spending; protracted consolidation in global information and communication technology (ICT); and deflated equity prices, have not improved at all; some have, in fact, deteriorated even further.

During the past six months, a few more adverse factors have come to the fore, including rising geopolitical tensions; an increasing number and an enlarged scale of revealed corporate scandals in major industrial countries, particularly in the United States; and worsening fiscal predicaments in Latin America. These new factors, plus the havoc wreaked by unusually large natural disasters such as floods and drought in a number of economies, have exacerbated the original weaknesses in the world economy. In fact, in mid-2002 these developments almost aborted the tentative global economic recovery.

Aside from non-economic factors, the far-from-buoyant global macroeconomic environment is currently principally due to the problem of excess investment in the developed economies in the late 1990s. It is also associated with debt overhang and asset price deflation, notably in major equity markets. A marked proportion of these excesses still remains to be worked off. For example, in telecommunications as the most beleaguered sector during the present phase of the evolving global economic cycle, even after two years of consolidation, capacity utilization is estimated to be running at only 35 per cent in the United States and many European countries. From a global perspective, the excess manufacturing capacity in developed economies reflects not only relatively lacklustre effective demand within these economies, but it also results from mediocre effective demand emanating from the rest of the world, particularly from the lower-income developing economies. In today's more globalized constellation of production, trade, and financing, capacity built in individual economies has become much more dependent on aggregate demand worldwide, rather than primarily on the state of the home economy. This holds especially for the high-technology sector with its large scope for economies of scale.

In light of the above, to resolve the overcapacity in manufacturing in core developed economies, it may be necessary for policymakers to focus on boosting their respective domestic demand in the short run. However, it will be even more crucial in the longer run to promote growth in a large number of developing countries, where potential demand remains well below satiation.

For many developing economies, the weakness of global demand has also exerted downward pressures on prices of many commodities that form the backbone of their export earnings and it has tended to shrink private capital flows, which has proven once again to be highly pro-cyclical. As a result, many developing countries with a high external debt burden have experienced either pressure on their exchange rates when adhering to a fixed-rate regime or weaker exchange rates when adhering to floating rates, and deteriorating debt-to-GDP and, for many economies, debt-to-export revenue ratios. Especially vulnerable have been countries with large current-account and fiscal deficits. The diminution in capital inflows into these countries has necessitated a contraction in economic activity, which in turn has entailed a deterioration in the fiscal outlook, eroded investor confidence, and led to further shrinkage in capital flows and a rise in the cost of external financing. A number of economies in Latin America were mired in such a vicious cycle in 2002, and remain quite vulnerable. Though the dynamics of public debt in Argentina and Brazil are not quite the same, in both countries it had major adverse impact on the health of public finances in general.

The current LINK baseline outlook shows that the economy of the United States will continue to lead the global recovery, but with not much momentum. Economic recovery in Japan and Western Europe continues to rely chiefly on external demand. With domestic demand lacking vigour, recovery in these economies will remain fragile. While the economy of Japan continues to be dragged down by fiscal and debt difficulties, most economies in Western Europe will be tightly constrained, on both the fiscal and monetary sides, by their adopted policy frameworks, leaving little scope for expansionary macroeconomic policies.

The economic rebound in several Asian developing economies is expected to continue, but it remains vulnerable to any relapse in the pace of the economic recovery sustained by major developed economies. On average, GDP for Latin America is expected to decline in 2002 and the outlook for 2003 remains cautious. While an increasing number of countries in Africa are expected to grow by 4 per cent or higher due mainly to strengthened domestic economic factors, many economies in the region are still not expected to gain any tangible growth in per capita income. Despite a significant rebound in oil prices, the benefit for most oil-exporting developing economies in West Asia and elsewhere has been confined at best. However, the group of economies in transition is likely to continue to exhibit fairly stable growth.

The key downside risks for the global economic outlook are rooted in the rising geopolitical tensions and the rise in deflationary pressures due to the protracted decline in equity prices. In such an inauspicious environment, macroeconomic policies are expected to remain accommodative. The current stance on economic stimuli may well fail to be sufficiently strong, however. . . .

Challenges for macroeconomic policies

The April 2002 LINK global outlook was predicated on the view, among others, that the global monetary easing cycle, which began in early 2001, would soon end. While a few central banks such as those of Australia, Canada, New Zealand, and Sweden raised interest rates somewhat, the majority of central banks decided to leave interest rates at low levels. Not only that, several central banks in developing countries and economies in transition continued to reduce their policy interest rates.

Expansionary monetary policies have pumped excess liquidity into the global economy: nominal money supply grew on average by 7–8 per cent in 2002 for the world economy and at double-digit rates in some developed economies.

Low interest rates so far seem to have had more salutary effects on the household sector than on businesses. The observed strong housing market and resilient consumption of durable goods in a large number of economies owe much to low interest rates. However, business capital spending has on the whole remained insensitive to the monetary easing, although low interest rates have, of course, also ameliorated corporate financial conditions. Excess capacity, depressed equity prices, rising risk premia for corporate borrowing due to heightened uncertainties, the lacklustre outlook for profit growth, and financial scandals may have offset the beneficial effect that the monetary stimulus for the business sector, particularly in major developed economies, would otherwise have imparted.

On the other hand, fragility in banking and non-banking financial systems such as large non-performing loans in a number of economies, developed as well as developing, may have dampened the effects of monetary easing from being properly channelled into the real sector. At the same time, inflation-targeting policy rules adopted by a number of economies may have prevented some central banks from reducing interest rates low enough to generate, given the prevailing circumstances, adequate stimulus for the real economic growth.

In the outlook, most central banks are expected to maintain an accommodative stance at the current level until mid-2003. Room for further monetary easing remains in many economies should the recovery turn sour.

Fiscal policy in the world economy is at a subtle juncture. While the sluggish economic recovery definitely calls for more fiscal stimulus, the majority of world economies are facing growing difficulties in strengthening their policy stance. The recent global slowdown worsened budget balances in almost all economies, albeit to varying degrees, due to the diminution in tax revenues or the rise in government expenditures or both.

Government accounts in most developed economies have turned from surplus registered in 2000 to deficits. In the United States, fiscal stimulus has been a major driver for the economic recovery, amounting in all to an estimated 1.5 to 2 per cent of GDP, taking the form of a combination of tax reduction and increased spending since the 11 September 2001 events. Real government spending is estimated to grow by 7 per cent in 2002. Although another extra stimulus package is not expected in 2003, the lagged multiplier effects of the pro-growth measures enacted since early 2001 are likely to continue to work through the economy into 2003. The balance of the government budget is estimated to register a deficit of more than $100 billion in 2002 and about $200 billion in 2003, compared with a surplus of more than $200 billion in 2000.

In Western Europe, the automatic stabilizers, in a few cases combined with moderate discretionary stimulus, has functioned in such a way as to generate broad deterioration in budget deficits; only a few countries such as Austria, Finland, and Spain are exceptions. Portugal was the first country to exceed the Stability and Growth Pact limit of 3 per cent deficit-to-GDP, while France, Germany, and Italy risk such an outcome over the next year or so. As a result, the budget goals embodied in the most recent revised stability programmes for all EU countries to achieve budget balance by 2004 are no longer within reach and measures are currently being contemplated to defer that deadline until 2006. Meanwhile, political pressure for further tax reduction remains in many European economies. The outlook assumes no major fiscal consolidation in 2003, but a gradual fiscal tightening in the farther horizon is reckoned with.

In Japan, any further government stimulus is limited by the already large fiscal deficit and high public debt level.

Fiscal deficits and government debts in many developing countries and economies in transition have worsened substantially—with Argentina being the extreme case when it declared sovereign default and some others near the brink of a debt crisis. In the past year, only a few developing economies in Asia have been able to adopt expansionary fiscal policy to counter the global slowdown and to stimulate the recovery. Most other developing countries and economies in transition are already facing a tight fiscal constraint. The fiscal situation for these economies will remain severe in the outlook, and for some it may even worsen further.

Uncertainties and forecasting risks

The baseline outlook is subject to a plethora of uncertainties and encompasses a number of risks, mostly on the downside. Major caveats include: (1) any military operation in the Middle East might lead to a disruption in oil supply, thus provoking an oil-supply shock to the world economy or exacerbating the effect of the run-up in oil prices recently experienced; (2) a further prolonged depression in major equity markets may send the global economy into another downturn or trap it into a protracted period of low growth well below the potential pace; (3) an abrupt adjustment in large trade imbalances across the world economies with a sharp reversal of the United States external deficits and accompanied by a substantial devaluation of the U.S. dollar could trigger financial and real economic shocks in the rest of the world; and (4) and financial and fiscal fragility in a number of economies could set off further debt crises.

Military confrontation in the Gulf

No specific military operation in the Middle East is included in the basic assumptions for the LINK baseline forecast—it is not prudent to do so even if it were possible. Some "war-danger premium" is, however, implicitly built into the baseline, such as higher prices of oil and lower business and consumer confidence than posited in the previous forecast. Risks do exist for a lingering standoff or a military operation with much higher costs than those subsumed under the premium included here.

The economic consequences of any military operation in the Gulf will depend on the kind of open confrontation that will materialize. It could have a wide range of plausible outcomes of substantially different magnitudes. Not only that, opinions are also widely split on the impact on the world economy of even a well-defined scenario of a military operation. For example, some commentators believe that a repeat of "Desert Storm" could boost economic growth of the United States, as well as of the world economy, by lifting consumer and investor confidence, propping up equity markets, and lowering the prices of oil. Dissenters argue, however, that new uncertainties will continue to depress confidence and that the financial costs of such a military operation will crowd out business investment, leading to lower potential growth. Nevertheless, the outcome could be well outside any presently conceivable scenario, rendering any serious configuration of its economic impact too complicated or beyond the realm of the plausible.

With simple assumptions on the outcome of a military operation in the Middle East, an analysis of the global economic impact would focus, in addition to human casualties; capital destruction; and infrastructure disruptions for the countries and regions directly involved, on the prices and supply of oil, the attendant changes in consumer and business confidence, and the modifications in macroeconomic policies. In this case, some of the earlier simulation exercises done with the LINK system may shed some light on the analysis. For example, a study executed two years ago indicated that a rise in the prices of oil will normally have a limited impact on the world economy, in terms of welfare losses, but an "oil shock," that is, a higher price of oil sustained for six months or longer, will be recessionary for the world economy, not only through welfare losses, but also through the erosion of consumer and business confidence.

In general, a military operation in the Middle East should be considered as a net drag to the world economy, no matter its merits or demerits on other grounds. It could have a substantial impact on the pace of economic activity in many countries of the Middle East, even if not directly involved in military operations.

Longer-term consequences of the protracted and severe contraction in equity prices

As a second major downside risk, the protracted fall in world equity markets over the past several years has increasingly inflicted downward pressure on world economic growth. After the incipient recovery following the 11 September 2001 terrorist attacks petered out in the second quarter of 2002, volatility in and downward pressure on equity markets have once again taken centre-stage since mid-2002 in all major economies. For example, this is the third year in a row of marked declines in broad indices of shares in the United

States. Such a drawn-out contraction has been rare; in fact, it has occurred only twice in stock-market history. Not only that, the cumulative falls have been large: The S& P 500 was down by 45 per cent in September 2002 from its peak of 2000, the largest fall since the Great Depression. Moreover, the erosion has continued despite the very substantial easing of monetary policy.

Equity markets elsewhere have also weakened considerably in a high degree of synchronicity. As shown by figure 3, all major indices have completely reversed to the levels of five years ago, with the core Japanese stock index having fallen to a 19-year low.

The impact of depressed equity prices on the buoyancy of the global economy has also been previously studied in LINK exercises and elsewhere over the past few years. A LINK simulation study reported in *World Economic and Social Survey 1999* showed that a 40 per cent drop in major equity markets of the United States and of Western Europe would lead to a decline of GWP by 1.7 percentage points from the baseline in two years. This simulation result coincides well with what has since materialized in the global economy in 2001–2002, with the actual growth in GWP remaining below its potential rate by about 1.5 to 2 percentage points.

One should contemplate whether, if equity markets continue to be depressed for even longer, the recovery in the pace of global growth to potential forecast in the baseline for 2003 will be feasible at all.

The sustainability of the external deficits of the United States

Another downside risk for the world economy is associated with the sustainability of the large trade deficit in the United States and the value of the U.S. dollar. This issue too has been repeatedly discussed in previous LINK meetings and other studies. The threat of a marked reversal in the external deficits of the United States in conjunction with a sharp erosion in the value of U.S. dollar against major currencies cannot be ruled out in what lingers on the horizon.

There seems to be a dilemma about the United States external deficits. It is well understood that the more the deficits expand, the higher the probability of an abrupt correction later, which will lead to larger shocks for both the financial markets and the real sectors of the world economy. Yet, paradoxically, for the sake of the global economic recovery in the short run, strong import demand from the United States, thus a further widening of the country's trade and current-account deficits, remains desirable.

As considered in the cited past study, there are a myriad of scenarios by which the trade deficit can be reversed. Three typical approaches are: (1) an abrupt adjustment driven by sentimental plunge in the value of the U.S. dollar; (2) structural adjustment in the economy of the United States, with a rise of domestic savings to narrow the saving-investment gap; and (3) structural adjustment in the world economy, with new growth engines coming to the fore and taking the relay of that of the United States, and more balanced investment portfolio across countries. The most perilous one would be an abrupt adjustment—the earlier simulation, as already noted, showed that halving the trade deficit in the United States within two years would lead to a drop in GWP by 1.7 percentage points. Therefore, it remains a challenge for policymakers worldwide to ensure a gradual and orderly adjustment. The recent return of the twin deficits in the United States, namely, a government deficit and a trade deficit, may, however, render the adjustment process more complicated than what was earlier considered.

Other risks

Other risks may arise from the financial fragility and the debt overhang in a number of economies. The latest debt crisis in Argentina has already underlined the severity of the issue. The probability of other countries falling into such a situation is by no means nil.

Conclusion

A global environment of low growth, low inflation, low interest rates, and worsened fiscal balances, combined with depressed equity prices and heighten geopolitical uncertainties, poses new challenges for macroeconomic policymakers. Bringing about a robust and sustained recovery in world economic growth should be the top priority for macroeconomic policies in most economies in 2002–2003. Further structural reforms, in some cases quite incisive ones, will, however, be needed for both national economies and international trade and financial systems to be able to support more balanced growth in the longer run.

AUSTRALIAN PRIME MINISTER ON TERRORIST BOMB IN INDONESIA
October 14, 2002

A terrorist bombing in Bali that killed more than 180 people—nearly all of them Australians and other foreigners—forced a reluctant Indonesia to confront the danger of Islamic extremism. The world's most populous Muslim country, Indonesia long had been considered by Western and Asian security experts as a potential breeding ground for the terrorism of extreme Islamist groups. That prediction appeared to come true on October 12, 2002, when a bomb exploded outside two nightclubs in a beachfront town on the resort island of Bali. An estimated 184 people—the exact total was unclear—were killed and dozens more were severely wounded in the explosion and a resulting fire.

In the weeks before the bombing the United States had tried persuasion and even threats to try to force Indonesian president Megawati Sukarnoputri to take action against known terrorist groups, to no avail. After the bombing, Megawati, famous for her passivity, continued to hesitate but eventually issued a decree giving security services leeway to go after extreme Islamic groups. By year's end the government claimed to have arrested the major planners of the Bali bombing and had taken into custody a cleric who allegedly headed one of Southeast Asia's most important terrorist groups.

In the immediate period after the bombing, perhaps the most important development was what did not happen: a sudden upsurge of public support in Indonesia for Islamic extremism. The country remained calm, and there were only scattered protests among followers of some of the radical Islamic groups. The bombing was one of two major bombings in 2002 with possible links to the terrorist organization al Qaeda. The other took place in Mombassa, Kenya. (Terrorism, p. 740)

The Bombing

It was a busy Saturday evening in the town of Kuta Beach, a popular destination on Bali for young people from Australia, New Zealand, the United States, and other countries. The Australian government later said some

20,000 of its citizens were on the island, attracted by the beaches and informal lifestyle. Apparently no one paid attention to a minivan that pulled in between two crowded bars, the Sari Club and Paddy's, frequented by "bules"—the Indonesian term for white foreigners. Suddenly a bomb in the vehicle exploded with a tremendous force, destroying the buildings and setting fire to their thatched roofs.

According to most estimates, 184 people were killed and several dozen were wounded, most with severe burns. Eighty-seven of the identified dead were Australians, twenty-six were British, seven were U.S. citizens, and the rest were from other countries. Both bars had a foreigners-only policy.

The investigation into the explosion got off to a rocky start when local police failed to secure the scene, allowing what might have been crucial evidence to be destroyed by curiosity seekers. Recognizing the shortcomings of local security services, Indonesia eventually allowed a joint team of Australian, British, and U.S. police officials to help investigate the bombing.

The heavy toll of Australian citizens was a severe shock to that country and represented the worst attack on Australian interests since the Japanese air force bombed the city of Darwin during World War II, killing 243 people. It also was a rude reminder that Australia's isolation in the South Pacific did not protect it from the cares of the world. Some Australians angrily blamed the government for siding with the George W. Bush administration in its antiterrorism war following the September 11, 2001, attacks on the United States. That step made Australia a target for terrorism that it might not otherwise have been, the critics said. Australian prime minister John Howard brushed off such criticism, saying that trying to avoid taking sides in the war against terror was "moral bankruptcy" that "will not purchase immunity." (September 11 attacks, Historic Documents of 2001, p. 614)

Addressing the Australian parliament two days after the bombing, Howard called the bombing "barbaric, brutal mass murder without justification." Howard said the event reminded Australians that "in this time of a borderless world with a particularly mobile, young population, Australia can scarcely imagine that it can be in any way immune from such horrible attacks."

U.S. Actions in Indonesia

The bombing came after the United States had made an unprecedented effort to get Megawati's government to take action against several extremist groups that intelligence services said were operating in her country. The U.S. diplomatic efforts—kept secret at the time—began shortly after the September 11, 2001, attacks and continued throughout 2002. In August Secretary of State Colin Powell visited Indonesia and made a personal appeal to Megawati. During his visit Powell announced a $50 million, three-year antiterrorism aid package for Indonesia.

On September 16, according to later news reports, Karen B. Brooks, a White House National Security Council staff member, met with Megawati in Jakarta and gave her detailed information about terrorist groups in the country. One source of the information reportedly was Omar al-Farouq, a

703

Kuwaiti citizen said to be an operative of the al Qaeda terrorist network that planned the September 11 attacks. Al-Farouq had been arrested in Indonesia the previous June and turned over to U.S. authorities for questioning; the United States was holding al-Farouq at an air base outside of Kabul, Afghanistan. Also in September the United States closed its embassy in Jakarta for five days because of a warning of a possible bombing. Indonesian authorities criticized the United States for that action, which they said undermined international confidence in the country.

On October 11, the day before the Bali bombing, U.S. ambassador Ralph Boyce met with Megawati to pass on urgent warnings that groups associated with al Qaeda were planning attacks against Western interests in Indonesia. Boyce reportedly insisted that Megawati act against these groups before her planned meeting in late October with President Bush at a Pacific regional summit meeting in Mexico. If no action had been taken by then, Boyce reportedly told Megawati, the United States would order its nonessential personnel to leave Indonesia—a step that would have sent a damaging message about security in the country. But then the Bali bombing intervened, and the United States took that threatened step, ordering about 90 embassy employees and 250 family members out of the country.

Later in the year numerous, often conflicting, reports emerged about how much information the Central Intelligence Agency (CIA) and other international intelligence services had collected prior to the Bali bombing about possible terrorist attacks in Indonesia. Some reports insisted that intelligence agencies had picked up warnings specifically mentioning Bali as a potential target. U.S. officials heatedly denied that, saying all suggestions they had received were that a terrorist attack could occur anywhere in southeast Asia. Boyce reportedly told Australian officials that some U.S. embassy employees were vacationing in Bali at the time of the bombing; they would have been warned to stay away if the embassy had more specific information, he said.

Indonesian Groups

Indonesia had a population of about 225 million, of whom an estimated 88 percent (or about 198 million) were Muslim, making it the most populous Muslim nation in the world. The country's authoritarian governments since independence in 1945 had kept a lid on dissent, and Islamic extremism had grown much more slowly in Indonesia than in the Middle East or South Asia. Suharto, the autocratic leader from 1968 to 1998, had allowed several moderate Muslim groups to operate as part of the political system, and those groups remained in parliament under the three presidents who succeeded Suharto—including Megawati. When Megawati took office in 2001 parliament elected as her vice president Hamzah Haz, the head of one of the Islamic parties. (Suharto overthrow, Historic Documents of 1998, p. 284; Megawati inauguration, Historic Documents of 2001, p. 562)

Despite that history of Islamic moderation, several radical groups had operated in Indonesia since the 1990s, taking advantage of the fact that the government in Jakarta could not possibly control all the country's 13,000 is-

lands. One Islamist group, Laskar Jihad, for several years used terrorist tactics in a campaign to drive out Christian communities on the Moluccan islands; the government's attempts to control that situation had only modest success.

Intelligence services in other Asian countries, as well as the CIA, had long been most concerned about a group called Jemaah Islamiyah ("Islamic community"), which reportedly had cells throughout Southeast Asia. The group's ideological leader—who denied any connection with it—was reported to be Abu Bakar Bashir, the principal of an Islamic school for boys in central Java. Terrorism experts said Jemaah Islamiyah's operational head was Riduan Isamuddin, a shadowy character also known as Hambali, who remained at large as of the end of 2002. The United States claimed Hambali was a close associate of Ramzi Yousef, who had been convicted for his role in 1993 bombing of the World Trade Center.

Jemaah Islamiyah had been linked to several small-scale terrorist attacks in Southeast Asia since the late 1990s, and it reportedly had a goal of merging Indonesia, Malaysia, Singapore, and possibly other countries into one large Islamic state. Most reports indicated the group was a loose network of local cells, rather than a tightly knit organization—a structure that made it difficult for intelligence agencies to track it. According to news reports, the intelligence services of Malaysia and Singapore had tried to monitor the group for years and had insisted that it had common cause with al Qaeda in the late 1990s. The Singapore government in December 2001 reportedly disrupted a plot by Jemaah Islamiyah to blow up several embassies there, including those of Australia and the United States.

At the time of the Bali bombing the Bush administration had been planning to add Jemaah Islamiyah to its list of international terrorist organizations but had delayed doing so reportedly because of Indonesian concerns about the negative publicity that would result. The State Department listed the group on October 22 but insisted the designation of the group was not directly related to the Bali bombing because it was not yet clear the group was responsible.

In addition to its worries about gaining a reputation as a terrorist haven, the Indonesian government objected to the United States naming Jemaah Islamiyah as a terrorist group because the group's leader, Abu Bakar Bashir, had several high-level allies, notably Vice President Hamzah. He reportedly had warned Megawati against challenging Bakar Bashir and had publicly criticized her for supporting the United States following the September 11 attacks.

Under intense international pressure following the Bali bombing, Megawati finally acted on October 18, issuing a decree authorizing the police to arrest and hold for seven days anyone strongly suspected of involvement with terrorism and imposing a penalty of death by firing squad for those convicted of terrorism. The decree was made retroactive to apply to the Bali bombing.

The government also announced that Bashir would be detained for questioning in connection with the bombing of several churches in Jakarta in

December 2000 that killed nineteen people. Bashir at first attempted to evade arrest by declaring he was ill and checking into a local hospital—a common tactic in the country—but he eventually was placed in a hospital run by the police. The government on November 6 filed charges against him in the 2000 bombings; the charges were still pending at the end of 2002.

The first big break in the Bali bombing case came November 8, when police arrested a man known as Amrozi, who admitted buying materials for the bomb and who said he knew both Jemaah Islamiyah leaders: Bashir and Hambali. Amrozi told investigators that the group had hoped to kill Americans, and he said he regretted that so many Australians died.

Police quickly rounded up others named by Amrozi as having been involved in the plot, including Iman Samudra, a computer engineer who was arrested on November 21 and readily confessed to having helped organize the bombing. Finally, on December 4 police arrested Amozi's older brother, Ali Ghufron, also known as Mukhlas, who was said to be one of the top commanders of Jemaah Islamiyah. Independent terrorism experts said the arrest of Mukhlas was a major coup for Indonesian police and the Western intelligence services that were aiding in the case because he presumably had important information about Jemaah Islamiyah operations throughout Southeast Asia.

At year's end the investigation into the Bali bombing was still under way, and international intelligence services were searching for other suspects with links to Jemaah Islamiyah and the al Qaeda network. The Indonesian government said it hoped to begin trials in the case early in 2003.

Impact of the Bombing on Indonesia

The Bali bombing exposed yet again how weak the Indonesian government had become since Suharto's fall from power in 1998. The long-time ruler had collected all political power into his own hands and those of close family members and friends—many of whom became extraordinarily wealthy through the country's pervasive system of corruption. Suharto had been succeeded by two weak presidents, the second of whom was ousted from office by the parliament on corruption charges. Megawati, the vice president at the time, was elected president despite her reputation for extreme caution and the general lack of knowledge about her positions on the central issues of the day in Indonesia. Her popularity was based almost entirely on the fact that her father was Sukarno, the country's founding president after World War II.

Megawati remained a passive leader during her first year in office, apparently not wanting to antagonize any of the country's numerous special interest groups. Her actions immediately after the Bali bombing were characteristic. Although she visited the scene of the attack a few days later, Megawati made no attempt to rally the country behind an antiterror campaign, to explain why Indonesia had become a terrorist target, or even to head off rapidly spreading rumors that the bombing was a U.S. plot to discredit Indonesia and its Islamic groups.

In addition to Megawati's inherent caution, analysts said the president's unwillingness to take strong actions stemmed from the fact that she headed a coalition that included most of the parties in parliament. She apparently felt the need to consult with a broad range of political leaders before taking any action, whether controversial or not. Despite widespread agreement, both inside and outside Indonesia, that one of the country's most urgent task was dealing with systemic corruption in government and business, Megawati took no action because it would have put her in conflict with important interest groups. With the next presidential elections scheduled for 2004, Megawati's main campaign tactic appeared to be avoiding controversy. In an October 22 policy brief for the Australian parliament, Indonesia expert Stephen Sherlock said Megawati's slow response to the Bali bombing was "just one manifestation of a general policy immobility that affects her entire administration."

If any one faction seemed bound to benefit from the bombing it was the Indonesian army, which for years had been under domestic and international pressure because of its reputation for corruption, cronyism, and human rights abuses. The army's sponsorship of paramilitary groups in East Timor that carried out extreme violence following a 1999 independence referendum brought widespread criticism and forced the government to take unprecedented steps to curtail its independence. Megawati already had moved to give the army more authority, and the Bali bombing offered a security rationale for a further loosening of restrictions. (East Timor, p. 256)

In addition to political considerations, the Bali bombing seemed certain to have serious long-term economic consequences for Indonesia. The country had never fully recovered from the battering it received during the 1997–1998 Asian financial crisis, an episode that was a major factor in Suharto's ouster. Although blessed with natural resources, including large gas and oil deposits, Indonesia had not been able to develop its economy to keep pace with many other countries in the region. Indonesia was heavily dependent on foreign investment, but investors had been scarce since the Asian crisis; in fact, the country was still losing foreign capital, at the rate of $5.7 billion in 2001, according to government estimates. (Asian financial crisis, Historic Documents of 1998, p. 722)

In the days after the bombing the government bought up millions of dollars worth of rupiahs to prevent the currency from collapsing. But the long-term challenge was convincing foreign companies—already nervous about insecurity, potential political instability, corruption, and a malfunctioning legal system—not to flee. Tourism, the main industry in Bali, dried up for the rest of the year, and analysts said it might be months or even years before the island would regain its status as a tropical paradise for the young and romantic.

Indonesia's one bit of good news late in the year was the signing, on December 9, of a cease-fire agreement with guerrillas who had been fighting for a separate homeland in the province of Aceh, on the extreme northwest tip of Sumatra island. A conflict between the government and the guerrillas had been under way since 1976, and an estimated 12,000 people, most of them civilians, had died as a result.

International mediators—including retired U.S. general Anthony C. Zinni—had been working for nearly two years to resolve the conflict. The key issues were control of revenues from the substantial oil and gas production in the region and the rebels' demand for the right to implement Islamic law, known as sharia. *To encourage the rebels to give up their struggle, Megawati agreed to allow a new provincial government in Aceh to control about 70 percent of the oil and gas revenues and to implement Islamic law. While it fell short of complete independence, that offer appeared to satisfy key guerrilla leaders, who agreed to the cease-fire. Despite continued low-level clashes, international cease-fire monitors took up their posts on December 28.*

Following are excerpts from a speech to the Australian parliament on October 14, 2002, by Australian prime minister John Howard about the October 12 bombing in Bali, Indonesia, that had claimed the lives of more than 180 people, nearly half of them Australian citizens.

The document was obtained from the Internet at www .pm.gov.au/news/speeches/2002/speech1913.htm; accessed January 27, 2003.

I move that this House:

1. expresses its outrage and condemnation at the barbaric terrorist bombings which took place in Bali on 12 October 2002;
2. extends its deepest and heartfelt sympathy to the families and loved ones of those Australians killed, missing or injured in this brutal and despicable attack;
3. offers its condolences to the families and friends of the Indonesians and citizens of other countries who have been killed or injured;
4. condemns those who employ terror and indiscriminate violence against innocent people;
5. commits the Australian government to work with the Indonesian government and others to bring those who are guilty of this horrendous crime, and all those who harbour and support them, to justice;
6. reaffirms Australia's commitment to continue the war against terrorism in our region and in the rest of the world.

For the rest of Australian history, 12 October 2002 will be counted as a day on which evil struck, with indiscriminate and indescribable savagery, young innocent Australians who were engaging in an understandable period of relaxation and whose innocence was palpable and whose death and injury we join the rest of the Australian community in marking and mourning today.

In many respects the word terrorism is too antiseptic an expression to describe what happened. It is too technical and too formal. What happened was barbaric brutal mass murder without justification. It is seen as that by the people of Australia and it is seen as that by the people of the world. It is a terrible reminder that terrorism can strike anyone anywhere at any time. Nobody anywhere in the world is immune from terrorism. It is a reminder that, in this time of a borderless world with a particularly mobile young population, Australia can scarcely imagine that it can be in any way immune from such horrible attacks.

I know that the thoughts of everyone in this parliament—and, indeed, the thoughts of millions of Australians—are with those of our fellow countrymen and women who still do not know whether their daughter or their son or their brother or their sister or their lover or their mother or their father or their mate is alive or dead. The agony of waiting at the end of a mobile telephone for a call is an anxiety that we can only begin to think about and try in our own inadequate way to share, and we hope that that effort is of some comfort to them. I know that the hearts of every man and woman in this parliament will go out to them and to those who know the worst already, and our thoughts and prayers are with those who are coping with injuries, many of them horrendous burns as a result of the flames that followed the bombing of the nightclub.

At present, the best advice I have is that there is a total of 181 dead. Very few of these have been identified. According to advice from the Indonesian authorities and our Consulate-General in Bali, 14 Australians are now confirmed among the dead and at least 113 Australians have been hospitalised following the attacks. We are still trying to establish the precise number of people evacuated to Australia, but the best advice is that it is in the order of 67 to 70. There are still 220 Australians unaccounted for. It should not be automatically assumed that all of those are dead but, given the very high percentage of Australians who were in the nightclub at the time of the bombing, we should as a nation prepare ourselves for the very real likelihood that the death toll of Australians will climb significantly when the final tally and identity of the fatalities is known.

As the House and, I am sure, the nation will be aware, a major rescue and medical evacuation operation has been under way since news of the attack came through. On behalf of this parliament and all of the Australian people, I want to express our gratitude to and admiration for the officers of the Department of Foreign Affairs and Trade; the men and women of the Australian Defence Force, particularly the Royal Australian Air Force; and the doctors, nurses and paramedics, many of whom have worked in very difficult circumstances. I also record my thanks to the various state governments that have offered help, to Qantas and to many other private individuals who have provided help and assistance. The willingness of the government to provide evacuation facilities for all Australians and, indeed, others in need of medical attention remains. No expense will be spared and no limitation will be placed upon our willingness to do that.

This foul deed—this wicked, evil act of terrorists—has not only claimed the lives of Australians but also claimed the lives of many of the innocent people of Bali, a beautiful, hitherto peaceful part of Indonesia. Bali is much loved by so many Australians. In many cases, it is the first place that young Australians visit. Many of us will feel the poignancy of this attack coinciding with the end of the football season in Australia. So many of the young people in that club that night were members of Australian rules football teams, rugby league teams and rugby union teams. They were having a bit of fun at the end of a hard season. It is that connection with the everyday occurrences of life which we know so well and embrace so lovingly, that cruel conjunction, which makes something such as this that much more despicable and something that all Australians will utterly repudiate to the depths of their being.

We must remember, though, that this will have an enormous impact on the people of Indonesia and the economy of Bali. The Indonesian economy is a fragile economy. It relies very heavily on tourism. Those who did this are no friends of Indonesia. Those who did this sought to inflict misery on and deliver hatred to not only the people of Australia and the people of the other nations who lost their sons and daughters but also the people and the government of Indonesia. We must understand essentially what has happened. This is a vile crime which has claimed the lives of an as yet uncounted number of Australians on Indonesian soil.

All of us have a right to feel a sense of deep anger and a deep determination to do everything we can, as a nation and as a community, working with the government and the people of Indonesia, to bring to justice those who are responsible for this crime. We owe it to those who died, we owe it to those who have been injured and we also owe it to a proper sense of justice. Nothing can excuse this behaviour. No cause—however explained, however advocated, however twisted, however spun—can possibly justify the indiscriminate, unprovoked slaughter of innocent people. That is what has occurred here. We must do all we can, as a nation and as a community, to mete out a proper response—a measured, sober, effective response—which brings to justice, if we can, those who are responsible.

It is necessary, in the course of this, for us to cooperate with the government and the people of Indonesia. Yesterday I spoke by telephone to President Megawati. She expressed her horror at what had occurred. She agreed with me that, on all the evidence available to us, this was clearly the act of terrorists. There can be no other explanation. Both of us agreed that every effort should be made to bring those responsible for this act to justice. . . .

I can also inform the House that this morning the National Security Committee of cabinet met in the wake of this outrage. . . . We also decided to institute a review of the adequacy of domestic terrorist legislation. It is inevitable that, in the wake of what occurred in Bali over the weekend, the thoughts of Australians will turn to the potential vulnerability of our own soil, our own mainland, to a possible terrorist attack. There is no point in ignoring that. I do the Australian people no service if I pretend that, in some way, it cannot happen on the Australian mainland. In a sense, this is sequential. I do not think any of us believed that something like 11 September 2001 would happen until it really happened. We might have intellectualised afterwards and said, 'Oh yes, we thought that might happen,' but in our hearts we did not really believe it was going to happen.

Equally, I do not think many Australians contemplated that what happened at the weekend in Bali would in fact occur. It is therefore very important that we disabuse ourselves for all time if any of us entertain the notion that something like that cannot happen in one of our cities and on our own mainland. We must dedicate and commit ourselves to doing all we can to guard against such an event. We therefore need to again assess the adequacy of our domestic law. I know it has been only recently reviewed, but further events have occurred and we are required as a matter of responsibility to almost 20 million Australians to do that. It is also necessary that we review the adequacy, which I have asked be done, of our counter-terrorism capacity. Once again, that was the subject of significant review after 11 September 2001 and major augmentation of the assets followed as a result of that review. It is therefore timely that those assets and that capacity also be reviewed.

I do not say these things lightly or in any sense of overdramatising the situation, but we are living in different circumstances and different times. That has been the case since 11 September last year; it is dramatically more so the case now, because what happened at the weekend claimed our own in great numbers, was on our own doorstep and touched us in a way that we would not have thought possible a week ago or even three days go. It has been the case that all the world, including Australia, has been more vulnerable to potential terrorist attacks since 11 September last year. In relation to the events in Bali, it is obvious that the Australian government has been concerned for some considerable time about the existence of extremist groups in the region, especially in Indonesia, with links to al-Qaeda and the real possibility of terrorist attacks against Western interests. That has been not only a concern of the Australian government but also a constant concern of the government of the United States. That concern, and the concern of our American friends, has been regularly communicated to the Indonesian authorities. . . .

I can inform the House that the intelligence available to the government highlighted the general threat environment but was at no time specific about Saturday night's attack in Bali. Indeed, the Department of Foreign Affairs and Trade's travel advice reflected the heightened level of concern which followed the terrorist attacks in September of last year. It was very much against the background of the general threat disclosed by intelligence that the government issued its alert in early September about the possible threat to Australian interests in the region around 11 September 2002.

It is apparent from the words of the resolution and from what has been said over the last 36 hours and what is self-evident from an examination of the realities that confront Australia and the rest of the civilised world today that the war against terrorism must go on in an uncompromising and unconditional fashion. Any other course of action would be folly. Retreat from the war against terrorism will not purchase for the retreaters immunity against the attacks of the terrorists. That has been the experience of the last year; that has been the experience of mankind through history. You will not escape the reach of terrorism by imagining that if you roll yourself into a little ball you will not be noticed, because terrorism is not dispensed according to some hierarchy of disdain; it is dispensed in an indiscriminate, evil, hateful fashion. Those who imagine that it is dispensed according to a hierarchy of disdain do not understand history and are deluding themselves.

The war against terrorism is not, as has frequently been said in this place, a war against Islam. People of good Islamic faith will abhor what happened in Bali. They will find it as despicable to the tenets of their faith as Christians, Jews and many others will find it despicable to the tenets of their faith. It is therefore important that we reaffirm again our commitment to a tolerant Australian community—an Australian community that, while embracing all, is an Australian community bound together by common values of openness, individual liberty and individual freedom. We fight terrorism because we love freedom; we fight terrorism because we want to preserve the way of life that this country has; we fight terrorism because we share the values of other countries that are in the war against terrorism; and we fight terrorism because it is intrinsically evil and you do not seek to covenant with evil and you do not seek to reach an accommodation with those who would destroy your sons and daughters and take away the security and the stability of this country.

In the hours that have followed this terrible outrage—this dark day for the people of Australia—there have been many expressions of concern from world leaders. I spoke at length this morning to President Bush of the United States and I received a call last night from British Prime Minister Tony Blair and the Prime Minister of New Zealand, Helen Clark. Her Majesty The Queen has sent a message of sympathy and condolence and I have received messages from many world leaders. All of them have a common theme and a common resonance, and that is that, in the world in which we live, our problems are the problems of others and the problems of others are so often ours as well. We live in a globalised world. We live in a world in which the young, in particular, are more footloose and more mobile than even their mobile parents and grandparents, and there is no escape in those circumstances from the reaches and the ravages of terror.

I want to thank the Leader of the Opposition for the constructive way in which we have been able together to discuss these challenges to our country. Our country belongs to all of us, and this is a challenge to the fabric of this country and what it stands for. . . .

In different ways, different communities in different parts of our country will mourn the abrupt and brutal deaths of so many and reflect on their own lives. In our own way we must try to offer comfort, care and hope to their bereaved friends, lovers and relatives. It is a very sad time for our country but it is a time—as always in cases like this—that has brought forth heroism, decency and goodness. Already stories of people assisting others at enormous risk to themselves are emerging, as are stories of the dedication of the staff of the hospitals and the commitment of so many. We think also of the lovely people of Bali who have been such friends to so many Australians of so many generations on so many occasions. We extend our thanks, our warmth and our affection to them.

I am saddened beyond words of proper description by what has happened. I hope I speak for all Australians in sending my and their love to those who are grieving and in expressing the fierce determination to do everything I and we can to bring to justice those who have done such evil things to our people.

U.S. AND UN RESOLUTIONS ON IRAQ AND IRAQI RESPONSE

October 16, November 8, and November 13, 2002

Eleven years after the United Nations Security Council first demanded that Iraq give up its weapons of mass destruction, President George W. Bush in late 2002 forced the Security Council to return to the unfinished business of Iraq's disarmament. Bush used patient diplomacy, coupled with an even more potent threat of a U.S.-led invasion of Iraq, to win an extraordinary unanimous resolution from the council on November 8 insisting that Iraqi leader Saddam Hussein finally keep his promise to surrender the weapons he had built to embellish his standing in the Middle East.

The Iraqi government responded with a claim that it no longer had the weapons, but it did allow UN inspectors to return to Iraq for the first time since Saddam forced them out in December 1998. At year's end about 100 inspectors were beginning the painstaking task of poking through warehouses, factories, defense installations—and even some of Saddam's palaces—in search of biological and chemical weapons, medium-range missiles, and the remaining elements of Iraq's past program to develop nuclear weapons.

Overhanging the diplomacy that led to the return of the inspectors was Bush's stated willingness, some said determination, to go to war in Iraq. The president offered two main rationales for such a war: disarming Iraq, if the inspections failed to finish the task, and ousting Saddam and his dictatorial regime from power (a task euphemistically referred to as "regime change"). Bush found broad international support for the disarmament goal. The UN Security Council had demanded Iraq's disarmament in ten resolutions passed since 1991, most of which Iraq had ignored or managed to evade. But there was much less enthusiasm in world capitals for the more daunting task of invading Iraq for the purpose of changing the government. One of the world's most brutal dictators, Saddam Hussein appeared to have little genuine popular support in Iraq and was sustained in power by a small entourage from his home base of Tikrit, south of Baghdad. Internationally, Saddam was considered a pariah in most capitals and was tolerated, at best, by his fellow Arab leaders. Even so, British Prime Minister Tony Blair seemed to be the only major world leader who readily embraced Bush's call for regime change in Iraq, by force if necessary.

Congress Responds

President Bush opened his campaign against Iraq in November 2001 with a statement equating that country's weapons program with terrorism. The president raised the stakes in his January 29, 2002, State of the Union address, in which he linked Iraq with Iran and North Korea as part of an "axis of evil." In subsequent months Bush and his aides made it clear that Iraq was the next target in the U.S. war against terrorism. The primary question was whether the administration would act on its own or seek the support of allies and other nations through the United Nations. Bush answered that question with an emphatic speech to the UN General Assembly on September 12, calling on the Security Council to take unspecified action to disarm Iraq. (State of the Union, p. 33; Bush speech to the UN, p. 612)

The president's next step was to seek support from Congress. Although Bush insisted he did not need congressional authorization to go to war, a vote of support on Capitol Hill would bolster his case internationally and offer him a measure of political protection at home should a war turn out badly. One week after his UN speech, Bush on September 19 sent Congress a proposed resolution that declared Iraq to be in "material and unacceptable breach" of UN Security Council resolutions and gave him virtually unlimited authorization to use military force to thwart "the threat posed by Iraq" and to "restore international peace and security in the [Middle East] region."

The president found broad support in Congress for confronting Iraq but also resistance to his request for unconditional authorization to go to war. Opinion polls also showed that the public was divided on the question, with many Americans expressing uncertainty about the need to take on Iraq while the United States was still battling the al Qaeda terrorist network that carried out the September 11, 2001, attacks in New York and Washington. Bush's key step on Capitol Hill was to secure the endorsement, on October 2, of House Minority Leader Richard A. Gephardt, D-Mo., a potential presidential candidate who had voted against a similar resolution in 1991 authorizing Bush's father to conduct the first Persian Gulf War. Gephardt convinced Bush to accept several procedural changes requiring him to continue consulting with Congress. In turn, Gephardt's endorsement undercut Democratic opposition to Bush's request and ensured its passage by a broad margin in both chambers.

But one more step was required before Congress would vote. Leaders in both parties expressed concern that Bush had not adequately explained to the public why Iraq posed a threat to U.S. interests and why it was urgent to confront that threat sooner rather than later. In response, Bush on October 7 delivered a nationally televised speech to an audience in Cincinnati arguing that Iraq "on any given day" could attack the United States or its allies with biological or chemical weapons and could decide to give these weapons to terrorist groups. The president offered no new evidence to sup-

port this assertion, but he did claim that Iraq ultimately could use its fleet of unmanned aerial vehicles to attack U.S. cities with biological or chemical weapons. He did not explain how those planes (modified L-29 trainer planes obtained from Czechoslovakia, with a range of less than 600 miles) could reach the United States from Iraqi territory. "Understanding the threats of our time, knowing the designs and deceptions of the Iraqi regime, we have every reason to assume the worst, and we have an urgent duty to prevent the worst from occurring," Bush said. Saddam must disarm, the president said, and if he refused the United States "will lead a coalition to disarm him."

The president's speech came as the Senate was debating the use-of-force resolution and the House was preparing to do so. Clearly, the alarmed tone of that speech helped convince any wavering members. The House acted first, approving the resolution (H J Res 114) on October 10 by a vote of 296– 133; all but 6 Republicans voted for the measure, and Gephardt was among the minority of 81 Democrats who supported it. The Senate acted the next day, approving the resolution by an even broader 77–23 vote; only 1 Republican voted no, while 29 Democrats—a majority, including leader Tom Daschle of South Dakota—voted in favor. Bush signed the resolution into law (PL 107–243) on October 16.

Negotiating a UN Resolution

There never was much doubt that Bush would be able to get congressional support for his get-tough stance against Iraq, but it was much less clear that all fourteen other members of the UN Security Council were prepared to launch a challenge that might lead to war. Immediately after Bush's September 12 speech to the General Assembly, Secretary of State Colin Powell began a series of consultations with diplomats from other countries represented on the Security Council. Powell had guaranteed support from Britain but the three other countries with veto power (China, France, and Russia) were much more skeptical, and only some of the ten other nations represented on the council seemed likely to endorse a step toward possible war against Iraq.

Diplomats on the council did agree quickly to an approach demanding that Iraq accept a return of UN weapons inspectors, who had been ousted during a previous dispute at the end of 1998. The question was whether the resolution making this demand of Iraq would also state the consequences of Iraq's failure to comply. The U.S. position was that the UN Security Council should adopt a single resolution that both demanded the return of the weapons inspectors and warned that "serious consequences" (diplomatic code language for war) would result if Iraq refused to cooperate. The key resistance came from France, which often tried to act as a counterweight to what it perceived as U.S. domination of world affairs and which, not coincidentally, also had substantial commercial interests in Iraq. French diplomats held out for a two-step process: one resolution demanding that Iraq allow the weapons inspectors to return, to be followed by a second resolution spelling out consequences if Iraq refused. In effect, the U.S. proposal would

715

have given Bush the advance blessing of the council to launch a war if he de-
termined that Iraq was balking, while the French plan would have required
Bush to return to the council for that authorization.

Behind-the-scenes diplomatic negotiations on the wording of the resolu-
tion dragged on for several weeks. The debate came into the open on Octo-
ber 16 when the UN Security Council began a two-day public session
requested by the "nonaligned movement," a coalition of developing nations.
Most of the diplomats who spoke represented nations that did not sit on the
council, but their speeches echoed the same conflicting positions of those
that would have to vote on a resolution. In a bid for unity, Secretary
General Kofi Annan reminded the diplomats that Iraq had violated many
previous resolutions and should be required to comply with the UN's disar-
mament ban or "face its responsibilities"—in other words, be prepared for
a war. But Annan also warned the diplomats, especially those from France
and the United States, to reach a consensus. "If you allow yourselves to be
divided, the authority and credibility of this organization [the UN] un-
doubtedly will suffer."

After nearly two months of diplomatic haggling, agreement came in early
November on a compromise approach. The text of a resolution, introduced
by the United States and Britain on November 6, declared that Iraq "has
been and remains in material breach of its obligations" under previous
UN resolutions; demanded that Iraq submit, within thirty days, a "cur-
rently accurate, full, and complete declaration" of its prohibited weapons
programs; warned that any future false statements or omissions by Iraq
would "constitute a further material breach" of its obligations; demanded
that Iraq give UN weapons inspectors "immediate, unimpeded, uncondi-
tional, and unrestricted access" to all sites and records they wished to in-
spect; and reminded Iraq that it would "face serious consequences" if it
continued to violate its obligations.

This resolution gave Bush his explicit demand for action by Iraq and
warned Baghdad, in diplomatic language, that it would risk a war if it did
not comply. John Negroponte, the U.S. ambassador to the United Nations,
assured his colleagues that United States would return to the council for an-
other debate before going to war. But, he insisted, the resolution's reference
to "serious consequences" meant that another resolution authorizing war
would not be necessary. China, France, Russia, and other reluctant coun-
tries interpreted the resolution differently. The UN weapons inspectors—
not the United States—would determine whether Iraq was cooperating,
China, France, and Russia said in a statement. If Iraq did not cooperate, the
UN Security Council would need to "take a position," in other words decide
whether to adopt a follow-up resolution authorizing war.

The council adopted the compromise resolution (number 1441) unani-
mously on November 8. Passage had not been in doubt once the principal
powers reached an agreement, but the unanimous vote came as a surprise to
most observers. According to news reports, the last two holdouts—Russian
president Vladimir Putin and Syrian president Bashar al-Assad—bowed to
U.S. lobbying in favor of the resolution during last-minute bargaining im-

mediately before the council acted. Syria's approval was of special signifi-cance because it was the only Arab nation represented on the Security Council. Relations between Iraq and Syria had been strained for decades, but so had relations between Syria and the United States.

Bush hailed the council's vote as representing a "final test" for Saddam. "Any act of delay or defiance will be an additional breach of Iraq's obligations, and a clear signal that the Iraqi regime has once again abandoned the path of voluntary compliance," he said.

The unanimous action by the Security Council also represented a major achievement by Secretary of State Powell. In terms of sheer negotiating legerdemain, Powell's negotiation of the resolution rivaled the two most important U.S. diplomatic feats of the previous decade: the first Bush administration's assembling, in late 1990 and early 1991, of a broad coalition that carried out the Persian Gulf War and forced Iraq to abandon its invasion of Kuwait; and the 1995 negotiations in Dayton, Ohio, mediated by diplomat Richard Holbrooke, that ended the bloody civil war in Bosnia and established a cumbersome but effective system of multiethnic government there. (Gulf War negotiations, Historic Documents of 1990, p. 716, and Historic Documents of 1991, p. 191; Bosnia agreement, Historic Documents of 1995, p. 735)

Despite Powell's success, the agreement reached at the UN contained the seeds of discord that was almost certain to arise as the confrontation with Iraq moved into 2003. Most important, the resolution left to the eye of the beholder the question of whether Iraq was fully complying with the disarmament demand. As of late 2002 it appeared almost certain that the Bush administration would accept nothing short of the complete destruction, within a few months at most, of every illegal missile that Iraq had built during the 1990s and every canister of biological and chemical weapons it had developed and kept hidden over the previous decade. The leaders of some other countries represented on the UN Security Council, however, indicated that they might well be satisfied with achievement of a less ambitious goal, such as Iraq's apparent cooperation, however grudging and limited, with the work of the UN weapons inspectors. As a result, it seemed likely that Bush once again would be faced with the choice of heading to war on his own—with possible support from Britain and only a few other countries—or returning to the council for another divisive debate on whether to give Iraq one more "final" chance to comply with the disarmament demand.

Iraq's Response

Iraq's first official response to the UN Security Council resolution came within the prescribed seven-day limit. In a nine-page letter delivered to the UN on November 13, Iraqi foreign minister Naji Sabri said his country "will deal with Resolution 1441 despite its bad contents." More important, the letter said: "We are prepared to receive the inspectors, so they can carry out their duties, and make sure that Iraq had not developed weapons of mass destruction during their absence since 1998."

Using language that diplomats said reflected Saddam's often blustery tone, the letter blasted Bush's "wicked slander" and "malicious intent" against Iraq. The president's charges that Iraq was developing weapons of mass destruction were baseless "fabrications," the letter said. Mimicking the language Bush used in his State of the Union speech, the letter said Bush and "his lackey Tony Blair" were a "gang of evil." To reinforce the point, the letter used the word evil *ten times—every one a reference to Bush or the United States.*

Despite its overheated tone, that letter set in motion a series of steps envisioned by the resolution. On November 18, just ten days after the council acted and four years after the previous inspectors left Iraq, the first advance team of UN weapons inspectors arrived in Baghdad. Leading the thirty inspectors were the two men who would have the initial task of assessing for the UN Security Council the degree of Iraq's cooperation: Hans Blix, a Swedish diplomat who headed the UN Monitoring, Verification, and Inspection Commission (UNMOVIC), which had the task of examining Iraq's missiles and its stocks of biological and chemical weapons; and Mohamed El Baradei, an Egyptian diplomat who directed the International Atomic Energy Agency and was charged with determining whether Iraq had attempted to restart its nuclear weapons program.

The UN resolution required Iraq to give a "full and complete" declaration of its banned weapons programs by December 8. One day ahead of time, Iraq delivered to the UN inspectors in Baghdad boxes and bags containing an estimated 12,000 pages of material. Major General Hussam Muhammad Amin, Iraq's liaison to the inspectors, said the documents showed that "Iraq is empty of any weapons of mass destruction." Saddam Hussein had personally ordered a "full and frank" declaration, Amin said, adding: "That means that when we say we have no weapons of mass destruction, we are speaking the truth."

Within days, UN and U.S. officials said most of the Iraqi declaration appeared to consist of information that Iraq had given previous weapons inspectors during the 1990s. Indeed, hundreds of pages appeared to be identical to earlier reports that also claimed Iraq had never developed biological or biological weapons or made any progress toward nuclear weapons. In many instances during the 1990s Iraq had made such claims even though UN inspectors had uncovered evidence that such weapons did exist.

In a preliminary assessment given to the UN Security Council on December 19, Blix said his "overall impression" was that Iraq's declaration contained "not much new significant information" about weapons programs. In particular, he said, Iraq had not provided "supporting documentation or other evidence" to back up its claims that it did not possess banned weapons. The inspectors had some evidence "that would appear to contradict Iraq's account," he said, noting only that the Iraq's claims that it had destroyed its anthrax weapons by 1991 "may not be accurate."

At year's end the UN inspectors were continuing to work their way through hundreds of buildings in Iraq to verify, or disprove, Baghdad's claims that it no longer had any banned weapons. As this work continued, the Bush administration continued its diplomatic efforts to build support for a military attack against Iraq, on the assumption that the government there ultimately would be found in violation of the UN Security Council's resolution that demanded full and complete cooperation with the inspectors.

Following are three documents: The text of the joint congressional resolution (PL 107–243) authorizing the use of U.S. armed forces against Iraq, signed into law by President George W. Bush on October 16, 2002; the text of UN Security Council Resolution 1441, adopted on November 8, 2002, demanding that Iraq disarm itself of all missiles and biological, chemical, and nuclear weapons it still possessed in violation of previous resolutions; and excerpts from a letter, dated November 13, 2002, from Iraqi foreign minister Naji Sabri to UN Secretary General Kofi A. Annan stating that Iraq agreed to the return of UN weapons inspectors.

The documents were obtained from the Internet at *frwebgate.access.gpo.gov/cgi-bin/getdoc.cgi?dbname = 107_cong_public_laws&docid =f:publ243.107; usinfo.state .gov/topical/pol/terror/02110803.htm; www.iraqi-mission .org/s-2002-1242.htm; accessed January 4, 2003.*

CONGRESSIONAL RESOLUTION

Joint Resolution

To authorize the use of United States Armed Forces against Iraq.

Whereas in 1990 in response to Iraq's war of aggression against and illegal occupation of Kuwait, the United States forged a coalition of nations to liberate Kuwait and its people in order to defend the national security of the United States and enforce United Nations Security Council resolutions relating to Iraq;

Whereas after the liberation of Kuwait in 1991, Iraq entered into a United Nations sponsored cease-fire agreement pursuant to which Iraq unequivocally agreed, among other things, to eliminate its nuclear, biological, and chemical weapons programs and the means to deliver and develop them, and to end its support for international terrorism;

Whereas the efforts of international weapons inspectors, United States intelligence agencies, and Iraqi defectors led to the discovery that Iraq had large stockpiles of chemical weapons and a large scale biological weapons program, and that Iraq had an advanced nuclear weapons development program that was much closer to producing a nuclear weapon than intelligence reporting had previously indicated;

Whereas Iraq, in direct and flagrant violation of the cease-fire, attempted to thwart the efforts of weapons inspectors to identify and destroy Iraq's weapons of mass destruction stockpiles and development capabilities, which finally resulted in the withdrawal of inspectors from Iraq on October 31, 1998;

Whereas in Public Law 105-235 (August 14, 1998), Congress concluded that Iraq's continuing weapons of mass destruction programs threatened vital United States interests and international peace and security, declared Iraq to be in "material and unacceptable breach of its international obligations" and urged the President "to take appropriate action, in accordance with the Constitution and relevant laws of the United States, to bring Iraq into compliance with its international obligations";

Whereas Iraq both poses a continuing threat to the national security of the United States and international peace and security in the Persian Gulf region and remains in material and unacceptable breach of its international obligations by, among other things, continuing to possess and develop a significant chemical and biological weapons capability, actively seeking a nuclear weapons capability, and supporting and harboring terrorist organizations;

Whereas Iraq persists in violating resolution of the United Nations Security Council by continuing to engage in brutal repression of its civilian population thereby threatening international peace and security in the region, by refusing to release, repatriate, or account for non-Iraqi citizens wrongfully detained by Iraq, including an American serviceman, and by failing to return property wrongfully seized by Iraq from Kuwait;

Whereas the current Iraqi regime has demonstrated its capability and willingness to use weapons of mass destruction against other nations and its own people;

Whereas the current Iraqi regime has demonstrated its continuing hostility toward, and willingness to attack, the United States, including by attempting in 1993 to assassinate former President Bush and by firing on many thousands of occasions on United States and Coalition Armed Forces engaged in enforcing the resolutions of the United Nations Security Council;

Whereas members of al Qaida, an organization bearing responsibility for attacks on the United States, its citizens, and interests, including the attacks that occurred on September 11, 2001, are known to be in Iraq;

Whereas Iraq continues to aid and harbor other international terrorist organizations, including organizations that threaten the lives and safety of United States citizens;

Whereas the attacks on the United States of September 11, 2001, underscored the gravity of the threat posed by the acquisition of weapons of mass destruction by international terrorist organizations;

Whereas Iraq's demonstrated capability and willingness to use weapons of mass destruction, the risk that the current Iraqi regime will either employ those weapons to launch a surprise attack against the United States or its Armed Forces or provide them to international terrorists who would do so, and the extreme magnitude of harm that would result to the United States and its citizens from such an attack, combine to justify action by the United States to defend itself;

Whereas United Nations Security Council Resolution 678 (1990) authorizes the use of all necessary means to enforce United Nations Security Council Resolution 660 (1990) and subsequent relevant resolutions and to compel Iraq to cease certain activities that threaten international peace and security, including the development of weapons of mass destruction and refusal or obstruction of United Nations weapons inspections in violation of United Nations Security Council Resolution 687 (1991), repression of its civilian population in violation of United Nations Security Council Resolution 688 (1991), and threatening its neighbors or United Nations operations in Iraq in violation of United Nations Security Council Resolution 949 (1994);

Whereas in the Authorization for Use of Military Force Against Iraq Resolution (Public Law 102-1), Congress has authorized the President "to use United States Armed Forces pursuant to United Nations Security Council Resolution 678 (1990) in order to achieve implementation of Security Council Resolution 660, 661, 662, 664, 665, 666, 667, 669, 670, 674, and 677";

Whereas in December 1991, Congress expressed its sense that it "supports the use of all necessary means to achieve the goals of United Nations Security Council Resolution 687 as being consistent with the Authorization of Use of Military Force Against Iraq Resolution (Public Law 102–1)," that Iraq's repression of its civilian population violates United Nations Security Council Resolution 688 and "constitutes a continuing threat to the peace, security, and stability of the Persian Gulf region," and that Congress, "supports the use of all necessary means to achieve the goals of United Nations Security Council Resolution 688";

Whereas the Iraq Liberation Act of 1998 (Public Law 105–338) expressed the sense of Congress that it should be the policy of the United States to support efforts to remove from power the current Iraqi regime and promote the emergence of a democratic government to replace that regime;

Whereas on September 12, 2002, President Bush committed the United States to "work with the United Nations Security Council to meet our common challenge" posed by Iraq and to "work for the necessary resolutions," while also making clear that "the Security Council resolutions will be enforced, and the just demands of peace and security will be met, or action will be unavoidable";

Whereas the United States is determined to prosecute the war on terrorism and Iraq's ongoing support for international terrorist groups combined with its development of weapons of mass destruction in direct violation of its obligations under the 1991 cease-fire and other United Nations Security Council resolutions make clear that it is in the national security interests of the United States and in furtherance of the war on terrorism that all relevant United Nations Security Council resolutions be enforced, including through the use of force if necessary;

Whereas Congress has taken steps to pursue vigorously the war on terrorism through the provision of authorities and funding requested by the

President to take the necessary actions against international terrorists and terrorist organizations, including those nations, organizations, or persons who planned, authorized, committed, or aided the terrorist attacks that occurred on September 11, 2001, or harbored such persons or organizations;

Whereas the President and Congress are determined to continue to take all appropriate actions against international terrorists and terrorist organizations, including those nations, organizations, or persons who planned, authorized, committed, or aided the terrorist attacks that occurred on September 11, 2001, or harbored such persons or organizations;

Whereas the President has authority under the Constitution to take action in order to deter and prevent acts of international terrorism against the United States, as Congress recognized in the joint resolution on Authorization for Use of Military Force (Public Law 107–40); and

Whereas it is in the national security interests of the United States to restore international peace and security to the Persian Gulf region: Now, therefore, be it

Resolved by the Senate and House of Representatives of the United States of America in assembled,

SECTION 1. SHORT TITLE.

This joint resolution may be cited as the "Authorization for Use of Military Force Against Iraq Resolution of 2002".

SEC. 2. SUPPORT FOR UNITED STATES DIPLOMATIC EFFORTS.

The Congress of the United States supports the efforts by the President to—

(1) strictly enforce through the United Nations Security Council all relevant Security Council resolutions regarding Iraq and encourages him in those efforts; and

(2) obtain prompt and decisive action by the Security Council to ensure that Iraq abandons its strategy of delay, evasion and noncompliance and promptly and strictly complies with all relevant Security Council resolutions regarding Iraq.

SEC. 3. AUTHORIZATION FOR USE OF UNITED STATES ARMED FORCES.

(a) AUTHORIZATION.—The President is authorized to use the Armed Forces of the United States as he determines to be necessary and appropriate in order to—

(1) defend the national security of the United States against the continuing threat posed by Iraq; and

(2) enforce all relevant United Nations Security Council resolutions regarding Iraq.

(b) PRESIDENTIAL DETERMINATION.—In connection with the exercise of the authority granted in subsection (a) to use force the President shall, prior to such exercise or as soon thereafter as may be feasible, but no later than 48 hours after exercising such authority, make available to the Speaker of the House of Representatives and the President pro tempore of the Senate his determination that—

(1) reliance by the United States on further diplomatic or other peaceful means alone either (A) will not adequately protect the national security of the United States against the continuing threat posed by Iraq or (B) is not likely to lead to enforcement of all relevant United Nations Security Council resolutions regarding Iraq; and

(2) acting pursuant to this joint resolution is consistent with the United States and other countries continuing to take the necessary actions against international terrorist and terrorist organizations, including those nations, organizations, or persons who planned, authorized, committed or aided the terrorist attacks that occurred on September 11, 2001.

(c) WAR POWERS RESOLUTION REQUIREMENTS.—

(1) SPECIFIC STATUTORY AUTHORIZATION.—Consistent with section 8(a)(1) of the War Powers Resolution, the Congress declares that this section is intended to constitute specific statutory authorization within the meaning of section 5(b) of the War Powers Resolution.

(2) APPLICABILITY OF OTHER REQUIREMENTS.—Nothing in this joint resolution supersedes any requirement of the War Powers Resolution.

SEC. 4. REPORTS TO CONGRESS.

(a) Reports.—The President shall, at least once every 60 days, submit to the Congress a report on matters relevant to this joint resolution, including actions taken pursuant to the exercise of authority granted in section 3 and the status of planning for efforts that are expected to be required after such actions are completed, including those actions described in section 7 of the Iraq Liberation Act of 1998 (Public Law 105–338).

(b) SINGLE CONSOLIDATED REPORT.—To the extent that the submission of any report described in subsection (a) coincides with the submission of any other report on matters relevant to this joint resolution otherwise required to be submitted to Congress pursuant to the reporting requirements of the War Powers Resolution (Public Law 93-148), all such reports may be submitted as a single consolidated report to the Congress.

(c) RULE OF CONSTRUCTION.—To the extent that the information required by section 3 of the Authorization for Use of Military Force Against Iraq Resolution (Public Law 102-1) is included in the report required by this section, such report shall be considered as meeting the requirements of section 3 of such resolution.

Approved October 16, 2002.

UN SECURITY COUNCIL RESOLUTION 1441

The Security Council,

Recalling all its previous relevant resolutions, in particular its resolutions 661 (1990) of 6 August 1990, 678 (1990) of 29 November 1990, 686 (1991) of 2 March 1991, 687 (1991) of 3 April 1991, 688 (1991) of 5 April 1991, 707 (1991) of 15 August 1991, 715 (1991) of 11 October 1991, 986 (1995) of 14 April 1995, and 1284 (1999) of 17 December 1999, and all the relevant statements of its President,

Recalling also its resolution 1382 (2001) of 29 November 2001 and its intention to implement it fully,

Recognizing the threat Iraq's noncompliance with Council resolutions and proliferation of weapons of mass destruction and long-range missiles poses to international peace and security,

Recalling that its resolution 678 (1990) authorized Member States to use all necessary means to uphold and implement its resolution 660 (1990) of 2 August 1990 and all relevant resolutions subsequent to Resolution 660 (1990) and to restore international peace and security in the area,

Further recalling that its resolution 687 (1991) imposed obligations on Iraq as a necessary step for achievement of its stated objective of restoring international peace and security in the area,

Deploring the fact that Iraq has not provided an accurate, full, final, and complete disclosure, as required by resolution 687 (1991), of all aspects of its programmes to develop weapons of mass destruction and ballistic missiles with a range greater than one hundred and fifty kilometres, and of all holdings of such weapons, their components and production facilities and locations, as well as all other nuclear programmes, including any which it claims are for purposes not related to nuclear-weapons-usable material,

Deploring further that Iraq repeatedly obstructed immediate, unconditional, and unrestricted access to sites designated by the United Nations Special Commission (UNSCOM) and the International Atomic Energy Agency (IAEA), failed to cooperate fully and unconditionally with UNSCOM and IAEA weapons inspectors, as required by resolution 687 (1991), and ultimately ceased all cooperation with UNSCOM and the IAEA in 1998,

Deploring the absence, since December 1998, in Iraq of international monitoring, inspection, and verification, as required by relevant resolutions, of weapons of mass destruction and ballistic missiles, in spite of the Council's repeated demands that Iraq provide immediate, unconditional, and unrestricted access to the United Nations Monitoring, Verification and Inspection Commission (UNMOVIC), established in resolution 1284 (1999) as the successor organization to UNSCOM, and the IAEA, and regretting the consequent prolonging of the crisis in the region and the suffering of the Iraqi people,

Deploring also that the Government of Iraq has failed to comply with its commitments pursuant to resolution 687 (1991) with regard to terrorism, pursuant to resolution 688 (1991) to end repression of its civilian population and to provide access by international humanitarian organizations to all those in need of assistance in Iraq, and pursuant to resolutions 686 (1991), 687 (1991), and 1284 (1999) to return or cooperate in accounting for Kuwaiti and third country nationals wrongfully detained by Iraq, or to return Kuwaiti property wrongfully seized by Iraq,

Recalling that in its resolution 687 (1991) the Council declared that a ceasefire would be based on acceptance by Iraq of the provisions of that resolution, including the obligations on Iraq contained therein,

Determined to ensure full and immediate compliance by Iraq without conditions or restrictions with its obligations under resolution 687 (1991) and other relevant resolutions and recalling that the resolutions of the Council constitute the governing standard of Iraqi compliance,

Recalling that the effective operation of UNMOVIC, as the successor organization to the Special Commission, and the IAEA is essential for the implementation of resolution 687 (1991) and other relevant resolutions,

Noting the letter dated 16 September 2002 from the Minister for Foreign Affairs of Iraq addressed to the Secretary General is a necessary first step toward rectifying Iraq's continued failure to comply with relevant Council resolutions,

Noting further the letter dated 8 October 2002 from the Executive Chairman of UNMOVIC and the Director General of the IAEA to General Al-Saadi of the Government of Iraq laying out the practical arrangements, as a follow-up to their meeting in Vienna, that are prerequisites for the resumption of inspections in Iraq by UNMOVIC and the IAEA, and expressing the gravest concern at the continued failure by the Government of Iraq to provide confirmation of the arrangements as laid out in that letter,

Reaffirming the commitment of all Member States to the sovereignty and territorial integrity of Iraq, Kuwait, and the neighbouring States,

Commending the Secretary General and members of the League of Arab States and its Secretary General for their efforts in this regard,

Determined to secure full compliance with its decisions,

Acting under Chapter VII of the Charter of the United Nations,

1. *Decides* that Iraq has been and remains in material breach of its obligations under relevant resolutions, including resolution 687 (1991), in particular through Iraq's failure to cooperate with United Nations inspectors and the IAEA, and to complete the actions required under paragraphs 8 to 13 of resolution 687 (1991);

2. *Decides*, while acknowledging paragraph 1 above, to afford Iraq, by this resolution, a final opportunity to comply with its disarmament obligations under relevant resolutions of the Council; and accordingly decides to set up an enhanced inspection regime with the aim of bringing to full and verified completion the disarmament process established by resolution 687 (1991) and subsequent resolutions of the Council;

3. *Decides* that, in order to begin to comply with its disarmament obligations, in addition to submitting the required biannual declarations, the Government of Iraq shall provide to UNMOVIC, the IAEA, and the Council, not later than 30 days from the date of this resolution, a currently accurate, full, and complete declaration of all aspects of its programmes to develop chemical, biological, and nuclear weapons, ballistic missiles, and other delivery

systems such as unmanned aerial vehicles and dispersal systems designed for use on aircraft, including any holdings and precise locations of such weapons, components, sub-components, stocks of agents, and related material and equipment, the locations and work of its research, development and production facilities, as well as all other chemical, biological, and nuclear programmes, including any which it claims are for purposes not related to weapon production or material;

4. *Decides* that false statements or omissions in the declarations submitted by Iraq pursuant to this resolution and failure by Iraq at any time to comply with, and cooperate fully in the implementation of, this resolution shall constitute a further material breach of Iraq's obligations and will be reported to the Council for assessment in accordance with paragraphs 11 and 12 below;

5. *Decides* that Iraq shall provide UNMOVIC and the IAEA immediate, unimpeded, unconditional, and unrestricted access to any and all, including underground, areas, facilities, buildings, equipment, records, and means of transport which they wish to inspect, as well as immediate, unimpeded, unrestricted, and private access to all officials and other persons whom UNMOVIC or the IAEA wish to interview in the mode or location of UNMOVIC's or the IAEA's choice pursuant to any aspect of their mandates; further decides that UNMOVIC and the IAEA may at their discretion conduct interviews inside or outside of Iraq, may facilitate the travel of those interviewed and family members outside of Iraq, and that, at the sole discretion of UNMOVIC and the IAEA, such interviews may occur without the presence of observers from the Iraqi government; and instructs UNMOVIC and requests the IAEA to resume inspections no later than 45 days following adoption of this resolution and to update the Council 60 days thereafter;

6. *Endorses* the 8 October 2002 letter from the Executive Chairman of UNMOVIC and the Director General of the IAEA to General Al-Saadi of the Government of Iraq, which is annexed hereto, and decides that the contents of the letter shall be binding upon Iraq;

7. *Decides* further that, in view of the prolonged interruption by Iraq of the presence of UNMOVIC and the IAEA and in order for them to accomplish the tasks set forth in this resolution and all previous relevant resolutions and notwithstanding prior understandings, the Council hereby establishes the following revised or additional authorities, which shall be binding upon Iraq, to facilitate their work in Iraq:

—UNMOVIC and the IAEA shall determine the composition of their inspection teams and ensure that these teams are composed of the most qualified and experienced experts available;

—All UNMOVIC and IAEA personnel shall enjoy the privileges and immunities, corresponding to those of experts on mission, provided in the Convention on Privileges and Immunities of the United Nations and the Agreement on the Privileges and Immunities of the IAEA;

—UNMOVIC and the IAEA shall have unrestricted rights of entry into and out of Iraq, the right to free, unrestricted, and immediate movement to and from inspection sites, and the right to inspect any sites and buildings, including immediate, unimpeded, unconditional, and unrestricted access to Presidential Sites equal to that at other sites, notwithstanding the provisions of resolution 1154 (1998);

—UNMOVIC and the IAEA shall have the right to be provided by Iraq the names of all personnel currently and formerly associated with Iraq's chemical, biological, nuclear, and ballistic missile programmes and the associated research, development, and production facilities;

—Security of UNMOVIC and IAEA facilities shall be ensured by sufficient UN security guards;

—UNMOVIC and the IAEA shall have the right to declare, for the purposes of freezing a site to be inspected, exclusion zones, including surrounding areas and transit corridors, in which Iraq will suspend ground and aerial movement so that nothing is changed in or taken out of a site being inspected;

—UNMOVIC and the IAEA shall have the free and unrestricted use and landing of fixed- and rotary-winged aircraft, including manned and unmanned reconnaissance vehicles;

—UNMOVIC and the IAEA shall have the right at their sole discretion verifiably to remove, destroy, or render harmless all prohibited weapons, subsystems, components, records, materials, and other related items, and the right to impound or close any facilities or equipment for the production thereof; and

—UNMOVIC and the IAEA shall have the right to free import and use of equipment or materials for inspections and to seize and export any equipment, materials, or documents taken during inspections, without search of UNMOVIC or IAEA personnel or official or personal baggage;

8. *Decides* further that Iraq shall not take or threaten hostile acts directed against any representative or personnel of the United Nations or the IAEA or of any Member State taking action to uphold any Council resolution;

9. *Requests* the Secretary General immediately to notify Iraq of this resolution, which is binding on Iraq; demands that Iraq confirm within seven days of that notification its intention to comply fully with this resolution; and demands further that Iraq cooperate immediately, unconditionally, and actively with UNMOVIC and the IAEA;

10. *Requests* all Member States to give full support to UNMOVIC and the IAEA in the discharge of their mandates, including by providing any information related to prohibited programmes or other aspects of their mandates, including on Iraqi attempts since 1998 to acquire prohibited items, and by recommending sites to be inspected, persons to be interviewed, conditions of such interviews, and data to be collected, the results of which shall be reported to the Council by UNMOVIC and the IAEA;

11. *Directs* the Executive Chairman of UNMOVIC and the Director General of the IAEA to report immediately to the Council any interference by Iraq with inspection activities, as well as any failure by Iraq to comply with its disarmament obligations, including its obligations regarding inspections under this resolution;

12. *Decides* to convene immediately upon receipt of a report in accordance with paragraphs 4 or 11 above, in order to consider the situation and the need for full compliance with all of the relevant Council resolutions in order to secure international peace and security;

13. *Recalls*, in that context, that the Council has repeatedly warned Iraq that it will face serious consequences as a result of its continued violations of its obligations;

14. *Decides* to remain seized of the matter.

IRAQI LETTER TO THE UN

Sir,

You may recall the enormous uproar created by the President of the United States of America in the greatest and most wicked slander against Iraq, in which he was followed in his malicious intent and preceded in word and infliction of harm by his lackey Tony Blair, when they spread the rumour that Iraq might have produced or might have been on the way to producing nuclear weapons during the period since 1998 in which the international inspectors were absent. They later asserted that Iraq had indeed produced chemical and biological weapons, though they know as well as we do, and other States are in a position to know, that this is a an utterly unfounded fabrication. But does knowledge of the truth even enter into the vocabulary of political interaction in our time, after evil has been unleashed to the fullest within the American administration and any hope of good has been dashed? Indeed, is there any good to be expected or hoped for from American administrations now that they have been transformed by their greed, by Zionism and by other well-known factors into the false god of our time? . . .

The influence of any international organization is based on the conviction and trust of the community in which it exists, once the organization declares that it has been established to serve goals important to that community. We fear that the United Nations will lose the trust and interest of peoples, if that has not already taken place, once it has been exhausted by powerful interests, wherever those interests converge at the expense of other peoples or flatter each other and haggle over what is false at the expense of what is true. Thus the United Nations and its agencies will collapse just as the League of Nations did before it. The responsibility for this will not rest on the American administration alone, but on all those who, in their weakness, work for its interests, yielding to its threats, enticements or promises. . . .

We know that those who pressed the case in the Security Council for the adoption of Security Council resolution 1441 (2002) have objectives other than to ascertain that Iraq has developed no weapons of mass destruction in the absence of the inspectors from Iraq since 1998. You are aware of how they left Iraq and who was the cause of their departure. Although we are aware that, following the widely known understanding between the representatives of Iraq and the Secretary-General and the press statement issued by [chief UN weapons inspector Hans] Blix, [director general of the International Atomic

Energy Agency Mohamed] El Baradei and the representatives of Iraq, there are no facts or principles of justice and fairness to necessitate the adoption of that resolution in the name of the Security Council, we hereby inform you that we will deal with resolution 1441 (2002), despite its iniquitous contents, even though it is to be implemented against the background of the intentions harboured by those of bad faith. Based as this is in an attempt to spare our people harm, we shall not forget, just as others should not forget, that the preservation of our people's dignity and of their security and independence within their homeland is a sacred and honourable national duty on the agenda of our leadership and our Government. The same is true of the protection of the homeland and its sovereignty, together with that of the people and their security, interests and high values, from antagonists and oppressors. Hence, as we said in the aforementioned agreement and press statement, we are ready to receive the inspectors so that they can perform their duties and ascertain that Iraq has produced no weapons of mass destruction in their absence from Iraq since 1998 under the circumstances known both to you and to the Security Council. We request you to inform the Security Council that we are ready to receive the inspectors in accordance with the established dates. All concerned parties should remember that we are in our holy month of Ramadan and that the people are fasting, and that after this month is a feast. The concerned bodies and officials, however, will cooperate with the inspectors against this entire background and that of the tripartite statement of France, the Russian Federation and China. The Government of Iraq will also take all of this into consideration when dealing with the inspectors and with all matters relating to their demeanour and the intentions of any one of them who demonstrates bad faith or an inappropriate approach to preserving the national dignity, independence and security of the people and the security, independence and sovereignty of the homeland. We are eager for them to accomplish their task in accordance with international law as soon as possible. If they do so in a professional and lawful manner, and without previously planned goals, the fabrications of the liars will be revealed to the public and the declared aim of the Security Council will be achieved. At that point, the Security Council will become legally obligated to lift the embargo from Iraq, failing which all persons of goodwill throughout the world, in addition to Iraq, will tell it to lift the embargo and all the other unjust sanctions from Iraq. Before the public and the law, the Council will be under obligation to apply paragraph 14 of its resolution 687 (1991) to the Zionist entity (Israel) and thereafter to the entire region of the Middle East so that it is free of weapons of mass destruction. The worldwide number of fair-minded persons will increase, together with Iraq's potential to drive from its environment the cawing of the crows of evil, who daily raid its lands, demolish its property and take the lives of those hit by their bombs, if not already claimed by the evil-doers themselves. When this happens, it will help to stabilize the region and the world, if accompanied by a solution not based on double standards to end the Zionist occupation of Palestine and if the aggressors desist from their attacks against Muslims and the world.

We therefore reiterate, through you, the same statement to the Security Council: send the inspectors to Iraq to ascertain as much and, if their conduct is thoroughly supervised to ensure that it is lawful and professional, everyone will be assured that Iraq has produced no nuclear, chemical or biological weapons of mass destruction, whatever allegations to the contrary are made by the evil pretenders. The fabrications of the liars and the deceit of the charlatans in the American and British administrations will be revealed before the world in contrast to the truthfulness of the proud Iraqis and the correctness of what they say and do. If, however, the opportunity is left for the whim of the American administration and the desires of Zionism, coupled with the followers, intelligence services, threats and foul inducements of each, to manipulate and play with the inspection teams and among their ranks, the picture will be muddled and the ensuing confusion will distort the facts and push matters in a dangerous direction, to the edge of the precipice, a situation wanted neither by the fair-minded nor by those, including my Government, who seek to uncover the facts as they stand. The fieldwork and the implementation will be the deciding factors as to whether the true intent was for the Security Council to ascertain that Iraq is free of those alleged weapons or whether the entire matter is nothing more than an evil cover for the authors of the resolution, with their vile slander and their shamelessness in lying to the public, including their own peoples.

So let the inspectors come to Baghdad to perform their duty in accordance with the law, whereupon we shall hear and see, together with those who hear, see and act, each in accordance with his obligations and rights as established in the Charter of the United Nations and international law. The final frame of reference continues to be resolution 687 (1991), which imposes obligations on the Security Council and Iraq, as well as the code of conduct contained in the agreement signed with the Secretary-General in New York on 16 September 2002 and the press statement issued jointly with Hans Blix and El Baradei in Vienna on 30 September-1 October 2002.

We hope that you will exercise your responsibilities by speaking to the oppressors and advising them that their unjust treatment of Muslims, faithful Arabs and all people has disastrous consequences and that God is omnipotent and capable of all things. Tell them that the people of Iraq are proud, faithful and militant, having fought and waged war against the former colonialism, imperialism and aggression, including that of the false god, for years and years. The price paid for the preservation of their independence, dignity and the high principles in which they believed was rivers of blood, together with a great deal of deprivation and damage to their wealth, alongside the immortal achievements and record in which they take pride. We hope that you will advise those who are ignorant not to push the situation to the edge of the precipice at the time of implementation, because the people of Iraq will not choose to live if the price is their dignity, their homeland, their freedom or the things sacrosanct to them. On the contrary, the price will be their lives if that is the only way forward to preserve what must be preserved. . . .

(Signed) Naji Sabri
Minister for Foreign Affairs of the Republic of Iraq
13 November 2002

U.S. AND IAEA ON NUCLEAR WEAPONS IN NORTH KOREA
October 16 and November 29, 2002

The United States and North Korea during late 2002 engaged in a bitter war of words—but as of year's end not a war in fact—over Pyongyang's reported admission that for several years it had secretly been attempting to develop nuclear weapons. The weapons program was in violation of a 1994 agreement (called the Agreed Framework) under which North Korea had pledged not to develop nuclear weapons in exchange for aid from the United States and its allies for its civilian energy needs.

The confrontation over North Korea's weapons program capped a year of hardened rhetoric between the two old enemies that began in January when President George W. Bush named North Korea as part of an "axis of evil," along with Iran and Iraq. The heightened tension with North Korea came as the Bush administration was focused on its campaign to disarm Iraq. As a result, the administration put its concerns about North Korea on the back burner until the Iraq matter was settled—in all probability by a war early in 2003. (Iraq, pp. 612, 713; North Korea background, Historic Documents of 2001, p. 267; Historic Documents of 1994, p. 602)

Despite the renewed dangers on the Korean peninsula, voters in South Korea on December 20 elected a new president, Roh Moo-hyun, who said he was committed to continuing a policy of working toward reconciliation with the North. Roh defeated a candidate who had advocated a tougher line toward North Korea. Roh succeeded Kim Dae Jung, who was elected in 1997 on a promise of improving relations with the communist north. Kim met in 2000 with North Korean leader Kim Jong Il and signed an agreement calling for the eventual reunification of the two Koreas. Kim Dae Jung was awarded that year's Nobel Peace prize for his efforts. (Background, Historic Documents of 2000, p. 359)

The crisis over their nuclear weapons program overshadowed a continuing humanitarian disaster in North Korea. The country was in its eighth year of a food emergency, initially caused by droughts during the mid-1990s but worsened by economic mismanagement by the communist government, according to international aid agencies. An estimated 2 million people—about 10 percent of the population—had starved to death during the 1990s. The United States for several years had been the single largest contributor of food aid to North Korea. But in December, after the Pyongyang government restricted access to the country by UN food monitors, the Bush administration in December said it was reconsidering the level of its donations.

Axis of Evil

President Bush had entered office in 2001 expressing a much more skeptical attitude toward the communist regime in North Korea than his predecessor, Bill Clinton (1993–2001), had adopted. Clinton had negotiated the 1994 agreement intended to halt North Korea's nuclear weapons program, had relaxed U.S. economic sanctions against that country, and even had considered visiting Pyongyang in the final months of his presidency. Bush reversed course, in March 2001 cutting off formal U.S. discussions with North Korea. Then, in his January 29, 2002, State of the Union address, Bush said the North Korean government was part of an "axis of evil" because of its ambitions to obtain nuclear weapons and the repression of its people. (State of the Union speech, p. 33)

Visiting South Korea on February 20, Bush sought to soften his tone against the north, saying the United States had "no intention of invading North Korea" and was interested in a "dialogue" with the north. Bush said he had made his "axis of evil" comment because he was worried "about a regime that is closed and not transparent. I'm deeply concerned about the people of North Korea." But two days later North Korea announced that it was rejecting Bush's offer for talks.

The first high-level contact between the Bush administration and North Korea took place on July 31 during an Asia-Pacific security forum in Brunei. At an informal conversation over coffee, Secretary of State Colin Powell and North Korean foreign minister Paek Nam Sun discussed the possibility of resuming the "dialogue" that had been suspended for most of the time since Bush took office in January 2001.

During the next several weeks the administration consulted with its key allies, especially Japan and South Korea, about the next steps in dealing with North Korea. In particular, Bush and his aides in mid-September told Japanese officials that U.S. intelligence agencies had determined that North Korea was pursuing a secret nuclear weapons program based on enriching uranium. This was a new program, different from North Korea's previous weapons effort that extracted weapons-grade plutonium from nuclear waste. The U.S. briefings of Japanese officials came in advance of the historic visit to Pyongyang by Japanese prime minister Junichiro Koizumi on September 17. Koizumi, however, reportedly did not raise the nuclear issue in his meetings with Kim Jong Il. Instead, the meetings focused on North Korea's admission that it had abducted Japanese citizens in the past.

On September 25 the White House announced that a delegation headed by a senior State Department envoy would travel to Pyongyang to reopen U.S.-North Korean talks. The envoy was James A. Kelly, the assistant secretary of state for East Asian and Pacific affairs, who on October 3–4 held a series of talks with senior officials in the North Korean capital. Kelly then went to South Korea and told reporters his meetings had been "frank" and "useful," but he added that no further talks were planned. On October 7 the North Korean foreign ministry issued a statement saying Kelly had exhibited an "arrogant attitude" during his visit, and that the United States was pursuing a "hardline policy of hostility to bring North Korea to its knees by force."

A Surprise Announcement

Apparently it took the Bush administration nearly two weeks to decide on its next move, which came on October 16 when State Department spokesman Richard Boucher announced that Kelly had brought back startling news from North Korea. Boucher said Kelly had gone to Pyongyang armed with an offer from Bush of "economic and political steps to improve the lives of the North Korean people." But at the outset of his visit, Kelly told North Korean officials that the United States had evidence the country was secretly continuing work to develop nuclear weapons, in violation of the 1994 agreement. The North Korean officials at first denied Kelly's assertion, but the next day deputy foreign minister Kang Sok Joo (who had negotiated the 1994 agreement) acknowledged that the secret weapons program had been under way for several years. Kang also told Kelly that North Korea had developed unspecified "more powerful" weapons—an apparent reference either to biological or chemical weapons or to the long-range missiles it had been working on for many years. U.S. officials later said Kang had been "belligerent" in his remarks and had declared that the 1994 agreement was no longer valid.

In his announcement of Kelly's findings, Boucher called the North Korean weapons program "a serious violation" of the 1994 agreement. But he said the United States sought a "peaceful resolution" of the situation, which he said presented "an opportunity for peace-loving nations in the region to deal, effectively, with this challenge." In the meantime, he said, the United States was consulting with its "friends and allies" and suspending further talks with North Korea.

Other officials told reporters that the administration had been stunned by the North Korean admission and was scrambling to decide on a next step. Reportedly, the administration had expected the North Koreans to deny the weapons program—at which point the United States would cut off further talks.

North Korea's willingness to admit its weapon program exposed long-standing divisions within the administration about how to deal with that regime. Some officials reportedly viewed North Korea's unusual frankness as a potentially positive development—a willingness "to come clean," as one official put it, that should be pursued in hopes the two sides finally were past the stage of trading harsh rhetoric. Others took the opposite view, that North Korea once again was demonstrating open hostility and was embarking on another round of confrontation in hopes of extracting more concessions from the United States. Defense Secretary Donald H. Rumsfeld appeared to be in the latter camp, saying of the North Korean statement: "I don't see how anyone could say that's a good sign."

In addition to its uncertainty about what to do next, the administration reportedly was unsure about how advanced or successful the secret North Korean weapons program had been. U.S. intelligence agencies had said for several years that North Korea probably had extracted enough plutonium from a different atomic energy facility to develop one or two small nuclear bombs; some estimates by nongovernment experts had suggested that North Korea might have developed as many as eight or nine weapons. The plutonium-extraction program had been halted by the 1994 agreement. While it had some hard information about that program, the administration did not have reliable intelligence about how much material North Korea had developed with its secret uranium enrichment program. "We're not sure it's been weaponized yet" was as much as one official was willing to tell reporters.

U.S. officials later said it appeared that Pakistan—a U.S. ally—had given North Korea equipment vital to its new weapons program in exchange for North Korean missile technology. Pakistan had tested its first nuclear weapons in 1998 after receiving help from China. North Korea was further along in developing ballistic missiles than was Pakistan, thus the two countries had a mutual interest in trading technology. Pakistan's nuclear aid to North Korea apparently began in 1997, U.S. officials said. (Pakistan weapons, Historic Documents of 1998, p. 326)

Mohammed El Baradei, director of the UN's International Atomic Energy Agency (IAEA), on October 17 expressed "deep concern" about the news and said his agency was seeking further information from both North Korea and the United States. The IAEA had been monitoring North Korea's compliance with the 1994 Agreed Framework but since 1993 had been barred by North Korea from inspecting other nuclear facilities in the country—apparently including the facilities that had produced the enriched uranium.

Diplomacy and Confrontation

It was at this point, on October 17, that the Bush administration signaled its approach to North Korea—a stance the administration maintained for the rest of the year. While denouncing the North Korean weapons program as violating the 1994 agreement, administration officials said the United States would use low-key diplomacy in hopes of convincing Pyongyang to back down. The United States would work with China, Japan, South Korea, and Russia to convince North Korea that it was not threatened by Washington. However, the administration said that although the United States would not negotiate with North Korea, it might talk but would not offer anything as an inducement for North Korea to stop its weapons program.

This apparent decision by the administration not to escalate the confrontation with North Korea stood in sharp contrast to the simultaneous U.S. approach to Iraq. In the latter case, Bush had explicitly threatened the overwhelming use of force to achieve his policy goals: the dismantling of Baghdad's programs to develop weapons of mass destruction, and possibly even the ousting of Iraqi leader Saddam Hussein.

The key difference between the two cases, U.S. officials told reporters, was that Iraq was the greater danger because it had used chemical weapons in the past and had invaded two neighboring countries (Iran in 1980 and Kuwait in 1990). Bush and his aides also accused the Iraqi government of aiding and cooperating with terrorist groups, including the al Qaeda network that had planned the September 11, 2001, attacks against the United States.

By contrast, the administration argued, North Korea appeared to be seeking nuclear weapons for defensive purposes—to deter what it saw as a possible U.S. invasion—and not as an active threat against any of its neighbors. From a practical point of view, the administration also admitted that the United States had no good military options in dealing with North Korea, as it did with Iraq. If the United States were to invade North Korea, or simply fire missiles at its military installations, that country probably would respond by firing its small arsenal of nuclear bombs at Seoul (which was just thirty-five miles south the border between the two countries) or even Tokyo; the North might also invade South Korea, as it had done in 1950 at the outset of the Korean War. About 35,000 U.S. troops were based in South Korea as a deterrent against another invasion by the North, but they also represented a potential target for a North Korean nuclear attack. While saying that Kim Jong Il was a repressive dictator, Bush's national security adviser Condoleezza Rice said "we do believe that we have other ways of dealing with North Korea" than threatening a military confrontation.

Chief among those other ways was the development of a unified diplomatic strategy with U.S. allies in the region (Japan and South Korea) and other nations that were presumed to have influence over North Korea (China and Russia). During late October and early November U.S. diplomats were busy in the capitals of all four countries.

A key question in all these diplomatic maneuvers was whether, and to what degree, the United States and its allies would continue providing aid to North Korea under the 1994 Agreed Framework. That aid was in two forms. For the long term, the United States and its allies were financing the construction in North Korea of two light-water nuclear reactors to supply electricity; those reactors were to be completed by 2003 (but as of 2002 construction was several years behind schedule, a major sore point with the North Koreans). In the meantime, Washington each year would give North Korea about 500,000 tons of surplus heavy fuel oil for its nonnuclear energy needs.

Late in October some U.S. officials said the 1994 agreement was "dead" because North Korea's nuclear program had eliminated the rationale for it. Continuing to give North Korea any fuel aid would amount to giving into blackmail, according to this argument. Others in the administration, however, said it was too early to abandon the agreement entirely, and this argument was adopted as well by Japan and South Korea.

Eventually a sort of compromise emerged. The Bush administration on November 13 announced that a shipment of heavy fuel oil to North Korea that was already under way would continue, but all future shipments would be canceled. The decision was endorsed the next day by the European Union, Japan, and South Korea, the other underwriters of the aid program. This action set off another round of accusations, with North Korea insisting that the United States was the party violating the 1994 agreement, and the Bush administration insisting that any failures under the agreement were solely the fault of North Korea.

Washington received important international support for its position on November 29, when the board of governors of the IAEA adopted a resolution denouncing North Korea's attempts to acquire nuclear weapons. The agency repeated its long-standing demand that North Korea allow IAEA inspectors to examine its nuclear facilities—as required by the Nuclear Nonproliferation Treaty, which North Korea had signed.

By this point both Washington and Pyongyang were insisting that the next step was up to the other party. The Bush administration said it would not hold any further talks with North Korea until Pyongyang abandoned its weapons program and allowed the IAEA to resume its inspections of all nuclear facilities in the country. North Korea on October 25 revealed its negotiating strategy on the issue, saying in a foreign ministry statement that the United States had to take three steps before the dispute could be resolved. Washington, the statement said, must recognize the North Korean sovereignty, sign a "nonaggression" agreement with North Korea, and promise not to "hinder" that country's economic development.

The war of words between Washington and Pyongyang escalated in December, starting with a December 2 statement by North Korean foreign minister Paek accusing the United States of manipulating the IAEA. The next day, Defense Secretary Rumsfeld denounced the "vicious" government of North Korea and said that "what it is doing to the people of North Korea is criminal."

North Korea then elevated the dispute to a more serious level, announcing on December 12 that it had asked the IAEA to remove its seals and monitoring cameras from the nuclear complex at Yongbyon. These security measures, in place since the 1994 agreement, had prevented North Korea from separating weapons-grade plutonium from about 8,000 spent fuel rods. The agency refused the request, and on December 21 North Korean technicians began removing the IAEA monitoring equipment.

As work at the nuclear complex was under way, North Korea issued one of its most belligerent statements to date. Speaking at a December 24 ceremony marking the eleventh anniversary of Kim Jong Il's appointment as supreme military commander, armed forces chief Kim Il Chol said it was the "U.S. hawks" who were pushing the situation "to the brink of a nuclear war. If they, ignorant of their rival, dare provoke a nuclear war, the army and people of [North Korea] led by Kim Jong Il, the invincible commander, will rise up to mete out determined and merciless punishment to the U.S. imperialist aggressors with the might of single-hearted unity more powerful than [an] A-bomb."

Apparently unwilling to match that style of rhetoric, the White House responded on December 27 with a statement that the United States would not negotiate in response to threats or broken commitments. Also on December 27 the IAEA said it had received a letter from North Korea asking for the removal of all agency inspectors at the Yongbyon facility. IAEA director El Baradei said: "Together with the loss of cameras and seals, the departure of inspectors would practically bring to an end our ability to monitor [North Korea's] nuclear program or assess its nature."

At year's end the standoff was still continuing: North Korea was refusing to renounce its weapons program, the United States was refusing to talk directly with North Korea, and other countries in the region were unsure how or when the situation could be resolved without negotiation. In the United States, the Bush administration calmly claimed the North Korea situation was not a "crisis"—and administration critics in Congress insisted it was.

Following are two texts: a statement issued October 16, 2002, by State Department spokesman Richard Boucher revealing that North Korea had acknowledged that it was attempting to develop nuclear weapons by enriching uranium, and a resolution adopted November 29, 2002, by the board of governors of the International Atomic Energy Agency calling on North Korea to give up any nuclear weapons program and allow IAEA inspectors back into the country.

The documents were obtained from the Internet at www .state.gov/r/pa/prs/ps/2002/14432pf.htm; www.iaea.org/ worldatom/Press/P_release/2002/med-advise_033.shtml; accessed December 7, 2002.

STATE DEPARTMENT PRESS RELEASE

Earlier this month, senior U.S. officials traveled to North Korea to begin talks on a wide range of issues. During those talks, Assistant Secretary James A. Kelly and his delegation advised the North Koreans that we had recently acquired information that indicates that North Korea has a program to enrich uranium for nuclear weapons in violation of the Agreed Framework and other agreements. North Korean officials acknowledged that they have such a program. The North Koreans attempted to blame the United States and said that they considered the Agreed Framework nullified. Assistant Secretary Kelly pointed out that North Korea had been embarked on this program for several years.

Over the summer, President Bush—in consultation with our allies and friends—had developed a bold approach to improve relations with North Korea. The United States was prepared to offer economic and political steps to improve the lives of the North Korean people, provided the North were dramatically to alter its behavior across a range of issues, including its weapons of mass destruction programs, development and export of ballistic missiles, threats to its neighbors, support for terrorism, and the deplorable treatment of the North Korean people. In light of our concerns about the North's nuclear weapons program, however, we are unable to pursue this approach.

North Korea's secret nuclear weapons program is a serious violation of North Korea's commitments under the Agreed Framework as well as under the Nonproliferation Treaty (NPT), its International Atomic Energy Agency safeguards agreement, and the Joint North-South Declaration on the Denuclearization of the Korean Peninsula.

The Administration is consulting with key Members of Congress, and will continue to do so. Under Secretary of State John Bolton and Assistant Secretary of State James Kelly are traveling to the region to confer with friends and allies about this important issue.

The United States and our allies call on North Korea to comply with its commitments under the Nonproliferation Treaty, and to eliminate its nuclear weapons program in a verifiable manner.

We seek a peaceful resolution of this situation. Everyone in the region has a stake in this issue and no peaceful nation wants to see a nuclear-armed North Korea. This is an opportunity for peace loving nations in the region to deal, effectively, with this challenge.

IAEA RESOLUTION ON SAFEGUARDS

The Board of Governors,

    a. *Recalling* its resolutions GOV/2636, GOV/2639, GOV/2645, GOV/2692, GOV/2711 and GOV/2742, and General Conference resolutions GC (XXXVII)RES/624, GC(XXXVIII)RES/16, GC(39)/RES/3, GC(40)/RES/4, GC(41)/RES/22, GC(42)/RES/2, GC(43)/RES/3, GC(44)/RES/26, GC(45)RES/16, and GC(46) RES/14,

    b. *Noting* that the Democratic People's Republic of Korea (DPRK) is a party to the Treaty on the Non-Proliferation of Nuclear Weapons (NPT) and *reaffirming* that the IAEA-DPRK safeguards agreement (INFCIRC/403) under the NPT remains binding and in force,

    c. *Recalling further* resolution 825 (1993) adopted by the Security Council of the United Nations on 11 May 1993 and 31 March 1994, 30 May 1994 and 4 November 1994 statements by the President of the United Nations Security Council, particularly the request to take all steps the Agency deems necessary to verify full compliance by the DPRK with its safeguards agreement with the Agency,

    d. *Noting with extreme concern* recent reports of an unsafeguarded DPRK uranium enrichment programme, and the DPRK statement of 25 October 2002 that it is "entitled to possess not only nuclear weapons but any type of weapon more powerful than that,"

    e. *Mindful* of the indispensable role of the IAEA in continuing to monitor the freeze on nuclear facilities in the DPRK as requested by the Security Council,

f. *Recognizing* the importance to the international community of maintaining peace, stability, and the nuclear weapons-free status of the Korean Peninsula, and declaring its readiness to promote a peaceful resolution of the DPRK nuclear issue,

g. *Noting* that the IAEA Secretariat has sent two letters (17 and 18 October 2002) to the authorities of the DPRK, asking them to cooperate with the Agency and seeking clarification of reported information about a programme to enrich uranium,

h. *Having considered* the report of the Director General at its meeting of 28 November 2002,

1. *Reiterates* its previous calls to the DPRK to comply fully and promptly with its safeguards agreement and to co-operate fully with the Agency to that end;

2. *Endorses* the statement by the Director General on 17 October 2002 in which he expressed "deep concern" regarding reported information that the DPRK has a programme to enrich uranium for nuclear weapons, and the action taken by the Director General to seek information from the DPRK on any such activity;

3. *Insists* that the DPRK urgently and constructively respond to letters from the IAEA Secretariat requesting clarification of the reported uranium enrichment programme;

4. *Calls upon* the DPRK to accept without delay the proposal of the Director General to despatch a senior team to the DPRK, or to receive a DPRK team in Vienna, to clarify the aforementioned uranium enrichment programme;

5. *Recognises* that such a programme, or any other covert nuclear activities, would constitute a violation of the DPRK's international commitments, including the DPRK's safeguards agreement with the Agency pursuant to the NPT;

6. *Deplores* the DPRK's repeated public statements that it is entitled to possess nuclear weapons, which runs contrary to its obligations under the NPT not to develop or possess nuclear weapons;

7. *Urges* the DPRK to provide to the Agency all relevant information concerning the reported uranium enrichment programme, and other relevant nuclear fuel cycle facilities;

8. *Urges* the DPRK to cooperate with the Agency with a view to opening immediately all relevant facilities to IAEA inspection and safeguards, as required under its comprehensive safeguards agreement;

9. *Urges* the DPRK to give up any nuclear weapons programme, expeditiously and in a verifiable manner;

10. *Requests* the Director General to transmit this resolution to the DPRK, to continue dialogue with the DPRK with a view toward urgent resolution of the issues above, and to report again to the Board of Governors on the matter at its next meeting or when deemed necessary; and

11. *Decides* to remain seized of the matter.

HART-RUDMAN TASK FORCE
ON TERROR THREATS
October 25, 2002

The September 11, 2001, terrorist attacks against the United States spurred an unprecedented burst of energy in the country to confront the immediate and long-term dangers posed by terrorism. President George W. Bush and Congress initiated a government reorganization, likely to require several years, to establish a new Homeland Security Department with the task of improving domestic security. One of the department's components was another new agency, the Transportation Security Administration (TSA), which hired some 50,000 people in less than a year and took over security at more than 400 commercial airports. Governments and private businesses at every level in the United States also began taking steps to reduce their risks and improve their responses to future terrorist attacks. They had plenty of advice to work from, as an ever-growing stack of reports assessed the nation's vulnerabilities and made recommendations for dealing with them.

The entire year passed without a terrorist attack in the United States, although individual Americans were killed abroad by terrorists, including Wall Street Journal *reporter Daniel Pearl in Afghanistan, diplomat Laurence Foley in Jordan, and several U.S. service personnel in Kuwait. Experts, including the head of the Central Intelligence Agency, were unanimous in predicting that terrorists would again attack the United States directly, possibly with even more dramatic and damaging force than the three airplanes that were flown into the World Trade Center towers and the Pentagon in September 2001. The al Qaeda terrorist network, which was responsible for those attacks, was still in existence even though its bases in Afghanistan had been destroyed by the United States military and dozens of people associated with it had been arrested in an international crackdown on terrorism. Al Qaeda's leader, Osama bin Laden, remained at large—possibly in hiding or killed by U.S. bombing in Afghanistan. Also still at large was whoever was responsible for mailing high-quality anthrax to U.S. media outlets and members of Congress in October and November 2001, an act that killed five people, injured more than a dozens others, and threw much of the country into panic for weeks.* (Terrorist attacks, Historic Documents of 2001, pp. 614, 624, 637; Anthrax mailings, Historic Documents of 2001, p. 672)

CIA Threat Assessments

For years the director of the CIA has provided the House and Senate Intelligence committees an annual review of the potential threats facing the United States. This review came in two forms: a classified version presented to members of the committees and a declassified version made public by the director during his first appearance of the year before each committee. The 2002 "threat assessment" by CIA director George Tenet took on special significance for two reasons: It came just four months after the September 11 terrorist attacks, and it followed by one week President Bush's State of Union address, in which the president declared that Iran, Iraq, and North Korea constituted an "axis of evil" threatening the United States and the rest of the world. In his February 6 testimony to the Senate Select Committee on Intelligence, Tenet noted the significance of his report, especially in relation to the terrorist attacks: "Never before has the subject of this annual threat briefing had more immediate resonance. Never before have the dangers been more clear or more present."

Tenet told the committee that the al Qaeda terrorist network remained "the most immediate and serious threat" to the United States. Tenet had used the same language a year earlier, almost nine months before the attacks in New York City and Washington.

Although the United States and its allies around the world had damaged much of al Qaeda's infrastructure, the group and other terrorist organizations "will continue to plan to attack this country and its interests abroad," Tenet told the committee. "Their modus operandi is to have multiple attack plans in the works simultaneously, and to have al Qaeda cells in place to conduct them." Tenet said the CIA had information suggesting that terrorist groups had considered attacks against "high profile" targets in the United States, such as famous landmarks, bridges, harbors, and dams—and possibly such major public events as the Olympics or the Super Bowl. Al Qaeda also planned to attack U.S. and allied targets in most other regions of the world, he said, adding that U.S. diplomatic and military installations, especially those in East Africa, Israel, Saudi Arabia, and Turkey, were at a "high risk" of a terrorist attack.

Al Qaeda and other terrorist groups had attempted, and would continue to attempt, to acquire biological, chemical, and nuclear weapons, Tenet said. Even if they failed to buy or develop these types of weapons, he added, the groups might try to launch a "conventional" attack (such as a bomb) against a chemical or nuclear facility in the United States "to cause widespread toxic or radiological damage." These groups also were looking into cyber warfare (attacking the Internet and telecommunications networks) as a "viable option," Tenet told the committee.

Tenet discussed each of the three members of Bush's "axis of evil" but did not attempt to link the three in any way other than describing efforts by each nation to obtain weapons of mass destruction. Tenet devoted more attention to Iran and Iraq than to North Korea. The Iranian reform movement headed by President Mohammed Khatami "may be losing its momentum" as a result of constant pressure by the hard-line religious officials who held ultimate power, Tenet said. "The hard-line regime appears secure for now because security forces have easily contained dissenters and arrested potential opposition leaders," he said. Even so, the reform movement in Iran "is not dead," he added, and the country's political balance was so fragile that it could be upset by miscalculation by either the reform movement or the hard-line clerics. Tenet said Iran had not reduced its long-time support for terrorist groups. He cited only one example: Tehran's reported shipment of weapons to a hard-line faction of the Palestinian Authority—a shipment that was intercepted by Israel. Iran also was continuing its pursuit of biological, chemical, and nuclear weapons, along with the ballistic missiles needed to deliver them to distant targets, Tenet said. (North Korea, p. 731; Middle East violence, p. 927)

Tenet's report to the committee on Iraq and its leader, Saddam Hussein, appeared to be somewhat more circumspect than the harsh rhetoric that came throughout the year from the White House and Defense Department. In particular, Tenet took a cautious approach to the question of a relationship between Iraq and al Qaeda; some administration officials alleged, without providing concrete evidence, that Baghdad supported the terrorist network. Iraq had a "long history of supporting terrorism" and had "contacts" with al Qaeda, Tenet said, but he did not attempt to establish any kind of relationship between them.

Despite UN sanctions against it, Iraq was "continuing to build and expand an infrastructure capable of producing" weapons of mass destruction, Tenet said. Specifically, he said Iraq was expanding its civilian chemical industry "in ways that could be diverted quickly" to produce chemical weapons; still maintained an "active and capable" biological weapons program; continued to pursue acquisition of medium-range and long-range ballistic missiles that the United Nations had prohibited in its 1991 sanctions against Iraq; and "never abandoned [its] nuclear weapons program" despite heavy damage to it during the 1991 Persian Gulf War and subsequent dismantlement of key components by UN inspectors during the 1990s. The CIA's major near-term concern, Tenet said, was that Iraq might be able to gain access to the weapons-grade plutonium or uranium that would be needed to build a nuclear bomb. (Iraq issues, pp. 612, 713)

Hart-Rudman Task Force

Between 1998 and 2001 former senators Gary Hart, D-Colo., and Warren Rudman, R-N.H., cochaired a blue ribbon commission established by the Pentagon to examine challenges to U.S. national security in the twenty-first century. The commission issued its first report in 1999 and subsequent reports in 2000 and 2001. The panel's final report, released in March 2001, warned that a major terrorist attack was likely in the United States and that the country's ability to respond to the threat was fragmented and inadequate. In July 2002 the Council on Foreign Relations—an influential for-

eign policy think tank based in New York City—established a new task force headed by Hart and Rudman to take a look at the nation's ability to deal with terrorism in the wake of the September 11 attacks. Among the panel members were two former secretaries of state (Warren Christopher and George Shultz), two former chairmen of the joint chiefs of staff (William J. Crowe and John W. Vessey), former CIA and FBI director William H. Webster, and several leaders from business and academia. The panel issued its report, "America Still Unprepared—America Still in Danger," on October 25. (Hart-Rudman commission report, Historic Documents of 1999, p. 500)

As its unambiguous title indicated, the report argued that the nation "remains dangerously unprepared to prevent and respond to a catastrophic attack on U.S. soil." The next attack probably would result in greater casualties and more widespread disruption than did the September 11 attack, the panel said. Furthermore, the need for action was made more urgent by the prospect—then pending—of a war against Iraq, during which Iraq might respond by using biological or chemical weapons against the United States.

Hart and Rudman released the report shortly after Congress recessed for the midterm elections without having passed a final version of a bill establishing the Homeland Security Department. While widely supported by both parties, the proposal had become bogged down in a partisan dispute over labor issues. The former senators heatedly chastised their former colleagues for the delay. "It's time for action, and if you don't like it, there will be hell to pay for anyone who looks like an obstructionist," Rudman said. Hart added that the government "teeters on the brink of not being functional, and I think in this case particularly the executive branch." Congress passed the homeland security bill a month later, following midterm elections in which President Bush successfully used the delayed action on the bill as a partisan issue against Democrats, who were the majority in the Senate. (Homeland security issue, p. 530)

The Hart-Rudman panel's report consisted of two parts: a review of U.S. vulnerabilities to terrorist attacks and a series of recommendations for short-term and longer-term steps to reduce those vulnerabilities. Most of the panel's findings were similar to those of numerous other groups that studied the issues, but the political stature of the task force members and their blunt language drew special attention to their report.

The panel cited several vulnerabilities as particularly urgent, among them the prospect that a weapon of mass destruction could be hidden aboard any one of the tens of thousands of containers, ships, trucks, and trains that entered the United States each day—only a few of which were examined for contraband. The report also said that state and local police officials operated in a "virtual intelligence vacuum" because they did not have access to the State Department's terrorist "watch lists" used by federal immigration and consular officials; that firefighters, policemen, emergency medical personnel, and other first responders lacked the training, protective gear, and even the communications equipment needed to deal with attacks by biological or chemical weapons; and that the nation's energy infrastructure "remains largely unprotected" against sabotage.

To deal with these and other weaknesses, the panel offered several dozen specific and general recommendations, including establishing a full-time operations center in each state that could provide updated information about terrorist threats to local law enforcement agencies; providing immediate federal funding to clear a large backlog of state and local requests for equipment and training for first responders; adopting a new approach to transportation security, for example by abandoning the "assumption that every [airline] passenger and every bag of luggage poses an equal risk" and instead screening passengers and cargo on the basis of intelligence information and other factors indicating potential risks; and conducting immediate assessments of the vulnerability of energy distribution systems within the United States and stockpiling backup components "to quickly restore the operation of the energy grid should it be targeted."

Other Studies

As could be expected, fighting terrorism and improving homeland security became popular topics during 2002 for study by government agencies, academic institutions, and special interest groups. Several dozen reports on these topics were made public during the year, among them:

- **Warnings.** *A panel of emergency experts on November 26 urged the government to develop a high-technology system to warn the public of national emergencies, such as threats of terrorist attacks. The Partnership for Public Warning, which included representatives from government and independent agencies, said the existing Emergency Alert System, created during the cold war, was outdated. The panel also said a color-coded terrorism alert system adopted by the White House in March 2002 was confusing to the public. As a long-term alternative to these systems, the panel suggested that the government should adapt existing technology to create a system in which computer chips embedded in electronic devices (such as cell phones, television sets, and computers) would give off broadcast warnings of terrorist threats, natural disasters, or similar dangers.*

- **Slow government response.** *The* New York Times *reported on May 12 that security audits conducted in late 2001 and early 2002 found that several federal government agencies failed to take immediate security steps following the September 11, 2001, terrorist attacks and the outbreak of anthrax poisonings later that year. A study by the inspector general of the Agriculture Department found that several of the agency's laboratories failed to keep accurate records of potentially dangerous biological agents. Inspectors found that security was inadequate at nearly half of the department's 124 labs; some lacked such simple security devices as alarm systems or security fences. The Centers for Disease Control and Prevention on December 5 issued new guidelines intended to tighten security at all laboratories—whether run by the government or independent authorities such as universities—that handled any of forty-two pathogens and toxins. An audit by the Energy*

Department's inspector general found that the department had lost records of small amounts of nuclear material, including fuel rods, that the United States had loaned to several other countries, starting in the 1960s, for nonmilitary uses. Among the countries that had borrowed nuclear material was Iran—at the time a U.S. ally but in later years a country that successive administrations declared to be a threat to U.S. interests.

- **Scientific studies.** *Two panels of scientists issued reports on June 24 calling on the government to recognize the complexity of terrorist threats and to develop priorities for attacking them. One study, by the National Academy of Sciences, suggested specific improvements in such areas as protecting and accounting for nuclear weapons and weapons-grade materials, producing and distributing treatments for victims of biological weapons, improving ventilation systems of office buildings to filter out chemical or biological agents, and improving security for transportation of toxic or flammable materials. Another set of papers sponsored by the American Association for the Advancement of Science offered suggestions for countering biological weapons by focusing on a small number of the most dangerous pathogens and for conducting research into methods of securing computer networks from catastrophic attacks.*

- **First responders.** *Numerous studies dealt with the challenges faced by the firemen, policemen, emergency medical technicians, and others who were the first to reach disaster scenes. Most studies reported that, despite the expenditure of millions of dollars on training and aid programs during the previous decade, many first responders still were incapable of dealing with a major terrorist event. In one study released on September 9, the Federation of American Scientists reported that law enforcement officers, doctors, nurses and other emergency personnel said they were unprepared to handle the consequences of an attack by a biological, chemical, or nuclear weapon. The report recommended that the federal government develop a joint program with states and localities to train first responders on how to deal with such attacks. These training courses should be reinforced with frequent refresher courses, the federation's report said.*

- **Intelligence assessment.** *In its fourth annual report to the president and Congress, a congressionally mandated panel on November 15 urged creation of an independent agency to analyze all U.S. intelligence information about potential terrorist threats. Such an agency was needed because experience had shown that the FBI, the CIA, and other intelligence agencies did not always share the information they collected—depriving law enforcement agencies and policymakers of a complete picture of terrorist threats, the panel said. The Bush administration was considering such a proposal and appeared likely to adopt a version of it early in 2003. Formally known as the Advisory Panel to Assess Domestic Response Capabilities for Terrorism Involving Weapons of Mass Destruction, the committee of current and former government officials* *and independent experts was better known as the Gilmore commission, after its chairman, former Virginia governor James S. Gilmore.*

- **Cyber terrorism.** *Federal government agencies were making very little progress in protecting their computer systems against cyber terrorism, fraud, and misuse, according to an evaluation issued November 19 by the House Government Reform subcommittee on government efficiency. The subcommittee cited a study by the General Accounting Office (GAO) that found "significant weaknesses" in the security of computer systems at twenty-four agencies. According to the study, most agencies had inadequate controls on access to sensitive computer systems, making them vulnerable to misuse by disgruntled employees or even a malicious attack by terrorists. Vulnerable systems included those with confidential financial or medical records on individuals and documents needed for the regular functioning of government agencies. The agencies with the most serious problems were the Departments of Defense, Justice, State, and Transportation, the House subcommittee said.*

- **Access to federal buildings.** *Another investigation by the GAO raised serious questions about security at federal office buildings. In an April 30 report, the GAO said its investigators gained unauthorized access to four federal buildings in Atlanta. Investigators were able to obtain security badges (including one permitting the carrying of a firearm) without having proper authorization. The investigators then counterfeited the badges with commercial software and gained access to the buildings with the phony identification. Investigators also were able to sneak packages into buildings by avoiding x-ray machines and other security devices. The General Services Administration, which handles security at federal buildings, took "corrective action" when told about the lapses, the GAO said.*

Aviation Security

The year after the September 11 attacks was one of the most traumatic ever for the U.S. aviation industry, which witnessed the bankruptcies of two major airlines (US Air and United) and a radical transformation in airport security measures. The tightening of security at airports created confusion and long lines in many cases, further discouraging air travel by millions of people already frightened by the September 11 attacks.

The year's main aviation security event was not another tragedy but a bureaucratic and logistical process: the creation of a gigantic federal agency, the Transportation Security Administration, to take over major security functions at all of the nation's commercial airports. Mandated by Congress after a political battle with President Bush in late 2001, the TSA started early in 2002 at Baltimore-Washington International airport and quickly expanded nationwide. In little under a year the agency hired nearly 50,000 security workers and placed them at 424 commercial airports. The new government workers replaced employees of private companies that had been hired by airlines; many of them low-paid and ill-trained, the private work-

ers frequently had been held responsible for airport security lapses. (Airport screener issue, Historic Documents of 2001, p. 650)

In establishing the new agency, Congress had set a November 19, 2002, deadline for all private security screeners to be replaced. The agency met that deadline, but some critics said the speed of the hiring blitz prevented it from adequately checking the qualifications of its new employees. Another deadline posed an even more difficult problem: a requirement that, by December 31, 2002, all baggage checked by passengers had to be screened by explosive-detection equipment. This congressional mandate turned out to be unrealistic because the new high-technology equipment was in short supply and each piece was so large that many airports had to rebuild their concourses to make room for it. Congress ultimately gave the agency a one-year extension on the requirement.

Congress initially placed the TSA within the Transportation Department. Within a year of its founding, the new agency was moved to the new Homeland Security Department, where it was the single biggest component, in terms of number of employees.

The nation's new focus on aviation security brought continuing problems to light. For example, more than a year after the September 11 attacks, tens of thousands of passengers were still attempting to carry knives, guns, and other weapons aboard airplanes. Many of the weapons were caught by screeners at airports, but several investigations showed that it was still possible to get weapons onto airplanes. In a March report the Transportation Department's inspector general found that in tests at thirty-two airports screeners failed to catch knives 70 percent of the time, simulated explosives 60 percent of the time, and guns 30 percent of the time. The tests were conducted when private contractors hired by the airlines still staffed nearly all the airport security stations. In late August and early September, after the new Transportation Security Administration had begun staffing the airports, reporters for the New York Daily News succeeded in carrying small knives, razor blades, and even pepper spray through checkpoints at eleven airports. CBS News employees also carried bags lined with lead (to block x-rays) past about 70 percent of screeners at several airports around the country.

Also during the year federal authorities continued a nationwide crackdown on airport workers who had used phony identifications, had lied about their backgrounds, were in the United States illegally, or had otherwise obtained their jobs illegally. Operation Tarmac, launched by the Justice and Transportation departments after the September 11 attacks, resulted in the arrest and firing of several hundred airport employees around the country—many of whom had access to high-security areas. The majority of those arrested had committed immigration violations, but some were charged with making false statements when they were hired about criminal backgrounds, in some cases for drug offenses, burglary, and robbery. None of those arrested during the crackdown were linked to terrorist groups. In ordering the investigations, Jane Garvey, administrator of the Federal Aviation Administration, said about 750,000 airline and airport employees had access to secure areas at airports.

Following is the "Issues and Recommendations" chapter of "America Still Unprepared—America Still in Danger," a report released October 25, 2002, by an independent task force sponsored by the Council on Foreign Relations and cochaired by former U.S. senators Gary Hart, D-Colo., and Warren B. Rudman, R-N.H.

The document was obtained from the Internet at www.cfr .org/publication.php?id=5099; accessed February 8, 2003.

1. Tap the Eyes and Ears of Local and State Law Enforcement Officers in Preventing Attacks; Make First Responders Ready to Respond.

"Today, we are fighting a different kind of war—on two fronts. One front is Afghanistan, where we have the best technology, the best equipment, the best intelligence being sent right to the front, and no expense is spared. But for the first time in nearly 200 years, the second front is right here at home. And to date, it's where we've seen the greatest loss of life. Yet we have insufficient equipment, too little training, and a lack of intelligence sharing with federal authorities."
—Martin O'Malley, Mayor of Baltimore, April 10, 2002

There are an estimated 8.5 million illegal aliens living in the United States, including nearly 300,000 fugitive aliens who have opted for life as a fugitive rather than submitting to a final order of deportation. Stowaways arriving in U.S. ports and jumping ship are almost a daily occurrence. These illegal migrants find it easy to blend in among the tens of millions of foreigners who arrive legally in the United States each year to travel, study, or work. Compounding the problem is widespread trafficking in forged or fraudulently obtained passports, licenses, and other identification documents. Baseline documents such as social security cards, birth certificates, and driver's licenses are particularly subject to abuse.

With just fifty-six field offices around the nation, the burden of identifying and intercepting terrorists in our midst is a task well beyond the scope of the Federal Bureau of Investigation. This burden could and should be shared with 650,000 local, county, and state law enforcement officers, but they clearly cannot lend a hand in a counterterrorism information void.

When it comes to combating terrorism, the police officers on the beat are effectively operating deaf, dumb, and blind. Terrorist watch lists provided by the U.S. Department of State to immigration and consular officials are still out of bounds for state and local police. In the interim period as information sharing issues get worked out, known terrorists will be free to move about to plan and execute their attacks. And if a catastrophic terrorist attack occurred today, emergency first responders—police, firefighters, and emergency medical personnel—in most of the nation's cities and counties are no better prepared to react now than they were prior to September 11. The tools of emergency preparedness are in very short supply. For instance, according to a survey done by the U.S. Conference of Mayors earlier this year:

- 79% of mayors reported a funding shortfall for necessary threat detection equipment; 77% for emergency response equipment; and 69% for personal protective apparel.
- 86% said they did not have adequate personal protective apparel and only 10% were satisfied with the protective equipment they had in the event of a biological attack."

Communications

In virtually every major city and county in the United States, no interoperable communications system exists to support police, fire departments, and county, state, regional, and federal response personnel during a major emergency. Radio frequencies are not available to support the post–incident communication demands that will be placed on them, and most cities have no redundant systems to use as backups. Portable radios will not work in highrise buildings unless the buildings are equipped with repeater systems. Most U.S. cities have separate command-and-control functions for their police and fire departments, and little to no coordination exists between the two organizations. Furthermore, with few exceptions, first-responder commanders do not have access to secure radios, telephones, or video-conferencing capabilities that can support communications with county, state, and federal emergency preparedness officials or National Guard leaders.

Protective Gear

In the event of a chemical attack, a window of a few minutes to two hours exists to respond to the incident before morbidity and mortality rates skyrocket. Yet protective gear is often available only to a few specialized incident response teams. Most communities will run short of even the most basic emergency response resources (e.g., life-saving equipment, personal protection suits, oxygen, respirators, etc.) in six hours. Federal agency response teams can help but they will invariably arrive too late (i.e., no earlier then twelve hours after the attack).

Detection Equipment

Portable and hand-held detection equipment for highly explosive, chemical, biological, and radiological materials is in short supply and notoriously unreliable in urban environments. Department of Defense and Department of Energy sensors deployed to local first responders have been issued without adequate personnel training on use and maintenance of the equipment, or guidance on what to do should the detection equipment register an alarm.

Training

Major field exercises are important tools to test the adequacy of contingency plans, equipment, command-and-control procedures, and training. In all but America's largest cities, there is a paucity of resources and expertise to organize and conduct these large scale exercises. For example, from 1996 to 1999, the federal government was able to provide WMD response training to only 134,000 of the nation's estimated nine million first responders. Furthermore, only two percent of these 134,000 responders received hands-on training with live chemical agents. The Center for Domestic Preparedness in Anniston, Alabama, is the only facility in the nation where first responders can train with and gain first-hand knowledge of chemical agents. At peak capacity, it can train only 10,000 responders per year.

Recommendations

Our nation would not send its armed forces into harm's way without outfitting them with the right tools and skills. Our first responders and local law enforcement officers deserve the same investment—their lives and our lives depend on it. Therefore, the Task Force makes the following recommendations:

- Establish a twenty-four–hour operations center in each state that can provide a real time intergovernmental link between local and federal law enforcement. Field-level police would contact this center when they apprehend suspects to receive a red or green light to hold or release them based on a check of federal and Interpol databases.
- Step up efforts to rein in identity fraud by strengthening the anti-counterfeit safeguards in state driver's licenses and passports, passing state laws criminalizing identity theft, and mobilizing 120-day joint local, state, and federal agency task forces to investigate and target phony identification traffickers.
- Provide grants for states and cities to hire retired first responders on ninety-day renewable contracts to conduct comprehensive assessments on the status of urban emergency preparedness, including the state of protective gear, communications plans and equipment, and the availability of chemical antidotes.
- Fund the backlog of protective equipment and training requests by urban fire departments. This is a case where an immediate infusion of resources can make an immediate difference in reducing the risks to first responders and the morbidity and mortality of incident victims.
- Fund and deploy commercial off-the-shelf technologies that can integrate multiple radio platforms to support interoperable communications, including the ability to coordinate the flow of voice, image, and electronic information among responding agencies.
- Provide the national research labs with adequate funding to develop, field-test, and widely distribute new portable and hand-held sensor equipment suitable for urban environments.
- Ensure that the distribution of new technologies to first responders is supported by training and long-term maintenance contracts.
- The Federal Emergency Management Agency (FEMA) and the National Guard should collaborate with state and local officials to deploy threat-based simulation models and training modules to support local emergency operations center training. WMD field exercises should be funded in all the nation's major urban areas over the next eighteen months. Senior police and fire officials from smaller cities and localities should be included in these exercises.

2. MAKE TRADE SECURITY A GLOBAL PRIORITY.

"There is virtually no security for what is the primary system to transport global trade. The consequence of a terrorist incident using a container would be profound. . . . If terrorists used a sea container to conceal a weapon of mass destruction and detonated it on arrival at a port, the impact on global trade and the global economy could be immediate and devastating—all nations would be affected. No container ships would be allowed to unload at U.S. ports after such an event."
—Robert Bonner, Commissioner, U.S. Customs Service, August 26, 2002

Immediately following the September 11 attacks, federal authorities ordered the closing of U.S. airspace to all flights, both foreign and domestic, shut down the nation's major seaports, and slowed truck, automobile, and pedestrian traffic across the land borders with Canada and Mexico to a trickle. Nineteen men wielding box-cutters forced the United States to do to itself what no adversary could ever accomplish: a successful blockade of the U.S. economy. If a surprise terrorist attack were to happen tomorrow involving the sea, rail, or truck transportation systems that carry millions of tons of trade to the United States each day, the response would likely be the same—a self-imposed global embargo.

Vulnerable Seaports

Ninety-five percent of all non-North American U.S. trade moves by sea and arrives in 361 ports around the nation. Despite the vital role seaports play in linking America to the world, both economically and militarily, port vulnerability studies for the nation's fifty largest ports are not scheduled to be completed for five more years. Over the past few decades, container traffic and energy imports increasingly have been concentrated in just a handful of ports, making them inviting targets. For instance, forty-three percent of all the maritime containers that arrived in the United States in 2001 came through the ports of Los Angeles and Long Beach. As the recent West Coast port closures demonstrated, the cost to the economy of closing these ports totals approximately $1 billion per day for the first five days, rising exponentially thereafter. Nearly one-quarter of all of California's imported crude oil is offloaded in one geographically confined area. A USS Cole–style incident involving a ship offloading at that locale could leave Southern California without refined fuels within just a few days. The American Association of Port Authorities estimates the cost of adequate physical security at the nation's commercial seaports to be $2 billion. So far only $92.3 million in federal grants have been authorized and approved. Even then, the grants have not been awarded on the basis of a port's relative importance to the nation. The ports of Los Angeles and Long Beach requested $70 million in post–September 11 grants and were awarded just $6.175 million. The adequacy of such grant levels needs urgent reexamination.

Trade Dependency on the Intermodal Container

There are an estimated eleven million containers worldwide that are loaded and unloaded ten times per year. Ninety percent of the world's general cargo moves in these boxes. The architects of the intermodal revolution in transportation never considered security as a criterion—lower transport costs and improved speed and efficiency were the driving forces. For example, a new 40' container costs on average $2,500 to build and holds up to thirty tons of freight. The cost of the ocean voyage for a full container from Europe or Asia is approximately $1,500. There are no required security standards governing the loading or transport of an intermodal container. Most are "sealed" with a numbered fifty-cent, lead tag.

If an explosive device was loaded in a container and set off in a port, it would almost automatically raise concern about the integrity of the 21,000 containers that arrive in U.S. ports each day and the many thousands more that arrive by truck and rail across U.S. land borders. A three-to-four-week closure of U.S. ports would bring the global container industry to its knees. Megaports like Rotterdam and Singapore would have to close their gates to prevent boxes from piling up on their limited pier space. Trucks, trains, and barges would be stranded outside the terminals with no way to unload their boxes. Boxes bound for the United States would have to be unloaded from their outbound ships. Service contracts would need to be renegotiated. As this system becomes gridlocked, so would much of global commerce.

Trade Dependency on a Small Number of Border Crossings

The five major bridges and one tunnel that link Ontario to Michigan and New York account for seventy percent of all the trade between the United States and Canada—America's largest trading partner. The Ambassador Bridge, between Detroit, Michigan, and Windsor, Ontario, alone carries $250 million per day, which is twenty-seven percent of the total U.S.-Canada daily trade in merchandise. When these border crossings were effectively closed following the September 11 attacks, many of the "big three" automakers' assembly plants went idle within two days (the average assembly plant produces $1 million worth of automobiles per hour). Manufacturers and retailers depend on the unimpeded cross-border flow of trade to respond to "just-in-time" delivery imperatives. Despite this dependency, the U.S. and Canadian governments provide no security to these structures because they are either privately owned or controlled by binational bridge authorities. Since border inspections are done after vehicles cross the bridge or emerge from the tunnel, these inspections provide no protective value for these vital trade lines.

Recommendations

The Task Force makes the following recommendations:

- Develop a layered security system that focuses on the entire logistics and intermodal transportation network rather than on an unintegrated series of tactics aimed at addressing vulnerabilities at arrival ports or at already congested land borders.
- Develop standards for security at loading facilities for an intermodal container. Require certification of these standards and periodic independent

audits for compliance as a condition for gaining access to an international transportation terminal.

- Identify and test commercial off-the-shelf sensors and tracking devices to assure in-transit visibility and accountability of container movements and conduct demonstration projects using volunteer commercial shippers to test their technological and commercial viability.
- Improve the accuracy, timing, and format for transmitting and sharing data about the contents, location, and chain of custody involving a container shipment.
- Accelerate the time table for the action plans agreed to in the U.S.-Canada and U.S.-Mexico "smart-border" accords.
- Work with Canada to implement adequate security measures for cross-border bridges and the Detroit-Windsor tunnel.
- Task the U.S. Department of State, U.S. Department of Commerce, and U.S. Trade Representative to actively promote rapid adoption of security standards governing surface and maritime transportation in bilateral and multilateral arrangements with America's trading partners. Work to advance these standards within appropriate international organizations such as the International Standards Organization, International Maritime Organization, and the World Customs Organization. Retrofitting security into the global trade system is not only about mitigating the risk of terrorists exploiting these systems to target the United States, but also about sustaining the system that underpins global commerce.

3. SET CRITICAL INFRASTRUCTURE PROTECTION PRIORITIES.

"We are convinced that our vulnerabilities are increasing steadily, that the means to exploit those weaknesses are readily available and that the costs associated with an effective attack continue to drop. What is more, the investments required to improve the situation—now still relatively modest—will rise if we procrastinate."
—The Report of the President's Commission on Critical Infrastructure Protection, 1997

Our adversaries can attempt to strike anywhere, but their choice of target will likely not be indiscriminate. There are some targets in the United States that are more high-value than others in terms of visibility and the disruptive potential. Not all critical infrastructure is equally critical. Decisions about what warrants the most immediate attention must be made on the basis of relative vulnerability and consequence. Many of the critical infrastructures that underpin our national economy and support our modern way of life remain as vulnerable to attack today as they were a year ago. In some instances, the U.S. government is just beginning the process of undertaking an initial inventory of these vulnerabilities. Greater attention has been paid to physical security—gates, guards, and guns—but few resources are focused on preparing to respond and restore critical systems should these protective measures fail. The Task Force reviewed the June 30, 2002, findings and recommendations contained within the National Academies' report, *Making the Nation Safer*. The areas that the Task Force finds most worrisome include:

Vulnerable Energy Distribution Systems

Crude oil must be refined and distributed if it is to be a meaningful source of energy. Power generation plants are worthless if the electricity cannot be transmitted to the factories, office buildings, and households that need it to power equipment and provide lighting and climate control. An adversary intent on disrupting America's reliance on energy need not target oil fields in the Middle East. The infrastructure for providing energy to end users is concentrated, sophisticated, and largely unprotected. Further, some infrastructure lies offshore in the Gulf of Mexico, on the continental shelf, and within the territories of our North American neighbors.

Sixty percent of the Northeast's refined oil products are piped from refineries in Texas and Louisiana. A coordinated attack on several key pumping stations—most of which are in remote areas, are not staffed, and possess no intrusion detection devices—could cause mass disruption to these flows. Nearly fifty percent of California's electrical supply comes from natural gas power plants and thirty percent of California's natural gas comes from Canada. Compressor stations to maintain pressure cost up to $40 million each and are located every sixty miles on a pipeline. If these compressor stations were targeted, the pipeline would be shut down for an extended period of time. A coordinated attack on a selected set of key points in the electrical power system could result in multistate blackouts. While power might be restored in parts of the region within a matter of days or weeks, acute shortages could mandate rolling blackouts for as long as several years. Spare parts for critical components of the power grid are in short supply; in many cases they must be shipped from overseas sources.

Vulnerable Food and Water Supplies

The nation's food and agriculture industry represents a substantial sector of our economy and presents an inviting opportunity for biological attacks. As the recent foot-and-mouth disease outbreak among livestock in Great Britain illustrated, once a diagnosis of a contagious disease is made, the effect on domestic and export markets can be devastating. Similarly, there are vast numbers of pathogens that have the potential to wreak havoc on crops. Public anxieties over food contamination can undermine the demand for major foodstuffs for years. Yet, there is no CDC equivalent to provide a shared communications network among states and the U.S. Department of Agriculture. Nor is there an effective means to communicate and coordinate internationally. Confusion over reporting obligations, who has jurisdiction, and to what extent they can provide adequate response to a potential attack promises to seriously compromise America's ability to contain the consequences of attacks on U.S. crops and livestock. For example, one recent exercise found that by the time the Agriculture Department's foreign-disease laboratory on Plum Island, N.Y., would have confirmed the first case of foot-and-mouth cross-border contamination, the disease would likely have spread to twenty-eight states.

The system that provides Americans with a basic element of life—water—

remains vulnerable to mass disruption. Water systems are generally owned and maintained by local water companies and authorities that are slow to adopt new technologies and protocols. America's water supply is extremely vulnerable to contamination. This problem is compounded by the fact that extremely limited laboratory capacity and legal liability issues have made the routine monitoring of public water supplies for dangerous contaminants the exception rather than the rule. This lack of testing and monitoring capability can compound the consequences of a localized attack since there is no means to quickly reassure an anxious public across America that their drinking water is safe once a highly publicized incident takes place.

Vulnerable Clearinghouse Infrastructure to Support Financial Markets

Over the past two decades, the securities and banking industries have moved toward relying on a small number of core organizations for their post–trade clearing and settlement activities. If these systems were targeted by terrorists, the concentrated nature of these essential services could translate into profound disruption of daily economic life, both inside the United States and abroad. For example, clearing and settlement activities for the proper functioning of the government securities markets are essentially managed by just two banks, JP Morgan Chase and the Bank of New York. These two banks each extend approximately $1 trillion in intraday credit to their dealer and clearing customers each day. The sudden loss of these services could create a serious liquidity problem and likely damage public confidence in America's financial institutions and the systems upon which they borrow, invest, spend and save.

Recommendations

The Task Force makes the following recommendations:

- Set critical infrastructure priorities by moving beyond a ranking of vulnerabilities within each sector. Instead, conduct a cross-sector analysis, placing a premium on addressing vulnerabilities that present the greatest risk of cascading disruption and losses across multiple sectors.
- Fund energy distribution vulnerability assessments to be completed in no more than six months.
- Fund a stockpile of modular backup components to quickly restore the operation of the energy grid should it be targeted.
- Work with Canada to put in place adequate security measures for cross-border pipelines.
- Bolster the capacity for the U.S. Department of Agriculture (USDA) to exercise control over detection and incidence management of plant and animal disease, drawing upon the best practices developed by the Center for Disease Control (CDC) for managing human disease. Task USDA with immediately bringing online a shared communications network to link it with states and U.S. trade partners.

- Provide adequate funding to significantly enhance USDA's training in identifying foreign diseases and assume global leadership in devising a robust international system for monitoring the outbreak of animal and plant disease.
- Identify and remove legal liability constraints to routinely testing public water supplies for dangerous contaminants. Accelerate the development of adequate laboratory testing to serve local water companies and commissions.
- Create common integrated communication networks and real-time data/software backup repositories among the clearing banks, the Depository Trust and Clearing Corporation, dealers, and other key participants in the government securities market. Routinely test for recovery and resumption operations. The goal is to ensure that there are sufficient funds and securities available to market-makers in times of market stress so as to support the high level of liquidity required for trading.

4. BOLSTER PUBLIC HEALTH SYSTEMS.

"Our concern is that bioterrorism preparedness funding must be adequate, lasting, and reliable to enable local public health agencies to build and sustain permanent improvements in their ability to protect their communities twenty-four hours a day, seven days a week. Most communities do not now have this level of protection."

—Thomas L. Milne, Executive Director
National Association of County and City Health Officials, April 18, 2002

Agents used in biological attacks often require several days before victims start exhibiting acute symptoms. Early detection is key to stemming morbidity and mortality rates. Yet, with the possible exception of New York City, America's urban areas lack the advanced public health warning systems or specialized equipment to make this determination. There are simply not enough resources available within existing state and local budgets to remedy this situation in a timely way. Most local public health departments are barely funded and staffed to run during a normal 9 A.M. to 5 P.M. work week. Medical professionals often lack the training to properly diagnose and treat diseases spawned by biological agents. Many of the states' public health reporting systems are antiquated, slow, and outmoded. It can routinely take up to three weeks for a public health department to register a disease incident report in the national database. And there is no consensus on which language and diagnostic coding system should be used for a national database or how to safeguard that information.

Recent efforts in the federal government to respond to the bioterrorism threat may only add to confusion over responsibility and accountability. Responsibility for direction and coordination of public health efforts should rest with a substantially bolstered Centers for Disease Control with clear lines of communication to other departments and agencies such as the National Institutes of Health. Since much of the nation's research and most of the treatment capacity lie in the private sector, outreach is essential.

Chemical Versus Biological Attacks Have Different Imperatives

In chemical terrorism, detecting an attack is generally not a problem. People will show symptoms immediately: vomiting, suffering from seizures, experiencing respiratory distress, etc. The real challenge is deciphering which antidotes are appropriate and delivering them to the victims. The window of opportunity to mitigate the consequences of these attacks is very small—between a few minutes and two hours.

Detecting that there has been a biological attack can be far more problematic since symptoms in a person do not show up right away. The window of opportunity for responding to the biological agent anthrax ranges from thirty-six to forty-eight hours and for small pox nine to eleven days. For hemorrhagic fever viruses such as Ebola, an outbreak can range from two to twenty-one days after the attack is launched. The problem of discerning the difference between flu-like symptoms and the onset of a deadly disease is compounded when physicians are unfamiliar with diagnosing and treating such diseases and lack the medications to prescribe in any event.

Little to No Capacity to Conduct Outbreak Investigations

Medical care providers who come in contact with victims are the first line of defense. Few of these professionals have received training on how to diagnose, treat, and report symptoms that are associated with a biological attack.

Most city and county public health agencies currently lack the resources to support emergency hotlines twenty-four hours a day. The National Association of City and County Health Officials estimate that localities need 10,000 to 15,000 new employees to work in public health preparedness functions. Given these shortages, few localities have the ability to assemble a team to conduct an outbreak investigation.

Public health laboratories cannot support a surge in the number of tests to verify the existence of a biological agent. Seven months after the anthrax mailings, there was a backlog of thousands of unexamined specimens suspected of being contaminated with anthrax powder around the United States.

Recommendations

The Task Force makes the following recommendations:

- Ensure that major cities and counties plan and train for truly catastrophic attacks. While these scenarios strike many as too horrific to contemplate, imagining and planning for them can potentially make the difference between a twenty percent casualty rate and an eighty percent or higher casualty rate.
- Make emergency federal funding available to address the highest priority state, county, and city public health needs.
- Develop public health surveillance systems built around monitoring ambulance calls, pharmacies reporting an upsurge in the purchase of certain over-the-counter drugs, corporations and schools reporting a surge

in worker or student absenteeism, and doctors and hospitals reporting
an increase in walk-in patients.

- Develop and maintain call lists of retired nurses, doctors, and emergency
  medical technicians living in the community who can be mobilized in an
  emergency. Provide annual training for these nonpracticing professionals and create a process for activating a "good Samaritan" clause to over-
  ride malpractice issues.
- Identify and maintain call lists of knowledgeable experts who can au-
  thoritatively speak to the media about nuclear, chemical, or biological
  agents, symptoms of exposures, and recommended safeguards. Develop
  communications strategies and prepare educational materials and media
  guides for radio and TV on survival fundamentals for attacks involving
  weapons of mass destruction.
- Recruit major corporations and schools to help provide medications during an emergency. While the federal government will soon have the capability to ship antibiotics 32 and vaccines from the twelve national
  pharmaceutical stockpiles to urban areas within six hours, there are currently no local distribution plans to get these medicines to the general
  population.
- Provide funding to hospitals to pre-wire and outfit certain common areas
  such as lobbies, cafeterias, and hallways to support a surge in patients.
  Negotiate arrangements with hotels and conference centers to provide
  bed space for spillover patients.

5. REMOVE FEDERAL GOVERNMENT OBSTACLES TO PARTNERING.

*Obstacles for using our most potent resources for countering catastrophic ter-
rorism must be identified and overcome.*
— Committee on Science and Technology for Countering Terrorism
National Research Council, June 30, 2002

The burden of preparing and responding to catastrophic terrorist attacks
lies primarily outside the federal government at the local and state levels and
with the private sector companies that own and operate much of the nation's
critical infrastructure. Most of the expertise about both the vulnerabilities and
the most practical protective measures to save lives and avert mass societal
and economic disruption rests at this level as well. The federal government
must provide leadership by issuing the call to action, supporting forums convened to address these issues, and supplying as much specific information as
possible to key decision-makers on the nature of the threat.

Engaging the Private Sector

The barriers to greater information-sharing between the public and private
sector are not simply bureaucratic and cultural. Private sector leaders have
legal concerns with respect to liability. They also worry about violating antitrust laws and are apprehensive that sensitive security information may be
publicly disclosed by way of the FOIA. For their part, government agencies
find it almost impossible to discuss matters that may involve classified secu-

rity information. Protecting the public's right to know and ensuring free and competitive markets are cornerstones of our democracy. Safeguarding classified material is essential to protecting sources and methods. As a practical matter, however, the current rules confound the ability of the private sector to share information with public authorities on vulnerabilities within critical infrastructure, and preclude the ability of federal government officials to share anything but the most generic security and threat information.

The real value of sharing information is that it can encourage efforts to develop innovative security measures that involve all the relevant stakeholders. But innovation also generally requires the infusion of federal resources to support research and development. Here the sense of urgency required by the homeland security mission collides with the lethargic and arcane system governing federal procurement—the Federal Acquisition Rules (FAR). These rules, which run literally into the thousands of pages, may be tolerable for routine government purchases, but without a more streamlined process to move federal resources, change will be measured in terms of years, not in the weeks and months that taking emergency measures to address our most serious vulnerabilities requires. Also, private companies that agree to work with the public sector to assist in developing and providing security measures will require legal safeguards that appropriately reduce their liability exposure. Good faith efforts to advance security should not result in a risk of bankruptcy or huge litigation costs should these measures ultimately fail to deter or prevent terrorist attacks.

Tap International Expertise

While terrorism may be a new and painful experience for most Americans, regrettably many American allies such as Britain, France, Spain, and Israel have been confronted by this challenge for some time. Countries such as Switzerland provide a model for how civil defense efforts can be coordinated and largely resourced at the national level and adapted and managed at the local level. The United States does not have a monopoly on insight and ingenuity. It should be keen to learn from others' experience by sending research teams abroad to identify the best practices that could be implemented quickly here in the United States.

Recommendations

The Task Force makes the following recommendations:

- Draw on private sector experts who are involved in the design and operations of critical infrastructures such as the electric-power grid, telecommunications, gas and oil, banking and finance, transportation, water supply, public health services, and emergency services. Enlist their participation to conduct government-sponsored vulnerability assessments and to participate in red-team activities.
- Enact an "Omnibus Anti-Red Tape" law with a two-year sunset clause for approved private-public homeland security task forces to include: (1) a fast-track security clearance process that permits the sharing of "secret-

level" classified information with non-federal and industry leaders; (2) a FOIA exemption in instances when critical infrastructure industry leaders agree to share information about their security vulnerabilities with federal agencies, (3) exemption of private participants in these task forces from antitrust rules; (4) permitting homeland security appropriations to be managed under the more liberal rules governing research and development programs in the Department of Defense rather than according to the customary Federal Acquisition Rules; and (5) liability of safeguards and limits.

- Fund and deploy survey teams in Britain, France, Spain, and Israel to conduct studies on managing urban terrorism, evaluating European airline security procedures, and examining private-public intelligence sharing arrangements.

6. FUND, TRAIN, AND EQUIP THE NATIONAL GUARD TO MAKE HOMELAND SECURITY A PRIMARY MISSION.

The National Guard will play a critical role when the next catastrophic terrorist attack happens on American soil, and it must be well trained and equipped. Governors will expect National Guard units in their states to help with detecting chemical and biological agents, treating the victims, managing secondary consequences, and maintaining civil order. The National Guard has highly disciplined manpower spread throughout the nation in 5,475 units. The men and women who make up its ranks often come from the local community in which their unit is based. When called up by governors, the National Guard can be used to enforce civil laws—unlike regular forces which are bound by *posse comitatus* restrictions on performing law enforcement duties. The National Guard's medical units, engineer units, military police units, and ground and air transport units will likely prove indispensable in helping to manage the consequences of a terrorist attack.

Adapting to the New Homeland Security Imperative

Governors, charged with developing state homeland security plans, will look to their National Guard units to fulfill such needs as:

- State-of-the-art communications systems necessary for command-and-control during the chaos of a terrorist attack;
- Manpower in order to evacuate, quarantine, and protect residents as need be;
- Knowledge of chemical, biological, and radiological attacks and the capability to respond to them;
- The capacity to provide local medical centers with additional trauma and triage capabilities. The National Guard is currently equipped and trained primarily for carrying out its role in supporting conventional combat units overseas. The homeland security mission can draw on many of these capabilities but requires added emphasis on:
- Responding to a biological attack—the National Guard's focus in recent years has been primarily on surviving and fighting in a battlefield where chemical weapons have been deployed.

- Acquiring protection, detection, and other equipment that is tailored for complex urban environments.
- Training to provide civil support in the aftermath of a large-scale catastrophic attack.

Recommendations

An aggressive approach to revamping the capabilities of National Guard units designated to respond to domestic terrorist attacks can in the short-term provide a more robust response capability while states and localities work to bring their individual response mechanisms up to par. In order for the National Guard to fulfill this mission, the Task Force recommends:

- Congress should authorize and fund additional training for National Guard units to work with state civil authorities and to conduct exercises with local first responders in support of the new homeland security plans being developed by each governor.
- Triple the number of WMD-Civil Support Teams from twenty-two to sixty-six teams, develop capabilities so that response times are reduced to within the narrow window where their presence is still valuable, and reevaluate equipment and training programs in order to develop response capabilities for the full range of WMD threats in urban environments.
- Bolster the National Guard's "train the trainers" programs to quickly bring baseline training on the recognition and response to WMD events to localities around the country.
- Move away from using National Guard resources where their deployment has a minimal impact. National Guardsmen are too valuable to be assigned to borders and airports where they are limited in the functions they can perform. Instead, the agencies with the mandate in these areas need to be given the necessary resources to perform their missions without National Guard help.
- Redress the pay and job protection discrepancies between when National Guard units are called up by the president and when they are called up by a governor. When governors order an activation, guardsmen receive no protection that allows them to return to their civilian jobs as provided under the Soldiers and Sailors Civil Relief Act. In addition, when on state active duty they may be paid as little as $75 a day.

Conclusion

Quickly mobilizing the nation to prepare for the worst is an act of prudence, not fatalism. In the twenty-first century, security and liberty are inseparable. The absence of adequate security elevates the risk that laws will be passed immediately in the wake of surprise terrorist attacks that will be reactive, not deliberative. Predictably, the consequence will be to compound the initial harm incurred by a tragic event with measures that overreach in terms of imposing costly new security mandates and the assumption of new government authorities that may erode our freedoms. Accordingly, aggressively pursuing America's homeland security imperatives immediately may well be the most important thing we can do to sustain our cherished freedoms for future generations.

Preparedness at home also plays a critical role in combating terrorism by reducing its appeal as an effective means of warfare. Acts of catastrophic terrorism produce not only deaths and physical destruction but also societal and economic disruption. Thus, as important as it is to try and attack terrorist organizations overseas and isolate those who support them, it is equally important to eliminate the incentive for undertaking these acts in the first place. By sharply reducing, if not eliminating, the disruptive effects of terrorism, America's adversaries may be deterred from taking their battles to the streets of our nation's homeland.

RUSSIAN PRESIDENT PUTIN
ON THEATER HOSTAGE RESCUE
October 28 and November 10, 2002

A dramatic hostage-taking at a theater in Moscow in October 2002 drew renewed international attention to the guerrilla war in Chechnya, which was still under way more than two years after the Russian military had proclaimed victory. The Russian government successfully dealt with the hostage crisis, although at a price of killing 129 of the approximately 750 people who had been captured at the theater by Chechen rebels. The hostage crisis, coupled with several major bombings, served as grim reminders that Moscow had not yet succeeded in gaining total control over the breakaway province.

Chechnya, a province in southern Russia at the edge of the Caucasus Mountains, had tried to secede from Moscow's control after the Soviet Union collapsed in late 1991. A brutal war starting in 1994 essentially led to an inglorious defeat for the Russian army, which was withdrawn in 1996, leaving Chechnya in the hands of pro-independence leaders and guerrillas who wanted to make the province a Muslim state. Blaming the guerrillas for a series of bombings in Russia that killed about 300 people, the Russian government sent the army back into Chechnya in late 1999. After a fierce assault that destroyed much of the Chechen capital, Grozny, and drove several hundred thousand people from their homes, the army declared early in 2000 that it had broken the insurgency. Fighting continued at a low level, however, and a series of bombings and shootings in 2002 preceded the takeover of the Moscow theater by a band of guerrillas demanding Chechen independence. (Chechen war background, Historic Documents of 1999, p. 909; Historic Documents of 2000, p. 175)

Russian president Vladimir Putin on December 12 announced plans for a referendum in March 2003 on a new constitution reaffirming the province's status as part of Russia. That vote was to be followed by parliamentary and presidential elections. But that pledge of democracy was not enough to bring peace to Chechnya. A little more than two weeks later, on December 28, twin suicide bombings destroyed the main government building in Grozny, killing nearly 60 people and wounding about 120.

The Theater Hostage Crisis

On the evening of Wednesday, October 23, during the second act of a popular musical, Nord-Ost (German for "northwest") staged at a Moscow theater, about forty camouflaged and heavily armed men and women rushed onto the stage and into the audience. The guerrillas warned the actors, musicians, and audience members that they had bombs and would blow up the building if anyone tried to leave or a rescue was attempted. That set off a three-night, two-day hostage ordeal that brought the Chechen war into the eyes of the world and posed the greatest challenge yet to Putin's presidency, which began in 2000.

Speaking on cell phones from inside the theater—still known by its Soviet-era name, the House of Culture for the State Ball-Bearing Factory—the guerrillas demanded the withdrawal of Russian troops and government from Chechnya and threatened to begin executing their hostages if the government did not comply within seven days. Mediation attempts over the next two days by a prominent Russian journalist, Ana Politkovskaya, and several politicians resulted in the release on Friday of nineteen hostages, including eight children, but the guerrillas stuck to their demand and made increasingly dire warnings about shooting the hostages.

At about 2:30 A.M. on Saturday at least one shot was heard in the theater. Within two hours Russian commandos began carrying out a rescue attempt that had been rehearsed the night before in another theater. They started by pumping an opium-derived gas into the building through its air conditioning system. At that point many of the guerrillas reportedly were in the theater's control room, watching a videotape of their raid. Just before 5:30 A.M., about 200 commandos broke into the theater complex from underground tunnels and through holes in a wall and the roof. Most of the hostages and guerrillas had passed out from the effect of the gas, but several of the guerrillas remained conscious and engaged in a fierce firefight with the commandos. Several grenades were exploded in the confusion but none of the bombs that were strapped to the bodies of some of the guerrillas or planted in the auditorium.

By mid-morning the hostage crisis was over. Ambulances carried away hundreds of dazed hostages sickened by the gas; dozens of them would never recover, most having choked to death on their own vomit. Moscow area hospitals were overwhelmed by the number of people suffering from gas poisoning. The government had made available some supplies of an antidote but not nearly enough for the sudden demand. The final death toll among the hostages was 129, all but two of whom died from the after-effects of the gas.

The forty-one guerrillas were all dead. Among them was the commander, Mosvar Barayev, the nephew of a famous Chechen warlord who was killed by Russian security forces in 2001. Many of the guerrillas had been shot by the commandos, including some of the dozen or more female guerrillas who had bombs strapped to their bodies. None of the commandos were killed in the raid, although the gas reportedly sickened several.

Putin went on national television to announce the end of the siege and that "hundreds, hundreds of people" had been saved. Regrettably, he said, "we were unable to save all. Forgive us."

In the days immediately after the rescue, Russians were seized by conflicting emotions. According to opinion polls, most Russians were relieved that the hostage crisis had been resolved quickly and that most of the hostages had been rescued. But many were angered by the government's conflicting explanations of the raid, its refusal—for three days—to reveal what type of gas had been used, and the apparent incompetence in the arrangements for treating the victims. "I am no longer 100 percent sure what they did was right," Andrei Borisenok, a young Muscovite told the Washington Post two days later. "They say that if they didn't do it, the terrorists would have blown up the building. Everyone would have died. But who really knows?"

For Russians, the initial announced death toll of hostages—117—was hauntingly close to the 118 sailors who had died just two years earlier when their submarine, the Kursk, was ripped apart by an explosion as it traveled deep beneath the surface of the Barents Sea. Then, as with the hostage crisis, the government offered conflicting explanations of what had happened. (Kursk sinking, Historic Documents of 2000, p. 635)

Putin ultimately survived the storm of public criticism from his government's handling of the Kursk disaster, and he moved quickly to stem any political damage resulting from the deaths of so many hostages. On October 28, the day after the rescue, Putin held a public meeting with senior government officials and announced that the military would be given new orders to pursue terrorists "wherever they may be." Echoing the public posture of President George W. Bush following the September 11 terrorist attacks in the United States just a year earlier, Putin said Russia would not make any deals with terrorists "and won't yield to any blackmail."

The government continued to face criticism over the hostage deaths at the Moscow theater, which grew to a total of 129 at year's end after several victims died in hospitals. The government promised to pay $3,500 to the families of each of the hostages who were killed and one-half that amount to those who survived. In addition, the government paid for hospitalization and follow-up medical care. But in December more than forty former hostages and relatives of those who died filed an unusual lawsuit demanding $40 million in compensation. A court in Moscow was scheduled to hold hearings on the suit in January 2003.

Continued Fighting in Chechnya

The current war in Chechnya had stirred strong international reactions during 1999 and 2000 because of the brutal tactics of both the guerrillas and the Russian army. The guerrillas used bombings, night-time raids, and other terrorist actions to attack Russian security forces, government officials, and Chechen civilians who were believed to collaborate with Moscow. The Russian army responded with harsh repression, starting with the destruction of most of Grozny at the outset of the war and continuing with dragnet raids that caught up hundreds of civilians as well as guerrillas.

Amnesty International, Human Rights Watch, and other international agencies repeatedly denounced severe human rights abuses by both sides in the conflict. Partly in response to such criticism, Moscow kept a tight lid on information about Chechnya and made it almost impossible for outsiders—including journalists and human rights investigators—to determine what actually was happening in the war.

In his annual state of the nation address on April 18, Putin offered Russians what sounded like good news about Chechnya: "The military stage of the conflict may be considered concluded," he said. "It has been concluded owing to the courage and heroism of army and special units of Russia." But Russian soldiers on the ground in Chechnya might have been forgiven for thinking that their president spoke too soon. Just one day earlier six Russian soldiers were killed by a bomb in a village near Grozny; and just a few hours before Putin's speech seventeen policemen and soldiers were killed when bombs ripped apart two troop-carrying buses in Grozny. Two weeks later, on May 3, a bomb exploded during a World War II memorial parade in the south Russian town of Kaspiisk, near the border with Chechnya. Forty-one people died, including seventeen children. The government blamed the Chechen guerrillas for the bombing, which was the most serious attack on Russian civilians since the series of bombings in late 1999.

Despite the continuing violence, Moscow kept up its public relations campaign to demonstrate that the war was winding down. Starting in May the government began closing some of the camps that had been built for some 20,000 of the 100,000 Chechens who had taken refuge in the neighboring province of Ingushetia. The government stepped up this effort in December, according to Human Rights Watch, forcing several thousand refugees to leave the sparse camps and face a harsh winter without guaranteed housing in their former home regions in Chechnya. Relief workers said the government's message was that the departure of refugees from Ingushetia proved the war was over.

During the summer Putin briefly tried a new tactic for dealing with Chechnya. He acknowledged at a June 25 news conference that failures by the Russian government during the mid-1990s had allowed the guerrillas to gain the upper hand there. "The state proved incapable of protecting the interests of the Chechen people," who were used by the "fanatics" as "a living shield," he said. Putin also promised to end dragnet operations run by the military and known as "mop-ups"; human rights organizations had long said the operations punished many more civilians than guerrillas. In addition, the army announced plans to scale back its 80,000-troop presence in the province. Putin in July also appointed a Chechen, Abdul-Khakim Sultygov, as his personal envoy to investigate human rights abuses in the province.

The Chechen war's ability to embarrass Moscow surfaced again on August 26, when a Russian military transport helicopter crashed in a minefield outside Grozny, killing 119 soldiers. It was army's biggest single loss of life during the war. Despite initial reports that the helicopter had been overloaded or malfunctioning, investigators ultimately concluded that it had been brought down by a surface-to-air missile, confirming a claim by

Chechen guerrillas. Two other army helicopters were shot down in subsequent weeks.

Within days after the Moscow theater hostage crisis ended, the army stepped up its attacks in Chechnya and canceled the earlier plans to cut back the number of troops there. Defense Minister Sergei Ivanov said on November 5 that Putin had authorized military strikes against Chechen terrorists wherever they might be—even in foreign countries—just as Bush had sent the U.S. military in search of terrorists in Afghanistan, the Philippines, and other countries.

Putin also abandoned any pretense of moderate talk about Chechnya, even in the presence of international diplomats who in the past had criticized Russian human rights abuses in the province. The Russian president caused quite a diplomatic stir on November 11, when he used a joint news conference in Brussels with European Union leaders to launch a harsh verbal attack on Chechen rebels. Rhetorically addressing the guerrillas, who he noted had a goal of establishing an Islamic state, Putin said: "If you want to become a complete Islamic radical, and are ready to undergo circumcision, then I invite you to Moscow. We are multi-confessional. We have experts in this sphere. . . . I will recommend [they] conduct the operation so that nothing on you will grow again." An official Russian government translation of Putin's remarks, made in Russian, omitted the threatening last sentence.

On December 12 Putin announced plans for the referendum on a new constitution giving Chechnya increased autonomy from Moscow but retaining it as an "integral" part of Russia. Adoption of the constitution would be followed by elections. But such plans were widely considered unlikely to bring a sudden birth of peace and democracy to Chechnya. Any candidate allowed to run for the presidency almost certainly would be seen by many Chechens as a puppet for Moscow, as was the current nominal head of the administration installed by Moscow, Akhmad Kadyrov. Aslan Maskhadov, the Chechen leader who had signed an earlier peace agreement with Moscow but was then ousted from power when Russian troops returned in 1999, reportedly still enjoyed broad popular support in the province. But in a November 10 speech to pro-Moscow Chechens, Putin had said that "those who choose Maskhadov are choosing war"—a clear signal that the former Chechen president would not be welcome on any ballot sponsored by the Kremlin.

The year closed with yet another major bombing in Chechnya. On December 28 two suicide bombs destroyed the main government building in Grozny, killing 72 people and wounding more than 200. The building was one of the few in the city to have been repaired since the Russian army demolished most of the city during the two wars.

Yet another worrisome development were reports late in the year that the Chechen rebels were continuing their efforts to obtain nuclear weapons—or at least the radioactive material to make a "dirty bomb"—from Russia's vast arsenal inherited from the Soviet Union. Most Western experts said it was unlikely that the guerrillas actually had succeeded in obtaining a nuclear bomb, but they warned that the prospect was a dangerous one that could not be ignored.

The year's bombings and other guerrilla actions brought the government's official total for the number of Russian soldiers, officers, and policemen killed in Chechnya since the war started in 1999 to 4,705; most independent observers said this figure was low and estimated the real death roll at two or three times the official estimate. The Kremlin said another 13,000 troops and security officers had been wounded. The government also claimed more than 14,000 guerrillas had been killed. Several human rights organizations estimated that some 80,000 Chechen civilians had died since the fighting began; tens of thousands remained homeless, according to reports by relief agencies.

Following are two statements by Russian president Vladimir Putin in response to the hostage crisis at a Moscow theater: First, a nationally broadcast statement October 28, 2002, announcing that the government had rescued most of those who had been held hostage for more than two days by Chechen rebels; second, a speech delivered in Moscow on November 10, 2002, to a group of Chechen citizens who had been organized by the government to propose a new constitution for the province of Chechnya.

The documents were obtained from the Internet at www.ln .mid.ru/bl.nsf/8bc3c105f5d1c44843256a14004cad37/23129 9ac0942d01843256c6000424438?OpenDocument; 14004cad37/ebfb65a429c46e5443256c6f00286479?Open-Document; accessed December 14, 2002.

PUTIN STATEMENT, OCTOBER 28

Dear compatriots,

In these days we together went through a horrible ordeal. All our thoughts were about the people who had found themselves in the hands of the armed riff-raff. We had hoped for the freeing of those in trouble, but each of us understood that we had to be ready for the worst.

Early this morning an operation to free the hostages was carried out. Almost the impossible had been accomplished: saving the lives of hundreds, hundreds of people. We have proved that Russia can't be brought to its knees.

But now I primarily wish to address the kith and kin of those who died.

We were unable to save all.

Forgive us.

The memory of the dead ought to unite us.

I thank all the citizens of Russia for the self-possession and unity. My special thanks to all who participated in the freeing of the people. First of all, to the members of the special units who without hesitation, risking their own lives, fought to save the people.

We are grateful also to our friends throughout the world for the moral and practical support in the fight against a common enemy. This enemy is strong and dangerous, inhumane and cruel. It is international terrorism. Until it is defeated, nowhere in the world can people feel safe. But it must and will be defeated.

Today in hospital I spoke to one of the sufferers. He said, "I wasn't terrified—there was the confidence that the terrorists had no future all the same."

And this is true.

They have no future.

And we do.

PUTIN SPEECH, NOVEMBER 10

Let me first say a few words, and then we will move to a discussion of the issues which you consider advisable to discuss today. Two days ago you as part of a broad circle of representatives of the Chechen public came up with an appeal to the Chechen people. Much in this appeal is absolutely consonant with my own stand, and with that of the entire Russian leadership.

Your initiative [for a constitutional referendum] appears timely, and I today spoke about this at a meeting with senior Government members. Only recently I thought that maybe it wasn't worthwhile to hurry but rather to prepare adequately. But if you yourselves feel the time has come to step up these processes, I agree with you.

I agree with you that the terrorist act in Moscow was directed in the first place to exacerbate the situation in Chechnya. Terrorists are afraid that in Chechen society itself there have begun important, I would say—systemic changes.

People there have come to believe in the processes of the establishment of a normal, peaceful, human life. Hospitals, polyclinics, kindergartens have begun working. After many years, the children of Chechnya are again going to school. Institutions of higher learning are now operating, and the competition for entry into Chechen higher schools is growing, which was simply unthinkable some time ago.

This year in the Republic an all-time bumper grain crop was gathered in, even for the Soviet period. Industrial plants are being restored and are beginning to function. In the law enforcement sphere the Chechen militia is taking over an increasingly large part of functions and real work. I want to inform you that today the Minister of Internal Affairs of the Russian Federation signed an order on the establishment of a Ministry of Internal Affairs of the Chechen Republic.

The constitutional process under way in Chechnya presents a special danger to terrorists and their accomplices. The possibility of political normalization cuts the ground from under their feet. It does not suit them that the republic's people is consistently moving matters to the restoration of full-fledged and lawful authority.

And you are right, absolutely right in that precisely in this political process lies the key to a way out of the vicious circle of pointless and ruinous bloodshed.

And once again I repeat, responding to your initiative, I responsibly declare—federal authorities are ready together with you for this political process.

Of course, in such conditions terrorists and their accomplices—including those abroad—are compelled to engage in a substitution of notions. Instead of the real political process already going on in Chechnya, they are trying to impose on us dubious negotiators. Those who not so long ago were staging public executions in the city squares, engaging in the slave trade, taking hostages, killing Russian and foreign journalists—implanting medieval ideas in Chechnya and discrediting the Chechen people.

What are these bandits "resisting" today? Civilized laws of life? What are their foreign partners in crime trying to help? And with whom are they urging us to establish contacts and dialogue?

In this connection I do not regard it correct to bypass the figure of [Aslan] Maskhadov [a former Chechen leader who favored independence from Russia] in silence. This man in the conditions of Russia's de facto recognition in 1996 of the independence of Chechnya, I want to stress this—a de facto recognition—got power in the Republic. How did he use this power? What did he do? What did he do with Chechnya? Where did he lead the Chechen people?

He led the Republic to an economic collapse, hunger, a total disruption of the social and cultural spheres. To genocide against members of other peoples who had earlier lived in Chechnya. To a great loss of life among the Chechens themselves. It was he who led Russia and Chechnya to war.

Yet, despite all the political costs, the Russian leadership up to quite recently, I want to inform you about this, had contacted with him. Up to the summer of 1999 for the rendering of economic assistance to the people of the Republic federal authority sent the Maskhadov administration financial and material resources. Those funds were intended to be used for pensions, wages, benefits. But ordinary peaceful people did not receive them.

Whereas Maskhadov, in his turn, now spoke of the destruction of odious terrorists, and I want to tell you about this (not many know that) called upon us to destroy these people; now, all of a sudden, unexpectedly, appointed them to be his deputies. Now he himself organized bandit-like attacks, now condemned the perpetrators after the failure of those actions.

In September last year we directly invited him to resume the negotiation process. He sent for semblance to Moscow his representative, but again refrained from further contacts. Instead of negotiations he chose the path of terror and stood behind the riff-raff who took hundreds of people hostage on October 23 in Moscow.

And today, after the tragic events in Moscow, I especially declare: those who choose Maskhadov are choosing war. All these people, wherever they are—on the territory of Russia or outside it—will be regarded by us as the accomplices of terrorists.

And to those who because of thoughtlessness or deliberately, out of fear before bandits or by following the tenacious European tradition of appeasing them, will continue to urge us to sit down at the negotiating table with the murderers—I suggest that they should set an example for us: sit down at the negotiating table and come first to terms with [Osama] bin Laden [leader of the al Qaeda terrorist network] or Mullah Omar [former head of the Taliban regime in Afghanistan].

Those figures also not because of pleasure are killing innocent people by the hundreds and the thousands, they're also putting forward political demands. Demands against the United States and against European and Arab states and with regard to the Middle East and Kashmir, and in our case—Chechnya. They also have claims against other regions of the world.

We are not opposed to settlement of outstanding issues by political means. We are in favor. Yet, I want simultaneously to say: to us, terrorists and their accomplices are a separate thing. And the political process is a separate development.

Those who today hinder the restoration in the republic of a peaceful and civilized life—just as years ago, are just using the slogans of independence and so-called free self-determination as a cover. So let us discuss that also both honestly and frankly.

In this context I would like to recall how the degeneration of separatism into terrorism proceeded in Chechnya. That did not happen overnight. A seat and at the same time a victim of international terrorism, Chechnya also didn't become today.

Yes, the beginning of this way was paved by separatists. And I even assume that the people who were bearers of separatist ideas initially acted in accordance with absolutely good intentions. They, just as many others who sought in the early '90s their own ways to get out of the whole tangle of contradictions and crisis phenomena with which Russia was faced at that period of time. And I assume that they did that quite sincerely.

But it was others who then took advantage of the difficulties of the most complicated transitional period in Russian history—and not at all for noble aims. The ideas of separatism and of the so called independence of Ichkeria were quickly taken up by Wahhabites [followers of the conservative Wahhabi sect of Islam, dominant in Saudi Arabia], of the worst kind at that, by nationalists and in the end—by international terrorists. They used these ideas as a cover for their own ideological and aggressive intentions having nothing in common with the interests of the Chechen people. Actually, that was used to turn Chechnya into a bridgehead of international terrorism, for subsequent ambitious plans of attack on fraternal Dagestan [a province neighboring Chechnya, from which Chechen guerrillas operated in 1999], to create a medieval caliphate from the Black to the Caspian Sea. What does that have to do with the interests of the Chechen people?

In this connection I want to stress the importance for Russia of the resolution of the Chechen problem. And to say bluntly to where political irresponsibility, laxity or weakness might lead Russia.

When I am speaking of the need to unconditionally ensure the territorial integrity of Russia, I am convinced of the following. Unless today we solve the problem of Chechnya, tomorrow, just as in 1999, new attempts will be made to create the notorious "caliphate" according to the design of extremists, and they—you know about that—speak absolutely straightforwardly and openly, they do not conceal their plans that this "caliphate" must incorporate not only the entire North Caucasus, but also a part of Krasnodar and Stavropol Territories [a reference to the reported goal of some Islamic groups in Russia to recreate the Islamic empire that ruled parts of Russia during the Middle Ages].

Neither is this the whole story. That will inevitably be followed by attempts to undermine the situation in Russia's multinational Volga area. All of this is designed to steer the development of the situation in our country according to the "Yugoslav scenario." No way. I responsibly declare: there won't be a second Khasavyurt.

I want that not only those sitting in this hall but also every citizen of Russia, wherever he may live—in a large city or small settlement—would know and understand what is at issue when we're speaking of a settlement in the Chechen Republic. The issue is not only about the struggle against separatism and about a local conflict in a region of the Russian Federation. Fighting extremism and terrorism is today for us a struggle to preserve Russian statehood. That is the price of the question, that's what it is all about.

I want today to refer to another thing. Now in Chechnya it is not simple at all, I would say that the situation is very complicated. And it's not only political problems, of course. It is difficult, first of all, in human terms. The crisis has exhausted in the first place the Chechen people itself.

The destinies of very many Russian citizens have found themselves in a tight knot of problems—both Chechens and members of other nationalities. The long years of conflict have led to a multitude of human dramas, to losses among the kith and kin. Sometimes brothers turned out to be, as they say, on the different sides of the barricades. Citizens of non-Chechen nationality were being intimidated, plundered, killed. They were practically fully driven outside the Republic.

But all this makes us treat with even greater care the already tangible shifts towards a peaceful life in Chechnya. Makes us together, jointly help people who were drawn into this severe confrontation return to a normal, human life. This is our main task.

And here your position and your active support are extremely important. Important is your work inside the Republic. I know that you sincere want well-being for Chechnya and its people. I am absolutely convinced that without your civic stance, the complex problems of Chechnya can't be solved today, the economy can't be raised, refugees can't be returned.

You and we must help all who are prepared to show their civic stance, who would like to put their labor and their money in the economy of Chechnya, who can influence the solution of its complex social problems. For nowhere in the world have poverty, and the lack of economic rights ever contributed to either peace or stability.

In the final analysis, it is our common principal task to give the people in Chechnya an opportunity to work calmly, to normally earn a living for themselves and their children, to have prosperity in the home and peace in the family. We all want this—we have come to this desire through suffering, and in this aspiration of ours—we are sincere.

Together we must do all to ensure that the citizens of Russia—I want to stress this especially—regardless of nationality: whether they live in its central part or in the North Caucasus or in any other corner of our country—that everywhere in our country they feel confident and comfortable. It is equally advantageous for terrorists, the fomenting of anti-Chechen sentiments in Russia and the whipping up of tensions, of social instability within the republic itself.

And, finally, I would like to again return to the initiative for speeding the constitutional process. I agree with you that it is within the framework of this political process that we must find agreed-upon decisions and enlist new supporters for the establishment of a peaceful life in the long-suffering Chechen land.

LULA DA SILVA ON HIS ELECTION AS PRESIDENT OF BRAZIL
October 28, 2002

Brazilians on October 27 handed the government of Latin America's largest country to a leftist former union leader whose appeal was fueled, in large part, by broad popular discontent with the failure of free-market economic reforms to produce more jobs and reduce poverty. Workers Party candidate Luiz Inacio Lula da Silva, known universally as Lula, won the presidency with a record 61 percent of the vote in a second-round runoff on October 27 against the governing party's lackluster candidate, Jose Serra. Lula had finished just below the simple majority required for victory in the first round held on October 6.

Earlier in the campaign the prospect of a Lula victory had frightened many of Brazil's business elite and foreign investors. The currency, the real, *was pummeled as a result of concerns that Lula would default on the country's huge $260 billion public debt so he could pay for the social programs he was promising voters. But by the time of the second round of voting, Lula's newly moderated positions and reassuring demeanor—plus the near certainty of his victory—brought him substantial support from the business leaders who had once scorned him.*

The election was a personal triumph for Lula, who spent much of his childhood in the streets of Sao Paolo's slums, then worked in a factory for two decades, earned a reputation as a fiery labor union leader, and unsuccessfully sought the presidency in the three previous elections. More broadly, Lula's election was a clear manifestation of public unease with the results of free-market economic reforms that governments in Brazil, along with many other developing countries, had adopted over the previous decade— and that had delivered a decidedly mixed picture of prosperity.

Although its economy had grown rapidly during the early 1990s, Brazil in 2002 was in the fourth year of economic stagnation that stemmed, in part, from the lingering affects of the 1997–98 Asian financial crisis that had damaged developing economies worldwide. Like many of its neighbors, Brazil was reeling under an enormous debt, had seen the value of its cur-

rency plunge, and was suffering rising unemployment and the threat of inflation. (Asian financial crisis, Historic Documents of 1998, p. 722)

In his campaign, Lula offered two somewhat contradictory promises. To business leaders and foreign investors worried about his leftist leanings, Lula promised to maintain the free-market economic policies of his two-term predecessor, Henrique Cardoso, who in August had secured a record $30 billion loan from the International Monetary Fund. To get that loan, Cardoso had pledged to keep a tight reign on government spending, a pledge that Lula adopted as well. But to his core supporters among the 40-some million Brazilians living in poverty, Lula promised to create 10 million new jobs and provide improved social services, such as food subsidies, better schools and medical care, and a doubling (over four years) of the $56 monthly minimum wage. His campaign song summed up his message: "All you have to do is want it, to make it happen tomorrow. Vote and say, 'Lula, I want Lula.'" Speaking at an election-night victory rally in Sao Paolo, Lula promised again to "create a country that is more just, a country of brotherhood and solidarity."

In fiscal terms, Lula's challenge would be to pay for his promises without busting the budget and running up Brazil's already huge public debt. Since it was clear that he could not deliver on all his promises all at once, and almost certainly would have to scale back on many of them, perhaps his chief political task would be to manage the expectations of change that his overwhelming victory created among his supporters. "Lula promised me a raise, and I'm expecting to get it," Leila Maria Oliveria, who collected bus fares in Rio de Janeiro, told the Los Angeles Times. *"If he doesn't give it to me, I'm going to have to go to his office to collect it."*

A timely illustration of what could happen when a leftist president got elected on a social justice platform but failed to keep his promises was readily available in nearby Venezuela. There, Hugo Chavez made extravagant promises to the poor but could not deliver on them, and in the process alienated virtually every other sector of society. He was briefly ousted in a coup in April, then returned to office only to face massive street demonstrations during much of the rest of the year. Most observers predicted Lula would be able to avoid the many mistakes that got Chavez in trouble. (Venezuela, p. 201)

Lula and the Workers Party

Lula and his Workers Party had a radical image both domestically and internationally. Lula himself had fostered that image during the 1980s with his often-heated rhetoric against capitalists, especially the foreign capitalists who controlled much of Brazil's economy. The party was founded in 1979 as an alliance of trade unions, former leftist guerrillas, and social activities driven by the "liberation theology" preached by many leading Roman Catholic priests and scholars of the era. At the time Brazil was under the repressive control of a right-wing military regime that had seized power in 1964. As the leader of the 100,000-member metal workers union in the foreign-owned automobile industry, Lula was a key figure in several contentious strikes and became one of many radicals imprisoned by the generals.

The military dictatorship ended in 1985 when the generals stepped down in disgrace, having driven up the national debt, run the economy to ground, and severely damaged democratic political institutions. The following year Lula won election to Congress with the most votes of any candidate in the country. He served in Congress for four years but otherwise never held elected office—and never held a senior administrative post except for his union leadership.

Lula and other party leaders complained of the inequities of capitalism, but most of them, and the party itself, never adopted the formal Marxist ideology that inspired many leftist parties worldwide during much of the twentieth century. As some of its leaders became successful politicians at the local and state levels, the party moderated its image during the 1990s to attract broader support. The key figure in the transformation of the party was Jose Dirceu, Lula's closest adviser who took over as chairman in 1994 and shunted aside the most radical elements. Workers Party members gained reputations for running relatively efficient and corruption-free governments in the five states and nearly 200 localities they governed.

Lula's victory in 2002 came in his fourth run for the presidency. In each of his first three attempts (1989, 1994, and 1998), Lula was a dark-horse candidate generally considered too far to the left to win a majority among Brazil's polarized electorate. The timing was better for him in 2002. Cardoso's free-market economic policies during the previous eight years had spurred foreign investment in Brazil and opened the country's economy to international trade to a greater degree than ever before. Brazil's economy grew steadily, but not spectacularly, during the 1990s, benefiting primarily a growing middle class. Although the poverty rate fell, by the end of the decade about a third of the country's 175 million people were still living on less than $1 a day.

As happened in other developing countries, Brazil also discovered the downside to the open-economy trend known as globalization: Foreign investors can pull their money out of a country just as fast as they put it in. After the Asian financial crisis and resulting economic turmoil in Russia during 1998 investors began worrying about Brazil and many moved their money elsewhere. Brazil's economic growth slowed starting in 1999. By 2002 the country was facing a dangerous combination of high interest rates, high unemployment, a vulnerable currency, rising public and private debt—and presidential and legislative elections.

As the campaign season got under way early in the year, Lula was riding high in most opinion polls, generally in first or second place. Lagging far behind was Jose Serra, a government minister who Cardoso had handpicked as his successor. By May Lula was appearing more and more to be the strongest candidate in the field. With each new poll confirming his front-runner status, the real took a beating on international currency markets, losing nearly half its value against the dollar between late May and the first round of elections in October. Business leaders became even more worried when Serra fell into the number three position in the polls behind another leftist candidate, Ciro Gomez of the Labor Front coalition.

Lula repeatedly insisted that he was no longer the radical labor organizer of the past but was a respected political leader able both to represent his constituency and work with the business community. Lula also reached out to Brazilian business leaders with assurances that he would continue Cardoso's moderate economic policies. An important step in that direction was his choice of a vice presidential running mate: Jose Alencar, a business leader from the conservative state of Minas Gerais.

By late July many economists were predicting that a default by Brazil on its debt was inevitable, given the continuing fall of the currency and the high interest rates that foreign lenders were demanding from Brazilian borrowers. A default in Brazil—coming on top of neighboring Argentina's fiscal meltdown at the end of 2001 and deep trouble in Uruguay—would have spelled long term economic disaster for all of Latin America. (Argentina, p. 80)

On August 7 the International Monetary Fund (IMF) intervened in an effort to stabilize the situation before it got out of hand. At the conclusion of a visit to the region by U.S. Treasury Secretary Paul O'Neill, the IMF announced a $30 billion loan to Brazil. The loan was the largest ever by the IMF to any country. The size of the loan was especially noteworthy because just a few weeks earlier O'Neill had suggested that the United States was reluctant to support any new lending to Brazil, in part because the money might end up in Swiss bank accounts.

The IMF tied its loan to a promise by Cardoso to maintain a "primary budget surplus"—a surplus in government spending before interest payments—of at least 3.75 percent of Brazil's gross domestic product. Keeping such a surplus, especially when the currency was falling and interest rates were rising, would mean tight limits on government spending. And to ensure that the new Brazilian government would keep the promise, the IMF said 80 percent of the $30 million loan would be disbursed during 2003. Cardoso persuaded Lula and other presidential candidates to support the loan agreement, including the commitment to restrain spending but even that step failed to calm the fears of business leaders about what a Lula presidency would mean.

In the first round of voting on October 7, Lula captured more than 38 million votes, about twice as many as Serra, who finished second. But Lula fell short of the required majority for an outright victory, thus forcing a second round on October 27. Lula quickly won endorsements from the other left-of-center candidates and became the odds-on favorite. In perhaps the most remarkable sign of how much had changed, key business leaders abandoned Serra's sinking candidacy and endorsed Lula, perhaps in hopes of influencing his policies once he took office.

Lula's landslide victory on October 27—coincidentally his fifty-seventh birthday—was a personal triumph for him but, in a sign of potential trouble, his popularity outran that of his Workers Party colleagues. The party won 20 percent of the seats in the two chambers of Congress, making it the largest single party but still far short of a majority, even with the likely support of other center-left parties. Workers Party candidates for state governorships also lagged behind Lula, winning only three of the twenty-seven races and losing in several areas where it had been strong in the past.

Economic Challenges Ahead

In the two months after his victory and before his January 1 inauguration, Lula worked to moderate the expectations of his domestic supporters and put to rest the fears of the world's financial markets. He made an important start with a speech on October 28 that reiterated his pledge of social justice but offered just one specific proposal: Creation of a new agency to help ensure that "each Brazilian is able to eat three times a day." Lula also pledged that he would not default on Brazil's public debt or spend the country into bankruptcy. "Our government will honor established contracts, will not neglect the control of inflation, and will maintain a posture of fiscal responsibility," he said.

Internationally, Lula's most-awaited appointments were those of his economic team, the officials charged with formulating the specifics of the new president's wide range of promises. World financial markets were reassured by the appointment of Antonio Palocci as finance minister and Henrique Meirelles as head of the central bank. Both men had broad experience in the private sector and had played a significant role in assuring investors that Lula did not intend to transform Brazil into a communist state. Another key move was Lula's adoption of a plan by Cardoso to grant autonomy to the central bank; economists said that step signaled Lula's determination not to play political games with the bank and monetary policy.

But even with experienced administrators at the helm of his departments, Lula faced a series of daunting economic challenges. Most worrisome was Brazil's public debt burden, which had risen from 30 percent of gross domestic product in 1994 to 60 percent in late 2002—a level many economists considered unsustainable over the long haul. One illustration of Brazil's predicament was that in July, before the IMF stepped in, international lenders required borrowers there to pay interest rates higher than those in any other major developing country except Argentina, which had defaulted on its commercial debt a half-year earlier.

By the end of the year, with his January 1 inauguration approaching, Lula was still promising to stick with Cardoso's general economic policies and to keep the promise to the IMF to restrain government spending. In the first meeting of the cabinet members he had appointed, Lula acknowledged the difficult choices the new government would face. "We may not be able to complete our project. It takes more than four years," he said. "The situation is not good in almost any aspect, except for the consolidation of democracy."

Lula and the United States

As a candidate Lula took several positions that put him at odds with U.S. policy. Most important, he was a fierce critic of a proposed Free Trade Area of the Americans, a free-trade zone for the entire Western Hemisphere that Presidents Bill Clinton (1993–2001) and George W. Bush had championed. Lula complained that the proposed zone would represent an effective U.S. "annexation" of Brazil and other Latin countries. Lula also opposed the longtime U.S. economic embargo of Cuba and Washington's military aid to the government of Colombia, which was fighting narcotics traffickers, left-wing guerrillas, and right-wing paramilitaries. Bush called Lula to congratulate him on his victory but White House press secretary Ari Fleischer on October 28 issued a restrained statement that "we look forward to working with Brazil. We consider our relations with Brazil to be good relations." (Cuba embargo, p. 232; Colombia aid, p. 569)*

Lula went to Washington in mid-December for meetings with Bush, members of Congress, and the country's opinion leaders. Bush and Lula praised each other after an hour-long meeting at the White House on December 10. "My impression of Bush was the best possible," Lula said.

> *Following is the text of a speech given October 28, 2002, by Luiz Inacio Lula da Silva following his second-round runoff victory in elections held October 27 for president of Brazil. The speech was translated from the Portuguese by Liv Sovik and Liliana Krawczuk and supplied by the AFL-CIO.*

The document was not available on the Internet at the time of publication.

Yesterday, Brazil voted for change. Hope vanquished fear and the electorate decided to set a new path for the country. We gave the world a beautiful show of democracy. One of the greatest peoples in the world decided, peacefully and calmly, to chart a new direction for itself.

The elections that have just taken place were, above all, a victory for Brazilian society and its democratic institutions, given that they brought with them rotation in power, without which democracy loses its very essence.

We have been through an excellent election process, in which citizens demanded and obtained a clean, frank and high-level debate about the immediate and historic challenges our country faces. The attitude of the electoral authorities and the President of the Republic contributed to this, as they played their constitutional role in an even-handed way.

The great virtue of democracy is that it allows a people to change its horizon as it deems necessary. Our victory means the choice of an alternative project and the beginning of a new historical cycle for Brazil.

Our arrival to the Presidency of the Republic is the fruit of a vast collective effort, made over decades, by countless people engaged in democratic social struggle. Unfortunately, many of them were not able to witness Brazilian society, especially the oppressed, reaping the fruits of their hard work, dedication and militant sacrifice.

Wherever you are, brothers and sisters that death has harvested before this hour, know that we are the heirs and carriers of your legacy of human dignity, personal integrity, love for Brazil and passion for justice. Know too that your work is still with us, as if you were alive, and that we are inspired by it to continue to fight the good fight, the fight in favor of the excluded and those who suffer discrimination. The fight for the dispossessed, humiliated and affronted.

I want here to pay homage to the anonymous activists, to those who gave their labor and dedication, over years, for us to arrive at this place. In the most faraway regions of the country, they never lost heart. They learned, as I did, with defeat. They became more competent and effective in the defense of a sovereign and just country.

I celebrate today those who, at difficult times in the past, when the cause of a country of justice and solidarity seemed impossible, did not become indifferent, did not give way to selfishness and acute individualism. I celebrate all those who kept hold of their capacity to become indignant in the face of others' suffering. They resisted and kept the flame of social solidarity burning. I celebrate all of those who did not desert our dream, who were sometimes alone in the squares of this immense Brazil, hoisting high the starred flag of hope.

But the victory is, above all, that of thousands, millions of people who have no party affiliation and became engaged in this cause. It is the victory of working-class people, of the middle classes, of substantial parts of business, of social movements and union organizations that understood the need to combat poverty and defend the national interest.

In order to achieve yesterday's result, it was essential for the PT [Workers Party], a Left party, to build a broad alliance with other parties. . . .

There is no question that the majority of society voted to adopt another ideal for the country, in which everyone's basic rights are guaranteed. The majority of Brazilian society voted to adopt a different economic and social model, able to ensure renewed growth, economic development with job creation and income distribution.

The Brazilian people know, however, that what was undone or not done over the last decade cannot be solved by magic trick. Historic privations of the working population cannot be overcome overnight. There is no miraculous solution to a social debt of these dimensions, which have worsened in recent years. But it is possible and necessary to make a start, from the very first day in government.

We will face resolutely the current external vulnerability of the Brazilian economy—a crucial factor in the financial turbulence of recent months. As we said during the campaign, our administration will honor the contracts signed by the government, it will not overlook the control of inflation and will maintain—as has always been the case of PT administrations—a position of fiscal responsibility. That is why all Brazilians must be told clearly: the hard crossing that Brazil faces requires austerity in the use of public money and an implacable fight against corruption.

But even with budgetary restrictions, imposed by the difficult financial situation we will inherit, we are convinced that it will be possible to act with creativity and determination on social questions, from the first day of our administration. We will appease hunger, create jobs, attack crime, combat corruption and create better education conditions for the low-income population, from the very start of my administration.

My first year in office will have the seal of the combat against hunger and an appeal for solidarity with those who have nothing to eat. To that end, I announce the creation of a Secretariat for Social Emergencies, with a budget and a mandate to begin to fight the scourge of hunger, starting in January. I am certain that, today, this is the greatest demand of society as a whole. If, at the end of my term of office, every Brazilian can eat three times a day, I will have fulfilled my life's mission.

As I said when I launched my Program of Government, creating jobs will be my obsession. To this end, we will immediately mobilize public resources available in state banks—and through partnerships with private enterprise—to activate the civil construction and sanitation sector. Besides creating jobs, this measure will contribute to a gradual return to sustained growth.

The country has been concerned about the international financial crisis and its implications for the Brazilian situation, especially the instability of the exchange rate and inflationary pressures caused by it.

However, even with all the international adversity, we have a trade surplus of more than US$10 billion this year. This can be expanded in 2003 with an aggressive export policy, by incorporating more added value in our products, making our economy more competitive and promoting a judicious policy of competitive import substitution.

Brazil will do its part to overcome the crisis, but it is essential that, besides the support of multilateral bodies like the IMF [International Monetary Fund], IDB [Inter-American Development Bank] and World Bank, lines of credit for companies and international trade be reestablished. It is equally important to make progress in international trade negotiations, so that rich countries effectively lift protectionist barriers and subsidies that penalize our exports, particularly of agricultural products.

Over the last three years, with the end of the exchange rate anchor, we increased our agricultural product by more than 20 million tons. We have enormous potential in this sector to launch a broad program to combat hunger and export food products; this potential continues to run into obstacles in the form of unjust protectionism by the major economic powers, obstacles we will spare no effort to remove.

Work is the path to our development and to overcoming the historic legacy of inequality and social exclusion. We want to build a broad mass consumer market that provides security for corporate investment, attracts international investments in production, represents a new model for development and makes income distribution and economic growth compatible.

The construction of this new perspective of sustained growth and job creation will require increased and cheaper credit, development of capital markets and careful investment in science and technology. It will also demand an inversion of priorities in finance and public expenditures, to value family farming, cooperatives, micro and small businesses and the different forms of the economy of solidarity.

The National Congress has an immense responsibility in providing for the changes that will promote social inclusion and sustained growth. For that reason, I will endeavor personally to send Congress the major reforms that society is calling for: reforms of the social security system, tax reform, labor legislation and trade union structure reform, land reform and political reform.

The world is paying attention to the spectacular demonstration of democracy and popular participation in yesterday's election. It is a good time to reaffirm the commitment to a courageous defense of our national sovereignty. We will go forward in the search to build a culture of peace among nations, increasing the economic and commercial integration of countries, renewing and broadening Mercosul as an instrument of regional integration and implementing effective negotiations of the FTAA proposal. We will stimulate bilateral trade agreements and struggle for a new international economic order that diminishes injustice, closes the broadening gap between rich and poor countries, as well as reducing the international financial instability that has imposed so many losses on developing countries.

Our government will be a guardian of the Amazon and its biodiversity. Especially in that region, our development program will be marked by environmental responsibility.

We want to stimulate all forms of integration of Latin America that strengthen our historical, social and cultural identity. It will be particularly important to seek partnerships that permit an implacable opposition to traffic in drugs, which lures away part of our youth and fosters organized crime.

Our government will respect and seek to fortify international organizations, especially the United Nations, and support important international conventions, like the Kyoto protocol and the International Criminal Tribunal, as well as non-proliferation treaties on nuclear and chemical weapons. We will encourage the idea of a globalization of solidarity and humanism in which the peoples of poor countries can reverse the unjust international structure of exclusion.

I will not disappoint the Brazilian people. The expression that sprang from the bottom of the souls of my compatriots yesterday will be my inspiration and my compass. I will be, starting on January 1st, the president of all Brazilians because I know that is what the voters who chose me expect.

We are living in a decisive, unique moment for the changes we all desire. They will come without surprises or shocks. My government will carry the mark of understanding and negotiation. Of firmness and patience. We are fully aware that the greatness of the task goes beyond the limits of one party. This was why we have tried, since the campaign, to bring together unionists, NGOs [nongovernmental organizations] and businessmen from all segments in common action for the country.

We will continue to act decidedly to unite a range of political and social forces to build a nation that benefits all of the people. We will promote a National Pact for Brazil, establish the Council on Economic and Social Development and choose among the best-qualified people in Brazil to participate in a broad-based administration that can begin to pay back historical social debts. This cannot be done without the active participation of all living forces in Brazil, workers and entrepreneurs, men and women of good will.

My heart beats strongly. I know that it beats with the hope of millions and millions of other hearts. I am optimistic. I feel that a new Brazil is being born.

FBI REPORT ON CRIME
IN THE UNITED STATES
October 28, 2002

The crime rate in the United States began to creep upward in 2001, rising 2.1 percent over the level in 2000. The increase was the first since 1991 but the overall rate was still 10.2 percent lower than it had been in 1997 and 17.9 percent lower than in 1992. Preliminary figures for 2002 indicated that the rate of serious crime was continuing to rise. Several factors accounted for the rise in crime, but most experts cited the faltering economy as the main contributing factor

The growth in the prison population continued to slow, reflecting not only a decrease in crime throughout the latter half of the 1990s but also a trend among the states to find alternatives to imprisonment, such as drug treatment programs. The prison population rose by 1.1 percent in 2001, a small drop from its 1.3 increase in 2000 but well below its peak of 8.7 percent in 1994.

Rising Crime Rate

According to the FBI's annual report, Crime in the United States, 2001, *three of the four categories of violent crime—murder, forcible rape, and robbery—and all three categories of property crime showed increases. There were 15,980 murders, a 2.5 percent increase over 2000 (the figures did not include those killed in the terrorist attacks on the World Trade Center and the Pentagon). Although the number of forcible rapes increased slightly over 2000, the rate per 100,000 women continued to decline to 62.2 percent, from 62.7 percent. The number of robberies increased 3.7 percent over 2000. The only Crime Index offense to show a decrease was aggravated assault, which fell by half a percent. Aggravated assaults accounted for more than three-fifths of all violent crimes. Firearms were involved in more than a quarter of all violent crimes and two-thirds of all murders.* (Crime in 2000, Historic Documents of 2001, p. 746; terrorist attacks, Historic Documents of 2001, p. 614)

Both the number and rate of property crimes—burglary, larceny-theft, and motor vehicle theft—increased over their levels in 2000. There were an *estimated 10.4 million offenses for an estimated dollar loss of the $16.6 billion.*

The South still had the highest rate of crime of any of the four regions, but the crime rate in 2001 increased the most in the West, where it was up 3 percent, followed by the Midwest at 1.1 percent, and the South at 0.3 percent. The crime rate fell 1.9 percent in the Northeast. Serious crimes increased 4.1 percent in cities with 250,000 to 499,000 population, but only 0.5 percent in cities with populations over 1 million. The volume of crime in suburbs and rural areas rose 2.4 percent and 1.9 percent, respectively.

The increase in the Crime Index did not come as a surprise to most criminologists, who had been warning for several years that several factors were likely to cause a reversal in the ten-year decline. These included an increase in the teenage population, the age group most likely to commit crime, and the fact that after ten years of decreases, which brought the crime rate to its lowest level since the 1960s, it could not be expected to fall much further.

Experts cited the faltering economy as a main culprit in the increase in crime. Lack of jobs, particularly for young people and inmates leaving prison, was a likely contributor to the increase. Some experts and politicians also cited reduced budgets for policing and a shift in emphasis from fighting traditional crime to combating terrorism as contributing factors. "You can't take forces away from traditional street crime fighting and put it into homeland security and think there won't be an impact," said James Alan Fox, a professor of criminal justice at Northeastern University. "This is a slight increase . . . it should be a wake-up call. We have to pay for programs now or pray for the victims later."

Sen. Charles Schumer of New York agreed. "This report is a shot across the bow. To make people more safe from terrorists as they become less safe from criminals is counterproductive." Schumer and other Democrats were critical of President George W. Bush's administration for proposing to transfer more than $300 million from community policing programs into the Federal Emergency Management Agency as part of the war on terrorism.

Identity Theft

Perhaps the fastest-growing crime, and one that was not directly broken out in the FBI report, was identity theft. Identity theft was defined as stealing someone's personal information, such as a Social Security number, date of birth, and mother's maiden name, and then using that information to create a false identity to drain bank accounts or to obtain credit or run up debt, sticking the victim with the bills. In 1998 Congress made identity theft against an individual a federal crime with the penalty for conviction ranging from a fine to fifteen years in prison. Since then, most states had also designated identity theft as a crime.

No one knew for certain the number of victims of identity theft or the amounts that had been stolen. According to a report released in March by the General Accounting Office (GAO), two credit card companies, Visa and MasterCard, had fraud losses of about $1 billion in 2000, up 45 percent since 1996. Claims of fraudulent use of Social Security numbers increased to

*65,000 in 2001, from 11,000 in 1998. A separate report by the inspector
general of the Social Security Administration estimated that one in twelve
foreigners had used fake documents to obtain Social Security numbers. Although the vast majority of immigrants then used the Social Security numbers for legal purposes such as getting jobs or driver's licenses, federal
officials were investigating hundreds of people, including some terrorist
suspects, believed to use the fraudulently obtained numbers in subsequent
criminal activities such as credit card fraud.* (Immigration, p. 842)

*In November, federal law enforcement officials arrested two men who
were alleged to have stolen the personal information of 30,000 people over
three years and then sold the lists to scam artists for $60 a name. One of the
men arrested was a computer help-desk employee who had access to sensitive passwords from banks and credit companies. Federal prosecutors said
it was the largest case of identity fraud ever uncovered. But for many state
and local law enforcement agencies, identity theft was not a high priority.
A GAO report released in July found that although many state law enforcement agencies had improved their responses to claims of identity theft, some
were still refusing to take reports of identity theft, let alone investigate them.
Funding shortages, lack of training in handling the often-complex cases,
and the fact that the thefts often involved several jurisdictions were cited as
the reasons.*

Slowing Growth in the Prison Population

*The Bureau of Justice Statistics reported July 31 that the total federal,
state, and local "correctional population," including those in prison, on probation, or on parole, grew by 148,000 in 2001, to a total of 6,594,000. Of that
total, about 2 million were in prison or jail, 732,000 were on parole, and 3.9
million were on probation. Fifty-three percent of those on probation had
been convicted of felonies.*

*The prison population rose by 1.1 percent, the smallest annual increase
in nearly three years. The number of state prison inmates grew by only 0.3
percent, to 11.2 million, while the federal prison population grew by 8 percent to 157,000. Nearly 60 percent of the new federal inmates had been convicted on drug charges, whereas the states were more likely to imprison
people who committed violent crimes. "It appears the state prison population has reached some stability," Allen Beck, a statistician with the Bureau
of Justice Statistics, said in April when preliminary data were released.
Beck added that the federal prison population rate could continue to grow
at current rates as drug, immigration, and weapons cases flooded federal
courthouses.*

*The states, however, were beginning to reverse three decades of tough sen-
tencing policies. The Sentencing Project, a group advocating alternatives to
incarceration, found that five states had expanded drug treatment as a sentencing option, while seven states had passed laws to ease prison crowding
through early paroles for nonviolent offenders, eliminating mandatory
minimum sentences, and other alternatives. A review by the Justice Policy
Institute found that tight state budgets had forced the governors in Florida,*

Illinois, Michigan, and Ohio to close prisons. "Increasingly, policymakers recognize that prisons are expensive," said Marc Mauer, assistant director of the Sentencing Project.

Another report by the Bureau of Justice Statistics, released in June, found that two-thirds of inmates released from prison in fifteen states in 1994 were rearrested for a new offense within three years and nearly half were returned to prison, either for a new crime or for failing to fulfill a condition of their release. Released prisoners with the highest rearrest records were robbers, burglars, larcenists, auto thieves, and those imprisoned on illegal weapons charges.

The new data on recidivism were viewed by some persons as justification for keeping tough sentencing laws and by others as an indicator that the emphasis should shift to rehabilitation programs. "Many states are being pressured to relax or abandon their habitual criminal sentencing laws. This report shows that would be exactly the wrong approach," said Michael Rushford, president of the Criminal Justice Legal Foundation in Sacramento. Vincent Schiraldi, president of the Justice Policy Institute, disagreed. In the 1980s prisons "were at least attempting to turn these guys' lives around. They've stopped attempting to do that [in the 1990s] and we are suffering for it now," he said.

Following is the text of a news release issued October 28, 2002, by the Federal Bureau of Investigation summarizing the findings of its annual report, Crime in the United States, 2001.

The document was obtained from the Internet at www .fbi.gov/pressrel/pressrel02/clus2001.htm; accessed October 29, 2002.

The Nation's Crime Index increased 2.1 percent in 2001 from the 2000 number, the first year-to-year increase since 1991, the Federal Bureau of Investigation reported today. However, final data released by the FBI's Uniform Crime Reporting (UCR) Program in the annual publication Crime in the United States, 2001, indicated that, when looking at 5- and 10-year trends, crime was down 10.2 percent when compared to 1997 data and down 17.9 percent when compared to 1992 statistics.

The Crime Index is composed of four violent crimes (murder and non-negligent manslaughter, forcible rape, robbery, and aggravated assault) and three property crimes (burglary, larceny-theft, and motor vehicle theft). The Crime Index offenses plus the arson offenses form the Modified Crime Index. Index crimes serve as a measure of the level and scope of the Nation's crime experience.

In 2001, the nearly 17,000 city, county, and state law enforcement agencies that provided data to the UCR Program represented 92 percent of the total United States population as established by the Bureau of the Census. Population estimates were included for nonreporting areas. Because of the many variables that affect crime in a city, county, state, or region, data users are cautioned against comparing or ranking locales. Valid assessments are possible only with careful study and analysis of the various conditions affecting each law enforcement jurisdiction.

Crime Volume

- The estimated 11.8 million Crime Index offenses in the Nation in 2001 represented a 2.1-percent increase over the 2000 estimate.
- In 2001, estimated violent crime showed a 0.8-percent increase over the 2000 estimate. Five- and 10-year trends revealed that the estimated number of violent crime offenses decreased 12.2 percent from the 1997 estimate and 25.7 percent from the 1992 estimate.
- Estimated property crime was up 2.3 percent from the prior year's estimate. Property crime trends for the 5- and 10-year period showed a 9.9-percent decrease from the 1997 level and a 16.7-percent decrease from the 1992 level.
- Collectively, the Nation's cities reported an increase of 2.0 percent in the total number of crimes reported. Cities with populations of 250,000 to 499,999 recorded the largest increase of reported crime offenses at 4.1 percent. The smallest increase in volume (0.5 percent) occurred in cities with 1 million or more inhabitants. Suburban and rural counties had increases in the volume of crimes reported of 2.4 percent and 1.9 percent, respectively.

Crime Index Rate

- The Crime Index rate measures the total estimated volume of the seven Index offenses per 100,000 United States population. In 2001, the Crime Index rate was 4,160.5 estimated offenses per 100,000 inhabitants, 0.9 percent higher than the 2000 estimated rate. However, the rate was 15.6 percent lower than the 1997 rate and 26.5 percent lower than the 1992 rate.
- By region, the South had a Crime Index rate of 4,760.9; the West, 4,354.9; the Midwest, 3,981.1; and the Northeast, 3,006.9 offenses per 100,000 inhabitants. The Northeast was the only region to have a decrease (1.9 percent) in the Crime Index rate when compared to the previous year's rate. The West's rate increased 3.0 percent, the Midwest's rate rose 1.1 percent, and the South's rate was up 0.3 percent when compared to rates in 2000.
- Metropolitan Statistical Areas (MSAs) had a rate of 4,474.9 offenses per 100,000 inhabitants. Cities outside the Nation's MSAs recorded a rate of 4,450.4 per 100,000 population. Rural counties reported a Crime Index rate of 1,892.4 per 100,000 in population.

Violent Crime

Data reported in 2001 indicated a 0.8-percent increase in the estimated volume of violent crime from the 2000 estimate, or an estimated 1.4 million violent crimes. However, the rate of violent crime (504.4 offenses per 100,000 inhabitants) decreased 0.4 percent from the 2000 data.

Personal weapons, such as hands, fists, and feet, were used in 31.1 percent of violent crimes. Firearms were involved in 26.2 percent of violent crimes, and knives and other cutting instruments in 14.9 percent. Other dangerous weapons were used in 27.8 percent of violent crimes reported in 2001.

Property Crime

- Both the volume and rate per 100,000 inhabitants of all property crime offenses increased in 2001. With an estimated 10.4 million offenses, the property crime total was 2.3 percent higher than the 2000 total. The estimated property crime rate of 3,656.1 per 100,000 inhabitants was 1.0 percent higher than the previous year's rate.
- The estimated dollar loss attributed to property crime (excluding arson) was $16.6 billion, a 5.6-percent increase from the 2000 estimate.

Hate Crime

- Hate crime data were provided by 11,987 law enforcement agencies. The 9,726 hate crime incidents reported in 2001 involved 11,447 separate offenses, 12,016 victims, and 9,231 known offenders.
- Of all reported single-bias incidents, 44.9 percent were motivated by racial bias, 21.6 percent were motivated by an ethnicity or national origin bias, 18.8 percent were based on a religious bias, 14.3 percent were based on a sexual-orientation bias, and 0.3 percent were based on a disability bias.
- A review of the hate crime victims showed that 64.6 percent of reported victims were targets of a hate crime against persons; 34.7 percent of victims were targets of a hate crime against property. The remaining 0.6 percent of victims were targets of crimes against society.
- Intimidation accounted for 55.9 percent of hate crimes directed against persons. Destruction, damage, or vandalism was reported in 83.7 percent of hate crimes against property.

Index Crime Clearances

- Nationally, 19.6 percent of all Crime Index offenses were cleared by arrest or exceptional means in 2001. Of violent crimes, 46.2 percent were cleared, and 16.2 percent of property crimes (excluding arson) were cleared. In addition, 16.0 percent of arson offenses were cleared.
- Of all Crime Index offenses, murder was the offense most likely to be cleared-62.4 percent. Burglary had the lowest percentage (12.7 percent) of clearances among the Crime Index offenses.
- Of the Crime Index offenses cleared in 2001, 18.6 percent involved only juveniles (persons under the age of 18). Juvenile clearances accounted for 12.1 percent of the overall violent crime clearances and 21.1 percent of property crime clearances.

Arrests

- Law enforcement made an estimated 13.7 million arrests for criminal offenses (excluding traffic violations) in 2001, a 2.1-percent decline from the 2000 estimated total.

- Approximately 2.2 million of the estimated arrests involved Crime Index offenses, accounting for 16.4 percent of the total arrests. A look at the two categories of Index crime showed that violent crime arrests increased 0.1 percent, and property crime arrests decreased 1.0 percent when comparing 2000 and 2001 data.
- A review of Crime Index offense data showed that 73.8 percent of those arrested were adults. A breakdown of Index crime categories showed that 84.6 percent of arrestees for violent crime were adults as were 69.9 percent of arrestees for property crime.
- A review of violent crime arrest data by age showed that 44.2 percent of the arrestees were persons under 25 years of age, and 15.4 percent were under age 18. Arrest data for property crimes showed that 58.3 percent of those arrested were under 25 years of age, and 30.4 percent of arrestees were under age 18.
- An analysis of total arrests showed that 83.3 percent of arrestees were adults. Of total arrests nationwide, 45.9 percent involved persons under the age of 25, and 16.7 percent involved persons under the age of 18.
- An analysis of arrest data by gender showed that approximately 77.5 percent of all arrestees were male; 69.5 percent of all arrestees were white. By volume, males were most often arrested for drug abuse violations; females were most often arrested for larceny-theft offenses.
- The Nation's smallest cities, those with fewer than 10,000 inhabitants, had the highest arrest rate per 100,000 population, 6,308.4. Among cities, the lowest arrest rate (4,482.5 per 100,000 inhabitants) was reported in cities with populations of 25,000 to 49,999. Rural counties had an overall arrest rate of 3,968.3 and suburban counties a rate of 3,801.5 arrests per 100,000 inhabitants.

Murder

- An estimated 15,980 murders occurred in the United States in 2001, a 2.5-percent increase over the 2000 estimate. However, a 5-year trend reflected a 12.2-percent decline from the 1997 estimate. The rate of 5.6 murders per 100,000 in population was 1.3 percent higher than the 2000 rate of 5.5, but 17.5 percent lower than the 1997 rate.
- Supplemental data such as the age, sex, and race of the victim and offender, the type of weapon used, and the circumstance of the incident were provided for 13,752 murders. Based on those reports, 76.6 percent of murder victims were male and 89.6 percent were adults (those aged 18 and over). By race, 49.8 percent of murder victims were white, 47.5 percent were black, and the remainder were persons of other races.
- Approximately 42.3 percent of murder victims knew their assailants. Nearly a third of all female victims were slain by a husband or boyfriend.
- Supplemental homicide data revealed that 90.3 percent of murder offenders were male, and 91.7 percent were over the age of 18. Of the incidents in which the race of the offender was known, 50.3 percent of the offenders were black, 47.2 percent were white, and 2.5 percent were of other races.

- In 2001, of murders with a single victim and a single offender, 93.6 percent of black homicide victims were killed by black offenders; 85.4 percent of white homicide victims were killed by white offenders.
- For those incidents in which the murder weapon was known, 69.5 percent were committed with a firearm. Knives or cutting instruments were employed in 14.3 percent of murders in 2001. Personal weapons, such as hands, fists, feet, etc., were used in 7.4 percent, blunt objects were used in 5.3 percent, and other dangerous weapons (e.g., poisons or explosives) were used in the remainder of the homicides.
- Twenty-eight percent of homicide victims were involved in an argument with the offender. More than 16 percent (16.6) of murders occurred in conjunction with another felony, such as robbery or arson. Circumstances were unknown in 32.4 percent of murders.

Forcible Rape

- There were an estimated 90,491 forcible rapes in the United States in 2001, an increase of 0.3 percent when compared to the 2000 estimate.
- In 2001, there were 62.2 forcible rapes per 100,000 females in the Nation, which continued a downward trend. In 2000, there were an estimated 62.7 rapes per 100,000 females. A review of 5- and 10-year trend data showed that in 1997 the estimated rate was 70.3 rapes per 100,000 females; and in 1992, the estimated rate was 83.7.

Robbery

- The estimated 422,921 robberies reported in 2001 represented the first increase of this offense (up 3.7 percent) in year-to-year comparisons since 1991. The rate of robberies nationwide was 148.5 offenses per 100,000 inhabitants, a 2.4-percent increase from the 2000 rate.
- Robbery accounted for 3.6 percent of all Crime Index offenses and 29.4 percent of all violent crimes in the United States in 2001.
- Robbery resulted in an estimated $532 million loss in 2001, or an average dollar loss of $1,258. Bank robberies had the highest average loss at $4,587 per offense.
- During 2001, firearms were used in 42.0 percent of the reported robbery offenses, and strong-arm tactics were used in 39.0 percent of robberies. Offenders used knives or cutting instruments in 8.7 percent of robbery offenses; the remaining 10.4 percent involved other weapons.

Aggravated Assault

- The only Crime Index offense to show a decrease (0.5 percent) in estimated volume when compared to the 2000 estimate, aggravated assaults accounted for 63.1 percent of violent crimes in 2001, or an estimated 907,219 aggravated assault offenses.
- Five- and 10-year trends indicated that the estimated volume of aggravated assaults was down 11.3 percent from the 1997 estimate and was down 19.5 percent from the 1992 estimate.
- The rate of aggravated assaults per 100,000 inhabitants for the Nation was

318.5, which was 1.7 percent less than in 2000, 16.6 percent lower than in 1997, and 27.9 percent lower than in 1992.

- Personal weapons, such as hands, fists, and feet, were used in 27.9 percent of aggravated assaults in 2001. Firearms were used in 18.3 percent of the offenses. Knives or cutting instruments were used in 17.8 percent of the incidents, and blunt objects or other dangerous weapons were used in 36.0 percent of aggravated assaults in 2001.

Burglary

- There were an estimated 2.1 million burglaries in 2001, a 2.9-percent increase from the previous year's data.
- In 2001, burglary data showed an estimated $3.3 billion in losses in the Nation with an average loss per incident of $1,545. Most burglaries (65.2 percent) were residential in nature.
- Forcible entry was involved in 63.3 percent of burglaries. Unlawful entry without the use of force comprised 30.2 percent of burglaries, and attempted forcible entry accounted for 6.5 percent.

Larceny-theft

- There were more than 7.0 million estimated larceny-theft offenses in 2001, an increase of 1.5 percent from the 2000 estimate.
- Larcenies accounted for 59.7 percent of all Crime Index offenses and 68.0 percent of all property crimes.
- Data reported for larceny-theft offenses showed an estimated $5.2 billion in losses nationwide. The average monetary loss per offense was $730.

Motor Vehicle Theft

- There were more than 1.2 million estimated motor vehicle thefts in 2001, a 5.7-percent increase over the 2000 estimate. This translated into a rate of 430.6 motor vehicle thefts per 100,000 United States inhabitants.
- By vehicle type, motor vehicles were stolen at a rate of 336.9 per 100,000 inhabitants during 2001; trucks and buses were stolen at a rate of 86.5 per 100,000 persons.
- Based on the more than 1.2 million estimated motor vehicles stolen in 2001, the estimated dollar value of vehicles stolen nationwide was almost $8.2 billion. Approximately 62.0 percent of that amount was recovered. The estimated average value of stolen motor vehicles was $6,646.

Arson

- A total of 76,760 arson offenses were reported in 2001.
- For the 68,967 arson offenses for which supplemental data were provided, the average monetary value of property loss for arson was $11,098 per incident. The average loss for structural properties was $20,128, and the average loss for mobile properties was $6,974 per incident. Other property types had an average dollar loss of $1,361 per incident.
- Structural arson was the most frequently reported arson category in 2001 and accounted for 42.2 percent of the arson offense total. Mobile proper-

ties were the target of 32.5 percent of reported arson offenses, and other property types accounted for the remaining 25.4 percent.

- The offense of arson had a higher percentage of juvenile involvement than any other Index offense. Of all arson offenses cleared in 2001, 45.2 percent involved only juvenile offenders.

Law Enforcement Employees

- The 13,530 city, county, and state police agencies that reported 2001 personnel data collectively employed 659,104 officers and 279,926 civilians and provided law enforcement services to approximately 268.1 million United States inhabitants.
- In 2001, law enforcement agencies in the Nation employed 2.5 full-time officers per 1000 inhabitants. Cities collectively employed 2.4 officers per 1,000 inhabitants. Suburban counties had a rate of 2.7 officers per 1,000 inhabitants; rural counties had 2.5 full-time officers per 1,000 population.
- Males comprised 88.8 percent of all sworn officers, and females accounted for 62.7 percent of all civilian employees. Civilians made up 29.8 percent of the total law enforcement employee force in the Nation in 2001.

Terrorist Attacks of September 11, 2001

Most of the data associated with the events of September 11, 2001, were included only in a special report published in Section V of Crime in the United States, 2001. As of the date of publication, the report revealed that:

- In all, there were 3,047 deaths as a result of the events of September 11, 2001: 2,823 homicide victims were attributed to the attacks on the World Trade Center, 184 murder victims to the Pentagon, and 40 murder victims to the airliner crash site in Somerset County, Pennsylvania.
- The vast majority, 99.7 percent, of victims were over age 18 in those cases when the age of the victim was known. Most victims were between the ages of 35 and 39.
- All of the offenders were white males. Four offenders were under age 22. The oldest offender was in the 30-34 age group.

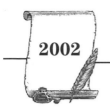

November

U.S. DISTRICT COURT ON MICROSOFT SETTLEMENT
November 1, 2002

One of the federal government's biggest antitrust cases ever ended on November 1, 2002, with a major victory for Microsoft Corporation, the giant software manufacturer that earlier had been accused of holding an illegal monopoly on operating systems for personal computers. A federal judge in Washington, D.C., ended the case with a decision that required Microsoft to make minor changes in its business practices but that posed no risk to the company's near-total domination of the personal computer industry.

Just two years earlier, Microsoft had faced the prospect of becoming the third major monopoly in a century to be broken up by the federal courts. The Standard Oil Company was broken into smaller companies in 1911 because of its illegal monopoly of the oil industry, and AT&T was broken into seven "baby Bells" in 1982 because of its illegal monopoly of long-distance telephone services. (AT&T breakup, Historic Documents of 1982, p. 17)

A federal judge in 2000 ordered Microsoft broken in two because it had used its monopoly to block competition in some elements of personal computer software. But Microsoft escaped that fate in 2001 when an appellate court overturned the penalty aspect of the judge's ruling but retained his finding that Microsoft engaged in illegal monopolistic behavior. The Bush administration's new top leadership at the Justice Department then negotiated a settlement requiring Microsoft to make modest concessions to its competitors. After further negotiations, nine states that had been part of the suit against Microsoft won several additional requirements, which Microsoft and the Justice Department accepted as part of a proposed "final" settlement in November 2001; several additional changes were adopted in March 2002. Nine other states and the District of Columbia, which also had been plaintiffs against Microsoft, refused to accept that settlement and asked for more serious restrictions on Microsoft's behavior.

U.S. District Court Judge Colleen Kollar-Kotelly in Washington resolved the issue with her ruling on November 1 that essentially accepted the Bush administration's deal with Microsoft as being in the public interest. The judge imposed limited restrictions on Microsoft's behavior, which were to remain in effect for five years.

"We're pleased to put another step of this case behind us," said a jubilant William H. Gates, Microsoft's founder and chairman. Most of Microsoft's competitors expressed little disappointment, having long since given up hope that the government or courts would act to curtail the company's monopoly. Two of the states that had been active in the case, Massachusetts and West Virginia, vowed to pursue an appeal but were given little chance of success. "There was nothing [in the government's settlement with Microsoft] that will change Microsoft's business practices in any substantial way," Massachusetts attorney general Thomas Reilly said in explaining his decision to appeal. (Microsoft case background, Historic Documents of 1999, p. 654; Historic Documents of 2000, pp. 105, 308; Historic Documents of 2001, p. 775)

Microsoft still faced a series of more than 100 private lawsuits that had been consolidated before another federal judge, sitting in Baltimore. That judge, Frederick Motz, took two significant steps during the year that appeared to indicate that he was taking a tougher line against Microsoft than either the Bush administration or the courts in Washington. First, on January 11, he blocked a settlement of the case that would have required Microsoft to give about $1 billion worth of computers, software, and technical support to some of the nation's poorest school systems. Judge Motz said the deal would not have represented a fair settlement of the cases. The deal also was opposed by Apple Computer, which said it would have given Microsoft an unfair advantage in the schools—one of the few settings where Apple's Macintosh computers were competitive with Windows-driven computers. Second, on December 24 Motz ruled that the Java programming language of a competitor, Sun Microsystems, must be included in Microsoft's dominant Windows operating systems for personal computers. Microsoft said it would appeal that ruling, and other aspects of the private lawsuits remained before Judge Motz.

Also still on the table at the end of 2002 was a possibility that the European Union (EU) would pursue antitrust charges against Microsoft. EU regulators for four years had been investigating Microsoft's behavior, especially its use of its Windows systems to control world markets for video software and servers used to access the Internet.

Hearings in 2002

In earlier stages, court hearings in the Microsoft antitrust case were significant public events that drew wide media coverage and even affected the stock prices of Microsoft and its competitors. But by 2002, with nearly all the potential sting having been taken from the government's case against Microsoft, a final eight-week series of hearings before Judge Kollar-Kotelly attracted little attention. The basic question before the judge in those hearings was whether she should approve the settlement between Microsoft and the Justice Department, as modified by several small changes requested by the states that had accepted it. The states that had rejected the settlement pre-

sented the judge with an alternative that would have stiffened some of the requirements on Microsoft.

The hearings drew wide attention only once, on April 22, when Gates appeared on the witness stand in defense of his company. Generally deferential and subdued, Gates for two days directly answered questions and took care to explain complex technical issues in everyday language. His live appearance was in marked contrast to a videotape of his deposition shown during hearings in 1999. Gate's evasive answers on that occasion clearly offended Judge Thomas Penfield Jackson, who later ruled that Microsoft was an illegal monopoly that had to be broken in two. The appellate court that overturned Jackson's ruling in 2001 harshly criticized him for interviews he later gave reporters, in which he denounced Gates's "arrogance."

Judge Kollar-Kotelly's Ruling

In her ruling, Kollar-Kotelly accepted the basis of the settlement between Microsoft and the Justice Department and rejected all but a handful of the proposed alternatives that the dissenting states had wanted to impose on the company. The essence of the judge's ruling was that the settlement satisfied most of the government's complaints against Microsoft that had been upheld by the appellate court decision. Moreover, she said, the additional requirements proposed by the states would have gone far beyond the limits of that decision. An important effect of her decision was that the settlement's restrictions on Microsoft's behavior would apply only to software written for personal computers—not for newer technologies such as interactive television or handheld devices that mimicked some computer functions.

Perhaps the judge's most important rebuff to the dissenting states was her rejection of their request that Microsoft be forced to offer a stripped-down version of Windows that was simply an operating system. Such a version would not have included such items as the Internet Explorer browser or the Media Player audio/video device, features that competitors complained were not necessary for Windows and that Microsoft added solely to thwart competing products. Rather than creating a basic version of Windows, the judge said, Microsoft had to make it possible for users to hide programs such as Internet Explorer if they wanted to use a competing product instead.

Similarly, Judge Kollar-Kotelly rejected an appeal by the states that Microsoft be required to offer versions of its other software programs, such as the Office suite of word processing and business applications, that would run on operating systems other than Windows. Microsoft already offered such a version of Office for Apple's competing Macintosh system but did not provide one for Linux, another operating system that was growing in popularity.

The judge also dismissed the demand by the dissenting states that Microsoft be punished for its continued behavior that, the states said, compounded the monopoly that had been found to be illegal. An example cited by the states was Microsoft's release of a new operating system, Windows XP, that appeared aimed at extending the same degree of control over software for new technologies—such as audio and video players, handheld devices, and other

*computer-related appliances—that the company held in personal comput-
ers. Acknowledging that these steps by Microsoft could be considered "bad,"
Judge Kollar-Kotelly noted that Judge Jackson had mentioned some of them
in his earlier decisions but neither he, nor the appellate court, had used
them as the basis for finding Microsoft's monopoly to be illegal. In addition,
she chastised the states for bringing up new allegations at such a late stage
in the legal process.*

*Microsoft already had implemented some of the changes required by the
settlement. Many of them were included in a large software package, called
a "Service Pack," which corrected dozens of mistakes ("bugs") in Windows
XP. As part of the Service Pack—but in a format so difficult to find that few
consumers were likely to take advantage of it—was an option allowing installation on Windows XP of Internet browsers, music players, or other
"middleware" offered by Microsoft competitors. Critics said this was a typical move by Microsoft—appearing to comply with a court ruling but in such
a way that the original intent of the ruling was undermined.*

Judge's Changes from the Agreement

*Judge Kollar-Kotelly ordered several changes to the original settlement as
it had been modified by some of the states in late 2001. Most of her changes
posed no threat to Microsoft's continuing domination of the computer software market—or its plans to extend that domination into related fields. Instead, most experts said, her changes responded to some of the complaints
competitors had about Microsoft's behavior and tried to ensure that the
company would comply with the settlement.*

*According to most observers, one of Kollar-Kotelly's orders had potential
to strengthen the Microsoft settlement: a requirement that Microsoft share
technical information with competitors in the field of software for servers,
the computers that acted as the relay points, or hubs, for the Internet and
other computer networks. The development of server software had become
one of the most important and competitive aspects of the high-technology
business since the government first investigated Microsoft in the mid-1990s
but before Judge Kollar-Kotelly's ruling that the field had played only a secondary role in the antitrust case. A key factor had been the growing popularity of server software based on the Linux operating system, an alternative
to Windows that users could obtain for free over the Internet but that was
used primarily by computer professionals.*

*In her ruling, Kollar-Kotelly required Microsoft to disclose to competitors
the programming language known as communications protocols that were
embedded in the Windows operating systems. With that information, Microsoft's competitors—such as IBM, Sun Microsystems, and the developers of
Linux-based programs—could make their server software work just as well
with Windows as did Microsoft's own server software.*

*Kollar-Kotelly called her decision in this area one of the more "forward
looking" elements of the ruling, and most observers agreed. "That is a real
effort to do something procompetitive," Timothy Bresnahan, a Stanford Uni-*

versity professor and former Justice Department official, told the New York Times. *Bresnahan otherwise was extremely critical of the ruling, which he called a missed opportunity to stimulate competition in the software industry.*

The judge also tightened a provision that required Microsoft to modify Windows to make it easier for consumers to have competitors' software programs start running (or "launch") automatically when a personal computer was started. In the past, Microsoft had designed Windows so that only Microsoft products would automatically appear on the computer screen; changing this start-up sequence required a degree of expertise that few computer users had.

Another change dealt with the issue of who would oversee Microsoft's compliance with the settlement. The original agreement would have established a "technical oversight board" of software industry professionals to monitor the company's future actions. Instead, Judge Kollar-Kotelly created a compliance committee of three Microsoft board members who were not company employees or officers. The committee's day-to-day activities would be run by a full-time compliance officer who would be on Microsoft's payroll but was to have a "significant amount of autonomy and independence" from the company, the judge said. That officer would be responsible for reporting violations to the compliance board, to the Justice Department, and to the states that had participated in the suit.

In addition, Kollar-Kotelly said she would continue to monitor Microsoft's compliance herself. "The court will hold Microsoft's directors, particularly those who testified before this court [a reference to Gates], responsible for implementing each provision of this remedial decree," she wrote. In a clear reference to complaints by Microsoft's competitors that the company had evaded past court rulings, the judge said she would exercise her "full panoply of powers to ensure that the letter and spirit of this remedial decree are carried out." In a similar vein, the judge ordered Microsoft not to threaten retaliation for the suit against its competitors, and she ordered Microsoft to pay the multimillion dollar legal fees of the states that had sued it.

How Microsoft Escaped

Legal experts and software industry observers offered several explanations for Microsoft's ultimate victory over those who sought more stringent regulation of its behavior. Perhaps most important, the high-technology industry evolved so quickly that it left behind the cumbersome legal and political processes of government. When the Clinton administration filed its suit against Microsoft in May 1998, the Internet browser market was still competitive, with Netscape Corporation's Navigator program holding a slight edge over Microsoft' Internet Explorer. But by the end of that year, Microsoft had taken the lead because of its decision to distribute Internet Explorer for free as part of its Windows operating system. That move ultimately cost Netscape nearly all its market share and forced the company to sell out to America Online. By the time of Judge Jackson's rulings in 1999 and 2000 and the appellate court decision in 2001, no conceivable action by the courts—not even the breakup of Microsoft—would have reversed Microsoft's newly established monopoly on Internet browsers.

Microsoft also benefited from the political calendar. The Justice Department under the Clinton administration viewed the Microsoft case as an important test of whether antitrust laws could still play a role in promoting competition. Moreover, President Bill Clinton (1993–2001) and his vice president, Al Gore, both had important political ties to many of Microsoft's competitors headquartered in the region south of San Francisco known as "Silicon Valley." George W. Bush, during his 2000 campaign, suggested the suit against Microsoft should never have been filed, and he expressed "great fear" about the prospect of Microsoft being broken in two. His administration, which took office in 2001 just as the Microsoft case was reaching a crucial stage, clearly had less interest than had the Clinton administration in government regulation of any type, including antitrust laws, to influence the behavior of private companies. Bush's Justice Department therefore took a much more conciliatory approach toward Microsoft.

In addition, Microsoft was far from passive in the political arena. Starting in the late 1990s company executives made large campaign donations to candidates for statewide and national offices, most of them Republicans, in states such as North Carolina that had taken part in the antitrust case. North Carolina was among the states that accepted the Justice Department's settlement in 2001.

Finally, Microsoft benefited from developments that were beyond its control. One example was Judge Jackson's decision in late 2000 to tell reporters about his anger at Microsoft and Gates. Jackson's intemperate remarks resulted in the removal from the case of a judge who had steeped himself in the arcane issues of antitrust law and computer technology and who clearly had come to view Microsoft as an unrepentant corporate bully that needed to be restrained by government action. Jackson also had previous run-ins with the appellate court that ultimately removed him from the case; in several rulings over the past decade the circuit court had demonstrated an extreme reluctance to challenge Microsoft in any serious way.

Another significant development that affected the case in Microsoft's favor was the September 11, 2001, terrorist attack against the World Trade Center towers in New York and the Pentagon near Washington. Meeting with the competing sides after that attack, Judge Kollar-Kotelly, who had no prior experience in antitrust cases, suggested the Microsoft case paled in significance compared to the threat of terrorism faced by the United States, and she demanded a new agreement among them. The states that held out did themselves no favors with Kollar-Kotelly in 2002 when they sought to introduce new evidence and new complaints about Microsoft. In scathing remarks, she wrote that they had "shown little respect" for the limits in the case that had been established by the appellate court in 2001.

Following are excerpts from the executive summary of the decision issued November 1, 2002, by U.S. District Court Judge Col-

leen Kollar-Kotelly in the case State of New York v. Microsoft Corporation, *which accepted the essential features of a settlement of the antitrust case reached in 2001 among Microsoft, the U.S. Justice Department, and nine states that had been plaintiffs in the case. Nine other states, plus the District of Columbia, had not accepted that settlement and had sought additional remedies, which were the subject of Kollar-Kotelly's decision.*

The document was obtained from the Internet at www.dcd .uscourts.gov/microsoft-2001.html; accessed November 9, 2002.

I. Appellate Opinion & Antitrust Law of Remedies

- The appellate court stated unambiguously that "we have *drastically* altered the scope of Microsoft's liability, and it is for the District Court in the first instance to determine the propriety of a specific remedy for the *limited* ground of liability we have upheld."
- The monopoly in this case was not found to have been illegally acquired, but only to have been illegally maintained. Therefore, rather than termination of the monopoly, the proper objective of the remedy in this case is termination of the exclusionary acts and practices related thereto which served to illegally maintain the monopoly.
- Ultimately, the goal of a remedy in an equitable suit is not the "punishment of past transgression, nor is it merely to end specific illegal practices." Rather, the remedy should "effectively pry open to competition a market that has been closed by [a] defendant['s] illegal restraints." Equitable relief in an antitrust case should not "embody harsh measures when less severe ones will do," nor should it adopt overly regulatory requirements which involve the judiciary in the intricacies of business management. In crafting a remedy specific to the violations, the Court "is not limited to prohibition of the proven means by which the evil was accomplished, but may range broadly through practices connected with acts actually found to be illegal."
- The "causal connection between Microsoft's exclusionary conduct and its continuing position in the operating systems market" was established "only through inference." In fact, the district court expressly determined as a factual matter that there was "insufficient evidence to find that, absent Microsoft's actions, Navigator and Java already would have ignited genuine competition in the market for Intel—compatible PC operating systems." The appellate court advised that the strength of the causal connection is to be considered "in connection with the appropriate remedy issue, i.e., whether the court should impose a structural remedy or merely enjoin the offensive conduct at issue." As a result, the Court's determination of the appropriate remedy in this case reflects, among other

considerations, the strength of the evidence linking Defendant's anticompetitive behavior to its present position in the market. It is noteworthy, however, that Plaintiffs have not persisted in their request for a structural remedy of dissolution ("a break-up of Microsoft") and instead have proposed a remedy which focuses on regulating Microsoft's behavior.

II. Theory of Liability

- The appellate court concluded that the district court properly identified the relevant market as the market for Intel-compatible PC operating systems and properly excluded middleware products from that market.
  - Operating systems perform many functions, including allocating computer memory and controlling peripherals such as printers and keyboards. Operating systems also function as platforms for software applications. They do this by "exposing"—i.e., making available to software developers—routines or protocols that perform certain widely-used functions. These are known as Application Programming Interfaces, or "APIs."
  - Because "[e]very operating system has different APIs," applications written for one operating system will not function on another operating system unless the developer undertakes the "time consuming and expensive" process of transferring and adapting, known in the industry as "porting," the application to the alternative operating system.
  - Both the district and appellate courts noted that Microsoft's lawfully-acquired monopoly is naturally protected by a "structural barrier," known as the "applications barrier to entry."
- Plaintiffs proceeded under the theory that certain kinds of software products, termed "middleware" [Such software takes the name "middleware" because "it relies on the interfaces provided by the underlying operating system while simultaneously exposing its own APIs to developers" and, therefore, is said to reside in the middle], could reduce the "applications barrier to entry" by serving as a platform for applications, taking over some of the platform functions provided by Windows and thereby "weaken[ing] the applications barrier to entry." Eventually, reasoned Plaintiffs, if applications were written to rely on the middleware API set, rather than the Windows API set, the applications could be made to run on alternative operating systems simply by porting the middleware. Ultimately, by writing to the middleware API set, applications developers could write applications which would run on any operating system on which the middleware was preset.
- Plaintiffs focused their attention primarily upon two such middleware threats to Microsoft's operating system dominance—Netscape Navigator and the Java technologies. The district and appellate courts accepted Plaintiffs' theory of competition despite the fact that "neither Navigator, Java, nor any other middleware product could [at that time], or would soon, expose enough APIs to serve as a platform for popular applications."

III. Scope of the Remedy

A. Middleware

- Integral to understanding the two remedies proposed in this case is a preliminary understanding of the manner in which the two remedies treat middleware. In simple terms, the treatment of middleware in the two remedies plays a significant role in defining the scope of products which will receive various protections under the terms of the respective remedies.

- The Court ultimately concludes that Plaintiffs' proposed definition of "middleware" is inconsonant with the treatment of the term during the liability phase of this case. Plaintiffs include in their definition of "middleware" almost any software product, without regard to the potential of the product to evolve into a true platform for other applications.

  - Plaintiffs' definition of "middleware" is irreparably flawed in its attempt to capture within their parameters all software that exposes even a single API. Plaintiffs fail to adduce evidence sufficient to establish that these various pieces of software, which often lack robust platform capabilities but expose at least one API, have the capacity to lower the applications barrier to entry, and thereby promote competition in the monopolized market. As a result, to label such software as "middleware" is not consistent with the manner in which middleware was discussed during the liability phase of this case.

  - A further flaw in Plaintiffs' treatment of middleware is the inclusion of technologies which fall outside of the relevant market and which do not pose a threat to Microsoft's monopoly similar to the threat posed by nascent middleware. While the Court does not fault Plaintiffs' general approach in looking beyond the relevant market to search for the new nascent threats, the Court is unable to conclude that Plaintiffs have established that all of these technologies have the capacity to increase competition within the relevant market.

  - The Court observes in addition that Plaintiffs' middleware definition, because of its use throughout their proposed remedy, frequently renders various provisions of Plaintiffs' remedy to be ambiguous and, therefore, unenforceable.

- Conversely, the Court finds that the treatment of middleware and the related definitions in Microsoft's proposed remedy more closely reflect the meaning given to the term from the inception of this proceeding. Microsoft's treatment of middleware appropriately expands beyond the specific middleware addressed during the liability phase to address new potential platform threats which possess many of the defining characteristics of the middleware identified by Judge Jackson. The Court's remedial decree reflects this determination, adopting the treatment of middleware advanced by Microsoft in its remedy proposal.

  - **"Non-Microsoft Middleware,"** as that term is defined in Microsoft's remedy proposal, captures the essence of the middleware threats which were discussed during the liability phase. The definition of "Non-Microsoft Middleware" expands beyond the middleware discussed at the liability phase in that it does not require that the software products already run on multiple PC operating systems, only that they have the potential, if ported to such operating systems, to serve as platforms for applications. In this regard, the term "Non-Microsoft Middleware" is noteworthy for the breadth of its coverage of software products without limitation as to specific types of functionality.

- Microsoft's proposed remedy also uses the term **"Non-Microsoft Middleware Product,"** which is defined similarly to "Non-Microsoft Middleware," but adds a requirement that "at least one million copies" of the product "were distributed in the United States within the previous year." The one-million-copies distribution requirement in the definition of "Non-Microsoft Middleware Products" is reflective of the treatment of middleware threats in this case because the district and appellate courts did not merely focus on any software with the potential to serve as a multi-purpose platform, but specifically focused upon middleware which could "gain widespread use based on its value as a complement to Windows." Because a certain portion of Microsoft's proposed remedy requires Microsoft to undertake the redesign of its own product, the one-million- copies threshold relieves Microsoft of the obligation to redesign its product to accommodate a particular piece of software with extremely limited use.

- In contrast to the broad definitions of "Non-Microsoft Middleware" and "Non-Microsoft Middleware Products," the term **"Microsoft Middleware Product"** is defined according to a specific set of existing Microsoft functionalities, as well as future Microsoft functionality. The existing set of functionalities which are included in "Microsoft Middleware Product" are those provided by Internet Explorer, Microsoft's Java Virtual Machine, Windows Media Player, Windows Messenger, Outlook Express, and their successors in Windows. The future technologies captured by the definition of "Microsoft Middleware Product" encompass software included in Windows that provides the functionality of Internet browsers, email client software, networked audio/ video client software, and instant messaging software. Other future technologies captured in the definition of "Microsoft Middleware Product" are those functionalities which are both distributed as part of Windows and distributed separately from Windows by Microsoft, trademarked by Microsoft, and which compete with third-party middleware products.

- In portions of Microsoft's proposed remedy, there is a need to identify the specific code in Windows. Hence, Microsoft's remedy proposal uses term **"Microsoft Middleware,"** which is largely reflective of the definition of "Microsoft Middleware Product," but which is further limited to the code separately distributed and trademarked or marketed as a major version of the Microsoft Middleware Product. The term "Microsoft Middleware" is used sparingly in Microsoft's remedy proposal, with its most significant and prominent use arising in conjunction with a provision that requires Microsoft to disclose very specific APIs and related technical information

B. New Technologies

- Plaintiffs have identified certain technologies which, prior to this remedy proceeding, had not been addressed by the district and appellate courts in detail in conjunction with this case. Plaintiffs identify these technologies as the new frontier in "middleware platform threats" and, therefore, seek to include these technologies in the definition of "middleware" and related definitions. The Court examined four categories of technologies in order to determine if Plaintiffs' proposal to encompass these technologies within the remedy is appropriate: (1) network and server-based applications; (2) interactive television middleware and set-top boxes; (3) handheld devices; and (4) Web services.
- The Court concludes that **server/network computing** has the capacity to function in a role akin to middleware, and therefore, over Microsoft's objection, the Court addresses this technology in a portion of the remedy.
- The potential "threat" posed by **interactive television software** is almost entirely hypothetical. However, the Court notes that, if interactive television software is proven, in the future, to have been ported from TV set-top boxes to run on a Microsoft PC operating system and expose a range of functionality to ISVs [a software company other than Microsoft—independent software vendor] through published APIs, such technology would be included automatically in a number of the Court's remedy provisions.
- Plaintiffs advance four theories pursuant to which **handheld devices** pose a "platform threat to the Windows operating system." The Court rejects each of these theories as either logically flawed or unsupported by the evidence. In short, the technology associated with handheld devices has not been shown to have the potential to function in a manner similar to "middleware" consistent with the liability phase.
- Plaintiffs argue that **Web services,** which are entirely distinct from Web browsing, carry the potential to decrease reliance upon personal computers while increasing reliance upon other computing devices, emphasizing that a number of non-PC devices will have the capacity to access Web services. The Court rejects this argument on the grounds that Plaintiffs have not explained how the increase in the use of non-PC devices in conjunction with Web services will reduce Microsoft's monopoly in the market for PC operating systems.
  - The Court's rejection of Plaintiffs' inclusion in the remedy of handheld devices and Web services is based, in part, upon the conclusion that mere reduction in the popularity of the PC and the ensuing reduction in the absolute demand for Microsoft's Windows operating system does not necessarily "pry open to competition" the market for PC operating systems.

IV. Alleged "Bad" Acts by Microsoft

- Throughout this phase of the proceeding, Plaintiffs have recited for the Court's benefit countless findings of fact entered by Judge Jackson during the liability phase regarding actions taken by Microsoft. These findings recount various actions taken by Microsoft which can be characterized as improper or unsavory in one respect or another and, at the very least, harmful to its competitors. Significantly however, many of these findings were ultimately not relied upon by the district and appellate courts in conjunction with the imposition of liability for violation of § 2 of the Sherman Act [the Sherman Antitrust Act, under which the suit against Microsoft was filed].

- As the appellate court observed, "[e]ven an act of pure malice by one business competitor against another does not, without more, state a claim under the federal antitrust laws . . . ." The federal antitrust laws "do not create a federal law of unfair competition or 'purport to afford remedies for all torts committed by or against persons engaged in interstate commerce.' " Harm to "one or more competitors," *however severe*, is not condemned by the Sherman Act in the absence of harm to the competitive process and thereby harm to consumers. Because no court has yet found that the acts identified in Judge Jackson's *Findings of Fact*, but not relied upon for the imposition of liability, visited *any* harm upon competition, let alone a harm which was not outweighed by the simultaneous procompetitive effect, this Court cannot presume that each of the acts identified in the *Findings of Fact* merits consideration equal with those acts which were found to be anticompetitive, nor that these acts merit any special weight.

- The parties have agreed throughout this proceeding that it would be inappropriate now, during the remedy phase of this proceeding, for the Court to consider and evaluate for anticompetitive effect new allegations against Microsoft.

- Nevertheless, Plaintiffs identify a number of new and, for lack of a better term, allegedly "bad" acts, relating predominantly to interoperability, taken by Microsoft both prior and subsequent to the imposition of liability. Upon review of Plaintiffs' allegations of "bad" conduct by Microsoft relating to interoperability and the liability findings in this case, the Court concludes that Plaintiffs' allegations in this area bear only a remote relationship to the liability findings. In this regard, the Court has rejected Plaintiffs' suggestion that the imposition of liability, in any way, condemns decisions to depart from industry standards or to utilize a proprietary standard in the absence of deception regarding the departure. In fact, Microsoft's alteration or proprietary extension of industry standards more closely resembles conduct for which Microsoft was absolved of liability; the appellate court absolved Microsoft of liability for its development of a Java implementation incompatible with Sun's Java Implementation

- Moreover, despite Plaintiffs' protestations to the contrary, the Court finds that Plaintiffs' allegations with regard to Microsoft's conduct in the area of interoperability are, at their core, new allegations of anticompetitive conduct. As a result, Plaintiffs' reliance upon this series of allegedly new "bad" acts by Microsoft carries little weight, if any, in the Court's determination of the appropriate remedy in this case.

V. Remedy-Specific Conclusions

A. Original Equipment Manufacturer ("OEM") Configuration Flexibility

1. *Windows Licenses*

- The remedy imposed by the Court will provide substantial freedom to OEMs in their configuration of Microsoft's Windows operating system by lifting Microsoft's illegal license restrictions.

- The Court rejects the third-party licensing portion of Plaintiffs' proposal that would permit such third parties to "customize" the appearance of Windows to reflect the third party's input. Plaintiffs have failed to establish that such licensing will actually benefit or promote competition. Additionally, Plaintiffs' proposal for third-party licensing does not reflect the appellate court's recognition that, to the extent that Microsoft's license restrictions prevented drastic alteration of the user interface, they did not violate the Sherman Act.

2. *Installation and Display of Icons, Shortcuts, and Menu Entries*

- Microsoft will be enjoined from restricting by agreement any OEM licensee from installing an icon, menu entry, shortcut, product, or service related to "Non-Microsoft Middleware."

- The remedy imposed by the Court will secure for OEMs the general ability to install and display icons, shortcuts, and menu entries for middleware—the type of software disfavored by Microsoft's anticompetitive restrictions—on the Windows desktop or in the Start menu.

- However, the Court will not prevent Microsoft from imposing nondiscriminatory limitations on the specific areas in which icons may be displayed, provided that such limitations cannot be used to favor Microsoft and, instead, exist as part of the Windows product design. The Court's remedy will also permit Microsoft to protect the design of its product from drastic alteration in a manner which is the substantial equivalent of a launching of a new user interface, such as OEM designation of an icon in such an extreme size or shape that it obscures the crucial elements of the Windows user interface.

3. *Insertion of Internet Access Provider ("IAP") Registration Offers*

- The remedial decree imposed by the Court will enjoin Microsoft from imposing license restrictions on the ability of OEMs to insert offers of service from IAPs during the initial boot sequence. The insertion of these offers was found to provide an opportunity for the promotion of alternative middleware. Microsoft's limitation on the ability of OEMs to insert such offers was found to have an anticompetitive effect in violation of antitrust law.

- The Court rejects Microsoft's argument that the insertion of IAP registration sequences should be subject to the imposition of Microsoft's "reasonable technical requirements" on the rationale that such requirements preserve a consistent user experience.

4. *Automatic Launching of Applications*

- It is appropriate for the remedy in this case to permit the automatic launch of non-Microsoft programs upon the completion of the initial boot sequence where the automatically launched program does not substitute the Windows user interface for a different interface or otherwise drastically alter Microsoft's copyrighted work.
- The Court has tailored its remedy to permit the automatic launch of such programs because the ability to launch programs automatically will assist in the promotion of non-Microsoft software and middleware, resulting in an increased likelihood that a particular piece of middleware will reach its potential to serve as a multi-purpose platform for applications.
- The Court, therefore, specifically rejects the contention by Microsoft that automatic launching of software products should be limited to circumstances in which Microsoft has chosen to launch automatically a competing middleware program.

B. End-User Access

- The Court's remedial order will require Microsoft to alter its Windows technology to ensure that OEMs and end users may disable end-user access to various types of Windows functionality. In addition, the Court will prohibit Microsoft from designing its operating system product so as to induce reconfiguration of an OEM's or consumer's formatting of icons, shortcuts, and menu entries in an attempt to favor Microsoft's own software.
- Plaintiffs have advanced a remedy that requires the removal of Windows software code. Yet, Plaintiffs' remedy proposal does not offer a reasonable way for Microsoft to separate the code in order to comply with the code removal requirements therein. More importantly, the evidence does not indicate that the removal of software code is beneficial from an economic perspective. The Court also finds that the forced removal of software code from the Windows operating system will disrupt the industry, harming both ISVs and consumers.
- Nothing in the rationale underlying the commingling liability finding requires removal of software code to remedy the violation. To the contrary, the evidence presented to the Court indicates that the ability to remove end-user access to any commingled functionality would sufficiently address the anticompetitive aspect of the conduct and would prove far less disruptive to consumers and industry participants. In the case of com-

mingling, therefore, the most appropriate remedy must place paramount significance upon addressing the exclusionary effect of the commingling, rather than the mere conduct which gives rise to the effect.

C. Additional Protection for OEM Flexibility

- Because the OEM channel is such a significant channel of distribution for middleware, the remedy in this case can further unfetter the market from the effects of Microsoft's unlawful anticompetitive behavior by protecting OEMs from retaliation by Microsoft based upon an OEM's support for alternative middleware or operating systems. Nevertheless, restrictions on Microsoft's freedom to retaliate or threaten retaliation must be carefully drawn so as not to unduly restrict legitimate business practices.
- Over Microsoft's objection, the Court finds that protection of OEMs against threats of retaliation as well as acts of retaliation will have an effect similar to a ban on actual retaliation and, thus, will further the ultimate goal of promoting competition.
- Further protection for OEMs as a middleware channel of distribution is available through the implementation of uniformity in the licenses Microsoft provides in the monopoly market. To tailor the uniform licensing provision so as to provide OEMs with the greatest security, while minimizing the less desirable collateral effects of uniformity, the Court's order of remedy will not prohibit Microsoft's practice of awarding "market development allowances, programs, or other discounts" ("MDPs"), provided that the award of such benefits is based upon reasonable, objective criteria, which are enforced uniformly and without discrimination.
- Additional protection for OEMs and their ability to exercise their rights under the remedy imposed in this case can be derived from limited regulation of Microsoft's ability to terminate an OEM's Windows license. Microsoft shall not be permitted to terminate an OEM's license without having first provided the OEM with notice and opportunity to cure. When Microsoft has provided two such notices, Microsoft may terminate the license without any further notice or opportunity to cure.

D. Other Participants in the Ecosystem

1. *Ban on Retaliation*

- Microsoft is not permitted to retaliate against ISVs and Independent Hardware Vendors ("IHVs") for their support of platform software that competes with Microsoft's PC operating system software. In addition, the Court will prohibit threats of retaliation, which have the capacity to chill ISV and IHV support for competing products even where the retaliation itself is prohibited.

2. *Agreements Limiting Support for Competing Products*

- The Court's remedy will preclude Microsoft from entering into agreements predicated upon an ISV's promise to refrain from developing, promoting, or distributing any software which competes with the platform capabilities of Microsoft software. Such a provision will ensure that Microsoft is unable to chill the development of competing software products which may provide a platform for PC applications.

- Because a remedy which "dampen[s] . . . technological innovation would be at cross-purposes with antitrust law," and because Plaintiffs have not offered any valid justification for prohibiting such agreements, the remedy in this case is carefully tailored so as not to hinder Microsoft's ability to enter into legitimate joint ventures and work-for-hire agreements.

3. *Exclusive Agreements*

- The Court's remedial decree will limit Microsoft's ability to enter into agreements in which the other party agrees to support Microsoft's operating system products exclusively or in a fixed percentage. This provision will address those industry participants with whom Microsoft entered into unlawful and anticompetitive exclusive agreements, namely ISVs, IAPs, and OEMs, as well as those industry participants, such as Internet Content Providers ("ICPs") and IHVs, who are ready targets for the imposition of similarly unlawful exclusive agreements.
- Again, in recognition of the benefit to technology and to competition derived from cooperative agreements between industry participants, the Court's remedy takes pains not to discourage Microsoft from entering into legitimate joint ventures and joint development agreements. In this regard, Microsoft will have some limited ability to prohibit competition with the object of the joint venture or joint agreement, where both parties have contributed significant resources to the venture.

4. *Agreements Regarding Placement on the Desktop*

- The Court's remedy will include a provision which addresses the particular means of leverage Microsoft used to induce IAPs to enter into these agreements; namely, special placement on the desktop or elsewhere in Microsoft's PC operating system products of a visible means of end-user access to the third-party product. Therefore, the remedy imposed by the Court shall prohibit Microsoft from granting special placement within the Windows operating system on the condition that the IAP refrain from support of software which competes with not merely Microsoft's Web-browsing technology, but also a number of technologies incorporated into Windows which portray middleware characteristics such that they are properly treated as "Microsoft Middleware." This provision applies to ICPs as well as IAPs, notwithstanding the fact that the appellate court declined to impose liability for Microsoft's exclusive agreements with ICPs.

E. Explicitly Forward-Looking Remedies

1. *API Disclosures (Interoperation between Windows and Microsoft Middleware)*

- The remedy imposed by the Court with regard to the disclosure of APIs shall require Microsoft to disclose those APIs, along with related technical information, which "Microsoft Middleware" utilizes to interoperate with the Windows platform.

2. *Communications Protocols (Interoperation Between PC Operating Systems and Server Operating Systems)*

- The remedy imposed by the Court will mandate disclosure and licensing of protocols used by clients running on Microsoft's Windows operating system to interoperate with Microsoft servers.
- In all likelihood, the requirement that Microsoft disclose and license the communications protocols utilized by its PC operating systems to communicate with Microsoft's servers is the most forward-looking provision in the Court's remedy.

3. *Plaintiffs' Flawed Arguments for Overly Broad Disclosures*

- Plaintiffs are unable to establish a satisfactory link between the interoperability disclosures they seek and the liability in this case.
- Over-broad disclosure, such as that proposed by Plaintiffs, must also be avoided because it will likely enable wholesale copying or cloning By cloning, the Court means the creation of a piece of software which replicates the functions of another piece of software, even if the replication is accomplished by some means other than the literal repetition of the same source code] of Windows without violating Microsoft's intellectual property rights. The cloning of Microsoft's technology carries the potential to hinder some aspects of competition and discourage innovation. As antitrust law does not exist for the protection of competitors, but for the protection of competition, the Court does not regard this end as a legitimate one.
- The Court finds that there is sufficient harm which flows from the mandated disclosure of a vast quantity of internal interfaces which is not countermanded by competitive benefit such that it is best not to require Microsoft to disclose a multitude of internal interfaces. There exist a number of technical justifications for operating system vendors to decline to make such internal interfaces public. For example, internal interfaces are often unstable, meaning that they will not perform effectively when relied upon by third-party applications.

4. *Reasonable, Non-Discriminatory Licenses*

- Although the Court has rejected Plaintiffs' request for the broad disclosure of technical information relating to Microsoft's products, the Court's remedial decree will require Microsoft to make more limited disclosures of APIs, communications protocols, and related technical information in order to facilitate interoperability.
- The Court will prohibit Microsoft from imposing unreasonable or discriminatory license terms, but will permit Microsoft to require a reasonable royalty for the licenses necessary to exercise the rights guaranteed by the final judgment.

5. *Protection Against Hackers, Viruses and Piracy*

- The Court's remedy will exempt certain material from disclosure in order to preserve the security of Microsoft products against hackers and viruses. Similarly, Microsoft will not be forced to disclose valuable information to firms with a history of piracy, so long as Microsoft does not use claims of piracy as a means by which to discriminate.

F. Compliance and Enforcement Provisions

- The scheme envisioned by Plaintiffs for enforcing the injunctive decree entered as the remedy in this case is marked by its reliance upon a special master. In light of the applicable law, the Court harbors serious concerns as to the propriety of Plaintiffs' proposed use of a special master. Even if the Court were confident that Plaintiffs' proposed use of a special master was legally sound, such a conclusion would not allay the Court's remaining concerns with regard to the logistical difficulties in Plaintiffs' special master proposal. Accordingly, the Court declines to appoint a special master at this time.

- The remedy in this case will charge Plaintiffs with the obligation of monitoring Microsoft's compliance. While Plaintiffs may rely upon the views of third parties to guide them in this task, the duty of enforcement belongs to Plaintiffs. To ease the burden on the Court and on Microsoft in addressing Plaintiffs' concerns, the Court will require Plaintiffs to form a committee to coordinate enforcement of the remedial decree. Such a committee will serve to minimize duplication of enforcement activities and requests of the Court and Microsoft.

- Plaintiffs have been unwaveringly critical of Microsoft's proposal for a technical committee. As the technical committee provision exists largely to assist Plaintiffs in enforcing the provisions of the final judgment in this case, if Plaintiffs do not want to rely upon a technical committee, the Court will not require them to do so.

- The Court adopts Plaintiffs' proposal for selecting a compliance officer who serves as a high-level Microsoft employee, but retains a significant amount of autonomy and independence from the corporation.

- The Court adopts Microsoft's proposal that the compliance officer distribute the decree and obtain a certification of understanding and compliance only from Microsoft's officers and directors.

- The remedy adopted by the Court will provide Plaintiffs, acting only after consultation with their enforcement committee, reasonable access to Microsoft's source code, books, ledgers, accounts, correspondence, memoranda, and other correspondence, access to Microsoft employees for interview, and the right to request and receive written reports from Microsoft on any matter contained in the Court's remedial decree. Plaintiffs will, of course, be bound to limit any use of information obtained through these means for the purpose of ensuring Microsoft's compliance with the remedial decree, or as otherwise required by law. Similarly, should information and documents provided to Plaintiffs be subject to disclosure to a third party, Microsoft will not be deprived of the opportunity to claim protection pursuant to Federal Rule of Civil Procedure 26(c)(7).

G. Term of the Decree

- The Court's remedial decree shall persist for five years from its effective date.
- As an incentive for Microsoft to comply with the terms of the decree, however, the Court specifically reserves the right to extend the term of the decree for up to two years upon a finding that Microsoft has engaged in a pattern of willful and systemic violation of the Court's decree.

Conclusion

Recognizing, as they must, the confluence of the rapid pace of change in the software industry and the delays inherent in antitrust litigation, Plaintiffs sought to gather all existing complaints regarding Microsoft's business practices and bring them before the Court at this late stage in the case. In doing so, Plaintiffs attempted to circumvent the arduous process which necessarily precedes the imposition of antitrust liability and, instead, proceeded directly to seek a remedy for the readily identifiable aspects of Microsoft's business conduct that other industry participants find objectionable. Though an appropriate remedy may be forward-looking and address conduct beyond the specific acts found to be anticompetitive, Plaintiffs are mistaken in thinking that the imposition of Section 2 liability under the Sherman Act for unlawful monopoly maintenance in the market for Intel-compatible PC operating systems permits the Court to impose a remedy in areas unrelated to the monopoly market. This suit, however remarkable, is not the vehicle through which Plaintiffs can resolve all existing allegations of anticompetitive conduct which have not been proven or for which liability has not been ascribed.

The appellate court could not have been clearer in its admonition that this Court's decree should be "tailored to fit the wrong creating the occasion for the remedy." Yet despite this admonition, in their request for relief, Plaintiffs have shown little respect for the parameters of liability that were so precisely delineated by the appellate court. In many instances, therefore, this Court has had little choice but to reject Plaintiffs' remedial suggestions on the grounds that they are unjustifiably in conflict with the imposition as well as the rejection of liability in this case.

Additionally, the Court observes that a number of the remedial provisions proposed by Plaintiffs would require drastic alterations to Microsoft's products, as well as to aspects of its business model which do not involve illegal conduct. Plaintiffs present little, if any, legitimate justification for these remedies, and in most instances, these proposals are not supported by any economic analysis. Instead, it appears that these types of remedial provisions seek to convert certain legitimate aspects of Microsoft's business model and/or product design into a model which resembles that of other industry participants simply for the sake of changing the status quo. Certain of Microsoft's competitors appear to be those who most desire these provisions and, concomitantly, are the likely beneficiaries of these provisions, while other competitors in the relevant market would not necessarily benefit. In bringing these types of proposals before the Court, Plaintiffs again misunderstand the task presently before the Court—to remedy Microsoft's antitrust violations. General changes to the lawful aspects of Microsoft's business model or product design of the type proposed by Plaintiffs do not themselves provide a remedy, nor have Plaintiffs established that such changes are required, or even appropriate, in conjunction with a remedy. Accordingly, the Court has rejected those aspects of Plaintiffs' remedy proposal which would impose such changes.

Instead, the appropriate remedy, which the Court has devised and explained at length in the full Memorandum Opinion, is carefully tailored to fit the wrong creating the occasion for the remedy. The Court's remedy exceeds a mere proscription of the precise conduct found to be anticompetitive and is forward-looking in the parameters of the relief provided. Moreover, the remedy imposed by the Court is crafted to foster competition in the monopolized market in a manner consistent with the theory of liability in this case.

In particular, the Court's remedy addresses, to the extent appropriate, Plaintiffs' desire that Microsoft disclose technical information to foster interoperation between Microsoft's PC operating system software and third-party products, as well as between Microsoft's PC operating system products and server operating systems. The mandatory disclosures between Microsoft's monopoly product and server operating systems acknowledge the competitive significance of server/ network computing as the most significant "platform threat" to Microsoft's dominance in the relevant market. The disclosures mandated by the Court will likely prove beneficial to the development of middleware platforms and the functional equivalent of the middleware platform provided by server operating systems.

Likewise, the Court's remedy satisfies Plaintiffs' demand for remedial provisions which address OEM flexibility in the configuration of Microsoft's operating system products, but is tempered by the necessary respect for Microsoft's intellectual property rights. In this regard, the Court has largely rejected Microsoft's paternalistic view that it can determine what is best for consumers with regard to the configuration of the Windows operating system. In rejecting this view, the Court's remedy affords OEMs the freedom to configure Microsoft's operating system products in a manner which promotes third-party middleware through the prominent display of icons, shortcuts, and menu entries, and such configuration will be protected against automatic alteration resulting from Microsoft's product design. In addition, OEMs will have the freedom to remove all prominent means of end-user access to portions of middleware functionality integrated into Microsoft's operating system so as to encourage the installation of third-party middleware. The Court's remedial decree also ensures that OEMs may introduce subscription services during the boot sequence without restriction by unjustified Microsoft technical requirements. Further secured by the terms of the Court's decree is the automatic launching of innovative software programs limited only by the requirement that the programs not drastically alter the Windows user interface.

In its order of remedy, the Court has heeded Plaintiffs' call for broad protection for OEMs, ISVs, and IHVs against retaliation and threats of retaliation by Microsoft for the support of products that compete with Microsoft's monopoly product. The Court's remedy further curtails Microsoft's ability to enter into agreements that have the effect of excluding competitors from the marketplace. The Court's prohibition on exclusionary contracts is carefully drawn, however, so as to foster, rather than prohibit, procompetitive joint ventures, work-for-hire agreements, and intellectual property licenses. Notwithstanding these affirmative measures, the Court's remedy, of necessity, stops short of any measure which will substantially discourage procompetitive joint ventures, require the substantial redesign of Microsoft's products, or otherwise interfere in Microsoft's lawful use of proprietary technology.

Throughout all of its provisions, the Court's remedial order is generous in its treatment middleware platform threats. The defined terms in the Court's order are appropriately grounded in the theory of liability and the treatment of middleware platform threats during the liability phase, while simultaneously prescient in that they are not confined to technology which exists today. Most notable is the scope of the term "Non-Microsoft Middleware," which captures a wide array of existing platform technology, as well as technology not yet developed. In this regard, even the technologies which Plaintiffs have identified as future potential platform threats, such as interactive television middleware—whose success is but a prediction, will be addressed by the Court's remedial order, provided the aspirations of these technologies become reality.

Plaintiffs are correct that Microsoft has a tendency to minimize the effects of its illegal conduct. Yet this minimization, however frustrating, does not require a remedy which prodigiously exceeds even an expansive view of the illegal conduct. The remedy in this case addresses the conduct found by the district and appellate courts to violate the antitrust laws and is imposed without regard to Microsoft's minimalist view of its own illegal conduct. More importantly, the behavioral remedy imposed by this Court neither bends nor softens simply because Microsoft refuses to acknowledge the extent of its own wrongdoing.

During this litigation, promises have been made on behalf of Microsoft that the company will change its predatory practices which have been part of its competitive strategy in order to comply with the remedial decree. The Court will hold Microsoft's directors, particularly those who testified before this Court, responsible for implementing each provision of this remedial decree. Let it not be said of Microsoft that "a prince never lacks legitimate reasons to break his promise," [a quote from Machiavelli, *The Prince*] for this Court will exercise its full panoply of powers to ensure that the letter and spirit of this remedial decree are carried out.

PRESIDENT BUSH DELIVERS A MIDTERM CAMPAIGN SPEECH
November 4, 2002

Although his name did not appear on any election ballot, President George W. Bush was the big winner of the 2002 midterm congressional elections when his Republican Party regained control of the Senate it had lost to the Democrats in 2001 and added to its slim majority in the House of Representatives. The president had put his prestige on the line by campaigning nearly nonstop for GOP candidates in close races in the weeks running up to the November 5 election. The victories strengthened not only Bush's ability to control the legislative agenda but also his own political position going into the 2004 presidential election campaign. "We made history tonight. It was a great win for the president of the United States," chortled Rep. Thomas M. Davis III, R-Va., chairman of the Republican Congressional Campaign Committee.

Democrats, who had hoped to increase their majority in the Senate and possibly even win control of the House, were stunned by their losses—a net total of two in the Senate and six in the House. Political analysts agreed that the party and its candidates had failed because they offered no clear or convincing alternatives to Republican policies. "Democrats pawed and slapped and poked at Bush, but they never really expended the effort to take a good shot at him," said Dan Schnur, a Republican consultant in California. Analysts also agreed that the dismal midterm election results, together with the lack of any clear party leaders, dimmed Democratic hopes of taking back the White House in 2004.

One immediate consequence of the elections was the resignation of Democrat Richard A. Gephardt of Missouri as House minority leader. Gephardt said he was stepping down to prepare for a possible run for the Democratic presidential nomination, but others suggested he was also seeking to avoid a challenge to his position from Democrats disgruntled by the elections results and by Gephardt's early decision to back Bush on his request for authorization to use force in Iraq. Another immediate consequence was passage of a bill creating a Department of Homeland Security that was to be responsible for counterterrorism. The bill had been stalemated in the Senate over a controversy between Bush and Democrats on personnel rules for employees of the new department—a stalemate that Bush and the Republicans were able to turn to their advantage in several close election races.

Bush's victories did not stop with the elections. On November 8 he won unanimous approval from the United Nations Security Council for a resolution calling on Iraqi dictator Saddam Hussein to get rid of his weapons of mass destruction or face the consequences. Congress had already given Bush the go-ahead on the use of force, although a majority of Democrats in the House voted against the president and their own party leader. Bush was also reported to be satisfied by the resignation in late December of Trent Lott as Republican leader in the Senate and the election of Bill Frist of Tennessee as Lott's replacement. Lott was forced to resign after making remarks that appeared to lament the passing of the era of racial segregation. (Iraq resolution, p. 713; Lott resignation, p. 969)

Bush was only the second president in the last hundred years to make midterm gains in both chambers and only the third to gain midterm seats in the House. Franklin D. Roosevelt gained Democratic seats in both chambers in 1934; Bill Clinton won Democratic seats in the House in 1998, while sustaining no gains or losses in the Senate. Political commentators were uncertain, however, whether congressional Republicans would be able to form a strong enough majority to enact Bush's agenda. The GOP had only fifty-one seats in the Senate, not enough to stop any filibuster if the Democratic opposition stayed united. Although the GOP had margin of twenty-four votes over the Democrats in the House, philosophical differences among House Republicans threatened the party from acting cohesively. Conservative Republicans, who dominated the leadership and held most other key positions, were expected to push legislative proposals that more centrist members feared would alienate moderate voters. Democrats were expected to have little incentive to cooperate under any circumstances. Still Bush interpreted the victory as a mandate and began laying plans accordingly.

The Midterm Campaign

The Republican election victories were based on a combination of carefully chosen candidates, abundant campaign financing, and a strong get-out-the-vote drive. Chief White House political strategist Karl Rove was instrumental not only in recruiting candidates (and discouraging some deemed too weak to stand up against the Democratic opponent) but also in determining when and where the president and other key administration officials would appear and in shaping the message they delivered. As he put it the day before the election, "If we win, it'll be because of the president and the quality of our candidates and our campaigns. If we lose, it will be because of me."

Bush appeared at sixty-seven fund-raising events all over the country, raising more than $144 million for GOP candidates, including $8 million for his brother, Gov. Jeb Bush of Florida. Republican campaign committees *had more than $525 million in their campaign coffers, compared with less than $350 million for the Democrats. Special interest groups spent far less than the two parties. The organization that spent the most was the United Seniors Association, a group composed mainly of pharmaceutical companies that spent an estimated $12 million, primarily on Republican candidates who supported the drug company position on prescription drug pricing.* (Prescription drug advertising, p. 945)

The Republican Party also mounted a massive voter registration drive early in the year and a get-out-the-vote drive that used modern technology and old-fashioned door-to-door footwork to identify specific voters and get them to the voting booth. Texas Republican Tom DeLay, the House whip in line to become majority leader in the 108th Congress, set up his own voter turnout project to help House candidates. With the support of the Republican National Committee, DeLay asked Republican legislators in safe seats to bring volunteers to help turn out the vote in nearby congressional districts where the Republican was in a close race. In the last three days before the election DeLay moved 8,000 volunteers to targeted districts. The voter turnout efforts appeared to work. Overall turnout was up from the 1998 midterm elections, with slightly more than 39 percent of all eligible voters going to the polls. Democratic turnout was down 1.3 percentage points, while Republican turnout increased by 0.5 percentage point, according to an analysis by the Committee for the Study of the American Electorate.

The catalyst in the days before the election was the president himself. During the final week of campaigning, Bush made seventeen stops in fifteen states on behalf of Republican Senate candidates in tight races. At each stop he delivered a fairly standard stump speech that acknowledged but deemphasized the nation's economic problems; called for enactment of popular programs, such as prescription drug pricing for seniors, without going into details; and blamed the Democrats—"the bunch running the Senate"—for not approving his judicial nominees or passing legislation creating a homeland security department. "Here we are with an enemy lurking out there, and the bill got stuck in the Senate" because the Democrats refused to allow him to put "the right people at the right place at the right time to protect you," Bush said at a stop in Dallas on November 4, on behalf of Republican Senate candidate John Cornyn. Bush then typically appealed to the patriotism of his audience, asking listeners to support him in the war on terrorism and his efforts to rid Iraq of weapons of mass destruction.

Democrats were reluctant to challenge Bush on Iraq—many of them had supported the president in his call for authority to use force if necessary— and they were unable to swing the electorate's attention away from Iraq and the war on terror to domestic issues, including the souring economy. "The national Democratic Party never defined the Democratic agenda," Dick Harpootlian, chairman of the South Carolina Democratic Party, told the New York Times. *"Other than being sort of whiney as we got dragged into the Iraq war, we never really defined our position on the economy, we never said what we would do differently. We [had] no message this year other than we're not Bush. Well, guess what? Eighty percent of the people like Bush."*

The Results

The Democrats lost Senate seats in Georgia, Minnesota, and Missouri and failed to win against vulnerable Republicans in Colorado and New Hampshire. Democrats picked up one Senate seat in Arkansas and held onto seats in South Dakota and Louisiana, where Bush had campaigned hard for the Republican challengers. That put the party breakdown at fifty-one Republicans, forty-eight Democrats, and one independent, James M. Jeffords of Vermont, whose switch from the Republican Party in May 2001 had given Democrats control of the Senate for most of Bush's first two years in office. (Jeffords switch, Historic Documents of 2001, p. 377)

The attack on the Democrats' stand on homeland security was widely seen as the key factor in the defeat of Democratic senators Max Cleland of Georgia and Jean Carnahan of Missouri. Bush appeared twice in Georgia to stump for Cleland's opponent, Rep. Saxby Chambliss, and Chambliss was aided by a negative ad campaign that accused Cleland—a triple amputee veteran of the Vietnam War—of being unpatriotic. Chambliss's victory helped Republicans oust the Democratic governor, a surprise upset. It was the first time since Reconstruction that Georgia had elected a Republican governor. Carnahan had been appointed to the Senate in 2000 for two years after her husband, Mel Carnahan, won the Senate election that year even though he had been killed in a plane crash three weeks before the election. The winner of the 2002 race, Jim Talent, was to complete the four years remaining in that Senate seat.

Republicans also won in another race where the Democratic candidate died just before the election. In Minnesota, Sen. Paul Wellstone was locked in a tight race with former St. Paul mayor Norm Coleman when Wellstone, his wife, daughter, and several campaign workers were killed in a plane crash less than two weeks before the election. The state Democratic Party enlisted former vice president and senator Walter Mondale to run in Wellstone's place, but Coleman won the election with barely more than 50 percent of the vote.

In New Jersey, however, former Democratic senator Frank J. Lautenberg handily won election after entering the race in early October to replace New Jersey senator Robert Torricelli. Torricelli had suddenly withdrawn from the race on September 30 after polls showed him losing to a Republican who constantly pummeled Torricelli on allegations that he had accepted improper campaign gifts and was thus unfit to hold public office. Torricelli, who had survived a criminal probe of his campaign finances and an admonishment from the Senate Ethics Committee for using "poor judgment," denied Douglas Forrester's allegations but apparently could not deny the polling data. "I will not be responsible for the loss of the Democratic majority of the U.S. Senate," Torricelli said as he announced he was leaving the campaign. Republicans challenged the last-minute substitution all the way to the Supreme Court, perhaps hoping for a repeat of the 2000 presidential election when the Court intervened to rule against a recount of several thousand disputed ballots in Florida, thus handing the election to George Bush. In 2002, however, the Court refused to review the New Jersey supreme court's ruling allowing Lautenberg's name to go on the ballot. (2000 election controversy, Historic Documents of 2000, p. 999)

One of the newly elected members of the House was Katherine Harris, the former Republican secretary of state in Florida who was at the center of the ballot controversy between Bush and Democrat Al Gore in 2000. Only sixteen House incumbents who ran for reelection in 2002 lost, eight in the primaries and eight in the general election. In four House races redistricting forced two incumbents to face each other. Republicans won three of those races, Democrats the fourth. Overall, redistricting, which was required by the 2000 census, benefited the Republicans, who picked up a majority of the new seats and stabilized many of the Republican incumbents who had been elected by narrow margins in previous elections. The biggest change facing House members of both parties was likely to be in their leadership. In addition to Gephardt's decision to step down as House minority leader, House majority leader Dick Armey of Texas and Republican conference chairman J.C. Watts Jr. of Oklahoma were both retiring from Congress.

Perhaps the sweetest election victory for Bush was neither a Senate nor a House race but the reelection of his brother Jeb to the governorship of Florida. Democrats had targeted Jeb Bush as payback for the ballot confrontation in Florida that gave George Bush the presidential election in the electoral college even though Vice President Gore had won the popular vote. Both former president Bill Clinton (1993–2001) and Gore campaigned in the state for Tampa lawyer Bill McBride, who had defeated Janet Reno, attorney general in the Clinton administration, in the Democratic primary. But it was not enough to overcome the Bush brothers. The governor mounted the most expensive gubernatorial campaign in Florida history and, helped by strategically timed campaign appearances by the president, handily defeated McBride. Florida had installed new voting equipment to replace the punch-card ballots that had created the deadlock in 2000, and numerous malfunctions and confusion occurred during the trial run in the September primaries. But the balloting went reasonably smoothly in November, as it did in the rest of the nation.

Another sign that the Republicans had deepened their appeal came at the state level. Republicans held onto more of their governorships than had been expected, maintaining a 26–24 lead over the Democrats. For the first time since 1954 more Republicans held state legislative seats than Democrats. After the elections, the GOP controlled the legislature in twenty-one states, up from seventeen. Democrats controlled seventeen, down one. Control was split in eleven states, and Nebraska was unicameral and nonpartisan. "Presidential and congressional returns may bounce around in response to national events, but if you are looking for the plate tectonics of American politics, look to the statehouses. Right now, the geology favors Republicans," Jack Pitney, a political scientist at Claremont McKenna College in California, told the Christian Science Monitor.

Seizing a Mandate

Bush wasted no time in taking advantage of the election night momentum. Following the GOP victory, Bush declared that the bill creating the homeland security department was the "single most important item of unfinished business" for Congress and told the lame-duck Congress not to go home until they had passed it. With that, a small group of Senate moderates, who had been working for months to find a middle ground on the work rules issue, reluctantly threw in the towel and accepted GOP language allowing the new department to write its own personnel rules. Senate Democratic leader Tom Daschle made one final attempt to put a Democratic stamp on the bill by offering an amendment ridding it of several Republican-sponsored provisions favoring corporations. That amendment failed, 47–52, and the Senate then passed the bill, 90–9. (Homeland security department, p. 530)

Before adjourning, Congress gave Bush two more victories. The first was passage of an administration-sponsored bill setting up a federal program to help private insurance companies cover claims in any future terrorist attack. The second was Senate confirmation of U.S. District Judge Dennis W. Shedd to a seat on the U.S. Court of Appeals for the Fourth Circuit. The vote was 55–44. Shedd, a former aide to retiring Republican senator Strom Thurmond of South Carolina, was opposed by civil rights organizations. Shedd's nomination was one of several controversial judicial nominations that Bush had pointed to during the campaign when he charged the Democrats with delaying action on his nominees. Bush also promised that he would renominate two nominees that the Senate had rejected, Priscilla R. Owen and Charles W. Pickering Sr., both nominees to the Fifth Circuit.

Bush also took several executive actions in the last days of the year that had been long sought by Republicans but opposed by most Democrats. On December 12 Bush announced that he was issuing an executive order directing federal agencies to give equal treatment to social service organizations without regard to religious affiliation. Bush said the action would bring to an end "a pattern of discrimination" against faith-based charities. Bush said religious organizations and other faith-based organizations should be allowed to compete for federal grants so long as they provided their services to anyone qualified for them without regard to religious affiliation. He also said that his action was intended "to ensure that religious organizations receiving federal contracts are able to take their faith into account in making employment decisions." Bush's broader Faith-Based and Community Initiative had stalled in the Senate, in part because some senators were concerned that it would allow religious organizations to discriminate in their hiring practices. (Faith-based initiative, Historic Documents of 2001, p. 132)

Under another new regulation, the government would be able to open up several "commercial activities" it currently conducted for competition from private industry. Commercial activities included a broad range of activities from ground and building maintenance to secretarial services and covered an estimated 850,000 federal jobs, about half of the government's civilian workforce. Such a move had long been opposed by labor unions.

The Bush administration also issued new rules easing regulations on pollution by old industrial plants—something that manufacturers had long requested. Environmental groups said it was just the latest in a series of steps the administration had taken to relax standards meant to safeguard the nation's air, land, and water from pollution and environmental degradation. They were anticipating renewed attempts by Republicans and the energy industry in 2003 to open the Arctic National Wildlife Refuge to oil drilling. Bush had already made that his top energy priority. (Environmental issues, p. 894)

Meanwhile business lobbyists and economic conservatives were gearing up to push for several items on their agenda. Chief among these was likely to be a new campaign to make the massive tax cuts Congress passed in 2001 permanent and to lobby for new tax cuts they fully expected the president to offer in his budget for 2003. Other priority items were expected to be prescription drug coverage for senior citizens, caps on medical malpractice lawsuits, and a revival of a long-stalled measure overhauling bankruptcy laws. Conservatives were expected to try again to push their social agenda, including placing limits on abortions and increasing funding for sexual abstinence programs.

Following are excerpts from a campaign speech by President George W. Bush on November 4, 2002, at an appearance at Southern Methodist University in Dallas, Texas, for Republican Senate candidate John Cornyn.

The document was obtained from the Internet at www .whitehouse.gov/news/releases/2002/10/20021028-1.html; accessed November 4, 2002.

Thank you, all. It's nice to be home. I want to thank you all for coming. Laura and I are working are way across the country to get back to Texas so we can vote, and I want to tell you, we're not undecided. For the sake of Texas and for the sake of America, vote John Cornyn for the United States Senate.

And for the sake of the taxpayers of Texas and for the sake of the school children of Texas, elect Rick Perry as the governor of Texas. . . .

I want to thank you all for what you have done. I want to thank you for what you're going to do, which is to find good Texans and get them to vote, turn them out to vote and get them to vote for this ticket.

These are candidates we can be proud of. These are people that you can have confidence in. So work hard. And, by the way, I'm pretty familiar with Texas politics. You know, there's a lot of discerning Democrats who are going to support this ticket. Don't be afraid to talk to those good Democrats. Don't be afraid to talk to independents. Our candidates can reach across party line, because they've got a positive vision for the future of this state and for the future of our country. . . .

. . . And we can work together on some big issues on behalf of all of Texas and all of America. And there are some big hurdles facing this country.

First of all, this economy isn't doing as good as it should be doing. It's bumping along. And, therefore, there's some people looking for work who can't find work. And any time somebody is looking for work who can't find work, it says to me that we've got to figure out how to continue to increase the job base of America.

But there's a fundamental difference of opinion in Washington, D.C., as to how to do that. The page of the economic textbook that we've read from says that if you let a person keep more of their own money, they're more than likely to demand an additional good or a service. They're likely to demand a good or a service, and when they do that, somebody is likely to produce the good or a service. And when somebody produces the good or a service, it's more likely somebody is going to be able to find a job.

And, therefore, the tax cuts we pass in Washington came at the exact right time in economic history. And I need a senator who will stand strong on this issue. I need a senator with whom we can work to make the tax cuts permanent. And that senator is John Cornyn.

I look forward to working with John on a lot of issues. On education, and on Medicare. Listen, medicine has changed and Medicare hasn't. Medicine has become modern; technologies have changed, there's new discoveries. But Medicare is stuck in the past. I need to work with [Texas senator] Kay Hutchison and John Cornyn and members of the Congress to modernize Medicare, which means prescription drug benefits for our seniors.

And we've got another problem with health care. There's too many lawsuits. There's too many junk lawsuits that are running up the cost of medicine. They're filing suits all over this country, which means good, honest people who have got a claim can't get to the judges, can't get into the courthouse. It means that people aren't going to have accessible and affordable health care. Excessive lawsuits run up the cost of medicine, and they're driving docs out of the practice of medicine. We need a Senate who will join me in passing federal medical liability reform.

And I need a senator from Texas with whom I can work, to help fulfil one of my most serious responsibilities, and that is to put good people on the federal bench. There is a vacancy on our benches. There is vacancies all around the country, because the bunch that's running the Senate right now won't give my nominees a fair hearing. And when they do give them a hearing, some of them have their records distorted. I need a United States senator who will stand strong for what most Texans want, and that is a judiciary full of honest and honorable people who will not use their bench from which to legislate, but to interpret the Constitution of the United States.

You may remember what happened to one of our finest Texans, Priscilla Owen. I picked Priscilla to serve on one of our top benches. I did so because she's a brilliant lady, she's an honest person, she finished tops in her law school, she was ranked by the ABA [American Bar Association] as one of the top picks. She is backed by Republicans and Democrats from the state of Texas. She ran statewide and was overwhelmingly elected. I put her up there. Because these people are playing politics, petty politics, with the nominees I've picked, her record was distorted and she was denied a seat. She was grossly treated. I can assure you that with John Cornyn in the Senate he would be a strong supporter of Priscilla Owen and my judges.

There's a big difference in this race between the two running for the United States Senate. And that Priscilla Owen case is a clear example of what I'm talking about. There's going to be a lot of issues we'll work on together. The biggest issue we've got is to protect America, to protect you from further attack, to do everything we can to prevent an enemy from hitting this country again.

It's still a problem for us, because there's an enemy lurking out there which hates us. And they hate us because of what we love—we love our freedom. We love the fact that people can worship freely in America. We love the fact that people can speak their mind in this country. We love a free press. We love every aspect of our freedom, and we're not going to change.

So long as we take that stand, they're going to try to hurt us. And therefore, we've got to do everything we can to protect you. And there's a lot of good people doing that. I mean, listen, we're on notice. We remember, we remember, remember what happened. And therefore, there's a lot of good people working overtime to run down every hint, any idea, any suggestion that somebody is fixing to or thinking about doing something to America, we're moving on it. It is our most solemn obligation.

I think we can do a better job of protecting you, and that's why I went to the United States Congress, to join me in the creation of a Department of Homeland Security. It needs to be a department that brings agencies together, to focus their attention, to change [the] culture if need be, so that people who are working hard on your behalf get the message that this is our number one job and number one priority.

And the House of Representatives responded. And I want to thank the House members who are here. But the bill got stuck in the Senate. Here we are with an enemy lurking out there, and the bill got stuck in the Senate because some Senators want to take away power from the Presidency. They want to take away what every President since John F. Kennedy has had, and that is the capacity to suspend certain collective bargaining rules for the sake of national security. In other words, if there's some rules that prevent me from putting the right place—people at the right place at the right time, to protect you, I ought to be able to suspend those rules. But not according to these people.

No, the special interests have grabbed them up there. They want to micromanage the process. I need John Cornyn in the Senate to make sure we get us a good homeland security bill.

But the best way to protect the homeland is to hunt these killers down, one at a time, and bring them to justice. That's what we have to do. And that is what we're going to do. And that is why I went to the Congress and asked for a substantial increase in defense spending, as a matter of fact, the largest increase since Ronald Reagan was the President. And I want to thank Senator Hutchinson, and I want to thank the members of Congress for backing me on that request. And there's two messages in that bill that I want to share with you. One, any time this country puts any of our youngsters into harm's way, they deserve the best pay, the best training and the best possible equipment.

And the second message is equally important. And that is, we're in this deal for the long haul. See, when it comes to the defense of our freedoms, it doesn't matter how long it takes. We're going to do the job. We're going to defend freedom. We're going to do a responsibility so future generations of Americans will know we answered the call. It just doesn't matter how long it takes. There's not a calendar on my desk in that wonderful Oval Office that says on such-and-such a date, haul them home. That's not the way I think.

And we're making progress in this different kind of war. In the old days, if you knocked down an airplane or sunk a ship, you could say you're making progress. This group we fight now hides in caves or kind of slithers around the dark corners of the world and they send their youngsters to their suicidal deaths. We value life in America. We say everybody is precious. These folks have hijacked a great religion and don't care who they kill. And that's the nature of the enemy. They're tough—we're tougher.

Slowly but surely—slowly but surely we're dismantling the terrorist network. It's important for us to be realistic here in America about the threats we face. It's essential we see the world the way it is, not the way we hope it would be. Because the stakes changed dramatically after September the 11th, 2001. Prior to that date, we had oceans that we thought protected us; that if there was a gathering threat somewhere around the world we could either deal with that threat or ignore it, because we were safe at home. Geography kept us safe. After September the 11th, 2001, geography doesn't keep us safe. And, therefore, in my judgment, we've got to be cold-eyed realists about threats as they emerge and deal with each one of them according to the level of threat.

There is a threat to the United States and our close friends and allies in Iraq. The leader of Iraq is a man who for 11 years has deceived the world. He said he wouldn't have weapons of mass destruction—he has weapons of mass destruction. At one time we know for certain he was close to having a nuclear weapon. Imagine Saddam Hussein with a nuclear weapon. Not only has he got chemical weapons, but I want you to remember, he's used chemical weapons.

He's used weapons on people in his neighborhood, he's used weapons on people in his own country. This is a man who cannot stand America, he cannot stand what we stand for, he can't stand some of our closest friends and allies.

This is a man who has got connections with al Qaeda. Imagine a terrorist network with Iraq as an arsenal and as a training ground, so that a Saddam Hussein could use his shadowy group of people to attack his enemy and leave no fingerprint behind. He's a threat.

I went to the United Nations to make clear a couple of things. One, he's a threat. And, secondly, that this august body has a chance to keep the peace. And yet for 16 resolutions—resolution after resolution after resolution—Saddam Hussein has defied the United Nations. It is now time for the United Nations to choose whether it's going to be an effective peacekeeping organization, or whether it's going to be like one of its predecessors, the League of Nations, an empty debating society. It is their choice to make.

It is Saddam Hussein's choice to make. He's told the world he would not have weapons of mass destruction, and in the name of peace, we expect him to honor that commitment. Should he choose not to honor the commitment, the U.N. is incapable of acting, the United States in the name of peace, in the name of freedom, will lead a coalition and disarm Saddam Hussein.

I say, "in the name of peace," because that's what's going to happen, in my judgment. See, out of the evil done to America is going to come some good. I don't know what got into the minds of the terrorists when they hit us, I guess they assumed our national religion was materialism, that we were so selfish, self-absorbed that after 9/11/2001 we might take a step back and file a lawsuit or two.

They don't understand the nature of this great country. They don't understand the depth of our passion for freedom. If we stay tough when we need to be tough; stay strong when we need to be strong; speak clearly about good and evil; if we remember that freedom is not America's gift to the world, but God's gift to the world, we can achieve peace.

We can achieve peace here at home, we can achieve peace here at home. We can achieve peace in parts of the world which have quit on peace. I believe it. I believe out of the evil done to America is going to come good abroad, in the form of peace. And I believe it's going to make America a better place.

I believe I know a lot of our citizens have taken a step back and taken an assessment about that which is important in their lives. A lot of people have asked that question, how can I help. Well, I've got some ideas for you. First, it's important to remember that in the land of plenty there are people who hurt. There's pockets of despair and hopelessness and addiction. People, when you say, the American Dream, they have absolutely no idea what you're talking about. We've got to remember in this country, when some of us hurt, we all hurt. And therefore we've got to try to make a difference to improve the lot of everybody's lives.

And government can help. We'll work on Medicare and we'll work on education. And government can pass out money. But I want you to remember what government cannot do is to put hope in people's hearts, or a sense of purpose in people's lives. People's lives change when somebody puts their arm around them, and says, I love you, can I help you, what can I do to make your life a better life?

And that's happening all across America. I'm sure there's mentors here, people who are saving one child's life at a time. I know there are people here who feed the hungry, provide housing for the homeless, or run a Boy Scouts troop or a Girl Scouts troop, or Big Brothers and Big Sisters.

There's all kinds of ways that you can help change America, one heart, one conscience, one soul at a time. No, the spirit of America is strong; it's alive and well. It's a spirit that says, when it comes to the defense of our freedom, it doesn't matter how long it takes, we'll defend freedom.

It also says that a true American is somebody who serves a cause greater than themselves. I want the high school students and youngsters here to always remember the story of Flight 93. These are people flying across the country, what they thought was going to be just an average trip. They learned that the airplane they were on was going to be used as a weapon. They told their loved ones goodbye. They said a prayer, asking for guidance from the Almighty. One guy said, let's roll. They took the plane into the ground to save lives, and to serve something greater than themselves.

The enemy hit us, the enemy hit us. They had no earthly idea who they were hitting. They didn't have any idea that the spirit of this country is strong and alive and vibrant, which allows me to boldly predict that out of the evil done to America is going to come a more peaceful world, and out of the evil done to America will come a more hopeful America, where the great sunshine of hope of this country shines its light into every corner of this land.

And I can say that with confidence, because this is the greatest country, full of the most decent and honorable people on the face of the earth.

Thanks for coming. May God bless.

BRITISH COURT ON DETENTIONS AT GUANTANAMO BAY
November 6, 2002

The Bush administration found itself at odds with civil liberties advocates and many legal experts during the year because of its use of secret detentions in its all-out campaign to battle terrorism. In the months after the September 11, 2001, terrorist attacks in New York and Washington, U.S. law enforcement and military authorities arrested nearly 2,000 men, both in the United States and overseas, and held many of them secretly for months at a time without the customary legal rights guaranteed under U.S. law. Administration officials said its extraordinary measures were justified by the need to confront shadowy terrorist groups that continued to threaten the country's security. "The single most important priority is to protect the homeland now in America [because] we're at war," President George W. Bush said.

Critics questioned the necessity of weakening traditional legal rights and challenged some of the administration's actions in courts, where judges rendered conflicting opinions. One of the strongest opinions criticizing the government's actions came from a senior court in Great Britain, which found "legally objectionable" the U.S. military's indefinite detention of a British citizen at a prison in Guantanamo Bay, Cuba.

In an extensive report issued on August 15, 2002, Human Rights Watch, which normally focused on human rights abuses in other countries, documented dozens of cases in which the Bush administration had restricted the civil liberties of people in the United States, most of them immigrants. Since the September 11 attacks, the report said, "the country has witnessed a persistent, deliberate, and unwarranted erosion of basic rights against abusive governmental power that are guaranteed by the U.S. Constitution and international human rights law. Most of those directly affected have been non-U.S. citizens. Under Attorney General John Ashcroft, the Department of Justice has subjected them to arbitrary detention, violated due process in legal proceedings against them, and run roughshod over the presumption of innocence." Human Rights Watch and other organizations had similar criticisms of other administration initiatives, including stepped-up surveillance of Americans thought to have ties to terrorism. (Civil liberties issues, p. 559)

Prisoners at Guantanamo and Bagram

During 2002 U.S. military and intelligence agencies held large groups of prisoners at two facilities: the U.S. naval base at Guantanamo Bay in Cuba, and a former Soviet air base at Bagram, Afghanistan, just north of Kabul. All those held in both facilities had been captured in Afghanistan or Pakistan; some were captured during the fighting in late 2001 when the United States invaded Afghanistan to oust the ruling Taliban regime and the al Qaeda terrorist network, but others were captured during subsequent military operations in 2002 against the pockets of resistance by Taliban and al Qaeda fighters.

In most cases, according to news reports, captured fighters were first taken to the Bagram base where they were subjected to intense interrogation by U.S. intelligence and military officers. Those considered to be the most valuable detainees, because of their rank in or knowledge of the Taliban or al Qaeda organizations, were kept at Bagram. Some detainees were released and sent home because they had no valuable information to offer, and the rest were sent to Guantanamo Bay.

The first prisoners arrived at Guantanamo Bay in January and were placed in a makeshift, open-air prison called Camp X-Ray. Photographs of the men, heavily shackled and wearing orange jump suits, brought international protests about their treatment. The military then built a new, more permanent, facility known as Camp Delta, which had a capacity of about 800 prisoners in individual cells, each with a cot, sink, and toilet.

Under pressure from human rights groups to declare the detained men as prisoners of war, the White House announced on February 7 that it would apply the principles of the Geneva Convention to those men who had been captured with the Taliban but would not consider them as actual prisoners of war, a status that would give them rights—such as housing in conditions similar to those of their captors. Men captured with al Qaeda would not be treated in accordance with the Geneva Convention, but would be treated humanely, the White House said.

The administration drew a distinction between the Taliban and al Qaeda fighters because the former technically fought on behalf of the Afghanistan government, while the latter were part of a nongovernmental terrorist organization. While it went part of the way toward satisfying critics, the administration's distinction between different prisoners brought continuing complaints. Amnesty International, for example, on April 15 released a sharply worded report denouncing the secrecy surrounding the Guantanamo Bay detentions. "The U.S.A.'s pick and choose approach to the Geneva Conventions is unacceptable, as is its failure to respect fundamental international human rights standards," the report said.

Four prisoners—three Afghans and one Pakistani—were released in late October and sent home. Upon arrival back in Kabul, two of the Afghan men told reporters they had been treated well but had never understood why they were held. As of late 2002 about 625 men from forty-three countries were still being held at Camp Delta. According to press reports about 60 of the *men were held in isolation; the others were allowed to speak to one another. The International Committee of the Red Cross monitored the treatment of these detainees but made no public statements about its findings. The men were held without being charged with any crimes or having the benefit of legal advice.*

The Los Angeles Times *reported on December 22 that U.S. intelligence officials had determined that at least 59 of those held at Guantanamo Bay had no real information to offer but were still being held, in part because of "a pervasive fear of letting a valuable prisoner go free by mistake." These men were farmers, taxi drivers, or common laborers, not regular fighters for the Taliban or al Qaeda. Among those held at Guantanamo Bay, according to the* Times *report, was an Arab who had fought for the Taliban but suffered a massive head injury that destroyed his reasoning ability and led interrogators to refer to him as "half-head Bob." Pentagon officials defended their decisions about who was detained at the facility: "We're sending the right folks" to the Guantanamo Bay prison, Army Colonel Michael T. Flynn told the newspaper.*

As of late 2002 the U.S. military held about 100 other men at the Bagram air base, reportedly in conditions that would not pass legal muster in the United States. In a detailed report published on December 26, the Washington Post *described "brass-knuckled" interrogation techniques, including extreme verbal abuse and sleep deprivation, intended to break prisoners' resistance to providing information. In some cases, prisoners were turned over to intelligence officers from other countries—such as Egypt, Jordan, and Morocco—who were "known for using brutal means," the newspaper said. Among the prisoners held at Bagram were several senior leaders of al Qaeda and other terrorist organizations thought to be associated with al Qaeda.*

The Post's *description of conditions at Bagram brought a stiff protest from Human Rights Watch, which on December 27 sent the White House a letter saying the use of strong-arm interrogation methods amounted to torture and "would place the United States in violation of some of the most fundamental prohibitions of international human rights law." White House spokesman Scott McClellan rejected that assertion, saying that "we believe we are in full compliance with domestic and international law," including laws dealing with torture.*

Legal Challenges to Guantanamo Detentions

The administration faced two legal challenges to its detentions at Guantanamo Bay, one filed in the United States and the other in Britain. In practical terms, the more serious of the two was a suit filed in federal court in Washington by lawyers for twelve Kuwaitis, two Australians, and two Britons who had been captured in Afghanistan or Pakistan and then transferred to Guantanamo Bay. Judge Colleen Kollar-Kotelly, of the U.S. District Court in Washington, rejected that challenge on July 31, ruling that U.S. courts did not have jurisdiction in cases of noncitizens held outside of U.S. territory. The plaintiffs appealed that ruling, and the circuit court heard arguments in the case on December 2 but had not rendered a decision by the end of 2002. During the hearing, however, the three appellate judges asked questions that led observers to believe they would side with the government.

Another challenge came from London, where the mother of Feroz Abbasi—one of seven British citizens held at Guantanamo—filed suit seeking to force the British government to intervene on behalf of her son. The government said it had no power to influence the U.S. handling of prisoners at Guantanamo. In a ruling on November 6, a senior appellate court agreed that neither the government nor courts in Britain had any legal standing to act on behalf of Abbasi. But in unusually harsh language, the three-judge panel denounced as "legally objectionable" the U.S. policy of holding prisoners indefinitely on foreign soil without any legal rights. "What appears to us objectionable is that Mr. Abbasi is subject to indefinite detention in territory over which the United States has exclusive control, with no opportunity to challenge the legitimacy of his detention before any court or tribunal," the panel said. Lord Phillips, one of Britain's senior judges, wrote the decision.

U.S. and British legal experts said the decision obviously was intended as a public rebuke to the United States from a friendly country with a similar legal tradition. The judges said as much themselves in their decision: "It may be the anxiety that we have expressed will be drawn to their [U.S. officials'] attention."

Domestic Detentions and Criminal Cases

The Bush administration used new powers granted it by the USA Patriot Act—as well as new interpretations of previous laws and regulations—to arrest and jail, often for months, hundreds of immigrants from Middle Eastern and South Asian countries. Although Ashcroft and other officials said these detentions were part of the antiterrorism campaign, only a handful of those caught in the dragnet were charged with crimes having to do with terrorism by the end of 2002. The administration's approach was articulated at an American Bar Association meeting in Philadelphia on February 1. Assistant Attorney General Viet Dinh told an audience of lawyers and human rights activists that terrorist suspects would be arrested on any possible grounds—even if they "so much as spit on the street"—just to get them behind bars. "If we suspect you of terrorism, we will arrest you, no matter how minor the violation, so that you are removed from the street and from the people that you wish to harm," he said. "By the time we wait to investigate, prosecute, and then incarcerate the persons, the damage is already done."

The USA Patriot Act said the government could hold noncitizens for up to seven days without charges if the attorney general "certifies" that they were terrorist risks. In the weeks after September 11, the FBI and other law enforcement agencies detained 1,182 immigrants—nearly all of them Muslim men from Middle Eastern or South Asian nations. In most cases the immigrants were held without charge for much longer than seven days, although the government did not release exact details. After announcing that tally of 1,182 in November 2001, the Justice Department refused to give a precise count of how many more immigrants had been detained. On December 11,

2002, however, the department told the Associated Press (AP) that 756 of those who had been detained were held on immigration charges, such as overstaying a visa. Of the total, 469 were deported, 281 were released in the United States without being charged, and only 6 remained in detention. The government released 281 people without charging them. Another 134 people detained after September 11 had been charged with various federal and state crimes, such as theft, credit card fraud, or illegal weapon possession; of these 99 had been found guilty through pleas or trials. The AP said an undisclosed number, probably in the dozens, were still held as material witnesses— people who might have information about criminal activity and who the government feared might flee if allowed to go free. After reviewing federal records, the Washington Post *on November 24 estimated that at least 44 people had been held as material witnesses; in 20 cases, those held had never been brought before a grand jury, the* Post *reported.*

Only one of the detainees was charged with a crime directly connected to the September 11 terrorist attacks. He was Zacarias Moussaoui, a French citizen of Moroccan descent who had been detained in Minnesota in August 2001 for immigration violations. Officials later declared that Moussaoui would have been the twentieth member of the four crews of hijackers who carried out the September 11 attacks. The administration reportedly considered trying Moussaoui before one of the military tribunals authorized by President Bush in late 2001 but ultimately decided to try him in the civilian court system. Moussaoui was transferred to prison in Virginia and charged with six felony conspiracy crimes. His case was still pending at the end of 2002.

The only other detainees charged with a terrorism-related crime were four men arrested in the Detroit area in late 2001 and then indicted, on August 28, 2002, on charges of planning terrorist attacks in the United States. Two of the men were Moroccan, one was Algerian, and the nationality of the fourth was not known.

In at least 611 detention cases it defined as being of "special interest," the government conducted all proceedings in extraordinary secrecy, refusing to make public the names of those being held, to confirm that any specific individuals were in detention, or to describe what made these cases of special interest. In effect, the government said it could hold these men until it discovered whether they had committed crimes, an action that Human Rights Watch said amounted to "turning the presumption of innocence on its head." These secret proceedings were authorized by the chief judge for the Immigration and Naturalization Service, Michael J. Creppy, on September 21, 2001.

Friends and relatives of several of those detained filed suits that, in some cases, resulted in court orders reversing the secrecy. In response, the government argued that immigration hearings were not trials, which are normally open to the public, but were administrative hearings that the public had no right to observe. The government also argued that releasing information about the detainees would damage its post-September 11 investigations. "If these proceedings are opened to the public during the critical phase of the ur-

gent threat to national security, terrorist organizations will have direct access to information about the government's ongoing investigation," Solicitor General Theodore Olsen wrote in a brief to the Supreme Court in June.

Several separate court rulings reached conflicting conclusions on the constitutionality of secret detentions—leaving the administration free, for the time being, to continue the practice and setting the stage for possible action by the Supreme Court. In the most widely watched case, U.S. district court judge Gladys Kessler, in Washington, ruled on August 2 that the identities of most of those still being held should be made public under the Freedom of Information Act. "Secret arrests are a concept odious to a democratic society," she said in her ruling, which allowed the government to keep secret other details, such as the reasons for the detentions. The Justice Department refused to abide by the ruling, which it said "increases the risk of future terrorist threats to our nation," and filed an appeal.

On August 26 an appeals court in Cincinnati ruled in a separate case that the immigration hearings should be open unless the government demonstrated a valid reason for closing them. "The executive branch seeks to uproot people's lives, outside the public eye and behind a closed door," Judge Damon Keith wrote for the unanimous circuit court. "Democracies die behind closed doors."

The U.S. Supreme Court got involved in just one of the detention cases during 2002. In June the high court temporarily blocked an order issued in May by Judge John W. Bissell, chief judge of the Newark district, demanding that all deportation hearings nationwide be opened to the public unless the government was able to show the need for a closed hearing on a case-by-case basis. Bissell's ruling came in response to a suit by several newspapers. In appealing the ruling, the Bush administration argued that opening the hearings would give terrorist organizations "direct access to information about the government's ongoing investigation." Along with the other cases, that one was pending at year's end.

Enemy Combatants

The government accused three American citizens of being "enemy combatants" because of their alleged involvement with terrorists. The only case to reach a conclusion during 2002 was that of John Walker Lindh, often called the "American Taliban" because he had gone to Afghanistan to support the Taliban regime that had hosted the al Qaeda terrorist network. Lindh was captured during the fighting in Afghanistan in late 2001 and transferred to prison in Virginia, where in February he was indicted on ten felony counts of aiding the enemy. To avoid a trial—and thus risk disclosure of potentially embarrassing information about alleged mistreatment of Lindh in the early stages of his detention—the Justice Department agreed to a plea bargain under which Lindh pleaded guilty on July 15 to two charges of supplying services to the Taliban and carrying explosives in the commission of a felony. He was sentenced on October 4 to twenty years in prison, the maximum penalty for those charges.

Another case involved Yasser Esam Hamdi, a Saudi national born in

Louisiana, who also was captured among Taliban forces in Afghanistan. Hamdi was first transferred to the military's detention center at Guantanamo Bay in Cuba, but when interrogators discovered that he was a U.S. citizen, Hamdi was jailed in a naval brig in South Carolina as an enemy combatant. Hamdi was kept incommunicado and denied access to an attorney on the basis of an administration decision that enemy combatants were under the jurisdiction of the U.S. military, not the civilian courts. Judge Robert G. Doumar, of the Eastern Virginia district court, ruled in June that Hamdi had a right to counsel. The Fourth District appellate court overturned that ruling on July 12, but that court objected to what it called the government's "sweeping proposition" that civil courts could be excluded from any involvement in enemy combatant cases. Later in the year Judge Doumar and government prosecutors sparred over that issue, which remained unresolved.

The third enemy combatant case was that of Jose Padilla, a former Chicago gang member who also called himself Abdullah al-Muhajir. He was arrested on May 8 at Chicago O'Hare Airport after returning from Pakistan and held as a material witness because of suspicions that he had tried to obtain information about building a radiological bomb (a conventional bomb that dispersed radioactivity). On June 9, two days before Padilla was scheduled to appear in federal court in New York, Bush signed an order designating Padilla as an enemy combatant and ordering him transferred to the naval brig in South Carolina and held without access to a lawyer. Bush declared Padilla to be "a threat to the country who is now off the street, where he should be." At year's end a U.S. district court judge in New York was considering a plea by Padilla's attorney for a writ of habeas corpus in the case.

Although not directly related to September 11, another terrorist case involved Richard Reid, also known as the "shoe bomber," a British citizen who was arrested at Boston Logan Airport on December 22, 2001, after he tried to ignite bombs hidden in his shoes during a flight from London to Miami. Reid boasted of his affiliation with al Qaeda, and on October 4 pleaded guilty to eight charges, including attempted homicide and attempted use of a weapon of mass destruction (an airplane).

As of the end of 2002 the government had not made use of another extraordinary legal process stemming from the September 11 attacks: special military commissions. In November 2001 Bush signed an order establishing a procedure for military courts to try terrorism cases, totally outside of the review of civilian courts. Bush's order brought an outcry from many legal experts, who said it was vague, poorly drafted, and overly broad. The Defense Department redrafted the rules and issued revised regulations in March that offered some legal protections to the accused (such as setting a "reasonable doubt" standard for guilt or innocence) but retained the original provision that put the tribunals outside the review of civilian courts. News reports late in the year indicated that the administration was considering using the tribunals to handle the cases of at least some of the prisoners held at Guantanamo Bay and the Bagram air base. One option reportedly under consideration was defining membership in al Qaeda as a war crime — a step that would make it easier for the administration to prosecute the detainees who were captured in Afghanistan.

Following are excerpts from a decision handed down November 6, 2002, by the British Court of Appeal of the Supreme Court of Judicature in the case of an application for intervention by the British government on behalf of Feroz Abbasi, a British citizen held in detention by the U.S. military at Guantanamo Bay, Cuba.

The document was obtained from the Internet at www .courtservice.gov.uk/judgmentsfiles/j1354/abassi_ judgment.htm; accessed February 6, 2003.

This is the judgment of the Court to which all members have contributed.

Introduction

1. Feroz Ali Abbasi, the first claimant, is a British national. He was captured by United States forces in Afghanistan. In January 2002 he was transported to Guantanamo Bay in Cuba, a naval base on territory held by the United States on long lease pursuant to a treaty with Cuba. By the time of the hearing before us he had been held captive for eight months without access to a court or any other form of tribunal or even to a lawyer. These proceedings, brought on his behalf by his mother, the second claimant, are founded on the contention that one of his fundamental human rights, the right not to be arbitrarily detained, is being infringed. They seek, by judicial review, to compel the Foreign Office to make representations on his behalf to the United States Government or to take other appropriate action or at least to give an explanation as to why this has not been done.

2. On 15 March 2002 Richards J. [Justice Richards of the High Court of Justice] refused the application for permission to seek judicial review. However, on 1 July 2002 this court granted that permission, retained the matter for itself, and directed that the substantive hearing commence on 10 September 2002. It did so because the unusual facts of this case raise important issues. To what extent, if at all, can the English court examine whether a foreign state is in breach of treaty obligations or public international law where fundamental human rights are engaged? To what extent, if at all, is a decision of the executive in the field of foreign relations justiciable in the English court? More particularly, are there any circumstances in which the court can properly seek to influence the conduct of the executive in a situation where this may impact on foreign relations? Finally, in the light of the answers to these questions, is any form of relief open to Mr Abbasi and his mother against the Secretary of State for Foreign and Commonwealth Affairs?

Mr Abbasi's predicament

3. Mr Abbasi was one of a number of British citizens captured by American forces in Afghanistan. He was, with others, transferred to Guantanamo Bay. Those currently detained there include seven British citizens. As soon as she learned what had happened to her son, Mrs Abbasi made contact with the Foreign Office. Through lawyers, she pressed the Foreign Office to assist in ensuring that the conditions in which her son was detained were humane. She has also pressed the Foreign Office to procure from the United States authorities clarification of her son's status and of what is to be done with him in the future.

4. Evidence of action taken by the United Kingdom Government in relation to Mr Abbasi and the other British detainees in Guantanamo Bay has been provided in a witness statement by Mr Fry, a Deputy Under-Secretary of State for Foreign and Commonwealth Affairs. He speaks of close contact between the United Kingdom Government and the United States Government about the situation of the detainees and their treatment and of the consistent endeavour of the government to secure their welfare and ensure their proper treatment. To that end, we are told, the circumstances of the British detainees have been the subject of regular representations by the British Embassy in Washington to the United States Government. They have also been the subject of direct discussions between the Foreign Secretary and the United States Secretary of State as well as 'numerous communications at official level'.

5. The government was able to obtain permission from the United States Government to visit detainees at Guantanamo Bay on three occasions, between 19 and 20 January, between 26 February and 1 March and between 27 and 31 May. These visits were conducted by officials of the Foreign and Commonwealth Office and members of the security services. The former were able to assure themselves that the British prisoners, including Mr Abbasi, were being well treated and appeared in good physical health. By the time of the third visit, facilities had been purpose built to house detainees. Each was held in an individual cell with air ventilation, a washbasin and a toilet. It is not suggested by the claimants that Mr Abbasi is not being treated humanely.

6. The members of the security services took advantage of these visits to question Mr Abbasi with a view to obtaining information about possible threats to the safety of the United Kingdom. Initially this was the subject of independent complaint by the claimants, but before us the argument has focussed on the allegation that the Foreign and Commonwealth Office is not reacting appropriately to the fact that Mr Abbasi is being arbitrarily detained in violation of his fundamental human rights.

7. The position of the Foreign and Commonwealth Office is summarised by Mr Fry in the following terms:

"In cases that come to us with a request for assistance, Foreign and Commonwealth Ministers and Her Majesty's diplomatic and consular officers have to make an informed and considered judgement about the most appropriate way in which the interests of the British national may be protected, including the nature, manner and timing of any diplomatic representations to the country concerned. Assessments of when and how to press another State require very fine judgements to be made, based on experience and detailed information gathered in the course of diplomatic business.

In cases where a person is detained in connection with international terrorism, these judgements become particularly complex. As regards the issue of the detainees now at Guantanamo Bay, as well as satisfying the clear need to safeguard the welfare of British nationals, the conduct of United Kingdom international relations has had to take account of a range of factors, including the duty of the Government to gather information relevant to United Kingdom national security and which might be important in averting a possible attack against the United Kingdom or British nationals or our allies; and the objectives of handling the detainees securely and of bringing any terrorist suspects to justice."

8. In or about February 2002 the claimants initiated habeas corpus proceedings in the District Court of Columbia. As we shall explain, rulings in proceedings brought by other detainees in a similar position demonstrate that Mr Abbasi's proceedings have, at present, no prospect of success. . . .

[Paragraphs 9 through 57 reviewed the position of the U.S. government that detainees at Guantanamo Bay were "enemy combatants" who were being held "for the duration of the hostilities," the status of court cases in the United States concerning the detainees at Guantanamo Bay and other locations, the expressions of concern by the United Nations High Commissioner for Human Rights and the Inter-American Commission on Human Rights about the status of those detainees, and the legal questions involved in the issue of whether the British government or courts could intervene on behalf of Mr. Abbasi].

Our view of Mr Abbasi's predicament

58. Mr Blake [the attorney for the claimant] has founded his case upon Mr Abbasi's predicament as it currently appears. If the decision of the District Court of Columbia accurately represents the law of the United States, then the United States executive is detaining Mr Abbasi on territory over which it has total control in circumstances where Mr Abbasi can make no challenge to his detention before any court or tribunal. How long this state of affairs continues is within the sole control of the United States executive. Mr Blake contends that this constitutes arbitrary detention contrary to the fundamental norms of international law. It is not the fact that Mr Abbasi is detained on which Mr Blake relies—it is the fact that Mr Abbasi has no means of challenging the legality of his detention. It is this predicament which, so Mr Blake contends, gives rise to a duty on the part of the Foreign Secretary to come to Mr Abbasi's assistance. That assistance is claimed as a matter of last resort. We do not consider that we can deal satisfactorily with this appeal without addressing those submissions and we consider, in the light of the jurisprudence discussed above, that it is open to us to do so.

59. The United Kingdom and the United States share a great legal tradition, founded in the English common law. One of the cornerstones of that tradition is the ancient writ of habeas corpus, recognised at least by the time of Edward I, and developed by the 17th Century into "the most efficient protection yet developed for the liberty of the subject". . . . [The remainder of paragraph 59 and paragraphs 60 through 62 cite English and U.S. court cases setting out the writ of habeas corpus].

63. The recognition of this basic protection in both English and American law long pre-dates the adoption of the same principle as a fundamental part of international human rights law. Of the many source documents to which we have been referred, it is enough to cite the International Covenant of Civil and Political Rights, to which the United Kingdom and the United States are parties. Article 9, which affirms "the right to liberty and security of person" provides:

> "4. Anyone who is deprived of his liberty by arrest or detention shall be entitled to take proceedings before a court, in order that a court may decide without delay on the lawfulness of his detention and order his release if the detention is not lawful."

By Article 2, each state party undertakes to

> "ensure to all individuals within its territory and subject to its jurisdiction" the rights recognised by the Covenant "without distinction of any kind, such as . . . national origin. . . ."

64. For these reasons we do not find it possible to approach this claim for judicial review other than on the basis that, in apparent contravention of fundamental principles recognised by both jurisdictions and by international law, Mr Abbasi is at present arbitrarily detained in a 'legal black-hole'.

65. That is not to say that his detention as an alleged "enemy combatant" may not be justified. This court has very recently had occasion to consider the legitimacy of legislation that empowers the Secretary of State to detain within this jurisdiction aliens who are suspected of being international terrorists—*A, X and Y and Others v Secretary of State for the Home Department* [2002] EWCA Civ 1502. We would endorse the summary of the position under international law of Brooke LJ at paragraph 130:

> "What emerges from the efforts of the international community to introduce orderly arrangements for controlling the power of detention of non-nationals is a distinct movement away from the doctrine of the inherent power of the state to control the treatment of non-nationals within its borders as it will towards a regime, founded on modern international human rights norms, which is infused by the principle that any measures that are restrictive of liberty, whether they relate to nationals or non-nationals, must be such as are prescribed by law and necessary in a democratic society. The state's power to detain must be related to a recognised object and purpose, and there must be a reasonable relationship of proportionality between the end and the means. On the other hand, both customary international law and the international treaties by which this country is bound expressly reserve the power of a state in time of war or similar public emergency to detain aliens on grounds of national security when it would not necessarily detain its own nationals on those grounds."

These comments can be applied with equal force to those suspected of having taken part in military operations involving terrorist organisations.

66. What appears to us to be objectionable is that Mr Abbasi should be subject to indefinite detention in territory over which the United States has exclusive control with no opportunity to challenge the legitimacy of his detention before any court or tribunal. It is important to record that the position may change when the appellate courts in the United States consider the matter.

The question for us is what attitude should the courts in England take pending review by the appellate courts in the United States, to a detention of a British Citizen the legality of which rests (so the decisions of the United States Courts so far suggest) solely on the dictate of the United States Government, and, unlike that of United States' citizens, is said to be immune from review in any court or independent forum.

67. It is clear that there can be no direct remedy in this court. The United States Government is not before the court, and no order of this court would be binding upon it. Conversely, the United Kingdom Government, which, through the Secretaries of State is the respondent to these proceedings, has no direct responsibility for the detention. Nor is it suggested that it has any enforceable right, or even standing, before any domestic or international tribunal to represent the rights of the applicant, or compel access to a court. . . .

[The balance of the decision explained why the court was unable to support the claimant's request for a directive for the British government to intervene on behalf of Mr. Abbasi.]

ATTORNEY GENERAL ON
SCREENING IMMIGRANTS
November 7, 2002

The federal government took several steps in 2002 to tighten its scrutiny of foreign visitors and immigrants to the United States in its efforts to prevent terrorists from coming into the country. The most controversial step was a requirement that nonimmigrant men coming into or already in the United States from twenty predominantly Muslim countries be fingerprinted and registered with the Immigration and Naturalization Service (INS). Other programs tightened procedures for granting visas to foreign travelers from those twenty countries and for all student visas, set up a program to track foreigners on student visas to make sure they were actually attending school, and required all noncitizens—in the country legally or illegally—to report a change of address within ten days or face possible fines, jail time, or even deportation.

The new restrictions were all intended to prevent another terrorist attack similar to the one that occurred on September 11, 2001, when nineteen Arab Muslims commandeered four American commercial airliners and crashed three of them into the World Trade Center and the Pentagon, killing some 3,000 people. The fourth crashed in the Pennsylvania countryside. "On September 11th, the American definition of national security changed and changed forever," Attorney General John Ashcroft said on June 6, 2002, while announcing the fingerprinting and registration plan. (September 11 attack, Historic Documents of 2001, p. 614)

Congress also split the INS into separate agencies. One would police the country's borders and enforce immigration laws; the other would assist immigrants who were in the country legally to work their way through the cumbersome process to become citizens. The two agencies were then folded into the new Department of Homeland Security. Long regarded by many as "dysfunctional," the INS was further embarrassed in 2002 by several incidents that showed its ineptness in one way or another. By far the most embarrassing moment for the INS came on March 11, when a Florida flight school received student visas for two of the terrorists who exactly six months earlier had piloted the planes that crashed into the twin towers of the World Trade Center. (Homeland Security Department, p. 530)

The registration requirements, in particular, were sharply criticized by Muslim and immigrant rights groups, who said the procedure amounted to racial profiling, would further alienate Muslims around the world, and was unlikely to be very effective. Still others questioned whether the federal government had the infrastructure and personnel necessary to process all the new information it was requiring. Throughout the year, the General Accounting Office and other investigatory agencies repeatedly found evidence that the recordkeeping systems of the federal agencies involved in detecting and dealing with illegal immigrants and suspected foreign terrorists were out of date, uncoordinated, and already backlogged even before September 11.

Although several organizations questioned how effective the new immigration restrictions would be in actually keeping would-be terrorists out of the country, the regulations did not generate as much opposition as similar proposals had before September 11. Still, combined with other actions the federal government was taking or planning—such as secretly detaining hundreds of men, mostly Muslims from the Middle East and South Asia, and building a computer system to search vast quantities of personal information about Americans—the tightened immigrations policies aroused widespread concerns that the war on terrorism was resulting in a reduction of the civil liberties that undergirded American freedoms. (Civil liberties, 559; detentions, p. 830)

Tracking Foreign Students

Although the young Middle Eastern men who carried out the September 11 attacks all entered the United States legally, it was inevitable that the federal government would tighten its scrutiny of people coming into the country. Within two months of the attacks, President George W. Bush had ordered a crackdown on the abuse of student visas, Congress had ordered the implementation by 2005 of a new system to track the entry and exit of all foreign visitors to the United States, and the State Department had announced plans to subject men from twenty-five Arabic and Islamic countries to more rigorous screening when they applied for U.S. visas. Under the new procedures, the names of men ages sixteen to forty-five from those countries would be submitted to the FBI for background checks when they applied for visas. (Tightening immigration policy, Historic Documents of 2001, p. 764)

Attention focused on student visas in part because one of the hijackers had come into the country on a student visa but never showed up at the school he was supposed to attend. The Justice Department speeded up its efforts to clamp down on student visa abuses in March after a flight school, Huffman Aviation International of Venice, Florida, revealed that it had received notice of a change in visa status for two of the September 11 hijackers—Mohamed Atta, the presumed ringleader of the terrorists, and Marwan Al-Shehhi. Atta had a business visa and Al-Shehhi a tourist visa when they arrived at Huffman for flight training in July 2000. The school's student coordinator submitted applications in August 2000 seeking a change in the status of their visas, as required under INS regulations.

At a news conference on March 13, President Bush said he "was stunned and not happy" about the incident. "Let me put it another way: I was plenty hot," he continued. "We've got to reform the INS, and we've got to push hard to do so." INS officials quickly pointed out that the change of status had been approved before September 11, and that neither of the men appeared on any watch list at the time. Atta's visa change was approved on July 17, 2001, and Al-Shehhi's on August 9, 2001, nearly a fully year after Huffman had applied for the change in status and long after both men had completed the course.

After investigating the incident, Glenn A. Fine, inspector general of the Justice Department, reported on May 20 that the INS should never have issued the student visas for Atta and Al-Shehhi because both men had left the United States twice while seeking the change in their visa status. INS policy stipulated that an application for a visa change was considered "abandoned" if the applicant left the country while it was pending. Fine's investigation also found that the INS had sent the files it had on Atta and Al-Shehhi to the FBI after the hijackings, but that "no one in the INS located—or even considered locating—the notification forms that were being processed" by a private contractor for the INS. Fine said problems with student visas predated September 11. "The INS's foreign student program historically has been dysfunctional, and the INS has acknowledged for several years that it does not know how many foreign students are in the United States."

Even before the investigation was complete, INS announced on April 8 that, effective immediately, any foreigner wanting to study in the United States had to obtain a visa before beginning classes and that anyone wanting to switch from a tourist or business visa to a student visa had to return home to apply. On May 10 the Justice Department announced that it was speeding up the timetable for a computerized tracking system for foreign students that had been in the works since 1996. Under the new system, foreign students could not apply for a visa until they had been accepted for admission by a specific school, which would then have to enter the students' names and other identifying information into the computerized database. Schools would have to inform the INS within twenty-four hours if a student dropped out or did not show up within thirty days of entering the country. Schools would also have to report the status of foreign students to the INS every term. Schools were required to begin the reporting procedures by January 30, 2003.

When fully operational, the system was supposed to provide up-to-date information on 1 million nonimmigrant foreign students at any given time. There was widespread agreement that the computerized tracking system would be more effective than the existing paper system. But there were also lingering questions about whether the new system would help the INS perform better in other areas, including ensuring whether the schools applying for the student visas were in fact bona fide, and finding students who jumped their visas.

Colleges and universities had initially been cool to the tracking system when it was first proposed in 1996, but their opposition waned in the wake of September 11. In contrast, criticism from American colleges and universities led the Bush administration to scale back plans announced in 2001 to limit or prohibit foreign students from studying science and technology subjects that could assist them in building weapons of mass destruction. Instead the White House said it would set up a screening process to evaluate the visa applications of about 2,000 foreign graduate and postgraduate students, as well as visiting scholars. The goal of the screening process, said a spokesman, "would be to ensure that international students or visiting scholars do not acquire uniquely available education or training in U.S. educational institutions that may be used against us in a terrorist attack."

Targeted Registration and Fingerprinting

A month after he announced the new regulations on student visas, Ashcroft announced a new program to register and fingerprint certain foreign visitors determined to be a possible threat to American security. The National Security Entry-Exit Registration System (NSEERS) required certain foreign visitors to be fingerprinted when they arrived at customs. Those fingerprints would then be compared with those of suspected terrorists, previous violators of immigration regulations, and others provided by the INS, the military, and law enforcement agencies such as the FBI. The fingerprint database would include those of the Afghan and other prisoners held at Guantanamo Bay, Cuba, and latent prints collected from abandoned terrorist training camps and safehouses in Afghanistan. If the fingerprints of a would-be foreign visitor matched any in the database, the FBI would step in.

Registered foreign visitors would be required to report their whereabouts periodically to the INS while they were in the country and to complete exit control forms upon departure. Ashcroft said that all adult men and women (except for some diplomats) from Iran, Iraq, Libya, Sudan, and Syria would be subject to the new procedures. All five countries were on the State Department's list of countries that supported terrorist activities. Visitors from other countries, especially Muslim and Arab countries, were also likely to be subject to the registration and fingerprinting, but Ashcroft refused to disclose the criteria by which the government would determine who was a potential threat. "We will be able to stop terrorists from entering the country," Ashcroft said, announcing the program June 5. "Fingerprints don't lie," he said.

The plan was immediately attacked by some legislators. "It is as though the equal protection clause had no meaning or context whatsoever to the authors of this Orwellian proposal," Rep. John Conyers, D-Mich., said. "We have long fought repressive and totalitarian regimes that sought to register their people, ban them from public places, and eventually incarcerate them based solely on their race or religion." Sen. Edward M. Kennedy, D-Mass., added that the plan would "further stigmatize innocent Arab and Muslin visitors . . . who have committed no crimes and pose no danger to us." In contrast, House Judiciary committee chairman F. James Sensenbrenner, R-Wis., said it was "a reasonable first step in regaining control over illegal immigration in the United States, which is out of control." He also said his committee would conduct "'all necessary oversight" to prevent abuses by the Justice Department.

The program began on a test basis on September 11, 2002, the one-year anniversary of the terrorist attacks on New York and Washington. On October 1 the registration program was extended to include men ages sixteen to forty-five from at least ten additional countries, including Saudi Arabia, Pakistan, and Yemen. On November 7 Ashcroft announced in a speech in Niagara Falls that NSEERS was "up and running at every port of entry into the United States." Ashcroft said that the system was "performing extremely well." The INS had already fingerprinted 14,000 visitors from 112 different countries and used the information to arrest 179 aliens at the border.

Ashcroft's remarks did not apply to an even more controversial aspect of the NSEERS program—a requirement that certain men ages sixteen to forty-five already in the United States register at their local INS office. The program initially covered men from Iran, Iraq, Libya, Sudan, and Somalia who had been in the country before September 11, 2001, and was quickly extended to men from Afghanistan, Algeria, Bahrain, Eritrea, Lebanon, Morocco, North Korea, Oman, Qatar, Somalia, Tunisia, the United Arab Emirates, and Yemen who entered the country before September 30, and then to men from Saudi Arabia and Pakistan.

Those who failed to register would be subject to fines, imprisonment, and deportation. However, hundreds of men who showed up to register were arrested when their papers were found to be out of order. The detentions resulted in demonstrations in several cities. Demonstrators said the detainees were victims of entrapment and that many of the men's papers were out of order because of government backlogs in processing them. Signs carried sentiments such as "What's Next? Concentration Camps?" and "Detain Terrorists, Not Innocent Immigrants." Lawsuits were filed in at least three cities. A suit filed in Los Angeles in late December said that "the effort to deport law abiding people who could just as easily be allowed to continue the immigration process seriously undermines prospects for future compliance and constitutes an absurd waste of resources."

Following are remarks made November 7, 2002, by Attorney General John Ashcroft at Niagara Falls, New York, announcing the full implementation of the National Security Entry-Exit Registration System to register and track certain foreign visitors while they were in the United States.

The document was obtained from the Internet at www.usdoj.gov/ag/speeches/2002/110702agremarksnseers_niagarafalls.htm; accessed February 8, 2003.

It is fitting that this event take place at the edge of Niagara Falls—a majestic setting that has drawn visitors to this land for centuries. But Niagara is more than just a wonder of nature.

The Falls stand as an imposing sentinel on our northern border; a physical reminder of the importance that national boundaries play in securing free peoples. When our nation was founded, the raging waters of the Niagara River served as a barrier that protected Americans against hostile British troops on the other side.

Two and a quarter centuries later, on September 11, 2001, we saw just how much things had changed. The physical borders of the United States are no longer sufficient to prevent our nation's enemies from treading on American soil and endangering our freedoms. We are confronted with a new adversary—one whose platoons seek to enter the country quietly, disguised in the form of legitimate tourists, students, and businessmen. The challenge that we face is to identify and apprehend such individuals while maintaining the free flow of goods and people across the border that is so important to us and to our neighbors.

As part of our ongoing efforts to meet this challenge, five months ago, I announced that the Department of Justice and the Immigration and Naturalization service would develop and deploy the National Security Entry-Exit Registration System, or "N-SEERS," as it has come to be called. On September 11, 2002, a year to the day after terrorists declared war on the United States, NSEERS began operation at selected ports of entry.

Today, I am here at Niagara Falls to announce that the NSEERS system is up and running at every port of entry into the United States. We have increased our capacity intercept terrorists or criminals who attempt to enter the country, to verify that foreign visitors who may present national security concerns stick to their plans while they are here. And we have elevated substantially our ability to know instantly when such visitors overstay their visas.

NSEERS has three fundamental components:

- *The first is fingerprinting at the border. Using state-of-the-art computer technology, we can obtain digital fingerprints from a visitor's index fingers in seconds.* We then run those prints against a digital database of tens of thousands of individuals who are wanted for committing felonies in the United States and a database of thousands of known terrorists—a process that typically takes fewer than three minutes. We can also run the fingerprints of these visitors against a database of "latent" or unidentified fingerprints that our military has collected from terrorist training camps in Afghanistan and elsewhere.

- *The second component of NSEERS is periodic registration and confirmation of visitors' activities while they are within our borders.* Our European allies have had similar registration systems in place for decades and know the value of ensuring that foreign visitors are doing what they said they would do and living where they said they would live. The NSEERS system takes the European model and combines it with a modern intranet system so that files may be updated in real time at any INS office in the country.

- *The third component of NSEERS is a system of exit controls.* Visitors who are enrolled in the program must complete a departure check when they leave the country. Now, the INS can know immediately when a high-risk alien overstays his visa.

These NSEERS requirements apply to all non-immigrant adult aliens from five state sponsors of terrorism: Iran, Iraq, Libya, Sudan, and Syria. In addition, aliens from other countries who warrant extra scrutiny when they visit the United States are subject to the NSEERS requirements. INS inspectors are applying intelligence-based criteria to identify aliens who may pose an elevated national security risk, and registering them in the system.

Today, I am pleased to report that the system is performing extremely well. In the eight weeks since the operation of NSEERS commenced, the INS has fingerprinted and registered more than 14,000 visitors to the United States. A significant portion of those aliens came from those nations that sponsor terrorism, but NSEERS applies to visitors from every corner of the globe.

So far, the INS has fingerprinted and registered individuals from 112 different countries. From the Baltic to the Balkans and from the Cape of Good Hope to the Rock of Gibraltar, visitors who may present elevated national security concerns will be included. No country is exempt. In the war against terrorism, we cannot afford to have tunnel vision.

NSEERS has already paid large dividends in national security and law enforcement. The fingerprint matching technology has provided a basis for the arrest of 179 aliens at the border. Some were wanted felons who fled law enforcement during a prior visit to the United States. Others were aliens who had serious criminal records and were therefore inadmissible. And others were attempting to enter the United States under false pretenses or with fraudulent documents. These arrests would not have occurred without NSEERS. And let me also add that, if today or tomorrow a suspected terrorists is identified through NSEERS, it will not be the first time that such an apprehension has been made. In this way, NSEERS protects both the United States and Canada. Each time a dangerous individual, a wanted criminal, or a terrorist is stopped at the border, both countries are made more secure.

Congress has mandated that a comprehensive entry-exit system applicable to virtually all aliens be built by 2005. NSEERS is the first, crucial step toward that goal. It has allowed us to close the entry-exit loop for those aliens who present the highest national security risks. Part of its success lies in the cutting-edge technology that makes it possible to intercept terrorists and criminals at our borders by scanning fingerprints and searching databases in a matter of seconds. But a more important aspect of the system's success lies in its human dimension.

The INS inspectors who serve on the front lines—literally—of our national defense have proven extremely capable in operating the system, and have been vigilant in applying the intelligence-based criteria to identify aliens for inclusion in the program. At the same time, they have been courteous to our foreign guests, and have made every effort to minimize any delay or inconvenience. These Americans play a crucial role in the defense of our homeland, and I am grateful for their service.

Deploying this system so rapidly was a Herculean task. I want to thank the dedicated team of INS and Department of Justice officials who worked around the clock to make sure that this vital national security shield was raised as quickly as possible. Their unwavering commitment has made America more secure. The Buffalo District was a crucial testing ground for the system before NSEERS was implemented nationwide, and I want to thank especially the INS employees of Buffalo. Your ingenuity and can-do attitude have served our country well.

And finally, I want to thank the U.S. Attorney's Office, the Anti-Terrorism Task Force, and the larger law enforcement community of the Buffalo area, whose diligent work led to the arrest and arraignment of six individuals in Lackawanna for knowingly providing or attempting to provide material support to al Qaeda. These arrests sent an unambiguous message that we will track down terrorists wherever they hide.

Over two centuries ago, patriots stood on this riverbank defending a new nation's freedom. They recognized that freedom requires vigilance and security if it is to flourish. Today, a new group of patriots stands guard. On behalf of all Americans, I thank them for the sacrifice they have made, the security they provide, and the freedom they defend.

CHINESE PRESIDENT JIANG ZEMIN ON LEADERSHIP TRANSITION
November 8, 2002

The Chinese Communist Party selected a new generation of leadership in late 2002. It was a generation that was expected to broaden and deepen China's transformation into a country with an economy driven by capitalism but with a rigid political system still dominated by a tiny elite. The younger generation's greatest challenge would be to keep these two contradictory elements in balance, with neither destroying the other.

Jiang Zemin, 76, who had taken over the party following the massacre of prodemocracy protesters at Tiananmen Square in 1989 and guided China through a period of stunning economic growth, gave up his position as party general secretary on November 14, 2002. He was succeeded the next day by Hu Jintao, 59, a bureaucrat who also was expected to assume Jiang's government post as president of China in March 2003. (Tiananmen Square, Historic Documents of 1989, p. 275)

In the smoothest transition of power since the party took control of China in 1949, eight other men of Hu's generation were named in November to the powerful Standing Committee of the Politburo during the week-long Sixteenth National Congress of the Communist Party. Among them were those expected to succeed Prime Minister Zhu Rongji, 74, who had overseen many of China's economic reforms, and Li Peng, 74, head of the National Congress (the parliament) who had been the most visible symbol of government's use of force at Tiananmen Square. Dozens of other officials in their forties, fifties, and early sixties were named to the Central Committee, a body of 356 members from which the twenty-four-member Politburo and the nine-member Standing Committee were drawn. The Standing Committee basically ran the country on a day-to-day basis.

Although he was giving up most of his formal positions, Jiang was expected to remain a significant influence in Chinese affairs for some time to come. At least for the time being he remained chairman of the party's military commission (which controlled the armed forces), and he maneuvered appointments to the Standing Committee of several protégés. In the one visible sign of power struggle, Jiang forced off the Standing Committee a per-

sonal rival, Li Ruihuan, considered by many to be among the most liberal of the leaders who had served with Jiang.

Jiang also ensured his place in history by winning formal adoption of his contribution to Communist Party dogma to take place beside theories of Mao Zedong and Deng Xiaoping. Jiang's "Three Represents" theory said the party represented the best elements of modern China: the workers, the "broad interests of the entire society," and "advanced forces." The new element was the third, which referred to the capitalists, who were engineering the country's economic growth, and the emerging middle class, who were in the vanguard of that change. Putting substance to the theory, the Party Congress welcomed its first-ever members from the capitalist community—owners and executives of private businesses, once condemned as "exploiters" and worse.

In a ninety-minute speech to the Congress on November 8, accompanied by a lengthy written report, Jiang urged continued reforms and said China's future depended on its economic relations with the rest of the world. "All investors at home or from overseas should be encouraged to carry out business activities in China's development," he said. "All legitimate income, from work or not [a reference to investments], should be protected." Even so, there were limits to reform, particularly in politics, Jiang said: "We must never copy any models of the political system of the West."

Jiang's Legacy

Jiang represented the third generation of China's top communist leadership, following Mao and Deng. Mao led the party in its long battle to take control of China during the first half of the twentieth century and then struggled to control both the party and China after victory came in 1949. As was the case with many revolutionary leaders, Mao proved to be less capable as an administrator than as an ideological inspiration. Deng, who took over after Mao's death in 1976, had a career that spanned the revolution, the excesses of the postrevolutionary years, and then China's coming to terms with the rest of the world. Perhaps more than any other figure in modern-day China, Deng was responsible for recognizing that communist dogma could not lift an entire country of more than 1 billion people out of poverty. (Deng's death, Historic Documents of 1997, p. 94)

While he never inspired either the frenzied adoration or the vituperative hatred that occasionally attended his more famous predecessors, Jiang did leave a permanent mark on his country. At the time of the Tiananmen Square protests, Jiang was Communist Party secretary in Shanghai. Following that trauma, Deng moved Jiang from Shanghai to take over the national party and to carry out Deng's plan for introducing capitalism into China. Jiang, according to most experts, ensured that old-line party leaders could not derail such steps as the creation of private corporations controlled by both the government and foreign investors and the reform or even closing of some of the giant state-run industrial firms that were unprofitable. Most important for the long term, Jiang and Prime Minister Zhu oversaw China's entry into the World Trade Organization in 2001, an action that ultimately would force the country to adopt world business standards if it was to continue attracting the foreign investment needed for economic growth.

Politically, Jiang's years in power saw the continued evolution of China away from a totalitarian state that was firmly under the Communist Party's grip in every respect. Instead, China was becoming an authoritarian state, in which the party no longer was able to control every aspect of the economy and peoples' lives. The elements of control—the huge army and ubiquitous security services, the state-controlled media, a judiciary system that did not recognize personal liberties—remained in place to guarantee that Western-style democracy would not take root. But a people who were now able to think about bettering their lives through capitalism also had a limited degree of freedom to think new political thoughts, so long as they did not express them too publicly.

The Communist Party also changed substantially during Jiang's thirteen years at the helm. The party was no longer a revolutionary band of uneducated workers and peasant farmers united by Marxist and Maoist ideology. Of the 2,114 delegates who attended the Sixteenth Party Congress, more than 90 percent held college degrees. That figure was an important symbol that the party had evolved into a leadership elite of government officials, professional army generals, and business entrepreneurs, with a few token workers as a reminder of the past. At the beginning of the twenty-first century, Chinese sought membership in the party not because of Mao's ideals but because it guaranteed them access to privileges, such as better jobs or a chance to obtain financing and contracts for a business they wanted to start.

By the time Jiang stepped down, millions of Chinese men and women had begun to experience the benefits of capitalism and a few new personal freedoms. Incomes were up dramatically in many urban areas (especially Shanghai, Shenzhen, Guangzhou, and other coastal cities), consumer goods were more available than ever before, and parents could realistically hope that their children would have even better lives. But that picture of progress was not uniform. Tens of millions of workers had lost their jobs when state-run industries were forced to close or limit production, and income in rural areas was falling because of inefficient agricultural production.

The New Leadership

Hu Jintao was the most visible, but also one of the least known, of the new inner circle of Chinese leaders. Trained as a hydroelectric engineer, Hu in 1982 became the youngest member of the party's Central Committee at age thirty-nine. He served as party secretary in remote Guizhou province and later in Tibet, where he imposed martial law to quell riots in 1988 protesting Chinese rule. Hu's rise in the party leadership was accelerated in 1992 when Deng put him on the Politburo and designated him as the successor to Jiang. So powerful was Deng's continuing influence that Hu was made vice president in 1998, a year after Deng died. Hu gradually stepped into the limelight, visiting Europe in 2001 and the United States in 2002, when he met with President George W. Bush. All descriptions of Hu portrayed an extremely cautious man who left few fingerprints but possessed the intelligence (in-

cluding a reported photographic memory) and self-confidence necessary for such a rapid rise to the top of China's conservative hierarchy. Analysts said it was possible that Hu would try to force dramatic changes, but it would be a surprise. Hu's public pronouncements were as bland as his bespectacled, dark-suit personal appearance. In his comment November 15 on the results of the Party Congress, perhaps his most memorable line was: "This is a meeting which has carried on the past and opened a new chapter for the future."

Analysts who studied the closely held Chinese leadership predicted that one of Hu's chief tasks would be to develop a working relationship with several of Jiang's loyalists who also had been named to the Standing Committee of the Politburo. Probably most important among them was Zeng Qinghong, 63, who had been Jiang's chief aide and was known for his use of sharp elbows in the party's bruising behind-the-scenes squabbles. Wen Jiabao, an aide to outgoing Prime Minister Zhu, was expected to inherit that post in March 2003. In China's system, the prime minister was in charge of daily government affairs while the president represented China to the world—especially when he also happened to be general secretary of the party.

Hu and most of his new colleagues on the Standing Committee represented the first generation of Chinese leaders who were too young to have participated in the long civil war leading to the communist takeover in 1949 and therefore grew to maturity in a China dominated by the party. All rose to their positions because of their ability to stand out in a political system that was extremely competitive behind the scenes, not in the public setting of a democracy. All of them appeared to be committed to continuing the economic reforms instituted by Deng and advanced by Jiang. But analysts said the new leaders also were aware of the many failings of the communist system and were prepared to take gradual steps to modernize it, without adopting either the trappings or the substance of democracy. These leaders were "aware of popular dissatisfaction with the Communist Party but not intimidated by it," China specialists Andrew J. Nathan and Bruce Gilley wrote in the October 10 edition of the New York Review of Books.

Challenges Ahead

As the new leaders prepared to assume power, there seemed little question that economic growth would continue as China opened itself to increased investment from and trade with the outside world. What was in question was the government's ability to manage the growth by carrying out economic reforms that were necessary for the long term but could cause severe social upheaval over the short term.

Since it first experimented with capitalism in 1979, China's economic growth averaged more than 9 percent annually, according to official figures. Even discounting for a degree of exaggeration on the government's part, China experienced the strongest sustained economic growth of any major country in the world at the close of the twentieth century. China's overall economy was still relatively small—at $1.2 trillion in 2001, about the same size as Italy's—but its rate of growth, if continued, put it on course to surpass even the United States in size some time in the twenty-first century.

Despite this economic growth, China remained a poor country for the most part. The World Bank estimated in 2002 that nearly one-third of China's 1.3 billion people lived in what the bank defined as extreme poverty, with a per capita income of less than $1 a day. Even as capitalist enterprises were creating China's first millionaires, the vast majority of peasants and workers still eked out a living just above the level of subsistence. According to unofficial estimates, the per capita income in rural China had fallen for the previous four years in a row.

Economic dislocation was common in the cities, as well. An estimated 30 million urban workers had lost their jobs since 1997 as money-losing industries owned by the state closed their doors or sharply cut back production. According to official estimates, more than 170,000 state-owned enterprises accounted for about one-fourth of China's industrial production and employed about two-thirds of urban workers. But about one-half of those companies were unprofitable, producing bicycles, air conditioners, and other goods that were in oversupply domestically and were too shoddy to market overseas.

Past job cutbacks in state industries, and other economic privations, had led to numerous social disturbances but to date all had been suppressed at the local level. Over the longer term, however, most experts and even many Chinese officials said the country would have to quell unrest with better jobs, schools, and health care, not just with the policeman's truncheon.

China's banking system also presented a worrisome picture for the new leaders. For years the four major state-owned banks had been required to pump about two-thirds of their lending into the unprofitable state-owned industries—money that could have been put into more efficient operations. By 2002, according to most estimates, the banks held at least $250 billion in bad loans that were unlikely to be repaid, a figure that technically made three of the four banks insolvent by world standards of accounting.

In his final report to the Party Congress, Jiang acknowledged another issue that was often on the minds of Chinese citizens and foreigners alike: corruption. After five decades in power, the Communist Party had developed many aspects of a mafia, with party functionaries both high and low using their positions to extract bribes and other favors as payment for doing their jobs. Western businesses, while attracted to China by the low wages of workers and the enormous potential market there, repeatedly complained that corruption and uneven enforcement of the country's arcane bureaucratic rules seemed to trump the free market. Even the government admitted that capital flight was costing China an estimated $40 billion each year—not the usual problem of private investors fleeing a risky situation but of party bureaucracies shipping the fruit of corrupt practices to foreign bank accounts for safekeeping.

Jiang said corruption also endangered the party's standing with the people. "If we do not crack down on corruption, the flesh-and-blood ties between the party and the people will suffer a lot and the party will be in danger of losing its ruling position, or possibly heading for self-destruction," Jiang wrote. In keeping with the party line, Jiang suggested that the prob-

*lem was the result of misbehavior by individual party members, not a con-
sequence of the party's long-term control of power. He offered few specific
cures but said senior party leaders had to lead by example by "exercising the
power in their hands correctly."*

*The health of China's 1.3 billion people was another issue that govern-
ment officials were just beginning to address at the turn of the century. The
country's headlong rush into industrial development had severely damaged
the environment, making the air and rivers in Chinese cities among the most
polluted in the world. The United Nations Environment Program estimated,
in its 2002 Global Environmental Outlook, that more than 20 million urban
residents in China lacked access to safe water supplies. Poor air quality
contributed to a tuberculosis epidemic in parts of the country.*

*China also had one of the world's fastest-growing problems with the AIDS
virus. In its 2002 report, the UN's AIDS agency said that China was on the
verge of a "catastrophe that could result in unimaginable suffering, economic loss, and social devastation" unless the government acted quickly
with programs of education and treatment. While the government had begun
to take notice of the AIDS epidemic, it was still uncertain in 2002 that the issue had captured much attention at the highest levels. For example, Jiang's
21,000-word report discussed many problems facing the country—but AIDS
was not among them.* (AIDS issue, p. 469)

China-U.S. Relations

*Ever since President Richard M. Nixon (1969–1974) traveled to China in
1972, the two countries had engaged in a diplomatic dance that brought
them ever closer, while still maintaining a respectful distance. Jiang had
continued his predecessors' policy of seeking better relations with Washington without limiting China's freedom to take positions at odds with U.S. policy. He was China's most-traveled leader ever, visiting the United States
repeatedly for meetings with presidents Bill Clinton and George W. Bush,
traveling widely throughout Europe and Asia, and regularly attending summits of such groups as the Asia-Pacific Economic Cooperation Forum.*

*Relations between China and the new Bush administration got off to a
rocky start in April 2001 when a Chinese fighter plane collided with a U.S.
spy plane off southern China. The U.S. plane was forced to make an emergency landing on Hainan Island, and the twenty-four crew members were
detained by China for eleven days. The heated rhetoric that accompanied a
tense diplomatic standoff before China released the plane's crew gradually
gave way to business as usual, which meant focusing on expanded economic ties between the two countries.* (Spy plane standoff, Historic Documents of 2001, p. 247)

*Later in 2001 and throughout 2002, Jiang carefully aligned China with
important elements of U.S. foreign policy. After the September 11, 2001, terrorist attacks against the United States, China supported the U.S. military
response, which centered on an invasion of Afghanistan to root out the al
Qaeda terrorist network headquartered there. In November 2002, less than a
week before the Party Congress convened, China joined a unanimous United*

Nations Security Council in adopting a U.S.-requested resolution demanding that Iraq keep its promise to disarm. In years past, China might, reflexively, have taken positions at odds with U.S. interests. (Iraq resolution, p. 713; Afghanistan invasion, Historic Documents of 2001, p. 686)

In late October, Jiang paid one last visit to the United States as president and was invited to President Bush's ranch at Crawford, Texas. Jiang and Bush, in their third meeting since Bush took office in January 2001, reportedly focused on North Korea's admission earlier in the month that it had started a secret program to develop additional nuclear weapons. Jiang said he and Bush agreed to work toward a peaceful resolution of what he acknowledged was a "problem." (North Korea issue, p. 731)

Taiwan remained the one issue with the greatest potential for a dangerous miscalculation that might lead to conflict between the United States and China. While both countries accepted the concept of "one China" that included Taiwan, they had radically different visions of what that meant. Beijing's leaders clearly were determined to assert de facto control over Taiwan at some point, with the question being one of timing. After the election in 2001 of a new president in Taiwan committed to the island's independence, Beijing issued threats that backfired by reinforcing the independence movement on the island and leading Bush to toughen the U.S. commitment to defend Taiwan by force, if necessary. Even so, China continued to build its military position in such a way that gave it potential strengthen to seize Taiwan by force or coercion, according to a Pentagon report released in mid-July.

Following are excerpts from a report submitted by President Jiang Zemin on November 8, 2002, to the Sixteenth National Congress of the Communist Party of China, in which he summarized progress during his years in power and urged continued economic reforms under his successors.

The document was obtained from the Internet at www .16congress.org.cn/english/features/49007.htm; accessed November 17, 2002.

The theme of the congress is to hold high the great banner of Deng Xiaoping Theory, fully act on the important thought of Three Represents, carry forward our cause into the future, keep pace with the times, build a well-off society in an all-round way, speed up socialist modernization and work hard to create a new situation in building socialism with Chinese characteristics.

As human society entered the 21st century, we started a new phase of development for building a well-off society in an all-round way and speeding up socialist modernization. The international situation is undergoing profound changes. The trends toward world multipolarization and economic globalization are developing amidst twists and turns. Science and technology are advancing rapidly. Competition in overall national strength is becoming increasingly fierce. Given this pressing situation, we must move forward, or we will fall behind. Our Party must stand firm in the forefront of the times and unite with and lead the Chinese people of all ethnic groups in accomplishing the three major historical tasks: to propel the modernization drive, to achieve national reunification and to safeguard world peace and promote common development, and in bringing about the great rejuvenation of the Chinese nation on its road to socialism with Chinese characteristics. This is a grand mission history and the era have entrusted to our Party.

I. Work of the Past Five Years and Basic Experience of 13 Years

... The national economy has maintained a sustained, rapid and sound development. By pursuing the principle of stimulating domestic demand and adopting the proactive fiscal policy and the sound monetary policy in good time, we overcame the adverse effects the Asian financial crisis and world economic fluctuations had on China, and maintained a relatively rapid economic growth. The strategic adjustment of the economic structure has been crowned with success. The position of agriculture as the foundation of the economy has been strengthened. Traditional industries have been upgraded. High and new technology industries and modern services have gained speed. A large number of infrastructure projects in such areas as water conservancy, transportation, telecommunications, energy and environmental protection have been completed. Significant headway has been made in the large-scale development of China's western region. Economic returns have further improved. National revenue has kept growing. The Ninth Five-Year Plan (1996-2000) was fulfilled and the Tenth Five-Year Plan has seen a good start.

Reform and opening up have yielded substantial results. The socialist market economy has taken shape initially. The public sector of the economy has expanded and steady progress has been made in the reform of state-owned enterprises. Self-employed or private enterprises and other non-public sectors of the economy have developed fairly fast. The work of building up the market system has been in full swing. The macro-control system has improved constantly. The pace of change in government functions has been quickened. Reform in finance, taxation, banking, distribution, housing, government institutions and other areas has continued to deepen. The open economy has developed swiftly. Trade in commodities and services and capital flow have grown markedly. China's foreign exchange reserves have risen considerably. With its accession to the World Trade Organization (WTO), China has entered a new stage in its opening up. . . .

On the whole, the people have reached a well-off standard of living. The income of urban and rural residents has gone up steadily. The urban and rural markets have been brisk, and there has been an ample supply of goods. The quality of life of the residents has been on the rise, with considerable improvement in food, clothing, housing, transport and daily necessities. There has been marked progress in building the social security system. The seven-year program to help 80 million people out of poverty has been in the main fulfilled. . . .

We must be clearly aware that there are still quite a few difficulties and problems in our work. The income of farmers and some urban residents has increased only slowly. The number of the unemployed has gone up. Some people are still badly off. Things have yet to be straightened out in the matter of income distribution. The order of the market economy has to be further rectified and standardized. Public order is poor in some places. Formalism, the bureaucratic style of work, falsification, extravagance and waste are still serious problems among some leading cadres in our Party, and corruption is still conspicuous in some places. The Party's way of leadership and governance does not yet entirely meet the requirements of the new situation and new tasks. Some Party organizations are feeble and lax. We must pay close attention to these problems and continue to take effective measures to solve them. . . .

Over the past 13 years, with clearly defined objectives, we worked with one heart and one mind and scored historic achievements. In 2001, China's GDP reached 9.5933 trillion yuan, almost tripling that of 1989, representing an average annual increase of 9.3 percent. China came up to the sixth place in the world in terms of economic aggregate. On the whole, the people made a historic leap from having only adequate food and clothing to leading a well-off life. As is universally recognized, the 13 years have been a period in which China's overall national strength has risen by a big margin, the people have received more tangible benefits than ever before, and China has enjoyed long-term social stability and solidarity and had a good government and a united people. China's influence in the world has grown notably, and the cohesion of the nation has increased remarkably. The hard work of our Party and people and their great achievements have attracted worldwide attention and will surely go down as a glorious page in the annals of the great rejuvenation of the Chinese nation.

A review of these 13 years shows that we have traversed a tortuous course and that our achievements are hard won. We have responded confidently to a series of unexpected international events bearing on China's sovereignty and security. We have surmounted difficulties and risks arising from the political and economic spheres and from nature. We have gone through one trial after another and removed all kinds of obstacles, thus ensuring that our reform, opening up and modernization drive have been forging ahead in the correct direction like a ship braving surging waves. We have attained these successes by relying on the correct guidance of the Party's basic theory, line and program, on the high degree of unity and solidarity of the Party and on the tenacious work of the whole Party and the people of all ethnic groups around the country. . . .

II. Implement the Important Thought of Three Represents in an All-Round Way

. . . We must be aware that China is in the primary stage of socialism and will remain so for a long time to come. The well-off life we are leading is still at a low level; it is not all-inclusive and is very uneven. The principal contradiction in our society is still one between the ever-growing material and cultural needs of the people and the backwardness of social production. Our productive forces, science, technology and education are still relatively backward, so there is still a long way to go before we achieve industrialization and modernization. The dual structure in urban and rural economy has not yet been changed, the gap between regions is still widening and there are still quite a large number of impoverished people. China's population continues to grow, the proportion of the aged is getting larger, and the pressure on employment and social security is mounting. The contradiction between the ecological environment and natural resources on the one hand and economic and social development on the other is becoming increasingly conspicuous. We still feel pressure from developed countries as they have the upper hand in such fields as the economy, science and technology. The economic structure and managerial systems in other fields remain to be perfected. There are still some problems we cannot afford to overlook in improving democracy and the legal system as well as the ideological and ethical standards. We need to work hard over a long period of time to consolidate and uplift our current well-off standard of living.

An overview of the situation shows that for our country, the first two decades of the 21st century are a period of important strategic opportunities, which we must seize tightly and which offers bright prospects. In accordance with the development objectives up to 2010, the centenary of the Party and that of New China, as proposed at the Fifteenth National Congress, we need to concentrate on building a well-off society of a higher standard in an all-round way to the benefit of well over one billion people in this period. We will further develop the economy, improve democracy, advance science and education, enrich culture, foster social harmony and upgrade the texture of life for the people. The two decades of development will serve as an inevitable connecting link for attainting the third-step strategic objectives for our modernization drive as well as a key stage for improving the socialist market economy and opening wider to the outside world. Building on what is achieved at this stage and continuing to work for several more decades, we will have in the main accomplished the modernization program and turned China into a strong, prosperous, democratic and culturally advanced socialist country by the middle of this century.

III. The Objectives of Building a Well-off Society in an All-Round Way

— On the basis of optimized structure and better economic returns, efforts will be made to quadruple the GDP of the year 2000 by 2020, and China's overall national strength and international competitiveness will increase markedly. We will in the main achieve industrialization and establish a full-fledged socialist market economy and a more open and viable economic system. The proportion of urban population will go up considerably and the trend of widening differences between industry and agriculture, between urban and rural areas and between regions will be reversed step by step. We will have a fairly sound social security system. There will be a higher rate of employment. People will have more family property and lead a more prosperous life. . . .

IV. Economic Development and Restructuring

. . . State-owned enterprises are the pillar of the national economy. We should deepen the reform of state-owned enterprises and further explore diversified forms for effectively realizing public ownership, especially state ownership. We should promote institutional, technological and managerial innovations in enterprises. Except for a tiny number of enterprises that must be funded solely by the state, all the others should introduce the joint-stock system to develop a mixed sector of the economy. Sources of investment must be diversified. The controlling shares in lifeline enterprises must be held by the state. Large and medium state-owned enterprises must continue their reform to convert themselves into standard companies in compliance with the requirements of the modern enterprise system and improve their corporate governance. Monopoly industries should carry out reforms to introduce competition mechanisms. We should form large internationally competitive companies and enterprise groups through market forces and policy guidance. We should give a freer rein to small and medium state-owned enterprises to invigorate themselves. We should deepen the reform of collective enterprises and give more support and help to the growth of the various forms of the collective sector of the economy.

We must give full scope to the important role of the non-public sector of self-employed, private and other forms of ownership of the economy in stimulating economic growth, creating more jobs and activating the market. We should expand the areas for the market access of domestic nongovernmental capital and adopt measures with regard to investment, financing, taxation, land use, foreign trade and other aspects to carry out fair competition. We should strengthen the supervision and administration of the non-public sectors according to law to promote their sound development. We should improve the legal system for protecting private property.

5. Improve the modern market system and tighten and improve macroeconomic control. We should give a fuller play to the basic role of the market in the allocation of resources and build up a unified, open, competitive and orderly modern market system. We should go ahead with reform, opening up, stability and development of the capital market. We should develop markets for property rights, land, labor and technology and create an environment for the equal use of production factors by market players. We must deepen the reform of the distribution system and introduce modern ways of distribution. We must rectify and standardize the order of the market economy and establish a social credit system compatible with a modern market economy. We must get rid of trade monopolies and regional blockades to allow free movement of goods and production factors on markets around the country.

We must improve the government functions of economic regulation, market supervision, social administration and public services, and reduce and standardize administrative procedures for examination and approval. We must stimulate economic growth, create more jobs, stabilize prices and maintain balance of international payments as the main macroeconomic control objectives. Stimulating domestic demand is an essential and long-standing factor underlying China's economic growth. We must stick to the policy of stimulating domestic demand and implement corresponding macroeconomic policies in light of actual needs. We must adjust the relationship between investment and consumption to raise the proportion of consumption in GDP gradually. We should improve the macroeconomic control system featuring the coordination of state planning and fiscal and monetary policies to give play to economic leverage. We should deepen the reform of the fiscal, taxation, banking, investment and financing systems. We should improve the budgetary decision-making and management system, step up the supervision of revenue and expenditures and intensify tax administration. We should carry out the reform steadily to deregulate interest rates to leave them to market forces, optimize the allocation of financial resources, strengthen regulation and prevent and defuse financial risks so as to provide better banking services for economic and social development.

6. Deepen the reform of the income distribution system and improve the social security system. Rationalizing the relations of income distribution bears on the immediate interests of the general public and the display of their initiative. We should adjust and standardize the relations of distribution among the state, enterprises and individuals. We should establish the principle that labor, capital, technology, managerial expertise and other production factors participate in the distribution of income in accordance with their respective contributions, thereby improving the system under which distribution according to work is dominant and a variety of modes of distribution coexist. We should give priority to efficiency with due consideration to fairness, earnestly implementing the distribution policy while advocating the spirit of devotion and guarding against an excessive disparity in income while opposing equalitarianism. In primary distribution, we should pay more attention to efficiency, bringing the market forces into play and encouraging part of the people to become rich first through honest labor and lawful operations. In redistribution, we should pay more attention to fairness and strengthen the function of the government in regulating income distribution to narrow the gap if it is too wide. We should standardize the order of income distribution, properly regulate the excessively high income of some monopoly industries and outlaw illegal gains. Bearing in mind the objective of common prosperity, we should try to raise the proportion of the middle-income group and increase the income of the low-income group. . . .

V. Political Development and Restructuring

Developing socialist democracy and establishing a socialist political civilization are an important goal for building a well-off society in an all-round way. Adhering to the Four Cardinal Principles, we must go on steadily and surely with political restructuring, extend socialist democracy and improve the socialist legal system in order to build a socialist country under the rule of law and consolidate and develop the political situation characterized by democracy, solidarity, liveliness, stability and harmony.

Our Party has always deemed it its duty to realize and develop people's democracy. Since the beginning of reform and opening up, we have pressed on with political restructuring and improved socialist democracy. The key to developing socialist democracy is to combine the need to uphold the Party's leadership and to ensure that the people are the masters of the country with the need to rule the country by law. Leadership by the Party is the fundamental guarantee that the people are the masters of the country and that the country is ruled by law. The people being the masters of the country constitutes the essential requirement of socialist democracy. Ruling the country by law is the basic principle the Party pursues while it leads the people in running the country. The CPC is the core of leadership for the cause of socialism with Chinese characteristics. Governance by the Communist Party means that it leads and supports the people in acting as the masters of the country and mobilizes and organizes them on a most extensive scale to manage state and social affairs and economic and cultural undertakings according to law, safeguarding and realizing their fundamental interests. The Constitution and other laws embody the unity of the Party's views and the people's will. All organizations and individuals must act in strict accordance with the law, and none of them are allowed to have the privilege to overstep the Constitution and other laws.

Political restructuring is the self-improvement and development of the socialist political system. It must help enhance the vitality of the Party and state, demonstrate the features and advantages of the socialist system, give full scope to the initiative and creativity of the people, safeguard national unity, ethnic solidarity and social stability and promote economic development and social progress. We must always proceed from our national conditions, review our experience gained in practice and at the same time learn from the achievements of political civilization of mankind. We should never copy any models of the political system of the West. We must concentrate on institutional improvement and ensure that socialist democracy is institutionalized and standardized and has its procedures. . . .

2. Improve the socialist legal system. We must see to it that there are laws to go by, the laws are observed and strictly enforced, and law-breakers are prosecuted. To adapt to the new situation characterized by the development of a socialist market economy, all-round social progress and China's accession to the WTO, we will strengthen legislation and improve its quality and will have formulated a socialist system of laws with Chinese characteristics by the year 2010. We must see to it that all people are equal before the law. We should tighten supervision over law enforcement, promote the exercise of administrative functions according to law, safeguard judicial justice and raise the level of law enforcement so that laws are strictly implemented. We must safeguard the uniformity and sanctity of the legal system and prevent or overcome local and departmental protectionism. We will extend and standardize legal services and provide effective legal aid. We should give more publicity to the legal system so that the people are better educated in law. In particular, we will enhance the public servants' awareness of law and their ability to perform their official duties according to law. Party members and cadres, especially leading cadres, should play an exemplary role in abiding by the Constitution and other laws. . . .

VIII. "One Country, Two Systems" and Complete National Reunification

To achieve complete reunification of the motherland is a common aspiration of all sons and daughters of the Chinese nation both at home and abroad. We have successfully resolved the questions of Hong Kong and Macao and are striving for an early settlement of the question of Taiwan and for the accomplishment of the great cause of national reunification.

The return of Hong Kong and Macao to the motherland has enriched the concept of "one country, two systems" in both theory and practice. Facts prove that "one country, two systems" is a correct policy and has strong vitality. We will resolutely implement this policy and act in strict accordance with the basic laws of Hong Kong and Macao special administrative regions. We will render full support to the chief executives and governments of the two regions in their work and unite with people from all walks of life there in a joint effort to maintain and promote the prosperity, stability and development of Hong Kong and Macao.

We will adhere to the basic principles of "peaceful reunification" and "one country, two systems" and the eight-point proposal on developing cross-straits relations and advancing the process of peaceful national reunification at the present stage. We will work with our compatriots in Taiwan to step up personnel exchanges and promote economic, cultural and other interflows between the two sides and firmly oppose the Taiwan separatist forces. The basic configuration and development trend of the cross-straits relations remain unchanged. The desire of our Taiwan compatriots for peace, stability and development is growing stronger day by day. The splitting activities by the Taiwan separatist forces are unpopular.

Adherence to the one-China principle is the basis for the development of cross-straits relations and the realization of peaceful reunification. There is but one China in the world, and both the mainland and Taiwan belong to one China. China's sovereignty and territorial integrity brook no division. We firmly oppose all words and deeds aimed at creating "Taiwan independence", "two Chinas" or "one China, one Taiwan". The future of Taiwan lies in the reunification of the motherland. To conduct dialogue and hold negotiations on peaceful reunification has been our consistent position. Here we repeat our appeal: On the basis of the one-China principle, let us shelve for now certain political disputes and resume the cross-straits dialogue and negotiations as soon as possible. On the premise of the one-China principle, all issues can be discussed. We may discuss how to end the cross-straits hostility formally. We may also discuss the international space in which the Taiwan region may conduct economic, cultural and social activities compatible with its status, or discuss the political status of the Taiwan authorities or other issues. We are willing to exchange views with all political parties and personages of all circles in Taiwan on the development of cross-straits relations and the promotion of peaceful reunification.

We place our hopes on the people in Taiwan for the settlement of the Taiwan question and the realization of the complete reunification of China. Our compatriots in Taiwan have a glorious patriotic tradition and are an important force in developing cross-straits relations. We fully respect their life style and their wish to be the masters of our country. The two sides should expand mutual contacts and exchanges and work together to carry forward the fine tradition of the Chinese culture. As the direct links of mail, air and shipping services, and trade across the Taiwan Straits serve the common interests of the compatriots on both sides, there is every reason to take practical and positive steps to promote such direct links and open up new prospects for cross-straits economic cooperation.

"One country, two systems" is the best way for the reunification between the two sides. After its reunification with the mainland, Taiwan may keep its existing social system unchanged and enjoy a high degree of autonomy. Our Taiwan compatriots may keep their way of life unchanged, and their vital interests will be fully guaranteed. They will enjoy a lasting peace. Taiwan may then truly rely on the mainland as its hinterland for economic growth and thus get broad space for development. Our Taiwan compatriots may join the people on the mainland in exercising the right to administer the country and sharing the dignity and honor of the great motherland in the international community.

The 23 million Taiwan compatriots are our brothers and sisters of the same blood. No one is more eager than we are to resolve the Taiwan question through peaceful means. We will continue to implement the basic principles of "peaceful reunification" and "one country, two systems" and act on the eight-point proposal. We will work in utmost sincerity and do all we can to strive for a peaceful reunification. Our position of never undertaking to renounce the use of force is not directed at our Taiwan compatriots. It is aimed at the foreign forces' attempts to interfere in China's reunification and the Taiwan separatist forces' schemes for "Taiwan independence". To safeguard national unity bears on the fundamental interests of the Chinese nation. We Chinese people will safeguard our state sovereignty and territorial integrity with firm resolve. We will never allow anyone to separate Taiwan from China in any way.

China will be reunified, and the Chinese nation will be rejuvenated. The Taiwan question must not be allowed to drag on indefinitely. We are convinced that with the concerted efforts of all sons and daughters of the Chinese nation, the complete reunification of the motherland will be achieved at an early date. . . .

X. Strengthen and Improve Party Building

In a large multi-ethnic developing country like ours, we must spare no efforts to strengthen and improve the Party's leadership and fully advance the great new undertaking of Party building if we are to rally the entire people to work heart and soul in building a well-off society in an all-round way and speed up the socialist modernization drive. . . .

6. Strengthen and improve the Party's style of work and intensify the struggle against corruption. The key to improving the Party's style of work lies in keeping the flesh-and-blood ties between the Party and the people. The biggest political advantage of our Party lies in its close ties with the masses while the biggest potential danger for it as a ruling party comes from its divorce from them. We must at all times and under all circumstances adhere to the Party's mass line, and to the purpose of serving the people heart and soul and

regard the people's interests as the starting point and goal of all our work. We must carry forward the fine tradition and style of our Party, bearing in mind the fundamental principle that the Party is built for the public and that it exercises state power for the people. We must make effective efforts to resolve the outstanding issues in respect of the way of thinking, study and work of our Party, its style of leadership and its cadres' way of life and especially to prevent and overcome formalism and bureaucracy by acting on the principle of the "eight do's" and "eight don'ts" [1. Emancipate the mind and seek truth from facts; do not stick to old ways and make no progress. 2. Combine theory with practice; do not copy mechanically or take to book worship. 3. Keep close ties with the people; do not go in for formalism and bureaucracy. 4. Adhere to the principle of democratic centralism; do not act arbitrarily or stay feeble and lax. 5. Abide by Party discipline; do not pursue liberalism. 6. Be honest and upright; do not abuse power for personal gains. 7. Work hard; do not indulge in hedonism. 8. Appoint people on their merits; do not resort to malpractice in personnel placement.] put forward by the Party Central Committee, by resorting to both educational and institutional means and by correctly conducting criticism and self-criticism. Closely following the new changes in social activities and carefully studying the new features of our mass work, we must strengthen and improve such work throughout the process of building the Party and political power. All Party members, primarily leading cadres at all levels, must do mass work well in light of the new situation and, by persuading, setting examples and providing services, unite and lead the masses in making progress.

To combat and prevent corruption resolutely is a major political task of the whole Party. If we do not crack down on corruption, the flesh-and-blood ties between the Party and the people will suffer a lot and the Party will be in danger of losing its ruling position, or possibly heading for self-destruction. Against the background of its long-term governance and China's opening up and development of the socialist market economy, the Party must be on full alert against corrosion by all decadent ideas and maintain the purity of its membership. Party committees at all levels must fully recognize the urgency as well as the protracted nature of the fight against corruption. They should enhance confidence, do a solid job, take a clear-cut stand and never waver in carrying on the fight in depth. We should work still harder to make sure that our leading cadres are clean, honest and self-disciplined, and see to it that major corruption cases are investigated and dealt with. Malpractices in departments and trades and services must be corrected. We must adhere to the principle of addressing both symptoms and root causes of corruption and taking comprehensive measures to rectify both while devoting greater efforts gradually to tackling the latter. We must strengthen education, develop democracy, improve the legal system, tighten supervision, make institutional innovation and incorporate counter-corruption in all our major policy measures so as to prevent and tackle corruption at its source. We must uphold and improve the leadership system and working mechanism against corruption and earnestly implement the responsibility system for improving the Party's work style and building clean government, in a concerted effort to prevent and punish corruption. Leading cadres, particularly senior ones, should play an exemplary role in exercising the power in their hands correctly. They must always be honest and upright and take the initiative to crack down on all forms of corruption. All corruptionists must be thoroughly investigated and punished without leniency.

So long as all Party comrades always maintain the vigor and vitality, dashing spirit and integrity as Communists and have the people at heart, the foundation of our Party's governance will remain rock solid. . . .

CATHOLIC BISHOPS ON
SEXUAL ABUSE BY PRIESTS
November 13, 2002

Widespread allegations of child sexual abuse by priests, and revelations that some church officials covered up many of those activities, engulfed the Roman Catholic Church in a bitter controversy in 2002 that undermined the authority of the religious hierarchy in the United States and caused a deep breach within the clergy. By the end of the year, American bishops had adopted a national policy that barred abusive priests from parish work. However, advocates for the abused, many parishioners, and even some priests and other church officials said that changes demanded by the Vatican had weakened the original policy and would allow church officials to continue to cover up cases of sexual abuse.

The scandal was touched off in January when Cardinal Bernard F. Law of Boston was forced to admit he had moved a priest from parish to parish despite evidence that the priest was a child molester. Evidence released later in the year showed that Law had handled several other abuse cases similarly, moving priests to other parishes without notifying either the parish or law enforcement officials of the suspected abuse.

Similar revelations quickly came from other Catholic dioceses around the country. Over the next few months at least 200 priests suspected of sexual abuse had either resigned or been removed from their duties in parishes in more than half the states, and most of the remaining states were actively reviewing their personnel files and turning the names of suspected abusers over to law enforcement officials. By the end of May a bishop and an archbishop had resigned, at least two priests accused of abuse had committed suicide, and another was shot and seriously wounded by his accuser. Hundreds of lawsuits alleging abuse and seeking financial settlement had been filed, and thousands of Catholic parishioners had joined reform groups demanding changes within the church, including ending the celibacy requirement and allowing the ordination of women.

In June, after an emotional two-day meeting where victims tearfully testified to their abuse at the hands of priests, the U.S. Conference of Catholic Bishops approved a policy that would require the removal from public ministry of any priest convicted of molesting a child, even if the abuse had occurred only once many decades earlier. The Vatican, which had to approve the policy before it could take effect, said it did not afford the accused priests their due process rights under canon law and demanded changes. The bishops asserted that the changes adopted in November made the policy stronger, but many in the victims rights and reform groups were unpersuaded, arguing that the disciplinary proceedings would still be behind closed doors and the bishops who had sought to hide the extent of the problem for so long had not been brought to account for the suffering they had caused.

Even the December resignation of Cardinal Law as archbishop of Boston appeared to do little to quell the outrage that had been unleashed. Victim's rights groups immediately turned their sights on other bishops that the groups said had been equally insensitive in their zeal to protect the church from scandal and from financial losses stemming from settlement of legal suits.

Spreading Allegations of Abuse

Neither allegations of sexual abuse nor assertions that church officials tried to hide it were new. National attention had focused on the abuse problem in 1985, when a priest in Louisiana pleaded guilty to molesting eleven boys. In 1992 the Archdiocese of Chicago adopted a policy setting out measures to protect children from sexual abuse by priests. The policy was issued after parishioners learned that the church had kept secret previous allegations of abuse against a priest who had been accused of molesting a young girl and propositioning a young man. "Very often, allegations of sexual abuse have not been handled well in the Church because the overriding concern has been to do everything possible to protect the rights of priests, at times leading to an infringement of the rights of the victims," wrote the church commission that drafted the policy. (Chicago policy, Historic Documents of 1992, p. 507)

An overriding concern to protect the Catholic Church was at the heart of the controversy that exploded in Boston on January 6, when the Boston Globe *published a front-page story alleging that the Boston Archdiocese had moved the Rev. John J. Geoghan from parish to parish over a thirty-year period knowing full well that Geoghan had been accused of molesting children. (On January 18 Geoghan was sentenced to up to ten years in prison on charges of molesting a young boy, but attorneys involved with the case said he may have had as many as 130 victims.) Law, who in the past had staunchly defended his handling of sexual abuse allegations, acknowledged on January 9 that he been aware of the allegations against Geoghan but still kept him in parish work rather than removing him from the ministry. Law apologized to Geoghan's victims and to parishioners for secretly paying $10 million to settle some fifty cases against him. The Archdiocese also reportedly began turning over to law enforcement officials the names of other priests who had been accused of sexual abuse during the last four decades.*

For many Catholics in the Boston area, Law's apologies were too little too late. Many parishioners called on Law to resign, and a few Catholic priests *were reported to be ashamed to wear their collars in public. The outcry surrounding the Boston revelations prompted church officials in New York, Philadelphia, and elsewhere to begin to turn over names of alleged offenders to authorities. The Boston scandal also encouraged other victims of sexual abuse to take their allegations public. By the end of the year nearly 300 priests suspected of abuse had either resigned or been removed from their duties. Among those who resigned were three bishops. In addition, Archbishop Rembert Weakland of Milwaukee, a leading liberal in the American Catholic hierarchy, resigned after it was revealed that his archdiocese had paid $450,000 to a man alleging that Weakland had tried to sexually assault him. Weakland admitted having an "inappropriate relationship" with the man but denied that it was abusive.*

The revelations of widespread abuse renewed calls in some quarters for the Catholic Church to abandon its celibacy requirement and to permit women to be ordained as priests. Others tried to put the allegations in perspective, noting that the number of priests accused of abuse was a very small percentage of the more than 46,000 priests working in the United States and that many of the allegations involved incidents that had occurred years in the past and apparently had not been repeated. But the most pressing calls were for new church policies that would ensure that abusive priests were prevented from continuing to harm children and were prosecuted openly for their crimes. Many looked not only to their own church officials but to the Vatican for a response.

Initial Response

In the past the Vatican had tended to deny the substance of abuse allegations, saying that they were lodged to discredit the church or as a part of a campaign to end the celibacy requirement. By March 2002 some Vatican officials were changing that stance and saying that seminaries had to do a better job of screening applicants for the priesthood, perhaps through psychological testing. On March 21 Pope John Paul II broke his silence on the subject and said the "grave scandal" was casting a "dark shadow of suspicion over all the other fine priests who perform their ministry with honesty and integrity and often with heroic self-sacrifice." The pope's brief comments, embedded in a letter to priests that addressed several topics, did little to assure those who thought the church was turning a blind eye to the allegations.

The Vatican summoned U.S. cardinals to a meeting on April 23 after many cardinals specifically asked for guidance about how they should proceed. The extraordinary meeting was said to signal the Vatican's realization of the seriousness of the crisis in the United States. Four days before the meeting, the pope set the parameters for the discussion when he reaffirmed the necessity of celibacy and said bishops must "diligently investigate accusations of any" sexual abuse, "taking firm steps to correct it where it is found to exist." At the meeting itself, the pope seemed to signal little tolerance for abusive priests. "There is no place in the priesthood and religious life for those who harm the young," he said.

Six weeks later a committee of the United States Conference of Catholic Bishops released a draft recommendation pledging to defrock all priests found guilty of abuse in the future as well as those priests found to have committed more than one act against a minor at any time in their career. It also pledged that church officials would report all allegations of abuse to civil authorities. But the document did not call for the automatic expulsion of priests found to have committed only a single act of abuse in the past. For many Catholics, priests as well as laypeople, the draft fell short of the zero tolerance they were seeking. "The bishops say zero tolerance, sort of, kind of, maybe, sometimes, and only for those who molest tomorrow," complained David Clohessy, national director of Survivors Network of Those Abused by Priests (SNAP), one of the most active victims' rights organizations.

Meeting in Dallas in June, the bishops listened to testimony from witnesses who described how abuse had affected their lives and heard conference president, Bishop Wilton Gregory, acknowledge that the church had let down its parishioners. They then voted, 239–13, for a zero tolerance policy. In addition to barring all priests who committed sexual abuse from parish work and the public ministry, the policy adopted by Catholic bishops on June 14 set up a procedure for deciding whether to defrock abusive priests and created a review board to annually assess how bishops were responding to abuse. The bishops also pledged that they would no longer keep settlement agreements with abuse victims secret unless requested to do so by the victims. The church would also require background checks for all diocesan and parish workers who came into contact with children.

Revised Draft

To make the new rules, known as "norms," enforceable under canon law the bishops needed approval from the Vatican. But the rules quickly ran afoul of canon lawyers both in the United States and at the Vatican who said the policy denied accused priests due process and ignored the statute of limitations in canon law. Vatican officials were also said to be concerned that American bishops were responding to the crisis by ceding some of their authority to laypeople and inviting scrutiny of their actions by people outside the Catholic Church hierarchy. On October 18 the Vatican refused to approve the new rules unless they were revised.

The rejection pleased Catholics who agreed with the Vatican that the new rules might treat unfairly those priests who were falsely accused or who had been rehabilitated and no longer posed a threat to children. "As a matter of fact, I've been hoping that there would be a refinement of the Dallas charter and the norms, and I welcome what's been called for," said one archbishop. Clohessy, the director of SNAP, expressed outrage, however. "Fundamentally, we're almost back to square one, where each bishop handles it however he deems best, which is precisely what got us into this mess to begin with," he said.

On November 13 the conference of bishops overwhelmingly approved revisions to the plan, which they said would protect children from abuse but also ensure due process for accused priests. The revised policy retained the rule that barred any priest, deacon, or church volunteer from continuing in his or her duties after a conviction of abuse, even if there was only one occurrence many years in the past. But the new rules applied the canonical statute of limitations, which meant that victims had to make their allegations before they turned twenty-eight. Bishops could apply to the Vatican to set aside the statute of limitations in specific cases. The revised rules also prohibited the transfer of any abusive priest to another diocese and required church officials to report allegations of abuse to civil authorities in accordance with applicable civil law. In perhaps the most controversial change, the revised rules established a procedure for hearing allegations of abuse under canon law. Such hearings would be kept confidential, and the accused could appeal their treatment to the Vatican. The new rules took effect after they were approved December 16 by the Vatican.

Healing Expected to Be a Slow Process

The revisions did little to appease victims' rights organizations or others who said the policy would continue the secrecy of the past and contained no procedures for holding accountable bishops who did not follow the rules. A measure of the depth of the anger could be seen in the response to remarks Bishop Gregory made on November 11 opening the meetings to discuss the revised norms. In that speech Gregory acknowledged that the controversy had fractured relations within the church. But he also cautioned his fellow bishops about "extremes within the church who have chosen to exploit the vulnerability of the bishops in this moment to advance their own agendas." Told of that remark by a reporter for the New York Times, *a Kentucky priest, who had been victimized as a child and was protesting the meeting from across the street, said, "Oh my God! Exploit the vulnerability of bishops? This is not now, never has been, and never will be about the vulnerability of bishops. It's about the vulnerability of thousands of innocent children and young people. That he [Gregory] would dare to characterize the bishops as victims in this is deplorable."*

In the wake of the revisions, several victims' rights advocacy groups formed a Coalition of Catholics and Survivors to lobby state legislatures for protections, including mandatory reporting requirements, they said the church was not providing. The group said it would seek the repeal of state statutes of limitation on abuse cases and prison time for people, including church officials, who did report allegations of abuse to the police. Meanwhile lawyers in California were readying hundreds of civil suits for filing on January 1, 2003, when a state law dropping the statute of limitations that had prevented abuse victims from suing the church. The Roman Catholic Diocese of Manchester, New Hampshire, became the first diocese to settle a criminal case when it publicly acknowledged that it had failed to protect children from abusive priests. Grand juries were conducting similar investigations in Arizona, California, Maryland, Massachusetts, Missouri, New York, Ohio, Pennsylvania, and South Carolina.

As the year ended, Massachusetts was still the focal point of attention. On December 3 thousands of personnel files were made public under court order. They showed that priests in the Boston Archdiocese had been accused not only of molesting boys but also of abusing woman and girls as well as taking drugs. The following day Cardinal Law was given permission by church officials to seek bankruptcy protection for the archdiocese from more than 400 plaintiffs who were seeking monetary settlement of their sexual abuse cases from the church. On December 13 Law gave into overwhelming pressure and resigned as archbishop of Boston. Speaking from the Vatican, where he had been meeting for a week with senior officials, Law again apologized for the way he handled the abuse allegations. "To all those who have suffered from my shortcomings and mistakes, I both apologize and from them beg forgiveness," Law said.

How quickly and thoroughly the Catholic Church and its parishioners would be able to put the crisis behind them remained to be seen. Russell Shaw, a former spokesman for the U.S. Conference of Catholic Bishops, summarized the situation well. "The problems this crisis has brought to the surface, or created, are so large, so complex, there's no way this crisis can be quickly solved," he said in November. "Restoring confidence in the bishops, the priesthood, and the authority structures of the church will take a long, long time."

> *Following is the text of "Essential Norms for Diocesan/Eparchial Policies Dealing with Allegations of Sexual Abuse of Minors by Priests or Deacons," the revised policy setting out the procedures for Roman Catholic bishops to follow in dealing with allegations of sexual abuse of minors by clergy, adopted by the United States Conference of Catholic Bishops on November 13, 2002, at a meeting in Washington, D.C.*
>
> ***The document was obtained from the Internet at www.nc-cbuscc.org/bishops/normsrevised.htm; accessed November 21, 2002.***

Preamble

On June 14, 2002, the United States Conference of Catholic Bishops approved a *Charter for the Protection of Children and Young People.* The charter addresses the Church's commitment to deal appropriately and effectively with cases of sexual abuse of minors by priests, deacons, and other church personnel (i.e., employees and volunteers). The bishops of the United States have promised to reach out to those who have been sexually abused as minors by anyone serving the Church in ministry, employment, or a volunteer position, whether the sexual abuse was recent or occurred many years ago. They stated that they would be as open as possible with the people in parishes and communities about instances of sexual abuse of minors, with respect always for the privacy and the reputation of the individuals involved. They have committed themselves to the pastoral and spiritual care and emotional well-being of those who have been sexually abused and of their families.

In addition, the bishops will work with parents, civil authorities, educators, and various organizations in the community to make and maintain the safest environment for minors. In the same way, the bishops have pledged to evaluate the background of seminary applicants as well as all church personnel who have responsibility for the care and supervision of children and young people.

Therefore, to ensure that each diocese/eparchy in the United States of America will have procedures in place to respond promptly to all allegations of sexual abuse of minors, the United States Conference of Catholic Bishops decrees these norms for diocesan/eparchial policies dealing with allegations of sexual abuse of minors by diocesan and religious priests or deacons. These norms are complementary to the universal law of the Church, which has traditionally considered the sexual abuse of minors a grave delict and punishes the offender with penalties, not excluding dismissal from the clerical state if the case so warrants.

Sexual abuse of a minor includes sexual molestation or sexual exploitation of a minor and other behavior by which an adult uses a minor as an object of sexual gratification. Sexual abuse has been defined by different civil authorities in various ways, and these norms do not adopt any particular definition provided in civil law. Rather, the transgressions in question relate to obligations arising from divine commands regarding human sexual interaction as conveyed to us by the sixth commandment of the Decalogue. Thus, the norm to be considered in assessing an allegation of sexual abuse of a minor is whether conduct or interaction with a minor qualifies as an external, objectively grave violation of the sixth commandment. . . . A canonical offence against the sixth commandment of the Decalogue . . . need not be a complete act of intercourse. Nor, to be objectively grave, does an act need to involve force, physical contact, or a discernible harmful outcome. Moreover, "imputability [moral responsibility] for a canonical offense is presumed upon external violation . . . unless it is otherwise apparent. . . ."

Norms

1. Having received the *recognitio* of the Apostolic See on _____, 2002, and having been legitimately promulgated in accordance with the practice of this Episcopal Conference on _____, 2002, these Norms constitute particular law for all the dioceses/eparchies of the United States of America. Two years after *recognitio* has been received, these norms will be evaluated by the plenary assembly of the United States Conference of Catholic Bishops.

2. Each diocese/eparchy will have a written policy on the sexual abuse of minors by priests and deacons, as well as by other church personnel. This policy is to comply fully with, and is to specify in more detail, the steps to be taken in implementing the requirements of canon law, particularly CIC, canons 1717-1719, and CCEO, canons 1468-1470. A copy of this policy will be filed with the United States Conference of Catholic Bishops within three months of the effective date of these norms. Copies

of any eventual revisions of the written diocesan/eparchial policy are also to be filed with the United States Conference of Catholic Bishops within three months of such modifications.

3. Each diocese/eparchy will designate a competent person to coordinate assistance for the immediate pastoral care of persons who claim to have been sexually abused when they were minors by priests or deacons.

4. To assist diocesan/eparchial bishops, each diocese/eparchy will also have a review board which will function as a confidential consultative body to the bishop/eparch in discharging his responsibilities. The functions of this board may include

   A. advising the diocesan bishop/eparch in his assessment of allegations of sexual abuse of minors and in his determination of suitability for ministry;

   B. reviewing diocesan/eparchial policies for dealing with sexual abuse of minors; and

   C. offering advice on all aspects of these cases, whether retrospectively or prospectively.

5. The review board, established by the diocesan/eparchial bishop, will be composed of at least five persons of outstanding integrity and good judgment in full communion with the Church. The majority of the review board members will be lay persons who are not in the employ of the diocese/eparchy; but at least one member should be a priest who is an experienced and respected pastor of the diocese/eparchy in question, and at least one member should have particular expertise in the treatment of the sexual abuse of minors. The members will be appointed for a term of five years, which can be renewed. It is desirable that the Promoter of Justice participate in the meetings of the review board.

6. When an allegation of sexual abuse of a minor by a priest or deacon is received, a preliminary investigation in harmony with canon law will be initiated and conducted promptly and objectively. . . . All appropriate steps shall be taken to protect the reputation of the accused during the investigation. The accused will be encouraged to retain the assistance of civil and canonical counsel and will be promptly notified of the results of the investigation. When there is sufficient evidence that sexual abuse of a minor has occurred, the Congregation of the Doctrine of the Faith shall be notified. The bishop/eparch shall then apply the precautionary measures mentioned in CIC, canon 1722, or CCEO, canon 1473—i.e., remove the accused from the sacred ministry or from any ecclesiastical office or function, impose or prohibit residence in a given place or territory, and prohibit public participation in the Most Holy Eucharist pending the outcome of the process.

7. The alleged offender may be requested to seek, and may be urged voluntarily to comply with, an appropriate medical and psychological evaluation at a facility mutually acceptable to the diocese/eparchy and to the accused.

8. When even a single act of sexual abuse by a priest or deacon is admitted or is established after an appropriate process in accord with canon law,

the offending priest or deacon will be removed permanently from ecclesiastical ministry, not excluding dismissal from the clerical state, if the case so warrants. . . .

    A. In every case involving canonical penalties, the processes provided for in canon law must be observed, and the various provisions of canon law must be considered . . . . Unless the Congregation for the Doctrine of the Faith, having been notified, calls the case to itself because of special circumstances, it will direct the diocesan bishop/eparch to proceed. . . . If the case would otherwise be barred by prescription, because sexual abuse of a minor is a grave offense, the bishop/eparch shall apply to the Congregation for the Doctrine of the Faith for a dispensation from the prescription, while indicating appropriate pastoral reasons. For the sake of due process, the accused is to be encouraged to retain the assistance of civil and canonical counsel. When necessary, the diocese/eparchy will supply canonical counsel to a priest. The provisions of CIC, canon 1722, or CCEO, canon 1473, shall be implemented during the pendency of the penal process.

    B. If the penalty of dismissal from the clerical state has not been applied (e.g., for reasons of advanced age or infirmity), the offender ought to lead a life of prayer and penance. He will not be permitted to celebrate Mass publicly or to administer the sacraments. He is to be instructed not to wear clerical garb, or to present himself publicly as a priest.

9. At all times, the diocesan bishop/eparch has the executive power of governance, through an administrative act, to remove an offending cleric from office, to remove or restrict his faculties, and to limit his exercise of priestly ministry. Because sexual abuse of a minor by a cleric is a crime in the universal law of the Church . . . and is a crime in all jurisdictions in the United States, for the sake of the common good and observing the provisions of canon law, the diocesan bishop/eparch shall exercise this power of governance to ensure that any priest who has committed even one act of sexual abuse of a minor as described above shall not continue in active ministry.

10. The priest or deacon may at any time request a dispensation from the obligations of the clerical state. In exceptional cases, the bishop/eparch may request of the Holy Father the dismissal of the priest or deacon from the clerical state ex officio, even without the consent of the priest or deacon.

11. The diocese/eparchy will comply with all applicable civil laws with respect to the reporting of allegations of sexual abuse of minors to civil authorities and will cooperate in their investigation. In every instance, the diocese/eparchy will advise and support a person's right to make a report to public authorities.

12. No priest or deacon who has committed an act of sexual abuse of a minor may be transferred for ministerial assignment to another diocese/eparchy or religious province. Before a priest or deacon can be transferred for residence to another diocese/eparchy or religious province,

his bishop/eparch or religious ordinary shall forward, in a confidential manner, to the local bishop/eparch and religious ordinary (if applicable) of the proposed place of residence any and all information concerning any act of sexual abuse of a minor and any other information indicating that he has been or may be a danger to children or young people. This shall apply even if the priest or deacon will reside in the local community of an institute of consecrated life or society of apostolic life (or, in the Eastern Churches, as a monk or other religious, in a society of common life according to the manner of religious, in a secular institute, or in another form of consecrated life or society of apostolic life). Every bishop/eparch or religious ordinary who receives a priest or deacon from outside his jurisdiction will obtain the necessary information regarding any past act of sexual abuse of a minor by the priest or deacon in question.

13. Care will always be taken to protect the rights of all parties involved, particularly those of the person claiming to have been sexually abused and of the person against whom the charge has been made. When an accusation has proved to be unfounded, every step possible will be taken to restore the good name of the person falsely accused.

FEDERAL RESERVE CHAIRMAN ON THE STATE OF THE ECONOMY
November 13, 2002

The fragile American economy grew in fits and starts in 2002, buffeted by a year-long slump on the stock market, corporate accounting scandals that sapped investor confidence, fears of more terrorist attacks, and preparations in Washington for war in Iraq. Although interests rates and inflation remained low, the jobless rate stood at or near 6 percent throughout the year. Declining revenues forced state and local governments to begin to slash social programs to keep their budgets in balance, as most state constitutions required, and poverty, homelessness, and the number of those without health insurance—all indicators of economic well-being—continued to rise. By year's end concern was mounting that the economy might fall back into the recession from which it was slowly emerging. (Status of economy, p. 51)

Although public opinion polls showed the economy to be high on voters' list of concerns, President George W. Bush suffered little apparent political damage from its faltering performance. His folksy acknowledgement that the economy was just "bumping along" and that it needed to do better suggested that he had learned the lesson of 1992 when the widespread perception that his father, then President George H. Bush, was out of touch on the economy helped propel Democrat Bill Clinton into office. The younger Bush blamed the lackluster economy on the uncertainty caused by the terrorist attacks on New York and Washington in September 2001, on the Clinton administration, and on Senate Democrats for blocking his agenda—including his proposal to make the massive tax cuts enacted in 2001 permanent.

For their part Democrats tried to blame Bush for the country's economic woes. But with little agreement on an economic agenda of their own, Democratic efforts met with little success, at least as measured by the congressional election results in November. Republicans regained control of the Senate and added to their narrow majority in the House, clearing the way for the president to push for a new round of tax cuts in 2003.

With Republicans in control of the White House and Congress going into the 2004 presidential campaign season, it was clear that Bush could no longer escape blame if the economy did not begin to pick up. That perception seemed implicit in the December firings of two prominent members of his economic team and their replacement with individuals who were considered likely to be more persuasive spokesmen for the president's economic agenda.

Staying on Message

Although homeland security, the war on terrorism, and the potential war with Iraq appeared to occupy most of Bush's attention in 2002, he took care throughout the year to assure the public that he was concerned about the economy. At appearances with workers, frequently scheduled to coincide with the release of major economic indicators, Bush repeatedly said he would not be satisfied until every American who wanted a job had one. In August the White House staged a day-long campaign-style economic forum at Baylor University in Waco, Texas, designed to showcase Bush's concern about people hurt in the downturn. The forum was filled with conversations between the president, cabinet officers, and a carefully chosen audience of workers, corporate executives, and GOP donors.

The administration also took quick action to shore up public support whenever it appeared to be slipping. For example, in mid-July, with the stock market plummeting to its lowest levels in decades, GOP pollsters began to warn the White House that the economy could be a problem in the elections. Although about two-thirds of those surveyed approved Bush's performance, more than half said they thought the country was moving in the "wrong direction," and they pointed specifically to the faltering economy and the corporate accounting scandals. Although Bush had initially been lukewarm about legislation setting new penalties for wrongdoers and tightening corporate accounting regulations, he changed course in mid-July and demanded that Congress get the legislation to his desk before leaving on its August recess. (Corporate accounting scandals, p. 391)

In mid-October, as his pollsters told him that the economy was the most important issue to voters, ahead of both terrorism and education, Bush began nearly full-time campaigning, focusing blame for the flagging economy on congressional Democrats. He accused them of slowing things down by failing to pass his legislative requests on terrorism insurance and homeland security, and by not making the large tax cuts enacted in 2001 permanent. (The law enacting the cuts also specified that they would expire automatically at the end of the decade.) Throughout the year, the administration had used the nation's economic woes as a justification for the policies it wanted on trade, energy and the environment, and the war against terrorism. The administration argued, for example, that looser environmental restrictions that were less costly to industries would allow larger investment in business. It also contended that special authority for the president to negotiate trade agreements, known as fast-track, would keep the nation competitive in international markets. (Midterm elections, p. 818; environmental regulations, p. 894)

The centerpiece of Bush's economic policy in 2002 remained tax cuts. Bush and his administration repeatedly argued that the ten-year, $1.35 tril-

lion tax cut enacted in 2001 (PL 107–16) helped jump-start the economy in 2002 and should be made permanent. The Republican-controlled House voted six times in 2002 to extend indefinitely all or some of the tax cuts, which were set to expire on December 31, 2010. But Senate Democrats blocked all but the least costly and least controversial of the tax breaks—tax-free treatment of restitution payments made to Holocaust survivors. Democrats argued that making the tax cuts permanent would do almost nothing to stimulate the currently wobbly economy and would, instead, have a long-term negative effect by forcing the government back into deficit spending, which in turn would raise interest rates and weaken the economy. Senate Republicans abandoned the effort for the year in June, after they fell short of the sixty votes needed to bring up a bill that would have made repeal of the estate tax permanent. (2001 tax cuts, Historic Documents of 2001, p. 400)

Political differences also kept the two parties at loggerheads over legislation to provide immediate economic stimulus. Both Republicans and Democrats began the year replaying debates that had left a House-passed economic stimulus bill stalled at the end of 2001. Republicans proposed to rev up the economy with broad tax relief for individuals and businesses, including acceleration of the 2001 tax cut package. Democrats wanted to provide more aid to the unemployed and spend more on infrastructure and homeland security.

Unable to get either plan to the floor, Senate leaders from both parties agreed in February to give up on a broad stimulus package. Instead they passed a stripped-down bill containing only a thirteen-week extension of unemployment benefits. House GOP insistence on a broad stimulus bill, however, forced Senate Democrats to accept some of the GOP tax cuts in order to pass the jobless benefits extension. The final version (PL 107–147) included tax breaks designed to help businesses recover from the September 11 terrorist attacks as well as several routine business tax breaks, most of which had expired at the end of 2001.

In the lame-duck session after the November elections, Republicans and Democrats again wrangled over extending jobless benefits. This time they were unable to reach an agreement and left an estimated 2.1 million workers without benefits, starting just days after Christmas.

Positioning for the 2004 Campaign

With the elections successfully behind it and Republicans in control of both chambers of Congress, the White House began preparing its economic agenda for the remaining two years of Bush's term. That seemed certain to include proposals to make the 2001 tax cut permanent; enact additional tax cuts to help investors, including reducing the tax stockholders paid on dividends; and reduce federal spending in most domestic areas.

At least one influential person, however, was urging caution on additional tax cuts. In response to questioning by members of the Joint Economic Committee on November 11, Federal Reserve Board Chairman Alan Greenspan said he "doubted" that making the tax cuts permanent would "add stimulus to the economy." Greenspan also cautioned Congress to keep the long term in view in making spending and tax-cut decisions. The impending retirement of the baby-boom generation, with its attendant call on the Treasury both for Social Security and Medicare payments, should be uppermost in Congress's mind as it weighed decisions that could increase the federal budget deficit, Greenspan said.

Democrats, too, were likely to raise concerns about the burgeoning federal budget deficits. After four years of running surpluses, the federal budget was projected to return to deficit starting in fiscal 2002, and many economists expected the deficit to reach record levels in 2003 and 2004 as the result of declining tax revenue and increased spending on national security, the war on terrorism, and the impending war in Iraq. Republicans, who in the 1980s and 1990s argued that budget deficits slowed growth by keeping interest rates high, were now brushing aside those concerns and instead insisting that tax cuts were the answer for both the slow economy and the deficit.

To help carry that message to the voters, the White House decided to make key changes in its economic team in preparation for the 2004 presidential election campaign. On election day, the chairman of the Securities and Exchange Commission, Harvey L. Pitt, announced his resignation after a series of political gaffes made it untenable for him to remain as head of the agency charged with cleaning up the corporate accounting mess. (SEC problems, p. 1032)

A month later, on December 6, Treasury Secretary Paul H. O'Neil and Lawrence B. Lindsey, director of the White House National Economic Council, announced their resignations. Both men had become liabilities to the White House. O'Neill was criticized for gaffes that shook the markets, for not being around at crucial times, and for insulting important legislators and corporate executives. He was also resisting some of the president's tax cut proposals and was said to be worried about the rising budget deficit. Lindsey was Bush's economic tutor during the 2000 presidential campaign and the chief architect of the 2001 tax cut, but his overly optimistic economic forecasts and his later advice made him seem out of step with reality. Lindsey was said, for example, to have advised Bush to stop the corporate accountability bill passed by the Senate, even though it passed unanimously. Lindsey was also criticized for publicly predicting that the cost of a war with Iraq could reach $200 billion, which was much higher than other administration officials were saying at the time.

John W. Snow, chairman of the railroad company CSX Corp, was named to be Treasury secretary. Stephen Friedman, a former cochairman of Goldman-Sachs, the investment firm, was tapped to fill Lindsey's slot. Both men were expected to have smoother relations with Wall Street and Congress than their predecessors.

With a new economic team and Republicans in control of Congress and the White House, Bush was now under pressure to make good on his economic promises. "Republicans say all they want to do is stimulate the economy, create jobs, and put money in people's pockets. They have an ambitious agenda. And they have two years to do whatever they want to do. But now they have to deliver," said William G. Gale, an economist at the Brookings

Institution. "If they don't deliver, they will have no one to blame but themselves."

> *Following is the text of testimony before the Joint Economic Committee on November 13, 2002, by Federal Reserve Board Chairman Alan Greenspan on the state of the U.S. economy.*

The document was obtained from the Internet at http://www.federalreserve.gov/BoardDocs/testimony/2002/20021113/default.htm; accessed December 11, 2002.

The past year has been both a difficult and a remarkable one for the United States economy. A year ago, we were struggling to understand the potential economic consequences of the events of September 11. At that time, it was unclear how households and businesses would react to this unprecedented shock as well as to the declines in equity markets and cutbacks in investment spending that had already been under way. Economic forecasts were lowered sharply, and analysts feared that even these downward-revised projections might be undone by a significant retrenchment in aggregate demand. The United States economy, however, proved to be remarkably resilient: In the event, real GDP over the past four quarters grew 3 percent—a very respectable pace given the blows that the economy endured.

Although economic growth was relatively well maintained over the past year, several forces have continued to weigh on the economy: the lengthy adjustment of capital spending, the fallout from the revelations of corporate malfeasance, the further decline in equity values, and heightened geopolitical risks. Over the last few months, these forces have taken their toll on activity, and evidence has accumulated that the economy has hit a soft patch. Households have become more cautious in their purchases, while business spending has yet to show any substantial vigor. In financial markets, risk spreads on both investment-grade and non-investment-grade securities have widened. It was in this context that the Federal Open Market Committee further reduced our target federal funds rate last week.

The consumer until recently has been the driving force of this expansion. Faced with falling equity prices, uncertainty about future employment prospects, and the emergence of the terrorist threat, consumer spending has slowed over the course of the past year but has not slumped as some had earlier feared it might. Tax cuts and extended unemployment insurance provided a timely boost to disposable income. And the deep discounts offered by many businesses on their products were most supportive.

In particular, automotive manufacturers responded to the events of September 11 with cut-rate financing and generous rebates. These incentives were an enormous success in supporting—indeed increasing—the demand for new cars and trucks. Sales surged each time the incentive packages were sweetened and, of course, fell back a bit when they expired. Some decline in sales was to be expected in recent months after the extraordinary run-up recorded in the summer. However, it will bear watching to see whether this most recent softening is a payback for borrowed earlier strength in sales or whether it represents some weakening in the underlying pace of demand.

Stimulated by mortgage interest rates that are at lows not seen in decades, home sales and housing starts have remained strong. Moreover, the underlying demand for new housing units has received support from an expanding population, in part resulting from high levels of immigration.

Besides sustaining the demand for new construction, mortgage markets have also been a powerful stabilizing force over the past two years of economic distress by facilitating the extraction of some of the equity that homeowners had built up over the years. This effect occurs through three channels: the turnover of the housing stock, home equity loans, and cash-outs associated with the refinancing of existing mortgages. Sales of existing homes have been the major source of extraction of equity. Because the buyer of an existing home almost invariably takes out a mortgage that exceeds the loan canceled by the seller, the net debt on that home rises by the amount of the difference. And, not surprisingly, the increase in net debt tends to approximate the sellers' realized capital gain on the sale. That realized capital gain is financed essentially by the mortgage extension to the homebuyer, and the proceeds, in turn, are used to finance some combination of a down payment on a newly purchased home, a reduction of other household debt, or purchases of goods and services or other assets.

Home equity loans and funds from cash-outs are generally extractions of unrealized capital gains. Cash-outs, as you know, reflect the additional debt incurred when refinancings in excess of the remaining balance on the original loan are taken in cash.

According to survey data, roughly half of equity extractions are allocated to the combination of personal consumption expenditures and outlays on home modernization. These data and some preliminary econometric results suggest that a dollar of equity extracted from housing has a more powerful effect on consumer spending than does a dollar change in the value of common stocks. Of course, the net decline in the market value of stocks has greatly exceeded the additions to capital gains on homes over the past two years. So despite the greater apparent sensitivity of consumption to capital gains on homes, the net effect of all changes in household wealth on consumer spending since early 2000 has been negative. Indeed, the recent softness in consumption suggests that this net wealth erosion has continued to weigh on household spending. That said, it is important to recognize that the extraction of equity from homes has been a significant support to consumption during a period when other asset prices were declining sharply. Were it not for this phenomenon, economic activity would have been notably weaker in the wake of the decline in the value of household financial assets.

In the business sector, there have been few signs of any appreciable vigor. Uncertainty about the economic outlook and heightened geopolitical risks have made companies reluctant to expand their operations, hire workers, or buy new equipment. Executives consistently report that in today's intensely competitive global marketplace it is no longer feasible to raise prices in order to improve profitability.

There are many alternatives for most products, and with technology driving down the cost of acquiring information, buyers today can (and do) easily shift to the low-price seller. In such a setting, firms must focus on the cost side of their operations if they are to generate greater returns for their shareholders. Negotiations with their suppliers are aimed at reducing the costs of materials and services. Some companies have also eschewed the traditional annual pay increment in favor of compensation packages for their rank-and-file workers that are linked to individual performance goals. And, most important, businesses have revamped their operations to achieve substantial reductions in costs.

On a consolidated basis for the corporate sector as a whole, lowered costs are generally associated with increased output per hour. Much of the recent reported improvements in cost control doubtless have reflected the paring of so-called "fat" in corporate operations—fat that accumulated during the long expansion of the 1990s, when management focused attention primarily on the perceived profitability of expansion and less on the increments to profitability that derive from cost savings. Managers, now refocused, are pressing hard to identify and eliminate those redundant or nonessential activities that accumulated in the boom years.

With margins under pressure, businesses have also been reallocating their capital so as to use it more productively. Moreover, for equipment with active secondary markets, such as computers and networking gear, productivity may also have been boosted by a reallocation to firms that could use the equipment more efficiently. For example, healthy firms reportedly have been buying equipment from failed dot-coms.

Businesses may also have managed to eke out increases in output per hour by employing their existing workforce more intensively. Unlike cutting fat, which permanently elevates the levels of productivity, these gains in output per hour are often temporary, as more demanding workloads eventually begin to tax workers and impede efficiency.

But the impressive performance of productivity also appears to support the view that the step-up in the pace of structural productivity growth that occurred in the latter part of the 1990s has not, as yet, faltered. Indeed, the high growth of productivity during the past year merely extends recent experience. Over the past seven years, output per hour has been growing at an annual rate of more than 2½ percent, on average, compared with a rate of roughly 1½ percent during the preceding two decades. Although we cannot know with certainty until the books are closed, the growth of productivity since 1995 appears to be among the largest in decades.

Arguably, the pickup in productivity growth since 1995 reflects largely the ongoing incorporation of innovations in computing and communications technologies into the capital stock and business practices. Indeed, the transition to the higher permanent level of productivity associated with these innovations is likely not yet completed. Once the current level of risk recedes, businesses will no doubt move to exploit the profitable investment opportunities made possible by the ongoing advances in technology.

However, history does raise some warning flags concerning the length of time that productivity growth remains elevated. Gains in productivity remained quite rapid for years after the innovations that followed the surge in inventions a century ago. But in other episodes, the period of elevated growth of productivity was shorter. Regrettably, examples are too few to generalize. Hence, policymakers have no substitute for continued close surveillance of the evolution of productivity during this current period of significant innovation.

In summary, as we noted last week, "The [Federal Open Market] Committee continues to believe that an accommodative stance of monetary policy, coupled with still-robust underlying growth in productivity, is providing important ongoing support to economic activity. However, incoming economic data have tended to confirm that greater uncertainty, in part attributable to heightened geopolitical risks, is currently inhibiting spending, production, and employment. Inflation and inflation expectations remain well contained." In these circumstances, the Committee believed that the actions taken last week to ease monetary policy should prove helpful as the economy works its way through this current soft spot.

NATO LEADERS ON EXPANDING THE ALLIANCE
November 21, 2002

The NATO alliance in 2002 continued its search for relevance and a role in the post-cold war world. The alliance in May formally embraced Russia as a quasi-member, inviting into its highest councils the country formerly at the core of the Soviet Union—NATO's enemy and raison d'être *for four decades after its founding in 1949. Just as remarkable, NATO in November invited into full membership seven countries that had been dominated by the Soviet Union during the cold war: Bulgaria, Estonia, Latvia, Lithuania, Romania, Slovakia, and Slovenia. Three of those countries, the Baltic states of Estonia, Latvia, and Lithuania, had formally been part of the Soviet Union until they declared independence in 1991. When they took their seats in 2004, the new allies would put NATO's total membership at twenty-six, not counting Russia as an almost-member.*

Despite these signs of growth and renewal, and the past success of its central mission of confronting communism, NATO faced an uncertain future. Increasingly the alliance had become unbalanced, with the United States as a military giant that overshadowed all the other members combined. This disequilibrium led to resentment and misunderstanding on both sides of the Atlantic, creating a strong impression that the United States had come to view the alliance as an afterthought at best, or a hindrance at worst. Rather than keeping the United States involved in Europe, which had been one of the original purposes of NATO, it seemed possible in 2002 that new tensions within the alliance might ultimately pull Washington farther away.

In public statements, President George W. Bush and his chief aides insisted that the United States still viewed NATO as an essential component of U.S. security. But key administration officials—especially in the Pentagon —derided the alliance in private and expressed growing frustration with the reluctance of many European countries to follow the U.S. lead on important issues. "NATO: Keep the myth alive!" was a joke uttered repeatedly by Douglas J. Feith, the undersecretary of defense for policy. The humor thinly masked a conviction by some of Bush's senior aides that the alliance had become more of a burden than a help to the United States.

Russia's New Role

When it began its eastward expansion in the mid-1990s, NATO confronted determined resistance from Russia, which continued to view the alliance as a potential threat to its interests. Largely to calm such fears, NATO in 1997 signed an agreement, called a charter, declaring that Russia was no longer an enemy but rather a "partner" of the West. Russian diplomats and military officers were invited to participate in regular meetings with the NATO counterparts, along with representatives from Eastern European nations that aspired to membership in the alliance. Three of those countries—the Czech Republic, Hungary, and Poland—in 1999 became the first NATO members that formerly had been part of the Soviet bloc. (NATO-Russia charter, Historic Documents of 1997, p. 514; NATO expansion, Historic Documents of 1999, p. 119)

Starting in 2001 Britain and several other European members of NATO began advocating an even closer relationship between the alliance and Russia. No one was yet advocating full membership for Moscow, but there was growing support for giving Russia a seat at the table so it could express its views when the alliance considered major decisions. After months of discussion, NATO leaders in November 2001 agreed to establish a NATO-Russia Council. Replacing a "Permanent Joint Council" established by the 1997 charter but rarely used afterward, the new body was supposed to hold monthly meetings to which Russia was invited as an equal participant, except that it would not have a formal veto power. The meetings would discuss such issues as terrorism, regional crises, and the control of weapons of mass destruction.

Despite general agreement on a format, NATO leaders in late 2001 could not agree on all the details about the operation of a NATO-Russia Council, thereby requiring more negotiations early in 2002. The core issue, according to diplomats, was a concern by the new members from Eastern Europe that their views might be overwhelmed by those of Russia. (Council proposal, Historic Documents of 2001, p. 892)

A final deal, reached by NATO foreign ministers at a meeting in Iceland in April, created a "safeguard" mechanism under which any member could withdraw an issue from consideration by the NATO-Russia Council and refer it instead to NATO's regular board, on which Russia was not represented. With that compromise in place, NATO leaders formally adopted the plan for the new council at a May 27 summit meeting held at an airbase near Rome. A declaration issued by the leaders said that a "qualitatively new relationship between NATO and the Russian federation will constitute an essential contribution" to the goal of security for the European-Atlantic area.

Symbolically, on that same day an Italian admiral and other officers representing NATO opened the alliance's first military mission in Moscow. The office was supposed to have been established as part of the 1997 NATO-Russia agreement but was delayed for five years because of disagreements over Yugoslavia and Russia's continued resistance to NATO expansion.

NATO Expands Eastward

NATO's expansion eastward paralleled a similar step by the European Union (EU). Both organizations had their origins in Western Europe (NATO also included the United States and Canada), but the end of the cold war presented an opportunity for both to renew themselves with newer members from Eastern Europe, now called Central Europe by most countries in the region. As of the start of 2002 more than a dozen countries had applied for membership in either NATO or the EU, or both. Five countries that wanted to join both organizations succeeded in winning membership invitations during the year: Estonia, Latvia, Lithuania, Slovakia, and Slovenia. Two other countries, Bulgaria and Romania, received invitations to join NATO but were told by the EU that their applications would be considered later, perhaps in time for membership by 2007. (EU expansion, p. 679)

At their summit meeting in Prague in mid-November, NATO leaders extended invitations to the seven new members who were expected to formally join in May 2004. President Bush called the invitation a "bold decision to guarantee the freedom of millions of people." NATO put on hold three other countries that had applied: Albania, Croatia, and Macedonia.

None of the new NATO members could even remotely be considered an important military or political power. Romania was by far the most populous of the group, with about 22 million people. The others ranged in size from Estonia's 1.4 million to Bulgaria's 7.7 million. All seven were relatively poor by NATO's standards and were still struggling to establish working market economies in place of the ill-functioning communist systems that had been imposed during the Soviet era. None of the countries could fully afford the large cost of modernizing their militaries to bring them up to NATO standards, and all looked westward for help. At least some help came from the United States, which in 2002 budgeted $55.5 million in military aid for the seven countries. Bulgaria and Romania also were burdened with ethnic disputes inherited from the collapse of the Ottoman empire and the frequent redrawing of European borders as a consequence of twentieth century wars. In short, these countries offered NATO little except the symbolic importance of expanding the alliance boundaries eastward and the possibility that NATO membership would help guarantee their futures as stable democracies.

For the applicant countries, NATO membership offered a psychologically important measure of prestige. Whether their political orientation was center-right, center-left, or simply centrist, the governments of these countries viewed membership in the world's most powerful military alliance as a sign of acceptance in the modern world and as a rejection of the communist past. Just as important, the leaders of countries once suppressed by the Soviet Union were eager to demonstrate their recently won independence from Moscow. In an interview with the Washington Post, *Latvian president Vaira Vike-Freiberga summarized membership in NATO as representing "the fact that you can go to bed and not worry about somebody knocking on the door and putting you on a train to Siberia."*

Still Searching for a New Role

The basic question faced by NATO as it expanded eastward was whether it should attempt to remain a muscular alliance capable of fighting major wars in unison—as was the intention of its post-World War II founders— or should it embrace a more modest role, perhaps as an emergency firefighting and peacekeeping force to quell small regional conflicts, such as the Balkan wars of the 1990s. Officially, the alliance adopted policies pledging a capability to do both of these things. Secretary General Lord Robertson (a former British defense minister) was NATO's most prominent advocate of this view, traveling among the alliance capitals with a message that members needed more planes, ships, and high-tech weaponry to keep a military edge against all possible foes.

Unofficially, however, the squabbles between Washington and some of the European capitals seemed to indicate that ultimately the alliance might have to choose either a grand or a scaled-back role for itself. This choice was complicated by the emergence in 2001 of terrorism as the focal point of U.S. security concerns. Nothing in NATO's past equipped it to concentrate on shadowy networks of terrorists whose weapons were suicide bombs and hijacked airplanes, rather than the battalions of tanks or fleets of aircraft carriers that NATO's armies were positioned against.

Two recent conflicts—the 1999 air war against Yugoslavia and the 2001 operation to dislodge the Taliban regime and the al Qaeda terrorist network in Afghanistan—had demonstrated the enormous gap between the military capability of the United States and all its allies combined. In both cases the United States carried the overwhelming burden of the fighting, largely because it possessed high-technology tools—such as precision-guided bombs and unmanned surveillance planes that also could fire missiles—that the allies lacked. The buildup to the Afghanistan fighting during 2001 even resulted in an unusual dispute in which the Bush administration spurned offers of help from some allies, arguing that it would be more trouble than it was worth. In addition to its technological edge, the United States towered over its allies militarily simply because it was willing to spend more; during the decade after the 1991 collapse of the Soviet Union, the United States spent about 3 percent of its gross domestic product—that is, more than $300 billion annually—on its military while the European members of NATO spent an average of about 1.8 percent of their GDP—a combined total of about $150 billion annually. (Yugoslavia war, Historic Documents of 1999, p. 134; Afghanistan war, Historic Documents of 2001, p. 686)

Early in 2002 Lord Robertson used his position to push both the United States and its allies to address the growing imbalance in the alliance's military capabilities. "America's critics of Europe's military incapability are right," Robertson said on February 3 at an annual security conference in Munich. "So, if we are to ensure that the United States moves neither toward unilateralism nor isolation, all European countries must show a new willingness to develop effective crisis management capabilities." But Robertson also said the United States needed to recognize that NATO remained an im-

portant alliance that could support Washington's interests in the world. The war to oust terrorists from Afghanistan, he said, "reinforces the fact that no modern military operation can be undertaken by a single country. Even superpowers need allies and coalitions to provide bases, fuel, airspace, and forces. And they need mechanisms and experience to integrate these forces in a single coherent military capability." Washington could help its allies meet their responsibilities by providing them with some of the modern military technologies it had developed but so far refused to export, Robertson added.

Rapid Deployment

A specific issue facing the alliance as it considered these broader questions involved the creation of a "rapid deployment force" that could respond quickly to emergencies, such as the outbreak of ethnic conflict in the Balkans in 1992. NATO officials for years had talked about setting up a highly mobile unit of a few thousand troops that could be airlifted to trouble spots within a matter of a few days, as opposed to NATO's cumbersome structure of heavily armored divisions that could take weeks or even months to mobilize.

Largely as a result of Europe's inability to deal with the Balkan wars, the European Union in 1999 agreed to establish a quick-reaction force throughout Europe. But disagreements among European leaders had delayed those plans, and it appeared that such a force would not become operational until 2003 at the earliest. In the meantime U.S. officials expressed some misgivings about a Europe-only military force, fearing that it might undermine NATO. (European force, Historic Documents of 1999, p. 817)

U.S. defense secretary Donald H. Rumsfeld revived the idea of a NATO rapid reaction force during the June 2002 meeting of the NATO defense ministers. Noting that he also was trying to reshape the U.S. military to make it better able to respond quickly, Rumsfeld said he envisioned a military unit for NATO with "the kind of ability to deal with the types of problems that exist today," such as terrorism.

At their November summit meeting in Prague, the NATO leaders accepted the proposal for a "Response Force" of 21,000 troops. The leaders called for the force to begin operations by October 2004 and to be fully operational within two more years. In their closing declaration, the leaders said NATO "must be able to field forces that can move quickly to wherever needed." That open-ended statement marked a significant break from past policy of the alliance, which since its founding had been focused on defending the specific locations of Europe and the North Atlantic—not "wherever."

> *Following is an excerpt from the "Prague Summit Declaration," issued November 21, 2002, by the leaders of the NATO alliance after their meeting in Prague, Czechoslovakia. The declaration invited seven countries to join NATO in 2004 and called for the formation of a new Response Force to deal with emergencies anywhere in the world.*

*The document was obtained from the Internet at www
.nato.int/docu/pr/2002/p02-127e.htm; accessed November 30, 2002.*

We, the Heads of State and Government of the member countries of the
North Atlantic Alliance, met today to enlarge our Alliance and further
strengthen NATO to meet the grave new threats and profound security challenges of the 21st century. Bound by our common vision embodied in the
Washington Treaty, we commit ourselves to transforming NATO with new
members, new capabilities and new relationships with our partners. We are
steadfast in our commitment to the transatlantic link; to NATO's fundamental
security tasks including collective defence; to our shared democratic values;
and to the United Nations Charter.

Today, we have decided to invite Bulgaria, Estonia, Latvia, Lithuania, Romania, Slovakia and Slovenia to begin accession talks to join our Alliance. We
congratulate them on this historic occasion, which so fittingly takes place in
Prague. The accession of these new members will strengthen security for all
in the Euro-Atlantic area, and help achieve our common goal of a Europe
whole and free, united in peace and by common values. NATO's door will remain open to European democracies willing and able to assume the responsibilities and obligations of membership, in accordance with Article 10 of the
Washington Treaty.

Recalling the tragic events of 11 September 2001 and our subsequent decision to invoke Article 5 of the Washington Treaty, we have approved a comprehensive package of measures, based on NATO's Strategic Concept, to
strengthen our ability to meet the challenges to the security of our forces, populations and territory, from wherever they may come.

Today's decisions will provide for balanced and effective capabilities
within the Alliance so that NATO can better carry out the full range of its missions and respond collectively to those challenges, including the threat posed
by terrorism and by the proliferation of weapons of mass destruction and their
means of delivery.

We underscore that our efforts to transform and adapt NATO should not be
perceived as a threat by any country or organisation, but rather as a demonstration of our determination to protect our populations, territory and forces
from any armed attack, including terrorist attack, directed from abroad. We
are determined to deter, disrupt, defend and protect against any attacks on us,
in accordance with the Washington Treaty and the Charter of the United Nations. In order to carry out the full range of its missions, NATO must be able to
field forces that can move quickly to wherever they are needed, upon decision
by the North Atlantic Council, to sustain operations over distance and time, including in an environment where they might be faced with nuclear, biological
and chemical threats, and to achieve their objectives. Effective military
forces, an essential part of our overall political strategy, are vital to safeguard

the freedom and security of our populations and to contribute to peace and security in the Euro-Atlantic region. We have therefore decided to:

a. Create a NATO Response Force (NRF) consisting of a technologically advanced, flexible, deployable, interoperable and sustainable force including land, sea, and air elements ready to move quickly to wherever needed, as decided by the Council. The NRF will also be a catalyst for focusing and promoting improvements in the Alliance's military capabilities. We gave directions for the development of a comprehensive concept for such a force, which will have its initial operational capability as soon as possible, but not later than October 2004 and its full operational capability not later than October 2006, and for a report to Defence Ministers in Spring 2003. The NRF and the related work of the EU Headline Goal should be mutually reinforcing while respecting the autonomy of both organisations.

b. Streamline NATO's military command arrangements. We have approved the Defence Ministers' report providing the outline of a leaner, more efficient, effective and deployable command structure, with a view to meeting the operational requirements for the full range of Alliance missions. It is based on the agreed Minimum Military Requirements document for the Alliance's command arrangements. The structure will enhance the transatlantic link, result in a significant reduction in headquarters and Combined Air Operations Centres, and promote the transformation of our military capabilities. There will be two strategic commands, one operational, and one functional. The strategic command for Operations, headquartered in Europe (Belgium), will be supported by two Joint Force Commands able to generate a land-based Combined Joint Task Force (CJTF) headquarters and a robust but more limited standing joint headquarters from which a sea-based CJTF headquarters capability can be drawn. There will also be land, sea and air components. The strategic command for Transformation, headquartered in the United States, and with a presence in Europe, will be responsible for the continuing transformation of military capabilities and for the promotion of interoperability of Alliance forces, in cooperation with the Allied Command Operations as appropriate. We have instructed the Council and Defence Planning Committee, taking into account the work of the NATO Military Authorities and objective military criteria, to finalise the details of the structure, including geographic locations of command structure headquarters and other elements, so that final decisions are taken by Defence Ministers in June 2003.

c. Approve the Prague Capabilities Commitment (PCC) as part of the continuing Alliance effort to improve and develop new military capabilities for modern warfare in a high threat environment. Individual Allies have made firm and specific political commitments to improve their capabilities in the areas of chemical, biological, radiological, and nuclear defence; intelligence, surveillance, and target acquisition; air-to-ground surveillance; command, control and communications; combat effectiveness, including precision guided munitions and suppression of enemy air defences; strategic air and sea lift; air-to-air refuelling; and deployable combat support and combat service support units. Our efforts to improve capabilities through the PCC and those of the European Union to enhance European capabilities through the European Capabilities Action Plan should be mutually reinforcing, while respecting the autonomy of both organisations, and in a spirit of openness. We will implement all aspects of our Prague Capabilities Commitment as quickly as possible. We will take the necessary steps to improve capabilities in the identified areas of continuing capability shortfalls. Such steps could include multinational efforts, role specialisation and reprioritisation, noting that in many cases additional financial resources will be required, subject as appropriate to parliamentary approval. We are committed to pursuing vigorously capability improvements. We have directed the Council in Permanent Session to report on implementation to Defence Ministers.

d. Endorse the agreed military concept for defence against terrorism. The concept is part of a package of measures to strengthen NATO's capabilities in this area, which also includes improved intelligence sharing and crisis response arrangements. Terrorism, which we categorically reject and condemn in all its forms and manifestations, poses a grave and growing threat to Alliance populations, forces and territory, as well as to international security. We are determined to combat this scourge for as long as necessary. To combat terrorism effectively, our response must be multi-faceted and comprehensive. We are committed, in cooperation with our partners, to fully implement the Civil Emergency Planning (CEP) Action Plan for the improvement of civil preparedness against possible attacks against the civilian population with chemical, biological or radiological (CBR) agents. We will enhance our ability to provide support, when requested, to help national authorities to deal with the consequences of terrorist attacks, including attacks with CBRN against critical infrastructure, as foreseen in the CEP Action Plan.

e. Endorse the implementation of five nuclear, biological and chemical weapons defence initiatives, which will enhance the Alliance's defence capabilities against weapons of mass destruction: a Prototype Deployable NBC Analytical Laboratory; a Prototype NBC Event Response team; a virtual Centre of Excellence for NBC Weapons Defence; a NATO Biological and Chemical Defence Stockpile; and a Disease Surveillance system. We reaffirm our commitment to augment and improve expeditiously our NBC defence capabilities.

f. Strengthen our capabilities to defend against cyber attacks.

g. Examine options for addressing the increasing missile threat to Alliance territory, forces and population centres in an effective and efficient way through an appropriate mix of political and defence efforts, along with deterrence. Today we initiated a new NATO Missile Defence feasibility study to examine options for protecting Alliance territory, forces and population centres against the full range of missile threats, which we will continue to assess. Our efforts in this regard will be consistent with the indivisibility of Allied security. We support the enhancement of the role of the WMD Centre within the International Staff to assist the work of the Alliance in tackling this threat. We reaffirm that disarmament, arms control and non-proliferation make an essential contribution to preventing the spread and use of WMD and their means of delivery. We stress the importance of abiding by and strengthening existing multilateral non-proliferation and export control regimes and international arms control and disarmament accords.

Admitting Bulgaria, Estonia, Latvia, Lithuania, Romania, Slovakia and Slovenia as new members will enhance NATO's ability to face the challenges of today and tomorrow. They have demonstrated their commitment to the basic principles and values set out in the Washington Treaty, the ability to contribute to the Alliance's full range of missions including collective defence, and a firm commitment to contribute to stability and security, especially in regions of crisis and conflict. We will begin accession talks immediately with the aim of signing Accession Protocols by the end of March 2003 and completing the ratification process in time for these countries to join the Alliance at the latest at our Summit in May 2004. During the period leading up to accession, the Alliance will involve the invited countries in Alliance activities to the greatest extent possible. We pledge our continued support and assistance, including through the Membership Action Plan (MAP). We look forward to receiving the invitees' timetables for reforms, upon which further progress will be expected before and after accession in order to enhance their contribution to the Alliance.

We commend Albania for its significant reform progress, its constructive role in promoting regional stability, and strong support for the Alliance. We commend the former Yugoslav Republic of Macedonia for the significant progress it has achieved in its reform process and for its strong support for Alliance operations, as well as for the important steps it has made in overcoming its internal challenges and advancing democracy, stability and ethnic reconciliation. We will continue to help both countries, including through the MAP, to achieve stability, security and prosperity, so that they can meet the obligations of membership. In this context, we have also agreed to improve our capacity to contribute to Albania's continued reform, and to further assist defence and security sector reform in the former Yugoslav Republic of Macedonia through the NATO presence. We encourage both countries to redouble their reform efforts. They remain under consideration for future membership.

Croatia, which has made encouraging progress on reform, will also be under consideration for future membership. Progress in this regard will depend upon Croatia's further reform efforts and compliance with all of its international obligations, including to the International Criminal Tribunal for the former Yugoslavia (ICTY).

The Membership Action Plan will remain the vehicle to keep aspirants' progress under review. Today's invitees will not be the last. . . .

EPA ON REGULATING
INDUSTRIAL POLLUTION
November 22, 2002

*The Bush administration during 2002 stepped up its comprehensive ef-
fort to loosen environmental regulations that administration officials and
corporations viewed as hindering economic development. In nearly every
area of environmental policy the administration took actions that reduced
the legal and bureaucratic hurdles faced by business such as the oil and gas
industry, loggers and miners, and electric power producers.*

*President George W. Bush had barely taken office in 2001 when he became
embroiled in a series of disputes over environmental policy. A former oil
industry executive, Bush had long advocated relaxing government regulations and instead allowing what he called "market forces" to set the pace
on protecting the environment. Bush put like-minded officials—many of
them from industries affected by environmental regulations—in charge
of most agencies responsible for environmental policies. In 2001 these officials spent much of their time attempting to roll back regulations that President Bill Clinton (1993–2001) and his administration had put in place,
many of them at the very close of Clinton's second administration.* (Bush's
first-year environmental policies, Historic Documents of 2001, p. 212)

*By 2002 the nation's debate over environmental issues had settled
into a regular pattern. A Bush administration agency would announce—
generally with little fanfare—a plan to change environmental regulations
and would describe the change as an improvement or a reform. In several
cases the administration gave its new policy a name—such as "Clear Skies"
or "Healthy Forests"—that put the change in the most "eco-friendly" light.
Major business organizations and leading Republicans in Congress would
endorse the proposal as creating the proper "balance" between environmental and economic concerns. Almost invariably, major environmental advocacy organizations and their allies on Capitol Hill would denounce the
administration's approach and insist that the supposed reform actually was
the granting of yet another item on the deregulatory wish list of corporate
America. These groups also insisted that the administration was attempting to mislead the public about its true intentions. Polls consistently showed*

that a strong majority of Americans wanted stronger, rather than weaker, federal policies to protect the environment.

Some of these disputes were then taken to Congress or the courts, but most were still unresolved at the close of the year. The battles were expected to intensify in 2003 when Republicans would control both houses of Congress as well as the White House. Several of Bush's most controversial changes in environmental laws failed in Congress during 2001 and 2002 because Democrats controlled key Senate committees.

"New Source Review" Dispute

In terms of public attention, the hottest dispute between the Bush administration and environmental organizations concerned regulations governing air pollution by some of the country's oldest and dirtiest factories. The issue also was one of the few environmental questions on which the Bush administration had limited support from environmental advocacy organizations.

The bureaucratic and legal policy at stake was a provision of the 1970 Clean Air Act called "new source review." In general terms, that provision allowed industrial plants, many of which used coal, to continue polluting at their historic levels. But if the plants' owners made major repairs or changes, the plants' emissions controls would have to be modernized to meet current pollution requirements, which had been raised in 1990. The general assumption at the time the law was enacted was that older, less efficient, and more polluting plants would be phased out and replaced with new ones better equipped to control pollution. In many cases that did not happen. As of 2002, according to figures compiled by the Natural Resources Defense Council, more than 17,000 oil refineries, chemical plants, power plants, incinerators, iron and steel foundries, paper mills, cement plants, and other industrial facilities still did not meet air quality standards enacted three decades earlier.

In 1999 the Clinton administration filed lawsuits against nine electric utility companies that owned a combined total of fifty-one aging power plants, charging that the companies had upgraded output of the plants under the guise of "routine maintenance" but had failed to make the required emission control improvements. Twenty-nine of the plants were owned by just three companies: American Electric Power, based in Ohio; the Southern Co., based in Atlanta; and the Tennessee Valley Authority (TVA). The Clinton administration also sued several dozen oil refineries. In addition, attorneys general in several northeastern states also had filed suits against industries whose plants spewed pollutants that fouled the air over those states.

Some of the lawsuits were settled over the next two years, but most remained pending at the time Bush took office. In the meantime, the utilities launched a major public relations and political campaign to overturn the rules on which the lawsuits were based. The Southern Co., which faced lawsuits against eight of its plants, was the most assertive, hiring as its lobbyists several leading Republicans, including Haley Barbour, the former national Republican Party chairman; Marc Racicot, the current party chairman and former governor of Idaho; and C. Boyden Gray, who had been White House counsel when Bush's father, George H. Bush, was president.

Shortly after taking office the Bush administration announced that it would review the issue. That review resulted in a determination by the Justice Department in January 2002 that the Clinton administration's lawsuits were valid under the Clean Air Act. But officials made it clear that they planned a new approach, giving polluters more incentive to clean up their plants without the threat of legal action.

On March 5 EPA administrator Christine Whitman signaled that the Bush administration was preparing to reverse course, telling the Senate Governmental Affairs Committee that if she were a lawyer for one of the utilities involved in the lawsuits, "I wouldn't settle anything" with the government until a decision was reached in a pending case involving seven coal-fired power plants in Alabama, Kentucky, and Tennessee owned by the TVA. Critics said Whitman was, in effect, telling the utilities to wait until the administration proposed rules more to their liking. After resulting negative publicity, the administration said in May it was considering filing new suits against polluters—a step it did not take during the rest of the year.

Whitman announced the administration's proposed new policy on June 13. Although providing few specifics, Whitman said the administration would revise such regulations as the definition of "routine maintenance" to enable industries to modernize and expand their plants without having to comply with more recent and rigorous air pollution requirements. Whitman called the original new source review requirement a "valuable program" but said "the need for reform is clear and has broad-based support." She said the regulation had "deterred companies from implementing projects that would increase energy efficiency and decrease air pollution." As was the case with other administration actions on environmental issues, Whitman's announcement was welcomed by representatives of public utility companies. Representatives of many environmental groups agreed with the administration that current regulations offered companies little incentive to upgrade their pollution control equipment. But most of these groups characterized the administration's approach as rewarding those companies for their failure to act.

The administration on November 22 announced its "final" proposed changes in the new source review regulations, including some, but not all, of the specifics that had been lacking in its June 13 proposal. Apparently because of the furor that the previous announcement had generated, the administration took a low-key approach. It waited until after the midterm congressional elections to make the announcement, which was presented by an assistant administrator of the Environmental Protection Agency in a news conference at which television cameras were banned. Although the decision involved one of the EPA's most important policy changes in years, Whitman did not appear and was simply quoted in the agency press release.

The EPA's announcement was in two parts. The first changed specific new source review requirements for most industrial plants, although only some of the changes applied to power plants. This was a "final" rule that would go into effect immediately. The rule included four changes that would make it easier for most industrial plants to continue operating at old levels of air pollution. One change, called a "plantwide applicability limit," would allow a company to modernize some equipment at a facility with many smoke-stacks or pollution sources, without having to upgrade all of the plant's pollution controls, so long as the overall pollution emissions from the total facility did not exceed certain levels. Another change gave most industrial companies (except power plants) greater flexibility in choosing the "baseline" level of pollution that was used in determining whether pollution control upgrades would be needed. A company could pick any two-year period during the previous decade as its pollution baseline, even if its pollution increased later in the decade. EPA officials said these changes would allow companies to upgrade their plants without having to spend millions or even billions of dollars on new pollution control equipment. The EPA also insisted the changes, over time, would reduce pollution levels.

The administration's second key rule change announced on November 22 was a revised definition of the types of "routine maintenance" that companies could perform on their plants without having to upgrade air pollution controls. Under the new definition, repairs made to promote the "safe, reliable, and efficient operation" of plants or that replaced existing equipment with "functionally equivalent new equipment" would be defined as routine maintenance. This proposal was not final but was subject to additional scrutiny, including public hearings.

Industry spokesmen welcomed the EPA announcement but expressed frustration that it still did not provide all the specific details of the new regulations. In particular, representatives of the power industry said they were disappointed that the new definition of routine maintenance could take a year or more to complete. "We obviously don't think we've won anything," Frank Maisano, a spokesman for the Electric Reliability Coordinating Council, a power industry group, told the Washington Post.

Reaction from environmental groups and their allies on Capitol Hill was immediate and fierce. Sen. Joseph I. Lieberman, D-Conn., who was expected to seek his party's presidential nomination in 2004, called on Whitman to resign. Whitman had "good intentions," he said, but she had repeatedly been overruled by the White House.

Opposition also came from northeastern states whose air had long been polluted by power plants and factories located in other regions. The attorneys general of nine states—the six New England states, plus Maryland, New Jersey, and New York—announced plans to sue the EPA to overturn the new rules. A major reason for the concern of the states was that the Clean Air Act required them to meet new air quality standards, even though much of the pollution in their skies was generated by plants in the Midwest or the Appalachian region.

Administration's "Clear Skies" Initiative

In a related air pollution issue, the Bush administration on February 14 announced plans for a gradual phase-in of reductions in industrial emissions of three types of pollutants: sulfur dioxide, which created fine particles of soot and contributed to the phenomenon known as acid rain, which poisoned lakes and rivers; nitrogen oxide, a major component of smog, which was harmful to people with respiratory diseases; and mercury, a toxic metal. The White House called the plan "Clear Skies" and said it would result in "rapid and certain improvements in air quality." Bush's aides said the plan was intended to encourage industries to reduce their emissions voluntarily. It would allow companies that could not meet the new standards to trade "rights" to pollute with other companies that could meet the standards. That aspect of his plan would amend the Clean Air Act and therefore would need approval by Congress. Bush announced his Clear Skies proposal in conjunction with another plan on global warming. (Global warming, p. 298)

Environmental advocates said the plan—far from promoting clear skies—actually would delay and reduce air clean-up requirements under the existing law. The Natural Resources Defense Council said the plan would allow 50 percent higher emissions of sulfur dioxide and postpone further cleanup requirements until 2018—six years later than under current law. It also would allow increased emissions of nitrogen oxide pollution and delay its tougher standards for ten years. And, critics said, the plan would postpone by ten years pending regulations on mercury emissions and triple the allowed emission limits in those regulations.

The New York Times *reported on April 28 that the White House, in writing the Clear Skies proposal, had rejected a tougher alternative advocated by the EPA. The newspaper cited administration documents showing that the EPA plan "would have reduced air pollution further and faster" than the one Bush adopted. Jeffrey R. Holmstead, an EPA assistant administrator, said the agency's proposal was found to be "not feasible" because the government lacked the manpower to enforce it.*

The administration's plan made no headway on Capitol Hill, in part because of resistance in the Democratic-controlled Senate. Administration officials also had trouble defending the plan because of a lack of studies showing its potential impact on emissions. Officials said Bush would ask the Republican-controlled Congress to act on the proposal in 2003.

The Bush administration sided with environmentalists on another controversial clean air policy involving tougher standards for diesel engines. In his final weeks in office, President Clinton had imposed regulations requiring all new trucks and buses with diesel engines to begin meeting new emissions standards by October 1, as part of a long-term plan to cut diesel emissions by 90 percent by 2007. Diesel engines were a major source of nitrogen oxide emissions.

The trucking industry and some manufacturers of heavy equipment opposed the rules and went to court to overturn them. The Bush administra-

tion defended Clinton's rules, however, and a panel of the U.S. Court of Appeals for the District of Columbia upheld them on May 3. Opponents of the rule then sought help from Congress and won backing from House Speaker J. Dennis Hastert, whose state, Illinois, was the home of Caterpillar Inc., a major heavy equipment manufacturer that had fought the rules and faced heavy fines because its fleet would not meet the new standards by the October 1 deadline. At least two competing firms, Cummins Engine and Mack Trucks, had complied with the rules. The White House on July 31 rejected Hastert's plea to delay the rules.

Logging and Development in National Forests

Control of mining, logging, and other industrial uses of the national forests had been an especially contentious issue in recent years. The Clinton administration in 1999 announced plans to curtail development in nearly 60 million acres of forest lands—about one-third of the total—by prohibiting construction of new roads. This "roadless" initiative was broadly supported by environmental advocates but bitterly opposed by commercial interests and by states and localities, especially in western states, that relied on the forests for jobs in the extraction industries. Clinton issued his final rules barring road construction in those forest lands shortly before he left office. (Roadless background, Historic Documents of 1999, p. 592)

After taking office, the Bush administration said it supported the Clinton rules in principle but then took several steps that, environmentalists said, effectively undercut enforcement of them. One major action by the Bush administration was to refuse to defend the Clinton rules in court. The state of Idaho and logging interests challenged the rules in 2001 and quickly won a ruling from a federal district judge in Boise blocking their enforcement. That judge's ruling was overturned on December 12, 2002, by the Ninth District Court of Appeals in San Francisco, which said Clinton's rules had met all legal requirements. That decision left the ultimate fate of Clinton's rules uncertain.

In the meantime, the Bush administration had taken three other major steps that had the potential to increase commercial uses of the forests. First, on May 16, the Forest Service announced plans to open about 10 million acres of the 17-million acre Tongass National Forest in Alaska to logging and mining, while setting aside a much smaller portion of the Chugach National Forest, also in Alaska. Clinton had included Tongass—the nation's largest remaining forest wilderness area—in his roadless regulations, and so the December 12 reinstatement of those regulations raised questions about the Forest Service's new plan to develop that forest.

Second, the administration on August 22 announced plans to speed up logging in several million acres of national forest land as a means of reducing the risk of wildfire. Major wildfires had hit several western states earlier than usual in the summer and spawned a public uproar in the region. The administration's plan, called "Healthy Forests," would exempt from environmental reviews and legal challenges the logging of forest land for the purpose of preventing fires. The plan allowed logging companies to take large, commercially valuable trees (which generally were resistant to fire) as an incentive to remove the more fire-prone underbrush and small trees that had little commercial value. Administration officials said this step was necessary because court challenges had stymied previous plans to reduce fire risks in the forests. Environmentalists countered that very few fire-prevention plans had been blocked by environmental reviews, and they said the administration was using the fire issue as an excuse to open previously off-limit areas of forests to logging companies. Congress did not act on the administration's plan, and the White House in December acted administratively by broadening the categories of logging that would be attributed to fighting fires. The Natural Resources Defense Council called Bush's action a "thinly veiled giveaway to the timber industry."

Third, the administration on November 27 issued proposed rules giving local managers of the 155 national forests increased discretion to make major decisions determining how the land would be used. The new rules would eliminate several environmental requirements under regulations the Clinton administration had adopted. Sally Collins, the Forest Service associate chief, said the new rules would "better harmonize the environmental, social, and economic benefits" of the forests. Environmental advocates said the rules would reduce public and scientific scrutiny of commercial uses of the forests. Moreover, they said, the administration was putting decisions about the use of some 190 million acres of forests and grasslands in the hands of local Forest Service officials who, in many cases, had close ties with logging, mining, and other business interests.

Other Contentious Issues

Following are some of the other controversial environmental issues dealt with by the Bush administration and Congress during 2002:

- *Arctic drilling. One of Bush's highest legislative priorities was his proposal, announced in May 2001, to open the Arctic National Wildlife Refugee in Alaska to oil production. Bush said the refuge could produce up to 16.5 billion gallons of oil without causing undue damage to the region's fragile environment. Environmentalists said Bush's estimate of the oil potential in the region was wildly exaggerated and they insisted that drilling would cause irreparable harm to one of the country's last remaining pristine ecosystems. The House in 2001 passed energy legislation approving Bush's proposal with modest restrictions, but the Senate rejected the plan on April 18, 2002, by a 54–46 vote. Bush said he would resubmit the proposal to Congress in 2003.*

- *Superfund. The Bush administration and environmental groups continued to spar over the administration's use of the Superfund law to force and pay for cleanups of toxic waste sites. With more than 1,200 toxic sites remaining on the national priority list, and money in the Superfund rapidly running out, the administration said it was concentrating on the most dangerous sites containing toxic chemicals. A*

July report by the EPA inspector general said the agency was stretching out cleanups at thirty-three sites because of a lack of funds and was failing to address some serious health risks. Administration officials rejected both charges, saying cleanups were being handled as quickly as possible. (Superfund cleanup, Historic Documents of 1999, p. 40)

- ***Environmental reviews.*** *One of the administration's least noticed major actions had the potential of affecting nearly all the nation's environmental policy making. In August White House officials announced a "review" of the National Environmental Policy Act, a 1970 law that established the requirement for "environmental impact" studies of major commercial developments and other activities, such as logging and mining, that had potential to damage the environment. Commercial interests had long claimed the law posed unnecessary legal and bureaucratic hurdles and had been misused by environmentalists to oppose land uses they did not like. Environmental groups expressed fear that Bush would use little-noticed administrative rule changes to weaken or eliminate one of the most important legal tools at their disposal to force developers to address the long-term consequences of their projects.*

- ***EPA enforcement.*** *For the second year in a row, Congress in 2002 rejected Bush's plan to transfer to the states much of the environmental enforcement work that had been handled for decades by the EPA. Bush proposed eliminating the jobs of about two hundred EPA officials who enforced federal air and water laws and regulations; individual states would have taken up the task. Bush said enforcement was better handled at the state level, but environmentalists noted that many states had poor enforcement records because they lacked the necessary expertise and their governments were heavily influenced by local industries. Two senior EPA enforcement officials resigned during the year to protest the administration's policies. One of them, Eric V. Schaeffer, the director of regulatory enforcement, said in a letter to Whitman that the White House "seems determined to weaken the rules we are trying to enforce." Sylvia Lowrance, another senior enforcement official, retired in August and later told a Senate committee that the administration's policies gave polluters reason to believe they would not have to abide by environmental regulations.*

- ***Mining waste.*** *Siding with coal companies in West Virginia and other Appalachian states, the EPA on May 3 reversed a previous interpretation of the Clean Water Act that prohibited the dumping of mining wastes into rivers and wetlands. During the process of strip mining in the region, coal companies removed tons of rock and dirt from mountaintops to expose seams of coal. For decades the companies had simply dumped the waste into streams, hollows, and wetlands. Environmentalists and local community groups said the practice created health risks by polluting streams with toxic chemicals. A federal district judge in West Virginia overturned the Bush administration's rule* *allowing coal companies to resume the dumping of wastes, but that decision was on appeal at the end of the year and seemed unlikely to survive.*

- **Wetlands.** *Late in 2002 the Bush administration made its second effort to deal with the disputed topic of wetlands, the natural systems of bogs, marshes, and swamps that absorbed runoff from storms and provided important habitat for wildlife. In 2001 the Army Corps of Engineers, which regulated development of wetlands by homebuilders and other commercial interests, appeared set to abandon a 1989 policy (called "no net loss") that had declared that any natural wetlands lost to development should be replaced by a comparable amount of new wetlands. Responding to a furor created by the corps's position, the administration developed a new position, which was announced by the EPA's Whitman on December 27. Whitman said the administration was affirming the "no net loss" policy but was adopting guidelines stressing the ecological value of replacement wetlands as opposed to the amount of acreage involved. In other words, a developer might not have to replace destroyed wetlands on an acre-for-acre basis if he could prove that a smaller replacement would serve the same environmental function. The administration's new policy appeared to satisfy neither environmentalists, who wanted tougher regulations to stem the rapid loss of the nation's wetlands, nor developers, who had lobbied for an easing of current regulations.*

- **Snowmobiles in parks.** *One of the most controversial disputes involved relatively few people but did affect two of the country's most important national parks. The Clinton administration had planned a gradual prohibition on the use of snowmobiles in Yellowstone and Grand Teton national parks, saying recreational use of the machines caused severe air pollution and distressed the wildlife. The Bush administration on November 12 reversed the ban but limited the number of vehicles allowed on peak weekends and holidays and required a gradual shift to less-polluting machines. Even so, the administration plan allowed an overall increase in the number of snowmobiles allowed in the parks each season from about 64,000 to about 80,000.*

Following is the text of an announcement issued November 22, 2002, by the Environmental Protection Agency detailing plans for new regulations governing the installation of air pollution equipment at thousands of industrial plants in the United States. The regulations concerned a program known as "new source review," which determined when owners of polluting facilities would be required to upgrade their pollution-control equipment.

The document was obtained from the Internet at www.epa .gov/nsr/press_release.html; accessed November 24, 2002.

In a move to increase energy efficiency and encourage emissions reductions, the U.S. Environmental Protection Agency (EPA) announced today that it has finalized a rule to improve the New Source Review (NSR) program. EPA also announced a proposed rule to provide a regulatory definition of "routine maintenance, repair and replacement." These actions will offer facilities greater flexibility to improve and modernize their operations in ways that will reduce energy use and air pollution, provide incentives to install state-of-the-art pollution controls and more accurately calculate actual emissions of air pollution. These improvements will also remove perverse and unintended regulatory barriers to investments in energy efficiency and pollution control projects, while preserving the environmental benefits of the NSR program.

"EPA is taking actions now to improve NSR and thereby encourage emissions reductions," said EPA Administrator Christie Whitman. "NSR is a valuable program in many respects but the need for reform is clear and has broad-based support. The steps we are taking today recognize that some aspects of the NSR program have deterred companies from implementing projects that would increase energy efficiency and decrease air pollution."

After a comprehensive review of the program, EPA issued a Report to the President on NSR in June 2002. This report concluded that the program as currently administered has impeded or resulted in the cancellation of projects that would maintain or improve the reliability, efficiency or safety of existing power plants and refineries. EPA also concluded that, at existing industrial facilities outside the energy sector, NSR discourages projects that improve capacity or efficiency and do not increase emissions. Instead of being a tool to help improve air quality, the report indicated that NSR has stood in the way of making numerous environmental improvements at many facilities across the nation. Based on these findings, EPA recommended a series of improvements to help address these problems. The final and proposed rules implement these recommendations.

The final rule improvements are the culmination of a 10-year process. During this period, EPA implemented pilot studies and engaged state and local governments, environmental groups, private sector representatives, academia and concerned citizens in an open and far-reaching public rulemaking process. Last summer the nation's governors and environmental commissioners, on a bipartisan basis, called for NSR reform.

The final rule implements the following major improvements to the NSR program:

Plantwide Applicability Limits (PALs): To provide facilities with greater flexibility to modernize their operations without increasing air pollution, facilities that agree to operate within strict site-wide emissions caps called PALs will be given flexibility to modify their operations without undergoing NSR, so long as the modifications do not cause emissions to violate their plantwide cap.

Pollution Control and Prevention Projects: To maximize investments in pollution prevention, companies that undertake certain specified environmentally beneficial activities will be free to do so upon submission to their permitting authority of a notice, rather than having to wait for adjudication of a permit application. EPA is also creating a simplified process for approving other environmentally beneficial projects. Current elements of the NSR program can actually hinder pollution prevention projects.

Clean Unit Provision: To encourage the installation of state-of-the-art air pollution controls, EPA will give plants that attain "clean unit" status flexibility in the future if they continue to operate within permitted limits. This flexibility is an incentive for plants to voluntarily install the best available pollution controls. Clean units must have an NSR permit or other regulatory limit that requires the use of the best air pollution control technologies.

Emissions Calculation Test Methodology: To provide facilities with a more accurate procedure for evaluating the effect of a project on future emissions, the final regulations improve how a facility calculates whether a particular change will result in a significant emissions increase and thereby trigger NSR permitting requirements. Also, to more accurately represent a facility's actual emissions before a change, to account for variations in business cycles, and to provide a bright-line test for measuring pre-change emissions levels, industrial facilities will be allowed to use any consecutive 24-month period in the previous decade as a baseline, as long as all current emission limitations are taken into account. (This "baseline emissions" provision does not apply to power plants.)

Proposed Rule

The proposed rule would make improvements to the "routine maintenance, repair and replacement" exclusion currently contained in EPA's regulations. These proposed improvements will be subject to a full and open public rulemaking process. Since 1980 EPA regulations have excluded from NSR review all repairs and maintenance activities that are "routine," but a complex analysis must be used to determine what activities meet that standard. This has deterred companies from conducting repairs and replacements that are necessary for the safe, efficient and reliable operation of facilities, resulting in unnecessary emissions of pollution and less efficient, safe and reliable plant processes.

Routine Maintenance, Repair and Replacement: To increase environmental protection and promote the implementation of necessary maintenance, repair and replacement projects, EPA proposes to revise the existing routine maintenance, repair and replacement exemption contained in EPA's regulations to make clear that two categories of activities automatically constitute routine maintenance, repair and replacement. The proposal sets out a range of options for particular features of each approach, and seeks public comment on these options:

Annual Maintenance, Repair and Replacement Allowance: would provide a facility-wide annual allowance for maintenance activities. Activities undertaken to promote the safe, reliable and efficient operation of a plant, whose costs fall within the allowance, would constitute routine maintenance, repair and replacement. The allowance would be set on an industry-specific basis so as to cover the capital and non-capital costs that an owner or operator of a stationary source in a particular industry would typically incur in maintaining, replacing and repairing equipment at the source in order to promote the safe, reliable and efficient operation of the source.

Equipment Replacement Approach: would provide that most projects involving the replacements of existing equipment with functionally equivalent new equipment would constitute routine maintenance, repair and replacement. That would be determined by comparing the cost of the components being replaced with the cost of replacing a production unit at the plant. If the cost of the replaced components is below a specified threshold, then the replacements would qualify as routine maintenance, repair and replacement. The threshold would be set so as to allow replacement of components that are typically replaced at sources in the relevant industrial category in order to promote the safe, efficient and reliable operation of such sources, but not to include major renovations or rehabilitations. . . .

NEW TURKISH GOVERNMENT ON ITS LEGISLATIVE PROGRAM
November 23, 2002

Angry over a failing economy and the inability of their traditional political leaders to set it right, the voters of Turkey on November 3, 2002, gave an overwhelming electoral victory to an openly Islamic party. The Justice and Development Party (known by its Turkish initials AKP) took office on November 18 as only the second nonsecular government in the country's eighty-year history. The first Islamic government, narrowly elected in 1996, lasted in power for less than a year. But the AKP's broad victory—coupled with the depth of public dissatisfaction with the leaders who had run the country in previous years—appeared to usher in a new era in the country of 70 million people that occupied a crucial juncture between Europe and Asia.

At least for the first few months, Turkey's de facto leader would be an unelected one, in fact a man who held no formal government post. Recep Tayyip Erdogan, a charismatic former mayor of Istanbul, was the undisputed leader of the AKP but had been barred from running for parliament because he had been stripped of his political rights after serving time in prison for "religious incitement" in a 1997 political speech. In the meantime his place as prime minister was taken by Abdullah Gul, the party's deputy chairman and a Western-educated economist.

Erdogan in late November made a triumphant tour of European capitals, pleading Turkey's case for admission to the European Union (EU) and making the case that his party did not intend to turn the country into an Islamic state. EU leaders rebuffed his membership plea and instead said Turkey's application would be considered again in late 2004. But Erdogan succeeded in reassuring world leaders—and just as important the international financial markets—that the new government would retain the generally secular nature of the largest Islamic country on Europe's borders. (EU membership, p. 679)

A Political Earthquake

The November 3 election represented a near-total repudiation of the centrist political parties that had governed the country for much of the period since World War II. In recent decades a handful of political leaders had dominated the country's leadership, often at the head of coalition governments—ten of them since the last majority government was elected in 1987. For example, the aging prime minister, Bulent Ecevit, had held that post five times over a forty-five-year political career and appeared incapable of making some of the tough decisions necessary to pull the country out of its economic morass. Several younger centrist political leaders, notably the former economics minister Kemal Dervis, quit the government in disgust after they were unable to win enactment of economic reforms. The resignations cost Ecevit his coalition majority and forced him to call elections for November, eighteen months ahead of time.

From the outset of the campaign it was clear that Erdogan's AKP was the front-runner. The only question was whether it could win a majority enabling it to govern, given that fifteen other parties were contesting legislative seats, including the three mainstream parties that each held more than one hundred seats in the outgoing parliament.

The results on election day were shocking. The old mainstream parties of the past failed to win a single seat in the parliament. Ecevit's party, for example, captured just 1 percent of the vote. Those parties were shut out of parliament because they failed to secure the minimum threshold of 10 percent of the national vote introduced by the military during the 1980s in hopes of ending the political gridlock that had resulted from the presence of numerous parties in parliament. Under the rules, the votes of parties that fell below the 10 percent level were distributed to those parties that finished above that threshold. In 2002 the net effect was to give the AKP, which won just 34 percent of the popular vote, 363 of the 550 seats in the parliament. The official opposition would be the party founded by Kemal Ataturk, the Republican People's Party, led in 2002 by Deniz Baykal, Dervis, and other politicians on the center-left of Turkey's political spectrum; that party won 19.4 percent of the vote and 178 seats in parliament. In effect, the new parliament would have the first two-party division since the introduction of multiparty democracy in 1954.

During the campaign Erdogan had been the AKP's clear leader and had never said who would become prime minister if the party won, since Erdogan himself was barred even from running for parliament. After the election Erdogan tapped Gul, a choice that reassured world financial and political leaders because of his economic expertise.

An Islamist Party?

Since Ataturk's modernization of Turkish society in the 1920s and 1930s, the majority of Turks had become cautious and conservative, apparently viewing their country as an island of secular stability in a turbulent region of religious conflict. Turkey's political scene had not been stable, however, and had suffered from the result of numerous failed coalition governments and three military coups since 1950. For the most part Turkey was governed by a succession of generally colorless political leaders who were committed to the status quo and respected the de facto limits on their discretion that had been established by the military.

The one exception was a brief-lived one. Necmittin Erbakan, founder of the avowedly Islamist Welfare Party, became prime minister in June 1996 because of gridlock among the traditional secular parties. He was forced out in February 1997 by the military, which banned the Welfare Party and other Islamic parties.

Erdogan himself was elected mayor of Istanbul in 1994, serving one four-year term. He stirred fears among many nonreligious Turks with such steps as banning alcohol in the city's restaurants. At the time Erdogan also opposed Turkey's membership in the EU, a position he later reversed. The government in 1998 imprisoned Erdogan for reciting a poem in public that included the lines: "The mosques are our bayonets, the domes our helmets, and the believers our soldiers." He served four months in prison for the crime of "religious incitement" and, more important, was stripped of his rights to vote and hold public office. Parliament on December 13 approved constitutional amendments clearing the way for Erdogan to run for office early in 2003.

In 2001 Erdogan and others who had been members of the banned Islamic parties formed the AKP with the aim of contesting the next elections, then scheduled for 2004. The AKP worked hard to portray itself as a moderate party that would make changes to improve peoples' lives but would not push through a radical agenda. As its symbol, the AKP used a light bulb emitting seven rays, one for each of the country's major regions.

Just like any political party in an advanced democracy, the party conducted public opinion surveys and tailored its campaign to appeal to the broadest possible segment of the electorate. The party deliberately chose to play down controversial issues that might stimulate its religious base but at the expense of antagonizing the majority of voters. For example, party leaders did not take a stance on the question of removing Ataturk's ban on the wearing of head scarves by women in public places; because of the ban, thousands of women had been dismissed from or denied admission to high schools and colleges. The wives of Edogan and Gul both routinely wore head scarves.

At least to Western audiences, Erdogan resolutely insisted that the AKP had no intentions or plans to transform Turkey into an Islamic state. "We do not accept being characterized as an Islamist party," he told the Financial Times *in an interview just before the election. "That carries with it too many misinterpretations and antidemocratic associations. If you call yourself an Islamist, it suggests you are trying to impose some sort of Jacobin and intolerant uniformity." Religion, he added, is a personal issue. "Just as no race is better than any other, so no one religion is superior to any other."*

Turkey's Economic Troubles

Turkey's economy had sunk for the three years before 2002, a victim of the worldwide malaise in developing countries resulting from the 1997–1998 Asian financial crisis. The worst year was 2001, when the Turkish currency, the lira, collapsed (falling 50 percent against the dollar). Turkey's overall economy shrank by 7.4 percent; along with Argentina, this was one of the worst economic performances in the world. (Argentina, p. 80; Asian financial crisis, Historic Documents of 1998, p. 722)

By 2002 Turkey's economy had started to recover, but more than 2 million people were still without jobs, putting the unemployment rate at about 20 percent. Inflation was running about 30 percent, and interest rates on some forms of debt ran as high as 50 percent during the year. As with many developing countries, one of Turkey's greatest long-term problems was its debt. As of late 2002 domestic debt was about $85 billion and foreign debt was more than $120 billion; the combined total of more than $200 billion was quite large, by international standards, in comparison to Turkey's overall economy of just about $300 billion.

The International Monetary Fund (IMF) in 1999 extended Turkey a $16.3 billion, multiyear loan program to help ease its debt burden. As with all IMF loans, this one came with conditions: Turkey agreed to reduce the government's fiscal deficit, to ease regulations that discouraged investment, and to fight corruption, which had become endemic both within the government and the private economy. Ecevit's government cut back the government deficit by raising taxes, but other IMF conditions were far from being met as of late 2002.

In times past, the election of an Islamic-based government in Turkey might have frightened foreign investors and international institutions such as the IMF and sent the economy into another tailspin. But Erdogan's reassuring demeanor and pledges, coupled with the presence in the government of respected figures such as Gul and the government's strong majority in parliament, appeared to offer some hope for progress on economic reform. The financial markets gave the new government some breathing room by cutting interest rates for Turkey following the election. The questions were how much of a honeymoon the new government would have and how successful it would be in meeting voters' expectations for economic improvements while cutting spending to meet IMF conditions on debt reduction.

Political, Legal Issues for EU Membership

In addition to the economic conditions imposed by the IMF, Turkey faced conditions for its hoped-for membership in the European Union. Turkey had been trying since the late 1950s to join the EU's predecessor organizations, only to be rebuffed repeatedly because it was too poor, too unstable politically, too repressive—and too Islamic, which was always the unstated reason. In 2002 Turkey for the first time had a reasonable expectation that the EU might set a date to start the process leading to membership.

To get to that point, Ankara had been making numerous political reforms to meet EU criteria on such measures as democracy and human rights. In one of its most important steps, the parliament in August abolished the death penalty for peace-time offenses. EU treaties prohibited any member state from imposing the death penalty, and the issue had become a central one to the European view of Turkey as a modern democracy. Following the elimination of the death penalty, the government commuted the sentences of eighty-seven prisoners on death row to life imprisonments. Turkey's last execution was in 1984. Also in August the Turkish parliament lifted a ban on Kurdish-language broadcasting and education. During the previous year more than one thousand students had been arrested for circulating petitions calling for optional courses in Kurdish.

A related issue of great symbolic importance was torture. Turkish police were notorious for their use of torture to extract confessions and information from criminal suspects. The European Court of Human Rights, an affiliate of the EU, had ordered Turkey to prohibit the use of torture by the police, but the government still had not enacted the demanded legislation as of 2002.

Iraq and the United States

As if a failing economy and the demands of the European Union for political reforms were not enough of an agenda for Turkey's new leadership, another major crisis was barreling down the road and likely to confront the country early in 2003. That was the matter of a likely U.S.-led war to unseat Saddam Hussein, the dictatorial leader of neighboring Iraq. Pentagon officials in late 2002 began the process of seeking Turkey's permission to use the country's air bases, port facilities, and roads to move the tens of thousands of troops who would be making a northern thrust into Iraq.

The U.S. request put the new government in a difficult position. On the one hand, Turkey and the United States were NATO allies, Washington was a major factor in deciding the fate of Turkey's loans from the IMF and likely would be offering Turkey new aid in exchange for the use of its territory, and there was little popular sympathy within Turkey for the Iraqi regime. All these factors argued in favor of Turkey's agreeing to the U.S. request. If a war was going to occur, some Turkish officials said, the country might as well be on the likely winning side and get paid for being there.

On the other hand, Iraq was a fellow Muslim country, and a substantial portion of the Turkish population could be expected to oppose U.S. military action there on religious and cultural grounds despite Saddam's unpopularity. In addition, Turkey's leaders believed they were never adequately compensated by the United States for their economic losses during and after the 1991 Persian Gulf War. Turkey supported that U.S.-led war against Iraq but then lost billions of dollars worth of trade with Iraq when the United Nations imposed stiff economic sanctions against Baghdad.

Even more important, a war in Iraq was almost certain to destabilize the existing status of the region's Kurds, who were a large minority population in Turkey, Iraq, and Iran. Iraq's Kurds had established a successful self-governing zone in northern Iraq since the 1991 Persian Gulf War. That development increased agitation among the region's Kurds for a broader homeland that they wanted to call Kurdistan. Ankara feared that once a new war began in Iraq, tens or even hundreds of thousands of Iraqi Kurds likely would flee, or be pushed, across the border into Turkey, creating an enormous refugee problem. Such a development would be a repeat of what happened after the 1991 war, when Iraq's Kurds (with U.S. encouragement) rose up against Saddam and were crushed; thousands fled into Turkey. That crisis fanned the flames of a separatist rebellion by Turkey's Kurds, which Ankara was able to break only in 1999. Since then Turkey had kept several thousand troops in northern Iraq to secure its borders against another Kurdish uprising. The prospect of another Kurdish refugee crisis—coupled with a possible move by Kurds to declare an independent homeland— terrified leaders in Turkey and heightened their nervousness about another war in Iraq.

> *Following are excerpts from the program submitted November 23, 2002, to the Turkish parliament by the newly elected government headed by Prime Minister Abdullah Gul of the Justice and Development Party.*

> **The document was obtained from the Internet at http:// www.byegm.gov.tr/hukumetler/58hukumet/government programme.htm; accessed November 30, 2002.**

Turkey, in the aftermath of the November 3 General Elections, has achieved stability with a bipartisan parliament and a one-party government. We, as the Parliament and the Government, are well aware of our responsibility to do our best in order to introduce genuine and swift solutions to the problems which have been confronting us. While we try to find urgent solutions to problems, we will also undertake structural changes and reforms to make sure that such problems would never face us again. We are well aware of the fact that the current conditions cannot be overcome by superficial measures.

Both our Electoral Manifesto and the Emergency Action Plan, which was announced by our leader Recep Tayyip Erdogan, the result of a coherent, responsible and reformist understanding, were appreciated by the public opinion. Therefore, our Government Programme has been prepared along these lines to fulfil the commitments we had given to the people before the elections.

The Government will not get involved into unnecessary political discussions and polemics and it expects to receive the trust and support of the nation. We will work in dialogue and cooperation with the opposition party and all sectors of the society in a democratic and transparent way. We will respect pluralistic democracy, human rights and the supremacy of law and we will do our best to achieve social consensus when tackling with important issues, for we know very well that numerical superiority does not mean everything.

We will strengthen the ties between the state and the society, broaden the political field, reinstall the trust between the politics and the society and respond to the demands of the people.

Following the announcement of the November 3 election results, interest rates began to decrease, the stock exchange began to rally and foreign exchange rates started to fall down because of the positive expectations and the climate of confidence in both domestic and international markets. It is imperative to maintain this climate of confidence to solve urgent social and economic problems. We will never forget the demands and expectations of the people. Our success will not only belong to us, it will be the success of all political and state institutions, and, above all, it will belong to the nation.

While the world was undergoing radical transformations, Turkey, unfortunately, has wasted her time and energy tackling internal problems. Although multiparty system was adopted 50 years ago, Turkey is still among the countries which could not become fully democratic, where basic rights and freedoms cannot be fully enjoyed. Despite its young and dynamic population and rich natural sources, Turkey has been unable to increase her level of welfare and establish a truly competitive production sector.

The state's role in the economy could not conform with the changing conditions due to wrong policies that were being implemented and the injustice in the distribution of wealth among the parts of the community and regions could not be corrected. A sound privatization scheme could not be carried out. The country could not rid itself of cumbersome, overcentralist administrative system, impoverishment and political corruption.

The economic policies of recent coalition governments have failed and the worst economic crisis in its history hit the country. As a result, unprecedented poverty has struck our people. Hundreds of thousands have lost their jobs and tens of thousands of business had to be closed down. People have lost their hope for the future.

The government, however, believes that Turkey has the potential to be a rightful member of the new world with its young population, unique geographical location, rich natural resources and cultural aspects. The government has set off a course to establish a secure future and meet the people's demands with a comprehensive program, an honest leadership and well-educated and experienced personnel.

Most of the issues mentioned in the program are actually those which have been discussed for long time. These issues will be taken up in an atmosphere of social dialogue and constructive relations between the government and the opposition. The motto of Mustafa Kemal Atatürk, the founder of the Republic and our great leader, to surpass the level of contemporary civilization, will form the basis of the steps we will take.

The government will create a democratic, credible and dynamic Turkey enjoying economic stability, competitive market structure, sustainable development environment, justice in welfare, peace, freedom and integration with the modern world. We will make this vision come true.

Basic Rights and Freedoms

People enjoy inalienable and nontransferable basic rights and freedoms. The individual will be the center of our policies which will take all international democratic standards as a basis.

Our country, which made European Convention on Human Rights and Universal Declaration of Human Rights a part of its internal law, will put these values into practice and reach universal standards in the field of basic rights and freedoms, under our leadership.

Therefore, we will introduce all necessary amendments to the Constitution and the laws to upgrade the basic rights and freedoms to the level in international conventions and the Copenhagen criteria [conditions for membership in the European Union], in particular.

We will put these basic rights and freedoms into practice and make them an established dimension of our political culture.

No double standards and political manipulation will be permitted in basic rights and freedoms of individuals.

We will wage a determined struggle against violations of human rights and torture in particular. . . .

We will also prepare a new Constitution which will underline freedoms and participatory aspects. The new Constitution will enjoy powerful social legitimacy and conform with the international norms. It will feature the understanding of the democratic rule of law based on individual rights and freedoms as well as pluralist and participatory democracy. . . .

A New Economic Programme To Be Implemented

Taking into account the deficient and problematic aspects of the current economic program, the Government will implement a new economic programme, which would receive the support of the people, to order to reach a high and stable growth performance to decrease public debt stock and to reduce inflation rate.

It is evident that a growth model based on foreign loans and public deficits can no longer be sustained. Therefore, the finance policy of our Government will aim to reduce the debt stock and ensure non-interest surplus which would protect macro stability. The scale of non-interest surplus would be formed by taking its composition, economic feasibility as well as the growth and social policies into consideration. The public debt stock would be reduced to a sustainable level.

The public sector will be restructured, privatization will be speeded up, and an encouraging atmosphere will be created for domestic and foreign investors. We will also see to it that the productivity in the agriculture sector would be restructured as well.

The Government will continue the floating exchange rate policy but Central Bank would intervene in a more sensitive way in case of speculative floatings which have no macro economic bases.

The Government will implement the economic development policies in a balanced way together with social policies.

We believe that it is necessary to put individuals at the centre of economic development in order to have successful policies to fight with poverty and to improve the distribution of income.

The basic priority in removing poverty will be to clean the politics and public administration from corruption. On the other hand, the tax burden on employees will be lessened gradually. . . .

Education and Secularism

The government will make the principle of secularism as well as the freedom of religion and conscience defined in the Constitution more tangible and functional. We will attach importance to a religious education and teaching which will prevent manipulation of religion, religious feelings, and things considered "holy" by the religion for political and individual interests. Thus, the expectations of the citizens in the field of religious education and teaching will be met and also manipulations in this field will be over.

The government will lift the impediments in front of exercising the right to education and be educated. Universities will turn into free forums where there are no prohibitions and restrictions. . . .

Despite the most difficult economic problems, we have managed to survive. This is mainly due to our strong family structure. The Government will support efforts which aim to protect the family.

The women will have the equal status which would provide them to have social responsibility in every field with that of men. Violence against women will be prevented.

The youth, besides the treasure of the country, is the source of our dynamism and potential for change. We will support cultural, artistic and supporting activities for our youth. The central administration should play a regulating and coordinating role in such services. Local administrations, cooperating with the private sector and volunteer organisations will provide these services. . . .

Foreign Policy

The government will pursue an objective, unbiased and realist foreign policy based on reciprocal interests, and it will respect the territorial integrity and sovereignty of all countries.

Turkey has to redefine its foreign policy priorities in line with changing regional and global realities and set up a new balance with these realities and national interests.

Turkey has close relations with Europe both in respect of geography and also in respect of history. Therefore, the relations with European countries will continue to occupy the highest level at Turkey's foreign policy agenda.

Turkey's full EU membership is the fundamental goal of our administration. Therefore, the government will endeavour to start accession talks with the EU after Turkey's candidacy in EU enlargement process is reconfirmed. It is without doubt that Turkey's getting the place it deserves in the EU family will bring benefits to both sides and create positive results for the peace, stability and security beyond the European continent as well.

Within this framework, the EU adjustment laws adopted by the Parliament will be strengthened in respect to basic rights and freedoms. We will also attach importance to training studies to fully put these reforms into practice. . . .

The government will launch efforts to decrease the tension between religions and cultures which started to escalate following the September 11 attack and it will actively be involved in endeavours to form an atmosphere of global peace.

Our cooperation with the U.S. which exists for a long time and which deals mainly with defense issues, will continue. This cooperation will also spread to economy, investment, science and technology. . . .

Turkey has concerns regarding the uncertainty vis-a-vis its neighbour Iraq. The government attributes particular importance to the territorial integrity of Iraq and the protection of its political unity. Spoiling Iraq's territorial integrity will change all the balances in the Middle East. The Government wants Iraqi administration to fully implement the U.N. resolutions and a peaceful solution to this problem. . . .

UN SECRETARY GENERAL ON
NATIONS USING CHILD SOLDIERS
November 26, 2002

The nations of the world took a small step forward in 2002 when a treaty outlawing the use of children in armed combat went into force. Later in the year United Nations Secretary General Kofi Annan took the unusual action of naming twenty-three parties, including insurgent groups and governments, in five countries that continued to recruit and use children in warfare. Annan also named nine other countries where either the government or insurgent groups were known or thought to use child soldiers.

Olara A. Otunnu, Annan's special representative for children and armed conflict, said the list was an important political signal. "First, it indicates that the international community is becoming serious in moving to translate norms, standards, declarations, resolutions into applications on the ground. And secondly, it signals the parties in conflict that the international community is watching and will hold you responsible for what you do to children in situations under your control," he said.

The treaty outlawing child soldiers and Annan's report were just two of several steps the international community took in 2002 to protect children from predators and to ensure that they enjoyed basic rights, such as access to education and health care. A second treaty barring the sale of children, child pornography, and child prostitution took effect on January 18. In May delegates to the UN General Assembly's Special Session on Children rededicated themselves to improving the well-being of children. But a measure of how difficult that task could be came in early March when it was revealed that aid workers hired by international relief organizations, including the United Nations, were demanding sex from young girls in refugee camps in West Africa in exchange for food and other assistance. (UN Special Session on Children, p. 221; Internet pornography, p. 287; human trafficking, p. 332; sexual exploitation of children, Historic Documents of 2001, p. 955)

An "Intolerable" Practice

Overall, an estimated 300,000 young boys and girls were thought to be involved in armed conflicts in more than thirty-five countries, serving as sol-

diers, runners, guards, sex slaves, spies, cooks, decoys, and mine clearers. Some youngsters joined one or another side in an armed conflict to serve a cause, such as fighting the oppression of their people, religion, or culture. It was thought, however, that most child soldiers were forcibly recruited, often drugged and then kidnapped into service. Many children were orphans who had nowhere else to go. Once they were recruited, children were often forced to watch or commit atrocities, including murder and rape, sometimes against their own tribes and villages. Many, especially young girls, were victims of sexual abuse, often made to serve as "wives" to rebel soldiers. Children were routinely beaten or killed if they tried to escape. Children who escaped or were demobilized often had difficulty adjusting to civilian life. Many suffered from psychological trauma.

A study of child soldiers in East Asia and the Pacific region found that the average age of child soldiers in that region was thirteen, but armed soldiers as young as five had been reported. In the study, conducted by the United Nations International Children's Emergency Fund (UNICEF) and released October 30, sixty-nine current and former child combatants from six countries—Cambodia, East Timor, Indonesia, Myanmar, Papua New Guinea, and the Philippines— gave chilling firsthand accounts of their experiences. "The voices of these children constitute a cry for help on behalf of all child soldiers, a cry that we cannot ignore," said Carol Bellemy, UNICEF executive director. "They provide compelling evidence on why children must not be allowed to become combatants and why every effort needs to be made to ensure that those still serving are demobilized and reintegrated into society," she said.

Other former child soldiers described their experiences to delegates attending the UN's Special Session on Children in May as part of an effort by the UN to increase financial support for pilot rehabilitation projects for newly surrendered and demobilized child soldiers in Congo, Sierra Leone, and Sri Lanka. "It becomes a normal thing—killing someone was as easy as doing anything," said a twenty-year-old from Sierra Leone, who was forced to serve as a rebel soldier for three years. "I kept pulling the trigger for three years. I ran out of tears to shed." Listening to this testimony, Annan declared, "Those who practice this form of child abuse must be held accountable. For far too long, the use of child soldiers has been seen as merely regrettable. We are here to ensure it is recognized as intolerable."

Another facet of the problem involved Western soldiers who found themselves in combat with child soldiers. American troops, for example, sent to help quell rebellions in the Philippines could encounter boy soldiers recruited by the Abu Sayyaf rebel group. Iraqi dictator Saddam Hussein had trained thousands of ten- to fifteen-year-olds, known as Ashbal Saddam (Saddam's Lion Cubs), in small arms and infantry tactics. Should the United States find itself in a ground war there, as seemed possible at the end of the year, American military personnel might find themselves in a direct confrontation with these young troops. (Iraq, p. 713)

In one of first engagements between Western troops and child soldiers, a patrol of British soldiers was taken hostage in late 2000 in Sierra Leone by

917

a rebel militia made up primarily of children. The squad commander reportedly refused to fire on "children armed with AK-47s." The patrol was rescued more than two weeks later by an assault team that left 25 to 150 of the rebel soldiers dead. A British military officer suggested that at least some of the men would probably require psychological counseling to help them deal with the trauma of firing on and killing youngsters.

Protocol Barring Child Soldiers

The Optional Protocol of the Convention on the Rights of the Child regarding children involved in armed conflict entered into force on February 12. It forbid signatory members to compel children under eighteen to serve in the military and to engage in direct hostilities. The minimum age for voluntary recruitment was set at sixteen. Under no circumstances were insurgent forces permitted to recruit children under eighteen or use them in hostilities. "There can no longer be any excuses for using children for war," said Mary Robinson, UN High Commissioner for Human Rights during a ceremony in Geneva. "Children have no place in war," said Otunnu, the UN's special representative for children and armed conflict. "This new treaty is a victory for children who have been neglected, abused, and sexually exploited by warring factions for decades."

Ninety-six countries had signed the protocol, which went into force when the requisite fourteen countries had ratified it. The United States officially became a party to the treaty on December 23. The Defense Department, which allowed seventeen-year-olds to fight, initially opposed the protocol but signed on after it determined that it could meet its military recruitment and readiness goals without using combatants younger than eighteen. The United States had sent seventeen-year-olds into armed conflict in Somalia, Bosnia, and the Persian Gulf War.

A second treaty, the Rome Statute of the International Criminal Court, which entered into force on July 1, made conscription, enlistment, or the use in hostilities of children under age fifteen a war crime in both international and internal conflicts. The United States was not a signatory to the treaty.
(International Criminal Court, p. 605)

Naming Names

In submitting his report on the countries that continued to recruit and use child soldiers, Secretary General Annan said the list represented "an important step forward in our efforts to induce compliance by parties to conflict with international child protection obligations." Annan said he listed only those countries "on the agenda" of the Security Council, that is, where the Security Council had taken some action that was still pending to deal with an armed conflict in that country. The five countries named were Afghanistan, Burundi, the Democratic Republic of the Congo, Liberia, and Somalia. Most of the twenty-three parties listed were rebel groups, but government armed forces in the four African countries were also listed. Congo was a party to the optional protocol on child soldiers. (Afghanistan, p. 15; Congo, p. 546)

Annan also listed several other "situations of concern" around the world. These included the recruitment and use of children by paramilitary groups in Northern Ireland, the use of children to plant landmines and explosives by insurgents in Chechnya, and forced recruitment by rebel or independence movements in Colombia, Myanmar, Nepal, the Philippines, Sri Lanka, the Sudan, and Uganda. Annan also said that the United Nations and other organizations were closely monitoring demobilization and reintegration into civil society of child soldiers in several countries, including Angola, Kosovo, and Sierra Leone. Annan's report was dated November 26, but it was not made public until December 16. (Sri Lanka, p. 92; Angola, p. 151; Sierra Leone, p. 247; Colombia, p. 569)

Abuses in Refugee Camps

Many of the demobilized child soldiers, as well as hundreds of thousands of children and their parents uprooted by armed conflicts around the world, were living in refugee camps. In March the UN High Commissioner for Refugees (UNHCR) revealed that children in refugee camps in Guinea, Liberia, and Sierra Leone had been sexually exploited by aid workers and others. The shocking findings were uncovered during an investigation by the UN agency and the British-based charity, Save the Children. "Sexual violence and exploitation of children appears to be extensive in the communities visited and involves actors at all levels, including those who are engaged to protect the very children they are exploiting," the two agencies reported. The findings were based on 1,500 interviews. About 600,000 people were living in refugee camps in the three countries, which had been the sites of civil war and cross-border conflicts for the past decade. Another 700,000 people were estimated to be internally displaced within the three countries.

The main victims of abuse were girls ages thirteen to eighteen. Children interviewed made specific allegations against sixty-seven individuals from more than forty organizations. Most often the accused were male workers hired by international aid agencies, but UN peacekeepers, local government officials, teachers, and even community leaders in the camps themselves were named. According to the study, several of the victims said that giving in to demands for sex "was often the only option they had" if they wanted to receive food and medicine and to pay for education. Others said their parents encouraged them to offer themselves to aid workers to get basic necessities. Apart from the human rights aspect of the abuse, there was also concern about the spread of HIV, the virus that caused AIDS. (AIDS, p. 469)

The report said poor management, the vulnerability and poverty of the refugees, and the relative power and wealth of the aid agency staff were the leading causes of the abuse. "The problem arises directly from a combination of poor management, poor oversight, and insufficient allocation of resources," said Jeff Drumtra, senior Africa policy analyst with the U.S. Committee for Refugees.

The report recommended that security be increased and that more international supervisors and more female staff be deployed at the refugee camps. UNHCR also said it was implementing a plan to inform all staff members about their expected conduct, increasing support to the girls most at risk of exploitation, and opening channels for refugees to lodge complaints about abuses. Various nongovernmental organizations were also investigating ways to improve distribution methods to minimize opportunities for abuse. One senior aid worker suggested that ending the exploitation could be a difficult task because of the gender discrimination built into cultures not only in West Africa but elsewhere in the world.

Following are excerpts from a report, dated November 26, 2002, to the United Nations Security Council by Secretary General Kofi Annan, in which he listed twenty-three parties in five countries that were still recruiting and using child soldiers in violation of international standards. Annan also expressed concern about the situation in nine additional, named countries.

The document was obtained from the Internet at www .reliefweb.int/w/rwb.nsf/9ca65951ee22658ec125663300408 599/bbb6c3c3a12d265a85256c9100729a9e?OpenDocu ment; accessed January 6, 2003.

[Parts I–IV omitted.]

V. Child soldiers

Preparation of the list annexed to the report

27. As requested by the Security Council, the annex to the present report contains a list of parties to armed conflict that recruit or use children in violation of the international obligations applicable to them, in situations that are on the Security Council's agenda or that may be brought to the attention of the Security Council by the Secretary-General, in accordance with Article 99 of the Charter of the United Nations, which in his opinion may threaten the maintenance of international peace and security (resolution 1379 (2001)).

28. Factual information for the preparation of the list was sought from and verified with a wide range of sources, including entities of the United Nations system such as peace operations and country teams, international and local non-governmental organizations, and individual academics and experts. The preparation of the list posed numerous challenges; nevertheless the final product represents an important step forward in our efforts to induce compliance with international child protection obligations by parties to conflict. The Security Council is encouraged to consider the information provided in the list in its deliberations and actions on specific country situations.

29. In preparing the list it was decided to include (a) only those current armed conflict situations of which the Security Council was seized at the time of writing of the report; (b) identifiable parties to such a conflict; and (c) those

parties that continue to recruit or use children in violation of international obligations applicable to them.

30. The minimum international standard to which all Member States on the list are held is the Convention on the Rights of the Child. When appropriate, the conduct of States was also assessed in accordance with the Optional Protocol to the Convention on the Rights of the Child on the involvement of children in armed conflict, Additional Protocol II to the Geneva Conventions, International Labour Organization (ILO) Convention No. 182 concerning the elimination of the worst forms of child labour, and the African Charter on the Rights and Welfare of the Child.

31. The conduct of non-State armed groups was assessed in accordance with the widely accepted minimum international standard that children under age 15 shall not be conscripted or enlisted into armed forces or groups or used by them to participate actively in hostilities in either international or internal armed conflicts. This standard echoes the Convention on the Rights of the Child, Additional Protocol II to the Geneva Conventions, the Rome Statute of the International Criminal Court, and the statute of the Special Court for Sierra Leone. In States that have ratified the Optional Protocol to the Convention on the Rights of the Child on the involvement of children in armed conflict, non-State armed groups are held to that higher standard, prohibiting all recruitment and use of children under 18. Commitments made in peace agreements or to my Special Representative were also taken into account.

Parties on the list

32. Applying the above criteria to the information that has been gathered, 23 parties to conflict were found to be engaged in the recruitment or use, or both, of children in the conflicts. These 23 parties to conflict are involved in five situations of which the Security Council is seized . . . : Afghanistan, Burundi, the Democratic Republic of Congo, Liberia and Somalia.

33. In Afghanistan, over the past 20 years of conflict, various State and non-State actors conscripted child soldiers. Following the fall of the Taliban government, there was significant demobilization of soldiers, including children. Recent reports indicate, however, that some armed groups in various parts of the country have resumed recruitment, including under-age boys. The new Afghan National Army, which is designed to replace all other armed groups, will not be employing underage soldiers.

34. In Burundi and the Democratic Republic of the Congo, members of the United Nations country teams are working with relevant government departments, and when possible with non-State armed groups, to facilitate the demobilization of child soldiers.

35. In Burundi, the Government has requested the assistance of UNICEF to conduct a census of child soldiers and to prepare a demobilization plan; this process is currently under way.

36. In the Democratic Republic of the Congo, the Pretoria and Luanda Agreements with the Governments of Rwanda (July 2002) and Uganda (September 2002), which support the principles laid down in the Lusaka

Agreement of 1999, provide a concrete opportunity to move forward with disarmament, demobilization and reintegration and the withdrawal of Rwandan and Ugandan forces, coordinated by MONUC. In May 2001, several parties appearing on the list in the Democratic Republic of the Congo made commitments to my Special Representative to refrain from recruiting children into their armed forces or groups. These same parties are also signatories to the Lusaka Agreement, which imposes a similar restriction. In addition, in November 2001, the Democratic Republic of the Congo ratified the Optional Protocol on the involvement of children in armed conflict, setting 18 as the age limit for all recruitment into the armed forces. A disarmament, demobilization and reintegration process for child soldiers has been initiated with the Government and RCD-Goma.

37. In Liberia, while United Nations and civil society partners are engaged in advocacy to convince the Government to acknowledge the problem of child recruitment, there are indications that renewed fighting has led to new recruitment of children by armed forces and groups.

38. In Somalia, the United Nations has limited ability to monitor recruitment or mount responsive interventions because of insecurity and lack of access. A small pilot demobilization project is under way in Mogadishu for 120 children, including 20 girls.

39. Three parties included in the list are Government armed forces, of which one is legally obliged not to recruit or enlist persons under age 18. The Democratic Republic of the Congo is a party to the Optional Protocol on the involvement of children in armed conflict and has declared an age limit of 18 for voluntary enlistment in the armed forces. The Democratic Republic of the Congo is also a party to ILO Convention No. 182 concerning the elimination of the worst forms of child labour.

Situations of concern not included in the list

40. Other situations of concern with regard to recruitment and use of children in armed conflict, which are not included in the list, are described below.

Conflict situations not on the agenda of the Security Council

41. Such situations include that in Colombia, where armed groups like the FARC (Fuerzas Armadas Revolucionarias de Colombia), ELN (Ejercito de Liberación Nacional) and paramilitaries AUC (Autodefensas Unidas de Colombia), AUSC (Autodefensas Unidas del Sur del Casanare) and ACCU (Autodefensas Campesinas de Córdoba y Uraba) continue their decades-long practice of recruiting boys and girls for use in combat. In Northern Ireland, paramilitaries continue to recruit and use children. In the Republic of Chechnya of the Russian Federation, insurgency groups continue to enlist children and use them to plant landmines and explosives.

42. In Myanmar, Human Rights Watch has reported that large numbers of children are forcibly recruited into the national armed forces, as well as by armed groups. Testimonies received by UNICEF confirm this. In his report to the General Assembly . . . the Special Rapporteur of the Commission on Human Rights on the situation of human rights in Myanmar expressed concern

about reports of abuses on the part of armed opposition groups, notably the Karenni National Liberation Army, which is accused of forced conscription of male villagers, including under-age youths.

43. In Nepal, the United Nations country team and non-governmental organizations report forced and involuntary recruitment by the Communist Party of Nepal (Maoist), although access to the relevant areas of the country is restricted.

44. In the Philippines, the United Nations country team reports recruitment of children by several armed groups, including the New People's Army, the Moro Islamic Liberation Front, the Moro National Liberation Front, and Abu Sayyaf.

45. In the Sudan, the Sudan People's Liberation Army (SPLA) has released some children since March 2001, but the number of children remaining in its ranks is unknown. The Machakos peace process should facilitate the demobilization of child soldiers.

46. In northern Uganda, the Lord's Resistance Army (LRA) continues to use children to fight and as sexual slaves. Some 100 children were recently released by LRA and several others escaped, but hundreds more have been abducted since April 2002, when fighting intensified in the southern Sudan and northern Uganda following the Government of Uganda's launch of Operation Iron Fist. It is believed that a large number of children remain in the ranks of LRA, while many children abducted by LRA over the last decade are still missing.

47. In Sri Lanka, the current peace negotiation under the auspices of Norway is a welcome development. The commitment made to my Special Representative by the Liberation Tigers of Tamil Eelam (LTTE) during his visit to Sri Lanka in 1998 not to recruit or use children has been formally accepted in the current round of negotiations. Demobilization and reintegration of child soldiers from the ranks of LTTE should be accorded priority attention.

Situations on the agenda of the Security Council where conflicts have recently ended

48. Situations of which the Security Council is seized where conflicts have recently ended, and where there is no evidence of either recruitment or use of children at this time, have not been included in the list. In some situations, such as those in Angola, Guinea-Bissau, Kosovo, the Republic of the Congo and Sierra Leone, demobilization and/or reintegration programmes are under way.

49. Other situations where conflicts have been over for some time and peace is being consolidated, as in Cambodia, El Salvador, Guatemala, Honduras, Mozambique and Nicaragua, have not been included in the list. Nonetheless, the legacy of the recruitment and use of child soldiers remains and their full rehabilitation and integration is still a challenge.

Situations of conflict where children have not been recruited or used

50. My Special Representative reported after his visit to Ethiopia and Eritrea that there had been no recruitment or use of children in either country

during the border conflict. This is good news and lessons should be learned from this example.

Demobilization of child soldiers

51. In Sierra Leone, education, family and community support programmes and continued monitoring are essential for more than 6,850 demobilized child ex-combatants, 6,500 of whom have been reunited with their families. These children remain at risk of being recruited again to fight across the border in Liberia.

52. In Guinea-Bissau, since the cessation of the armed conflict two years ago, UNICEF and the United Nations Peace-building Support Office continue to work with the Government to demobilize children from the armed forces.

53. In Angola, following a ceasefire in April 2002 and progress in negotiating a permanent peace, the need for the demobilization and reintegration of ex-combatants is urgent. It is estimated that between 6,000 and 8,000 children under the age of 18 served in the ranks of UNITA.

54. In the Republic of the Congo, those who fought as children in armed groups, a small number of whom were recently demobilized, are considered by the United Nations country team to be at risk of being recruited again in renewed fighting. In the Democratic Republic of the Congo, some of the children from Bunia, who were released and reunited with their families in 2001, were reportedly recruited again in the Iturri region in North Kivu.

55. In the Great Lakes region, the World Bank and donor Governments have undertaken to provide resources ($500 million) to support the demobilization and reintegration of combatants, including child soldiers. This joint international effort—involving donors and United Nations funds and programmes—was launched by the World Bank in December 2001, in support of a regional Multi- Country Demobilization and Reintegration Programme for the Greater Great Lakes Region. The Programme involves nine countries—Angola, Burundi, the Central African Republic, the Democratic Republic of the Congo, the Republic of the Congo, Namibia, Rwanda, Uganda and Zimbabwe—and includes a regional disarmament, demobilization and reintegration strategy and programme with a multi-country approach, to provide a mechanism that will allow demobilization to occur simultaneously in countries affected by regional conflicts. The World Bank and Programme partners have made a commitment to give priority to the unconditional and urgent demobilization of child soldiers.

56. Demobilization and reintegration programming is central to breaking the cycle of violence for children and the provision of adequate resources for such programming is crucial. The Security Council and Member States are urged to provide sustained and adequate resources to all relevant actors, in particular peace operations, United Nations entities and non-governmental organizations, engaged in implementing demobilization and reintegration programmes for children. . . .

[Part VI omitted.]

VII. Observations

68. Since my first report to the Security Council, impressive gains have been made in codifying international norms and standards for the protection and well-being of children. As requested by the Council, a list of violators of those norms and standards is annexed to the present report, demonstrating clearly the will of the international community that those who violate the standards cannot do so with impunity. More needs to be done; there is a need to promote and disseminate these standards and norms, and to raise awareness about them on the ground. Similarly, there is a need to put in place strengthened monitoring and reporting mechanisms to identify the violators and take measures against them. Dissemination, advocacy, monitoring and reporting are the key components that an "era of application" must encompass. My Special Representative will be devoting particular attention to these issues. I also urge the members of the Security Council to reflect upon them during their deliberations.

Annex

Parties to armed conflict that recruit or use child soldiers

The situation in Afghanistan

1. Remnants of the Taliban
2. Factions associated with the former Northern Alliance
3. Factions in the south of Afghanistan

The situation in Burundi

1. Government of Burundi
2. PALIPEHUTU/FNL (Parti pour la libération du peuple hutu/Forces nationales pour la libération)
3. CNDD/FDD (Conseil national pour la défense de la démocratie/Front pour la défense de la démocratie)

The situation in the Democratic Republic of the Congo

1. Government of the Democratic Republic of the Congo
2. Mouvement national de libération du Congo (MLC)
3. Rassemblement congolais pour la démocratie (RCD)-Goma
4. Rassemblement congolais pour la démocratie (RCD)-National
5. Rassemblement congolais pour la démocratie (RCD)-Kisangani/ML
6. Union des patriotes congolais (UPC) (Hema militia)
7. Masunzu's forces
8. Lendu militias
9. Ex-FAR/Interahamwe
10. Mai-Mai

The situation in Liberia

1. Government of Liberia
2. Liberians United for Reconciliation and Democracy (LURD)

The situation in Somalia

1. Transitional National Government
2. Juba Valley Alliance
3. Somali Reconciliation and Restoration Council
4. Somali Reconciliation and Restoration Council—Mogadishu
5. Rahanwein Resistance Army (RRA)

UN SECRETARY GENERAL ON ISRAELI-PALESTINIAN VIOLENCE
November 26, 2002

Violence between Israel and the Palestinians escalated during 2002, the second full year of a Palestinian intifada, *or uprising. More than 1,400 people, most of them Palestinians, died during the year in a continuing cycle of violence that featured Palestinian suicide bombings and other attacks on Israelis, followed by harsh reprisals by Israeli security forces. Israel occupied most of the major Palestinian cities in the West Bank for much of the year, reversing the results of a peace process during the 1990s that had given Yasir Arafat's Palestinian Authority control of about 40 percent of the West Bank and Gaza strip. Arafat himself spent most of 2002 under virtual house arrest by Israeli forces at his compound in the West Bank town of Ramallah.*

The violence caused great harm to the societies and economies of both Israel and the Palestinians. As the toll of dead and wounded mounted, attitudes hardened on both sides, undermining the prospect of an eventual compromise solution of two states living peacefully side by side. In a significant step to isolate itself from Palestinian violence, Israel began construction of a security fence around the West Bank. The Israeli economy, for years the most vibrant in the Middle East, was in deep recession. The Palestinian economy had nearly ceased to exist, with well over half of all Palestinians in the occupied territories out of work and forced to survive on international aid handouts.

The Palestinian intifada *began in September 2000. It followed the failure of a high-stakes gamble by U.S. president Bill Clinton (1993–2001) to negotiate a comprehensive settlement of the competing claims by Israel and the Palestinians to the territories that Israel had occupied since the 1967 Arab-Israeli war. The violence at first pitted stone-throwing Palestinian youths against heavily armed Israeli security forces, but it quickly escalated into a war in which Palestinian suicide bombers and gunmen attacked Israeli military and civilian targets, and the Israeli army responded with broad attacks on entire Palestinian communities.*

In a November 26 report to the UN Security Council on the violence, Secretary General Kofi Annan expressed outrage at the killings by both sides, which he said violated international law and would prove counterproductive. "Illegitimate or illegal means cannot be justified by reference to legitimate objectives—whether they be an end to occupation and statehood for Palestinians or security for Israelis," Annan said. "Beyond the question of legality, surely we need no further reminder of the ultimate futility of the present course than the hundreds of deaths, thousands of injuries and tens of thousands of grieving families and friends of the victims of this conflict. The parties are on a path leading to further pain and suffering—a path that will bring neither closer to achieving its stated goals." (Middle East diplomacy, p. 369; Background, Historic Documents of 2000, p. 930; Historic Documents of 2001, p. 360)

The Toll of Dead and Wounded

As with nearly everything else about the Israeli-Palestinian conflict, the two sides disputed key aspects of the human toll of the intifada. Palestinian groups asserted that the vast majority of those killed and injured were innocent Palestinian victims of Israeli aggression. While acknowledging that many more Palestinians than Israelis had been killed and wounded, the Israeli government insisted that most Palestinians had put themselves in harm's way, whether they were teenagers who threw stones at Israeli tanks or suicide bombers. The language each side used also was important. Palestinians referred to their dead as "martyrs," while Israel called the suicide bombers "terrorists" and considered its own dead to be "heroes."

The Israeli government, private organizations, and the news media compiled statistics about the intifada, but no two sets of statistics agreed because of differing definitions. The most comprehensive statistics were compiled by B'Tselem, an Israeli human rights organization that frequently was at odds with the government. That organization counted a total of 1,755 Palestinians killed as a result of the intifada between September 2000 and December 2002, of whom 1,018 were killed in 2002. Of the total, 316 were age eighteen or younger. B'Tselem said nearly all the Palestinians had been killed in the West Bank and Gaza; only thirty-nine died within Israel proper. March and April 2002 were by far the most violent months of the entire intifada to date; 493 Palestinians were killed in just those two months. B'Tselem's total figures were slightly lower than those of the Palestinian Red Crescent Society (the equivalent of the Red Cross), which counted 1,973 Palestinians killed and 21,371 wounded between September 2000 and the end of 2002. About one-fifth of the wounded had been injured by live ammunition, the Red Crescent Society said, and the rest were injured by rubber or plastic bullets, tear gas, or other causes.

B'Tselem counted a total of 647 Israeli deaths during the intifada, of whom 419 died during 2002. Of the 647 total, 83 were minors (eighteen or younger) and 204 were members of Israeli security forces. The Israeli government counted a total of 700 Israelis killed since the intifada began.

The Red Crescent Society and other Palestinian organizations said few of the Palestinian casualties had done anything to put themselves at risk— they were neither suicide bombers nor gunmen who deliberately attacked

Israelis and Israeli targets. The Israeli government disputed this claim, arguing that the proportion of noncombatants among the Palestinians was "no more than 45 percent" and that many of those had "engaged in stone-throwing, rioting, and other acts of violence." By contrast, the government said, 80 percent of the Israeli victims were "going about their daily lives—traveling to work, shopping, eating out, or participating in a family or religious celebration."

One of the year's most prominent victims was a senior United Nations refugee official—Iain Hook of Britain—who on November 22 was shot to death by the Israeli military while he was in his office at the Palestinian refugee camp in Jenin. A majority of UN Security Council members on December 20 approved a Syria-sponsored resolution condemning Israel for the killings of Hook and several other UN employees and for the army's destruction of a World Food Program warehouse, which contained 537 metric tons of food, in Gaza on November 30. The United States vetoed the resolution, arguing that it "would not contribute to an environment" of promoting peace.

The Violence Continues

By 2002 the violence between Israelis and Palestinians had settled into several categories. The most dramatic and attention-getting were the suicide bombings, in which Palestinians strapped explosives to their bodies, got as close as possible to groups of Israelis on buses, at shopping areas, or in other public locations, and then exploded their bombs. Several dozen suicide bombers—among them, for the first time, several teenage girls—had struck by the end of 2002, most of them killing a few Israelis but several killing twenty or more people and wounding dozens others.

In other cases, Palestinians used guns and grenades to attack Israeli targets, including police and army outposts, settlements of Israeli Jews in the West Bank and Gaza, and even civilian communities within Israel proper. One such attack came on July 16 when Palestinians disguised in Israeli army uniforms set off a bomb as a bus traveled along a road in the West Bank; they then attacked occupants of the damaged bus with grenades and rifles. Seven people were killed, including an eleven-month-old baby and her father and grandfather, and seventeen were wounded. The attackers escaped.

The Palestinian attackers often sought to heighten the shock value by going after symbolically important targets or events. Perhaps the most provocative attack during 2002 was the suicide bombing on March 27 at a hotel in the seaside resort of Netanya where scores of Israelis and tourists were celebrating the first night of Passover. The bombing also came on the eve of an Arab summit meeting in Beirut, called to discuss a Saudi Arabian peace plan that was opposed by Palestinian extremists. Twenty-nine people died and more than 140 were wounded. Israel responded with its biggest military operation of the intifada.

The suicide bombings were not spontaneous events but rather the result of a deliberate strategy of terrifying the Israeli public and government.

Some Palestinian groups sought to drive Israel out of existence, while others had a more limited goal of pushing Israel out of all the territories it had occupied since the 1967 war.

The bombings were sponsored primarily by three extremist groups: the Islamic Resistance Movement, best known as Hamas, which arose in the late 1980s as a radical alternative to Arafat's Palestine Liberation Organization (PLO); Islamic Jihad, another extremist group with links to Iran; and the al-Aqsa Martyrs Brigade, a wing of Arafat's Fatah movement within the PLO. The Israeli newspaper Haaretz *reported in September that during the first two years of the intifada Israeli intelligence officials had counted two suicide bombings sponsored by Hamas, thirty-five bombings sponsored by Islamic Jihad, and forty bombings sponsored by the al-Aqsa Martyrs Brigade. Those figures, along with failed bombing attempts, totaled 145, a considerably higher figure than most other tabulations. The Associated Press, for example, by November 1 had counted 80 suicide bombings since September 2000 that killed 294 people.*

The official Israeli response to Palestinian attacks fell into two broad categories. The most damaging retaliations were large-scale military occupations of the West Bank cities and towns that Israel had turned over to Palestinian control in the mid-1990s. In each of these operations the Israeli army and other security forces arrested thousands of Palestinians (typically all males ages fifteen to forty-five) and detained them for days or weeks; bulldozed houses, shops, and fruit or olive trees belonging to suspected militants or their families and neighbors; and imposed twenty-four-hour curfews that effectively shut down all Palestinian activity. The government also shut off all border crossings between Israel proper and the occupied territories, preventing Palestinians from reaching their jobs within Israel. Except for Jericho, all of the eight largest Palestinian towns in the West Bank were occupied, or at least surrounded, by the Israeli army for most of 2002. These mass-scale operations disrupted what Israeli officials called the "terrorist infrastructure" but generally led only to brief respites in suicide bombings. The operations resulted in hundreds of deaths and injuries among Palestinians; the government said most were terrorists or armed collaborators, but Palestinians said nearly all the victims were unarmed civilians, including many children.

The government's other form of official retaliation involved carefully targeted assassinations—which Israel called "liquidations"—of Palestinians suspected of organizing the suicide bombings or other terrorist attacks. In some cases, Israeli helicopters or warplanes fired missiles at or dropped bombs on the homes, offices, or cars of suspected militants, often killing bystanders as well as the targeted militants. The most controversial assassination was the July 23 bombing of the house in Gaza of Hamas military leader Sheik Salah Shehadeh. The one-ton bomb killed the intended target but also fourteen others (including eight children) and wounded about 140. International human rights organizations condemned the bombing as indiscriminate, but Sharon praised the operation as "a great success." Israel used more precise high-tech devices for several other assassinations, such a bomb implanted in a Bethlehem-area pay phone that killed Mohammad Shtawi Abayat, a suspected leader of the al-Aqsa Martyrs Brigade.

Unofficial Israeli retaliation against the Palestinians came primarily from the residents of Jewish settlements in Gaza and the West Bank. Most of the settlements had been founded by religious zealots who insisted they had been ordered by God to "reclaim" from Arabs the land known in biblical times as Judea and Samaria. Nearly all adults in the settlements carried weapons for protection against Palestinians, all of whom viewed the settlements as infringements on Palestinian land and some of whom attacked the settlements with guns or bombs. Only three Palestinians were killed by Israeli civilians during the first twenty-eight months of the intifada. One case that drew international attention was an October 5 attack by Jewish settlers on Palestinians harvesting olives at the village of Akraba, near Nablus. One Palestinian was killed and another injured.

International human rights organizations accused both Israel and the Palestinian extremist groups of committing numerous human rights violations, including war crimes. In a report issued on November 1, Human Rights Watch said the Palestinian suicide bombings met the international legal definition of "crimes against humanity." The group said Arafat bore "significant political responsibility" for not doing enough to stop the attacks. Human Rights Watch also issued reports highly critical of Israeli military suppression of the Palestinians. Amnesty International on November 3 published a report detailing its investigation into Israel's large invasion of the West Bank in March and April. The group said it found "clear evidence" that the army committed war crimes by killing and torturing civilians, destroying homes, and using civilians as "human shields." Amnesty International in July had issued reports denouncing the Palestinian suicide bombings and other terrorist attacks as crimes against humanity. Israeli officials and representatives of various Palestinian groups rejected the characterization of their actions as human rights violations or war crimes. Each side argued that its actions were justified responses to provocations by the other.

Israel's Military Operations

Along with the suicide bombings, the most important actions of 2002 were the four waves of Israeli occupations of West Bank cities and towns. Each wave came in response to one or more terrorist incident but had far-reaching consequences for hundreds of thousands of Palestinians.

The first broad Israeli military attack started on February 27, when the army invaded two large West Bank refugee camps in pursuit of Palestinian gunmen who had killed Israelis in attacks during the previous week. The army pulled back on March 14 after arresting hundreds of Palestinians and engaging in numerous battles.

The second Israeli offensive was launched on March 29 in response to the bombing in Netanya. Called Operation Defensive Shield, it was Israeli's largest military offensive since the 1982 invasion of Lebanon. A reported 30,000 Israeli soldiers swept into the major Palestinian cities, towns, and refugee camps, rounded up hundreds of people, and destroyed houses and even entire neighborhoods where suspected militants lived. President Bush on April 6 demanded that Israel withdraw its forces from the Palestinian areas "without delay," but Sharon ignored the demand and said he would continue the operation as long as necessary. (Lebanon war, Historic Documents of 1982, p. 741)

This operation resulted in two related stand-offs that received worldwide attention. In Ramallah, Israeli tanks surrounded and systematically destroyed most of the large complex of buildings that served as headquarters for Arafat's Palestinian Authority. While held as a virtual hostage, Arafat met in mid-April with U.S. secretary of state Colin Powell during his failed mission to secure a cease-fire in the intifada. *Israel said it was holding Arafat captive until he arranged for the handover of six suspected Palestinian militants who were among about 100 people who had taken refuge at the Church of the Nativity in Bethlehem. The Israeli army laid siege to the historic church for thirty-nine days, allowing only minimal supplies of food and water to reach those inside. Israel on May 2 lifted the sieges in Ramallah and Bethlehem as a result of a U.S.-mediated compromise under which the militants at the church were placed in a Palestinian prison under U.S. and British supervision. Israel already had begun withdrawing some troops from other Palestinian areas on April 21 but remained on the outskirts of the cities it had occupied, effectively keeping them under a tight grip.*

A third wave of occupation came in response to back-to-back suicide bombings on June 18–19 that killed twenty-eight people. By June 25 Israel had fully occupied seven of the eight largest West Bank towns (except Jericho) and placed them under curfew, preventing some 700,000 people from leaving their homes. The government also announced a new policy in which it would hold onto Palestinian-administered territory indefinitely in retaliation for attacks.

Israel's fourth broad-scale military action began September 20 after two suicide bombings, the first in more than six weeks. Israeli bulldozers again demolished buildings at Arafat's Ramallah compound and attacked Palestinian targets in Gaza, including an October 7 raid on the town of Khan Yunis that killed thirteen Palestinians and wounded about 100 others. The White House called the attack in Ramallah "unhelpful" but on September 24 abstained from a UN Security Council resolution demanding an immediate end to Israel's occupation. Israel lifted its siege of Arafat on September 29, but army troops continued to encircle Ramallah.

At year's end the Israeli army remained on the outskirts of most large Palestinian towns on the West Bank and occupied all or part of several others, including Bethlehem, Hebron, and Nablus. The army withdrew from Bethlehem for two days at Christmas but reoccupied the town on December 26. An average of 500,000 Palestinians were under an army curfew at any given time, and some 1,000 Palestinians remained in government custody, according to a report by the Israeli human rights group B'Tselem.

Throughout the intifada *the Israeli military focused most of its attention on Arafat's Palestinian Authority and made only isolated attempts to target* the two groups that organized most of the bombings: Hamas and Islamic Jihad. In repeated attacks during 2001 and 2002, the military destroyed nearly all of Arafat's complex in Ramallah but never attacked the homes in Gaza of Hamas's intellectual leader, Sheik Ahmed Yassin, or its most visible spokesman, Abdul Aziz Rantisi. Israel's most important attack against Hamas was the July 23 bombing in Gaza that killed Sheik Salah Shehada, the leader of the Hamas military wing.

The government's justification for its focus on the Palestinian Authority was that Arafat had the influence to halt all Palestinian attacks, including those by the rival groups. "The Palestinian Authority continues to pour terror into Israel," Sharon's spokesman, David Baker, said after a series of attacks in early August. Most neutral observers expressed doubt that Arafat could halt all the attacks even if he wanted to, in part because of growing support among Palestinians for the more radical groups, and also because Israel had methodically dismantled the Palestinian Authority security services that Arafat would have needed for any crackdown on extremists. Arafat reportedly negotiated with Hamas in September about limiting the terrorist attacks to Israeli security forces and settlers in the occupied territories, but nothing came of the talks. Some critics suggested that Israeli prime minister Sharon considered Arafat—who had at least some credibility in world capitals—to be a greater danger to Israel's international standing than the more radical Palestinian leaders who were popular in the refugee camps and in many Arab countries but had no support in the West.

"Massacre" in Jenin?

Perhaps the most controversial of Israel's actions during the year was its takeover in April of the Palestinian refugee camp at Jenin, about forty-five miles north of Jerusalem. The camp, home to some 14,000 Palestinians, was one of several makeshift facilities established on the West Bank for Palestinians who fled Israel following the establishment of the Jewish state in May 1948. Over the following decades Jenin and the other camps had developed into permanent, impoverished towns managed by the United Nations Relief and Works Agency (UNRWA).

The Israel government for years had charged that the Jenin camp was a breeding ground for Palestinian extremists, and early in 2002 officials said twenty-eight suicide bombings had been planned or launched from there. As part of its West Bank offensive following the bombing in Netanya, the Israeli army moved into the Jenin camp on April 3 and during the next few days engaged in house-to-house gun battles with Palestinian fighters. According to the army, about 11,000 of the camp's residents fled as these battles raged, but about 3,000 remained. On April 9 thirteen Israeli soldiers were killed when they entered a building that had been booby-trapped with bombs; it was the army's single greatest loss of life since the war in Lebanon two decades earlier. In retaliation the army stepped up its attacks and bulldozed a large section of the camp equivalent to about two football fields. Palestinian resistance collapsed by April 11 and Israeli forces withdrew from the heavily damaged camp on April 18.

Officials of Arafat's Palestinian Authority immediately charged that the Israelis had "massacred" hundreds of people in Jenin, possibly as many as 500. The Palestinians and representatives of some international human rights organizations said soldiers deliberately bulldozed houses they knew to be occupied by civilians and then refused to allow rescue workers to retrieve the dead and or help the wounded. The government vehemently denied these and other charges of abusing civilians, saying that fewer than 100 Palestinians died at the camp, most of whom were armed extremists. Army officials also insisted that soldiers had repeatedly warned residents to get out of the way, but some ignored the warnings. If anyone was to blame, the government said, it was the Palestinian extremists who took refuge in a civilian camp. The army said it lost twenty-three soldiers during the operation.

Two senior diplomats toured the camp after Israel withdrew and expressed horror at the extent of the damage caused to buildings and the suffering of refugees. Terje Roed-Larsen, the UN special envoy to the Middle East, walked through the camp hours after Israeli tanks pulled out and said: "What we are seeing here is horrifying—horrifying scenes of human suffering." Roed-Larsen later accused Israel of using "morally repugnant" tactics in its assault on the camp—a charge that infuriated Israeli officials, who threatened to cut off his access to government agencies. William Burns, the U.S. assistant secretary of state for the Near East, visited the camp on April 20 and also said he was disturbed by what he found. "It's obvious that what happened here in the Jenin camp has caused enormous human suffering for thousands of Palestinian civilians," he said. Burns called on Israel to grant free access to the camp by relief agencies—a step the government earlier had refused on the grounds that it could not guarantee security for relief workers.

Roed-Larsen's findings—coupled with televised images of Palestinians furiously picking through the debris of flattened buildings in hopes of finding relatives—led the UN Security Council on April 19 to authorize an investigation of the assault on the Jenin camp. Israeli foreign minister Shimon Peres agreed to the probe, but dissension within the government coalition became visible on April 23 when aides to Prime Minister Sharon raised objections. Sharon's aides complained that Annan, the UN secretary general, had not consulted with Israel about the composition of the investigating team, which was to be headed by former Finnish president Martti Ahtisaari. Israel also strenuously objected to Annan's statement that the group might investigate army operations in other places, not just Jenin.

Unable to overcome Israeli resistance to the planned investigation, Annan announced on May 1 that he was disbanding the team even before it began work. By this point most journalists, humanitarian agencies, and other independent observers who had visited Jenin had concluded that a few dozen Palestinians probably died in the fighting, but not the several hundred that Palestinian officials had charged. Human Rights Watch said on May 2 that the killings at Jenin did not appear to justify the term massacre, *al-*

though the Israeli army might have killed civilians in violation of international law.

The UN General Assembly on May 7 asked Annan for a report on the Israeli assault on Jenin and other Palestinian towns and cities. Annan on August 1 submitted a report based on news reports and information provided by UN agencies, various governments, and independent organizations; Israel refused to provide information. Annan said at least fifty-two Palestinians, up to half of whom might have been civilians, were killed in the Jenin camp during the Israeli operations. But, he said, Palestinian allegations of a massacre "were not substantiated by the evidence that subsequently emerged." Annan noted but did not comment on several other allegations that Palestinians and human rights organizations had lodged against the Israeli army, including indiscriminate destruction of Palestinian homes and businesses, arbitrary arrest and detention of Palestinian males, and the use of civilians as human shields during gun battles. Israel denied these charges and said its actions had been justified responses to the suicide bombings and other acts of Palestinian terrorism.

Economy Plummets, Palestinians Suffer

While disputing who was to blame, both sides in the conflict agreed that the Israeli and Palestinian economies had tumbled during the intifada and that tens of thousands of people had suffered severe deprivation. The Israeli economy, which had boomed throughout the 1990s, fell into a deep recession by 2001 and remained stuck there through 2002. Tourism, one of Israel's prime sources of cash, was especially hard hit because prospective visitors feared being caught in the crossfire.

Serious as it was, the damage caused to the Israeli economy paled next to the consequences for Palestinian communities in Gaza and the West Bank. Tens of thousands of Palestinians were thrown out of work by Israeli travel restrictions during the intifada. These restrictions included the closing of border crossings between Israel proper and the occupied territories, numerous military checkpoints on most roads within the territories, and curfews in most major Palestinian cities and towns. Catherine Bertini, a special UN humanitarian envoy appointed by Anna, visited the region in August and estimated that the Palestinian unemployment rate had reached 65 percent in the West Bank and 70 percent in Gaza. Bertini said Israeli government officials had acknowledged to her that the travel restrictions had caused hardships for Palestinians and had agreed to ease the restrictions.

In a report covering the first half of 2002, the Office of the United Nations Special Coordinator said the Palestinian economy was "near collapse" and would not be able to rebound quickly if the violence ended and Israel lifted its travel restrictions. The economy was being sustained primarily by humanitarian aid and emergency donations from other countries, principally the European Union and Arab nations.

With more than one-half of the population living in poverty (defined locally as an average daily income of $2 or less), Palestinians were increasingly

*suffering from malnutrition and consequent health problems. A study com-
missioned by the U.S. Agency for International Development showed that
22 percent of Palestinian children under the age of five suffered from acute
or chronic malnourishment, and nearly all the underfed had some form of
anemia, which could harm their physical and mental development. UNRWA,
the UN refugee agency in the occupied territories, announced in November
that it planned to feed about 1.3 million Palestinians in 2003, compared to
about 11,000 people who needed food aid before the* intifada *began.*

Building a Fence

*Polls showed that by 2002 most Israelis had given up on the decades-long
"peace process" and had concluded that the only long-term solution was
segregation—in some way keeping the Palestinians in the occupied territories and out of Israel proper. The government in late 2001 and early 2002
resurrected long dormant plans for a "security barrier," or fence, surrounding the West Bank and began construction in June. The fence consisted of
twenty-five-foot-high concrete slabs topped by razor wire, electronic monitors, and a cleared buffer zone on the Israeli side. If completed, the 210-mile-
long fence would surround all the West Bank bordering Israel proper. The
government's plans for the fence approximated but did not entirely follow
the "green line"—what had been the internationally recognized boundary
between Israel and the then Jordanian-controlled West Bank before Israel
captured the territory in the 1967 war. In numerous places the fence would
veer east of the green line to take in what had been Palestinian land, cutting
Palestinian farmers off from their fields or orchards and in some cases
dividing Palestinian villages.*

*While it was intended to offer urban Israelis a sense of security, the fence
was highly controversial among Israelis. Most opposed were those who believed in a "greater Israel" including the West Bank. Among these were the
380,000 Israeli Jews who had settled in the West Bank and East Jerusalem,
the formerly Arab-dominated part of the city that Israel had occupied since
1967 and had annexed over international opposition. Settlers said they
feared the fence ultimately would become the de facto border between Israel
and the West Bank, thus cutting them off from Israel proper, ending any
prospect of formally incorporating the West Bank into Israel and isolating
them among the 2.4 million Palestinians in the territory. Although his
government initiated the construction, Sharon clearly was among those Israelis who had mixed feelings about the fence because of the possibility that
it would isolate the West Bank settlements, which he had championed.*

In a related development, the Israeli newspaper Haaretz *reported on December 26 that the Israeli army was building security zones around some
of the West Bank settlements to protect them from Palestinian attacks. The
settlements were to be surrounded by fences with watchtowers.*

Israeli Government Collapses

During the first two years of the intifada, *Israel had a "national unity"
government that included representatives from the two major parties—*

Likud, the largest right-wing party, and Labor, the largest left-wing party—as well as several smaller factions in the Knesset. Likud leader Ariel Sharon was the prime minister, and two senior Labor leaders held key posts, Shimon Peres as foreign minister and Benjamin Ben-Eliezer as defense minister.

That political marriage of convenience began to fall apart in mid-2002 as politicians to both the left and right of Sharon threatened to revolt because of policy differences or his tendency to act before consulting with cabinet colleagues. The first break came October 30 when the Labor Party withdrew from the cabinet, leaving Sharon with a minority government of 55 seats in the 120-seat Knesset. Labor leaders said the key issue forcing the break was Sharon's budget, which increased spending on behalf of Jewish settlers in the occupied Palestinian territories while cutting social services within Israel. Most political analysts said internal Labor Party factors—including Ben-Eliezer's hope to retain the party chairmanship—were important factors behind the pullout from the coalition government.

Unable to form a majority government, Sharon announced on November 5 that he was calling early elections in January 2003. Sharon also appointed as interim foreign minister the former prime minister Benjamin Netanyahu, his longtime rival who was expected to challenge Sharon for the Likud Party leadership. Although both men were solidly positioned in the right-wing of Likud, Netanyahu immediately staked out a position to the right of Sharon, saying that he would never accept a Palestinian state. Sharon had said he would allow Palestinians to form a state only if it was disarmed.

In intraparty primaries, Labor members on November 19 dumped Ben-Eliezer in favor of Amram Mitzna, a former general and war hero who was mayor of Haifa, and Likud members on November 28 overwhelmingly stuck with Sharon, rejecting Netanyahu's bid to return to leadership. The election was scheduled for January 2003.

> *Following are excerpts from a report submitted to the United Nations Security Council on November 26, 2002, by Secretary General Kofi Annan, in which he gave an overview of the conflict in 2002 between Israelis and Palestinians.*
>
> ***The document was obtained from the Internet at daccess-ods.un.org/access.nsf/Get?OpenAgent&DS=S/2002/1268&Lang=E&Area=UNDOC; accessed January 22, 2003.***

II. Observations

5. Over the past year, the Israeli-Palestinian conflict has deteriorated further, eroding many of the achievements of the peace process. The ongoing cycle of violence and retaliation has further inflamed political tensions and

caused a significant death toll on both sides. The international community, united in its support for the vision of two States living side by side in peace and security, has continued to develop initiatives aimed at stopping the violence and bringing the parties back to the negotiating table.

6. Since the outbreak of the *intifada* at the end of September 2000, more than 1,800 Palestinians have been killed and some 25,000 injured. On the Israeli side, more than 600 people have been killed and over 4,000 injured. I have urged both sides to live up to their obligations under international humanitarian law to ensure the protection of civilians. Illegitimate or illegal means cannot be justified by reference to legitimate objectives—whether they be an end to occupation and statehood for Palestinians or security for Israelis.

Beyond the question of legality, surely we need no further reminder of the ultimate futility of the present course than the hundreds of deaths, thousands of injuries and tens of thousands of grieving families and friends of the victims of this conflict. The parties are on a path leading to further pain and suffering—a path that will bring neither closer to achieving its stated goals.

7. The situation reached a particularly dangerous point at the end of March 2002, following a Palestinian suicide bomb attack in the Israeli city of Netanya. After that terrorist attack, which left 28 persons dead and 140 injured, the Israel Defence Forces (IDF) launched a massive military operation in the West Bank, leading to the reoccupation of cities under full Palestinian control (Area A). That operation, called "Defensive Shield" by Israel, inflicted severe damage on the Palestinian security and civilian infrastructure and created a humanitarian and human rights crisis. To address the sharpening trend towards greater violence and the attendant consequences for both sides, in April 2002 I proposed the deployment of a multinational force to help provide security for Israeli and Palestinian civilians, and to promote an environment conducive to the resumption of negotiations. This proposal remains on the table.

8. The Israeli incursion into the Jenin refugee camp in April led to allegations of human rights abuses and violations of international humanitarian law. Following consultations with, inter alia, members of the Security Council and the Government of Israel, I offered to send an impartial fact-finding team to compile an accurate account of what had occurred. In resolution 1405 (2002), the Security Council unanimously accepted that offer, and I then named a team headed by former President Martti Ahtisaari of Finland. Israel subsequently raised objections to the implementation of resolution 1405 (2002) that were fundamental in nature and which effectively precluded the team's visit to the region. With great regret, I found it necessary to disband the team. In May 2002, the General Assembly at its resumed emergency special session requested me to submit a report on the events in Jenin and other Palestinian cities on the basis of available resources and information. My report (A/ES-10/186) was issued on 30 July 2002.

9. A particularly worrying trend was the rapid expansion of Israeli settlements in the West Bank, including those around East Jerusalem, despite repeated international calls for a freeze on all such activity and an end to land

confiscations. These settlements, and the road networks that serve them, are enveloping East Jerusalem, cutting it off from other Palestinian areas in the West Bank, which would be split into two. Other new settlement projects would bisect the northern West Bank and encircle both Bethlehem and Hebron to the south. Such settlement activity is illegal under international law and should be halted.

10. The escalating confrontation has had a devastating impact on the humanitarian and economic situation in the occupied Palestinian territory. The Palestinian economy has virtually ceased to function in some areas, owing largely to the Israeli policy of curfews and closures. More and more people are living below the poverty line. In August, I sent Ms. Catherine Bertini to the region, as my Personal Humanitarian Envoy, to review humanitarian needs in the light of recent developments. As Ms. Bertini noted in her report, this is not a "traditional" humanitarian crisis. It is inextricably linked to the conflict and to the measures imposed by Israel in response to terrorist and other attacks: closures, curfews and tight restrictions on the movement of goods and people. On 17 September 2002, the Quartet [a diplomatic effort by the European Union, Russia, the United Nations, and the United States] reviewed the recommendations contained in Ms. Bertini's report and urged the parties to recognize and act upon their respective responsibilities. In particular, it urged Israel to take measures to improve the lives of Palestinians, by, inter alia, allowing the resumption of normal economic activity, facilitating the movement of goods, people and essential services and lifting curfews and closures. In addition, the members of the Quartet agreed that Israel must ensure full, safe and unfettered access for international and humanitarian personnel.

11. The growing humanitarian needs of the Palestinian population must be met. At the same time, in doing so the international community should not lessen its efforts to revive a sustainable peace process. It cannot be overemphasized that there is no military solution to this conflict. The realization of legitimate Palestinian national aspirations and genuine security for Israel can only be achieved through compromise and a negotiated settlement. The road map being set out by the Quartet offers a way forward (see para. 14 below).

12. Over the past year, the situation in the Middle East, including the Palestinian question, has been the subject of extensive consultations and debates in the Security Council. Since January 2002, regular briefings have been held in order to update the Council on the latest developments in the Middle East. Five new resolutions were adopted by the Security Council, in particular resolution 1397 (2002), affirming the Council's vision of a region where two States, Israel and Palestine, would live side by side within secure and recognized borders. This vision of a two-State solution has gained universal support in the international community.

13. It is a matter of particular regret to me that so little remains of the mutual trust that had been so painstakingly built between the parties. Regular and consistent third-party involvement and encouragement is needed to help them find a way out of the current vicious cycle of destruction. To this end, I personally and my representatives in the region have continued to devote a great

deal of attention to this issue. I have maintained close and regular contacts with the parties and other leaders in the region and the international community to try to find a way forward.

14. As part of this effort, the United Nations, the United States, the Russian Federation and the European Union came together to form a new coordinating mechanism for international peace efforts known as the Quartet. The Quartet met for the first time at the principals' level at United Nations Headquarters in New York in November 2001. At a principals' meeting in Madrid in April 2002, the Quartet called for a three-pronged approach to address comprehensively security, economic and political concerns. In May 2002, in Washington, D.C., the Quartet announced its intention to work with the parties to hold an international peace conference focused on attaining the two-State goal set forth in Security Council resolution 1397 (2002). In July 2002, in New York, the Quartet agreed to pursue the following goals: two democratic States living side by side in peace and security; a complete and lasting halt to violence and terrorism; an end to the occupation that began in 1967; a halt to settlements; reform of the Palestinian Authority's security and civilian institutions; the holding of Palestinian elections; and the conclusion of permanent settlement negotiations on the outstanding issues within three years. In September 2002, the Quartet agreed on a three-year, three-phase implementation road map to achieve a comprehensive settlement.

Progress would be based on compliance with specific performance benchmarks to be monitored and assessed by the Quartet. The details of that road map are being worked out. In this context, I am very encouraged by the growing involvement of the parties and neighbouring Arab States in a direct dialogue with the Quartet.

15. In March 2002, the Summit of the League of Arab States unanimously adopted—as the Arab Peace Initiative—the plan proposed by Crown Prince Abdullah bin Abdul Aziz of Saudi Arabia calling for full Israeli withdrawal from all the Arab territories occupied since June 1967 and for Israel's acceptance of an independent Palestinian State with East Jerusalem as its capital, in return for the establishment of normal relations with the Arab countries in the context of a comprehensive peace with Israel. This initiative introduced a new and important element in the search for a lasting political solution: the collective political commitment of the Arab world to long-term peace with Israel. The Arab Peace Initiative will remain a crucial element in future peace efforts.

16. As the General Assembly has underscored on many occasions, the achievement of a final and peaceful settlement of the question of Palestine— the core issue of the Arab-Israeli conflict—is imperative for the attainment of a comprehensive and lasting peace in the Middle East. I hope that there will also be movement on the Syrian and Lebanese tracks so that peace, security and stability will be achieved for all people in the region on the basis of Security Council resolutions 242 (1967) and 338 (1973). It is my considered view that our common vision for a truly comprehensive peace can only be realized if all concerned, namely the parties, the key regional players, and the wider international community, live up to their respective responsibilities and work together to make it possible.

17. For its part, the United Nations will continue to support the resumption of a meaningful peace process and will remain at the forefront of efforts to alleviate the severe economic and social hardships of the Palestinian people. I call on the international community to provide the necessary resources in support of United Nations programmes to address the deteriorating economic and humanitarian situation of the Palestinian people, and especially to provide adequate funding for UNRWA [United Nations Relief and Works Agency, which ran Palestinian refugee camps] so that it can continue to deliver the necessary services to Palestinian refugees. Donor assistance is especially crucial at a time when the humanitarian situation is so critical.

18. I should like to pay special tribute to Terje Roed-Larsen, United Nations Special Coordinator and my Personal Representative, and to the staff of the Office of the Special Coordinator, as well as to Peter Hansen, Commissioner-General of UNRWA and the staff of that Agency and all other United Nations agencies, who have rendered sterling service while working under the most demanding and difficult circumstances.

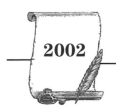
December

GAO ON PRESCRIPTION
DRUG ADVERTISING
December 3, 2002

*The high and rising cost of prescription drugs continued to be a con-
tentious political issue in 2002. Spending on prescription drugs jumped
17 percent in 2001 and was increasingly cited as a significant factor in rising health insurance premiums. Higher premiums in turn were forcing
employers to raise the share of health insurance costs paid by their employees and causing some individuals and families to forgo health insurance
altogether. After falling for two years in a row, the number of Americans
without health insurance rose in 2001, to nearly 42 million, and the number was expected to be even higher in 2002.* (Health insurance, p. 666)

*One of the population groups most affected by the high price of pharma-
ceuticals was the elderly, who accounted for about half of all spending on
prescription drugs. The need for prescription medications was a considerable financial burden on many elderly persons because drug purchases were
not covered under the federal Medicare program. Although legislators in
both political parties had hoped to pass a drug benefit program for the elderly before the November 2002 congressional elections, major differences
over the size and scope of the program prevented its enactment.*

*The pharmaceutical industry found itself under attack on many fronts.
Consumer groups and advocates for the elderly castigated the manufacturers for the high price of drugs, which some critics said bordered on price
gouging. In addition, the industry was widely criticized for using aggressive marketing practices, frequently in television commercials. Several
studies showed that direct-marketing campaigns to consumers were creating a demand that not only pushed up spending on drugs but also increased
usage. Although drug makers justified the broadcast and print advertising
as providing useful information, some consumer groups argued that the
ads were promoting unnecessary or inappropriate prescriptions. Closer
scrutiny was also being given to marketing practices directed at doctors. In
October the Bush administration, usually a strong supporter of the pharmaceutical industry, warned drug companies to alter some of the practices*

*they used to get the attention of physicians, such as lavish dinners and out-
ings to sports events.*

*The pharmaceutical industry—for years the most profitable industry in
the nation and one of the most politically powerful—was running into other
problems. For more than a decade drug makers had brought one blockbuster
drug after another to the marketplace as research led to new and innovative
chemical breakthroughs for a variety of common ailments and illnesses. By
the late 1990s, however, the pipeline had begun to slow, in part because the
innovations still needed were for difficult illnesses such as cancers and in
part because research was turning to genetic therapies, which were still
in the development stage and unlikely to come to market for some years. In
addition many of the most profitable drugs were nearing the end of their
patent protection and soon to encounter competition from generic drugs,
which were usually cheaper.*

*Merck & Co. and Bristol-Myers Squibb Co. were caught up in the corpo-
rate accounting scandals. Wyeth, makers of the most popular hormone replacement therapy, was rocked by a study finding that, rather than reducing
the risk of heart disease, the drugs actually increased it. Several states had
filed suit against various drug makers, alleging antitrust violations and illegal actions to manipulate drug prices. The largest was a lawsuit filed by
twenty-nine state attorneys general against Bristol-Myers Squibb, charging
that it had acted illegally to keep cheaper generic versions of its anticancer
drug Taxol off the market.*

The Rising Price of Prescription Drugs

*Retail and mail order sales of outpatient prescription drugs rose 17.1 per-
cent in 2001 to a total of $175.2 billion. It was the fourth year in a row that
the increase had exceeded 17 percent, according to the National Institute for
Health Care Management, a private nonprofit research organization funded
by the federal government, insurance companies, and private health care
foundations. Overall, 3.1 billion prescriptions were written in 2001, up
from 2.9 billion in 2000. Retail drug sales had nearly doubled since 1997.*

*Most of the increase in spending was on a small group of high-profile,
heavily advertised brand-name drugs. Out of 9,482 drugs, just 50 accounted
for 62 percent of the $22.5 billion increase in retail sales, the research or-
ganization said. Although the cholesterol-reducing drugs Lipitor and Zocor
were the best-selling drugs in the United States in 2001, antidepressants
remained the top-selling category of drugs, with sales of $12.5 billion. Anti-
ulcer drugs were the second biggest category, with $10.8 billion in sales.*

*The drug makers had long argued that the high prices of their brand-
name products were justified by the high costs of researching, developing,
and testing new and innovative drugs. According to the Tufts Center for the
Study of Drug Development, bringing a new drug to market cost an average
of $805 million and took between ten and fifteen years, yet only three of ten
drugs recouped that average cost. The pharmaceutical industry also argued
that drug pricing needed to be kept in perspective. "In many cases a medicine is going to be the most cost-effective treatment, a much cheaper alter-*

native than surgery or hospitalization or long-term care," a spokeswoman for the Pharmaceutical Research and Manufacturers' Association of America told the Washington Post.

Consumer organizations, insurers, and others were increasingly skeptical of that argument, arguing that the drug makers were spending more money on marketing and on developing slightly different versions of popular drugs whose patents were expiring to keep generics off the market. For example, Families USA, a health advocacy group, reported that Merck spent less than $2.5 billion on research in 2002 but more than $6 billion on marketing, advertising, and administration. According to the industry's own data, as reported December 3 by the General Accounting Office (GAO), the investigative arm of Congress, drug manufacturers spent $30.3 billion on research and development in 2001 and $19.1 billion on promotion, including $2.7 billion on direct-to-consumer advertising, most of it for broadcast ads.

Increased Drug Advertising

Buying television advertising for prescription drugs was a relatively new phenomenon, made possible in 1997 when the Food and Drug Administration (FDA) revised the guidelines. Before then, drug makers generally had to list all the risks associated with a particular drug, often making the ad too long—and too dull—to be effective. Under the new guidance, the ads had only to list the major risks and side-effects and tell consumers how to obtain additional information. That made broadcast advertising attractive to drug manufacturers, as figures provided in the GAO report made clear. Between 1997 and 2001 spending on direct-to-consumer advertising increased 145 percent, compared with a 59 percent increase in spending for research and development. About 5 percent of consumers (8.5 million people) said they requested and received a prescription for a drug as a direct result of seeing advertising for that drug.

The GAO study found that the number of prescriptions written for the most heavily advertised drugs—such as Claritin, an antiallergen; Lipitor; Vioxx, for arthritic pain; and Prilosec, for heartburn—had increased 25 percent, while the number of prescription for less heavily advertised drugs had gone up only 4 percent. This increased utilization of heavily advertised and more expensive drugs troubled consumer groups, insurers, employers, unions, and others who argued that many of these drugs were no more effective than older and cheaper drugs. Where equivalent drugs already existed, the demand stimulated by the advertising for newer, more expensive drugs was thus inflating health care costs while offering little improvement in overall health, they argued.

The GAO study also reviewed FDA oversight of television drug ads and found its effectiveness limited. The FDA reviewed all broadcast ads and issued warning letters for those that contained misleading claims. Between August 1997 and August 2002 the FDA had issued eighty-eight letters, and FDA officials said the pharmaceutical companies "invariably" stopped disseminating the misleading ads. But oversight had not prevented companies

*from releasing new misleading ads for the same drug, or from submitting
"in a timely manner" all ads to FDA for review, according to the GAO study.
Furthermore, a procedural change implemented in January 2002 had "significantly increased the time" between the FDA's identification of a misleading ad and the issuing of the letter asking that the ad be stopped, "with
the result that some regulatory letters may not be issued until after the advertising campaign has run its course."*

*Sen. Susan Collins, R-Maine, who was one of five members of Congress
who requested the study, called its findings "troubling" and said it showed
that "the FDA is unable to keep pace with those pharmaceutical companies
that are bent on bad-faith advertising while seeming to comply with the
rules." Bruce Kuhlik, general counsel for the Pharmaceutical Research and
Manufacturers of America, countered that the "story is how few advertisements the FDA has identified as having any issue at all."*

*On December 11 the newly appointed FDA commissioner, Mark McClellan,
referred to the delays in reviewing warning letters and said: "Let me be
clear. We are not backing off on our policy of enforcing the law here. . . . We
will not be afraid to go to court if necessary." McClellan, a physician and an
economist who had been a White House adviser to President George W. Bush
on health issues until his appointment to the FDA, also suggested that issuing warning letters might not be enough in cases where drug companies
repeatedly ran misleading ads for the same drug. He declined, however, to
say what other steps the FDA might take.*

*Although much attention was focused on direct-to-consumer drug adver-
tising, nearly 80 percent of drug promotion was aimed directly at physicians. In 2000, for example, the industry gave $8 billion worth of free
samples to doctors and spent $4.8 billion on visits to hospitals, nursing
homes, and doctors' offices to persuade physicians to prescribe their products, according to an article in the* New England Journal of Medicine. *The
major pharmaceutical companies routinely held "educational" dinners and
conferences for physicians where other doctors, usually paid by the drug
companies, touted the effectiveness of specific drugs for specific conditions,
with the information often based on research ghostwritten by researchers
paid by the drug companies. Drug companies also routinely gave discounts
and incentive payments to health plans and pharmacy benefit managers
that shifted their purchases to the promoted brand-name drugs.*

*To counter those practices and hold down drug costs, some states and
insurers were beginning to send out their own salesmen to doctors and hospitals to encourage the use of generics and cheaper drugs. AARP, the advocacy group for seniors, and the FDA both began campaigns explaining that
generics were as safe and effective as brand-name drugs. In October the Department of Health and Human Services weighed in with a warning to drug
companies that their financial incentives to doctors, pharmacists, and others to prescribe or recommend particular drugs could violate prohibiting
fraud and kickbacks and improperly raise the costs for Medicare and Medicaid, the federal health care programs for the elderly, disabled, and poor.*

The warning came in the form of proposed guidance on ethical marketing practices.

The drug industry defended its practices, noting that in April it had adopted a new set of voluntary guidelines aimed at eliminating some of the more questionable marketing tactics, such as treating doctors to meals in expensive restaurants or providing tickets to sports events. Others said that the threat of federal ethical guidelines would help clean up some of the more egregious practices but added that financial incentives were so ingrained in the industry that removing them could be extremely disruptive.

Prescription Drug Benefit for Seniors

Once again Congress was unable to pass legislation giving a prescription drug benefit for seniors covered under the Medicare program. Medicare usually covered only the cost of prescription drugs used in the hospital. About two-thirds of Medicare recipients had coverage for drugs used outside the hospital under supplemental insurance policies, although many living on fixed incomes found it difficult to meet the required copayments. Roughly 11 million had no drug coverage under retiree health plans and either had to pay for their medicines out of pocket or go without.

Both political parties had made enactment of Medicare coverage for prescription drugs a high priority in the 2000 presidential elections, but divisions over who should set premiums, determine benefits, and deliver coverage prevented the legislation from moving forward in 2001. Republicans generally favored private insurers, who had flexibility to offer varying coverage at differing premium costs. Most Democrats wanted the government-run Medicare program to offer a standard drug benefit to all Medicare recipients.

With seniors clamoring for help with paying for drugs and congressional elections coming up in November, both parties were eager to pass legislation in 2002. House Republican leaders pushed a bill through in June that passed on a party-line vote, 221–208, after Democrats were unable to win approval for a far more generous plan. The Senate faced a procedural problem that required any prescription drug legislation to win sixty votes rather than a simple majority. The chamber voted on four proposals offered as floor amendments to a bill designed to make it harder for band-name drug makers to head off competition from cheaper generic versions. None of the four alternatives were able to garner the necessary sixty votes.

The Senate passed the underlying bill to make it easier for generic drugs to reach the market after patent protection had expired on the brand-name version of a drug, but the legislation died at the end of the congressional session. On October 21 the Bush administration proposed new regulations that would achieve largely the same goal. Under the proposed regulations, holders of an expiring drug patent would be permitted only one thirty-month stay of a generic drug application while it moved to protect its patent rights in court. Current regulations allowed drug manufacturers to seek repeated thirty-month stays, effectively blocking generic competition. The proposed *regulation also limited the kinds of patents the drug maker could file in its effort to block generic drug approvals. In general, new patent protection would not be allowed for changes that did not represent significant innovation in the underlying product. "The message to the big brand drug companies is clear," President Bush said announcing the proposed regulation. "You deserve the rewards of your research and development, but you do not have the right to keep the generic drugs off the market for frivolous reasons." Tommy G. Thompson, secretary of health and human services, said the new regulation could save consumers approximately $3.5 billion a year.*

Patents for about 200 drugs were scheduled to expire over the next three years, including patents on best-selling drugs such as Prilosec; Cipro, an antibiotic used to fight anthrax; Paxil, an antidepressant, and Flonase, an antiallergen. Generic drugs, the chemical equivalents of brand-name drugs, were almost always cheaper than the patented drug they imitated. In his statement, Bush said the average prescription price for generic drugs was $17, compared with $72 for the branded versions. But there was some evidence that the cost of generics was rising, both because new generics for drugs that had recently gone off patent always tended to be more expensive in the first few months and because generic drug makers were raising the prices of some of their older products. As a result, makers of generics were increasing their profits while still offering prices that were well below those of the best-selling brand-name drugs. According to IMS Health, a pharmaceutical information company, generic drug prices grew more slowly than prices for brand-name drugs until 2001 when they rose twice as fast, a trend that appeared to continue in 2002.

> *Following are excerpts from "FDA Oversight of Direct-to-Consumer Advertising Has Limitations," a report issued December 3, 2002, by the United States General Accounting Office.*

> **The document was obtained from the Internet at www.gao .gov/new.items/d03177.pdf; accessed December 8, 2002.**

Results in Brief

Pharmaceutical companies spend more on research and development initiatives than on all drug promotional activities, including DTC [direct-to-consumer] advertising. According to industry estimates, pharmaceutical companies spent $30.3 billion on research and development and $19.1 billion on all promotional activities, which includes $2.7 billion on DTC advertising, in 2001. Pharmaceutical companies have increased spending on DTC advertising more rapidly than they have increased spending on research and development. Between 1997 and 2001, DTC advertising spending increased 145 percent, while research and development spending increased 59 percent. Promotion to physicians accounted for more than 80 percent of all promotional spending by pharmaceutical companies in 2001. Total promotional spending was equivalent to 12 percent of drug sales in the United States in 2001.

DTC advertising appears to increase prescription drug spending and utilization. Drugs that are promoted directly to consumers often are among the best-selling drugs, and sales for DTC-advertised drugs have increased faster than sales for drugs that are not heavily advertised to consumers. Most of the spending increase for heavily advertised drugs is the result of increased utilization, not price increases. For example, between 1999 and 2000, the number of prescriptions dispensed for the most heavily advertised drugs rose 25 percent, but increased only 4 percent for drugs that were not heavily advertised. Over the same period, prices rose 6 percent for the most heavily advertised drugs and 9 percent for the others. The concentration of DTC spending on a small number of drugs for chronic diseases that are likely to have high sales anyway and the simultaneous promotion of these drugs to physicians may contribute to increased utilization and thereby increase sales of DTC-advertised drugs. The recent research literature shows that DTC advertising may cause increases in drug utilization and sales in some cases. In addition, consumer surveys have consistently found that about 5 percent of consumers (or, by our estimate, about 8.5 million consumers annually) have both requested and received from their physician a prescription for a particular drug in response to seeing a DTC advertisement.

While generally effective at halting the dissemination of advertisements it reviews and identifies as misleading, FDA's oversight of DTC advertising has limitations. DDMAC [the Division of Drug Marketing, Advertising, and Communications] focuses on advertisements that will be widely circulated or that are the most likely to impart misleading impressions of a drug to consumers. For example, DDMAC reviews all broadcast DTC advertisements because of the large number of people who will see them. FDA issues regulatory letters for a small percentage of the advertisements it reviews. From August 1997 through August 2002, FDA issued 88 regulatory letters for violative DTC advertisements. FDA officials told us that pharmaceutical companies that have received regulatory letters have invariably ceased dissemination of the misleading advertisement. However, FDA's oversight has not prevented some pharmaceutical companies from repeatedly disseminating new misleading advertisements for the same drug, and some pharmaceutical companies have failed to submit in a timely manner all newly disseminated advertisements to FDA for review. Furthermore, FDA's oversight has been adversely affected by a January 2002 change in its procedures for reviewing draft regulatory letters that was directed by the Department of Health and Human Services (HHS). This change has significantly increased the time between DDMAC's identification of a misleading advertisement and FDA's request to remove it from dissemination, with the result that some regulatory letters may not be issued until after the advertising campaign has run its course.

In light of the delay caused by the change in policy for review of draft DTC regulatory letters, we are recommending that HHS expedite the review of these letters to ensure that misleading DTC advertisements are withdrawn as soon as possible once identified. In its comments on a draft of this report, HHS explained that the purpose of the change in procedure was to ensure that the letters are based on a solid legal foundation and promote voluntary compliance. HHS agreed that it is important to issue regulatory letters quickly and said that it intends to reduce the number of days that the letters are under review. . . .

FDA's Requirements for the Content of DTC Advertising

FDA regulations describe several types of prescription drug advertisements, including DTC advertisements, and the extent to which they are subject to regulation. One type, product claim advertisements, usually mentions a drug's name and the condition it is intended to treat and describes the risks and benefits associated with taking the medication.

The regulations specify, among other things, that product claim advertisements (1) cannot be false or misleading; (2) must present a fair balance between the risks and the benefits of a drug product; (3) must reveal facts that are material to the representations made in the advertisement or the consequences of using the product as advertised; and (4) must, depending on the medium, either disclose all the risks listed in the product's labeling or make "adequate provision" to disseminate the approved product labeling through other means to the advertisement's audience. . . .

In 1997, FDA issued draft guidance on how broadcast product claim DTC advertisements could communicate information about the risks of using a drug by finding mechanisms by which to get the product labeling information to consumers, and thereby meet the adequate provision portion of its regulations. Before this provision of the regulation was clarified in 1997, pharmaceutical companies generally had to provide all of the risk information associated with the medication during the broadcast advertisement. Including all of this risk information in a broadcast DTC advertisement increased the length of the advertisement to the point that such advertising was largely impractical. After the guidance was issued, pharmaceutical companies had an alternative to the requirement that all risks in broadcast advertisements be disclosed. Pharmaceutical companies could meet the regulatory requirements by presenting the major side effects, either in audio or in audio and visual form, and by telling consumers where to find additional information, including how or where to obtain the approved product labeling.

A second type of advertisement is reminder advertisements. These may disclose the name of the product and dosage form (e.g., tablet, syrup) or cost information, but they are not permitted to present its intended use or to make any claims or representations about the product. Under FDA regulations, reminder advertisements are exempt from the risk disclosure requirements.

A third type of advertisement is help-seeking advertisements, which are not regulated by FDA. They do not identify drugs by name and generally discuss a disease or condition and advise the print or broadcast audience to "see your doctor" for possible treatments.

FDA Regulatory Letters

In an effort to stop dissemination of misleading DTC advertisements, FDA sends regulatory letters to companies that are in violation of its regulations. These letters are of two types—untitled letters and warning letters. Untitled letters address violations such as overstating the effectiveness of the drug, suggesting a broader range of indicated uses than the drug has been approved for, and making misleading claims because of inadequate context or lack of balanced risk information. Warning letters address more serious violations, including safety or health risks, or continued violations of the act. Warning letters advise a pharmaceutical firm that FDA may take further enforcement actions, such as seeking judicial remediation, without notifying the company, and generally ask the firm to conduct a new advertising campaign to correct inaccurate impressions left by the advertisement. A company that receives either type of letter from FDA is asked to submit a written response to the agency within 14 days describing the remedial actions it has taken. . . .

Research Studies Suggest that DTC Advertising Has Increased Utilization and Sales of Advertised Drugs

Researchers have only recently begun to examine the effects of DTC advertising on drug utilization and sales. The few studies we identified have conflicting findings but, on the whole, suggest that DTC advertising may increase drug utilization and sales. One study looked at the utilization of an injectable migraine headache treatment in cities in which a DTC advertising campaign was conducted and cities with no advertising. During the first year the drug was marketed, February 1993 to February 1994, the drug was dispensed nearly 10 percent more in cities in which DTC advertisements were disseminated. Additionally, three recent studies that examined the joint effects of DTC advertising and promotion to physicians all found that DTC advertising significantly increased drug sales. Each of the studies found that DTC advertising increased sales within the advertised drug's class (implying, for example, that advertising for one antihistamine increased sales for other antihistamines as well). Two of the studies estimated that each 10 percent increase in DTC spending within a drug class increased sales in that class by 1 percent. An exception to this pattern of findings is a study on the effects of fluctuations in the intensity of DTC advertising on sales of cholesterol-lowering drugs from 1995 to 2000. While sales of cholesterol-lowering drugs increased substantially over that period, this study found that variations in the amount of DTC advertising were not statistically related to either sales of particular brand-name drugs or sales of cholesterol-lowering drugs as a class. Unlike the studies described above, this research did not consider the effects of promotion to physicians.

Consumer Surveys Have Found That DTC Advertisements Influence Consumers to Ask Physicians for Brand-name Drugs

Surveys conducted by FDA and private organizations consistently show that DTC advertisements have an impact on whether consumers request and receive a specific brand-name prescription from their physician. . . . In several of these surveys, consumers were asked whether they had seen an advertisement for a prescription drug and whether seeing the advertisement resulted in discussing the medication with their doctor and receiving the prescription. Most consumers (65 to 85 percent) remembered seeing a DTC advertisement. A subset of consumers who saw an advertisement discussed the medication with their doctor. The percentage of patients asking their physicians about a prescription for a specific drug was consistent across studies, about 30 to 35 percent of those who remembered seeing a DTC advertisement. One study estimated that the 32 percent of consumers in a 2001 survey who had discussed a DTC advertisement with their doctor translated into approximately 61.1 million consumers asking about specific medications. In the consumer surveys we examined, the percentage of consumers who, in response to a DTC advertisement, requested and received a prescription from their physician for a drug they were not currently taking was generally about 5 percent (ranging from 2 percent to 10 percent). By our estimate, this means that about 8.5 million consumers received a prescription after viewing a DTC advertisement and asking their physician for the drug in 2000.

FDA's Oversight of DTC Advertising Has Limitations

FDA's oversight of DTC advertising is focused on advertisements that have the greatest exposure or the greatest potential to be misleading. Pharmaceutical companies comply with FDA's requests to cease dissemination of misleading DTC advertisements. However, some pharmaceutical companies have repeatedly disseminated misleading advertisements for the same drug, and pharmaceutical companies have failed to submit, or to submit in a timely manner, all newly disseminated advertisements to FDA for review. A recent change in the procedures for reviewing draft regulatory letters has adversely affected FDA's ability to issue regulatory letters in a timely manner.

DDMAC Targets Reviews

As of June 2002, five DDMAC staff were dedicated to reviewing DTC advertisements, and two DTC review slots were vacant. DDMAC's reviewers focus on advertisements that will receive the greatest exposure or have the most potential to impart misleading impressions of a drug to consumers. These include broadcast advertisements, print advertisements appearing in high-circulation periodicals, initial advertising campaigns for newly marketed drugs, and new advertisements from pharmaceutical companies that have previously been cited for disseminating misleading advertisements. DDMAC officials told us that 248 broadcast advertisements and an unknown number of DTC print advertisements were submitted to it at the time of their dissemination in 2001. DDMAC staff reviewed all the broadcast advertisements it received in 2001. DDMAC does not keep track of the number of print advertisements it reviewed. DDMAC also received and reviewed 230 complaints about allegedly misleading advertisements (for both consumer-directed and health professional-directed materials) in 2001, the majority of which were submitted by competing pharmaceutical companies. DDMAC investigates all tips concerning potentially misleading advertisements. Although FDA generally does not have the authority to preapprove advertisements before they are disseminated, companies may voluntarily submit their materials to FDA for advisory comments before launching an advertisement. DDMAC gave advisory comments on 128 broadcast advertisements in 2001. In addition to monitoring and review activities, DDMAC conducts research to better understand consumer and physician behavior related to DTC advertising.

FDA Sends Regulatory Letters When It Identifies a Violation

When FDA identifies a violative DTC advertisement, it sends a regulatory letter to the company responsible for the advertisement asking that the company cease disseminating the advertisement. FDA issues regulatory letters for only a small percentage of the advertisements it reviews. For example, FDA has issued letters for about 5 percent of the broadcast advertisements it reviewed between 1999 and 2001. In total, FDA issued 88 regulatory letters for DTC advertisements between August 1997 and August 2002—44 for broadcast advertisements, 35 for print advertisements, and 9 for both broadcast and print advertisements. 28 Almost all of the regulatory letters were untitled letters, which are for less serious violations. . . ; for more serious violations, FDA issued three warning letters for broadcast advertisements and one for a print advertisement.

FDA's warning letters often cite multiple, serious offenses or violations that raise public health issues. For example, FDA's January 21, 1999, warning letter to Novartis Pharmaceuticals Corporation about the marketing of Lescol, a cholesterol-lowering drug, described four violations: (1) Novartis did not submit the broadcast advertisement to FDA when it was disseminated, as required by the regulations, resulting in "violative messages being disseminated to a far larger consumer audience than might have otherwise occurred"; (2) the advertisement falsely stated that treatment with Lescol was as effective as treatment with other cholesterol-lowering agents named in the advertisement; (3) the advertisement falsely stated that treatment with Lescol was less expensive than treatment with other named cholesterol-lowering agents; and (4) the advertisement minimized the risk of potentially serious side effects, including liver function abnormalities and muscle pain or weakness.

[The FDA issued 14 DTC regulatory letters in 2001.] One-half of the letters cited advertisements that made misleading claims about a drug's efficacy. For example, FDA's August 2001 letter concerning Luxiq, a cream for the treatment of psoriasis and eczema, noted that the advertisement claimed "highly effective relief in three out of four patients," even though the clinical trial described on the product labeling found that Luxiq's success at improving various symptoms ranged from 41 percent to 67 percent. The Luxiq advertisement also claimed that it reduced symptoms "within days," even though the clinical trial results were for patients who used it for 4 weeks. Similarly, in November 2001, FDA cited an advertisement for Protopic Ointment, a treatment for allergic dermatitis, which included models with completely smooth skin. FDA concluded that this implied that patients would experience 100 percent improvement of their symptoms with the ointment, even though the product labeling noted that only one-tenth of the patients taking the drug showed complete improvement. Regulatory letters have also cited advertisements for minimizing risk information. For example, FDA's October 2001 letter about an advertisement for Differin Gel, an acne medication, claimed that risk information was inadequately presented because, "During the audio presentation of the major risk information, there are numerous visual distractions that interfere with the viewer's ability to listen to . . . the information . . . [including] numerous scene changes and quick camera movements." Still other advertisements have been cited because FDA identified them as being a different type of advertisement than apparently intended by the pharmaceutical firm. FDA's January 2001 letter concerning an advertisement for the acid reflux medication Prilosec, for instance, noted that the advertisement did not mention the drug by name and did not include information about the drug's approved indication and usage. The manufacturer apparently intended it to be a help-seeking advertisement that did not require such information. However, FDA found that, in essence, the advertisement was a product claim advertisement because it discussed acid reflux in conjunction with "the purple pill," and at the time Prilosec was the only purple pill that treated acid reflux.

FDA's Regulatory Letters Are Effective in Halting Dissemination of Misleading Advertisements

FDA officials told us that pharmaceutical companies have complied with FDA's requests to cease dissemination of misleading DTC drug advertisements in every case to date. For that reason, and because FDA does not want to remove a beneficial drug from the market, FDA has yet to employ any of the harsher remedies available to it. FDA, through the Department of Justice, can initiate court action to seize drugs for which advertisements are false or misleading. FDA may also ask a court to stop the advertisement and request the company to run a corrective campaign. FFDCA provides for criminal penalties for violative prescription drug advertising.

Some Pharmaceutical Companies Have Been Cited for Repeatedly Disseminating Different Misleading Advertisements

FDA's regulatory letters do not completely deter pharmaceutical companies from making misleading claims in subsequent advertisements. Since 1997, FDA has issued repeated regulatory letters to several pharmaceutical companies, including 14 to GlaxoSmithKline, 6 to Schering Corporation, and 5 to Merck & Co. Some companies have received multiple regulatory letters over time for new advertisements promoting the same drug. For example, FDA issued four separate regulatory letters, one of which was a warning letter, to stop misleading advertisements for the allergy drug Flonase marketed by Glaxo Wellcome in 1999 and 2000. The untitled letters were for unsubstantiated efficacy claims and for lack of fair balance. The warning letter was for failure to provide any risk information on the major side effects and contraindications of the drug, failure to make adequate provision for disseminating the product labeling, and failure to submit the advertisement to FDA. In the past 4 years, FDA has issued four regulatory letters to Pfizer regarding broadcast and print advertisements for its cholesterol-lowering drug, Lipitor. Among other infractions, FDA noted that the advertisements gave the false impression that Lipitor can reduce heart disease and falsely claimed that Lipitor is safer than competing products.

Effectiveness of FDA's Oversight of DTC Advertising Is Limited in Two Ways

While FDA's enforcement actions have succeeded in removing from dissemination misleading DTC advertisements, the effectiveness of its oversight is limited in two respects. First, FDA's ability to assess the compliance of pharmaceutical companies with its DTC advertising regulations is compromised because FDA cannot verify that it receives all newly disseminated advertisements from pharmaceutical companies. FDA has issued six regulatory letters for misleading advertisements since 1997 that cited pharmaceutical companies for failing to submit their advertisements to the agency when they were first disseminated.

FDA officials told us that the agency contracts with a commercial service that monitors television advertising placement to find advertisements that pharmaceutical companies have failed to submit to the agency. The service monitors six cable television networks and the New York City affiliates of the four major networks and PBS. This service does not identify all advertisements that are broadcast on smaller networks, such as some cable television stations, or in some local markets. Indeed, in one case a misleading advertisement was broadcast in 2 calendar years in Puerto Rico before FDA became aware of it.

Second, a recent change in the Department of Health and Human Services policy for reviewing regulatory letters has sharply reduced FDA's effectiveness in issuing untitled and warning letters in a timely manner. The ability to issue regulatory letters quickly after an advertising violation is identified is a key component of FDA's oversight of DTC advertising. Any inaccurate impressions of a drug that are caused by a misleading advertisement are minimized if the advertisement is quickly removed from dissemination. Prior to the policy change, FDA officials told us that regulatory letters were issued directly by DDMAC within several days of its receipt of an advertisement that it identified as misleading. On November 29, 2001, HHS instructed FDA that no untitled or warning letters could be issued until FDA's Office of the Chief Counsel (OCC) reviewed them. HHS implemented this new policy to ensure that all draft warning and untitled letters from FDA were reviewed for "legal sufficiency and consistency with agency policy." FDA officials told us that OCC implemented this policy for regulatory letters on January 31, 2002, and that OCC set the goal of reviewing all draft regulatory letters from DDMAC within 45 working days.

Since the policy change, OCC's reviews of draft regulatory letters from FDA have taken so long that misleading advertisements may have completed their broadcast life cycle before FDA issued the letters. FDA provided us with information indicating that DDMAC submitted five draft DTC regulatory letters between January 31, 2002, and September 5, 2002. All of the letters have been issued. The letters were issued from 13 to 78 calendar days after they were first submitted to OCC by DDMAC. . . . [M]any television DTC advertisements are on the air for only a short time—about one-fifth of them for 1 month, and about one-third for 2 months or less. Although we do not know the broadcast status of the advertisements targeted by DDMAC's draft regulatory letters, there is a possibility that misleading advertisements could remain on the air after they are identified by DDMAC if FDA maintains its current review policies.

Conclusions

DTC advertising prompts millions of consumers to ask their doctors for prescriptions for specific brand-name drugs. As a result, it is important that FDA act effectively to minimize the public's exposure to misleading DTC advertisements. We found that FDA's oversight is generally effective at halting the dissemination of advertisements it reviews and identifies as misleading. The recent change directed by HHS in FDA's procedures for reviewing draft regulatory letters has adversely affected FDA's ability to enforce compliance with its regulations. Without more timely action, DTC advertisements that DDMAC has identified as misleading can remain on the air too long.

Recommendation for Executive Action

To ensure that FDA's enforcement actions are timely, we recommend that HHS reduce the amount of time for internal review of draft regulatory letters. . . .

FEDERAL COURT ON MEANING OF THE SECOND AMENDMENT
December 5, 2002

The debate over whether the Second Amendment gave individuals a constitutional right to keep and bear arms heated up in 2002 after the Justice Department, at the prompting of Attorney General John Ashcroft, reversed decades of official government policy to hold that individuals did have the right to own guns, subject to reasonable restrictions. The policy was almost immediately challenged by a federal appeals court, which ruled on December 5, 2002, that the right to keep and bear arms applied only to state and federal militias and not to individuals.

Reversing the department's position on the Second Amendment was one of the first actions Ashcroft took upon becoming attorney general in 2001. Ashcroft also moved to reduce, from ninety days to one day, the amount of time the Federal Bureau of Investigation had to keep records of gun purchases. Although the Justice Department was reportedly prepared to implement that change, there was continued opposition to it from a variety of sources, and by the end of 2002 the ninety-day requirement was still in place.

One reason for not moving ahead with that change may have been the uproar that ensued in October when the Washington, D.C., metropolitan area was effectively held hostage for nearly three weeks by the so-called Beltway sniper, who shot at random targets in different locations at different times of the day. By the time the snipers, two men working together, were arrested ten people had been killed, three wounded, and area residents terrified, many of them too frightened to leave their homes to go about daily business.

The sniper incident provoked a widespread debate about the merits of requiring ballistic "fingerprinting" of every gun sold in the United States. Advocates of the program argued that, had such fingerprinting been in place, it might have helped police in their efforts to track the snipers. Opponents, led by the National Rifle Association (NRA), claimed that ballistic fingerprinting would be a gross invasion of the privacy of legitimate gun owners and of little use because most guns used in crimes were stolen. Although experts questioned the NRA's assertion that most guns used in crimes were stolen, that apparently turned out to be the case in the sniper incident. Using records from the manufacturer of the assault rifle found with the snipers when they were arrested, federal law enforcement officials were able to track the weapon to a gun shop in Takoma, Washington, where the snipers had once lived. But the gun shop had no sales records for the weapon (or for many others), and there was speculation that an employee may have sold the guns "off the books."

Competing Interpretations

The confrontation over the meaning of the Second Amendment began in May 2001, when Ashcroft, a long-time member of the NRA and a foe of most gun control laws, told the politically powerful pro-gun organization that he "unequivocally" believed that the Second Amendment to the Constitution protected the rights of individuals to keep and bear arms. "While some have argued that the Second Amendment guarantees only a 'collective right' of the states to maintain militias, I believe the amendment's plain meaning and original intent provide otherwise." The NRA and other advocates of gun rights had long supported Ashcroft's position, but it differed from the collective rights interpretation endorsed by most courts and attorneys general since 1939, when the Supreme Court last ruled on the issue.

In October 2001 the Court of Appeals for the Fifth Circuit, sitting in New Orleans, agreed with Ashcroft, finding that individuals had a right to possess guns subject to "limited, narrowly tailored specific exceptions." At issue in the case was a 1994 federal law prohibiting anyone under a domestic-violence restraining order from possessing a gun, and the appeals court agreed that law was a valid restriction on the individual right to bear arms. (Appeals court decision, Historic Documents of 2001, p. 722)

On May 7, 2002, the Justice Department used the appeals court formulation in footnotes in briefs in two separate cases filed with the Supreme Court, formally reversing official government policy on the meaning of the Second Amendment. In the footnotes Solicitor General Ted Olson wrote: "The current position of the United States . . . is that the Second Amendment more broadly protects the rights of individuals, including persons who are not members of any militia or engaged in any active military service or training, to possess and bear their own firearms, subject to reasonable restrictions designed to prevent possession by unfit persons or to restrict the possession of types of firearms that are particularly suited to criminal misuse." Olson's briefs argued that the Supreme Court should not hear the cases (one of which was an appeal of the Fifth Circuit's October decision) because the men involved had been properly charged under laws that placed reasonable restrictions on gun ownership. The Supreme Court declined to review.

The new policy was challenged almost immediately by a ruling from the Court of Appeals for the Ninth Circuit, sitting in San Francisco. On December 5 a three-judge panel upheld a California law that restricted the ownership of assault weapons, holding that there was no constitutional right for individuals to keep and bear arms. That law, adopted in 1989 and amended in 1999, was the most sweeping assault weapon ban in the country. It prohibited the manufacture, sale, or import of grenade launchers, semiautomatic pistols with a capacity to fire more than ten rounds, semiautomatic rifles that used detachable magazines, and guns with barrels that could be fitted with silencers. California residents who owned such guns or wanted to buy them challenged the law, claiming it violated their Second Amendment rights and raised other constitutional issues.

In a lengthy opinion, Judge Stephen Reinhardt reviewed the debates surrounding the drafting and ratification of the Second Amendment, much as the judges on the Fifth Circuit bench had a year earlier. But the Ninth Circuit judges came to an opposite conclusion. The amendment, Reinhardt wrote, "was adopted to ensure that effective state militias would be maintained, thus preserving the people's right to bear arms. The amendment was not adopted in order to afford rights to individuals with respect to private gun ownership." As a result, Reinhardt reasoned, the Second Amendment "imposes no limitation on California's ability to enact legislation regulating or prohibiting the possession or use of firearms, including dangerous weapons such as assault weapons."

Although the three judges were unanimous on this conclusion, one said that it was unnecessary to write a detailed opinion on the meaning of the amendment because the court had already done so in a case decided in 1996. Reinhardt disagreed, saying that the recent debate made it advisable to revisit the issue. Reinhardt, widely considered to be one of the most liberal judges on a liberal bench, was one of two appeals court judges who in June ruled that the pledge of allegiance was unconstitutional. Although the ruling was expected to be appealed to the Supreme Court, it was unclear whether the Court would agree to hear it. (Pledge ruling, p. 382)

Ballistic Fingerprinting

The Washington sniper case renewed interest, at least momentarily, in legislative proposals to create a nationwide database to collect the unique ballistic fingerprints that each firearm imprinted on the bullets fired from it. The proposals would require gun manufacturers to record the ballistic fingerprints of every weapon they made and file them in a database so that law enforcement agencies could match the ammunition used in a crime to a specific weapon whose ownership could then be traced through sales records. Only two states, Maryland and New York, already used ballistic fingerprinting to help in crime detection. Although ballistic fingerprinting was strongly supported by the federal Bureau of Alcohol, Tobacco and Firearms (BATF) as well as many other law enforcement agencies, it was just as staunchly opposed by the NRA, which said such a database would amount to gun registration by another name. Given the political power of the NRA, few in Congress were willing to push the legislation forward.

The Washington sniper incidents increased speculation that such a database might have helped police track the weapon and thus obtain information that could have aided the search for the elusive shooters. The Bush administration sparked increased—and unwanted—media attention to the ballistic fingerprinting proposals when it first denigrated the proposals but then softened its stance in the face of criticism that it was appearing to side with the gun lobby against law enforcement agencies that were trying to protect the public from an unknown and elusive menace.

The flap began October 15 when, in response to a question, White House press secretary Ari Fleischer dismissed the technology as unreliable and undesirable. Fleischer said such proposals were similar to arguing that "every citizen in the United States" should be fingerprinted "in order to catch robbers and thieves." Fleischer also said the fingerprints themselves could be changed too easily to be reliable. "The more a gun is used, the less accurate the tracing can become. A simple nail file put down the barrel of a gun can alter the amount of tracing that's on a bullet and therefore change the accuracy of the fingerprinting. . . ."

After White House officials met with BATF staff, Fleischer retreated from his previous remarks, announcing the next day that the BATF would study whether a national database would be an effective tool in fighting crime. "The president wants this issue explored," Fleischer said. "There are reasons people think that it could possibly move forward and other reasons that people think it may not be able to move forward. And so that's why it's going to be explored."

In January 2002 Americans for Gun Safety issued "Broken Records," a report that said the states' failure to computerize their records allowed nearly 10,000 convicted felons to pass background checks and buy guns despite being ineligible to purchase guns. The study found that twenty-five states had automated less than 60 percent of their felony conviction records, thirty-three states had not automated any records of those who were involuntarily institutionalized in mental health facilities, and fifteen states had no automated records of domestic violence misdemeanors. Individuals in all three categories were barred from possessing guns under federal laws.

Coming less than three weeks before congressional elections, the debate over ballistic fingerprinting legislation died almost as soon as the snipers were arrested, on October 24. The only other gun legislation that came before Congress in 2002 was a bill to provide states with more money to upgrade their systems for doing background checks for gun purchases. The House passed the measure by voice vote, but the Senate took no action on it.

Following are excerpts from the opinion issued December 5, 2002, by the United States Court of Appeals for the Ninth Circuit in the case of Silveira v. Lockyer, *holding that the Second Amendment right to keep and bear arms did not apply to individuals.*

The document was obtained from the Internet at www .ca9.uscourts.gov/ca9/newopinions.nsf/661116A4ECB1A7 BE88256C8600544DCB/$file/0115098.pdf?openelement; accessed December 9, 2002.

Opinion

REINHARDT, Circuit Judge:

In 1999, the State of California enacted amendments to its gun control laws that significantly strengthened the state's restrictions on the possession, use, and transfer of the semi-automatic weapons popularly known as "assault weapons." Plaintiffs, California residents who either own assault weapons, seek to acquire such weapons, or both, brought this challenge to the gun control statute, asserting that the law, as amended, violates the Second Amendment, the Equal Protection Clause, and a host of other constitutional provisions. The district court dismissed all of the plaintiffs' claims. Because the Second Amendment does not confer an individual right to own or possess arms, we affirm the dismissal of all claims brought pursuant to that constitutional provision. As to the Equal Protection claims, we conclude that there is no constitutional infirmity in the statute's provisions regarding active peace officers. We find, however, no rational basis for the establishment of a statutory exception with respect to retired peace officers, and hold that the retired officers' exception fails even the most deferential level of scrutiny under the Equal Protection Clause. Finally, we conclude that each of the three additional constitutional claims asserted by plaintiffs on appeal is without merit.

[Part I omitted]

II. Discussion

A. Background and Precedent.

A robust constitutional debate is currently taking place in this nation regarding the scope of the Second Amendment, a debate that has gained intensity over the last several years. Until recently, this relatively obscure constitutional provision attracted little judicial or scholarly attention. As a result, however, of increasing popular concern over gun violence, the passage of legislation restricting the sale and use of firearms, the cultural significance of firearms in American society, and the political activities of pro-gun enthusiasts under the leadership of the National Rifle Association (the NRA), the disagreement over the meaning of the Second Amendment has grown particularly heated.

[1] There are three principal schools of thought that form the basis for the debate. The first, which we will refer to as the "traditional individual rights" model, holds that the Second Amendment guarantees to individual private citizens a fundamental right to possess and use firearms for any purpose at all, subject only to limited government regulation. This view, urged by the NRA and other firearms enthusiasts, as well as by a prolific cadre of fervent supporters in the legal academy, had never been adopted by any court until the recent Fifth Circuit decision in *United States v. Emerson* ... (5th Cir. 2001), *cert. Denied* ... (2002). The second view, a variant of the first, we will refer to as the "limited individual rights" model. Under that view, individuals maintain a constitutional right to possess firearms insofar as such possession bears a

reasonable relationship to militia service. The third, a wholly contrary view, commonly called the "collective rights" model, asserts that the Second Amendment right to "bear arms" guarantees the right of the people to maintain effective state militias, but does not provide any type of individual right to own or possess weapons. Under this theory of the amendment, the federal and state governments have the full authority to enact prohibitions and restrictions on the use and possession of firearms, subject only to generally applicable constitutional constraints, such as due process, equal protection, and the like. Long the dominant view of the Second Amendment, and widely accepted by the federal courts, the collective rights model has recently come under strong criticism from individual rights advocates. After conducting a full analysis of the amendment, its history, and its purpose, we reaffirm our conclusion in *Hickman v. Block* . . . (9th Cir. 1996), that it is this collective rights model which provides the best interpretation of the Second Amendment.

Despite the increased attention by commentators and political interest groups to the question of what exactly the Second Amendment protects, with the sole exception of the Fifth Circuit's Emerson decision there exists no thorough judicial examination of the amendment's meaning. The Supreme Court's most extensive treatment of the amendment is a somewhat cryptic discussion in *United States v. Miller* . . . (1939). In that case, a criminal defendant brought a Second Amendment challenge to a federal gun control law that prohibited the transport of sawed-off shotguns in interstate commerce. The Court rejected the challenge to the statute. In the only and oft-quoted passage in the United States Reports to consider, albeit somewhat indirectly, whether the Second Amendment establishes an individual right to arms, the *Miller* Court concluded:

> In the absence of any evidence tending to show that possession or use of a 'shotgun having a barrel of less than eighteen inches in length' at this time has some reasonable relationship to the preservation or efficiency of a well regulated militia, we cannot say that the Second Amendment guarantees the right to keep and bear such an instrument. Certainly it is not within judicial notice that this weapon is any part of the ordinary military equipment or that its use could contribute to the common defense.

. . . Thus, in *Miller* the Supreme Court decided that because a weapon was not suitable for use in the militia, its possession was not protected by the Second Amendment. As a result of its phrasing of its holding in the negative, however, the Miller Court's opinion stands only for the proposition that the possession of certain weapons is not protected, and offers little guidance as to what rights the Second Amendment does protect. Accordingly, it has been noted, with good reason, that "[t]he Supreme Court's jurisprudence on the scope of [the Second] [A]mendment is quite limited, and not entirely illuminating.". . . What *Miller* does strongly imply, however, is that the Supreme Court rejects the traditional individual rights view.

The only *post-Miller* reference by the Supreme Court to the scope of the amendment occurred in *Lewis v. United States* . . . (1980), in which the Court noted, in a footnote dismissing a Second Amendment challenge to a felon-in-possession conviction, that the federal gun control laws at issue did not "trench upon any constitutionally protected liberties," citing *Miller* in support of this observation. . . .

We also note that two of the Supreme Court's recent decisions that limit the power of the federal government to regulate activities of the states relate to firearms restrictions. . . . In neither case did the Court address a Second Amendment issue directly; however, in each case a currently-sitting Justice expressed his individual view of the amendment's scope, directly or indirectly, but from radically different standpoints. In his dissent in [*United States v.*] *Lopez* [(1995)], Justice Stevens, although not mentioning the Second Amendment, strongly implied that he believes that it offers no obstacles to the federal government's ability to regulate firearms. . . .

Justice Thomas spoke to the Second Amendment issue more directly in his concurrence in *Printz* [*v. United States* (1997)], in words that suggested that he may well support the traditional individual rights view. . . .

Finally, we note that, after his retirement, Chief Justice Warren Burger uttered one of the most widely publicized comments about the Second Amendment ever made by a Justice inside or outside the context of a judicial opinion. In an interview, former Chief Justice Burger stated that the traditional individual rights view was:

> one of the greatest pieces of fraud, I repeat the word 'fraud,' on the American public by special interest groups that I've ever seen in my lifetime. The real purpose of the Second Amendment was to ensure that state armies—the militia—would be maintained for the defense of the state. The very language of the Second Amendment refutes any argument that it was intended to guarantee every citizen an unfettered right to any kind of weapon he or she desires.

. . . Although we in no way share Chief Justice Burger's view that Second Amendment enthusiasts are guilty of fraud, we do generally agree with his statements regarding the Amendment's purpose and scope.

Our court, like every other federal court of appeals to reach the issue except for the Fifth Circuit, has interpreted *Miller* as rejecting the traditional individual rights view. In *Hickman v. Block*, we held that "the Second Amendment guarantees a collective rather than an individual right.". . . Like the other courts, we reached our conclusion regarding the Second Amendment's scope largely on the basis of the rather cursory discussion in *Miller*, and touched only briefly on the merits of the debate over the force of the amendment. . . .

In light of the United States government's recent change in position on the meaning of the amendment, the resultant flood of Second Amendment challenges in the district courts, the Fifth Circuit's extensive study and analysis of the amendment and its conclusion that *Miller* does not mean what we and other courts have assumed it to mean, the proliferation of gun control statutes both state and federal, and the active scholarly debate that is being waged across this nation, we believe it prudent to explore Appellants' Second Amendment arguments in some depth, and to address the merits of the issue, even though this circuit's position on the scope and effect of the amendment was established in *Hickman.* Having engaged in that exploration, we determine that the conclusion we reached in *Hickman* was correct.

B. Appellants Lack Standing to Challenge the Assault Weapons Control Act on Second Amendment Grounds.

[2] Appellants contend that the California Assault Weapons Control Act and its 1999 revisions violate their Second Amendment rights. We unequivocally reject this contention. We conclude that although the text and structure of the amendment, standing alone, do not conclusively resolve the question of its meaning, when we give the text its most plausible reading and consider the amendment in light of the historical context and circumstances surrounding its enactment we are compelled to reaffirm the collective rights view we adopted in *Hickman:* The amendment protects the people's right to maintain an effective state militia, and does not establish an individual right to own or possess firearms for personal or other use. This conclusion is reinforced in part by *Miller*'s implicit rejection of the traditional individual rights position. Because we hold that the Second Amendment does not provide an individual right to own or possess guns or other firearms, plaintiffs lack standing to challenge the AWCA. . . .

[Detailed discussion of the historical context of the Second Amendment omitted.]

An examination of the historical context surrounding the enactment of the Second Amendment leaves us with little doubt that the proper reading of the amendment is that embodied in the collective rights model. We note at the outset that the interpretation of the Second Amendment lends itself particularly to historical analysis. The content of the amendment is restricted to a narrow, specific subject that is itself defined in narrow, specific terms. Only one other provision of the Bill of Rights is similarly composed—the almost never-used Third Amendment. The other eight amendments all employ broad and general terms, such as "no law respecting" (the Free Exercise Clause), "unreasonable" (searches and seizures), "due process of law" (for deprivations of life, liberty, and property), "cruel and unusual" (punishments). Even the Ninth and Tenth Amendments speak vaguely of "other" rights or unenumerated "reserved" rights. The use of narrow, specific language of limited applicability renders the task of construing the Second Amendment somewhat different from that which we ordinarily undertake when we interpret the other portions of the Bill of Rights.

What our historical inquiry reveals is that the Second Amendment was enacted in order to assuage the fears of Anti-Federalists that the new federal government would cause the state militias to atrophy by refusing to exercise its prerogative of arming the state fighting forces, and that the states would, in the absence of the amendment, be without the authority to provide them with the necessary arms. Thus, they feared, the people would be stripped of their ability to defend themselves against a powerful, over-reaching federal government. The debates of the founding era demonstrate that the second of the first ten amendments to the Constitution was included in order to preserve the efficacy of the state militias for the people's defense—not to ensure an individual right to possess weapons. Specifically, the amendment was enacted to guarantee that the people would be able to maintain an effective state fighting force—that they would have the right to bear arms in the service of the state. . . .

[Discussion of drafting and ratification of Second Amendment omitted.]

[9] In sum, our review of the historical record regarding the enactment of the Second Amendment reveals that the amendment was adopted to ensure that effective state militias would be maintained, thus preserving the people's right to bear arms. The militias, in turn, were viewed as critical to preserving the integrity of the states within the newly structured national government as well as to ensuring the freedom of the people from federal tyranny. Properly read, the historical record relating to the Second Amendment leaves little doubt as to its intended scope and effect.

3. Text, History, and Precedent All Support the Collective Rights View of the Amendment.

We reaffirm our earlier adherence to the collective rights interpretation of the Second Amendment, although for reasons somewhat different from those we stated in *Hickman*. Hick-man rested on a canvass of our sister circuits and a summary evaluation of *Miller*. *Miller* did not, however, definitively resolve the nature of the right that the Second Amendment establishes. As we observed earlier, the relevant statements in *Miller* are all expressed in negative terms. Although those negative statements rule out the traditional individual rights model, the Court took no specific affirmative position as to what rights the amendment does protect. Thus, our decision regarding the nature of the rights guaranteed by the Second Amendment must be guided by additional factors—the text and structure of the amendment, an examination of the materials reflecting the historical context in which it was adopted, and a review of the deliberations that preceded the enactment of the amendment— considered in a manner that comports with the rationale of *Miller*.

[10] After conducting our analysis of the meaning of the words employed in the amendment's two clauses, and the effect of their relationship to each other, we concluded that the language and structure of the amendment strongly support the collective rights view. The preamble establishes that the amendment's purpose was to ensure the maintenance of effective state militias, and the amendment's operative clause establishes that this objective was to be attained by preserving the right of the people to "bear arms"—to carry weapons in conjunction with their service in the militia. To resolve any remaining uncertainty, we carefully examined the historical circumstances surrounding the adoption of the amendment. Our review of the debates during the Constitutional Convention, the state ratifying conventions, and the First Congress, as well as the other historical materials we have discussed, confirmed what the text strongly suggested: that the amendment was adopted in order to protect the people from the threat of federal tyranny by preserving the right of the states to arm their militias. The proponents of the Second Amendment believed that only if the states retained that power could the existence of effective state militias—in which the people could exercise their

right to "bear arms"—be ensured. The historical record makes it equally plain that the amendment was not adopted in order to afford rights to individuals with respect to private gun ownership or possession. Accordingly, we are persuaded that we were correct in *Hickman* that the collective rights view, rather than the individual rights models, reflects the proper interpretation of the Second Amendment. Thus, we hold that the Second Amendment imposes no limitation on California's ability to enact legislation regulating or prohibiting the possession or use of firearms, including dangerous weapons such as assault weapons. Plaintiffs lack standing to assert a Second Amendment claim, and their challenge to the Assault Weapons Control Act fails. . . .

[Remainder of opinion dealing with other challenges to the California law omitted.]

TRENT LOTT ON
HIS RACIAL BELIEFS
December 5, 13, and 20, 2002

A careless remark appearing to endorse the past segregationist policies of a retiring colleague cost Sen. Trent Lott, R-Miss., his job as Senate majority leader, inflamed old wounds from the civil rights era, and threatened to set back President George W. Bush's efforts to make the Republican Party more inclusive of African Americans and other minorities. The outcry against Lott's remarks, which occupied national media attention for nearly three weeks, took the senator by surprise. Lott repeatedly apologized for his insensitivity, disavowed segregationist policies, and even endorsed affirmative action. But the apologies could not overcome Lott's voting record opposing civil rights measures and evidence that Lott had expressed similar segregationist sentiments in the past.

Although his colleagues on both sides of the aisle did not rush to condemn Lott's remarks, neither did many rush to his defense. Lott was openly denounced by civil rights leaders and a handful of Democrats, but he was also criticized by many conservative commentators outside of Congress who brought the story to the attention of the national media in the first place and who helped keep the controversy alive until Lott's resignation on December 20, 2002. Some conservatives said that Lott's remarks were reminiscent of a bygone era and not the current stance of the Republican Party. Observers also suggested that conservatives—long annoyed with what they saw as Lott's willingness as Republican leader to accommodate Senate Democrats—were taking advantage of the situation to try to force Lott out.

Any hope Lott had of retaining his position began to fade on December 12, when President Bush signaled that he would not come to Lott's defense. Although Bush said repeatedly through aides that he did not think it was necessary for Lott to resign, it was clear that the White House was maneuvering behind the scenes to force Lott from the leadership role and to replace him with Sen. Bill Frist, R-Tenn., a heart surgeon in his second term in the Senate. Frist had worked closely with the White House on the midterm Senate election campaign. His demeanor, background, and political philosophy more closely represented the image of Republicanism the White House was seeking to advance.

The Lott controversy erupted at an awkward time for the White House. On December 2 the Supreme Court announced that it would hear arguments in an affirmative action case involving the University of Michigan's admissions policies. The case was likely to pit conservatives who opposed affirmative action and were the core supporters of the Republican Party against blacks and other racial and ethnic minorities who generally supported affirmative action and whose votes the party was trying to woo. By year's end the Bush administration had not announced its position on the case.

A "Terrible" Remark

When he attended a party on December 5 celebrating the 100th birthday of Sen. Strom Thurmond, R-S.C., Lott could have been forgiven for doing a little celebrating on his own behalf. Lott's Republican Party had regained control of the Senate in the November 5 election and he was set to become majority leader when the 108th Congress convened in January. Lott was first elected by Senate Republicans to that position in 1996, but until 2001 he had faced a Democratic president, Bill Clinton (1993–2001), who had proved exceedingly effective at thwarting the legislative aspirations of Republicans, especially in the Senate. With Bush's election in 2000 Lott was working with a Republican president, even if a 50–50 split between the parties in the Senate made compromise with the Democrats a prerequisite for passing any controversial legislation. Then in May Sen. James M. Jeffords, R-Vt., announced that he was leaving the Republican Party to become an independent and that he would caucus with the Democrats, giving them the power to organize the Senate, take control of committees, and select the majority leadership. With the unprecedented power-switch during a session, Lott—whom many blamed for Jeffords's defection—was relegated to minority leader. Now, as the 107th Congress drew to a close, Lott was getting ready to assume the Senate's top leadership position once again in the wake of the 2002 elections. (2002 elections, p. 818; Jeffords's switch, Historic Documents of 2001, p. 377)

Then came the comment, which was no doubt intended as a compliment to the retiring Thurmond, that undid Lott's plans. Thurmond, once a Democrat himself, had run for president in 1948 on a segregationist platform as the candidate of the States Rights Party. Lott's comment paid tribute to that campaign. "I want to say this about my state," Lott told the gathering in a Washington hotel. "When Strom Thurmond ran for president, we voted for him. We're proud of it. And if the rest of the country had followed our lead, we wouldn't have had all these problems over all these years."

Although there were audible gasps in the room at Lott's statement, the comment went largely unnoticed publicly until conservative commentators began to call attention to it. Soon questions and criticisms were coming from several quarters. Commentators such as William Kristol, editor of the Weekly Standard, *and Charles Krauthammer, writing in the* Washington Post, *as well as the editors of the* National Review *and the* Wall Street Journal *called directly for Lott's resignation or indicated unhappiness with him. Jack F. Kemp, a former secretary of housing and colleague of Lott's when both men were in the House of Representatives, called the remarks "inexplicable, indefensible, and inexcusable." Leaders of the Congressional Black Caucus, whose members were all Democrats, called on the Senate to censure Lott. NAACP president Kweisi Mfume said Lott's statement was "the kind of callous, calculated bigotry that has no place in the halls of Congress."*

Lott initially sought to deflect the criticism. "This was a lighthearted celebration of the 100th birthday of legendary Sen. Strom Thurmond. My comments were not an endorsement of his positions of over 50 years ago, but of the man and his life," he said on December 9. Later in the day Lott issued a brief, written statement apologizing for any offense his remarks may have given. Two days later, Lott offered two more apologies, one in an interview with conservative radio show host Sean Hannity and another on CNN's "Larry King Live." On the Hannity show, Lott said that his remarks had been "terrible" and "insensitive" and that he did not "accept those policies of the past at all." He explained that he had not been referring to Thurmond's past segregationist stance but to his staunch opposition to communism and support for a strong national defense. On the Larry King show, he again disavowed segregationist policies and turned aside calls from Democrats and civil rights leaders that he resign. Lott's office also released a three-page list of his legislative achievements in education, trade with Africa, economic development, and community health care. The release noted that while Lott was majority leader the Senate had honored civil rights activist Rosa Parks, the nine black students that integrated Little Rock schools, and Jackie Robinson, the first black player in major league baseball, as well as minority veterans of World War II.

By that time, however, reporters had dug into Lott's legislative background and found that he had voted against several measures supported by civil rights groups, including an extension of the Voting Rights Act in 1981 and a bill to make Martin Luther King Day a federal holiday. It was also widely reported that Lott had made several appearances before the Council of Conservative Citizens, a white supremacist group in Mississippi, in the late 1980s and early 1990s, and that he had once applauded the organization's members for having "the right principles and the right philosophy." The most damaging revelation was that Lott in 1980 had made a comment virtually identical to his remarks at Thurmond's party. For Rep. John Conyers Jr., D-Mich., an African American, that fact was "chilling confirmation" that Lott's remarks on December 5 "were not an inadvertent slip of the tongue."

Beginning of the End

On December 12, the White House, which had been quiet on the controversy, decided it was to time to speak up. Appearing before a group of religious leaders in Philadelphia, most of them African American, President Bush said: "Any suggestion that the segregated past was acceptable or positive is offensive, and it is wrong. Recent comments by Senator Lott do not reflect the spirit of our country. He has apologized, and rightly so. Every day our nation was segregated was a day that America was unfaithful to our founding ideals. And the founding ideals of our nation and, in fact, the founding ideals of the political party I represent was, and remains today, the equal dignity and equal rights of every American."

Bush's comments were construed not only as an effort to divorce the president from any association with Lott's remarks but also as a signal that the White House had determined that Lott's continuing presence as Senate majority leader could hurt the Republican Party. Party strategists in the White House and elsewhere were beginning to worry that a lingering controversy would both intensify black mistrust of the GOP and turn off Republican voters who did not regard themselves as racist and did not want to be associated with those who were or appeared to be.

Lott tried twice more to defuse the situation by apologizing, but to little avail. At a news conference in his hometown of Pascagoula, Mississippi, on December 13, Lott said: "I apologize for opening old wounds and hurting many Americans who feel so deeply in this area. I take full responsibility for my remarks. . . . I only hope that people will find it in their heart to forgive me for that grievous mistake on that occasion." Lott also said that he had no plans to step down. "I'm not about to resign for an accusation that I'm something I'm not," he said. On December 16 Lott appeared in a thirty-minute interview on Black Entertainment Television, where he again apologized and asked for forgiveness. In statements that some observers later described as "groveling," Lott also said that he had changed his mind about the King holiday and that he supported affirmative action. "I'm for that. I'm for affirmative action, and I've practiced it."

After Lott's December 13 news conference about twenty Republican senators held a conference call in which several expressed concern about keeping Lott in the leadership position. On December 15 Don Nickles of Oklahoma, the assistant GOP leader, who was leaving that office under party term limits, became the first Republican senator to suggest that Lott step down as leader. In a statement Nickles said that he accepted Lott's apology but added that "there are several outstanding senators who are more than capable of effective leadership and I hope we have an opportunity to choose." Sen. John Warner , R-Va., quickly agreed that the Republican caucus should meet soon to decide the matter. "The party's been hurt by it. We're going to be judged by how we handle this," Warner said on CNN.

On December 18 the White House signaled that the controversy had gone on long enough. Secretary of State Colin Powell, who had quietly declined to support Lott several days earlier, now said publicly that he "deplored the sentiments" of Lott's comment. Florida Gov. Jeb Bush, the president's brother, said the controversy was hurting the GOP. "This can't be the topic of conversation over the next week," the governor said. Lott on December 20 conceded the inevitable and announced he was stepping down as majority leader but that he would remain in the Senate.

By that time much of the focus had already turned to choosing his likely successor. Nickles had long wanted to be leader, but his civil rights voting record was nearly identical to Lott's and he was not particularly popular with many of his colleagues. Nickles also had the disadvantage of being opposed by the White House, which had indicated its strong preference for Frist. "Nickles is a traditional Southern conservative who is against everything," an influential Republican told the New York Times. *"The problem with Nickles is that he's not Frist. He's not urbane, he's not sophisticated." Mitch McConnell of Kentucky and Rick Santorum of Pennsylvania had also been known to be interested in the leadership position, but they too gave way in the face of growing support for Frist. By December 20, the day of Lott's resignation, more than half of all Senate Republicans had endorsed Frist, and he was easily elected in a conference call on December 23.*

Lott did not go peacefully. Even before his resignation he railed at the White House for not supporting him. In an interview with the Associated Press on December 22 he said again that his own "inappropriate remark" had caused his downfall. However, he added, "there are people in Washington who have been trying to nail me for a long time. When you're from Mississippi and you're a conservative and you're a Christian, there are a lot of people that don't like that. I fell into their trap and so I have only myself to blame." Lott refused to say exactly who he meant.

African American organizations indicated that they would not abandon the attack on the GOP in the wake of Lott's resignation. The NAACP, the Congressional Black Caucus, the Leadership Conference on Civil Rights, and others all said they were looking to the Republicans to take the next step in dismantling their negative racial attitudes. Lott's resignation was "a good first step for the Republican Party," said Mfume of the NAACP. "Now they've got to reverse four decades of dependence on racial elements in their base. They can do this by embracing the generally accepted remedies for racial discrimination and by replacing the rhetoric of outreach with reality."

Affirmative Action

The Bush administration was given an opportunity to take a stand on one of those remedies for racial discrimination—affirmative action— perhaps sooner than it would have liked. On December 2 the Supreme Court announced that it would hear arguments in two cases challenging the University of Michigan's policy of considering race and ethnicity as a factor in its admission policies. The university argued that the policy was intended to promote racial and ethnic diversity on campus. The challenge came from two prospective white students who said they were illegally discriminated against when the university passed over their applications in favor of blacks and other minorities with the same or lower grades and tests scores. The question concerned whether racial diversity was a "compelling government interest" that could justify consideration of race and ethnicity as factors in admission.

The case—and the Supreme Court decision—were seen as likely to reopen old and divisive debates about affirmative action and as a potential minefield for the Bush administration, which was actively reaching out for support from minority groups and trying to change the party's image

*among African Americans even as its core conservative constituency gen-
erally opposed affirmative action. Bush had tried to skirt the issue by calling for a policy of affirmative access in higher education admissions. In
1997, when Bush was governor of Texas, that state initiated a practice of
granting admission to state public colleges to all high school students who
graduated in the top 10 percent of their classes. The program was set up
after a federal circuit court rejected the University of Texas's affirmative
action program in a case that the Supreme Court did not hear. Fleischer on
December 17 said the "affirmative access" program in Texas "has actually
resulted in a nice increase in minority participation and enrollment at
universities and post-graduate studies. That's what the president has done,
and that's what he supports."*

*The United States was not a party to the Michigan case and was under
no obligation to file a brief. The administration had not intervened at the
appeals level, but there was a strong presumption that the administration
should make its views known on a case of such importance. By year's end,
however, the administration was apparently still debating what to do. Solicitor General Ted Olson, Attorney General John Ashcroft, and Ralph Boyd,
head of the civil rights division in the Justice Department, were said to be
eager to argue against the university policy. White House counsel Alberto R.
Gonzales reportedly cautioned that such a stance would hurt the president's
efforts to draw Hispanics and other minorities into the Republican Party.
Observers suggested that White House political strategist Karl Rove was
likely to resolve the debate, just as he had shaped the White House strategy
regarding Lott. Briefs were due in the case by January 16, 2003.*

> *Following are texts of three statements made by Sen. Trent Lott,
> R-Miss., the first on December 5, 2002, in which he appeared to
> endorse segregationist policies of the past; the second on Decem-
> ber 13, in which he apologized for that comment during a news
> conference in his home town of Pascagoula, Mississippi; and the
> third on December 20, when he announced that he would step
> aside as Senate Republican leader.*

> **The documents were obtained from the Internet at
> congressionaltranscripts&pub=congressionaltranscripts;
> accessed January 3, 2003.**

STATEMENT ABOUT STROM THURMOND

I want to say this about my state. When Strom Thurmond ran for president,
we voted for him. We're proud of it. And if the rest of the country had followed
our lead, we wouldn't have had all these problems over all these years, either.

NEWS CONFERENCE STATEMENT

Well, first, thank you for being here and giving me an opportunity to comment further on a number of things that have occurred and been said over the past few days. I have a prepared statement, and then I have a brief announcement, and then I'd be glad to take your questions.

Segregation is a stain on our nation's soul. There's no other way to describe it. It represents one of the lowest moments in our nation's history, and we can never forget that.

I grew up with segregation here in these communities, but I want to note that in these communities of Pascagoula and Moss Point, Gautier and Ocean Springs, Mississippi, we worked hard to overcome that and to bring about reconciliation and to work together.

I grew up in an environment that condoned policies and views that we now know were wrong and immoral, and I repudiate them.

Let me be clear: Segregation and racism are immoral.

I feel very strongly about my faith. I grew up in a local church here. I actively participate. And as I've grown older, I have come to realize more and more, if you feel strongly about that, you cannot in any way support discrimination or unfairness for anybody. It's just not consistent with the beliefs that I feel so strongly about.

I've seen what that type of thing in the past can do to families, to schools and to communities. I've seen personally the destruction it's wrought on lives and good people. I've known many of them personally. And I know that there are terrible harms that have come out of that era.

The president was right when he said that every day our nation was segregated was a day that America was unfaithful to our founding principals and our founding fathers. I lived through those troubled times in the South. And along with the South, I have learned from the mistakes of our past.

I've asked and I'm asking for forbearance and forgiveness as I continue to learn from my own mistakes, and as I continue to grow and get older. But as you get older, you hopefully grow in your views and your acceptance of everybody, both as a person and certainly as a leader.

With regard to my remarks about Strom Thurmond, Senator Thurmond is a friend. He's a colleague. And if no other reason, because he's a 100 years old and still a member of the Senate, he's legendary.

But he came to understand the evil of segregation and the wrongness of his own views. And to his credit, he's said as much himself.

Last week, I was privileged to join hundreds of others to honor him.

It was a lighthearted affair. But my choice of words were totally unacceptable and insensitive, and I apologize for that.

Let me make clear, though, in celebrating his life, I didn't mean in any way to suggest that his views of over 50 years ago on segregation were justified or right. It was wrong and immoral then, and it is now.

By the time I came to know Strom Thurmond, some 40 years after he ran for president—I knew of him when I was in the House of Representatives; I didn't really get to know him until I started running for the Senate and moved over to the Senate—he had long since renounced many of the views of the past, the repugnant views he had had, and he made public himself.

That said, I apologize for opening old wounds and hurting many Americans who feel so deeply in this area.

I take full responsibility for my remarks. I can't say it was prepared remarks. As a matter of fact, I was winging it. I was too much into the moment.

But I only hope that people will find it in their heart to forgive me for that grievous mistake on that occasion.

Not only have I seen the destruction by these immoral policies of the past, I have tried to and will continue to do everything in my power to ensure that we never go back to that type of society again.

I have worked in this town, in this county and in this state to try to help people, to bring about reconciliation, to reach out to people of all race, colors, religions, to give them a chance to get a better education, to get a job. That's the best way I can think of to help liberate people, to help them be able to get a good paying job.

And this is a blue collar, working-class community, and we've been blessed with the opportunities we've had here because we're a blue collar, working-class community.

Now, there'll be some disagreement on the best ways to ensure that every American—every American—of every color and race and ethnic background has a fair and equal chance in life. But our goals are the same, even though we'll debate it on philosophical or partisan lines.

We want a color-blind society that every American has an opportunity to succeed; an end to the entrenched poverty and joblessness that has plagued minority communities and communities of all kinds in this state and across this nation; a good education for every child, that gives him a real chance for a good life and that rejects the soft racism of low expectations.

I benefited from a public education in this state. I was able to go on to college and to get a law degree. So did my wife and so did both of my children, both in public schools in Virginia and in Mississippi. And it gave us the chance that we want everybody to have to get a good education and then go on to have a profession and get a job.

We need strict enforcement of civil rights laws on the books and all laws on the books to guarantee equality and punish racism.

Government does best when it helps people help themselves. You've heard that phrase before. Human dignity is found not in a handout but a hand up to help people to be able to do more for themselves and their children and their grandchildren and their future.

Government should be about giving people a real chance to do for themselves and help themselves to live the American dream. I believe this because I have lived it.

My father, when I was born, was a sharecropper—yes, a sharecropper. He raised cotton on somebody else's land in a county where everybody was poor, regardless of race or anything else. Almost everybody was barely making it.

And then, of course, we came to down Pascagoula. My dad was a shipyard worker, and my mother taught school. So I have lived this dream.

I was their only son; the first to earn a graduate degree. And I feel so strongly that everything I've been able to do, in my education, in my opportunities in life and in my political career, is evidence that, no matter where you're from or what your background of your parents or what your race is, you can, if you work hard and take advantage of the opportunities, get a good education, you can live this American dream.

To those who believe that I was implying that this dream is for some and not for all, that's just not true. But I apologize for those that got that impression.

I work in this state to try to make sure that all Mississippians have a chance at the American dream. And I will continue to do that as long as I live.

In the days and months to come, I will dedicate myself to undo the hurt I have caused and will do all that I can to contribute to a society where every American has an opportunity to succeed.

As a man of faith in a local church here, I read the Bible all of my life. I now more fully understand the psalm that says, "a broken spirit, a contrite and humbled heart."

One final point: The next step to make sure that these are not just words here today is I am talking to and working with African-American leaders like Roy Innis, of the Congress of Racial Equality, and Bob Johnson, of Black Entertainment Television.

And in that vein we are working to get the final agreement on a time next week—early next week when, for a full hour, I will talk about my hopes and dreams for the people in this state and this country regardless of their race, and to make sure that African-Americans have the opportunities that they deserve.

That was the announcement I was going to make. Now I would be glad to take your questions. . . .

Question: Senator Lott, a lot of conservative commentators have called for you to step down as Senate Republican leader. Have any Senate Republicans come to you privately and asked you to step down or perhaps talked to you about a Senate censure for what you said, even though you've already apologized?

Lott: No senator has spoken to me about the possibility of me stepping down directly, publicly or privately; certainly not any Republican senator. A lot of senators have called to say they're—frankly, they're praying for me, to offer suggestions and ideas of what we can do to, you know, have something positive come out of all of this.

But, you know, I'm not about to resign for an accusation that I'm something I'm not.

And my colleagues have been very good about calling. Even, you know, Senator Paul Simon from Illinois from was at the event. He's a Democrat, ran for president, a pretty liberal Democrat, really nice guy. I'm crazy about him too. He brought over and introduced me to his wife, because his first wife I had known and passed away a couple of years ago.

He called and said, "Look, I was there. I saw the tone of the event. I heard what you said. I in no way, you know, read into it what has been inferred." And so, I mean, that's what a Democrat said.

Some people might be surprised that Jim Jeffords hadn't exactly made my life a, you know, bowl of cherries the last year and a half, but Jim Jeffords put out a statement saying, "I know this guy. I have been in 15 or so states with him around the country. Never did he utter one word"—these are not his words, but basically saying, "This is not the Trent Lott I know. I may not agree with him on how much funding for that, you know, some education program, but I know the man." And I appreciate him doing that.

Yes?

Question: Mr. Leader, you said you were winging it last week. You winged it in the same way in 1980 (inaudible) the same comment in the newspaper here. And even regarding issues like Martin Luther King's birthday, the Voting Rights Act, Strom Thurmond voted for Martin Luther King holiday. You voted against it. I wonder if you could see how your actions don't inspire a lot of confidence in some people, particularly in the African-American community.

Lott: Well, I've heard about the 1980 incident, and I don't deny that that, you know, almost the same words were used.

I mean, for many years I'd go up to Senator Thurmond—some of you know where he sits there on the floor, and, you know, we've had—I'd kid with him and say, "Strom, you'd have made a great president." And he always looked up and smiled big. And it was just that kind of a, you know, platonic, almost father/son relationship that we had.

But you know, there are a number of issues that I have voted for and supported over the years. Look, Martin Luther King Jr. was a premiere civil rights leader in this country a little over the last 50 years.

And while I have never supported additional holidays, because I think they are—they cost a huge amount of money—$325 million is the statistic I have—one of the things I have done, for instance, is I did vote to put a bust in the Capitol because there was a lot of support for it, and I thought that that was something that would help bring about reconciliation.

Also, I was the author of the resolution commemorating Juneteenth Independence Day—June 19, 1865, the day on which slavery finally came to an end in the United States. I did that.

And some people were surprised about it, but, you know—and I've been working with a number of African-American leaders to try to get a suitable memorial, a monument on the Mall.

I made the point in an interview three weeks ago, well before this developed, that I had seen some leaders over the year that, you know, might surprise you. And one of them was Charlie Rangel of New York who worked with me when we passed the Africa free trade bill. And at one point, it was about to die. And I talked with him, and he said, "No, I don't want to blame anybody for what we didn't get done. Let's get this done."

He and I worked together. We passed a bill. It will be a bill in the end that will help the people in Africa and that will help the people in America, because trade is good.

Somebody will argue with me about that in this state, but I think that free trade, like freedom and free enterprise, is what America is based on. . . .

Question: (Off-mike.)

Lott: You know, when I see Strom Thurmond, the Strom Thurmond I have known, this is a man that was chairman of the Armed Services Committee, so I see strong national defense.

He was chairman of the Judiciary Committee. I remember when I first moved over to the Senate, I thought, "Gosh, can he still give a—you know, a strong speech." He got in the center aisle, gave a strong speech about how unfair crime is and the need for strong law enforcement. I presume it was a crime law reform; I don't remember the particular bill.

This is a man that has always said that, "Look, we got to encourage growth, but we got to have fiscal responsibility; we need to look at the bottom line, make sure that we don't create long-term problems for ourselves by overspending or any other practice that will cause problems for our children." That's the guy I knew.

But instead of that, really, it was just an effort to help—encourage an elderly gentleman to feel good on that occasion of his 100th birthday.

So there were no venal thoughts in my mind. But those are the things I thought about. . . .

Question: Senator, you and your office have issues several apologies and clarifications over the last several days. Why did you feel the need to come here and expound upon that? Were you pressured by anyone in Washington to come here today?

Lott: No, first of all, I was in Washington last week. I can't remember what day this birthday party was—Wednesday or Thursday. I was there Thursday, Friday, Saturday—events, went to events Saturday, Sunday, Monday.

I left Tuesday afternoon and had lots of, you know, contacts with the media, and there was not much being said about it. And then, all of a sudden, of course, when (inaudible) got, you know, quite active and I was in a remote area, and the only way I could communicate was in writing or in—at that point, this was Wednesday and Thursday—or by radio hookup with Larry King and Sean Hannity.

But the main reason I'm here today is because I'm home, I'm in Mississippi. And the first person I called on was local media.

I knew I needed to do this with my local people anyway. And so since I had not actually stood up and taken questions from the national media because of my location for the last three days, it seemed like the logical thing to do. I didn't want to, you know, be running back and forth doing one, two or 100 interviews. This seemed like a better way to do it. . . .

Question: Senator, before the president publicly denounced your comments, did he contact you, did he say anything?

Lott: I did receive a call, and his remarks were read to me. I said, "That sounds fine." You know, they were terrible words. I apologized, and rightly so, that's what he said.

And I talked to him after his trip to Philadelphia yesterday. And we have a very close relationship, and we talked about it. And, you know, it was a very positive conversation. I'm not going to quote him, because you're not supposed to.

But, look, I've talked to everybody that I can get on the phone, the president, the vice president, the president's chief of staff. Probably 50 or 55 senators that are strung all across the country and the world and a lot of individuals, leaders in Congress, in Washington, African-American leaders and others. . . .

RESIGNATION ANNOUNCEMENT

In the interest of pursuing the best possible agenda for the future of our country, I will not seek to remain as Majority Leader of the United States Senate for the 108th Congress, effective January 6, 2003. To all those who offered me their friendship, support and prayers, I will be eternally grateful. I will continue to serve the people of Mississippi in the United States Senate.

JIMMY CARTER ON RECEIVING THE NOBEL PEACE PRIZE
December 10, 2002

Jimmy Carter, who was turned out of the presidency by American voters in 1980 and then became the country's foremost international advocate of democracy and human rights, received the 2002 Nobel Peace Prize. Carter used his speech accepting the prize, on December 10, 2002, to promote the causes to which he had devoted his life after the presidency, including the peaceful resolution of international disputes. Many observers, including the chairman of the Norwegian committee that awarded the prize, drew a contrast between Carter's passionate advocacy of peace and the steady buildup toward war in Iraq by one of his successors, the current president, George W. Bush.

Carter was just the third U.S. president to win the honor, after Theodore Roosevelt and Woodrow Wilson. Roosevelt was honored in 1906 for his successful mediation of a peace agreement ending the 1905 war between Japan and Russia. Wilson was honored in 1919 for his advocacy of the League of Nations, an organization the United States never joined because Wilson failed to win support for it in the Senate.

Carter served as president from 1977 to 1981, leaving office after he lost his bid for reelection to Ronald Reagan (1981–1989). The conventional wisdom in the subsequent two decades was that Carter's presidency was a failure on many counts but his postpresidency was among the most successful ever. The Nobel Peace Prize committee chose to highlight Carter's greatest success as president: his mediation of the September 1978 Camp David peace agreement that led six months later to a formal peace treaty between Egypt and Israel. Carter did not receive the peace prize in 1978 because his nomination had not been made in time—a rebuff that aides later said was deeply disappointing to him. The 1978 prize went instead to the two leaders who Carter had persuaded to take the political risks of accepting the Camp David accord, Egyptian president Anwar al-Sadat and Israeli prime minister Menachem Begin. (Camp David agreement, Historic Documents of 1978, p. 605; Historic Documents of 1979, p.223)

The Award to Carter

In recent decades the annual awarding of the Nobel Peace Prize often had been widely interpreted as a political statement by the Norwegian parliamentary committee that made the selection. Several recent prizes had gone to dissidents in authoritarian countries—such as former South African archbishop Desmond Tutu in 1984 and Myanmar's opposition leader Aung San Suu Kyi in 1991—or to groups that pushed for peaceful causes in opposition to government policy, such as the U.S.-based International Campaign to Ban Landmines in 1997.

The choice of Carter was widely viewed as a statement of concern by the committee about Bush's evident determination to press for war against Iraq. Carter had said little about Bush's policy on that issue, but Gunnar Berge, chairman of the Nobel committee, explicitly contrasted Carter's long-term advocacy of peace with the Bush administration's actions. "It should be interpreted as a criticism of the line that the current administration has taken," Berge said of the award to Carter on October 11. "It's a kick in the leg to all that follow the same line as the United States." Other committee members distanced themselves from that interpretation, but the language used by the committee seemed to lend some support to Berge's comment. "In a situation currently marked by threats of the use of force, Carter has stood by the principles that conflicts must as far as possible be resolved through mediation and international cooperation based on international law, respect for human rights, and economic development," the committee's citation said.

Carter took a diplomatic approach when asked, at an October 12 news conference, about the "message" the Nobel committee was sending the world through the award. "My hope is that the message that I've been delivering in the last few months, in a very small way—that we should work through the United Nations in dealing with crises on earth, like the Iraq issue—will be heard clearly," Carter said. Carter added that he expected the UN Security Council to "take strong action" demanding that Iraqi leader Saddam Hussein comply with longstanding requirements that he give up illegal biological and chemical weapons and other armaments. The Security Council did adopt such a resolution on November 8. (Iraq resolution, p. 713)

In addition to Carter's mediation of the Camp David agreement, the Nobel committee cited the former president for his seemingly tireless work on behalf of human rights and democracy around the world. As president, Carter had formally adopted the promotion of human rights as a major element of U.S. foreign policy, the first time that goal had been elevated alongside such traditional standards as fighting communism and protecting U.S. commercial interests overseas.

After leaving the presidency Carter in 1982 founded the nonprofit Carter Center in Atlanta, Georgia, which he used as the base for his campaigns on behalf of his causes around the world. Carter was particularly interested in promoting free and open elections in countries just beginning to embrace democracy. Between 1989 and late 2002 the Carter Center monitored forty-five elections in twenty-three countries, setting what was to become the international standard for independent scrutiny of the political process. In many cases Carter's personal stamp of approval—or disapproval—meant the difference in whether the rest of the world accepted the legitimacy of an election. After the political and legal crisis over the handling of 2000 U.S. presidential election results in Florida, Carter wryly noted that he had witnessed better management of elections in several poor countries that had experienced democracy for the first time. In 2001 Carter and former president Gerald R. Ford led an independent commission that recommended sweeping electoral reforms in the United States. (Florida election, Historic Documents of 2000, p. 999; election reforms, Historic Documents of 2001, p. 522)

One of Carter's most important achievements of recent years appeared to be in the process of coming undone during 2002—his 1994 intervention in a crisis in North Korea, which at the time was threatening to build nuclear weapons with plutonium it was processing from a power plant. Carter made the initial diplomatic contacts that led to an "agreed framework" under which North Korea agreed to halt its nuclear weapons program in exchange for aid for its energy needs from the United States, Japan, and South Korea. The Bush administration in 2002 developed evidence that North Korea was violating that agreement; pressed on the matter, Pyongyang late in the year said it would withdraw from the 1994 accord and restart the reactor that had been shut down. (North Korea weapons issue, p. 731; Agreed framework, Historic Documents of 1994, p. 603)

Two other high-profile efforts by Carter had yet to bear fruit as of the end of 2002. In May Carter visited Cuba and pressed that country's dictator, Fidel Castro, to take a step toward democracy by acting on a petition signed by more than 11,000 people calling for free elections. Castro allowed Carter to address the Cuban people over national television, a radical step in a country where the public's access to news was tightly controlled. Castro did not schedule the free elections, however. Carter also flew to Venezuela in July for meetings with President Hugo Chavez and a coalition of business and labor leaders who were trying to oust him from power. Carter failed to bring the two sides together for negotiations, however, and Venezuela fell into a near anarchic state later in the year when opposition groups mounted a series of general strikes. (Venezuela crisis, p. 201; Carter in Cuba, p. 232)

Yet another Carter passion was promoting education and health initiatives in developing countries. Many observers said his greatest single success in that regard was a battle against the parasitic disease known as guinea worm infection, which endangered millions of people in Asia and Africa. The Carter Center in 1986 launched a campaign to wipe out the disease. By 2002 the number of reported cases had been reduced by about 98 percent.

The Nobel committee selected Carter from a record 156 nominees. Another leading candidate reportedly was Hamid Karzai, the new president of Afghanistan who was attempting to restore peace and stability there. Karzai congratulated Carter, saying "he had many, many years of work for peace in a very concerted way, in a very human way. . . . He deserved it better than I, and he won it, and I'll try for next year." Other serious candidates included rock star Bono, who was leading an international campaign for increased Western aid to impoverished countries in Africa and other regions; and the UN War Crimes Tribunal for the former Yugoslavia, which was hearing cases against former Yugoslav leader Slobodan Milosevic and others accused of widespread killings during the Balkan wars of the 1990s. (Afghanistan recovery, p. 15; Milosevic case, Historic Documents of 2001, p. 826)

Carter's Nobel Speech

Carter formally accepted the Nobel Peace Prize at the traditional ceremony in Oslo on December 10, the anniversary of the death in 1896 of the prize's benefactor, dynamite manufacturer Alfred Nobel. Although much of the talk surrounding Carter's prize dealt with his advocacy of peace in a time of gathering war, Nobel chairman Berge noted another aspect of the former president's work on behalf of his causes. "Every year we see pictures of Jimmy and Rosalynn [Carter's wife] in a slum somewhere or other, busy building housing for and together with the poor," Berge said in introducing Carter. "While there must have been good opportunities for an expresident to make money for himself, Carter has instead through Habitat for Humanity and the Atlanta Project [two agencies that provided housing for the poor] wielded hammer and saw for the benefit of others."

Berge also lamented the panel's failure to award the prize to Carter in 1978 or in the many intervening years when he was nominated. "It became increasingly obvious that the bypassing of Carter had been one of the real sins of omission in Peace Prize history," he said. "This year we can finally put all that behind us."

Carter used his acceptance speech to plea for international action on behalf of peace and human rights, and to gently prod the Bush administration to continue working through the United Nations as it sought to disarm Iraq. "It is clear that global challenges must be met by an emphasis on peace, in harmony with others, with strong alliances and international consensus," he said. "Imperfect as it may be, there is no doubt that this can best be done through the United Nations." War, Carter said in concluding his speech, "may sometimes be a necessary evil. But no matter how necessary, it is always an evil, never a good. We will not learn how to live together in peace by killing each other's children."

Following is the text of Jimmy Carter's speech on December 10, 2002, upon his acceptance of the Nobel Peace Prize.

The document was obtained from the Internet at www .cartercenter.org/viewdoc.asp?docID=1233&submenu= news; accessed February 18, 2003.

It is with a deep sense of gratitude that I accept this prize. I am grateful to my wife Rosalynn, to my colleagues at The Carter Center, and to many others who continue to seek an end to violence and suffering throughout the world. The scope and character of our Center's activities are perhaps unique, but in many other ways they are typical of the work being done by many hundreds of nongovernmental organizations that strive for human rights and peace.

Most Nobel laureates have carried out our work in safety, but there are others who have acted with great personal courage. None has provided more vivid reminders of the dangers of peacemaking than two of my friends, Anwar Sadat and Yitzhak Rabin, who gave their lives for the cause of peace in the Middle East.

Like these two heroes, my first chosen career was in the military, as a submarine officer. My shipmates and I realized that we had to be ready to fight if combat was forced upon us, and we were prepared to give our lives to defend our nation and its principles. At the same time, we always prayed fervently that our readiness would ensure that there would be no war.

Later, as President and as Commander-in-Chief of our armed forces, I was one of those who bore the sobering responsibility of maintaining global stability during the height of the Cold War, as the world's two superpowers confronted each other. Both sides understood that an unresolved political altercation or a serious misjudgment could lead to a nuclear holocaust. In Washington and in Moscow, we knew that we would have less than a half hour to respond after we learned that intercontinental missiles had been launched against us. There had to be a constant and delicate balancing of our great military strength with aggressive diplomacy, always seeking to build friendships with other nations, large and small, that shared a common cause.

In those days, the nuclear and conventional armaments of the United States and the Soviet Union were almost equal, but democracy ultimately prevailed because of commitments to freedom and human rights, not only by people in my country and those of our allies, but in the former Soviet empire as well. As president, I extended my public support and encouragement to Andrei Sakharov, who, although denied the right to attend the ceremony, was honored here for his personal commitments to these same ideals.

The world has changed greatly since I left the White House. Now there is only one superpower, with unprecedented military and economic strength. The coming budget for American armaments will be greater than those of the next fifteen nations combined, and there are troops from the United States in many countries throughout the world. Our gross national economy exceeds that of the three countries that follow us, and our nation's voice most often prevails as decisions are made concerning trade, humanitarian assistance, and the allocation of global wealth. This dominant status is unlikely to change in our lifetimes.

Great American power and responsibility are not unprecedented, and have been used with restraint and great benefit in the past. We have not assumed that super strength guarantees super wisdom, and we have consistently reached out to the international community to ensure that our own power and influence are tempered by the best common judgment.

Within our country, ultimate decisions are made through democratic means, which tend to moderate radical or ill-advised proposals. Constrained and inspired by historic constitutional principles, our nation has endeavored for more than two hundred years to follow the now almost universal ideals of freedom, human rights, and justice for all.

Our president, Woodrow Wilson, was honored here for promoting the League of Nations, whose two basic concepts were profoundly important: "collective security" and "self-determination." Now they are embedded in international law. Violations of these premises during the last half-century have been tragic failures, as was vividly demonstrated when the Soviet Union attempted to conquer Afghanistan and when Iraq invaded Kuwait.

After the second world war, American Secretary of State Cordell Hull received this prize for his role in founding the United Nations. His successor, General George C. Marshall, was recognized because of his efforts to help rebuild Europe, without excluding the vanquished nations of Italy and Germany. This was a historic example of respecting human rights at the international level.

Ladies and gentlemen:

Twelve years ago, President Mikhail Gorbachev received your recognition for his preeminent role in ending the Cold War that had lasted fifty years.

But instead of entering a millennium of peace, the world is now, in many ways, a more dangerous place. The greater ease of travel and communication has not been matched by equal understanding and mutual respect. There is a plethora of civil wars, unrestrained by rules of the Geneva Convention, within which an overwhelming portion of the casualties are unarmed civilians who have no ability to defend themselves. And recent appalling acts of terrorism have reminded us that no nations, even superpowers, are invulnerable.

It is clear that global challenges must be met with an emphasis on peace, in harmony with others, with strong alliances and international consensus. Imperfect as it may be, there is no doubt that this can best be done through the United Nations, which Ralph Bunche described here in this same forum as exhibiting a "fortunate flexibility"—not merely to preserve peace but also to make change, even radical change, without violence.

He went on to say: "To suggest that war can prevent war is a base play on words and a despicable form of warmongering. The objective of any who sincerely believe in peace clearly must be to exhaust every honorable recourse in the effort to save the peace. The world has had ample evidence that war begets only conditions that beget further war."

We must remember that today there are at least eight nuclear powers on earth, and three of them are threatening to their neighbors in areas of great international tension. For powerful countries to adopt a principle of preventive war may well set an example that can have catastrophic consequences.

If we accept the premise that the United Nations is the best avenue for the maintenance of peace, then the carefully considered decisions of the United Nations Security Council must be enforced. All too often, the alternative has proven to be uncontrollable violence and expanding spheres of hostility.

For more than half a century, following the founding of the State of Israel in 1948, the Middle East conflict has been a source of worldwide tension.

At Camp David in 1978 and in Oslo in 1993, Israelis, Egyptians, and Palestinians have endorsed the only reasonable prescription for peace: United Nations Resolution 242. It condemns the acquisition of territory by force, calls for withdrawal of Israel from the occupied territories, and provides for Israelis to live securely and in harmony with their neighbors. There is no other mandate whose implementation could more profoundly improve international relationships.

Perhaps of more immediate concern is the necessity for Iraq to comply fully with the unanimous decision of the Security Council that it eliminate all weapons of mass destruction and permit unimpeded access by inspectors to confirm that this commitment has been honored. The world insists that this be done.

I thought often during my years in the White House of an admonition that we received in our small school in Plains, Georgia, from a beloved teacher, Miss Julia Coleman. She often said: "We must adjust to changing times and still hold to unchanging principles."

When I was a young boy, this same teacher also introduced me to Leo Tolstoy's novel, "War and Peace." She interpreted that powerful narrative as a reminder that the simple human attributes of goodness and truth can overcome great power. She also taught us that an individual is not swept along on a tide of inevitability but can influence even the greatest human events.

These premises have been proven by the lives of many heroes, some of whose names were little known outside their own regions until they became Nobel laureates: Albert John Lutuli, Norman Borlaug, Desmond Tutu, Elie Wiesel, Aung San Suu Kyi, Jody Williams, and even Albert Schweitzer and Mother Teresa. All of these and others have proven that even without government power—and often in opposition to it—individuals can enhance human rights and wage peace, actively and effectively.

The Nobel prize also profoundly magnified the inspiring global influence of Martin Luther King, Jr., the greatest leader that my native state has ever produced. On a personal note, it is unlikely that my political career beyond Georgia would have been possible without the changes brought about by the civil rights movement in the American south and throughout our nation.

On the steps of our memorial to Abraham Lincoln, Dr. King said: "I have a dream that on the red hills of Georgia the sons of former slaves and the sons of former slaveowners will be able to sit down together at a table of brotherhood."

The scourge of racism has not been vanquished, either in the red hills of our state or around the world. And yet we see ever more frequent manifestations of his dream of racial healing. In a symbolic but very genuine way, at least involving two Georgians, it is coming true in Oslo today.

I am not here as a public official, but as a citizen of a troubled world who finds hope in a growing consensus that the generally accepted goals of society are peace, freedom, human rights, environmental quality, the alleviation of suffering, and the rule of law.

During the past decades, the international community, usually under the auspices of the United Nations, has struggled to negotiate global standards

987

that can help us achieve these essential goals. They include: the abolition of land mines and chemical weapons; an end to the testing, proliferation, and further deployment of nuclear warheads; constraints on global warming; prohibition of the death penalty, at least for children; and an international criminal court to deter and to punish war crimes and genocide. Those agreements already adopted must be fully implemented, and others should be pursued aggressively.

We must also strive to correct the injustice of economic sanctions that seek to penalize abusive leaders but all too often inflict punishment on those who are already suffering from the abuse.

The unchanging principles of life predate modern times. I worship Jesus Christ, whom we Christians consider to be the Prince of Peace. As a Jew, he taught us to cross religious boundaries, in service and in love. He repeatedly reached out and embraced Roman conquerors, other Gentiles, and even the more despised Samaritans.

Despite theological differences, all great religions share common commitments that define our ideal secular relationships. I am convinced that Christians, Muslims, Buddhists, Hindus, Jews, and others can embrace each other in a common effort to alleviate human suffering and to espouse peace.

But the present era is a challenging and disturbing time for those whose lives are shaped by religious faith based on kindness toward each other. We have been reminded that cruel and inhuman acts can be derived from distorted theological beliefs, as suicide bombers take the lives of innocent human beings, draped falsely in the cloak of God's will. With horrible brutality, neighbors have massacred neighbors in Europe, Asia, and Africa.

In order for us human beings to commit ourselves personally to the inhumanity of war, we find it necessary first to dehumanize our opponents, which is in itself a violation of the beliefs of all religions. Once we characterize our adversaries as beyond the scope of God's mercy and grace, their lives lose all value. We deny personal responsibility when we plant landmines and, days or years later, a stranger to us—often a child—is crippled or killed. From a great distance, we launch bombs or missiles with almost total impunity, and never want to know the number or identity of the victims.

At the beginning of this new millennium I was asked to discuss, here in Oslo, the greatest challenge that the world faces. Among all the possible choices, I decided that the most serious and universal problem is the growing chasm between the richest and poorest people on earth. Citizens of the ten wealthiest countries are now seventy-five times richer than those who live in the ten poorest ones, and the separation is increasing every year, not only between nations but also within them. The results of this disparity are root causes of most of the world's unresolved problems, including starvation, illiteracy, environmental degradation, violent conflict, and unnecessary illnesses that range from Guinea worm to HIV/AIDS.

Most work of The Carter Center is in remote villages in the poorest nations of Africa, and there I have witnessed the capacity of destitute people to persevere under heartbreaking conditions. I have come to admire their judgment and wisdom, their courage and faith, and their awesome accomplishments when given a chance to use their innate abilities.

But tragically, in the industrialized world there is a terrible absence of understanding or concern about those who are enduring lives of despair and hopelessness. We have not yet made the commitment to share with others an appreciable part of our excessive wealth. This is a potentially rewarding burden that we should all be willing to assume.

Ladies and gentlemen:

War may sometimes be a necessary evil. But no matter how necessary, it is always an evil, never a good. We will not learn how to live together in peace by killing each other's children.

The bond of our common humanity is stronger than the divisiveness of our fears and prejudices. God gives us the capacity for choice. We can choose to alleviate suffering. We can choose to work together for peace. We can make these changes—and we must.

Thank you.

CONGRESSIONAL PANEL ON INTELLIGENCE FAILURES
December 11, 2002

A special congressional panel investigating the September 11, 2001, terrorist attacks against the United States found that U.S. intelligence and law enforcement agencies had collected bits of information ahead of time that might have alerted them that a major attack was imminent. That information had not been examined in such a way to give decision makers an adequate warning. In one step to prevent such problems in the future, the committee recommended a revamping of government intelligence services, including the appointment of a cabinet-level director with real control over all agencies that collected and analyzed intelligence.

A joint inquiry by the House and Senate intelligence committees held hearings during the year and issued its final report on December 11, 2002. The inquiry was the first major investigation into why the government failed to detect plans by four teams of men from Arab countries to hijack airplanes and fly them into the World Trade Center towers in New York City, the Pentagon near Washington, and another building in Washington, probably the White House. (September 11 attacks, Historic Documents of 2001, p. 614)

Another panel mandated by Congress to investigate broader issues surrounding the September 11 attacks got off to a rough start later in December when its two senior leaders resigned to avoid potential conflicts of interest. Henry A. Kissinger, former secretary of state for presidents Richard M. Nixon and Gerald R. Ford, nominated by President George W. Bush to chair the panel, and George Mitchell, former Democratic senator from Maine, nominated by congressional Democrats as vice chairman, both resigned shortly after they were appointed. After accepting the posts both men had learned they might have to give up their private work that might conflict with the panel's inquiry. Bush then named former New Jersey governor Thomas Kean to take Kissinger's place, and Democrats named former representative Lee Hamilton, an Indiana Democrat.

Committee's Hearings and Investigation

The joint investigating committee was cochaired by the chairmen of the House and Senate intelligence committees: Rep. Porter J. Goss, R-Fla., a former CIA agent, and Sen. Bob Graham, a Democrat who previously was governor of Florida. The committee's investigation was in some respects the most important probe of U.S. intelligence-gathering since the 1975 hearings chaired by Sen. Frank Church, D-Idaho, which revealed failed CIA plots to assassinate Cuban leader Fidel Castro and other foreigners and the government's spying on U.S. citizens. Those hearings led to legislation curbing domestic espionage and imposing ethical restraints on CIA activities overseas. (Church committee investigations, Historic Documents of 1975, pp. 709, 799)

The September 11 committee itself hit a rough patch even before its work got under way. Its first staff director, L. Britt Snider, a former CIA inspector general, was forced to resign after only two months on the job because he had hired a staff aide who had once failed a CIA polygraph test. The choice of Snider had been criticized by some conservatives in Washington because of his ties with the intelligence community, particularly CIA director George Tenet. To replace Snider the committee hired Eleanor Hill, who also had years of experience in intelligence work.

After several months of exploratory work by a staff of thirty experts, the panel began its inquiry on June 4 with closed-door hearings. The hearings also followed several months of news reports that raised questions about how much the Bush administration—and the Clinton administration before it—knew of, but did not understand, the planning for the September 11 attacks. "Connecting the dots" became the panel's theme question: Why hadn't intelligence agencies put together the bits of information they had collected to form a rough picture of the al Qaeda terrorists' plans?

The committee opened its public hearings on September 18 with a lengthy statement by Hill detailing the preliminary results of the staff's investigations. The bulk of Hill's statement dealt with a history of operations by the al Qaeda terrorist network, headed by Saudi Arabian exile Osama bin Laden, and the efforts of the U.S. intelligence agencies to track those operations. The inquiry had produced no smoking gun pointing to one or more specific failures that made the United States vulnerable to the September 11 attacks. Hill told committee members: "No one will ever know if September 11 could have been avoided. It's one 'if' after another."

In their testimony before the joint committee on October 17, senior officials of the intelligence services acknowledged shortcomings in their operations before the September 11 attacks but defended their agencies' overall operations and efforts to deal with terrorism and said problems were being corrected. For example, Lieutenant General Michael V. Hayden, director of the National Security Agency, acknowledged criticism that his agency did not have enough linguists in Arabic and other languages , saying the "downsizing" of his staff was a result of budget cuts during the 1990s. "I am not *really helped by being reminded that I need more Arabic linguists or by someone second-guessing an obscure [communications] intercept sitting in our files that may make more sense today than it did two years ago," he said.*

Responding to allegations that the Federal Bureau of Investigation and the Central Intelligence Agecny had engaged in turf battles that limited their cooperation, FBI director Robert S. Mueller III told the panel, also on October 17, that the relationship between the two agencies "has never been stronger or more productive." Tenet said the CIA had disrupted numerous terrorist plots before and after September 11, but he acknowledged that more terrorism could be expected. "It is important for the American people to know that despite the enormous successes we've had in the past year, indeed over many years, al Qaeda continues to plan and will attempt more deadly strikes against us," Tenet said. "There will be more battles won and, sadly, more battles lost."

Committee Findings

After the hearings, the joint panel began work on its report, which was completed in draft form in late November, submitted to the administration for review, approved by the committee on December 10, and made public in final form the next day. In essence, the panel found that U.S. intelligence had not shifted enough attention from threats of the past to current threats, notably terrorism. Graham gave this summary conclusion: "The intelligence community was not properly postured to meet the threat of global terrorism against the people of the United States."

In its key findings of systemwide failures, the panel said the intelligence agencies had not paid enough attention to the potential for terrorist attacks inside the United States; had not developed a "comprehensive strategy" for dealing with bin Laden, even though his capabilities and intentions were well known; had not been able to coordinate in one place all the available information about terrorist threats; and did not share information.

Although the intelligence agencies had collected large quantities of information about bin Laden and his al Qaeda organization, the panel said, "none of it identified the time, place, and specific nature of the attacks that were planned for September 11, 2001." But the agencies did collect information that in hindsight was "clearly relevant" to the attacks. Among those bits of information were:

- *Early in 2000 the CIA identified two of the men who would become hijackers (Khalid al-Mihdhar and Nawaf al-Hazmi) as having attended a meeting of al Qaeda operatives that January in Malaysia. That information "lay dormant within the intelligence community for eighteen months"—the period when the September 11 attacks were being planned, the report said. The names of the two men were not placed on the State Department's "watch list" (used by U.S. immigration authorities to identify security risks) until a few weeks before the Septem-*

ber 11 attacks. In the meantime, the two men had entered the United States, and no effort was made to track their movements or activities.

- *FBI agents in Minneapolis and Phoenix sent memos to FBI headquarters in Washington and other offices suggesting a possible connection between terrorism and civil aviation in the United States, but adequate follow-up action was not taken. In August 2001 the FBI and the Immigration and Naturalization Service detained Zacarias Moussaoui, a French citizen of Algerian heritage, because of suspicions that he was involved in a hijacking plot. But because of bureaucratic mistakes, the FBI did not obtain a warrant to search Moussaoui's belongings and he was never linked with other information about potential terrorism. After September 11 the FBI concluded that Moussaoui was to have been the twentieth hijacker.*

  Perhaps even more perplexing, in retrospect, was the fate of a July 10, 2001, memo from a FBI agent in Phoenix suggesting that bin Laden was trying to "establish a cadre of individuals in civil aviation who would conduct future terrorist activity." The agent suggested several specific steps to pursue his theory, but none of them had been taken before September 11 because, the congressional panel said, his memo "generated little or no interest" at FBI headquarters or the New York field office that handled many terrorism issues.

- *The intelligence community misunderstood the importance of Khalid Sheikh Mohammed, who later was identified as al Qaeda's "mastermind" of the September 11 attacks. Intelligence agencies had information linking him "to terrorist plans to use aircraft as weapons, and to terrorist activity in the United States," the panel said. But the agencies did not recognize the significance of his role nor did they try to collect information that might have shed light on his planning of the attacks.*

- *In the three days just before the attacks, the National Security Agency intercepted "some communications that indicated possible impending terrorist activity." But the agency did not translate or disseminate that information until after the attacks.*

Reflecting on the totality of such bits of information, plus others that remained classified, the panel said the intelligence agencies "missed opportunities to disrupt the September 11 plot" through investigative work and such actions as detaining the hijackers. "No one will ever know what might have happened had more connections been drawn between these disparate pieces of information," the panel said.

Committee Recommendations

The special panel made nineteen specific recommendations for improving U.S. counterterrorism operations. Some involved systemwide changes, such as putting one director in charge of all the intelligence agencies, and others dealt with such specific steps as the hiring of more linguists and other specialists by the agencies.

Because of its ramifications for Washington politics and the bureau-cracy, the recommendation for a higher level intelligence director was by far the most controversial of the panel's findings. A director of national intelli-gence, the panel said, should have "the full range of management, budgetary, and personnel responsibilities needed to make the entire U.S. Intelligence Community operate as a whole." The director should be a member of the president's cabinet and should not be the same person who headed the CIA or any other intelligence agency, the panel said. In terms of ensuring that the director had real clout in Washington's bureaucracy, the panel's most important recommendation was that he or she control the budgets of all in-telligence agencies.

In effect, the recommendation would revise and give substance to what had been a theoretical proposition for many years—that a director of cen-tral intelligence would supervise and coordinate all the intelligence ser-vices. Under the current system, that position was held by the CIA director, who had little influence over the other intelligence agencies. Similar recom-mendations to give a single intelligence director real power over all the agencies had been proposed by other panels and considered by Congress over the years but had never gone anywhere. A principle reason was that the De-fense Department resisted putting its intelligence responsibilities under the supervision of a non-Pentagon official. Although the CIA was the best known of the U.S. intelligence agencies, more than three-fourths of the govern-ment's estimated $38 billion intelligence budget was controlled by several Pentagon agencies, including the Defense Intelligence Agency (which was responsible for tactical intelligence about enemy military capabilities), the National Security Agency (which intercepted and analyzed foreign tele-phone, broadcast, and Internet communications), and the National Recon-naissance Office (which ran spy satellites). One apparent sign that the Pentagon still was resisting such a plan was a decision late in the year by Secretary of Defense Donald H. Rumsfeld to appoint a high-level under-secretary of defense for military intelligence. Congress approved creation of the position with no formal debate, and Rumsfeld filled the slot with Richard L. Haver, who had been his special assistant for intelligence.

A related recommendation was that the White House speed up its plans to "examine and revamp existing intelligence agencies." The panel offered no specific information about those plans or their status, but it did say that the president needed to establish "clear, consistent, and current priorities" for the work of the intelligence agencies; those priorities, which would includ-ing battling terrorism, should be updated at least annually, the panel said.

The panel did not take a formal stand on the controversial question of establishing a new agency to collect intelligence information within the United States. In the past that task fell to the FBI, but the panel questioned whether the agency had moved quickly enough to focus more of its efforts on combating terrorism. The panel said Congress should study the "best way to structure" domestic intelligence gathering, specifically including whether a new agency was needed. In response the Justice Department issued a state-

ment defending its handling of terrorism investigations—including the actions of the FBI, a component of the department. The statement also argued against taking domestic intelligence gathering away from the FBI and giving it to a new agency. FBI director Mueller later took the same position, saying his agency was beginning to do a good job on domestic intelligence issues.

Other recommendations clearly were aimed at improving the ability of the intelligence agencies to communicate with one another and to give more resources and greater stature to counterterrorism work. One specific proposal that was bound to raise some hackles, if carried out, was for an aggressive investigation of whether foreign governments had provided support for or been involved in terrorism against the United States. This was widely seen as a call for a probe of possible financing of al Qaeda activities by individuals in Saudi Arabia. Bin Laden was from Saudi Arabia, as were fifteen of the nineteen hijackers on September 11. Some panel members had hinted that the United States in the past had been reluctant to press for information about the involvement of Saudi citizens in terrorism because that country was a major source of oil and was host to several major bases used by the U.S. military.

Punishing Individuals

One of the most contentious issues the panel faced in its closed-door deliberations was whether to recommend that specific individuals within the government be punished for their actions—or inactions—in the months before September 11. Alabama senator Richard Shelby, the ranking Republican on the Senate Intelligence committee, argued strenuously for citing individuals who should be punished. Shelby had been a frequent critic of CIA director Tenet and made no secret of his belief that Tenet—a former Democratic staff member of the Senate Intelligence Committee—had been a failure as an administrator and should resign or be fired. "There have been more massive failures in intelligence on his watch as director of the CIA than any director in the history of the agency," Shelby said. In a minority report, Shelby also cited what he said were failures by the leaders of other agencies, including one of Tenet's predecessors, John Deutch; former FBI director Louis Freeh; and NSA director Hayden. All, including Tenet, had been appointed by former president Bill Clinton (1993–2001).

Other panel members said naming and punishing individuals was not as important as identifying systemic problems that could be fixed and thereby increase the chances of averting another major terrorist attack. "There was a systemic failure of the Congress and the executive branch over a long period of time to supply the resources and supply the direction" to the intelligence agencies, said Sen. Mike DeWine, R-Ohio. "That had better be the lesson we learn, and if the lesson we learn is [that] one guy at the FBI or CIA messed up, that's not the real lesson."

Several committee members said they also feared that focusing on individuals might exacerbate an existing tendency at the intelligence agencies *known as "risk aversion." In too many cases, the panel found, employees had avoided taking what might be considered risky steps because they feared getting into trouble.*

Broader Investigating Commission

Shortly after the September 11 attacks, leaders of the intelligence committees from both parties began calling for an independent investigation into why the government had been unprepared for such an attack using commercial airliners. They ran into an important obstacle, however: the Bush administration. The White House made it clear that Bush opposed such an investigation as a diversion from the U.S. war against terrorism and as a potentially divisive intrusion into his responsibilities as president. Administration officials also feared that an investigation could give Democrats a soap box from which to attack Bush's handling of terrorism issues.

After months of wrangling, the White House agreed in late September to support a bipartisan investigation, but attempts to craft an agreement between Congress and the administration on the details fell apart in less than a week. A final agreement came after the November midterm elections when Bush agreed to support a proposal for an investigation that was incorporated into the annual authorizing legislation for the intelligence agencies. The bill provided for a ten-member commission to be equally divided between Republicans and Democrats. The president would name the chairman and congressional Democrats the vice chairman. A majority of six commission members would be required to issue subpoenas.

Bush signed the bill into law (PL 107–306) on November 27 and named Kissinger as its chairman. As one of the most influential U.S. diplomats of the previous half century, Kissinger automatically added prestige to the new commission, but he also brought controversy because of lingering resentment in the country over his role in prolonging the Vietnam War in the late 1960s and early 1970s. Representatives of the families of people killed in the September 11 attacks expressed dismay at Kissinger's appointment, saying controversy over his background might undermine the panel's findings. Congressional Democrats named Mitchell as the vice chairman. The selection of Mitchell brought little controversy; since leaving the Senate he had helped broker peace talks between the warring sides in Northern Ireland and headed an international commission that made recommendations— never adopted—for peace steps between Israel and the Palestinians. (Northern Ireland peace accord, Historic Documents of 1998, p. 204; Mitchell commission report on the Middle East, Historic Documents of 2001, p. 360)

Controversy over the Kissinger appointment built quickly, with critics demanding that he make public the list of clients of his consulting firm, Kissinger Associates, which reportedly provided "risk analysis" services for multinational corporations. Kissinger at first refused, then agreed to provide such a list in confidence to a third party chosen by the group of September 11 victims' relatives.

The first blow to the new commission came on December 11, when Mitchell announced that he was withdrawing because of time pressure and potential conflicts with his law practice, which had international clients. The next day lawyers for the Senate Ethics Committee produced a legal opinion saying all members of the commission would have to comply with Senate ethics rules, which would require disclosure of clients of their private firms. Kissinger resigned a day later, saying he was unwilling either to make public a list of his clients or to sever all ties with his firm.

The White House and Democrats quickly came up with substitutes—two men who were widely respected in Washington but lacked the high profiles of those they replaced. Former New Jersey governor Kean, Bush's choice as chairman, was a moderate Republican who was president of Drew University. Hamilton, chosen by the Democrats as vice chairman, represented an Indiana district in the House from 1965 to 1999 and served as chairman of the House Intelligence Committee in the 1980s, was cochairman in 1987 of the special congressional committee that investigated the Iran-contra affair, and briefly served as chairman of the House Foreign Affairs Committee in 1994. He was director of the Woodrow Wilson Center in Washington. Under the new leadership, the commission was scheduled to begin its investigations in 2003, with a deadline of early 2004.

Following are excerpts from part 1 of the final report of the joint inquiry of the House and Senate intelligence committees into the September 11, 2001, terrorist attacks against the United States, made public on December 11, 2002. The report included findings of fact concerning what the U.S. government knew of potential terrorist attacks before September 11, as well as recommendations for reforming government intelligence agencies to help thwart future attacks.

The documents were obtained from the Internet at intelligence.senate.gov/findings.pdf; intelligence.senate .gov/recommendations.pdf; accessed January 22, 2003.

Findings and Conclusions

Factual Findings

1. *Finding:* While the Intelligence Community had amassed a great deal of valuable intelligence regarding Usama Bin Ladin and his terrorist activities, none of it identified the time, place, and specific nature of the attacks that were planned for September 11, 2001. Nonetheless, the Community did have information that was clearly relevant to the September 11 attacks, particularly when considered for its collective significance.

2. *Finding:* During the spring and summer of 2001, the Intelligence Community experienced a significant increase in information indicating that Bin Ladin and al-Qa'ida intended to strike against U.S. interests in the very near future.

3. *Finding:* Beginning in 1998 and continuing into the summer of 2001, the Intelligence Community received a modest, but relatively steady, stream of intelligence reporting that indicated the possibility of terrorist attacks within the United States. Nonetheless, testimony and interviews confirm that it was the general view of the Intelligence Community, in the spring and summer of 2001, that the threatened Bin Ladin attacks would most likely occur against U.S. interests overseas, despite indications of plans and intentions to attack in the domestic United States.

4. *Finding:* From at least 1994, and continuing into the summer of 2001, the Intelligence Community received information indicating that terrorists were contemplating, among other means of attack, the use of aircraft as weapons. This information did not stimulate any specific Intelligence Community assessment of, or collective U.S. Government reaction to, this form of threat.

5. *Finding:* Although relevant information that is significant in retrospect regarding the attacks was available to the Intelligence Community prior to September 11, 2001, the Community too often failed to focus on that information and consider and appreciate its collective significance in terms of a probable terrorist attack. Neither did the Intelligence Community demonstrate sufficient initiative in coming to grips with the new transnational threats. Some significant pieces of information in the vast stream of data being collected were overlooked, some were not recognized as potentially significant at the time and therefore not disseminated, and some required additional action on the part of foreign governments before a direct connection to the hijackers could have been established. For all those reasons, the Intelligence Community failed to fully capitalize on available, and potentially important, information. The sub-findings below identify each category of this information.

Terrorist Communications in 1999

5.a. During 1999, the National Security Agency obtained a number of communications—none of which included specific detail regarding the time, place or nature of the September 11 attacks—connecting individuals to terrorism who were identified, after September 11, 2001, as participants in the attacks that occurred on that day.

Malaysia Meeting and Travel of al-Qa'ida Operatives to the United States

5.b. The Intelligence Community acquired additional, and highly significant, information regarding Khalid al-Mihdhar and Nawaf al-Hazmi in early 2000. Critical parts of the information concerning al-Mihdhar and al-Hazmi lay dormant within the Intelligence Community for as long as eighteen months, at the very time when plans for the September 11 attacks were proceeding.

The CIA missed repeated opportunities to act based on information in its possession that these two Bin Ladin-associated terrorists were traveling to the United States, and to add their names to watchlists.

Terrorist Communications in Spring 2000

5.c. In January 2000, after the meeting of al-Qa'ida operatives in Malaysia, Khalid al-Mihdhar and Nawaf al-Hazmi entered the United States. Thereafter, the Intelligence Community obtained information indicating that an individual named "Khaled" at an unknown location had contacted a suspected terrorist facility in the Middle East. The Intelligence Community reported some of this information but did not report all of it. Some of it was not reported because it was deemed not terrorist-related. It was not until after September 11, 2001 that the Intelligence Community determined that these contacts had been made by future hijacker Khalid al-Mihdhar while he was living within the domestic United States.

5.d. [Redacted for national security reasons.]

The Phoenix Electronic Communication

5.e. On July 10, 2001, a Phoenix FBI field office agent sent an "Electronic Communication" to 4 individuals in the Radical Fundamentalist Unit (RFU) and two people in the Usama Bin Ladin Unit (UBLU) at FBI headquarters, and to two agents on International Terrorism squads in the New York Field Office. In the communication, the agent expressed his concerns, based on his first-hand knowledge, that there was a coordinated effort underway by Bin Ladin to send students to the United States for civil aviation-related training. He noted that there was an "inordinate number of individuals of investigative interest" participating in this type of training in Arizona and expressed his suspicion that this was an effort to establish a cadre of individuals in civil aviation who would conduct future terrorist activity. The Phoenix EC requested that FBI Headquarters consider implementing four recommendations:

- accumulate a list of civil aviation university/ colleges around the country;
- establish liaison with these schools;
- discuss the theories contained in the Phoenix EC with the Intelligence Community; and
- consider seeking authority to obtain visa information concerning individuals seeking to attend flight schools.

However, the FBI headquarters personnel did not take the action requested by the Phoenix agent prior to September 11, 2001. The communication generated little or no interest at either FBI Headquarters or the FBI's New York field office.

The FBI Investigation of Zacarias Moussaoui

5.f. In August 2001, the FBI's Minneapolis field office, in conjunction with the INS, detained Zacarias Moussaoui, a French national who had enrolled in flight training in Minnesota because FBI agents there suspected that

Moussaoui was involved in a hijacking plot. FBI Headquarters attorneys determined that there was not probable cause to obtain a court order to search Moussaoui's belongings under the Foreign Intelligence Surveillance Act (FISA). However, personnel at FBI Headquarters, including the Radical Fundamentalist Unit and the National Security Law Unit, as well as agents in the Minneapolis field office, misunderstood the legal standard for obtaining an order under FISA. Therefore FBI Minneapolis field office personnel wasted valuable investigative resources trying to connect the Chechen rebels to al-Qa'ida. Finally, no one at the FBI apparently connected the Moussaoui investigation with the heightened threat environment in the summer of 2001, the Phoenix communication, or the entry of al-Mihdhar and al-Hazmi into the United States.

Hijackers In Contact With Persons of FBI Investigative Interest in the United States

5.g. The Joint Inquiry confirmed that at least some of the hijackers were not as isolated during their time in the United States as has been previously suggested. Rather, they maintained a number of contacts both in the United States and abroad during this time period. Some of those contacts were with individuals who were known to the FBI, through either past or, at the time, ongoing FBI inquiries and investigations. Although it is not known to what extent any of these contacts in the United States were aware of the plot, it is now clear that they did provide at least some of the hijackers with substantial assistance while they were living in this country.

Hijackers' Associates in Germany

5.h. Since 1995, the CIA had been aware of a radical Islamic presence in Germany, including individuals with connections to Usama Bin Ladin. Prior to September 11, 2001, the CIA had unsuccessfully sought additional information on individuals who have now been identified as associates of some of the hijackers.

Khalid Shaykh Mohammad

5.i. Prior to September 11, the Intelligence Community had information linking Khalid Shaykh Mohammed (KSM), now recognized by the Intelligence Community as the mastermind of the attacks, to Bin Ladin, to terrorist plans to use aircraft as weapons, and to terrorist activity in the United States. The Intelligence Community, however, relegated Khalid Shaykh Mohammed (KSM) to rendition target status following his 1996 indictment in connection with the Bojinka Plot and, as a result, focused primarily on his location, rather than his activities and place in the al-Qa'ida hierarchy. The Community also did not recognize the significance of reporting in June 2001 concerning KSM's active role in sending terrorists to the United States, or the facilitation of their activities upon arriving in the United States. Collection efforts were not targeted on information about KSM that might have helped better understand al-Qa'ida's plans and intentions, and KSM's role in the September 11 attacks was a surprise to the Intelligence Community.

Terrorist Communications in September 2001

5.j. In the period from September 8 to September 10, 2001 NSA intercepted, but did not translate or disseminate until after September 11, some communications that indicated possible impending terrorist activity.

Conclusion—Factual Findings

In short, for a variety of reasons, the Intelligence Community failed to capitalize on both the individual and collective significance of available information that appears relevant to the events of September 11. As a result, the Community missed opportunities to disrupt the September 11thplot by denying entry to or detaining would-be hijackers; to at least try to unravel the plot through surveillance and other investigative work within the United States; and, finally, to generate a heightened state of alert and thus harden the homeland against attack.

No one will ever know what might have happened had more connections been drawn between these disparate pieces of information. We will never definitively know to what extent the Community would have been able and willing to exploit fully all the opportunities that may have emerged. The important point is that the Intelligence Community, for a variety of reasons, did not bring together and fully appreciate a range of information that could have greatly enhanced its chances of uncovering and preventing Usama Bin Ladin's plan to attack these United States on September 11th, 2001.

Systemic Findings

Our review of the events surrounding September 11 has revealed a number of systemic weaknesses that hindered the Intelligence Community's counterterrorism efforts before September 11. If not addressed, these weaknesses will continue to undercut U.S. counterterrorist efforts. In order to minimize the possibility of attacks like September 11 in the future, effective solutions to those problems need to be developed and fully implemented as soon as possible.

1. *Finding:* Prior to September 11, the Intelligence Community was neither well organized nor equipped, and did not adequately adapt, to meet the challenge posed by global terrorists focused on targets within the domestic United States. Serious gaps existed between the collection coverage provided by U.S. foreign and U.S. domestic intelligence capabilities. The U.S. foreign intelligence agencies paid inadequate attention to the potential for a domestic attack. The CIA's failure to watchlist suspected terrorists aggressively reflected a lack of emphasis on a process designed to protect the homeland from the terrorist threat. As a result, CIA employees failed to watchlist al-Mihdhar and al-Hazmi. At home, the counterterrorism effort suffered from the lack of an effective domestic intelligence capability. The FBI was unable to identify and monitor effectively the extent of activity by al-Qa'ida and other international terrorist groups operating in the United States. Taken together, these problems greatly exacerbated the nation's vulnerability to an increasingly dangerous and immediate international terrorist threat inside the United States.

2. *Finding:* Prior to September 11, 2001, neither the U.S. Government as a whole nor the Intelligence Community had a comprehensive counterterrorist strategy for combating the threat posed by Usama Bin Ladin. Furthermore, the Director of Central Intelligence (DCI) was either unwilling or unable to marshal the full range of Intelligence Community resources necessary to combat the growing threat to the United States.

3. *Finding:* Between the end of the Cold War and September 11, 2001, overall Intelligence Community funding fell or remained even in constant dollars, while funding for the Community's counterterrorism efforts increased considerably. Despite those increases, the accumulation of intelligence priorities, a burdensome requirements process, the overall decline in Intelligence Community funding, and reliance on supplemental appropriations made it difficult to allocate Community resources effectively against an evolving terrorist threat. Inefficiencies in the resource and requirements process were compounded by problems in Intelligence Community budgeting practices and procedures.

4. *Finding:* While technology remains one of this nation's greatest advantages, it has not been fully and most effectively applied in support of U.S. counterterrorism efforts. Persistent problems in this area included a lack of collaboration between Intelligence Community agencies, a reluctance to develop and implement new technical capabilities aggressively, the FBI's reliance on outdated and insufficient technical systems, and the absence of a central counterterrorism database.

5. *Finding:* Prior to September 11, the Intelligence Community's understanding of al-Qa'ida was hampered by insufficient analytic focus and quality, particularly in terms of strategic analysis. Analysis and analysts were not always used effectively because of the perception in some quarters of the Intelligence Community that they were less important to agency counterterrorism missions than were operations personnel. The quality of counterterrorism analysis was inconsistent, and many analysts were inexperienced, unqualified, under-trained, and without access to critical information. As a result, there was a dearth of creative, aggressive analysis targeting Bin Ladin and a persistent inability to comprehend the collective significance of individual pieces of intelligence. These analytic deficiencies seriously undercut the ability of U.S. policymakers to understand the full nature of the threat, and to make fully informed decisions.

6. *Finding:* Prior to September 11, the Intelligence Community was not prepared to handle the challenge it faced in translating the volumes of foreign language counterterrorism intelligence it collected. Agencies within the Intelligence Community experienced backlogs in material awaiting translation, a shortage of language specialists and language-qualified field officers, and a readiness level of only 30% in the most critical terrorism-related languages.

7. *Finding:* Prior to September 11, the Intelligence Community's ability to produce significant and timely signals intelligence on counterterrorism was limited by NSA's failure to address modern communications technology aggressively, continuing conflict between Intelligence Community agencies, NSA's cautious approach to any collection of intelligence relating to activities

in the United States, and insufficient collaboration between NSA and the FBI regarding the potential for terrorist attacks within the United States.

8. *Finding:* The continuing erosion of NSA's program management expertise and experience has hindered its contribution to the fight against terrorism. NSA continues to have mixed results in providing timely technical solutions to modern intelligence collection, analysis, and information sharing problems.

9. *Finding:* The U.S. Government does not presently bring together in one place all terrorism-related information from all sources. While the CTC does manage overseas operations and has access to most Intelligence Community information, it does not collect terrorism-related information from all sources, domestic and foreign. Within the Intelligence Community, agencies did not adequately share relevant counterterrorism information, prior to September 11. This breakdown in communications was the result of a number of factors, including differences in the agencies' missions, legal authorities and cultures. Information was not sufficiently shared, not only between different Intelligence Community agencies, but also within individual agencies, and between the intelligence and the law enforcement agencies.

10. *Finding:* Serious problems in information sharing also persisted, prior to September 11, between the Intelligence Community and relevant non-Intelligence Community agencies. This included other federal agencies as well as state and local authorities. This lack of communication and collaboration deprived those other entities, as well as the Intelligence Community, of access to potentially valuable information in the "war" against Bin Ladin. The Inquiry's focus on the Intelligence Community limited the extent to which it explored these issues, and this is an area that should be reviewed further.

11. *Finding:* Prior to September 11, 2001, the Intelligence Community did not effectively develop and use human sources to penetrate the al-Qa'ida inner circle. This lack of reliable and knowledgeable human sources significantly limited the Community's ability to acquire intelligence that could be acted upon before the September 11 attacks. In part, at least, the lack of unilateral (i.e., U.S.-recruited) counterterrorism sources was a product of an excessive reliance on foreign liaison services.

12. *Finding:* During the summer of 2001, when the Intelligence Community was bracing for an imminent al-Qa'ida attack, difficulties with FBI applications for Foreign Intelligence Surveillance Act (FISA) surveillance and the FISA process led to a diminished level of coverage of suspected al-Qa'ida operatives in the United States. The effect of these difficulties was compounded by the perception that spread among FBI personnel at Headquarters and the field offices that the FISA process was lengthy and fraught with peril.

13. [Redacted for national security reasons.]

14. [Redacted for national security reasons.]

15. *Finding:* The Intelligence Community depended heavily on foreign intelligence and law enforcement services for the collection of counterterrorism intelligence and the conduct of other counterterrorism activities. The results were mixed in terms of productive intelligence, reflecting vast differences in the ability and willingness of the various foreign services to target the Bin Ladin and al-Qa'ida network. Intelligence Community agencies sometimes

failed to coordinate their relationships with foreign services adequately, either within the Intelligence Community or with broader U.S. Government liaison and foreign policy efforts. This reliance on foreign liaison services also resulted in a lack of focus on the development of unilateral human sources.

16. *Finding:* The activities of the September 11 hijackers in the United States appear to have been financed, in large part, from monies sent to them from abroad. Prior to September 11, there was no coordinated U.S. Government-wide strategy, and reluctance in some parts of the U.S. Government, to track terrorist funding and close down their financial support networks. As a result, the U.S. Government was unable to disrupt financial support for Usama Bin Ladin's terrorist activities effectively.

Related Findings

17. *Finding:* Despite intelligence reporting from 1998 through the summer of 2001 indicating that Usama Bin Ladin's terrorist network intended to strike inside the United States, the United States Government did not undertake a comprehensive effort to implement defensive measures in the United States.

18. *Finding:* Between 1996 and September 2001, the counterterrorism strategy adopted by the U.S. Government did not succeed in eliminating Afghanistan as a sanctuary and training ground for Usama Bin Ladin's terrorist network. A range of instruments was used to counter al-Qa'ida, with law enforcement often emerging as a leading tool because other means were deemed not to be feasible or failed to produce results. While generating numerous successful prosecutions, law enforcement efforts were not adequate by themselves to target or eliminate Bin Ladin's sanctuary. While the United States persisted in observing the rule of law and accepted norms of international behavior, Bin Ladin and al-Qa'ida recognized no rules and thrived in the safe-haven provided by Afghanistan.

19. *Finding:* Prior to September 11, the Intelligence Community and the U.S. Government labored to prevent attacks by Usama Bin Ladin and his terrorist network against the United States, but largely without the benefit of an alert, mobilized and committed American public. Despite intelligence information on the immediacy of the threat level in the spring and summer of 2001, the assumption prevailed in the U.S. Government that attacks of the magnitude of September 11 could not happen here. As a result, there was insufficient effort to alert the American public to the reality and gravity of the threat.

Recommendations

Since the National Security Act's establishment of the Director of Central Intelligence and the Central Intelligence Agency in 1947, numerous independent commissions, experts, and legislative initiatives have examined the growth and performance of the U.S. Intelligence Community. While those efforts generated numerous proposals for reform over the years, some of the most significant proposals have not been implemented, particularly in the areas of organization and structure. These Committees believe that the cataclysmic events of September 11, 2001 provide a unique and compelling mandate for strong leadership and constructive change throughout the Intelligence

Community. With that in mind, and based on the work of this Joint Inquiry, the Committees recommend the following:

1. Congress should amend the National Security Act of 1947 to create and sufficiently staff a statutory Director of National Intelligence 2 who shall be the President's principal advisor on intelligence and shall have the full range of management, budgetary and personnel responsibilities needed to make the entire U.S. Intelligence Community operate as a coherent whole. These responsibilities should include:

- establishment and enforcement of consistent priorities for the collection, analysis, and dissemination of intelligence throughout the Intelligence Community;
- setting of policy and the ability to move personnel between elements of the Intelligence Community;
- review, approval, modification, and primary management and oversight of the execution of Intelligence Community budgets;
- review, approval, modification, and primary management and oversight of the execution of Intelligence Community personnel and resource allocations;
- review, approval, modification, and primary management and oversight of the execution of Intelligence Community research and development efforts;
- review, approval, and coordination of relationships between the Intelligence Community agencies and foreign intelligence and law enforcement services; and
- exercise of statutory authority to insure that Intelligence Community agencies and components fully comply with Community-wide policy, management, spending, and administrative guidance and priorities.

The Director of National Intelligence should be a Cabinet level position, appointed by the President and subject to Senate confirmation. Congress and the President should also work to insure that the Director of National Intelligence effectively exercises these authorities.

To insure focused and consistent Intelligence Community leadership, Congress should require that no person may simultaneously serve as both the Director of National Intelligence and the Director of the Central Intelligence Agency, or as the director of any other specific intelligence agency.

2. Current efforts by the National Security Council to examine and revamp existing intelligence priorities should be expedited, given the immediate need for clear guidance in intelligence and counterterrorism efforts. The President should take action to ensure that clear, consistent, and current priorities are established and enforced throughout the Intelligence Community. Once established, these priorities should be reviewed and updated on at least an annual basis to ensure that the allocation of Intelligence Community resources reflects and effectively addresses the continually evolving threat environment. Finally, the establishment of Intelligence Community priorities, and the justification for such priorities, should be reported to both the House and Senate Intelligence Committees on an annual basis.

3. The National Security Council, in conjunction with the Director of National Intelligence, and in consultation with the Secretary of the Department of Homeland Security, the Secretary of State and Secretary of Defense, should prepare, for the President's approval, a U.S. government-wide strategy for combating terrorism, both at home and abroad, including the growing terrorism threat posed by the proliferation of weapons of mass destruction and associated technologies. This strategy should identify and fully engage those foreign policy, economic, military, intelligence, and law enforcement elements that are critical to a comprehensive blueprint for success in the war against terrorism.

As part of that effort, the Director of National Intelligence shall develop the Intelligence Community component of the strategy, identifying specific programs and budgets and including plans to address the threats posed by Usama Bin Ladin and al Qa'ida, Hezbollah, Hamas, and other significant terrorist groups. Consistent with applicable law, the strategy should effectively employ and integrate all capabilities available to the Intelligence Community against those threats and should encompass specific efforts to:

- develop human sources to penetrate terrorist organizations and networks both overseas and within the United States;
- fully utilize existing and future technologies to better exploit terrorist communications; to improve and expand the use of data mining and other cutting edge analytical tools; and to develop a multi-level security capability to facilitate the timely and complete sharing of relevant intelligence information both within the Intelligence Community and with other appropriate federal, state, and local authorities;
- enhance the depth and quality of domestic intelligence collection and analysis by, for example, modernizing current intelligence reporting formats through the use of existing information technology to emphasize the existence and the significance of links between new and previously acquired information;
- maximize the effective use of covert action in counterterrorist efforts;
- develop programs to deal with financial support for international terrorism; and
- facilitate the ability of CIA paramilitary units and military special operations forces to conduct joint operations against terrorist targets.

4. The position of National Intelligence Officer for Terrorism should be created on the National Intelligence Council and a highly qualified individual appointed to prepare intelligence estimates on terrorism for the use of Congress and policymakers in the Executive Branch and to assist the Intelligence Community in developing a program for strategic analysis and assessments.

5. Congress and the Administration should ensure the full development within the Department of Homeland Security of an effective all-source terrorism information fusion center that will dramatically improve the focus and quality of counterterrorism analysis and facilitate the timely dissemination of relevant intelligence information, both within and beyond the boundaries of

the Intelligence Community. Congress and the Administration should ensure that this fusion center has all the authority and the resources needed to:

- have full and timely access to all counterterrorism-related intelligence information, including "raw" supporting data as needed;
- have the ability to participate fully in the existing requirements process for tasking the Intelligence Community to gather information on foreign individuals, entities and threats;
- integrate such information in order to identify and assess the nature and scope of terrorist threats to the United States in light of actual and potential vulnerabilities;
- implement and fully utilize data mining and other advanced analytical tools, consistent with applicable law;
- retain a permanent staff of experienced and highly skilled analysts, supplemented on a regular basis by personnel on "joint tours" from the various Intelligence Community agencies;
- institute a reporting mechanism that enables analysts at all the intelligence and law enforcement agencies to post lead information for use by analysts at other agencies without waiting for dissemination of a formal report;
- maintain excellence and creativity in staff analytic skills through regular use of analysis and language training programs; and
- establish and sustain effective channels for the exchange of counterterrorism-related information with federal agencies outside the Intelligence Community as well as with state and local authorities.

6. Given the FBI's history of repeated shortcomings within its current responsibility for domestic intelligence, and in the face of grave and immediate threats to our homeland, the FBI should strengthen and improve its domestic capability as fully and expeditiously as possible by immediately instituting measures to:

- strengthen counterterrorism as a national FBI program by clearly designating national counterterrorism priorities and enforcing field office adherence to those priorities;
- establish and sustain independent career tracks within the FBI that recognize and provide incentives for demonstrated skills and performance of counterterrorism agents and analysts;
- significantly improve strategic analytical capabilities by assuring the qualification, training, and independence of analysts, coupled with sufficient access to necessary information and resources;
- establish a strong reports officer cadre at FBI Headquarters and field offices to facilitate timely dissemination of intelligence from agents to analysts within the FBI and other agencies within the Intelligence Community;
- implement training for agents in the effective use of analysts and analysis in their work;

- expand and sustain the recruitment of agents and analysts with the linguistic skills needed in counterterrorism efforts;
- increase substantially efforts to penetrate terrorist organizations operating in the United States through all available means of collection;
- improve the national security law training of FBI personnel;
- implement mechanisms to maximize the exchange of counterterrorism-related information between the FBI and other federal, state and local agencies; and
- finally solve the FBI's persistent and incapacitating information technology problems.

7. Congress and the Administration should carefully consider how best to structure and manage U.S. domestic intelligence responsibilities. Congress should review the scope of domestic intelligence authorities to determine their adequacy in pursuing counterterrorism at home and ensuring the protection of privacy and other rights guaranteed under the Constitution. This review should include, for example, such questions as whether the range of persons subject to searches and surveillances authorized under the Foreign Intelligence Surveillance Act (FISA) should be expanded.

Based on their oversight responsibilities, the Intelligence and Judiciary Committees of the Congress, as appropriate, should consider promptly, in consultation with the Administration, whether the FBI should continue to perform the domestic intelligence functions of the United States Government or whether legislation is necessary to remedy this problem, including the possibility of creating a new agency to perform those functions.

Congress should require that the new Director of National Intelligence, the Attorney General, and the Secretary of the Department of Homeland Security report to the President and the Congress on a date certain concerning:

- the FBI's progress since September 11, 2001 in implementing the reforms required to conduct an effective domestic intelligence program, including the measures recommended above;
- the experience of other democratic nations in organizing the conduct of domestic intelligence;
- the specific manner in which a new domestic intelligence service could be established in the United States, recognizing the need to enhance national security while fully protecting civil liberties; and
- their recommendations on how to best fulfill the nation's need for an effective domestic intelligence capability, including necessary legislation.

8. The Attorney General and the Director of the FBI should take action necessary to ensure that:

- the Office of Intelligence Policy and Review and other Department of Justice components provide in-depth training to the FBI and other members of the Intelligence Community regarding the use of the Foreign Intelligence Surveillance Act (FISA) to address terrorist threats to the United States;

- the FBI disseminates results of searches and surveillances authorized under FISA to appropriate personnel within the FBI and the Intelligence Community on a timely basis so they may be used for analysis and operations that address terrorist threats to the United States; and
- the FBI develops and implements a plan to use authorities provided by FISA to assess the threat of international terrorist groups within the United States fully, including the extent to which such groups are funded or otherwise supported by foreign governments.

9. The House and Senate Intelligence and Judiciary Committees should continue to examine the Foreign Intelligence Surveillance Act and its implementation thoroughly, particularly with respect to changes made as a result of the USA PATRIOT Act and the subsequent decision of the United States Foreign Intelligence Court of Review, to determine whether its provisions adequately address present and emerging terrorist threats to the United States. Legislation should be proposed by those Committees to remedy any deficiencies identified as a result of that review.

10. The Director of the National Security Agency should present to the Director of National Intelligence and the Secretary of Defense by June 30, 2003, and report to the House and Senate Intelligence Committees, a detailed plan that:

- describes solutions for the technological challenges for signals intelligence;
- requires a review, on a quarterly basis, of the goals, products to be delivered, funding levels and schedules for every technology development program;
- ensures strict accounting for program expenditures;
- within their jurisdiction as established by current law, makes NSA a full collaborating partner with the Central Intelligence Agency and the Federal Bureau of Investigation in the war on terrorism, including fully integrating the collection and analytic capabilities of NSA, CIA, and the FBI; and
- makes recommendations for legislation needed to facilitate these goals.

In evaluating the plan, the Committees should also consider issues pertaining to whether civilians should be appointed to the position of Director of the National Security Agency and whether the term of service for the position should be longer than it has been in the recent past.

11. Recognizing that the Intelligence Community's employees remain its greatest resource, the Director of National Intelligence should require that measures be implemented to greatly enhance the recruitment and development of a workforce with the intelligence skills and expertise needed for success in counterterrorist efforts, including:

- the agencies of the Intelligence Community should act promptly to expand and improve counterterrorism training programs within the Community, insuring coverage of such critical areas as information sharing among law enforcement and intelligence personnel; language capabilities; the use of the Foreign Intelligence Surveillance Act; and watchlisting;

- the Intelligence Community should build on the provisions of the Intelligence Authorization Act for Fiscal Year 2003 regarding the development of language capabilities, including the Act's requirement for a report on the feasibility of establishing a Civilian Linguist Reserve Corps, and implement expeditiously measures to identify and recruit linguists outside the Community whose abilities are relevant to the needs of counterterrorism;

- the existing Intelligence Community Reserve Corps should be expanded to ensure the use of relevant personnel and expertise from outside the Community as special needs arise;

- Congress should consider enacting legislation, modeled on the Goldwater-Nichols Act of 1986, to instill the concept of "jointness" throughout the Intelligence Community. By emphasizing such things as joint education, a joint career specialty, increased authority for regional commanders, and joint exercises, that Act greatly enhanced the joint warfighting capabilities of the individual military services. Legislation to instill similar concepts throughout the Intelligence Community could help improve management of Community resources and priorities and insure a far more effective "team" effort by all the intelligence agencies. The Director of National Intelligence should require more extensive use of "joint tours" for intelligence and appropriate law enforcement personnel to broaden their experience and help bridge existing organizational and cultural divides through service in other agencies. These joint tours should include not only service at Intelligence Community agencies, but also service in those agencies that are users or consumers of intelligence products. Serious incentives for joint service should be established throughout the Intelligence Community and personnel should be rewarded for joint service with career advancement credit at individual agencies. The Director of National Intelligence should also require Intelligence Community agencies to participate in joint exercises;

- Congress should expand and improve existing educational grant programs focused on intelligence-related fields, similar to military scholarship programs and others that provide financial assistance in return for a commitment to serve in the Intelligence Community; and

- the Intelligence Community should enhance recruitment of a more ethnically and culturally diverse workforce and devise a strategy to capitalize upon the unique cultural and linguistic capabilities of first-generation Americans, a strategy designed to utilize their skills to the greatest practical effect while recognizing the potential counterintelligence challenges such hiring decisions might pose.

12. Steps should be taken to increase and ensure the greatest return on this nation's substantial investment in intelligence, including:

- the President should submit budget recommendations, and Congress should enact budget authority, for sustained, long-term investment in counterterrorism capabilities that avoid dependence on repeated stop-gap supplemental appropriations;

- in making such budget recommendations, the President should provide for the consideration of a separate classified Intelligence Community budget;
- long-term counterterrorism investment should be accompanied by sufficient flexibility, subject to congressional oversight, to enable the Intelligence Community to rapidly respond to altered or unanticipated needs;
- the Director of National Intelligence should insure that Intelligence Community budgeting practices and procedures are revised to better identify the levels and nature of counterterrorism funding within the Community;
- counterterrorism funding should be allocated in accordance with the program requirements of the national counterterrorism strategy; and
- due consideration should be given to directing an outside agency or entity to conduct a thorough and rigorous cost-benefit analysis of the resources spent on intelligence.

13. The State Department, in consultation with the Department of Justice, should review and report to the President and the Congress by June 30, 2003 on the extent to which revisions in bilateral and multilateral agreements, including extradition and mutual assistance treaties, would strengthen U.S. counterterrorism efforts. The review should address the degree to which current categories of extraditable offenses should be expanded to cover offenses, such as visa and immigration fraud, which may be particularly useful against terrorists and those who support them.

14. Recognizing the importance of intelligence in this nation's struggle against terrorism, Congress should maintain vigorous, informed, and constructive oversight of the Intelligence Community. To best achieve that goal, the National Commission on Terrorist Attacks Upon the United States should study and make recommendations concerning how Congress may improve its oversight of the Intelligence Community, including consideration of such areas as:

- changes in the budgetary process;
- changes in the rules regarding membership on the oversight committees;
- whether oversight responsibility should be vested in a joint House-Senate Committee or, as currently exists, in separate Committees in each house;
- the extent to which classification decisions impair congressional oversight; and
- how Congressional oversight can best contribute to the continuing need of the Intelligence Community to evolve and adapt to changes in the subject matter of intelligence and the needs of policy makers.

15. The President should review and consider amendments to the Executive Orders, policies and procedures that govern the national security classification of intelligence information, in an effort to expand access to relevant information for federal agencies outside the Intelligence Community, for state

and local authorities, which are critical to the fight against terrorism, and for the American public. In addition, the President and the heads of federal agencies should ensure that the policies and procedures to protect against the unauthorized disclosure of classified intelligence information are well understood, fully implemented and vigorously enforced.

Congress should also review the statutes, policies and procedures that govern the national security classification of intelligence information and its protection from unauthorized disclosure. Among other matters, Congress should consider the degree to which excessive classification has been used in the past and the extent to which the emerging threat environment has greatly increased the need for real-time sharing of sensitive information. The Director of National Intelligence, in consultation with the Secretary of Defense, the Secretary of State, the Secretary of Homeland Security, and the Attorney General, should review and report to the House and Senate Intelligence Committees on proposals for a new and more realistic approach to the processes and structures that have governed the designation of sensitive and classified information. The report should include proposals to protect against the use of the classification process as a shield to protect agency self-interest.

16. Assured standards of accountability are critical to developing the personal responsibility, urgency, and diligence which our counterterrorism responsibility requires. Given the absence of any substantial efforts within the Intelligence Community to impose accountability in relation to the events of September 11, 2001, the Director of Central Intelligence and the heads of Intelligence Community agencies should require that measures designed to ensure accountability are implemented throughout the Community.

To underscore the need for accountability:

- The Director of Central Intelligence should report to the House and Senate Intelligence Committees no later than June 30, 2003 as to the steps taken to implement a system of accountability throughout the Intelligence Community, to include processes for identifying poor performance and affixing responsibility for it, and for recognizing and rewarding excellence in performance;
- as part of the confirmation process for Intelligence Community officials, Congress should require from those officials an affirmative commitment to the implementation and use of strong accountability mechanisms throughout the Intelligence Community; and
- the Inspectors General at the Central Intelligence Agency, the Department of Defense, the Department of Justice, and the Department of State should review the factual findings and the record of this Inquiry and conduct investigations and reviews as necessary to determine whether and to what extent personnel at all levels should be held accountable for any omission, commission, or failure to meet professional standards in regard to the identification, prevention, or disruption of terrorist attacks, including the events of September 11, 2001. These reviews should also address those individuals who performed in a stellar or exceptional manner, and the degree to which the quality of their performance was re-

warded or otherwise impacted their careers. Based on those investigations and reviews, agency heads should take appropriate disciplinary and other action and the President and the House and Senate Intelligence Committees should be advised of such action.

17. The Administration should review and report to the House and Senate Intelligence Committees by June 30, 2003 regarding what progress has been made in reducing the inappropriate and obsolete barriers among intelligence and law enforcement agencies engaged in counterterrorism, what remains to be done to reduce those barriers, and what legislative actions may be advisable in that regard. In particular, this report should address what steps are being taken to insure that perceptions within the Intelligence Community about the scope and limits of current law and policy with respect to restrictions on collection and information sharing are, in fact, accurate and well-founded.

18. Congress and the Administration should ensure the full development of a national watchlist center that will be responsible for coordinating and integrating all terrorist-related watchlist systems; promoting awareness and use of the center by all relevant government agencies and elements of the private sector; and ensuring a consistent and comprehensive flow of terrorist names into the center from all relevant points of collection.

19. The Intelligence Community, and particularly the FBI and the CIA, should aggressively address the possibility that foreign governments are providing support to or are involved in terrorist activity targeting the United States and U.S. interests. State-sponsored terrorism substantially increases the likelihood of successful and more lethal attacks within the United States. This issue must be addressed from a national standpoint and should not be limited in focus by the geographical and factual boundaries of individual cases. The FBI and CIA should aggressively and thoroughly pursue related matters developed through this Joint Inquiry that have been referred to them for further investigation by these Committees.

The Intelligence Community should fully inform the House and Senate Intelligence Committees of significant developments in these efforts, through regular reports and additional communications as necessary, and the Committees should, in turn, exercise vigorous and continuing oversight of the Community's work in this critically important area.

UNITED NATIONS PANEL ON SANCTIONS AGAINST AL QAEDA
December 17, 2002

Significant terrorist bombings in Indonesia and Kenya late in 2002 appeared to indicate that the al Qaeda terrorist network and groups allied with it remained active despite an extensive U.S.-led international war against terrorism. Both bombings were against what experts called "soft targets"—a pair of nightclubs on the Indonesian island of Bali and a resort hotel in Kenya. The combined total death toll of more than 200 people, all civilians, was small compared to the nearly 3,000 people who died in the September 11, 2001, attacks against the World Trade Center towers in New York City and the Pentagon near Washington, D.C. But the bombings demonstrated that terrorist groups retained the capability to plan and carry out attention-getting attacks on opposite sides of the world. (Terrorist attacks, Historic Documents of 2001, p. 764)

Counterterrorism officials in the United States and other countries said the Indonesia and Kenya bombings both appeared to be the work of radical Islamist groups directly or indirectly affiliated with al Qaeda, the network that sponsored the September 11 attacks. In Indonesia authorities arrested key leaders of a group that may have received support from al Qaeda. A statement allegedly from al Qaeda claimed responsibility for the Kenya bombing. (Indonesia bombing, p. 702)

The United States and its allies made some progress during 2002 in their campaign to disrupt the al Qaeda network, said to have at least some presence in several dozen countries. But Osama bin Laden, al Qaeda's charismatic leader, and most of his top deputies remained at large. After the September 11 attacks, President George W. Bush had made the capture of bin Laden "dead or alive" a key test of the success of a war against terrorism but the Saudi exile continued to taunt the United States with tape recordings threatening more attacks.

Kenya Bombing

Thursday, November 28, 2002, was a busy day at the Paradise Hotel, an Israeli-owned beachfront resort just outside of Mombasa, Kenya, that ca-

tered almost exclusively to Israeli tourists. Each Thursday a new group of Israelis arrived at the hotel for a week of sun and relaxation on the Indian Ocean beaches. In midmorning, traditional African dancers were just beginning to sing and clap for the benefit of arriving guests in the hotel lobby when a jeep crashed into the front of the building, setting off explosives that ripped apart much of the glass, wood, and steel structure and set fire to all that remained. Two men driving the jeep were killed instantly. Nine Kenyans, including seven of the dancers, and three Israelis also died. More than eighty people were injured in the explosion and the resulting fire.

A few minutes before that attack, someone stationed near the Mombasa airport fired two portable antiaircraft missiles into the air, just missing an Israeli-chartered Boeing 757 airliner that was headed back to Tel Aviv.

The double attacks fit the pattern of al Qaeda's operations. Four years earlier, in August 1998, al Qaeda terrorists drove bomb-laden vehicles toward the U.S. embassies in Nairobi, Kenya, and Dar es Salaam, Tanzania, killing about 230 people and wounding approximately 5,000, most of them Africans. The September 11 attacks in the United States involved the near-simultaneous hijacking of four airplanes, three of which hit their intended targets (the fourth crashed hundreds of miles away). (Embassy bombings, Historic Documents of 1998, p. 555)

Investigations failed to turn up solid evidence about who was responsible for the October 17 attacks, but on December 2 a Web site used by al Qaeda contained a statement claiming responsibility. "The Jewish crusader coalition [an apparent reference to Israel and the United States] will not be safe anywhere from the fighters' attacks," the statement said. It was attributed to Sulaiman Abu Ghaith, a cleric said by Western intelligence services to be associated with al Qaeda. President Bush had previously blamed al Qaeda for the attacks.

If al Qaeda was in fact responsible, the attacks demonstrated the network's continuing ability to carry out high visibility operations in countries, such as Kenya, that had porous borders and weak law enforcement. U.S. intelligence officials had warned since the 1998 embassy bombings that al Qaeda cells likely would continue to operate in Kenya, Tanzania, and other countries in the Horn of Africa region that had large Muslim populations and visible Western targets.

Several other terrorist attacks in the latter half of 2002 also appeared to bear the hallmarks of al Qaeda or groups aligned with it. They included three events in October: the fatal shooting of a U.S. Marine in Kuwait, the assassination of U.S. diplomat Laurence Foley in Jordan, and an unsuccessful bomb attack against a French oil tanker near Yemen.

Bin Laden's Whereabouts

The United States and its allies managed to capture several high-level operatives in the al Qaeda network during 2002—but bin Laden, if he was still alive, remained elusive. Also at large was Mullah Omar, the leader of Afghanistan's Taliban regime before it was knocked from power by a U.S.-led invasion in October 2001. Some 600 former Taliban and al Qaeda fighters captured in late 2001 and early 2002 were sent to a U.S. detention facility at Guantanamo Bay, Cuba, where they underwent interrogation. Another 100 or so men thought to have ranked higher in the organizations were kept in U.S. detention at the Bagram airbase just north of Kabul, Afghanistan. (Guantanamo detentions, p. 830)

At least three senior al Qaeda figures were captured during 2002: Abu Zubaida, described by U.S. officials as al Qaeda's chief field commander, was captured in Pakistan in March; Ramzi Binalshibh, an alleged coordinator of the September 11 attacks, was captured in Pakistan in September; and Abd al-Rahim al-Hashiri, described as al Qaeda's senior planner in the Persian Gulf region, was captured at an undisclosed location in November.

The United States used a less conventional approach against another senior al Qaeda figure, Abu Ali al-Harithi, who was said to be one of the network's top representatives in Yemen. On November 3 a CIA-operated unmanned drone, known as a Predator, fired Hellfire missiles at a vehicle traveling along a highway in Yemen. The missiles killed six occupants, including al-Harithi, the CIA said. U.S. officials later said Bush had authorized the CIA to assassinate about two dozen senior al Qaeda figures, including al-Harithi, bin Laden, and others, despite a longstanding presidential ban on CIA assassinations.

U.S. officials said the capture or killing of these key al Qaeda leaders created important gaps in the al Qaeda power structure and might make it somewhat more difficult for the network to plan, finance, and coordinate major terrorist attacks in the future. Even so, the top leadership of al Qaeda remained at large, notably bin Laden, the Saudi exile who had used his share of a large family fortune and his considerable motivational skills to build al Qaeda into the most formidable terrorist network of modern times. U.S. and Pakistan intelligence officials had said bin Laden almost certainly was in the mountainous Tora Bora region of eastern Afghanistan in late 2001 when the U.S. military bombed caves and encampments used by al Qaeda. But an intensive manhunt in the region turned up no sign of bin Laden. Bin Laden appeared on a videotape sent to the al Jazeera satellite television network in December 2001; in that tape he was characteristically defiant in his denunciations of the United States but appeared haggard and possibly wounded because he did not move his right arm.

In subsequent months intelligence officials debated whether bin Laden was alive or dead, but no one could show any conclusive evidence either way. Then on November 12 al Jazeera broadcast a four-minute audiotape with a message attributed to bin Laden and given in a voice that U.S. experts said appeared to be that of the al Qaeda leader. The taped message made references to several events in previous weeks, including the October 12 bombing in Bali. "We had warned Australia about its participation in [the war in] Afghanistan," the voice said. "It ignored the warning until it woke up to the sound of explosions in Bali." Most of those killed in the Bali bombing were Australian citizens. The taped message also threatened renewed attacks against the United States and any of its allies who might participate in Bush's threatened invasion of Iraq. (Iraq, p. 713)

The purported bin Laden tape followed by about one month a broadcast by al Jazeera of another audiotape said to be of Aymn Zawahiri, an Egyptian generally considered bin Laden's chief deputy. The message on that tape also referred to events in 2002 and threatened new attacks on the United States.

These tapes—coming on top of the Indonesia and Kenya bombings and the other terrorist attacks late in the year—led some U.S. officials and many independent terrorism experts to conclude that al Qaeda was successfully regrouping just one year after losing its operational base in Afghanistan. General Richard B. Myers, chairman of the Joint Chiefs of Staff, acknowledged on November 5 that the U.S. military momentum against al Qaeda in Afghanistan was faltering because of the organization's resilience. "They've made lots of adaptations to our tactics, and we've got to continue to think and try to out-think them and to be faster at it," Myers told a Brookings Institution audience. Testifying on October 17 before a joint congressional committee investigating the September 11 attacks, CIA director George Tenet said that "al Qaeda continues to plan and will attempt more deadly strikes against us. There will be more battles won and, sadly, more battles lost."

Other experts said al Qaeda was continuing to attract new recruits to its cause—generally young men alienated from the generally repressive governments of most Muslim-majority countries. Michael Chandler, chairman of the United Nations monitoring group on terrorism, told reporters on December 17 that support for al Qaeda was undiminished in much of the world. "What is actually happening is, more young men who are disillusioned and perhaps have a feeling for al Qaeda—and let's face it, the sympathy for this organization is actually quite widespread in many countries—are happy to turn up and be trained," Chandler said. "They believe it's the thing they should be doing."

Tenet was among the handful of senior Bush administration officials who repeatedly said that even the successful dismantling of al Qaeda would not be enough to win the war against terrorism. "To claim victory, we and our allies will need to address the circumstances that bring peoples to despair, weaken governments, and create power vacuums that extremists are all too ready to fill," Tenet said in a December 11 speech at the Nixon Center in Washington. A recipe for that larger strategic fight against terrorism, he said, would require the United States and its allies "to enlarge the opportunities within the Muslim world to embrace democratic norms, to encourage open, constructive political discussion in closed, reserved societies, to support experiments in improved governance, to promote opportunities for Muslim women to participate more broadly in the life of their societies."

Tracking al Qaeda's Money

In addition to capturing top al Qaeda officials, a chief focus of international antiterrorism efforts during the year was the network's access to money. According to most experts, bin Laden had used much of his inherited fortune—estimated at somewhere between $30 million and $300 million—as seed money for al Qaeda. Bin Laden also had succeeded in raising *millions more from Muslims in countries around the world, including the United States. After the September 11 attacks the U.S. government targeted charitable organizations that reportedly had raised money for al Qaeda. Among the charities was the Benevolence International Foundation, which moved from Saudi Arabia to Chicago in the 1990s. A federal grand jury in October indicted the foundation's U.S. director, Enaam M. Arnaout, on criminal charges of serving as a conduit for al Qaeda fund raising.*

The United Nations also attempted to organize a worldwide freeze on bank accounts and other assets held by al Qaeda. By December, according to U.S. figures, 166 countries had seized or frozen about $121 million in "terrorist-related financial assets," most of it reportedly associated with al Qaeda. All but about $10 million of that total was seized late in 2001. International efforts to track al Qaeda's money reportedly slowed during 2002 for several reasons, including the organization's apparent success in shifting its assets from cash bank accounts to gold, diamonds, and other commodities that were more difficult for investigators to locate.

Another problem, according to a report issued October 17 by the Council of Foreign Relations, was the reluctance of authorities in some countries, notably Saudi Arabia, to cooperate in the search for al Qaeda's assets. "For years, individuals and charities in Saudi Arabia have been the most important source of funds for al Qaeda," the council's report said. "And for years Saudi officials have turned a blind eye to the problem." Responding to the report, U.S. government officials agreed with that assessment and said the Saudi Arabian government was still uncooperative on the matter.

Al Qaeda and Iraq

In addition to the question of bin Laden's whereabouts, one of the year's most discussed issues was the extent, if any, of the relationship between al Qaeda and the Iraqi regime of Saddam Hussein. As part of his bill of particulars against the government of Iraq, President Bush frequently accused it of supporting terrorism and occasionally made a more specific charge that Baghdad had links to al Qaeda. On September 25, for example, Bush said that Iraq and al Qaeda "work in concert. The danger is that al Qaeda becomes an extension of Saddam's madness and his hatred and his capacity to extend weapons of mass destruction around the world."

Bush offered no specific evidence to support such statements, and most other administration officials acknowledged that the United States had no hard intelligence information pointing toward direct cooperation between Iraq and al Qaeda. Government officials backed away from the one specific allegation made after the September 11 attacks: that Mohammed Atta, the presumed leader of those attacks, had met earlier in 2001 with an Iraqi intelligence official in Czechoslovakia.

During much of 2002 officials in the White House and other government agencies suggested a danger of future cooperation between Iraq and al Qaeda—specifically the possibility that Iraq might turn over to the terrorist network some of its presumed arsenals of biological and chemical weapons. Bush cited such a danger in his request to Congress in September for authorization to take military action against Iraq if that country refused to allow resumption of United Nations weapons inspections.

Following are excerpts from the third annual report submitted December 17, 2002, to the United Nations Security Council by the monitoring group that was appointed by the council in 1999 to review the implementation of UN sanctions against the al Qaeda terrorism network.

The document was obtained from the Internet at daccess-ods.un.org/TMP/6975236.html; accessed March 22, 2003.

II. The al-Qa'idah network

7. The Bali bombing [a terrorist bombing on October 12, 2002, on the island of Bali, Indonesia, killing more than two hundred people] has confirmed the extent of the relationship between al-Qa'idah and the loose coalition of extremist groups in South-East Asia. A concerted effort by the Governments of Malaysia, the Philippines and Singapore, dating back to the autumn of 2001, led to the identification of a number of cells in the area linked to Jemaah Islamiyah, which had been planning terrorist attacks. More and more information is coming to light. Much of this information was obtained as a result of the successful break-up by the Singaporean authorities of a major operational cell. In addition, the recent arrests in Indonesia, arising from the investigation by the authorities there into the Bali incident, have provided further evidence of the dangers posed by al-Qa'idah and Jemaah Islamiyah in the region. The cooperation between these Governments represents a major step forward in the fight against al-Qa'idah. There are signs that law enforcement authorities around the world are increasingly successful in identifying and detaining members of al-Qa'idah and their associates. Some of the key suspects recently arrested are Ramzi bin al-Shibh, Abd al-Rahim al-Nashiri and Imam Samudra.

8. The Mombasa attacks [two attacks in the vicinity of Mombasa, Kenya on November 28, including a bombing at a resort hotel] have been attributed by many States to al-Qa'idah. However, even if some may not perceive the individuals responsible to be a component part of al-Qa'idah, those involved have clearly drawn on the pronouncements of Osama bin Laden for their inspiration. Thus, by default, those responsible for these latest outrages in Kenya fall into the category of associates and associated entities as defined in resolution 1390 (2002), as do those connected with the Bali bombings. Together these incidents appear to indicate a shift in tactics by the al-Qa'idah network. Soft targets, preferably with maximum casualties, would now appear to be the order of the day. The success of the al-Qa'idah network's loosely affiliated cell system has again been demonstrated; a reminder, if one should be needed, of how this global scourge is manifesting itself. But the most important point that

arises from these horrendous events is the need for even greater and more determined action, collectively, by all States of the United Nations to eradicate al-Qa'idah and all its manifestations.

9. One aspect of the al-Qa'idah phenomenon that is a major area of concern is the number of operatives that were trained in Afghanistan during the years that the training camps existed. These operatives have returned to their countries of origin or gone to others. They have been likened to time bombs— when the time comes they will "explode". By this the Group means that, following extensive planning and preparation of identified targets, they then act on receipt of the appropriate signal or the presentation of the appropriate opportunity. Most of these operatives remain at large. The authorities in the States where they are in waiting possibly know some of them. Many others are "dormant", and their identities and whereabouts are unknown.

10. One of the most recent developments to come to light is the apparent activation of new, albeit simple, training camps in eastern Afghanistan. Particularly disturbing about this trend is the fact that new volunteers are making their way to these camps, swelling the numbers of would-be al-Qa'idah activists and the longer-term capabilities of the network.

III. General observations

11. The representatives of all of the Governments with whom the Group met reiterated their Governments' commitment to discharging their responsibilities as Members of the United Nations in the fight against terrorism, and in particular in complying with resolution 1390 (2002). At the time of writing, only 79 States have submitted their 90-day reports, as requested in paragraph 6 of the resolution. The Group has not been able to assess the level of compliance of the States that have not responded. The Committee may wish to address this matter, as it is a fundamental aspect of compliance.

12. The fight against the al-Qa'idah network is proving to be a difficult and drawn-out undertaking. Al-Qa'idah is more than a terrorist organization that can be identified and eliminated. It is an insidious mass movement that must be dealt with using a broad range of tactics. This includes intelligence and information-gathering, military action, financial countermeasures, police investigation, travel restrictions and an arms embargo. It requires constant security consciousness and vigilance. Perhaps most importantly, it requires concrete international cooperation. No country or group of countries can handle the problem alone. Without broad information-sharing, police investigative cooperation and the application of international system-wide financial controls, al-Qa'idah will continue to be able to resist, recruit and rearm, and will continue to pose a danger to international peace and security in every region of the world. It is up to each country to take the measures necessary within its borders to deal with al-Qa'idah and its support mechanisms. Countries that fail in this endeavour undermine the efforts made elsewhere.

13. One of the most significant failings observed by the Group to date is the apparent reluctance of many countries, for various reasons, to submit the names of persons or entities they have identified as al-Qa'idah members, associates or associated entities. This includes all those individuals who, over

time, have returned from training camps in Afghanistan and are known to the authorities. These individuals should be regarded as terrorists and treated accordingly. This failing has seriously degraded the value of the United Nations consolidated list, one of the key instruments supporting international cooperation. The list, in conjunction with resolution 1390 (2002), provides the only internationally recognized mechanism that assures that common steps are taken to deal with those designated. . . .

V. Freezing of financial and economic assets . . .

35. The funding of al-Qa'idah and associated terrorist groups through charitable and other non-governmental organizations continues to pose one of the greatest challenges to the financial war on terrorism. The line between fund-raising activities for legitimate purposes and those related to terrorist recruitment, maintenance, indoctrination and training is often blurred. In some cases the charities and non-governmental organizations have been only "shell", or front, organizations intended to funnel money to al-Qa'idah or its associated groups or cells. However, in many cases, otherwise legitimate charities have been infiltrated or used by al-Qa'idah and its associates to obtain, transfer or divert money to support their activities.

36. The capture of al-Qa'idah operatives and the dismantling of the organization's camps and bases in Afghanistan has provided substantial information on al-Qa'idah financial operations and the emphasis it placed on fund-raising through charities and other non-governmental organizations. It also used these organizations for logistic support, as a cover for employment, false documentation, travel facilitation and training. This information has focused a greater international effort on closely monitoring and regulating the potential use of charities and other associations for these purposes. Several charities and organizations have been investigated for possible al-Qa'idah ties, and freezing orders have been issued in several instances.

37. International standards regulating charities, non-governmental organizations and associations vary significantly between jurisdictions and between different legal systems. Charities in many countries have gone largely unregulated, except with regard to questions related to possible tax exemption status. In many cases charities come under official scrutiny only if accusations of fraud or embezzlement arise. . . .

38. Several of the charities and non-governmental organizations implicated in channelling funds, knowingly or unwittingly, to al-Qa'idah or associated groups or entities are based in the Middle East, Africa, South Asia and South-East Asia. In recognition of the religious and cultural importance given to acts of anonymous charity, the relevant Governments were reluctant to tightly oversee these charities. This has particularly been the case regarding charitable programmes operating outside their jurisdiction. Several of these countries have now pledged to more closely regulate and scrutinize the activities of these charities. The Group recommends that all States establish a charities commission or similar regulatory body.

39. The Government of Saudi Arabia issued new regulations earlier this year tightening up charity oversight. It has required all charities based in Saudi

Arabia since 1999 to be registered. The new requirements provide for the creation of a special oversight commission. They also require Saudi charities and other non-governmental organizations to report to the Saudi Government all activities that extend beyond Saudi Arabia. Such activities are to be closely monitored. The new regulations also encourage donations to be made only through established Saudi groups. Unfortunately, some of these approved groups have, in the past, been alleged to have provided funds, directly or indirectly, to al-Qa'idah operatives. On 23 October 2002, the Saudi Government hosted a special forum on Islamic charities to discuss new regulatory measures as well as new coordinated investment and programme strategies.

40. The Government of Pakistan has also initiated several new measures to regulate charities and non-governmental organizations, including madrasas. The Pakistan Government has pledged to reform the madrasa system. The Group was informed that the new laws will provide for changes in curriculum, registration and the monitoring of finances.

41. The fight against the financing of terrorism has also benefited significantly from increased intelligence, including information obtained from captured al-Qa'idah operatives. Government sources have told the Group that these intelligence and information-gathering efforts are starting to pay off. Considerable information on al-Qa'idah operations and financing, and the operations and financing of related organizations and entities, has been obtained and analysed by intelligence services in several countries. This includes information gleaned from forensic banking investigations, from suspicious transaction reports, from seized computers and documents and from information obtained from captured al-Qa'idah associates or operatives. Some of this information has been disclosed publicly, including information obtained from Omar al-Faruq, a key financial operative in South-East Asia who was captured recently in the Philippines.

42. The information gathered has proved very useful in tracking down and unmasking al-Qa'idah and related terrorist cells in the United States of America, Europe, Pakistan, North Africa and South-East Asia, leading to a number of arrests. It has also hampered the transfer of terrorism-related funds. However, few of the bank accounts identified contained any significant amounts, and few additional assets of any value have been frozen. Nevertheless, this approach has had a major impact on the financing of terrorism and has forced al-Qa'idah to develop new strategies to hide the identity of its resources and to store and transfer funds.

43. As al-Qa'idah cells have moved towards greater decentralization, their leaders have sought also to disseminate their previously established financial networks in favour of local or regionally based systems. They are believed to have sequestered at least some of their assets in gold and other precious commodities. They may also be using gold and precious commodities as a medium of transfer. Such transactions have been reported in the press and have been given credence in official statements by American and other government officials. However, few details have been given, and the Group has been unable to obtain any further information concerning such transactions. These assets are reportedly being stored for future requirements, such as the pos-

sible re-establishment of training and recruitment centres, if and when appropriate new "safe areas" become available to them. Reports indicate that such centres are being considered in some remote areas of South-East Asia. Other assets are believed to remain in the hands of unidentified al-Qa'idah sympathizers and supporters in Afghanistan, Pakistan, the Middle East and Central and South-East Asia. There are also suggestions that some major financial donors and supporters may have broken off their ties, at least temporarily, with al-Qa'idah to avoid detection.

44. Information obtained through investigations of the attacks of 11 September 2001, from captured al-Qa'idah members and from seized records and documents, showed clearly that al-Qa'idah traditionally relied on an international network of financing that had originally been established to support the "holy war", or jihad, that was fought against the Soviet occupation of Afghanistan. With the crackdown taking place against this network, through increased pressure on Governments and banking institutions around the world to block such transactions, al-Qa'idah, and its associated entities, have increasingly turned to local sources of funding. Local affiliated groups and al-Qa'idah cells have become increasingly reliant on their own funding, maintenance and support. Many of the extremist fundamentalist and nationalist groups associated with al-Qa'idah were already handling their finances in this manner. They rely on local community solicitations, tap local charities (both overtly and covertly), conduct small business operations and often engage in street or petty crime. In addition, local groups have on occasion been asked to raise funds for al-Qa'idah by offering training courses for payment. Such courses included indoctrination and training in camps set up by al-Qa'idah for this purpose, including former camps operated in Mindanao (Philippines) and Poso, Sulawesi (Indonesia).

45. While al-Qa'idah's principal financial support network may appear somewhat dormant, it still remains operational. Al-Qa'idah appears to still have access to substantial funding from its previously established investments, non-governmental organization and charitable support network, and deep-pocket supporters. Al-Qa'idah funds are still being generated to support major operations, such as the Bali bombing 10 and the plot to blow up embassies in Singapore. In addition, the traditional network of non-governmental organizations, charities and private donors that supported extremist institutions and proselytizing activities in support of al-Qa'idah and its objectives in the past remains active. While these latter funds are ostensibly for (and do go largely to) legitimate religious, humanitarian, social and educational purposes, they are also being used to fund radical extremist movements that support al-Qa'idah recruitment and indoctrination efforts.

46. Intelligence information has also provided a clearer picture of al-Qa'idah's involvement in developing or aligning itself with other radical extremist groups in South-East Asia, including Jemaah Islamiyah, Abu Sayyaf and the Moro Islamic Liberation Front. This has included substantial financial assistance and terrorism-related expertise. Relationships were first established in the late 1980s, followed by the establishment of a logistics base in the Philippines in the early 1990's. This base was believed to have been

financed in large part by funds received through charities and specially established front companies, allegedly set up by Osama bin Laden's brother-in-law, Mohammed Jamal Khalifa. Khalifa, a regional director for the Saudi-based charity International Islamic Relief Organization (IIRO), was married to a Filipina from Mindanao. Subsequent intelligence reports indicated that IIRO was used as a "pipeline" for bankrolling local militants. It is estimated that a substantial amount of IIRO funding to the region was diverted to terrorist-related activities. This included support for fundamentalist schools and centres and for recruiting promising young cadres who were then sent to centres in Pakistan and Afghanistan for further indoctrination. Al-Qa'idah is also alleged to have provided funding for training and arms.

47. External funding and support from legitimate charities and illicit funding channelled through al-Qa'idah operations and front companies continue to flow to groups linked to radical elements throughout the South-East Asia region. Regulating this funding is a very delicate and difficult issue. South-East Asia is home to about a fifth of the world's Muslim population, and many areas rely heavily on funding from local and international charities to support their religious, humanitarian, economic, social and educational activities. The population and local governments are likely to be wary of any attempts to interfere with the local work of such charities or organizations. The answer must therefore lie in more intense self-regulation supported by national and local government authorities. There will also have to be more careful oversight of sources of funding from outside the region.

48. Financial regulatory authorities have also focused greater attention on informal transfer mechanisms, such as *hawala*. Al-Qa'idah is believed to rely increasingly on such informal mechanisms to transmit funds for support and operational purposes. This is a result, in part, of increased vigilance over traditional bank transfers and the increased ability of law enforcement agencies in a number of countries to trace such transactions. It is also attributable to the absence of formal banking mechanisms in a number of areas in Pakistan and Afghanistan and remote areas of South-East Asia where al-Qa'idah and related organizations are now operating.

49. The legal status of *hawala* systems differs from country to country. Several countries treat *hawala* and similar transfer arrangements under their regular banking regulations or under a special regulatory category reserved for such transfer facilities. They are subjected to registration requirements and reporting and oversight rules. Many countries require such transfer agencies to "know their customers" and to file suspicious transaction reports. This is usually the case in North America and Europe. Some countries have established more liberal regulatory regimes for such informal transfer mechanisms. Others do not regulate *hawala* or have simply declared such systems illegal.

50. Whatever the regulatory regime, there is growing recognition that unregulated *hawala*-like operations exist in many countries. It is estimated that, at a minimum, tens of billions of dollars flow through *hawala* and other informal value transfer systems on an annual basis. Many countries have therefore stepped up their policing and enforcement of such practices. Others are now

taking the first step to regulate such activities. As an example, the Group has noted the announcement by the Central Bank of the United Arab Emirates, on 5 November 2002, that all *hawala* transfers would be subject to reporting requirements. Each such transaction would have to be recorded and reported to the United Arab Emirates Government banking regulatory authority. *Hawala* operators or *hawaladars* will be required to provide the Central Bank with details regarding those sending and receiving money transfers both originating in and coming into the country. The Group also noted the regulations that the Pakistan Government indicated it intends to implement with respect to *hawala* transfer systems. . . .

VIII. Conclusions

86. After a year of monitoring the implementation by States of resolution 1390 (2002) and discussing with Governments the measures imposed under the resolution, the Group has come to the following conclusions:

87. The effective implementation by a number of States of some of the measures in resolution 1390 (2002) has had a positive impact in terms of reducing the operational capability of al-Qa'idah.

88. Al-Qa'idah appears to have suffered some significant disruption to its infrastructure, but due to its decentralized, loose and relatively simple command and control system and inherent flexibility, it continues to pose a substantial threat, globally, to peace and security.

89. The United Nations consolidated list suffers from a number of inadequacies, which require rectification in order for States to comply more effectively. Similarly, States as a whole need to be more proactive in submitting names and supporting information to the Committee established pursuant to resolution 1267 (1999).

90. The measures to freeze financial and economic assets have had a positive impact in terms of disrupting al-Qa'idah's financial support, forcing al-Qa'idah to find alternative methods of funding and move its finances. Consequently, it has become more difficult to trace and identify the network's assets. Greater reliance is being placed on intelligence-gathering and the sharing of information, and this is beginning to produce positive results.

91. The travel ban under resolution 1390 (2002) is based predominantly on previously established United Nations travel bans. It is not configured to counter a global terrorist network such as al-Qa'idah.

92. The arms embargo, when initiated, had a geographical visibility. The global dispersion of the al-Qa'idah network has significantly changed the scale of the arms embargo that has to be implemented, to such an extent that the stipulated measures now fall short of the target.

93. The resolution has provided a good foundation for international cooperation in the fight against al-Qa'idah, and significant progress has been achieved. Nevertheless, the implementation of the measures contained in the resolution does not appear to have been sufficiently effective. Countering the al-Qa'idah network effectively will demand a more proactive approach to the formulation and implementation of the resolution by all Member States. . . .

PRESIDENT BUSH ON PLANS FOR
A MISSILE DEFENSE SYSTEM
December 17, 2002

Any lingering doubt that President George W. Bush was determined to build a multibillion-dollar system to defend the United States against missile attacks vanished in 2002. Bush convinced Congress to appropriate all but $14 million of the $7.4 billion he had requested for the system in fiscal year 2003. With that success in hand, the president announced on December 17, 2002, that the first elements of the missile defense system would be put in place in 2004.

Some members of Congress, most of them leading Democrats in the Senate, continued to oppose Bush's missile defense concept as flawed, unnecessary, and excessively expensive. But Bush capitalized on continuing security fears among the American public resulting from the September 11, 2001, terrorist attacks against the United States. The missile defense system was not intended to counter typical terrorist threats, such as bombings or even the hijacking of airplanes for the purpose of flying them into buildings. Even so, Bush insisted that there was a link between the war against terrorism and his missile defense system. "I have made clear that the United States will take every necessary measure to protect our citizens against what is perhaps the gravest danger of all: the catastrophic harm that may result from hostile states or terrorist groups armed with weapons of mass destruction and the means to deliver them," Bush said in his December 17 announcement.

The president's announcement came just days before a sharp escalation of tension over North Korea's threat to expand its apparent program to build nuclear weapons. Bush and others had long cited North Korea—which also was developing long-range ballistic missiles—as the principle threat justifying a U.S. missile defense program. Pyongyang's actions during 2002 considerably strengthened Bush's hand in pressing forward with such a program. (North Korea issue, p. 731)

The war against terrorism and the North Korean threat also put to rest most of the anxiety that missile defense critics had expressed about Bush's decision in 2001 to abandon the 1972 Anti-Ballistic Missile (ABM) treaty, which for three decades had barred the United States and the Soviet Union (later Russia) from developing nationwide missile defense systems. The U.S. withdrawal from the treaty became effective in June. (Missile defense and ABM treaty background, Historic Documents of 2001, p. 927)

Congress Approves Funding

Congress had been funding research on a missile defense since the mid-1990s, when key Republicans pushed President Bill Clinton (1993–2001) into supporting a plan to base interceptor missiles in Alaska that could shoot down incoming missiles from North Korea or other possible enemies. Numerous tests of that system produced mixed results. The Pentagon insisted that most tests were successful, but several academic experts produced evidence showing that some of the Pentagon's reports were overly optimistic or misleading. Clinton in September 2000 postponed a decision on deploying the Alaska system then being tested, saying a final decision should be made by his successor, who was to be elected two months later. That successor turned out to be Bush, who had made the building of a missile defense system one of the few specific planks of his defense and foreign policy platform. (Clinton action, Historic Documents of 2000, p. 677)

By the time Clinton announced the postponement the Pentagon had spent an estimated $5.7 billion on development and testing for missile defense. The Congressional Budget Office estimated in 2000 that the system Clinton was working on would have cost a total of $56 billion to $64 billion by 2025. Congress approved another $4.8 billion for missile defense research in fiscal year 2001, which started when Clinton was in office and continued for the first eight-plus months of Bush's term.

After taking office in 2001 Bush said he favored a much broader missile defense system than the land-based system Clinton had pursued. Bush said he also was directing the Pentagon to investigate placing antimissile systems at sea (onboard ships and submarines) and in space (using high-powered lasers mounted on satellites). The idea, Bush said, was to create a "layered" system that would be able to shoot down a threatening missile in each phase of its flight toward the United States: the "boost" phase in the first few minutes after launch, the "mid-course" phase as it traveled through space, and the "terminal" phase as it dived toward its target. Bush planned to investigate two or three different types of defense for each of those phases.

Bush and his aides refused to give total cost estimates for this complex system, arguing that it was too early to name a price tag because some of the elements to be tested would prove to be successful and then would be adopted, while others might fail and be discarded. For fiscal year 2003, the first budget year totally under his control, Bush requested just under $7.4 billion and Pentagon projections indicated plans to spend another $30 billion in the following four fiscal years. In a controversial move, Defense Secretary Donald H. Rumsfeld in January 2002 exempted the missile defense program from most of the routine oversight by independent Pentagon analysts. Rumsfeld said the move was necessary because the program needed flexibility as it conducted fast-paced research; critics said Rumsfeld

*was merely allowing a politically favored program to escape the analysis
that would expose flaws to Congress and the public.*

*The administration's attempt to dampen interest in the long-term costs
of missile defense suffered a modest blow on January 31 when the Congressional Budget Office produced cost ranges for each of the three major components of Bush's proposed land-, sea-, and space-based system. The study
said missile interceptors based on land—the first ones to be deployed—
could cost between $26 billion and $74 billion through 2015; interceptors
based on ships could cost between $50 billion and $64 billion during the
same period; and a space-based laser system could cost between $82 billion
and $100 billion through 2025. The study gave a longer-term estimate for
the space system because it likely would be the last component deployed.*

*The total of the low-range estimates for the three components was
$158 billion; the total of the high-range estimates was $238 billion. However, the budget office warned against simply adding the figures in that way
to come up with the totals, noting that some technological elements were
common to all three components of the system, so the actual combined costs
might be lower. A Pentagon spokesman also cautioned against the figures,
saying the administration had not decided which components of the system
ultimately would be deployed. Despite those caveats, critics noted that the
estimated costs far exceeded any numbers, in the tens of billions of dollars,
that administration officials had talked about when selling the missile defense program to Congress in 2001.*

*As Congress worked on Bush's requests for missile defense in 2002, one
aspect of his plan became an early casualty: the proposal for lasers, based
on orbiting satellites, that would destroy missiles aimed at the United States
right after they were launched. Bush requested $35 million for research on
that idea in fiscal year 2003 and said he would spend another $50 million
in each of the next four years. Arguing that this program would take too
long, Congress in 2001 and again in 2002 made cuts in Bush's request for
it, effectively shutting it down for the time being. Congress approved nearly
all of Bush's other requests, totaling about $7.4 billion for missile defense
spending in fiscal year 2003. The largest single item included in that total
was about $2.6 billion for the land-based missiles that would be based in
Alaska and would attack threatening missiles in mid-flight.*

*The Pentagon began work on six underground silos for those missiles at
Fort Greely, near Fairbanks, Alaska, on June 15, immediately after the U.S.
withdrawal from the ABM treaty (which had barred such work) became effective. That work was expected to take two years and would take place even
as the Pentagon continued testing the ability of interceptor missiles to
detect and destroy incoming missiles. This was the system Bush said on December 17 would be ready for initial deployment in 2004 even though testing had not yet proven it would work. In addition to the interceptors based
in Alaska, Bush said some would be based at Vandenberg Air Force Base in
California. Also in mid-June the Pentagon said it hoped to be able to deploy
its first sea-based defensive missiles as early as 2004.*

Explaining Bush's decision to deploy the ground-based system in 2004, Rumsfeld described the overall missile defense concept as an "evolutionary" one. "When it finishes some day out there in the years ahead, it will very likely look quite different than it begins," he said. "And it very likely will involve a variety of locations. And it will very likely involve the participation of a number of countries." Administration officials were negotiating with Denmark and Great Britain for the right to use their communications facilities as part of the missile defense system.

Some longtime critics of the missile defense concept said Bush's decision was premature and likely would waste billions of dollars. The president's action "violates common sense by determining to deploy systems before they have been tested and shown to work," said Carl M. Levin, D-Mich., the ranking Democrat on the Senate Armed Services Committee.

The Russian government, which had opposed the U.S. missile defense system and reluctantly acceded to Bush's decision to scrap the ABM treaty, reacted cautiously to Bush's announcement. The Russian Foreign Ministry expressed "regret" and warned that U.S. planning for missile defense had entered "a new destabilizing phase." Even so, Moscow said it expected to be consulted by Washington in the future and might even want to participate in the missile defense plan. The Japanese government also had expressed interest in being covered by a U.S. missile defense system because North Korea's missiles could deliver a nuclear weapon to any of Japan's islands.

Testing Continues

Because the missile defense program was expensive and still had a number of influential critics in and outside Congress, the Pentagon's testing of various components drew widespread scrutiny. During the Clinton administration, scientists who opposed the missile defense concept—notably Theodore A. Postal of the Massachusetts Institute of Technology—had used the Pentagon's data to demonstrate that several claimed test successes actually were failures. After Bush took office the Pentagon conducted three new tests of the ground-based system and claimed all were successful. Then in June the Pentagon announced that it would no longer make public specific data about its tests, arguing that enemies could make use of the information to counter the U.S. program. Critics said the administration was merely trying to hide its missile defense program from public scrutiny. "You get the suspicion this is as much to avoid scrutiny of the program as to shield it from adversaries," Sen. Jack Reed, D-R.I., told the Washington Post *in response to the Pentagon's announcement.*

The Post *on August 5 reported problems with one of the systems for which the Pentagon had expressed the most hope. Called the Patriot Advanced Capability-3 (or PAC-3, in Pentagon language), the system used a version of the Patriot antimissile missile that the Pentagon had deployed during the 1991 Persian Gulf War. The new version was intended to shoot down incoming missiles during the final stage of their flights. Four tests of the new system between February and May 2002 failed for various reasons, the* Post *reported, forcing the Pentagon to delay for about a year its decisions about deploying the system. Even so, Bush mentioned the PAC-3 system as one he wanted to have deployed by 2004.*

In a related development, the Post *reported on September 3 that a Pentagon advisory board urged the administration to narrow the number of missile defense options under consideration. The Defense Science Board, made up of independent experts, reportedly said the administration had enough information to concentrate on two options for intensive research and development. The* Post *said that board favored the land-based system then being built in Alaska and a fleet of missile interceptors based aboard the navy's Aegis cruisers and destroyers.*

> *Following is the text of a statement by President George W. Bush on December 17, 2002, announcing plans to deploy the first elements of a missile defense system in 2004.*
>
> **The document was obtained from the Internet at www .whitehouse.gov/news/releases/2002/12/20021217.html; accessed January 23, 2003.**

When I came to office, I made a commitment to transform America's national security strategy and defense capabilities to meet the threats of the 21st century. Today, I am pleased to announce that we will take another important step in countering these threats by beginning to field missile defense capabilities to protect the United States, as well as our friends and allies. These initial capabilities emerge from our research and development program and build on the test bed that we have been constructing. While modest, these capabilities will add to America's security and serve as a starting point for improved and expanded capabilities later, as further progress is made in researching and developing missile defense technologies and in light of changes in the threat.

September 11, 2001 underscored that our Nation faces unprecedented threats, in a world that has changed greatly since the Cold War. To better protect our country against the threats of today and tomorrow, my Administration has developed a new national security strategy, and new supporting strategies for making our homeland more secure and for combating weapons of mass destruction. Throughout my Administration, I have made clear that the United States will take every necessary measure to protect our citizens against what is perhaps the gravest danger of all: the catastrophic harm that may result from hostile states or terrorist groups armed with weapons of mass destruction and the means to deliver them.

Missile defenses have an important role to play in this effort. The United States has moved beyond the doctrine of Cold War deterrence reflected in the 1972 ABM [Antiballistic Missile] Treaty. At the same time we have established a positive relationship with Russia that includes partnership in counterterrorism and in other key areas of mutual concern. We have adopted a new concept of deterrence that recognizes that missile defenses will add to our ability to deter those who may contemplate attacking us with missiles. Our withdrawal from the ABM Treaty has made it possible to develop and test the full range of missile defense technologies, and to deploy defenses capable of protecting our territory and our cities.

I have directed the Secretary of Defense to proceed with fielding an initial set of missile defense capabilities. We plan to begin operating these initial capabilities in 2004 and 2005, and they will include ground-based interceptors, sea-based interceptors, additional Patriot (PAC-3) units, and sensors based on land, at sea, and in space.

Because the threats of the 21st century also endanger our friends and allies around the world, it is essential that we work together to defend against them. The Defense Department will develop and deploy missile defenses capable of protecting not only the United States and our deployed forces, but also our friends and allies. The United States will also structure our missile defense program in a manner that encourages industrial participation by other nations. Demonstrating the important role played by our friends and allies, as part of our initial missile defense capabilities, the United States will seek agreement from the United Kingdom and Denmark to upgrade early-warning radars on their territory.

The new strategic challenges of the 21st century require us to think differently, but they also require us to act. The deployment of missile defenses is an essential element of our broader efforts to transform our defense and deterrence policies and capabilities to meet the new threats we face. Defending the American people against these new threats is my highest priority as Commander-in-Chief, and the highest priority of my Administration.

GENERAL ACCOUNTING OFFICE ON FAILURES BY THE SEC
December 19, 2002

A wave of corporate scandals that began with the collapse of Enron Corporation in late 2001 and continued through 2002 exposed fundamental weaknesses in the federal government's regulation of American business practices. Investigative reports by news organizations and government and private agencies painted a portrait of the government's chief corporate watchdog—the Securities and Exchange Commission (SEC)—as understaffed, mismanaged, and ill-equipped to ferret out corporate wrongdoing.

The SEC's problems became painfully evident in October as it struggled to appoint a new board to oversee the accounting industry, according to a hard-hitting report issued December 19, 2002, by the General Accounting Office (GAO), the investigative arm of Congress. The GAO portrayed a commission that functioned just above the level of chaos as it bungled its way through the politically sensitive task of naming the board, which Congress had recently created. The SEC's failures led to the resignation of its chairman, Harvey L. Pitt, and of the man Pitt chose to head the accounting board, former FBI and CIA director William H. Webster.

The bankruptcy of Enron in December 2001 was the first of more than a dozen major corporate scandals that damaged an already weak economy and severely undermined public confidence in American business. Throughout the year a parade of revelations brought on by bankruptcies and investigations showed that some leaders of large corporations had misled investors and the public with false financial reports and enriched themselves with corporate spending and stock options In a few cases, individual corporate executives found themselves arrested on criminal charges. (Corporate scandals, p. 391; Enron bankruptcy, Historic Documents of 2001, p. 857)

Accounting Board Upheaval

Responding to an almost daily barrage of bad news about misdeeds in corporate suites and boardrooms—and a resulting plunge in the stock markets—Congress in July pushed through legislation reforming major elements of government regulations that had been enacted since the 1930s to protect investors and the general public. The legislation was known as the Sarbanes-Oxley Act (PL 107–204), after the chairmen of the two banking committees who were its main sponsors: Paul S. Sarbanes, D-Md., of the Senate Banking Committee, and Michael G. Oxley, R-Ohio, of the House Financial Services Committee. President George W. Bush, who initially had been reluctant to support tough regulatory changes, eventually endorsed the bill when it gathered wide bipartisan support on Capitol Hill.

The bill toughened laws against securities fraud by adding a maximum prison sentence of up to twenty-five years and barred accounting firms from performing tasks (such as internal auditing and management consulting) at companies for which they performed outside audits. The bill also required chief executive officers and chief financial officers of publicly traded companies to certify their official financial statements filed with the SEC and face fines and prison sentences for willful violations.

The centerpiece provision of the bill was the creation of a new Public Company Accounting Oversight Board to police the accounting industry. The five-member board was to be appointed by the SEC, and at least two of its members were to be accountants. Sarbanes and Oxley said this new board would have strong powers to prevent a recurrence of problems that became evident after the Enron collapse. Enron's auditor, the Arthur Andersen accounting firm, had engaged in several questionable activities, including helping the company create off-the-books partnerships that were intended to disguise its financial losses. A federal grand jury in June found the Arthur Andersen firm guilty of obstruction of justice because of its shredding of documents in late 2001. Its once-vaunted reputation shattered and its clients gone, Arthur Andersen went out of business.

The creation of the accounting board set in motion a series of events that left the reputation of the SEC and its chairman little better off than that of Arthur Andersen. Faced with an October 28 deadline under the law for naming the accounting board's new members, Pitt began looking for candidates. His goal, according to the GAO report on the selection process, "was to find an outstanding candidate as chairman, an individual of great stature who could reassure investors and receive unanimous support from the commission [the SEC]."

Pitt conducted the initial stage of his search with the help of the SEC's chief accountant, Robert K. Herdman, and a Democratic member of the SEC. Pitt first approached former Federal Reserve Board chairman Paul A. Volcker, who declined the job in early September. Attention then shifted to John H. Biggs, chairman of the TIAA-CREF pension fund and a longtime critic of the accounting industry. By late September Pitt and at least two other SEC members had agreed on Biggs as chairman. But after October 1 news reports suggested that Biggs had been selected, dissension over the choice grew within the commission and in Republican circles, according to the GAO report, and Pitt began looking elsewhere for a chairman. Democrats in Congress then accused Pitt of caving into the accounting industry, which opposed Biggs. In an October 9 letter to Bush, several leading Democrats demanded that Pitt be fired, saying his "repeated insensitivity suggests an arrogant indifference to the appearance of conflicts of interest."

Pitt's search for a chairman then focused quickly on Webster, a man with an extraordinarily long resume of service at high levels of government. Webster had been a federal district court judge as well as director of the CIA and FBI (at different times) and was highly regarded in Washington for his independence and honesty. Although he had served on corporate boards, Webster was not well known for his experience or acumen in business or accounting matters—and that is where the problem arose. Webster later told the GAO that early in the selection process he had told Pitt that he had served as the chairman of the audit committee of a small firm, U.S. Technologies, that was on the brink of bankruptcy. SEC officials then checked the commission's records about that firm and, according to the GAO report, turned up no evidence that appeared to disqualify Webster.

The full SEC held an open meeting on October 25 to consider the appointment of Webster and four other nominees for the accounting board. One commissioner, Democrat Harvey J. Goldschmid, voted against all five candidates on the grounds that the selection process was "inept" and "seriously flawed," the GAO said. The other Democratic commissioner, Roel C. Campos, voted against Webster, saying he was not as qualified as Biggs, but supported the other four candidates. Webster's nomination was approved by a vote of 3–2—not the unanimous vote Pitt had hoped for—and the others were approved by a 4–1 vote.

Six days later, on October 31, the New York Times *reported that Pitt had not told his fellow commissioners about Webster's involvement with U.S. Technologies, a company the newspaper said had been accused of fraudulent activities. That story set off a flurry of reports about the selection process at the SEC, none of them particularly complimentary either to the SEC or to Pitt. Seeking to head off the controversy, the White House sent a senior public relations specialist to help dig Pitt out of his hole.*

The White House advice failed to stem the torrent of criticism of Pitt's handling of the accounting board nominations and his general stewardship of the SEC during the previous fifteen months. Pitt announced on the evening of November 5—the day of midterm congressional elections—that he was resigning. Three days later Herdman, the SEC chief accountant who had handled most of the staff work in the selection process, announced his resignation as well. Finally, on November 12 Webster said that he had resigned, effective with the appointment of his successor. As of the end of the year, the SEC had not named a replacement for Webster, and the new accounting board was not expected to begin its operations until January 2003.

Pitt said he would stay on as SEC chairman until his successor was named and confirmed. Bush on December 10 announced the nomination of William H. Donaldson, head of the New York investment firm Donaldson, Lufkin, and Jenrette and a former chairman of the New York Stock Exchange, as Pitt's replacement. Donaldson was expected to win easy confirmation by the Senate in 2003.

In its detailed report on the SEC's selection of Webster, the GAO flagged serious mistakes at nearly every point of the process. At the outset, the GAO said, the commissioners failed to agree on formal responsibilities for themselves and their staff members. The commission also failed to establish specific criteria for candidates, and they did not communicate among themselves. As the deadline set by Congress for selection of the board approached, the GAO said, the SEC rushed to a decision without adequately reviewing the background of the candidates, particularly Webster. "The overall process that emerged was neither consistent nor effective and changed and evolved over time," the report said.

Systematic Failures at the SEC

Even before the uproar over the Webster appointment, newspaper reports and analyses by independent investigators portrayed a SEC that lacked the resources to carry out its primary job of policing thousands of public companies on behalf of the investing public. Many of these same reports painted Pitt as a regulator who failed to understand some of the fundamental principles of government regulation.

Testifying before the Senate Banking Committee on March 5, the GAO's chief, Comptroller General David M. Walker, said the SEC suffered from severe staff shortages, high turnover among personnel, and a lack of a plan to deal with its problems. "There is a growing mismatch between the SEC's responsibilities and their resources," Walker testified. The GAO and other observers noted that the SEC lacked the staff to examine in any detail the numerous financial reports that more than 17,300 public companies were required, by law, to file each year. One study found that each SEC auditor was responsible for reviewing an average of six corporate reports daily. That figure helped explain the agency's trouble in catching false or misleading reports from companies such as Enron that were determined to hide losses from shareholders and the public.

As part of the Sarbanes-Oxley corporate reform act, Congress authorized the biggest single increase ever in the SEC's budget—a 77 percent boost to $776 million a year. Months later the Bush administration quietly cut more than $200 million from what Congress had approved. Pitt acknowledged the cut would prevent him from carrying out new enforcement plans but reportedly made no serious effort to get the money restored.

Pitt emerged in published reports as a brilliant lawyer who was incapable of managing a large and complex agency such as the SEC. He started his legal career with the SEC in the 1970s, then went into private practice and became one of the country's most successful corporate lawyers. Bush appointed him as chairman in August 2001 to succeed Arthur Levitt, who had served in the post throughout the Clinton administration and had fought numerous battles, only some of them successful, to enhance the agency's oversight functions. With his experience, contacts, and reported analytical ability, Pitt was widely expected to be one of the best SEC chairmen ever.

Pitt's understanding of corporate law and finances may have prepared him for some tasks, but navigating the politically treacherous waters of government regulation during a time of crisis was not one of them. Within months of taking office Pitt found himself the subject of unflattering media reports. The collapse of Enron, followed by numerous failures at other corporations large and small, elicited few indications of concern from Pitt's SEC, which said it had matters in hand and was taking care to protect the public's interest. In the first of many demonstrations of his inability to recognize political danger signals, Pitt refused to recuse himself from an SEC investigation into Enron's auditor, the Arthur Andersen accounting firm, which he had represented in private practice. Pitt's explanation that he had no role in the probe other than voting for it caused outrage in Washington and sent his reputation plummeting. Pitt also became the subject of ridicule in July when he tried, unsuccessfully, to get a provision in the pending Sarbanes-Oxley bill to raise his pay and elevate his position to cabinet level.

Within the agency, SEC staff members reportedly were dismayed by Pitt's repeated meetings with the executives of companies that were being investigated by the agency. As calls mounted for tougher scrutiny of the accounting industry, Pitt in January announced a new plan for regulations; he developed the plan after consulting with the accounting trade group but not with key staff or an oversight board that had limited clout to police the industry.

In April, with increasing evidence pointing to conflicts of interest among leading Wall Street stock analysts, the SEC at first stood by as attorneys general in New York and other states launched their own investigations. Pitt ultimately opened his own inquiry and proposed modest rule changes, but New York attorney general Eliot Spitzer had moved so aggressively that the SEC found itself in a supporting role. Spitzer eventually forced Merrill Lynch and Wall Street's other major investment houses to sign agreements barring their analysts from the lucrative practice of advising companies on their stock offerings even while giving the investing public supposedly independent advice about those offerings. The contrast between Spitzer's actions and those of the SEC made it appear that the federal agency "was in the rearguard, not the vanguard, of reform" and that Pitt was "embarrassingly inept," the Economist *magazine said in November.*

A broad analysis of the SEC's failures—especially in relation to Enron— came in an October 8 report by the bipartisan staff of the Senate Governmental Affairs Committee. The 127-page report detailed numerous instances in which the SEC, over a period of years, failed to hold Enron to standards that might have prevented the company from misleading investors, and itself, about its financial health. For example, the report said the SEC gave full-scale reviews to only three Enron annual reports during the 1990s and conducted no reviews of any kind after 1997. It was in the latter period that Enron developed most of the off-the-book partnerships, disguising its losses, that eventually got the company into trouble. The SEC's failure to review Enron's statements was not unusual, the committee report said, because the SEC lacked the staff to regularly review the financial reports even of large companies. What was "troubling," the report noted, was that several factors—notably Enron's "astonishingly rapid growth" and its transformation into the new field of energy trading—should have triggered greater interest by the SEC in the company's reports. Enron hid its wrongdoing so well, the committee report said, that only a much more detailed analysis than the SEC's superficial reviews could have uncovered it.

Overall, the committee staff said, its investigation showed a "fundamental breakdown" in the system in which the government relied primarily on the private sector to ensure that companies complied with laws mandating honest financial disclosures. "Thus, although our investigation found no willful malfeasance by the commission with respect to Enron, committee staff has concluded that the commission's largely hands-off approach to the company—combined with the failure of the auditors and the board of directors to do their jobs—allowed inaccurate and incomplete information to flood the market, leading to significant financial losses for thousands of Enron employees and an even greater number of investors," the report said.

The Senate committee report also criticized actions in the Enron case by the three major private-sector credit rating agencies, Moody's Investor Service, Standard & Poor's, and Fitch Ratings. Those agencies, the report said, failed to understand Enron's financial weaknesses until it was too late. While all three lowered their ratings of Enron in 2001 as the company's stock was declining, none dropped Enron below the "investment grade" rating until just days before the company filed for bankruptcy in December 2001.

Following are excerpts from "Securities and Exchange Commission: Actions Needed to Improve Public Accounting Oversight Board Selection Process," a report issued December 19, 2002, by the General Accounting Office.

The document was obtained from the Internet at www.gao .gov/new.items/d03339.pdf; accessed February 10, 2003.

Initial Strategy for the Selection and Vetting Process

In requiring SEC to appoint members to the PCAOB [Public Company Accounting Oversight Board] within 90 days, the act posed a unique challenge for SEC. SEC had not in recent history conducted a similar selection process; therefore, it lacked formalized and tested procedures that were familiar to the Commissioners and SEC staff. The actual process used to appoint PCAOB members was not documented and evolved as the statutory deadline for appointing members approached. Upon passage of the act, the Chairman designated the SEC's Chief Accountant to lead the search for and identification of PCAOB nominees, with assistance from the General Counsel, who was assigned to vet the candidates. The Chief Accountant began identifying potential candidates for the PCAOB from a wide range of sources, including current and prior Commissioners, Members of Congress, government officials, regulatory organizations, trade associations, and industry leaders. SEC also solicited input from the public through an August 1, 2002, release asking for nominations and applicants willing to serve on the PCAOB. As required by the act, early in the process, the SEC Chairman began to consult with the Chairman of the Board of Governors of the Federal Reserve System and the Secretary of the Treasury to obtain their input and suggestions for potential PCAOB candidates.

Early in the selection process, the SEC Chairman's goal was to find an outstanding candidate as chairman, an individual of great stature who could reassure investors and receive unanimous support from the Commission. The SEC Chairman initially planned that he, along with a Democratic Commissioner and the Chief Accountant, would approach candidates for the chairmanship. The Chairman said that he believed this would help make the process bipartisan. The SEC Chairman wanted the Chief Accountant to participate because he was the person within SEC who would have the most contact with the PCAOB chairman; therefore, he needed to be comfortable with the selection. However, at least one Commissioner told us that the reason for this approach was neither communicated to him nor fully understood by him.

Given that the nominees were being considered for service on a board that was designed to help restore investor confidence in financial reporting systems and to clean up perceived problems in the accounting profession, the SEC Chairman said that the PCAOB, and thus each of its members, must be beyond reproach. To achieve that end, the Chairman asked the General Counsel to vet nominees and, at a minimum, identify any significant potential problems or conflicts, real or perceived, involving accounting and other related issues. The General Counsel said that he saw his role as working with the Office of the Chief Accountant to develop an application to collect financial and background information from appointees, to select a contractor to conduct background checks on the appointees, and to identify other steps to vet the slate of candidates selected by the Commission. The staff initially planned to have the slate of potential PCAOB candidates determined by the end of September, which the General Counsel thought would have provided time to do at least some vetting of the appointees before the October 28 deadline. It is unclear whether the other Commissioners were informed of or fully endorsed this plan; some of the Commissioners wanted more involvement in the process and thought it best for each Commissioner independently to do due diligence on potential candidates. This selection strategy broke down when the Commissioners, lacking a documented and formalized process, were unable to agree upon and follow a strategy to identify, vet, and select members to the PCAOB and attract a consensus candidate to serve as chairman.

Major Events Leading to the Appointment of the First PCAOB

In August 2002, according to those involved in the process, Paul A. Volcker, the former Chairman of the Board of Governors of the Federal Reserve System, emerged as the consensus choice for PCAOB chairman. The SEC Chairman, a Democratic Commissioner, and the Chief Accountant tried throughout

August to persuade Mr. Volcker to consider serving as PCAOB chairman. The SEC Chairman also asked the Secretary of the Treasury, the Chairman of the Board of Governors of the Federal Reserve System, and others to assist him in persuading Mr. Volcker. In early September, Mr. Volcker declined to be considered for appointment, in part because the full-time nature of the position required him to give up outside interests that were important to him. In September, the SEC Chairman, the Democratic Commissioner, and the Chief Accountant shifted their focus to Mr. Biggs, the retiring Chief Executive Officer of Teachers Insurance and Annuity Association-College Retirement Equities Fund (TIAA-CREF).

On September 11, the Chairman, the Democratic Commissioner, and the Chief Accountant met with Mr. Biggs to discuss his interest in serving on the PCAOB. According to those involved, the purpose of the meeting was to persuade Mr. Biggs to agree to be considered for the chairmanship of the PCAOB. At this meeting, the Chairman and the Democratic Commissioner in attendance told Mr. Biggs that he would have their support. However, the SEC Chairman also stated that his final decision would rest in what he hoped would be a unanimous decision by the Commission. Mr. Biggs said that he told the SEC Chairman that he would only serve on the PCAOB if he were appointed its chairman. The following week, Mr. Biggs called the Chairman and the Chief Accountant to say that he was willing to be considered. On September 24, Mr. Biggs met with a third Commissioner who also gave his support, thereby giving Mr. Biggs enough votes for a majority. Mr. Biggs subsequently met with the remaining two Commissioners and other SEC staff on September 27. For the Chairman, support of Mr. Biggs was contingent upon another specific individual being appointed to the PCAOB. Therefore, when one of the Commissioners informed the Chairman (around Sept. 27) that another Commissioner might not be willing to support that individual, the Chairman became less willing to support Mr. Biggs.

The SEC Chairman continued to discuss throughout September other candidates who could potentially serve as chairman or members of the PCAOB. Although potential appointees to the PCAOB had been the subject of ongoing media speculation, on October 1, a newspaper article indicated that Mr. Biggs had "agreed to be the first head of a new regulatory oversight board for the accounting profession." According to those we interviewed, this article upset some of the Commissioners because it said that the job had been offered to Mr. Biggs. Some of the Commissioners said that the article made them feel that their vote was irrelevant to the selection of the chairman. The SEC Chairman telephoned Mr. Biggs on October 2 and informed him that the October 1 article had "complicated things" and threatened the Chairman's desire to achieve a unanimous vote. Although the article reported that Mr. Biggs declined to be interviewed, the article, together with a subsequent article that appeared on October 4, led some of the Commissioners to believe that Mr. Biggs was the source of the information included in the articles, directly or indirectly. As a result, some of the Commissioners raised serious questions about Mr. Biggs's independence, judgment, and ability to effectively work on the PCAOB. At this point, the Commission became divided, with at least one Commissioner willing to support only Mr. Biggs as the chairman and others who strongly opposed Mr. Biggs's nomination as chairman.

SEC's Chairman and Chief Accountant said that they originally planned for the Commissioners to meet with only about five to seven PCAOB candidates, who would be identified by the Chief Accountant. Again, this approach was not communicated to or endorsed by all of the Commissioners. Therefore, in late September, with time running out and little progress made in selecting candidates, the selection process changed. At the urging of one of the Commissioners, the Chief Accountant and each of the Commissioners began to interview candidates. In total, each Commissioner interviewed about 25 candidates for the PCAOB from late September to October. Although the SEC Chairman and the Chief Accountant were considering a number of candidates, Judge Webster, former Director of the Federal Bureau of Investigation (FBI) and the Central Intelligence Agency, emerged as a leading candidate for PCAOB chairman. Although his name had surfaced in early August along with others, he was not seriously pursued at that time. According to Judge Webster, the SEC Chairman first contacted him on September 27 about considering a position on the PCAOB and later sent him some background material. On October 15, Judge Webster met with the SEC Chairman, the Chief Accountant, and the SEC Chairman's Chief of Staff, who urged Judge Webster to consider serving as PCAOB chairman. They discussed a number of items at this meeting. At some point during the meeting, the Chairman said that there was one reason for Judge Webster not to consider the position, which was that Judge Webster's nomination would be criticized by some and that he could be attacked in the media. According to those in attendance, Judge Webster said that he had been confirmed by the Senate for other federal posts on five occasions and nothing in his past would pose a problem. He added that people might make something out of the fact that he was the former chairman of the audit committee of the board of directors of U.S. Technologies, a company that he described as on the brink of failure. According to Judge Webster, he also asked the SEC officials at that meeting to check SEC's records to see if they indicated any problems relating to U.S. Technologies. As discussed in detail in the next section, an initial review of this matter conducted by staff in SEC's Office of the Chief Accountant did not reveal, in the Chief Accountant's opinion, any disqualifying problems involving Judge Webster's role in the company. Based on the information he obtained, the Chief Accountant passed along information to the Chief of Staff, indicating that there was no problem with Judge Webster's involvement in U.S. Technologies. The Chief of Staff communicated that message to the SEC Chairman. Neither the information provided by Judge Webster nor collected by the Chief Accountant was provided to SEC's General Counsel for vetting purposes.

On October 21, Judge Webster met with the SEC Chairman and the Chief Accountant to discuss the position further. According to Judge Webster, the Chief Accountant and the SEC Chairman independently told Judge Webster on October 22 or 23 that his involvement with U.S. Technologies would not be a problem. Judge Webster also spoke, in person or on the telephone, with the other Commissioners and the General Counsel on or around October 22, but U.S. Technologies was not mentioned or discussed. Late in the afternoon of October 23, Judge Webster agreed to have his name considered for PCAOB chairman. The SEC Chairman and the Chief Accountant finalized the choices for the other members of the PCAOB and developed a five-member slate on October 24. On that day, in part due to concerns about a leak to the press, the draft slate was not shared with the full Commission. However, the Secretary of the Treasury and the Chairman of the Board of Governors of the Federal Reserve System were informed of the draft slate on October 24, and at the request of the SEC Chairman, they signed a joint letter endorsing Judge Webster and the other members on the slate.

There was additional research into Judge Webster's involvement with U.S. Technologies after Judge Webster agreed to have his name submitted for consideration on October 23. On October 24, the Chief Accountant received a draft newspaper article, which mentioned that Judge Webster had served on the board of directors of several companies, including U.S. Technologies. This prompted the Chief Accountant to ask one of his staff to do some additional follow up on any open or closed enforcement activity concerning U.S. Technologies. This review also included a review of certain corporate disclosures filed with SEC by U.S. Technologies, including documents indicating that the company had dismissed its external auditor a month after material internal control weaknesses were reported. The Chief Accountant received this information on the morning of October 25, a few hours before the scheduled open meeting of the Commission. Again as discussed in detail in the next section, in the opinion of the Chief Accountant, this review revealed nothing that would have disqualified Judge Webster as a nominee. Therefore, the Chief Accountant did not pass on any information about U.S. Technologies or Judge Webster's role to the SEC Chairman or the other Commissioners to consider prior to their vote to appoint members to the PCAOB. He also did not share this information with the General Counsel.

The SEC Chairman said that he and the Commissioners had planned to vote seriatim—whereby the slate of nominees would be passed among the Commissioners for signature—on Thursday, October 24, rather than holding an open Commission meeting. However, on October 23, one of the Commissioners requested an open meeting. On the morning of the October 25 vote, the Office of the Chief Accountant provided the Commissioners with the slate of names for the PCAOB and formally notified them that vetting would occur post-appointment. At the open meeting, one Commissioner voted against all of the board nominees, stating that the selection process was inept and seriously flawed. Another Commissioner voted against Judge Webster, stating that he was not as qualified for the post as Mr. Biggs, but voted in favor of the remaining slate. The SEC Chairman and the remaining two Commissioners voted in favor of the slate of five. Judge Webster therefore was approved by a vote of three to two, and the remaining PCAOB nominees were approved by a vote of four to one.

Staff in the Office of the Chief Accountant continued to research matters associated with U.S. Technologies from the morning of the vote into the week of October 28. On October 31, allegations emerged that the SEC Chairman, before the October 25 vote, withheld from his fellow Commissioners material information about Judge Webster's role at U.S. Technologies, which was relevant to the appointment of Judge Webster as chairman of the PCAOB. Later that same day, the SEC Chairman and another Commissioner separately called the SEC Inspector General to investigate these allegations. The SEC Chairman also asked the SEC Office of the General Counsel to conduct an investigation into Judge Webster's involvement with U.S. Technologies.

Amid the subsequent controversy, the SEC Chairman announced his intention to resign on November 5, the Chief Accountant announced his resignation on November 8, and Judge Webster resigned from the PCAOB on November 12, effective upon the appointment of a new chairman. To date, the PCAOB has had two planning meetings, which have included Judge Webster. The PCAOB is expected to hold its first official meeting on January 6, 2003, at which time members' terms officially begin. At this time, no acting chairman or replacement chairman has been appointed to the PCAOB. . . .

Conclusions

Given the short time frame to appoint members and the lack of an existing formalized process, the PCAOB selection process was a difficult undertaking for SEC. Based on our reviews of various correspondence and extensive interviews with the principals involved, it is clear that the Commissioners never collectively discussed establishing a process nor reached consensus on how best to proceed in selecting members for the PCAOB. This lack of consensus was evidenced by a fundamental disagreement about whether the Commissioners should have played a lead role in identifying potential PCAOB candidates or whether the process should have been staff-driven as envisioned by the Chairman. Although Sunshine Act requirements may have made it more difficult for the Commission to reach this much needed consensus, SEC did not identify effective alternative methods for ensuring that the views of all the Commissioners were reflected in the process. As a result, the process changed and evolved over time and was neither consistent nor effective. Although the Commission was informed that background checks and vetting had not occurred before the vote on October 25, the Chairman and Commissioners generally believed that the Office of the General Counsel and/or the Office of the Chief Accountant was undertaking some type of vetting of candidates throughout the process. Given the highly scrutinized, political nature of the appointment process, any decisions had to be able to withstand intense public scrutiny and, hence, the lack of vetting proved to be a significant flaw in the selection process.

Based on our reviews of thousands of pieces of correspondence and comprehensive interviews, we found no evidence that the SEC Chairman knew anything before the October 25 vote other than that Judge Webster had once been chairman of the audit committee of the board of directors of U.S. Technologies, a company on the brink of failure. This information, which the SEC Chairman heard from Judge Webster on October 15, was not detailed and did not raise a major concern at that time, and prior to the vote, the Chairman's

Chief of Staff had told the Chairman that Judge Webster's involvement in U.S. Technologies was not a problem. However, in making this conclusion, insufficient due diligence was performed by the Office of the Chief Accountant. In addition, the Chief Accountant's failure to communicate any information to the General Counsel, who had responsibility for the vetting process, could have contributed to this incomplete assessment.

When staff in the Office of the Chief Accountant conducted further analysis into U.S. Technologies on October 25, they became aware that the company's 2001 filings disclosed that the company had dismissed its external auditor a month after that external auditor reported material internal control weaknesses related to the company's accounting and financial reporting infrastructure resulting from the lack of an experienced chief financial officer. Based on the factors previously discussed including his experience as an auditor, his knowledge of Judge Webster's long and prominent record of public service, and an understanding that additional vetting would take place post-appointment, the Chief Accountant concluded that this matter did not raise a concern and decided that it was not necessary to inform the Chairman, the other Commissioners, or the Office of the General Counsel of these issues. In light of the current environment surrounding auditors, the role played by audit committees of boards of directors of publicly held companies and the expectation that new members of the PCAOB be beyond reproach, it is clear from our review of the relevant documents that these matters, especially when viewed in the current environment, should have prompted SEC to perform additional, in-depth evaluation before reaching a conclusion about U.S. Technologies and Judge Webster's involvement. Further, in our view, the information concerning Judge Webster's role as chairman of the audit committee of the board of directors of a company that had dismissed its external auditor after the auditor had found material internal control weaknesses should have been shared by the Chief Accountant with the SEC Chairman and other Commissioners prior to the vote.

SEC was under enormous pressure in selecting the PCAOB members and had little time to do so. SEC also had difficulty getting certain outstanding individuals to agree to be PCAOB members because of the full-time service requirement and the need for members to give up certain forms of income and other professional or business activities. However, going forward, the Commission will be tasked with establishing a more credible process to replace individual PCAOB members, starting first with selecting a replacement for the chairman and then conducting annual staggered reappointments. . . .

KIBAKI ON HIS INAUGURATION
AS PRESIDENT OF KENYA
December 30, 2002

Kenyan president Daniel Arap Moi, one of the last of the "Big Men" who had long ruled African countries with an authoritarian hand, reluctantly stepped aside in 2002 and allowed an opposition party to win elections for the first time since Kenya gained independence in 1963. Mwai Kibaki, a former vice president who had broken with Moi, led an opposition coalition to an overwhelming victory in presidential and parliamentary elections held December 27, 2002. Taking office three days later before a jubilant crowd of a half-million people, Kibaki pledged to end the corruption and tribal-influenced infighting that had severely damaged the economy and the political life of the country, which was once considered among the most likely to succeed in all of Africa.

Kibaki faced enormous challenges, starting with the need to revive an economy that had been sluggish for more than a decade. He also would be hard pressed to meet the expectations of Kenyans who were exhilarated by the country's rebirth as a real democracy after long years of one-party—indeed, one-man—rule. Leaders of minority tribes that had not participated in government appeared to expect favors for their support of the new government. Millions of voters also seemed ready to hold Kibaki to his promises of free schooling for their children and other improved social services.

A Break with the Past

With a population of 31 million, Kenya in 2002 was one of the largest and most important countries in Sub-Saharan Africa that had never experienced a truly competitive election, one in which the opposition had a realistic chance to win. After independence, Jomo Kenyatta—leader of the main political party, the Kenya African National Union (KANU) and a member of the largest tribe, the Kikuyu—was elected president without real opposition. Kenyatta died in 1978 and was succeeded by Moi, his vice president, who was a member of the smaller Kalenjin tribe. Moi amended the constitution in 1982 to make Kenya officially what it had been in practice, a one-party state. He was reelected without opposition in 1983 and 1988.

Moi ruled autocratically, using the tools of government to reward his supporters and punish his enemies. Britain, the colonial power, left behind in Kenya one of Africa's best-developed infrastructures of roads and other public services, but by the 1980s much of it had deteriorated from lack of investment and maintenance. Tourism, mining, agriculture, and small-scale industry sustained economic growth for the first three decades after independence, until crime and violence frightened away many of the tourists and pervasive corruption undermined the incentive for foreigners to invest in Kenya. Hundreds of thousands of refugees from conflicts and famines in neighboring Ethiopia, Somalia, and Sudan crowded into Kenya, stretching the country's already thin resources.

An outbreak of urban violence in 1991 led to an upsurge in government repression but also to the formation of an illegal opposition party led by Oginga Odinga, an old foe of Kenyatta. Western nations and the International Monetary Fund (IMF), which had helped keep the Kenyan economy afloat, exerted strong pressure on Moi to allow political reform. In response he allowed opposition parties to challenge him in the December 1992 elections, but a split among the opposition, which Moi encouraged, enabled the president to win a fourth term.

Political violence, much of it tribally based, continued to build during the 1990s, and Moi stepped up his repression, throwing opposition leaders into jail and using government security services to break up large antigovernment demonstrations in mid-1997. Moi again agreed to hold multiparty elections, which he won in January 1998 after a surge of preelection violence and another failure by the opposition to unite behind a challenger.

Under the constitution, which he wrote, Moi was forbidden to seek another term as president. But as the time for new elections approached in 2002, Moi kept the nation guessing as to his intentions and many believed he would find a way to hold onto power.

On February 14 seven of Kenya's fractious opposition parties offered up a surprise: an agreement to form an alliance to challenge Moi and his long-dominant KANU party. The parties called their new alliance the National Rainbow Coalition, or NARC. Opposition leaders, including Kibaki, said they realized that anti-Moi factions had won a combined total of more than 60 percent of the votes cast in the previous two elections but had lost because of their divisions. Many of these same opposition leaders had made similar attempts to patch up their differences before the previous elections, but they eventually fell back into their tribal- and personality-based disputes, enabling Moi to win.

Moi came up with his own surprise a month later, saying he would step aside, after all, in favor of Uhuru Kenyatta, the forty-one-year-old son of the country's first president. Moi pushed aside his vice president, George Saitoti, who had hoped to inherit the party leadership. Moi's announcement also antagonized Raila Odinga, son of the former opposition leader, who had merged his own party with KANU and taken a government post in hopes of grabbing the top spot. One by one, Odinga and other cabinet ministers quit KANU and went over to the opposition.

After several more months of wrangling, Moi solidified his party's choice of Kenyatta, and the opposition alliance on October 22 agreed on Kibaki as its candidate. As Moi's vice president during the 1980s, Kibaki had resisted multiparty elections. But after Moi dumped him from that post, Kibaki went into opposition and ran unsuccessfully against Moi in 1992 and 1998. Kibaki, 71, and Moi, 77, were of the same generation of Kenyan leaders. One of the reasons Kibaki won support from potential rivals was that he was expected to serve only one term, creating an opportunity in five years for younger leaders.

Suddenly, the real prospect of a change in government control generated widespread excitement in Kenya and offered hope in place of long-held cynicism about the political process. Some Kenyans said they were even willing to set aside their old grievances against Moi. "We are so happy that he is leaving that we forgive him," Ferdinand Watirla, a clock salesman in Mombasa told the Washington Post. *"We need to move on. He's been in office so long that he's too old even to put in jail."*

The new hopefulness about Kenya's future was momentarily shattered on November 28, when a terrorist car bomb exploded at a seaside resort hotel in Mombasa, killing twelve people, plus the two bombers. The hotel was owned by and patronized almost exclusively by Israelis but nine of the dead were Kenyans. The bombing was Kenya's second major experience with terrorism in four years. In 1998 a massive truck bomb exploded outside the U.S. embassy in Nairobi, killing more than 200 people, most of them Kenyans, and injuring several thousand more. Both bombings were the work of the al Qaeda terrorist network, a group of Islamist extremists who targeted U.S. and other Western interests but killed many others in the process. (Al Qaeda, p. 740)

A much smaller tragedy befell Kibaki on December 3 when he was involved in a serious car accident while campaigning. He sustained a broken arm, a severely sprained ankle, and a hairline fracture in his neck and was sent to a hospital in London for treatment. His running mate, Michael Wamalwa, was stricken with gout while visiting Kibaki in the hospital; for a few days, as the campaign proceeded back in Kenya, both were in the same London hospital. The director of the Kenyatta National Hospital in Nairobi later described Kibaki's decision to seek treatment in London, rather than at home, as a "huge metaphor for the state of every service in the country." Kibaki returned to the campaign trail just before the December 27 election, making the rounds in a wheelchair.

Both Kibaki and Kenyatta campaigned on a theme of change. Kibaki portrayed Kenyatta as a puppet of Moi and insisted the longtime president would remain in charge if his young protege won. Kenyatta sought at every point to distance himself from the man who had chosen him as his successor, insisting that it was Kibaki and the aging generation of politicians associated with him who represented "continuity with Moi's and KANU's ways."

On election day, December 27, Kibaki's claim to represent change proved to be the more credible with the 5.4 million voters who went to the polls for

Kenya's freest election ever and its most peaceful one in years. Kibaki won with a landslide 62 percent of the vote, with Kenyatta capturing 31 percent, about the same as Moi received in his minority victory over a divided opposition nearly five years earlier. The opposition NARC alliance also won 124 of the 210 seats in the parliament, soundly routing the long-ruling KANU party, which won 64.

In a December 29 editorial celebrating the election, the Sunday Nation *newspaper wrote: "Never has the nation spoken with such clarity. Never has a tired people, burdened with the cares of decades of bad government, slipped off the yoke with such a determined, steady hand."*

Promising Change

Moi had been scheduled to step aside early in January, but he moved up the handover of power to December 30. Speaking to an enormous crowd packed into a park in central Nairobi for Kibaki's inauguration, Moi acknowledged that he had mixed feelings about leaving office but said "the people of Kenya have spoken." As Moi spoke, many jeered him with taunts of "go away" and "bye-bye," and some threw bits of dirt in his direction.

Kibaki delivered his inaugural address seated in a wheelchair, just a few feet from Moi. But Kibaki never directly addressed his one-time mentor and later rival. "Fellow Kenyans, I am inheriting a country which has been badly ravaged by years of misrule and ineptitude," Kibaki said, as Moi sat slumped in his chair. "There has been a wide disconnect between the people and the government, between people's aspirations and the government's attitude toward them."

Kibaki promised to root out corruption, which had become embedded in the government during the four decades of one-party rule. "I call upon all those members of my government and public offices accustomed to corrupt practices to know and clearly understand that there will be no sacred cow under my government," he said. Among specific promises, Kibaki said the government would immediately end the practice of charging parents for primary school education for their children.

Political analysts said Kibaki would face many problems, starting with finding the money to pay for the basic education, health, and other social services he had promised during his campaign and that Kenyans now expected to receive. Western governments and the IMF, relieved to see the end of the Moi era, were expected to provide some support, but it was clear that most of the burden of reviving the economy and paying for new social programs would fall on Kibaki and his new government. As a president widely expected to serve just one term, Kibaki also faced power struggles within the alliance-of-convenience that had worked to put him in office. Fellow leaders who had been in opposition to Moi, notably Raila Odinga, were said to be angling for cabinet posts that would give them a head start in the campaign five years hence. Moreover, rivalries among Kenya's seven major tribes—which Moi had exploited for his own purposes—could easily pose a danger to the new government.

Following is the text of the address delivered December 30, 2002,
by Mwai Kibaki, upon his inauguration as president of Kenya.

The document was obtained from the Internet at www
.kenyaembassy.com/articles/kibakispeech.htm; accessed
January 3, 2003.

I feel extremely happy to address you today. I am overwhelmed by your love. I am emboldened by your support and enthusiasm. I am thrilled by your sense of dedication and commitment to this country. You have renewed my hope and strengthened my belief in the greatness of this country.

Now, all of us, both young and old, men and women, Kenyans of every ethnic group, race or creed, have embarked on a journey to a promising future with unshakable determination and faith in God and in ourselves.

I would like, on behalf of myself, my family and the entire leadership and supporters of the National Rainbow Coalition (Narc), to express my sincere appreciation to all Kenyans for giving me the mandate to preside over the affairs of this great country for the next five years.

I am greatly honoured for the confidence you have extended to me and I promise not to let you down. You have asked me to be your chief servant and I accept it with humility and gratitude. I would like to congratulate all our elected parliamentary and civic leaders who will also be servants of the people.

Future of Kenyan Politics

The National Rainbow Coalition represents the future of Kenyan politics. Narc is the hope of this country. Our phenomenal success in so short a time is proof that working together in unity, we can move Kenya forward.

Look around you, see what a gorgeous constellation of stars we are, and just look at this dazzling mosaic of people of various ethnic backgrounds, race, creed, sex, age, experience and social status.

Never in the history of this country have its leaders come together and worked so hard together as one indivisible entity with one vision. It is the love of Kenya that has brought us together. We chose to let go our individual differences and personal ambitions in order to save this nation.

Some prophets of doom have predicted a vicious in fighting in Narc following this victory. I want to assure you that they will be disappointed. When a group of people comes together over an idea or because of a shared vision, such a group can never fail or disintegrate. Narc will never die as long as the original vision endures. It will grow stronger and coalesce into a single party that will become a beacon of hope not only to Kenyans, but also to the rest of Africa.

This is a critical moment in the history of our country. The task ahead is enormous, the expectations are high, and the challenges are intimidating. But

I know that with your support and co-operation, we shall turn all our problems into opportunities.

Sacred Duty

You have asked me to lead this nation out of the present wilderness and malaise onto the Promised Land. And I shall. I shall offer a responsive, transparent and innovative leadership. I am willing to put everything I have got into this job because I regard it as a sacred duty.

I offer our competitors a hand of friendship. We have been through a long and sometimes bitter electioneering campaign. Now, the elections are over, there should be no bitterness. Let us all unite in forgiveness, reconciliation, and hard work to rebuild Kenya. Nation building requires joint efforts of all Kenyans. Let us work for our common destiny and advance our common aspiration to bequeath a better country to our children.

I salute the efforts of the gallant freedom fighters and builders of modern Kenya. I salute my worthy predecessors for their contribution to this nation. The mistakes people have made in the past should not distract us from confronting the enormous challenges ahead.

One would have preferred to overlook some of the all too obvious human errors and forge ahead, but it would be unfair to Kenyans not to raise questions about certain deliberate actions or policies of the past that continue to have grave consequences on the present. We are, however, not going to engage in witch-hunting. Our task will be to advance Kenya's interests and ensure they are well served.

We want to bring back the culture of due process, accountability and transparency in public office. The era of "anything goes" is gone forever. Government will no longer be run on the whims of individuals. The era of roadside policy declarations is gone. My government's decisions will be guided by teamwork and consultations. The authority of Parliament and the independence of the Judiciary will be restored and enhanced as part of the democratic process and culture that we have undertaken to bring to foster.

Fellow Kenyans, I am inheriting a country, which has been badly ravaged by years of misrule and ineptitude. There has been a wide disconnect between the people and the government, between people's aspirations and the government's attitude toward them. I believe that government exists to serve the people and not the people to serve the government. I believe that government exists to chart a common path and create an enabling environment for its citizens and residents to fulfill themselves in life.

Government is not supposed to be a burden on the people, it is not supposed to intrude on every aspect of life, and it is not supposed to mount roadblocks in every direction we turn to in life. The true purpose of government is to make laws and policies for the general good of the people, maintain law and order, provide social services that can enhance the quality of life, defend the country against internal and external aggression, and generally ensure that peace and stability prevails.

These will be the aims and objectives of the government under my leadership. My government will promote the creative potential of the Kenyan people. My government will adhere to the principles and practice of the rule of law in a modern society. My government will conserve national environment, develop Kenya's resources, and protect our national heritage.

Corruption will now cease to be a way of life in Kenya, and I call upon all those members of my government and public officers accustomed to corrupt practices to know and clearly understand that there will be no sacred cows under my government.

The economy, which you all know has been under-performing since the last decade, is going to be my first priority. There is deepening poverty in the country. Millions of our people have no jobs. School enrolment has been declining. In fact, the agricultural sector, like all other sectors, is steadily deteriorating. Majority of our people do not have access to basic and affordable health services. Our roads and other infrastructures are dilapidated. Most of our institutions are failing and basic road services are crumbling. There is growing insecurity in our cities and towns. The list is endless.

My government will embark on policies geared to economic reconstruction, employment creation and immediate rehabilitation of the collapsed infrastructure. We shall restructure public institutions to match them with demands of a modernizing society. A new development plan will be produced soon in order to give expression to the promises we made in our Election Manifesto. Provision of free primary education for all our children will be our immediate goal. Other areas to receive our immediate attention include:

- Provision of greater access to affordable healthcare. Reform in the delivery of social services.
- Refocus on agriculture and tourism as growth drivers of the economy.
- Privatization of non-performing public enterprises in a transparent manner, and
- Improvement of security through the retaining, re-equipping and re-orientation of the security and armed forces of our country.

My government will work closely with the private sector and with our external partners to fulfill these promises. We need the support and understanding of the international community to succeed in the task we have embarked on to recreate our beloved country.

On our part, my government will use tax revenues transparently, effectively and efficiently. We shall streamline procurement procedures and close all loopholes that have in the past led to massive wastage of national public resources.

Terrorist Attacks

My government will continue to play a leading role in East Africa, Africa and the world. It will support and facilitate all positive efforts to resolve the conflicts in Somalia, Sudan, Burundi, the Democratic Republic of Congo and other trouble spots in Africa.

Kenya continues to bear a heavy burden of these regional conflicts with hundreds of thousands of refugees in our land. As a country, which has suffered two devastating terrorist attacks, we shall work closely with others to root out causes of terrorism in the world. We desire to live in a peaceful world, united by a common sense of purpose in pursuit of a safe common future.

Once again, I call on all Kenyans to work with my government to realize the enormous potential of this country. We invite all those who have been hounded out of our shores by repressive policies of our predecessors to come back home and join us in nation building. Kenya needs the genius of its citizens wherever they are. It is time for healing, and we need every hand on deck.

Face-Lift

I was woken up this morning by rays of sunlight, which had bathed my room in such brilliance that it felt completely new. I began to notice things around me in greater details. It was as if the room had been given a face-lift. I looked out of the window and, behold a cloudless sky. The trees danced lazily enjoying the early morning breeze. I looked far into the horizon and the beauty of what I saw around me stirred my soul. It was as if I was standing atop Mount Kenya surveying the landscape. I said to myself "Oh, what a beautiful country!"

Indeed, we are so blessed, so endowed. Poverty, skepticism and despondency are not supposed to be our lot. Ours is a land of unparalleled beauty and promise. It is a land of laughter and hope.

My fellow Kenyans, I will strive to lead you to create a country you can be proud of again. Let us join hands and remain united for the sake of our country. That way Kenya will be a happy place for all of us. That is my dream.

God bless you all. God bless Kenya.

Thank you.

CUMULATIVE INDEX, 1998–2002